Let's Go writers travel on your budget.

"Guides that penetrate the veneer of the holiday brochures and mine the grit of real life."

—*The Economist*

"The writers seem to have experienced every rooster-packed bus and lunar-surfaced mattress about which they write."

—*The New York Times*

"All the dirt, dirt cheap."

—*People*

Great for independent travelers.

"The guides are aimed not only at young budget travelers but at the independent traveler; a sort of streetwise cookbook for traveling alone."

—*The New York Times*

"Flush with candor and irreverence, chock full of budget travel advice."

—*The Des Moines Register*

"An indispensible resource, *Let's Go*'s practical information can be used by every traveler."

—*The Chattanooga Free Press*

Let's Go is completely revised each year.

"Only *Let's Go* has the zeal to annually update every title on its list."

—*The Boston Globe*

"Unbeatable: good sightseeing advice; up-to-date info on restaurants, hotels, and inns; a commitment to money-saving travel; and a wry style that brightens nearly every page."

—*The Washington Post*

All the important information you need.

"*Let's Go* authors provide a comedic element while still providing concise information and thorough coverage of the country. Anything you need to know about budget traveling is detailed in this book."

—*The Chicago Sun-Times*

"Value-packed, unbeatable, accurate, and comprehensive."

—*Los Angeles Times*

Let's Go Publications

Let's Go: Alaska & the Pacific Northwest 2000
Let's Go: Australia 2000
Let's Go: Austria & Switzerland 2000
Let's Go: Britain & Ireland 2000
Let's Go: California 2000
Let's Go: Central America 2000
Let's Go: China 2000 **New Title!**
Let's Go: Eastern Europe 2000
Let's Go: Europe 2000
Let's Go: France 2000
Let's Go: Germany 2000
Let's Go: Greece 2000
Let's Go: India & Nepal 2000
Let's Go: Ireland 2000
Let's Go: Israel 2000 **New Title!**
Let's Go: Italy 2000
Let's Go: Mexico 2000
Let's Go: Middle East 2000 **New Title!**
Let's Go: New York City 2000
Let's Go: New Zealand 2000
Let's Go: Paris 2000
Let's Go: Perú & Ecuador 2000 **New Title!**
Let's Go: Rome 2000
Let's Go: South Africa 2000
Let's Go: Southeast Asia 2000
Let's Go: Spain & Portugal 2000
Let's Go: Turkey 2000
Let's Go: USA 2000
Let's Go: Washington, D.C. 2000

Let's Go *Map Guides*

Amsterdam
Berlin
Boston
Chicago
Florence
London
Los Angeles
Madrid
New Orleans
New York City
Paris
Prague
Rome
San Francisco
Seattle
Washington, D.C.

Coming Soon: *Sydney* and *Hong Kong*

2000

PERÚ & ECUADOR

Rolán Solís Hernández
Editor

Taylor M. Bollman
Esti M. Iturralde
Associate Editors

Researcher-Writers:
Eduardo Carvajal **Rachel Mason**
Adam E. Cohen **Emilia Petersen**
Esti Iturralde **Micaela Root**
Timothy Warren

Macmillan

HELPING LET'S GO If you want to share your discoveries, suggestions, or corrections, please drop us a line. We read every piece of correspondence, whether a postcard, a 10-page email, or a coconut. Please note that mail received after May 2000 may be too late for the 2001 book, but will be kept for future editions. **Address mail to:**

Let's Go: Perú & Ecuador
67 Mount Auburn Street
Cambridge, MA 02138
USA

Visit Let's Go at **http://www.letsgo.com,** or send email to:

feedback@letsgo.com
Subject: "Let's Go: Perú & Ecuador"

In addition to the invaluable travel advice our readers share with us, many are kind enough to offer their services as researchers or editors. Unfortunately, our charter enables us to employ only currently enrolled Harvard students.

Published in Great Britain 2000 by Macmillan, an imprint of Macmillan Publishers Ltd, 25 Eccleston Place, London, SW1W 9NF, Basingstoke and Oxford
Associated companies throughout the world
www.macmillan.co.uk

Published in the United States of America by St. Martin's Press.

ISBN: 0 333 77994 0
First edition
10 9 8 7 6 5 4 3 2 1

Let's Go: Perú & Ecuador is written by Let's Go Publications, 67 Mount Auburn Street, Cambridge, MA 02138, USA.

Printed in the USA on recycled paper with biodegradable soy ink.

ADVERTISING DISCLAIMER All advertisements appearing in Let's Go publications are sold by an independent agency not affiliated with the production of the guides. Advertisers are never given preferential treatment, and the guides are researched, written, and published independent of advertising. Advertisements do not imply endorsement of products or services by Let's Go. If you are interested in purchasing advertising space in a Let's Go publication, contact: Let's Go Advertising Sales, 67 Mount Auburn St., Cambridge, MA 02138, USA.

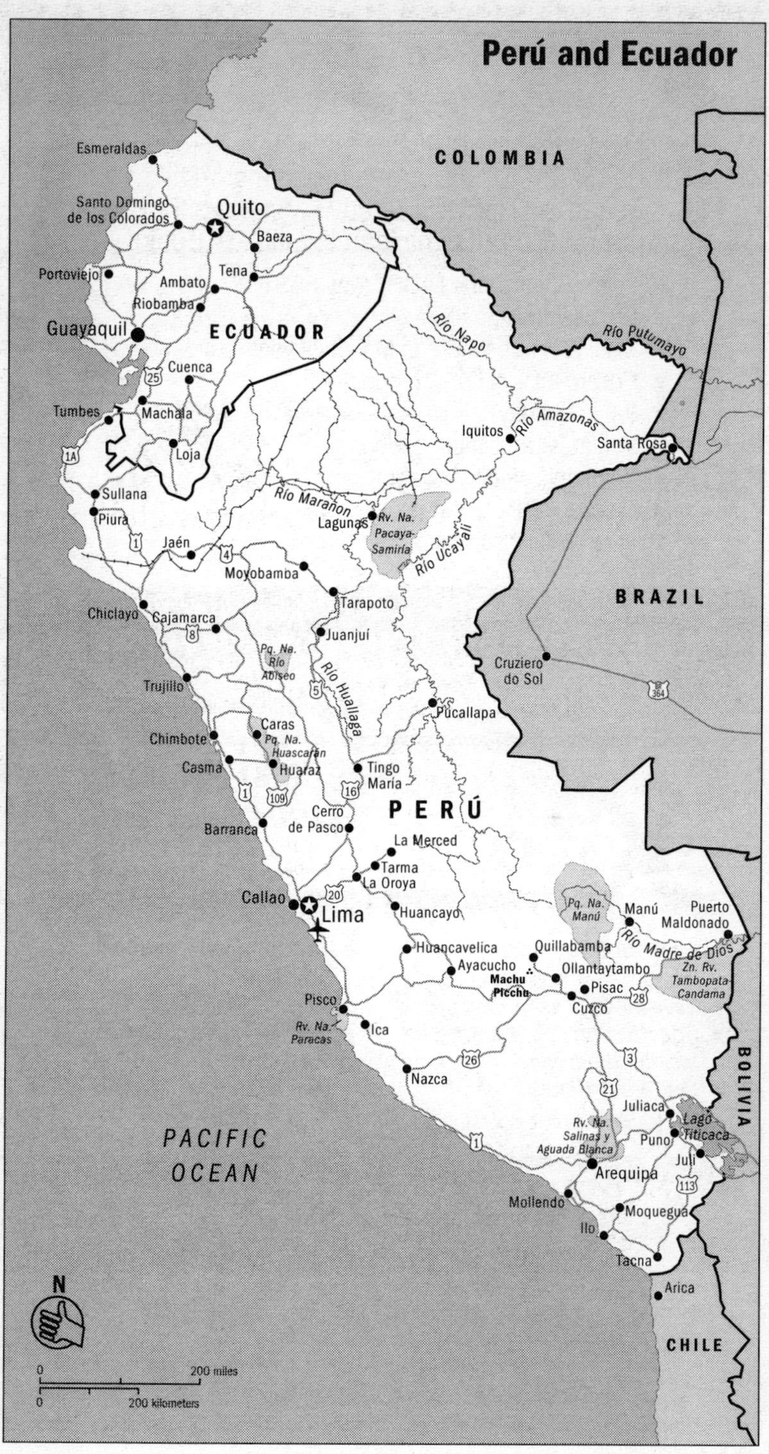
Perú and Ecuador
COLOMBIA
ECUADOR
BRAZIL
PERÚ
BOLIVIA
CHILE
PACIFIC
OCEAN
Esmeraldas
Santo Domingo
de los Colorados
Quito
Baeza
Tena
Portoviejo
Ambato
Riobamba
Guayaquil
Cuenca
Machala
Tumbes
Loja
Sullana
Piura
Jaén
Moyobamba
Tarapoto
Chiclayo
Cajamarca
Juanjuí
Trujillo
Chimbote
Casma
Caras
Huaraz
Barranca
Tingo
María
Cerro
de Pasco
La Merced
Tarma
La Oroya
Callao
Lima
Huancayo
Huancavelica
Ayacucho
Machu
Picchu
Quillabamba
Ollantaytambo
Pisac
Cuzco
Pisco
Ica
Nazca
Juliaca
Puno
Juli
Arequipa
Mollendo
Moquegua
Ilo
Tacna
Arica
Manú
Puerto
Maldonado
Iquitos
Santa Rosa
Lagunas
Pucallapa
Cruziero
do Sol
Río Napo
Río Putumayo
Río Amazonas
Río Marañon
Río Ucayali
Río Huallaga
Río Madre de Dios
Rv. Na.
Pacaya-
Samiría
Pq. Na.
Río
Abiseo
Pq. Na.
Huascarán
Pq. Na.
Manú
Zn. Rv.
Tambopata-
Candama
Rv. Na.
Paracas
Rv. Na.
Salinas y
Aguada Blanca
Lago
Titicaca
1A
1
4
8
5
109
16
20
25
26
28
3
21
113
364
N
0
200 miles
0
200 kilometers

CONTENTS

MAPS

COLOMBIA
Quito
ECUADOR
Guayaquil
Tumbes
THE AMAZON BASIN pp. 214–234
Iquitos
Santa Rosa
Piura
NORTHERN PERÚ pp. 176–199
Lagunas
Moyobamba
Tarapoto
BRAZIL
Chiclayo
Cajamarca
Juanjuí
Cruziero do Sol
Trujillo
Pucallapa
Chimbote
Casma
Huaraz
Tingo María
THE CORDILLERA BLANCA pp. 200–213
Barranca
La Oroya
CENTRAL HIGHLANDS pp. 156–175
THE SACRED VALLEY pp. 142–155
Callao
LIMA pp. 65–86
Puerto Maldonado
Ayacucho
Machu Picchu
CUSCO pp. 123–141
Pisco
SOUTHERN COAST pp. 87–100
Nazca
SOUTHERN PERÚ
TITICACA REGION pp. 115–122
PACIFIC OCEAN
Arequipa
Juli
AREQUIPA TO CHILE pp. 101–114
BOLIVIA
Tacna
N
Arica
0
200 miles
0
200 kilometers
CHILE

Regions of Perú

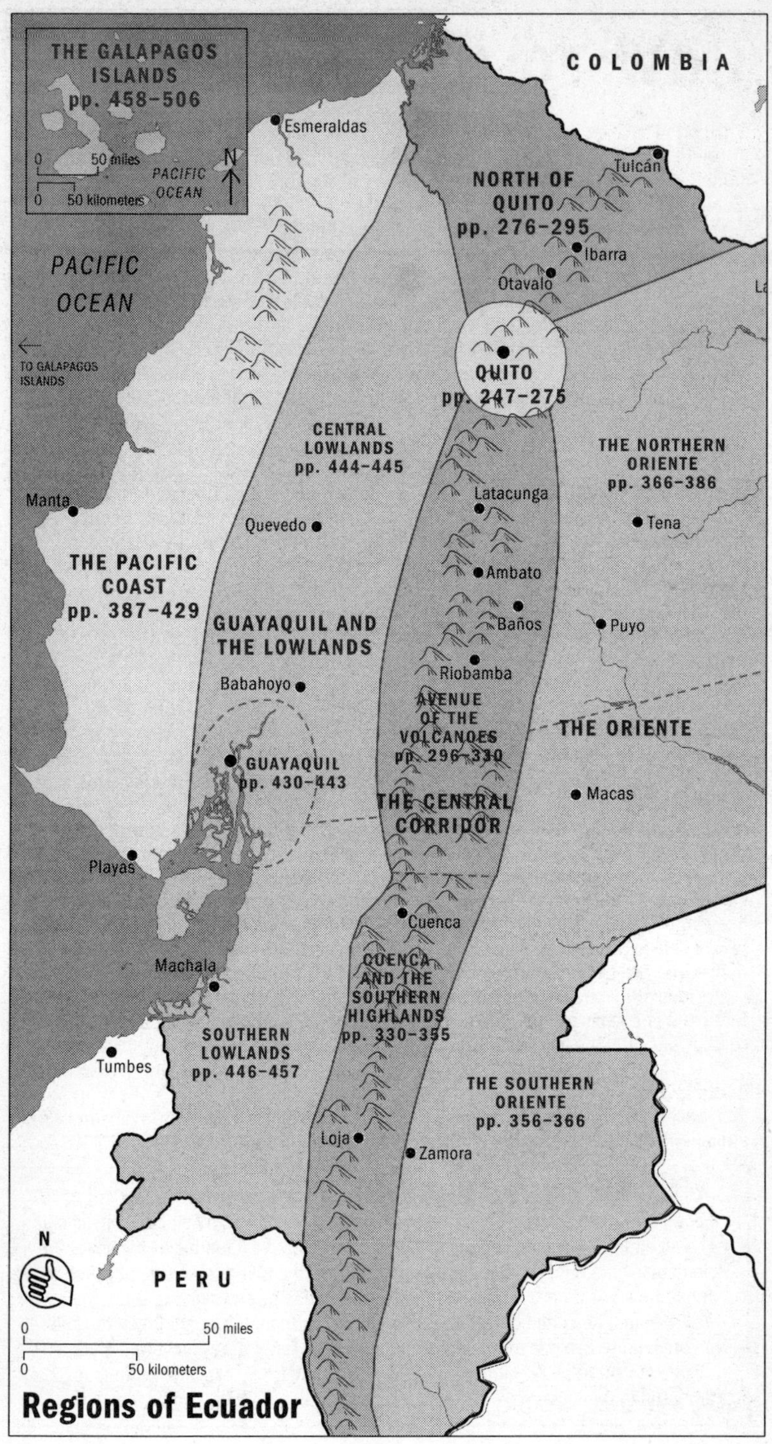
THE GALAPAGOS ISLANDS
pp. 458–506
0 50 miles
0 50 kilometers
PACIFIC OCEAN
N
COLOMBIA
Esmeraldas
Tulcán
NORTH OF QUITO
pp. 276–295
Ibarra
Otavalo
PACIFIC OCEAN
TO GALAPAGOS ISLANDS
QUITO
pp. 247–275
CENTRAL LOWLANDS
pp. 444–445
THE NORTHERN ORIENTE
pp. 366–386
Latacunga
Manta
Quevedo
Tena
THE PACIFIC COAST
pp. 387–429
Ambato
Baños
Puyo
GUAYAQUIL AND THE LOWLANDS
Babahoyo
Riobamba
AVENUE OF THE VOLCANOES
pp. 296–330
THE ORIENTE
GUAYAQUIL
pp. 430–443
THE CENTRAL CORRIDOR
Macas
Playas
Cuenca
Machala
CUENCA AND THE SOUTHERN HIGHLANDS
pp. 330–355
SOUTHERN LOWLANDS
pp. 446–457
Tumbes
THE SOUTHERN ORIENTE
pp. 356–366
Loja
Zamora
N
PERU
0 50 miles
0 50 kilometers

Regions of Ecuador

HOW TO USE THIS BOOK

Perú and Ecuador are the kinds of places that don't follow the rules. When it takes "between 12 and 36 hours" to get there, stop looking at your watch. What's the point? That volcano overhead might **erupt** any second. *Let's Go: Perú and Ecuador 2000* is not a manual; it's an adventure companion.

Let's Go has been publishing an Ecuador guide for several years now, and we've been dabbling in Perú for a while. This year's expansion into the entire country comes only after years of conspiring with our staff and readership to learn what combination of Andean nations are most desirable in an expanded guide. Essentially, we think Ecuador is a wonderful country, and that we cover it very well. But, we also realize that most travelers visit Andean countries in groups. Those who visit Ecuador also visit Perú, and vice versa. These travelers want our guides, and so now (drumroll, please), we deliver them. It's all of Perú—the sacred ruins of the Incas, the splendor of Lake Titicaca, the jungle fastness of Manú, the otherworldly lines of the Nazca—and it's all been included to complement what we already knew about Ecuador. This is a momentous occasion, kind of like a birth in the family. So sit back, have a cigar (or carrot), and watch the plan unfold.

As you may have already noticed, our new and improved book begins with a short **Discover** section, which is kind of like travel propaganda for travelers unfamiliar with what the region has to offer. Next comes the traditional **Essentials** section, which contains all of those less-than-obvious tips on how to navigate throughout Perú and Ecuador, including a comparison of their similarities and differences. We follow this with **A Regional Overview,** introducing some cultural information common between both countries (hence, the region). But if Perú and Ecuador were identical, who would need two of them in the same book? That's why we provide separate **Perú** and **Ecuador** chapters, which outline more modern, distinct histories of the two countries.

The book itself is divided into **regional chapters,** adjacent areas that are most often along major transportation routes. Though it may be confusing, this organizational scheme made sense to us. More important, the size of each **town write-up** corresponds to that town's relative importance to tourists and is composed of several components: an **Introduction**, which usually is a frank irreverent description of a town or city; **Practical Information,** which is helpful tourist info; **Food** and **Accommodations** listings, written from the most to least impressive establishment (at least in our biased, subjective opinion), and **Sights** and **Entertainment,** which are pretty self-explanatory. One tip, if there is an exceptionally great place, it may be displaying the Let's Go pick symbol, ☒, next to their name.

Besides all of the regular boring tourism stuff, this book has some really **exciting** features. The **glossary** specializes in local expression, **grayboxes** point out important or peculiar facts about Perú, Ecuador, and their culture.

Embedded in these pages, you will also find: a cyclops dog and orifice fish, a madman in love, a well-cut, five-foot phallus, a place called Willy's, the world's biggest wave, aliens in the Peruvian desert, lovely lady tortoises, a puya raimondi in your pocket, and Lorena Bobbit. Happy hunting and *¡buena suerte!*

A NOTE TO OUR READERS The information for this book was gathered by *Let's Go*'s researchers from May through August. Each listing is derived from the assigned researcher's opinion based upon his or her visit at a particular time. The opinions are expressed in a candid and forthright manner. Those traveling at a different time may have different experiences since prices, dates, hours, and conditions are always subject to change. You are urged to check beforehand to avoid inconvenience and surprises. Travel always involves a certain degree of risk, especially in low-cost areas. When traveling, especially on a budget, always take particular care to ensure your safety.

RESEARCHER-WRITERS

Eduardo Carvajal *Quito, North of Quito, and North Pacific Coast*
Sustained by his dashing good looks, super-*suave* personality and cool, cool wit, Mr. Carvajal was truly undaunted in the face of seemingly insurmountable adversity. Operating under his covert Colombian pseudonym, "Fast Eddy C," he rarely blew his cover—or his top—without a very good reason. Stranded in Otavalo by a crippling transportation strike, our intrepid hero completed his coverage by mountain bike before hiking back to Quito. Upon arriving, flanked by an Ecuadorian exodus of 40 fellow pilgrims, he was greeted by wild cheers and crowds of adoring *quiteñas*. Selflessly, he traded in this fanfare for an unforgettable birthday celebration in Esmeraldas. You see, for Fast Eddy C, work always comes first, deadlines are just that, and there's always one more stop on the itinerary.

Adam E. Cohen *Central Corridor and Northern Oriente*
As the bookteam's resident scientist, Mr. Cohen took a naturalist approach to his Ecuadorian adventures—Darwin meets Don Quixote, if you will. Fortunately, this crazy gamble paid off. As comprehensive and painstakingly detailed as an organic chemistry lab report, Adam's copy faithfully recorded all that he encountered in the line of duty while his comprehensive coverage earned him both journalistic credibility and the undying respect of his editors. As was his brother-in-arms Eduardo, Mr. Cohen was unavoidably detained by an 11-day *paro*, as well as by more pleasant distractions. Stranded in the gringo hotbed of Baños, Adam worked diligently to expand the inadequate coverage of excellent international restaurants and rockin' *discotecas*. After an aborted Tungurahua attempt, a near car-jacking by angry protestors, and several narrowly missed mailstops, our hero emerged from the jungle, intact and unphased, with stellar copy in hand.

Esti Iturralde *Central Highlands, Cusco, and Lake Titicaca*
A former Spain R-W and the editor of *Let's Go: Ecuador 1999*, Ms. Iturralde is a veritable guru on format, etiquette on the road, and all things Let's Go. Esti successfully complements her hard-nosed investigative instinct with the good cheer and good looks truly befitting an R-debutante. This year's research brought her perilously near bodily harm—on the beach of Barranco, in the goat-gutting district of Huancavelica, and on the frenzied whitewater rapids of the Apurimac—but her cool head and Quechua colloquialisms staved off danger. Our temptress emerged unscathed and in plenty of time to redefine travel guide coverage of Cusco and the Sacred Valley. Not only did she script this flagship section from scratch, but she went above and beyond the call of duty by unearthing an Inca ruin near Puno. Unbelievably, hers were the first eyes to gaze upon the 5-foot phallus of the Chucuito fertility temple in over 500 years. Later, she picked up the peculiarly hushed voice and drop-spinning method of the women of Isla Taquile, which eventually wore off once she ran out of precious *vicuña* wool. Esti was last seen working as an office assistant somewhere in New England.

Rachel Mason *Southern Oriente, Southern Lowlands, Northern Coastan Perú, Southern Perú*
A *bandita* in disguise, Rachel turned out to be as tough as nails and at least six times as smart. Mud-soaked clothing, a banana strike, benign bacterial infections, and vast stretches of uninhabited coastal desert were thrust in her path, and Ms. Mason responded in kind by transmogrifying into a post-apocalyptic doomsday-machine-like researcher. And once she did that, she became unstoppable. Of course, her copybatches also became radioactive, but the editorial staff wore black spandex, knotted polo cardigans on their shoulders, and "Risky Business" sunglasses while handling them. After two half-lives, Rachel was allowed back in the States, where she promptly warped back to Beantown in order to unleash her bionic gamma rays upon Let's Go headquarters.

Emilia Petersen *Galápagos, Guayaquil, and Southern Pacific Coast*

Externally as mild and demure as her name might imply (say it out loud a few times), Emilia turned out to be a fiercely persistent researcher. She began by taking the Galápagos by storm, sending back almost more material than we could organize and edit. Furthermore, she seemed to be having a pretty good time, following a rigorous daily regimen of tour boats, beaches, snorkeling, and observing the incredible wildlife that comes along with the Galápagos. Like a blue-footed booby, she navigated the volcanic islands adroitly and with style. Though problems with boat schedules, island accessibility, and renegade sea lions plagued part of her journey, she dismissed them all in the same nonchalant manner as her myriad prospective suitors. Back on the mainland, Emilia re-assumed her human persona and completed her coverage on her natural, un-webbed feet. When the dust settled, she survived the test and will be "naturally selected" as a return RW.

Mica Root *Central Highlands, Amazon*

A cool mist seeps up from the liquefied ground, patrolling the first light of another sweltering day. Somewhere along the Ucayali, a combat-seasoned jungle vet stirs in her hammock. The river is low; this journey will be longer than she had anticipated. Her rations are nearly exhausted and that unsavory sailor is still waiting for her on the deck below. As she carefully removes her bowie knife from under her pillow, she asks herself, "Why did I take this job again...?" We never questioned Mica's motivation for returning as an RW; we were just ecstatic to have her on board. Sure, she's not fluent in Quechua, but after her stellar research in Thailand and Laos last year, we sensed Mica's jungle savvy and didn't hesitate to send her to write new coverage of the Amazon Basin. She did so in a manner as straightforward, seething, and gritty as the region itself—a style that seems to be more *of* the jungle than *about* it. Along the way, our heroine evaded cocaine traffickers, machine-gun-toting hostal employees, and malaria-carrying mosquitoes. She slept on a police station bench in Quillabamba, gained quite a reputation among the backpacking elite of the new SAEC in Cusco, and surprised us all with her totally incredible work ethic.

Timothy Warren *Lima, Cordillera Blanca, Arequipa to Chile*

Tim was budget: his pack was light, his lodgings spartan, and his prose economical. That is to say that we couldn't get enough of his lean, athletic coverage of Perú's Andean playgrounds. Tim began in Lima, where he followed in the path of legends and, with every step, came nearer to fulfilling the duties of his post. His insightful additions are seen here: more comprehensive, more clear, and more concise coverage of the capital. As are many "budget boys," Tim was a tireless tightwad who survived on the bare essentials for most of the time. Look for his upcoming appendix, "Tim's Two-Dollar Travel Tips," which is currently being considered for series-wide implementation in 2001. By the time he got to Arequipa, he had endured a gun-wielding assailant, several short-term liasions, a roaming band of rogue delinquents, and an accident in an airport taxi. He shrugged these off resiliently, living each day in Perú as if it were his last. And, with his fickle stomach and penchant for melodrama, we sometimes thought it was.

ACKNOWLEDGMENTS

TEAM THANKS: Alex Bayro & José Chocano, our 2 Spanish muses, for all the late laughs; Poverland, Poversea, we'll find you wherever you may be...

ROLÁN THANKS: My family: Kathy, Sonia, Steve, for understanding my preoccupation, indifference, and wayward nature throughout this project; Jodi, my Siberian Siren, who's bound to bring a little bit of Sun to some otherwise gloomy lives; G-luv, for getting me to leave the office and see more movies; Dylan, the best muse a man could ask for; Brotiv, in hope that we can use this guide sometime; T-Bonk, Maria, Jon, things were crazy, but it was a fun summer; Taylor, I wasn't sure at first, but things couldn't have been better; the Hindu lush, for making an otherwise daunting, painful task bearable *Sabemos la verdad: lo más importante es que el trajabo es solo para la oficina, no? ¡Palabra!*; the temptress, without whom none of this would have happened, it was an honor watching your magic; the last-minute help, especially Bede, Kate, and Mad Dog Rudy *¡gracias!*

TAYLOR THANKS: Peter, Rolán, and Sonesh for their tremendous effort and constant support; Eddy, Emilia, Mica, Adam, Rachel, Esti, and Tim for their dedication and excellent copy; Esti, Rachel, Bede, and Kate for all their help in the last days before our deadline; mom, Portishead, and dad for their love and for mixin' good music the nights before our deadline; all the people in the salsa pod for not always sticking me with the really low, kind of uncomfortable chair; and marisa and brinkly for being my sister and my dog, respectively.

ESTI THANKS: Whoa, here I am again! A dedication to the beautiful people: Sonesh and Erin (Christian, too). Bede: wow, that was so cool of you. Rachel: many, many thanks. To my darlings, please open that other yellow book for proper attention. And, to Alex Bayro, without whom this last week could not have happened. Until the day we finally meet...

Editor
Rolán Solís Hernández
Associate Editors
Taylor M. Bollman, Esti M. Iturralde
Managing Editor
Sonesh S. Chainani

Publishing Director
Benjamin Wilkinson
Editor-in-Chief
Bentsion Harder
Production Manager
Christian Lorentzen
Cartography Manager
Daniel J. Luskin
Design Managers
Matthew Daniels, Melissa Rudolph
Editorial Managers
Brendan Gibbon, Benjamin Paloff, Kaya Stone, Taya Weiss
Financial Manager
Kathy Lu
Personnel Manager
Adam Stein
Publicity & Marketing Managers
Sonesh Chainani, Alexandra Leichtman
New Media Manager
Maryanthe Malliaris
Map Editors
Kurt Muller, Jon Stein
Production Associates
Steven Aponte, John Fiore
Office Coordinators
Elena Schneider, Vanessa Bertozzi, Monica Henderson

Director of Advertising Sales
Marta Szabo
Associate Sales Executives
Tamas Eisenberger, Li Ran

President
Noble M. Hansen III
General Managers
Blair Brown, Robert B. Rombauer
Assistant General Manager
Anne E. Chisholm

LET'S GO PICKS

From the Amazon to the Andes to the isles of Galápagos, here's the scoop straight from the notebooks of our intrepid researchers:

BEST TREKS. The Inca Trail (p. 147) is more than a hike; it's a pilgrimage. **The Colca Canyon** (p. 108) has condors and trails. **Parque Podocarpus** (p. 349).

BEST MOUNTAIN-CLIMBING: In Ecuador: **Volcán Cotopaxi** (see p. 304), because the tallest active volcano in the world demands respect. **Volcán Chimborazo** (see p. 326), whose towering summit is farther away from the earth's core than any other. In Perú: the big climbs start and end in the **Parque Nacional Huascarán** (see p. 200).

BEST RUINS. Machu Picchu (p. 150); **Nazca** (p. 98); **Chavín** (p. 202).

BEST JUNGLE. Iquitos (p. 221); **Manú** (p. 232); **Coca** (p. 379); **Macas** (p. 364).

BEST RAFTING. Río Apurimac (p. 139). With a rapid called "Odyssey in Space" you'd better hang on. Bruise your butt in the whitewater rapids of **Tena** (p. 372).

BEST "GALÁPAGOS EXPERIENCE": The Galápagos Islands (p. 458), the genuine article, the cream of the crop, a bunch of finches. **Isla de la Plata** (p. 418) in Parque Nacional Machalilla—Galápagos, budget-style.

BEST NIGHTLIFE: Lima (p. 81). **Cusco** (p. 138), where fleece is chic. **Guayaquil** (p. 430), with 6,000 grooving bodies in one disco. **Quito** (p. 264) offers sierran salsa.

BEST SURFING. Puerto Chicama (p. 195). **Montañita** (p. 419), a mecca for bronzed skin, unclad torsos, and killer swells.

BEST SPOILED-ROTTEN PAMPERING: Baños (p. 311), the original and still champion. The **Baños de San Vicente** (p. 427) will provide masseuses and aloe goop.

BEST SHOPPING: Otavalo (p. 280) attracting those from far and wide on Saturday. **Saraguro** (p. 345), filled with blankets and beaded shawls on Sundays. **Pisac's market** (p. 143) has alpaca sweaters three days a week!

BEST ARTESANÍA: The **Río Mantaro Valley** (p. 167), your best source for carved gourds. **Ayacucho** (p. 156), world-class tapestries at discount prices. **Montecristi** (p. 406), where hats show Panamá who's boss. **Cotacachi** (p. 284), with more leatherwork than you'd see in your wildest dreams.

BEST PRESERVED MUD-BRICK CITY. Chan Chan (p. 195). The key word is **preserved.**

BEST EXPLOITATION OF A GEOGRAPHICAL FEATURE: Mitad del Mundo (p. 271). Not the best theme park, but Disney ain't got the equator.

BEST (QUESTIONABLE) RUIN. Huge Penis Outside Chucuito (p. 119). Who cares if the Inca queen sat on it or not?

WORST IDEA. Living on islands built out of reeds (p. 121).

MOST ADORABLE WILDLIFE: Iguanas, flightless cormorants, boobies, waved albatrosses, frigatebirds, and those ever-talented tool-using finches (p. 468).

LEAST ENDEARING WILDLIFE: Fire ants, vampire bats, anacondas, and our favorite: orifice fish (p. 232).

DISCOVER PERÚ AND ECUADOR

Traveling in South America is a lesson in flexibility. In Perú and Ecuador, buses have no permanent schedules, prices are not posted and subject to negotiation, and hot water is considered a carnal luxury in remote areas. For rigid, unadventurous types, this not acceptable. They can go to Scandinavia. Other, more foolhardy travelers thrive on the uniquely Latin American ability to place more importance on the championship *futból* game than on mail circulation, telephone networks, or emergency health care service. They are content to enjoy afternoon *siestas*, stroll through town plazas, perfect their Spanish, and live, at least temporarily, without the myriad and mindless distractions of home.

Though the first-world media makes much of the fact that several Latin American countries, including Ecuador in the last year, have experienced severe recessions and virtual economic collapse, these countries are not nearly as "poor" as they are depicted to be. In many ways, the culture and lives of Latin Americans are more complete, perhaps even happier, than their more affluent counterparts in other countries. In exchange for stressful careers and consumerism, many Peruvians and Ecuadorians have family, friends, and the best fresh fruit in the world. We're not trying to suggest that every traveler pull up the proverbial tent stakes, sell all of their worldly possessions, and go live the simple life. But, if you'd like to at least try it temporarily, there's a warm, welcoming community awaiting to receive you. So, grab your Spanish-English dictionary, a sturdy pair of hiking boots, and some anti-diarrhea medication. Get ready to roll.

PERÚ	ECUADOR
■ **Capital:** Lima. ■ **Land Area:** Peru 1,285,220 sq. km (just smaller than Alaska). ■ **Highest Point:** 6768m, Huascarán. ■ **Price of a budget hotel room:** US$5, US$8 with bath.	■ **Capital:** Quito. ■ **Land Area:** Ecuador 283,560 sq. km (the size of Oregon). ■ **Highest Point:** 6267m, Chimborazo. ■ **Price of a budget hotel room:** US$4, US$6 with bath.

JOE VERSUS THE VOLCANO

Absolutely gargantuan mountains scrape the sky of these Andean countries. We're talking volcanic peaks so tall that you get dizzy spells from just looking at their sheer faces. Many people visit Perú and Ecuador just for this reason, determined to conquer these untamed behemoths. Others are content to enjoy the view from the valley floor. The Andes of Perú and Ecuador not only contain the highest tropical peaks in the world but also boast a higher density of summits than just about anywhere on the planet. In the highlands, you can't look out a bus without spying a silent, snow-capped cone looming high overhead. Many mountains are big enough to warrant their own park, including the highest active volcano in the world, Ecuador's **Volcán Cotopaxi** (5897m; p. 304). The tallest mountain in Perú, **Volcán Huascarán** (6768m; p. 200), and **Volcán Chimborazo** (6267m; p. 326) in Ecuador, whose summit, because of the equatorial bulge, is the farthest point from the center of the earth. Other popular snow-capped playgrounds in Ecuador include: **Tungurahua** (p. 319), **Pichincha** (p. 269), **Los Altares** (p. 319), and **Sangay** (p. 319). In Perú head for: **Alpamayo** (p. 200), **Ampato** (p. 200), **Chachani** (p. 108), **El Misti** (p. 108), and **Picchu Picchu** (p. 108).

BEACH BLANKET BINGO BASH

Perú and Ecuador occupy one-third of South America's vast Pacific coast, yet few people think of them as maritime nations. Don't be fooled by common ignorance, this is the place to come for pristine natural **beaches,** world-class **surfing,** and some of the best **seafood** on the continent. On the mainland, solitude awaits at the beaches of **Alandaluz** (p. 415) and the **Paracas National Reserve** (p. 93). If it's drinking and dancing you're after, head to **Atacames** (p. 391), **Salinas** (p. 422), and **Punta Hermosa** (p. 88). To tempt surfers, **Montañita** (p. 419) has consistent year-round swells and beach-front fiestas, while **Pico Alto** (p. 88) is South America's tallest wave (12-15 ft. faces), and **Puerto Chicama** (p. 195) boasts one of the longest lefts in the world. Better yet, most breaks see little traffic, which means more rides for everyone. As for the seafood menu, *ceviche* (a chilled, spicy, raw seafood dish) is the undisputed regional champion. It's a lot tastier than it sounds: sushi with a twist of lemon, salsa, and spice.

WELCOME TO THE JUNGLE...

As abruptly as the western edge of the Andes erupts from the lowlands of the Pacific, the chain's eastern edge plunges thousands of meters to the sweltering, seething immensity of the Amazon Basin. This is not a manicured tourist "rainforest"; this is tropical jungle at its most feral. The untamed expanse of northeastern Perú alone is larger than Germany. Though most people think of it simply as a geographic region, those who have visited know that the jungle is our planet at its most alive. It certainly has the wildlife to support that claim. Created by a chorus of howler monkeys, toucans, crocodiles, jaguars, the mighty anaconda, and thousands of insects, some of the nocturnal noises that travels through the darkness of the jungle are best left unrepeated. Spend a few days exploring its depths from **Puerto Moldanado** (p. 226) and **Iquitos** (p. 221) in Perú, or **Coca** (p. 379) in Ecuador, and you'll likely feel the same. If unsettled wilderness sounds a little bit too foreboding, take refuge in a **jungle lodge,** most of which offer the basic comforts of civilization, but still make visitors feel hard-core. Many of these guided excursions in Ecuador leave from **Macas** (p. 364), **Tena** (p. 372), and **Misahuallí** (p. 376).

REMAINS OF THE DAY

Five hundred years ago, before Spanish conquistadors "discovered" the new world, numerous native tribes controlled the land. One of them, the Incas, developed advanced agricultural methods and masonry, and subjecting neighboring tribes, rose above the rest to establish a mighty empire. At the height of their influence, the Incas dominated the Andean and coastal region from present-day Chile to northern Ecuador. Cusco, in southern Perú, was their imperial capital, and is now the site of most significant ruins. The highlights are pretty obvious to most visitors. Though over-touristed, the sacred city of **Machu Picchu** (p. 150) is an unforgettable experience. Many intrepid visitors arrive by foot, over the legendary **Inca Trail** (p. 147) Numerous other ruins await around **Cusco** (p. 141).

TABLOID TOUR

There is a Latin American way of doing things. You'll probably notice it the first time you ride on a bus, try to make an international call from a phone office, or visit a livestock market full of squealing pigs and spitting llamas. After a while, you may find the mentality has infected you, too. Perhaps you'll begin arriving at public functions in a Batman suit, backed up by a Uruguayan rock band. Then, maybe you'll even release a CD called "Madman in Love." Sound crazy? Well, it happened to supposedly distinguished public figures (see **¿Y Este Hombre Quiere Ser Presidente?,** p. 242). For more displays of bizzare behavior, head no farther than the **world's largest ceviche,** a collaborative project by the restauranteers of **Salinas** (p. 422). If the highlands are becoming a bore, try spending six days floating down the **Río Ucayalí** between Pucallpa and Iquitos in Perú (p. 231). From the jungle, hop right onto the **highest-altitude railway in the world** (see p. 172). Sit in on the judges' panel for the **Machala Banana Queen pageant** (p. 446). Don't be skeptical, it's a lot larger than it sounds.

VOYAGE OF THE BEAGLE: THE GALÁPAGOS

Fundamentalist Christians may want to steer clear of the birthplace of evolutionary theory. Other visitors will invariably be captivated by the ecosystem that compelled Charles Darwin to formulate his groundbreaking theory of natural selection. The quality of a Galápagos experience is reflected in its price tag, but the opportunity to interact with so many fascinating species, most of which have no fear of man, is well worth it. Here, visitors are greeted by absolutely pristine beaches, ample opportunities for snorkeling and dayhikes, and the opportunity to learn about ecosystems that exist nowhere else in the world. Some particularly outstanding sight in the islands are: the spectacle of **Puerto Ayora** and tortoise reserve of **Isla Santa Cruz** (p. 475); the still-evolving geology and magnificent wildlife of **Isla Isabela** (p. 492); and the endemic birds and tranquil beauty of **Isla Esañola** (p. 503).

SUGGESTED ITINERARIES

PERUVIAN OUTDOOR ADVENTURES (A 3-WEEK TOUR) On this short jaunt through central and southern Perú, you'll find major thrills about every ecosystem in the country. For the ultimate in alpine adventure, begin with Peru's **Parque Nacional Huascarán** (p. 200). From the highland town of **Caraz** (p. 211), make a 4-day trek through the Santa Cruz Valley (p. 209), passing some of Perú's tallest peaks along the way. Head south to **Huaraz** (p. 203), where you can hike up and ski or snowboard down the **Pastoruri Glacier** (p. 208). Catch a flight to **Cusco** (p. 123) for a little bit of highland cultural enrichment. Take it easy and get your feet wet while rafting for a day on the **Río Urubamba** (p. 139). Then, set out on a pilgrimage to the tourist mecca of **Machu Picchu** (p. 150). Travel in style by hiking the **Inca Trail** (p. 147), and **camping** for 3 nights at **ruins** along the route. Catch the sunrise over the Sacred City and then beat the tra in-riding tourists back to **Aguas Calientes** (p. 154). From there, head up to **Quillabamba,** from which you can brave the broiling rapids of **El Pongo de Mainique** (p. 224), a 3-day round trip. Return to Cusco and arrange a week-long tour to the **Manú Biosphere Reserve** (p. 232), where over 1,000 species of birds and countless mammals and reptiles await naturalists of all temperaments. After all this highland exertion, unwind for a few days on the coast by **camping** at the **Reserva Nacional de Paracas** (p. 93).

ECUADORIAN HIGHLANDS (A 3-WEEK TOUR) Beginning in the capital of **Quito** (p. 247), head north to the world-famous Saturday market of **Otavalo** (p. 280), where high-quality textiles, wood carvings, and even livestock are for sale. Name your price. From here, head south and take a 3-day trip on the **Latacunga Loop** (p. 302), a welcome respite from the heavy traffic and bustling cities along the Panamerican Highway. Along the loop, stay at the **Black Sheep Inn** in the small town of **Chugchilán** (p. 303). From there, rent a horse and ride to the majestic **Laguna Quilotoa** (p. 302), a topaz-blue lake hidden within an extinct volcanic crater. Spend the night in the tiny hamlet of **Quilotoa** (p. 302) and sample *cuy* (guinea pig), a traditional

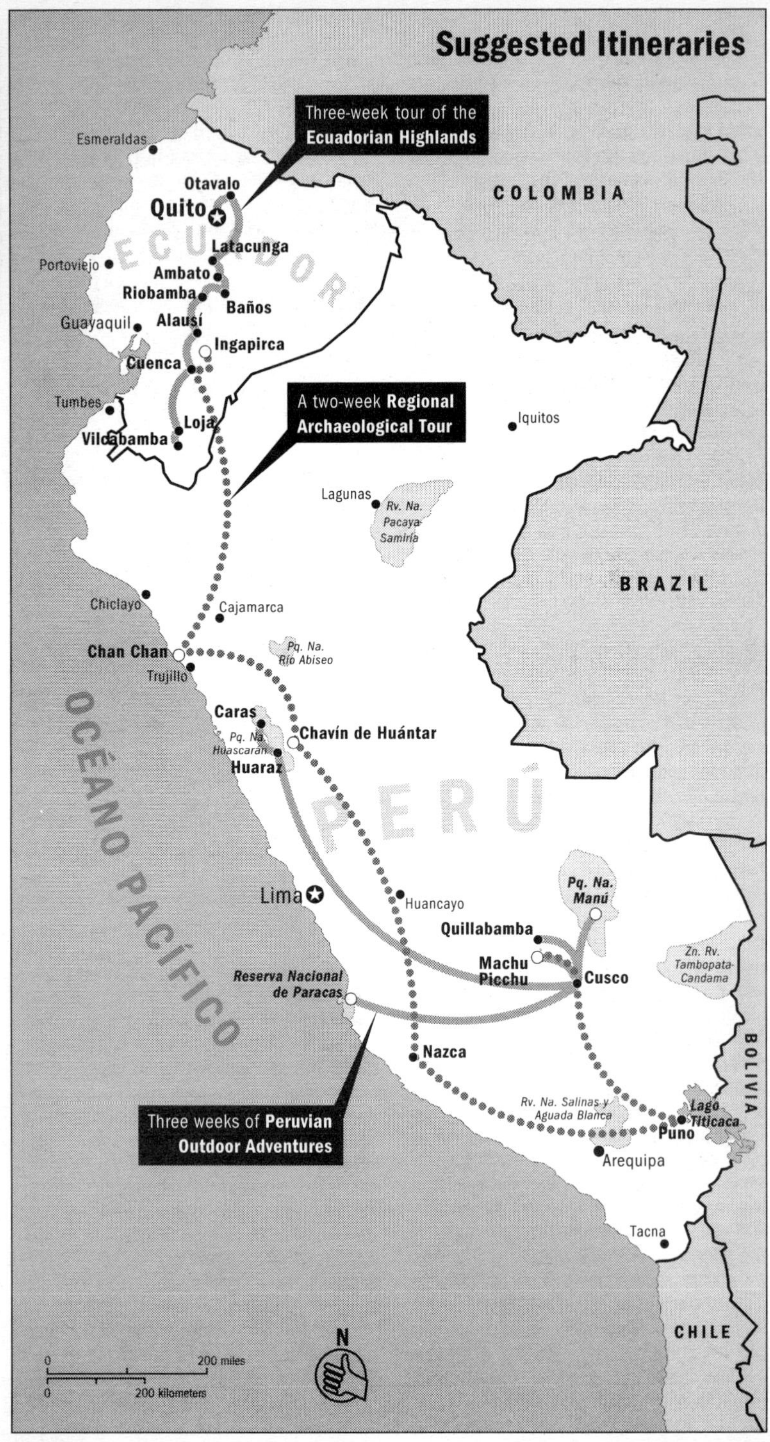

Suggested Itineraries
Three-week tour of the Ecuadorian Highlands
A two-week Regional Archaeological Tour
Three weeks of Peruvian Outdoor Adventures
COLOMBIA
BRAZIL
BOLIVIA
CHILE
ECUADOR
PERÚ
OCÉANO PACÍFICO
Esmeraldas
Otavalo
Quito
Latacunga
Portoviejo
Ambato
Riobamba
Baños
Guayaquil
Alausí
Ingapirca
Cuenca
Tumbes
Loja
Vilcabamba
Iquitos
Lagunas
Rv. Na. Pacaya-Samiria
Chiclayo
Cajamarca
Chan Chan
Trujillo
Pq. Na. Río Abiseo
Caras
Pq. Na. Huascarán
Huaraz
Chavín de Huántar
Lima
Huancayo
Pq. Na. Manú
Quillabamba
Machu Picchu
Cusco
Zn. Rv. Tambopata-Candamo
Reserva Nacional de Paracas
Nazca
Rv. Na. Salinas y Aguada Blanca
Lago Titicaca
Puno
Arequipa
Tacna
N
0
200 miles
0
200 kilometers

delicacy. From there, return to Latacunga and catch the Thursday morning market at **Saquisilí** (p. 304). Hop back on the Panamerican Highway and head south to **Ambato** (p. 306). Don't forget to check out the city's famous **clown trash cans** (p. 309). From there, take a side trip east to **Baños** (p. 311), the hot spring capital of Ecuador. There, soak in one of the city's four baths, hike in the verdant hills surounding the city, or dine in one of the many fine gourmet restaurants operated by the thriving ex-patriate community. Hop back on the Panamerican Highway and head to **Riobamba** (p. 319), where you can buy carved tagua nuts and ride a mountain bike down Volcán Chimborazo. Head south to **Alausí** (p. 328), where a trip down the railroad tracks leads to the spectacular **Nariz del Diablo** (p. 327), an easy hike or "train" ride from town. **Cuenca** (p. 332) is the next stop on the highland circuit, and it may well be the most attractive city on the tour. Spend a few days visiting the city's various museums and getting to know its friendly locals. Make an overnight **camping** trip to **El Cajas Recreation Area** (p. 340) if you grow tired of the urban atmosphere. From Cuenca, the Panamerican leads south again. **Loja** (p. 341), though rather quiet and unremarkable, does provide an ideal base from which to explore the **Parque Nacional Podocarpus** (p. 349). Hike for a day or a week; maybe even see an Andean speckled bear along the way. To recuperate from the sometimes cold and rainy weather of the sierra, head for **Vilcabamba** (p. 351), a southern town in the mystical **Valle del Juventud Eternal** (Valley of Eternal Youth). Here, you'll find one of the most unique mixes of people in Ecuador, as natives, vacationing Cuencans, and residential ex-patriates all mix in the town plaza. Chat with a **100-year-old man** as he smokes an unfiltered cigarette and explore nearby Podocarpus by horseback.

REGIONAL ARCHAEOLOGICAL TOUR (2-WEEK TOUR) Most tours of ruins and remnants of cultures past will begin in **Cusco** (p. 123), Perú, the archaeological capital of the region, with more ruins than you can shake a stick at. From here, the major ruins of **Sacsayhuaman, Qenco, Pisac,** and, of course, **Machu Picchu** (p. 150) are all very nearby. From here, head south to **Puno** (p. 115). Surrounding majestic **Lake Titicaca** (p. 120), at the top of the world, lie numerous burial **chullpas** of the **Colla** culture. Also nearby, in the town of **Chucuito** (p. 119), decide for yourself whether the 5 ft. phallus belonged to the Inca or not. If you're dying from altitude sickness, sick of cold nights, and ready to see some of the coastal cultures, head to **Nazca** (p. 96), on Perú's southern coast. Here, you'll find a truly incredible specimen of geoglyph in the form of the **Nazca Lines** (p. 98), giant formations in the arid land near town. The origins of these lines are still a great mystery. Continuing up the coast, head inland to the impressive ruins at **Chavín de Huántar** (p. 202). These are remnants of the **Chavín** culture, which occupied the region before the rise of the Inca. Further up the coast lie the impressive ruins of **Chan Chan** (p. 195), which have the distinction of being the **oldest preserved mudbrick city in the world.** Northward-bound and across the border into Ecuador, the **Wall of Three Cultures** in **Cuenca** (p. 332) preserves ruins from the pre-Inca **Cañari** tribe, the **Inca**, and, finally, the **Spanish.** From Cuenca, it's a two-hour journey to Ecuador's most significant Inca ruins, **Ingapirca** (p. 329). Though they pale in comparison to the major ruins to the south, the site is quite well-preserved and gives a real idea of the territorial reach of the empire at the height of its power.

ESSENTIALS

WHEN TO GO

Despite the region's proximity to the equator, the climate varies greatly across the three geographical regions. On the Pacific coast and in the jungle regions (called the Oriente in Ecuador) you'll find sweltering heat typical of the tropics, but in the sierra (highlands), the higher you get, the cooler you'll be. The seasons don't cycle from summer to winter as in temperate regions, but instead from wet to dry. **Coastal** and **lowland** weather is affected by the currents of the Pacific. Warm waters bathe the coastal shores from January to April, bringing torrential downpours and daytime temperatures around 31°C (88°F). In May, cooler currents from the Antarctic mean less heat and less rainfall for the rest of the year.

Sun worshippers and beach crawlers come and go with the seasons. Expect crowds during the *temporada alta* (high season) from December to April, especially on weekends and holidays. Despite the rains, many locals swarm to the beaches to find solace from the higher temperatures. The rest of the year you'll most likely have the beach to yourself; skies are cloudy and temperatures cooler. In the **sierra,** temperatures remain more or less constant all year, averaging 21°C (70°F) during the day and 8°C (47°F) at night. The driest time of year in the highlands is from June to September, but precipitation variation from season to season is not extreme. Variation in rainfall in the **Amazon Basin** and **Oriente** is not extreme either; it rains year-round, especially heavily from June to August. As long as you bring adequate rain gear, a shower or two won't ruin your trip—rain makes jungle tours more authentic. Year-round temperature and humidity approximates that of the coast during the wet season.

In short, there is no perfect time to visit. Unlike the coast, seasonal variation is less marked in the highlands and the jungle. Keep local festivals and holidays in mind when planning your trip. The most important nationwide holidays are Christmas, *Semana Santa* (Easter week), and Independence Day. (May 24 in Ecuador and July 28-29 in Perú.) For info on other festivals and holidays see the **Appendix.**

CLIMATE

To convert from °C to °F, multiply by 1.8 and add 32. For a rough approximation, double the Celsius and add 25. To convert from °F to °C, subtract 32 and multiply by 0.55. For a rough approximation, subtract 25 and cut it in half.

°CELSIUS	-5	0	5	10	15	20	25	30	35	40
°FAHRENHEIT	23	32	41	50	59	68	77	86	95	104

AVERAGE TEMPERATURE (LO/HI) AND PRECIPITATION

	January			April			July			October		
	°C	°F	mm	°C	°F	mm	°C	°F	mm	°C	°F	mm
Galápagos	22/30	72/86	20	24/31	75/88	18	21/27	70/81	0	19/27	66/81	0
Guayaquil	21/31	70/88	239	22/32	72/90	117	19/29	66/84	5	20/30	68/86	8
Quito	8/22	46/72	99	8/21	46/70	175	7/22	45/72	20	8/22	46/72	112
Lima	19/28	66/82	0	17/26	63/79	0	14/21	57/70	1	15/23	59/73	0
Cusco	7/20	45/68	163	4/22	39/72	51	-1/21	30/70	5	6/22	43/72	66

DOCUMENTS AND FORMALITIES

ENTRANCE REQUIREMENTS FOR PERÚ AND ECUADOR.
Passport (p. 8). Required for all visitors.
Visa (p. 9). Required for stays of over 90 days.
Inoculations: (p. 18).
Work Permit (p. 9). Required for those planning to work in Perú and Ecuador.
Driving Permit (p. 33). Required for all those planning to drive.

PERUVIAN AND ECUADORIAN EMBASSIES AND CONSULATES

For most questions about documentation, contact the nearest Ecuadorian or Peruvian consulate before you depart. Embassies can provide you with the address and phone number of the consulate nearest you.

PERÚ

Australia: Embassy of Perú, 43 Culogoa Cct., O'Malley, Canberra ACT 2606 (tel. (02) 6290 0922; fax 6290 0924).

Canada: Embassy of Perú, 130 Albert St. #1901, Ottawa, ON K1P 5G4 (tel. (613) 238 1777; fax 232 3062).

United Kingdom: Embassy of Perú, 52 Sloane St., London SW1X 9SP, United Kingdom (tel. (0171) 235 1971; fax 235 4463).

United States: Consulate General of Perú, 1625 Massachusetts Ave. NW. Washington, D.C. 20036 (tel. (202) 462 1084; fax 659 9124).

ECUADOR

Australia: Consulate of Ecuador, Suite 1702-A, American Express Tower, 388 George St., Sydney NSW 2000 (tel. (06) 273 4437; fax 273 4279).

Canada: Embassy of Ecuador, 50 O'Connor St. #131, Ottawa, ON K1P 6L2 (tel. (613) 563 8206; fax 235 5776).

United Kingdom: Embassy of Ecuador, Flat 3B, Hans Crescent, London SW1X 0OI, United Kingdom (tel. (0171) 584 1267; fax 823 9701).

United States: Embassy of Ecuador, 2535 15th St. N. W., Washington, D.C. 20009 (tel. (202) 234 7200; fax 667 3482; www.ecuador.org).

EMBASSIES AND CONSULATES IN ECUADOR

Canada: 6 de Diciembre 2816 and Paul Rivet, 4th floor, Quito (tel. (02) 232 114; fax 503 108). Open M-F 9am-noon.

Ireland: Antonio de Ulloa 2651 and Rumipamba, Quito (tel. (02) 451 577; fax 269 862). Open M-F 9am-1pm.

United Kingdom: Gonzales Suárez 111 and 12 de Octubre, Quito (tel. (02) 560 670; fax 560 730; after-hours emergencies tel. (09) 723 021). Open M-F 8:30am-12:30pm and 2-5pm.

United States: Patria 120 and 12 de Octubre, Quito (tel. (02) 562 890; fax 502 052; 24hr. emergency tel. 561 749). Open M-F 8am-12:30pm and 1:30-5pm.

EMBASSIES AND CONSULATES IN PERÚ

Canada: Libertad 130, Miraflores, Lima 18 (tel. (01) 444 40 15; fax 444 4347).

United Kingdom: Natalio Sánchez 125, Plaza Washington, Lima (tel. (01) 433 47 38; 433 47 35).

United States: Ave. La Ecalada, cdra. 17 s/n, Surco Lima 33 (tel. (01) 434 3000; fax 434 3037).

PASSPORTS

All visitors need valid passports to enter Perú and Ecuador and to re-enter their own country. Perú and Ecuador do not allow entrance if the holder's passport expires in under six months; returning home with an expired passport is illegal, and may result in a fine.

PHOTOCOPIES. It's important to photocopy the page of your passport that contains your photograph, passport number, and other identifying information, along with other important documents such as visas, travel insurance policies, airplane tickets, and traveler's check serial numbers, in case you lose anything. Carry one set of copies in a safe place apart from the originals and leave another set at home. Consulates also recommend that you carry an expired passport or an official copy of your birth certificate in a part of your baggage separate from other documents.

LOST PASSPORTS. If you lose your passport, immediately notify the local police and the embassy or consulate of your home government. To expedite its replacement, you will need to know all information previously recorded and show identification and proof of citizenship. In some cases, a replacement may take weeks to process, and it may be valid only for a limited time. Any visas stamped in your old passport will be irretrievably lost. In an emergency, ask for temporary traveling papers that will permit you to re-enter your home country. Your passport is a public document belonging to your nation's government. You may have to surrender it to a foreign government official, but if you don't get it back within a reasonable amount of time, inform the nearest embassy or consulate of your home country.

NEW PASSPORTS. All applications for new passports or renewals should be filed in advance of your departure date—remember that you are relying on government agencies to complete these transactions. Most passport offices do offer emergency passport services for an extra charge. Citizens residing abroad who need a passport or renewal should contact their nearest embassy or consulate.

Australia: Citizens must apply for a passport in person at a post office, a passport office, or an Australian diplomatic mission overseas. Passport offices are located in every capital city. New adult passports cost AUS$126 (for a 32-page passport) or AUS$188 (64-page), and a child's is AUS$63 or AUS$94. Adult's passports are valid for 10 years and children's for 5 years. For more info, call 13 12 32, or visit www.dfat.gov.au/passports.

Canada: Application forms are available at all passport offices, Canadian missions, and many travel agencies. Passports cost CDN$60, plus a CDN$25 consular fee, are valid for 5 years, and are not renewable. For additional info, contact the Canadian Passport Office, Department of Foreign Affairs and International Trade, Ottawa, ON K1A OG3 (tel. (613) 994-3500; www.dfait-maeci.gc.ca/passport); or call 800-567-6868; in Toronto, (416) 973-3251; in Vancouver, (604) 586-2500; in Montreal, (514) 283-2152.

Ireland: Citizens can apply by mail to either the Department of Foreign Affairs, Passport Office, Setanta Centre, Molesworth St., Dublin 2 (tel. (01) 671 16 33; fax 671 10 92; www.irlgov.ie/iveagh), or the Passport Office, Irish Life Building, 1A South Mall, Cork (tel. (021) 27 25 25). Obtain an application at a local Garda station or post office, or request one from a passport office. Passports cost IR£45 and are valid for 10 years. Citizens under 18 or over 65 can request a 3-year passport that costs IR£10.

New Zealand: Application forms for passports are available from most travel agents. Applications may be forwarded to the Passport Office, P.O. Box 10526, Wellington (tel. 0800 22 50 50; www.govt.nz/agency_info/forms.shtml). Standard processing time is 10 working days. The fees are adult NZ$80, and child NZ$40. Children's names can no longer be endorsed on a parent's passport–they must apply for their own, which are valid for up to 5 years. An adult's passport is valid for up to 10 years.

South Africa: South African passports are issued only in Pretoria. However, all applications may still be submitted or forwarded to the applicable office of a South African consulate. Tourist passports, valid for 10 years, cost SAR80. Passports for children under 16, valid for 5 years, cost SAR60. Time for the completion of an application is normally 3 months or more. For further information, contact the nearest Department of Home Affairs Office (www.southafrica-newyork.net/passport.htm).

United Kingdom: Passports are valid for 10 years. Application forms are available at passport offices, main post offices, and many travel agents. Apply by mail or in person to one of the passport offices, located in London, Liverpool, Newport, Peterborough, Glasgow, or Belfast. The fee is UK£31, UK£11 for children under 16. The process takes about 4 weeks, but the London office offers a 5-day, walk-in rush service; arrive early. The U.K. Passport Agency can be reached by phone at (0870) 521 04 10, and more information is available at www.open.gov.uk/ukpass/ukpass.htm.

United States: Citizens may apply for a passport at any federal or state courthouse or post office authorized to accept passport applications, or at a US Passport Agency, located in most major cities. Refer to the "US Government, State Department" section of the telephone directory or the local post office for addresses. Passports are valid for 10 years (5 years if under 18) and cost US$60 (under 18 US$40). Passports may be renewed by mail or in person for US$40. Processing takes 3-4 weeks. Rush service is also available for an extra fee. For more info, contact the US Passport Information's 24-hour recorded message (tel. (202) 647-0518) or look on the web at http://travel.state.gov/passport_services.html.

VISAS AND WORK PERMITS

VISAS. Visas are not required for tourists staying less than 90 days. For information about visas for stays longer than 90 days, consult your nearest consulate. US citizens can take advantage of the **Center for International Business and Travel** (CIBT) (tel. 800-925-2428), which will secure visas for travel to almost all countries for a variable service charge.

WORK PERMITS. Admission as a visitor does not include the right to work, which is authorized only by a work permit, and entering Perú or Ecuador to study requires a special visa. For more information, see **Alternatives to Tourism.**

IDENTIFICATION

When you travel, always carry two or more forms of identification on your person, including at least one photo ID. A passport combined with a driver's license or birth certificate usually serves as adequate proof of your identity and citizenship. Many establishments, especially banks, require several IDs before cashing traveler's checks. Never carry all your forms of ID together, however; you risk being left entirely without ID or funds in case of theft or loss.

STUDENT IDENTIFICATION. Although international student discounts are not as common in Ecuador and Perú as in the US or European countries, it is still worth your while to flash your student ID whenever you get the opportunity, even if no discount is advertised. The the **International Student Identity Card (ISIC)** is the most widely accepted form of student identification. The international identification cards are preferable to institution-specific cards because the tourism personnel in Perú and Ecuador are taught to recognize ISIC. For US cardholders traveling abroad, the ISIC also provides insurance benefits, including US$100 per day of in-hospital sickness for a maximum of 60 days, and US$3,000 accident-related medical reimbursement for each accident (see **Insurance,** p. 23). In addition, cardholders have access to a toll-free 24-hour ISIC helpline with multilingual staff that can provide assistance in medical, legal, and financial emergencies overseas (tel. 800-626-2427 in the US and Canada; elsewhere call collect 44 181 666 90 25).

Many student travel agencies around the world issue ISICs, including STA Travel in Australia and New Zealand; Travel CUTS in Canada; USIT in Ireland and

Northern Ireland; SASTS in South Africa; Campus Travel and STA Travel in the U.K.; Council Travel, STA Travel, and via the web (www.counciltravel.comg/idcards/index.htm) in the US; and any other travel agency with a student focus. The card is valid from September of one year to December of the following year and costs AUS$15, CDN$15, or US$20. Applicants must be at least 12 years old and degree-seeking students of a secondary or post-secondary school. Because of the proliferation of phony ISICs, many airlines and other services require additional proof of student identity (e.g. a signed letter from the registrar attesting to your student status that is stamped with the school seal or your school ID card).

YOUTH IDENTIFICATION. The International Student Travel Confederation also issues a discount card to travelers who are 25 years old or younger, but not students. Known as the **International Youth Travel Card (IYTC)** (formerly the **GO25** Card), this one-year card offers many of the same benefits as the ISIC, and most organizations that sell the ISIC also sell the IYTC. The fee is US$20.

CUSTOMS

When entering Ecuador or Perú, customs is generally a pretty laid-back process. Officials are more likely to stop Ecuadorian and Peruvian nationals returning with loads of foreign merchandise than backpacking gringos. Nevertheless, they do sometimes search bags and you don't want to get busted: you may not enter or leave with firearms, ammunition, narcotics, fresh meat, or live plants or animals. You may bring in 300 cigarettes, 50 cigars, and a bottle of liquor tax-free. Visitors to Perú can be even more debaucherous while still being tax-free, with a limit of 400 cigarettes or 50 cigars, and three liters of booze.

Upon returning home, you must declare all articles acquired abroad and pay a **duty** on the value of articles that exceed the allowance established by your country's customs service. Goods and gifts purchased at **duty-free** shops abroad are not exempt from duty or sales tax at your point of return; you must declare these items as well. "Duty-free" means that you need not pay a tax in the country of purchase. For more specific information on customs requirements, contact the following information centers:

Australia: Australian Customs National Information Line (tel. 1 300 363); www.customs.gov.au.

Canada: Canadian Customs, 2265 St. Laurent Blvd., Ottawa, ON K1G 4K3 (tel. (613) 993-0534 or 24hr. automated service 800-461-9999; www.revcan.ca).

Ireland: The Collector of Customs and Excise, The Custom House, Dublin 1 (tel. (01) 679 27 77; fax 671 20 21; email taxes@revenue.iol.ie; www.revenue.ie/customs.htm).

New Zealand: New Zealand Customhouse, 17-21 Whitmore St., Box 2218, Wellington (tel. (04) 473 6099; fax 473 7370; www.customs.govt.nz).

South Africa: Commissioner for Customs and Excise, Private Bag X47, Pretoria 0001 (tel. (012) 314 99 11; fax 328 64 78).

United Kingdom: Her Majesty's Customs and Excise, Custom House, Nettleton Rd., Heathrow Airport, Hounslow, Middlesex TW6 2LA (tel. (0181) 910 36 02/35 66; fax 910 37 65; www.hmce.gov.uk).

United States: US Customs Service, Box 7407, Washington D.C. 20044 (tel. (202) 927-6724; www.customs.ustreas.gov).

MONEY

If you stay in hostels and prepare your own food, expect to spend anywhere from US$10-15 per person per day in Perú. **Accommodations** start at about US$6 per night for a single, while a basic sit-down meal costs US$3. Ecuador is slightly less expensive: expect to spend from US$8-12 per person per day. Accommodations in Ecuador start at about US$4 per night for a single, and a basic sit-down meal goes for around US$2. Carrying cash with you, even in a money belt, is risky but necessary; personal checks from home are usually not accepted, but most large banks do accept traveler's checks.

CURRENCY AND EXCHANGE

All prices in this book are listed in local currency, except where payment is expected in US dollars. Prices were accurate in the summer of 1999, but due to high inflation rates and frequent devaluation (as with the *sucre* in Ecuador), they may have changed since and should thus be used for comparative purposes only. A useful currency converter web site is www.oanda.com/cgi-bin/ncc.

The currency chart below is based on published exchange rates from August 1999.

THE PERUVIAN NUEVO SOL	
US$1 = 3.40 SOLES	1 SOL = US$0.29
CDN$1 = 2.28 SOLES	1 SOL = CDN$0.44
UK£1 = 5.45 SOLES	1 SOL = UK£0.18
IR£1 = 4.58 SOLES	1 SOL = IR£0.22
AUS$1 = 2.19 SOLES	1 SOL = AUS$0.46
NZ$1 = 1.76 SOLES	1 SOL = NZ$0.57
SAR1 = 0.56 SOLES	1 SOL = SAR1.77

THE ECUADORIAN SUCRE	
US$1 = 11,160 SUCRES	10,000 SUCRE = US$0.90
CDN$1 = 7,495 SUCRES	10,000 SUCRE = CDN$1.33
UK£1 = 17,895 SUCRES	10,000 SUCRE = UK£0.56
IR£1 = 15,042 SUCRES	10,000 SUCRE = IR£0.67
AUS$1 = 7,204 SUCRES	10,000 SUCRE = AUS$1.39
NZ$1 = 5,795 SUCRES	10,000 SUCRE = NZ$1.74
SAR1 = 1,843 SUCRES	10,000 SUCRE = SAR5.42

In Ecuador and Perú, as in many Latin American countries, US currency is widely accepted and, in many cases, is even preferred over the local currency. Other foreign currency is difficult or impossible to change. Even dollars with rips or stains may not be accepted. Upon arrival it is a good idea to have mostly US dollars and then convert them gradually. Despite the versatility of US dollars, consider avoiding using them. First, there is a potential risk of being overcharged if you don't pay in the *sucres* or *soles*. Second, throwing dollars around to gain better treatment is offensive and can attract theft.

As a general rule, it's cheaper to convert money in Perú and Ecuador. It's good to bring enough foreign currency to last for the first several days of a trip to avoid being penniless after banking hours or on a holiday. Travelers living in the US can get foreign currency from the comfort of their home; **Capital Foreign Exchange** (tel. 888-842-0880) or **International Currency Express** (tel. 888-278-6628) will deliver foreign currency (for over 120 countries) or traveler's checks overnight (US$15) or second-day (US$12) at competitive exchange rates.

Watch out for commission rates and check newspapers for the standard rate of exchange. Banks generally have the best rates. A good rule of thumb is only to go to banks or *casas de cambio* that have a 5% margin or less between their buy and sell prices. Also, using an ATM card or a credit card (see p. 13) will often get you the best possible rates.

If you use traveler's checks or bills, carry some in small denominations (US$50 or less), especially for times when you are forced to exchange money at disadvantageous rates. However, it is good to carry a range of denominations since charges may be levied per check cashed.

TRAVELER'S CHECKS

Traveler's checks are one of the safest and least troublesome means of carrying funds, since they can be refunded if stolen. Several agencies and banks sell them, usually for face value plus a small percentage commission. (Members of the American Automobile Association, and some banks and credit unions, can get American Express checks commission-free.) **American Express** and **Visa** are the most widely recognized. If you're ordering checks, do so well in advance, especially if you are requesting large sums. Each agency provides refunds if your checks are lost or stolen, and many provide additional services, such as toll-free refund hotlines in the countries you're visiting, emergency message services, and stolen credit card assistance. In order to collect a **refund for lost or stolen checks,** keep your check receipts separate from your checks and store them in a safe place or with a traveling companion. Record check numbers when you cash them, leave a list of check numbers with someone at home, and ask for a list of refund centers when you buy your checks. Never countersign your checks until you are ready to cash them, and always bring your passport with you when you plan to use the checks.

American Express: In Australia call 1800 251 902; in New Zealand 0800 441 068; in the U.K. (0800) 52 13 13; in the US and Canada 800-221-7282. Elsewhere, call US collect 1-801-964-6665; www.aexp.com. Checks can be purchased for a small fee (1-4%) at American Express Travel Service Offices, banks, and American Automobile Association offices. AAA members (see p. 33) can buy the checks commission-free. American Express offices cash their checks commission-free (except where prohibited by national governments), but often at slightly worse rates than banks.

Visa: Call 800-227-6811 in the US; in the U.K. (0800) 895 078; from elsewhere, call reverse charges to the U.K. 44 1733 318 949. Call to find their nearest office.

CREDIT CARDS

Credit cards are generally accepted in all but the smallest businesses and very rural areas. Major credit cards—**MasterCard** and **Visa** are welcomed most often—can be used to extract cash advances in *soles* and *sucres* from associated banks and teller machines throughout Perú and Ecuador. Credit card companies get the wholesale exchange rate, which is generally 5% better than the retail rate used by banks and other currency exchange establishments. **American Express** cards also work in some ATMs, as well as at AmEx offices and major airports. You must ask your credit card company for a **Personal Identification Number (PIN)** before you leave; without it, you will be unable to withdraw cash with your credit card outside your home country. If you already have a PIN, check with the company to make sure it will work in Perú and Ecuador. Credit cards often offer an array of other services, from insurance to emergency assistance. Check with your company to find out what is covered.

Visa (U.S. tel. 800-336-8472) and **MasterCard** (U.S. tel. 800-307-7309) are issued in cooperation with individual banks and some other organizations. **American Express** (U.S. tel. 800-843-2273) has an annual fee of up to US$55, depending on the card. AmEx also offers student cards that don't have a fee, but charge interest on the balance. Cardholder services include the option of cashing personal checks at AmEx offices, a 24-hour hotline with medical and legal assistance in emergencies (tel. 800-554-2639 in US and Canada; from abroad call US collect 1-202-554-2639), and the American Express Travel Service. Benefits include assistance in changing airline and car rental reservations, baggage loss and flight insurance, sending mailgrams and international cables, and holding your mail at one of the more than 1700 AmEx offices around the world.

CASH CARDS

ATMs (Automated Teller Machine)—known as *cajeros automáticos*—are common in the urban areas of Perú and Ecuador. Depending on the system that your home bank uses, you may be able to access your own personal bank account whenever you need money with your regular ATM card (also called cash cards). Happily, ATMs get the same wholesale exchange rate as credit cards. Despite these perks, do some research before relying too heavily on automation. There is often a limit on the amount of money you can withdraw per day (usually about US$500, depending on the type of card and account), and computer networks sometimes fail. Be sure to memorize your PIN code in numeral form since machines elsewhere often don't have letters on their keys. Also, if your PIN is longer than four digits, ask your bank whether the first four digits will work, or whether you need a new number. The two major international money networks present in Perú and Ecuador are **Cirrus** (US tel. 800-4-CIRRUS (424-7787)) and **PLUS** (US tel. 800-843-7587 for the "Voice Response Unit Locator"). To locate ATMs around the world, use www.visa.com/pd/atm or www.mastercard.com/atm.

GETTING MONEY FROM HOME

American Express: Cardholders can withdraw cash from their checking accounts at any of AmEx's major offices and many of its representatives' offices–up to US$1000 every 21 days (no service charge, no interest). AmEx also offers Express Cash at any of their ATMs in Perú and Ecuador. Express Cash withdrawals are automatically debited from the Cardmember's checking account or line of credit. Green card holders may withdraw up to US$1000 in a 7-day period. There is a 2% transaction fee for each cash withdrawal, with a US$2.50 minimum/$20 maximum. To enroll in Express Cash, Cardmembers may call 800-227-4669 in the US; outside the US call collect 1-336-668-5041.

Western Union: Travelers from the US, Canada, and the U.K. can wire money abroad through Western Union's international money transfer services. In the US, call 800-325-6000; in the U.K., call (0800) 833 833; in Canada, call 800-235-0000. The rates for sending cash are generally US$10-11 cheaper than with a credit card, and the money is usually available at the place you're sending it to within an hour. There are numerous Western Union agents located throughout Perú and Ecuador. In Perú, call (01) 421 9089 or (01) 422 0014; in Ecuador, call (02) 565 059 or (04) 287 044 for agent locations and services.

US State Department (US Citizens only): In emergencies, US citizens can have money sent via the State Department. For US$15, they will forward money within hours to the nearest consular office, which will disburse it according to instructions. The office serves only Americans in the direst of straits abroad; non-American travelers should contact their embassies for information on wiring cash. Check with the State Department or the nearest US embassy or consulate for the quickest way to have the money sent. Contact the Overseas Citizens Service, American Citizens Services, Consular Affairs, Room 4811, US Department of State, Washington, D.C. 20520 (tel. (202) 647-5225; nights, Sundays, and holidays 647-4000; fax (on demand only) 647-3000; travel.state.gov).

TIPPING, BARGAINING, AND TAXES

Relatively affluent foreigners are generally expected to **tip.** At fancier restaurants a 10% tip is included on the bill. When it is not included, consider leaving that much anyway. Tips may also be expected for other services, such as guided tours or maid service; in many cases, these people count on a small bonus.

In some places it's okay to **bargain,** and a little practice at playing "the game" can make it worth the effort. Bargaining for rooms works best in the low season, and it's not hard to get prices lowered at markets or from street vendors. It is also acceptable to bargain with taxi drivers, though an excessively low first bid may send the *taxista* on his way without you. The basic technique is to expect the first offered price to be higher than what the seller actually wants; pick a lower price, and marvel at the magic of compromise. However, it is vulgar for travelers to bargain down to a price that is clearly unreasonable. In countries where the cost of living is already dirt cheap, the s/1000 (measly pennies) discount received by a foreigner might have meant a great deal more in the pocket of a local vendor.

Upscale restaurants, hotels, and shops charge a **10% sales tax (IVA),** which you should expect to appear on the bill. The real whammy, though, hits the traveler on the way out—there is a US$25 **airport/departure tax** in Ecuador, and US$10 from regional airports in Perú, and US$25 from Lima.

SAFETY AND SECURITY

PERSONAL SAFETY

BLENDING IN. Tourists are particularly vulnerable to crime because they often carry large amounts of cash and are not as street-savvy as locals. To avoid unwanted attention, try to blend in as much as possible. Respecting local customs (e.g., in many cases, dressing more conservatively) may placate would-be hecklers. The gawking camera-toter is a more obvious target than the low-profile traveler. Familiarize yourself with your surroundings before setting out; if you must check a map on the street, duck into a cafe or shop. Carry yourself with confidence, your visible attitude can be very protective. If you are traveling alone, be sure that someone at home knows your itinerary and **never admit that you're traveling alone.**

TERRORISM. The **Sendero Luminoso** and the **Tupac Amaru Revolutionary Movement,** the two major terrorist organizations active in Perú, are a less potent force now than they have been in previous years, and terrorist attacks have not occurred in traditional tourist destinations for a number of years. But the Department of State warns that these organizations are still capable of terrorist actions. The Sendero Luminoso continues to operate in rural provinces of the Junin, Huanuco, San Martín, and Ayacucho of Perú. Adventure travelers are encouraged to contact the US Embassy in Lima for current security information.

GETTING AROUND. Traveling within Perú and Ecuador can be extremely dangerous. Roads are often in very poor condition, especially since the El Niño weather phenomenon, and potholes, sharp curves, lane ends, and construction sites are often unmarked. Travel only by day if possible, and use bus companies that take special precautions, such as frequent driver-changing, to ensure your safety. The extra money you pay to travel with the slightly better bus lines could be the most important investment you make. Drivers should not travel alone in rural areas, even during the day; sticking with convoy travel is the safest way to go. If you do choose to rent a **car,** learn local driving signals and wear a seatbelt. If you plan on spending a lot of time on the road, you may want to bring spare parts, carry a cellular phone, and invest in a roadside assistance program (see p. 33). Be sure to park your vehicle in a garage or well-traveled area, and use a steering wheel locking device in larger cities. **Sleeping in your car** is one of the most dangerous (and often illegal) ways to get your rest. If your car breaks down, wait for the police to assist you. *Let's Go* does not recommend **hitchhiking** under any circumstances, particularly for women—see **Getting Around,** p. 31 for more information.

SELF DEFENSE. There are no precautions that will protect you from every situation you might encounter when you travel. A good self-defense course will give you more concrete ways to react to different types of aggression. **Impact, Prepare, and Model Mugging** can refer you to local self-defense courses in the United States (tel. 800-345-5425) and Canada (tel. (604) 878-3838). Workshops (2-3hr.) start at US$50 and full courses run US$350-500. Both women and men are welcome.

FURTHER INFORMATION. The following government offices provide travel information and advisories by telephone or on their web sites:

Australian Department of Foreign Affairs and Trade. Tel. (02) 6261 1111; www.dfat.gov.au.

Canadian Department of Foreign Affairs and International Trade (DFAIT). Tel. 800-267-8376 or (613) 944-4000 from Ottawa; www.dfait-maeci.gc.ca.

United Kingdom Foreign and Commonwealth Office. Tel. (0171) 238 4503; www.fco.gov.uk.

United States Department of State. Tel. (202) 647-5225; http://travel.state.gov. For their publication *A Safe Trip Abroad,* call (202) 512-1800.

FINANCIAL SECURITY

Visitors to Andean countries often return with magical tales of unexpected theft: handbags carefully slit and emptied of valuables, hats deftly snatched from the tops of heads, cameras that vanished into thin air. Quito and Guayaquil in Ecuador, and Lima and Cusco in Perú have the worst reputations. While careful attention may save the tourist from most sets of sticky fingers, it may be reasonable to **expect to be robbed.** When packing, weigh the necessity of each object against the anguish you'll experience should it be taken. While most victims of robbery are not physically harmed, almost everybody sustains wounded pride. Having reasonable expectations may speed recovery time.

PROTECTING YOUR VALUABLES. Theft is a danger throughout Perú and Ecuador, but its prevalence varies greatly with location. Crime is especially prevalent in crowded urban areas as well as deserted streets of rural towns. You're often safest where there are people around but you're not trapped in a crowd. To prevent easy theft, don't keep all your valuables (money, important documents) in one place. Label every piece of luggage both inside and out. **Don't put a wallet with money in your back pocket.** Never count your money in public and carry as little as possible. If you carry a purse, buy a sturdy one with a secure clasp, and carry it crosswise on the side, away from the street with the clasp against you. Secure packs with small combination padlocks which slip through the two zippers. A **money belt** is the best way to carry cash; you can buy one at most camping supply stores. A nylon, zippered pouch with a belt that sits inside the waist of your pants or skirt combines convenience and security. A **neck pouch** is equally safe, although far less accessible. Refrain from pulling out your neck pouch in public. Avoid keeping anything in a fanny-pack: your valuables will be easy to steal. Keep some money separate from the rest to use in an emergency or in case of theft.

CON ARTISTS AND PICKPOCKETS. Among the more colorful aspects of large cities are **con artists.** Con artists and hustlers often work in groups, and children are among the most effective. They possess an innumerable range of ruses. Be aware of certain classics: sob stories that require money, rolls of bills "found" on the street, mustard spilled (or saliva spit) onto your shoulder distracting you for enough time to snatch your bag. Be especially suspicious in unexpected situations. Do not respond or make eye contact, walk away, and keep a solid grip on your belongings. Contact the police if a hustler is particularly insistent or aggressive.

In city crowds and especially on public transportation, **pickpockets** are amazingly deft at their craft. If someone stands uncomfortably close, move to another car and hold your bags tightly. Also, be alert in public telephone booths. If you must say your calling card number, do so very quietly; if you punch it in, make sure no one can look over your shoulder.

ACCOMMODATIONS AND TRANSPORTATION. Never leave your belongings unattended; crime occurs in even the most demure-looking hostel or hotel. If you feel unsafe, look for places with either a curfew or a night attendant. *Let's Go* lists locker availability, but you'll need your own **padlock.** Lockers are useful if you plan on sleeping outdoors or don't want to lug everything with you, but don't store valuables in them. Be particularly careful on **buses,** carry your backpack in front of you where you can see it, don't check baggage on trains, and don't trust anyone to "watch your bag for a second." Thieves thrive on **trains;** professionals wait for tourists to fall asleep and then carry off everything they can. When traveling in pairs, sleep in alternating shifts; when alone, use good judgement in selecting a train compartment: never stay in an empty one, and use a lock to secure your pack to the luggage rack.

DRUGS AND ALCOHOL

A meek "I didn't know it was illegal" will not suffice. Remember that you are subject to the laws of Perú or Ecuador, not to those of your home country, and it is your responsibility to familiarize yourself with these laws before leaving. Those caught in possession of drugs in Perú or Ecuador can expect **extended pre-trial detention** in poor prison conditions and a **lengthy prison sentence** if convicted. If you carry **prescription drugs** while you travel, it is vital to have the prescriptions themselves and a note from a doctor, both readily accessible at country borders. Also beware that some prescription drugs and traditional herbal remedies readily available in Perú and Ecuador may be illegal in your home country. Coca-leaf tea, for example, though easy to acquire in Perú, is highly illegal in many nations.

Drinking in Latin America is not for amateurs; non-gringo bars are often strongholds of *machismo.* When someone calls you *amigo* and orders you a beer, bow out quickly unless you want to match him glass for glass in a challenge. **Avoid public drunkenness;** it can jeopardize your safety and earn the disdain of locals.

HEALTH

Common sense is the simplest prescription for good health while you travel. Travelers complain most often about their feet and their gut, so take precautionary measures: drink lots of fluids to prevent dehydration and constipation, wear sturdy, broken-in shoes and clean socks, and use talcum powder to keep your feet dry. To minimize the effects of jet lag, "reset" your body's clock by adopting the time of your destination as soon as you board the plane.

BEFORE YOU GO

Preparation can help minimize the likelihood of contracting a disease and maximize the chances of receiving effective health care in the event of an emergency. For minor health problems, bring a compact **first-aid kit,** including bandages, aspirin or other pain killer, antibiotic cream, a thermometer, a Swiss army knife with tweezers, moleskin, decongestant for colds, motion sickness remedy, medicine for diarrhea or stomach problems (Pepto-Bismol tablets or liquid and Immodium), sunscreen, insect repellent, burn ointment, and a syringe for emergency medical purposes (get a letter of explanation from your doctor). **Contact lens** wearers should bring an extra pair, a copy of the prescription, a pair of glasses, extra solution, and eyedrops. Those who use heat disinfection might consider switching to chemical cleansers for the duration of the trip.

In your **passport,** write the names of any people you wish to be contacted in case of a medical emergency, and also list any **allergies** or medical conditions you have. Allergy sufferers might want to obtain a full supply of any necessary medication before the trip. Matching a prescription to a foreign equivalent is not always easy, safe, or possible. Carry up-to-date, legible prescriptions or a statement from your doctor stating the medication's trade name, manufacturer, chemical name, and dosage. While traveling, be sure to keep all medication in your carry-on luggage.

IMMUNIZATIONS. Take a look at your immunization records before you go. Travelers over two years old should be sure that the following vaccines are up to date: MMR (for measles, mumps, and rubella); DTaP or Td (for diptheria, tetanus, and pertussis); OPV (for polio); HbCV (for haemophilus influenza B); and HBV (for hepatitus B). Adults should consider an additional dose of Polio vaccine if they have not already had one during their adult years.

INOCULATIONS. The Centers for Disease Control (CDC) maintains a very comprehensive and detailed database of information for people traveling abroad. As of August 1999 they recommend protection against the following diseases:

Hepatitis A: ask your doctor about Harvix or an injection of **Immune Globulin.**

Hepatitis B: if you might be exposed to blood, have sexual contact on the road, stay more than 6 months in the region, or be exposed through medical treatment. The vaccine is also now recommended for all infants and children ages 11-12 who did not complete the series as infants.

Malaria: travelers to the coast, jungle, or rural areas, may want to take weekly **anti-malarial** drugs.

Rabies: if you might be exposed to animals through your work or recreation.

Typhoid: particularly if you are visiting rural areas in this region.

Yellow fever vaccination: if you will be traveling outside urban areas.

Tetanus-diptheria and **measles:** booster doses as needed.

USEFUL ORGANIZATIONS. The US **Centers for Disease Control and Prevention** (CDC; tel. 888-232-3299; www.cdc.gov) is an excellent source of information for travelers around the world and maintains an international fax information service for travelers. The CDC also publishes the booklet "Health Information for International Travelers" (US$20), an annual global rundown of disease, immunization, and general health advice, including risks in particular countries. This book may be purchased by sending a check or money order to the Superintendent of Documents, US Government Printing Office, P.O. Box 371954, Pittsburgh, PA, 15250-7954. Orders can be made by phone (tel. (202) 512-1800) with a major credit card (Visa, MasterCard, or Discover). The **United States State Department** (http://travel.state.gov) compiles Consular Information Sheets on health, entry requirements, and other issues for all countries of the world. For quick information on travel warnings, call the **Overseas Citizens' Services** (tel. (202) 647-5225; after hours tel. 647-4000). To receive the same Consular Information Sheets by fax, dial (202) 647-3000 directly from a fax machine and follow the recorded instructions. The State Department's regional passport agencies, field offices of the US Chamber of Commerce, and embassies and consulates abroad provide the same data, or send a self-addressed, stamped envelope to the Overseas Citizens' Services, Bureau of Consular Affairs, #4811, Department of State, Washington, D.C. 20520.

MEDICAL ASSISTANCE ON THE ROAD. The quality of medical care in Perú and Ecuador varies enormously. The best hospitals in major urban centers such as Lima, Quito, and Guayaquil offer well-trained doctors, some of whom know English, and have much better resources than their small-town counterparts. Even here, however, the quality of the care will likely not be on a par with the care you have become accustomed to at home. The caliber of the medical care in smaller towns is often significantly lower, and an English-speaking doctor is by no means guaranteed. Doctors in smaller towns are sometimes not as well trained and often lack the resources to provide quality health care. In both major cities and smaller towns the best health care locally available is generally provided by private **clínicas** (clinics). Public hospitals are often less expensive but less reliable. Many hospitals and clinics will not accept your insurance from home and will demand cash or, in urban centers, credit cards.

If you are concerned about being able to access medical support while traveling, contact one of these two services: **Global Emergency Medical Services (GEMS)** has products called *MedPass* that provide 24-hour international medical assistance and support coordinated through registered nurses who have online access to your medical information, your primary physician, and a worldwide network of screened, credential-holding English-speaking doctors and hospitals. Subscribers also receive a personal medical record that contains vital information in case of emergencies, and GEMS will pay for medical evacuation if necessary. Prices start at about US$35 for a 30-day trip and run up to about $100 for annual services. For more information contact them at 2001 Westside Dr. #120, Alpharetta, GA 30004 (tel. 800-860-1111; fax (770) 475-0058; www.globalems.com). The **International Association for Medical Assistance to Travelers (IAMAT)** has free membership and offers a directory of English-speaking doctors around the world who treat members for a set fee schedule and detailed charts on immunization requirements, various tropical diseases, climate, and sanitation. Chapters include: **US,** 417 Center St., Lewiston, NY 14092 (tel. (716) 754-4883, 8am-4pm; fax (519) 836-3412; email iamat@sentex.net; www.sentex.net/~iamat); **Canada,** 40 Regal Rd., Guelph, ON, N1K 1B5 (tel. (519) 836-0102) or 1287 St. Clair Ave. West, Toronto, ON M6E 1B8 (tel. (416) 652-0137; fax (519) 836-3412); **New Zealand,** P.O. Box 5049, Christchurch 5 (fax (03) 352 4630; email iamat@chch.planet.org.nz).

If your regular **insurance** policy does not cover travel abroad, you may wish to purchase additional coverage. With the exception of Medicare, most American health insurance plans cover members' medical emergencies during trips abroad; check with your insurance carrier. For more information, see **Insurance,** p. 23.

MEDICAL CONDITIONS. Those with medical conditions (e.g., diabetes, allergies to antibiotics, epilepsy, heart conditions) may want to obtain a stainless steel **Medic Alert** identification tag (US$35 the first year, and $15 annually thereafter), which identifies the condition and gives a 24-hour collect-call information number. Contact the Medic Alert Foundation, 2323 Colorado Ave., Turlock, CA 95382 (tel. 800-825-3785; www.medicalert.org). Diabetics can contact the **American Diabetes Association,** 1660 Duke St., Alexandria, VA 22314 (tel. 800-232-3472), to receive copies of the article "Travel and Diabetes" and a diabetic ID card, which carries messages in 18 languages explaining the carrier's diabetic status.

FURTHER READING. For detailed information and tips on travel health, including a country-by-country overview of diseases, check out the *International Travel Health Guide*, by Stuart Rose, MD (Travel Medicine, $20). Information is also available at Travel Medicine's web site (www.travmed.com). For general health information, contact the **American Red Cross.** The ARC publishes *First-Aid and Safety Handbook* (US$5) available by calling or writing to the American Red Cross, 285 Columbus Ave., Boston, MA 02116-5114 (tel. 800-564-1234).

ENVIRONMENTAL HAZARDS

Heat exhaustion and dehydration: Heat exhaustion, characterized by dehydration and salt deficiency, can lead to fatigue, headaches, and wooziness. Avoid heat exhaustion by drinking plenty of clear fluids and eating salty foods, like crackers. Always drink enough liquids to keep your urine clear. Alcoholic beverages are dehydrating, as are coffee, strong tea, and caffeinated sodas. Wear a hat, sunglasses, and a lightweight longsleeve shirt in hot sun, and take time to acclimate to a hot destination before seriously exerting yourself. Continuous heat stress can eventually lead to **heatstroke,** characterized by rising body temperature, severe headache, and cessation of sweating. Heatstroke is rare but serious, and victims must be cooled off with wet towels and taken to a doctor as soon as possible.

Sunburn: If you're prone to sunburn, bring sunscreen with you, and apply it liberally and often to avoid burns and risk of skin cancer. If you get sunburned, drink more fluids than usual and apply Calamine or an aloe-based lotion.

Hypothermia and frostbite: A rapid drop in body temperature is the clearest sign of overexposure to cold. Victims may also shiver, feel exhausted, have poor coordination or slurred speech, hallucinate, or suffer amnesia. Seek medical help, and **do not let hypothermia victims fall asleep**–their body temperature will continue to drop and they may die. To avoid hypothermia, keep dry, wear layers, and stay out of the wind. In wet weather, wool and synthetics retain heat. Most other fabrics, especially cotton, make you colder. When the temperature is below freezing, watch for **frostbite.** If a region of skin turns white, waxy, and cold, don't rub it. Drink warm beverages, get dry, and slowly warm the area with dry fabric or steady body contact, until a doctor can be found.

High altitude: The extreme variation in altitude in Ecuador and Perú means that **altitude sickness** is a risk. Travelers to high altitudes must allow their bodies a couple of days to adjust to lower oxygen levels in the air before exerting themselves. Ignoring this advice can result in symptoms such as headaches, nausea, sleeplessness, and shortness of breath, even while resting. It is best treated with rest, deep breathing, and moving to a lower altitude. If the symptoms persist or worsen, or if the victim begins to turn blue, **immediately descend to a lower altitude** and proceed to a hospital if necessary. Those planning to climb some of the region's taller peaks should take a week in the Sierra to adjust to the altitude before attempting the climb.

PREVENTING DISEASE

INSECT-BORNE DISEASES

Many diseases are transmitted by insects—mainly mosquitoes, fleas, ticks, and lice. Be aware of insects in wet or forested areas, while hiking, and especially while camping. **Mosquitoes** are most active from dusk to dawn. Use insect repellents, such as DEET. Wear long pants and long sleeves (fabric need not be thick or warm; tropic-weight cottons can keep you comfortable in the heat) and buy a mosquito net. Wear shoes and socks, and tuck long pants into socks. Soak or spray your gear with permethrin, which is licensed in the US for use on clothing. Natural repellents can be useful supplements: taking vitamin B-12 pills regularly can eventually make you smelly to insects, as can garlic pills. Calamine lotion or topical cortisones (like Cortaid) may stop insect bites from itching, as can a bath with a half-cup of baking soda or oatmeal.

Malaria is transmitted by *Anopheles* mosquitoes that bite at night. Incubation period varies; it could take months for an infected person to show symptoms. Early symptoms include fever, chills, aches, and fatigue, followed by high fever and sweating, sometimes with vomiting and diarrhea. See a doctor for any flu-like sickness that occurs after travel in a risk area, and get tested immediately. Left untreated, malaria can cause anemia, kidney failure, coma, and death, and is an especially serious threat to pregnant women. The least danger exists in more urbanized areas. It is advisable to use mosquito repellent in the evenings and when visiting jungle regions. There are a number of oral prophylactics to protect against the disease. Western Doctors typically prescribe **mefloquine** (sold under the name Lariam) or **doxycycline.** Both these drugs and other malaria treatments can have very serious side effects, including slowed heart rate and nightmares, which your physician can explain.

Dengue fever is an "urban viral infection" transmitted by *Aedes* mosquitoes, which bite during the day. Dengue has flu-like symptoms and is often indicated by a rash 3-4 days after the onset of fever. Symptoms for the first 2-4 days include chills, high fever, headaches, swollen lymph nodes, muscle aches, and in some instances, a pink rash on the face. Then the fever quickly disappears, and profuse sweating follows. For 24 hours there is no fever, but a rash appears all over the body. If you think you have contracted dengue fever, see a doctor, drink plenty of liquids, and take fever-reducing medication such as acetaminophen (Tylenol). Never take aspirin to treat dengue fever.

Other insect-borne diseases: Leishmaniasis is a parasite transmitted by sand flies. Common symptoms are fever, weakness, and swelling of the spleen. **CHAGAS disease**

(American trypanomiasis) is another relatively common parasite transmitted by the cone nose or kissing bug, which infests mud and thatch. Its symptoms are fever, heart disease, and later on, an enlarged intestine. Avoid staying overnight in infested buildings. There is no vaccine.

FOOD- AND WATER-BORNE DISEASES

Prevention is the best cure: be sure that everything you eat is cooked properly and that the water you drink is clean. You should never drink unbottled water which you have not treated yourself. To purify your own water, bring it to a rolling boil or treat it with **iodine tablets,** available at any camping goods store. Don't brush your teeth with tap water or rinse your toothbrush under the faucet, and keep your mouth closed in the shower. Ice cubes are just as dangerous as impure water in liquid form. Salads and uncooked vegetables (including lettuce and coleslaw) are full of untreated water. Other culprits are raw shellfish (used in *ceviche*), unpasteurized milk, and sauces containing raw eggs. Peel all fruits and vegetables yourself, and beware of watermelon, which is often injected with impure water. Watch out for food from markets or street vendors that may have been washed in dirty water or fried in rancid cooking oil, such as juices and peeled fruits. Always wash your hands before eating, or bring a quick-drying purifying liquid hand cleaner like Purrell. Your bowels will thank you.

Traveler's diarrhea results from drinking untreated water or eating uncooked foods. It is usually an indication of your body's temporary reaction to the bacteria in unfamiliar food ingredients. It can last three to seven days. If the nasties hit you, have quick-energy, non-sugary foods with protein and carbohydrates to keep your strength up. Over-the-counter remedies (such as Pepto-Bismol or Immodium) may counteract the problems, but they can complicate serious infections. Avoid anti-diarrheals if you suspect that you are risk for other diseases. The most dangerous side effect of diarrhea is dehydration; the simplest and most effective anti-dehydration formula is 8 oz. of (clean) water with a ½ tsp. of sugar or honey and a pinch of salt. Soft drinks without caffeine or salted crackers are also good. If you develop a fever or your symptoms don't go away after 4-5 days, consult a doctor. You may have dysentery (see below). If children develop traveler's diarrhea, consult a doctor, since treatment is different.

Dysentery results from a serious intestinal infection caused by certain bacteria. Symptoms include bloody diarrhea or bloody stools mixed with mucus, fever, and abdominal pain and tenderness. Bacillary dysentery generally only lasts a week, but it is highly contagious. However, it is a more serious disease, and may cause long-term damage if left untreated. A stool test can determine which kind you have, so you should seek medical help immediately. In an emergency, the drugs norfloxacin or ciprofloxacin (commonly known as Cipro) can be used. If you are traveling in high-risk regions (especially rural areas) consider obtaining a prescription before you leave home.

Cholera is an intestinal disease caused by a bacteria found in contaminated food and water. The disease has recently reached epidemic stages in South America. The first severe symptoms of cholera are lots of watery diarrhea, dehydration, vomiting, and muscle cramps. Untreated cholera can cause death very quickly. See a doctor immediately. Antibiotics are available, but the most important treatment is rehydration. Consider getting a (50% effective) vaccine if you have stomach problems (e.g. ulcers), or if you will be camping a good deal or living where water is not reliable.

Hepatitis A (distinct from B and C, see below) is a high risk in this region. Hep A is a viral infection of the liver acquired primarily through contaminated water, ice, shellfish, or unpeeled fruits, and vegetables, but also from sexual contact. Symptoms include fatigue, fever, loss of appetite, nausea, dark urine, jaundice, vomiting, aches and pains, and light stools. Ask your doctor about the vaccine called Havrix, or ask to get an injection of immune globulin (IG; formerly called gamma globulin). Risk is highest in rural areas and the countryside, but is also present in urban areas.

Parasites such as microbes and tapeworms also hide in unsafe water and food. **Giardia,** for example, is acquired by drinking untreated water from streams or lakes all over the world. Symptoms of parasitic infections in general include swollen glands or lymph nodes, fever, rashes or itchiness, digestive problems, eye problems, and anemia. Boil your water, wear shoes, avoid bugs, and eat only cooked food.

Schistosomiasis is another parasitic disease, caused when the larvae of the flatworm penetrates unbroken skin, and is a risk when swimming in fresh water, especially in rural areas. If your skin is exposed to untreated water, the CDC recommends immediate and vigorous rubbing with a towel and/or the application of rubbing alcohol. If infected, you may notice an itchy localized rash; later symptoms include fever, fatigue, painful urination, diarrhea, loss of appetite, night sweats, and a hive-like rash on the body. Schistosomiasis can be treated with prescription drugs once symptoms appear.

Typhoid fever is common in villages and rural areas. While mostly transmitted through contaminated food and water, it may also be acquired by direct contact with another person. Symptoms include fever, headaches, fatigue, loss of appetite, constipation, and a rash on the abdomen or chest. Antibiotics can treat typhoid, but the CDC recommends vaccinations (70-90% effective) if you will be hiking, camping, or staying in small cities or rural areas.

OTHER INFECTIOUS DISEASES

Rabies is transmitted through the saliva of infected animals. It is fatal if untreated. Avoid contact with animals, especially stray dogs. If you are bitten, wash the wound thoroughly and seek immediate medical care. Once you begin to show symptoms (thirst and muscle spasms), the disease is in its terminal stage. If possible, try to locate the animal that bit you to determine whether it does indeed have rabies. A rabies vaccine is available but is only semi-effective. Three shots must be administered over one year.

Hepatitis B is a viral infection of the liver transmitted through the transfer of bodily fluids, by sharing needles, or by having unprotected sex. Its incubation period varies and can be much longer than the 30-day incubation period of Hepatitis A. A person may not begin to show symptoms until many years after infection. The CDC recommends the Hepatitis B vaccination for health-care workers, sexually active travelers, and anyone who may need medical treatment abroad. Vaccination consists of a 3-shot series given over a period of time, and should begin 6 months before traveling.

Hepatitis C is like Hepatitis B, but the modes of transmission are different. Intravenous drug users, those with occupational exposure to blood, hemodialysis patients, or recipients of blood transfusions are at the highest risk, but the disease can also be spread through sexual contact and sharing of items like razors and toothbrushes, which may have traces of blood on them.

AIDS, HIV, STDS

Acquired Immune Deficiency Syndrome (AIDS) is a growing problem around the world. The World Health Organization estimates that there are 30 million people infected with the HIV virus, and women now represent 40% of all new HIV infections. The easiest mode of HIV transmission is through direct blood-to-blood contact with an HIV-positive person; *never* share intravenous drug, tattooing, or other needles. The most common mode of transmission is sexual intercourse. Health professionals recommend the use of latex condoms. Since it isn't always easy to buy condoms when traveling, take a supply with you before you depart for your trip. For more information on AIDS, call the **US Center for Disease Control's** 24-hour hotline at 800-342-2437. In Europe, contact the **World Health Organization,** Attn: Global Program on AIDS, Ave. Appia 20, 1211 Geneva 27, Switzerland (tel. 44 22 791 21 11; fax 791 31 11), for statistical material on AIDS internationally. Council's brochure, *Travel Safe: AIDS and International Travel,* is available at all Council Travel offices and at their web site (www.ciee.org/study/safety/travelsafe.htm).

Sexually transmitted diseases (STDs) such as gonorrhea, chlamydia, genital warts, syphilis, and herpes are easier to catch than HIV, and some can be just as deadly. **Hepatitis B** and **C** are also serious sexually-transmitted diseases (see **Other Infectious Diseases,** above). Warning signs for STDs include: swelling, sores, bumps, or blisters on sex organs, rectum, or mouth; burning and pain during urination and bowel movements; itching around sex organs; swelling or redness in the throat; flu-like symptoms with fever, chills, and aches. If these symptoms develop, see a doctor immediately. When having sex, condoms may protect you from certain STDs, but oral or even tactile contact can lead to transmission.

WOMEN'S HEALTH

Women traveling in unsanitary conditions are vulnerable to **urinary tract** and **bladder infections,** common bacterial diseases that cause a burning sensation and painful and sometimes frequent urination. To try to avoid these infections, drink plenty of vitamin-C-rich juice and plenty of clean water, and urinate frequently, especially right after intercourse. Untreated, these infections can lead to kidney infections, sterility, and even death. If symptoms persist, see a doctor.

Women are also susceptible to **vaginal yeast infections,** a treatable but uncomfortable illness likely to flare up in hot and humid climates. Wearing loosely fitting trousers or a skirt and cotton underwear will help. Yeast infections can be treated with an over-the-counter remedy like Monostat or Gynelotrimin. Bring supplies from home if you are prone to infection.

Tampons and **pads** are sometimes hard to find when traveling, and your preferred brands may not be available, so you might want to take supplies along. **Reliable contraceptives** may also be difficult to find in some areas. Women on the pill should bring enough to allow for possible loss or extended stays. Bring a prescription, since forms of the pill vary a good deal. Though condoms are increasingly available, bring your favorite brand along as availability and quality vary.

Women who need an **abortion** while abroad should contact the **International Planned Parenthood Federation,** European Regional Office, Regent's College Inner Circle, Regent's Park, London NW1 4NS (tel. 44 171 487 7900; fax 487 7950), for more information.

INSURANCE

Travel insurance generally covers four basic areas: medical/health problems, property loss, trip cancellation/interruption, and emergency evacuation. Although your regular insurance policies may well extend to travel-related accidents, you may consider purchasing travel insurance if the cost of potential trip cancellation/interruption or emergency medical evacuation is greater than you can absorb.

Medical insurance (especially university policies) often covers costs incurred abroad; check with your provider. Medicare does not cover foreign travel. Canadians are protected by their home province's health insurance plan for up to 90 days after leaving the country; check with the provincial Ministry of Health or Health Plan Headquarters for details. **Homeowners' insurance** (or your family's coverage) often covers theft during travel and loss of travel documents (passport, plane ticket, etc.) up to US$500.

ISIC provide basic insurance benefits, including US$100 per day of in-hospital sickness for a maximum of 60 days, US$3000 of accident-related medical reimbursement, and US$25,000 for emergency medical transport (see **Identification,** p. 9). **American Express** (tel. 800-528-4800) grants most cardholders automatic car rental insurance (collision and theft, but not liability) and ground travel accident coverage of US$100,000 on flight purchases made with the card. Prices for travel insurance purchased separately generally run about US$50 per week for full coverage, while trip cancellation/interruption may be purchased separately at a rate of US$5.50 per US$100 of coverage.

INSURANCE PROVIDERS. **Council** and **STA** (see p. 30 for complete listings) offer a range of plans that can supplement your basic insurance coverage. Other private insurance providers in the **US and Canada** include: **Access America** (tel. 800-284-

8300); **Berkely Group/Carefree Travel Insurance** (tel. 800-323-3149; www.berkely.com); **Globalcare Travel Insurance** (tel. 800-821-2488; www.globalcare-cocco.com); and **Travel Assistance International** (tel. 800-821-2828; www.worldwide-assistance.com). Providers in the **U.K.** include **Campus Travel** (tel. (01865) 258 000; fax 792 378) and **Columbus Travel Insurance** (tel. (0171) 375 0011; fax 375 0022). In **Australia,** try **CIC Insurance** (tel. (02) 9202 8000; 9202 8220).

PACKING

Pack according to the extremes of climate you may experience and the type of travel you'll be doing. **Pack light:** a good rule is to lay out only what you absolutely need, then take half the clothes and twice the money. It's always a good idea to bring a rain jacket (Gore-Tex is a miracle material that's both waterproof and breathable), a warm jacket or wool sweater, and sturdy shoes and thick socks. You may also want to add one outfit beyond the jeans and t-shirt uniform, and maybe a nicer pair of shoes if you have the room. Remember that wool will keep you warm even when soaked through, whereas wet cotton is colder than wearing nothing at all. Also remember that the weather at high altitudes can be very unpredictable, even in tropical areas. If you plan to do a lot of hiking, see **Outdoors,** p. 25.

Washing Clothes: *Let's Go* attempts to provide information on laundromats in the **Practical Information** listings for larger cities, but sometimes it may be cheaper and easier to use a sink. Bring a small bar or tube of detergent soap, a small rubber ball to stop up the sink, and a travel clothes line.

Electric current: In Perú and Ecuador, electricity is 110V. This is the same as in North America, but is not compatible with Europe and Australia. Ask first though, as some places might have alarm-clock-melting 220V outlets. If necessary visit a hardware store for an adapter (which changes the shape of the plug) and a converter (which changes the voltage). Don't make the mistake of using only an adapter (unless appliance instructions explicitly state otherwise).

Other Useful Items: No matter how you're traveling, it's always a good idea to carry a first-aid kit including sunscreen, insect repellent, and vitamins (see **Health,** p. 17). Other useful items include: an umbrella; sealable plastic bags (for damp clothes, soap, food, shampoo, and other spillables); alarm clock; waterproof matches; sun hat; moleskin (for blisters); needle and thread; safety pins; sunglasses; pocketknife; plastic water bottle; compass; string (makeshift clothesline and lashing material); towel; padlock; whistle; rubber bands; flashlight; cold-water soap; electrical tape (for patching tears); tweezers; garbage bags; a small calculator for currency conversion; a pair of flip-flops for the shower; a money-belt; deodorant; razors; tampons; and condoms.

ACCOMMODATIONS

HOTELS

Most budget accommodations in Perú and Ecuador are in the form of basic hotels. Rooms are usually small and simple, bathrooms may be private or communal, and there is often a lounge area, be it a plant-filled courtyard, sparsely-decorated TV-room, or dining area. These places may offer laundry service for a fee, they may have a place where guests can do their own laundry (sometimes simply a washtub and a clothes line), or there may be no laundry facilities at all. It is expected everywhere that after you've finished your business, you throw your toilet paper into the waste basket—*not* the toilet. It's also a good idea to carry tissues or a small roll of toilet paper with you; some places don't provide it. Otherwise, the rules vary at hotels. There is generally a lockout time before which you must return to the hotel. If you get locked out, you can try to wake the owner or receptionist, but don't expect their usual cheerful greeting.

HOSTELS

There are also numerous hostels in Ecuador and Perú that are often more like dormitories. Multiple guests may have to sleep in the same room, perhaps on bunkbeds, sometimes in mixed-gender groups. A bed in a hostel will average around US$3-5. A few of these hostels are part of **Hostelling International (HI),** a worldwide hostel organization that guarantees a certain level of quality in terms of cleanliness, comfort, and friendliness. HI's umbrella organization web page lists the web addresses and phone numbers of all national associations and can be a great place to begin researching hostelling in a specific region (www.iyhf.org). In Perú, the hostel association is called **Asociación Peruana de Albergues Turisticos Juveniles**, Av. Casimiro Ulloa 328, San Antonio, Miraflores, Lima 18 (tel. (01) 242 30 68; fax 444 81 87; email: hostell@mail.cosapidata.com.pe). In Ecuador, the hostel association is called **Asociación Ecuatoriana de Albergues**, Pinto 325 y Reina Victoria, Quito (tel. (02) 543 995; fax 508 221; email ecuatori@pi.pro.ec). To apply for an HI membership, contact your local branch: in **Australia,** 422 Kent St., Sydney NSW 2000 (tel. (02) 9261 1111; email yha@yhansw.org.au); **Canada,** 400-205 Catherine St., Ottawa, ON K2P 1C3 (tel. 800-663-5777; email info@hostellingintl.ca); **Ireland,** 61 Mountjoy St., Dublin 7 (tel. (01) 830 4555; email anoige@iol.ie); **New Zealand,** P.O. Box 436, 173 Cashel St., Christchurch (tel. (03) 379 9970; email info@yha.org.nz); **South Africa,** P.O. Box 4402, Cape Town 8000 (tel. (021) 24 2511; email info@hisa.org.za); **England** and **Wales,** 8 St. Stephen's Hill, St. Albans, Hertfordshire AL1 2DY (tel. (01727) 855 215; email yhacustomerservices@compuserve.com); and **United States,** 733 15th St. NW #840, Washington, D.C. 20005 (tel. (202) 783-6161 ext. 136; email hiayhserv@hiayh.org).

CAMPING AND THE OUTDOORS

Camping is definitely possible in Perú and Ecuador, even though it is neither terribly common nor very well-organized. Some parks and reserves have designated camping areas, and some more frequently climbed mountains have *refugios* (rustic shelters) at various elevation levels. Some landowners may allow camping on their property, but be sure to ask. Be cautious camping in non-designated spots, especially in isolated areas.

The non-profit **South American Explorers Club (SAEC)** is widely recognized as a wonderful source of travel information on Perú and Ecuador. With clubhouses in Lima and Cusco, Perú; Quito, Ecuador; and Ithaca, New York; the club provides members with reliable, up-to-date information on discount airfares, trip planning, travel conditions, and everything else you need to know for your trip or expedition. This outfit is well respected and is the ultimate resource for information about outdoor experiences in Perú and Ecuador. If you only make one call (or surf one web site) this should be it. Contact them at 126 Indian Creek Rd., Ithaca, NY 14850 (tel. (607) 277-0488; fax 277-6122; email explorer@samexplo.org; www.samexplo.org).

CAMPING AND HIKING EQUIPMENT

It's best to bring equipment with you, since buying it in Ecuador will be much more expensive. There are shops in Quito, Guayaquil, and Lima if you need to replace or fix equipment.

Sleeping Bag: Most good sleeping bags are rated by "season," or the lowest outdoor temperature at which they will keep you warm ("summer" means 30-40°F at night and "four-season" or "winter" often means below 0°F). Sleeping bags are made either of down (warmer and lighter, but more expensive, and miserable when wet) or of synthetic material (heavier, more durable, and warmer when wet). Prices vary but might range from US$80-210 for a summer synthetic to US$250-300 for a good down winter bag.

Sleeping bag pads, including foam pads (US$10-20) and air mattresses (US$15-50) cushion your back and neck and insulate you from the ground. **Therm-A-Rest** brand self-inflating sleeping pads are part foam and part air-mattress and partially inflate when you unroll them, but are costly (US$45-80). Bring a **"stuff sack"** or plastic bag to store your sleeping bag and keep it dry.

Tent: The best tents are free-standing, with their own frames and suspension systems; they set up quickly and only require staking in high winds. Low-profile dome tents are the best all-around. When pitched, their internal space is almost entirely usable, which means little unnecessary bulk. If you're traveling by car, go for the bigger tent, but if you're hiking, stick with a smaller tent that weighs no more than 5-6 lbs (2-3kg). Good 2-person tents start at US$90, 4-person tents at US$300. Seal the seams of your tent with waterproofer, and make sure it has a rain fly.

Boots: Be sure to wear boots with good **ankle support** which are appropriate for the terrain you plan to hike. Your boots should fit snugly and comfortably over one or two wool socks and a thin liner sock. Breaking in boots before setting out requires wearing them for several weeks; doing so will spare you from painful and debilitating blisters.

Other Necessities: Raingear in two pieces, a top and pants, is far superior to a poncho. **Synthetics,** like polypropylene tops, socks, and long underwear, along with a pile jacket, will keep you warm even when wet. When camping in autumn, winter, or spring, bring along a **"space blanket,"** which helps you to retain your body heat and doubles as a groundcloth (US$5-15). Plastic **canteens** or water bottles keep water cooler than metal ones do, and are virtually shatter- and leak-proof. Large, collapsible **water sacks** will significantly improve your lot in primitive campgrounds and weigh practically nothing when empty, though they are bulky and heavy when full. Bring **water-purification tablets** for when you can't boil water, unless you are willing to shell out money for a portable water-purification system. Though most campgrounds provide campfire sites, you may want to bring a small **metal grate** or **grill** of your own. The classic Coleman **camp stove** starts at about US$40. You will need to purchase a **fuel bottle** and fill it with propane to operate it. A **first aid kit, swiss army knife, insect repellent, calamine lotion,** and **waterproof matches** or a **lighter** are other essential camping items.

WILDERNESS SAFETY

Stay warm, stay dry, and stay hydrated. The vast majority of life-threatening wilderness situations result from a breach of this simple dictum. On any hike, however brief, you should pack enough equipment to keep you alive should disaster befall. This includes raingear, hat and mittens, a first-aid kit, a reflector, a whistle, high-energy food, and extra water. Dress in warm layers of synthetic materials designed for the outdoors, or wool. Pile fleece jackets and Gore-Tex raingear are excellent choices. Never rely on cotton for warmth. This "death cloth" will be absolutely useless should it get wet. Make sure to check all equipment for any defects before setting out, and see **Camping and Hiking Equipment,** above, for more information. Check **weather forecasts** and pay attention to the skies when hiking. Weather patterns can change suddenly. Whenever possible, let someone know when and where you are going hiking, either a friend, your hostel, a park ranger, or a local hiking organization. Do not attempt a hike beyond your ability—you may be endangering your life. See **Health,** p. 17 for information about outdoor ailments such as heatstroke, hypothermia, giardia, rabies, and insects, as well as basic medical concerns and first-aid.

JUNGLE TOURS

Tourists mainly visit Ecuador and Perú's rainforests to take a jungle tour through the Amazon basin. While the different tours vary greatly, they typically include treks through dripping rainforests, canoe rides down muddy rivers, visits to remote indigenous communities, and overnight stays in *cabaña* outposts or jungle lodges. Some regions of the jungle have less primary growth and smaller wildlife populations than others, mainly because oil companies have built roads opening the jungle up to colonization, deforestation, and the destruction of native habitats. Other sections remain more or less intact, but this is precisely because they are more isolated and harder to reach.

Tours operate out of just about every town in and around Ecuador's Oriente, but to reach the most remote parts, you'll want to head out of either **Coca** or **Lago Agrio.** These northern Oriente towns sit just west of Ecuador's most undeveloped rainforests and provide access to the country's most impressive protected jungle areas, including the prominent **Cuyabeno Reserve** and the enormous, remote **Parque Nacional Yasuní.** To the south and west of Coca, the pleasant town of **Tena** and the tourist village of **Misahuallí** send trips into the less pristine but still impressive jungle wilderness that stretches out just to the east of them. The undisputed base for southern Oriente jungle tours is **Macas,** which offers access to remote Shuar villages, the nearby Cueva de los Tayos, and the rugged expanse of the *zona baja* of **Parque Nacional Sangay.** A number of jungle tours can also be taken from cities in Perú. Although not actually situated in the jungle, Cusco promises numerous touring options out to Perú's highly revered **Manu Biosphere Reserve.** Within the rainforest, Iquitos makes a fabulous base for tours to the Pacaya-Samiria Reserve. **Tambopata-Candamo Reserve** is another promising area for exploration and is accessible from Puerto Maldonado.

After deciding which area you want to explore, you must make the equally important decision of who will guide you through it. You might end up having an excellent time with a tour guide who knows what he's doing, points out interesting wildlife, and respects the land and the people—or you could go along silently as your guide mentally counts his profits and stares out into a jungle he doesn't know much about. SAEC (see p. 25) can be helpful in avoiding such a situation; they provide trip reports that offer recommendations and warnings about various companies. The companies listed in this guide are generally quite reliable, but they don't come guaranteed. In general, it pays to ask a lot of questions and follow your gut feeling; after all, there are plenty of companies to choose from. If you plan on visiting any nationally protected areas, make sure the company is approved by the National Park Administration (INEFAN) to lead tours through those areas.

ENVIRONMENTALLY RESPONSIBLE TOURISM. The idea behind responsible tourism is to leave no trace of human presence behind. A campstove is the safer (and more efficient) way to cook than using vegetation, but if you must make a fire, keep it small and use only dead branches or brush rather than cutting vegetation. Make sure your campsite is at least 150 ft. (50m) from water supplies or bodies of water. If there are no toilet facilities, bury human waste (but not paper) at least four inches (10cm) deep and above the high-water line, and 150 ft. or more from any water supplies and campsites. Always pack your trash in a plastic bag and carry it with you until you reach the next trash can. For more on ecotourism in Ecuador and Perú, see p. 55, or contact one of the organizations listed below.

Earthwatch, 680 Mt. Auburn St., Box 403, Watertown, MA 02272 (tel. (617) 776-0188; fax 926-8532; email info@earthwatch.org; www.earthwatch.org).

Ecotourism Society, P.O. Box 755, North Bennington, VT 05257-0755 (tel. (802) 447-2121; email ecomail@ecotourism.org; www.ecotourism.org/tesinfo.html)

EcoTravel Center: www.ecotour.com.

National Audobon Society, Nature Odysseys, 700 Broadway, New York, NY 10003 (tel. (212) 979-3066; email travel@audobon.org; www.audobon.org).

Tourism Concern, Stapleton House, 277-281 Holloway Rd., London N7 8HN, England (tel. (0170) 753 3330; www.gn.apc.org/tourismconcern.

KEEPING IN TOUCH

MAIL

SENDING MAIL TO AND RECEIVING MAIL IN PERÚ AND ECUADOR

Airmail letters under 1 oz. between North America and Perú or Ecuador take 15 to 30 days and cost US$0.75 or CDN$0.95. Allow at least 20 days from Australia (postage AUS$1.20 for up to 20 grams) and 15 days from Britain (postage £0.65 for up to 20 grams). Envelopes should be marked "air mail" or "por avión" to avoid having letters sent by sea. There are several ways to arrange pick-up of letters sent to you by friends and relatives while you are abroad.

General Delivery: Mail can be sent to Perú and Ecuador through **lista de correos** (or by using the international phrase **Poste Restante**) to almost any city or town with a post office. Address letters to: Joe GARLAND, *Lista de Correos,* Quito, ECUADOR. The letter should also be marked *Favor de retener hasta la llegada* (please hold until arrival). The mail will go to a special desk in the central post office, unless you specify a post office by street address or postal code. As a rule, it is best to use the largest post office in the area, and mail may be sent there regardless of what is written on the envelope. When picking up your mail, bring a form of photo ID, preferably a passport. There is generally no surcharge; if there is a charge, it generally does not exceed the cost of domestic postage. If the clerks insist that there is nothing for you, have them check under your first name as well. *Let's Go* lists post offices in the **Practical Information** section for each city and most towns.

American Express: AmEx's travel offices will act as a mail service for cardholders if you contact them in advance. Under this free **Client Letter Service,** they will hold mail for up to 30 days and forward upon request. Some offices will offer these services to non-cardholders (especially those who have purchased AmEx Traveler's Cheques), but you must call ahead to make sure. Check the **Practical Information** section of the countries you plan to visit; *Let's Go* lists AmEx office locations for the large cities in Perú and Ecuador. A complete list is available free from AmEx (tel. 800-528-4800).

If regular airmail is too slow, **Federal Express** (US tel. for international operator 800-247-4747) can get a letter from New York to Quito or Lima in two days for a whopping US$41. By **US Express Mail,** a letter from New York would arrive within four days and would cost US$14. When ordering books and materials from abroad, always include one or two **international Reply Coupons (IRCs)**—a way of providing the postage to cover delivery. IRCs should be available from your local post office and those abroad (US$1.05).

SENDING MAIL HOME FROM PERÚ AND ECUADOR

The Ecuadorian postal service is notoriously slow and insecure, though the Peruvian system has a better reputation. **Aerogrammes,** printed sheets that fold into envelopes and travel via airmail, are available at post offices. Most post offices will charge exorbitant fees or simply refuse to send aerogrammes with enclosures. **Airmail** from Perú or Ecuador averages 10 to 18 days, but can take a month or more; times are more unpredictable from smaller towns. It helps to mark *Por Avión,* though *Par Avion* is universally understood. **Surface mail** is by far the cheapest and slowest way to send mail. Official estimates average 40 days, but in reality, it may takes months—appropriate for sending large quantities of items you won't need to see for a while.

TELEPHONES

CALLING PERÚ OR ECUADOR FROM HOME

To call Perú or Ecuador direct from home, dial:

1. The international access code of your home country. **International access codes** include: Australia 0011; Ireland 00; New Zealand 00; South Africa 09; U.K. 00; US 011.
2. 593 for Ecuador or 051 for Perú
3. The city code (see the city's **Practical Information** section). These are sometimes listed with a zero in front (e.g., 02), but after dialing the international access code, drop successive zeros (with an access code of 011, e.g., 011 2).
4. The local number.

CALLING HOME FROM PERÚ OR ECUADOR

A **calling card** is probably your best and cheapest bet. Calls are billed either collect or to your account. **MCI WorldPhone** also provides access to MCI's Traveler's Assist, which gives legal and medical advice, exchanges rate information, and offers translation services. Other phone companies provide similar services to travelers. **To obtain a calling card,** and the appropriate **access number** for both Ecuador and Perú, contact your national telecommunications service before you leave home: in the **US** there's AT&T (tel. 888-288-4685), Sprint (tel. 800-877-4646), or MCI (tel. 800-444-4141); in **Canada,** Bell Canada's Canada Direct (tel. 800-565-4708); in the **U.K.,** British Telecom BT Direct (tel. (0800) 34 51 44); in **Ireland,** Telecom Éireann Ireland Direct (tel. 800 250 250); in **Australia,** Telstra Australia Direct (tel. 13 22 00); in **New Zealand,** Telecom New Zealand (tel. 0800 000 000); and in **South Africa,** Telkom South Africa (tel. 09 03).

Calling home is difficult from **Ecuador.** The infamous national phone company, known as **PACIFICTEL** on the coast and **ANDINATEL** in the interior, has inspired public fury for being slow, unreliable, and pathetically backwards. Public telephones are nonexistent, even in Quito, and many telephone offices are not equipped to handle calling card, collect, or sometimes even international calls. Telephone offices are usually open daily from 8am to 10pm though times may vary slightly from town to town. Those offices that can handle international calls sometimes do them for exorbitant rates, others allow collect and calling cards calls for a fee or with the use of tokens *(fichas)*, and a very few, kindly offices, allow collect and calling card calls for free.

Things get easier across the border in **Perú,** where the whole wondrous show is run by the Spanish firm **Telefónica del Perú.** To make a calling card call, keep your eyes peeled for the newer blue public phones that often have a slot for both phone cards and coins. These public phones are a better bet than the telephone offices which sometimes only have old phones too senile to cope with the concept of toll-free calls. **Prepaid phonecards** are available in various denominations starting at s/5. Although incredibly convenient, in-room hotel calls invariably include an arbitrary and sky-high surcharge.

EMAIL AND INTERNET

Fax service and email are starting to become available in Perú and Ecuador. Not only are these services increasingly common in the larger cities, but it is even possible to now find e-communication opportunities in rural areas. Places like the SAEC, embassies, and Internet cafes can all provide a good fix for your online addictions. One strategy is to befriend college students as you go and ask if you can use their email accounts. Other free, web-based email providers include Hotmail (www.hotmail.com), RocketMail (www.rocketmail.com), Yahoo! Mail (www.yahoo.com), Operamail (www.operamail.com), and gURLmAIL (www.gurlmail.com). Many free email providers are funded by advertising (both on their pages and inserted at the end of outgoing messages) and some may require subscribers to fill out a questionnaire. Almost every Internet search engine has an affiliated free email service.

GETTING THERE

BY PLANE

When it comes to airfare, a little effort can save you a bundle. Call every toll-free number and don't be afraid to ask about discounts. Have a knowledgeable **travel agent** help you. Students, seniors, and those under 26 should never pay full price.

DETAILS AND TIPS

Timing: Airfares to Perú and Ecuador peak between mid-June and early September and holidays are also expensive periods in which to travel. Midweek (M-Th morning) round-trip flights run US$40-50 cheaper than weekend flights, but the latter are generally less crowded and more likely to permit frequent-flier upgrades. Return-date flexibility is usually not an option for the budget traveler; traveling with an "open return" ticket can be pricier than fixing a return date when buying the ticket and paying later to change it.

Route: Round-trip flights are by far the cheapest; "open-jaw" (arriving in and departing from different cities) and round-the-world, or RTW, flights are pricier but reasonable alternatives. Patching one-way flights together is the least economical way to travel. Flights between capital cities or regional hubs will offer the most competitive fares.

Boarding: Whenever flying internationally, pick up tickets for international flights well in advance of the departure date, and confirm by phone within 72 hours of departure. Most airlines require that passengers arrive at the airport at least 2 hours before departure. One carry-on item and 2 pieces of checked baggage is the norm for non-courier flights. Consult the airline for weight allowances.

Fares: Round-trip from gateway cities in the US to Quito or Lima can be as low as US$300-700, but flight quotes are usually much more (expect to pay quite a bit more for flights to the Galápagos). Connections are usually made through New York, Atlanta, Miami, Houston, Los Angeles, or Mexico City.

BUDGET AND STUDENT TRAVEL AGENCIES

A knowledgeable agent specializing in flights to Perú and Ecuador can make your life easy and help you save, too, but agents may not spend the time to find you the lowest possible fare—they get paid on commission. Students and those under 26 holding **ISIC** and **IYTC cards** (see **Identification,** p. 9), respectively, qualify for big discounts from student travel agencies.

Campus/Usit Youth and Student Travel (www.usitcampus.co.uk). In the U.K. call (0870) 240 10 10; in North America call (0171) 730 21 01; worldwide call 44 171 730 81 11. Offices include: 19-21 Aston Quay, O'Connell Bridge, **Dublin** 2 (tel. (01) 677 8117; fax 679 8833); 52 Grosvenor Gardens, **London** SW1W 0AG; New York Student Center, 895 Amsterdam Ave., **New York,** NY, 10025 (tel. (212) 663-5435; email usitny@aol.com).

Council Travel (www.counciltravel.com). US offices include: 273 Newbury St., **Boston,** MA 02116 (tel. (617) 266-1926); 1160 N. State St., **Chicago,** IL 60610 (tel. (312) 951-0585); 10904 Lindbrook Dr., **Los Angeles,** CA 90024 (tel. (310) 208-3551); 205 E. 42nd St., **New York,** NY 10017 (tel. (212) 822-2700); 530 Bush St., **San Francisco,** CA 94108 (tel. (415) 421-3473); **Washington, D.C.** 20007 (tel. (202) 337-6464). **For US cities not listed,** call 800-2-COUNCIL (226-8624). Also 28A Poland St. (Oxford Circus), **London,** W1V 3DB (tel. (0171) 287 3337).

CTS Travel, 44 Goodge St., **London** W1 (tel. (0171) 636 00 31; fax 637 53 28; email ctsinfo@ctstravel.com.uk).

STA Travel, 6560 Scottsdale Rd. #F100, Scottsdale, AZ 85253 (tel. 800-777-0112 fax (602) 922-0793; www.sta-travel.com). A student and youth travel organization with over 150 offices worldwide. Ticket booking, travel insurance, railpasses, and more. US offices include: 297 Newbury St., **Boston,** MA 02115 (tel. (617) 266-6014); 429 S.

Dearborn St., **Chicago,** IL 60605 (tel. (312) 786-9050); 7202 Melrose Ave., **Los Angeles,** CA 90046 (tel. (323) 934-8722); 10 Downing St., **New York,** NY 10014 (tel. (212) 627-3111); 4341 University Way NE, **Seattle,** WA 98105 (tel. (206) 633-5000); 2401 Pennsylvania Ave., Ste. G, **Washington, D.C.** 20037 (tel. (202) 887-0912); 51 Grant Ave., **San Francisco,** CA 94108 (tel. (415) 391-8407). In the U.K., 6 Wrights Ln., **London** W8 6TA (tel. (0171) 938 47 11). In New Zealand, 10 High St., **Auckland** (tel. (09) 309 04 58). In Australia, 222 Faraday St., **Melbourne** (tel. (03) 9349 2411).

Travel CUTS (Canadian Universities Travel Services Limited), 187 College St., Toronto, ON M5T 1P7 (tel. (416) 979-2406; fax 979-8167; www.travelcuts.com). 40 offices in Canada. Also in the U.K., 295A Regent St., **London** W1R 7YA (tel. (020) 7255 1944).

Travel Avenue (tel. 800-333-3335) rebates commercial fares to or from the US and offers low fares for flights anywhere in the world.

COMMERCIAL AIRLINES

Both US and Latin American commercial airlines fly to Ecuador. While the US airlines are typically more expensive, they allow you to fly from anywhere in the United States. The Latin American airlines, on the other hand, fly only to and from Miami, Houston, Los Angeles, and sometimes New York. US airlines that fly to Ecuador and Perú are **American** (US tel. 800-433-7300; www.americanair.com), **Continental** (US tel. 800-231-0856; www.flycontinental.com), and **United** (US tel. 800-538-2929; www.ual.com); the Latin American options come from **AeroContinente** (US tel. (323) 852-0549 or (305) 436-9400; www.aerocontinente.com.pe), **LASCA** (US tel. 800-225-2272; www.flylatinamerica.com), and **SAETA** (tel. US 800-827-2382).

AIRCRAFT SAFETY. The airlines flying to Perú and Ecuador are very reliable but third-world nations do not always meet safety standards for domestic flights. The *Official Airline Guide* (www.oag.com) and many travel agencies can tell you the type and age of aircraft on a particular route. The **International Airline Passengers Association** (US tel. (972) 404-9980; U.K. tel. (181) 681 65 55) provides region-specific safety information.

The commercial airlines' lowest regular offer is the **APEX** (Advance Purchase Excursion) fare, which provides confirmed reservations. Generally, reservations must be made 7 to 21 days in advance, with 7- to 14-day minimum and up to 90-day maximum-stay limits, and hefty cancellation and change penalties (fees rise in summer). Book peak-season APEX fares early, since by May you will have a hard time getting the departure date you want. Although APEX fares are probably not the cheapest possible fares, they will give you a sense of the average commercial price, from which to measure other bargains. Specials advertised in newspapers may be cheaper but have more restrictions and fewer available seats.

GETTING AROUND

BY BUS

While the cheapest and most reliable way to get around Perú and Ecuador, bus travel can still be daunting. Buses along the well-paved Panamerican Highway that hugs the Peruvian coast promise a reasonably tame journey. Elsewhere, prepare for anything. Coaches crammed with people and luggage whip around hairpin turns through thick clouds on the edges of cliffs. And once you muster up enough courage to open your eyes again, another bus coming in the opposite direction swerves past on a one-lane dirt highway overlooking oblivion. Cope with the impending doom by giving in to the experience. Consider it a ride at an amusement park; no matter how scary the ride becomes, the car is still attached (theoretically) to the tracks. Whether or not this strategy works, every budget traveler will eventually have to accept the realities of bus travel for the sake of necessity.

Buses leave town from the **terminal terrestre** (bus station), or from a particular street with a high density of *cooperativos* (bus companies). In Ecuador, the bus fare is usually paid upon entering the bus or collected en route by an *ayudante* (helper). Occasionally, tickets must be purchased in advance at the *cooperativo* office. The reverse is true in Perú, where the norm is to buy tickets from the *empresa* (bus ticket office) before boarding, or well in advance for common routes and during the holiday season. Departure times are usually approximate, and buses run between most destinations frequently enough that it is practical just to show up at the *terminal terrestre* and board the next bus headed your way. The destination is usually indicated on the bus itself, as well as advertised by a man yelling the town's name over and over and over again. The vehicles themselves vary greatly in quality, from *camionetas* (open-air trucks) to second-hand school buses to sparkling new Mercedes-Benz mega-buses. A general guideline: the longer the route, the nicer the bus will be, so it may be worthwhile to board a long-distance bus even if you plan to get off before the final destination. One peculiar aspect of bus travel is that the buses rarely get "full." Drivers are often happy to pack as many passengers/chicken crates as they can into the aisles or even hanging out the doors and windows. If the buses get really full, Ecuadorian drivers will let passengers ride on the roof, an especially amazing (and certainly dangerous) experience in the mountains. It is a good idea to keep your bags and belongings with you if at all possible.

BY PLANE

Air travel within and between Perú and Ecuador is definitely more expensive than bus or train travel, but it's also much quicker and more comfortable. Moreover, flights between most destinations on the mainland are usually cheap (US$30-80), though they can be higher between the capital cities. Expect flights to the Galápagos to be very expensive (US$350-450). Flying into Cusco, and then traveling overland back to Lima is a particularly common itinerary. *Let's Go* lists the relevant airport and airline information for each town or city with an airport. As a general guideline, purchase tickets a few days before departure and at least a week ahead of time for flights between large destinations. Often, flights are overbooked and, despite holding a *billete* (ticket), a passenger may be bumped off the flight for not having *cupo*, roughly translated as "a reservation." Ask the ticketing agent if you have both. If you don't have *cupo* it is still possible to fly standby if you arrive three hours early and hope for the best. Check for specific airline service and fares in a city's **Practical Information** or **Transportation** sections.

BY TRAIN

Railroad travel is not the most convenient, cheapest, nor quickest way to get around. Some are willing to make these kinds of sacrifices for the strangely soothing sensation of traveling by train. Not only do the trains travel through some of the most spectacular terrain in the world, but in Ecuador roof-riding is also permitted. While the tracks run the length of Ecuador, much of this distance is in disrepair due to mudslides, El Niño, and other natural damage. Nevertheless, there are several stretches that have been repaired and maintained. The most well-traveled stretches lie between Guayaquil and Alausí in the south (see **The Riobamba-Alausí-Bucay-Durán Railway,** p. 327), and Ibarra and San Lorenzo in the north (see **Ibarra: Practical Information,** p. 287). Both of these routes travel from the coast into the Sierra and give passengers the opportunity to see the land change with the altitude. Another train also runs between Quito and Riobamba. In Perú, trains cover the route from Arequipa to Cusco through Puno and Juliaca. Trains run roughly every other day, but weather often causes the tracks to be inoperable for a day or two. The Peruvian rail system operates two classes (and prices) of trains: local trains cost a lot less than tourist trains, but are more crowded, less comfortable, and slower. For info on prices and travel times, check the **Practical Information** sections of these towns.

BY BOAT

In the Oriente and Peruvian jungle, motorized dugout canoes travel the murky, winding rivers that connect many towns. While this may seem like a glamorous way to travel, hours under the hot equatorial sun and the constant threat of torrential downpours add up. Also, since the riverbanks are the most accessible parts of the jungle, hopes of seeing more isolated and untouched areas by river are rarely realized. On top of these minor inconveniences, traveling by river is more expensive than going by bus on roads that now connect many jungle towns. If you still want to travel by river, ask about regular boat schedules and prices at a local marina. Public transportation boats regularly run up and down the **Río Napo** between Tena and Coca. You can also charter a canoe and customize your itinerary although this is only economically feasible for larger groups.

Roads run along most of the **Pacific Coast,** making boat travel unnecessary and thus quite rare. One exception is the stretch between the undeveloped northern coast towns of Muisne and Cojimíes; the only way to travel between these is a cheap and frequent, one-and-a-half-hour, wet-and-wild boat trip. Boats can also be a popular means of transport in the Amazon basin, and are the only way to reach places like Iquitos without flying.

BY TAXI AND CAR

Taxis can be a convenient way to get around, especially when you are in a hurry or traveling to places where buses don't venture. They are commonly used for travel between towns or to outlying destinations. It is usually cheaper to arrange for a taxi to drop you off and pick you up at an out-of-the-way spot than it is to rent a car yourself. If you do decide to take a taxi, try to settle on a fair price before entering; if you don't, the driver might try to take advantage of you by charging more than the ride is worth and even cranking up the speed on the meter. You can also travel by *colectivo;* the VW vans travel regular routes and pick up numerous passengers, falling in-between taxis and buses in price, speed, and size.

Car rental can be a real nightmare. It will cost between US$30-80 a day (try Budget for good deals), the roads and drivers can be very scary, and a car is one more thing to worry about getting stolen. If you plan to drive a car you should have an **International Driving Permit** (IDP). It will be indispensable if you're in a situation (e.g. an accident or being stranded in a smaller town) where the police do not speak English, as information on the IDP is printed in Spanish. Your IDP, valid for one year, must be issued in your own country before you depart. A valid driver's license from your home country must always accompany the IDP. An application for an IDP usually needs to include one or two photos, a current local license, an additional form of identification, and a fee. Contact your local Automobile Association of America for an application. Most credit cards cover standard insurance. If you rent, lease, or borrow a car, you will need a **green card,** or **International Insurance Certificate,** to prove that you have liability insurance. Obtain it through the car rental agency; most include coverage in their prices. If you lease a car, you can obtain a green card from the dealer.

BY THUMB

Let's Go urges you to use common sense if you decide to hitch, and to seriously consider all possible risks before you make that decision. The information listed below and throughout the book is not intended to recommend hitchhiking; Let's Go does not recommend hitchhiking as a means of transportation.

Buses travel almost everywhere in Perú and Ecuador and cost very little, so it is rarely worthwhile to hitchhike. However, there are more remote places where buses don't travel. Trucks will often pick up passengers to make a little extra money. Usually they cost about the same as taxis, but may charge a little more; most passengers settle on a price before getting in.

SPECIFIC CONCERNS

WOMEN TRAVELERS

Women exploring on their own inevitably face some additional safety concerns, but it's easy to be adventurous without taking undue risks. If you are concerned, you might consider staying in hotels which offer single rooms that lock from the inside or in religious organizations that offer rooms for women only. Communal showers in some hostels are safer than others; check them before settling in. Stick to centrally located accommodations and avoid solitary late-night treks. When traveling, always carry extra money for a phone call, bus, or taxi. **Hitching** is never safe for lone women, or even for two women traveling together. Look as if you know where you're going (even when you don't) and consider approaching older women or couples for directions if you're lost or feel uncomfortable.

Generally, the less you look like a tourist, the better off you'll be. Dress conservatively, especially in rural areas. Shorts and t-shirts, even if unrevealing by Western standards, will clearly identify you as a foreigner. As it is, many Latin Americans believe foreign women have looser sexual morals and will consider skimpy clothing an invitation. Wearing a conspicuous **wedding band** may help prevent unwanted overtures. Some travelers report that carrying pictures of a "husband" or "children" is extremely useful to help document marriage status. Even a mention of a husband waiting back at the hotel may be enough in some places to discount your potentially vulnerable, unattached appearance.

In cities, you may be harassed no matter how you're dressed. *Machismo* is very common among Peruvian and Ecuadorian men, and they will often express their manliness with a kind of stuttered hissing or, sometimes, by yelling vulgarities. The best answer to such harassment is no answer at all; feigned deafness, sitting motionless and staring straight ahead at nothing in particular will do a world of good that reactions usually don't achieve. The extremely persistent can sometimes be dissuaded by a firm, loud, and very public "*¡Déjame!*" (DEH-ha-me, "leave me alone!") or "*¡no molestes!*" (no mole-EST-ace, "don't bother me!"). If need be, turn to an older woman for help; her stern rebukes will usually be enough to embarrass the most determined jerks. Don't hesitate to seek out a police officer.

Let's Go: Perú and Ecuador lists emergency numbers in the Practical Information listings of cities. Memorize these numbers in the places you visit. Carry a **whistle** or an airhorn on your keychain, and don't hesitate to use it in an emergency. An **IMPACT Model Mugging** self-defense course will not only prepare you for a potential attack, but will also raise your level of awareness of your surroundings as well as your confidence (see **Self Defense,** p. 15). Women also face some specific health concerns when traveling (see **Women's Health,** p. 23).

TRAVELING ALONE

There are many benefits to traveling alone, among them greater independence and challenge. As a lone traveler, you have greater opportunity to interact with local Peruvians and Ecuadorians, who are generally enthusiastic about making a new foreign *amigo*.

On the other hand, any solo traveler is a more vulnerable target of harassment and street theft. Lone travelers need to be well-organized and look confident at all times. Try not to stand out as a tourist, and be especially careful in deserted or very crowded areas. If questioned, never admit that you are traveling alone. Maintain regular contact with someone at home who knows your itinerary. A number of organizations supply information for solo travelers, and others find travel companions for those who don't want to go alone. A few are listed here.

Connecting: Solo Traveler Network, P.O. Box 29088, 1996 W. Broadway, Vancouver, BC V6J 5C2, Canada (tel. (604) 737-7791; email info@cstn.org; www.cstn.org). Bi-monthly newsletter features going solo tips, single-friendly tips, and travel companion ads. Annual directory lists holiday suppliers that avoid single supplement charges. Advice and lodging exchanges facilitated between members. Membership US$25-35.

Travel Companion Exchange, P.O. Box 833, Amityville, NY 11701 (tel. (516) 454-0880 or 800-392-1256; www.travelalone.com). Publishes the pamphlet *Foiling Pickpockets & Bag Snatchers* (US$4) and *Travel Companions*, a bi-monthly newsletter for single travelers seeking a travel partner (subscription US$48).

OLDER TRAVELERS

Agencies for senior group travel are growing in popularity. These are only a few:

ElderTreks, 597 Markham St., Toronto, ON, Canada, M6G 2L7 (tel. 800-741-7956 or (416) 588-5000; fax 588-9839; email passages@inforamp.net; www.eldertreks.com).

Elderhostel, 75 Federal St., Boston, MA 02110-1941 (tel. (617) 426-7788 or (877) 426-8056; email registration@elderhostel.org; www.elderhostel.org). Programs at colleges, universities, and other learning centers in Perú and Ecuador on varied subjects lasting 1-4 weeks. Must be 55 or over (spouse can be of any age).

Walking the World, P.O. Box 1186, Fort Collins, CO 80522 (tel. (970) 498-0500; fax 498-9100; email walktworld@aol.com; www.walkingtheworld.com), sends trips to Perú.

BISEXUAL, GAY, AND LESBIAN TRAVELERS

Homosexuality is not socially accepted in Perú or Ecuador, partly due to the influence of the Catholic church. The derogatory term, "*maricón*," is used more frequently than the proper "*homosexual*," and homosexuals are sometimes subject to ridicule. Homosexual acts are, however, legal in Perú and were legalized just last year in Ecuador. For more information, contact **Movimiento Homosexual de Lima,** Mariscal Miller 828 (tel. (02) 433 63 75; fax 433 55 19) in Jesús María, Lima. Listed below are contact organizations, mail-order bookstores and publishers which offer materials addressing some specific concerns.

Gay's the Word, 66 Marchmont St., London WC1N 1AB (tel. (0171) 278 7654; email gays.theword@virgin.net; www.gaystheword.co.uk). The largest gay and lesbian bookshop in the U.K. Mail-order service available. No catalogue of listings, but they will provide a list of titles on a given subject.

Giovanni's Room, 345 S. 12th St., Philadelphia, PA 19107 (tel. (215) 923-2960; fax 923-0813; email giophilp@netaxs.com). An international feminist, lesbian, and gay bookstore with mail-order service which carries the publications listed here.

International Gay and Lesbian Travel Association, 4331 N. Federal Hwy. #304, Fort Lauderdale, FL 33308 (tel. (954) 776-2626 or 800-448-8550; fax 776-3303; email IGLTA@aol.com; www.iglta.com). An organization of over 1350 companies serving gay and lesbian travelers. Call for lists of travel agents, accommodations, and events.

FURTHER READING. *Spartacus International Gay Guide*, by Bruno Gmunder Verlag (US$33). *Ferrari Guides' Gay Travel A to Z, Ferrari Guides' Men's Travel in Your Pocket*, and *Ferrari Guides' Women's Travel in Your Pocket*, by Ferrari Guides (US$14-16; tel. (602) 863-2408; www.q-net.com).

TRAVELERS WITH DISABILITIES

Travelling with a disability through Perú and Ecuador may be difficult. The more upscale hotels will generally be able to meet your needs, but the public transportation system and most hostels are ill-equipped to handle the needs of travelers with a disability. Those with disabilities should inform airlines and hotels of their disabilities when making arrangements for travel; some time may be needed to prepare special accommodations. Call ahead to restaurants, hotels, parks, and other facilities to find out about the existence of ramps, the widths of doors, the dimensions of elevators, etc. The following organizations provide information or publications that might be of assistance:

Moss Rehab Hospital Travel Information Service (tel. (215) 456-9600; www.mossresourcenet.org). A telephone and Internet information resource center on travel accessibility and other travel-related concerns for those with disabilities.

Society for the Advancement of Travel for the Handicapped (SATH), 347 Fifth Ave. #610, New York, NY 10016 (tel. (212) 447-1928; fax 725-8253; email sathtravel@aol.com; www.sath.org). Advocacy group publishing a quarterly color travel magazine *OPEN WORLD* (free for members or US$13 for nonmembers). Also publishes a wide range of information sheets on disability travel facilitation and accessible destinations. Annual membership US$45, students and seniors US$30.

DIETARY CONCERNS

In larger cities, vegetarians shouldn't have too much trouble finding amenable cuisine. However in smaller towns—where every restaurant seems to serve a fixed *menú*—vegetarians may have to resort to a monotonous diet of rice. One way to escape is by visiting the local market and stocking up on fruits and vegetables. Those planning to keep kosher will probably find most meat unsuitable in Perú and Ecuador, so vegetarian dishes might be best. There are several Jewish centers in both Quito and Lima; see the **Practical Information** sections of both towns.

The Jewish Travel Guide lists synagogues, kosher restaurants, and Jewish institutions in Ecuador and Perú. Available from Vallentine-Mitchell Publishers, Newbury House 890-900, Eastern Ave., Newbury Park, Ilford, Essex, U.K. IG2 7HH (tel. (0181) 599 88 66; fax 599 09 84). It is available in the US ($16) from ISBS, 5804 NE Hassallo St., Portland, OR 97213-3644 (tel. 800-944-6190).

ALTERNATIVES TO TOURISM

STUDY

Many students come to Ecuador and Perú to learn Spanish from one of the language schools around the region. Programs vary, but they generally include four to seven hours of daily instruction and a homestay with a local family. In Quito, these schools are as abundant as shoeshiners, and they flourish in Lima and Cusco as well. Sifting through the available opportunities can be a daunting task. Cost, duration, intensity, and availability of extracurricular programs are a few of the variables to be considered. The **South American Explorers Club** (see p. 25) can help narrow down the options, as can the resources listed below. Arrangements can be made before leaving your home country or after you arrive. In addition to local language schools, American universities and other more global organizations have different academic programs in Perú and Ecuador. Local libraries and bookstores can be useful sources for current info on study abroad. The Internet has a study abroad web site at www.studyabroad.com/menu.html. You will need to acquire a student visa if you are planning to stay longer than 90 days.

LANGUAGE SCHOOLS

Programs vary significantly in cost, duration, and inclusions. A few are listed below. See **Further Reading** to find out about more.

American Field Service (AFS), 310 SW 4th Ave. #630, Portland, OR 97204-2608 (tel. (800) 237-4636; fax (503) 241-1653; email afsinfo@afs.org; www.afs.org/usa). AFS offers summer, semester, and year-long homestay international exchange programs in Ecuador for high school students and graduating high school seniors. Financial aid available.

Language Liaison, 1610 Woodstead Court #130, The Woodlands, TX 77380 (tel. 800-284-4448; fax (281) 367 4498; email learn@languageliason.com; www.languageliaison.com), offers language programs of varying duration for ages 16 and over.

Amerispan Unlimited, P.O. Box 40007, Philadelphia, PA 19106 (tel. (215) 751-1100; fax (215) 751-1986; email info@amerispan.com; www.amerispan.com), offers language immersion programs (ranging in price from US$300-2000) in Quito, Cuenca, Cusco, and Huancayo. Also offers educational travel programs, volunteer and internship opportunities, and links for Ecuador-related web resources.

School for International Training, College Semester Abroad, Admissions, Kipling Rd., P.O. Box 676, Brattleboro, VT 05302 (tel. 800-336-1616 or (802) 257-7751; fax 258-3248; www.worldlearning.org). Runs semester- and year-long programs in Quito. Programs cost US$8200-10,300, all expenses included. Financial aid available and US financial aid is transferable. Also runs the **Experiment in International Living,** Summer Programs (tel. 800-345-2929; fax (802) 258-3428; email eil@worldlearning.org). Founded in 1932, it offers cross-cultural, educational homestays, community service, ecological adventure, and language training in Quito and Riobamba (Ecuador). Programs are 3-5 weeks long and run from US$1800-5000. Positions as group leaders are available worldwide for college graduates with strong in-country experienced language skills for the host country and experience working with students.

FURTHER READING. *Academic Year Abroad*, by the Institute of International Education Books (US$45). *Vacation Study Abroad*, also from the Institute of International Education Books (US$40). *Peterson's Study Abroad Guide*, by Peterson's (US$30).

VOLUNTEER AND WORK

Volunteering is an excellent way to immerse yourself in Latin American culture, becoming familiar with the people and language while giving back to the place you are visiting. The good news is that it's very easy to find volunteer positions, especially if you are willing to shell out a few bucks for program fees; the bad news is that paid work can be exceedingly difficult to find. Countries are reluctant to give up precious jobs to traveling gringos when many of their citizens are unemployed. It's not impossible, though. Friends in Perú or Ecuador can help expedite work permits or arrange work-for-accommodations swaps, and some businesses are eager to hire English-speaking personnel for prestige or for the convenience of their patrons. The following is a list of useful publications and organizations.

For the most part, it is easiest for foreigners to find employment teaching English in Perú and Ecuador, where many professionals and students are eager to learn but there is often a shortage of instructors. Pay is meager, but bilinguals with some teaching experience or certification can earn considerably more.

TEACHING ENGLISH

International Schools Services, Educational Staffing Program, P.O. Box 5910, Princeton, NJ 08543 (tel. (609) 452-0990; fax 452-2690; email edustaffing@iss.edu; www.iss.edu). Recruits teachers and administrators for American and English schools in Perú and Ecuador. All instruction in English. Applicants must have a bachelor's degree and 2 years of relevant experience. Nonrefundable US$100 application fee. Publishes *The ISS Directory of Overseas Schools* (US$35).

Office of Overseas Schools, A/OS Room 245, SA-29, Dept. of State, Washington, D.C. 20522-2902 (tel. (703) 875-7800; fax 875-7979; email overseas.school@state.gov; www.state.gov/www/about_state/schools/). Keeps a list of schools abroad and agencies that arrange placement for Americans to teach abroad.

World Teach, Harvard Institute for International Development, 14 Story St., Cambridge, MA 02138 (tel. (617) 495-5527; fax 495-1599; email info@worldteach.org; www.worldteach.org). Volunteers teach mostly English, but also math, science, and environmental education to students of all ages in Ecuador. Bachelor's degree required for 6-month and year-long programs. Room and board are provided during the period of service, but volunteers must pay a fee covering transportation, health insurance, and training. (There is currently no progam in Perú.)

ARCHAEOLOGICAL DIGS

Archaeological Institute of America, 656 Beacon St., Boston, MA 02215-2010 (tel. (617) 353-9361; fax 353-6550; email aia@bu.edu; www.archaeological.org), puts out the *Archaeological Fieldwork Opportunities Bulletin* (US$16 for nonmembers), which lists field sites in Perú and Ecuador. This can be purchased from Kendall/Hunt Publishing, 4050 Westmark Dr., Dubuque, IA 52002 (tel. 800-228-0810).

VOLUNTEER

Volunteer jobs are readily available almost everywhere. You may receive room and board in exchange for your labor. You can sometimes avoid the high application fees charged by the organizations that arrange placement by contacting the individual workcamps directly; check with the organizations.

Peace Corps, 1111 20th St. NW, Washington, D.C. 20526 (tel. 800-424-8580; www.peacecorps.gov). Write for their "blue" brochure, which details application requirements. They have opportunities in a variety of fields in Ecuador (there is currently no program in Perú). Volunteers must be US citizens, age 18 and over, and willing to make a 2-year commitment. A bachelor's degree is usually required.

Volunteers for Peace, 1034 Tiffany Rd., Belmont, VT 05730 (tel. (802) 259-2759; fax 259-2922; email vfp@vfp.org; www.vfp.org). A nonprofit organization that arranges speedy placement in 2-3 week workcamps in Ecuador comprising 10-15 people. Most complete and up-to-date listings provided in the annual *International Workcamp Directory* (US$15). Registration fee US$195. Free newsletter.

OTHER RESOURCES

USEFUL PUBLICATIONS

Latin American Travel Consultants, P.O. Box 17-17-908, Quito, Ecuador (fax (5932) 562-566 or USA/CDA toll-free fax 1-888-215-9511; email latc@pi.pro.ec; www.amerispan.com/latc). Publishes quarterly newsletter on 17 countries in Latin America (Latin American Travel Advisor), focusing on the public safety, health, weather, natural phenomena, travel costs, politics, and economy of each country. US$39 for one-year newsletter subscription. Sells road, city, and topographic maps. Organizes small-group expeditions and multilingual private guides. Complete travel information service.

Specialty Travel Index, 305 San Anselmo Ave. #313, San Anselmo, CA 94960 (tel. (415) 455-1643 or 888-624-4030; fax 459-4974; email spectrav@ix.netcom.com; www.spectrav.com). Published twice yearly, this is a listing of "off the beaten track" and specialty travel opportunities. One copy US$6, one-year subscription (2 copies) US$10.

Hippocrene Books, Inc., 171 Madison Ave., New York, NY 10016 (tel. (212) 685-4371; orders (718) 454-2366; fax 454-1391; email contact@hippocrenebooks.com; www.netcom.com/~hippocre). Publishes travel reference books, travel guides, foreign language dictionaries, and language learning guides which cover over 100 languages.

THE WORLD WIDE WEB

Perú Online Networks (www.peruonline.com) provides a very comprehensive set of links and search engines for everything Peruvian.

Ecuaworld (http://ecuaworld.com) provides historical, cultural, geographical, and other useful information about Ecuador. Includes chat room and links to all kinds of resources useful to travelers.

Latinworld (www.latinworld.com) provides information on Latin America with links to specific countries including Perú and Ecuador.

South American Explorers Club (www.samexplo.org) has all you ever need. For a list of services see p. 25.

Microsoft Expedia (expedia.msn.com) has everything you'd ever need to make travel plans on the web: compare flight fares, look at maps, make reservations. FareTracker, a free service, sends you monthly mailings about the cheapest fares to any destination.

Foreign Language for Travelers (www.travlang.com) helps you brush up on your Spanish.

Let's Go (www.letsgo.com) is where you can find our newsletter, information about our books, up-to-the-minute links, and more.

A REGIONAL OVERVIEW

THE LAND

The **Andes Mountains** span the entire western side of South America, cutting the Perú and Ecuador region into two lopsided halves. The extraordinary mountain range was formed by the brutal collision of two tectonic plates several million years ago. The mountains' relatively young age has prevented wind and water from working their erosive magic on the rugged peaks. However, the region's geology is far from static; the entire South American coast lies on the edge of a continental plate that is being subducted by the oceanic plate of the Pacific. The interaction of the two plates causes volcanic activity and relatively frequent **earthquakes.** All along the Ecuadorian and Peruvian Andes, active and extinct volcanoes mingle with long stretches of arable highlands (or **sierra**), which are cultivated with barley, wheat, and corn. In Perú, other important crops are the potato and the extremely hardy quinoa, dubbed the "miracle grain" for its high nutritive content. The southern highlands of Ecuador and the Sacred Valley in Perú feature the typical sierra landscape of patchwork fields dominated by snow capped mountains, with an occasional sparkling lake thrown in for good measure. Farther south in Perú, near Lake Titicaca, high altitude plains (or **altiplano**) are extraordinarily desolate, too high up to support anything but scrub grass.

Yet Perú and Ecuador possess more than just stunning mountain landscape. Most of the land area of the two countries is occupied by sparsely populated, hot and humid tropical rainforest, found to the east of the central corridor formed by the Andes. Called the **Oriente** in Ecuador and the **Amazon basin** in Perú, this is where much of the region's extraordinary biodiversity can be found. In Perú, the high jungle is the choice climate for growing coca, a sacred crop since Inca times, but lately used for less holy purposes—to produce cocaine for export. On the opposite side of the Ecuadorian Andes, along the coast, mountains give way to fertile **lowlands** where coffee and bananas thrive. Also in Ecuador, swampy areas that once served as a breeding ground for many wildlife species follow the coastline, though some of these are now being replaced by shrimp and fish farms. As one moves towards the Peruvian coast, the Andes become scorched foothills, then arid **desert.** In some sections (like Nazca along the southern coast), the surrounding desert is among the driest in the world.

The **Galápagos Islands** (controlled by Ecuador) are in an ecological niche all their own. Formed over the past five million years from the eruptions of underwater volcanoes, the islands began as barren masses of lava. Today, they are covered with the animal and plant species that were able to cross the water from the continent to the islands. The warm waters of El Niño and the cold ones of the Humboldt stream battle to keep temperatures on the warm side but replete with rain, rain, and more rain. The first half of the year is the wet season; the air dries out and cools off noticeably during later months, when temperatures fall below 21°C.

FLORA AND FAUNA

As one might expect from an area extending across coastal, sierra, and tropical zones, the region encompassed by Perú and Ecuador hosts an extremely diverse range of plants and animals. Of the various constituent ecological zones, the rainforest has by far the greatest biodiversity: of the two million plant and animal species known to exist in the world today, half live exclusively in **rainforests.** Activists

South America
Gulf of Mexico
Caribbean Sea
ATLANTIC OCEAN
PANAMÁ
VENEZUELA
GUYANA
SURINAME
FRENCH GUIANA
COLOMBIA
Galápagos Islands
Quito
Guayaquil
ECUADOR
Amazon River
PERÚ
Lima
BRAZIL
BOLIVIA
PARAGUAY
CHILE
PACIFIC OCEAN
URUGUAY
ARGENTINA
ATLANTIC OCEAN
N
0
600 miles
0
600 kilometers
ANTARCTICA

around the world have recently stepped up efforts to protect the biodiversity of these forests, where tall trees form a several-story-high canopy under which smaller ferns, palms, and other plants grow. Thousands of animal species thrive in the Amazon basin, from the familiar deer, squirrels, and bats, to the powerful tapirs and jaguars, to the comically exotic guatusa, capybaras, and three-toed sloths. The high-altitude cloudforests of the **sierra** are remarkable for their strange combinations of cool, moist air and fairy tale flora. The only species of bear found in South America, the spectacled bear, resides in the highland region, as do domesticated llamas and alpacas. The vicuña, a relative of these last two, can only be found in areas above 3500m altitude. Ecuador has over 1,600 bird species—Perú over 1,700—each more than twice as many as all of North America. Both countries also boast several hundred species of mammals and fish. Of course, these only include the identified species. Within the six distinct zones of vegetation on the Galápagos (supporting mangroves, cacti, ferns, orchids, coffee plants, pineapple trees, and much more), numerous animal populations evolved in isolation, becoming unique to these islands. Some 30 endemic species of birds, various iguanas, sea lions, penguins, and the endangered giant tortoise from which the archipelago derives its name are all unique to the islands.

THE PEOPLE

The first peoples to inhabit the region of present-day Ecuador and Perú migrated from the north to the coastal regions over 12,000 years ago. The most notable migration of the modern era was the 15th-century conquest of much of the region by the Cusco-based **Incas.** Over the course of a few decades, the Incas spread their language (Quechua) and culture to many previously disparate social groups. No external invasions, however, occurred until the momentous invasion in 1526 by Spain's Francisco Pizarro. Since the infusion of **Spanish** blood and culture, other groups, too, have been mixed into the picture: **African slaves** were brought to work plantations on the coast, and small but thriving communities of **Chinese** and **Japanese** live in the region today. The majority of Ecuador's 12 million and Perú's 26 million inhabitants live in the highland and coastal regions; the Amazon remains little populated. A significant percentage of the region's population is centered in the urban centers of Quito and Guayaquil (home to over 2 million) and Lima (with a population surpassing 7 million). Issues of race and ethnicity are closely intertwined; an individual's identity as white, black, *mestizo* (mixed white and indigenous), or *indígena* (indigenous) is a combination of biological and social factors. Since the elite class has always been predominantly white and the working class mainly *mestizo* and *indígena*, a biological *mestizo* of high social rank may be called white, while a biological white with a low social rank may be called *mestizo*. This kind of ambiguity makes it impossible to know exactly how the population breaks down racially. The current estimate for Ecuador is 55% *mestizo*, 25% *indígena*, 10% white, and 10% black. A recent estimate for Perú is 45% *indígena*, 37% *mestizo*, 15% white, and 3% black, Japanese, Chinese, and other ethnicities.

Descendants of slaves who arrived in the 17th and 18th centuries, the **black population** of the region clearly maintains a distinct culture and ethnicity. The black peoples of Ecuador live primarily in the northern coastal province of Esmeraldas and in the Chota Valley of the northwest. Perú's small black population is centered along the coast between Lima and Ica. The country's **white population** is predominantly made up of descendants of Spanish conquistadors and colonists. Like their ancestors, they make up the majority of the country's elite and are concentrated primarily in the urban centers. **Mestizos** make up the bulk of Ecuador and Perú's urban population but also inhabit rural zones, often overlapping with indigenous communities. Far from a homogenous group, the cultures and lifestyles of *mestizo* groups are the complex result of varying influences, and they vary greatly from the coastal lowlands to the highlands to the jungle.

Indígenas are usually divided into two major groups, highlanders and lowlanders. Highland *indígenas* predominate in both countries; lowland groups generally reside in the western Amazon basin and Oriente, and constitute only 5% of Perú's and 2.5% of Ecuador's indigenous population. The *indígenas* are the poorest and least educated sector of the population. They generally occupy rural zones: only 17% of Perú's indigenous peoples live in cities. The indigenous population is also a highly **heterogeneous** group, divided into numerous distinct tribes and linguistic groups. There are over 80 extant language families in Perú alone, and several others in Ecuador. By far the most commonly spoken indigenous languages are **Quechua** (called Quichua in Ecuador) and **Aymara**—though these are divided into numerous regional dialects.

HISTORY

THE EARLIEST INHABITANTS

While the Inca culture has left the most visible mark on the region today, earlier pre-Hispanic civilizations thrived in the area long before the Incas arrived. Archaeological evidence shows that the earliest cultures lived over 12,000 years ago in the coastal regions of present-day Perú and Ecuador. In general, the ancient coastal inhabitants were hunter-gatherers and fishermen whose descendants gradually learned to practice sustainable agriculture. Auspicious ocean currents and winds made the coast ideal for farming, and for 8,000 years industrious settlements thrived there. There are few remains from these early civilizations, so little is known of them today. The oldest extensive archaeological findings are from the **Valdivia culture,** a people who lived along the coast of Ecuador's Santa Elena Peninsula roughly between 3500 and 1500 BC. The earliest known site is **Loma Alta,** where impressive pottery and female figurines were produced as early as 3500 BC. Another ancient town, **Real Alto,** reached its peak by 1500 BC. The site is scattered with more female figurines and remnants of over 100 households. Villages consisted of wood and straw huts arranged in a semi-circle around a central plaza, paved with shells for ceremonial purposes. By the variety of the materials used in their construction, these sites suggest the existence of trade networks connecting the coast, highlands, and jungle.

Other cultures also arose in the coastal areas over time, including the **Esmeralda, Manta, Huancavilca, Puná, Paracas, Mochica, Nazca,** and **Chimú** tribes. These groups also traded with tribes from the sierra, and as they eventually developed oceanic travel, trans-coastal trade became increasingly important. Several of these groups left remarkable accomplishments. The Nazca are famous for the gigantic, cryptic etchings they left on the dry soil of southern Perú (see p. 98), as well as for the high quality of their pottery. The Mochica of Northern Perú constructed lofty pyramids to their gods and an extensive irrigation system that allowed an otherwise barren valley to sustain a population of more than 50,000. In the same region, the Chimú built the great city of Chan Chan, which still stands outside of Trujillo and was also once home to about 50,000 residents. Farther north, **La Tolita,** a civilization that reached its peak around 700 BC, produced some of the most remarkable gold work known from Ecuador, most notably the famous mask of the Sun god whose image is frequently replicated in Ecuadorian literature and culture. Slowly, these early coastal cultures expanded and developed, creating a background against which later cultures would flourish.

By about the first century AD, various erstwhile coastal tribes had moved into the Andes region. These sedentary and mainly agricultural tribes—among them the **Pasto, Cara, Quitu, Cañari, Palta, Chavín, Huari (Huari),** and **Tiahuanuco**—used irrigation to cultivate corn, quinoa, beans, many varieties of potatoes and squash, and fruits such as pineapples and avocados. Local chieftains raised armies, distributed communal lands, and united different villages in political confederations headed by a single monarch. Several of these highland cultures have left lasting impressions on the region. The Cañari culture, which occupied the Cuenca region of southern Ecuador, developed an extensive irrigation system that came to support large cities and a military strong enough to fiercely resist the Inca expansion of the 15th century. In the Ancash region of northern Perú, the Chavín culture diffused its own set of ideas, rituals, and religious art across a fairly extensive empire. They are best known for their stylized religious iconography, which included depictions of various animals—particularly the jaguar. These early cultures persisted and maintained their autonomy for over 1000 years, but that independence was destined to end with the rise of an overwhelmingly powerful military force based in the southern sierra...

THE INCA EMPIRE

The Inca culture made a more extensive and profound impact on the region than did any other pre-Hispanic society. With meager beginnings as a small tribe centered around **Cusco** (or *Qosqo* in the Inca tongue of Quechua) in southern Perú, the Inca Empire expanded rapidly in the mid-15th century; within a century, it controlled nearly one-third of South America and more than 10 million people. Remarkably, this was accomplished without the use of the wheel or a developed system of writing (records were kept with an elaborate system of knot-tying). In the process of expanding their empire out from its capital in Cusco, the Incas moved north through Perú and into Ecuador in the late 15th century. The Inca conquest was executed mostly under the leadership of the warrior **Pachacuti Inca Yupanqui** (1438-71). Several tribes, including the Cañari from southern Ecuador, met the Inca troops with fierce resistance, and it took nearly four decades before both the sierra and coastal populations surrendered. **Huayna Cápac,** grandson of Pachacuti Inca Yupanqui and son of a Cañari princess, became ruler of the entire extended Inca empire, *Tawantinsuya* ("four corners" in Quechua), which spanned from present-day Northern Chile to what is now Southern Colombia.

A few aspects of life among the conquered tribes, such as their traditional religious beliefs, were left largely intact, but most areas of society were significantly changed by the conquering Incas. In addition to new foods (such as yucca, sweet potatoes, and peanut) and agricultural techniques (such as irrigation and terracing, in a planned exportation known as the *mitmaq* system), new land-ownership patterns were also introduced by the Incas. Instead of the previous system of private ownership, land became property of the Inca emperor (referred to as "the Inca") and was divided up into units for collective farming by **ayllu,** kinship-based clans. Each *ayllu* consisted of a number of individual families who, though allowed to consume a portion of their produce, were required to give tribute payments to an Inca **kuraka,** or chieftain.

Huayna Cápac grew up in the area occupied by modern-day Ecuador. Enamored of his homeland, he named Quito the second capital of the Inca empire. Fearful of unrest in his ever-expanding kingdom, he traveled all over the empire putting down uprisings and strengthening unions whenever he could—sometimes by marriage, other times by replacing troublesome populations with colonists from more peaceful parts of the empire. These colonizations helped spread the traditional Inca language of Quechua, which is still widely spoken today in many indigenous communities throughout Perú and Ecuador (now called "Quichua" in the latter).

Huayna Cápac's sudden death in 1526 (possibly from measles introduced by European explorers) brought on a bitter power struggle that became a devastating civil war. Rather than leaving the empire to one heir, he split the kingdom between two sons: Cusco and the southern empire were left to **Huáscar,** a son by Huayna Cápac's sister and therefore the legitimate heir; while Ecuador and the northern empire went to **Atahuallpa,** born by a lesser wife but his father's favorite. In 1532, Atahuallpa decisively defeated Huáscar near Riobamba in central Ecuador. Though the civil war was over, the Inca empire was left weakened and divided, unprepared for the arrival of the Spanish conquistadors a few months later.

THE SPANISH CONQUEST

As the Inca empire thrived in South America, Spain was rising in prominence and power in the New World. After pillaging and subjecting the peoples of Mexico and Central America, Spanish *conquistadores* moved south to the vast continent beyond. One of these conquerors was **Francisco Pizarro,** who had become a rich *encomendero* (landowner) in Panamá after leading the conquest of Nicaragua in 1522. Starting in 1524, he began lead several financed expeditions to the west coast of South America. After several failed journeys, Pizarro solicited King Carlos I for more funding and manpower from Spain. His request was granted, and the reinforced Spanish troops landed on the shores of northern Perú late in 1531. They reached Tumbes in mid-1532, where Pizarro left **Sebastián de Benalcázar**—who would later lead the conquest of Ecuador—to develop the Spanish base of San Miguel. Although the Incas received news of the foreigners' arrival, they failed to realize the threat they represented.

Fueled by stories of great Inca riches, Pizarro pushed inland to Cajamarca, the Inca summer residence in the highlands of northern Perú. He arrived in November 1532, and immediately demanded an audience with recently victorious Inca ruler **Atahuallpa,** who was resting in the *Baños del Inca* thermal baths (see p. 191). Accompanied by several thousand troops, Atahuallpa met the Spanish explorers in the plaza of Cajamarca. There, he was confronted by a priest, who ordered him to renounce his gods and swear allegiance to the King of Spain. He refused and threw a Spanish prayer book to the ground, an offense that inflamed the tempers of the Spanish soldiers surrounding the plaza. They opened fire on the Inca envoy, killing several thousand of Atahuallpa's men and taking the Inca emperor captive. Atahuallpa feared that the Spanish planned to depose him in favor of his brother, so he ordered the execution of Huáscar along with several hundred military leaders and members of the ruling family. Ironically, this action further weakened the Inca empire and facilitated the Spanish conquest in the months and years to come. According to legend, Pizarro offered to free Atahuallpa if he could raise a **King's ransom,** filling his prison cell once with gold and twice with silver (yielding a total of nearly 15,000kg of precious metals). Atahuallpa complied, but instead of releasing him, the Spanish held a mock trial that called for the execution the Inca emperor.

The strength and cohesion of the Inca nation died with Atahuallpa. Nevertheless, some Inca warriors continued to defend their empire. In Quito, the general **Rumiñahui,** with the help of Cañari tribesmen from southern Ecuador, engaged in a struggle with the Spanish. Sebastián de Benalcázar, one of Pizarro's lieutenants, defeated Rumiñahui near Mount Chimborazo and began pushing the Incas north. In mid-1534, when Rumiñahui realized that the Spaniards would soon conquer Quito, he set it ablaze, preferring to destroy this secondary Inca capital rather than surrender it to the conquistadors. Quito was refounded by the Spaniards on **December 6, 1534,** a day still celebrated with parades, bullfights, and dances in the modern city.

Meanwhile, the Spanish initiated a march of conquest on the Inca capital of Cusco. To aid in their assault, they enlisted the support of other native groups eager to end years of subjugation by the Incas. Even Manco Capac II, half-brother of the slain Inca leader, agreed to collaborate with the Spanish after Pizarro promised to install Manco as the ruling Inca. Eventually Manco realized that he was little more than a puppet, and instigated an indigenous revolt against his erstwhile ally in 1536. Though they had superior numbers, the Inca forces were unable to eject the conquistadors, and set their sacred capital ablaze in desperation. Following his defeat, Manco Capac II retreated to Vilcabamba, a town deep in the rugged Andean interior, and established an Inca kingdom that would remain autonomous and continue to resist Spanish rule until 1572.

THE COLONIAL ERA

After the Conquest, Pizarro assumed the role of governor of **New Castile,** as the area was first known. Unfortunately, he had neither the vision nor the ability to establish a peaceful society, and fighting and civil strife prevailed. During this time, the native population was grossly exploited, serving as a slave labor force for **encomenderos,** conquistadors given control of the land and (in exchange for Christianizing them) its residents. These *encomenderos* created huge plantations for themselves on land obtained by making deals with the *kurakas* (local chieftains). The *kurakas* acquiesced to the more powerful Spaniards and agreed to hand over their *ayllu*'s tribute payments, supposedly in exchange for the order that Spanish Christianity brought to them. The era of *encomiendas* was one of extreme civil unrest, with fighting between *indígenas* and colonists as well as violent power struggles among the Spanish landowners.

Originally, both Perú and Ecuador were part of the **Viceroyalty of Perú,** administered by the *audencia* (high court) and *cabildo* (municipal court) in Lima. As the colonial population grew, the *audencia* in Lima could no longer exert adequate control over its sprawling area of responsibility, so in 1563 the **Audencia de Quito** was established. This allowed Spain to better exercise its control of the entire region and finally bring a civil order that would last for several centuries. In 1720, in a further attempt to tighten Spanish control over the colonies, Ecuador was made part of the **Viceroyalty of Nueva Granada,** and central authority shifted from Lima to Bogotá, Colombia. The viceroy and *audencias* enforced the New Laws of 1542, which officially abolished slave labor and *encomiendas*, though both continued throughout most of the colonial period. Later viceroys established a social system known as the *repartamiento de indios*, which made the entire indigenous population vassals of the Spanish crown. They also introduced the *mita*, a system of forced labor that required all men between the ages of 18 and 50 to work for the Spanish crown for at least two months each year. Overseen by *corregidores*, new Spanish officials in charge of administering the *mita*, *mitayos* (workers) labored on huge agricultural *haciendas* or in *obrajes* (primitive textile sweatshops). As treacherous as the *mita* was for Ecuadorian workers, they were fortunate relative to their Peruvian counterparts. In Perú, where there were much heftier deposits of valuable minerals, miner *mitayos* experienced even more brutal conditions in the dark and dangerous quarries. The largest threat to the *indígenas*, however, was disease. **Smallpox** and **measles** brought by the colonists virtually wiped out the coastal population and drastically reduced the population of the sierras, especially during an epidemic in the 1690s. In the first century of Spanish rule, the indigenous population of Perú and Ecuador was reduced by 80%, plummeting from over 20 to around four million.

THE INDEPENDENCE MOVEMENT

Over the course of the 18th century, tensions escalated as the newly ascendant Bourbon dynasty (established in Spain in 1700) progressively tightened its control over the colonies. *Criollos* (people of European descent born in the New World) ever more ardently resented their high taxes, limited access to indigenous labor, and trade restrictions, as well as the privileges the Spanish-born *peninsulares* had in gaining political office. The relation between the Crown and the *criollos* was further strained when, after Europe's Seven Years' War (1756-63), the defeated and bankrupt Spanish kingdom passed the **Bourbon Reforms,** which greatly increased Spain's control over colonial surpluses.

IN PERÚ. The paths of Perú and Ecuador diverged in 1808, when Napoleon invaded Spain and deposed King Ferdinand VII. While local *criollos* were a driving force for independence in Ecuador, their Peruvian counterparts, under royalist Viceroy **José Fernando Abascal** (1806-16), remained loyal to the motherland. This reluctance to rebel was in part due to *criollo* fears inspired by the **Great Rebellion,** an indigenous and *mestizo* uprising led by **Túpac Amaru II** in 1780. Though officially not a racial movement, the rebellion involved significant violence along race lines, and many *criollos* preferred continued colonial status over the possibility of racial revolt. Since *criollos* were the most unified, as well as the most politically and economically potent, sector of the New World populace, a movement without their support would be destined for failure. Though Ferdinand VII's severe treatment of the American colonies somewhat weakened the loyalist cause, Perú's independence movement was primarily a movement imposed from the outside, rather than an expression of local sentiment. Argentine General **José de San Martín** believed Argentina's recently attained independence would remain insecure until Perú too achieved liberation. In 1819, San Martín thus launched a campaign against Perú's royalist forces. After taking Lima, he declared Perú independent on **July 28, 1821.** The declaration, however, was not the deed: a formidable royalist force remained to oppose San Martín in the southern sierra. To defeat the remaining royalist forces, San Martín enlisted the aid of liberator **Simón Bolívar,** arriving from the north, at a historic meeting in Guayaquil. Following the meeting, San Martín returned to Europe and Bolívar took charge of the struggle. Victory followed upon victory, and on **December 9, 1824,** Bolívar's forces, led by José Antonio de Sucre, struck the final blow against troops loyal to the Crown at the **Battle of Ayachuco.**

IN ECUADOR. Ecuadorian local *criollos*, unlike their Peruvian counterparts, were a driving force for independence. After King Ferdinand was deposed in 1808, colonists banded together in support of Ferdinand to form **cabildos abiertos** (town councils), which in some areas even seized authority. One of the first patriot uprisings in all of Latin America is believed to have occurred when a group of leading citizens took control of Quito in August 1809. However, as troops threatened the city, the rebels returned power to the *audencia* authorities. After Ferdinand VII returned the throne in 1814, his severe restriction of colonial autonomy caused even the most conservative Ecuadorians to turn against him. In Guayaquil, a patriotic *junta* under the leadership of poet **José Joaquín Olmedo** proclaimed the city's independence in October 1820. Troops from the independence movements of both the Argentine José de San Martín in the south and the Venezuelan Simón Bolívar in the north helped Ecuador in the fight against the royalist forces. Led by Lieutenant **Antonio José de Sucre,** a string of patriotic victories culminated in the decisive victory at the **Battle of Pichincha,** just outside Quito, on May 24, 1822. The next year, Ecuador joined the **Confederation of Gran Colombia,** uniting with the modern-day nations of Colombia and Venezuela under Bolívar's grand plan to unite Latin America. Plagued by regional rivalries, this tumultuous confederation split up in 1830; a small section in its southwest corner became today's independent Republic of Ecuador.

RELIGION

One important repercussion of the Spanish Conquest was the conversion of the *indígenas* to **Catholicism.** The earliest colonists were granted the labor of indigenous groups by the Spanish monarchy on the condition that they convert them to Christianity before working them to death. The Spanish justified this cruelty by reasoning that they had saved the *indígenas'* souls before they took their lives. As indigenous labor became more scarce, missionaries headed into the wilderness and established missions there. This often resulted in peaceful conversion, but *encomenderos* often used the newly blazed trails to enslave and exploit the native populations. Today's Perú and Ecuador, like the rest of Latin America, has a mostly Roman Catholic population. As a result of missionary activities during this century, a small percentage of the population is also **Protestant.** Even these modern-day missions can be quite coercive, offering medical services or other aid only to those who visit their churches. In recent years, **Mormon** and **Seventh Day Adventist** missionaries have been traveling to the region in ever greater numbers.

In many cases, the indigenous populations have not given up their own traditions but have simply incorporated Catholicism into their earlier belief systems. The resulting **hybrid religions** intertwine identities of indigenous gods and spirits with those of Christian saints. Indigenous celebrations are now often held on Saints' Days; for instance, the June 24 festival of St. John the Baptist is thought to have replaced the Inca festival of *Inti Raymi*, held on the summer solstice. In other cases, a given situation (e.g. an illness) requires an offering to a certain saint instead of to an indigenous spirit. Other traditions have remained completely distinct from Catholicism. Many indigenous peoples in the Andes still worship mountains, as they traditionally have, which they believe are the homes of mighty spirits (or *apus*) that control fertility and the rain. In addition, **shamans** (*curanderos* in Spanish) are often called upon to cure the sick. Many techniques are used to diagnose and treat illnesses. One ritual involves rubbing a disemboweled guinea pig all over a sick person's body, then using the convoluted pattern of its entrails to learn something about the ailment; another process involves rubbing the person with a whole raw egg and then interpreting the noise the egg makes when shaken.

FESTIVALS AND HOLIDAYS

Semana Santa, the Holy Week immediately preceding Easter, occasions the most parties in Perú and Ecuador. Ayacucho and Cusco in the Peruvian highlands are regarded as the best places to experience this celebration; in Ecuador, Quito is the popular point of pilgrimage for Good Friday. However, large festivals can be found in most cities, especially in the highlands. As one would expect, **Navidad** (Christmas) on December 25 is another religious holiday of great importance. However, instead of a capitalist onslaught of Christmas trees and clearance sales, processions of the Christ child largely predominate. Although the celebration of **Carnaval,** the week before Lent, does not reach Mardi Gras proportions, it takes on its own flare: in Ambato, the streets are filled with a cornucopia of flowers and fruit; while in Cajamarca and other highland cities, townspeople run around flinging water, paint, oil, and other liquids at each other (and especially at gawking tourists). **Día de los Difuntos** (Day of the Dead; Nov. 2) combines the Catholic tradition of All Souls' Day with *indígena* burial rituals. Offerings of food, along with little bread renditions of people and animals, are laid on top of the graves of relatives. Many highland towns also hold a **Corpus Cristi** (Body of Christ) celebration around the second week of June, most notably in Cuenca in southern Ecuador. Though the religious significance is vague at best, the week-long festival has enough sweet pastries, fruit candies, and *castillos* (large towers of fireworks that explode every night with dangerous vigor) to supersede any traditional explanation.

Not all fiestas in Perú and Ecuador have their roots in Catholicism; especially in the highlands and in the jungle regions, locals continue to celebrate holidays dedicated to non-Christian deities. The most famous of these is undoubtedly the festival of **Inti Raymi** ("Festival of the Sun" in Quechua), celebrated in Cusco on June 24. A tribute to the Inca sun god Inti, the solstice festival involves colorful parades, traditional dances, live music, diverse expositions, and an oration in Quechua given at the archaeological complex of Sacsayhuaman. This celebration, attracting hordes of tourists to the Andean city, is reputedly the second biggest festival in Latin America after the carnival of Rio de Janeiro. Most towns celebrate an **Independence Day** associated with the date on which they were liberated from Spain. Quito's (August 10), Guayaquil's (October 9), and Cuenca's (November 3) are Ecuadorian national holidays and entail concerts, sporting events, parades, and other spectacles. Peruvians go all out for their **Fiestas Patrias** on July 28-29; even in the smallest towns, schoolchildren begin practicing weeks in advance for the parades.

Many of the lesser-known celebrations take on more of a local flavor. Chincha Alta, on Perú's southern coast, is known for its colorful **Verano Negro** festival at the end of February, featuring all sorts of displays of local and cultural pride. In Ecuador, Esmeraldas's festivities (Aug. 3-5) include African music and *marimba* dancing. **Regional festivals,** such as those dedicated to patron saints, often originated as indigenous feast days before they were assimilated into the Catholic tradition. They are usually celebrated with drinking, dancing to local music, and sometimes a beauty pageant or two. In the Peruvian capital, the residents have been paying homage to **Santa Rosa de Lima,** the patron saint of the city, every August 30th since 1671. In Ecuador, men doll up in drag and blackface for Latacunga's **La Virgen de las Mercedes** holiday on September 24, in honor of the city's dark-skinned statue of the Virgin Mary, known as La Mama Negra (see p. 301).

Check in tourist offices when you get to a new city or town, since there's almost always bound to be some sort of festival going on in the area. When traveling on or around major festival days, reserve accommodations well in advance.

CUSTOMS AND MANNERS

Traveling in the region of Perú and Ecuador, it doesn't take long to figure out that local customs and manners aren't always what you're used to. No one bats an eye when an elderly woman spits a huge blob on a public bus, but a traveler might be frowned upon for having a stubbly beard. The people you encounter will pay particular attention to you, as a foreigner, and you'll be more likely to earn their respect if you take a moment to familiarize yourself with their social norms.

Foreign visitors are often shocked by the overwhelming **machismo** in some parts of Latin America. Women in bars—and foreign women in general—are often regarded as lascivious. Females who drink and act rowdy, or even just express their opinions, will shock men who prize meekness in women. Whether you're male or female, be sensitive to rising testosterone levels. Never say anything about a man's mother, sister, wife, or girlfriend.

Personal hygiene and **appearance** are often difficult to maintain while traveling, but they are very important in Perú and Ecuador. Your appearance affects how you are treated by locals: clean-shaven men with short hair and women who don't show much skin are more likely to receive respect than scruffies and smellies or women without bras. Men should remove hats when entering a building.

Punctuality isn't as important as it is in Europe and the U.S. (as you'll quickly confirm), but there are, of course, limits. A different perspective on time is apparent during meals, which are rarely hurried in Perú and Ecuador. After a big meal, enjoy the ingenious tradition of *siesta*, a time in the afternoon when it's just too hot to do anything but relax, have a drink, or maybe nap. Don't expect much to happen during the mid-afternoon, as banks and shops often shut their doors. Latin Americans hold **politeness** in high esteem, both in acquaintances and strangers. Jaded foreign travelers who consider urban indifference the highest virtue need to adjust if they expect to be treated with respect. When meeting someone for the first time, shake hands firmly, look the person in the eye, and say *"Mucho gusto de conocerle"* ("Pleased to meet you."). When entering a room, greet everybody, not just the person you came to see. Females often greet each other with a peck on the cheek or a quick hug. Sometimes men shake hands with women in a business situation, but the standard greeting between a man and a woman—even if they are meeting for the first time—is a quick kiss on the cheek.

Salutations in passing are considered common courtesy in small towns, particularly in the Oriente. *"Buenos días"* in the morning, *"buenas tardes"* after noon, and *"buenas noches"* after nightfall should be said to almost anyone with whom you come into contact. This charming Latin American custom epitomizes a general feeling of *amistad* on the streets, even between strangers. A similar custom is saying *"buen provecho"* ("bon appetit") to everyone in a restaurant upon entering or leaving. The American "OK" symbol (a circle with the thumb and forefinger) is considered vulgar and offensive—move your hand rapidly towards and away from yourself, and you'll understand why. Finally, be sensitive when taking **photographs.** Devotees at a shrine may be interesting to look at, but their piety is no novelty. If you must take pictures of locals, first ask if they mind—they may object strongly to being photographed.

FOOD

From conventional standbys to exotic local dishes, Perú and Ecuador satisfy people of all tastes. The fruits encountered here are some of the most succulent in the world. Distinctive grains and tubers abound, and a plethora of vegetables are cultivated and cooked. As for meat, just about any animal—and any part of its body—is considered fair game, from hoof to heart, tentacle to testicle. For the most part, your culinary experience will be determined by the region you're in and the type of restaurant you choose to visit.

Eating in a hotel or in a pricier restaurant allows you to sample finely prepared cuisine native to regions other than the one you're visiting, as well as hard-to-find desserts like the exquisite *dulce tres leches* (three-milk dessert). But chances are you'll do most of your eating in small, family-owned local diners, sometimes referred to as **comedores.** Unequivocally the most economical way to acquire your daily sustenance, and certainly the most popular way to eat out among locals, is to order the **menú del día** (meal of the day) that most *comedores* offer. Sometimes referred to as *el almuerzo* (the lunch) during the day or *la merienda* (the dinner) at night, this is a set platter, usually with two courses and various extras. It is prepared in advance and served at a special price (US$1-3, a little more in Perú). The first course consists of soup; you may be served a succulent *chupe de pescado* (a popular fish and vegetable soup), a hearty *caldo de res* (beef stew), or *caldo de patas* (pig- or cow-hoof stew). The second course (*segundo* or *plato fuerte*) is almost always based upon some kind of *carne* (meat), often smothered in a savory sauce appealing to the tastes of the locals. Popular traditional *platos fuertes* include *lomo saltado* (a stir-fried meat dish), *seco de pollo* (a thick chicken stew), *chicharrón* (deep-fried meats, usually pork), and *pescado sudado* (traditionally flavored steamed fish; mainly eaten along the coast). Along with the *carne* generally comes rice, fried potatoes, vegetables, or *menestre* (lentils or beans). Occasionally you'll luck into *choclo* (large-kernel native corn), yucca, a *tamal* (like a tamale), or an *humita* (also like a tamale; sometimes sweet). Fancier restaurants sometimes offer a *menú del día* as well, always at significantly higher prices, often with extras like coffee, dessert, cloth napkins, and uniformed waters. If the *menú del día* doesn't do the trick, check out the menu for **à la carte** selections. These will almost always cost more and provide less nourishment, but sometimes it's worth the extra cash to be able to choose your own meal.

To diversify your diet you may decide to dine at three other types of restaurants that are both inexpensive and abundant. **Chifas** (Chinese restaurants), present in even the smallest of towns, are generally very clean and serve scrumptious and filling *chaufas* (fried-rice dishes) and *tallarines* (noodle dishes). **Parilladas** (grills) serve meat—and nothing but meat—of all kinds: steak, pork chop, liver, and more unusual but very popular cuts such as intestine, tripe, udder, heart, and blood sausage (mmmmm). **Cevicherías** (sometimes called *picanterías* in Perú) serve seafood, especially *ceviche* (or *cebiche*), an popular dish made from raw seafood marinated in lemon and lime juice (whose acids partly cook the meat) with cilantro and onion (served extra spicy in Perú.) Larger and more touristed cities also offer all the fast food, international food, and vegetarian options you're accustomed to at home.

But ceviche and blood sausage just don't satisfy first thing in the morning. Luckily, breakfast food can be found in most any *comedor*, though *desayuno* (breakfast) is usually light. Most common are bread, juice, coffee, eggs, and sometimes rice and beans, as well as plantain dishes such as *chirriados* in certain regions (see p. 452). Well-touristed areas may offer a *desayuno americano*, which includes a bit more food for voracious American appetites. If you don't mind a light breakfast or want a midday snack, a quick and easy way to grab a bite is to buy fruit at the local **mercado** (market): papayas, passion fruit, avocados, tangerines, pineapples, tamarinds, *naranjilla*, and *tomate de árbol* are just a few of the possibilities. Or visit a **panadería** (bakery): *empanadas de queso* (bread stuffed with cheese), *pan dulce* (sugar-coated rolls), and *pan de sal* (salted rolls) all go unbelievably cheap.

TRADITIONAL FOODS

PERÚ. Perú has a culinary history equaled in richness only by its assortment of delectable **desserts:** *picarones* (deep-fried bread in a golden syrup); *mazamorra* (a sweet purple pudding); *helado de lúcuma* (ice cream made with a local fruit); and, in Lima, *suspiro de limeña* ("sigh of a Liman woman," made with sugar and condensed milk). But resist, if you can, the temptation to skip right to the sweets. Start instead with the succulent and ubiquitous **papa a la huancaína** (potato covered in a special creamy sauce). Originating in Huancayo, this simple but delicious dish is wildly popular throughout most of the country. Another light and simple plate loved by locals is **palta rellena,** consisting of an avocado stuffed with a chicken and vegetable mix. For something a bit heartier, try **anticuchos de corazón** (kabob of cow heart). Equally scrumptious is **encocado de mariscos** (seafood in coconut milk), often served in a coconut shell. Peruvians also enjoy a good plate of *cuy* (see below). If you don't have the cash to eat these relative delicacies, sample a **bistec a lo pobre,** "poor man's steak," mixed with bananas and egg. Maximally filling and a perennial side dish is the national specialty, **tacu-tacu,** a dense mix of mashed beans and rice served with anything and everything: don't leave Perú without trying it.

ECUADOR. Most dishes popular in Ecuador can be found in Perú and vice-versa, but some foods are more particular to one country or the other. **Tronquito** (bull penis) and **yaguarlocro** (soup with blood-sprinklings) are among Ecuador's most exotic (and erotic) dishes. Equally shocking to foreigners but extremely popular among locals is the mouth-watering delicacy known as **cuy** (guinea pig). A specialty dating back to Inca times, the dish gets its name from the sound the animal makes just before getting skewered and roasted: "cuy, cuy, cuy...." The more vegetarian-friendly **llapingachos** (Andean potato and cheese pancakes) also date back to ancient times and get their name from the sound the potatoes make when being boiled and mashed: "llapingacho, llapingacho, llapingacho...." Andean natives really know their potatoes, first cultivated in the Andes before becoming a starch staple the world over. Perhaps the easiest way to get your daily intake of non-meat foods, though, is to order a few of the myriad banana and plantain dishes that constitute a mainstay of the *costeño* (coast-dweller) diet. **Patacones** (deep fried plantain slices) are a favorite side dish, divine as an accompaniment to *ceviche.*

DRINK

If urgent visits to the nearest restroom are not your idea of fun, avoid drinking tap water. Water advertised as **purificada** (purified) may have only been passed through a filter, which does not necessarily catch all of those diarrhea-causing demons. Water that has been boiled or treated with **iodine** is safe to drink; otherwise, **bottled water** is best. Make sure the cap is sealed and wipe the rim before taking a sip.

Sweeter, more effervescent options also abound. Popular soft drinks, always called *colas*, include the worldwide brands Coca-Cola, Sprite, and Fanta, as well as **Fiorivanti** in Ecuador (with strawberry, apple, and pineapple flavors) and **Inca Kola,** found everywhere in Perú. **Juices** made from the region's abundance of exotic fruits are common and delicious, but almost always made with water; before drinking up, make sure the water used was purified. **Coffee** is not as good as it should be, considering that the beans come from the region. It is usually served as *esencia* (boiled-down, concentrated grinds mixed with water or milk). You might also be served hot water with a can of Nescafé instant coffee. **Milk** is also readily available, but is much creamier than the low-fat milk to which many foreigners may be accustomed. A favorite dairy drink is **yogur,** a cold drink made with thin, sweetened yogurt, often flavored with fruit. Before downing a tall, cold glass of the white stuff, make sure it's been pasteurized.

If you're looking for something a bit more intoxicating, sample a local lager. **Pilsener** and **Club** predominate in Ecuador; **Cristal** and **Cusqueña** abound in Perú. One of these beers will set you back a fraction of a U.S. dollar—at these prices, why hold back? If you really want to drown your sorrows, liquor is readily available at almost every corner store at absurdly cheap prices (around US$2 for a liter of decent rum). If you wish to imbibe in a nice bar or restaurant, prices rise dramatically. Many a tasty drink is made from **aguardiente,** an extremely potent sugarcane alcohol. **Caneliza,** made by boiling together water, *aguardiente*, cinnamon, and lemon juice, will warm your insides on cool, misty highland evenings. Another enticing intoxicant is Perú's **pisco,** a clear, brandy-like liquor. You'll most often find it in the form of a *pisco sour*, a mixed drink made with *pisco*, lemon juice, and sugar. **Alcoholic chicha,** popular in Ecuador's Oriente, is a liquor made from the yucca plant and fermented with the saliva of elderly *Shuar* women. **Non-alcoholic chichas** (also non-saliva) come in myriad varieties throughout the region. Especially popular in Perú is **chicha morrada,** a sweet purple beverage made from corn.

SPORTS AND RECREATION

When they're not working, the people of Perú and Ecuador love to play. As is the case in the rest of Latin America (and the world, for that matter), soccer, or **fútbol,** reigns supreme. Fútbol fields dot the countryside and urban areas and are heavily used by *jugadores* (players) of all shapes, sizes, and ability levels. For a slightly less strenuous activity, many people also enjoy **foosball,** the analogous table sport that relies more on hand-eye coordination than strength and stamina. But don't be fooled by its tranquil appearance; although the game involves minimal physical movement, some matches can become as heated as any World Cup final.

Basketball has become quite popular in Latin America in recent years. This is largely because of the global attention that the sport receives and the hero-god role that its finest players and teams have assumed in North American pop culture. Perhaps more unexplainable is the increasing popularity of **volleyball** in some parts of the region. The courts are usually rather makeshift, often marked off by articles of clothing in an open lot or field, but the rules are basically the same as elsewhere in the world. The play of the games differs slightly; since most residents are under six feet tall, most of the action takes place *below* the net.

For the slightly more adventurous (and wealthier) visitor, there is a multitude of activities that will quench any adrenaline craving. Because of the, well, *extreme* geography of the region, thrill-seeking opportunities abound. The Andes mountain range, which bisects the region from north to south, provides not only incredible scenery but also some of the best **trekking** and **mountaineering** in the world. With dozens of peaks over 5000m high, Perú and Ecuador have become prime destinations for serious mountain climbers from around the world. For more sedate activity, the passes and valleys created by the volcanic peaks provide perfect conditions for short- or long-distance hikes through pristine countryside.

If you'd rather swim than walk, check out the excellent **whitewater rafting** and **kayaking.** Raging rivers run rapidly from the mountains to either the Pacific or the tropical Amazon basin, creating plenty of aquatic turbulence along the way. A word of caution: since rafting is a fairly new industry in Latin America, those interested should check equipment ahead of time and ask tourist authorities to recommend reputable operators. Some companies just want to attract tourists, even if that means using outdated equipment, incompetent guides, or dangerous rapids. At the very least, make sure they provide everyone with a life jacket and helmet. Try to find out which rivers are safe during the rainy or dry seasons and plan your trip accordingly. The accomplished will find surprisingly good **surfing** along most of the Pacific coast. The central coast of Ecuador, especially Montañita, and most of the Peruvian coast have recently developed local surfing communities, with the occasional foreigner "dropping in" with little or no problem. Some surf shops have sprung up, many of which repair dings and rent boards to visitors. If you bring your own equipment, consult with the airline first to make sure that you can check it as regular baggage or sporting equipment rather than freight. Because of the Humboldt current, the water in central and southern Perú may be surprisingly chilly despite the latitude.

THE ARTS

Peruvian and Ecuadorian arts reveal a complex blend of influences—indigenous and European, ancient and modern. The legacy was laid down by the Incas and other pre-Hispanic groups with their **artesanía** (arts and crafts) and distinctive Andean music. When the Spanish arrived, the artistic influences and technology of the Old World mixed with indigenous art styles. In particular, the religious art so well known in the Old World developed a distinct new style. With time, the art of this region followed modern trends more and more. Indigenous artisans, combining ancient and modern techniques, began making products for an international market. A number of talented painters, in touch with worldwide artistic currents, started producing modern art with South American subject matter. Today's art scene in Perú and Ecuador is as active as ever, and numerous museums, festivals, and markets celebrate the countries' artistic traditions. Whether you seek the holy splendor of a colonial cathedral or the mellifluous notes of the Andean *zampoñas*, the region has the cultural color to further decorate your cerebral canvas.

ARTESANÍA

Crafts of all kinds are produced in Perú and Ecuador, but the region is best known for its large variety of **handmade textiles,** almost all of which are produced by various indigenous groups. In Ecuador, the most prolific and well-known center of textile production is **Otavalo,** an indigenous community 96km north of Quito. *Otavaleños* have been in the textile business for centuries. When the Incas conquered the area in the late 15th century, they forced the inhabitants to pay tribute with their textiles. A few decades later, the Spanish brought new technologies in the forms of treadle looms and hand carders, and new materials like silk and sheep's wool. Under one guise or another, they forced the *indígenas* to work under horrible conditions in *obrajes* (textile workshops) well into the 19th century. In the early 1900s, the *otavaleños* got their start in the modern textile industry by producing imitations of British tweeds (called *casimires*). Since then, the region has continued to put out quality textiles, with almost all production taking place in indigenous households. Most weaving is done with the treadle loom, but some families still use the backstrap loom, a pre-Hispanic design, with one end attached to the weaver's back. All kinds of indigenous products, from *ponchos* to belts and tapestries, are exported to markets around the world.

In Perú, the best textiles can be found in the highlands, particularly in the **Ayacucho** area (known for its weavings) and in **Huancayo** and the surrounding **Río Mantaro** region. On Lake Titicaca, the **Isla Taquile** is the place to go for famous fine-spun products. The most common medium is wool, whether from sheep (generally referred to simply as *lana*, sometimes as *lana de oveja*), llama, or alpaca. Occasionally soft vicuña wool is also used; however, because vicuña are extremely difficult to raise domestically, their wool is rare and quite expensive. In addition to the practical items of clothing that many tourists buy as protection from the cold, artisans sell a wide selection of tapestries with scenes of the mountains or local life.

A major center for **leatherwork** exists in **Cotacachi,** Ecuador, just north of Otavalo. Wallets, purses, belts, whips, and even leather underwear can all be found in the many shops lining the town's main street. The handiwork of the Cotacachicans is of excellent quality. The people of Perú and Ecuador carve **wood products** of all kinds, from intricate wooden boxes and sculptures to furniture. Many artisans work and sell goods right out of their homes, hence the sounds of saws and chisels, and the trails of sawdust. In Perú's Río Mantaro region, **carved gourds** known as *matés burilados* also make popular gifts.

Pre-Hispanic **metalwork** was highly skilled, and in some places the tradition of hand-crafting jewelry lives on. Elaborate shawl pins (called *tupus*) are made and worn by *indígenas*, often as family heirlooms passed from one generation to the next. Much Ecuadorian and Peruvian jewelry incorporates beads into its design, a tradition that began before the Spanish conquest. Beads made of red Spondylus shell were traded throughout the Andes, and to this day, red is the favored bead color. Ceramics are also made throughout the region. The Quichua *Sacha Runa* (jungle people) who inhabit the Ecuadorian Oriente produce fine hand-coiled pots with paintings of Quichua life and mythology on the sides. Other well-respected Ecuadorian ceramics are made in the area around Latacunga. The small town of **Pujilí** is known for its painted ceramic figurines. In Perú, ceramics are produced all along the coast, displaying the same designs and made with techniques similar to those used by the region's ancient cultures. **Ayacucho** and **Cajamarca** are good places to find reputable ceramics, as are many shops in Quito and Lima.

MUSIC

The music of Perú and Ecuador is the result of the confluence of two distinct musical streams: Spanish and pre-Hispanic. This tranquil hybrid music of the Andes, rife with fife, strings, and other things, has been popularized around the world by traveling musicians from Ecuador, Perú, and Bolivia. Often the music is just instrumental, but when there's singing, it is usually in Quechua. One of the most popular songs in the Andes is "El Cóndor Pasa," whose tune was made internationally famous by **Simon and Garfunkel.** Bands frequently play at festivals, and recently people have begun holding music competitions. Get into the groove at one of the many folk music clubs (called *peñas*), where locals get together to celebrate and have a good time. Indigenous contributions to the typical Andean band include wind instruments, drums, and rattles. The first instrument that pops into most people's minds when thinking of Andean music is the **panpipe** or *rondador*, which is believed to be over 2,000 years old. A relative of the *rondador*, originating from the southern Andes but commonly played in Ecuador and Perú, is the **zampoña,** with two rows of pipes instead of just one. This instrument, along with the five-note scale on which the tunes are based, gives the Andean music its distinctively haunting sound. Two flutes of different sizes are also quite often used—the larger **quena** and the smaller *pingullu*. The flutes and panpipes are both carved from bamboo. Bells, drums, and **maracas** (rattles made from gourds) comprise the rest of the indigenous contribution to the modern Andean band.

When the Spanish arrived, they brought with them **stringed instruments** of all shapes, sounds, and sizes, including the *guitarra* (guitar), *violín, bandolín* (mandolin), *charango* (a ukulele-type instrument commonly made from an armadillo shell), and *arpa* (harp). These added more variety and texture to the already rich local music; today's sounds reflect the continued use of both breeds of sound.

ARCHITECTURE

The oldest large-scale architecture in the region is that which the Incas left behind. **Machu Picchu,** near the highland city of Cusco in Perú, reigns as the most famous and majestic example of Inca ruins in all of South America. Unknown to the outside world until 1911, the site may have been a ceremonial center. The ruins of **Ingapirca,** just north of Cuenca, are Ecuador's best. Located on an old Inca road, the complex is believed to have served as an inn, a fortress, a temple, or some combination of the three. Both of these ruins exhibit the fine stonework and carving for which the Incas were famous. Much of what the Incas built no longer stands, primarily because the Spanish either destroyed or co-opted their buildings. A number of important towns are built on the rubble of the Inca civilization; in many cases, the Spaniards even re-used Inca building stones. Many colonial churches are on hilltops because they were built over foundations of Inca temples.

Colonial architecture is a blend of the Old and New Worlds; the style of religious art and architecture that resulted from the mix is called the **Quito School.** The Spaniards commissioned works to be done in the popular Baroque style, but the indigenous peoples who executed them added their own distinctive touches. Churches and convents in older towns are decorated with intricately carved facades, ornate interiors sparkling with gilt, and leafy stone vines wrapping around classically styled columns. Municipal buildings and private residences are usually more modest. Large wooden doors open onto blocky two-story buildings with high ceilings, interior courtyards, and covered verandas. Simple stonework and elegant wrought iron decorate white-washed interiors, while ancient wooden beams and weathered red tiles make up the roofs above. Much of the region's built environment has been erected in the 20th century, a time when building costs assumed primary importance in the architectural mind. Blocky concrete and rebar buildings predominate in the downtown areas of the region's larger cities.

ECOTOURISM

As recently as a decade ago, tourism to Perú, Ecuador, and the Galápagos was destroying natural resources at an alarming rate. Cruise ships brought litter to beaches, tourists bought trinkets fashioned from the shells of endangered tortoises, developers paved roads through the jungle, and scuba resorts encouraged divers mistreat the coral. Since then, countries around the world have faced strong demands for more responsible, sustainable tourism—"ecotourism" is the pop-name for this trend. The fastest-growing sector of the tourist industry, ecotourism is intended to encourage enjoyment and appreciation of an ecosystem while contributing to its continued existence. While few can object to these goals in theory, ecotourism in practice has garnered its share of criticism. Some say "eco" has come to stand for economics rather than ecology, pointing to greedy entrepreneurs who lead eco-tours with little concern for nature. Others warn that increased traffic in natural settings, no matter how "low-impact" it is, can only harm the ecology in the long run. The **Inca Trail** to Machu Picchu, for example, sees so many tourists each year that even responsible visitors who do not leave litter have still had a devastating cumulative effect, and recently rumors have been circulating that the trail might soon close to visitors to prevent further damage.

Since the early days of the movement, ecotourists have flocked to Perú and Ecuador for the bevy of natural beauties. In 1991, some 365,000 foreign visitors to Ecuador alone handed over nearly US$200 million in revenues. The **Jatún Sacha Biological Station** in Ecuador was founded in 1986 with the intent of conserving the incredible biodiversity of the land and providing a window for researchers. Located on the Río Napo, this tropical rainforest has 70% primary growth forest. In Perú, the extensive **Manú Biosphere Reserve** has been divided into three zones, one of which is entirely off-limits to everyone but scientists and native residents; the other two allow restricted access only. While Jatún Sacha and Manú limit the number of human visitors, the hundreds who cannot enter look elsewhere for an environmental experience. Such numbers tantalize entrepreneurs and tour leaders alike, who readily grasp that tagging their services as "eco" could yield huge profits. The most legit tour companies have government-issued licenses, but no certification is required to simply call oneself an "environmental" tour guide. True eco-devotees should seek out organizations that actively support conservation efforts and strive to minimize their impact on the environment.

Recently, the risk to the rainforest has been heightened by the discovery of oil in the Oriente region of Ecuador. For the first time, water and air pollution are serious threats outside of the cities. The effects of oil drilling have been destructive to the regional wildlife and environment. Indigenous peoples living in the rainforest have allies with the environmentalists, as their lands and lifestyles have been pillaged by the multi-national oil companies. Political protests have been enough to save some areas—the **Limoncocha Biological Reserve,** downriver from Coca, Ecuador, was founded with the help of angry birdwatchers determined to push oil companies away from their haven. "Debt-for-nature swaps," in which foreign creditors allow lending nations to pay off their debts by protecting areas of the rainforest, has also helped save parts of the environment. But the **Parque Nacional Yasuní** has been the source of the most controversy; while it houses hundreds of bird, animal, and fish species, it is also potentially one of the most valuable oil-drilling areas—a serious consideration in a region with a dwindling economy. Though progress may occur slowly, awareness is on the rise. Overall, environmental consciousness has been immensely rewarding for the region's economy, for tourists with a thirst for adventure and immersion in nature, and most importantly, for the environment itself.

PERÚ

HISTORY SINCE INDEPENDENCE

PERÚ

POST-INDEPENDENCE CAUDILLISMO (1824-45)

The immediate effect of Independence was the transfer of power from *peninsulares* (Spanish mainlanders) to elite Peruvian *criollos*. This entrenched elite tenaciously, and often unscrupulously, tried to safeguard and increase their social and economic privileges. Following liberation, Simón Bolívar maintained power for two years before events in Colombia led him to return to Bogotá. After Bolívar's departure there followed a long series of short-lived military administrations headed by *caudillos*, military strongmen who often seized power by force or by manipulation of intricate political alliances. In their struggle for power these *caudillos* played upon and deepened divisions among the populace. Some particularly divisive issues included qualifications for citizenship, the proper role of the church, tariffs, and the proper organizational structure of the government and economy. Heated struggles among rival *caudillos* made the period between 1826 and 1845 one of severe sociopolitical instability and—a natural result of such instability—economic stagnation.

In the late 1830s, after a five year interlude of relative stability under **General Agustín Gamarra** (1829-34), the struggle for power transcended the realm of elite political maneuverings, inciting a series of short but serious civil wars among regions supporting opposing military factions. The chaos opened the country to an invasion by Bolivia in 1836 which forced Perú into the **Perú-Bolivia Confederation,** a complete political union with Bolivia. The forced confederation, unwelcome in Peru, lasted until Chile—threatened by the resulting disruption to the balance of power—ended the union of Perú and Bolivia by military force in 1839. Heightened factional strife followed Perú's defeat by Chilean troops.

GUANO BOOM AND BUST (1845-86)

BOOM AND POLITICAL STABILIZATION. Two events conspired in 1845 to initiate a period of relative peace and stability. The first was the so-called "guano boom." A huge deposit of the potent fertilizer, guano, Quechua for "bird droppings," was discovered on the Chincha Islands, and over the next couple of decades Perú accrued close to US$500 million from its exportation. The second event was intimately related to the first: **General Ramón Castilla** rode the guano-driven economic upsurge to power in 1845 and used his popular support to end the factional conflict that had wracked Perú since independence. In addition to terminating years of political strife, Castilla instituted a number of social and economic reforms. Among the most important were the abolition of the remaining vestiges of slavery and the termination of native tribute. Unquestionably the most successful element of his economic program was the rapid repayment of Perú's internal and external debt—a move which greatly improved the country's credit rating.

ECONOMIC MISMANAGEMENT AND BUST. Unfortunately, Castilla and his successors later committed a number of economic policy blunders and failed to capitalize on the opportunities presented by the guano boom and the early repayment of all foreign debt. The sound credit rating established by Castilla was used for massive borrowing of funds from Great Britain, which—in combination with revenue from guano—were invested in an overly ambitious program of railroad- and road-building. Additionally, Castilla's and subsequent administrations proved unable to prevent the elite business class from securing the majority of the profits brought in from guano sales. In fact, Castilla's administration significantly

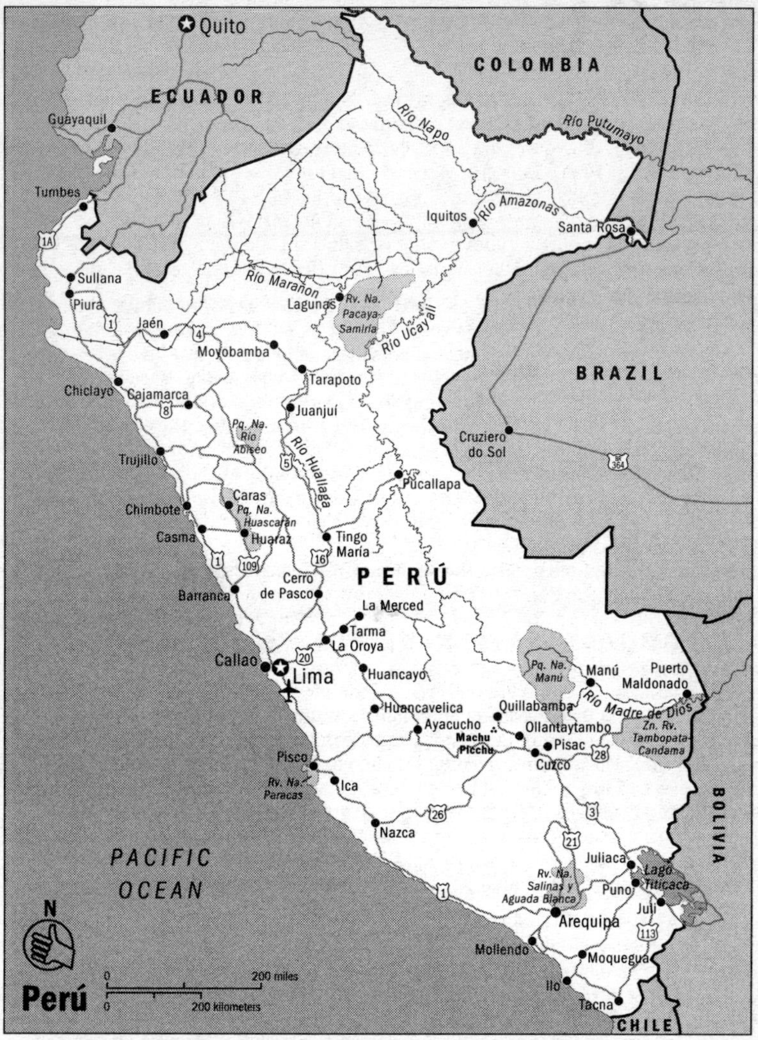

strengthened the political and economic position of the wealthy by consigning much of the commercialization of guano to elite merchants in Lima. Elected in 1865 and again in 1875, military hero **Mariano Ignacio Prado** attempted to undo the economic damage inflicted by the flawed policies of his predecessors, but Prado's reforms came too late. Insufficient returns on the massive investment in transportation infrastructure, two successful but costly wars—a border dispute with Ecuador and a dispute with Spain over the Chincha Islands—and the world-wide depression of 1873 together forced Perú to default on its newly accumulated foreign debt. A final blow was struck to the economy by the **War of the Pacific** (1879-83), a war with Chile over a border region rich in nitrates (another fertilizer in high demand). Perú suffered a humiliating defeat and was forced to sign the **Treaty of Ancón,** which committed Perú to ceding the nitrate-rich Tarapacá Province and relinquishing the provinces of Tacna and Arica to Chile for a period of ten years—after which a plebiscite would return Tacna but not Arica. A three-year period of economic decline and civil unrest followed the signing of the Ancón Treaty.

ECONOMIC RECOVERY AND DEVELOPMENT (1886-1919)

RESUSCITATING THE ECONOMY. In the late 1880s British creditors cast out a life-raft to the sinking Peruvian economy in which they had invested so much. This took the form of the **Grace Contract,** negotiated by Michael Grace. The offer was simple: British creditors would cancel Perú's foreign debt in exchange for complete control over Perú's railroad system for sixty-six years and annual payments of funds and goods for thirty years. Despite opposition to foreign control over such a large portion of Perú's economy, General **Andrés Avelina Cáceres** (1886-90, 1894-5) seized the opportunity for economic salvation and made it the core of his relatively successful program for initiating export-led economic growth.

"ARISTOCRATIC REPUBLIC" (1895-1919). In what has been dubbed the **Revolution of 1895, José Nicolás Piérola** seized power from an increasingly dictatorial Cáceres. Piérola quickly forged an alliance with the **Civilista Party (PC),** a party supported primarily by elite merchants and businessmen who had accrued extraordinary wealth during the period of the guano boom. With the political ascension of this elite band of business magnates began the period dubbed the "Aristocratic Republic." Overseeing the repeated elections of Civilista candidates, these economic oligarchs directed economic policy and virtually monopolized political power for the next two decades. Ardent anti-militarists—a policy that reassured foreign investors seeking stability—and resolutely committed to the development of Perú's export economy, the Civilistas' successful program fueled rapid export-led economic development until the advent of WWI, when a temporary economic slump precipitated the PC's fall from power.

THE POPULARIZATION OF POLITICS (1919-30)

NEW IDEAS. The post-WWI period was one of intense intellectual ferment. Writers such as **Manuel González Prada** and **Clorinda Matto de Turner** advanced new, liberal thought and helped increase awareness of and sympathy for the extreme poverty of rural Perú. Radical ideologues such as **José Carlos Mariátegui** and **Víctor Raúl Haya De La Torre** politicized these liberal perspectives. They and their followers denounced vestiges of the colonial social structure, the elitism of the oligarchy, militarism, the political powerlessness of indigenous groups, and the increasing level of economic and social inequality. This movement for radical social change and greater equality became known as the **indigenista movement.**

ORGANIZATION OF THE MASSES. The economic development of the 1900s and 1910s initiated and propelled mass migration from rural areas in the Sierra to urban centers along the coast. Aggregated in urban centers, former rural workers had better access to newly developing liberal ideologies and were more easily organized and led. This massive influx of rural poor into the cities helped facilitate the rise of mass-based labor and social-reform movements. Tapping energy and guided by the new wave of liberal ideas, Haya De La Torre founded the **Alianza Popular Revolucionaria Americana** (APRA) in 1924. The APRA appealed to the urban poor and, gaining strength, successfully sought to incorporate the rural masses into the move for socioeconomic change.

THE "ONCENIO" (1919-30). In the 1919 presidential election, the first election after the fall of the Civilista Party, **Augusto Leguía** appealed for support to the increasingly powerful lower- and middle-class workers. Once elected to office, Leguía initiated his *oncenio*, or "eleven-year rule," by drafting a new, progressive **constitution** (1920) that centralized political power. This centralization facilitated Leguía's execution of the numerous economic and social programs pushed for by his economically disadvantaged constituency. Leguía's social programs included reforms in education, banking, and urban housing. These programs improved the condition of the middle class—especially the education reforms and the construction of sorely needed urban housing—but failed to provide significant relief to the most impoverished sectors of society.

To stimulate the economy and sustain costly social programs, Leguía sought to attract foreign capital by granting virtual *carte blanche* to overseas investors. This gambit, though controversial, initiated a long period of export-led economic growth. Unfortunately, the benefits of this growth were, again, distributed very unevenly; the wealthiest classes reaped the greatest rewards. And once again, economic success led to excessive government spending. In the face of temporary economic decline engendered by the **Great Depression** in 1929, the *oncenio* of the increasingly dictatorial Leguía came to an abrupt halt.

SUPPRESSION AND RADICALIZATION (1930-68)

MILITARY RULE (1930-56). With the exception of the three-year rule of the APRA-friendly **José Luís Bustamente** (1945-8), the period from 1930 to 1956 saw a series of military administrations antagonistic to the APRA. These governments, despite enacting some legislation for social reform, were politically repressive; they outlawed the APRA and many trade unions, banned strikes, and forcefully suppressed opposition. Political oppression reached its apogee with the eight-year dictatorship of **Manuel A. Odría** (1948-56).

THE "CONVIVENCIA" (1956-68). In 1956 the APRA and the conservative **Manuel Prado** forged an awkward, opportunistic alliance dubbed the *convivencia* ("living together"). The purpose of the Convivencia was straightforward: to ensure the election of Prado and to guarantee the legitimation of the previously outlawed APRA. The APRA, working with Prado, proved much less progressive than its radical propaganda and years of underground agitation had led its supporters to expect. Many supporters became severely disaffected and shifted their support to smaller, more militant groups that had been overshadowed by the mammoth APRA. The **Acción Popular (AP)** of **Fernando Belaúnde Terry**, taking advantage of frustration with the APRA, gained power in 1963, but it too proved too moderate for its own constituency and relinquished power at the end of Belaúnde's term. Disillusionment with the ostensibly progressive parties of previous decades, higher levels of social awareness, frustration with the extreme inequality of economic growth, and a rapid slow-down in economic growth in the 1960s made disadvantaged populations more politically active and radical.

RADICAL MILITARY REGIMES (1968-80)

In 1968 a group of radical military officers trained at the prestigious Center for Advanced Military Studies and committed to radical change decided the time was ripe for the establishment of a new order. Taking advantage of increasingly ardent popular dissatisfaction, they staged a coup under the leadership of General **Juan Velasco Alvarado** (1968-75). Velasco, frustrated with the APRA and AP and dedicated to mitigating long-standing inequalities, instituted a revolutionary socialist program. This program involved the nationalization of large industry, the coopertivization of agriculture, and the inauguration of new agencies dedicated to carefully regulating prices and wages. Velasco's program, however, like so many other socialist movements, soon lead to over-bureaucratization, corruption, economic stagnation, and soaring inflation. General **Francisco Morales Bermúdez Cerrutti** (1975-80), Velasco's appointed successor, reversed much of Velasco's legislation, but proved incapable of halting the downward spiral.

RETURN OF DEMOCRACY AND CAPITALISM (1980-90)

BELAÚNDE. Acknowledging the failure of their program, the military arranged for democratic elections in 1980. The relatively conservative ex-president **Fernando Belaúnde** (1980-5), supported by discontented business interests, emerged victorious and began laying the foundations for a return to a free-market system. The Belaúnde administration made significant progress in the privatization of business

GUERRILLAS IN THE MIST The bombing of ballot boxes on May 17, 1980 in Chuschi, Perú was the first of many terrorist acts committed by the **Sendero Luminoso (Shining Path).** Founded and led by **Abimael Guzmán,** a philosophy professor in Ayacucho, the Sendero has directed a brutal campaign against all vestiges of bourgeois capitalism, seeking to advance its own Maoist, communist ideology.

In all, 30,000 people have died in Sendero violence. While most deaths have occurred in the Central Sierra near the towns of Ayacucho and Huancayo, Lima was also scarred by the terrorist attacks. In July of 1992, a car bomb on Av. Tarata, in Lima's affluent suburb of Miraflores, killed 23 people. Other Sendero attacks targeted the city's electrical transformers, leaving the city in the dark. Finally, the Peruvian government took action. They captured Guzman in 1992 and eventually (after a much-televised manhunt in July 1999) captured his successor, Oscar Alberto Ramírez Durand (a.k.a. **Feliciano**), in Jauja, a small town near Huancayo. Since these events, the influence and activity of the Sendero Luminoso and a later faction, the Sendero Rojo, have been minimal.

In the early 1990s, near the end of the Shining Path's reign of terror, Perú constructed an enormous cross on the edge of a cliff in Barranco. **La Cruz de Morro,** which separates Barranco from Chorrilos, was constructed from scrap debris collected from the bombing sites. Brightly illuminated at night, the cross serves as a conspicuous reminder of the country's recent bloodshed. The Sendero, its ideals, and its actions influenced every Peruvian old enough to remember the violence. The experience is captured by Perú's most famous author, Mario Vargas Llosa, in his evocative novel, *Death in the Andes.* Gustavo Gorriti provides an excellent historical account of the era in *The Shining Path: A History of the Millenarian War in Perú.*

and the opening the economy to foreign imports. Unfortunately some misguided policy—a combination of a devaluation of the *sol*, the creation of an imbalance of imports over exports, and excessive government spending at home—triggered soaring inflation (163% a year by 1985.) A series of natural disasters and a drop in international commodity prices to the lowest level since the Great Depression only compounded the government's difficulties.

RETURN OF THE APRA. In the face of his failure to tame the economy, Belaúnde had little hope for re-election. Victory in the 1985 election went instead to the APRA's **Alan García Pérez** (1985-90). For the first time in its history the APRA ruled the country by itself. This time the APRA was not constrained by an alliance with a conservative partner. However, it once again proved unable to meet the high expectations aroused by decades of radical rhetoric. It both proved more moderate than expected and ended up exacerbating the country's economic crisis. For two years the García administration's economic policy was moderately successful. The new administration, with their program of *concertación* ("national understanding"), managed to mitigate the trade imbalance created under Belaúnde, channeled badly needed funding to Perú's agricultural sector, reduced government spending, and curtailed inflation by fixing prices and wages.

Increased imports triggered by the economic boom, however, resulted in a trade imbalance; imports increased and exports were consumed at home. Lamentably, the government failed to take appropriate counter-measures; instead, it allowed the exchange rate to fall and resorted to massive borrowing from the Central bank. Finally, in 1987, with the economy already severely stressed, García committed a calamitous and difficult-to-explain blunder: he nationalized the country's banking system. This action clearly conveyed that the presidency held virtually unchecked control over economic policy and thus undermined the confidence of private business—ever wary of unilateral and capricious policy shifts. Private investment plummeted, inflation continued its upward march, and by the 1990 election the economy lay in ruin.

FUJIMORI'S ELECTION AND REFORMS

THE ELECTIONS OF 1990. In 1990 the APRA was eliminated in the first round of elections. Conservative **Mario Vargas Llosa** (see p. 64), a prominent writer and head of a political party called the Liberty Movement, and **Alberto Fujimori,** a university president of Japanese decent, remained for a run-off. Fujimori was supported by a strong grass-roots campaign conducted by **Cambio '90**, a highly diverse political party formed expressly for the purpose of electing Fujimori. On June 10th, with the support of Cambio '90, Fujimori emerged victorious. How such a relative unknown rose so quickly to the nation's highest office is a difficult question. Profound distaste for all things representative of the status quo was probably the primary contributor to Fujimori's success. The conservative Llosa was viewed as a politically connected member of the elite. Fujimori, referred to as "El Chinito," was seen as both untainted by politics and representative of the common man.

FUJIMORI'S REFORMS. The most pressing concern for the newly elected Fujimori was Perú's sky-rocketing inflation. Under pressure from abroad and on the advice of his staff, Fujimori completely reversed his promised plan for a gradual recovery and instituted the type of economic shock program favored by Llosa. Dubbed **"Fujishock,"** this program sought to control inflation by expanding and eliminating controls on the private sector while increasing prices in the public sector. Additionally, Fujimori repaid outstanding national debts, lowering tariffs, and liberalized trade. The program was Fujishockingly successful: inflation was reduced from 2300% in 1990 to below 10% in 1992. Growth began somewhat slowly but followed an upward path and reached a whopping 12% of GDP in 1994. Growth was very uneven, however, and Fujishock resulted in severe hardship for the nation's poorest. A common feature of orthodox economic shock programs is the establishment of a parallel program to cushion the injury to those left devastated by the shock. Here, there was a conspicuous gap in Fujimori's policy; it included no such parallel program. Despite this, broad support for the new president continued long after his election.

EL AUTOGOLPE: FUJIMORI'S COUP

Cambio '90, an eclectic hodge-podge of interests, failed to maintain unity and secure seats in Congress following Fujimori's election. Fujimori held an awkward alliance with the APRA through 1991, but without a stable basis of political support in the Congress, he was forced to rely ever more heavily on the military. Confronting an increasingly hostile congress and intolerant of dissent, Fujimori thus staged a successful coup—the *autogolpe*—on April 5, 1992. Dissolving the Congress and suspending the constitution, he initiated a brief period of rule-by-personal-decree.

Soon placed under sanctions by economically important foreign powers, Fujimori was quickly forced to restore democratic rule. He was not, however, about to restore the very congress he had abolished. In November 1992, he held elections for an entirely new congress, his "Democratic Constituent Congress," composed of 80—instead of the previous 240—members. The opposition parties boycotted the elections, calling them unconstitutional, and the result was a congress loyal to Fujimori. The new Congress quickly drafted a new **constitution** which, in accordance with the president's wishes, centralized power, increased presidential authority, and allowed a single person to hold the presidency for two consecutive terms. Fujimori continued to maintain popularity despite his Machiavellian manipulation of the governmental structure, and the newly drafted constitution was approved by a referendum on October 31, 1993. In spite of the obvious underhandedness involved in Fujimori's reestablishment of a democratic structure, the international community responded by lifting economic sanctions. With sanctions lifted and with the powers of the presidency augmented, Fujimori continued to promote his orthodox economic policy popular with big business at home and major capitalist economies abroad.

FUJIMORI'S CURRENT TERM

The economy continued to grow, Fujimori's approval rating continued to remain high, and on April 16, 1995 Fujimori was vindicated by a free election that resoundingly demanded his continued occupation of the presidency.

THREE MAJOR ACHIEVEMENTS. Since Fujimori's re-election in 1995, his administration has been achieved resounding success on a number of fronts. One outstanding triumph has been Fujimori's campaign against radical, terrorist guerrilla organizations such as the **Sendero Luminoso** and the **Tupac Amaru Revolutionary Movement.** Critical victories against these rebels were the arrest of Abimael Guzmán, leader of the Sendero, in late 1992 (see **Guerrillas in the Mist,** p. 60) and the successful recovery of all 72 occupants of the Japanese embassy taken hostage on December 17, 1997 (see **It's My Party and I'll Die if I Want to,** p. 70). Another historically pivotal achievement was Fujimori's October 1998 negotiation with Ecuadorian president Jamil Mahuad of a peace treaty ending a longstanding border dispute with Ecuador (see p. 240). A somewhat lesser known success is the Fujimori administration's war against drug cultivation and export. Fujimori has pursued a two-pronged approach: severe police crack-down combined with significant aid to coca producers who shift to legal cash crops. This policy has made Perú's anti-drug campaign one of Latin America's most successful; nearly half of Peru's coca fields have been eliminated in the past few years.

EL NIÑO AND ECONOMIC RECESSION. In 1997-98, Perú was left devastated by a period of massive flooding brought on by the weather patterned known as **El Niño** (see p. 415). Homes and roads were destroyed, potable water became scarce, and the population suffered epidemics of cholera and other infectious diseases. Not only did the flooding lead to horrendous human tragedy, it was also highly detrimental to the economy. In combination with the Asian recession and the worldwide crisis provoked by turmoil in Russia. El Niño made 1998 a year of economic stagnation and decline. GDP growth was near zero, and unemployment hit a new high, rising close to 50%. Not surprisingly, Fujimori's approval rating suffered a corresponding deterioration, falling to around 35% in early 1999.

LAST YEAR. The economy has improved somewhat in the first half of 1999: GDP growth for the year is predicted to be around 4.5%, relatively high for the region; the country successfully completed a three year **International Monetary Fund program,** entitling it to a loan of around US$1.3 billion; and the cancellation of an agreement for the mutual opening of the Peruvian and Ecuadorian economies is expected to bring significant economic rewards.

However, all is not well. Unequal growth has preserved and fostered extreme inequality, unemployment remains high, and a burgeoning trade imbalance has forced Perú to increase its borrowing from abroad. Fujimori—having pressed for an exemption to the two-term limit in 1997—will run for re-election in 2000. But his popularity is not what it once was. In an effort to recoup waning support, he initiated a populist campaign requiring significant backpedaling on an important plan for increased privatization. This shift in policy is predicted to cost the country hundreds of millions of dollars over the course of the year—money sorely needed to pay off debts and, by so doing, preserve investors' interest in Perú.

INDIGENOUS PERÚ

The majority of indigenous people come from the highland Andean regions of Perú in the central and southern parts of the country. They number approximately nine million, or 38% of Perú's total population. Of indigenous people in the highlands, 30% speak **Quechua** and 22% speak **Aymara** (or local variations of these languages). Both Aymara and Quechua are officially recognized languages of the government in areas where they are predominantly spoken, but Spanish is the official national language. Social prejudice in society leads many indigenous people to resort to speaking their native tongue at home, while speaking Spanish in public. There are clear differences between the indigenous people of the Andes and the coastal region from those of the **Amazon.** All have different languages, customs, and lifestyles, and, because they lived in relative isolation for many centuries, even neighboring tribes are likely to have little in common. Traditionally, the Andean peoples were referred to by outsiders as "indios," while those from the Amazon were referred to as "savages." As in many societies in Latin America, most of the indigenous people of Perú are in the lowest socio-economic and political tier. Most earn their incomes from agricultural work, mining, and heavy industrial labor. Illiteracy is high; they are often taught in Spanish (not their native tongue) and the school year is not coordinated with the agricultural labor cycle. As a result, many children do not attend classes regularly.

From 1919 until 1930, the government modernized the economy and tried to include indigenous groups in the market. In 1926, 59 indigenous communities were officially recognized; this number steadily increased throughout the next several decades. In 1958, the first indigenous union was formed to mobilize against the selling of indigenous territories. During the 1960s many Quechua speakers protested the government through marches and various acts of vandalism. Since 1969, indigenous people have been given autonomy regarding internal organization and the administration of their own communities. In 1979, the Peruvian constitution was reformed to include the protection of all ethnicities in the country and recognize the right of people to adhere to their own "cultural identities." By the 1980s, peasant organizations had formed, composed of both Indians and non-Indians, as a form of grassroots mobilization against agrarian reform and development of indigenous lands. These include the **Peasant Confederation of Perú** and the **National Agrarian Confederation,** which offer small loans and credit to indigenous farmers.

Despite the political gains of the last few decades, the indigenous people of Perú still suffer from widespread discrimination and, at times, outright persecution by *mestizos* or Peruvians of European descent.

FINE ARTS

The people of Perú have been producing exquisite works of art since long before the arrival of the Europeans. Although much pre-Columbian art was destroyed in the Conquest—including the priceless pieces of gold and silver that were acquired by the Spaniards as Atahuallpa's ransom and then melted down to bullion—or were stolen by looters or *huaqueros* (grave robbers), many fine examples are still visible in Perú's numerous museums. Along the coast, beautifully decorated pre-Inca ceramics and textiles reveal much about the lifestyles of the ancient Chimú, Moche, Paracas, and Nazca cultures, while in the Huaraz area the Chavín left finely detailed carved rock figures.

In the 17th century, Spanish colonization was accompanied by the arrival of European art to the New World, especially Flemish, Italian, and Spanish religious paintings that were used to illustrate the teachings of Christianity. In the highlands, newly converted natives were trained in contemporary styles of painting but soon began to add local touches to their works of art. The tradition that developed, known as the **Cusco School,** reflects the mixture of European and Peruvian influences. A famous painting of *The Last Supper* by acclaimed artist **Marcos Zapato,** for example, depicts the well-known religious scene with a distinctly Andean twist—the subjects of the painting are feasting on *cuy* (guinea pig). The Cusco School style is still popular today, as groups of indigenous and *mestizo* painters continue to mix the traditional with the Peruvian to produce unique works of art.

One interesting example of the Peruvian fascination with historical and cultural artistic roots is the **Usko-Ayar Amazonian School of Painting** in Pucallpa. The works produced by the artists of Usko-Ayar (meaning "Spiritual Prince" in Quechua) exist as a celebration and documentation of the flora, fauna, and culture of the Amazon and its native peoples. Founded in 1988 by visionary painter and *shaman*

Pablo Amaringo, the school is made up entirely of local artists mostly between the ages of 8 and 24 years. Paintings from Usko-Ayar have received international acclaim and have toured to countries around the world.

LITERATURE

The ancient civilizations of Perú had a long tradition of storytelling, but the lack of a written language meant that stories and historical accounts were passed down to future generations only in oral and pictographic forms. After the Spanish Conquest, however, a rich body of literature developed out of the folklore and history of the region. The earliest written material from Perú consists of the detailed historical accounts of the Conquest as recorded by Pizarro and his men. One important chronicler was **Garcilaso de la Vega,** the son of an Inca noblewoman and a Spanish conquistador whose writing recorded the last days of the Incas. Inca folklore, mythology, and history continue to play major roles in the literary traditions of modern-day Perú. These foundational elements and the country's diverse ethnic make-up have led to an equally diverse (and difficult to quantify) body of literature that has long been the subject of intense intellectual and academic interest.

CONTEMPORARY LITERATURE

Easily the most famous—and most notorious—of the Peruvian writers in the 20th century is **Mario Vargas Llosa;** he epitomizes the nation's literary tradition over the last 35 years. His literary career has been closely intertwined with political commentary and criticism right from the beginning: his first novel, *La ciudad y los perros* (1963), used conflicts rising between school boys and the faculty of a Peruvian boarding school to comment indirectly on unjust political treatment. Many of his works have been stylistically experimental as well as controversial (e.g. *Conversión en la Catedral* (1969) and *La Casa Verde* (1966). Along with Gabriel García Márquez, Carlos Fuentes, and Julio Cortázar, Vargas Llosa is one of the great Latin American Boom novel pioneers. Vargas Llosa's influence extends beyond the literary world into current events and politics; in 1990, representing the Liberty Movement Party, Llosa unsuccessfully ran against **Alberto Fujimori** for the presidency of Perú. In his 1993 memoirs, *El Pez en el Agua*, Vargas Llosa refers to this campaign as seeking "the most dangerous job in the world." Fortunately, the loss of the election has not affected the quality of his writing—one of his newer works, *Lituma en los Andes* (1993), is regarded as one of his best. In 1999, Vargas Llosa received an honorary degree from **Harvard University.**

The most celebrated poet from Perú is **César Vallejo** (1892-1938), whose modernist works deal with issues of humanity and historical realism. Born in Santiago de Chuco, Perú, Vallejo published his first book of poetry, *Los Heraldos Negros*, in 1918. The nature of his writing changed following a 112-day incarceration in 1920; the influences of his experiences are reflected in his widely acclaimed *Trilce*, published in 1922. Vallejo left Perú for Paris shortly thereafter, where he became involved in politics and was ultimately exiled from France. His final collection of *Poemas Humanos* was published posthumously in 1939.

Although not as well-known as Vargas Llosa or Vallejo, **José Santos Chocano** (1875-1934) was a Peruvian writer who led a more colorful life than some of his colleagues. Chocano traveled throughout Latin America writing poetry, prose, journalism, and political criticism. In Mexico, he met the revolutionary leader **Pancho Villa,** who admired Chocano and his poetry; he nominated the writer to be a special advisor. Chocano returned to Perú in 1924 after splitting with Villa. In his home country, Chocano found himself constantly under attack for his revolutionary ideas, and in 1925, he killed one of his critics in a duel. During his imprisonment, he wrote *El Libro de Mi Proceso*, his most famous work. In 1934, Chocano was brutally stabbed to death in Chile, where he had been attempting to solve his financial problems by hunting for lost treasures.

LIMA

All purveyors of Peruvian literature could be divided into two tendencies: those who sanctify Lima and those who criticize her. The real city is probably not as beautiful as some say or as dreadful as others proclaim.

—Mario Vargas Llosa, Peruvian novelist

Lima began its life as a quietly prosperous Inca city on the banks of the Río Rímac; it was not the center of the empire but had its share of gold, silver, and impressive architectural masterpieces. When the Spanish conquered the city, they stripped it of its gold and destroyed most of the Inca buildings. The next cycle of Lima's history began as the Spanish built their city on top of the Inca ruins. The Spanish cathedral arose atop the Inca temple; the Palacio de Gobierno took root on the Inca emperor's house. The city became the commercial and administrative center of the Spanish empire in South America—Chinese silks, fine furniture, and exotic spices flowed through the city's rich markets, and *criollos* spent fortunes on palatial mansions. South America's first university, the University of San Marcos, was founded in Lima in 1551; the continent's first printing press went into action in 1594. Lima was the headquarters of the Spanish conquistadores in Perú for a generation or so—beginning when Francisco Pizarro founded the city in 1535—during which time the Spanish accumulated a sizeable stash of human bones (now in the catacombs of the San Franciscan monastery). Lima experienced a period of prosperity until an earthquake devastated the city in 1746.

Lima embarked on the next stage of its history near the end of the 18th century under Viceroy Amat. The governor saw the rubble as an opportunity to rebuild his city in as ornate a manner as many a baroque European city. Lima's wide streets, old houses with elaborately carved balconies, and immense plazas are Amat's legacy. Over the course of the 19th century Lima prospered as the main port in mineral-rich Perú and slowly accustomed itself to its new economic stature.

HIGHLIGHTS OF LIMA

- Lima Centro's grandiose **Plaza de Armas** (p. 77) combines Inca and Spanish influences and comprises the historical center of the city.
- The **Iglesia de la Merced** (p. 78) is one spectacular example of Lima's many ornate, gold-encrusted Roman Catholic cathedrals.
- The **Museo del Arte** (p. 79) exhibits its extensive collection of national and international art in a tremendous 19th-century palace.
- The well-polished, glitzy neighborhood of **Miraflores** (p. 72) hosts Lima's trendy and affluent citizens, as well as many fine shops and restaurants.
- From **Miraflores** to **Barranco, Lima's nightlife** (p. 81) goes on and on.

The good times didn't last forever, though; in the last half of this century, Lima has suffered political and economic crises, rising poverty, and overly rapid urbanization. The problems of overpopulation—the proliferation of smog-emission, strained public utilities, and the struggle for scarce jobs—have taken their toll. In the past decade, generally considered one of the low points of recent history, Lima has been pounded by terrorist bombs, shamed by a hostage crisis in the Japanese Embassy, impoverished by the severe hyperinflation of the late 1980s, overwhelmed by immigrants from Perú's interior provinces, and beset by an epidemic of cholera. The results of these events—aggressive street vendors, highly visible poverty, and frequent petty crime—earned the city the reputation of a necessary evil: a gateway to Perú, but not a great place to visit.

The last decade, however, is coming to a close, and Lima's fortunes are once again on the rise: the historic center is being restored, parks have been replanted,

Lima Overview
TO ANCÓN
INDEPENDENCIA
Av. Canto Grande
Río Rímac
Vía de Evitamiento
Av. Atarjea
Cerro San Cristóbal
Av. Alcazar
Carretera Panamericana Norte
Carretera a Canta
Av. Universitaria
LOS OLIVOS
RÍMAC
Pizarro
García Rivero
Cajamarca
Av. 9 de Octubre
SEE LIMA CENTRO DETAIL MAP
Av. Abancay
Av. Grau
Manco
Av. Tomás Valle
LIMA CENTRO
Estadio Nacional
SAN MARTÍN DE PORRES
Av. Universitaria
Av. Arequipa
Av. Arica
Colonial
Av. Peru
Av. Salaverry
BREÑA
Av. Tingo María
Av. Brasil
CARMEN DE LA LEGUA REYNOSO
JESÚS MARÍA
Aeropuerto Internacional Jorge Chavéz
PUEBLO LIBRE
Museo de Antropología y Arqueología
Museo de la República
Av. República de Argentina
Av. República de Venezuela
Av. Bolívar
CALLAO
Av. Universitaria
Museo Rafael Larco Herrera
Parque las Leyendas
Av. M. Benavides
Av. Elmer Faucett
SAN MIGUEL
Av. Sucre
MAGDALENA
Río Rímac
BELLAVISTA
Av. de la Marina
Terminal Marítimo
Av. la Paz
LA PERLA
Av. Guardia Chalaca
Av. José Gálvez
Playa Mar Brava
OCEANO PACIFICO
La Punta

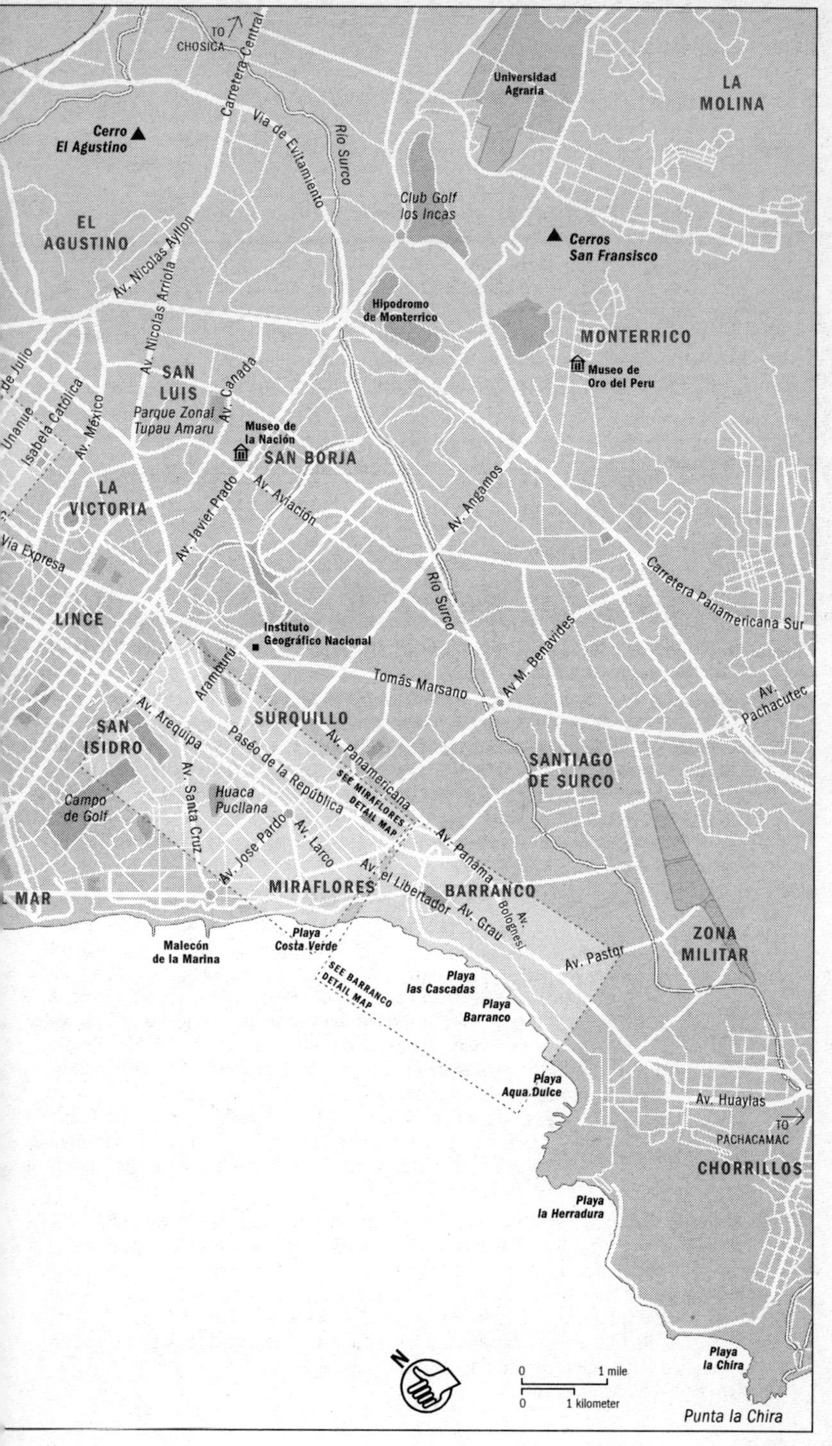
TO CHOSICA
Carretera Central
Universidad Agraria
LA MOLINA
Cerro El Agustino
Via de Evitamiento
Rio Surco
Club Golf los Incas
Cerros San Fransisco
EL AGUSTINO
Av. Nicolas Ayllon
Av. Nicolas Arriola
Hipodromo de Monterrico
MONTERRICO
Museo de Oro del Peru
de Julio
SAN LUIS
Av. Canada
Parque Zonal Tupau Amaru
Unanue
Isabela Católica
Av. México
Museo de la Nación
SAN BORJA
LA VICTORIA
Av. Javier Prado
Av. Aviación
Av. Angamos
Via Expresa
Carretera Panamericana Sur
Rio Surco
LINCE
Instituto Geográfico Nacional
Av. M. Benavides
Tomás Marsano
Aramburú
Av. Pachacutec
SURQUILLO
SAN ISIDRO
Av. Arequipa
Paséo de la República
Av. Panamericana
SEE MIRAFLORES DETAIL MAP
SANTIAGO DE SURCO
Campo de Golf
Av. Santa Cruz
Huaca Pucllana
Av. Jose Pardo
Av. Larco
Av. Panama
Av. el Libertador
MIRAFLORES
BARRANCO
MAR
Av. Grau
Av. Bolognesi
Malecón de la Marina
Playa Costa Verde
SEE BARRANCO DETAIL MAP
Av. Pastor
ZONA MILITAR
Playa las Cascadas
Playa Barranco
Playa Aqua Dulce
Av. Huaylas
TO PACHACAMAC
CHORRILLOS
Playa la Herradura
Playa la Chira
N
0
1 mile
0
1 kilometer
Punta la Chira

terrorist activity has been nearly eradicated, police vigilance has increased, and the cholera plague has retreated. As Lima's older sections gradually repair themselves, the city's suburbs to the south, Miraflores and Barranco, continue to function as a cultural center filled with glitzy establishments and fashionable residents. The city's rich history and cosmopolitan atmosphere are redefining Lima as a deserving destination city, rather than a grimy portal into Perú.

ORIENTATION

Lima is huge—if you spend any time here, it's well worth your *soles* to buy a map. The main tourist districts are **Lima Centro, San Isidro, Miraflores,** and **Barranco. Av. Arequipa** connects the center to the southern suburbs of San Isidro and Miraflores. **Av. Larco** runs into **El Libertador** to connect Miraflores to Barranco. The **Vía Expresa,** parallel to the slower **Paseo de la República,** runs north-south to provide a quick, direct route from Lima Centro to the southern suburbs.

PRACTICAL INFORMATION

TRANSPORTATION

Airport: Aeropuerto Internacional Jorge Chávez is located north of Lima on Faucett in Callao. It is a relatively unsafe area; taxis are the recommended mode of transportation (s/20 to Miraflores, s/13 to Lima Centro). Beware of advice given by taxi driver–they are often biased in recommending accommodations, and they may be lying if they tell you your chosen lodging is full. Several of the *colectivos* (s/1) that run along Benavides and Brasil go to the outside gate of the airport.

Airlines: Copa, Dos de Mayo 741 (tel. 444 97 78); **Iberia,** Camino Real 390 (tel. 421 46 16); and **Lan Chile,** José Pardo 805 (tel. 446 69 95), in Miraflores, have frequent flights to other Latin American countries. **Continental,** 147 Victor Andrés Belaúnde (tel. 221 43 40); **United Airlines,** Camino Real 390 (tel. 421 33 34); **Delta,** 147 Victor Andrés Belaúnde (tel. 421 12 75); and **American Airlines,** Juan de Arona 830 (tel. 211 70 00), in San Isidro, serve the U.S. and Europe but usually have higher prices for flights within Latin America. **AeroContinente,** José Pardo 651 (tel. 242 42 60), in Miraflores, is the principal domestic carrier.

Long-Distance Buses: There is no *terminal terrestre,* so you'll have to go to the individual bus terminals. Call for times, which are subject to change. **Cruz del Sur,** Jr. Quilca 531 (tel. 424 00 40), goes to: **Arequipa** (14hr., s/60); **Chiclayo** (10hr., s/55); **Chimbote** (5hr., s/30); **Chincha** (2hr., s/10); **Huancayo** (7hr., s/25); **Huaraz** (7hr., s/35); **Ica** (4hr., s/10); **Nazca** (8hr., s/20); **Piura** (17hr., s/40); **Puno** (21hr., s/60); **Sullana** (16hr., s/60); **Tacna** (22hr., s/45); **Trujillo** (9hr., 6 per day, s/25); and **Tumbes** (20hr., s/30). **Ormeño,** Javier Prado Este 1059 (tel. 472 17 10), and **Carlos Zavala** (tel. 427 56 79) have buses to **Arequipa** (14hr., s/40); **Chiclayo** (12hr., s/35); **Chincha** (2hr., s/7); **Cusco** (32hr., s/85); **Huaraz** (8hr., s/20); **Ica** (4hr., s/12); **Nazca** (8hr., s/17); **Pisco** (4hr., s/10); **Puno** (21hr., s/60); **Sullana** (18hr., s/45); **Tacna** (20hr., s/50); **Trujillo** (8hr., s/40); and **Tumbes** (21hr., s/50). **Rodríguez,** Roosevelt 354 (tel. 428 05 06), specializes in trips to **Huaraz** (8hr., s/20) and the smaller towns near it, as well as **Caraz** (9hr., 8am and 9pm, s/23).

Local Buses: Buses and *colectivos* (s/0.80-1) are the cheapest way to get around the city between 6am and 1am. They are easy to use–all post their routes on the sides and will let you off upon request (just say *"bajo aquí"*). The main *colectivo* routes are: **Arequipa/Tacna/Wilson** from Miraflores to San Isidro to Lima Centro; and **Brasil/La Marina/Faucett** from Miraflores to the market along La Marina, and then to the airport. Any bus marked **Chorrillos/Barranco** will go to the southern nightlife district via Larco or Arequipa. Many *colectivos* run east-west along Javier Prado from La Molina to San Isidro and Magdalena del Mar.

Taxis: Calling a **taxi company** (tel. 446 39 53, 470 62 63, or 438 72 10) for a taxi is the safest way to go. A cheaper, but not as safe, alternative to standard taxis are the independent VW bugs and small Ticos with flourescent stickers, but these can be dangerous. If you do take a VW/Tico, bargain—a ride from Lima Center to Miraflores should cost s/7; within the Miraflores/San Isidro/Barranco area, it should be s/3-4.

Car Rental: Avis (tel. 434 11 11); **Budget** (tel. 441 04 93); **Dollar** (tel. 452 67 41); **Hertz** (tel. 442 44 75); and **National** (tel. 433 37 50) all have offices at the airport. Rates change frequently, but expect to pay US$40-50 per day for a compact car. Min. age 23, but younger drivers can sometimes pay an extra fee to rent.

USEFUL ORGANIZATIONS

Visitor Information: PROMPERU, (tel. 224 31 25 or 224 32 79), Corpac, Calle 1, in San Isidro, on the 14th floor of the Ministerio de Industria building, has a binder full of tourist info, a few glossy maps and brochures, and a lot of posters. Open W-Sa 10am-noon and 3-6pm. Lima's **tourist office** (tel. 427 48 48), Conde de Superunda, near the Plaza de Armas, offers info on the city's attractions and tour companies. Open M-F 9:30am-5pm. The **Biblioteca Nacional,** 4th block of Abancay, has more in-depth info (in Spanish) on Lima's history. You must leave some form of I.D. to enter the PROMPERU office and the Biblioteca. Open M-Sa 8am-8pm and Su 9:30am-1:30pm. Private tourist resources are generally better-stocked. Tourist agencies can be very helpful, as is the **South American Explorers Club,** República de Portugal 146 (tel. 425 01 42; email montagne@amauta.vcp.net.pe), off Ugarte near the 13th block. Their clubhouse is a hub of gringo activity in Perú. Friendly, English-speaking staff members will offer advice on all things Peruvian and South American, up-to-date info binders, and trip report files. Message boards, a book exchange, equipment storage, mail, phone, fax, and email service round out the list of SAEC amenities. Membership costs US$40 per year. Open M-F 9:30am-5pm. While the free tourist maps available at the SAEC and some tourist agencies are helpful, anyone staying in Lima for more than a couple days will want to buy a more complete map. **Guía 2000** or **Guía Inca de Lima** (s/40 in any bookstore) are both detailed, laminated, and easy to carry.

Travel Agencies: Lima Tours, Belén 1040 (tel. 424 75 60), sets the standard for *agencias de viaje* with its wide selection of city and department tours and comprehensive travel services. Open M-F 8:30am-5:15pm and Sa 9am-noon. One of the highest densities of travel agencies is on Larco near the Ovalo of Miraflores. When visiting tourist agencies, beware of unbelievably cheap packages. If your tour guide abandons you in the middle of the Andes, call the 24hr. hotline (tel. 224 7888) for the **Tourist Bureau of Complaints. Intej** (477 2864; intej@amauta.rcp.net.pe), San Martín 240 in Barranco, two blocks from the Plaza de Armas, is the official ISIC site, affiliated with student tickets from both **STA** and **Council Travel** agencies.

Embassies: For the embassies of **Canada, United Kingdom,** and **United States,** see p. 7. **Israel,** Natalio Sanchez 125, 6th floor (tel. 433 4431; fax 433 8925; email emisrael@electrodata.com.pe).

Immigration Office: Dirección General de Migraciones (tel. 330 41 14 or 330 40 30), España and Huaraz, can extend your visa and issue new tourist cards.

FINANCIAL SERVICES

Currency Exchange: There are *casas de cambios* and money-changers all over the city, but the best place to do your banking is in Miraflores, where most banks have offices on Larco (blocks 5-8). Also, the money changers are regulated in central Miraflores, so you are less likely to be robbed. **Banco de Crédito,** Larco 1099, in Miraflores, has **Visa ATMs. Banco Wiese** and **Banco Latino** allow withdrawals on MC with a long wait. **Cirrus** service does not work in Perú, but **Plus** cards work in Banco de Crédito's Unicard machines at Lampa 499 and at Larco 1099, in Miraflores. Banks above change traveler's checks and cash and are open M-F 9:15am-6pm, Sa 9:30am-12:30pm.

American Express: Belén 1040 (tel. 424 75 60), in the Lima Tours office.

IT'S MY PARTY AND I'LL DIE IF I WANT TO

On December 17, 1996, during an elaborate soirée at the Japanese ambassador's residence in Lima, a group of **Tupac Amaru** (formally known as the Movimiento Revoluionario de Tupac Amaru, or **MRTA**) guerillas blew a hole in the back of the ambassador's home and crashed the party. Once inside, they set off explosives and took hundreds of hostages, initiating what would turn into an interminable stand-off between the rebels and Peruvian **President Alberto Fujimori.** The rebels demanded the release of their jailed comrades, captured earlier in the year. In spite of the fact that his mother and younger brother were among the hostages, Fujimori took a characteristically hard line, refusing outright to free any Tupac Amaru prisoners. In the first few weeks, the rebels let many of the hostages go, but negotiations failed to bring about a solution. While the crisis initially attracted international attention, the affair dragged on and even many Peruvians started to lose interest. The Tupac Amaru Movement, which was founded in 1984 to defend the rights of Perú's indigenous underclass, found little sympathy even among those it claimed to be fighting for—after years of civil war, Perú's poor were tired of fighting and bloodshed.

In March 1997, the hostage situation found its way back into the headlines, with rumors that the Peruvian military was excavating a tunnel under the ambassador's residence in preparation for a rescue attempt, a claim that was vigorously denied by Fujimori. The rumors turned out to be true—on April 22, with a negotiated settlement apparently near, a team of Israeli-trained Peruvian commandos stormed the building, freeing the hostages and killing the rebels.

In the immediate aftermath, Fujimori was hailed around the world as a hero—the only hostage that died during the operation had succumbed to a heart attack, rather than to shrapnel or gunfire. Only days later, stories of surrendering rebels being executed by the rescue team began to appear in the press, bringing Fujimori's stance on human rights under public scrutiny once again.

LOCAL SERVICES

Bookstores: Most English-language bookstores are in Miraflores near the Ovalo/Parque Kennedy. **Mosca Azul,** Malecón Armendariz 713 (tel. 445 62 64), has used non-Spanish books. Open M-Sa 10am-9pm, Su 3-10pm. The **South American Explorers Club** (see p. 69) has an impressive selection of English-language books for exchange or rental. They also sell many useful regional guidebooks. The **Instituto Geográfico Nacional,** Aramburu 1190 (tel. 475 30 85), near the 9th block of República de Panamá, sells maps and has a **book exchange.** Open M-F 8:30am-5:30pm.

Cultural Centers: Find home country newspapers, film screenings, and cultural events at the **Alliance Française,** Arequipa 4595 (tel. 241 70 14); **Centro Boliviano,** Valles del Sur 350 (tel. 438 23 34) in Surco; **Centro de Estudios Brasileños,** Grau 270 (tel. 328 35 30); the **Instituto Cultural Peruano-Norteamericano,** Arequipa 4798 (tel. 446 03 81); **Goethe Instituto,** Nazca 722 (tel. 433 31 80) in Jesus María district; and the **British Council**, A. Lynch 110 (tel. 221 75 52).

Jewish Centers: There are 3 synagogues: the conservative **Unión Israelita Sharon,** Maimonides 610 (tel. 440 02 90), in San Isidro by the 14th block of Pezet; the reform **Sociedad de 1870** (tel. 445 10 09); and an **Orthodox congregation** (tel. 471 72 30). Visitors must ahead of time with a passport number and bring a passport for verification. There is also a **Club Hebraica** (tel. 437 23 95) farther from the city, and even a small **Delicatessen Minimarket Kosher,** Pezet 1472 (tel. 264 21 87), around the corner from the synagogue, with possibly the only Kosher meat in Perú.

Gay and Lesbian Organizations: Movimiento Homosexual de Lima, Mariscal Miller 828 (tel. 433 6375; fax 433 5519), in Jesús María, provides lots of information. They also have a *taller libre* (discussion group) for women M and men for men Tu (7:30-9pm).

Outdoor Gear: Alpamayo, Larco 345 (tel. 445 16 71) in Miraflores, has high quality, though very expensive, camping gear. Open M-Sa 10am-8pm.

Supermarkets: Wong, Augusto Angulo 130 in Miraflores, and Av. Santa Cruz 771, and **Santa Isabel,** Javier Prado Este 2030, José Pardo 707, and San Felipe Tolas 74-75 in Jesus María, dominate the *supermercado* scene. All are open approximately 8am-9pm; Sta. Isabel's Benavides 467 location is open 24hr. **Hipermercado Metro,** Venezuela and Alfonso Ugarte, Breña, is one of the few supermarkets near Lima Centro.

Laundry: Laverap, Schell 601 (tel. 241 07 59), in Miraflores. **Lavandería Burbujitas,** Porta 293 (tel. 444 95 06).

Pharmacies: Abundant all over the city. **Farmacia Deza** (tel. 440 89 11), Conquistadores in Miraflores, and **Farmacia Moretti,** Benavides 1741 (tel. 241 63 88), are both well-stocked and offer 24hr. service.

EMERGENCY AND COMMUNICATIONS

Emergency: Police 105. Fire 116.

Police: In **Miraflores:** tel. 445 65 83, 445 42 16, or 445 35 37; **San Isidro:** tel. 421 25 00; **Barranco:** tel. 477 00 88; **Breña:** tel. 431 14 25.

Clinics: The **Clínica Anglo-Americana** (tel. 221 36 56), on Salazar in San Isidro, has the best selection of immunizations (but no typhoid vaccine). **Clínica Internaccional,** Washington 1475 (tel. 433 43 06). **Clínica Ricardo Palma,** Javier Prado Este 1066 (tel. 224 22 24) in San Isidro.

Post Office: The postal system has recently been privatized and is supposedly more reliable. You can mail letters from the **Wong** and **Santa Isabel** supermarkets (see above) and from the **Central Post Office** (tel. 427 93 70), Piura near the Plaza de Armas in Lima (open M-Sa 8am-8pm, Su 8am-2pm). It's quicker and more certain to send packages via **DHL,** Los Castaños 225 (tel. 954 43 45) in San Isidro (open M-F 8am-9pm and Sa 9am-5pm); **EMS** (tel. 225 47 09), across from the Central Post Office (open M-Sa 8am-8pm); or **FedEx,** Pasaje Olayo 260 (tel. 242 22 80) in Miraflores (open M-F 8:30am-6pm). The **South American Explorers Club** (see p. 69) is one of the best places to receive mail in Lima if you are a member.

Faxes: You can send and receive faxes at the **South American Explorers Club** (fax 425 01 42; see p. 69) or at the many internet cafes in the city.

Internet Access: Cybersandeg Internet, Unión 853, inside the shopping center. Fast storefront internet access with friendly owners ready to help (s/4 per hr.). Also offers cheap phone and fax services via internet. Open M-Sa 8:30am-10pm, Sun 10am-5pm. There are *cabinas de internet* popping up all over the city. The pedestrian walkway, Tarata, off Larco in Miraflores, has more than 5 internet cafes (s/6 per hr.).

Telephones: You can dial the MCI (tel. (0 800) 50 010) and AT&T (tel. (0 800) 50 000) operators from most **Telefónica del Perú** phones, found on many street corners. The call is usually free but occasionally requires a small fee (s/0.30). For regular international calls, dial 108 to reach an operator. Telefónica del Perú or Telepoint cards are convenient and sold by pharmacies and street vendors.

TELEPHONE CODE	01

ACCOMMODATIONS

LIMA CENTRO

Casas antiguas are by far the most attractive and affordable options in Lima Centro. If you ignore the concave iron beds, uneven floor boards, and occasional errant paint chip, you can live like a conquistador in rooms with private balconies, elaborately painted ceilings, and arched doorways. The rambling old mansions are usually filled with a young, international crowd. While staying in Lima Centro is convenient and will give you a better sense of Lima's colonial history than living in modern Miraflores, the area can be unsafe at night and noisy during the day.

Hotel España, Azángaro 105 (tel. 428 55 46). This light, lively, statue-filled colonial house echoes with the constant commotion of European, Israeli, and U.S. backpackers. Plants grow, birds fly, tortoises crawl, international travelers meet, greet, and plan future adventures. Hot water, laundry, message board, tourist info, cafe, and locked storage facilities. Dorms US$2.75; singles US$5.55; doubles US$8; triples US$11.

Familia Rodríguez, Nicolás de Piérola 730 (tel. 423 64 65), 2nd floor. This house is almost as congenial as the caring family that runs it. The Rodríguezes invite guests to eat with them in thier cozy dinning-room. US$6 per person includes breakfast.

La Casona, Moquegua 289 (tel. 426 65 52). A white, plant-filled colonial house with a restaurant in the blue-tiled inner courtyard and rooms that open onto ornate wooden balconies. Dorms US$5; singles US$7.50; doubles US$9; triples US$13.

Roma, Ica 326 (tel. 427 75 76), is a rare find, with skylights and angel paintings on the ceiling. Rooms vary in attractiveness–ask to see one before paying. Single s/30, with bath s/40; doubles s/47, with bath s/60; triples s/66, with bath s/84.

Hostal de Los Artes, Chota 1460 (tel. 433 00 31; email artes@telematic.com.pe). A Dutch-owned, cultured old house near the Museo de Arte and SAEC. Rooms are well-decorated, with unbelievably high ceilings. One caveat: the neighborhood isn't particularly safe, so take a taxi here at night. Singles s/20; doubles with bath s/30.

Hotel Europa, Ancash 376 (tel. 427 33 51). This large, rambling *casa antigua* needs some more open windows, but it offers a slightly more serene setting than its neighbor, Hotel España. No phones, only common bath, occasional carved wood paneling. Dorms s/10; singles s/10; doubles s/23; triples s/30.

Hotel Wiracocha, Junín 284 (tel. 427 11 78), just down from the Plaza de Armas, offers a central location. Large halls and high-ceilinged rooms ensure a colonial feel. Singles s/18, with bath s/30; doubles s/31, with bath s/35.

Pensión Ibarra, Tacna 359 (tel. 427 86 03), on the 14th and 15th floors. Spacious rooms with an *impresionante* view of Lima. The very amiable owner offers breakfast, laundry, phone, and free kitchen access. There's even a *bidet* in one of the bathrooms! Dorms US$12; singles US$7. Discounts for long stays.

SOUTH OF CENTER

Hotels get larger, more modern, and more expensive as you move from Lima Centro to the San Isidro/Miraflores area. The area is generally safer, quieter, cleaner, and more convenient for seaside nightlife, but all advantages have a price. You'll have to take a bus or cab to see the sites in Lima Centro, and budget accommodations are less abundant. Nevertheless there are a few more affordable options in case you've left your Platinum card at home.

NEAR LIMA CENTRO

Hostal Renacimiento, Parque Hernán Velarde 51 (tel. 433 19 17), near the first block of Arequipa. A large, white *casa antigua* in a quiet, tree-filled park. Simple, well-lit rooms, most with attractive views. Convenient for buses to Chosica, Lurín, and other near-Lima excursions; also near main route (Arequipa) to southern suburbs. The vegetarian cafeteria serves breakfast and lunch. Singles US$15, with bath US$25; doubles US$30.

Hotel Columbus, Arequipa 1421 (tel. 471 73 71). Dimly-lit hallways with suspiciously threadbare carpets belie the light, airy rooms, most of which have a private balcony and TV. Singles s/60; doubles s/75.

SAN ISIDRO/MIRAFLORES/BARRANCO

Mochilero's Backpackers (tel. 477 4506; backpacker@amauta.rcp.net.pe), Pedro de Osma 135 in Barranco, two blocks form the main plaza. A great deal for students, this converted, cavernous mansion has 40 beds, mostly in dorms that are so big, you'll forget you're sharing a room. Other services include internet access, a large, fully-equipped kitchen, and cable TV. An adjoining pub, Dirty Nelly's, gets rowdy on the weekends (open M-Sa). Dorms are US$10 per person, with ISIC US$6.

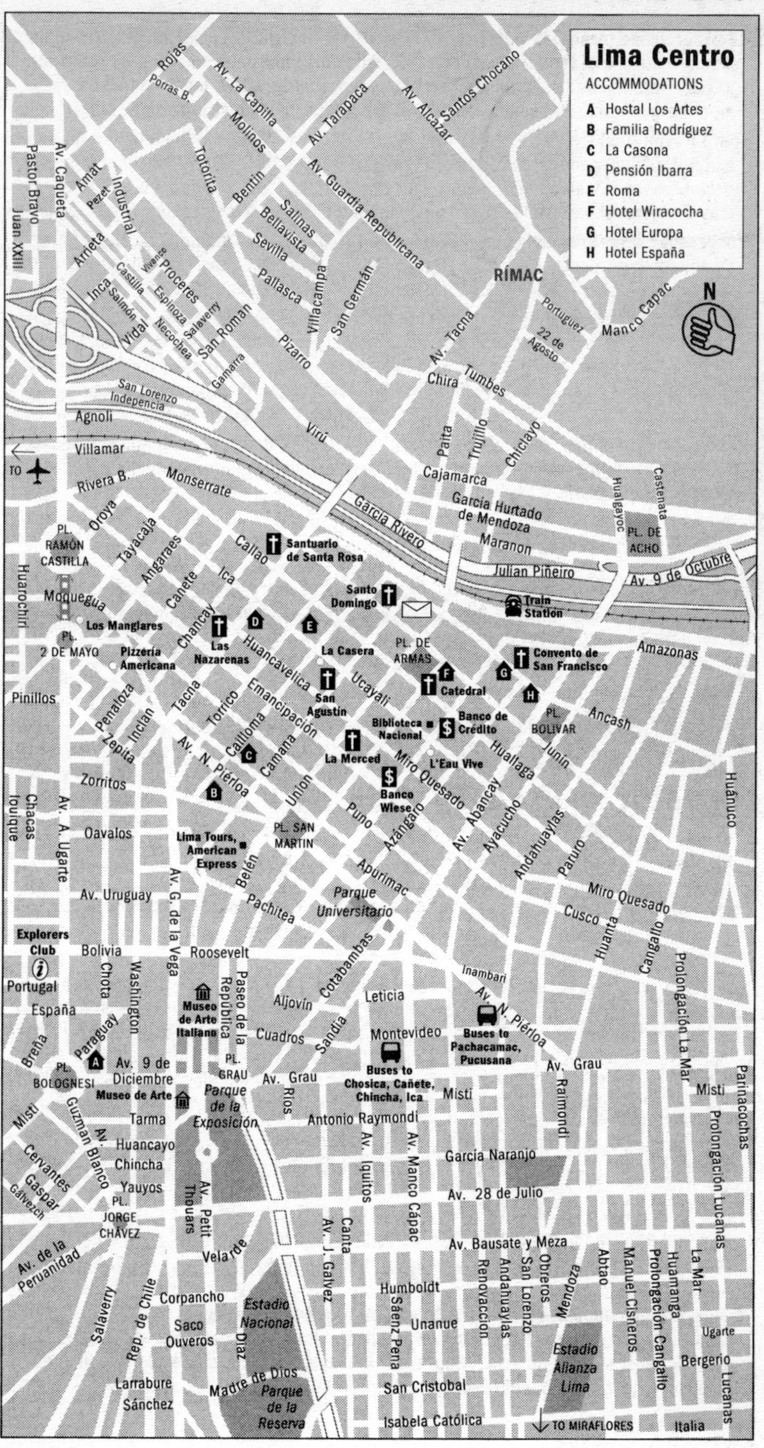
Lima Centro
ACCOMMODATIONS
A Hostal Los Artes
B Familia Rodríguez
C La Casona
D Pensión Ibarra
E Roma
F Hotel Wiracocha
G Hotel Europa
H Hotel España
N
RÍMAC
Santuario de Santa Rosa
Santo Domingo
Train Station
Convento de San Francisco
Los Manglares
Las Nazarenas
Pizzería Americana
La Casera
PL. DE ARMAS
Catedral
San Agustín
Biblioteca Nacional
Banco de Crédito
La Merced
L'Eau Vive
Banco Wiese
Lima Tours, American Express
PL. SAN MARTIN
PL. BOLIVAR
PL. RAMÓN CASTILLA
PL. 2 DE MAYO
PL. DE ACHO
Parque Universitario
Explorers Club
Museo de Arte Italiano
Buses to Pachacamac, Pucusana
Buses to Chosica, Cañete, Chincha, Ica
PL. BOLOGNESI
PL. GRAU
Museo de Arte
Parque de la Exposición
PL. JORGE CHÁVEZ
Estadio Nacional
Parque de la Reserva
Estadio Alianza Lima
TO MIRAFLORES
TO
Rojas
Porras B.
Av. La Capilla
Molinos
Av. Tarapaca
Av. Alcazar
Santos Chocano
Av. Guardia Republicana
Totorita
Bentin
Salinas
Bellavista
Sevilla
Pallasca
Villacampa
San Germán
Pastor Bravo
Juan XXIII
Av. Caqueta
Amat
Pezet
Industrial
Arrieta
Inca
Castilla
Salmón
Vidal
Vivanco
Proceres
Espinoza
Necochea
Salaverry
San Roman
Gamarra
Pizarro
Av. Tacna
Portuguez
22 de Agosto
Manco Capac
Chira
Tumbes
San Lorenzo
Indepencia
Agnoli
Villamar
Virú
Paita
Trujillo
Chiclayo
Cajamarca
Rivera B.
Monserrate
García Rivero
García Hurtado de Mendoza
Maranon
Julian Piñeiro
Av. 9 de Octubre
Hualgayoc
Castenata
Oroya
Tayacaja
Angaraes
Callao
Ica
Canete
Chancay
Huancavelica
Ucayali
Amazonas
Ancash
Junín
Huallaga
Moquegua
Huarochiri
Pinillos
Penaloza
Zepita
Inclan
Tacna
Torrico
Emancipación
Callloma
Camana
Av. N. Piérola
Union
Miro Quesado
Av. Abancay
Ayacucho
Andahuaylas
Paruro
Huánuco
Zorritos
Chacas
Iquique
Av. A. Ugarte
Oavalos
Puno
Azángaro
Belén
Apurimac
Av. Uruguay
Av. G. de la Vega
Pachitea
Miro Quesado
Cusco
Huanta
Cangallo
Prolongación La Mar
Bolivia
Roosevelt
Chota
Washington
Paseo de la República
Cotabambas
Inambari
Portugal
España
Aljovín
Leticia
Av. N. Piérola
Paraguay
Cuadros
Sandia
Montevideo
Breña
Av. 9 de Diciembre
Av. Grau
Ríos
Misti
Av. Grau
Raimondi
Misti
Parinacochas
Tarma
Antonio Raymondi
Prolongación Lucanas
Misti
Guzman Blanco
Huancayo
Av. Iquitos
Av. Manco Cápac
García Naranjo
Cervantes
Chincha
Gaspar
Gálvez
Yauyos
Av. Petit Thouars
Av. 28 de Julio
Av. J. Gálvez
Canta
Av. de la Peruanidad
Velarde
Av. Bausate y Meza
Renovacion
Andahuaylas
San Lorenzo
Obreros
Mendoza
Abtao
Manuel Cisneros
Prolongación Cangallo
Huamanga
La Mar
Salaverry
Rep. de Chile
Corpancho
Humboldt
Saco
Ouveros
Diaz
Sáenz Pena
Unanue
Ugarte
Bergerio
Lucanas
Larrabure
Sánchez
Madre de Dios
San Cristobal
Isabela Católica
Italia

LIMA

Pensión Jose Luís, Paula Ugarriza 727 (tel. 444 10 15), Miraflores. Pensión Jose Luís provides the low price of a hostel but none of the institutional feel. The English-speaking owner offers a winding old house with plants, parakeets, sunny patios, and cable TV. A great value. US$12 per person. Breakfast included. Must call ahead.

Youth Hostel Malka, Los Lirios 165 (tel. 442 01 62), near Javier Prado and Parodí, San Isidro. This *albergue juvenil* is a little out of the way, but finding this quiet, usually safe neighborhood is well worth the effort. Run by a climber, the hostel is filled with spectacular mountain photos and has a small climbing wall in the backyard. US$6 per person.

Hospedaje Yolanda, Domingo Elías 230 (tel. 445 75 65), near Arequipa block 47, offers small, spotless rooms in a private house. The amiable owner provides tea, coffee, and outdated English magazines in a small common room. Singles US$20; doubles US$30.

International Youth Hostel, Casimiro Ulloa 328 (tel. 446 54 88), is the largest hostel in the area. Tidy, spacious common areas, a kitchen, a dining room, tourist information, and hot-water baths are just a few of the amenities. It's hard to destroy the character of a charming old colonial house, but neatly lined-up bunkbeds and orange lockers come close to doing just that. Dorms US$11.50; singles with bath US$30.

Residencial El Castillo, Diez Canseco 580 (tel. 446 95 01). The elderly proprietress has adjusted well to the strangers living in her quiet, antique-filled house. Rooms are simple but attractive. Singles US$12; doubles US$24.

FOOD

Food in Lima is heavy on the fish and rice. *Criollo* food, often the substance of the economical set *menús*, is usually a sauce-covered or fried meat-and-potato dish with a side of rice. It's definitely worth a visit to one of the costlier restaurants to sample true *criollo* cuisine more lovingly prepared.

LIMA CENTRO

The lunchtime *menús* in Lima Centro offer the most calories per dollar. For US$2 you can buy a drink, soup, appetizer, and main course of *criollo* food.

L'Eau Vive, Ucayali 370 (tel. 427 56 12). The s/12 lunch *menú* is one of the best bargains in central Lima—carefully prepared French delicacies served by friendly nuns can't be found for this price (or any price) anywhere else. A la carte lunch s/10-20, dinner s/25-30. Open M-Sa 12:30-3pm and 7:30-9pm.

Restaurant La Casera, Huancavelica 244 (tel. 427 23 80), near the Teatro Principal, is one of the more popular places for a fast, cheap lunchtime *menú* (s/5.50) of meat, salad, and juice. Open daily 9am-10pm.

Los Manglares, Moquegua 266 (tel. 427 14 94), is a campy combination of a fishtank and Tumbes-style fisherman's restaurant. It's a bit disconcerting to eat *ceviche* (s/12-32) under the watchful gaze of the larger-than-life sea creatures painted on the walls, but the restaurant is one of the less risky places to eat seafood in Lima Centro. Live rock, *salsa*, and *criollo* music daily 3pm-Midnight. Open daily Noon-Midnight.

El Milagro de la Naturaleza, Chota 1462 (tel. 330 38 51). Another of Peru's Krishna-run Govindas, this "Centro de Medicina Natural" offers natural medicine consultations and will modify any of its dishes to suit particular dietary restrictions. Main dishes s/4-5. Open M-F 8am-8pm, Sa 8am-4pm.

Norky's, Unión 426 and another location at Abacay 210 (tel. 521 05 26). Extremely popular and fronting on an outdoor mall, Norky's bright neon lights contrast oddly with the slow-roasting rotisserie chicken, but such details matter little once you taste it. Chicken combo meals s/4-8. Open 11am-11pm.

Natur, Moquegua 132 (tel. 427 8281), one block from la Uníon. Saddle up to the counter at this small cafe and order a yogurt. The friendly owners offer a diverse selection, but with *todo vegetariano*. Soups are yummy (s/3), rice and lentils are, well, rice and lentils (s/6). Open M-Sa 8am-9pm, Su 10am-5pm.

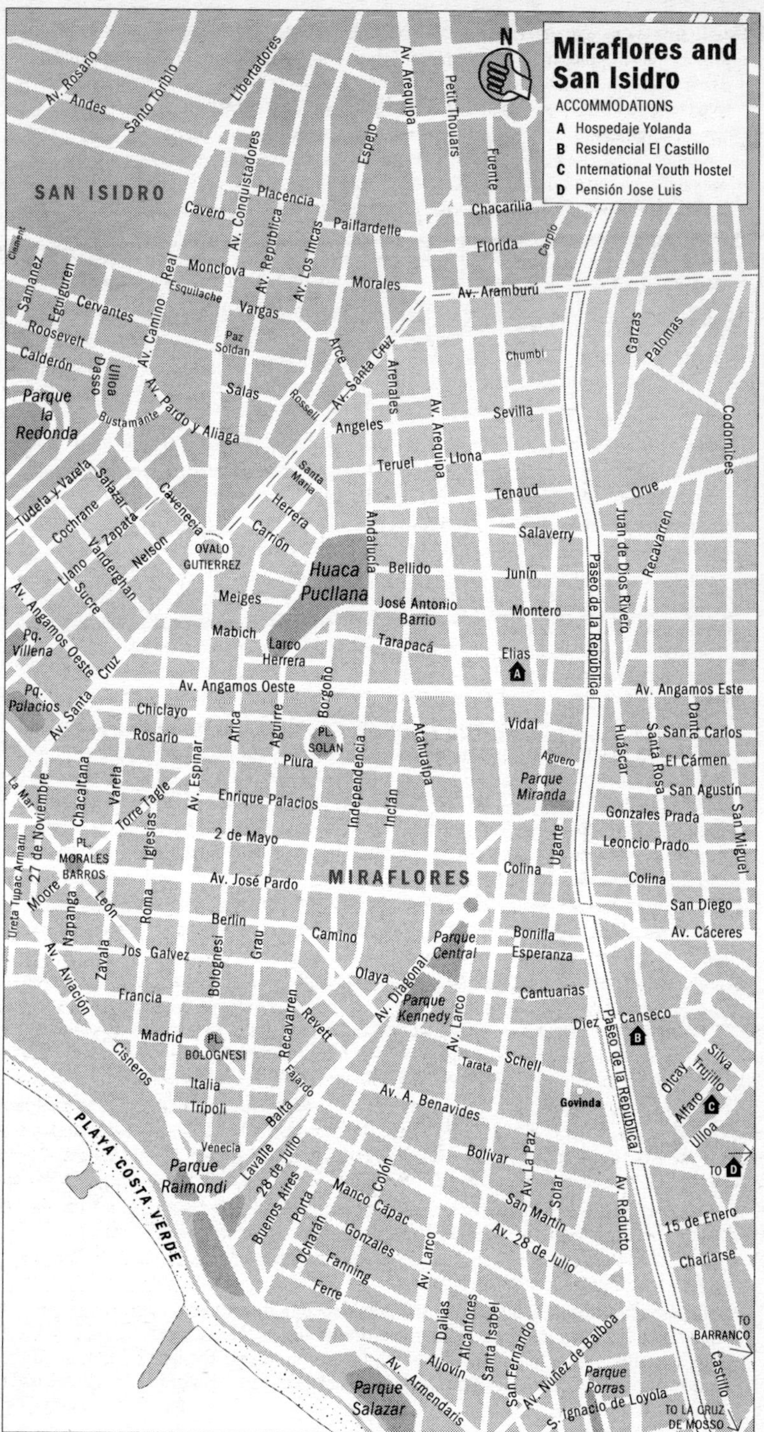
Miraflores and San Isidro
ACCOMMODATIONS
A Hospedaje Yolanda
B Residencial El Castillo
C International Youth Hostel
D Pensión Jose Luis
SAN ISIDRO
MIRAFLORES
Huaca Pucllana
Parque la Redonda
Parque Miranda
Parque Central
Parque Kennedy
Parque Raimondi
Parque Salazar
Parque Porras
PLAYA COSTA VERDE
OVALO GUTIERREZ
PL. SOLAN
PL. MORALES BARROS
PL. BOLOGNESI
Govinda
TO BARRANCO
TO LA CRUZ DE MOSSO

Restaurante Los Heraldos, Aucash 306 (tel. 427 40 44). Across from the Convento de San Francisco, and down the street from Hotel España, this friendly spot offers full portions of beef (s/10) and pitchers of *cerveza* (s/12). A special English menu includes all the ingredients in every dish. Open daily 8am-midnight. Live music Friday nights.

Pizzería Americana, Nicolás de Piérola 514. A predominantly Peruvian crowd munches on American-style pizzas with delicious chewy crusts. The cool, dark interior provides a welcome escape from the chaotic street outside. Pizza grande s/22-27, pizza individual s/12-17. Open daily 10am-midnight.

OUTSIDE LIMA CENTRO

Restaurants become more expensive as you move away from the tangled downtown area. With a few exceptions listed below, there are three types of restaurants in the San Isidro/Miraflores/Barranco area: cheap fast food; expensive cafes where the people are more beautiful than the food; and succulent, delicious, exquisite, and otherwise excellent *criollo* restaurants and *cevicherías*. The latter, although detrimental to your budget, are definitely worth the extra *soles*.

Govinda, Schell 630 (tel. 444 28 71) in Miraflores. One of several Hare Krishna, vegetarian eateries in Lima, Govinda's tasty cuisine offers a refreshing alternative to standard meat and fish fare. Divine juices s/3. Open M-F 10am-8pm, Su 10am-4pm.

Restaurante Rischbeck's, Porta 185-B (tel. 941 47 53) in Miraflores. Depending on your mood, you can dine in the light and breezy patio outside or under dim mystical blue lighting indoors. Regardless, the *mariscos* are delicious and relatively inexpensive for Miraflores (*menú* s/6). Open M-Th 10am-2am, F-Sa 10am-6am, Su 10am-1am.

Restaurant Bircher-Benner, Diez Canseco 487 (tel. 444 42 50) in Miraflores, between Laneo and La República, is another popular vegetarian restaurant. It offers a variety of dishes made with *gluten* meat, as well as tasty pizzas (s/34-50). *Postres* and fruit cups (s/10) are *muy ricos*. Open M-Sa 8:30am-10:30pm.

Tropicana, Schell 498 (tel. 444 56 26), in Miraflores. Bamboo and exotic fruit mixtures abound in this tropical-hut-styled eatery. The *menú* offers good *comida criolla* and *mariscos* for very few *soles* (s/6). Try the *Bistec a Tropicana* (s/15) for a hefty combination of eggs, beets, rice, plantains, and fries. Open M-Sa 8am-11pm.

Punta Sal, Conquistadores 948 (tel. 441 74 31) in San Isidro, 2nd location at Malecón Cisneros, Cdra. 3 (tel. 445 96 75) in Miraflores. Famous for its fresh *ceviche* (s/28.50). It's worth paying for quality preparation—after all, it is raw fish. Open daily 11am-5pm.

Palachinke, Schell 120 (tel. 447 26 01), Parque Kennedy in Miraflores, serves the best crepe-style *panqueques* in town. Have one with cheese and veggies for dinner and one with ice cream for dessert (s/17-26). Open Tu-Sa noon-11pm; Su-M 3-11pm.

CHEAP EATS

Most of the cheap food options in Miraflores are the fast food *pollo a la brasa* and pizza places. One notable exception is the Krishna-run **Vrinda,** Prado Este 185, off the 30th block of Arequipa. They serve a daily *menú* (s/5) and arrange Sunday excursions to "ecological communities" for yoga sessions. (Open M-Sa 9am-9pm.) Alternatively, **Bembo's,** on Benavides near Larco, across from the Santa Isabel Supermarket, will stuff you full of greasy sort-of-Peruvian fast food (s/5-15). **Super Rueda II,** Porta 133, is like Taco Bell with sandwiches (open daily 8am-12:30am). **El Peruanito,** Angamos 391, near the Vía Expresa, has some of the best sandwiches (s/6) in metropolitan Lima (open daily 7am-midnight).

CAFES

Feast your eyes, not your stomach, in San Isidro and Miraflores's overpriced cafes. A slice of tasteless quiche will cost more than a full meal in Lima Centro, but the drinks are affordable. **Ovalo Gutiérrez,** where Comandante Espinar, Conquistadores, and Santa Cruz all converge, has several overpriced, yuppified gathering places. **Mango's** (tel. 446 51 80) charges s/22 for a sandwich and pisco sour (open 7:30am-midnight). **Bohemia's** fare, while well-prepared, is very expensive (dinner s/40; open daily noon-3am).

Café Café, Mártir Olaya 250 (tel. 445 11 65), just off Parque, serves drinks, good coffee, munchies, and ice cream, and is supremely popular among chic 20-somethings. This is where it's at. Open Su-W 8am-1am; Th 8am-2am; Fr and Sa 8am-3am.

Gelatería Laritza D., Comandante Espinar 845, just off Ovalo Gutiérrez, additionally at Larcomar, is a popular hangout and offers some of the best ice cream in Lima (s/4 for two scoops). Open daily 9am-12:30am.

Phantom Café, Diagonal 344 (tel. 242 43 07), overlooks Parque Kennedy. Hyper-artsy, with multiple ultra-modern metal sculptures. The bright colors throughout are dulled by the even more brilliant bar. Exotic concoctions such as the *orgasmo múltiple* intoxicate with style. Open daily 6pm-1am.

THE BIG SPLURGE

Manos Morenas, Pedro de Osma Barranco 409 (tel. 467 04 21), serves *criollo* food at its best in a 19th-century mansion near the ocean. Live *criollo* music shows often accompany dinner (entrees s/20-25) Wed-Sat. Open M-Sa 12:30-4:30pm and 7:30-11:30pm, Su 12:30-4:30pm.

El Señorio de Sulco, Malecón Cisneros 1470 (tel. 445 66 40), close to the intersection with José Pardo. The Incas would have been obese if their food had been anything like Señorio's. Only traditional tools such as earthen pots are used to prepare exquisite fish, meat, and vegetarian dishes (s/25-35). Open noon-midnight.

Las Brujas de Cachiche, Bolognesi 460 (tel. 444 53 10), at Plaza Bolognesi in Miraflores, bewitches their clientele with their *tamales verdes* (s/8) and beguiles them with fish from the sea. Have no illusions, however; the bill for the meal (s/50-55 per person) will not disappear. Open M-Sa 12:30pm-12:30am, Su 12:30pm-4pm.

SIGHTS

Most of Lima's historic sights—plazas, museums, and *casas antiguas*—are clustered in the complicated maze known as Lima Centro. This district, bounded roughly by **Av. 28 de Julio** to the south, **Av. Alfonso Ugarte** to the west, **Río Rímac** to the north, and **Av. Abancay** to the east, was built on top of the old Inca city; today almost nothing remains of its pre-Hispanic architecture. A small part of Lima's historical center spills over into **Rímac** to the north of the river, across the 17th-century bridge, the **Puente de Piedra.** While the center shows what Lima was, the southern districts of **Miraflores** and **San Isidro** demonstrate what Lima might be in a few decades. The glittering, modern suburbs between the center and beach are home to fashionable, high-rent commercial and residential districts. **Barranco,** further south on the coast, was an outlying beach resort during colonial times, but modern transportation and urban sprawl have made it a popular and easily accessible nightlife district for young *limeños.*

PLAZAS

PLAZA DE ARMAS. Built squarely on top of an Inca temple dedicated to the Puma God, the last palace of the Inca emperor, and the mansion of an Inca envoy, the square now glorifies Spanish culture. An ornate fountain, beds of red and white flowers, and a larger-than-life statue of Francisco Pizarro on horseback dominate the square, while a large stone monument to the Inca emperor **Tauri Chusko** stands on a side street beside the **Palacio Municipal.** In the **Palacio de Gobierno** to the north, a replica of Pizarro's original house now displays a recreated baroque interior and some slightly mismatched colonial-style furniture. *(Free guided tours from entrance on Unión.)* A more impressive sight, the changing of the guard, takes place outside Monday through Friday at 11:45am. **The Palacio Municipal,** Unión, on the west side of the plaza, has a small Pancho Fierro art gallery that highlights the work of colonial Peruvian artists. *(Open M-F 10am-4pm. Admission free.)* **The Biblioteca Nacional** is on the 4th block of Abancay. *(Open M-Sa 8am-8pm, Su 8:30am-1:30pm.)* **The Correo Central,** Conde de Superunda, just off the plaza, is more of a stamp-collector's museum and stamp-trading locale than an important mail center since the privatization of the postal system. *(Exhibits open M-Sa 8:30am-6:30pm, Su 8:30am-noon. Admission free.)*

OTHER PLAZAS. Bounded by Nicolás de Piérola, Unión, and Carabaya, **Plaza San Martín** is the lesser of Lima's city plazas: it's a big square with some erratically working fountains in the center. The plaza is an attractive place to stroll or sit, and tourists in search of a glimpse of Lima's city politics can often find some kind of demonstration here. Three smaller, very similar plazas—**Dos de Mayo,** where Colmena and Ugarte intersect, **Plaza Castilla,** where Emancipación meets Oroya and Ugarte, and **Plaza Bolognesi,** where Brasil meets Guzman Blanco and 9 de Diciembre—round out central Lima's collection of open spaces. **Plaza Gran,** at the end of La República, offers little more, but the neighboring park between the Sheraton and Palacio de Justicia features more shrubs, flowers, and life-size animal statues. The **pedestrian mall** on Unión between the Plaza de Armas and Plaza de San Martín, has high concentrations of shoe and jewelry stores.

CHURCHES

The Spanish quest to save Inca souls resulted in the construction of numerous visible reminders of the three great motivators: gold, glory, and God. Lima's churches are artistic masterpieces and are almost invariably filled with ornate wooden carvings, gold- and silver-covered altars, and soulful paintings.

LA CATEDRAL DE LIMA. As you might expect, Lima's central cathedral is resplendent in gold, silver, and carved-wood glory. Home to the Catholic cardinal, Sunday mass at 11am is broadcast to the entire country. The glass coffin in the sacristy contains some gory remains which may or may not be Pizarro's. The attached **Museum of Religious Art and Treasures** contains more carved wood (choir stalls by Pedro Noguero) and a large collection of gilt-encrusted 17th- and 18th-century paintings. *(On the east side of the Plaza de Armas. Catedral open daily 8am-8pm. Admission free. Museum open M-Sa 10am-5pm. Admission s/5.)*

LA MERCED. The church, home to the massive, much-kissed silver cross of the Venerable Padre Uvraca, is built on the site of the first mass said in Lima. It has since been destroyed twice by earthquakes and once by fire, but its original appearance has been carefully restored. *(Unión Cdra. 6. Open M-Sa 8am-12:30pm and 4-8:30pm; Sunday 7am-1pm and 4-9pm.Admission free.)*

CONVENTO DE SAN FRANCISCO. San Francisco has the unique distinction of being a mass graveyard as well as museum and church. While the Sevillian tilework upstairs is standard church fare, the pits full of neatly-arranged bones in the catacombs downstairs are reminiscent of a B-grade horror movie—except they're real. Once a burial ground filled by victims of natural disasters or disease epidemics, the catacombs are reportedly haunted by a mischievous ghost who likes to scare tourists that stray from their group. *(Ancash 471, across from Hotel España. Open daily 9:30am-5:45pm. Admission s/5, students s/2.)*

IGLESIA DE SANTO DOMINGO. The church houses sainted *limeños* such as the ever-virginal Santa Rosa (see below) and San Martín de Porras. The tile mosaics of Santo Domingo's life have been well preserved and the cloisters offer a pleasant, dark retreat from the streets outside. *(Camaná 170, across from the Correo Central. Open M-Sa 9am-12:30pm and 3-5:30pm; Sunday 9am-1pm. Admission s/2.)*

SANTUARIO DE SANTA ROSA. This sanctuary glorifies Santa Rosa's ascetic life. Visitors can see the small adobe meditation/prayer hut she built with her own hands, the tree trunk bed where she allowed herself two hours of sleep with a stone for a pillow, and the well where she chucked the key to her chastity belt. There is also a small church on site. *(On the first block of Tacua. Open daily 5:30am-Noon and 3-8pm.)*

THE CONVENTO DE LOS DESCALZOS. The convent displays the spartan cells in which the pious Franciscan friars lived and worked. It also contains an art museum with examples of the Cusco, Quito, and Lima schools as well as a weighty gold altar. *(Alameda de los Descalzos, in Rímac. Open W-M 9:30am-1pm and 2-6pm.)*

OTHER CHURCHES. Las Nazarenas, on the corner of Huancavelica and Tacua, contains one of the oldest—some say miraculous—walls in Lima. It is currently under heavy construction. While the original church crumbled in the 1655 earthquake, one wall with a large mural of Christ on the cross, painted by an ex-slave, survived. *(Open M-Sa 6am-Noon and 4-8:30pm; Su 6am-1pm. Admission free.)* **Iglesia de San Pedro,** Azángaro 451, has gilded altars with Moorish-style balconies. *(Open daily 8:30am-1pm and 2-4pm. Admission free.)* **Iglesia de San Agustín,** Ica and Camaná, is full of carved effigies (*Death* is in storage now) and *churriguerresque* carving. *(Open M-F 7:30-10am and 4:30-7pm. Admission free.)* The **Iglesia de San Tomás'** unique circular cloister (now a school on Junín at Audahuaylas) completes Lima's show of religious finery. *(Free. Ask doorman on Audahuaylas to enter.)*

MUSEUMS

As with many large capital cities, Lima is home to some of the finest museums in Perú. Though the quality and variety of the displays may pale in comparison to those found in most European cities, the collections are always growing and may tell the observant visitor a lot about the history of the nation and people of Perú.

MUSEO DE ARTE. The art museum houses everything from Chavín ceramics and textiles to colonial silverware in a huge 19th-century palace. The collection spans 3000 years of Peruvian history, and the paintings of Apocryphal Gospel scenes will re-educate anyone who has been brought up believing in the King James Bible. The museum also shows films and has short-term art classes in subjects from singing to sculpture to computer literacy. *(Paseo Colón 125. Tel. 423 47 32. Open Tu-Su 10am-1pm and 2-5pm. Admission s/6, students s/3; admission free W.)*

MUSEO DE ORO DEL PERÚ Y ARMAS DEL MUNDO. As the name literally states, this museum displays gold from Perú and guns of the world. The basement vault overflows with gilded riches, but this gold has been used for ear plugs, jewelry, and ornate metal-plated capes. Upstairs, the improbable shapes and ridiculous decorations in the world's largest collection of firearms will intrigue even the most peaceable people. *(Alonso de Molina 1100, off block 18 of Primavera, in Monterrico. Tel. 435 07 91. Open daily 11:30am-7pm. Admission s/15, students s/7.)*

MUSEO DE LA NACIÓN. This museum's purpose is to offer an overview of Perú's archaeological heritage, focusing on the various cultures that have inhabited Perú over the centuries. *(Javier Prado Oeste 2465, San Borja. Tel. 476 98 75. Open Tu-Sa 9am-5pm, Su 10am-5pm. Admission s/10, students s/5.)*

BANK GALLERIES. Small galleries seem to be a fashionable accessory for banks in Lima, and it is worth calling to see what special collections the following banks are displaying: **Banco Central de Reserva del Perú** (*tel. 427 62 50, ext. 2660*), Ucayali and Lampa, has a permanent ceramics collection. *(Open Tu-F 10am-4:30pm, Sa-Su 10am-1pm. Admission free.)* **The Museo Numismático del Banco Wiese,** Cusco 245 (*tel. 428 60 00*), is a coin collector's dream. *(Open M-F 9:30am-5pm. Admission free.)*

OTHER MUSEUMS. There are smaller, more specific art museums scattered throughout the city. The **Museo de Arte Italiano,** La República 250, houses early 20th-century European art in an imposing neoclassical building. *(Tel 423 99 32. Open M-F 9am-4:30pm. Admission s/1, students s/0.50.)* The **Arte Popular de la PUC,** Camaná 459, shows more modern art. *(Tel. 427 92 75. Open Tu-Su 10am-7:30pm. Admission s/2.)* The **Museo Rafael Larco Henera,** Bolívar 1515, displays ceramic pots depicting everything from ancient medicine to the erotic sexual practices of pre-Hispanic cultures. *(Tel. 461 13 12. Open daily 9am-6pm. Admission s/20, students s/10.)* The **Museo Pedro de Osma,** Pecho de Osma 423 in Barranco, is much smaller and focuses on art, furniture, and artisanry from colonial Perú. *(Tel. 467 01 41. Open Tu-*

Su 10am-1:30pm and 2:30-6:30pm. Admission s/10, students s/5). The **Museo Nacional de Antropología, Arqueología, e Historia,** Plaza Bolívar in Pueblo Libre, lost some of its best pieces to the Museo de la Nación but retains an impressive collection. *(Tel. 463 50 70. Open M-F 9am-6pm, Sa 9am-1pm. Admission s/5, students s/2.)* The smaller **Museo Amano,** Retiro 160 in Miraflores, specializes in pieces from the Chancay culture. *(Tel. 441 29 09. Tours M-F 3, 4, and 5pm. Admission free.)* The **Museo de Cultura Peruana,** Alfonso Ugarte 650, offers smaller archaeological collections. *(Tel. 423 58 92. Open Tu-F 10am-4:30pm, Sa 10am-2pm. Admission s/2, students s/1.)* The gory **Museo de la Inquisición,** Junín 548 *(tel. 428 79 80; open daily 9am-1pm and 2:30-5pm; admission free)* and **Museo Taurino,** Plaza de Acho Hualgayoc 332, in Rímac *(tel. 482 33 60; open M-Sa 8am-4pm; admission s/5, students s/1),* exhibit Perú's bloodier history. The first displays torture instruments, the second bloody costumes from bull-gored matadors.

CASAS ANTIGUAS AND ANCIENT RUINS

While most of the old mansions in Lima Centro have been allowed to gradually rot away or have been converted into cheap *hostales*, some have been preserved in their original grandeur. The **Palacio Torre Tagle,** Ucayali 363, retains its colonial glory as the Office of the Foreign Ministry. (*Open to the public Sa. 9am-Noon*) The **Casa de las Trece Moredas,** Ancash 536, **Casa de Oquendo,** Conde de Superunda 298, and **Casa de Riva Agüero,** Camaná 459, are a few more impressive *casas antiguas*, but getting into them can be difficult.

The **Huaca Huallamarca,** on El Rosario at Nicolás de Riviera in San Isidro, and **Huaca Pucllana,** on the 4th block of Angamos in Miraflores, were pre-Inca centers of administration and ceremony. These ruins are minor compared to Machu Picchu in the mountains above, but admission is free, and they are conveniently near to Lima Centro. *(Open W-M 9am-5pm. Admission free.)*

OUTSIDE LIMA CENTRO

San Isidro's biggest attraction is its mall, **Centro Camino Real** on Camino Real. International mall rats won't want to miss the fountains, piped-in music, or overhyped international boutiques. The district also has a few discos and overpriced cafes, but they are scattered and not as pleasant as those in Miraflores or Barranco.

Miraflores fills the space between San Isidro and the beach with modern high-rises, glittering casinos, and well-kept oceanside parks. The **Ovalo Miraflores,** at the end of Arequipa, flanked by **Parque Kennedy** and **Parque Central,** is the focal point of people-watching and nightlife, although you'll have to go farther south along **Av. Larco** to lose your money in a casino. **Larcomar,** at the southern end of Av. Larco, is a modern, three-story mall which, because it is cleverly built into the side of an ocean-front hill, is nearly undetectable from the street above. The myriad, first-world shops, restaurants, and bars belong more to Southern California than South America, but the complex still offers breathtaking views of the cliffs and ocean below. St. Valentine would have a field day with the **Parque del Amor's** enormous statue of lovers embracing, real-life couples mimicking the statue, and love-poem-inscribed mosaics; but he would be a bit disturbed by the way the floodlights shine up the stone woman's skirt at night.

It's an easy *colectivo* ride (*take and marked "Chorrillos" of "Barranco"*) from the Ovalo Miraflores to the nightlife district of **Barranco.** The old mansions and seaside promenades that fan out from the **Parque Municipal** on Grau and Pedro de Osma are pleasant for walks during the day, but the crowds really come out at night to drink, dance, see, and be seen. The walk along the beach from Miraflores to Barranco takes about 15 minutes, but at night the area below the cliffs—except for the luxurious **La Rosa Náutica** restaurant on the pier—is dangerous and deserted.

The string of parks continues west to the middle class suburbs of **Magdalena del Mar, Pueblo Libre,** and **San Miguel.** Lima's zoo, the **Parque de Las Leyendas,** is in San Miguel on La Marina. (*Open daily 9am-5pm. Admission s/4, students s/2.*) Take the *colectivos* marked "La María" that run along Benavides or Javier Prado.

NIGHTLIFE

Lima comes alive at night and stays wide-eyed until 5 or 6am. The parks, large and small, fill with families, cruising teenagers, strolling couples, and attentive snack sellers. The clubs blare all varieties of music, and the energetic *salsa* away while the sedentary imbibe. While you can find "nightlife" and liveliness all over the city, it's safer to stick to the bars and clubs clustered in **Miraflores** and **Barranco.** Limeños refer to some *discotecas* in the Lima centro as *mala muerte,* bad death, because of the prostitution, drugs, and violence they sometimes contain. If going out in this area, take a cab, know the club's address, and don't start any trouble.

LIMA CENTRO

Las Brisas del Titicaca, Wakulsky 168 (tel. 332 18 81). A relatively inexpensive *peña* with enough pull to attract nationally-known folk, Andean, and *criollo* acts. Friday and Saturday shows usually s/20. Open Su-Th noon-9pm, F-Sa noon-3:30am.

Cerebro, Emancipación 119 (tel. 427 71 28), at the intersection with la Unión. The biggest and most widely-known *discoteca* in Lima Centro. Dance to rock and Latin music on the huge, underground dance floor. *Cervezas* go for s/15. Show your international passport, and receive a free drink. Cover s/5. Open daily from 5pm-the morning.

MIRAFLORES

For nighttime drinking and dancing, most skip Lima Centro and head straight to Miraflores and Barranco (below). Slick, wealthy limeños clad in designer attire swarm here en masse to groove to Latin, rock, and techno beats into the early hours. Most of Lima's gay and lesbian nightlife is in this area as well (see **Gay and Lesbian Nightlife,** below).

Tequila Rock, Caseco 146 (tel. 444 36 61). An intimate bar/dance club very close to Parque Kennedy. The music is unremarkable, but limeños and *extranjeros* alike crowd into the club on weekends.

Media Naranja Brasileiro, Schell 130, near Parque Kennedy. A good place to snack and imbibe tropical mixes (s/10-15) to constant Brasilian *samba* beats, before heading to the discos. Open daily 10am-1am.

Mamut/Blue Buddha, Berlin 438 (tel. 241 04 70). Two very different clubs sharing one huge converted theatre. Upstairs, in the **Blue Buddha,** trendy locals bust out their moves to blaring techno beats under, you guessed it, a large blue buddha. **Mamut,** on the first floor, is more upscale and plays the standard mix of rock, *salsa*, and *merengue*. s/15 for one club, s/25 for both. Open daily 10:30pm-5am.

Brick, Circuito de Playas Costa Verde, Bajado San Isidro, also plays a mix of music. Set in a large castle-like building with a pirate theme. Cover (*s/30*) includes one drink.

Hard Rock Cafe (tel. 446 84 00), in the LarcoMar mall in Miraflores. Whereas most Hard Rock Cafes are primarily tourist attractions, this one is very popular with locals. Even with two floors, many customers are left standing at the back on weekend nights, but they don't seem to mind. The main highlights are a pair of Bruce Springsteen's boots and a Madonna outfit. Burgers go for s/24. Open daily 11am-2am.

Sazú Jazz Bar (tel. 242 53 26), in Larcomar. This bar's blues on Tuesday nights and jazz on Wednesday and Thursday somehow clash with its super-sterile, mall-like decor. Well worth a visit if in LarcoMar. Open Tu-Sa 10pm-2am.

BARRANCO

The best way to choose where to go in Barranco is to stand in the middle of the Municipal Park and listen to the various strains of music and chatter. These include classical music, jazz, techno, folk (both Andean and Joan Baez-style), romantic whispers, and lively drunken chatter. There are a multitude of smaller discos along Pasaje Sánchez Carrión, but the bigger attraction is the variety of super-stylin', ever-so-artsy cafes in which each of the many wandering rooms has a new, funky, bright color scheme and nobody drinks coffee (unless perhaps mixed with an imported liquor). And the winners in this competition of drinking glitz and glamour are **La Noche,** Bolognesi 307 (tel. 477 41 54), the largest and busiest (open daily 8pm-3am); **La Democracía,** Bolognesi 660 (tel. 247 37 15; open M-Sa 8pm-4am); and the appropriately named **Kafe Kitsch,** Bolognesi 743 (tel. 247 33 25; open W-Sa from 9pm until late).

Barranco's walkway to the ocean and **Puente del Suspiros**—named for the lovelorn who sigh *(suspiran)* as they gaze at twinkling lights and waves below—are behind the parkside church and down the stone steps. Pounding surf replaces disco, *salsa,* and all other music. The bars near this seaside lookout are more romantic, and more expensive, than other bars in the area. The late-night revelers can always find a sandwich (s/5) along Piérola's first and second blocks.

Delirium, Sánchez Carrión 131 (tel. 477 98 19), is an elite private dance club—complete with security gate—but will let foreigners in with passport or international student ID card. Open M-Sa 9pm-4am.

Las Terrazas de Barranco, Grau 290 (tel. 477 55 33), on the park, offers a more civilized, tree-screened, candlelit meeting place during the week—until its Saturday metamorphosis into a towering, four-story disco.

La Posada del Angel, Pedro de Osmas 222 (tel. 247 03 41), has photos on the wall and a tranquil, softly chattering crowd, which gathers on the weekends to hear *trova,* Cuban folk music. Live music W-Sa. One drink minimum (s/3.50).

De Parranda, Grau 622 (tel. 247 20 36), offers a rousing 18-piece *salsa* orchestra. You can't help but get down at this brand new club. Cover s/20. Open F and Sa 10pm-4am.

De Rompe y Raja, Manuel Segura 127 (tel. 247 32 71). An old-school dance hall, with a stage, tables, and a dance floor in between. Music varies from Brazilian to *folklórica* to *salsa,* depending on the night. Cover s/20. Open W-Sa 10pm-4am.

GAY AND LESBIAN NIGHTLIFE

Although homosexuality isn't widely accepted in Perú, Lima has some excellent resources (see **Gay and Lesbian Organizations,** p. 70) and nightlife just as good as the best heterosexually oriented discos and bars. When looking for gay-friendly nightlife, the key phrase is "*al ambiente.*" Many of the buildings are unmarked on the outside but rocking inside, and most are not exclusively frequented by gays or lesbians. The best and most popular disco-bar is **Gitano,** Berlin 231 (tel. 446 34 35), in Miraflores, with a classy lounge and lively disco (open W-Su 10:30pm-6am; cover s/10 after midnight). Also in Miraflores, **Splash,** Los Pinos 181 (tel. 444 24 00), attracts an "open-minded" mixed crowd in a more upscale establishment (open W-Su 11pm-6am; cover Sa s/15, s/20 after midnight including one drink). **Voglia,** Ricardo Palma 336 (tel. 864 31 34), in Miraflores, attracts a similarly open-minded crowd and treats them to techno and *salsa* throughout the night (open Tu-Su 10pm-6am; cover s/5, F-Sa s/10).

ENTERTAINMENT

Lima is a veritable haven for all forms of entertainment, from thrilling *fútbol* matches to the raging nightlife for which the southern suburbs are famous. **El Comercio's** Friday supplement, **Visto y Bueno,** has excellent listings of concerts, sporting events, plays, movies, and other diversions.

SPORTS AND RECREATION

Fútbol (soccer) is more than a sport in Perú. It is a religion with the power to empty the streets, halt traffic, and drag even policemen away from their work. The **Estadio Nacional,** off blocks 7-9 of La República, and the nearby **Estadio Alianza Lima** host most of the important matches. If you can't make the game,

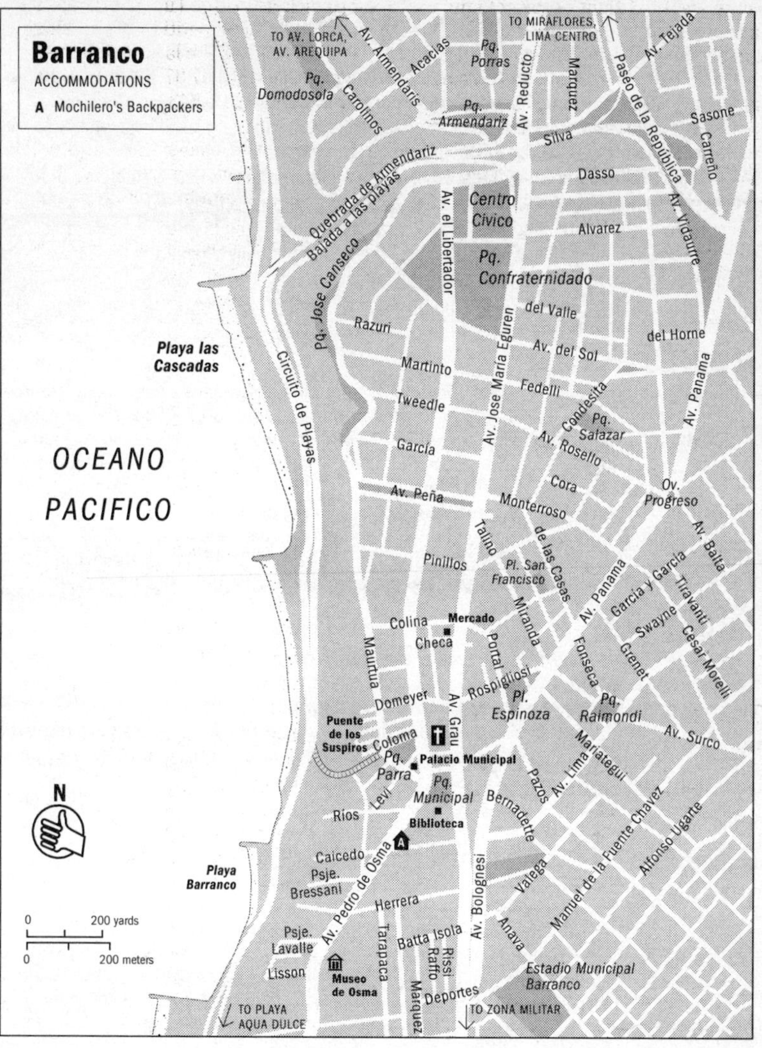

you can listen to it in *colectivos*, parks, and virtually any other public venue with a loudspeaker. (*For national matches, seats are s/25-45; for professional matches seats sell for as little as s/5.*) **Volleyball,** also played in the Estadio Nacional, comes in a distant second.

When you've tired of watching humans play, turn to the animals: **bullfighting, cockfighting** *(pelea de gallos)*, and **horse racing** are all popular spectator events. **The Plaza de Acho,** Hualgayoc 332 (*tel. 481 14 67*), in Rímac, hosts matadors during Fiesta Patrias in the last week of July, as well as during October and December. The chickens battle to the death in **La Chacra,** at the end of Tomás Marsano in Surco, and **Coliseo El Rosedal,** near the Plaza de Armas (*s/10 for national championships*). Watch horses and jockeys run in circles at the **Hipódromo de Monterrico** (*tel. 436 56 77*), on Javier Prado Oeste at the Panamericana Sur.

HANGIN' IN THE HOOD No matter how well you know Lima, walking on the streets the first day will be nerve wracking. President Fujimori's strict crackdown on street violence, though, has eradicated much criminal behavior in the last five years. Incidents of violence are very rare, but petty theft occurs frequently. Never leave bags unattended, avoid wearing conspicuous jewelry or watches (likely to be snatched off your wrist), and keep valuables protected in pouches.

Unlike those in other Latin American cities, the police (*la policia*) are a good resource in Lima. They are everywhere, and quite willing to help. If a situation appears unsafe, find a policeman and stand near him. Policia Nacional wear elaborate green uniforms. Unarmed Policia Municipal, *serenazgos*, who are specifically charged to stop street thievery, wear baggy, blue outfits. Private security guards, who are less helpful, generally wear brown outfits with matching bulletproof vests.

MOVIES

High-budget, flashy Hollywood films with Spanish subtitles are easy to find and are relatively cheap (*s/6-12*). The **Cine Pacífico** (*tel. 445 69 90*), on the Parque Kennedy, in Miraflores; **Cinemark** (*tel. 435 92 62*), in Jockey Plaza (see below); **Cine Orrantia** (*tel. 422 44 07*), on the corner of Javier Prado and Arequipa in San Isidro; **Excelsior,** Unión 762, Lima Centro; **Cine Plaza** (*tel. 428 60 42*), Plaza San Martín; and **Multicines UVK** (*tel. 446 75 88*), inside Larcomar (see below) have cleaner seats and better sound quality than most other locations. The **Cine Club de la Católica,** Camino Real 1075 (*tel. 422 33 05*), San Isidro; the **El Cinematógrafo,** Pérez Roca 196 (*tel. 477 19 61*), in Barranco; and the **Museo del Arte** (see p. 79) show artsier movies.

SHOPPING

The glitziest shopping is at the **Jockey Plaza** in Monterico and at the new **Larcomar,** cleverly constructed into the side of a cliff in Miraflores. The prices are far from bargains (and nearer to prices in the US and Europe), but the people-watching is interesting. In the center of Lima, the fifth block of **Unión** has been converted into an outdoor mall that overflows with shoes. Offering more variety, at rock-bottom prices, are the artisan markets along **La Marina** around blocks 800 to 900. The quality of the sweaters, wall hangings, and bags varies, but there are goods from all over Perú. More expensive artisan markets sell their wares in Miraflores' **Parque Kennedy** or around the 5200 to 5400 blocks of **Petit Thouars.**

THEATER

The **Teatro Principal Manuel Segura,** Huancavelica 265 (*tel. 428 74 27*), hosts most of the big name, professional operas, ballets, and plays. Call ahead for sometimes-available student discounts. Smaller plays with local actors can be found at the **Teatro Montecarlo,** Elías Aguirie 479 (*tel. 445 50 37*), Miraflores; **Teatro Real,** Belaúnde 180 (*tel. 421 46 89*), San Isidro; and the **Centro Cultural de PUC,** Camino Real 1075 (*tel. 222 68 09*), San Isidro.

NEAR LIMA

There are three main escape routes from Lima's honking horns, constant fog, and urban bustle: north to the tiny towns of Chancay, Churín, Ancón, and the Lomas de Lachay wildlife reserve; inland (and uphill) to Chosica and the Marcahuasi ruins; or south to the Pachacamac ruins and surf spots along the coast to Paracas.

NORTH OF LIMA

The Panamericana heads north to the seaside town of **Ancón** (40km). Weathered, wooden houses interspersed with box-like modern apartments testify to the town's past fame as an exclusive resort village for upperclass *limeños.* Most of today's visitors are less affluent daytrippers seeking a spot on the beach and a cheap seafood meal. The beaches are relatively clean, but check the ratings posted on large signs by the beach—avoid the *"muy malo"* (very bad) water. Because of Ancón's accessibility via *colectivo* from Plaza Dos de Mayo (45min., s/2), you will usually have to share your sand. Numerous pre-Inca ruins lie in the **Chillón Valley** near Ancón, but they have not been developed for inquisitive tourists; it's best to ask around in Ancón for a guide to visit the three pyramids of the **Templo El Paraíso.**

Farther north of Lima along the Panamericana, the **Chancay Valley** harbors more rarely visited ruins. You can take a northbound bus from the Plaza de Acho in Rímac to **Huaral,** the valley's gateway town. Once there, ask around for guides to take you to the **Añay** ruins near Huayopampa, the **Rupac** ruins near La Flonda, or the **Chiprac** ruins near Huasloy. There is very little tourist-oriented infrastructure here, so don't expect to spend the night, and try to start the trip early. The **Lomas de Lachay,** near Huacho, are a good excursion for the less adventurous. You can take an Empressa Huaral bus from Abancay 131 (2½hr., s/10) or a *colectivo* (3hr., s/9) to **Huacho;** the reserve's visitors center is 3km out of town along a well-marked access road. A resting place for migrating birds and an oasis in the middle of the northern desert, the reserve is at its best during the spring flowering (Sept.-Oct.), but trees are green between June and December. The sight has a useful interpretative center (open daily 7am-7pm). **Canta,** inland to the north of Lima, offers another breath of fresh air and an escape from Lima's smog. *Colectivos* (s/2.50) marked "Canta" leave along Lima's Tupac Amaru. The best time to catch them is early in the morning from Plaza Dos de Mayo.

LIMA

INLAND AND UPHILL FROM LIMA

It takes less than two hours to change seasons in Perú, as the journey inland replaces Lima's smog with **Chosica's** warmth. Chosica sees sun 365 days a year, making it a choice spot for the weekend getaway of *limeños*. The town offers nothing to tourists, but travelers must go toward Chosica in order to visit the nearby Puruchuco ruins and the more remote rock formations of Marcahuasi. Find *colectivos* marked "Chosica" constantly running inland along Grau from Plaza Grau in Lima Centro. The scenery provided by the bus trip from Lima is an interesting juxtaposition of the city's industrial parks and poster neighborhoods, and the scenic foothills of the Andes.

Puruchuco, a well-preserved adobe dwelling built in pre-Inca times, is a mere 5km on the way to Chosica on the Central Highway. Once home to an Inca noble, the site now hosts a very informative museum. (Open 9am-4pm. Admission s/4.) Take the Chosica *colectivo* 45-minutes from Plaza Grau, telling the driver to stop at Puruchuco (s/3). Look for the *zona arqueológica* sign on the right.

MARCAHUASI AND SAN PEDRO DE CASTA

An enigmatic collection of rock formations 90km east of Lima and 4000m up in the mountains, **Marcahuasi** makes for an excellent three-day camping excursion. These massive chunks of spookily eroded granite resemble figures such as a sphinx, a tortoise, a judge (or priest if you look just right), and even the Egyptian fertility goddess Thueris (with the head of a hippo and the belly of a pregnant woman). Who created these things? Man? God? Nature? Alien? The source is still unclear. At any rate, Marcahuasi is the site of weekend pilgrimages by Peruvians who speak of a powerful spiritual presence and can feel "magnetic forces" coursing through their fingertips. Cynics might call this "altitude sickness." Nevertheless, the dead silence of the plateau invites meditation, provided that one gets there before the weekend crowds do.

Getting to Marcahuasi is a full day's journey. Take the *colectivo* to Chosica and ask for Parque Echenique (1½hr., s/4), the town's central bus depot. From there, take a *colectivo* up to the small mountain village of **San Pedro de Casta** (3-4hr., 9am and 4pm, s/5). The Marcahuasi plateau is an uphill 3km hike from here, which could take four hours or longer for those not yet acclimatized—the altitude leaps from 3200 to 4000m. Those camping at the top should come prepared: bring a tent, a sleeping bag, food, rain gear, and a compass in the rainy season (since a dense fog rises by early afternoon).

Obtain a map (s/5) after registering at the **tourist office** in San Pedro de Casta, located in the **central plaza** along with a **clinic** and a store with the town's only **telephone**. The tourist office also rents horses and mules for the hike up (s/15). Those low on provisions can stay in the friendly and hard-working peasant community of Casta, at the lavender-colored house of **Manuel Olivares,** directly behind town hall. Sr. Olivares keeps two rooms with bunkbeds, wool blankets, and one of the town's only flushable toilets. (Rooms s/10.) The tourist office also rents rooms upstairs without beds or running water (rooms s/5). Next door, the store keeps canned staples, and a woman will cook rice, chicken, and eggs upon request.

On the plaza, ask at the school for a key to Casta's one-room collection of **mummified human remains** recovered from an ancient burial spot at Marcahuasi. They retain the fetal position in which they were buried as well as the ghastly looks they had on their faces when they died. Bring warm clothing for nighttime or risk ending up like one of the mummies.

SOUTH OF LIMA

Limeños head south for one reason: the beaches. Tourists head south for two: the **Pachacamac** ruins and the beaches. The coast south of Lima is more developed than that to the north, so it's easier to get there and easier for the rest of the world to follow. Pachacamac—roughly translated as "creator of land and time"—is the site of a Huari shrine so sacred that even the Incas didn't tamper with it when they razed the rest of the Huari settlement in 1470. Instead, they added their own theological input in the form of the Temple of the Sun, the top of which offers the best vantage point for viewing the ruins, the nearby ocean, and the house-covered hills of **Villa El Salvador.** You can get to the ruins easily by taking one of the brown and white *colectivos* marked "Lurín" and "Pachacamac" from the corner of Montevideo and Ayacucho in Lima Centro. To be dropped off at the small **museum** near the entrance, ask for *las ruinas.* (Open daily 7am-7pm. Admission s/5.)

SOUTHERN PERÚ

The route south from Lima takes in a variety of landscapes which are conveniently joined by the smoothly paved Panamerican Highway. During the first stretch along the coast, sweeping expanses of desert are spotted with city oases. A range of well-known attractions appeal to a variety of interests: wildlife enthusiasts stop at the Islas Ballestas, wine-drinkers find Ica's vineyards hard to resist, and Huancachina is popular for its immense sand dunes. Best of all, the gigantic, mysterious lines traced in the desert near Nazca continue to amaze visitors and defy explanation.The highway then ascends towards Arequipa, a fantastic colonial city perched above 2000m sea level which presents a drastic contrast to the flat, desert attractions of the coast. The city's trademark white buildings are infused with cosmopolitan charm, but Arequipa appeals to more than just city-slickers. Destinations for mountain climbing and trekking lie at a short distance, the most important being the extraordinarily deep Colca Canyon.

The Panamericana abandons the tourist at this point, but thanks to a frequently running rail line, Puno has become the next logical stop in the usual tourist circuit. The train from Arequipa climbs more than 1000m higher to the stark plateau surrounding Lake Titicaca. Puno is the main port town on the Peruvian side of the lake and sends constant motorboats out to Titicaca's many island sights, all of them distinct from the rest of Perú—even the parts on the edge of the lake. Those determined to continue their southward direction enter Bolivia by skirting the lake over land. But if Chile is the next country on your itinerary, a return trip is necessary to the Pacific coast where the border crossing awaits at Tacna.

SOUTHERN COAST

Most tourists traveling south along the Panamericana don't get off the bus until they reach Pisco, three and a half hours away. After visiting the Paracas Reserve, they make their way down to Ica and onto Nazca. However, with a little more time, one can stray from the beaten path and perhaps inspect the wineries of Lunahuaná, raft down the Río Cañete, participate in Chincha's Verano Negro festival, or wonder over the petroglyphs near Palpa. A little more money buys resort-style accommodations with special attractions: the sugar and cotton plantations at the Hacienda San José, the industrial-sized winery at Ocucaje, the Inca ruins at Puerto Inca. The trip between Nazca and Arequipa takes about nine hours and is most frequently done directly on an overnight bus. While you sleep, the Panamericana moves back out to the coast, hugging the shoreline as it passes through the intermediary towns of Chala and Camaná. From Camaná, the road again moves inland and starts to ascend toward Arequipa.

HIGHLIGHTS OF THE SOUTHERN COAST

- From Pisco, take a boat to see the boobies and sea lions at the **Islas Ballestas,** or camp at the **Paracas Reserve** (see p. 92).
- The many large and small **wineries** *(bodegas)* surrounding **Lunahuaná** (see p. 88) and **Ica** (see p. 94) make for intoxicating diversion.
- Try your skills at **sandboarding** at the sand dunes of **Huacachina** (see p. 95).
- From Nazca, take a flight over the fascinating **Nazca lines** (see p. 98), and come up with your own theory to explain them.

PUCUSANA AND PUNTA HERMOSA

In the summertime, surfers head to **Punta Hermosa,** 40km from Lima. While Puerto Chicama on the north coast is known for having the world's longest wave, Punta Hermosa boasts South America's tallest, a 12- to 15-foot wave called "Pico Alto." There are a number of restaurants, discos, and hotels open during the busy summer season, but during the rest of the year Punta Hermosa is a veritable ghost town. You'll find a few more permanent residents in the small fishing town of **Pucusana,** slightly farther south. Located in a bay, the beach of **Naplo** offers no waves for surfing but is nice for swimming. **Buses** to **Lima** leave Pucusana from Calle Lima whenever full. *Colectivos* leave from the lot next to the church and go north to Lima and south toward **Pisco.** Buses headed to Pucusana from Lima leave from the area near Ayacucho and Montevideo. There are no banks in Pucusana, although some stores will change dollars. **Emergency:** tel. 105. The **police** (tel. 430 9005) are on Calle Lima near the buses. Next door is a small **hospital** (tel. 430 9053), although for serious problems it is better to go Lima. **Farmacia YSA** (tel. 430 9063) is across the street (open daily 8am-10:30pm). There are a few **Telefónica del Perú** booths scattered near the beach and Plaza de Armas. **Telephone code:** 01.

Hostal Salon Blanco (tel. 430 9452), on the water, has spacious, well-lit rooms and a good restaurant (singles s/10, with bath s/15; doubles with bath s/25, with TV s/30). Another good place to sleep and eat is the **Hostal Restaurant Las Delicias** (tel. 430 9101), also on the water, lined with plants to keep the place cheerful. All rooms are doubles with cold-water private baths. (Rooms s/20.) The **Restaurant Turístico Bahia** (tel. 430 9023), near the impressive inlet with crashing waves, comes highly recommended for its excellent seafood (open daily 9am-10pm).

CAÑETE

Cañete is a small, pleasant town that sees few tourists. Residents are friendly, hotels are clean, and the Plaza de Armas is green and inviting. Travelers to Lunahuaná will have to stop in Cañete, as there are no direct buses; spending a night in Cañete, rather than switching buses immediately, may be a relaxing experience.

The **Plaza de Armas** is 2 de Mayo, a few blocks up from the point on the Panamericana where **buses** pause for passengers to get on or off. **Interbank,** 2 de Mayo 451, changes dollars and traveler's checks (open M-F 8:30am-6:15pm, Sa 9am-12:30pm). The **police** (tel. 581 2083) are farther up 2 de Mayo at the Plaza San Martín. Next door, the **Hospital de Apoyo** (tel. 581 2010) has 24-hour **emergency** and **pharmacy** service. **Telephone code:** 01. **Hostal La Casona** (tel. 581 3130), on the Plaza de Armas, has rooms decorated with Peruvian wall hangings or pictures of tourist sites (singles s/15; matrimonials s/20; doubles s/25). Slightly nicer rooms can be found closer to the highway at the **Hostal Casablanca,** 2 de Mayo 689 (tel. 581 2040). All rooms are doubles with private hot-water baths. (Rooms s/45.) The **Hostal Restaurant Manolo,** Santa Rosa 640-648 (tel. 581 2329), behind the police station, has more expensive rooms, but the restaurant is one of the best in town (meals s/12-20; open daily 8am-10pm). The **Restaurant Tun Tun,** on the Plaza de Armas, is also popular and is less expensive (*patita con mani* s/4; open daily 8:30am-11pm).

LUNAHUANÁ

Lunahuaná isn't so much a unified town as it is a series of small neighborhoods (or *anexos*) spread out along the road that runs above the Río Cañete. There are two main reasons to visit Lunahuaná: the wine and the whitewater—both of which are celebrated during the **Fiesta de la Vendimia y el Canotaje,** the first week in March. Both can be enjoyed the rest of the year as well.

The best food and some of the cheapest rooms can be found at the **Restaurant Hostal Campestre Mi Rosedal** (tel. 284 1177), on the main road in the *anexo* of Uchupampa. All rooms are clean and welcoming, with private hot-water baths. (Matrimonials s/35; doubles s/50.) The restaurant specializes in *camarones* and *platos típicos* (*arroz con pato* s/6.50; open daily 7am-11pm). **Las Viñas** (Lima tel. (01) 437

3187), nearby in the *anexo* of Condoray, offers beautiful *cabañas* with a tropical feel, pleasant balconies, and tastefully decorated rooms. Las Viñas also offers campsites and rafting trips known for their emphasis on safety. (Campsite s/10, with tent s/15; matrimonials s/60; doubles s/90; discounts on weekdays.) **El Guanabo,** in the Juta *anexo*, also offers camping, and their sites have views of the river (s/10, with tent s/20). The **Sol & Río Restaurant** (tel. 284 1078), in Lunahuaná proper, has good food and is yet another good place to find a whitewater rafting trip. Don't eat too much *ceviche* (s/15) before you head to the rapids. (Open daily 7am-10pm.)

RAFTING. Many hotels and restaurants (see above) offer **whitewater rafting** trips on the Río Cañete. The best season for rafting (*canotaje* in Spanish) is December through April, when the rapids reach a respectable Class IV. The rest of the year, the rapids are Class II-III—good for beginners but less exciting for more experienced paddlers. Kayaking is also possible if you can convince the agencies that you know what you're doing—there is no kayak instruction. Generally, 45 minutes are spent on the river. Most companies charge US$15, although this can vary with the seasons.

WINERIES AND RUINS. There are several small *bodegas* (wineries) in the Lunahuaná Valley that produce *pisco*, a white brandy-like alcohol, and *cachina*, a naturally fermented wine. The best time to visit the *bodegas* is from February to April, the season of the *vendimia*, when tourists can shed their shoes, roll up their pants, and help with the wine-making a la *I Love Lucy*. The best *bodegas* are **La Reyna de Lunahuaná** (tel. 449 9917), in the *anexo* of Catapalla across the river, and the closer **Viña Los Reyes** (tel. 284 1206), in the *anexo* of Condoray. You can buy the *pisco* (s/15) and wine (s/8-10) all year.

TRANSPORTATION. To get to Lunahuaná from Cañete, take a *colectivo* from the *ovalo* near Plaza San Martín to the small village of **Imperial** (10min., s/50); from there, catch another *colectivo* to Lunahuaná (1hr., s/2.50).

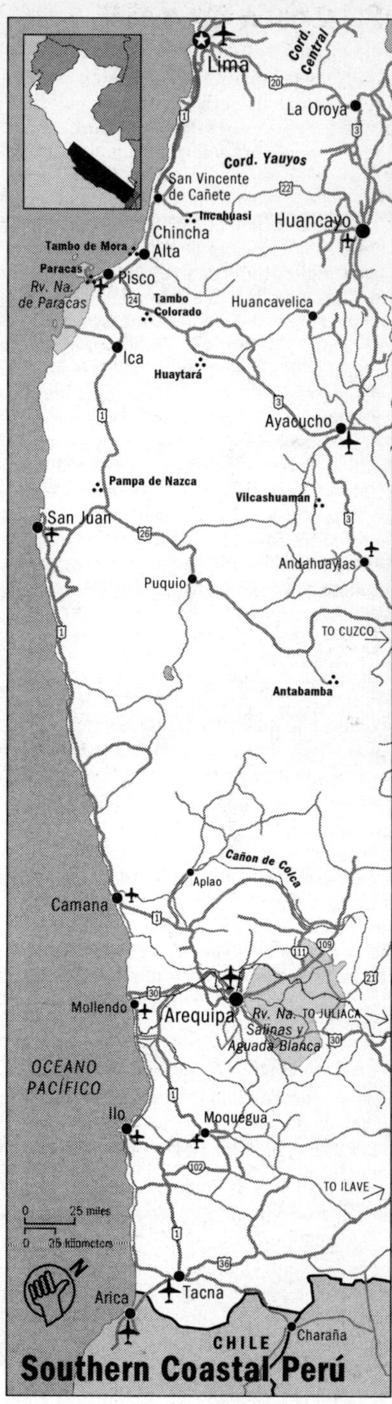

Southern Coastal Perú

CHINCHA ALTA

Chincha Alta is one of the larger cities on the southern coast, but it is not frequently visited by tourists on their way to the small towns of Pisco or Nazca. Chincha is famous in Perú for being a city that knows how to party. People come in droves for various *fiestas*, including the Verano Negro ("Black Summer;" Feb. 20-Mar. 5)—a celebration of art and culture featuring dancing, contests, *peñas*, and lots of local pride—and the similar Fiesta de Chincha (end of Oct.). Although these are the most exciting times to visit, hotel prices often double during *fiestas*.

The main street in town is the busy **Mariscal Benavides,** running between the palm tree-laden **Plaza de Armas** and the bus-laden **Plazuela Bolognesi.** The gigantic indoor and outdoor **market** covers several square blocks by the Plazuela Bolognesi. The **Ormeño** bus station, (tel. 261 301), also in the *plazuela*, sends buses to **Marcona:** (5:30, 9am, noon, and 9pm; s/10) via **Ica** (s/3), **Palpa** (s/7), and **Nazca** (s/8); **Arequipa** (11:30am, 4:30, 6:30, and 9:30pm; s/30) via **Camaná** (s/25); **Ilo** (daily 1:30pm, s/40) via **Moquegua** (s/35); **Tacna** (12:30 and 6pm, s/40); and **Lima** (every hr. 6:40am-6pm, s/5). Other bus companies and *colectivos* leave from the same area.

For **tourist information,** ask for Señor Javier Galvarez in the **Municipalidad** building on the Plaza de Armas. The **Banca de Crédito,** on Benavides and Mariscal Castilla, changes money (open M-F 9:30am-1:15pm and 4:30-6:30pm, Sa 9:30am-12:30pm). **Emergency:** Tel. 105. The 24-hour **police** (tel. 261 261) can be found by the Plaza de Armas. The **Farmacia Inmaculada** (tel. 267 070) is also on the plaza (open M-Sa 8am-11pm, Su 8am-1:30pm and 6-11pm). **Hospital San Jose** (tel. 269 006), several blocks from the center of town on Alva Maurtua, has 24-hour emergency service. The **post office** (tel. 261 141) is on the Plaza de Armas (open M-Sa 8am-8pm). There is also a store with **internet access,** at Italia 151 (tel./fax 262 670; email datanet98@hotmail.com; open M-Sa 9am-2pm and 4-9pm). **Telephone code:** 034.

There are plenty of hotels in Chincha, though most fill up quickly during the *fiestas*. **Hotel Sotelo,** Benavides 260 (tel. 261 681), has clean, pale blue rooms off a pale green hallway (doubles s/25, with bath s/35, with bath and TV s/40). The **Hostal Oriente,** Mariscal Castilla 211-223 (tel. 263 008), has boring decor, but all rooms come with TV and private hot-water bathrooms (doubles s/35). Across the street is the fancier **Hotel Embassy,** M. Castilla 218 (tel. 262 341), part of a small chain which also has hotels in Pisco and Lunahuaná (doubles s/60-75 during the *fiestas*, up to 50% discount the rest of the year). The cheapest meals are available from the food stands in and around the market, although sanitation here is not guaranteed. **Restaurante Cebichería Costa Marina,** Plaza de Armas 148 (tel. 262 700), is one of the best places in town for seafood or *criollo* cuisine (open daily 7am-11pm). Around the corner is **El Fogón,** Lima 144 (tel. 261 827), a red, rustic restaurant tastefully decorated with farming tools. The owner recommends a traditional Peruvian dish known as *lomo a lo pobre* (steak with fried eggs, plantains, potatoes, and rice s/19; open daily 10am-11pm).

NEAR CHINCHA ALTA: CASA-HACIENDA SAN JOSÉ

Ever wondered what it would have been like to have lived in the era of cotton and sugar plantations? You can get a taste of that 300-year-old lifestyle at the Casa-Hacienda San José, an estate dating back to 1688, just 30 minutes southeast of Chincha, in the district of El Carmen. At first only sugar and honey were produced; during the late 18th century, cotton was planted as well. At the height of productivity, more than 1,000 African slaves worked at the *hacienda*. Their influence is still highly visible in and around Chincha—in the music, art, dancing, and skin tone. Sugar and cotton are still harvested in the fields, but today San José is primarily known as a resort hotel. The beautiful gardens include a swimming pool, horses, tennis courts, ping-pong tables, and *sapo*, a traditional game similar to horseshoes. Every Sunday there is an elaborate *criollo* buffet and a colorful show. Although this isn't exactly "budget travel," their all-inclusive two to five day packages are a pretty good deal. It's also possible to come just for the day and take a tour of the estate, which includes a visit to the unusual catacombs. For information or to make reservations, contact the Lima office (tel. (01) 444 5242; fax 444 5524; email hsanjose@bellnet.com.pe).

Transportation: To get to the Hacienda, take a taxi from **Chincha** (30min., s/10).

PISCO

When most Peruvians hear the word "*pisco*," this small coastal town isn't the first thing that comes to mind. Sharing the name is the powerful white-grape brandy produced in the region, commonly served in the popular *pisco sour*. Still, although the town of Pisco (pop. 141,000) is not itself particularly interesting, dozens of Peruvian and foreign tourists veer off the Panamericana every day with Pisco as their destination. Are *pisco sours* so good that people should come simply to pay homage to the town that shares their name? Well, yes, but most tourists have another reason for coming to Pisco: unique and fascinating nearby sights such as the Islas Ballestas, the Paracas Reserve, and Tambo Colorado.

ORIENTATION AND PRACTICAL INFORMATION

As usual, most services cluster around the **Plaza de Armas.** On the north side of the plaza runs **San Fransisco.** On the southwest side of the plaza, a busy pedestrian boulevard leads to the smaller **Plaza Belén.**

Buses: Pisco is 10min. west of the Panamericana, so relatively few buses go directly to town. However, any bus heading to a destination beyond Pisco can drop you off at the turn-off (tell the bus driver, *"Bajo en la cruce para Pisco"*). From there, *colectivos* leave all the time for the center of town (10min., s/0.50). *Colectivos* are more convenient and you can avoid the mob of representatives from different hotels and tour agencies who often come to greet the Ormeño buses. **Ormeño** (tel. 532 762), San Fransisco and Ayacucho, is the biggest bus company in town. It serves **Lima** (3½hr., 10 per day 4:15am-8:10pm, s/8; Royal service 2 and 4:45pm, s/30); **Tacna** (18hr., 11am and 5pm, s/40); **Ica** (1hr., 9am and 12:30pm, s/2); **Nazca** (3hr., 9am and 12:30pm, s/10; Royal service 4:30pm, s/35); and **Arequipa** (12hr.; 11am, 3:30, and 6:30pm; s/30). **Colectivos** to **Chincha** leave regularly from near the Plaza Belén (1hr., s/2).

Tourist Agencies: Everywhere you look, especially on San Fransisco between the Ormeño station and the Plaza de Armas, there are agencies advertising trips to the Islas Ballestas, Paracas Reserve, and Tambo Colorado. While most agencies offer similar tours at the same price, only 3 are officially registered tour agencies: **The Zarcillo Connection,** San Francisco 111 (tel. 536 543; email zarcillo@cbd.com.pe); **Ballestas Travel Service,** San Francisco 249 (tel./fax 533 095; email jpacheco@net.telematic.com.pe); and **Paracas Tours,** San Fransisco 257 (tel./fax 533 630).

Banks: Banco Crédito, on the Plaza de Armas, will change your dollars and traveler's checks. Open M-F 9:15am-1:30pm and 4:30-6:30pm, Sa 9:15am-12:30pm.

Laundry: Lavandería Iris, Pedemonte 170 (tel. 532 285), has next-day service.

Emergency: Tel. 105.

Police: (Tel. 532 884), on the Plaza de Armas. Open 24hr.

Hospital: The **Hospital Antonio Skrabonja** (tel. 532 784), on San Fransisco's 3rd block, has 24hr. **emergency** service.

Post Office: On the Plaza de Armas. Open M-Sa 8am-8pm.

Internet Access: Computación e Informática Bill Gates, San Francisco 290 (tel. 533 616). Open daily 7am-11pm.

Telephones: Telefónica del Perú booths are around the Plaza de Armas.

TELEPHONE CODE 034

ACCOMMODATIONS

Thanks to the large number of budget travelers who pass through Pisco, there are many clean, comfortable, and low-priced options in town. Camping is possible on the beaches in the Paracas Reserve (bring your own supplies), but do not camp on the Pisco beach, as it is not a particularly safe area, especially at night.

Hostal San Isidro, San Clemente 103 (tel. 533 217), past the cemetery. The rooms, all with TVs, are clean and cheerful. Guests are welcome to use laundry and kitchen facilities, or just lounge in the courtyard and play foosball. The friendly, English-speaking family provides free coffee in the morning—necessary since the Islas Ballestas tours usually leave before 8am. Rooms s/10 per person, with bath s/15.

Hostal La Portada, Alipio Ponce 250 (tel. 532 098), is a new place with attractive rooms, a relaxed atmosphere, and private hot-water baths. Rooms s/20 per person.

Hostal Pisco, San Francisco 115 (tel. 532 018), right on the Plaza de Armas, has an excellent, central location. Rooms are simple but clean, and there's a bright courtyard, a large dining room, and a kitchen that guests can use (s/2). Singles s/10, with bath s/20; doubles with bath s/35.

Hostal Colonial, Comercio 194 (tel. 532 035), on the walkway near Plaza Belén. Basic rooms have only common baths, but the location is good, if a bit noisy. Some suites have small balconies overlooking the plaza. Rooms s/10 per person.

Hostal San Francisco, San Francisco 372 (tel. 534 035), has comfortable rooms with private baths, TVs, and fans, and is close to the Ormeño station (not that anything in Pisco is particularly far). Singles s/20; doubles s/35.

FOOD

Although the tourist industry is responsible for a plethora of good, affordable hotels in Pisco, the same cannot really be said about the restaurants. Nevertheless, there are enough decent restaurants to make sure that nobody goes away hungry.

Restaurant Turistico Ch'Reyes, Comercio 167 (tel. 534 678), on the pedestrian boulevard, serves good food at low prices. Among their varied selection is a vegetarian *menú* (s/10). Open daily 6:30am-10pm.

Don Manuel (tel. 532 035), also on the pedestrian boulevard across from Hostal Colonial, specializes in seafood and meat. This is a slightly more upscale option, and some of the waitstaff speak English and French. Open daily 10am-11pm.

As de Oro, San Martín 472 (tel. 532 010), serving local and international cuisine and a wide selection of alcoholic beverages, is even classier. It's also somewhat pricier than some of the restaurants closer to the center of town. Open Tu-Su noon-11pm.

NEAR PISCO: ISLAS BALLESTAS

The islands off the coast of the Paracas peninsula may not be the Galápagos, but only the toughest critics will be disappointed by the wildlife here. The main attraction is the abundance of sea lions and birds, including Peruvian boobies, three types of cormorants, Inca terns (*zarcillos*), pelicans, turkey vultures, Humboldt penguins, and a number of other migratory species. With all these birds around, there is also an abundance of you-know-what covering the islands, which locals exploit as a natural resource—every few years, the *guano* is collected and exported as fertilizer.

TOURING THE ISLANDS. Other than these guano-collectors, nobody is allowed on the islands, so all viewing of the marine animals is done from tour boats, the only boats allowed to go to the islands. Tours to the Islas Ballestas usually last two to three hours, cost US$10, and leave early (7:30am) since morning is the best time to see the wildlife. Sign up with an agency the night before to reserve a spot. Small motorboats leave from the port of El Chaco with a driver, an English-speaking guide, and about 12 tourists. Wear layers, since the temperature varies greatly. Also wear a hat to protect yourself from both the sun and the fertilizer.

EL CANDELABRO. Before heading to the islands, tour boats first stop in front of *el candelabro*, a mysterious figure etched in the sand on the northeast side of the Paracas Bay. The three-pronged geoglyph is 177m high, 54m wide, and up to 60cm deep. Nobody knows who made the figure or what its significance was. Some believe that it dates back to the Paracas culture (around 700 BC) and represents a hallucinogenic variety of cactus which was used in religious ceremonies. Others believe that it is related to the Nazca lines, which were probably constructed around 500 BC. Another theory is that it wasn't created by any ancient culture, but rather by the pirates who raided the area in the 17th century: it either marked the location of buried treasure or was used as an orientating landmark. Supporting this theory is the fact that earlier explorers in the region never mentioned the figure in any of their reports; the earliest record of the geoglyph dates from 1863.

NEAR PISCO: RESERVA NACIONAL DE PARACAS

In 1975, the National Reserve of Paracas was established to protect the ecological and archaeological splendor of the Paracas peninsula and the Islas Ballestas. The peninsula has a very long history; the first inhabitants arrived in the region about 9,000 years ago. The remains of some of these earliest inhabitants can be seen at the **Julio C. Tello Museum** in the reserve (admission s/2, students with ID s/1; open daily 9am-5pm). The museum is named for the man who is often referred to as the "father of Peruvian archaeology." Tello (1880-1947) led excavations at the sites of **Cerro Colorado** and **Cabezas Largas** in Paracas from 1924 to 1930, uncovering much of what we now know about the Paracas culture. The site of Cabezas Largas gets its name from the unusual custom of skull deformation practiced by the Paracas culture (see below). Both elongated and trepanned skulls can be seen in the museum.

TOURING THE RESERVE. It is possible to walk 5km from El Chaco to the museum—stick close to the water, and you'll probably get to see some flamingoes in the bay. Alternatively, you can take a taxi. However, most people visit the museum as part of an organized tour to the Paracas Reserve, often combined with the Islas Ballestas tour to make a full-day adventure. Tours generally also include a visit to **La Catedral,** a naturally eroded rock structure where you can see many birds and an occasional sea otter; allow time to explore some of Perú's prettiest beaches (because of the strong undertow, however, swimming is not recommended); and conclude with an hour or so in **Lagunillas,** a small port with good seafood restaurants. You can visit La Catedral, Lagunillas, and the beach without a tour, and it is possible to camp on the beach (it's safer than other beaches since it's in the reserve, but never camp alone; bring all supplies with you and don't leave anything behind). There's no public transportation, so hire a taxi and arrange for a pickup the next day, or arrange for a tour agency to leave you at the beach and let you return with them the next day. (Admission s/5; tours s/5-15 extra, usually 5hr.)

PARACAS BEAUTY AND HEALING The archaeological investigations in the Reserva Nacional de Paracas have revealed that the Paracas culture had some ideas about physical beauty and health that might today strike one as rather unusual. For example, skulls unearthed in the region suggest that infants of upper-class birth would have a special combination of boards and pads tied around their foreheads so that as they grew their skulls became elongated. A long sloped cranium was probably a sign of ethnic identity, beauty, and prestige. In addition to cranial elongation, the Paracas people also practiced an early form of brain surgery known as trepanation. The procedure involved removal of a piece of skull to relieve pressure on the brain following a severe head trauma. However, the large number of trepanned skulls discovered in Paracas suggests that this practice was used not just to cure head-trauma patients, but also to treat psychological or behavioral problems, perhaps by providing an escape route for evil spirits that might be residing in the brain. Astonishingly, a large majority of the patients survived the procedures, as evidenced by the signs of healing around the holes.

NEAR PISCO: TAMBO COLORADO

Although not as frequently visited as the Islas Ballestas or Paracas Reserve, Tambo Colorado is also easily accessible from Pisco, either with an organized tour or on your own. About 45km from Pisco, this is the site of some of the best preserved Inca ruins anywhere on the coast. It's not as splendid as Machu Picchu but is worth a visit if you have time. Tours from Pisco only leave with a minimum of three tourists (US$5).

ICA

A major transportation hub, Ica (pop. 245,000) is the capital of the eponymous department. The city is well-known for its wine and *pisco bodegas*—about 85 small *bodegas artesanales* and three large *bodegas industriales*. In the former, wine is still made by stomping on grapes, while in the industrial *bodegas* have replaced traditional methods with impressive looking machines. Wine harvesting is done once a year, around the beginning of March, and is celebrated throughout the city during the *Fiesta Internacional de la Vendimia*. Ica is a more dangerous city than many of the surrounding areas. Exercise considerable caution with all of your belongings, especially around bus terminals. It is not uncommon for hats and glasses to be snatched right off the heads of unsuspecting tourists.

ORIENTATION AND PRACTICAL INFORMATION

Ica is a fairly large city, but, like most cities, much of the activity centers near the **Plaza de Armas. Av. Municipalidad** runs between the north side of the plaza and many of the bus terminals. Bordering the plaza on the west side is **Bolívar,** which becomes **Tacna** when it crosses Municipalidad.

Airplanes: There is a small, private **airport** run by AeroCóndor, from which you can take expensive flights over the Nazca lines if you don't have enough time to go to Nazca. Inquire in the Hotel Las Dunas near the airport.

Buses: Transportes Soyuz, Matías Manzanilla 130 (tel. 224 138), sends buses to **Lima** (4hr., every 15min., s/13). **Cuz del Sur** (tel. 223 333), on Lambayeque and Municipalidad, goes to: **Arequipa** (11hr.; 5:30, 9, and 10pm; s/30); and **Tacna** (16hr., 3:30pm, s/40; imperial service 6pm, s/70). **Ormeño** (tel. 215 600), Lambayeque and Salaverry, serves: **Nazca** (3hr., 6 per day, s/5); **Lima** (4hr., every hr. 6:30am-7:45pm, s/10); and a dozen other locations. **Colectivos** also leave for **Pisco** or **Nazca** from the Lambayeque/Manzanilla area whenever full.

Tourist Information: The **tourist office,** Cabrera 426 (tel. 235 409), 15min. walk from the Plaza de Armas. Open M-F 7:45am-4pm.

Banks: Banco Latino, Cajamarca 170, will change dollars and traveler's checks. Open M-F 9:15am-1:30pm and 4:10-6:15pm, Sa 8:15am-1:30pm. Also has a 24hr. Cirrus/MC **ATM.** Open M-F 8:45am-1:30pm and 4-7pm, Sa 9am-1pm.

Emergency: Tel. 105.

Pharmacies: Farmacia Ayacucho, Grau 112, is well stocked. Open daily 8am-11pm.

Hospital: Hospital Felix Torrealva Gutierrez, Bolívar 1065 (tel. 234 450), has 24hr. **emergency** service.

Post Office: Serpost, Libertad 119-A (tel. 233 881), on the Plaza de Armas. Open M-Sa 8am-8pm.

Internet Access: ELW Services, Lima 276 (tel. 213 370), provides *cabinas de internet* (s/5 per hr.). Open daily 9am-midnight.

TELEPHONE CODE 034

ACCOMMODATIONS

Hotel La Viña, San Martín 256 (tel. 218 188), is close to the Plaza de Armas and clean. All rooms have private baths with electric hot water. Singles s/25; doubles s/35.

Hostal Oasis, Tacna 216 (tel. 234 767). This is no mirage; Oasis's open, airy, and clean rooms are quite real. To bask in the warm glow of television just ask; TVs provided upon request. Singles s/25; doubles s/35.

Hostal Lilias, Tacna 228 (tel. 233 910), next door to Oasis, has crimson-and-white rooms and a slightly odd smell. Singles s/15, with bath s/25; doubles s/20, with bath s/40.

Hotel Castilla, Ayacucho 317 (tel. 233 712), has a secure front gate and an attractive plant-lined main passage, but rooms are quite basic, with cold water only. Singles s/10, with bath s/15; doubles s/20, with bath s/25.

FOOD

Zambos Sandwichs, Libertad 173 (tel. 228 074), on the Plaza de Armas, decorated with posters of the Doors and Madonna. People come here for the mustard-yellow and ketchup-red tables but stay for the food. Combo meals s/7. Open daily 8am-midnight.

Velazco, Libertad 137 (tel. 218 182), also on the plaza, a few doors down from Zambos. Both a bakery and a restaurant, Velazco offers a decent selection of local and international food at affordable prices (*palta rellena* s/5). Open daily 8am-11pm.

Nueva Castilla Restaurant Bar, Libertad 252 (tel. 213 140), with *mucho* modern art decor, is a more upscale establishment. Dine inside or out for s/15. Open M-Sa 10am-4pm and 7:30pm-midnight, Su 9am-1pm.

El Otro Peñoncito, Bolívar 255 (tel. 233 921), has an enormous selection of food (including vegetarian options) and alcohol, served by candlelight in a classy dining room—sometimes to live music. Open daily 7am-midnight.

SIGHTS

The **Museo Regional María Reiche de Ica** (tel. 234 383), a short taxi ride (s/2) from the Plaza de Armas, has a small but interesting collection of artifacts from the region, including a "bioanthropology hall" with mummies and deformed and trepanned skulls. Many exhibits have English explanations. Behind the museum is a 1:500 scale model of the Nazca lines. (Open M-F 8am-7pm, Sa 8:30am-6:30pm, Su 9am-6pm. Admission s/5; camera permit additional s/4.)

NEAR ICA: HUACACHINA

Surf's up! But hey, where's the water? At Huacachina, the sport of choice is **sandboarding,** an exhilarating experience that will leave you covered in sand and gasping for breath. Rent sandboards and get a little bit of instruction (s/3 per hr.). Then climb up the enormous dunes (this place could really use a ski lift), stick your feet in the loops, and take off down the steep slopes. There's also a small lagoon that locals sometimes swim in, though it is not particularly inviting. You can rent pedal boats (s/6 for 30min.) or row boats (s/5 for 40min.). Hotel options are limited in Huacahina; the very fancy **Massone Hotel** is outside most backpackers' budgets, but you can use their swimming pool for s/15 (and they'll throw in a complimentary sandwich and drink). The **Hotel Salvatierra** (tel. 232 352) has basic rooms by the lagoon (s/10 per person). The **Restaurant Turístico La Sirena** (tel. 213 239) serves tourists generous, filling meals for s/5-15 (open daily 8am-10pm). On the way into "town" is the **Restaurant Curas** (tel. 236 134), which serves *platos típicos* such as *pallares con arroz* (lima beans and rice s/3; open daily 8:30am-8pm).

Transportation: Travel the 8km from Ica by **taxi** (10min., s/3).

NEAR ICA: OCUCAJE

Meaning "between hills" in Aymara, Ocucaje could also be described as being "in the middle of nowhere." About 30 minutes (taxis s/2.50) from Ica, the small desert town is best known for its **winery,** the most traditional of Ica's three industrial-sized *bodegas.* In addition to the standard *cachina* and *pisco,* the Ocucaje winery also produces a variety of white and red wines, dry and sweet. Some of their wines have been aging since 1940. A tour of the winery (with wine sampling) costs s/10 per person. (Open M-F 7am-noon and 1-4pm, Sa 7am-12:45pm.) Ocucaje also boasts a beautiful **resort hotel** (tel. 408 001; fax 408 003; email rubitours@ocucaje.com; www.ocucaje.com), next door to the winery, featuring a large, inviting swimming pool, horseback riding, a tennis court, ping-pong, foosball, and pool tables. All-inclusive package deals, including a tour of the winery (with sampling), are worth it if you can afford to splurge (2 nights with food US$130 per person).

PALPA

When traveling the Panamericana, almost nobody stops in Palpa. But Palpa officials are hoping this will change as more of a tourism infrastructure develops in the town. Indeed, it is not without attractions—the town publishes a map marking 28 sites that might be of interest to travelers.

There's a legend that the ancient inhabitants of Palpa once captured the sun and would only release it on two conditions: that it would never fail to shine on Palpa, and that the town's oranges would be the best in the country. It seems that the sun kept its promise on both counts; Palpa is now known as "*la tierra del sol y las naranjas*" (the land of sun and oranges). Food and accommodation options are somewhat limited in Palpa. The **Hostal San Francisco,** Lima 181 (tel. 404 043), one block north of the Plaza de Armas, offers simple rooms and cold-water baths (singles s/8; doubles s/14, with bath s/20). On the next block is the comparable **Hostal Villa Sol** (tel. 404 149), with only common baths (singles s/8; doubles s/10). The best place to eat is **El Monterrey** (tel. 404 126), on the Panamericana next to the Mobil station (vegetable omelette s/5; open daily 6am-10pm). Among the sights most worthy of a visit are the **Petroglifos de Chichictara,** figures carved into rocks scattered across the mountainside. Go with a knowledgeable guide who can explain the significance of the different designs and symbols (ask in the Municipalidad building). Also quite impressive are the **Líneas de Palpa,** which, like their better known counterparts in Nazca, were also studied by Maria Reiche and other scientists. The **Reloj del Sol,** a large, double-lined spiral, possibly used as a sun dial, is visible from a *mirador*. Outside Palpa, you can also visit the lost city of Huayuri, ruins from the Nazca period with influences from the Paracas culture. Nearby is a famous *huarango* tree that is over 1,000 years old.

NAZCA

Offering little of touristic interest besides its proximity to the world-famous Nazca Lines, this town of the same name nevertheless offers a wide variety of services, a testament to the popularity of its main attraction. At seven hours from Lima by bus, Nazca is the place to arrange a flight to the large-scale sand drawings and, along the way, design your own interpretation of who drew them.

ORIENTATION AND PRACTICAL INFORMATION

The small town has a simple layout: most hotels and restaurants are either on **Lima** or **Bolognesi,** which splits off from Lima and heads to the **Plaza de Armas.**

Airplanes: The small **airport** in Nazca is primarily used only for flights over the Nazca lines, but it may be possible to get expensive flights between Lima and Nazca on **Aero-Condor** (Lima tel. (01) 442 5215).

Bus: Ormeño (tel. 522 058) serves: **Lima** (7hr.; 9am, 10:45, and 11:30pm; s/27); **Arequipa** (9hr., 6 per day 1am-10pm, s/60); **Ica** (3hr., 6 per day 7:15am-6:45pm, s/5); **Pisco** (3½hr., 4:15 and 6:45pm, s/10); and **Puquio** (4hr., 4pm and 1am, s/10). Buy a ticket fast, especially for night buses to Arequipa, since they often sell out. **Colectivos** to **Ica, Chala,** and other locations leave from near the Ormeño station.

Tourist Information: Unfortunately, there is no official tourist office in Nazca, so you'll have to rely on one of the private tour agencies.

Tour Agencies: If you arrive in Nazca on a standard Ormeño bus from Lima, Pisco, or Arequipa, be prepared to be met upon your arrival by a dozen representatives of different hotels and tour agencies. While it is often perfectly fine to trust these people, there are always exceptions—people who lie about which agencies they represent, about prices, and about availability of tours. The best thing to do is to go to the offices themselves and, if possible, speak to the owner. **Alegría Tours,** Lima 168 (tel./fax 523 775; email info@nazcaperu.com; www.nazcaperu.com), run by the same owner of the Hotel Alegría next door, offers excellent tours with English-speaking guides. Try to make the arrangements directly through the friendly owner, Efraín Alegría, who speaks several languages including English, Hebrew, French, and German. They also show a Time/Life video about the lines every morning and night. **Nanasca Tours,** Lima 16 (tel./fax 522 917; email nanascatours@yahoo.com), is a fairly new agency run by the owners of the Cañada restaurant. People who sign up for tours here receive a complimentary *pisco sour.* **Nasca Trails Travel Agency,** Bolognesi 550 (tel. 522 858; email nasca@correo.dnet.com.pe), on the Plaza de Armas, is a helpful, independent agency.

Currency Exchange: The **Banco de Crédito,** at Grau and Lima, changes dollars and traveler's checks. Open M-F 9:30am-1pm and 4:30-6:30pm, Sa 9:30am-12:30pm. **Interbank,** on the Plaza de Armas, does the same. Open M-F 9am-1:15pm and 4-6:30pm, Sa 9am-12:30pm. There are also plenty of **money changers** wandering the streets.

Police: (Tel. 522 442), across from the Ormeño station on Lima.

Hospital: Hospital Apoyo de Nasca (tel. 522 586), Callao and Moresky, has 24hr. emergency service and a 24hr. **pharmacy.**

Post Office: Fermín del Castillo 279. Open M-Sa 9am-8pm.

Internet Access: The **Hotel Alegría** and **La Cañada Restaurant** (see below) both offer internet access (s/5 per hour).

Telephones: Local and international calls can be made from the **Telefónica del Perú booths** around town.

TELEPHONE CODE: 034

ACCOMMODATIONS

Many tourists arrive in Nazca early, take a flight over the Nazca lines, tour the cemetery, and leave town that evening. For those staying overnight, options range from basic (s/10 per person) hostels to the fancy Nazca Lines Hotel (tel. 522 293), which is definitely not a budget accommodation (but, for s/15, anyone can use the swimming pool and get a complimentary sandwich and soft drink).

Hotel Alegría, Lima 168 (tel./fax 522 444; email info@nazcaperu.com), is the most popular option among budget travelers—so popular that they recently opened a second hotel, Alegría II, across from the Ormeño station. If you take a tour with Alegría Tours, you can use the hotel's services—including a luggage storage room, hot shower, internet access, and book exchange—even if you don't spend the night in Nazca. The pleasant courtyard is a great place to hang out while you wait for a bus. Quarters are clean and comfortable. Rooms s/10 per person, with bath s/35.

Hostal Internacional, Av. María Reiche 112 (tel. 522 744), has attractive, peaceful bungalows with porches overlooking a not-as-attractive parking lot. There are also interior rooms that are not as nice but, also, not as expensive. All rooms have private bathrooms and TVs. In addition, the hotel boasts laundry service, a book exchange, and a *cafetería/pollería.* Single bungalow s/45; double bungalows/60; single interior room s/25; double interior room s/35.

Hostal Nasca, Lima 424 (tel./fax 522 085), has basic rooms and common bathrooms; the owners are congenial and the atmosphere a bit less hectic than at Alegría up the road. Singles s/12; doubles s/20.

Hotel El Mirador, Tacna 436 (tel. 523 121), on the Plaza de Armas, has a luxury-class feel and a rooftop restaurant with a view. All rooms come with TV, fan, and private hot-water bath. *Desayuno* included with price of a room. Singles s/40; doubles s/60.

FOOD

Plenty of Nasca's restaurants cater to tourists, which means a good selection, good food, and good atmosphere, but also relatively high prices. In addition to the nicer touristy restaurants, places that offer a set *menú* (s/5) are common.

La Cañada Restaurant, Lima 160 (tel. 522 917), has a romantic, thatched-roof decor and live traditional Peruvian music at night. Entrees aren't cheap (s/15-25), but they come with a complimentary *pisco sour.* Open daily 10am-11pm.

La Taberna (tel. 521 411), on Lima between Moresky and Fermín de Castillo, has a good selection of pastas, meat, and fish in a small dining room with walls completely covered in multilingual graffiti. Bring a marker and add your own message, signature, design, or sketch of the Nazca lines. Open daily 8am-4pm and 6-11pm.

El Puquio, Bolognesi 481 (tel. 522 137), is a popular pizzeria decorated with Roman busts that somehow avoid looking *too* tacky. Pizzas are creative and tasty—try a "*haway-ana*" (medium s/17.50). Open daily 5pm-midnight.

Restaurant Farita, next door to the Hotel Mirador on the Plaza de Armas, is a good place to go for a cheap and quick *desayuno* or *almuerzo* (tamales s/2.50) and is popular with locals. Open daily 7am-3pm.

SIGHTS

CEMETERY OF CHAUCHILLA. Although the lines are the most famous of Nazca's tourist attractions (see **Near Nazca,** below), there are many other sites worth visiting if you have the time. A trip to the Cemetery of Chauchilla is often combined with a flight over the lines to make a full-day trip. At the cemetery you'll find bones and skulls bleached so white by the sun that they almost look fake. But they're all real, as is the still-attached hair and the skin and textiles found on some. The bones' placement in the deep tombs is not quite as authentic; *huaqueros* (grave robbers) stole them from these tombs and left the bodies scattered about the desert; only a few years ago did archaeologists place them back in the graves as they might have originally been found. *(Admission s/5. Tours from Nazca US$5.)*

MUSEO DIDÁCTICO ANTONINI. Even if you don't have time for any of these excursions, you can get a good taste of the archaeological and anthropological wonders of the region at the Museo Didáctico Antonini. The museum, which just opened in July 1999, has excellent displays of ceramics, textiles, and other artifacts, as well as an authentic Nazca aqueduct in the back. *(A 10min. walk down Bolognesi from the Plaza de Armas. Tel. 523 100. Open M-Sa 9am-7pm. Admission s/10.)*

OTHER SIGHTS. Organized tours from Nazca often include a visit to a **pottery workshop** and a **goldsmith's workshop,** which some tourists find quite interesting and others find quite commercial. Also worth visiting in the Nazca area are the **aqueducts** at Cantalloc. An amazing example of the advanced hydraulic knowledge of the Nazca civilization, the aqueducts are still in use today. Two more interesting attractions are **Cahuachi,** a ceremonial center with burial grounds, and, farther away, the **Pampas Galeras Reserve,** one of the best places in Perú to see *vicuña.*

NEAR NAZCA: THE NAZCA LINES

These curious figures, drawn into the desert over 1,000 years ago, have become Perú's biggest tourist attraction after Machu Picchu. Attributed to the Paracas and Nazca cultures, the lines are best described as **geoglyphs,** hundreds of drawings such as birds, hands, monkeys, sharks, spiders, flowers, elongated trapezoids, and much more, etched into the desert by clearing away the rocky soil from the surface to reveal the white-colored dirt underneath. As one of the driest places on earth—only a few minutes of rain fall each year—and protected by a unique thermal air cushion, the desert surface has stayed nearly unchanged. Some conjecture that even a footprint in this desert would survive 1,000 years. Most amazingly, the designs extend hundreds of feet in length, indiscernible except when viewed from planes flying overhead. (The outside world only learned of their existence in the 30s.) By the time the lines gained international attention, one of the ancient lizards had already been cut in half by the Panamericana.

ARCHAEOLOGY. Many theories have been advanced about the purpose of the lines. The most esteemed authority on Nazca is **Maria Reiche** (see **graybox,** p. 99), who lived at the site for over 50 years, and believed that the lines were intended to map the movements of celestial bodies as a way of directing the cultivation of land. Reiche demonstrated that many lines pointed in the direction of the sun and moon as they would have risen and set 1,000 years ago. Other designs seemed to depict constellations. She believed that the Nazca culture used long ropes and sophisticated mathematics to create their extraordinarily straight figures and magnify their designs to a gargantuan scale. However, several scholars have shown that these kinds of coincidences don't occur frequently enough to be statistically significant. The British documentary-maker Tony Morrison has championed the theory that Nazca was a predecessor to the extensive Inca zodiac system, or **ceque.** The Incas conceived a great conceptual wheel centered on the Qorikancha in Cusco (see p. 134), with sight lines radiating out towards the horizon. Each line ran through some sacred spot, or **huaca.** Similarly, the Nazca lines may have delineated shrines of great importance.

ALIENS. Several observers feel uneasy with the notion that an ancient people with no aeronautical technology would spend so much time and energy constructing something they would never be able to see themselves. In 1969, Erich von Daniken thought he would solve this problem by asserting that the lines were actually constructed by extraterrestrial life forms to mark a landing site for their aircraft. Since then, Nazca has been regarded by many as an other-worldly energy center, attracting mystics who sometimes try to **camp** directly on the lines in order to absorb some of their power. This is prohibited, not to mention foolish and downright irresponsible. Driving or walking over the lines will help erase them for good. Some critics of the alien school are offended by the assumption that an indigenous people could not have the smarts to build the beautiful formations themselves.

LADY OF THE LINES When German mathematician **Maria Reiche** went to Perú in the 1940s to work as the tutor of a diplomat's son, she hardly expected to make South America a permanent home. But when a colleague introduced her to the enigmatic **Nazca lines**—hundreds of enormous designs of animals, symbols, and abstract figures etched into the nearby desert—Reiche began to see a mystery so great, it would consume all of her energies until the day she died. Reiche spent years in the desert alone, eating little besides fruit and sleeping under the stars, during which she measured the lines and cleaned the debris obscuring them. She became the major advocate of the **astronomical calendar theory:** the lines—marking celestial paths or copying the designs of constellations—were used by farmers when planting their crops.

Besides wrestling with ancient puzzles, Reiche also tackled the threat posed by a number of unsympathetic interests. This mathematician-turned-archaeologist became Nazca's fiercest guardian, thwarting plans to irrigate the desert for agriculture, construct highways through the plain, or dubiously "reconstruct" the lines. Revenues from Reiche's published works supported research projects and hiring a team of guards to patrol the grounds and keep vandals out.

In June 1998, at the age of 95, Maria Reiche died of ovarian cancer, leaving many to wonder who could possibly step in to continue her work. Since then, the occasional disturbance of the lines by careless tourists and treasure hunters has heightened fears. Fortunately, the extraordinary nature of the woman and her mission did not go unrecognized among most locals. Reiche is regarded as a national hero—some have even suggested that the Nazca site be renamed the Reiche Lines.

Others argue that the lines were not meant for mortal eyes; they were drawn at their huge size as a direct message for deities who, according to much pre-Columbian mythology, usually peered down from above.

TRANSPORTATION. Flights leave regularly throughout the day on very tiny planes (3-5 people) and can be arranged either through a group in town or directly at the airport, for about the same price. It's best to go in the morning. (Flights 35min. US$40. Departure tax s/5.) For those who want a different perspective, two of the figures can be seen from a *mirador* on the Panamericana. (Take any northbound bus out of Nazca, 15min., s/2; taxi s/10.)

CHALA AND PUERTO INCA

About three hours from Nazca is Chala, basically a one-road town (the road being the Panamericana) with a large, clean beach. Just north of the town is Puerto Inca, home to some relatively unknown but well-preserved Inca ruins. As the name implies, this was Inca seaport; there was a road (still visible in places) connecting it to Cusco (240km away), with runner stations every few kilometers so that messages and supplies, including fresh fish, could be speedily sent between coast and highlands. To catch a **bus** out of Chala, wait in front of the Hotel de Turistas or by the gas station *(grifo)* farther north. Today the small village is gone, and in its place is the resort-like **Hotel Puerto Inka** (tel. 271 663), with comfortable rooms and plenty of amenities, including water sports, and prices not *too* far out of budget travelers' range (US$25.50 per night, including food). In Chala, there are several less expensive places to stay, including the basic **Hostal Grau** (tel. 501 009) and **Hostal Evertyh** (tel. 501 095), both with ocean views and cold-water bath (s/10-15 per person). **Food** options are limited in Chala; the Hostal Grau has a restaurant, as does the pricier **Hotel de Turistas** (tel. 501 111).

CAMANÁ

Another three hours on the Panamericana will bring you to Camaná, a much bigger town with nice beaches nearby at **La Punta**—to which hordes of Arequipan youths flock during the summer months of December-March. The main streets in Camaná are **Lima** and **Mariscal Castilla,** neither of which borders the fairly quiet **Plaza de Armas. Buses** heading north or south stop at the **Ormeño office,** Lima 346 (tel. 571 376), or farther up the street at **Cruz del Sur. Tourist information** is available through the Relaciones Públicas department of the Municipalidad building on the Plaza de Armas. The **Banco de Crédito,** also on the plaza, changes dollars and traveler's checks (open M-F 9:15am-1:45pm and 4:30-6:30pm, Sa 9:30am-12:30pm). **Emergency** tel: 105. Other services include: the **police,** Castilla 600 (tel. 572 988); the **Bótica Belén,** Lima 101 (tel. 571 723), a well stocked **pharmacy** (open daily 8am-10pm); and the **post office,** Castilla 223. **Telephone code:** 054. During the summer, there are plenty of fun places to stay and eat by the beach at La Punta. The rest of the year, however, the beach area is deserted, and it's better to stay in Camaná. The **Hostal Plaza,** 28 de Julio 317 (tel. 571 051), on the Plaza de Armas, has nice comfortable rooms with TV and private hot-water bath, as well as a rooftop restaurant where a complimentary breakfast is served each morning (rooms s/20 per person). The **Hotel de Turistas,** Lima 138 (tel. 571 113), has a blue-and-white façade that displays an air of grandeur that the rooms themselves can't quite match (doubles s/70, including continental breakfast). The **Hotel Lima,** Lima 306 (tel. 572 901), is cheaper and closer to the Ormeño office. Rooms are simple but clean, and the showers are electrically heated. (Singles s/11, with bath s/15; doubles s/17, with bath s/23.) One of the best places to eat in Camaná is **Pollos Willy,** Lima 137 (tel. 571 028), serving delicious chicken, *parilladas*, and *anticuchos* (s/6; open daily 4pm-midnight). For a taste of the northern coast, head to the **Rinconcito Trujillano,** Pizarro 304 (tel. 571 252; open daily 9am-8pm).

AREQUIPA TO CHILE

The Panamerican Highway at first swerves inland towards Arequipa, but then seems to change its mind in favor of continuing its bee-line south. However, many tourists will depart from the highway in order to visit the polished, historic city of Arequipa—with nearby natural attractions that only add to its urban ones. After Arequipa, many will return to the road and continue south to the city of Tacna, unremarkable except for its gateway to Chile.

AREQUIPA

"Going to Arequipa?" someone from Cusco might ask, "Better bring your passport." It has been said that *arequipeños* consider themselves a nation distinct, classier, and more cosmopolitan than the rest of Perú. This reputation has historical roots: the city was built by colonial wealth and has remained a conservative stronghold ever since. People here prize formality, and may frown upon flamboyant or inappropriate behavior from visitors. For the most part though, this attitude lends the city a somewhat provincial air, which many tourists find quite charming. Arequipa is known for its glistening white buildings made from *sillar*, a white volcanic rock. That may explain the city's nickname, *"La Ciudad Blanca,"* but outsiders quip that it has more to do with Arequipa's European ancestry. Five-hundred years ago, the Incas came to Arequipa, a place where the living earth seemed all the more sacred for its nearby volcanoes. The city is framed by three fire-spewers: El Misti, still active at 5822m, the higher and extinct Chachani, and Pichu Pichu. The Incas were right to respect these peaks, as the runoff from their icecaps forms the headwaters of the mighty Amazon, thousands of kilometers away.

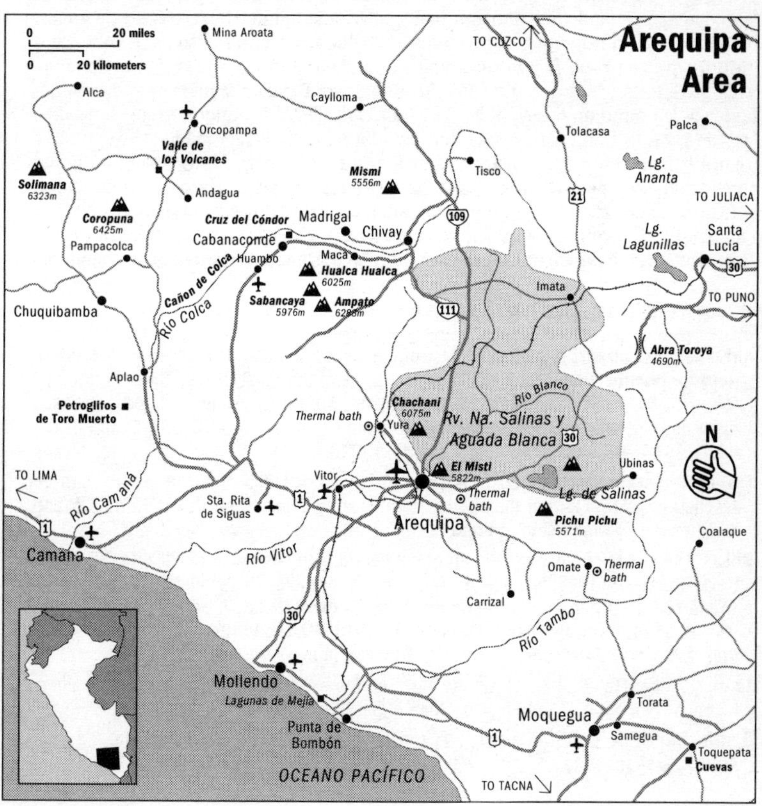

SOUTHERN PERÚ

AREQUIPA HIGHLIGHTS

■ Relax with a glass of fresh pineapple juice in a restaurant balcony overlooking Arequipa's beautiful **Plaza de Armas** (see p. 106).

■ Wander through the serene, colonial streets of the self-contained city of the **Monasterio de Santa Catalina** (see p. 107).

■ **The Colca Canyon** (see p. 108) offers an incredibly chance to see the majestic **Andean Condor** soaring freely above one of the deepest ravines in the world.

■ Challenge yourself to a climb up the virtually conical **Volcán El Misti** (see **p. 109**).

Other than from January to March (the rainy season), days in Arequipa tend to be sunny and warm. At 2380m, the quiet and prosperous city is well above the coastal fog of Lima. Peruvians, attracted by its warm climate, job opportunities, and calm, relatively safe atmosphere are immigrating to Arequipa en masse. The population has recently exploded, growing from 300,000 to over one million in the last 30 years, making it Perú's second largest city. Founded in 1540, the city itself does not feel nearly so large in its attractive, colonial center, which boasts several beautiful churches and the enormous, 16th-century Santa Catalina monastery. Arequipa serves as a convenient location from which to visit the nearby Colca and Cotahuasi canyons, two of the deepest in the world. The adventurous attempt trekking and rafting trips, while most are content to just view the canyon's depth and its wildlife from *miradores*.

ORIENTATION

Arequipa is conveniently laid out, with most services of interest to the tourist located near the handsome and compact **centro,** just uphill from the **Plaza de Armas.** The *centro* has three major thoroughfares, which run parallel to each other and uphill from the plaza. If you're facing the **cathedral** in the plaza, **Santa Catalina** forms the left-hand border and runs past the **Santa Catalina Monastery** and beyond. The plaza is bound on the right by **San Francisco.** The third major street, **Jerusalén,** is to the right of San Francisco. There is a large, daily **indoor market** three blocks downhill from the plaza, on the other side of Jerusalén. Many streets change names when they pass the plaza, but the city's regular grid pattern prevents much confusion. There are two separate **bus terminals** located next to one another 3km to the south of the city center. The **terminal terrestre** hosts the majority of bus companies, but long-distance or luxury coaches leave from the neighboring **terrapuerto.**

PRACTICAL INFORMATION

Airplanes: The **airport** is 9km northwest of the *centro* and can be reached by taxi (s/9). **AeroContinente,** Portal 113 (tel. 204 020), offers the most flights; **Tans,** Portal 119 (tel. 203 517); and **Lan Perú,** Portal 109 (tel. 102 200). All are located near each other on the Plaza de Armas. Flights go to **Lima** (9 per day, US$39-59), **Cusco** (2 per day, US$44-70), and **Tacna** (1 per day, US$39-59).

Trains: The **train station** (tel. 215 350), 6 blocks downhill from the *centro,* can be reached by taxi (s/2 from the *centro*). Comfortable trains go to: **Cusco** (20hr., W and Su 9pm, s/50) with a stop in **Puno** (11hr, s/30).

Buses: The bus terminals, 3km south of the *centro,* can be reached by taxi (s/3). Buses travel to: **Lima** (14-17hr., 15 per day 7am-9pm, s/25-85 depending on services); **Tacna** (6hr., 10 per day 7am-9:45pm, s/12); **Cusco** (12hr., 8 per day 7am-8pm, s/25); **Puno** (12hr., 6 per day 7:15am-6pm, s/20); **Mollendo** (2hr., 9 per day 6:30am-8pm, s/5); and **Cabanaconde** (6hr., 2:30am and noon, s/13) via **Chivay** (4hr., s/10).

Tourist Office: (Tel. 211 021), on the Plaza de Armas, across from the cathedral. Offers maps, advice, and broken English. Open M-Sa 8am-3:45pm.

Banks: Banco de Crédito, Moran 101 (tel. 212 112), a block away from the Plaza de Armas, exchanges cash and checks and has a VISA/Plus **ATM.** Open M-F 9:15am-

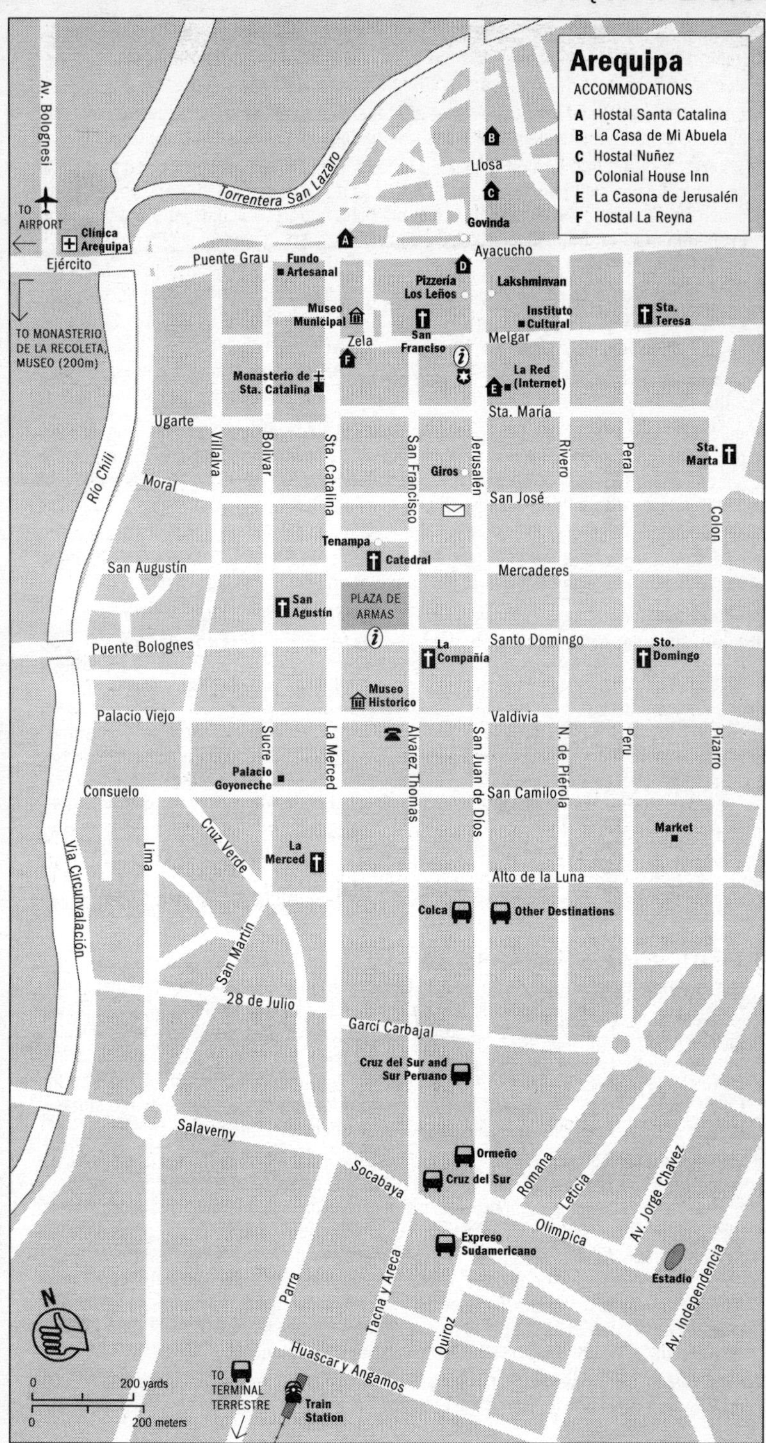
Arequipa
ACCOMMODATIONS
A Hostal Santa Catalina
B La Casa de Mi Abuela
C Hostal Nuñez
D Colonial House Inn
E La Casona de Jerusalén
F Hostal La Reyna
TO AIRPORT
Av. Bolognesi
Clínica Arequipa
Ejército
Puente Grau
TO MONASTERIO DE LA RECOLETA, MUSEO (200m)
Torrentera San Lazaro
Llosa
Govinda
Ayacucho
Fundo Artesanal
Pizzería Los Leños
Lakshminvan
Museo Municipal
San Francisco
Instituto Cultural
Sta. Teresa
Zela
Melgar
Monasterio de Sta. Catalina
La Red (Internet)
Sta. María
Ugarte
Villalva
Bolivar
Sta. Catalina
San Francisco
Jerusalén
Rivero
Peral
Sta. Marta
Moral
Río Chili
Giros
San José
Colon
Tenampa
Catedral
San Augustín
Mercaderes
San Agustín
PLAZA DE ARMAS
Puente Bolognes
Santo Domingo
La Compañía
Sto. Domingo
Museo Historico
Palacio Viejo
Valdivia
Sucre
La Merced
Alvarez Thomas
San Juan de Díos
N. de Piérola
Peru
Pizarro
Palacio Goyoneche
Consuelo
San Camilo
Market
Cruz Verde
Lima
La Merced
Alto de la Luna
Vía Circunvalación
Colca
Other Destinations
San Martin
28 de Julio
Garcí Carbajal
Cruz del Sur and Sur Peruano
Salaverry
Ormeño
Socabaya
Cruz del Sur
Romana
Leticia
Av. Jorge Chavez
Olimpica
Expreso Sudamericano
Estadio
Parra
Tacna y Areca
Quiroz
Av. Independencia
Huascar y Angamos
TO TERMINAL TERRESTRE
Train Station
0 200 yards
0 200 meters

1:15pm and 4:15-6:15pm, Sa 9:15am-noon. **Banco Continental,** San Francisco 108 (tel. 215 060), one block uphill from the Plaza de Armas, offers identical services. Open M-F 9:15am-12:45pm and 4-6:30pm, Sa 9am-12:30pm.

Money Exchange: Vendors on the street offer the best rates. There are several *casas de cambios* on the first block of San Francisco that change dollars and traveler's checks.

Markets: The **principal market** is located indoors at the corner of Pierola and San Camilo, 2 blocks downhill from the Plaza de Armas and across Jerusalén. Here, you can purchase exotic fruit (piled 3m high), young puppies, and fresh fish. Open 4am-5pm. The **artesanía market,** San Francisco 485 and Zela, consists of several shops on a tranquil square. The goods are high-quality but expensive. Open daily 10am-8pm.

Laundromat: Magic Laundry, Jerusalén 404-B, washes those dirties (wash and dry s/5 per kg). Open daily 9am-7pm.

Tourist Police: Jerusalén 315 (tel. 239 888).

Pharmacies: Botica del Pueblo, San Juan de Dios 200 and Moran (tel. 213 691). Open 24hr.

Medical Services: The principal hospital is **Hospital General** (tel. 233 812), on Av. Carrión, 1km to the south of Plaza de Armas. **Clínica Arequipa** (tel. 253 416), at the corner of Gau and Bolognesi. **Es Salud,** Santa Catalina 118-C (tel. 222 162), is a national health service with a 24hr. hotline. Open daily 7am-9pm.

Telephones: International and local calls are best made from one of several private agencies. One is located at Santa Catalina 118. Open daily 8:30am-1pm and 2-7pm. International calls can also be made at the corner of Catedral and San Francisco.

Mail: Serpost, Moral 118 (tel. 215 245). Open M-Sa 8am-8pm, Su 9am-1pm.

Internet: Internet cafes are sprouting up all over the place. Try **La Red,** Jerusalén 306 (tel. 287 600), for semi-reliable access (s/3 per hr.). Open daily 9am-9pm. **Chip's Internet,** San Francisco 202-A, has the same price. Open daily 9:15am-midnight.

TELEPHONE CODE	054

ACCOMMODATIONS

Arequipa has a plethora of hostels, hotels, and *casas de alojamiento*, so most visitors will probably find something that fits their taste and budget. There are a host of places that, while slightly more expensive, offer an exponential increase in comfort and security.

Hostal La Reyna, Zela 209 and Santa Catalina (tel. 286 578). This attractive *casa antigua* is newly incarnated as a popular backpacker's hostel. On the rooftop sun terrace, travelers swap stories while soaking up a few rays and devouring the view of the majestic peaks high above. Below, comfortable and spotless rooms are simple but sufficient. Both the shared and common baths pipe hot water, and there's a cozy cafeteria that serves a generous *desayuno americano* (s/3). The helpful owners offer tours to the Colca Canyon (US$20) as well as free tourist information and free luggage storage. Rooms s/12 per person, with bath s/15. Reservations recommended.

La Casa de Mi Abuela, Jerusalén 606 (tel. 241 206; email lperezwi@ucsm.edu.pe), uphill from the city center, is more like a full-service resort than your grandmother's house. The five-building complex consists of 2 restaurants, a library, a reputable travel agency, and almost 50 rooms, which range from simple singles to condo-style, 6-person suites. As if this weren't enough, there's a beautiful topaz swimming pool, competition-grade ping-pong table, a fish-filled fountain, and more lawn furniture than a Miami suburb. Breakfast (s/5) is served in one of the quiet, flowering gardens. This class of luxury comes at a price, however. Singles begin at US$10, with bath US$26; doubles US$17, with bath US$33. Reservations recommended.

Hostal Santa Catalina, Santa Catalina 500 (tel. 243 705), has spacious rooms with deliciously warm showers and a tranquil atmosphere. The genial owner serves breakfast in an attached cafeteria every morning and will purchase bus tickets and medication for ailing travelers. Always bold and pioneering, the Santa Catalina also offers tours to the Colca Canyon. Singles s/15, with bath s/25; doubles s/25, with bath s/35.

La Casona de Jerusalén, Jerusalén 306 (tel. 214 221), 2nd floor. Attractive, airy rooms surround a bright yellow courtyard. The centrally located hostel also offers laundry service, breakfast, and an onsite travel agency. Singles s/15, with bath s/35; doubles s/30, with bath s/55.

Colonial House Inn, Grau 114 and Jerusalén, 2nd floor (tel. 223 533). This small and unassuming bed and breakfast provides 5 very spacious rooms and refuge from the daily grind of gringo life. The gregarious hosts also offer washing facilities, access to a well-equipped kitchen, and plenty of meal time company and conversation. Check out the family cactus patch out back. Rooms s/15 per person, with bath s/28.

Hostal le Foyer, Ugarte 114 (tel. 286 473). Slightly similar to La Casona de Jerusalén, this hostel opens onto a central, sunny, 2nd-floor courtyard framed by several generously portioned rooms. In addition to the hot-water baths and funky bedspreads, the hostel boasts one of the best English-language book exchanges in Arequipa. Singles s/15, with bath s/25; doubles s/25, with bath s/35.

Hostal Nuñez, Jerusalén 528 (tel. 218 648). A sign on the hostel's front door reads "Be sure the door is closed to avoid strange people." Don't be fooled, though; even if the door is closed, you may still be susceptible to strange people. Heck, you might even be a strange person. If not, the hostel's staff is very welcoming, and the rooms are a good bargain. Attached cafeteria has terrace seating. Rooms s/14 per person.

FOOD

As with Arequipa's hotels, most of the city's restaurants are centered around the *centro* and Plaza de Armas. Many offer such regional specialties as **rocoto relleno,** meat (usually shredded beef) and vegetables stuffed into a spicy red bell pepper and then cooked; **adobo,** a dish of *chancho* (pig) only eaten on Sunday mornings; and, of course, *cuy* (guinea pig).

Sol de Mayo, Jerusalén 207 (tel. 254 148), in the nearby suburb of Yanahuara. An outstanding choice for sampling succulent, typical *arequipeñan* food. *Rocoto relleno* (s/13) and many fine seafood dishes are served in an atmospheric, outdoor courtyard. Near to the *mirador* of Yanahuara, it makes a perfect lunch spot year-round.

Govinda, Jerusalén 400-B (tel. 285 540). Govinda is an exceptional installation of the national Hare Krishna vegetarian consortium. This simple, sanitary, and serene sanctuary skillfully serves a scrumptious selection of substantial soul food for spare *soles*. Govinda's healthy variety of fixed-price *menús* (s/5-7) are both light and satisfying, great for soothing sensitive stomachs that may be rejecting the meat-and-potato fare of more traditional places. Open daily 7am-9:30pm.

Snack Vienticuatro Horas, Portal de Flores 122 (tel. 218 777), on the east side of the Plaza de Armas. A small, cheerful place with sunflower decor. The specialty here is the *pollo al spiedo,* quite possibly the tastiest chicken in all of Perú (s/5). They also serve sandwiches (s/4), omelettes (s/5), and various *platos del día,* including *conejo al ajo* (rabbit with garlic s/10) and *bisteck de alpaca* (s/10). Open 24hr.

Tradición Arequipeña, Canga 112 (tel. 452 987), off Av. Jesús. Don't be fooled by its younger, more expensive, and identically named sister. This location, the original, is reputedly the best. This place serves well-prepared traditional Arequipan specialties, such as *rocoto relleno,* to eager locals and a few tourists. Open daily noon-7pm.

Lakshmivan Restaurant, Jerusalén 402 (tel. 228 768). Either because of a diabolically competitive strategy or some wacky Peruvian zoning law, Arequipa's two Hare Krishna vegetarian eateries have chosen to operate next door to one another. Though its name is harder to pronounce than its neighbor's and its menu less comprehensive than Govinda's, this place is still exceptional. In fact, many loyal customers prefer Lakshmivan's hearty breakfasts, which taste even better under the morning sun of the restaurant's charming inner courtyard. For *almuerzo*, a *menú* offering bread, yogurt, fruit, soup, and main course (s/6.50) is sure to satisfy even the most discriminating of vegetarian tastebuds. Open daily 7am-9:30pm.

Pizzería Los Leños, Jerusalén 407-Cercado (tel. 289 179). Generous, piping-hot pizzas of varying shapes and sizes burst out of an authentic wood-brick oven, soar through a cavernous, picnic-tabled dining room and land tenuously on the plates of numerous hungry backpackers and locals alike. A ferocious fire and freely flowing fermentation (*cerveza* s/5) fuel the festive, funky feeling. Philosophical fodder for future friends is found in the form of fantastic graffiti framing the affair. Pizzas s/20-50.

Tenampa, Catedral 108 and San Francisco (tel. 202 313). A brief respite from traditional Peruvian food, Tenampa's Mexican menu retains some of the same spiciness in its succulent chicken, beef, and vegetable tacos (s/3). With tables on the pedestrian walkway of Catedral, this is a great place for lunchtime people-watching. Open daily 9am-9pm.

Giros, Jerusalén 207. Follow the locals to this cheap choice. The restaurant has saved money by keeping overhead costs low; it only offers 7 tables. But, those savings are passed on in the form of a generous, palatable *menú* (s/4.50). Open daily 9am-8pm.

ENTERTAINMENT

Though it is Peru's second-largest city, Arequipa's nightlife tends to disappoint when compared to its raging capital counterpart. Don't be discouraged; this city still knows how to party in its own highland manner, especially on weekends and holidays. There is a pretty healthy assortment of *discotecas*, *peñas*, and gringo rock clubs. Several local restaurants, especially near the Plaza de Armas, occasionally have live traditional music on weekend evenings. For that Hollywood fix, try one of the local theaters. **Cine Fenix,** Moran 104, and **Cine Portal,** Portal de Flores 112 (tel. 203 485), both screen recently-released international movies (s/8), many of which are in English with Spanish subtitles.

Daddy O's, Portal de Flores 112 (tel. 215 530), on the Plaza de Armas. As the name might suggest, this is a cheesy, Americanized bar. If you can overlook that, it's actually a lot of fun. This popular spot harkens back to 1977, with a brightly tiled dance floor, shimmering disco ball, and neon lights. Cover s/10. Open Th-Sa 9pm-4am.

Jenizaro, Melgar 119, at the intersection with Rivero. A good place for tourists who want to dance, it's popular with locals who want to dance with you. The music is mostly international, spiced up with a fair amount of Latin flavor. Open Th-Sa 10pm-4am.

Las Quenas, Santa Catalina 302 (tel. 281 115). A small, intimate venue where authentic *música folklorica* beckons visitors in for *Arequipeña* beer (s/4) and assorted mixed drinks. Open M-Sa 10am-1am.

Q'eros, Dolores 119 (tel. 651 266). Farther from the touristy center but well worth the trip. The large dance floor, which lies under a thatched roof, is a great place to swing those hips to primarily American rock. Live music F-Sa. Open daily 8pm-5am.

Forum, San Francisco 317, connected to the Bar Broccetta. This bi-level club, with plenty of room for dancing, provides a place to work off the dinner and drinks served next door. Live music F-Sa evenings. Open M-Sa 6pm-3am.

SIGHTS

THE PLAZA DE ARMAS. Arequipa's Plaza de Armas is one of the most attractive in Perú. The bronzed **Tuturutu,** named for the toot-toot of his horn, sits in the central fountain, keeping watch over the colonial center. On the north side of the plaza is the impressive, twin-towered **Catedral,** constructed out of white volcanic *sillar* in the 17th century. Since then, it has been repeatedly damaged in earthquakes, gutted by an 1844 fire, and rebuilt in the late 19th century. The cathedral's highlight is the enormous **Belgian organ,** the second largest in South America; two or three people can play at once. *(Open M-F 9-11:30am and 5-8pm, Sa-Su 7am-8pm.)*

LA COMPAÑIA. With intricately carved *sillar* adorning the entrance, this church, also on the Plaza de Armas, demands attention. Inside is an elegant yet sparse sanctuary, representative of the Baroque-Mestizo style—it's cedar altar is plated in gold. Next door lies the colorful **San Ignacio Chapel.** Though still very impressive, much of the chapel was ruined in an 1868 earthquake and was never properly restored. Adjacent to the chapel, attractive **cloisters** were constructed in 1738 around a square courtyard with a fountain and decorative columns. The original cloisters now house high-quality *artesanía* shops, which offer good bargains on woven wool products. *(Open daily 9-11:30am and 3-5:30pm. Chapel admission s/1.)*

SANTA CATALINA MONASTERY. Actually a functional convent, this enormous complex of cobblestone streets, chapels, artwork, and residences seems more like a city within walls than a religious installation. Five-hundred nuns once lived here; now only 20 live in a small, isolated section with the relative comforts of cable TV, modern kitchens, and washing machines. Guides who speak excellent English will accompany you, but feel free to move along at your own pace—the monastery is very navigable with several explanatory English signs.

A highlight of the monastery is **Calle Toledo,** the oldest part of the convent, a street lined with bright red stone buildings decorated with matching flower pots. The street ends at the lavandería, 20 huge stone basins on an incline, where the nuns could see other buildings but the high walls kept outsiders from peering in on them while they washed. Uphill from and parallel to Toledo, Calle Burgos passes a beautiful flower garden before reaching a *cafetería*, a good spot to grab a quiet snack. Continuing to the right, Calle Granada leads to the **Plaza Socodobe,** which holds a fish-filled fountain and an area where the nuns used to bathe. Then Granada leads to the *coro alto*, from which there is a beautiful view of Volcán Chachani. Next to it, the *coro bajo* is connected to the curtained-off main chapel. Tours conclude in the religious **art gallery,** which once served as a dormitory for the nuns and now houses many excellent examples of Peruvian artistic styles, including the syncretistic fusion of the Cusco School. *(Santa Catalina 301. Tel. 229 798. Open daily 9am-5pm; last admission 5pm. Tours last 1¼hr. Tip expected. Admission s/12.)*

MUSEO DE SANTUARIOS. Not just any other attraction, this is an archaeological museum that specializes in mummies dragged off nearby summits. The best preserved and most famous is **Juanita,** a 12-year-old girl sacrificed in the Inca ceremony of *Capac Cocha*. Discovered on the summit of Ampato by Johan Reinhard and Miguel Zarate in September 1995, "Juanita" is currently quite the jetsetter and will be touring Japan until July 2000. The museum screens a National Geographic documentary on the discovery of the mummy. There are also displays of Inca metals, ceramics, textiles, and a collection of several other recovered mummies. *(Santa Catalina 210. Tel. 200 345. Open daily 8am-5pm. Admission free.)*

LA RECOLETA. Originally a Franciscan convent, la Recoleta now contains a **museum** with exhibits on the Amazon River, pre-Columbian pottery, textiles, and ceramics. Most interesting is the 20,000-volume **library,** with a number of *incunables*, books printed during the 15th century. *(Recoleta 117. In a bright red building visible from the center of Arequipa, a 10-min. walk over the Río Chili. Tel. 270 966. Admission free.)*

LA CASA DEL MORAL. This *casa antigua* was built in 1730 for a Spanish viceroy, and many aspects of its design and decoration are good examples of the fusion of colonial and *mestizo* influences. Throughout, there are traditional paintings of the Cusco School, antique furniture, and ornate wood carvings. The highlights of the extensive library are the 3000 maps from that era. *(Moral 318. Open M-F 9am-5pm, Sa 9am-1pm. Admission s/15, students s/3.)*

YANAHUARA. This neighboring suburb has a *mirador* with an excellent view of Arequipa, El Misti, and Pichu Pichu. There is a small park near the Church of Yanahuara, noted for its elaborately decorated principal door. Nearby is the acclaimed restaurant Sol de Mayo. *(To reach the mirador, cross the Río Chili on Puente Grau from its intersection with Santa Catalina. Take Av. Ejército until Av. Lima and walk 5 blocks.)*

YURA. Yura is 30km northeast of Arequipa. Visitors come to visit the **four thermal baths,** which vary both in temperature and odor and reputedly have the power to heal various ailments. *(Buses to Yura leave from Puente Grau, at the bridge to Yanahuara (1hr., every 20min., s/1). Or go by taxi (25min., s/15). Open daily 7am-6pm.)*

SABADÍA. Sabadía is a tranquil small town 7km southeast of the city. The main attraction is the **Molino** (mill), Cesca 1621, which still grinds wheat by water power. The surrounding grounds are pleasantly decorated, and a lone alpaca patrols the grass. *(Buses to Sabadía leave from Independencia and Paveerpata, which is the eastern continuation of Mescaderes. The mill is off to the right of the main road, on the same road as the Holiday Inn. Open daily 9am-5pm. Admission s/5.)*

MOUNTAIN GUIDES AND TOUR AGENCIES

Some of the most exciting excursions around Arequipa may require special equipment or the expertise of a guide. When signing up with an agency, be sure to ask lots of questions and get answers in writing.

Zarate Expeditions, Ugarte 305 (tel. 463 624), is the best established climbing/trekking outfit in Arequipa. They lead conventional trips to local volcanoes, rent equipment, and also help plan extended trips to obscure archaeological destinations. Charged with mountain rescue in the region, Zarate's office is staffed 24hr.

Pablo Tour, Jerusalén 400-A (tel. 203 737), are specialists in trekking trips to the Colca. Climbing and rafting in the Colca during the safer dry season (one-day trips US$35 per person) and excursions to Toro Muerto and Valle de los Volcanos also offered. A good source of smart multilingual advice. Open daily 10am-1pm and 3-9pm.

Eco Tours, Jerusalén 402-A (tel. 200 516; email ecotours@peru.itete.com.pe). A complete tour agency with the standard Colca trip, rental gear (bicycles US$15 per day), and a 2-day trip that includes rafting, Toro de Muerto, and Valle de los Volcanos (US$80). Three-day whitewater kayaking course (US$150). Open daily 9am-10pm.

Campamento Base, Jerusalén 401-B (tel. 202 768). With possibly the best mountain equipment in Arequipa (for rental and purchase), "base camp" also leads climbs and treks in the Colca and Cotahuasi canyons. Vlado Soto, the agency's principal guide, is highly recommended. Open daily 10am-9pm.

Santa Catalina Tours, Santa Catalina 223 (tel. 218 994). This agency offers primarily conventional tourist trips, with English-speaking guides and comfortable tour buses. They also offer a 3hr. city tour (s/40). Open daily 8:30am-7pm.

EXCURSIONS FROM AREQUIPA

Arequipa offers magnificent excursions to nearby mountains, valleys, and a varied array of nearby tourist activities.

MOUNTAIN CLIMBING. El Misti (5822m) towers conspicuously over Arequipa, and is a popular two-day climb. The ascent, however, is physically demanding, and the route is somewhat unclear. Many tourists choose to make the trip with an agency or guide. To make the trip on your own, it is possible to take a private car (s/100) that will leave you seven hours from the campsite at the refuge. Alternatively, it's possible to take a taxi to Chiguata for around s/12.50, or the bus (s/2.50), which leaves hourly from Av. Sepuluecla, in the Miraflores district. From Chiguata, there is a more difficult nine-hour route to the first campsite. **Chachani** (6067m) is a challenging and isolated two-day climb. Private transport is required. For information on guided climbs, see above.

THE COLCA CANYON. Although no longer considered the world's deepest canyon—nearby Cotohuasi Canyon has that honor—the Colca is visited much more frequently by tourists. The cavernous fissure was formed by an enormous seismic fault between the Coropuna (6425m) and Ampato (6325m) volcanoes. Incredibly, the canyon was undiscovered by Western tourists until a Polish group navigated it in 1986. A standard two-day tour (US$20-35) from Arequipa stops in Chivay on the first day. On the second day, groups continue on to the nearby Cruz del Cóndor and then return to Arequipa. It is possible to reach all these destinations and Cabanaconde, a base for excursions into the canyon, with public transportation.

TORO MUERTO PETROGLYPHS. Before the Colca was "discovered," this was the original Arequipa tourist attraction. It consists of more than 5000 rocks engraved with petroglyphic images thought to be more than 1000 years old. The subjects vary from dancing people to the sun or animals such as dogs and snakes.

The easiest way to get there is a one-day tour with an agency in Arequipa *(US$16-50 per person).* Public buses depart frequently for Corire, from which the petroglyphs are a 30-minute walk. Although it is possible to make the return trip in the same day, Arequipa agencies recommend staying nearby, at a place called **Willy's.**

VALLE DE LOS VOLCANES. More than 80 small volcanic craters, none of which is more than 300m high, line this 65km valley. They can be visited in a multi-day trip with a tour group from Arequipa, or on your own, from the town of Andagua (see **Cabanaconde,** p. 109).

COTOHAUSI. Possibly the deepest canyon in the world, Cotohausi offers ample opportunities for rafting and trekking. Because of its remote location, many fewer tourists visit this canyon than the closer Colca. The town of Cotohuasi makes a good base to explore the Canyon if you choose to make the trip independently.

CHIVAY

The highland hamlet of Chivay (3633m) represents a green oasis after the mind-numbing bus ride from Arequipa. Tour groups often stay here for the night before continuing onto the Cruz del Cóndor, 35km from Chivay, along the road to Cabanaconde. As its name might suggest, it is home to some of the boldest, most exhibited condors in the world. Watching groups of them rise up the canyon and surf the morning air currents in the early morning is quite a beautiful show. The best time to see the soaring condors is between 8:30 and 10am during the drier months from April to December. At other times of the year, the show is less reliable. The **Calera Hot Springs,** 3km from Chivay, are very warm (up to 85°C) and surprisingly clean (open daily 5am-7pm; admission s/4). The town of Chivay is tiny and centered around the **Plaza de Armas,** where buses arrive and the site of affordable restaurants and hostels. **Buses** travel to **Arequipa** (4hr., 10am and noon, s/10) and **Cabanaconde** (2hr., 7am and 2pm, s/3). **Hostal Anita,** Plaza de Armas 607 (tel. 521 114), offers small, simple windowless rooms on a pleasant courtyard decorated with flowers (singles s/20; doubles s/36). **Hostal Municipal** (tel. 521 077), on the Plaza de Armas, has uninteresting motel decor, but the quarters are spacious and have large windows (s/20 per person). **Colca Inn,** Av. Salaverry 307 (tel. 521 088), is in a recently renovated building with small, carpeted rooms, and is very popular with tour groups (singles US$12; doubles US$18). **Casablanca,** Plaza de Armas 205, is one popular gringo choice for the *rocoto relleno* (s/15; open 7am-10pm). **Chositas,** Siglo Veinte, one block from the Plaza de Armas, serves a *menú* (s/12), that may include traditional dishes or standard fare like spaghetti (open daily 8am-10pm).

Transportation: A 2:30am bus leaves Arequipa for Chivay, arriving at 7am; the bus then continues on to the Cruz del Condor and Cabanaconde. It arrives just before the condors put on their daily exhibition. Another bus leaves Arequipa at noon, arriving at Chivay at 4pm and continuing on to Cadonaconde. In order to get to the hot springs from Chivay, take a *colectivo* (s/1) leaving from the Plaza de Armas. They return continually.

NEAR CHIVAY: CABANACONDE

A two-hour walk further down the road from Chivay, Cabanaconde is a very small town which serves as a good base for expeditions into the canyon. There are many relaxing and scenic **hikes** from Cabanaconde, including a 10-minute hike leading to a *mirador* that, locals claim, offers the best view of the Colca Canyon. A good one-day trip is to the bottom of the canyon, where there's an **oasis** perfect for swimming. Another popular trek is to **Andagua** (5-7days) and the spectacular **Valle de Los Volcanos.** July 14-18 is the most eventful time of the year to visit Cabanaconde: July 14, 15, and 16 bring dances and fiestas leading up to the **bullfights** of July 17 and 18, which are held in a specially constructed arena just outside of town. In town, the **Hostal Valle del Fuego** (tel. 280 367), on Calle de Los Palacios and Grau, is highly recommended for lodging, meals (s/5), and general information about treks into the canyon. The friendly family also rents equipment and makes arrangements with local guides and partners. (Rooms s/10 per person.)

Transportation: Buses go to Cabanaconde from Chivay (2hr., 7am and 2pm, s/3). They leave the Plaza de Armas for **Arequipa** (6hr., 7:30am and 9pm, s/13) via **Chivay** (2hr., s/3).

MOLLENDO

During the summer months (Jan.-Mar.), Peruvians, mostly *arequipeños*, flock to Mollendo's attractive beaches and calm currents. The rest of year, the small town of Mollendo (pop. 15,000), abandoned by the crowds from neighboring towns, is more subdued, but this can be a blessing for foreign tourists looking to repose on restful beaches or explore the nearby Mejía bird sanctuary.

The city center has two plazas, **Plaza Grau** and **Plaza de Bolognesi.** Grau is on the beach at the southern edge of town, and Bolognesi is two blocks up. Both are formed by the parallel north-south streets of Arequipa and Comercio. **Buses** and *colectivos* leave from Av. Mariscal Castillo, north of Plaza de Bolognesi. **Santa Ursula,** Castillo 824 (tel. 533 040), and **Carpio,** Castillo 818 (tel. 532 743), send buses to **Arequipa** (2hr., s/5). A **taxi** ride downhill to the beach should cost s/1. **Banco de Crédito,** Arequipa 330 (tel. 534 260), has a 24-hour Visa **ATM** (open M-Sa 9:15am-1:15pm and 4:30-6:30pm). Other services include: the **police** (tel. 534 242), on Av. Comercio along Plaza Grau; **Farmacia Milagros,** Arequipa 374 (tel. 534 601; open daily 8am-10pm); and **Serpost,** Arequipa 530 (tel. 532 264; open M-Sa 8am-1pm and 4-8pm). **Hostal Villa,** Castillo 366 (tel. 535 051), four blocks downhill from Plaza de Bolognesi, is the most attractive place in town. Inviting rooms have private baths, telephones, cable TV, and large windows, but the added luxury comes at a price. (Singles s/58; doubles s/69.) **Hostal Cabaña,** Comercio 240 (tel. 533 833), on the Plaza de Bolognesi, is less elegant but offers similar amenities and better views—every room overlooks the sea or the Plaza de Bolognesi—for a humbler price (singles s/15, with bath 38; doubles s/25, with bath s/38). As far as food goes, fresh fish wins hands down. **Restaurant Marco Antonio** offers tasty seafood at two locations: one at Castillo 366 (tel. 533 712), next to the Hostal La Villa (open daily 11am-10pm); and one on Conescio 258 (tel. 534 258; open 8am-11pm). The *corvina* (s/17) is the real delicacy, but the fish of the day (s/11) is tasty as well. **Chifa San Francisco,** Arequipa 385 (tel. 533 032), provides an alternative to seafood with *arroz chaufa* (s/6) and *sopa wanton* (s/4.50; open daily 9am-2:30pm and 4:30-10pm).

Mollendo's **beach,** which extends in either direction from town, is inviting and convenient but fails to compare to the more pristine, hotel-free **Mejía beaches,** 20km to the south. The beauty of the Mejía beach, in turn, pales in comparison to the natural splendor of the nearby **Mejía bird sanctuary.** The 690-hectare strip of unspoiled coastal marshlands is home to hundreds of species of tropical birds.

MOQUEGUA

Moquegua (pop. 10,000), the capital of its province, is on the border of the driest desert in the world, the Atacama. The center of this desert town is quaint and attractive, and the constant sun offers respite from coastal fog. There's not much of interest in Moquegua itself, but nearby ruins and a fascinating museum make Moquegua worth a multi-day visit for anyone at all interested in archaeology.

The Plaza de Armas, lush and overrun by pigeons, with a fountain designed by the famous **Gustav Eiffel,** marks the center of town. The **terminal terrestre** is a 10-minute walk downhill from the Plaza de Armas at Av. La Paz. **Buses** go to: **Lima** (15hr., 4 per day, s/40-70); **Tacna** (2hr., 4 per day 10am-5:30pm, s/5-6); **Arequipa** (3½hr., 5 per day, s/5); and **Ilo** (1½hr., 4 per day 7am-8:30pm, s/5). The **Dirección Regional de Turismo,** Moquegua 920, 2nd floor, is full of helpful advice (open M-F 7:30am-4:30pm). **Banco de Crédito,** Moquegua 861 (tel. 761 325), has the only 24-hour Visa **ATM** (open M-F 9:15am-1:30pm and 4:30-6:15pm, Sa 9:15-12:30pm). Other services include: the **police** (tel. 761 271), on Av. Ayacucho along the Plaza de Armas; **Farmacia Delgado,** Ayacucho 445 (tel. 761 949; open daily 9am-1pm and 4-9pm); the **post office,** Ayacucho 560 (tel. 762 551; open M-Sa 8am-12:30pm and 2:30-6:30pm); and **internet access,** at **Systems Service E.T.R.L.,** Moquegua 332 (tel. 763 758; open daily 9am-midnight). **Hotel los Limoneros,** Lima 441 (tel. 761 649), one of the best hostels in town, is designed with rooms laid out around an expansive courtyard enlivened by a colorful flower garden. All rooms have private baths and are equipped with cable TV. (Singles s/20, with bath s/42; doubles s/35, with bath s/53). **Hostal Piura,** Piura 255 (tel. 763 974), has very handsome rooms with orthopedic mattresses, elaborate bedspreads, and oriental rugs (singles s/25; doubles s/35; matrimonials s/30). *Palta* (avocado), wine, and *pisco* are local specialties. **Restaurante Palerma,** Moquegua 644 (tel. 764 072), has a popular lunchtime *menú* (s/15; open daily 8:30am-10pm).

The dry surrounding desert has preserved the possessions of earlier cultures—and sometimes their bodies—perfectly. The conduciveness of its environment to the preservation of ancient remains makes Moquegua and the surrounding lands an area of intense archaeological interest. A good source of initial information on the region and its history is the **Museo Contisuyo,** Tacna 194, near the Plaza de Armas. Opened in 1999, the exhibit shows a set of artifacts which traces cultural development from as far back as the Archaic period, 12,000 years ago. (Open W-M 10am-1pm and 3-5:30pm, Tu 10am-noon and 4:30-8pm.) A trip to the museum may interest you in a visit to one of the nearby archaeological sites. Most interesting are the **Paleolithic caves of Toquepala;** a visit to the caves must be arranged through the museum (guided trips s/50). **Cerro Baúl** ("Storage Trunk Hill"), named for its boxy appearance, is a large hill on which the pre-Inca Huari constructed a city in the years AD 600-750. Ruins of the sacked city can be visited on the flat summit. This excursion should only be attempted in the morning; it becomes very hot later in the day. *Colectivos* go past Cerro Baul frequently from the corner of Balta and Ancash, two blocks downhill from the Plaza de Armas (30min., s/1.5).

ILO

Ilo is a pleasant coastal town of 80,000 people, due west of Moquegua. The tankers and fishing boats one sees upon arrival are emblematic of Ilo's importance to the region; it's a major port not only for Perú but also for Bolivia. For the tourist, it is a relaxing place to enjoy decent beaches and fresh seafood.

Buses arrive at the corner of **Ilo** and **Matara.** The Plaza de Armas is two blocks from there; the water is four blocks downhill from the bus stop. The Plaza de Armas is formed by **Av. 28 de Julio** and **Av. Moquegua,** a street where many hostels and restaurants congregate. **Buses** go to **Tacna** (2hr, 16 per day, s/6); **Arequipa** (5hr., 12 per day, s/10); and **Moquegua** (1½hr., 11 per day, s/5). Helpful **tourist information** is offered at the municipal offices on Mirave 212 (tel. 781 141; open 7:30am-3pm M-F). **Banco de Crédito** (tel. 781 024), at the corner of Zepita and 28 de Julio, one block down from the Plaza de Armas, has a 24-hour **ATM.** Other services include: the **post office,** Marina Lino 311, a 10-minute walk from the *centro* (open M-Sa 8am-1pm and 4-7pm); **Farmacia San Luis,** Moquegua 602, (open daily 8:30am-12:30pm and 4-9:30pm); and the **police,** Pichincha 327 (tel. 781 021), at Moquegua.

The best value in town is at the **Hostal San Martín,** Matara 325 (tel. 781 082). This three-story hotel offers ocean views, spacious common areas, and a pool in the summer. (Singles s/20; doubles s/30.) **Hostal Paraíso,** Zepita 749 (tel. 781 432), has five floors and a lot of cute children prancing merrily around the common reception area. Rooms are very well kept. (Singles s/20, with bath s/35; doubles s/25, with bath s/45.) **Hotel El Pueblo,** Callao 523 (tel. 781 371), offers rooms with good lighting off a yellow-and-green hallway, and little else (singles s/15, with bath s/25; doubles s/25, with bath s/35). Seafood in town is as fresh as it gets; it alone almost merits a visit to Ilo. **La Estancia,** Moquegua 445, doesn't have a menu. Talk to the server about what's fresh, and they'll serve up a heaping plate of it at a very reasonable price (dinner s/6; open daily 6-11:30pm). **Corales,** Miranas 504 (tel. 783 466), with a view of the water, is very popular but more expensive than La Estancia (open daily 11am-3pm and 6-11pm). **Restaurant Veloso,** Miranas 108, closer to the Plaza de Armas, looks onto the water, but an enormous TV detracts from the tranquility of the view (*almuerzo* s/4.50; open daily 9am-10pm).

Local **beaches** are just beyond town. **Pozo de Lizos** beach is located to the south (taxi fare s/8). **Platanales** beach is more remotely located to the north (by taxi 30min., s/40). Camping on the beach is permitted and encouraged by town officials. During the summer, the beaches get somewhat crowded. Just 8km to the south, before the Pozo de Lizos, the **Punta de Coles Nature Reserve** hosts about 6000 sea lions, a variety of aquatic birds, and many large reptiles. Access to the park is a little difficult. The park officials (tel. 781 191) are happy to open the reserve to tourists free of charge, but they need a week's notice to make arrangements. The **Museo Algarrobal** is located on the main highway, 6km to the east in the suburb of Algarrobal. It principally exhibits artifacts of the pre-Inca culture Chiribaya, which lived in the area 1000 years ago. (Open daily 9am-1pm and 2-5pm. Admission s/2.)

TACNA

Tacna (pop. 170,000) is the southernmost city in Perú and the principal crossing point into Chile. The city is only 36km from the border and was actually part of Chile when Perú lost it in the 1879 War of the Pacific. On August 28, 1929, Tacna's citizens voted themselves back into Perú, earning the city the nickname, "Heroic Tacna." Tacna's well-maintained streets, relatively high prices, and good health care probably all stem from this Chilean influence. Barely any gringos stay more than a day in their rush to cross to Chile or pass deeper into Perú. But for those curious to explore or with some time before crossing into Chile, the city and its periphery offer hot springs and remarkable petroglyphs.

ORIENTATION AND PRACTICAL INFORMATION

Tourists arrive at the **terminal terrestre,** a 20-minute walk north of the **Plaza de Armas** (taxi s/3), where most hotels and restaurants cluster. **Av. San Martín** runs along the plaza. **Av. Bolognesi** and **Zela** run parallel to San Martín on opposite sides.

Airport: The **airport** is located 5km to the south (taxi fare s/10). **AeroContinente,** Arequipa 265 (tel. 721 775), at the intersection with San Martín, sends flights to: **Lima** (2 per day, US$59) and **Arequipa** (1 per day, US$39).

Trains: Alberacin and 2 de Mayo, beyond the cathedral in the Plaza de Armas. Trains are the slowest and most infrequently used way to get to **Arica, Chile** (1½hr.; M, W, F 6:30am; s/3.50).

Buses: The *terminal terrestre* is a 20min. walk north of the Plaza de Armas. There, you can find **Cruz del Sur** (tel. 726 921) which serves: **Lima** (standard 20hr., noon and 6pm, s/55; imperial 17hr., 3 and 8pm, s/75); **Arequipa** (6hr., every day 6:45am, 1:30, 4, and 9pm) via **Moquegua** (2hr.). Another company, **Flores** (tel. 723 376), has its own terminal on Av. Sarcini near the *terminal terrestre* and sends buses to **Ilo** (2hr., 16 per day, s/17) and **Arequipa** (6hr., 16 per day, s/17) via **Moquegua** (2hr., s/12). *Colectivos* to **Arica** (s/10) leave from the international end of the *terminal terrestre.*

Tourist Office: Blondel 50, 4th floor (tel. 722 784) in the municipal building to the side of the cathedral, will be happy to give tourist advice in Spanish. Open M-F 7am-1pm and 2-5pm.

Consulate: Chilean consulate (tel. 724 391), on Av. Abarracin near the train station.

Currency Exchange: Banco de Crédito, San Martín 574 (tel. 722 671), and **Banco Contintental,** San Martín 665 (tel. 726 279) both have 24hr. Visa **ATMs.** Both banks open M-F 9am-1pm and 4:30-6:30pm, Sa 9am-noon. **Money changers** seek both dollars and *pesos chilenos.*

Markets: The Mercado Central, Av. Bolognesi and Pillardelli. Open daily 6:30am-4pm. There are *artesanía* shops on Paillardelli. **Tacna Central,** on Leguía and Kennedy, has shoe repair, video games, and other services.

Police: (Tel. 714 141), Av. San Martín on the Plaza de Armas.

Pharmacy: Botica Lider, Bolognesi 612-A (tel. 721 855). Open 24hr.

Hospital: Hospital Unanue (tel. 733 431), on Av. Blondel beyond the cathedral.

Post Office: Serpost, Bolognesi 361 (tel. 724 641). Open M-Sa 8am-8pm.

Internet Access: *Tacneños* have no problem paying the local fee (s/2.50 per hr.), so the many cafes tend to be full, especially at night. **JM Data Internet,** San Martín 310 (tel. 711 246), has a fast connection. Open daily 8am-10pm.

ACCOMMODATIONS

SOUTHERN PERÚ

Just across the border from pricier Chile, Tacna offers underwhelming accommodations at prices higher than in the rest of Perú.

Hostal Lider, Zela 724 (tel. 715 441), offers quiet rooms with private bathrooms and black-and-white TVs. It's clean but unremarkable and they place an emphasis on safety. Singles s/20; doubles s/25.

Lido Hostal, San Martín 876-A (tel. 721 184), has several very basic rooms, but the price is right. Singles s/16; doubles s/28.

Hotel Lima (tel. 744 229), presents some of the trappings of a very elegant place; red carpet leads up the stairs and beds have faux-leather headboards. Don't be fooled by first impressions, though; rooms aren't particularly impressive. An adjoining restaurant serves tasty breakfasts. Singles s/25; doubles s/35; color TV s/5 extra.

Hospedaje San Diego, Ayacucho 86-A (tel. 712 398), 4 floors above street level, has a slightly cramped feeling. Singles s/15, with bath 20; doubles s/25, with bath s/30.

FOOD

El Viejo Almacen, San Martín 577 (tel. 714 471), painted in bright red, has an interesting barn-like interior. *Menú* s/15. Open daily 7am-1am.

Restaurant Peña Criollo, San Martín 1025, in the suburb of Pocollay, offers traditional dishes such as *cuy, choclo con queso,* and *papa a la huancaína.* Live *salsa* music converts this restaurant to a dancehall (Sa-Su 2-8pm). Open daily 11am-8pm.

Chifa May-Gen, Bolognesi 788 (tel. 713 513), serves the traditional Peruvian version of Chinese food. Open daily 11:30am-4:30pm and 6-11pm.

Restaurante Milanito, San Martín 271, across from the cathedral, prepares *almuerzos,* pizzas (s/16), and very tasty desserts. Open daily 9am-10pm.

SIGHTS

PLAZA DE ARMAS. A fountain called **Pilete,** designed by **Gustav Eiffel** in the 19th century but only completed in 1955, is very similar to the fountain Eiffel designed for Moquegua. Facing the plaza, the **cathedral,** finished in 1855, is small and ornate. The interior is painted in yellow and features a giant chandelier over the altar. On the other end of the plaza, a large arch commemorates two heroes from the War of the Pacific, Grau and Bolognesi. *(Cathedral's basilica open mornings and evenings.)*

OTHER SIGHTS IN TOWN. The **Museo Ferraviario** consists of two exhibit rooms right along the tracks at the train station. It's debatable whether the newspaper clippings and retired train parts are worth the admission fee. *(Tel. 215 350. Always open; just knock at the door to alert the guard. Admission s/1.)* **La Casa de Cultura** offers exhibits on local pre-Inca cultures and the War of the Pacific, as well as art exhibits. *(Apurimac 202. Exhibits open 9am-noon and 5-7pm).*

CALIENTES AND MICULLA. A paved road leaves Tacna and heads north to the town of Calientes (24km). The valley in which this town is situated is warmer and sunnier than Tacna. The town of Calientes has eight private **thermal baths,** *pozas*, which are kept very clean. *(Open daily 6am-6pm. Admission s/8 per person per 30min.)* From the nearby town of Miculla, you can walk 3km east to an area full of **petroglyphs,** where there are 400 rocks with over 2,000 engravings of animals and people. To get there, one must cross a 70m long and 1m wide suspended bridge—don't look down. *(To go to Miculla, take a colectivo from Tacna Central on Av. Leguea and Kennedy. Colectivos every 15min. until 7pm, s/1.50.)*

ENTERTAINMENT. Tacna has a couple of interesting places to have a drink and dance. One such locale is **La Taberna de 900** (tel. 726 657), San Martín, attached to El Viejo Almacen. They also offer some light *menús*. (Open daily 11pm-1am). **Manako's,** San Martín 781, is the most popular *discoteca* in town, but it only gets going at about 2am. There's an 11-sided dance floor in the center and a mural of John Lennon on the wall. (Cover s/5. Minimum bar tab s/5. Open Th-Sa 7pm-6am.)

 CROSSING THE BORDER

Everyone must pass through Peruvian and Chilean immigration to cross between Tacna and its Chilean counterpart, Arica. Giant American sedans from the 70s that seat eight cross the border both ways from dawn until 10pm. All you need is your **passport, tourist card,** and patience. The worst time to cross is during the middle of the day when lines are longest. Arica is a lively, active coastal town well connected to Chile's transportation infrastructure. There are a wide range of accommodations, and seafood is abundant, but be forewarned: everything is more expensive in Chile. It is wise to dump your *soles* by making purchases before entering the country. Ironically, even Chilean wine is cheaper in Tacna than Arica.

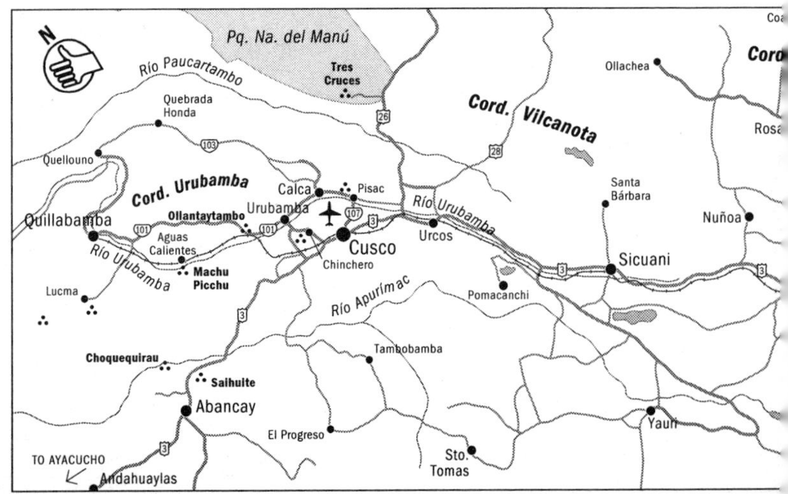

TITICACA REGION

More than just a body of water, Lake Titicaca is also a boundary—not only between Perú and Bolivia but also between two very different highland cultures, the Quechua and Aymara. With over 70 islands and spanning 8560 sq. km, the lake is a region all its own: a curious amalgam of customs, languages, and floating houses made of totora reeds. Because the islands lack many tourist services, most visitors opt to spend their nights in the dingy port town of Puno on the mainland. This coastal section around the lake—and "coast" hardly seems misused given Titicaca's enormous size—has its own appeal. Just a short *colectivo* ride out of Puno can bring you to the stunning *altiplano* around Silustani or, in the other direction, to the phallic wonders of Chucuito.

PUNO

Tourist authorities like to promote Puno as the Folkloric Capital of Perú, a title forged by the city's unique confluence of cultures: Aymara from the south and Quechua from the north. This city on the edge of Lake Titicaca can be proud of its region's many traditional dances—numbering in the hundreds—but few tourists get to see the dances performed except perhaps during festival days. To many visitors, Puno (3827m) is a bitterly cold, oxygenless place, which is not always a bad thing—the town is surrounded by rolling, desolate *altiplano* (high-altitude plain), at times resembling the surface of some bizarre and fascinating planet. Yet, Puno is still little more than a necessary stop on the way to the Titicaca islands or before crossing the border into Bolivia. Even a local in Puno might wistfully remark, "Been to Cusco yet? It sure is nice." (Most likely, the local is not from Puno but rather from next-door Juliaca, a much larger and even less appealing city.) Nevertheless, Lake Titicaca—despite all of its touristic excess—is reason enough to visit. And in the meantime, Puno offers all of the necessary resources and services.

SOUTHERN PERÚ

ORIENTATION

Trains from Arequipa and Cusco drop off their passengers just outside of the *centro* on **Av. La Torre,** which leads into **Jr. Tacna,** one of the main strips in town. Most buses stop along **Jr. Melgar,** which is perpendicular to Tacna. The **Plaza de Armas** marks the center of town and lies three blocks from Tacna along either **Jr. Puno** or

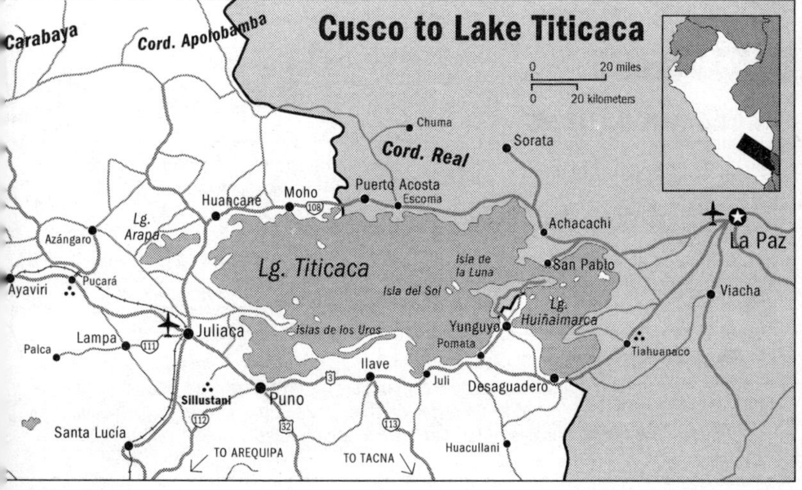

Jr. Deustua. The Plaza de Armas is connected to the artistically gardened **Parque Pino,** three blocks away, via the lively pedestrian street, **Jr. Lima.** Roughly 8 blocks from the center of town, **Lake Titicaca** can be seen from many streets in the *centro.*

PRACTICAL INFORMATION

Airplanes: Airport is 45km away in Juliaca. *Aeropuerto* buses leave along Tacna (45min., s/5-7). **Aerocontinente,** Tacna 301 and Melgar (tel. 354 870), sends flights to **Lima** (12:30, 3, and 4:30pm; US$89) with a stop in **Arequipa** (US$59). Open M-Sa 8am-6pm. **Tans,** San Román 153 in Juliaca (tel. 321 272), also flies to **Lima.**

Trains: Estación La Torre (tel. 351 041), sells tickets one day in advance to **Cusco** (10-11hr.; M, W-Th, and Sa 8am; s/25-US$20, depending on class). Some shorten the ride to Cusco and save money by taking a *colectivo* to **Juliaca** (30min., leaves from Tacna constantly, s/1) and catching the train there. For information, call the Juliaca station (tel. 321 036 or 321 112).

Buses: Buses leave from the streets around Melgar to: **Lima** (24-30hr., 6:30am and 5pm, s/45-60); **Cusco** (8hr.; 7:30am, 5:30, and 6pm; s/15); **Arequipa** (12hr., 4 per day, s/20); and **La Paz** (4hr.; M, W, and F 7:30am; s/20). A number of agencies along Tacna send buses to **Copacabana** (3hr., s/15), with a border passport stop in Yunguyo.

Boats: Motorized *lanchas* leave from the port on the edge of town (s/5 by taxi). *Lanchas* to **Los Uros** leave all day; to **Taquile** and **Amantaní,** they depart early in the morning. See **Lake Titicaca,** p. 120, for further information.

Tourist Information: Lima 549 (tel. 363 337), on the Plaza de Armas. A young, very helpful, mostly Spanish-speaking staff can provide a map and suggest sightseeing routes around the lake. Open M-Sa 8am-7pm.

Consulates: Bolivia, Jr. Arequipa, 2nd floor. Get your border-crossing questions answered. Open M-F 9am-noon and 4-6pm.

Money Exchange: Fairly easy within banks and *casas de cambio* along Jr. Lima.

ATMs: Machines on Lima. For Visa, try **Banco Continental;** for MC, **Telebanco.**

Tourism Police: (24hr. **emergency** tel. 357 100) on the Plaza de Armas.

Medical Services: Hospital Regional (tel. 353 780 or 369 286), 10th block of Sol, has ambulance service.

Post Office: SerPost, Moquegua 269 (tel./fax 351 141), has fax service. Open M-Sa 8am-8pm, Su 8am-3pm.

Internet Access: A number of places exist on Lima. **SurNet,** Lima 378, has plenty of fast computers and a cheerful staff. Open daily 8am-11pm.

Telephones: Telefónica, Lima 439, can place international calls.

TELEPHONE CODE	054

ACCOMMODATIONS

Even in high season, Puno seems to have more than enough room to house visitors. Hostels here are inexpensive, and when business is slow, most will offer hefty discounts. Puno can become creepy at night; it's a good idea to take a taxi.

Hostal Posada Real, Titicaca 156 and Tacna (tel. 351 701; email posadareal@hotmail.com), 3 blocks from the Plaza de Armas along Deustua, is a large hotel enhanced by big windows. Mattresses can be a little soft, but showers run hot 24hr. Singles s/20, with bath s/30; doubles s/30, with bath s/55; triples s/55, with bath s/70.

Hostal El Virrey, Tacna 510 and Puno (tel. 354 495), 3 blocks down Puno from the Plaza de Armas. Very spiffy carpeted rooms have firm beds, flowery bedspreads, and, in some cases, views of the lake. Most rooms also have cable TV. 24hr. hot water except in communal baths (7am-7pm). Singles s/15, with bath s/30; doubles with bath s/60; triples with bath s/80.

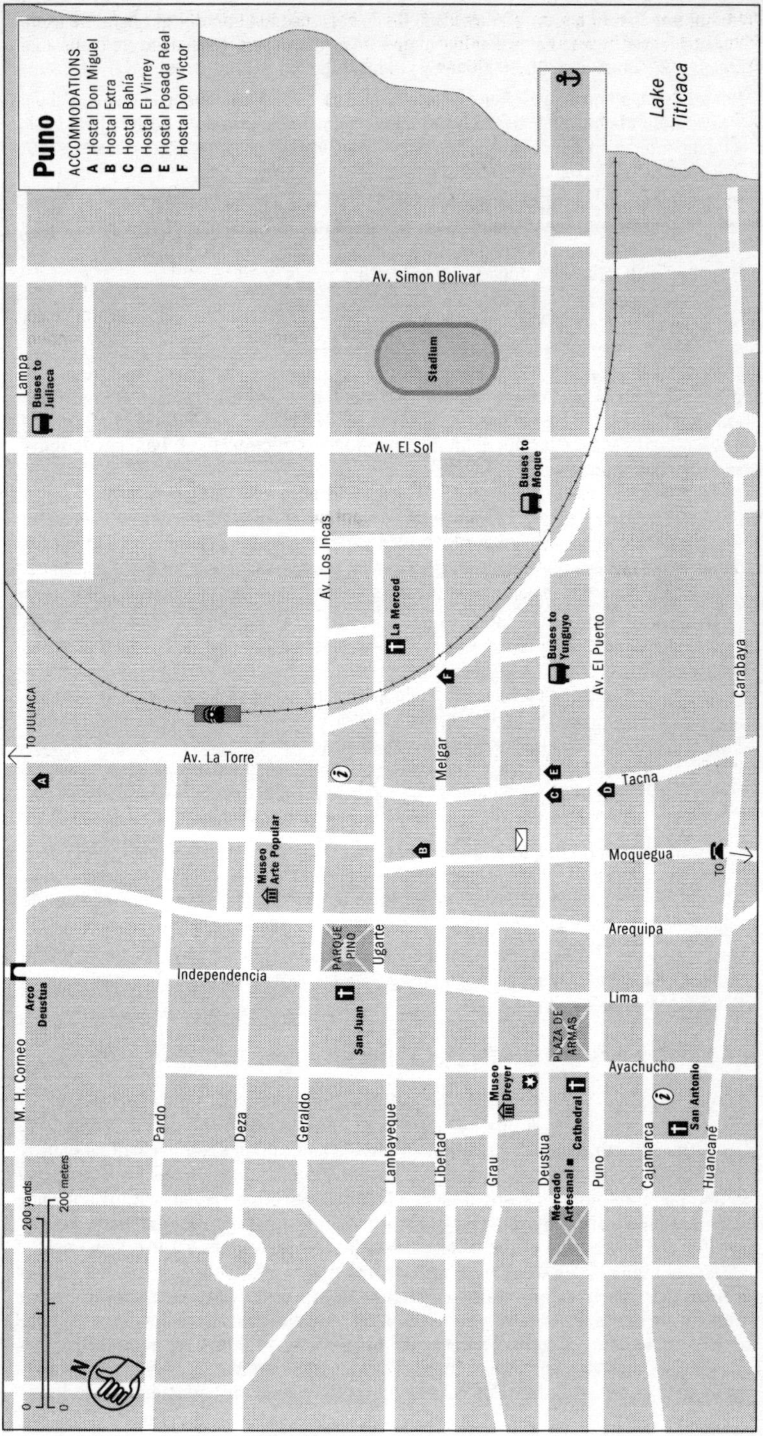

Puno

ACCOMMODATIONS
- **A** Hostal Don Miguel
- **B** Hostal Extra
- **C** Hostal Bahía
- **D** Hostal El Virrey
- **E** Hostal Posada Real
- **F** Hostal Don Victor

Lake Titicaca

Av. Simon Bolivar

Stadium

Lampa

Buses to Juliaca

Av. El Sol

Buses to Moque

Av. Los Incas

La Merced

Buses to Yunguyo

Av. El Puerto

Carabaya

TO JULIACA

Av. La Torre

Melgar

Tacna

Museo Arte Popular

Moquegua

TO

Arequipa

PARQUE PINO

Ugarte

Independencia

Arco Deustua

San Juan

Lima

PLAZA DE ARMAS

Ayachucho

M. H. Corneo

Museo Dreyer

Cathedral

San Antonio

Pardo

Deza

Geraldo

Lambayeque

Libertad

Grau

Deustua

Mercado Artesanal

Puno

Cajamarca

Huancané

0 200 yards

0 200 meters

N

Hostal Don Victor, Melgar 166 (tel. 366 087), near the train tracks. This bright, well-kept hostel leaves little to be desired. All rooms are comfortable and have private baths. Singles s/30; doubles s/50; triples s/65; TV s/5 extra.

Hostal Extra, Moquegua 124 and Libertad (tel. 351 123). From Parque Pino, take Arbulu away from the church 2 blocks and make a right. This ramshackle hostel offers basic rooms around an old courtyard. The grimy baths usually have hot water. Singles s/10; doubles s/18; triples s/25.

Hostal Bahía, Tacna 409 and Titicaca (tel. 352 655), 3 blocks from the Plaza de Armas on Deustua. A very friendly staff keeps well-sized rooms with plenty of light. Most rooms have private baths, although hot water can be erratic. Singles s/20, with bath s/25; doubles with bath s/40; triples with bath s/60.

FOOD

The always busy pedestrian strip, Jr. Lima, connecting the Plaza de Armas and Parque Pino, has a high concentration of decent, if somewhat touristy, restaurants, some of which have bad reputations for miscalculating their bills. Sitting on the shore of Lago Titicaca has its culinary advantages: delicious fresh fish, particularly *trucha* (trout) and *pejerrey* (kingfish).

Kröte Pizza Café, Tacna 336 and Melgar, 2nd floor. Infused with the charm of its owner and the younger family members who help run it, this small cafe prepares a medley of Italian and Peruvian dishes. "Only the freshest ingredients!" says the loveable *señora.* Generous rotating *menú* s/8. Amazing breakfasts s/5-10. Open daily 6am-11pm.

Restaurant El Portón Colonial, Lima 345 (tel. 351 214). Ambient yellow-green lighting, good music, and a very stylish waitstaff characterize this winning restaurant that serves typical dishes. A mind-bogglingly long menu of seafood platters and quick service makes one wonder if there's an army of pan-wielding cooks in the kitchen. Most entrées s/11-15. Savory *ceviche* s/6-8. Open daily 8am-11pm.

Café Restaurant Vegetarian Delisse, Moquegua 200. As the name would suggest, Delisse offers soy meat dishes, fresh juices, and vegetarian breakfasts, all at very inexpensive prices. Remarkably cheery waiters contrast with the ominous Seventh Day Adventist posters looming overhead. Open M-Th and Su 6am-6pm, Sa 6-10pm.

Cafetería Pastelería Baguetería Ricos-Pan, one at Lima 357 and another at Moquegua 330 (tel. 352 054). Cheap, cheap pastries, sandwiches, and drinks, and passionately red tablecloths make Ricos-Pan an upbeat place for breakfast or evening coffee. The blender in the back whirs out tall glasses of fresh juice (s/2-3). Open M-Sa 6am-10pm.

Govinda, Deusta 310 and Arequipa. This Hare Krishna restaurant can take credit for one of the cheapest set *menús* around (s/3-6). It's all pretty good and, of course, vegetarian. Open M-Sa 7am-9pm.

SIGHTS AND ENTERTAINMENT

Little in the town of Puno should distract visitors away from sights on the lake. A few minutes wander is enough to take in the **Museo Dryer,** Conde de Lemus 289, beside the cathedral, which maintains a small collection of pre-Inca artifacts and a couple of grisly mummies (open M-F 7:30am-3:30pm; admission s/2.50).

Puno has a number of festivals when locals take to the streets with traditional dance and music. Some dates to remember include January 6 for **Epiphany,** February 2 for the **Fiesta de la Virgen de la Candelaria,** and November 1-7 for **Puno week.**

Even on high-season weekends, **nightlife** in Puno is relatively tame. Streets in the center of town become desolate after 10pm, as locals return to the true population-center, Juliaca. A couple of nightspots exist on the ever-busy Jr. Lima, the best of which is **Café Video Discopub Apu Salkantay,** Lima 419, a good place to have coffee, order a beer, watch an MTV video, and dance, not necessarily in that order. **Kusillos Pub,** Libertad 265, 2nd floor, has a stylish bar and small dancefloor.

CROSSING THE BORDER INTO BOLIVIA

Getting to Bolivia is fairly straightforward. Travelers must go over land, following the coast of Titicaca. Many opt to cross the border at Yunguyo and then visit the charming Bolivian port town of **Copacabana,** from which a number of islands can be visited. Others skip this to head to the Bolivian capital of **La Paz,** through the town of Desaguaderos. (See **Buses,** p. 116, for specifics). Bolivia requires a visa from few English-speaking countries; check with the Bolivian consulate in Puno for more info (see p. 116). Usually, all one needs is a passport and tourist card.

NEAR PUNO: SILUSTANI

Silustani, 35km north of Puno, is a peninsula jutting into the Laguna Umayu, a salt lake completely separate from Titicaca and surrounded by stark *altiplano.* Silustani was sacred to the Colla people who chose it as a burial site for their most revered citizens. They constructed numerous stone tombs, called **chullpas,** in which whole families were buried accompanied by their riches. Most of the towers have since been broken open, either by lightning or grave-robbers looking for loot. It's a beautiful stroll through the park; you wander among various types of *chullpas*, ranging from the early "rustic" variety to more ambitious ones built by the Incas. Wild *cuy* (guinea pig) peek out from behind the stones, but don't try to make a meal of these little guys; hunting is forbidden on this sacred ground. An island in the Laguna Umayo serves as a more official reserve, this time for **vicuña.** Locals with totora reed boats give rides (s/8) to the island. (Silustani open daily 8am-6pm. Admission s/5.)

Transportation: To get to Silustani, most opt for a cheap agency-led tour. These usually leave around 2:30pm and cost as little as s/15, including admission cost. Alternatively, one could catch a *colectivo* bound for **Juliaca** and ask to be let off at the "*desvio a Silustani*" (s/1). From this fork, *colectivos* cover the remaining 14km to Silustani (s/2).

NEAR PUNO: CHUCUITO

Chucuito, 18km south of Puno along Titicaca, is a very small Aymara village. But really, **does size matter?** Sometimes it does. Aside from the town's two colonial churches and nearby fish farm, Chucuito is the proud site of the **Inca Uyo,** a pre-Columbian fertility temple housing some **80 big stone phalluses.** Most are a foot in length. All shock with their anatomical detail. About half point straight up (as a potent tribute to the Sun god, Inti), while the rest are rammed into the ground (to fertilize the Earth goddess, Pachamama). At the center stands the principal stone penis, about 5 feet in length. What appears at first glance to be its simple stone base is actually a carved figure lying down—a head, arms, and legs—the phallus's virile owner. As the story goes, the Inca ruler's wife and concubines would sit atop the giant phallus's mushroom head for three hours at a time to improve their chances of having male children. From the temple one can see the adjacent **Church of Santo Domingo,** and what's that on the tippy-top of its roof pointing straight to the sky? Hint: not a cross. The phallus has become something of a town emblem.

Not to ruin all of this phallic fun, but many discerning observers consider the Inca Uyo a **fake.** Several other Inca ruins feature large erect stones, possibly with phallic significance, but never with the kind of verisimilitude seen at Chucuito. Furthermore, the Spanish settled the area in the 17th century and probably would not have left such a temple intact. Inca ritual constructions suffered the most destruction from Spanish greed and religious convictions. (At the very least, the Spanish would have leveled it out of envy.) Even structures never seen by Spanish eyes—Machu Picchu for instance—don't look as complete as the Uyo. And if what locals say is true—that the Uyo has pre-Inca origins—Machu Picchu is a more recent construction. All phalluses should survive the wear of time so well.

Nevertheless, *puneños* don't even crack a smile when they insist that the penises are legit. Literature from the tourist office speaks of a temple belonging to a fertility cult, tour guides mention it freely, and Puno's Museo Dreyer has one of the phalluses on display. To be fair, the walls of the Uyo are undoubtedly Inca or Inca-influenced. Its massive stones show fine interlocking corners typical of sacred buildings. However, the phalluses seem to have only turned up in the last decade. They may have been carved a few decades beforehand and planted by a misfit with a chisel, or perhaps large phallic stones were found but later received a bit of reconstructive surgery. No one seems to know for sure. Real or not, Chucuito's temple is a good laugh, provides brilliant photographic opportunities, lies a few minutes by car from Puno, and costs close to nothing to visit.

Transportation: To get to Chucuito, catch a colectivo marked "Acora" around the 14th block of Av. Sol (20min., frequent, s/0.80). Ask to be let off at Chucuito. Walking uphill from the road, Santo Domingo is the first church one sees. Turn right to find the enclosed lot where the temple awaits. Young children play among the phalluses and can act as amateur guides. They also sell tourists fitting souvenirs—finger puppets. It's up to you where you wear them.

LAKE TITICACA

According to Andean myth, once upon a time, long before the Inca, the creator god Wiraccocha formed a world in shadow and populated it with great clumsy giants. These giant people stumbled around in the dark, becoming more and more irritated, and began to fight among each other. Wiraccocha erupted with anger, turning his large children to stone and flooding the world. With time, the water evaporated, the stone statues eroded, and Wiraccocha's temper diminished. He decided to give the creation business another try, this time stumbling upon the notion of light. He directed the Sun and Moon and Stars to rise out of Lake Titicaca and assume their rightful places in the sky. (At the last minute, the Sun, envious of the Moon's brighter light, scooped up a handful of ashes and cast them into her face, giving the Moon her permanently dull complexion.) In time, Lake Titicaca would also spawn the first Incas—the Ayar brothers—the eldest of whom, Manco Capac, would go on to found Cusco (see p. 123). According to Andean mythology, then, Lake Titicaca is the very cradle of civilization, even of life itself.

It's easy to see why Titicaca would inspire such epic legends. At 3827m altitude and extending across 8560 sq. km, it's the largest lake in South America and the largest in the world above 2000m. Traveling on its surface is like being on the open sea, except for the enormous peaks poking out of the horizon. The lake has 36 islands (not counting the floating ones made by the Uros people). Two of these are Isla del Sol and Isla de la Luna, the mythic birthplaces of the Sun and Moon. Popular tourist attractions, these islands fall on the Bolivian side of the lake and are usually visited from the port town of Copacabana.

Despite the Incas' tendency to take credit for all things civilized, in truth, a number of peoples preceded the Incas and remain a significant presence in the area. The Aymara culture, descended from the Colla, Lupaca, and Tiahuanuco, once dominated the area. (The word "Titicaca" itself is Aymara for "gray puma.") The expansion of the Inca empire in the 14th and 15th centuries brought Quechua customs to Titicaca but never succeeded in supplanting what formerly existed. To this day, Quechua and Aymara people prefer to live separately—Quechua north of the lake and throughout the Peruvian highlands, Aymara in the south and into Bolivia. Aymara women can be distinguished by their unique fedora, more bulbous than the Quechua version.

The best time to visit the lake is just after the dry season during the months of September through November, when increased rainfall revives some of the lake's surrounding vegetation and clouds mitigate the harshness of the sun. Starting in December, the lake is pounded by nearly ceaseless rainfall. Foreigners hit the scene in June, July, and August, and gather in herds to visit the man-made floating Uros Islands. Two more remote (natural) isles, Taquile and Amantaní, have been compared by some to paradise. They see fewer visitors and have managed to preserve centuries-old customs not witnessed anywhere else in Perú.

LOS UROS

Centuries ago, the Uros people lived along the shores of Titicaca. But faced with the gradual infiltration of the Aymaras and later the Incas, the Uros saw only one means of cultural preservation. They isolated themselves by constructing islands out of the totora reeds which grow throughout the lake. Today, over 40 islands still float in a cluster just a half-hour's motor boat-ride from Puno. The inhabitants build everything out of totora—houses, boats, souvenirs for the tourists—and constantly need to stack more reeds on the surface of the islands as old reeds rot underneath. Walking across an island is an eerie experience—the surface sinks slightly under each step. Many Uros people continue to support themselves by fishing, just as their ancestors once did.

Nowadays, however, the overwhelming majority of islanders subsist on tourism. True Uros customs, including the language, were lost long ago as inhabitants intermarried with Aymaras. Many of the people on the islands don't actually live there, but commute each morning to sell souvenirs. Upon landing at Los Uros, the visitor is immediately surrounded by local children asking for candy and peddling drawings. Adults hawk cheap souvenirs they couldn't have made themselves—how can one make ceramics when there's no earth? More and more it seems that the islanders are trapped in a self-perpetuating deal with the touristic devil.

The services of a tourist agency are unnecessary for visiting the Uros Islands; they are extremely easy to reach. Tour agencies charge little (around s/15), but anyone can go to the port in Puno and catch one of the frequent *lanchas* (motorboats; 40min., 8am-5pm, s/5). On some larger islands, locals offer short rides between individual islands of Los Uros on their long totora reed gondolas (s/3).

ISLA TAQUILE

This small island (pop. 3,000) is far enough from the shore that it has maintained a good deal of authenticity, despite the occasional interruption by curious visitors. People on Taquile speak Quechua but practice customs more similar to the Aymara. Women wear brightly colored skirts and cover themselves with black headscarves. Men don **floppy woolen caps** with colors that depend on the marital status of the wearer—red-and-white for bachelors, red-striped-with-black for husbands. Unmarried women are best recognized by their eerie manner of speaking only in whispers.

The people of Taquile subsist on agriculture, their main crops being quinoa and potatoes. Aside from that, they support themselves with the sale of exquisitely well-crafted **textiles.** All around the island, women can be seen spinning wool by using the drop-spool method, while men do all of the knitting. During high season (June-August), islanders set up stands in the Plaza de Armas (a breathless walk up hundreds of stone steps) to sell fine scarves, hats, belts, and gloves. Given the soundless customs of the people, this may be one of the more quiet markets you'll see. As boats arrive on the island, local women meet them down by the shore in order to offer tourists a place to stay. Most locals speak some Spanish. Accommodation tends to be rudimentary—no running water or electricity. If staying on the island, bring a flashlight and warm clothing or a sleeping bag. Families generally charge around s/10 for lodging and a little bit more for meals. It is customary to bring a gift of fruit to the family. As for food, islanders are chiefly vegetarian and limit themselves to a monotonous diet of eggs and potatoes. However, a slew of restaurants around the island can cook up seafood dishes as well. For information on transportation to the island, see **Isla Amantaní,** below.

ISLA AMANTANÍ

As pristine as Taquile is, Amantaní (pop. 4,000) is even more so and has gradually begun to cut into Taquile's share of the tourism industry. Also Quechua-speaking, Amantaní possesses its own set of customs, most notably, the beautifully embroidered shawls worn by island women.

Amantaní provides a good opportunity for dayhiking. The island is dominated by two hills each crowned by a temple, the taller hill being devoted to the **Pachatata** (Father Earth) and the shorter one to **Pachamama** (Mother Earth). No one is allowed to enter either except on the annual feast day (January 20), when the island's population splits in two, each half gathering at its own temple. A race is held from the summit of each to a designated point between them. One representative from each hill runs—if Mother Earth wins, the harvest will be a success; otherwise, the coming year will be stricken with scarcity. Pachamama always seems to end up victorious. Like Taquile, accommodation is basic and arranged by local families as boats arrive in the morning. Room and board normally costs about s/10, and some gift of food is expected. Unlike Taquile, very few restaurants exist on Amantaní, so you will probably eat whatever your family prepares.

Transportation: Lanchas (motorboats) to Taquile and Amantaní leave the port in Puno early in the morning (4hr., 8am, s/10). Boats returning to Puno leave each island around 2pm. A few boats travel between the two islands during the morning only. Puno agencies can also arrange transportation and accommodation for the two islands (sometimes combined with a tour of Los Uros) and charge as little as s/35 for a two-day trip, but only independent travelers can ensure that their money goes directly to the islanders. The services offered by tour agencies are not particularly special anyway—they use ordinary transportation and arrange lodging upon arriving on the islands, just as any regular traveler would.

CUSCO AND THE SACRED VALLEY

The Inca empire was founded in Cusco around AD 1100 by the first Inca, Manco Capac, both a historic and mythic figure. Legend has it that after the creator god Wiraccocha relieved the world from darkness by pulling the heavenly bodies out of Lake Titicaca (see p. 120), he created the first Incas in the same place. These were the four Ayar brothers—Manco Capac being the eldest—who together with their wives were called the Children of the Sun. Wiraccocha endowed them with a magical golden staff, the Tupayauri, a necessary tool for completing their mission: to found the capital of a new and powerful empire, the place where the mystical Tupayauri could be plunged fully into the earth. The four brothers walked many mountains and valleys, poking the ground with their Tupayauri every which way they went, but never seeing the sign. Along the way, the three youngest brothers misbehaved or otherwise got themselves turned to stone, leaving Manco Capac (and his brothers' wives) to search for the promised imperial ground themselves. They reached a fertile valley where the rivers Sapphi and Tullumayu flowed. Manco thrust his golden Tupayauri into the earth: when it was swallowed whole, Manco knew he had found his city. He called it "Qosco," or "Navel of the World."

The above may sound like a plausible history of Cusco, but more gullible people insist that the following story be told. Cusco was founded by a man named Manco Capac around AD 1100, but the Incas were just one of many small Andean states vying for control. Things changed in 1438 when the soon-to-become ninth Inca Pachacuti defeated the fierce Chanka people, opening the way for a massive expansion of the empire. Cusco became the center of Inca Perú, the building ground of great palaces and temples, and an administrative and religious headquarters. However, Pachacuti's influence extended far beyond his darling capital. The Pachacuti era saw the construction of great military and religious complexes at Pisac and Ollantaytambo, not to mention the extraordinary city of Machu Picchu—whose exact history still remains a tantalizing mystery. All of this took place alongside the Río Urubamba, an area now commonly known as the Sacred Valley. The valley's resplendent hills kept the Inca's dinner table overflowing with maize, fruit, and vegetables. Pachacuti kept the region surrounding Cusco under his sway with a shrewd policy of cultural unification: through language (Quechua), extraordinary public works projects, and an elaborately ritualistic religion.

Today, the name "Cusco" applies both to the city and its department. Not unlike Inca times, the region continues to revolve closely around its capital, but now the connection is based on a thriving tourist industry. A stay in Cusco is mandatory for anyone intending to explore the valley's many treasures, usually accessible as day-trips. Indeed, the city has become so tourist-friendly that it becomes hard not to spend all of one's time there. But the undeniable comforts of Cusco (the city) should not dissuade anyone from spending time in Cusco (the department). Extended stays in the serene Sacred Valley allow visitors to observe a relaxed lifestyle that the hustle and bustle of tourism still hasn't managed to corrupt.

CUSCO

Despite the popular mythology surrounding Manco Capac, Cusco owes most of its early development to the great Inca Pachacuti (Quechua for "Transformer"). Under his reign, Cusco supposedly took on the shape of a puma—a symbol of courage and commitment—with its head at the fortress of Sacsayhuaman, its heart in the main plaza, and its tail at the end of the sacred Qorikancha complex. Cusco thus became the capital of Tawantinsuyo, the vast empire that, in subsequent years, would stretch from southern Colombia to Chile and Argentina. However, with expansion also came division. The two sons of 11th Inca Huayna Capac waged civil war against each other, Huáscar in Cusco and Atahuallpa in the second capital of Quito. The Cusco faction lost, leaving the city in despair, but when a strange man named Pizarro landed on the coast and executed the usurping Inca Atahuallpa (then resting in Cajamarca), many in Cusco thought they were saved.

And so began the Spanish conquest of Perú. Francisco Pizarro entered the city a hero in 1533, looted Cusco's temples, and installed the puppet Inca Manco Capac II. Some of the best accounts of the epoch come from Garcilaso de la Vega, son of a Spanish conquistador and Inca noblewoman, who left for Spain at the age of 21 and wrote his *Comentarios Reales de Los Incas*. When Manco realized that the Spanish weren't leaving, he amassed an army of 150,000 and, in 1563, attacked the the colonists. During the siege, the Inca's army set fire to the city's thatched roofs, leaving Cusco in ruins. Manco's subsequent defeat at Sacsayhuaman sent him retreating to the jungle at Vilcabamba, the last capital of a then-shrunken empire. In 1572, after a number of costly attempts, the Spanish finally took Vilcabamba, bringing back the very last Inca, Tupac Amaru, whom they beheaded in the Cusco Plaza de Armas, extinguishing the once-great Inca empire for good.

HIGHLIGHTS OF CUSCO

- Cusco's **cathedral** (p. 133) is one of the best colonial churches in Perú.
- The **Museo Inka** (see p. 135) demands an afternoon of scrutiny.
- The fortress of **Sacsayhuaman** (p. 141) inspires awe with its huge stone ramparts.
- It's hard to spend less than a few hours in one of the city's soothing **cafes** (p. 132).
- Who *doesn't* want a hat with ten llamas knit into it? Go **shopping** (p. 138).
- Finally, a **club scene** (p. 138) that loves backpackers for themselves.

After smashing the Inca resistance, the Spanish let Cusco slip into colonial obscurity, a city with neither political nor economic significance. It briefly attracted attention in 1780 when the *mestizo* José Gabriel Condorcanqui, calling himself Tupac Amaru II, led a bloody rebellion out of Cusco. Like his namesake, though, he was defeated and horrifically executed in the Plaza de Armas.

Despite this long legacy of greatness, drama, violence, and tragedy, Cusco had was practically forgotten by the rest of the world until the American Hiram Bing-

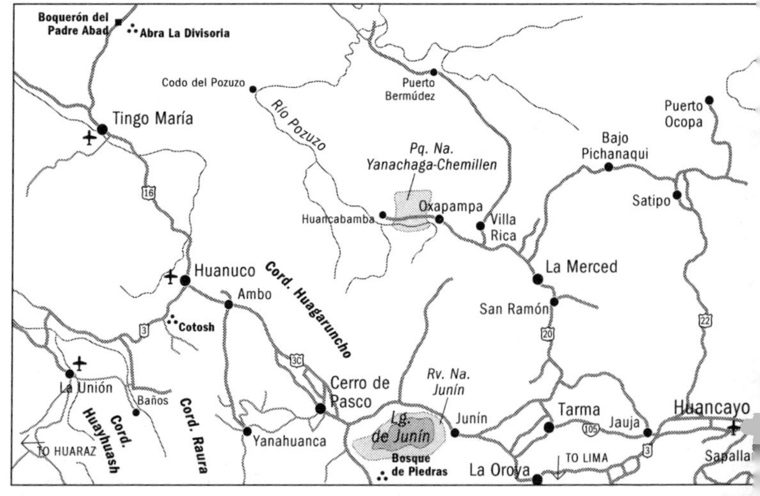

ham "discovered" Machu Picchu in 1911. The beautiful, enigmatic sacred city—untouched by the Spaniards (who were ignorant of its existence)—attracted armies of archaeologists and tourists, and consequently money. Cusco is now considered the archaeological capital of South America. It lies within a short distance of Machu Picchu and numerous other Inca treasures of the Sacred Valley—a region commanding awe for its exceptional natural beauty. But the city itself is exceptional and crawls with imperial legends hidden within the big, solemn stones comprising its Inca foundations. Earthquakes in 1650 and 1950 knocked down many of the Spanish constructions that had previously obscured this perfect stonework. Now *cusqueños* display their Inca facades with pride.

At 3400m high, Cusco is cold, especially during the sunny months of May to September. In rainy season, it's a bit warmer—but then again, it's raining. (Besides the weather, many visitors also notice a distinct lack of oxygen and develop mild altitude sickness.) The tourist business is lively year-round, but English speakers become impossible to avoid in July and August. Nevertheless, this is when nocturnal life in Cusco becomes its most energetic and begins to rival that of Lima.

ORIENTATION

Most everything in Cusco revolves around the **Plaza de Armas** with its two churches, **La Catedral** and **La Compañia.** The cathedral is slightly larger, with big front steps. The main avenue, **Av. Sol,** runs out of a corner of the Plaza de Armas towards the **airport,** the **terminal terrestre,** and **Huanchac train station** (sending trains to Puno and Arequipa). The other train station, **San Pedro,** located in the western part of town, sends trains to **Machu Picchu.**

Strict vigilance must be practiced over all valuables whenever in public, especially in crowded areas. While in the past, thievery in Cusco has been of a nonviolent nature, the city has recently experienced a rash of **strangle muggings.** These nighttime robbers work in gangs, and can, with alarming speed, find the right pressure point in the neck to knock someone unconscious. The victim wakes up seconds later stripped of all valuables, but otherwise unharmed. Men and women, even in groups, are advised to take a taxi after dark and not pay the driver until the front door of their hostel is opened.

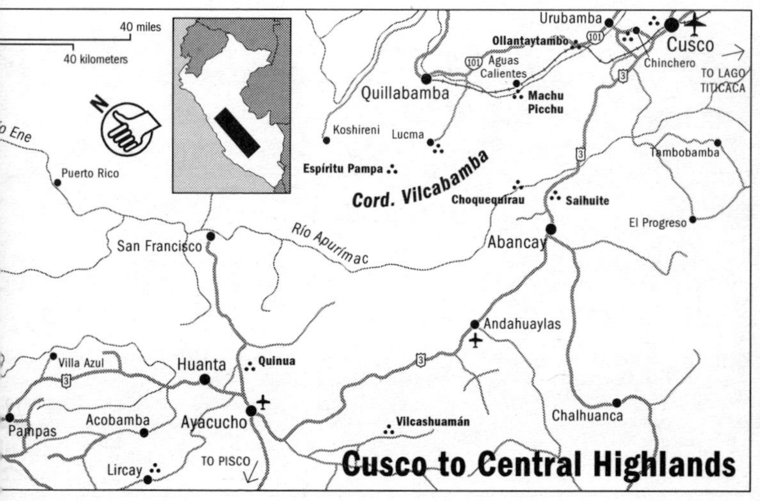

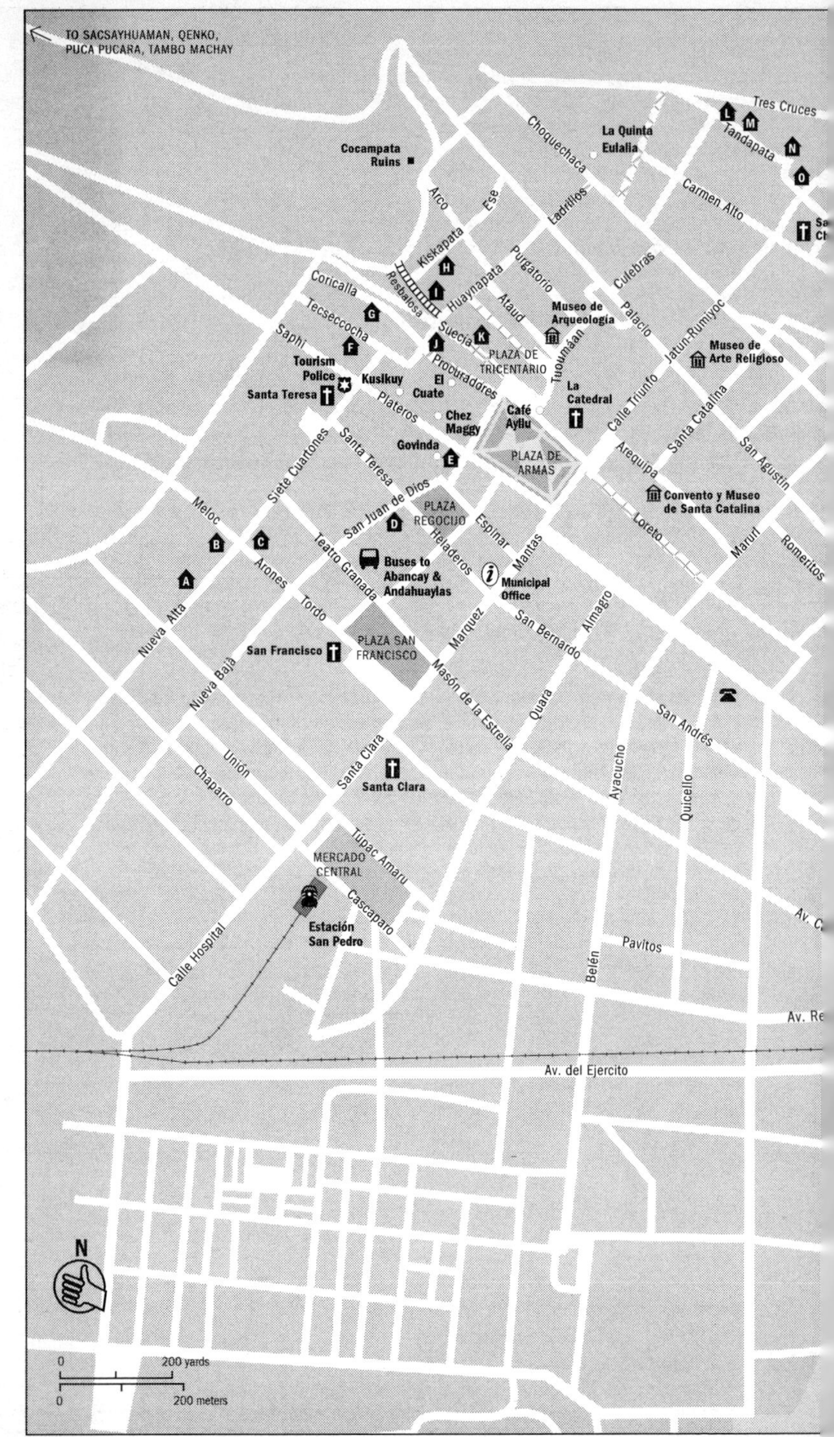
TO SACSAYHUAMAN, QENKO, PUCA PUCARA, TAMBO MACHAY
Cocampata Ruins
La Quinta Eulalia
Tres Cruces
Tandapata
Carmen Alto
Choquechaca
Arco
Ese
Ladrillos
Kiskapata
Resbalosa
Huaynapata
Purgatorio
Cuebras
Coricalla
Tecseccocha
Saphi
Suecia
Ataud
Museo de Arqueología
Palacio
Jatun-Rumiyoc
Museo de Arte Religioso
Tourism Police
Kusikuy
El Cuate
Procuradores
PLAZA DE TRICENTARIO
Tucumán
La Catedral
Santa Teresa
Plateros
Chez Maggy
Café Ayllu
Calle Triunfo
Santa Catalina
San Agustín
Govinda
PLAZA DE ARMAS
Arequipa
Siete Cuartones
Santa Teresa
San Juan de Dios
PLAZA REGOCIJO
Espinar
Convento y Museo de Santa Catalina
Meloc
Loreto
Maruri
Romeritos
Heladeros
Mantas
Teatro Granada
Buses to Abancay & Andahuaylas
Municipal Office
Arones
Tordo
Nueva Alta
San Bernardo
Almagro
Marquez
PLAZA SAN FRANCISCO
San Francisco
Nueva Baja
Masón de la Estrella
Quara
San Andrés
Unión
Chaparro
Santa Clara
Santa Clara
Ayacucho
Quicello
Túpac Amaru
MERCADO CENTRAL
Cascaparo
Estación San Pedro
Calle Hospital
Pavitos
Belén
Av. del Ejercito
N
0
200 yards
0
200 meters

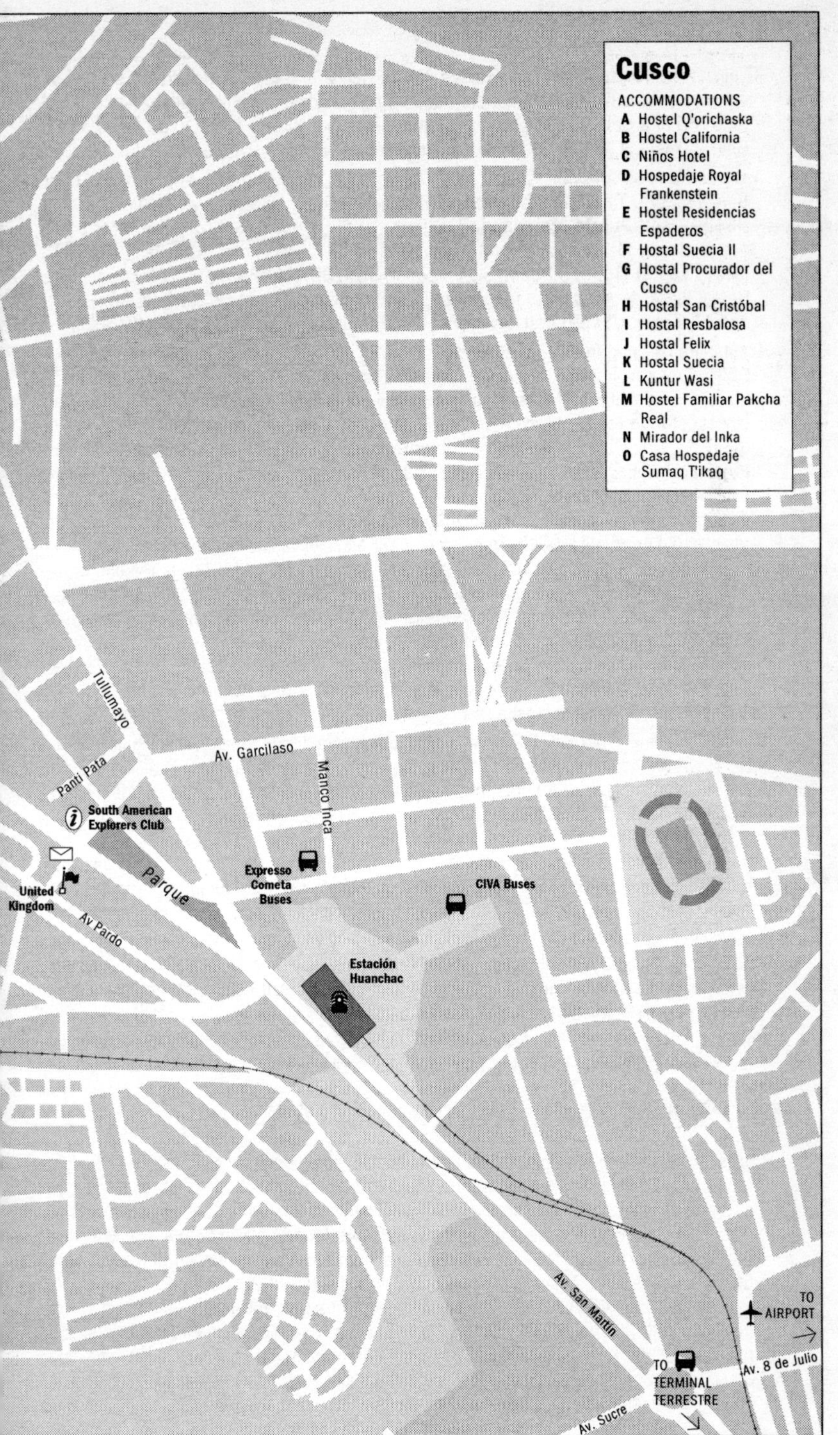
Cusco
ACCOMMODATIONS
A Hostel Q'orichaska
B Hostel California
C Niños Hotel
D Hospedaje Royal Frankenstein
E Hostel Residencias Espaderos
F Hostal Suecia II
G Hostal Procurador del Cusco
H Hostal San Cristóbal
I Hostal Resbalosa
J Hostal Felix
K Hostal Suecia
L Kuntur Wasi
M Hostel Familiar Pakcha Real
N Mirador del Inka
O Casa Hospedaje Sumaq T'ikaq
Tullumayo
Av. Garcilaso
Manco Inca
Panti Pata
South American Explorers Club
United Kingdom
Parque
Av Pardo
Expresso Cometa Buses
CIVA Buses
Estación Huanchac
Av. San Martin
TO AIRPORT
TO TERMINAL TERRESTRE
Av. 8 de Julio
Av. Sucre

TRANSPORTATION

Airport: Aeropuerto Alejandro Velasco Astete (tel. 222 611), located in the southeastern part of the city. Take one of the frequent *colectivos* along Sol marked "*Aeropuerto*" (s/0.50) or a taxi (s/3). Flights go to **Lima, Arequipa, Puerto Maldonado,** and **La Paz,** Bolivia. There is an international **departure tax** (US$10).

Airlines: AeroContinente, Carnes 254 (tel. 243 031), in Plaza de Armas. Open daily 8am-7:30pm. To: **Lima** (7 per day 7:30am-12:30pm, US$79); **Arequipa** (7:30am, US$59); and **Puerto Maldonado** (7:30am, US$59). **Tans,** Sol 526 (tel. 246 512), sends planes to **Lima** (7:20 and 11am, US$44-59). **LAB,** Prado 675 (tel. 222 990), flies to **La Paz** (Tu, Th 9:30am, Sa 11:20am; US$100). **LANPerú** (tel. 255 555), in the Hostal Plaza de Armas on the Plaza de Armas, travels to **Lima** (7:20, 8:20am, 12:10, and 12:35pm; US$59) and **Arequipa** (12:35pm, US$53). Open M-Sa 8:45am-7pm.

Trains: Trains chug from 2 different stations in town. The **Estación San Pedro** (tel. 224 552), 7 blocks from the Plaza de Armas walking along Mantas, Márquez, and Santa Clara, sells tickets to **Machu Picchu** (window open 8-11am and 3-4pm). For now, the closest station (called Machu Picchu) is at Aguas Calientes, from which buses run to the ruins. Trains also make stops in **Ollantaytambo.** One **local train** leaves for **Machu Picchu** (5hr., 6:30am, s/13-15) and stops at kilometer 88, at the start of the Inca Trail. **Tourist trains** to **Machu Picchu** consist of small *autovagons* (3½hr., every day 6 and 9am, US$55 round-trip). **Turismo Inka** (US$45 round-trip), **Pullman** (US$34 round-trip), and **Económico** (s/55 round-trip) cars also go to **Machu Picchu** (4hr., M-Sa 6:25am for all 3 companies). The **Estación Huanchac** (tel. 233 593), at the end of Av. Sol, sells tickets to **Puno** and **Arequipa** (M-F 7am-noon and 2-5pm, Sa 7am-noon, Su 8-10am). **Turismo Inka** (US$23), **Pullman** (US$19), and **Económico** (s/25) cars go to **Puno** (11hr.; M, W, F, and Sa 8am for all 3 companies). **Económico** cars leave for **Arequipa** (23hr.; M, W, F, and Sa 8am; s/40), as do **Pullman** cars (same times, US$29) with a stop in **Juliaca** (US$19). **Reservations** for all trains should be made 1 day in advance, especially in high season.

Buses: Conveniently, a new **terminal terrestre** has been opened several km southeast of the Plaza de Armas at the end of Sol (s/3 by taxi). Buses go to: **Lima** (24-30hr., 6 per day, s/50-60); **Arequipa** (12-13hr., 4 per day, s/20-25); **Ica** (22hr., 3 per day, s/50-55); **Nazca** (18hr.); **La Paz** (12-18hr., 8 per day, US$15); **Abancay** (5hr., 7 per day, s/12); **Juliaca** (9hr., 7 per day, s/15); **Puno** (9hr., 3 per day, s/15); **Quillabamba** (8hr., 8am and 5:30pm, s/15); **Andahuaylas** (11hr., 6am and 6pm, s/23); and **Copacabana** (4 per day, s/25-30). One major company has a separate *terminal*: **Cruz del Sur,** Pachacutec 303 and Huáscar (tel. 248 146), serves meals and plays bingo on heated buses to **Lima** (27hr., 4 per day, s/80), via **Arequipa** (12hr., s/40).

Taxis: (Tel. 222 222). Taxis surround the Plaza de Armas. They are a bit more expensive when called ahead of time. From the airport s/6. From the *terminal terrestre* s/4. Between most points in the city s/2, after 10pm s/3. Private hire s/15 per hr.

Colectivos: They run along Sol, Pardo, and Tullumayu (s/0.50). *Colectivos* to Pisac, Chinchero, and Urubamba run along Tullumayu 7am-6pm.

PRACTICAL INFORMATION

Tourist Information: Municipal Office, Mantas 188 and Heladeros (tel. 263 176), facing Iglesia La Merced. A very friendly, sometimes English-speaking staff offers free advice and maps of Cusco and the Inca Trail. They also sell tourist tickets (see p. 133). Open M-F 8am-6:30pm, Sa 8am-2pm. **South American Explorers Club,** Sol 930 and Garcilaso (tel./fax 223 102; email saec@wayna.rcp.net.pe), 6 blocks down Sol from the Plaza de Armas. This mighty non-profit organization of Latin America enthusiasts opened a Cusco clubhouse in June 1999. Members are welcome to this pretty little house to take advantage of the SAEC's many resources: recommendation lists, trip reports, bulletin boards, luggage storage, safe boxes, library, book exchange, and free email (at above address). The SAEC holds mail for members at Apartado 500, Cusco, Perú. Membership costs US$40 for individuals, US$70 for couples.

Consulates: United Kingdom, Pardo 895 and Garcilaso (tel. 226 671). Open M-F 9am-1pm and 3-6pm. **United States,** Tullumayo 127 (tel. 224 112). Open M-F 8am-noon and 3-6pm.

ATMs: Cusco *does* prefer Visa. **Banco Continental,** Sol 352 and Puluchapata, has a Visa ATM. **Banco de Crédito,** Sol 189 and Almagro, and **Bancosur,** Sol 459 and Arrayan-niyoq, have Visa/Plus **ATMs.** The 1 beacon of hope for MC/Cirrus users is **Banco Latino,** Sol 395 and Puluchapata.

Supermarket: Buy snacks for the Inca Trail at **El Chinito,** Sol and Almagro, or the larger **El Chinito Grande,** Matar 271 and Ayacucho. Both open daily 8am-2pm and 3-8pm.

Tourist Safety: Tourism Police, Saphy 510 and Siete Cuartones (tel. 232 221). English spoken. Open 24hr. To file complaints against fraudulent businesses or seek help if robbed, see the **Tourist Protection Bureau,** Carrizos 250 (tel. 252 974; **24hr. emergency** tel. (01) 224 78 88), on Plaza de Armas. English spoken. Open daily 8am-8pm.

Hospitals: Hospital Regional (**emergency** tel. 223 691), Av. de la Cultura, can send an ambulance. For medical complaints, visit **Clínica Pardo,** Av. de la Cultura 710 (tel. 240 387). **Dr. Oscar Tejada** (tel. 233 836) is available for emergencies 24hr.

Dentist: Dr. Virginia Valcarel Velarde, Panes 123 (tel. 231 558, **emergency** tel. 246 220), in the Plaza de Armas.

Post Office: Serpost (tel. 224 212), Sol and Garcilaso, 5 blocks from the Plaza de Armas. Fax services available. Open M-Sa 8am-8pm, Su 8am-2pm.

Internet Access: A number of cafes and bars (see below) have a cyber spin, but your typing may compete with loud music. For more no-nonsense bonding with email, try **Internet Station,** Teqsicocha 400. Access s/3 per hr. Open daily 8:30am-midnight. **Telser,** Medio 225 (tel. 242 424), off the Plaza de Armas. Charges s/4 per hr., s/3 per hr. 6:30-10am and 9pm-1am. Open daily 6:30am-1am.

TELEPHONE CODE: 084

ACCOMMODATIONS

Cusco swells with over 100 different hotels, hostels, *albergues*, and *casas de hospedaje*. Nevertheless, spaces fill quickly during the festival of **Inti Raymi** in late June, and during much of July and August. Reservations during the high season should be made, confirmed, and reconfirmed.

AROUND THE PLAZA DE ARMAS

The location can't be beat, but few truly good deals can be found. Beware of the *cusqueño* enemy to peaceful slumber: the all-night *disco-pub* on the second floor.

Hostal Suecia II, Teqsicocha 465 (tel. 239 757). Make a left at the top of Procuradores and follow the street around the corner. Cushier than the original (see below). A freshly painted inside courtyard invites with comfortable seating and leafy plants. Rooms are similarly welcoming, featuring neatly tiled bathrooms with hot water. Singles s/20, with bath s/30; doubles s/30, with bath s/50; triples s/45, with bath s/70.

Hostal Suecia, Suecia 332 (tel. 233 282), owned by the same people as Suecia II around the corner. Simple rooms surround a plant-filled courtyard and share communal hot-water baths. Dorms s/14 per person; singles s/20; doubles s/30; triples s/51.

Hostal Felix, Teqsicocha 171 (tel. 241 949), conveniently located right at the top of Procuradores. Hostal Felix can feel like a giant cave, probably because of the (literally) tons of exposed stone wall in this ancient house. Several rooms also preserve the wall-o'-boulders motif, softened a bit by a fireplace and furnishings. Decent bathrooms have hot water most of the time. Singles s/15, with bath s/20; doubles s/20, with bath s/24; triples s/30, with bath s/33.

Hostal Residencias Espaderos, Espaderos 136 (tel. 238 894), an adequate and cheap option for those who want to be very close to the Plaza de Armas. Dimly-lit rooms with old beds open onto a somewhat rustic courtyard. Hot water 6am-1pm and 4-8pm in communal baths. Singles s/13; doubles s/20; triples s/30; quads s/40.

Maison de la Tennesse (HI); (tel. 235 617), 5th block of Sol, on a little street slightly removed from the avenue. A tidy, family-run link in the worldwide HI web. Rooms may be a little cramped given the price, but everything's clean, the owners are nice, water runs hot 24hr., and guests can cook in the kitchen. HI membership not strictly necessary. Rooms US$8 per person, with bath US$10.

AROUND PLAZA REGOCIJO

Plenty of cheap beds lurk in charming colonial houses on the streets around this plaza, one block over from the Plaza de Armas. Shop around on Nueva Alta, Siete Cuartones, and Tambo de Montero.

Niños Hotel, Meloq 442 and Siete Cuartones (tel. 231 424; email ninos@correo.dnet.com.pe; www.targetfound.nl/ninos), 3 blocks from the Plaza de Armas. Started by a Dutch woman in 1998, revenues go toward caring for 12 little boys she found living on the street who now live with her. Large rooms surrounding a courtyard are painted with art deco furnishings, and bear the name of a boy and/or sponsor. Brand-new baths run hot water 24hr. A chic cafe-bar serves breakfast (s/5-10) and *sangría* (s/3.50). Look out for a Niños restaurant newly opened in summer 1999. Singles US$10, with bath US$15; doubles US$20, with bath US$25; triples with bath US$35.

Hostal California, Nueva Alta 444 and Meloq (tel./fax 242 997), 4 blocks from the Plaza de Armas. This beautiful old house with a sunny inner patio has a hot-water bath inside every room. Mattresses are a bit floppy, but guests have kitchen privileges. Dorms s/15 per person; doubles s/20-25.

Hostal Q'orichaska, Nueva Alta 458 (tel. 228 974). Plain, dimly-lit rooms surround the flower pots and seating area of the inner courtyard. Beds and furniture are a bit old, but there's an open kitchen. Clean bathrooms have 24hr. hot water. Breakfast included with price of room. US$5 per person, with bath US$7.

Hospedaje Royal Frankenstein, San Juan de Dios 260 (tel. 236 999), just off Plaza Regocijo. "Cold, dark rooms. German owned. What can you expect?" A jolly, multilingual staff maintains squeaky clean bedrooms and baths with electrically heated showers. Lively sitting rooms and a social kitchen can be found alongside near-windowless rooms dubbed "Mary Shelley" and "Frank 'n' Stoned." Handwash your clothes for free on the soaring roof, or send smellies away to the laundromat for s/3.50. Newcomers receive a free drink at Kamikaze (see p. 138). Singles US$10; doubles US$20, with bath US$30; triples US$30. Prices are often halved, so call ahead to find out.

SAN CRISTÓBAL

Calle Resbalosa ("Slippery Street"), a pedestrian stairway leading uphill from the top of Suecia (which in turn leads uphill from the Plaza de Armas), has some of the best hostels in this neighborhood. The following places are a bit of a hike, but the strenuous effort is rewarded by the outstanding vistas that take in the entire valley—including snow-capped Ausangate on clear days. Furthermore, prices are relatively low. On the downside, personal attacks have been reported in the area. Taxis and caution should be taken at night.

Hostal Resbalosa, Resbalosa 494 (tel. 240 461), on the right when scaling the slippery stairs on Resbalosa. Nice rooms with parquet floors and big windows. Shiny, clean baths run 24hr. hot water. The upstairs sunroom offers an astoundingly good view. Singles s/10; doubles s/25, with bath s/30; triples s/30, with bath s/36.

Hostal San Cristóbal, Kiscapata 242 (tel. 223 942). Make a right halfway up Resbalosa. A ramshackle but pleasant place run by a couple of sweet older ladies. Some rooms have great vistas, as does an upstairs terrace. Hot water most of the time. Communal kitchen. Rooms range from 1-6 beds, but always cost s/10 per person.

Hostal Procurador del Cusco, Coricalle 425 (tel. 243 559), on a narrow street 2 blocks over and parallel to Resbalosa. Spacious rooms usually with shared baths and 24hr. hot water. A pleasant, sunlit room and upstairs terrace take in the usual great views. Singles s/15; doubles s/30; triples s/40, with bath s/60; quads s/60.

SAN BLAS

This attractive whitewashed neighborhood on the hill behind the cathedral, a five-minute walk from the Plaza de Armas, is one of the quietest places to lodge. Recently the area has exploded with *casas familiares de hospedaje*, small family-run hostels where hospitality is included in the (slightly higher) price. While San Blas is one of the nicest places in town, it can become unpleasantly shady and secluded at night. Again, it's a good idea to take a taxi.

Hostal Familiar Pakcha Real, Tandapata 300 (tel. 237 484), one of the many family-run hostels on the street but cheaper than the others. Clean rooms go alongside clean baths which steam with 24hr. hot water. Kitchen privileges, sitting rooms, and a family dog round out the deal. Rooms s/15 per person, with bath s/20.

Kuntur Wasi, Tandapata 352-A (tel. 227 570). A very warm 3-generation family runs this clean, safe *casa de hospedaje* at the end of the street from Plaza San Blas. Comfy beds lend themselves to long nights of peaceful slumber. Bathrooms have electric showers. US$5 per person, with bath US$10.

Casa Hospedaje Sumaq T'ikaq, Tandapata 114 (tel. 229 127), a few paces from Plaza San Blas. A very outgoing landlady takes exceptional care of her visitors, serving a generous *desayuno* on the quiet patio (breakfast included in the price). Spacious rooms come with hot-water baths. The kitchen is open for guests' use. US$10 per person.

Hostal Choquechaka, Choquechaka 436B (tel. 237 265), is one of the cheaper options among other inexpensive choices on the same street. Decent rooms with 1-4 beds share the slightly dingy common baths, which have 24hr. hot water. A small kitchen has a stove. Rooms s/10 per person.

Mirador del Inka, Tandapata 160 (tel. 261 384). Extremely kind owners guarantee a safe and well-kept place to lodge. A number of courtyards and ancient walls add to the charm of this family-run hostel. US$5 per person, with bath US$15.

CUSCO AREA

FOOD

Cusco tempts the diner with a wide variety of cuisines. On **Espaderos, Plateros,** and **Procuradores** (a.k.a. Gringo Alley) alone, a multitude of tastes—Asian, Mexican, Italian, Peruvian, vegetarian—can find fulfillment at lower prices than elsewhere around the Plaza de Armas. Nevertheless, many Peruvians would not pay even these "low" prices for food, so expect foreign company. Should the choice between eateries seem impossible, roaming waiters with menus practice their English by trying to lure you. For traditional flavors, look farther afield to restaurants with less tourist packaging. Aside from *cuy* and *trucha* dishes, Cusco is known for its *lechón* (roast suckling pig) and *rocoto relleno* (chili pepper stuffed with meat, vegetables, and spices, and then fried in dough).

Chez Maggy, Plateros 339 (tel. 232 478). One of Cusco's many classic pizzerias, this small restaurant is a crossroads for wacky waiters, itinerant musicians, and travelers of every size, shape, origin, and ilk. Long tables necessitate elbow jostling and conversation with said travelers. Vague menu descriptions necessitate talking with said waiters. Everybody enjoys the freshly made pizzas (small s/10-12) and exquisite dessert *panqueques* (s/5-6). Because such merriment couldn't be contained, another pizzeria and a trattoria have sprouted on Procuradores. Open daily 11am-4pm and 6pm-midnight.

Govinda, Espaderos 128 (tel. 252 723). Hare Krishna in inspiration, vegetarian in cuisine, and very mellow in outlook. Experience spiritual uplift with their 2 pages of fruit salads and many yogurt dishes (s/5-7). *Arroz a la cabana* combines a tofu filet with rice and fried banana. Every meal should be accompanied with a piece of wholewheat *pan integral* (s/0.50). Open daily 8am-10pm.

Green's, Tandapata 700 (tel. 651 332), behind the church in Plaza San Blas. A very cosmopolitan European enclave in the center of San Blas, Green's is decorated with colorful abstraction. And with plentiful candles and a fireplace, Green's 2 rooms may be the warmest in all of Cusco. Soft couches, backgammon, and chess sets entertain insatiable loungers. For those who want to ingest more than ambiance, the menu serves a couple of subtle and satisfying steaks, chicken dishes, and curries (s/13-18). Reserve ahead of time for the Sunday roast: a feast of chicken, potatoes, vegetables, wine, and hot apple pie (s/25). Open daily noon-midnight. Food served noon-3pm and 6-11pm.

La Quinta Eulalia, Choquechaka 384 (tel. 241 380). With tented outdoor seating in the courtyard, metal tables and chairs, Andean music, a chalkboard menu, and crowing roosters, it doesn't get much more authentic than this. Specializing in *cuy* (s/20), *lechón* (s/14), and *rocoto relleno* (s/8), La Quinta Eulalia has served faithful locals *comida criolla* since 1941. Open daily 11am-6pm.

Kin Taro, Heladeros 149 (tel. 226 181), off Plaza Regocijo. It's probably for the best that they don't have sushi, but Kin Taro prepares a splendid array of *cooked* Japanese dishes, from terriyakies (s/10-15) to vegetarian tofu items. Open M-Sa noon-10pm.

Al Grano, Santa Catalina Ancha 398 (tel. 228 032), around the corner from the cathedral. A successful experiment in Pan-Asian cuisine, Al Grano rotates a menu that often features vegetarian curries, identified by country of origin and accompanied by chutney, yogurt with cucumber, peanut sauce, bread, and rice (s/13.50), none of which is too spicy. Open M-Sa 10am-9pm.

Kusikuy, Plateros 348 (tel. 262 870), A popular first testing ground for Peruvian dishes, Kusikuy specializes in *cuy al horno* (s/38), which emerges from the kitchen after an hour wearing a little hat of tomatoes and greeted by flashing cameras. None of the other dishes are nearly that elaborate (or expensive). *Trucha* (s/17-19), *bistec* (s/15-22), and sandwiches (s/4-6). Open M-Sa 8am-10:30pm, Su 7-10:30pm.

El Cuate, Procuradores 386 (tel. 227 003). Connoisseurs might scoff at the abundance of *papas fritas,* but El Cuate is good, cheap, and mostly Mexican. Enchiladas of all sorts (s/11-14) and burritos (s/8-13) are available. Open daily M-Su 11am-midnight.

CAFES

The foreign invasion of Cusco has made the brewing, selling, and consumption of java top priority. Those who had been suffering under a cruel addiction to coffee essences and Nescafé in more rural parts of Perú will find nirvana in Cusco. By day, cafes serve delicious breakfasts, sandwiches, and fruit salads. By night, they turn into smoky, multilingual dens for debate over variations in Quechua pronunciation and the moral implications of hiking the Inca Trail.

Many a coffee-drinker, however, has been converted by the discovery of *mate de coca,* a tea made from the coca leaf held so sacred by the Incas. Some may hope that the leaf has some of the same effects as its derivative, cocaine, but as a number of t-shirts will remind you: "Coca is not a drug!" Instead it is a mild stimulant, reputed to relieve altitude sickness.

La Tertulia, Procuradores 44, 2nd floor (tel. 241 422), makes a serious bid for the best breakfasts in town. Choose from a list of pancakes or the all-you-can-eat buffet of eggs, fruit, yogurt, granola, whole-wheat bread, and coffee (s/10-11). Salads, pizzas, Peruvian dishes, and fondue available. Also the home of the Amauta cultural center, which occasionally sponsors live performances. Open daily 6:30am-3pm and 3-11pm.

Café Ayllu, Carnes 208 (tel. 232 357), on the Plaza de Armas next to the cathedral, attracts both locals and tourists by offering cheerful and speedy service to the tune of classical music. Sip Ayllu's delicious coffee, cocoa, and steamed milk (s/2-5), or fill up on eggs and omelettes (s/6-10). Open M-Sa 6:30am-11pm, Su 6:30am-1:30pm.

Café Varayoc, Espaderos 142 (tel. 232 404), a small, smoky cafe-bar ideal for writing postcards while drinking *mate de coca.* Sandwiches (s/4-10) and cheese fondue (s/30) are on the menu, and there's a window of tasty deserts. Open daily 8am-11pm.

El Buen Pastor, Cuesta San Blas 579 (tel. 240 586), in San Blas. This bakery has a small seating area with few fancy touches, but entices with an exceptional array of pastries, croissants, and *empanadas* at a *sol* or 2 apiece. The coffee goes down even better knowing that all profits go towards an orphanage for girls. Open daily 7am-8pm.

Planeta Sur, Plateros 364. Good, medium-volume music and some reading materials accompany the computers in this small cyber-cafe (email s/4 per hr.). Crepes s/6-7, good coffee s/4-6, and should one receive an especially heartbreaking email, there's a good selection of liquors behind the bar. Open M-Sa 9am-midnight, Su 4pm-midnight.

SIGHTS

Serious time spent sightseeing in Cusco requires the purchase of a **tourist ticket** (*boleto turístico;* US$10, student US$5). In general, carrying an ISIC card entitles students to significant discounts in museums and tour agencies. The tourist ticket includes admission to the cathedral, the Iglesia de San Blas, the Museo de Arte Religioso del Arzobispado, the Museo de Arte y Monasterio de Santa Catalina, the site museum of the Qorikancha, the Museo Municipal de Arte Contemporáneo, the Museo Histórico Regional (Casa Garcilaso), and the nearby ruins of Sacsayhuaman, Qenco, Puca Pucara, Tambomachay, Pisac, Ollantaytambo, Chinchero, Tipón, and Pikillacta. The ticket *does not* include admission to the part of the Qorikancha belonging to the Convento de Santo Domingo (the best part), the Convento de la Merced, or the Museo Inka at the Casa del Almirante. Paying individual entrance fees is not allowed, but one can buy a **partial ticket** (*boleto parcial*) for just museums/churches or just ruins (each US$6, no student discount). All tickets are available at the **OFEC office** (tel. 226 919), Garcilaso and Heladeros, on Plaza Regocijo, or at the **tourist office** (see above), and sometimes at the sights themselves. Aside from tremendous Inca walls, many of the city's museums also feature paintings from the **Cusco School.** This prominent colonial school of art lasted 200 years and included *mestizo* as well as indigenous painters. As a result of this mixed heritage, even paintings on Christian themes incorporate a great deal of Andean symbolism. Common examples of such syncretism include backgrounds painted with local flora and fauna, and biblical figures wearing Inca costumes.

CATHEDRAL

Plaza de Armas. Open M-Sa 10-11:30am and 2-5:30pm, Su 2-5:30pm. Admission with tourist ticket only.

Built upon the foundations of the Inca Wiraccocha's palace, Cusco's cathedral took nearly a century to complete after it was begun in 1550. The church sustained serious damage in the earthquake of 1986; some parts are still blocked off or obscured by scaffolding. Although in need of restoration, the cathedral is fascinating in its subtle incorporation of Inca symbolism (explained by the large number of indigenous craftspeople who helped build it). The temple also boasts a collection of several hundred paintings from the Cusco School.

CAPILLA DE LA SAGRADA FAMILIA. Tourists enter through the Capilla de la Sagrada Familia. Passing into the central basilica, one can see the Renaissance-style main altar covered in silver plating. Next to it sits the notorious **Last Supper** attributed to **Marcos Zapata** of the Cusco School. A *mestizo* artist of the 18th century, Zapata borrowed from sacred Inca feasts when he made Christ's Last Supper a guinea-pig roast. Farther back from the altar resides the cathedral's finely carved wooden choir, considered one of the best in America. The choir was used as a didactic tool for the evangelization of the natives. Curiously, each seat has an armrest supported by the pregnant-bellied carving of the **Pachamama,** the Inca Earth goddess—yet another example of indigenous artistry. Mother Earth must have provided some diversion during those long hours of mass, considering certain well-rubbed parts of her anatomy.

CAPILLA DEL TRIUNFO. Passing into the Capilla del Triunfo, next door, one encounters the **Altar of Señor de los Temblores** (Lord of the Tremor). Reputedly, a procession of this crucified Christ in the Plaza de Armas brought a swift end to the earthquake of 1650. Blackened by centuries of candle smoke, el Señor makes a repeat appearance in the plaza on the Monday of Semana Santa. His altar is a magnificent work in stone covered in gold. A number of the other altars incorporate painted carvings of Peruvian jungle fauna. In a crypt under the chapel, one can view the ashes of Garcilaso de la Vega, *mestizo* chronicler of the Incas.

El Triunfo itself was the first Christian church built in Cusco. It was the site of **Suntur Wasi,** the Inca armory where Spanish troops took refuge during Manco Inca's attack in 1536. Like the rest of the city, the Incas set it on fire, but miraculously the flames did not persist. The Spaniards reported a vision of the Virgin Mary and St. James fighting the fire back, though the Incas said it was just slaves with buckets of water. After the "miracle," the Spanish broke out and won the battle; in honor of their victory, they dragged stones from Sacsayhuaman (see p. 141) to build El Triunfo. Later, the chapel was joined to the cathedral.

QORIKANCHA AND IGLESIA DE SANTO DOMINGO

Av. Sol and Arrayan. Archaeological site museum open M-Sa 10am-6pm. Admission with tourist ticket only. Santo Domingo and Sun Temple open M-Sa 8am-6pm, Su 2-4pm. Admission s/3, students s/1. Not included in Cusco tourist ticket.

THE HISTORY. In 1533, as the Inca Atahuallpa was held prisoner in Cajamarca, his captor, Francisco Pizarro, was promised roomfuls of ransom in gold and silver to be brought from Cusco. Pizarro, becoming impatient, sent three of his men to the Inca capital to hurry matters along. These three soldiers were quickly lured by the Qorikancha ("Court of Gold"), a massive construction extending from its present site down Av. Sol to the intersection with Av. Tullumayu. This important religious center left the three ruffians drooling at the sheer quantity of its exquisite treasure. In this first visit, they looted some 3,150 pounds of pure gold plating from the walls of the temples. In subsequent trips, Pizarro and his army joined the mayhem, dumping tons of precious Inca silver and gold objects into the melting pot. At around this time, an important golden disc belonging to the Temple of the Sun mysteriously disappeared. According to one Spaniard's boasting, he pinched the disc, but then lost it in a wager later that night. Other accounts relate that the Incas hid it away for permanent safe-keeping at the bottom of Lake Titicaca.

The Dominicans then built a Baroque church on the site. In an earthquake in 1950, when much of Santo Domingo toppled, unsympathetic archaeologists cheered as the Inca foundations emerged from the rubble. Studies of the ruins and contemporary accounts now give an idea of the marvel that the Qorikancha must have been. Its walls accommodated some 4,000 priests and attendants, who made daily offerings to gods and deceased royal ancestors. The great missing golden disc once deflected morning sunlight into a sun temple lined with gold. A silver-lined moon temple also had its own silver disc. Other temples were devoted to thunder, lightning, the rainbow, and various stars. At least one room held the captured idols of conquered tribes so that if subjugated peoples ever rebelled, they would see their gods desecrated in the public plaza. The Qorikancha also acted as an astronomical observatory where priests of a learned caste, the *amautas*, plotted the solstices and equinoxes, and predicted eclipses. These were intricately tied to both sacred and agricultural practices. Indeed, the Qorikancha was the geographical center of a large zodiac wheel (the *ceque*) with 41 spokes. On these rested 327 sacred sites, each guarded by its own *ayllu*, or clan.

VISITING THE SITE. Enter through the underground site museum on Av. Sol to see a small collection of ceramics, tools, jewelry, and some interesting old photographs of Cusco. Models give an idea of what the Qorikancha used to look like.

Exit past the bathrooms to the grounds upstairs, a graveyard of Inca building blocks. The remains of a pre-Inca fountain date to AD 800.

Far more interesting (and unfortunately not included in the tourist ticket) is the part of the Qorikancha belonging to the Church of Santo Domingo. This section is commonly called the Sun Temple, although its largest surviving shrines probably belonged to the Moon and Stars. Across the courtyard from these shrines stand temples to Lightning and the Rainbow. The Qorikancha's walls, with stones ever-so-finely fitting together, provide some of the best examples of Inca masonry. In the center of the courtyard resides a large stone receptacle, formerly covered in 120 pounds of gold, which is said to have held *chicha* for the libations of the Sun God. In odd competition, the sacristy of Santo Domingo holds the church's treasures, including ornate religious vestments.

MUSEO INKA (PALACIO DEL ALMIRANTE)

Cuesta del Almirante 103 (tel. 237 380), facing the cathedral, up the path to its left. Open M-Sa 8am-5pm. Admission s/5. Not included in Cusco tourist ticket.

Beautifully organized, taking the visitor from displays on pre-Inca peoples to the rebellious years after conquest, Museo Inka is a must-see for anyone curious about Andean civilization. The Universidad Nacional de San Antonio Abad maintains the collection, a combination of didactic displays, artifacts, artwork, and more.

This informative exhibit is housed in the magnificent 17th-century Palacio del Almirante, named for its first owner, Admiral Francisco Aldrete Maldonado. It later passed to the Count of Laguna, a man so despicable that he was hanged in his own courtyard after beating a priest who had come to file a complaint.

THINGS TO SEE. The **first floor** exhibits some remarkably well preserved ceramics and tools from the pre-Inca Nazca, Chimu, Mochica, Pukara, Tiahuanuco, and Huari cultures. Some neat pieces include great big Pukara monoliths and a funerary blanket dating from 900 BC. The **second floor** features colorful dioramas depicting Inca agricultural practices, as well as Inca jewelry, clothing, weapons, and huge ceremonial vases. Peek into a replicated burial crypt with real mummies inside. In an interesting demonstration, a map superimposes the Inca empire, Tawantinsuyo, on top of Europe, demonstrating the vastness of the former. Stretching from southern Colombia to central Chile, the Inca empire dwarfed Spain. Another room displays furniture from a salon belonging to post-conquest Inca royalty, including exquisite wooden tables and chests inlaid with tortoise shell and mother-of-pearl. Early copies of Garcilaso de la Vega's *Comentarios Reales* introduce an exhibit on *Inkanismo*, a movement of cultural preservation.

MUSEO DE ARTE RELIGIOSO DEL ARZOBISPADO

Hathrumiyoq and Herrajes (tel. 225 211). Open M-Sa 8-11:30am and 3-5:30pm. Admission with Cusco tourist ticket.

Before this mansion belonged to the archbishop, it was the house of the Marqués de Buenavista which had been built on the foundations of Inca Roca's palace. One of the immense walls of the Inca's palace survives along Hathrumiyoq, or "Street with the Big Stone." Its name refers to the great **12-sided stone** fitting harmoniously into the center of the wall. After the Marqués died, the building was turned over to the Archbishop, who still lives in the wing next to the museum. The exceptional courtyard is a sight in itself—covered over in blue-and-white tiles from Seville and featuring beautifully carved wooden doorways and grilles.

The paintings within come from the Cusco School, and although they form a smaller collection than elsewhere in town, they tend to be in better condition. One of the most interesting rooms is filled with paintings by Marcos Zapata, the 18th-century *mestizo* artist who often included native elements in his religious works (see **Cathedral**, p. 133). Zapata's unusual *Circumcisión* portrays the Christ child facing the blade while supported by an Inca ceremonial belt.

SAN BLAS

Formerly known in Inca Cusco as the district of Tococache, San Blas is one of Cusco's oldest and most picturesque neighborhoods. Its winding streets and footpaths extend uphill from behind the cathedral towards the Cristo Blanco statue, mounted atop the hill alongside Sacsayhuaman. This portion of Cusco (part of the puma's neck) is a thriving artistic community producing works ranging from traditional to contemporary. Wandering these cobblestoned streets not only allows time for idle window shopping and poking around in *talleres*, but also yields spectacular views of the city below.

ARTESANÍA. Hike up the steep Cuesta de San Blas to the Plaza de San Blas, surrounded by a number of famous *artesanía* workshops. **Antonio Olave** creates fine ceramics and oil paintings along both Andean and religious themes. *(Plaza San Blas 651. Tel. 231 835. Open daily 8am-6pm.)* **Pancho Mendivil** produces beautiful painted wood, ceramics, and mirrors, as well as his trademark long-necked ceramic dolls *(Plaza San Blas 619. Tel. 233 247. Open daily 8:30am-9pm.)* The plaza itself hosts a small **craft market** on Saturdays.

IGLESIA DE SAN BLAS. Also in the plaza one finds the Iglesia de San Blas, a small, attractive church dating from 1562, unremarkable except that it holds what many call the best **wood-carved pulpit** in all of America. The complicated and symmetrical pulpit is crafted from a single cedar trunk, and features the Virgin Mary, Apostles, and numerous angels and cherubs—all supported by the gut-wrenching efforts of eight heretics seen on the pulpit's underside. Legend has it that the carving was done by an Indian leper named Juan Tomás Tuirutupa. Supposedly the skull at St. Paul's feet belonged to Tuirutupa. *(Open M-Sa 10-11:30am and 2-5:30pm. Admission with Cusco tourist ticket only.)*

OTHER SIGHTS

IGLESIA DE LA COMPAÑIA AND MUSEO DE HISTORIA NATURAL. The cathedral should not be confused with the Iglesia de La Compañia, the other large church in the plaza which was constructed over Amarucancha, the palace of Inca Huayna Capac (one of the palace's walls still survives along Loreto). When the 17th-century Jesuits made plans for their church, a controversy broke out among *cuzqueño* clergy because La Compañia's size threatened to meet the cathedral's. Eventually, even Pope Paul III turned against the Jesuits, but by then most of the church had been built. Today, its rightmost wing belongs to the Universidad Nacional de San Antonio Abad. *(La Compañia open for mass M-Sa 7am, noon, 6, and 6:30pm, Su 7:30, 11:30am, 6, and 7pm. Admission free.)* The adjoining Museo de Historia Natural has several hundred stuffed animals on display from the Cusco region. *(Open daily 9am-noon and 3-6pm. Admission s/1.)*

THE CONVENTO DE SANTA CATALINA. The Convento de Santa Catalina is the home of cloistered nuns, but its foundations used to belong to a different kind of female residence, the **Acllahuasi** ("House of Chosen Women"). These women acted as virgin priestesses for the Sun god, Inti, or as the Inca emperor's concubines, and were responsible for making the ruler's *chicha* and woven garments. Weaving clothes made out of alpaca and vicuña was an interminable affair, as the Inca emperor burned his garments after one wearing. The Sun Virgins had the added responsibility of tending to the Sun Temple (see **Qorikancha,** p. 134), which meant answering the Sun God's every desire; they served as liaisons between Inti and the Inca, prepared offerings to Inti, and dressed provocatively for him in garments of tropical bird feathers. In addition to cloistering nuns, the Convento includes a **Museo de Arte,** a large collection of religious colonial paintings mostly from the Cusco School. An entire series on the ground floor captures the life of another "chosen woman," the self-flagellating **Santa Rosa de Lima,** whose suffering is offset by the harmonious sounds of singing nuns next door. *(Museum open M-Th 9am-6pm, F 9am-3pm, Sa 9am-6pm. Admission with Cusco tourist ticket only.)*

IGLESIA DE LA MERCED. The Iglesia de La Merced keeps a **Museo de Arte Religioso** around its dilapidated though charming and soon-to-be-restored courtyard. The collection may be small, but it includes a couple of notable works such as two Virgins by the *cuzqueño* painter Bitti and a crucified Christ by the Spanish Renaissance artist Zurbarán. The latter is known as the Cristo de Cuatro Clavos because of the extra hammered nail. Most impressive, however, is the Custodia de La Merced, a blinding, sparkling 18th-century monstrance rendered from 22kg of gold and encrusted with 1,518 diamonds and 615 pearls, not to mention other precious stones. Under the church rest the remains of Diego de Almagro, conquistador of Chile. *(Art museum open M-Sa 8am-noon and 2-5pm. Admission s/3, students s/2.)*

OTHER MUSEUMS. The **Museo Histórico Regional** is housed in the Casa Garcilaso de la Vega, home of the important *mestizo* Inca historian. Within, there's an uninspiring collection of pre-Inca ceramics and a mummy with braids extending a full 1½m. *(On Plaza Regocijo at Garcilaso and Heladeros. Tel. 223 245. Open M-Sa 8am-5:30pm. Admission with Cusco tourist ticket.)* Across the plaza sprawls the **Museo Municipal de Arte Contemporáneo,** which displays regional handicrafts and some modern painting. *(On San Juan de Dios. Tel. 240 006. Open M-Sa 9am-7pm. Admission free.)*

OTHER THINGS TO SEE IN CUSCO. Though not a conventional sight, many women and children roam around Cusco wearing fine ceremonial garments and leading **well primped llamas**–definitely camera-worthy. But most of these characters are models and their costumes rented; should you take a picture, you are expected to pay a *sol* or two in tip. Those who don't pay become public enemy number one. The most exciting **festivals** in Cusco are **Semana Santa,** when El Señor de los Temblores makes his procession in the Plaza de Armas (see **Cathedral,** p. 133); **Corpus Christi,** in early June, with its own fine processions and abundant feasting; and most importantly **Inti Raymi,** June 24, the world-famous festival of the Sun god held on the winter solstice.

ENTERTAINMENT

BARS

Around the Plaza de Armas, there's no loss for a place to have a beer, if your beverage of choice is Cusqueña. Despite the prevalence of foreign pub owners, import costs preclude most anything but domestic beers. However, Cusqueña, the region's pride, is a decent lager in its own right. Those suffering from altitude sickness should beware; alcohol tends to make matters worse.

Los Perros, Teqsicocha 436. Australian Tammy and Peruvian Guillermo own this young, artsy couch-bar. Assorted munchies, tea, and a full bar accompany some of the most inviting seating in town. Play board games and peruse magazines to the heartfelt lyrics of Cypress Hill or lighter meditation music. On Sunday nights, Tammy sings with her jazz band. Open daily 1pm-1am; in high season 11am-3am.

Paddy Flaherty's, Triunfo 124 (tel. 246 903), across the street from the cathedral. Small and warm, with good pub ambiance. The faithful gather to watch rugby and "other sports." Test your loyalty and wallet with a pint of Guinness (s/12). Draft beer s/5-7. Happy hour 7-8pm and 10-10:30pm. Open daily noon-1am.

Norton Rat's Tavern, Loreto 115 (tel. 246 204), overlooking the Plaza de Armas. American-owned, the Tavern still manages to count Peruvians among its clientele, and keeps a pool table. Spectacular balconies capture the nighttime lights. Specialty drinks includes Long Island Iced Tea (s/6) and Dirty Girl Scout (s/12). Mostly domestic beer (s/4-7). Happy hour usually 7-9pm. Open daily noon-1am.

Cross Keys, Confiturías 233, on the Plaza de Armas facing the cathedral. An old, well established English pub, Cross Keys fills with expats and travelers nightly. Pub grub served. A good *pisco sour* s/8. Happy hour 6-7pm and 9-9:30pm. 10% SAEC discount (on beer only). Open daily 11am-1am.

Rosie O'Grady's, Santa Catalina Anch 360 (tel. 247 935), around the corner from the Plaza de Armas. The owner, from County Cork, has opened pubs in Moscow and Siberia and wondered if it was any easier in Perú. This new Irish watering hole on the block eschews dark wooden interiors for light, upscale decor. TVs show live *fútbol* or rugby. Guinness s/12, Cusqueña s/4. Food served 11am-midnight. Live music Th-F. Happy hour 1-2pm, 6-7pm, and 11-11:30pm. 10% SAEC discount. Open daily 11am-1am.

DISCO-PUBS

Most nights of the week (especially June-Aug.), the streets around the Plaza de Armas thump with dance music and shimmer with disco lights. Calles Plateros, Procuradores, Suecia, and Teqsicocha are the places to find that curious hybrid: the **disco-pub**, not quite pub, not quite *discoteca*. New ones are spawned constantly, living or dying by the whim of fickle tourists. Most feature some sort of live performance and happy hour. On Friday and Saturday nights, some charge covers, which are either waived for tourists and women or avoided with easily found free passes (check around the Plaza de Armas in the evening). Leave the blue suede shoes back in San Blas—here, Gore-Tex rules. When foreigners hit the floor, dress code is dominated by nylon, fleece, and newly purchased alpaca-wear.

Mama Africa, Espaderos 135, 2nd floor (tel. 241 979), part of a multi-level disco-dancing complex with **Kerara** and **Wayruro.** Playing a mix of reggae and rock, with obligatory Bob Marley, Mama Africa mingles backpacker chic with beautiful young Peruvians. People pack this popular disco-pub all day and all night. Email (s/4 per hr.) and remarkably excellent food in a separate room. Movies and videos shown in the afternoon. Beer s/6. Live music 10:30pm. Happy hour 8-9:30pm. Cover s/10 F-Sa after 11pm. Open just about all the time.

Ukukus, Plateros 316 (tel. 242 951). Skeletons dance on the ceiling of this smoky, candle-lit disco-pub. Plenty of seating and a good-sized floor accommodate the crowds of international young 'uns. DJs play rock, pop, *salsa*, and techno. Cusqueña s/5. Live music 11pm-midnight. Good movies shown on afternoons. Happy hour 8-9:30pm. Cover s/10 F-Sa after 10pm; includes a drink.

Uptown, Suecia 302, 2nd floor (tel. 227 241). Newer than the rest and raging after midnight, with several levels and a distinctly thatched-hut motif. Lighting bounces with the reggae and funk. On the 1st floor, a separate club, **XCess,** plays Latin classics. *Cerveza* Cristal s/5. Happy hour 9-10pm and 11-11:30pm. Cover s/10 includes first drink.

Kamikaze, Plaza Regocijo 274, 2nd floor (tel. 233 865), now in its 15th year, is the oldest disco-pub in town but isn't as crowded as the rest. A young, foreign clientele dances to the standard reggae, disco, and classic 80s. A balcony looks out on Plaza Regocijo. Cusqueña s/5. Live music 11pm-midnight. Happy hour 8:30-9:30pm. No cover.

THEATER AND MUSIC

Cusco specializes in collecting aspects of different Peruvian regional cultures and wrapping them up for mass gringo consumption. Nightly around the Plaza de Armas, restaurants and bars host musicians playing traditional tunes. For a more formal exhibition of local dance and music, go to the **Centro Q'osqo,** Sol 604 (tel. 227 901), which features daily performances (6 or 7pm, s/10). The **Teatro Municipal,** Mesón de la Estrella 149 (tel. 221 847), occasionally exhibits traditional music concerts (shows 7 or 7:30pm, s/10).

SHOPPING

Cusco is the central exchange for handicrafts from all over Perú: carved gourds from Huancayo, *retablos* and tapestries from Ayacucho, weavings from the coast, *chompas* (sweaters) from all over the Andes, erotic ceramic keychains from... no one will admit where. Cusco's **mercado central** is devoted more to ordinary goods and produce, and is rife with pickpockets. A better bet for quality *artesanía* is one of the many private, enclosed markets, which can be found on Espinar (next to the tourist office), Palacios, Plateros, and elsewhere. Bargaining is expected and especially welcome if you're purchasing multiple items. The stores in **San Blas,** the neighborhood uphill from and behind the cathedral, may be more expensive, but they usually feature the original work of artists living in the *barrio*. This is the breeding ground for oil paintings, delicate ceramic dolls, and lively painted masks.

GUIDED TOURS FROM CUSCO

At the hub of the Sacred Valley and the Peruvian travel network, Cusco agencies offer a multiplicity of sightseeing opportunities, ranging from the easy and cheap (city and Sacred Valley tours) to the more rugged (Inca Trail) and expensive (Manú Biosphere). The longest guided treks offered by agencies are around the Cordillera Vilcanota and the Cordillera Ausangate (some of the snow-capped peaks seen from the Sacred Valley, usually 7 days), and along the Inca Trail from the glacier of Salcantay (also 7 days). Intrepid explorers can tackle these trips without an agency's help—look for maps, directions, and possible companions at the South American Explorers Club (see p. 128). One trip not allowed without a tour is a venture into the restricted sections of the Manú Biosphere Reserve.

THE INCA TRAIL

The most popular journey of the usually four-day hike along the Inca Trail (see p. 147) starts at kilometer 82 or kilometer 88 and terminates at the gates of Machu Picchu. A few agencies do an expensive, shortened trail starting at kilometer 104. As a number of agencies offer similar packages (and prices), it is important to ask specific questions and get all answers in writing. Some valid concerns include: group size (agencies may sign on 20 or more); language spoken; food; porters' responsibilities (most budget companies make you carry your own pack); and equipment (you will probably have to supply a sleeping bag). The quality of one's guide and equipment may make all the difference. Ask to meet the guide and see tents, etc. ahead of time. Ask if the guide for the Inca Trail and for Machu Picchu will be the same person. Some agencies save money by sending a less experienced (and less knowledgeable) guide on the Inca Trail and then hire a new one at Machu Picchu, since only certified guides are allowed into the ruins. Finally, make sure that porters and cooks will have a place to sleep each night. The South American Explorers Club in Cusco can provide reports on companies (see p. 128). The following specialize in the Inca Trail but also offer a number of other packages.

SAS Travel, Panes 143 (tel./fax 237 292), on the Plaza de Armas. One of the favorite tour operators among budget travelers, SAS promises to be eco-sensitive and treat its staff well. This service consequently comes at a slightly higher price. Group size for Inca Trail hikes generally ranges from 15 to 18 people. Good English is spoken in the office. Daily departures. All guides know Machu Picchu in addition to the Inca Trail. Kenny has been recommended. The 4-day, 3-night package costs US$88, students US$80. The standard Sacred Valley tour, the city tour, and rafting, horseback riding, and mountain-biking trips are also offered. Open daily 6am-10pm.

United Mice, Plateros 351 (tel. 221 139), is considered by some to be the premier budget tour agency for the Inca Trail. Efraín, Hamilton, and Salustio are certified to guide Machu Picchu, but others aren't. Groups can range from 10 to 22, sometimes larger. Fixed departures M, W, and F. The price for a 4-day, 3-night trek is US$85, students US$76. US$5 SAEC discount. Standard rafting, horseback riding, and city tours available as well. Open daily 9am-8:30pm.

Q'ente Adventure Trips, Plateros 365, 2nd floor (tel. 238 245) is another popular agency. Group size ranges 8-18 people in high season, 8-12 in low. All guides do both the Inca Trail and Machu Picchu. Roberto has received rave reviews. Q'ente offers 4-day, 3-night packages with daily departures for US$80, students US$71. A truncated 2-day, 1-night hike is US$65, students US$60. Treks to Ausangate and Salcantay are offered as well. 5% discount for SAEC members. Open daily 9am-2pm and 3-8pm.

Inca Explorers, Suecia 339 (tel. 239 669), one of the best agencies offering a "Class B" Inca Trail. The main difference (besides price) is that guides are more experienced and porters carry everything but you and your daypack. Groups are no more than 10 people. Guide Santiago has gotten a thumbs-up. For the 4-day, 3-night trip, the price comes to US$220, students US$212. SAEC discount 8%. Open daily 7am-9pm.

MANÚ BIOSPHERE RESERVE

Most of the nine companies that head to Manú (see p. 232) offer similar packages, with tours ranging from four to nine days. Trips that bus in and out cost less and witness all the heights of Manú's forest. Flying to **Boca Manú,** a town near the mouth of the reserve zone, saves only time. The reserve zone often closes January to April due to flooding.

Manú Nature Tours, Pardo 1046 (tel. 252 721; www.manuperu.com), offers mountain biking and whitewater rafting options (for extra) within their standard tours. 8-day, 7-night tours US$2,095 per person in the high season, US$1,633 in the low season; 5-day, 4-night trips US$1,625 or US$1,193.

Manú Expeditions, Pardo 895 (tel. 226 671), maintains a partnership with the non-profit Selva Sur Conservation Group. 9-day, 8-night tours US$1,595 per person. 6-day, 5-night trips US$1,119 per person.

Pantiacolla Tours, Plateros 360 (tel. 238 323; www.pantiacolla.com). Run by a biologist who worked for several years in Manú, Pantiacolla sends out camping tours as well as posher, lodge-based ones. 9-day, 8-night camping tours US$725 per person. 7-day, 6-night tours at the lodge US$795; 5-day, 4-night US$725. SAEC 10% discount; other mark-downs for groups of 4 or more.

Manú Ecological Adventures, Plateros 365 (tel. 261 640; www.cbc.org.pe/manu), sends the highest number of visitors to the park each year. As befits a cheaper alternative, their boats and tents tend to be more crowded than the other companies'. That said, the majority of their clients report relative satisfaction with their tours. 8-day, 7-night tours US$550; 7-day, 6-night US$646; 6-day, 5-night US$724. SAEC or student 10% discount.

MISCELLANEOUS ADVENTURES

Stints of adventure need not take four days: some operators offer fun, inexpensive one-day excursions for mountain biking, rock climbing, horseback riding, kayaking, and whitewater rafting. Of these, **rafting** on the **Río Urubamba** (class II-III in dry season, III-V in rainy) is most popular. A more lengthy expedition can be taken on the **Río Apurimac** (May-Sept. only, usually 3 days, class IV-V).

Instinct Back to Nature, Procuradores 50 (tel. 233 451), has record. Specializes in rafting trips on the Urubamba and Apurimac rivers. The 4-day Apurimac trip includes 1 day of training on the Urubamba in order to prepare for the class V Apurimac. US$140 includes food, transport, camping equipment, guides, and a home video of the trip. 3-day kayaking lessons on the Urubamba run US$120. Mountain biking, horseback riding, and rock climbing excursions also available. Open daily 9am-9pm.

Loreto Tours, Medio 111 (tel. 236 331). A one-day rafting trip on the Urubamba goes for US$20, 3 days on the Apurimac US$150. A guided mountain bike tour of Moray and Las Salineras is value for small groups (US$20 per person includes quality bikes). Open M-Sa 9am-1pm and 5-10pm, Su 5-10pm.

Eric Adventures, Plateros 324 (tel. 228 475), a long-time provider of rafting tours, as well as Inca Trail hikes. The popular 1-day rafting trip on the Urubamba costs US$25, students US$20, and departs daily. 2-day kayaking lessons also available (US$80). Groups for the Trail range from 12-15 people. Guides cover both Machu Picchu and the the Inca Trail. Julio César is a favorite. Inca Trail hikes US$75, students US$65. Open daily 8:30am-1pm and 4-9pm.

THE SOL STOPS HERE Perú's currency, the *nuevo sol*, may have stabilized in recent years, but not without a price: increased counterfeiting. Beware of shoddily molded and hammered "*cinco soles*" coins passed back at the market. Fake bills, in particular, are easy to avoid. Real ones printed relatively recently have iridescent drops painted on the front, and all bills should feature an inner plastic strip with a serial number. Also, hold the paper up to light in order to spot the watermark copy of the face (e.g., Raúl Porras Barrenechea on the 20). Dodge a phony right from the start; no savvy Peruvian will later accept it for payment.

NEAR CUSCO

Four nearby ruins along the paved road to Pisac make excellent destinations for a day-hike from Cusco. Each of the sites has prominent and clear signs pointing out its location. So many tourists walk this circuit that locals have set up souvenir stands along the road, and women do the usual posing for pictures (as if it were completely natural to sit in front of a spectacular backdrop with an alpaca and a Spanish loom). The most important of these ruins is **Sacsayhuaman** (pronounced "Sexy Woman"), located right beside a giant white statue of Christ the Redeemer that is visible from Cusco. Uphill from Sacsayhuaman lie the smaller sites of **Qenco, Puca Pucara,** and **Tambomachay.**

Transportation: Sacsayhuaman is a steep 30-minute hike from the center of town, either up Choquechaka in San Blas or meandering up Resbalosa in the neighborhood of San Cristóbal. Some like to view the ruins in reverse by taking a taxi (s/20) to Tambomachay, the most distant ruin, and walking downhill; one could also catch a *colectivo* on Tullumayu bound for Pisac and ask to get off at Tambomachay (s/2.50). Agencies in Cusco offer a tour on horseback of the route, and horses can be rented at Sacsayhuaman (see below).

NEAR CUSCO: SACSAYHUAMAN

Sacsayhuaman is believed to form the head of the Cusco puma, the figure in which the Inca Pachacuti is said to have designed his city. The name itself may come from the words "Sacsa Uma," Quechua for "speckled head." Sacsayhuaman was the site of a key battle in 1536 during the rebellion of the Inca **Manco Capac II** against the Spanish. The Incas claimed the fortress early in the struggle, using it as a headquarters from which to attack the conquered city of Cusco below. In an attempt on Sacsayhuaman, the conquistador **Juan Pizarro** (half-brother of Francisco) died from a slingshot wound. The bitter fighting that followed claimed thousands of Inca and Spanish lives, ending finally with the victory of the Spanish and the retreat of Manco to Ollantaytambo (see p. 145). Historians believe that this battle served as a turning point for the conquistadors—they had begun to lose their grip over Perú as the Inca's rebellion inspired open insurrection across the country. Manco's loss of Sacsayhuaman sealed the doom of his empire.

As a result of this grim history, most people think of Sacsayhuaman as purely a fortress. However, the original complex consisted of numerous buildings and towers, which probably served other functions besides the defensive. After the Spanish victory, most of these constructions were demolished and the site served as a municipal stone quarry until the looting was halted by excavations in 1935. By this point, most of the smaller structures which might have hinted at Sacsayhuaman's other purposes had long since disappeared.

Nevertheless, the parts still intact are among the most impressive Inca ruins in existence. Three tiers of gigantic **zig-zag stone ramparts** were too massive to be carried off; they amaze visitors with their precise interlocking edges. One estimate measures the biggest stone at 8.5m and 360 tons. On the hill behind these ramparts stood three towers, **Muyucmarca, Sayacmarca,** and **Paucarmarca.** The first two still have foundations intact. The circular base of Muyucmarca was recently re-excavated by Manuel Silva in August 1999. On the opposite hill facing the zig-zags, few structures remain, but just over the hill lies a round depression and clearing that may have served as a reservoir or site of water worship. A couple of short tunnels at the edge of the clearing dare giggling tourists to stumble through their pitch-black interiors. (Sacsayhuaman open daily 7am-5:30pm. Admission with the Cusco tourist ticket.)

The **Corcel Ranch** (tel. 245 878), just outside the ruins, rents horses for the ride up to the other sites (s/25 for 5hr.). A guide will go along for a tip.

NEAR CUSCO: QENCO

Close to kilometer 7 on the road to Pisac, Qenco ("zig-zag") is a natural formation altered by the Incas for religious purposes. This large limestone outcropping served as a *huaca* (shrine) and is carved with myriad figures. The site gets its name from the **zig-zag channels** carved into the top of the rock. Inca priests may have poured *chicha* or blood from sacrificed animals into the pools and then divined future outcomes from the path taken by the liquid. Some interesting carvings on top of the outcropping include a small llama in relief and an even smaller headless condor, both located on the side closest to the road. Further towards the interior of the plateau lies a mysterious stone topped with two fat cylinders and a little replica of a house. At the edge of the rock, a large **amphitheater** was constructed with 19 niches around a tall, vaguely **phallic rock.** Underneath the outcropping, a few caves probably held the mummified remains of Inca nobility. (Qenco open daily 7am-5:30pm. Admission with Cusco tourist ticket.)

NEAR CUSCO: PUCA PUCARA AND TAMBOMACHAY

About 5km beyond Qenco, these two ruins are on opposite sides of the road from each other. "Puca Pucara" means "red fort," but the building more likely served as a *tambo* ("resting house"), or perhaps as the hunting lodge of the Inca Pachacuti. "Tambomachay" means "cavern lodge," but is actually an ancient site of **ritual bathing.** Evidently, a water cult directed the hillside's underground stream through a series of stone fountains, which continue to work today. The site may have been surrounded by gardens and trees back in its glory days. (Qenco open daily 7am-5:30pm. Admission with Cusco tourist ticket.)

THE SACRED VALLEY

The term Sacred Valley refers to the area around the Río Urubamba (called the Río Vilcanota in parts upstream), which stretches northeast of Cusco. The Urubamba Valley was the breadbasket of imperial Cusco, with huge, rolling, fertile hills resplendent with maize, fruit, and vegetables. Inca engineers solved the problem of landslides and soil erosion by conceiving agricultural terraces (or *andenes*). These steps, a few meters in width and height, were sculpted from earth retained by stone walls. Many thousands of kilometers of these terraces are still used today. (Centuries after the Incas, Chairman Mao was so impressed with the idea that he had Chinese peasants do the same thing.) Another dazzling achievement of the Incas was the redirection of the Río Urubamba—the straightening of the waters near Pisac in order to allow for more efficient crop irrigation. The result of the Incas' labors was the longest pre-Columbian canal in the Americas. Besides this agricultural legacy, the Incas left the valley replete with sacred structures: the fortresses of Pisac and Ollantaytambo, and the sprawling city of Machu Picchu.

HIGHLIGHTS OF EL VALLE SAGRADO

- Buy the best souvenirs at **Pisac's market** and then make the scenic hike up to its glorious and well-preserved **ruins** (see p. 143).
- One of the best treks in South America, the **Inca Trail** makes an enchanting pilgrimage to the sacred city of the Incas (see p. 147).
- Egypt has its pyramids. China has its wall. Welcome to **Machu Picchu** (see p. 150).

The most visited part of the valley extends from Pisac to Ollantaytambo along a blissfully paved road and on to Aguas Calientes and the sacred city of Machu Picchu. Many visitors opt for the one-day tour out of Cusco or skip this in favor of directly hitting the Inca Trail or Machu Picchu. However, those who have the time often enjoy a few nights in the valley itself. A quilt of green and yellow fields fenced in by the snowy Cordillera Vilcanota offers idyllic charm. Judging by the growing expatriate population, some people visit and never leave.

PISAC

Pisac's **Sunday market** became so popular that the event is now repeated on Tuesdays and Thursdays as well. Sunday's market remains the largest affair; hundreds of canopied stands sell silver jewelry, ceramics, woven blankets, old coins, and other goods to herds of international visitors. One end of the market still caters mostly to villagers, who come dressed in traditional clothes to exchange bags of potatoes, grain, and fruit with each other according to the centuries-old *trueque*, or bartering system. Local notables join the fanfare once they emerge from Pisac's morning mass (11am), a service spoken entirely in Quechua. However, Pisac's charms go beyond the famous market. The hills above the town hold the **ruins** of Pisac; its well-preserved buildings enhanced by stunning mountain views make Pisac one of the most popular short hikes in the area (3hr.).

Colectivos drop passengers off just after crossing the Urubamba river at the edge of town. It's a three-minute walk into the **Plaza de Armas** where the **police, post office,** and other services can be found. **Buses** return frequently to **Cusco** (1hr., every 15min. 7am-8pm, s/2.50), while others continue through the valley to **Urubamba** (30min., s/1).

With Cusco so nearby, most people choose to return to the city for the night. However, a few good, cheap options exist in Pisac. **Kinsa Cocha Hospedaje,** Arequipa 307 (tel. 203 101), on a street parallel to the Plaza de Armas, keeps tidy dorm rooms and supplies hot water upon request (s/10 per person). For food, an expensive cafe and pizzeria sit on the plaza, but Peruvian places serve more economical fare near the bridge at the entrance of town. Of these, **Restaurante Valle Sagrado,** on Amazonas, prepares good *trucha* dishes (s/10; open daily 7am-10pm).

THE RUINS. Pisac is the largest Inca fortress still standing, but unlike those of Sacsayhuaman and Ollantaytambo, no famous battles with the Spanish ever took place here. Indeed, Pisac seems to have been abandoned before the Conquest. The Spanish never even bothered with Pisac (a good thing—many of the buildings have consequently stayed intact). Nevertheless, in its heyday, this highly inaccessible fort city occupied a key strategic point overlooking the valley. By guarding the entrance to the jungle region, which was inhabited by the indomitable Antis tribe, Pisac helped secure a vulnerable point in the Inca imperial domain.

From the Plaza de Armas, two trails lead up to the ruins. The one leading uphill from the right side of the plaza (when coming from the bus stop by the river) leads to a paved road used by tour groups. Most hikers take the steep path leading up from the left side. The trail loops through agricultural terraces that also served as defensive walls. Some say Pisac was designed to look like a massive condor, its terraces built as feathers. As the condor symbolized travel between the mortal and spiritual worlds, it seems appropriate that these hills hold the largest known **Inca cemetery.** Most of the tombs were robbed, leaving small holes in the mountainside, visible from many places on the trail. The path is fairly well-marked and weaves through a number of complexes, the most impressive of which is the **Intihuatana** (Temple of the Sun) sector, a triangle-shaped plateau. The Intihuatana itself is at the center, with a large sundial rock, and probably served as an astronomical observatory. Nearby lies a set of water channels and a ritual bath, which feed into the residential sector just downhill, called the **P'isaca.**

URUBAMBA AND YUCAY

Tranquil Urubamba and even sleepier Yucay rest side-by-side 40km and 37km, respectively, from Pisac on the road to Ollantaytambo. Neither seems much disturbed by the Sacred Valley tour groups rolling through from Cusco on Tuesdays, Thursdays, and Sundays. And despite the astounding density of three- to five-star hotels, local women still speak to their children in Quechua, and local men still plow their fields with oxen. Surrounded by cultivated green hills and snow-capped mountains, the two towns provide a markedly less gringo-ridden base than Cusco from which to explore the Sacred Valley.

Urubamba provides a wider range of services than does Yucay. Most everything revolves around **Av. Mariscal Castilla,** perpendicular to the main highway and recognizable by the taxis and *mototaxis* which congregate at the foot of the street. To reach the **Plaza de Armas,** walk up Castilla, make a left onto **Jirón Palacio,** and follow it two blocks. **Buses** terminate at the Urubamba bus station, 500m beyond Av. Castilla on the main highway. From here, *combis* go to **Ollantaytambo** (30min., s/1) and **Chinchero** (1hr., every 20min. 5am-7:30pm, s/2.50). To get to Urubamba and Yucay from Cusco, catch a **colectivo** along Tullumayu (s/2) or take a **Caminos del Inca** bus from the *terminal* at Huáscar and Garcilaso (1½hr., every 20min. 5am-7pm, s/2.50). Ask to be let off early at Av. Castilla in Urubamba or Plaza Manco II in Yucay. Yucay and Urubamba are a few minutes away from each other by taxi (s/2), *mototaxi* (s/1), or *colectivo* (s/0.50), all of which pass frequently along the highway. The **Banco de la Nación** on Castilla may change cash. Other services include: the **police** (tel. 201 092), at Palacio and Bolognesi; a **medical clinic** (tel. 201 334), along the highway at the end of Castilla; the **post office,** on the Plaza de Armas; and **phones,** found along Castilla. **Telephone code:** 084.

In Urubamba, accommodations can be found along Castilla and near the Plaza de Armas. The basic **Hostal Urubamba,** Bolognesi 605 (tel. 201 400), on a street right off Palacio between Castilla and the Plaza de Armas, is adequate, with thin mattresses and cold-water communal baths. Private baths have hot water in the mornings. (Dorms s/5 per person; singles s/10, with bath s/20; doubles s/16, with bath s/30; triples s/24.) Over in Yucay, the best budget option is the **Hostal Y'llary,** Pl. Manco II 107 (tel./fax 226 607), formed from the same 300-year-old *hacienda* as the next-door Posada del Inca Hotel. Y'llary offers much of the hotel's grandeur at a fraction of the price, with gorgeously furnished rooms and resplendent gardens. (Singles US$18; doubles US$30; triples US$42; includes breakfast; camping in the backyard with access to hot showers US$3 per person.) In Urubamba, restaurants along Castilla make mostly Peruvian dishes. **Hirano's,** on Castilla, prepares a stellar lunchtime *menú* (s/13). Up the street, **Café Nuevo Mundo,** Castilla and Comercio, is run by a couple of American ladies who serve vegetarian delights. In Yucay, the very cool **Casa Luna,** Plaza Manco II 107 (tel. 201 434), adjacent to Hostal Y'llary, is run by two international furniture designers and serves "the only pizza in town" (s/15-20). They also offer email (s/10 per hr.), long-term lodging, and a spin around the Valley in their four-wheel-drive vehicle. Sculptor José Antonio Paz Soldán plays drums and entertains after dark.

There's not much to see in Urubamba, but Yucay used to be the Inca Sayri Tupac's royal estate, a gift from the Spanish after the ruler agreed to leave the rebel capital of Vilcabamba and play puppet king. (The next Inca, Titu Cusi, remained in the jungle to keep the resistance alive.) His grounds occupied the site of the present-day Plaza de Armas and Plaza Manco II, which are now huge open fields of grass kept neatly cropped by munching goats and mules. At one end of Plaza Manco II remain the Inca Sayri Tupac's palacial walls; across from these, in the Plaza de Armas, stand the walls belonging to his Princess.

NEAR URUBAMBA: CHINCHERO

Somewhat removed from the valley, on a lofty plateau raised 3762m above sea-level, Chinchero (the mythical birthplace of the rainbow) gives way to gorgeous views of the surrounding plains and mountains. The town may have been a major city in Inca times; the most striking remnant of the period is the great stone wall in the main plaza. However, the town's major claim to tourism is its big **Sunday market,** the main competitor with Pisac's (see p. 143). Locals gather to barter goods in their Sunday best and sell stands upon stands of souvenirs to tourists.

Transportation: To get to Chinchero from Cusco, catch a *colectivo* along Tullumayu (1½hr., frequent, s/2.50). One can also get there from Urubamba (see p. 144).

NEAR URUBAMBA: MORAY AND LAS SALINERAS

Though a bit difficult to reach, the Inca terraces of Moray and the salt pans of Las Salineras (sometimes called Salinas) are well worth the effort. Both are visually stunning and testify to the ingenuity of pre-Columbian Andean peoples. Moray consists of two sets of concentric agricultural terraces sculpted from natural depressions in the earth. The changes in altitude from one step to the next create a multitude of different climatic conditions, allowing an assortment of crops to be planted in one place. Archaeologists believe that Moray was the site of agricultural experimentation dating to before the Incas. Andean peoples may have used the terraces to develop strains of corn that could grow at high altitudes, a crucial innovation for the flourishing of subsequent civilizations. (Admission s/5.) Las Salineras likewise took advantage of natural phenomena to produce something useful: salt. These Inca salt pans, still in use, are forged from shallow pools dug into the hillside. Over time they fill with the salty water that runs down from the mountain in underground streams. In the dry season, the water evaporates leaving a thin layer of sparkling white salt. Together, the pans look like row upon row of giant sugar cubes set against the scorched mountain landscape. (Admission s/3.)

Transportation: Moray and Las Salineras can be combined as a daytrip from Urubamba. Unfortunately, public transportation does not directly serve either site. From Urubamba, catch a *colectivo* headed for **Chinchero** (see p. 144) but ask to get off at the *"desvío a Maras."* From this turn-off, it's a one-hour walk to the tiny village of Maras, and then another two hours on a trail leading away from the town to Moray. One could also find a taxi in Maras to go to Moray (about s/20 round-trip). It is necessary to return to Maras in order to get to Las Salineras, which is a couple of kilometers downhill from the village on the way to Pichingoto. From the salt pans, a footpath leads further downhill to the paved road between Ollantaytambo and Urubamba, along the river. Cross the river and turn right onto the highway. Frequently passing *colectivos* can take you the rest of the 2km to Urubamba.

A number of agencies in Cusco can arrange a mountain biking excursion to the two sites for US$25 (see p. 139). These tours approach Moray and Las Salineras from a different angle, passing **Laguna Huaypo,** a picturesque lake reportedly visited by aliens on occasion.

OLLANTAYTAMBO

With a strong, Quechua identity, the people of Ollantaytambo cherish the long oral history associated with their town; they range from tales of former inhabitants to myths explaining the rock formations of surrounding mountains. In its day, the fortress looming in the hills above witnessed great acts of bravery, inspiring myriad tragic tales. One intriguing and true story concerns the Inca Manco Capac II, who retreated to the fortress here after his rebellion against the Spanish failed in Cusco. Pizarro's men chased him relentlessly, finally forcing the rebel Inca to build a new capital, Vilcabamba, in the depths of the jungle. Still, the invaders were not satisfied. If they couldn't assassinate the Inca ruler, they would do the next best thing. While stationed in Ollantaytambo, Spanish soldiers murdered Manco Capac's queen, Cura Ocllo, who had been captured earlier in battle. They tied her naked body to a raft and sent her floating down the Río Urubamba so that Manco would find her downstream and get the message.

Today, the fortress of Ollantaytambo lures troops of invading gringos fascinated by its colossal stone walls and fabulous vistas of the valley. However, the village below is a sight in itself: the best surviving example of what an Inca town looked like. Streets preserve a perfect grid pattern and are kept clean by waters diverted from the Río Patacancha into stone channels. Houses are arranged in enclosed blocks called *canchas*, and local men wear the *poncho* typical of the region.

ORIENTATION AND PRACTICAL INFORMATION. Buses arrive in the **Plaza de Armas,** from which one can see the ruined fortress stretching across the mountainside. The street extending to the entrance of the ruins crosses the narrow **Río Patacancha.** Make a left before crossing the river and walk downhill to reach the **train station** where daily trains to **Machu Picchu/Aguas Calientes** (8, 8:30, and 9am) stop in the morning and the local train back to **Cusco** (6:15pm) stops in the evening. The **bus** to **Cusco** (2hr., departs after the train arrives, s/10), which also departs from the train station, is much faster and cheaper (buy ticket at station). However, it's even cheaper to catch a bus to Urubamba, and from there take a *colectivo* to Cusco. Buses go to **Urubamba** (30min., s/1) from the plaza. There's no **bank** in Ollantaytambo; local businesses might be able to exchange dollars. The **police** (tel. 204 086) are also on the plaza. By the river on the way to the ruins stands the **Centro de Salud** (tel. 204 090) with 24-hour **emergency** service. The **post** and **telephone offices** are both located in the same building on the Plaza de Armas (open daily 7am-9pm). **Telephone code:** 084.

ACCOMMODATIONS AND FOOD. Lodging in Ollantaytambo is relatively expensive but of excellent quality. Right next to the train station, **El Albergue** (tel./fax 204 014), is run by friendly Americans and has comfortable, well-furnished rooms, handsome gardens, and even a sauna (US$15 per person; sauna US$5). **Hostal Las Orquideas** (tel. 204 032), on the way to the train station along the river, keeps clean, pleasantly rustic rooms around a grassy courtyard (singles US$10; doubles US$20; breakfast included). A cheaper option is **Hospedaje La Choza** (tel. 204 038), off the Plaza de Armas (look for the sign), with small, neat rooms and communal hot-water baths (singles s/15; doubles s/30; triples s/35; quads s/40). A couple of decent restaurants in the Plaza de Armas serve a variety of dishes, usually to tourists. Just off the plaza, the very friendly **Café Alcazar** (tel. 204 034), prepares mostly vegetarian soups, omelettes, and pastas (open 8am-8pm).

SIGHTS. One can imagine the fright experienced by Spanish soldiers as they rode up to the **fortress** at Ollantaytambo. Perched atop a set of steep terraces, the Inca army rained arrows and dropped boulders on the helpless invaders and their horses below. During one battle that forced Pizarro and his men to retreat, the Inca Manco Capac II flooded the courtyard at the foot of the fortress by diverting water from the Río Patacancha. Eventually, Ollantaytambo, like Cusco, would be abandoned. The Spanish Conquest might have interrupted the construction of certain parts of the fortress. Its foundation was made from enormous granite blocks dragged from the Cachicata quarry, 6km across the Río Urubamba and up a mountainside from Ollantaytambo. Three such stones were abandoned mid-haul and can be seen along the road into town. The stone courtyard (or **Plaza Manyaraqui**) where Pizzaro's men met watery failure now holds a tamer tribute to Inca engineering, a gushing channel leading into the **Baño de la Ñusta** (Bath of the Princess), where locals occasionally soak their feet. From here, over 200 stone steps climb up the terraces at the front of the fortress. At the top of the stairs to the left stands the unfinished complex known as the **Temple of the Sun,** with a number of tremendous stones notable for their carved faces. The zig-zag step design is a common symbol of the Andes. (Open daily 7am-5:30pm. Admission with Cusco tourist ticket.) The **Museo CATCCO,** just off the road leading to the Ollantaytambo ruins, was opened by a British group responsible for much of the archaeological excavation in the area. The collection is small but provides informative displays in English on local customs. (Open Tu-Su 10am-1pm and 2-4pm. Admission s/5.)

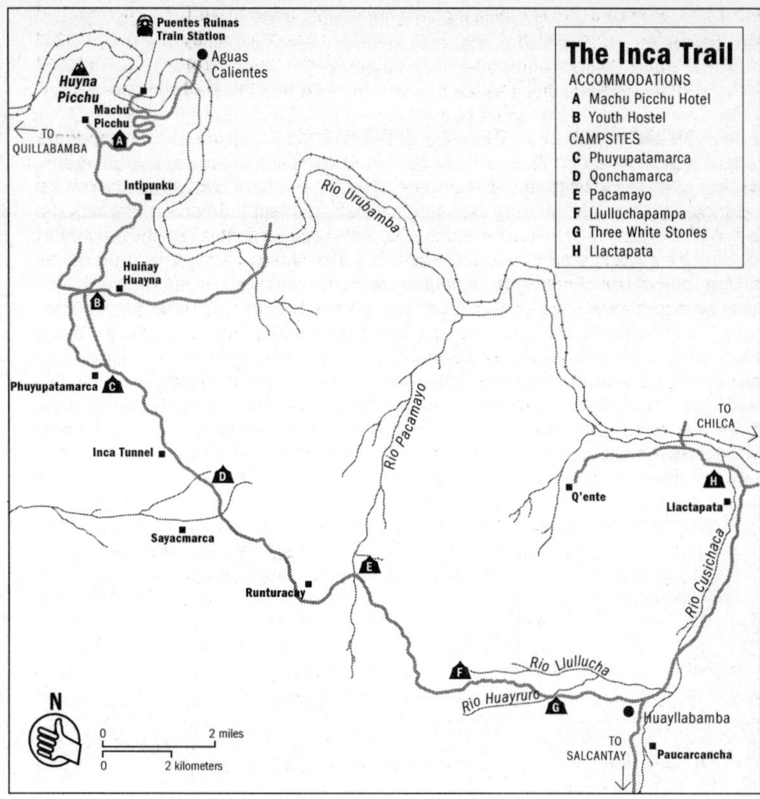

THE INCA TRAIL

Admission from kilometer 88 US$17, students US$8; from kilometer 104 US$12, students US$6.

Perhaps the best known hike in Perú, the Inca Trail weaves up mountainsides and winds down into cloudforests just like many other Inca highways built throughout the Sacred Valley. However, only *this* Inca Trail leads to the stony gates of Machu Picchu, which most consider the climax of the trek, perhaps even the highlight of their Peruvian experience. Little can match the wonder of reaching the final pass at daybreak and then descending upon the sacred city to wander around its temples and terraces. Yet, the two to four days preceding this point are filled with spectacular moments, too. The trail swings past a grand diversity of landscapes, and a number of impressive ruins, building anticipation for what lies ahead.

Given this, many many people attempt the Inca Trail and become impossible to avoid in the months of June through August. Even social hikers may become disillusioned by the decrepit condition of campsites and the accumulated trash. A further consideration besides season is preparation. Pack lightly but be smart: four days on the Inca Trail will involve extremes of temperature and weather. Most agree that any reasonably fit person should be able to cover the route, but it is challenging nevertheless, especially because of drastic changes in altitude. Therefore, doing some preparatory hiking around Cusco is a good idea.

HIKING THE TRAIL INDEPENDENTLY. As the number of tour groups on the Inca Trail multiplies, a heated debate has broken out among visitors to Cusco: follow the crowds or go it alone? One faction has made a strong case for the independent route. Solo hikers can do the trail at their own pace, make their own food, avoid the mindlessness and noise of large groups, make sure that campsites are left intact, and perhaps even save money. However, non-conformity has its drawbacks. Independent hikers must carry their own equipment (although porters can be found in the nearby town of Ollantaytambo or at the village of Huayllabamba, located along the trail). They will get the worst campsites, since agencies reserve the best ones ahead of time. (This is more of a problem in the crowded dry months of June-Aug. than during rainy Jan.-Mar.) Those short on time or experience may prefer the organization of a tour and the knowledge of a guide. Finally, the money one saves by not buying into a tour might be offset by transportation, admission, and equipment rental costs often included with the price of a group tour.

Those not discouraged by these last considerations must hike prepared: don't leave Cusco without a tent, a sleeping bag, raingear, rainproof coverings, warm (preferably wool) clothing, good hiking boots, a knife, a flashlight, matches, a water bottle, water purification tablets, a first-aid kit, toilet paper, bags for garbage, sunscreen, insect repellent, a stove, cooking utensils, and a change of clothing (since wet clothing won't dry). Food is rarely found along the trail, and where it is found, it's expensive; so hikers should bring enough for four to five days. A map and detailed guide to the trail are recommended. The classic source for the trail's historical background is Peter Frost's fascinating and excellent *Exploring Cusco.* Many of these items can be purchased or rented from outfitters around the Plaza de Armas. Per-day rental prices are US$2-3 per equipment piece. Occasional robberies suggest that hikers should camp in small groups and not alone.

INCA TRAIL ETIQUETTE. Thousands of people walk the Inca Trail each month and, especially in the high season, it shows. One can help preserve the delicate ecosystem of the Machu Picchu Sanctuary by following a few simple rules. Campfires are strictly prohibited. Trash should be deposited in designated places or carried in plastic bags; it should never be buried. Human waste should be disposed of away from the trail or in a public latrine, and never leave toilet paper behind.

On a human note: porters scramble up and down the Inca Trail, unceasingly putting up and taking down tents, hauling heavy equipment, sometimes carrying as much as 60kg on their backs, and all while wearing little more than sandals and *ponchos.* When hiring porters, either individually or through an agency, make sure they have a place to sleep on the trail and something to eat. Tip them well.

THE TRAIL

Traditionally, the Inca Trail begins at **kilometer 88,** scales four mountain passes, runs through several stretches of jungle, and climbs up and down several thousands of stone steps. Most tour companies cover the trek in three nights, spend the fourth morning in Machu Picchu, and return to Cusco by train in the evening. This itinerary is appropriate for hikers of most experience and fitness levels, but requires camping with large groups of people on the same schedule, especially during the high season. Fleet-footed hikers can scramble to Machu Picchu halfway into the third day, but they will probably have to spend an extra night anyway since Machu Picchu closes in early afternoon. Some extend their time to four nights or longer if their supplies hold out. An alternative to taking the kilometer 88 route is to ride the train from Cusco as far as **kilometer 104,** at the beginning of what is called the **Royal Trail.** Going at a completely different pace, the fastest hikers on this trail don't hike at all: they run—in a race held every September in which participants traverse the 33km to Machu Picchu in about four hours.

DAY I. The Inca Trail begins with the local train from Cusco (see **Cusco Transportation,** p. 128) to kilometer 88. (Some tour agencies choose to bus their groups to kilometer 82 instead.) Hikers cross the Río Urubamba and then pass the ruins of **Llactapata** ("Town on the Hill"), which appear on the right. The clearly marked path then crosses the Río Cusichaca ("River Happy Bridge") and follows the river's bank before beginning the 2½km climb towards the village of **Huayllabamba** ("Grassy Plain"), where many tour groups spend the night. There are a number of good campsites before and after the village, many with running water and toilets. In Huayllabamba, porters can be found to carry your stuff up to the towering first pass on the second day. Porters charge US$10-15 per pack per day.

DAY II. The main order of the day is scaling the steep incline (considered the hardest leg on the trail) to the **Abra de Huarmihuañusca,** better known as **Dead Woman's Pass,** the highest point on the Inca Trail. At a dizzying 4200m, the air feels much thinner up here than at the 3000m where most hikers woke up that morning. From Huayllabamba, it's a 2½hr., mostly uphill walk to a campground at **Llulluchapampa.** On the way, a stone stairway leads into a small patch of jungle with a green canopy offering momentary relief from the sun. At Llulluchapampa, one can finally see the course of the daunting climb ahead, along the left flank of the mountain. The gentle U-shape at the top is the pass. The next three hours expose hikers to the elements: first, scorching sun, then, closer to the pass, freezing winds whipping up over the mountaintops. Huarmihuañusca is met with great celebration, although sometimes it is cut short by extreme weather conditions.

Past the summit, it's a two-hour descent on stone steps to the Pacamayo Valley floor, where most groups spend the second night. There are limited toilet facilities.

DAY III, PART I. This is the longest day, with another two climbs, but neither as arduous as the first. Halfway up to the second pass rest the **Runkuracay ruins.** These were discovered by Hiram Bingham in 1915 as he traced the stone path from Machu Picchu. Runkuracay is noteworthy for being the only circular complex on the Inca Trail, and it may have served as a *tambo*, a resting house. Two ritual baths have been restored. A lookout surveys the Pacamayo valley below. Another 40 minutes uphill leads to the second pass: **Abra de Runkuracay** (4000m). Just over the pass, there's another official campsite.

From this point on, 80% of the Inca Trail is the real thing, original and unrestored. The footpath leads downhill through a natural tunnel and onwards towards the complex of **Sayacmarca** ("Inaccessible Town," 1hr.), an appropriate name given the sheer cliffs surrounding the town on three sides. The lack of nearby agricultural terracing suggests that no one actually lived here. Given the four ritual baths—three of which are found across the middle of the complex—Sayacmarca may have been a sacred spot for meditating pilgrims. Walk to the far end of the ruins to a triangular balcony overlooking the Aobamba valley. The sweeping view of the surrounding territory gives a hint at Sayacmarca's additional role: that of a control point for passing cargoes or persons on the highway. Backtrack and rejoin the trail as it passes **Conchamarca,** possibly another *tambo* for weary travelers. If you're feeling a bit weary yourself, you can stop at the small campsite.

From Conchamarca the path descends into dense jungle, meandering past orchids, wild daisies, bromeliads, and hanging mosses. This section is among the best preserved parts of the Inca Trail. An hour later, it passes a 20-meter-long **tunnel,** partly carved into the rock by the Incas as a shortcut to a more difficult route higher up. The trail then climbs to the third pass, **Abra de Phuyupatamarca** (3720m, 2hr.), offering exceptional views of Aguas Calientes below, the back side of Machu Picchu mountain (with its rainbow flag), and several snow-capped peaks including **Palcay** (5600m), **Salkantay** (6180m), and **Verónica** (5750m). Grounds near the pass are ideal for lunching or camping.

PART II. Descending a few minutes, one arrives at the ruins of **Phuyupatamarca** ("Town in the Clouds") and passes its six working ritual baths. The surrounding terraces, too high for crops, probably functioned instead as retaining walls. The top of the complex is dominated by a large slab of rock with mysterious dents carved into it. Some think these held sacrificial offerings. Locals like to say that Hiram Bingham pitched his tent here on stilts for fear of snakes. More likely, this was the base of an important building that was never completed.

A trail leads up and away from Phuypatamarca, bypassing the next two ruins to go directly to Machu Picchu. Most hikers take a stone staircase down instead. It is said that from the pass at Phuyupatamarca, 2,250 steps lead the way to Machu Picchu. Your knees will feel every one of these. After an hour or so of descent through now-familiar cloudforest flora, the path levels off a bit and forks near an electricity tower. The left path continues along the side of the mountain towards the terraces of Intipata. The right path descends to the ruins of Huiñay Huayna, which is next to a popular campsite and **hostel** offering hot showers (s/5), food, and beer. However, especially in high season, the grounds can end up looking (and smelling) like something akin to a Lima shantytown. As an alternative, some very coveted spots have been opened at the foot of Intipata, accessible from the main trail (as described above) as well as from a short path leading uphill from Huiñay Huayna.

Huiñay Huayna ("Forever Young"), discovered by Paul Fejos in 1941, was the last among the major complexes to be found and is named for the perpetually flowering orchid which grows nearby. Here, the number of ritual baths, all with flowing water, increases to 10. But, in addition to its role as spiritual purifier, Huiñay Huayna must have been a center of agricultural production; dozens of steep terraces cling to the mountainside. Some think the design of the complex resembles a river duck, with its terraces comprising the feathers. The terraces at **Intipata** mirror those of Huiñay Huayna in form and function. They also feature a wide central corridor appropriate for the procession of nobles inspecting the empire's bounty.

DAY IV. The Inca Trail is almost over at this point. Groups attempt to awaken at Huiñay Huayna at 4am in order to scramble to the pass over Machu Picchu in time for the legendary sunrise. To reach the pass, hikers must negotiate another hour of Inca stone pathways, culminating in a brief but near vertical set of 50 steps, probably a defensive measure securing this vulnerable edge of the sacred city. It's a few minutes climb to the fourth and final pass, **Intipunku** ("Sun Gate"), from which one can watch the morning's first rays of sunlight fall on Machu Picchu below. (The sky starts getting light by 6am; Machu Picchu is illuminated 1hr. later.) On the morning of the summer solstice, the sun's rays shine directly through a large stone "gate," and during the winter solstice they shine through another. Now the celebrating truly begins as you, weary pilgrim, descend to the promised sacred city of the Incas—Machu Picchu.

MACHU PICCHU

Open daily 5am-2:30pm. Admission US$10, students US$5, children US$2. Repeat admission US$5.

Guidebooks have been known to exaggerate, but the Inca ruins of Machu Picchu truly are among the most awe-inspiring sights in South America. Clinging to a vertiginous hillside surrounded by severe drops and towering green mountains and bathed in a near-constant stream of sunshine, it is surpassed by few other settings. The structures are as intact as Inca ruins come. Hundreds of fine stone constructions luckily had to contend only with natural forces; the invading Spaniards never knew Machu Picchu existed. One can only imagine what the city looked like with neighborhoods of adobe buildings that occupied the site during its use. The massive size of Machu Picchu comes close to absorbing the mobs of sunburnt tourists who visit annually, especially in the months of June through August. On average, 1,000 people visit Machu Picchu each day.

A DISCOVERY LONG OVERDUE. The American Hiram Bingham is commonly touted as the discoverer of Machu Picchu even though locals living nearby knew about the ruins long before Bingham explored the area and variations of the words "Machu Picchu" appeared all over property deeds and explorers' maps leading up to the 20th century. Nevertheless, Hiram Bingham was the first with the resources needed to expose the city's significance to the rest of the world. Ironically, he

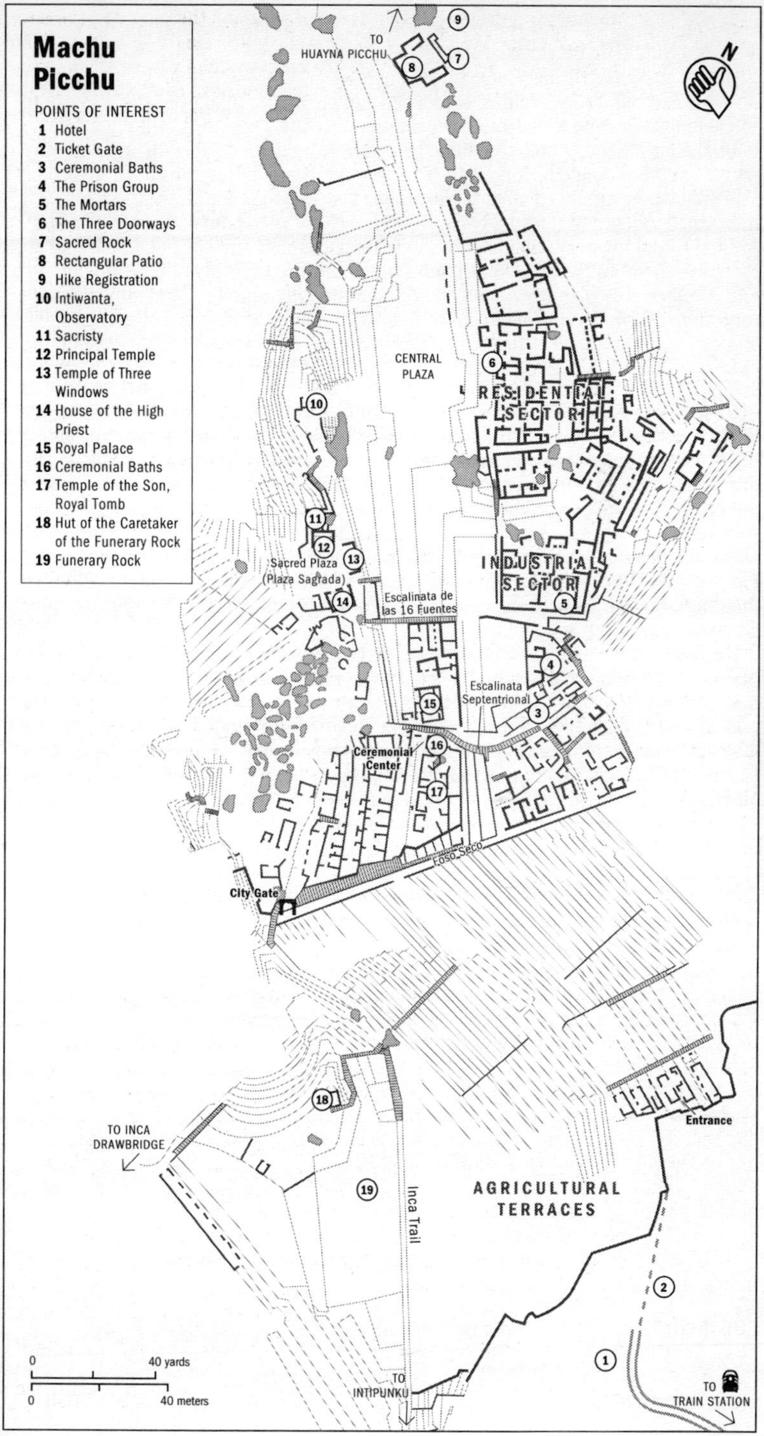

Machu Picchu

POINTS OF INTEREST
1 Hotel
2 Ticket Gate
3 Ceremonial Baths
4 The Prison Group
5 The Mortars
6 The Three Doorways
7 Sacred Rock
8 Rectangular Patio
9 Hike Registration
10 Intiwanta, Observatory
11 Sacristy
12 Principal Temple
13 Temple of Three Windows
14 House of the High Priest
15 Royal Palace
16 Ceremonial Baths
17 Temple of the Son, Royal Tomb
18 Hut of the Caretaker of the Funerary Rock
19 Funerary Rock

TO HUAYNA PICCHU
CENTRAL PLAZA
RESIDENTIAL SECTOR
INDUSTRIAL SECTOR
Sacred Plaza (Plaza Sagrada)
Escalinata de las 16 Fuentes
Escalinata Septentrional
Ceremonial Center
Foso Seco
City Gate
Entrance
TO INCA DRAWBRIDGE
Inca Trail
AGRICULTURAL TERRACES
TO INTIPUNKU
TO TRAIN STATION
0 40 yards
0 40 meters

completely mistook it for the long lost Inca capital of Vilcabamba, the city he had set out to find (see **Bingham's Folly,** p. 153).

However, what Hiram Bingham discovered in 1911—whether he knew it or not—turned out to be far more wondrous and enigmatic than even the lost city of Vilcabamba. Despite numerous excavations over the years, it is still unclear who built Machu Picchu, who lived there, and why. Nor can one say with any authority why it was abandoned or forgotten. This last detail may be the most disconcerting. The Spanish never got to Machu Picchu because they did not know it existed, and they failed to learn of the site, because even the *last Incas* did not know it existed. Adding to the mystery, Bingham and others discovered several ruins near Machu Picchu—now found on the Inca Trail—which are similar in style. Like Machu Picchu, these were carefully constructed, inhabited, abandoned, and subsequently forgotten. Machu Picchu seems to have been the administrative center of this network of complexes, an entire region never preserved in Inca memory, despite the existence of royal oral historians whose duty was to remember it.

FIGURING IT ALL OUT. The style and function of Machu Picchu's buildings place it within the reign of the **Inca Pachacuti,** also responsible for the flourishing of Cusco and the extension of the Inca empire towards Ecuador and Chile. The city was probably constructed shortly after the Incas defeated the rival Chanca people in 1438, an event which marked the beginning of the great Inca expansion. And yet, if one accepts that Machu Picchu had been laid to waste before the Conquest, that leaves less than a century for the city to have been built, populated, and left behind. Almost no one who has considered the grandeur of Machu Picchu's buildings, temples, and terraces is satisfied with this time frame, but few can offer a coherent alternative account.

Hiram Bingham's mistaken view that the city was built as a defensive post popularized the notion that Machu Picchu was a citadel. Its many lookout towers and one drawbridge seem to support this view. However, archaeologists have lately considered Machu Picchu more of a religious center than a fortress. Studies by Bingham's excavation crew of human remains revealed a large majority of women in Machu Picchu's population, suggesting the prominence of virgin priestesses. Machu Picchu may have been a holy city at the end of a long walk of pilgrimage. Evidence of habitation suggests that only around 1,000 people ever lived there at one time. Yet the surrounding terraces—in Machu Picchu and nearby at Huiñay Huayna and Intipata—would have fed many thousands. Perhaps then, Machu Picchu was a site of agricultural experimentation (which was intricately tied to sacred ritual), or maybe the city served as a jungle outpost guaranteeing a secure and constant supply of coca leaves. Given all of coca's uses in sacrifice, divination, and medicine, the Inca empire would have stood still without it.

The mystery of the region's abandonment inspires even more speculation. Some believe the site's population was decimated by an epidemic disease. Others point to hypothetical sieges by the Antis tribe from the jungle. It is possible Machu Picchu was a vacation estate for the Inca Pachacuti and populated by his own *ayllu* or clan. If true, the site's abandonment could be explained simply by the death of Pachacuti. One view conjectures that the entire region rebelled against the empire, and that to prevent a major uprising the Incas swept in and moved the population out. Peruvian archaeologist Marino Sánchez offers a vivid narrative according to which Machu Picchu was struck by torrential rains, the gold-covered principal temple was hit by lightning, and seeing this as a bad omen, everyone fled in tearful grief. Guides to Machu Picchu will present these accounts with varying degrees of factuality, but it's all speculation. Happily though, the great mystery of these walls only adds to Machu Picchu's mystique.

LOGISTICS. The nearest **train station** to Machu Picchu is at **Aguas Calientes** (see p. 154). **Shuttle buses** depart for Aguas Calientes from the Machu Picchu Hotel (20min., every 30min. 12:30-5:30pm, s/10). **Luggage storage,** mandatory for backpackers fresh off the trail, is located near the admission booth (s/2 per bag). **Guides**

BINGHAM'S FOLLY **Hiram Bingham,** "scientific discoverer" of Machu Picchu, was a doctor in philosophy and history at Yale and had already retraced the footsteps of Simón Bolívar in his study of the great liberator's military campaigns. This golden boy decided to try his luck at finding lost Inca ruins. In 1911, when the young son of a local family showed Bingham kilometers of terracing and walls of unmistakable Inca stonework, who could doubt the American when he declared Machu Picchu the very place he had wanted to find, the long lost Inca city of Vilcabamba the Old?

After the Conquest, the rebellious **Inca Manco Capac II** retreated into the jungle and built a town called Vilcabamba, which the last Incas used as a base to attack the Spaniards in Cusco for the next 36 years. The Spanish finally put an end to this pesky Inca resistance with a brutal invasion in 1572. They sacked Vilcabamba, brought the very last **Inca Tupac Amaru** (Manco's half-brother) back in chains, executed him in Cusco, and dispersed his relations, putting an end to the Inca dynasty for good. In time, Vilcabamba was abandoned and all but forgotten; no Spanish chronicler could pinpoint its location on the map. But then Bingham announced its discovery to the international press, brought in his team of scientists and archaeologists, and carted their findings back to Yale. Vilcabamba the Old was found.

Or was it? Bingham's "discovery" stood unchallenged for the next 50 years. Never mind that it didn't hold up to the simplest scrutiny. "Vilcabamba" means "Sacred Plain" in Quechua, but Machu Picchu is far from flat. Vilcabamba was attacked by the Spaniards, but Machu Picchu shows no signs of Spanish invasion. Vilcabamba was built after the Conquest, but Machu Picchu's architecture shows no Spanish influence. Finally, Vilcabamba was constructed in a hurry by a renegade set of Inca warriors. Machu Picchu was no rush job. Bingham's mistake was affirmed by Gene Savoy in 1964, when he discovered what most people agree are the true ruins of Vilcabamba the Old at Espíritu Pampa, four or five days by truck, horse, and foot into the jungle. Ironically, Hiram Bingham actually found part of these ruins in 1909, but passed over them, considering them unimportant. Bingham never lived to learn the tremendous significance of what he found at Machu Picchu.

can be hired on site for around US$12 per person. **Coin telephones** sit outside the Machu Picchu Hotel. Run to the **public toilet** beside the entrance to Machu Picchu. **Police** and **medical facilities** are situated outside the entrance as well.

SPENDING THE NIGHT. The only hotel at the sacred city is the luxurious **Machu Picchu Ruinas Hotel,** outside the main entrance. Camping is authorized at the bottom of Machu Picchu mountain by the banks of the Urubamba river. Lunch at the Machu Picchu Hotel costs a whopping US$18. Relatively cheap fast food can be found near the admissions booth. Better yet, bring your own snacks or wait to eat in Aguas Calientes.

IN THE RUINS. Spread out between two mountains, the sacred city sprawls along Machu Picchu mountain and faces Huayna Picchu mountain. Even those coming off the Inca Trail must exit Machu Picchu and re-enter, getting their ticket stamped in the process. The front entrance leads into what is called the agricultural sector of the city, great terraces which supported enough crops for the entire population. Those llamas munching on the grass have been installed for the tourists—they actually prefer to live at higher altitudes. At the very top of the terraces, one finds a carved granite slab known as the funeral rock, which may have been used to prepare the dead for burial. This upper part of the city seemed to function as a cemetery. Hikers emerge from the Inca Trail onto this hilltop. Those interested can follow the path in reverse to see **Intipunku** and the enormous terraces at **Huiñay Huayna** (admission US$2; see p. 150). Also from the cemetery hill, a road leads to the **Inca bridge,** a defensive drawbridge which has been restored with logs.

Back down the hill, starting at the front entrance, everyone walks across one of the large flat terraces to reach 16 lined-up ritual baths with water cascading from one to the next down the side of the mountain. On the left just before the baths is the **Sun Temple,** notable for its U-shaped wall which hardly betrays a flaw in its fine masonry. On the winter solstice, sunlight shines through one of the windows and falls exactly on the center of the rock in the middle of the temple. A carved cave underneath the temple might have held human remains. It is said that the large buildings across the baths on the other side of the Sun Temple once housed Inca nobility. Walk to the top of the staircase along the baths to reach the rock quarry.

Walking further into the city on the same level of terrace brings you to the three-walled **Temple with Three Windows,** which is beautifully symmetrical and carved from immense stones. Opening onto the same plaza, the three-walled **Principal Temple** has one droopy corner that has partially sunk into an underground chamber. In one wall, find the building block that is counted to have at least 32 edges around its various faces. Further beyond this and on top of a small hill resides the **Intihuatana,** another carved rock which may have been used to measure the movements of the sun. Look over at the flat grassy area dividing the city like a parade ground.

On the other side of this clearing, at the far edge of the city on the way towards Huayna Picchu mountain, another plaza with three-walled buildings centers on an erected rock. Called the **Sacred Rock,** it just happens to be shaped like the outline of the mountain behind it. A lot of visitors continue along this path in order to hike up the steep **Huayna Picchu,** which takes about two hours round-trip. The most interesting aspect of Huayna Picchu is its mountaintop terracing which seems to have been intended more for decoration than for agriculture. On the way up to Huayna Picchu, a trail splits off towards the fine **Temple of the Moon.** Walking back into the city, you'll find dozens of stone complexes, most of which seemed to comprise ordinary housing. Within one of these buildings, two circular pans are carved into the floor stone. Bingham called these **mortars,** which he thought were used to grind corn, but others have speculated that they were filled with water and used as mirrors to observe the night sky. A nearby staircase leads to the multi-level and intricately carved **Temple of the Condor.** Bingham incorrectly thought its inner chambers served as a jail, leading to the misnaming as the "Prison Sector." The temple's more recent name stems from the triangular stone thought to represent the condor's head and a carved rock face that looks like an extended wing.

AGUAS CALIENTES

The final tourist stop in the Sacred Valley, Aguas Calientes has lost some of the traditional charms more successfully preserved in other valley towns. The village derives its name from the warm waters emanating from its mineral hot springs—purported to possess curative powers—collected in a couple of baths uphill from town. Nevertheless, the main focus of this two-street village is undoubtedly that great tourist mecca nearby, Machu Picchu. Tourists going to the sacred city lodge in Aguas Calientes eat in Aguas Calientes, buy their souvenirs in Aguas Calientes, and at the end of the day, soak in Aguas Calientes's *aguas calientes.* Overpriced and quite artificial, Aguas Calientes can be bypassed almost entirely by making Machu Picchu a daytrip from Cusco. However, some choose to stay in this touristic village in order to visit the ruins first thing the following morning. Perhaps second only to hiking the Inca Trail, a stay in Aguas Calientes is one of the best ways to get to Machu Picchu before all of the tourists arrive by train from Cusco.

ORIENTATION AND PRACTICAL INFORMATION. The only two real streets in town are **Av. Imperio de Los Incas,** the street along the old train tracks, and **Av. Pachacutec,** extending uphill from the Plaza de Armas, around which most hotels and restaurants can be found. Only the **local train** leaves from the **old tracks** (5hr., 4:30pm, s/15). Buy tickets from a booth beside the train tracks starting at 2pm. **Tourist trains** all leave from the **Estación Nueva,** a walk through the market from the old tracks. In high season, getting a ticket on a tourist train in Aguas Calientes proves difficult, since many tourists reserve round-trip tickets in Cusco. Of the tourist trains, there's the small **autovagon** (3hr., M-Sa 3pm, US$28), and the three classes of regular train (3½hr., 4pm): **Inka** (US$23), **Pullman** (US$17), and **Económico** (s/27.50). Tickets are sold at the Estación Nueva for same-day departures starting at 10am. **Shuttle buses** to Machu Picchu leave from the market (30min., every hr. 6:30-11:30am, s/10).

A complete lack of **banks** makes money exchange difficult; small businesses on Pachacutec buy dollars at unappealing rates. The **police** (tel. 211 178) and **medical clinic** are both located on Imperio de Los Incas, beside the train tracks. The **post office** is in a souvenir store on Pachacutec, two blocks from Plaza de Armas (open daily 6:30am-10pm). A **telephone office** is located on Imperio de Los Incas. **Telephone code:** 084.

ACCOMMODATIONS AND FOOD. During the high season, almost all of the hostels in Aguas Calientes seem to be booked. Some travelers resort to making reservations through an agency in Cusco, but prices can become exorbitant. Those considering a stay in Aguas Calientes should make the phone call themselves well in advance. The best place to stay in town is **Gringo Bill's,** Colla Raymi 104 (tel./fax 211 046; email gringobills@yahoo.com), right on the Plaza de Armas. Highly comfortable rooms are decorated with trippy Andean murals. Travelers can gather in the excellent but expensive restaurant or the lively bar. Make reservations in Cusco at Garcilaso 265-3 (tel. 241 545), just off Plaza Regocijo. (Dorms US$8, with bath US$10; singles US$15, with bath US$18; doubles US$25, with bath US$30; triples US$36, with bath US$42.) **Continental Hostal,** Imperio de Los Incas 127 (tel. 211 065), along the train tracks, is more basic—shared baths only—but very tidy (singles s/15; doubles s/30; triples s/45). **Hostal Sinchiroca,** Pachacutec (tel./fax 211 033), is a great deal, with hot water and carpeted pastel-colored rooms (s/15 per person, with bath s/25). **Hostal Los Caminantes,** Imperio de Los Incas 114 (tel. 211 007; Cusco reservations tel. 237 497), in an old, very turquoise house, is somewhat rustic. Mattresses are sagging and hot water is available only in private baths upon request. (Rooms s/10 per person, with bath s/20.) For food, an endless number of restaurants line Pachacutec and Imperio de Los Incas. They're usually a bit overpriced and not of especially high quality. Gringo Bill's serves some of the best breakfasts (s/10-18). Those familiar with the renowned Cusco pizzeria will appreciate Aguas Calientes's very own **Chez Maggy,** on Pachacutec (see p. 131).

SIGHTS. Aguas Calientes's *baños termales*, located at the top of Av. Pachacutec, consist of a couple of steaming green pools and one cold pool, all surrounded by hills. The mineral waters soothe aching muscles fresh off the Inca Trail, but the whole experience is better in the morning before gangs of gringos show up. A bar next to the pool serves *pisco sours* in the evening, and has towels and swimsuits available for rent. (Baths open daily 5am-8:30pm. Admission s/5.).

CENTRAL HIGHLANDS

The overland route between Huancayo, Ayacucho, and Cusco was formerly stricken from most travelers' itineraries since this part of the sierra was overrun with peasant-based terrorist groups during the 80s and early 90s. In recent years, however, the relentless efforts of the army and shifting public opinion have forced most group members underground and on the run. The tide began to turn in 1992 with the official surrender of the Sendero Luminoso by its captivatingly persuasive leader Abimael Guzmán. Most recently, in July 1999, president Alberto Fujimori appeared very publicly on television leading the manhunt for Oscar Alberto Ramírez Durand (a.k.a. Feliciano), the leader of the persistent terrorist faction, Sendero Rojo. Dressed as a farm laborer and in poor health, he was apprehended just outside Huancayo.

Meanwhile, the lively, friendly towns of the central Andes, invigorated by growing tourism have pushed past their violent history. The region presents the Andes at its most authentic: a wealth of artistry, music, history, and interesting cuisine, without all of the touristic excess of Cusco. Huancayo also has the newly restored high-altitude train from Lima to recommend it—considered one of the great rail voyages of the world. Located 300km away, Ayacucho's graceful colonial architecture has put on a new, freshly painted finish, only further enlivened by the city's renowned handicrafts. Traveling by bus can be arduous at times, particularly on the unpaved stretch between Ayacucho and Cusco, a near 24-hour journey. However, it presents the advantage of acclimatizing oneself gradually. Bus travel in the central Andes is also one of the most *típico* experiences imaginable: locals overflow the aisles carrying goods both living and inanimate; stout women in their many-layered skirts hawk Inca Kola; and *salsa* tapes cycle endlessly.

HIGHLIGHTS OF THE CENTRAL HIGHLANDS

- Wander among graceful colonial mansions and world-renowned tapestry workshops in the warm highland sun of **Ayacucho** (see p. 156).
- Recently reopened, the breathtaking **Lima-Huancayo Railway** (see p. 172) climbs to a higher altitude than any other train in the world.
- The **Río Mantaro Valley** (see p. 166) overflows with the best handicrafts in Perú.

AYACUCHO

In 1540, the Spanish founded the city of Huamanga (later, Ayacucho), after they decided to pick up from their preliminary settlement nearby in rainy, cold Huamanguilla. Huamanga, on the other hand, was sunny, dry, and situated at a more reasonable 2761m, an ideal location for colonial mansions and churches built from the wealth sucked out of the mercury mines in Huancavelica. The Spanish also founded the Universidad Nacional de San Cristóbal de Huamanga in 1677, the second oldest university in South America. Prior to the Spanish, the major inhabitants of the region were the Huari, whose expansion in the years AD 700-1100 led to one of the great Andean confederations to precede the Inca. The Huari were renowned for their textiles and ruthless successes in combat. (They were so fierce that when they finally routed the Tiahuanuco people, the Huari supposedly decapitated their prisoners and hung their heads as trophies.) The Incas eventually took over, but Huari loyalties still run high—local weavings often copy ancient Huari designs, and when the final battle for Peruvian independence took place on the nearby Plain of Quinua, the victors swiftly proclaimed themselves the Huari Liberators. It was on this fateful occasion in 1824 that "Huamanga" became "Ayacucho," Quechua for "Corner of the Dead," in memory of the patriots who gave their lives.

In the 1980s, "Corner of the Dead" took on a whole other meaning as Ayacucho spawned the violent activity of Sendero Luminoso, masterminded by intellectual Abimael Guzmán, professor of philosophy at the University of Huamanga. With a penchant for Kantian theory and Marxist-Leninist-Maoist communism, Guzmán recruited his students into bringing the Revolution to Perú. In 1976, declaring violent struggle as the means necessary, the Sendero swept into sierra villages, armed the peasants, and executed government officials. The Peruvian army returned fire with secret missions and death squads. The total carnage—over 30,000 dead and disappeared—left a deep scar on the minds of *ayacuchanos*.

Guzmán's capture in 1992 ushered in a new period for Ayacucho. Many of the peasants who fled to Lima have returned to their villages in the sierra. The once-heavy military presence on the streets of Ayacucho has largely dissipated. Investment in the city's centuries-old facades has finally paid off, attracting a growing number of tourists each year. Ayacucho would now prefer to be known as a Peruvian capital of *artesanía*, producing unique tapestries and ceramics which sell internationally. Possibly the weightiest thing in Ayacucho's favor is its population of over 30,000 students, whose energy, many hope, will help transform the city.

ORIENTATION AND PRACTICAL INFORMATION

Following a fairly neat grid pattern, Ayacucho has the splendid garden of the Plaza Mayor at its center. Most everything of interest can be found nearby. Most buses stop along Jr. Mariscal Cáceres, two blocks over from the plaza.

Airport: 2km northeast of Plaza Mayor. To get there, catch a *colectivo* on Jr. Lima (s/0.50) or a taxi (s/3).

Airline Offices: Due to bankruptcy across the industry, **AeroContinente,** 9 de Diciembre 160 (tel. 813; fax 817 504), is the only airline flying out of Ayacucho. They go to **Cusco** (M, W-Sa 7am; US$118) with a stop in **Lima** (US$60). Open daily 8am-8pm.

Buses: A plethora of bus companies on Manco Capac and Mariscal Cáceres send buses to: **Lima** (10hr., 10 per day 8am-10pm, s/20-25); **Huancayo** (10hr., 8 per day 6:30am-9pm, s/15-18); and **Andahuaylas** (10hr; 6, 6:30am, and 7pm; s/18) on the way to Cusco. Most expensive ride to Lima is **Cruz del Sur** (tel. 818 908), on Plaza Mayor, departing from 9 de Diciembre and Mariscal Cáceres; service includes food, videos, and the chance to win return passage through Bingo (10hr., 9am and 9pm, s/45).

Tourist Information: On Plaza Mayor next to the cathedral. A helpful staff can provide maps and suggest itineraries. They promise to get an English speaker on staff soon.

Tour Agencies: Urpillay Tours (tel. 815 074), on Plaza Mayor, is the agency recommended by the tourist office for excursions to nearby sights. Offers a 4hr. trip to the Huari ruins and Quinua (s/20 per person including transportation and admission fees). A city tour and excursion to Vilcashuaman is also available. Little English is spoken.

Currency Exchange: Exchange travelers checks at the **Banco de Crédito** on Plaza Mayor. An **ATM** outside accepts MC. Open M-F 9:30am-12:30pm and 4:30-6pm, Sa 9:30am-12:30pm. **Casas de Cambio** buy dollars across Plaza Mayor from the cathedral.

Market: Located on the streets around 28 de Julio and Carlos Vivanco, overflows every day of the week–mostly with household items.

Police: Policía de Turismo, on the corner of 2 de Mayo and Arequipa in the Plaza Mayor. Open daily 7am-11pm, but knock on the door after hours in case of emergency.

Hospital: Hospital de Apoyo, Independencia 355 (tel. 812 380; **emergency** tel. 812 181).

Post Office: Serpost, Asamblea 293 and Mariscal Cáceres (tel. 812 224). Open M-Sa 8am-8pm.

Internet Access: Casa Don Bosco, Asamblea 120 and Cusco, on the corner with Plaza Mayor, offers email (s/3.50 per hr.). Open daily 8am-1pm and 2-8pm.

TELEPHONE CODE	064

ACCOMMODATIONS

The recent boom in tourism in Ayacucho has spawned a new breed of quality accommodation. Cheap hostels (about s/10 per person) can be found along the slightly dingy Jr. Mariscal Cáceres. Medium-priced but good-value lodgings line the streets around Plaza Mayor, usually in beautiful old colonial houses with courtyards and caged birds. Shower early; hot water often runs out by noon. Rooms may be full during weekends when tour groups from Lima come to town. Prices skyrocket and vacancies disappear during Semana Santa; the tourist office can place visitors in private homes.

Hotel Guzmán, Cusco 239-241 and Sol (tel. 816 262), 2 blocks from Plaza Mayor, has prettily painted, spacious rooms with good beds and, sometimes, balconies on the street. Great multi-room quads. 24hr. hot water. Singles s/15, with bath s/24; doubles s/20, with bath s/30; triples with bath s/60; quads with bath s/70; TV s/5 extra.

Hostal Mirador, Bellido 112 and Sucre (tel. 812 338), a steep hike up Bellido but worth the sweat for the outstanding views which come with each room. All 6 rooms are upstairs; some open onto balconies which let in sun and breeze. The rooftop patio (shortly to be turned into a restaurant) yields a fantastic 360° vista. Electric showers mean hot water all the time. Singles s/12, with bath s/16; doubles s/22, with bath s/30; triples s/30, with bath s/42.

Hotel Los Alamos, Cusco 215 and Tres Máscaras (tel. 812 782), 2 blocks down from Plaza Mayor. Spacious rooms on the 2nd floor open onto the patio terrace. Each one has firm beds and a brand-new bathroom, but hot water runs only in the morning. Teach the talking tropical birds all the words you hear men say on the street. Singles s/20; doubles s/40; triples s/60.

Hostal Central, Arequipa 188 and Tres Máscaras (tel. 812 144), a block away from Plaza Mayor, occupies a lovely old colonial house. Comfortable rooms open onto a sunny courtyard. Hot water in common baths 6-9am, evenings as well for private baths. Singles s/12, with bath s/20; doubles s/20, with bath s/30; triples s/30; quads s/40.

Hostal San Marcos, 9 de Diciembre 143 and Bellido (tel. 816 867), 2 blocks from Plaza Mayor, a new hostel at the end of a dark alley. Amiable owners keep beautifully furnished rooms with varnished hardwood floors, furniture, private hot-water baths, and cable TV, all with breakfast (including freshly baked bread still hot from the oven). Singles s/35; doubles s/55; triples s/70.

FOOD

Ayacucho demonstrates an impressive amount of culinary diversity in its many pizzerias, *pollerías*, *sandwicherías*, and *chifas*. Ayacuchan cooks take pride in their *mondongo*, a flavorful soup of lamb or pork boiled overnight with peeled corn. Another favorite, the *puca picante*, is a dish of potatoes in a spicy red sauce with rice and *chicharrones*.

La Casona, Bellido 463 and 9 de Diciembre (tel. 812 733), in an immaculate old colonial house, popular with locals and foreigners. The attentive staff will explain dishes (in Spanish). *Comida típica* ranges s/6-15, a *mondongo* (served on Sundays) is s/6. The *bistec a la Casona* is served over rice and cooked vegetables, topped with strips of cheese, avocado, banana, and a fried egg (s/15). Open daily 7am-11pm.

Vegetariano El Madero, Asamblea 131 and Cusco, right off Plaza Mayor. Usually populated with gringos, El Madero prepares a list of fresh juices and fruit salads (s/2.50-4). One of the few places in Perú you can get *bistec* and *lomo saltado* made out of soy meat (s/6.50-8). Open daily 7am-11pm or midnight.

Restaurante Los Alamos, Cusco 215 (tel. 812 782), in the hotel of the same name. With a floor so lovingly cleaned one could serve food on it, this patio restaurant serenaded by parrots ("*hola!*") keeps a book-length menu. One page is devoted to breakfast foods, including very eggy *panqueques* (s/7). A huge selection of *criollo* dishes is offered (s/7-15). Open daily 6:30am-10pm.

Mía Pizza, San Martín 420 and 2 de Mayo (tel. 815 407), prepares thick-crust pizzas in a brick oven using fresh ingredients. The simple decor makes tasteful use of wicker, Quinuan pottery, and picnic tables. Personal pizzas s/10-14, family-sized pies s/20-28. Open daily 5:30pm-midnight.

Chifa Taypa, Mariscal Cáceres 1131 and Garcilaso de la Vega (tel. 815 134). A *restaurante criollo* by day, Taypa whips up delicious shrimp and chicken stir-fries by night. *Arroz chaufa* s/5, a wonderful combination platter of wanton, fried rice, chicken, noodles, and vegetables s/7. A large-screen TV blasts the Discovery Channel or the latest *fútbol* match *en vivo.* Open daily 6pm-midnight.

SIGHTS

If doing serious sightseeing in Ayacucho, it may be a good idea to purchase a *boleto turístico* (s/5 or s/10) which provides admission to the city's attractions. The cheaper pass covers churches, colonial houses, and the Museo Mariscal Cáceres; the s/10 pass includes these, the Huari Ruins, and the Museo Hipólito Unanne. However, if short on time, it may prove more economical to pay each s/2 entrance fee (s/0.50 for students). Most of the colonial houses are free anyway.

CHURCHES. In the 16th and 17th centuries, the Catholic orders of Ayacucho built a slew of mostly Baroque churches, 33 in all. The tourist office can provide a map of many of them. Most important of these is the **cathedral,** on Plaza Mayor, first built in 1669, then partly destroyed and rebuilt after an earthquake in 1719. *(Cathedral open M-W and F-Sa 9am-noon and 3-5pm, Th 4-7pm. Mass daily 6pm and also Su 10am.)*

CASONA CHACÓN AND THE MUSEO JOAQUÍN LÓPEZ ANTAY. In the streets surrounding Plaza Mayor stand numerous restored **colonial mansions,** or *casonas*, many of which have been converted into municipal buildings or museums. (Again, ask the tourist office for a map.) Half of the Casona Chacón functions as the Banco de Crédito, the other half as the Museo Joaquín López Antay, dedicated to popular art forms from the region. Here's where to find a full explanation of Ayacucho's most typical handicraft, *retablos*, decorated wooden boxes which depict any number of scenes using painted and lacquered *papier maché*. The art form was adapted from the religious *retablos* in metal brought by Spaniards. The Ayacuchan version often depicts the Nativity, local customs, or much bawdier scenes of wild drunkenness and merrymaking. The exceptional mansion itself dates from the 17th century. *(On Plaza Mayor. Museum open M-F 9:30am-12:30pm and 4:30-6pm, Sa 9:30am-12:30pm.)*

OTHER CASONAS. The **Casona Boza y Solis,** now the police headquarters, was built in 1740. During the period of rebellion against the Spanish, the patriot martyr María Parado de Bellido was held captive here. *(On Plaza Mayor. Open daily 9am-5pm.)* A small collection of local artwork is on display at the **Casona Ruíz de Ochoa** (Banco Wiese), an elegant 18th century mansion *(2 de Mayo and San Martín. Open M-F 9:30am-12:30pm and 4:30-6pm, Sa 9:30am-12:30pm.)*

MUSEO MARISCAL CÁCERES. This was the magnificent home of military man and one-time president of Perú (1886-90 and 1894-5), General Cáceres (see p. 58). The small, attractive mansion displays a hodgepodge of colonial paintings, furniture, possessions of the general himself, and sometimes modern art. *(28 de Julio 508 and Chorro. Tel. 818 686. Open M-Sa 9am-12:30pm and 2-5pm.)*

BARRIO SANTA ANA. Atop a hill in the southern part of Ayacucho—at the end of Grau—resides the prolific artisan community of Barrio Santa Ana. Meander through its streets during daylight hours to peek into weaving and *retablo*-making workshops and see how the masters produce their works. Crafts here are also better and less expensive than what is sold in town. *Talleres* run by the **Sulca family** are renowned for their woolen tapestries, woven according to Huari designs painstakingly rendered with natural dyes. The master, **Edwin Sulca,** crafts tapestries which convey a poetic or political message and often goes on tour in the United States. He grants a special discount to those who visit him

BEAUTY AND THE BOLÍVAR Legend has it that after Perú finally won its Independence in the Battle of Ayacucho, **Simón Bolívar,** liberator of Venezuela and Colombia, paid a visit to the city to congratulate the victors. A great banquet was held, musicians entertained, and the liquor poured freely. As the merriment reached a heightened pitch, Bolívar looked over at a group of local women and called over the famous beauty, **Manuelita Toledo.** The two began to dance, and the great Latin American liberator, feeling especially liberated himself, swept the señorita up in a passionate embrace. Not sufficiently impressed by the drunken man's military accomplishments, Manuelita resisted, sending a great slap across the soldier's amorous face. Bolívar's men leaped to their feet and demanded that she be executed at once, but Bolívar raised one mighty martial hand and said, "No. This woman has defended her dignity. I praise her for it." And he proceeded to declare Ayacuchan women some of the most valiant in all of Perú.

directly—US$150, as opposed to the US$5,000 he may get abroad. *(Plaza Santa Ana 82. Tel. 814 242. Open 8am-7pm.)* On the corner of Plaza Santa Ana in a big yard (listen for the sound of chisels) can be found the *taller* of **Julio Gálvez Ramos,** also called "Master of the Region of Huari Libertadores," who creates brilliantly white statues from Huamanga stone (alabaster). He can present pictures of himself with foreign dignitaries and sells his wares for anywhere between s/2 and US$3,000.

OTHER SIGHTS AND FESTIVITIES. Housed in decidedly modern architecture, the **Museo Hipólito Unanue** displays some of the hefty monoliths recovered from the nearby Huari ruins and other sundry artifacts. *(On Independencia in the northern part of town. Tel. 812 056. Open M-Sa 8am-5pm, Su 8am-1pm. Admission free.)* On a neighboring hill sits a soaring lookout marked by a cross called the **Mirador Acuchimay** *(s/3 by taxi)*. A hilltop restaurant serves beer with a panoramic view of the city.

In recent years, Ayacucho's **Semana Santa** festivities have set records for attendance in Perú. Over 5,000 have crowded the Plaza on Easter Sunday to watch the magnificent procession of the Cristo de Resurrección.

ENTERTAINMENT

Ayacucho's young population goes dancing on Friday and Saturday nights, often in second-floor converted apartments overwhelmed by flashing strings of light and blasting *salsa.* Other nights, these places serve as mellower watering holes. On the same street, two choice spots are **Los Balcones,** Asamblea 187, and the live music club **Arco Blanco,** Alamblea 280. Also popular is **Caracol,** Arequipa 285.

NEAR AYACUCHO: HUARI RUINS

Twenty-two km from Ayacucho stand the remains of the capital of the Huari empire, which flourished around AD 1000. The site extends some 1600 hectares across cacti-studded mountain deserts and is divided into 15 districts, of which only three have been excavated. Within the excavated area can be found a large slab of rock, on which animals might have been sacrificed, and the circular **Templo Mayor** where offerings were left for the god Wiraccocha. Also here are the **Monoachayoq** funerary chambers which once held the headless remains of the Huari's vanquished. Further uphill along the highway, in the chambers of **Cheqo Wasi,** whole noble households were buried. Mysterious holes in the stone may have released the souls of those inside or allowed caretakers to pour in preservative mercury. A small **museum** gives a good chronology of the Huari civilization and its Tiahuanuco roots. (Complex open daily 8am-5:30pm. Admission free.)

Transportation: To get to Huari, catch one of the frequent *colectivos* at the bus stop downhill on Mariscal Cáceres (30min., s/2).

NEAR AYACUCHO: QUINUA

Pretty, whitewashed, cobblestoned little Quinua taps to its own beat 32km from Ayacucho and 3300m high. This cheerful village—polite salutations are nearly mandated by law—produces enchanting little ceramic statues and flower pots and sells them right out of the workshop. Most houses in town have these creations mounted on their rooftops to shoo away negative spirits.

In Quinua, follow the main street, Jr. Miller, through town and uphill, and then turn right onto a road curving up a hill (10min.) to get to the **Pampa de Quinua** and the obelisk commemorating the Battle of Ayacucho. This plain, covered with grass and surrounded by gorgeous mountain landscape, was the site of the bloody fight in 1824 between Spanish royalists led by Viceroy La Serna and the rebel army of Antonio José de Sucre. Despite numerical disadvantages (Perú's 6,000 men and one canon versus Spain's 10,000 men and 11 canyons), the patriots proved victorious, capturing La Serna in the process. The viceroy was compelled to approve an agreement guaranteeing Perú's liberty (though his wounded arm kept him from actually signing). The sparkling, pointy white **obelisk** atop the hill measures 44m, one meter for every year of armed conflict leading to Independence (starting from Tupac Amaru II's rebellion in 1780). (Pay s/1 to climb up halfway to the *mirador* and see much the same thing as from below.) Across the field, a comical, ceramic statue in Quinuan style freezes Sucre in the middle of a battle cry. Camping is authorized and free on the plain, ideal for unobstructed stargazing (though the field is muddy in rainy season and freezing cold in the dry season).

Back in Quinua, the **Museo y Casa de Capitulación** (tel. 810 207), in the main plaza, keeps a collection of 19th-century pistols, swords, bullets, and other relics from the battle. In a room across the courtyard, remains the cell where the captive La Serna surrendered the colony. The actual document he approved resides within. Tradition has it that, while wallowing in his cell, La Serna became enamored of a Quinua woman who nursed him back to health. But once booted back to Spain, La Serna lost both his sweetheart and his colonial possessions and most likely died a defeated and bitter man. (Open daily 8am-5pm. Admission s/2, students s/0.50.)

Transportation: The bus from Ayacucho to Huari also goes on to Quinua (1hr., s/4). Both Huari and Quinua are usually visited in a day.

NEAR AYACUCHO: VILCASHUAMAN

Considered the center of the Inca empire **Tawantinsayo,** Vilcashuaman was founded by the Inca Pachacuti as an administrative and religious center which oversaw the flow of goods between north and south. Just 120km from Ayacucho, the ruin retains the foundations of its Sun and Moon Temples and, notably, has the only surviving example of an *ushno*, or ceremonial pyramid. The Inca and his coya (queen) supposedly gave orders from the double throne atop the *ushno*—the seats were gilded and shielded from the sun by multicolored birds' feathers. To get to Vilcashuaman cheaply, take a minibus from **Chaski Tours,** Ramón Castilla 180 (tel. 815 433), downhill on Carlos Vivanco (4hr., every 2hr. 5am-4pm, s/7).

ANDAHUAYLAS

On the long road journey from Ayacucho to Cusco, all buses stop in Andahuaylas, which marks the halfway point. This small town (pop. 35,000) is largely Quechua-speaking and hosts a huge traditional **market** on Sundays in which locals use the old *trueque* system of bartering goods. The nearby lake, **Laguna Pacucha,** also offers an enjoyable detour from the taxing bus trip. Walk around the edge to reach the **Sondor ruins,** an eight-level pyramid built by the Chanka people for veneration and sacrifice. The warlike Chankas were the last major enemies of the Inca before the even more warlike Spaniards came along. To reach Pacucha and Sondor, catch a SerTur *combi* in front of the hospital on C. Hugo Pesce, eight blocks down from the Plaza de Armas (30min. s/3).

Buses pull up and depart from Av. Malecón Grau, which runs along the river. They go to: **Ayacucho** (10hr.; 6am, 6:30, and 7pm; s/10) and **Lima** (18hr., 8 and 9am, s/45). **San Jerónimo,** Andahuaylas 125 (tel. 721 400), on a street perpendicular to Grau and three blocks over from the Plaza de Armas, serves **Cusco** (12hr., 6pm, s/23) with a stop in **Abancay** (5hr., s/12). As a slow but frequent option, **Señor de Huanca,** Martinelly 170 (tel. 721 218), on the main street five blocks from the Plaza de Armas, sends cramped minibuses to **Abancay** (6hr.; 6am, 1, and 8pm; s/12).

Exchange traveler's checks at the **Banco de Crédito** or **casas de cambio** on Trelles, perpendicular to Grau, two blocks from the Plaza de Armas. Public **telephones** can be found along Martinelly. **Telephone code:** 084.

Cheap hostels linger around the Plaza de Armas, three blocks uphill from the river along Ricardo Palma. Walk a block further uphill and turn right to find **Hotel Cusco,** Casafranca 520 and Guillermo Cáceres (tel. 722 148), with grimy walls but good beds and electric showers (dorms s/5 per person; singles s/8, with bath s/15; doubles s/15, with bath s/22; triples with bath s/30). Down the street, **El Encanto de Oro Hotel,** Casafranca 424 (tel./fax 722 555), offers considerably more comfort: TVs, phones, hot water, and new furniture. (Singles s/35, with bath s/40; doubles s/55, with bath s/60; triples s/65; a suite for two with kitchen and bath s/75.)

As for food, a cheap chicken dish can be had around Plaza de Armas, but many consider the best place in town to be the Chinese **Chifa El Dragón,** Trelles 276 and Juan Ramos (tel. 721 641), serving chicken, shrimp, and duck dishes (s/6-9; open daily 8am-11pm).

LIMA-HUANCAYO RAILWAY

After being shut down in 1991, at the height of Shining Path activity in Huancayo, passenger service from Lima into the Andes was finally restored in late 1998. This extraordinary and famous train trip—the highest altitude standard gauge railway in the world—was considered one of the great feats of transportation technology when it was constructed between 1870 and 1908. President José Balta envisioned the **Ferrocarril del Centro** (F.C.C.) as a means of connecting the mining towns of La Oroya and the Mantaro valley to the coast.

The ride is stunning and severe in its scenery, winding around great rocky and snow-capped peaks, and traversing numerous ecological zones, from coastal desert to Andean *páramo*. Around the town of Ticlio, temperatures drop some ten degrees below zero. The rail line reaches its apex on the pass through the Galera Tunnel—a startling 4780m above sea level. During its 12-hour journey to Huancayo, the F.C.C. passes 27 stations, 58 bridges, 66 tunnels, and 9 switchbacks.

In its inaugural year, the Lima-Huancayo line ran once a month, departing Lima at 7:40am. The return trip left Huancayo several days later at 7am. It has been rumored that more service will be added. The round-trip price of s/60 covers onboard service including food, tourist information, oxygen bags, and medical attention if necessary. For exact departures inquire at the Lima train station, Jr. Ancash 201, next to the Palacio del Gobierno (tel. 427 43 87).

HUANCAYO

Right in the heart of the central highlands, Huancayo (pop. 350,000) has only recently emerged from the shadow of violence. In the late 80s and early 90s, terrorism in this part of the Andes closed the prospect of tourism to Huancayo, the capital of its department, culminating in the shutdown of the famed Lima-Huancayo rail line in 1991. Now, the train's back up and with it come hundreds of oxygen-deprived tourists monthly, gasping at the 4800m pass. Most return to Lima, but a few remain in Huancayo for weeks on end. As a city lacking major conventional attractions, Huancayo has become something of an alternative destination, promising an authentic Andean experience. Huancayo is the major city in the Río Mantaro Valley, cradle of Huanca culture and brimming with *artesenía*. The city itself hosts a thriving community of artists and artisans in its own right. Visitors can load

up on quality works as well as test the local claim that almost every day, there's a party going on somewhere, sometime, and somehow along the Río Mantaro.

ORIENTATION AND PRACTICAL INFORMATION

Most services of interest to tourists revolve around the always crowded **Plaza de Armas** (also called *Parque de la Constitución*), with gardens, fountains, and hi-fi speakers playing a steady flow of muzak seemingly timed to the rise and fall of the water. This splendor is bound by **Calle Real** and **Calle Ancash** (running more or less north-south), and **Calle Puno** and **Av. Giraldez** (running east-west). Giradez becomes **Paseo La Breña** west of the plaza. Most buses from Lima arrive nearby—keep an eye out for the adobe-red dome of the cathedral on the Plaza de Armas. From the Lima train station, exit and turn right, walk up about two blocks, and turn left at the big avenue, Giraldez, which leads into the Plaza de Armas.

Beware of scam artists and **thieves** (*rateros*) throughout Huancayo, especially on the side streets of Real. Other unsafe areas include the streets around the Calle Pachitea side of the train station (to Lima) and the market area framed by Calle Piura, Calle Huánuco, Calle Ancash, and Calle Amazonas.

Trains: The station for service to Lima is located on Pachitea. From the Plaza de Armas, walk 3 blocks down Giraldez and make a right. Currently the train runs infrequently and costs s/60 roundtrip (see **p. 172**). Service to **Huancavelica** runs from another station in the southern part of town, at Libertad and Prado. From the Plaza de Armas take Real 12 blocks down and then steer right a few (or take a taxi, s/2). Choices include **Expreso**

(5hr., 6:30am, s/8-12) and **Ordinario** (6hr., M-Sa 12:30pm, s/6-12). There's also a one-car train called the **Autovagon** (4hr., F 5:30pm and Su 6pm, s/17).

Buses: A number of bus companies go to **Lima,** the biggest ones being **Cruz del Sur,** Ayacucho 287 (tel. 235 650; 6hr.; 1 and 11:30pm, s/25); **ETUCSA,** Puno 220 (tel. 232 638; 6hr.; 11, 11:30, and 11:45pm; s/15-30); and Mariscal Caceres, Real 1241 (tel. 216 633; 6hr., 7 per day, s/20-25). **Molina,** Angaraes 334 (tel. 224 501) goes to **Ayacucho** (12hr., 5 per day, s/17). **San Juan,** Ferrocarril 161 (tel. 214 558) goes to **Tarma** (3hr., every hour 5:30am-6pm, s/7) and onto **La Merced. Turismo Central,** Ayacucho 274 (tel. 223 128) goes to jungle towns, including **Satipo** (8-10hr., 7pm, s/17); **Cerro de Pasco** (6hr., noon, s/10); **Tingo María** (12hr., 6:30pm, s/25), and **Huánuco** (8rh., 9pm, s/17). As an alternative to train, one can take **Expreso Huancavelica,** Tarapaca 391 (tel. 213 321) to **Huancavelica.**

Tourist Information: Located in the gigantic Casa del Artesano on the Pl. de Armas, the **oficina de turismo** (tel. 233 251) is under-resourced and Spanish-speaking only. They might be able to produce a free map of Huancayo and the surrounding region.

Tour agencies: **Incas del Perú,** Giraldez 652 (tel. 223 303; fax 222 395; email incacas&lucho@hys.com.pe), attached to Restaurante La Cabaña. Run by the inimitable Lucho Hurtado, who speaks near-flawless English and also owns La Casa de la Abuela and La Cabaña (see below), Incas is dedicated to promoting authentic cultural experiences in Huancayo and the Río Mantaro Valley. Lucho offers a crash course in Spanish, as well as classes in weaving, pan flute, and Quechua. A number of mountain-trekking and jungle excursions are available, as well as "Ethnical Journeys," which involve living with native families. Incas also rents high-quality mountain bikes (US$15 per day) and offers a good deal of free advice to travelers planning to stay a while. Open daily 9am-1pm and 2:30-7pm, but Lucho can be found hanging around La Cabaña and La Casa de la Abuela unless he's on the road. Discounts for SAEC members and students. **Peruvian Tours,** Puno 488 (tel. 213 069), on the Plaza de Armas. Spanish-speaking and catering mostly to Peruvian tourists, this operator does standard tours of Huancayo and the Río Manaro Valley. Open M-Sa 8am-1pm and 3-9pm, Su 9am-1pm.

Money Exchange: Try *casas de cambio* or banks on Real near the Plaza de Armas. Street dealers also lurk around, buying dollars at competitive rates.

ATMs: They're scarce. The one at Interbank, on Teal at Lima, accepts Visa. A Telebanco machine in Plaza de Armas, on the corner of Real and Breña, accepts MC.

Laundry: Lave-Rap, Breña 154 (tel. 231 107), 1 block down from the Plaza de Armas. An institutionally clean, self-service laundromat. Open M-Sa 8am-10pm, Su 10am-6pm.

Emergency: Tel. 105.

Police: At Ferrocarril and Cusco near the Huacavelica train station (tel. 234 714).

Hospital: Clínica Ortega, Carrión 1124 (tel. 232 921), has an ambulance service.

Post Office: In Pl. Huamancmarca, 3 blocks down from the Plaza de Armas on Real. Sends and receives faxes. Open M-Sa 8am-8pm, Su 8am-2pm.

Internet: A number of *cabinas de internet* can be found on Giraldez. Try **N@ve Net Plus,** Giraldez 304 (tel. 218 181), which charges s/3 per hr. Open daily 8am-11pm.

Telephones: Coin phones proliferate around Plaza de Armas; the calling-card phones can be found inside and around the post office.

TELEPHONE CODE: 064

ACCOMMODATIONS

Huacayo has scores of hotels throughout downtown. Decent, well-priced, and relatively safe hostels cluster around the Plaza de Armas, especially on Giraldez, Ancash, and Amazonas. Expect prices to rise during Semana Santa and in July. Reservations are necessary for when the train from Lima rolls into town.

La Casa de la Abuela, Giraldez 691 and Huancas (tel. 223 303; email incas&lucho@mail.hys.com.pe), 4 blocks down from Plaza de Armas. The delightful *abuela* who runs this popular backpackers hostel (Lucho Hurtado's mother; see above) races around with an energy that belies her years. She prepares scrumptious breakfasts and chats frequently with visitors in the backyard or in one of several game rooms (featuring foosball, darts, and ping pong). Well-swept dorm rooms, sparkling communal baths, 24hr. hot water, a full kitchen ("small charge for gas"), and breakfast are included. Six-bed dorms s/15 per person, doubles s/20, double with bath s/25.

Hostal Plaza, Ancash 171 (tel. 214 509), 2 blocks from the Plaza de Armas, has dainty, well-swept rooms with new showers and, sometimes, couches and dressing tables. All rooms have hot-water baths. Singles s/25; doubles s/35; triples s/45; TV s/5 extra.

Hotel Confort, Ancash 237 (tel. 233 601), right next to the cathedral in the Plaza de Armas. This enormous hotel with over 100 rooms—all with private baths and a decidedly pink motif—is a steal for the price. 24hr. hot water kicks in if one waits long enough. Singles s/20, doubles s/30.

Hostal Paraíso, Huánuco 351, located midway between both train stations and the Plaza de Armas. Friendly women run this small hostel with new, flashy furniture and a little bar which serves food. Rooms have cable TV and baths with electric showers. Singles s/25; doubles s/45, with king-sized bed s/30; triples s/65.

Hostal Pussy Cat, Giraldez 359 (tel. 231 565), a couple blocks down from the Plaza de Armas. Friendly, neat, and simple, this hostel is well-located and has 24hr. hot water. Ask that the free TV be placed in your room. Singles s/20, with bath s/25; doubles s/30, with bath s/40.

FOOD

Cheap *pollo a la brasa* joints and *chifas* can be found anywhere around the Plaza de Armas. For traditional meals, one must go farther afield. Particularly good *restaurantes típicos* await in the El Tambo district, a s/3 taxi ride up Real. Huancayo is the origin of *papa a la huancaína*, a cooked potato smothered in a dressing of butter, milk, and cheese, and has especially good *picante de cuy* (guinea pig). Nearby Ingenio (see below) provides the city with exceptional *trucha* (trout), which *huancaínos* like to prepare any way imaginable.

La Cabaña, Giraldez 652 (tel. 223 303), 4 blocks down from Plaza de Armas. This swinging dinner spot fills nightly with foreigners and well-dressed Peruvians. Decor ranges from the folkloric to the pop-cultural, and the multi-room restaurant is lit with candles the color of the strong sangría they pour (s/3 per glass). Sandwiches and hamburgers are s/3-7. Pizzas are pricier (s/18-25), and a generous fruit salad with ice cream goes for s/5. Happy hour (5-7pm) features half-price drinks, including a powerful *calientito*, hot tea with rum or *pisco*, a Cabaña specialty. Live bands play Th-Sa from 8pm. Open daily 5-11pm, later on weekends.

Huancahuasi, Mariscal Castilla 2222 (tel. 244 826), in El Tambo, directly up Real (which changes into Mariscal Castilla). Located in a large colonial house with skylights and wrought-iron chandeliers, this is the recommended place to go to satiate all *cuy* and *chicharrón* cravings. Peruvian families come here on Sundays and holidays to partake of *pachamanca* (meat, beans, and grains wrapped in leaves and baked in an earthen oven; s/15), one plate of which could easily feed two or three. A heaping serving of *papa a la Huancaína* goes for s/5. Traditional music F-Sa. Open daily 8am-7pm.

Pizzería Lalo's, Giraldez 365 (tel. 232 509), 3 blocks up from the Plaza de Armas, doubles as a delicatessen and pastry shop. Family-run and friendly, Lalo's serves quality breakfasts, a variety of tropical juices, and of course, pizzas—all at cheap, cheap prices. Lalo's own signature pizza combines pepperoni, ham, olives, peppers, mushrooms, and whatever other meats and veggies might be lying around the kitchen (s/15). Open daily 7am-10pm.

Nación Wanka, Breña 567 (tel. 225 432), 5 blocks from the Plaza de Armas. While lacking the ambiance of Huancahuasi and El Tambo establishments, Nación Wanka is a good place downtown to sample *papa a la huancaína* (s/5) in an open-air courtyard. They also specialize in trout dishes (s/7-10). Open daily 7am-8pm.

SIGHTS AND ENTERTAINMENT

MUSEO SALESIANO. If spending several days in Huancayo, it is worthwhile to take a look at the city's set of quirky tourist attractions. The most surprising might be the **Museo Salesiano,** Santa Rosa and Huancavelica, in El Tambo. Kept on the second floor of a boys' school, this two-room museum would tickle the fancy of the most hard-core taxidermist with over 14,000 insects and stuffed animals, including jungle mammals, birds, and piranhas. *(Taxi from centro s/3.)*

SUNDAY ATTRACTIONS. With little remarkable architecture or history, Huancayo is best known for its overflowing Sunday market, **Feria Dominical de Huancayo,** which has been a tradition since 1572 and now draws 50,000 from surrounding villages to hawk their wares. Most stands sell ordinary consumer goods, from cutlery to stationery to training bras, but good deals can be found on blankets and sweaters woven in the distinct local pattern. The market stretches for dozens of blocks down Huancavelica, four blocks over from the Plaza de Armas (with back to the cathedral).

PARKS. A number of beautiful, clean, and safe parks were constructed during the term of Huancayo's last mayor, Pedro Morales, and reflect the artistry and lifestyle of the Huanca people. The intricately crafted **Parque de la Identidad Huanca** in the northeastern San Antonio district, is formed by stone mosaics depicting local legends and traditions. Whimsical snakes, other animals, bridges, and statues beg an afternoon of scrutiny. Stands within sell *chicha* and local foods. *(Taxi fare s/2).* According to a similar motif, the **Cerrito de la Libertad** features a mosaic-covered playground, church, and outdoor acoustic theater (which occasionally hosts free performances) perched high above the *Huancaíno* landscape. A pleasant 30min. hike up Giraldez, this hill is where slavery was abolished throughout Perú by Ramón Castilla in 1854 (see p. 56). On the right one can see the eroded sandstone formations called **Torre Torre.**

OTHER ATTRACTIONS. Some pizzerias turn into cozy music halls on Thursday, Friday, and Saturday nights. The best is La Cabaña (see above), which plays Andean music, classic rock, or a pleasing fusion of the two. *(Starts at 8pm.)* **El Barullo,** Giraldez 369, and **El Espigón,** Giraldez 355, play traditional tunes *(9pm-3am).* One block from the Plaza de Armas, **Antojitos,** Puno 599, hosts a piano bar *(M-W)* and live music *(F-Sa after 9pm).* The plain **Iglesia de La Merced,** two blocks up from Plaza de Armas on Real and Ayacucho, is significant in that it hosted the signing of the first Peruvian Constitution. *(Open Tu, Th-Sa 8:30-11:30am and 2-5pm, W 8:30-11am. Admission s/2.50.)*

NEAR HUANCAYO

As the principle city in the Río Mantaro Valley, Huancayo makes a convenient base from which to visit numerous small villages ranging in attractions from fine handicrafts, to delicious trout, to a historic convent, to the sparkling blue **Laguna de Paca** near Jauja. Huancayo is the southern endpoint of the valley, Jauja is at the north, and the banks of the river are called left (east) and right (west). Most villages of interest are on the left side. A paved road goes past them on the way to Jauja, as do dirt roads which wind through the back country and allow for hiking and bike-riding. The tourist office and Incas del Perú offer free maps of the valley.

NEAR HUANCAYO: JAUJA AND LAGUNA DE PACA

The small town of Jauja was Pizarro's first choice for viceroyal capital, and the buildings still retain a colonial style, usually painted in white and light blue. Jauja makes a good afternoon's excursion from Huancayo, mostly because of the nearby Laguna de Paca, a pretty little lake surrounded by decks and lawn chairs. Boats jet visitors around in groups (20min., s/2) to sneak a look at the infinitesimal *Isla del Amor*, where sirens supposedly lure men and women out to their deaths. To get to the lake, walk 4km down the road or take a three-wheeled *mototaxi* (s/1).

Jauja's restaurants and lodging pale in quality when compared to that of Huancayo. Those staying in Jauja could try one of the hostel's on the lake, which have limited hot water and charge about s/5 a night. In town, there's **Hostal Santa Rosa,** Ayacucho 792 (tel. 362 225) in the Plaza de Armas, which keeps tired beds and furnishings but has hot water (singles s/15, with bath s/20; doubles with bath s/30).

Transportation: To get to Jauja, take a *combi* (marked "Jauja") from the corner of Calixto and Pachitea (45min., frequent, s/7). One can also take a bus headed for Tarma and get off early.

NEAR HUANCAYO: CONVENTO DE SANTA ROSA DE OCOPA

Near the town of Concepción—on peaceful, well-kept grounds—rests the Franciscan **Convento de Santa Rosa de Ocopa,** the starting point for the colonial settlement and evangelization of the Peruvian Amazon. Within its pristine white walls there's an impressive library of over 25,000 books and manuscripts, some dating from the 1500s; a number of stuffed jungle beasts and birds; and a collection of paintings from the Cusco school. (Open M, W-Su 9am-noon and 3-6pm. Guided tours in Spanish only. Admission s/4.)

Transportation: To get to the convent from Huancayo take a *combi* to Concepción from the corner of Calixto and Pachitea (s/1). From here, it's a short taxi ride to the convent.

NEAR HUANCAYO: INGENIO

If trout were a god, Ingenio would be its altar. The pride of this small, pleasant village is its trout farm or *criadero de trucha*, more formally known as the *Centro Pisicola del Ingenio*. A monument to the fish—with murals of trout anatomy and a trout-statue fountain with trout swimming in the water—the *criadero* produces 180,000kg of rainbow trout annually. Stroll along grassy paths winding among the many channels of swimming entrées-to-be. Spanish-only tours describe the 360-day reproductive cycle of rainbow trout in exhaustive detail. (Open daily 8am-noon and 1-5pm. Admission s/1.) Stands outside the *criadero* cook up its former inhabitants. Down the hill, the **Restaurante Avila,** with a pond, waterfall, and two tree houses, serves trout to Alberto Fujimori when he comes to town. Included among the sundry *trucha* dishes (s/7-15) are the classic *trucha al ajo* (trout in garlic sauce), and the spicy *trucha a la mexicana* (trout stuffed with cheese, onions, and peppers).

Transportation: To get to Ingenio, wait for one of the frequent *combis* headed to Concepción on the corner of Calixto and Pachitea. From Concepción, it's another short *colectivo* ride to Ingenio.

NEAR HUANCAYO: ARTESANÍA VILLAGES

Several pueblos in the valley specialize in a particular craft and open their homes to visitors wandering through town. No one speaks English, meaning that one should practice saying *buenos días* and *buenas tardes* ahead of time. Most townspeople are extremely receptive to foreigners and will eagerly point you in the right direction, especially if you drop the name of a specific workshop or family. If you express interest in a particular shop, the owners will normally demonstrate their craft using typical tools and then pull out stunningly crafted merchandise. This is the place to scoop up high quality *artesanía* before the exporters do.

The first areas of interest on the way north are the side-by-side villages of **Cochas Chico and Cochas Grande,** 11km from Huancayo, which produce nationally famous *mates burilados*—gourds which are carved to depict local legends, traditions, and symbols. The families **Veli, Medina,** and **Poma** open their houses to visitors.

The next craft village is **Hualhuas,** which specializes in alpaca rugs and blankets woven with a Spanish loom. Knock on the workshop door of **Faustino Maldonado**. Farther north, near Concepción, the town of **San Jerónimo de Tunan** creates delicate silver filigree jewelry, answering the demand for ceremonial pieces needed by the valley's many festivals. The shop of **Abelardo Cortez Turín** is recommended by a number of locals.

Transportation: Before setting out, get a map and instructions from one of the tourist authorities (see p. 164). One approach to the villages is by taking a *combi* towards Jauja and then asking to be dropped off near any one of the villages.

HUANCAVELICA

If Huancayo is on the ground floor, Huancavelica is the slightly eccentric relative living in the attic. This remote and small city (pop. 35,000), capital of its department, floats among Andean mountaintops at a no-nonsense altitude of 3680m. When mercury deposits were discovered here in the 16th century, Huancavelica got its colonial start. The indigenous population was ruthlessly exploited as workers in the Santa Barbara "mines of death," where they found themselves exposed to noxious gasses on a daily basis. Today, the railway constructed to haul the fruits of this morbid industry provides one of the few ways to access the town. The train from Huancayo chugs past picturesque farmland and dozens of rushing mountain streams. The town of Huancavelica itself, with the rustic feel of a still-young settlement, presents an interesting detour from the route through Huancayo, allowing for lazy hikes in the surrounding hills or friendly conversation with locals in the busy streets.

ORIENTATION AND PRACTICAL INFORMATION. Exiting the train station, it's a couple of blocks downhill to the main street, **Av. Muñoz.** Make a left to head into the pretty **Plaza de Armas** around which most services can be found. Running parallel to Muñoz across the plaza is **Calle Virrey Toledo,** another important street. Buses from Huancayo arrive in the Plazoleta de Santa Ana, at the end of Muñoz from the Plaza de Armas.

Trains (tel. 752 898) run to **Huancayo** only by *ordinario* (not *expreso*) service (5hr., 6:30am and 12:30pm, s/6-12). However, there is a faster one-car **Autovagon** (4hr., F 5:30pm, s/17). **Buses** leave to Huancayo (5hr., 6 per day, s/10) from offices in Pl. de Santa Ana. There is no direct bus to Ayacucho. However, instead of going all the way back to Huancayo, one can take the 6:30am train or an early bus as far as **Mejorada** (2½hr.). **Tourist Information** can be found at Victoria Garma and Nicolás de Pierola. They can provide a free map and advice in Spanish only. (Open M-F 8am-1pm and 2:15-4:45pm.) Buses and trucks bound for Ayacucho come by until 9 or 10am and again around 10pm. Change dollars or travelers checks at the **Banco de Crédito,** Arica and Nicolás de Pierola, further down Muñoz from the Plaza de Armas (open M-F 9am-1:15pm and 4:30-6:30pm). The **police** (tel. 753 041) take complaints at the Plaza de Santa Ana. The **Hospital del Ministerio,** (tel. 753 113 or 751 100), on Cáceres, is next door in the district of Yananaco and can send an ambulance. The **post office,** Muñoz 759 (tel. 752 750), sends faxes as well as mail (open M-Sa 8am-8pm). Check **email** at the Instituto Superior Pedagógico (tel. 752 959), a blue-and-white building on Toledo (s/7 an hr.; open M-F 10am-noon and 3-8pm, Sa 10am-noon and 3-6pm). **Telephones** can be found within and in front of Telefónica del Perú on Toledo and Carabaya. **Telephone code:** 064.

ACCOMMODATIONS AND FOOD. Cheap rooms can be found along Muñoz on the way to the Plaza de Armas. Check that a place has warm blankets since Huancavelica gets frigid at night. The **Hotel Camacho,** Carabaya 481 (tel. 753 298), a left turn before walking into the Plaza de Armas, has cheerful rooms with fine wood furniture. All bathrooms have 24-hour hot water, but only communal bathrooms are equipped with showers. (Singles s/8, with bath s/13; doubles s/14, with bath s/22; triples s/21, with bath s/30; TV s/7 extra.) The **Hotel Ascensión,** Manco Capac 481 (tel 753 103), on the Plaza de Armas has shoddier furniture and also offers communal showers only. Hot water 6-9am. (Singles s/10, with bath s/13; doubles s/16, with bath s/20; triples s/25.)

Great fans of *pollo* will love Huancavelica; the rest should stock up at the many general stores lining Muñoz. A local favorite which attempts some variety is **Restaurant Joy** (pronounced "Yoy"; tel. 752 826), Toledo and Manuel Segura, right off the Plaza de Armas. Joy serves simple sandwiches (s/1-4) as well as many traditional dishes. (Open daily 7:30am-10pm.)

SIGHTS. Huancavelica's one museum, the **Instituto Nacional de Cultura** (tel. 753 420), on Arica in Plaza San Juan de Dios, one plaza over from the Plaza de Armas, is housed in a charming colonial building with a gurgling fountain in the courtyard. Dedicated to displaying the natural and cultural history of the department, several small rooms display stone tools, human skulls, popular art, and modern paintings by local artists. Check out the traditional costumes (worn by disturbingly Caucasian mannequins) and the display on the Huancavelican *danza de tijeras* (scissors dance), witnessed on harvest holidays. (Building open daily 9am-9pm; museum opened upon request. Admission free.)

Huancavelica has several colonial **cathedrals** though most are desperately in need of renovation. None have tourist visitation hours. Instead, the curious must sneak in with a curator or awkwardly leer during mass. The **Catedral de San Antonio** on the Plaza de Armas was constructed in the 17th century in the Baroque style and has a collection of paintings from the Cusco school (open in the evenings and for Sunday mass). The **Iglesia de Santa Ana,** in the eponymous plaza, is Huancavelica's oldest, built in the 16th century. The oft-closed neoclassical 18th-century **Iglesia de San Sebastian** and 17th-century **Iglesia de San Francisco,** both in a plaza further down Arica from Plaza San Juan de Dios, preserve some of their former majesty in decorated whitewashed façades. San Francisco also has catacombs.

Huancavelica also holds a significant **Sunday market,** mostly with food, fruits, and vegetables but with many other goods as well. It stretches about seven blocks along Torre Tagle, the street parallel and uphill from Muñoz. Huancavelica's own **hot springs** have been turned into thermal baths located in a blue-and-white building up a set of stairs from the top of Manco Capac (which leads out of the Plaza de Armas). One can swim in the crowded pool or soak in private baths. The latter are housed in concrete cubicles which rob the bather of mountain views ignored by the adolescent boys splashing in the pool. (Open M-Th and Sa 5:30am-4pm, F 5:30am-noon. Admission to pool s/1, to private bath s/1.50. Towel, bathing suit, and soap available for rental.

TARMA

On the way to the jungle, Tarma is nevertheless called by locals "the pearl of the Andes." On the bus ride to this small, prosperous town (pop. 120,000), one can see a change in vegetation, from mountain cactus to eucalyptus, but at an altitude of 3050m, Tarma is still very much a part of the sierra. There is little to do in town; it makes a good stop on the way to the jungle. Currently, Peruvian tourists come here in order to tour nearby villages of local importance: Acobamba, for example, with its sanctuary to El Señor de Murahuay. Not far from Tarma, one can also find Perú's deepest explored cave, la Gruta de Guagapo.

ORIENTATION AND PRACTICAL INFORMATION. Buses from Lima arrive on **Jirón Callao** which can be followed into the center of town. The focal point of Tarma is its **Plaza de Armas** framed by the north-south streets **Jirón Moquegua** and **Jirón 2 de Mayo**, and east-west streets **Jirón Lima** and **Jirón Arequipa.** Look for the cathedral's two clock towers and red dome. Most buses from Huancayo arrive on

Av. Manuel Odria. Follow it towards the stadium, making a right to follow the Río Tarma. About three blocks later make a left onto Jr. 2 de Mayo which leads to the Plaza de Armas.

Several **bus** companies serve Tarma. **San Juan,** Odria 1047 (tel. 321 677), near the stadium, goes to: **Huancayo** (3hr, every hr. 5am-9pm, s/7); **La Merced** (3hr., every hr. 5:30am-8pm, s/5); and **Oxapampa** (10hr., 10am, s/10). Buses to **Lima** (6hr., 5 per day; s/15) depart from around the intersection of Callao and Vienrich. The cheerful people at the **tourist office,** 2 de Mayo 775 (tel. 321 010) on the Plaza de Armas, facing the cathedral, give out maps and loads of regional information in Spanish only (open M-F 8am-1pm, 3-6pm). **Exchange dollars** for *soles* on Moquegua near the corner with Pl. de Armas. Other services include: the **police** (tel. 321 222), first block of Callao; the **Hospital,** UTES (tel. 321 400), 3rd block of Av. Pacheco, which has ambulance service; the **post office,** Callao 356 and Moquegua (open M-F 8am-1pm and 3-6:30pm); and **telephones,** at the Telefónica del Perú office on the Plaza de Armas. **Telephone code:** 064.

ACCOMMODATIONS AND FOOD. Most lodging in Tarma is dilapidated and has limited hot water. One exception is **Hostal Tucho,** 2 de Mayo 561 and Callao (tel. 323 483), which keeps newly painted rooms, all with neat bathrooms running dependably hot water (singles s/20; doubles s/30; TV s/3 extra.) The shabbier **Residencial El Dorado,** Huánuco 488 and Paucartambo (tel. 321 598), surrounds a pleasant red-and-white courtyard with tables and chair. The rooms are clean and the mattresses soft. (Singles s/15, with bath s/20; doubles s/20, with bath s/30; triples with bath s/40. Hot water in private bath only.)

Cheap restaurants with set menus crowd the streets around the Plaza de Armas. For more variety, try the appropriately named **Lo Mejorcito de Tarma,** Huánuco 190 and Ucayali (tel. 321 766), three blocks downhill on 2 de Mayo from the Plaza de Armas and then one block to the right. Their dozen-page menu includes all manner of meat, seafood, and *comida criolla*. Sandwiches (s/2-3) and an array of meat-free pastas (s/10) are especially good. (Open daily 7am-11pm.) **La Cabaña,** Paucartambo 450 and Huánuco (tel. 653 364), two blocks down Paucartambo from the Plaza de Armas, also serves *comida típica* on green formica tables in what vaguely reminds one of a furniture showroom (open daily 7am-10pm).

SIGHTS. Tarma's **semana santa** festivities, the week before Easter, consist of legendary processions led over "the world's largest" carpet of flowers—over 3200 sq. m. (The tourist office is currently approaching the Guiness Book of World Records for official status.)

Tarma's most important sights are actually closer to other towns. Going to **Palcamayo**, 28km from Tarma, brings one nearer to la Gruta de Guagapo, possibly the largest cave in Perú, although no one has seen the end of it. Spelunkers using sophisticated underwater diving equipment have descended about 2700m into the cave. More amateur explorers can walk in about 300m to look at stalagmites, stalactites, and an ancient cave painting. A flashlight is necessary, and it is advised that one find a guide in Palcamayo. The best place to find one is by the mouth of the cave at the house of **Modesto Castro,** who has explored the gruta himself and can perhaps lend his son as a guide. The cave is a 5km hike from Palcamayo. Eight km further along the road from Palcamayo to the Gruta is the high altitude town of **San Pedro de Cajas** (about 4000m high). This small village produces renowned **tapestries** woven from alpaca wool and sells them right out of the workshop. However, getting to San Pedro is difficult since *colectivos* from Palcamayo are infrequent, usually leaving in the morning. A taxi to San Pedro costs roughly s/35. In order to reach Palcamayo from Tarma, catch one of the frequent *colectivos* from the corner of Huánuco and 2 de Mayo (90min., s/5).

An important site of pilgrimage near the town of **Acobamba,** 10km from Tarma, is the sanctuary of **El Señor de Murhuay.** The sanctuary is built on a hill where the image of Christ on the cross was etched into the rock, supposedly by a soldier during a battle of independence. A more religious local account holds that the carving appeared much earlier in 1756 and that at various times in can be seen bleeding. Whatever the origin, the holy outline has since been filled by paint, and nearby restaurants and food stands now feed *pachamanca* to hungry pilgrims. During the entire month of May, festivals are held in honor of El Señor. The sanctuary is 1.5km away from Acobamba and visible from town. To get to Acobamba from Tarma, take a *colectivo* from the corner of Huánuco and 2 de Mayo (30min., s/1).

LA MERCED

Avenida Circumvalacion's elementary schools let out for lunch around midday. The dust their students kick up while running home serves as a reminder of La Merced's separation from the verdant Chanchamayo Valley. Those surrounding hills have no time for the town's swarming *motos*; they're too busy brushing against the clouds. Despite La Merced's few opportunities for Amazon Basin adventures, however, it provides travelers with a bus-ride-from-Lima's taste of the frontier closing in on the Peruvian jungle—if any of them ever made it out there.

ORIENTATION AND PRACTICAL INFORMATION. The irregular oval of La Merced's center stretches out between the **Río Tambopata** and **Av. Circumvalación**, which runs under **Cerro la Cruz** at the top of the hill. Roughly parallel to them, **Jirón Tarma** bisects the oval lengthwise and borders the **Plaza de Armas** on the side farthest from the river. Also bordering the Plaza are **Jirón Palca** and, perpendicularly, **Jirón Ancash** and **Jirón Junín**. One block beyond the Plaza, **Jirón Dos de Mayo** runs parallel to Ancash and Junín.

Buses depart from the *terminal terrestre* to **Lima** (7-9 hr., 9 per day 7:45-11am and 8:30-9:45pm, s/15,000), usually via **Tarma** (1½-2 hr., s/5) and **La Oroya** (3-4hr., s/10); **Huancayo** (5-6hr., 5 per day 8:45-10:30am and 8:45-9:45pm, s/12-13); **Satipo** (3 hr., 12:30 and 1:30pm, s/8); **Huánuco** (8 hr., F-W 9:45pm, s/20); and **Tingo María** (10hr., Tu and Sa 9:45pm, s/25). Numerous van and minibus companies send vehicles out to towns along the edge of the jungle. **Colectivos** to **San Ramon** cluster on Jr. Junín, towards the hill. **Motos** cruise the streets; rides to most anywhere in town will probably cost less than s/1.

Banco de Crédito (tel. 531 005), on the Plaza de Armas at the intersection of Jr. Tarma and Jr. Junín, is the only bank in town that will exchange travelers checks—with an $11.50 minimum commission! They also have a 24hr. **ATM** that accepts Visa cards. (Open M-F 9:30am-1:15pm and 4:30-6:30pm, Sa 9:30am-1:15pm.) **Emergency:** (tel. 105). Other services include: the **police** station (tel. 531 292), three blocks down Jr. Junín, then two blocks to the left on Jr. Pirola (open 24hr); the **hospital,** Tarma 140 (tel. 531 002), two blocks down Jr. Tarma from the bank, away from the bus *terminal terrestre* (open 24hr., with a 24hr. **pharmacy**); the **post office** (tel. 531 174), on Jr. Dos de Mayo between Jr. Arica and Jr. Pirola (open M-Sa 8am-1pm and 3-6pm); and the **telephone office** (tel. 532 923), across the street from the post office, which features fax as well as telephone service (open M-F 8am-1pm). **Telephone code:** 064

ACCOMMODATIONS AND FOOD. There are many hostels in La Merced, but no great values. **Hostal Villa Dorada**, Julio Pirola 265 (tel. 531 221), three blocks toward the cross on the hill from the Banco de Crédito and one block to the left, has good-sized rooms with similarly large windows. Unfortunately, some windows open onto the hostel's hallways, which offer little but a dim fluorescent glow. Singles s/10, with bath s/20; doubles s/20, with bath s/25. **Hotel Cosmos** (tel. 531 051) can be found one block over, on Pirola, near the intersection with Jr. Pauni. Cosmos' modern façade hides wooden bed frames and almost-parquet floors. It also has the cleanest walls around. Doubles with bath s/20; triples with bath s/30. The private bathrooms at **Hostal Santa Rosa,** 2 de Mayo 447 (tel. 531 012), are a lot nicer than the common ones. Springing for a private bathroom will mean less time in

Santa Rosa's dank corridors and more in a room with a blood-red horse pattern dripping down its walls. Singles s/10, with bath s/14; doubles s/14, with bath s/18; triples s/19, with bath s/25. Laundry service is available (s/3 for 12 pieces).

Even if any of the hotels did have restaurants, you'd probably want to go out to eat. Small restaurants abound in and around the Plaza de Armas. La Mercedians recommend the brightly-painted **Los Koquis,** Tarma 381 (tel. 531 536), on the plaza. Two outdoor tables escape the blaring television, but don't let the bugs finish off your chicken (s/7-9) and *papas a la huancaína* (s/4; open M-Sa 6am-11pm, Su 8am-3pm.) **Chifa Tai-Pei,** Palca 229 (tel. 532 286), also draws a crowd, although television can dominate meals here as well. A variety of main dishes (s/7-8) and running *menú* (s/5) are available. Open Tu-Su 11am-3pm and 7-10:30pm. Cheaper, though not always safe, meals await at the **jugerías** in the market, two blocks down Jr. Tarma (with the hill on your left) from the plaza. Sandwiches (s/1-2), juices (s/1-2), and desserts (s/1) are easy to find. Open daily 6:30am-midnight.

NEAR LA MERCED: SAN RAMÓN

Slightly more than 10km back towards Lima, La Merced's little sibling city isn't all that different from its bigger sister. Though a little quieter and a little less vibrant, San Ramón does hold some potential points of interest for the traveler, and it's only a short *colectivo* ride away.

A visit to the 60m-high **Tirol Waterfall** near San Ramón provides a welcome excuse for a walk in the jungle, though it might not be a particularly peaceful one on weekends when more people visit the falls. The waterfall is a 20-minute walk, largely uphill, along a marked path (which can get prohibitively muddy during the rainy season). To get to the hike's starting point, hop in a *moto* to Puente Paloma (10min., not more than s/5). Perhaps equally as important, San Ramón has connections... to the internet, that is. **Info-Net**, Tarma 340 (tel. 331 349) may be a little pricey for some (s/6 per hr.). Open M-Sa 1-5pm, Su 9am-5pm.

If you wish to stay in San Ramón, the best value is probably **Hostel Chanchamayo,** Progreso 291 (tel. 331 008), two blocks from the Plaza de Armas. Chanchamayo's rooms are arranged motel-style around a pleasant but somewhat dimly lit garden. The rooms' real wooden doors almost make up for their lack of sunlight. Singles s/10, with bath s/30; doubles s/20; matrimonial s/15, with bath s/40; triples s/30.

Transportation Information: *Colectivos* to San Ramón depart from La Merced's Jr. Junín, a block up from the Banco de Crédito (15min., every 20min., s/1), and can be caught for the return trip at Junín's Plaza de Armas.

JUNÍN

Stretched flat along the Andes' barren plains, Junín does not see many visitors. The highway that passes through the center of town carries most of them along, far past the cold and sleepless nights one finds at 4105m above sea level. But while the treeless plazas and windy dirt streets may not merit much more than a glance, the stunning **Lago de Junín**, along with its attendant birds and neighboring village, lies a mere 20km away, just waiting to be discovered.

Buses and *colectivos* stop by the roadside market along **Av. Manuel Prado**, the highway that divides Junín in two. The town's center lies downhill from the highway—the two paved streets that head down from either side of the roadside snack stalls, **Jr. Simon Bolívar** and **Jr. San Martín**, travel several blocks to the **Plaza de Libertad** and then another six to the **Plaza de Armas**.

Buses go to: **Lima** (4-6hr., 9 per day, s/10-14); **Tarma** (1.5 hr., 8am, s/4); and to **Cerro de Pasco** (1½ hr., 7am, s/3), where one can get another bus (1½hr., s/3) or a *colectivo* (1 hr., s/12) to **Huánuco.** Other services include: the **police** (tel. 344 008), on Jr. Bernado Alcedo, just downhill of the intersection with Jr. Ramón Castilla; the **hospital,** Saez Pena 650 (tel. 344 159), 1km. downhill from Av. Manuel Prado (open 24hr., with 24hr. pharmacy); and the **post office,** San Martin 196, two blocks downhill from the Plaza de Libertad, on the right (open M-Sa 8am-12pm and 3-6pm). **Telephone Code:** 064.

Hostal San Cristobal, Manuel Prado 550 (tel. 344 215), provides charmingly ascetic accommodations: stone floors and walls, rough wool blankets, and cold (if any) water down the hall. The back rooms have mountain views and the proprietors will heat up some water upon request. (Singles s/12, doubles s/16.) The **Plaza de Libertad** sports several places with cheap *menús* (s/2-3), and, starting around 6pm, food stalls by the market building.

The road through the large **Reserva Nacional de Junín** passes many traditional stone houses and grazing alpacas before reaching the **Lago de Junín,** an ideal locale for strolling or lolling (provided you have warm clothing and watch out for the bulls). While not particularly impressive at first sight, the lookout point near km 25 offers glorious views of the lake and landscape. Plenty of blue-billed, red-faced and black-and-white spotted birds flap along the lake's periphery, but you should bring binoculars if you hope to glimpse one of the few remaining *parihuanas* (a bird native to the region). While the lake is renowned for its variety of feathered friends, however, it doesn't take a birding enthusiast to appreciate either the incredible scenery or the remote villages along its banks. The village of **Ondores,** at km 22, houses a lovely stone church that locals claim dates from 1550.

Transportation: Lago de Junín can be reached by *colectivos*, which leave from the end of Jr. Simon Bolívar in Junín (40min, 45min., s/1), or by taxi. *Colectivos* head back toward town frequently, so you shouldn't have a problem flagging one down.

HUÁNUCO

The original Huánuco was an Inca settlement, now a ruin 100km west of the modern city. Before them the Kotosh inhabited the area, and their nearby temples may be the oldest in the Americas. However, such historical currents don't much impact present-day Huánuco, with its concrete cathedral presiding over a leafy Plaza de Armas. On a stroll through the eminently walkable city center, for example, a pedestrian passes many a noisy *video pub* before stumbling upon the white-washed residential districts. Only the ramshackle settlements climbing the wrinkled gray hills on the outskirts of town seem like they too could have been here a long time ago.

ORIENTATION AND PRACTICAL INFORMATION

Bordered by the **Río Huallaga** to the east, the **Laguna Vina del Río** to the south and mountains all around, Huánuco is approximately 300km northeast of Lima. For the most part, streets in the city center follow a grid pattern.

Airport: T Doble A, 28 de Julio 1015 (tel. 517 439) flies to **Lima** (45min., M,W,F, noon, US$65) and to **Tingo María** (20min., 1 per day M and F, US$35). **AeroCondor,** Abtao 519 (tel. 517 090) also flies to **Lima** (45min., 1 per day Tu, Th, Sa, US$69). The airport (tel. 513 066) is 6km north of the city center. *Colectivos* to the airport leave from the intersection of Jr. Ituallayeo and Av. de La República (s/1). A taxi should cost s/5.

Buses: León de Huánuco, Malecón Aromias Robles 821 (tel. 512 996), runs to **Lima** (9hr., 10am, 8:30pm and 9pm; s/20-25), as does **Trans Rey,** 28 de Julio 201 (tel. 513 623 (8hr., 4 per day, s/22-30). Trans Rey also runs to **Huancayo** (7hr., 9:30pm, s/16) and **Pucallpa** (12hr., 8:30pm, s/25). **Transportes Perú,** Tarapaca 449 (tel. 512 333) goes to **Tantamayo** (8hr., 6:30am, s/17). **Transportes Vitor,** Tarapaca 413 (tel. 513 347), serves **La Union** (6hr., 7:30am, s/10). **Comite 5,** General Prado 1097 (tel. 518 346), sends *colectivos* to **Tingo Maria** (2hr., leaving when full, 4am-7pm, s/10). **ETNASA** minibuses also leave to **Tingo María** (3hr., every hr. on the half-hour, 6:30am-4:30pm, s/5), from the far side of the Río Huallaga.

Taxis: Taxis to anywhere in the city center (which, somehow, includes the university) should cost s/1, to the airport or the Kotosh temple s/5.

Tourist Office: General Prado 718 (tel. 512 980), on the Plaza de Armas. A municipal office with multiple functions, has some photocopied maps and pamphlets. Open M-F 8am-1pm and 3-7:30pm.

Currency Exchange: Banco de Crédito, Dos de Mayo 1005 (tel. 512 069), 1 block south of the Plaza de Armas, exchanges traveller's checks and has an 24hr. **ATM** which accepts Visa. Open M-F 9:15am-1:15pm and 4:30-6:30pm.

Markets: Mercado Modelo, bordered by San Martin and Huánuco; and **Mercado Antiguo**, 3 blocks away, fronting primarily on Huánuco and Valdizan, offer similar items: fruit, cassettes, underwear. The first tends to be more chaotic. Both open during daylight hours.

Emergency: tel. 105

Police: Jr. Constitución 105 (tel. 513 115), at the intersection with Jr. Abtao. Open 24hr.

Hospital: Hermilio Valdizan 950 (tel. 512 400), at Jr. Constitución. Open 24hr., with a 24hr. **pharmacy**.

Post Office: Serpost, Dos de Mayo 1157 (tel. 512 503), on the Plaza de Armas, has a *lista de correos*. Open M-Sa 8am-8pm, Su 8am-2pm.

Internet Access: (tel. 514 012) at the University, several kilometers from the Plaza de Armas, on the road to Lima. The computers are on the third floor of the building. Service costs s/2.5 per hr.; students with an ID may get a discount. Open M-F 7am-8pm, Sa-Su 8am-1pm.

Telephones: Telefónica del Perú, 28 de Julio 1135-1170 (tel. 512 232; fax 512 093), a block and a half north of the Plaza de Armas. Deals with international phone calls and faxes. Open daily 7:30am-10pm.

TELEPHONE CODE:	064

ACCOMMODATIONS

There will be no bed shortage in Huánuco any time soon. Fairly decrepit, yet very inexpensive lodgings choke the Mercado Modelo area; pricier rooms dot the Plaza de Armas. The following accommodations can be considered somewhere in between the two extremes.

Hostal Astoria, General Prado 984 at Jr. Bolívar, 2 blocks toward the river from the Plaza de Armas. Creaky floors and some initial mustiness are small prices to pay for a room in this charming old villa, with its mile-high ceilings and brightly-tiled courtyards. No private baths. Singles s/10; doubles s/15; triples s/20.

Hostal Trejo, Abtao 525, between Jr. Ayacucho and Jr. Aguilar, just opened in the spring of 1999. Some of the interior violet-colored walls already show scuffs, but otherwise this bright art-deco building seems in good condition. Singles with bath s/18; doubles with bath s/25.

Hostal Kotosh, Ayacucho 560 (tel. 517 341), between Jr. Huallayco and Jr. Abtao. As crisp and impersonal as the hospital green of its walls and sheets implies. Back rooms provide mountain views and less noise from the nearby market. Some rooms have televisions, and all have a private bathroom. Singles s/15; doubles s/26; triples s/36.

Hostal Viajero, 28 de Julio 820, between Jr. Prado and Jr. Huánuco. *El baño* crouches in a hut in the center of the courtyard around which the hostal is constructed. The rooms lack windows, but Viajero is one of the cheapest places in town. Singles s/8; doubles s/12.

FOOD

While the markets don't offer much beyond fruit, you can't go very far in this city without crossing a *panadería*, bread baskets just brimming with bargains (eight pieces of brown bread for s/1, anyone?). As usual, restaurants proliferate on the streets radiating from the Plaza de Armas. For *pollo al brasa*, try Jr. 29 de Julio.

Fuente de la Salud, Huallayco 1110, just north of Jr. Beraun. Not much more than a hole in the wall (albeit a healthful one), this *fuente* offers good vegetarian dishes at a great value (*menú s/3)*. Particularly tasty are the soy burgers (s/1), fresh juices (s/1-2.50) and appropriately tart natural yogurt (s/1-2). Open daily 8am-10pm.

Cevichería el Piurano, Beraun 821 (tel. 516 451), near the Plaza de Armas. The cool white tile makes for pleasant if somewhat incongruent meals, but it's the fresh *ceviche* (s/8-15) that draws the crowds. Open daily 7am-5pm.

SIGHTS

IN TOWN. Though not exactly a must-see on any Peruvian sightseeing tour, the city and its environs couch some gems. The Museo de Ciencias, General Prado 495 (tel. 518 104), houses nearly 10,000 stuffed animals, all dissected and prepared by the curator, Nester Armas Wenzel, who learned his taxidermy in Spain and Japan. 10,000 sounds like many more than it actually is, but the museum still merits a look, if only for the hilarious case at the front—also lovingly set up by Señor Wenzel—which features frogs doing aerobics, ducklings playing trombones and some sort of rodent "with cholera"—sitting on the toilet! Open daily 9am-12pm and 3-6pm. Admission s/1, children and students s/0.50. Half a block further up Jr. Huallayco from the market, is the Iglesia San Francisco, which dates to 1560. Simple wood benches lead back to an ornate gold altarpiece large enough to dwarf any priest. The best time to go is during their children's mass (Sunday, 10am). A joyful, song-filled event, the mass won't be wasted on anyone—no matter what age or religion.

KOTOSH TEMPLES. Five km from town, off the road to La Union, the pre-Inca (4,000 year-old in some parts) Kotosh Temples bake in the sun. One of the oldest Andean cultures, the Kotosh probably constructed their series of temples amidst cacti and butterflies similar to the ones surrounding the complex today. And while not much remains of the original structures, visitors can make out certain aspects of the temples' former stature. Following the marked path, the first site one reaches is thought to date from the Kotosh/Sajarupata period of around 300 BC. At that time the people lived communally, with many families sharing one building and yard—evident in the symmetrical compartments still discernible in the bases of the walls. The complex's oldest structure rests up at the top of the hill; its asymmetrical walls (now pretty crumbled) were 3m thick. Finally, the **Temple of the Crossed Hands** (the temple most people mean when they speak of "The Temple of Kotosh") rests under the archaeologists' shed. The temple actually housed two sets of crossed hands (representations of the Cruz del Sur constellation), a man's and a woman's, but the first has been destroyed and the second is in the National Museum in Lima. *(Open daily dawn to dusk. Admission s/2, children s/1, students s/0.50.)*

Transportation: To get out to Kotosh, head to the south of town (by the laguna Vina del Rio) and flag down a *colectivo* (s/1) heading down La Union, which is on the right if your back is to the city center. A taxi from the city costs s/5.

VICHAYCOTO'S DISTILLERIES. Modern-day earthly pleasures await at Vichaycoto's distilleries. The *aguardiente* produced here is sold all over Perú, but the workers at the factory will gladly give visitors a glass for free. And though the rusty old machines only set to work about once every fortnight, the huge metal vats keep a good reserve available all the time. *(Open M-Sa 7am-12:30pm.)*

Transportation: To get to Vichaycoto take an Ambo-bound bus (15-20 min., every 7min. 5:45am-9pm, s/0.50) from Cisne Alguilar 473 (tel. 516 199). The entrance to the factory faces the road.

NORTHERN PERÚ

The area of Perú extending from Tumbes at the Ecuadorian border to the Peruvian capital of Lima sees few foreign visitors on its long stretches of desert punctuated by rice and sugar plantations. Meanwhile, by the water, locals mainly occupy themselves with fishing and fish farming. Taking advantage of the busy port at Lima, most of Perú's economic activity takes place on the coast, adding to Lima's already formidable political responsibilities. But despite all of the serious business being handled in these parts, the coast is known for its generally laid-back and friendly attitude. And as one of the relatively undiscovered areas of the country, especially when compared to Machu Picchu and Lake Titicaca to the south, this northern section of the coast offers Perú at its most genuine.

Northern coastal Perú's attractions range from the natural to the architectural. This is where to find the country's most rugged and pristine beaches. Yet the splendor of the Andes is not far off, and jaunts to the highland towns of Cajamarca and Huancabamba are easy and pleasant excursions. Whether in Piura, Chiclayo, or Trujillo on the coast, or Cajamarca and Huancabamba farther inland, towns are characterized by well-swept plazas and gleaming white churches. These were built on top of the towns' pre-Hispanic foundations. These early founders have not been forgotten either: several important ruins still stand in this region, including the oldest site in Perú (Sechín), the largest preserved mud-brick city in the world (Chan Chan), and assorted other sites constructed by the Moche and Chimu peoples.

HIGHLIGHTS OF NORTHERN COASTAL PERU

- The **beaches near Tumbes** (see p. 180) are some of the prettiest on the northern coast, and provide some of the best **surfing** in South America.
- **Huancabamba** (see p. 183) is Perú's highland capital of mystical **faith healing.**
- **Cajamarca** (see p. 188), with its cathedrals and plazas, is one of the country's most beautiful colonial towns, with many nearby tourist attractions.
- **Chan Chan** (see p. 195), outside of Trujillo, is the largest preserved ancient mud-brick city in the world.

TUMBES

In Tumbes, the sun shines, and shines, and shines some more. It was shining on Pizarro when he sacked the then-Inca city. It was shining on the oil prospectors who discovered South America's first oil here in 1862. It was shining on the Ecuadorians who ruled the city for the first part of this century and continued to shine on the Peruvians who took it back during the Border War of 1941. Tumbes is a sun-lover's paradise. The nearby beaches, unspoiled by hordes of oil-smeared bathers, are some of the finest in South America and are complemented by the area's warm mineral mud baths, mangrove swamps and tropical rainforest. The city of Tumbes itself provides a perfect base for the exploration of these attractions. The center of town is lined with lovely *paseos* which, closed to cars, bustle with strolling *tumbeños.* Overspread with myriad brilliantly colored tiles, lined by pastel buildings, and filled with shining mosaic-covered fountains and monuments, these *paseos* are as attractive and aesthetically unique as they are lively and social.

ORIENTATION

The **Plaza de Armas,** on the southern edge of town, is the center of activity in Tumbes. Just south of the plaza's beautifully tiled walkways, the **Malecón Lishner** offers a shady walk along the **Río Tumbes.** On the cathedral end of the plaza, **Av. Tumbes** and **Calle Bolívar** are the two main northbound streets. Artisans and fruit-sellers hawk their wares at the **market** on **Mariscal Castilla** near the corner of **Ugarte.** The center of town, near the Plaza de Armas and **San Martín** (the pedestrian zone is called the **Paseo la Concordia**), is somewhat safer and better-maintained than the market area and the eastern end of the Malecón.

PRACTICAL INFORMATION

Airplanes: To get to the **airport** north of Tumbes, take a *colectivo* (s/1) from the market on the corner of Ugarte and Mariscal Castilla to the turn-off on Panamericana Norte, or ask for one of the travel agencies to arrange a shuttle. Flights go to **Lima** (2hr., M, W, F, and Su 1:30pm, US$89). Ask about special fares or promotions.

Long-Distance Buses: Most buses come in and go out along Av. Tumbes. They travel up and down the Panamerican highway, usually bound for **Lima** (18hr., 6 daily 11am-6pm, s/30). **Cruz del Sur**, on Tumbes next to Hotel Chicho, sends a luxury bus on the long trip to **Lima** (18 hr., 5pm, s/70 includes dinner and breakfast), as well as more regular buses to: **Chimbote** (13hr., 1:30 and 7pm, s/30) via **Trujillo** (10hr., s/25), **Chiclayo** (8hr., s/20), and **Piura** (5hr., s/15). The earlier **Lima** buses also stop in: **Sullana, Piura, Chiclayo, Trujillo, Chimbote, Casma, Huarmey, Barranca,** and **Huacho.** Buses heading for the **playas** south of Tumbes pass by the bridge on Av. Tumbes' south end.

Taxis: Local travel is generally done by **mototaxi,** s/1-2 for a spin around town.

Tourist Information: The Centro Cívico, on the Plaza de Armas, Room 204, offers various leaflets (mostly in Spanish) and local information for tourists. Open M-F 8am-4pm. **Tumbes Tours,**

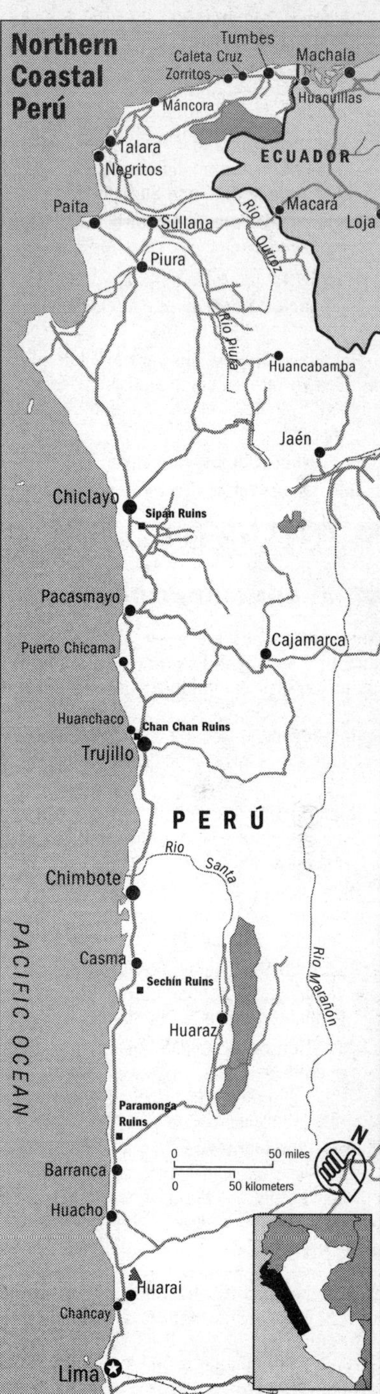

Tumbes 341 (tel. 524 837; fax 522 481), open M-Sa 8am-7:30pm, Su 8am-1pm. **Preference Tours** (tel. 525 518), Grau 427 near the Plaza de Armas.

Currency Exchange: Money-changers are far more common and flexible than banks near the Plaza de Armas. More secure, **Banco de Crédito,** behind the cathedral on the Paseo Los Libertadores, changes traveler's checks, U.S. dollars, and Ecuadorian *sucres*. Open M-F 9am-1pm and 4:30-6:30pm, Sa 8am-1pm. A **casa de cambio** next door to the bank also changes dollars and sucres and generally has much shorter lines. Open M-F 9am-1pm and 4-7pm, Sa 9am-1pm.

Laundromat: Lavandería Flash, Piura 1006 (tel. 523 231), has reasonable prices (s/12 for 4 kilos of clothes). Open M-Sa 8:30am-1pm and 3:30-8pm.

Emergency: Tel. 524 036.

Pharmacies: Tumbes has a *farmacia* on every corner. The **Farmacia San Vicente**, on Grau just off the plaza, is one of the best-stocked. Open M-Sa 9am-2pm and 4-9:30pm.

Hospitals/Clinics: The **Centro Médico San Jose** (tel. 523 873), next door to Farmacia San Vicente, caters to tourists and locals. Open M-Sa 8am-8pm. The **Hospital de Apoyo** (tel. 522 222), on Tumbes and 24 de Julio, has a 24hr. emergency room/ambulance service.

Post Office: Serpost San Martín 208. Open M-F 8am-8pm, Sa 9am-1pm.

Telephones: Telefónica de Perú on the 6th block of Piura. (Open daily 7am-11pm.)

TELEPHONE CODE	074

ACCOMMODATIONS

Most of Tumbes' budget hotels (called "two-star" hostels or hotels) are within several blocks of the Plaza de Armas. While all hotel owners post their rates at the front desk, most will bargain for a *descuento* of up to s/5.

Hotel César, Huáscar 311 (tel. 522 883). For three stars, César has tastefully furnished rooms with large wood closets, inlaid wooden floors, and cable TV. Singles with bath s/40; doubles s/50.

Hostal Tumbes, Grau 614 (tel. 522 203). Pass through an all-green court and all-salmon halls to reach a simple but comfortable room equipped with a fan and bath. Singles s/17; doubles s/25.

Hotel Roma (tel. 524 137), at the corner of Grau and Bolognesi, overlooks the Plaza de Armas. Roma's large, airy common balconies are great for people-watching. Rooms equipped with fan, TV, and private bath. Singles s/40; doubles s/60.

Hostal Chicho, Tumbes 327 (tel. 522 282), offers the most amenities: hot water, refrigerator, radio/cassette player, TV, and fan. It's also conveniently located near the bus terminals. Singles s/35; doubles s/50.

Hostal Cordova, Abad Puell 777 (tel. 523 981). Banal but clean rooms with windows and private baths line a long hallway. The management is friendly and helpful, and the price affordable—especially with the possible *descuento* that the manager is eager to offer. Singles s/19; doubles s/28.

Hotel Sudamericano, San Martín 130 (tel. 523 415), half a block from the Plaza de Armas, offers dimly-lit, somewhat shabby rooms, but the owner is friendly, the location convenient, and the price reasonable. Doubles s/12, with private bath s/17.

FOOD

You'll have no trouble finding *comida típica* in Tumbes. The *conchas negras* (black clams for which the region is famous), *ceviche*, and other seafood are universally fresh and well-prepared. **Panaderías** abound; **Mabrasa,** on the corner of Grau and Huáscar, offers fresh, warm rolls for pennies (multigrain pan s/0.10, cream-filled *churros* s/0.50; open M-Sa 8am-8pm, Su 9am-noon and 6-9pm).

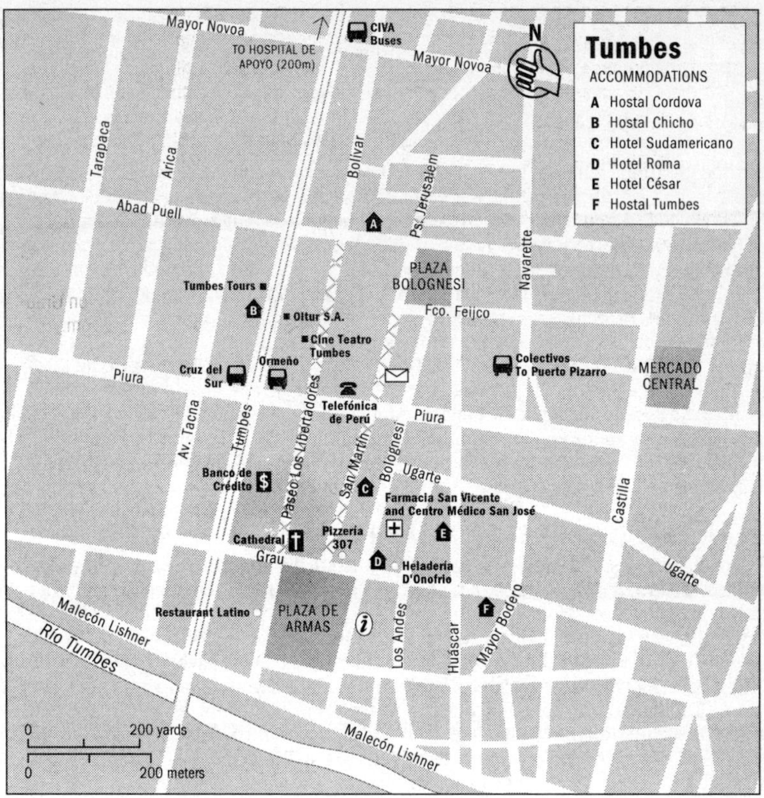

Pizzería 307 (tel. 524 052), on the cathedral side of Plaza de Armas, offers delectable pizzas (large vegetarian s/34) and much more. Impeccably polished bar replete with large TV and a *salsa*-blasting sound system keeps the atmosphere lively, as does the *sangría,* which locals imbibe by the pitcher (s/20). Open daily 8am-3am.

Restaurant Latino (tel. 523 198), on Bolívar on the Plaza de Armas, has a pleasant outdoor cafe, huge selection, and large *menu* portions (s/10-15). Open daily 7am-1am.

SIGHTS AND ENTERTAINMENT

Local residents emphasize that Tumbes is *muy tranquilo,* which translates not only as "safe and clean" but also as "dead at night." The *discotecas* near the Plaza de Armas are lively only on weekend nights, and even then most empty out by 1am. The **Restaurant Latino,** on the Plaza de Armas, has a large dance floor and *salsa* music on Saturdays. Smaller *discotecas* such as **La Cascada** along the **Paseo de los Libertadores,** off the Plaza de Armas, play the latest "techno-hits" from North and South America (open F and Sa 8pm-2am). The **Cine Teatro Tumbes,** on Bolívar near Piura, shows one movie nightly (s/2).

The **hervideros** (hot springs) in Bocapán, 35km south of Tumbes off the Panamericana Norte, will drown your dermatological and spiritual woes in a sea of warm mineralized mud. The hot springs are just beginning to be developed as a tourist attraction and are still hard to reach without a car or tour from Tumbes Tours. (US$20 per person; see **Tourist Information,** p. 177.)

NEAR TUMBES

The area surrounding Tumbes covers three completely different ecological zones, all easily accessible from Tumbes. First, there are the *playas*—100km of them. Take a *colectivo* south from Av. Tumbes near Piura (s/1-2) and find a spot on the arid white sand beaches that stretch out to the right of the Panamericana Norte. The villages of **Zorritos** (35min. south) and **Mancora** (1½hr. south) are popular destinations with a few small seafood restaurants, but you can ask the driver to drop you off at any point you want. To get back, flag down a north-bound *colectivo*. The second ecological zone, the **manglares** (mangroves), begins north of Tumbes at Puerto Pizarro. As swampy oases among the otherwise dry coastal landscape, the mangroves are densely populated by wildlife and leafy vegetation. Tumbes Tours (see **Tourist Information,** p. 177) has several excursions to the mangrove forests ($15-20 per person). If you're in a more independent mood, take a *colectivo* north to Puerto Pizarro and ask one of the local fishermen to take you up the Río Tumbes (s/60 per person). Two hours northeast of Tumbes, in the third ecological zone, await the orchids, butterflies, and savage beasts of the tropical rainforest **Bosque Nacional de Tumbes.** Any of the travel agencies along Tumbes can arrange tours for you, but Tumbes Tours offers a great 12-hour tour including transportation, meals, and an informative guide (about US$60 per person, less for larger groups).

NEAR TUMBES: PUERTO PIZARRO

Puerto Pizarro, a small fishing village 13km north of Tumbes, comes alive on weekends and *días de fiesta*. There isn't much of a town—just a few *barrios* on either side of the sandy road leading to the water—but it's the water that brings people to Puerto Pizarro anyway. Hop on a small boat and head over to the Isla del Amor (10min.) or another of the nearby islands for a picnic and a swim, or stay on the shore dancing with the *tumbeños* late into the night if you're lucky enough to be there during a holiday. The **Hotel Puerto Pizarro** (tel. 543 045) is the only place that offers resort-like perks (swimming pool, kayaking,, and trips to the islands) with clean but run-of-the-mill rooms with private baths, fans, and TV (US$20 per person). Eat there or in the **Bar Restaurante Venecia,** next door, which predictably specializes in seafood (*ceviche de conchas* s/7, *arroz con mariscos* s/5).

Transportation: Puerto Pizarro is easy to get to from Tumbes; *colectivos* leave from Piura near the *mercado central* (20min., s/1).

PIURA

Pleasingly cosmopolitan, Piura was founded in 1532 by Francisco Pizarro and enjoys the distinction of being Perú's oldest colonial city. Originally located in the Tangarará Valley, the town, evading pestilence and pirate attacks, moved three times before settling at its present site in 1588. Today, as the capital of its *departamento*, Piura hosts an impressive selection of fine hotels and restaurants and invites exploration of its lovely public squares. Take a contemplative rest on a bench by the La Pola statue in the Plaza de Armas and watch locals stroll and chat the night away under the light of the 16th century *catedral*. Or join strolling Piuran families and *enamorados* on the Plaza Pizarro. Nearby, the port town of Paita and the beach at Colán offer a refreshing escape from city life.

ORIENTATION AND PRACTICAL INFORMATION

Piura centers socially, if not geographically, around the **Plaza de Armas.** The always-busy **Av. Grau** runs west from the **cathedral** to the **Grau Monument. Tacna,** a major north-south street, intersects with Grau just between the church and the towering **Banco de Crédito,** which serves as an easy-to-spot landmark. The **Puente Peatonal**, on **Huancavelica** near the plaza, is one of the two main bridges in the city; the other, at **Sanchez Cerro** to the north, is closer to the **market** area.

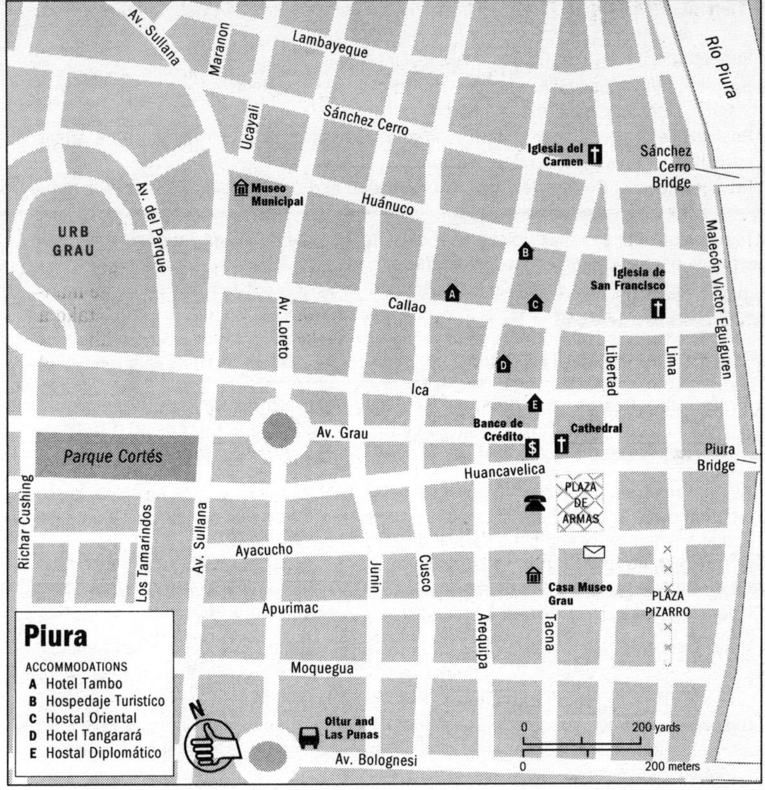

Airplanes: Piura's **Airport** (tel. 344 506), on Castillo, offers daily flights to **Lima** (1½-2hr., daily 9am and 7pm, US$79). Tickets can be purchased at **Aerocontinente,** Grau 110 (tel. 301 119). Open M-Sa 8:30am-1:30pm and 4-8pm, Su 9am-noon.

Buses: Oltur SA, Bolognesi 801 (tel. 326 666), sends a luxury bus to **Lima** (13hr., 6:30am and 6pm, s/50) The morning bus may also stop in the intermediate towns of **Trujillo** and **Chiclayo. Las Dunas** (tel. 321 973), across from Oltur, also sends luxury buses to **Lima** (13hr., 6pm, s/40) Buses also travel to **Huancabamba** (8hr., 3 per day 8am-9pm, s/20). Buses and *colectivos* heading north to **Tumbes** or **Sullana** (from which you can get to the Perú/Ecuador border crossing at Macará/La Tina) leave constantly from Sanchez Cerro between Sullana and the market.

Tourist Information: For lack of a real tourist office, consult with the many private tourist agencies. **Piura Tours,** Ayacucho 585 (tel. 328 873; fax 334 379; email piuratours@mail.udep.edu.pe), can provide information for tourists in English, French, or German. Open M-F 8:30am-1pm and 4-7:30pm, Sa 8:30am-1pm. **Tallán Tours,** Tacna 258 (tel. 334 647; fax 301 684; email tallantours@perumix.com), may also be of help. These companies can also arrange tours of Piura and surrounding areas such as Máncora, Paita, Colán, and Huancabamba.

Currency Exchange: Banco de Crédito (tel. 322 763), at the corner of Grau and Tacna. Open M-F 9:15am-1:15pm and 4:30-6:30pm, Sa 9:30am-12:30pm. Many **ATMs** congregate nearby. **Banco Latino,** Tacna 436 (tel. 335 858), also changes dollars and traveler's checks. Open M-F 8:45am-1:30pm and 4-7pm, Sa 8:45am-1pm. There are **casas de cambio** all along Arequipa between Ica and Grau.

Emergency: Tel. 113 or 105.

Pharmacies: All over the center of town. **Botica Central,** Grau 244 (tel. 334 869), is particularly well-stocked. Open daily 8am-midnight.

Supermarket: Costo, at Grau and Loreto. Open daily 8:30am-11pm.

Hospital: Clínica San Miguel, Cocos 153 (tel. 335 913). Offers 24hr. emergency service, ambulance, and a convenient pharmacy.

Post Office: At the corner of Ayacucho and Libertad across from the Plaza de Armas. Open M-Sa 8am-8pm, Su 8am-2:45pm.

Internet Access: GolNet (tel. 306 404), Libertad and Callao, offers *cabinas de internet* (s/3 per hr.). Open daily 8am-11pm.

Telephones: You can make credit card calls from any of the green **Telefónica del Perú** phone booths located on street corners.

TELEPHONE CODE 074

ACCOMMODATIONS

A great many of Piura's hotels and hostels offer both rooms with views of the street and rooms with views of, say, a cement wall. Usually, there is no difference in price, so try requesting one of the former *("con ventana a la calle")*.

Hostal Tangarará (tel. 326 450; fax 328 322), at the corner of Ica and Arequipa, is centrally located and has huge, functioning water heaters that your muscles will appreciate after a long day. TV and fan also included. Singles s/40; doubles s/60.

Hostal Oriental, Callao 446 (tel. 328 891). A 3-story lobby gives an open, airy feeling, and Chinese calligraphy adds to the charm of this budget find. Rooms are plain but sanitary. Singles s/13, with bath s/17; doubles s/24, with bath s/28.

Hotel Tambo, Callao 546 (tel. 322 312). As if the fan and telephone weren't enough, there's a comfy common TV-room and pieces of artwork everywhere to brighten things up. All rooms have cold water baths. Singles s/20; doubles s/30; TVs s/4.

Hospedaje Turístico, Arequipa 481 (tel. 334 520). A group of kind grandmotherly *señoras* run this hostel full of character and incongruous interior design. All rooms have private cold water baths. Singles s/25; doubles s/40.

Hospedaje Continental, on Junín between Ayacucho and Apurimac, may have peeling paint and worn furniture, but it's in a quiet location close to the plaza and very affordable. Singles s/14, with bath s/20; doubles s/20, with bath s/25.

FOOD

Tradiciones Piuranas, Ayacucho 565 (tel. 322 683). Pass a cast-iron gate and tiled patio to enter this alluring restaurant, decorated in the style of a traditional Piuran home and serving traditional Peruvian cuisine such as *palta rellena con pollo* (avocado stuffed with chicken s/8) and *pisco sour* (s/4). Open daily noon-3pm and 7-11pm.

Picantería la Santitos/Carburmer, Libertad 1014 (tel. 332 380), elegantly serves high-quality Italian food (personal pizza primavera s/15) as well as local specialties ("Gorden blue" s/27). Open daily 6pm-2am.

Pollo Dorado, Grau 267 (tel. 304 552), serves savory golden-brown rotisserie chicken to crowds of hungry locals. Fill up for cheap on a quarter chicken with french fries and salad (s/8). Open daily 6am-midnight.

Chifa San Gen, Grau 446 (tel. 332 415), is a popular restaurant serving chow mein, rice and noodle-based chinese food (*tallarines San Gen Especial* s/10.50). Open daily noon-3pm and 7pm-1am.

SIGHTS AND ENTERTAINMENT

CHURCHES AND PLAZAS. Piura provides the ingredients for long walks among colonial buildings and squares. The city takes great pride in its picturesque **Plaza de Armas,** in the center of which stands the liberty statue nicknamed **La Pola.** Off the plaza, the **catedral** was built in 1588 and contains an altar bathed in gold. Farther down at the end of Tacna, the **Iglesia del Carmen** now serves as a religious art museum. The independence of Piura was declared at the **Iglesia de San Francisco,** Lima and Callao, on January 4, 1821.

OTHER SIGHTS. Casa-Museo Grau, Tacna 662, displays the photographs, documents, and personal effects of the man who was born there, Admiral Miguel Grau, a naval hero from the 1879 war with Chile. The museum also exhibits a large collection of coins, which discusses the history of Peruvian currency. *(Open M-F 8am-1pm and 4-6pm, Sa-Su 8am-noon. Admission free.)* The **Museo Municipal,** Sullana and Huánuco, has a little bit of everything: anthropological, archaeological, and geological exhibits, as well as modern art, old photos of Piura, and even a small gift shop with books *(open daily 7am-7pm; admission free).*

There are a number of **discos** and **peñas** in Piura. **L'etage**, Ica 361 (tel. 992 354), is a trendy, upscale bar and disco attracting Piura's young and hip crowd (cover, including one drink, for men s/15, for women s/5; open Th-Sa 10:30pm-3am).

NEAR PIURA: PAITA AND COLÁN

Despite Piura's proximity to the sea, the city itself is landlocked. Most trade goes through the small port town of **Paita**, 57km northeast of Piura. Located in a natural bay, Paita is also a major center for fishing. The combination of small fishing boats and large cargo ships is somewhat disconcerting, but the activity and people are fun to watch from the palm tree-laden beach or lively pier.

Colán is one of the nicest beaches in northern Perú, with white sand and gentle waves. Colán is also famous for its church, which is an impressive stone Spanish structure said to be one of the oldest in South America.

Many people visit Paita and Colán as a day trip from Piura, but Paita has several decent hotels. The best is the **Hostal El Faro** (tel. 611 056), on Junín near Melendez, with clean, carpeted rooms with TVs, hot water, and private baths (singles s/50, doubles s/60). Less expensive is the **Kenco Hospidaje** (tel. 611 456) on Zanjon about 2 blocks from the water. A dimly-lit, dusty cement staircase gives way to surprisingly bright and cheerful rooms with cold-water private baths (singles s/25, double s/30). For food, try **N'Boga** (tel. 611 566), on Junín next door to El Faro, specializing in seafood (*ceviche* s/11; open daily 7am-4pm and 7-10pm). **Pattiburger** next to Kenco on Zanjon, is loud and lively (hamburgers s/3; open daily 8am-11pm).

Transportation: Buses to Paita leave frequently from Sanchez Cerro between Sullana and the market. From Paita, it is a 20-minute *colectivo* ride to Colán (s/2). Several tour companies in Piura offer organized trips to Paita and Colán; **Piura Tours** (see p. 181) has bungalows on the beach with a pool and restaurant.

HUANCABAMBA

As if consciously defying miles of coastal flatlands, the first towering peaks of the Andes shoot up with startling abruptness. Only by braving the narrow dirt road that winds up through a dense plain of clouds can one reach the lofty valley that cradles Huancabamba. Resist the urge to close your eyes and hold your breath as the bus winds its way along the steep cliffs—you'll miss the amazing scenery, and you'll need all the oxygen you can get, since the road climbs to 3000m above sea level before dropping to the city at just under 2000m. Think of the bus driver as a type of extreme tour guide; have complete faith in him and somehow, miraculously, you will arrive in Huancabamba safe and sound. The town serves as a gathering place for the farmers whose fields checker the sides of the surrounding mountains. It would be enough to visit Huancabamba for the town and surrounding landscape alone, but most come in search of spiritual healing. As one of Perú's major centers of traditional medicine, Huancabamba is renowned for its **chamanes** (spiritual healers, also known as *brujos*, *curanderos*, and *maestros*) and for the supposedly salubrious qualities of the nearby **Lagunas de Las Huaringas.**

ORIENTATION AND PRACTICAL INFORMATION. Activity centers around the colorful **Plaza de Armas** across from **La Iglesia San Pedro.** This square, one of the town's few level expanses, provides an excellent view of the hills above. For an even better view, ask someone in the church or tourist office to let you into the **Mirador** at the top of the bell tower. The town's **terminal terrestre** is as the end of **Centenario,** three blocks down from the Plaza de Armas.

Buses depart from the *terminal* to: **Piura** (9hr., 7:30am and 6pm, s/20) and **Chiclayo** (12hr.; Su, Tu, and Th 5:45pm; s/25). Huancabamba's helpful **tourist office,** at the *terminal terrestre*, dishes out information on nearby towns as well as on the curative powers of *chamanes* (open daily 8am-1pm and 3-8:30pm).

The **police** (tel. 473 010) are stationed on the plaza across from the cathedral (open 24hr.). **Botica Santa María,** 2 de Mayo 218 (tel. 473 018), is a 24-hour pharmacy. **Hospital Rural de Huancabamba** is at the entrance to the city. **Central Telefónica del Perú,** Unión 510 (tel. 473 144), can place your international call (open daily 8am-10pm). The **telephone code** is 074.

ACCOMMODATIONS AND FOOD. The best lodging is to be found on the plaza near the cathedral. **Hostal Dorado**, General Medina 116 (tel. 473 016), has 24-hour hot water in shared baths. Ask for a room with a window, or even better, a balcony. (Singles s/12; doubles s/22.) **Hospedaje San Pedro**, Centenario 206 (tel. 473 178), is right around the corner from the *terminal terrestre* and offers clean, basic rooms but has no water at night (singles s/10; doubles s/15, with bath s/25). **Hospedaje Danubio**, Grau 208 (tel. 473 200), offers good views of the mountains and sometimes has hot water (rooms s/10 per person).

WHAT A TRIP! Whether you suffer from arthritis or unrequited love, financial difficulty or fevers, the *maestros* of the **Huaringas** promise to provide a cure. The Huarinjas are comprised of about 250 *lagunas* of varying size, the largest of which is **El Shimbe,** at 3800m above sea level. The ceremony begins at the lagunas, where the *maestro* takes his patients to bathe in the purifying waters. The second part takes place at night and is known as *la mesada*. First, patients take a *remedia,* prepared from the hallucinogenic cactus known as the San Pedro or *huachumba*. After that has started to take effect, it is supplemented by *aguardiente* (sugarcane alcohol) and tobacco (absorbed through the nose). Next comes the invocations of various spirits and saints with the help of perfumes, incense, and special staffs, swords, and amulets depending on the nature of the ailment. This part of the ceremony lasts until 3 or 4 in the morning. While curious visitors are welcomed by locals, scorn or skepticism is not—these ceremonies are taken very seriously.

If you want to visit a *maestro,* ask around in Huancabamba to find out who the best ones are—not all of them work all the time, and some are specialists, only treating certain ailments. Then go to the tourist office and check in the official register to see how much each *maestro* claims to charge—usually around s/50. People in Huancabamba may offer to serve as guides to take you to your *maestro* of choice, but it may be better to find him on your own. To get to the *lagunas,* take a *colectivo* to **Salalá** from the plaza in Huancabamba, in front of CIVA (2½hr., 3-4am, s/10). From the drop-off point, you should be able to find a guide and continue by horseback (2hr., s/20). Alternatively, you can go the whole way with an English-speaking guide from one of the travel agencies in Piura.

The restaurants in town may be small and simple, but their proprietors are always friendly. **Poker de Aces**, around the corner from Hospedaje San Pedro, offers *criollo* food such as *cuy con papas* (guinea pig, s/15) and *rompopes* (a local libation made from *caña*—a strong sugarcane alcohol—with egg, sugar, honey, lemon, and vanilla, s/15; open daily 7am-11pm). **Restaurante El Artisia,** Centenario 180, serving *comida típica* in a covered dining area right next to the family's clothesline, bills itself as "*un lugar especialmente criollo.*" On occasion, local artists perform on El Artista's flashy stage. (Open daily 9am-9pm.) **Casa Blanca,** Unión 300 (tel. 473 137), is decorated with bright photos and walls painted to look like wood. The restaurant offers a wide selection of regional, Chinese, and vegetarian dishes (*menú* s/4; open daily 6am-9pm).

SIGHTS AND ENTERTAINMENT. As is often the case, the best sights in the area lie outside the city. The nearby ruins at the **Templo de los Jaguares** invite exploration, as do the waterfalls of **Citán** and **Los Peroles,** the **Baños del Inca,** the badland formations at the **Valle de los Infiernillos,** the **Lagunas de las Huaringas** (see graybox p. 184), and the traditional villages of **Sóndor** and **Canchaque.** The tourist office can tell you how to get to them, and they may also be able to provide a (Spanish-speaking) guide. Alternatively, go with an organized tour from Piura, which may be equipped with multilingual guides.

In the city itself, the small **Museo Municipal Mario Polia Meconi** houses artifacts from pre-Inca civilizations such as the Huancapampa, Chimu, Vicus, and Mochica, including two **mummies** found in Succhil (on Grau behind the Banco de la Nación; open M-F 8am-3pm).

The best times to visit Huancabamba are between June and November, particularly during the *fiestas*. The most important of these is the Festividad de la Virgen de Carmen, a four-day celebration beginning July 16, which features a group of *diablicos* in elaborate costumes who do a dance representing the struggle between good and evil.

CHICLAYO

Chiclayo, so close to several important archaeological sites, mostly attracts visitors with its prime location. The nearby ruins are among the oldest in South America, and have taught archaeologists much about elusive pre-Inca civilizations such as the **Mochica** and **Chimú.** Additionally, modern-day Chiclayo has earned recognition for its proud nickname of *La Ciudad de La Amistad* (The City of Friendship). Chiclayo's streets and well-maintained plazas buzz with amicable, curious and outgoing people. After a long day of exploring ruins, nothing could be more pleasant than a filling *criollo* meal and a long "Spanglish" conversation on Chiclayo's Plaza Cívica.

ORIENTATION AND PRACTICAL INFORMATION

Activity centers around the **Plaza de Armas. Av. Balta** is the major north-south street running through the plaza, and **Elias Aguirre** intersects Balta on the southern end of the plaza. The **Mercado Central** is on **Vicente de la Vega** one block from the plaza, but much more lively and colorful is the **Mercado Modelo**, five blocks north of the plaza on Balta and **Arica.** The **terminal terrestre** is at Bolognesi 338.

Airport: José A. Quiñones Airport, just south of the city, sends daily flights to **Lima** (1hr., 10am and 8pm, prices vary) and **Piura** (1hr., 8:15am, prices vary). Tickets can be purchased at **Aerocontinente,** Elias Aguirre 712 (tel. 209 916), on the Plaza de Armas. Ask about promotions or special fares. Open M-Sa 9am-8pm, Su 9am-1pm.

Long-Distance Buses: From the *terminal terrestre,* buses go to: **Lima** (12hr., 10 per day 6:30am-9:30pm, s/25-55); **Cajamarca** (7hr.: 7am, 2 and 9pm: s/15); **Jaen** (8:30am and 9pm, s/10); **Huancabamba** (12hr.; M, W, and F at 5pm; s/25); and **Tumbes** (8hr., 10pm, s/15) via **Piura** (4hr., s/10) and **Sullana** (5hr., s/12).

Tourist Information: For general information about Chiclayo and surrounding destinations, see the **Policía de Turismo,** Saenz Peña 830 (tel. 235 181; open 24hr.). **Quality Service Tours**, Balta 847 (tel. 221 963; fax 271 339; email quality@kipu.rednorte.com.pe) arranges tours to Sipán, Túcume, the Brüning museum,and nearby beaches. They have guides who speaks English, French, Italian, and German.

Currency Exchange: Interbank, Elias Aguirre 680 (tel. 238 361), on the plaza. Open M-F 9am-1pm and 4-6:15pm, Sa 9am-12:30pm.

Emergency: Tel. 114. The **tourist police** (tel. 236 700) can offer 24hr. assistance.

Pharmacies: Farmacia Solano, Balta 833 (tel. 236 632), is well-stocked and close to the plaza. Open M-Sa 8am-11pm, Su 8am-1pm and 4-8pm. Some 24hr. pharmacies can be found near the hospital.

Hospitals: Both **Hospital Las Mercedes,** Gonzales 635 (tel. 237 021) and **Clínica Lambayeque,** Vicente de la Vega 415 (tel. 237 961), provide 24hr. emergency service.

Post Office: The **post office,** at 140 Elias Aguirre (tel. 237 031). Open M-F 8am-9pm and Sa 8am-8pm.

Internet Access: Cibernet (tel. 222 791), on the Plaza Aguirre, offers reasonably-priced access in their *cabinas de internet* (s/3 per hr.) Open daily 8am-8pm.

Supermarket: If the *mercado modelo* doesn't have what you're looking for, the **Supermercado El Centro,** Aguirre and Luis Gonzales, is a well-stocked alternative. Open daily 9am-2pm and 4:30-10pm.

Telephones: Telefónica del Perú, Aguirre and 7 de Enero. Open M-F 8:30am-6pm, Sa 9am-1pm.

TELEPHONE CODE 074

ACCOMMODATIONS

Chiclayo offers numerous accommodations at reasonable prices. The cheapest ones (though not necessarily the best) are on Balta near the Mercado Modelo.

Royal Hotel, San Jose 787 (tel. 233 421), is in a grand old building with a winding staircase and a perfect location. Rooms have generous windows that open onto the plaza, as well as private, hot-water baths. Downstairs, there is a comfortable common room with a TV. Singles s/23; doubles s/35.

Hotel Oasis, Lora y Cordero 858 (tel. 272 700), is a newer establishment with clean, brightly-decorated rooms, big windows, and spotless, private hot-water baths. Singles s/20, with cable TV s/30; doubles s/40, with cable TV s/50.

Hostal Adriatico, 1009 Balta (tel. 221 873), is slightly less expensive but still loaded with character. The lobby has a huge pink vestibule with a crystal chandelier, and every room offers a colonial-style balcony overlooking bustling downtown Balta. Singles s/10; doubles s/18, with bath s/25.

Hostal Lido, Elias Aguirre 412 (tel. 232 810), has a friendly, multilingual sign by the door welcoming "travellers and friends" and wishing you a pleasant stay, which you likely will find here. Singles s/13, with bath s/20; doubles s/20, with bath s/30.

FOOD

Opportunities abound for fine dining. If you don't want to buy a cute, live guinea pig at the Mercado Modelo, you can find one on your plate at some of the restaurants specializing in *criollo* cuisine!

Pueblo Viejo, Izaga 900 (tel. 229 863), not only serves *comida criolla* at affordable prices, but is also an art gallery. The building's purple-and-green façade may not agree with its more rundown surroundings, but the pleasant interior is guaranteed to please. The staff recommends the popular *tollito a la plancha* (*tollo* is a fish native to the region, s/15). Open daily noon-5pm.

Parrillada Hebron, Balta and Izaga. Vegetarians beware: pleasant smells of grilled chicken and beef fill the air in this breezy and attractive carnivore's paradise. Artery-clogging offerings include the *menú ejecutivo* (roasted meat served with fresh juice and dessert s/6) and *costillas hebron* (ribs) with french fries and salad (s/12).

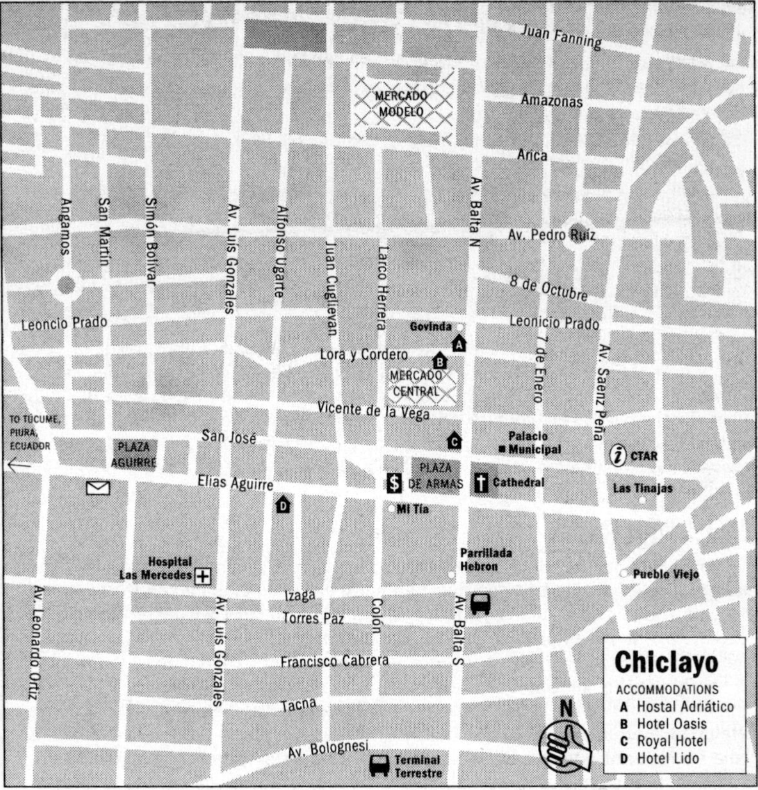

Govinda, 1029 Balta, another of Peru's Hare Krishna-run vegetarian restaurants, is Chiclayo's answer to traditional, meat-based *criollo* cuisine. Govinda serves delicious meat-free dishes, including healthy set menus (s/4.50) and strange-looking yogurt drinks topped with *kiwicha* and honey (s/7). Open M-Sa 8am-9:15pm, Su 8am-4pm.

Mi Tía, Elias Aguirre 662 (tel. 205 712), at the corner of the Plaza de Armas, offers tremendous selection and a great vantage for people-watching. *Arroz con pato* (duck with rice s/10) is a popular regional dish. Open M-Sa 8am-11pm.

SIGHTS

As mentioned earlier, most people come to Chiclayo to visit the area's many significant archaeological sights. Nearby ruins, including **Sipán, Túcume,** and **Lambayeque,** have yielded rare knowledge of pre-Inca civilizations such as the **Mochica** and **Chimú.** But you don't have to be an archaeologist or anthropologist to enjoy what the ancient sites have to offer; check with tourist agencies in Chiclayo (see p. 185) or at the ruins themselves to find pamphlets or guides that may help you (though not necessarily in English) unlock their secrets.

SIPÁN RUINS. Also known as the **Mochican tombs,** the ruins are of particular archaeological significance. They were discovered in 1987 near the town of Sipán and the site may still be visited today. *(Admission s/2.50.)* Most of the relics unearthed at the site have been moved to the archaeological and ethnographic **Brüning Museum** in Lambayeque, and only replicas remain at the Sipán site in a small one-room museum. *(Admission s/2.50.)*

CONGRATULATIONS, IT'S A GIRL Few would have imagined any benefits from the **El Niño** flooding of 1997-98. The northern coast of Perú was one of the worst-hit areas in the world, with hundreds dead and a half million homeless before the torment came to an end. The life-blood fishing industry of the region also faced near annihilation when processing plants were destroyed by flood waters, wreaking economic havoc.

However, once the clouds rolled away and Peruvians ventured out from underneath their tottering shelters, they found the sun shining on something born from the turmoil: a glistening, brand-new lake. Christened **La Niña,** the *laguna* spans over 4000 sq. km in the middle of the Sechura desert north of Chiclayo. The lake is so large that it will take up to five years for it to evaporate.

To see larger, more impressive edifices, head to **Túcume,** 33km north of Chiclayo, where the ancient **Sican** culture, and later the **Chimu,** dwelt and constructed 26 **pyramids** of varying size. Guided tours of these ruins can be arranged through any of Chiclayo's travel agencies. Guides can also sometimes be hired at the sites themselves (around s/5). *(To get to all of the ruins, take a colectivo (s/2-3) from the terminal terrestre in Chiclayo, near the junction of Saenz Peña and Pedro Ruíz.)*

CAJAMARCA

Up in the Sierra, the charming highland hamlet of Cajamarca has been the feather in many a warrior's cap. First home to various pre-Inca civilizations, the area was conquered in 1465 by the Incas and 67 years later witnessed an epoch-changing event: the imprisonment and execution of the great Inca Atahuallpa by Francisco Pizarro, an event which sparked a chain of battles that would ultimately lead to the Spanish conquest of the region in 1534 (see p. 45). Many remnants of these pre-Hispanic societies still remain and can be explored in the valley of Cajamarca. The town itself, however, displays a far more Spanish influence, a feature which has earned Cajamarca a reputation as one of the finest colonial cities in Perú. Cajamarca shares many of the qualities that tourists love about Cusco, yet the city remains relatively unvisited by travelers, and this gives it a more relaxed and authentic flavor than its more popular southern Andean cousin. And although the ruins near Cajamarca are not as magnificent as Machu Picchu, they are well worth the detour away from the dull and desertous Panamerican highway.

ORIENTATION AND PRACTICAL INFORMATION

At the heart of it all, the classical **Plaza de Armas** is large, green, and neatly kept. Most hotels and restaurants are nearby. **Amalia Puga** and **El Comercio** are major streets passing the plaza. Follow Amalia Puga away from the **Iglesia de San Francisco** to reach the **market.**

Buses: There are many bus companies on Atahuallpa's 300 and 400 blocks. This is not the same Atahuallpa that appears on the map; this is 1-2km east of the center of town. Take a **taxi** (s/2) or a **colectivo** headed toward the **Baños del Inca** (s/0.50). From this area on Atahuallpa, buses travel to: **Trujillo** (6hr.; 9:45am, 1, and 10pm; s/15); **Chimbote** (8hr., 10:15pm, s/20); **Chiclayo** (6 hr., 11am and 10pm, s/18); and direct to **Lima** (13hr.; 2, 5, and 6pm; s/25).

Tourist Information: ITINCI, Belén 600 (tel/fax. 822 903), on the first floor of the Belén complex, has helpful brochures and sells a detailed guidebook of the entire district (in Spanish, s/15). Open M-F 7:30am-1pm and 2:30-7pm. **Cajamarca Tours,** 2 de Mayo 323, can answer questions as well as arrange tours of town and nearby sights. Open M-Sa 7am-1pm and 2-7pm. **Cumbe Mayo Tours,** Amalia Puga 635 (tel. 822 938), offers information and tours with an English or French-speaking guide. Open daily 8am-10pm.

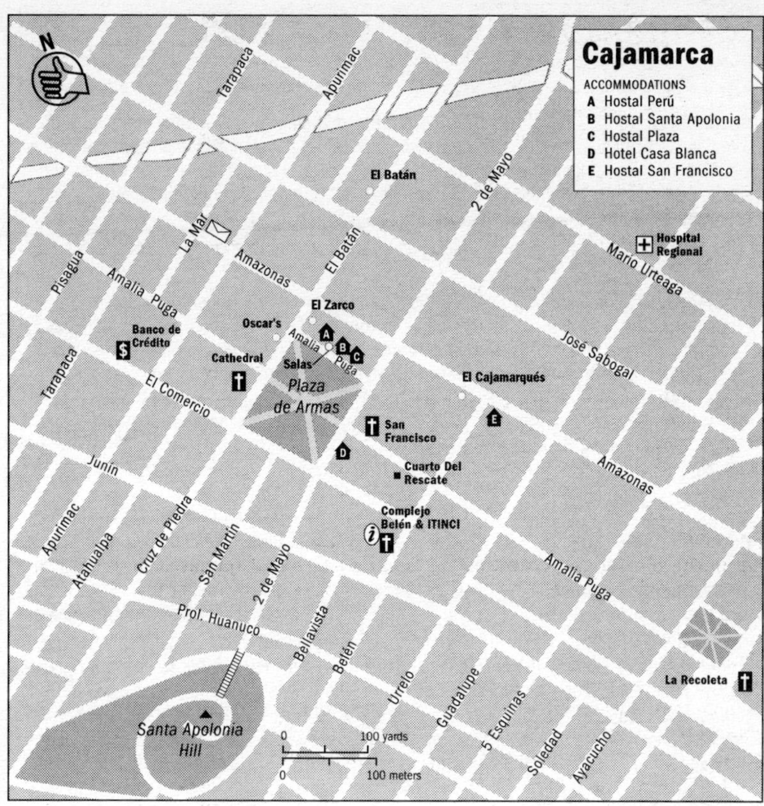

Currency Exchange: Interbank (tel. 822 460), 2 de Mayo, offers **ATMs** on the Plaza de Armas and will change dollars and traveler's checks. Open M-F 9am-1pm and 4-6pm, Sa 9am-12:30pm. Less reliable street money-changers roam near the plaza.

Laundry: Lavandería Dandy, Amalia Puga 545 (tel. 828 067), charges s/4 per kilogram of dirty laundry. Open daily 8am-7:30pm.

Police: Amalia Puga 807 (tel. 822 944).

Pharmacies: There is a multitude of pharmacies near the Plaza. **Botica 24 Horas,** Atahualpa 315 (tel. 820 644), is open around the clock.

Hospital: Hospital Regional Cajamarca, Marto Urteaga 500 (tel. 822 156), offers 24hr. emergency service and an in-hospital pharmacy.

Post Office: Amazonas 443 (tel. 822 206). Open M-Sa 8am-9pm, Su 8am-3:15pm. Additionally, **Cajamarca Tours** (see Tourist Information, above) provides **DHL** and **Western Union** service.

Telephones: Telefónica del Perú booths can handle collect and calling card calls.

TELEPHONE CODE	044

ACCOMMODATIONS

The best values are found on the Plaza de Armas. Searching hotels for an available room with a balcony onto the plaza is well worth the effort.

Hostal Santa Apolonia, Amalia Puga 649 (tel. 827 207). Rooms surround a clear, white-tiled courtyard illuminated by natural light filtered through a checkerboard of brightly-colored glass. Carpeted rooms are well-decorated. Singles s/20, with hot-water bath s/40; doubles s/40, with bath s/65.

Hostal Plaza, Amalia Puga 669 (tel. 822 058), located above two busy courtyards that house an artesanía shop and a restaurant. It has plain, basic rooms, many of which have balconies looking directly onto the plaza. Hot-water showers at certain hours of the day. Rooms s/15, with shower and plaza view s/25; group discounts available.

Hostal Perú, Amalia Puga 605 (tel. 824 030), offers accommodations similar to those of the Hostal Plaza at similar prices. All rooms have 24hr. hot-water private baths. Singles s/25; doubles s/50.

Hotel Casa Blanca, 2 de Mayo 442 (tel. 822 141). The "White House" is one of the more upscale hotels on the plaza, and most of its rooms surround a serene, beautifully decorated traditional courtyard. Carpeted rooms come fully equipped with TV, telephone, refrigerator, and hot-water bath. Singles s/50; doubles s/70.

Hostal San Francisco, Belén 790 (tel. 823 070), has less character and an inferior location but also costs less than its competitors. All rooms come with private, (electric) hot-water baths. Singles s/15; doubles s/25.

FOOD

Restaurant Salas, Amalia Puga 637 (tel. 922 867), in a large high-ceilinged dining area off the plaza. The decor is dull but the fabulous food attracts hordes of locals nonetheless. Open 9am-11pm.

El Batán, El Batán 369 (tel. 826 025; email kok.bolster@computextos.com.pe). Calling itself a "gran bufet de arte," El Batán is the classiest restaurant in town. Eat in the covered courtyard decorated with plants and paintings, or move inside to find a fireplace and small stage where different groups perform on F and Sa nights. They serve both a fancy set menu (s/26) and traditional *criollo* a la carte items (s/10-15). For a truly Peruvian experience, try an *algarrobina,* made from *pisco* brandy, creme cacao, algarrobina (a local fruit), milk, and egg white (s/11). Open daily 10am-11:30pm.

El Cajamarqués, Amazonas 770 (tel. 822 128). Not quite as upscale as El Batán, but still popular and impressive. Walk under white arches through an austere dining hall and into an interior garden courtyard filled with exotic birds. This is where to come for succulent *comida típica* (entrees around s/9). Open daily 9am-11pm.

Oscar's Restaurante Turístico, El Batán 149 (tel. 828 386). Oscar's offers a curious melange of food and atmosphere: barbecue, seafood, and Chinese fare is served between two big-screen TVs blasting music videos in a room with, strangely enough, a somewhat country-western flare. Open daily 9:30am-midnight.

Gran Restaurant El Zarco, El Batán 170 (tel. 820 561). Enter and pass through the restaurant's glass-enclosed kitchen area. This passage opens up onto a large dining space surrounded by a Peruvian mini-market selling drinks and snacks. A wide selection and reasonable prices abound (s/4-10). Open Su-F 7am-11pm.

SIGHTS

Though most of its tourist attractions lie outside of Cajamarca, there are some interesting things to see in town, including several cathedrals. One of the most noteworthy, the beautiful 17th-century **Iglesia de San Francisco,** contains a museum of religious art (museum open 3-6pm).

EL CONJUNTO MONUMENTAL BELÉN. The *conjunto* is a complex of colonial buildings the downtown Cajamarca. It includes the **Iglesia Belén,** built later in the 17th century, the small **Medical Museum,** and the **Museo Arqueológico y Etnográfico.** Along with the cathedral and museums, this small complex includes **El Cuarto del Rescate,** the room that, according to legend, was to be filled with the ransom—once with gold and twice with silver—for the last Inca emperor,

Atahuallpa. This is also the only remaining example of Inca architecture in Cajamarca; the rest of the Inca city was torn down by the Spanish conquistadors to make room and provide building material for their new colonial city. Spanish-speaking tour guides can be found at the complex; for an English-speaking tour go with a guide from **Cumbe Maya Tours.** *(The complex is located at Amalia Puga 750, on the 600 block of Belén. Open M and W-F 8am-1pm and 3-6pm, Sa-Su 9am-1pm. Admission s/3.20.)*

EL MIRADOR SANTA APOLONIA. For an excellent view of Cajamarca, visit this lookout which lies high above the city. It lies in a trim garden park at the crest of an Andean mountain just above the Santa Apolonia cathedral. The vista overlooks a vast, flat valley, set 2,700m above sea level amid towering peaks. In addition to the well-groomed gardens, the park houses a number of caged animals such as llamas, owls, hawks, and a cute little monkey. *(Park admission is s/1.)*

LOS BAÑOS DEL INCA. Beyond Cajamarca's borders lie Los Baños, a natural hot spring whose supposedly salubrious waters were the bathing place of the last Inca, Atahuallpa, shortly before his capture. Today, guests may enjoy private, indoor baths with water drawn from the springs (s/4), sit in the sauna (s/8), or go for a swim (s/2) in the outdoor pool. *(To get to the baños, take a taxi (s/5) or a colectivo (15min., s/0.80) from Amazonas in Cajamarca. Tel. 821 563. Baños complex open daily 5am-8pm. Admission s/3-4.)*

OTHER SIGHTS. The nearby sites of **Cumbe Mayo, Necropolis de Combayo, Ventanillas de Otuzco, Las Ruinas de Kuntur Wasi,** and numerous others are best visited through one of Cajamarca's tour companies. Cumbe Mayo, of particular interest, includes a "rock forest," caves covered with pre-Inca petroglyphs, ceremonial altars, and an ancient aqueduct. Most of the informative tours only take a few hours, are done in small groups, and are inexpensive (s/15-25).

TRUJILLO

The city of Trujillo, capital of the region of La Libertad, was founded in 1534 by Spanish conquistador Diego de Almagro and named for the birthplace of Francisco Pizarro. Of course, the Spanish weren't the first residents of this region: among others, the Mochica, Chimú, and Inca civilizations also inhabited these parts; remnants of their past splendor can be seen at the archaeological sites of Chan Chan, the Huacas del Sol y de la Luna, and El Brujo.

Depending on whether one is heading north or south, Trujillo is either an introduction to, or a reiteration of, the best qualities of Lima. In Trujillo, one gets the virtues of a sprawling metropolis without the vices: the noble, pedestrian-filled plazas are safer, the streets less disorienting, and the size less overwhelming. Gorgeous, colonial *casas antiguas* abound and appear just a touch brighter than those in Lima. Classy cafes and *discotecas* are here, but thick, choking pollution is not. Stroll along quiet *paseos*, go shopping, dine on exquisite *criollo* cuisine, or explore pre-Hispanic ruins. Trujillo is larger than many of its neighbors to the north but retains a small-town charm—a closeness and commonality—that its big brother to the south lacks.

ORIENTATION AND PRACTICAL INFORMATION

Most of the popular plazas, hotels, restaurants, and colonial houses are enclosed in the **old town** by the circular **Av. España,** which runs roughly the route of the wall that protected the city in colonial times. Remnants of that wall are located between blocks 11 and 17 of España. At the center of the old town lies the **Plaza de Armas.** The most frequented shopping and dining is along **Av. Pizarro** past the plaza in the direction of rising street numbers. At the terminus of this street, **La Plazuela El Recreo** stands witness to the promenades of many a passerby.

Airplanes: Getting to **El Aeropuerto Carlos Martínez de Pinillos,** 20min. from the *centro,* should cost s/10 by taxi. Flights go to: **Lima** (4:45 and 7pm, US$59). **AeroContinente**, 582 Orbegoso (tel. 200 775). Open M-Sa 9am-1pm and 4-8pm.

Buses: CIVA, Ejército 285 (tel. 251 402), sends buses to: **Lima** (8hr., 10:30pm, s/20) and **Tumbes** (9hr., 10pm, s/25) via **Sullana** (8hr., s/20). **Ormeño** (tel. 259 782), on the 2nd block of Ejército, serves: **Lima** (8hr., 8 per day, s/20-45 depending on quality of bus); **Tumbes** (11hr., *normal* 7pm, s/20; *especial* 10:45pm, s/35); as well as several points in Ecuador. **Cruz del Sur,** Amazonas 437 (tel. 261 801), sends comfortable night buses to **Lima** (8hr.; 4 per day; *bus-cama* at 11pm; s/60). **Vulkano,** Carrión 140 (tel. 235 847), serves **Cajamarca** (6hr.; 10:30am, 10, and 10:30pm; s/18-22) and **Piura** (6hr., 10:30pm, s/20).

Taxis: Within Trujillo, a ride should cost around s/2-3.

Tourist Information: The **Policía de Turismo**, Independencia 630 (tel. 291 705), in the 16th-century colonial house referred to as the Casa de la Portada de Leones. Available 24hr. Private tour companies can also provide general information.

Tour Agencies: The best are **Trujillo Tours,** Diego de Almagro 301 (tel. 233 091; email ttours@norteq.lima.net.pe; open M-F 9am-1pm and 4-7pm, Sa 9am-1pm); and **Guía Tours,** Independencia 580 (tel. 245 170; open M-F 9am-1pm and 4-7:30pm, Sa 9am-1pm). Both have English-speaking staff, offer inexpensive tours to nearby ruins and more distant sights, and arrange airline tickets for national and international flights.

Currency Exchange: Numerous street vendors circle the Plaza de Armas. **Banco de Lima,** Orbegoso 503 (tel. 261 030), is a secure alternative. Open M-F 9:15am-1pm and 4:30-6:30pm, Sa 9:15am-12:15pm. **Interbank,** Gamarra 469 (tel. 258 791), also changes cash and checks. Open M-F 9am-6:15pm, Sa 9am-12:30pm.

Supermarket: Meripsa, Iturregui and Pizarro, sells many essential items. Open M-Sa 9:15am-1:15pm and 4:30-9pm, Su 9:30am-1:30pm.

Laundry: Lavandería La Moderna, Orbegoso 270, has next-day (s/6 per kg) or same-day service (s/8.50 per kg). Open M-Sa 9am-1pm and 4-8pm.

Emergency: Tel. 105.

Police: Go to the Policía de Turismo (see above) for any problem. Open 24hr.

Pharmacy: There are many *farmacias* throughout old town. **Botica Arcangel** (tel. 291 805), Bolívar and Almagro, is near the Plaza de Armas. Open 24hr.

Hospital: Hospital Regional Docente (tel. 231 581), with 24hr. emergency service, is the best place to go in case of illness or accident.

Post Office: Bolognesi 410 (tel. 245 941). Open M-Sa 8am-8pm, Su 9am-1pm.

DHL: Almagro 579 (tel. 203 689), sends packages quickly and surely. Open M-F 9am-1pm and 4-8pm, Sa 9am-1pm.

Internet: There are a number of places around town advertising *cabinas de internet;* **El Navegante,** San Martín 626 (tel. 207 066), offers connections (s/3.50 per hr.) and is also a restaurant. Open daily 8am-midnight.

Telephones: Collect and calling card calls can be made from the green **Telefónica del Perú** phone booths on many street corners.

TELEPHONE CODE	044

ACCOMMODATIONS

Due to Trujillo's key location as the first major city to the north of Lima, accommodations are numerous. Places closer to the plaza are more convenient than elsewhere but are sometimes slightly noisier and more expensive.

Hostal Americano, Pizarro 764 (tel. 241 361). With old, faded walls that exude an air of past grandeur, Americano was probably once one of Trujillo's most upscale accommodations. High-ceilinged rooms are large and colorful. Singles s/20; doubles s/26, with bath s/30.

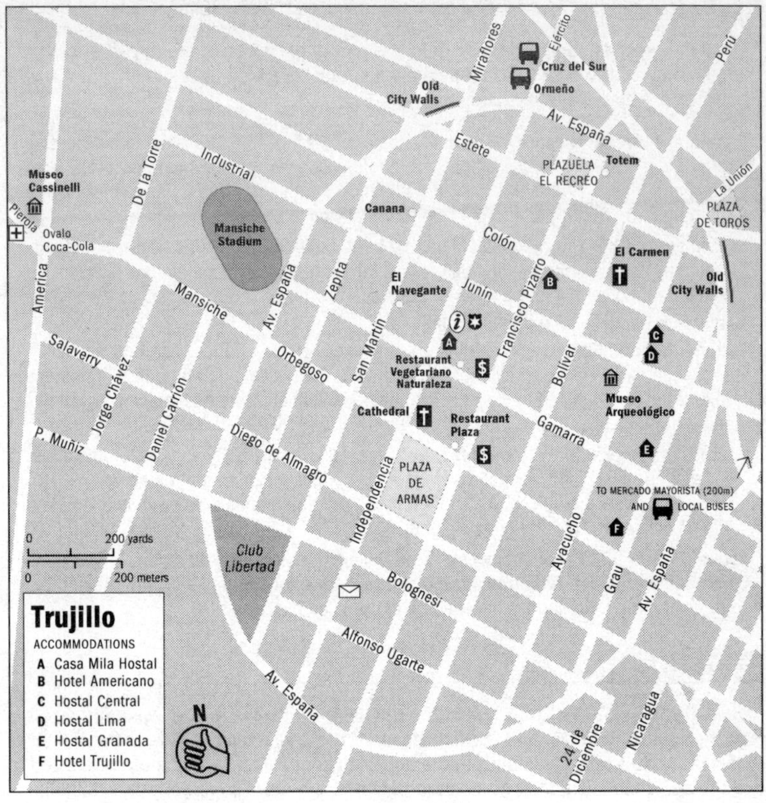

Casa Mila Hostal, Independencia 618 (tel. 291 133 fax 291 532), is a bit pricier but understandably so: modern, tastefully decorated rooms come with cable TV, phones (with which you can order room service), and immaculate hot-water baths. The adjoining restaurant and pub, *Mezzaluna,* offers a healthy selection that can be charged to your room, as well as live music shows on Friday and Saturday nights—don't try to go to sleep early! A nighttime guard provides added security. Singles s/50; doubles s/70.

Hotel Trujillo, Grau 581 (tel. 244 241), has a luxurious feel but offers very decent prices. Optional baths have hot water only during specific hours. Singles s/18, with bath s/22; doubles with bath s/35, with TV s/40.

Hostal Granada, Grau 611 (tel. 256 411), offers a large window to the street in every room, though this particular street doesn't offer particularly good views. Simple but attractively decorated rooms are all equipped with private hot-water baths. Matrimonial s/30; doubles s/35.

Hostal Central, Ayacucho 728 (tel. 205 745). Walk through a small stationery store and past arcade games to an open-air courtyard lined with small, simple, but sufficient rooms with optional hot-water baths. Singles s/12, with bath s/18; matrimonial s/14, with bath s/20; doubles s/18, with bath s/24.

Hostal Lima, Ayacucho 718 (tel. 232 499). This good budget find offers simple rooms lining a green-and-white open-air hallway. The security gate provides extra comfort. Common bath only. Singles s/11; doubles s/18.

FOOD

As you'd expect of a large city, Trujillo has plenty of delectable dining diversions, though some of the best food (especially seafood) is found in the nearby town of Huanchaco, a 20-minute bus ride away.

Restaurant Plaza, Orbegoso 491, on the corner of the Plaza de Armas, is an inexpensive diner where locals flock to snack on a *sandwich con pavo* (turkey sandwich s/4.50) for lunch and feast on rotisserie chicken (half-chicken with salad and fries s/8) for dinner. Open M-Sa 9am-3:30pm and 5-11pm, Su 2-11pm.

El Navegante Cafe Internet, San Martín 626 (tel. 207 066). Sticking to the theme suggested by its name and the computers lining the walls, the cybercafe offers dishes such as the *panqueque Microsoft* (s/6) or *sandwich wwwow* (s/2.50), as well as a standard set menú (s/4). Open daily 8am-Midnight.

Canana, San Martín 791 (tel. 257 788), presents polished wood, pastel colors, abundant vegetation, and a spacious open courtyard. Tasty *comida criolla,* including many varieties of *lomo* (grilled beef s/15-20). It has traditional music and dancing on Fridays and Saturdays after 11pm. Open M-Sa 9am-4:30am, Su 9am-5pm.

Restaurant Vegetariano Naturaleza, Gamarra 455, serves tasty vegetable omelettes. For a larger meal, try their delicious set menu, which includes fruit salad with yogurt, soup, and whole grain rice (s/3.50). They also sell natural products such as bee pollen and *uña de gato*. Open daily 7am-10pm.

Totem, Pizarro 922 in an anonymous blue building, mostly attracts groups of Trujillans who come to watch *fútbol* on TV and sip beer. But, for the traveler who doesn't like sports and beer, the food is also quite good (broiled *pescado* s/6).

SIGHTS

CHURCHES. Trujillo's churches and cathedrals invite visitors to casually stroll past their fancy façades. The **Basílica Menor** of the **Catedral de Trujillo,** at the corner of the Plaza de Armas, was built in the mid-17th century and is the most important cathedral in town. The attached **Museo Catedrálico** houses a collection of religious art, and its underground crypts feature the *martiros degollados* (decapitated martyrs), who died for their faith. *(Museum open M-Sa 8am-2pm and 4-8pm. Admission s/5. Guides available.)* **Monasterio El Carmen,** on the corner of Colón and Bolívar, is more architecturally impressive. Next door, **Pinacoteca Carmelita** also houses religious art. *(Pinacoteca open M-Sa 9am-1pm. Admission s/3; students with ID s/1.)*

CASAS ANTIGUAS. A number of beautiful colonial houses are scattered throughout old Trujillo. Some, such as the **Casa Bracamonte,** Independencia 441, are closed to the public and can only be appreciated for their spectacular façades. Others, such as the **Casa Calonge,** Pizarro 446, and **Casa de la Emancipación,** Pizarro 610, are now occupied by banks. Perhaps the most impressive *casa antigua*, **Palacio Iturregui,** Pizarro 688, has been converted into a private club, but much can be seen from the front court. The best time for visiting these and other houses is weekday mornings, when someone may be willing to let you inside. Guía Tours and Trujillo Tours offer tours of the city that include entrance into many of the *casonas*.

MUSEUMS. There are two decent archaeological museums in town. The **Museo Arqueológico de la Universidad Nacional de Trujillo** has the most varied collection and informative displays. *(Junín and Ayacucho. Open M 9:30-2pm, Tu-F 9:15am-1pm and 3-7pm, Sa-Su 9:30am-4pm. Admission s/5.)* **Museo Cassinelli's** has an incredible collection belied by its location—basically in the basement of a gas station. The museum also sells an informative book (s/15) which discusses the featured collection and pre-columbian Peruvian civilization. *(Nicolás de Piérola 601. Tel. 231 801. Open Su-F 9:30am-1pm and 3:30-7pm, Sa 10am-12:30pm. Admission s/5).*

CHAN CHAN. Touted as the **largest preserved mud-brick city in the world,** Chan Chan was once the glorious capital of the **Chimu** empire, which dominated the region around the turn of the first millennium. The mud metropolis consists of nine subcities. Today, visitors can investigate the winding passages, symbolic carvings, grand halls, and towering walls of the **Tschudi Palace,** the largest, best-preserved, and most fully-excavated sector of the site. Though Tschudi is definitely the main attraction, the other, significantly smaller structures are worth a visit and are accessible by taxi. The Chan Chan admission fee also includes entrance to the small **Museo de Sitio de Chan Chan,** the **El Dragon ruin,** the **Arco Iris ruin,** and the **Esmeralda temple.** *(The ruins are 10min. from Trujillo by taxi (s/5) or bus (s/1, take any bus headed to Huanchaco from the "Ovalo Coca Cola"). Site and museums open daily 9am-4pm. Admission s/10, s/5 with ISIC. Guides s/5-10.)*

MOCHICA RUINS. Though very different from Chan Chan, this set of ruins is equally spectacular. The main attractions are the **Huacas del Sol y de la Luna,** two mammoth temples that tower about 50m above the Moche Valley. These temples—one dedicated to the sun, the other to the moon—were built in stages around the middle of the first millennium by the **Mochica** empire, and may have served as administrative centers. A tour of the structures reveals grand halls, impressive colored carvings, and, from the temples' summits, awesome views of the surrounding lands. *(The temples are a 20min. (s/10) taxi ride from Trujillo. Open daily 9am-4pm. Admission s/5. Guided tours free with ticket. Guidebook s/10.)*

ENTERTAINMENT

Trujillo's nightlife can be slow during the week but comes alive on the weekend. Discos smoke all over town, especially **Crack Discoteca,** América Sur 2119 (tel. 242 182), at the Luna Rota complex, which also includes an excellent pub and a casino. Crack, which is especially popular with youthful yuppies, is bigger, brighter, and more glamorous than most of the competition. (Cover Sa s/6. Open W-Sa 8pm-5am.) **Millenium Drive Inn** (tel. 241 003), offers a novel concept: people come in their cars to enjoy big-screen music videos over a pitcher of beer (s/18)—just make sure you have a designated driver. For the pedestrians who just wanna dance, there is also a happening disco in the big, barn-like building in back. (Cover s/5. Open daily 7pm-5am.) **Las Tinajas,** Pizarro and Almagro, on the Plaza de Armas, offers a slick pub on weekdays and an even slicker disco playing all-English rock on weekends. Tinajas attracts a young and wealthy crowd. (Cover s/10. Disco open F and Sa 10pm-4am. Pub open M-Sa 8:30pm-3am.) **Star Light,** America Norte, is a gentlemen's nightclub for *los caballeros*, offering nightly entertainment (open 9:30pm-6am; shows start at 11pm).

There are also two **movie theaters** that often show English language movies with Spanish subtitles; one is at Pizarro 748 (movies 4:15, 7:15, and 10pm; s/6), and the other at Orbegoso 245 (4:15, 7:15, and 10:15pm; s/7).

NEAR TRUJILLO: PUERTO CHICAMA

The only reason to come to Puerto Chicama is the **surfing**—Chicama (also sometimes referred to as **Malabrigo**) supposedly has the longest wave in the world. According to some locals, rides of almost 2km are not unusual on a good day. Bring your own board and wetsuit, as there are no places to rent equipment here (though there are near Lima) and the water may be quite chilly depending on the swell direction.

In Chicama, the two principal hotels and the two best restaurants happen to coincide; most eat and lodge in the same edifice. **Hostal Restaurant El Hombre**, Progreso 200, at the end of the beach to the left when facing the water, is the most popular among surfers. It offers food and lodging and is run by a friendly family who look after their guests *con cariño*. Accommodations are basic, with rooms just large enough for you and your surfboard. (Rooms s/15 per person, prices are flexible.) The restaurant's daily *menú* specials usually feature fresh fish (s/6). **Hos-**

pedaje Restaurante Bar El Porteño, Tacna 269, offers simple but clean accommodations with common baths (singles s/15; doubles s/20, ask about discounts). The fairly large restaurant is lighter and airier than El Hombre's (tasty local fish dish s/6; open daily 7am-midnight).

Transportation: When full, *colectivos* depart for Puerto Chicama from Santa Cruz 290 in Trujillo (1½hr., s/3). It may be faster to take a *colectivo* from the "Ovalo Coca-Cola" to **Paijan** (1hr., s/2) and then another to Puerto Chicama (½hr., s/1.50). *Colectivos* return hourly from Chicama's Plaza de Armas between 5am and 8pm.

NEAR TRUJILLO: HUANCHACO

A popular weekend destination for Trujillans and tourists from surrounding towns, Huanchaco offers a long, clean beach, good-sized waves, an alluring artisan market (near the pier), magnificent *mariscos*, and enough visitors to keep the days and evenings exciting. Huanchaco is also one of the few places left in Perú where you can find *caballitos de totora* (fishing boats made from bundles of totora reeds) still in use. Far from being "just a daytrip", some tourists prefer to stay in Huanchaco and visit Trujillo during the day.

The more expensive accommodations are near the main *colectivo* drop-off point. The more interesting and affordable accommodations are a few minutes up the main walkway, set on the main beach (past the pier) amidst the restaurants, pubs, and people. **Naylamp** (tel. 461 022; email naylamp@ots.com.pe), on Victor Larco near the end of the beach to the right when facing the water, offers clean, bright rooms with hot-water baths. Other amenities include a communal kitchen, laundry facilities (s/3 per load), and relaxing hammocks. (Dorms s/10; singles s/20; doubles s/25.) Naylamp also offers clean, safe campsites with a view of the beach (s/5 with your own equipment, s/8 including rental of equipment). **Hospedaje Huanchaco's Garden** (tel. 461 194), Circunvalación, Lote 3, set back from the beach (look for the sign on the main walk), provides quiet, all-white, two-room matrimonial suites with private baths (s/30).

For some of the best seafood and beach views in town, stop in at the two-story, all-windows **Lucho del Mar,** Victor Larco 600 (tel. 461 460). Eat indoors or out, depending on the weather. (Meals s/15-20. Open daily 9am-6pm). **La Ola Marina**, right on the sand by the old pier, offers great seafood for less money (*ceviche de pescado* s/5). Although best known for its seafood, Huanchaco has several excellent establishments offering international alternatives. **Sabes?,** Victor Larco 920 (tel. 461 555; email yasabes@yahoo.com), is the place to be at night. In addition to the healthy and creative cuisine, including vegetarian fare and possibly the best hummus in northern Perú (all dishes s/10), the American owner also offers a well-stocked bar, **internet access** (s/6 per hr.), and an English-language book exchange. (Open daily 8pm-3am.) Closer to the center of town, **Mama Mía,** Victor Larco 538, offers a good selection of Italian food, vegetarian options, and burgers at reasonable prices (open daily 11am-11pm).

Transportation: To get to Huanchaco, take a *colectivo* from the so-called "Ovalo Coca-Cola" (15-20 min., s/1). To get back to Trujillo, catch a *colectivo* from Rivera. Late at night, a taxi (s/8) may be safer.

CHIMBOTE

The largest city between Lima and Trujillo, Chimbote is located on a beautiful bay—though the town itself is not quite as lovely. There are no major ruins in the area, but several natural attractions may spark the casual visitor's interest.

The main street is **J. Pardo,** two blocks from the water and parallel to the shore. One block closer to the water is **Bolognesi;** one block farther away is **L. Prado,** not to be confused with the parallel Pardo. The **Plaza de Armas** is between Pardo and Prado. **Manuel Ruiz** is the main street leading into town, running perpendicular to the water and two blocks east of the plaza.

Long-distance buses leave from Bolognesi or Manuel Ruiz. **Cruz del Sur** (tel. 331 021), on Bolognesi, goes to **Lima** (5hr., 11:30pm, s/35). **Las Dunas** (tel. 336 534) has buses heading south to **Lima** (5hr., 11am and 11:30pm, s/25) and north to **Trujillo** (4hr., 9am, s/30). **Transportes Yungay Express**, Elias Aguirre 264 (tel. 324 001), serves **Huaraz** (7hr.; 6, 9:30am, 1, and 7:30pm; s/18). Services include: **Banco de Lima**, Bolognesi and Villanicencio (open M-F 9:15am-1pm and 4:30-6:30pm, Sa 9:30am-12:30pm); the **police** (tel. 321 651), at Pardo 296 (open 24hr.); **Farmacia Chimbote,** at Bolognesi 404 (tel. 326 145; open M-Sa 9am-1pm and 5-10pm); and the **post office,** at Pardo 294 (open M-Sa 8am-8pm).

There is a wide range in quality and price among the hotels in Chimbote. **Hostal Bolognesi,** Bolognesi 596 (tel. 336 510), offers basic rooms with hot-water private baths (s/15 per person). **Hostal Chimbote**, Pardo 205 (tel. 344 721), is cheaper but with only cold water (rooms s/10 per person). For more of a splurge, try the **Hostal D'Carlo,** Villanicencio 384 (tel./fax 330 038), on the plaza. Carlo offers comfortable, carpeted rooms with cable TV, stocked refrigerators, and views of the plaza. A laundry service is also available. (Singles s/85; doubles s/105, includes breakfast.)

The **Chifa Canton**, Bolognesi 498 (tel. 344 388, fax 344 529), offers a wide selection of Chinese cuisine (meals s/10-20; open daily noon-3pm and 6:30-11pm). **Venecia** (tel. 325 490), on the corner of Bolognesi and Enrique Palacios, specializes in fish and *mariscos* and is recommended by locals (open daily 7am-1am). For a lighter meal, **La Casita de Hansel y Grettel**, Prado 523 (tel. 333 942), has delicious *tamales* (s/3), sandwiches, and desserts. Just look out for the child-eating witch...

As is the case with many small towns, most of Chimbote's visitor sights lie out of town and out-of-doors. **Aventurs Peru** (tel. 345 646), Enrique Palacios on the Plaza de Armas, arranges tours of nearby attractions, such as the **Isla Blanca** and **viveroforestal.** For more of an adventure, find a taxi driver willing to take you up to the top of the nearby mountain, **Cerro de la Juventud** (20min., s/15-20). Near the summit, the **Santuaría Señor de la Vida** offers incredible views of the city, bay, mountains, and Isla Blanca. Additionally, it is an impressive church, built into the side of the mountain and walled only with windows. The crypts beneath the sanctuary are reached by walking 15m in darkness through a tunnel dug into the mountain. A damaged statue of Christ resides there, left unrepaired to symbolize the effects of terrorism on Perú. From the church, it is a 30-minute climb to the summit and the **Cruz de la Paz,** which offers even more spectacular views. You can then walk back down the road to the highway (1hr.) and flag down a passing bus or taxi to take you back to town. Hiking from Chimbote to the church is not recommended without a knowledgeable guide, as the road is unmarked and a wrong turn could quickly get you lost in the surrounding high desert.

CASMA

The small town of Casma has been completely rebuilt since its utter devastation in 1970. The cause of the wreckage was a massive earthquake centered just off the coast. For a more in-depth—a *very* in-depth—description of the disaster, consult any Casma resident over forty. Despite the tremendous beauty of its post-1970 architecture, for most tourists, Casma is merely an overnight base for visiting the Sechín ruins, located just a few kilometers away.

Turismo Las Dunas, Tarapaca 439 (711 381), serves: **Lima** (5hr., 12:15am and noon, s/25); **Chiclayo** (6hr., 1:30am, s/25); and **Piura** (8hr., s/30). **Tepsa,** Luís Ormeño L16 (tel. 711 523), goes to: **Lima** (5hr.; 10am, 1pm, midnight; s/13); **Tumbes** (22hr., 2:30 and 10:30pm, s/40) via **Trujillo** (5hr., s/10), **Chiclayo** (6hr., s/15), and **Piura** (8hr., s/25); and **Cajamarca** (9hr., 10:30pm, s/23). **Banco de Crédito** is at Bolívar 181 and Cajamarca (tel. 711 314; open M-F 9:15am-1:15pm and 4:30-6:30pm). **Emergency** tel. 105. The **police** (712 199) are found at Magdalena 201 on the corner of the plaza. **Farmacia San Carlos,** Huarmey 372 (tel. 711 143), is well-stocked (open M-F 8am-11pm). **Hospital de Apoyo Casma,** (tel. 711 299), is on Mejía. The **post office** (tel. 711 067), is on Lomporte by the plaza (open M-Sa 8am-8pm). **Telephone code:** 044.

For an inexpensive room near the Plaza de Armas, head to **Hostal Indo Americano,** Huarmey 130 (tel. 711 395), which is extremely plain but safe and clean with sometimes-functioning hot water. All rooms have private bath. (Matrimonial s/20, doubles s/30.) Nicer rooms are further up the street at the **Rebecca Hostal** (tel. 711 143), Huarmey 370 next to the Farmacia San Carlos, where decorated rooms all have hot water private baths (singles s/30, doubles s/45). **Restaurante El Tío Sam,** Huarmey 138 (tel. 711 447), serves filling foods such as *pescado al ajo* (s/10) in a lush green, shady dining area (open daily 8am-3pm and 6-10pm). **Restaurante Picantería Ivans** (tel. 712 026), on Huarmey's second block, offers *comida criolla* such as *picante de cuy* (guinea pig s/5; open daily 7am-10pm).

THE RUINS. The only real attraction near Casma is the **Sechín ruins.** Some of the structures here were erected over three millenia ago. The great age of the sight makes it of vital importance for archeaologists trying to gain an understanding of the very ancient cultures of the Americas. (Open daily 8am-6pm. Admission s/5.) To learn more about the history of the ruins and those who built them, visit the **Museo Sechín,** at the site (info in Spanish). Knowledgeable guides will explain the site in detail (s/15). To get to the ruins, take a *mototaxi* (s/2-3). Ask the driver to wait for you or return to pick you up later, or take your chances and hope that a taxi or *colectivo* will stop to pick you up on the road to get back to Casma.

BARRANCA

Barranca is another small town that serves primarily as a base camp for exploring nearby ruins. In this case, the main attraction is the ancient **Paramonga Fortress,** built by the pre-Inca **Chimu Empire** at the southernmost extent of their expansive empire. (Open daily 8am-6pm. Admission s/3, students s/2.) Paramonga is a large ruin with walled passages winding their way up a somewhat steep incline. At the top, one can still find traces of colored murals, and the view from these heights is excellent. Although referred to as a fortress, the compound was most likely used as a ceremonial center. An aerial view of the ruins reveals their llama-like shape. A helpful information sheet can be purchased at the entrance (two very full pages in Spanish; s/0.50). The official working at the office is quite knowledgeable. The site lies right on the Panamerican Highway north of Barranca, so any north-bound bus can drop you off there (tell the driver to let you off at *la fortaleza*). Alternatively, take a *colectivo* from Jr. Lima in Barranca to the small Paramonga village (15min., s/1) and then take a *mototaxi* to the ruins (10min., s/3).

To catch a north or southbound bus from Barranca, go up to Jirón Lima (as the Panamerican Highway is known in town) and wait for one to come by. There are also several small companies in town that send buses to **Lima** (3hr., s/7-10). Services include: **Banco de Crédito,** Gálvez 330 (open M-F 9:15am-1:15pm and 4:30-6:30pm, Sa 9:30am-12:30pm); **Farmacia La Salud,** Ugarte 149 (tel. 235 2014; open M-Sa 8:30am-2pm and 3:30-9:30pm, Su 8am-1pm); the **Hospital de Apoyo** (tel. 235 2241), on the second block of Nicolás de Piérola, offering 24-hour emergency service.; and the **post office,** at Ugarte 114 (open M-Sa 8am-8pm). **Telephone code:** 01.

In general, accommodations in Barranca are basic and inexpensive. **Hostal Continental,** Alfonso Ugarte 190 (tel. 235 24 58), is a sizeable, modern building near the plaza. The halls are a bit dark, but the rooms have large windows looking onto the street. Rooms are equipped with fan and private hot-water baths. (Singles s/25; doubles s/40; cable TV s/5 extra.) **Hostal Pacífico,** Gálvez 115 (tel.

235 2526), has simple rooms with tiny windows too high to see out. But the old building is well maintained and the water hot. (Singles s/10, with bath s/13; doubles s/16, with bath s/19.)The town's **Plaza de Armas,** active and attractive, is highlighted by some delightful restaurants. **Fuente de Soda Alaska,** Alfonso Ugarte 194 (tel. 235 4125), is a cheerful place—lots of mirrors, music, and bright soda-fountain color (chicken sandwiches s/1.50; open daily 8:30am-2am). **Chifa La Unión,** Gálvez 159 (tel. 235 2340), serving no *comida típica,* is one of Barranca's fancier restaurants, with top-notch Chinese cuisine (open daily noon-midnight).

THE CORDILLERA BLANCA

Somewhere between the gringo-magnet culture of Cusco and the seaside desertscape of Cajamarca lies the gargantuan Cordillera Blanca, the most impressive expanse of mountain peaks in Perú and the second highest range in South America. The sheer splendor of these volcanic Andean peaks—19 of them are over 6000m in elevation and glaciated throughout the year—is magnified by their location. At only 10° south latitude and 150km from the Pacific Ocean, it's a remarkable place to find some of the Western Hemisphere's tallest peaks.

Between the Cordillera Blanca and the smaller Cordillera Negra lies El Callejón de Huaylas, a glacial valley that separates the mountain ranges and houses many towns. The largest of these is Huaraz, capital of the Ancash department and its tourism epicenter. The *callejón* runs north to several other towns which, though rendered nearly insignificant by the surrounding mountains, have their own distinctive charm. From this central, colonized valley, the *cordillera* lies just to the east, where exhilarating excursions await the region's adventurous guests.

THE CORDILLERA BLANCA

- Make a pilgrimage to the temple of the 3,000-year-old **Chavín de Huantar ruins,** and contemplate the symbolism of its ancient engravings (see p. 203).
- Hike around the lofty **Lagos Llanganuco,** raised high among the towering peaks of the Cordillera Blanca (see p. 208).
- Trek among the glaciated peaks and crystal-clear alpine lakes of the stunning **Santa Cruz Valley** (see p. 209).
- Attempt the six-day climb up Perú's highest mountain, **Volcán Huascarán,** a twin-peaked 6768m behemoth (see p. 209).

PARQUE NACIONAL HUASCARÁN

Remarkably, most of the Cordillera Blanca lies within the formidable 340,000 hectare Parque Nacional Huascarán, a nature reserve named for and centered around the highest peak in Perú. The official duty of the park is to preserve the area's natural beauty, but its practical function is to provide outdoor diversion to thousands of visitors each year. Among the attractions are brilliant alpine lakes, sprawling mountain passes left by the receding glaciers, and unlimited opportunities for outdoor adventure. There are countless treks to be made and mountains to be climbed, all of them best attempted during the (relatively) dry season from May to September and from the towns along the *callejón*. There, southern sights are reached via the numerous park entrances near **Huaraz** (p. 203), the region's major town. To the north, the Llanganuco Lakes and other popular excursions are most easily made from the small towns of **Yungay** (p. 210) or **Caraz** (p. 211). But, with such a dense concentration of attractions, any town in the *callejón* make a suitable base. (Park admission s/5 for one day; s/65 for multi-day excursions.)

CHIQUÍAN

Chiquían serves primarily as a staging area for treks in the neighboring Cordillera Huayhuash, a range that is more rugged and isolated than the Cordillera Blanca to the north. An incredible trail winds all the way around the range; the hike takes about 14 days. Besides the trailhead, Chiquían has little to offer the casual visitor.

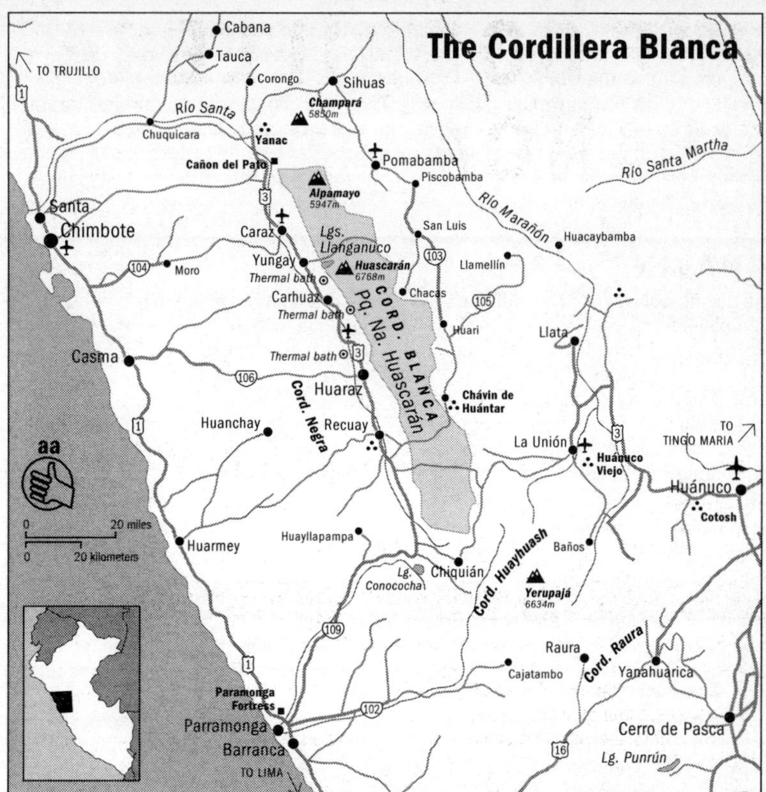

The **Parque Nacional Huascarán** is a mecca of Andean activity in Perú and, indeed, South America. Because of this, it receives very heavy visitor traffic from around the world. When exploring the park, please do your part to preserve its natural beauty. Always **pack out what you pack in,** including all refuse and extra food. Additionally, try to stay on marked trails to avoid harming the fragile alpine vegetation. Remember: take nothing but pictures, leave nothing but footprints.

The main thoroughfare in Chiquían is **Av. Comercio,** which runs by the **Plaza de Armas.** Here congregate most services of interest to visitors. Long-distance **buses** arrive and depart from near the Plaza de Armas, where most of the companies are headquartered. **El Rápido,** Figuevedo 216 (tel. 744 049), five blocks down Comercio and one to the left, travels to **Huaraz** (2hr., 5:30am and 2pm, s/7). **Mushca,** Comercio 904, and **Carassa,** Bolognesi 407 (tel. 747 036), both leave for **Lima** (4hr., 5pm, s/15). **Transfysa** departs from the Plaza de Armas for **Barranca** (3hr., 9am, s/10) and **Lima** (4hr., 8am and 5pm, s/15). **Banco de La Nación** (tel. 747 031) will exchange cash but may frown upon traveler's checks (open M-F 8:30am-noon and 2:30-4pm). **The Centro de Salud** (tel. 747 085), several blocks uphill from the Plaza de Armas, handles minor medical emergencies. Near the *centro* is the **police** station (tel. 747 124).

The **Hostal San Miguel,** Comercio 233 (tel. 747 001), is seven blocks from the Plaza de Armas. A reasonable choice in a town with few options, the hostel is basic but clean and comfortable, with occasional hot water. The staff has valuable trekking information and may be able to help in contracting an *arriero* (mule and porter). The hostal is near the Huayhuash trailhead, so you don't have to walk with mules through the center of town and risk making a mess of the streets. (Rooms s/10 per person, with bath s/15.) **El Rincón de Yerupaja,** 2 de Mayo 803, parallel to the Comercio, is a traditional restaurant near the *centro*. The menu contains few surprises (*pollo* s/9). They will also prepare a few vegetarian plates *al gusto*. (Open daily 7am-9pm.) **Restaurant Pizzería El Refugio,** 2 de Mayo 471 (tel. 747 086), offers more colorful and tourist-friendly selections. Choose from a fairly wide selection of juices, *pizza americana* (s/10), and tasty soups (s/3-5; open daily 8am-11pm).

CHAVÍN

As the closest town to the millennia-old Chavín de Huántar ruins, Chavín would be the place to spend the night. However, the vast majority of tourists arrive in the morning and leave by late afternoon. For those who want to stay, Chavín can't offer much besides dirt roads, an attractive Plaza de Armas, and countless little stores selling soup, Inca Kola, rice, and candy.

The **Río Mosna** runs north-south below Chavín. Another river, the **Quebrada Huachesa,** runs east-west. The **ruins** are located at the intersection of the two rivers, a five-minute walk uphill from the **Plaza de Armas** on **17 de Enero Sur,** the principal street. Most hostels and restaurants are close to the Plaza de Armas, which is adorned by a small church.

Most visitors come from Huaraz, usually in private tours, arrive at about noon, and leave at about 4pm. Even those who did not arrive by tour bus might prefer to return on one. Most tour guides will happily accommodate newcomers (s/10). Otherwise, it's a long wait for **buses** (3hr., every hr. midnight-3am, s/10). Another even lengthier option is to walk from **Olleros** (3 days, see p. 209), along the trail ending at the Chavín de Huántar ruins. Chavín has a small **tourist office,** Simón Bolívar 100, on the Plaza de Armas (open Tu-Su 11am-6pm).

La Casona (tel. 754 020), on Plaza de Armas, is probably the best place to stay in town, offering handsome rooms overlooking the lively plaza (singles s/13, with bath s/25; doubles s/22, with bath s/40). The **Hostal Chavín** (tel 754 055), San Martín 141, on the Plaza de Armas, is also comfortable and a slightly better deal (s/10 per person, with bath s/15). The **Hostal Inca** (tel. 754 021), on the Plaza de Armas, is being expanded to 30 rooms. Animal rights activists might object to the three deer fenced off in the backyard. (Rooms s/10 per person.) Most of Chavín's restaurants fill up with ruin-visiting tourists around lunch time. The popular **La Ramada** (tel. 754 005) is at 17 de Enero 577. Its menu features both

ANDEAN LOVE STORY Quechua, the language of the Incas, is still widely spoken in the Central Andes. At the very least, locals mix Quechua with their Spanish in everyday parlance. Throwing in certain words may seriously endear you to Peruvians: for example, asking for *la yapa* at the market (that extra little bit). But for more serous wooing, the following vocabulary is in order.

You might begin by asking *imamsutiqui* (what's your name)? and *maimanta jamunki* (where are you from)?, to which you yourself could answer *ñujapan sutii "Rolan"* and *ñuja kani "Oregon."* A good next move might be to ask *miknita munanqui* (would you like to eat)? Over a romantic dinner of *pachamanca*, inquire *sapaiki kanki* (are you single)? If the answer is *manan* (no), then it might be a little too late to ask *maiman rinqui* (where are you going)? which would shortly be answered with *ama rabiachihuachu* (leave me alone). On the other hand, if the answer is *ari* (yes), you could shortly hear panpipe music playing and be saying *muñayquiqi* (I love you). The two of you could become *huaylarsh* (young lovers) and maybe engage in a bit of *chanca kichachi* (opening of legs), resulting in a *wawa* (baby). But don't act too soon or risk being called *supaipa wawan* (son of the devil). Finally, take off running if your beloved says *ñuja majaruikiman.* It means "watch out before I hit you."

vegetarian potato dishes and not-so-vegetarian *cuy* (guinea pig), as well as the typical assortment of trout and chicken plates. (Open 7am-9pm.) Two blocks off 17 de Enero in the direction of the Río Mosna, **La Portada** (tel. 754 018), Julio C. Tello 276, is infrequently visited by tourists and offers an affordable *almuerzo* (s/3).

RUINS. The 3,000-year-old ruins of the Chavín, a.k.a. **Museo Arqueológico Chavín de Huántar,** stand as a testament to this extraordinary culture, which would come to influence peoples as far north as the Ecuadorian border and as far south as Ica. The Chavín lived here from 1300 to 400 BC. Their temple, constructed over eight generations, has endured the Recuay, Huaraz, and Inca cultures, not to mention the Spanish *conquistadores,* until its formal protection in 1956. Not exceptionally interesting to the untrained eye, the ruins might be better enjoyed if explained by one of the guides who work there. A number of the Chavín's stone carvings incorporate three **animal deities**—the bird (representing the afterlife), the feline (the mortal world), and the serpent (the underworld)—which were often depicted with their eyes wide open, a symbol of the hallucinogenic trance induced by the San Pedro cactus, which priests considered sacred.

In order to build the temple, workers flattened a steep hill and constructed 14 labyrinthine galleries (only four of which are open to the public). Formerly above ground, they were covered by a landslide in 1945 and are now viewed as tunnels. These amazingly well-engineered galleries once housed the Chavín's high priests. Outside of these, a **pyramid structure** built on a rectangular square is situated next to a smaller circular plaza. Large canals, which once carried rushing water, are visible beneath. Archaeologists speculate that those noisy canals might have mimicked the sound of thunder, revered by the Chavín. The most important artifact at Chavín, still in its original site inside a gallery, is the beautiful **Lanzón,** a tall, white granite carving of the feline, bird, and serpent. Two other famous artifacts, the Estela Raymondi and Tello Obelisk, were moved to the Museo de la Nación in Lima (see p. 79; ruins located uphill on the outskirts of town. Admission s/5. Spanish-only guide s/15 for 2hr.)

HUARAZ

People go to Huaraz for the mountains. At 3100m, it serves as a gateway to the Cordillera Blanca, Perú's best known mountain region. Huascarán, a twin-peaked 6768m behemoth visible from Huaraz, is Perú's highest mountain. Surprisingly—though it is a six-day journey—Huascarán is not as difficult as other climbs in the region. Constant chatter about alpine adventures overheard in bars may convince even the most ardent lounger to give trekking a try. The prevalence of travelers interested in outdoors experiences, combined with the amicable disposition of most people in town, makes it easy to find climbing, hiking, and traveling companions. Only eight hours by bus from Lima, this capital of the Department of Ancash offers more than just challenging climbs. Tranquil treks and bike rides wind through mountain passes, and nearby, thermal hot springs and the famous ruins of Wilcahuaín and Chavín provide calmer, more traditional excursions for tourists.

Locals refer to any event in the region's history as "*antes de*" (before) or "*después de*" (after) their catastrophic earthquake in 1970. On May 31, this earthquake measuring in at 7.7 on the Richter scale shattered all but one street of buildings and killed half of the city's population. Since then, Huaraz has recovered substantially, but hasty post-quake reconstruction led to a modern, architecturally uninteresting appearance.

The best time to visit Huaraz and the Cordillera Blanca is between the months of May and September, during the region's dry season, when the weather is much more hospitable to outdoor adventure. However, occasional rain, snow, and hail storms are still possible, though not nearly as common.

ORIENTATION AND PRACTICAL INFORMATION

Av. Luzuriaga, which runs north-south and connects the principal highways, is the main thoroughfare. The **Plaza de Armas,** where many of the businesses, hotels, and restaurants congregate, is on Luzuriaga, about seven blocks south of the **Río Quilcay.** Many tourists arrive at the **Cruz del Sur** bus terminal, on Lucar y Torre and Morales, one block uphill from Luzuriaga.

Transportation: Buses leave from **Av. Fitzcarraldo** (the northern end of Luzuriaga), near the bridge, and travel to: **Lima** (9hr., every hr. 8am-9pm, s/30); **Chimbote** (7hr., 5 per day 8am-10pm, s/25); and **Casma** (5hr., 7 per day 7am-6pm, s/18) Buses don't frequently navigate the mountain roads. Instead, **colectivos** travel along the central highway, bound for **Caraz** (2hr., every 30min. 6am-8pm, s/6) via **Carhuaz** (1hr., s/3) and **Yungay** (1½hr., s/5). *Colectivos* to the north leave from the other side of the bridge over the Río Quilcay, at the northern end of Fitzcarraldo. *Colectivos* to the south leave from Tarapaca and 28 de Julio.

Taxis: A ride between any two points in Huaraz generally costs s/2, and taxis can easily be found on Av. Luzuriaga.

Tourist Office: OPTUR (tel. 682 718), on Luzuriaga across from the Plaza de Armas. Open M-Sa 9am-1pm and 5-8pm. For info on technical mountain climbing, consult **La Casa de Guías,** Parque Ginebra 28 (tel. 721 811), one block from the Plaza de Armas.

Tour Companies: In Huaraz, companies offer everything from tame driving tours to adrenaline-pumping climbing packages. **Pyramid Adventures,** Luzuriaga 530 (tel. 721 864), is reputed to be a valuable source of information, equipment, and guides. They specialize in adventure tours and rarely open their office. **Outdoor Expeditions S.A.,** San Martín 659 (tel. 721 151), through the tunnel on the 4th block of Luzuriaga, specializes in guided treks and climbs. They also rent high-quality equipment at fair prices. Open M-Sa 8am-1pm and 4-9pm.

Banks: Most banks are clustered around the Plaza de Armas. **Banco de Crédito** (tel. 721 411), at the corner of Sucre and Luzureaga, has an **ATM** which accepts Visa. Open M-F 9am-1pm and 4-6:30pm, Sa 9am-12:30pm.

Market: The indoor market, at Raymondi and La Cruz Romero, has all the fruit, dry food, and shoe repair specialists you would ever need—for trekking or on-site consumption. Open daily 6am-9pm.

Laundromat: Lavandería Tintoreria, La Mar 674 (tel. 721 719), charges s/3.50 per kg. Open M-Sa 9am-1pm, 3-8pm. Many hostels also offer laundry service.

Equipment Rental: Almost anything can be rented in Huaraz; from head lamp batteries to camping stoves and sleeping bags, gear is readily available. Bargaining is expected, especially if renting more than one item, or for more than one day. **Outdoor Expeditions S.A.** (see **Tour Companies,** above) is one good source of quality outdoor gear.

Bike Rental: Mountain Bike Adventures, Larco y Torre 530 (tel. 724 259; email alaza2mail.cosapidata.com.pe), 2nd floor, between José de la Mar and Morales, has the best bikes, but you usually need to go on a guided tour (US$20 per day) to use them. For a much cheaper option—in both price and quality—try **Sobre Ruedas,** La Cruz Romero 593 (tel. 692 004). Open daily 6am-7pm.

Police: (Tel. 721 235), on San Martín, one block downhill from the Plaza de Armas.

Hospital/Medical Services: The **Regional Hospital** (tel. 721 290) is on Luzuriago, near the intersection with Pedro Villón. A number of **doctors** (tel. 725 702) have their offices on the second floor of the building at the corner of José de la Mar and Luzuriaga. Open daily 8am-8pm.

Pharmacies: The official pharmacy of the Ministerio de Salud is **Farmacia Diremid,** Luzuriaga 1076 (tel. 727 729). Open daily 9am-9pm. **Farmacia Recuay** (tel. 721 391) is slightly closer to the *centro,* but more expensive. Open daily 9am-9pm.

Post Office: Serpost (tel. 721 031), on the Plaza de Armas, at the corner of Sucre and Luzuriaga. Open M-Sa 8am-8pm, Su 8am-1pm.

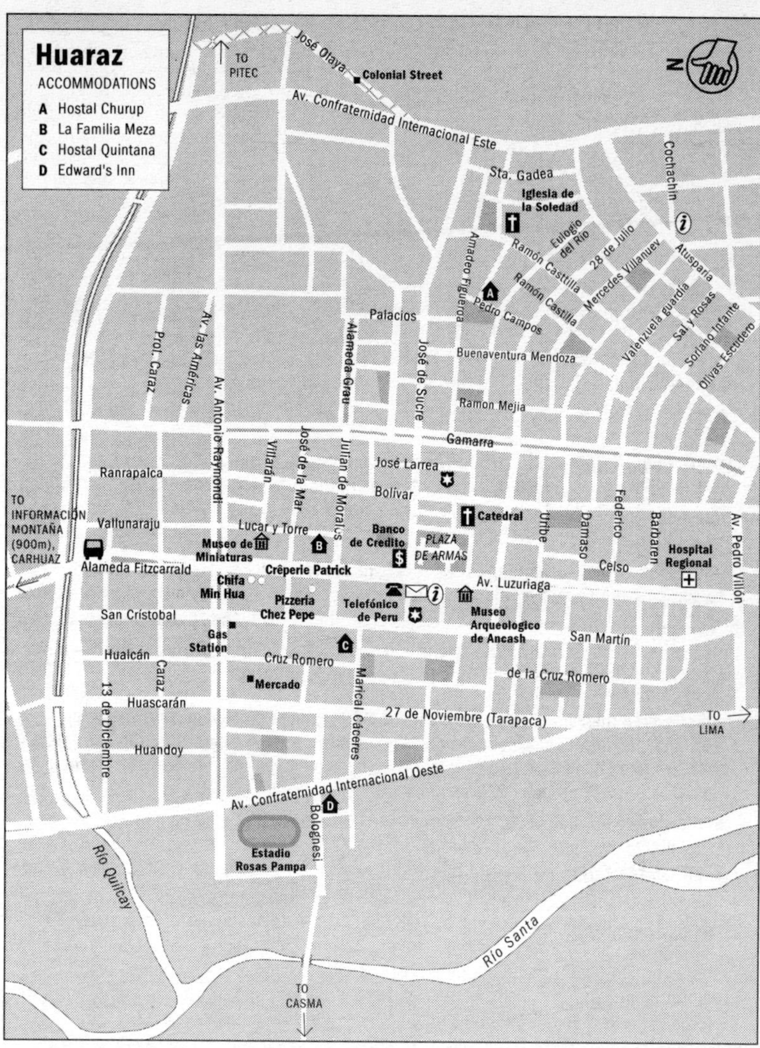

Internet Access: Parque Ginebra, on Parque Ginebra, offers full service (s/4 per hr.). Open daily 9am-11pm. **Avance S.R.L,** Luzuriaga 672 (tel. 726 690), offers private phone and internet access (s/6 per hr.). Open daily 7am-midnight.

Telephones: Public telephones are all around. **Telefónica del Perú** (tel. 723 525) has its main office at Luzuriaga and Sucre. Open M-F 8:30am-4:30pm.

TELEPHONE CODE 044

ACCOMMODATIONS

Since this relatively small town sees more than its share of tourists and adventure-seekers, it has a good variety of comfortable, affordable places to stay. Many of these establishments can also help guests arrange adventure tours.

Hostal Churup, Pedro Campos 735 (tel. 722 584), directly below the Iglesia de la Soledad. Every morning, the family who runs the hostel shares a heaping breakfast with their guests. The owner is eager to share some of his encyclopedic knowledge of the region's attractions, as well as how best to see them. Guests are free to play table tennis or just sunbathe in the spacious backyard. Dorms s/13 per person.

Hostal Quintana, Mariscal Cáceres 411 (tel. 726 060), 2 blocks from Luzuriaga, through the tunnel where vendors sell their wares. The two sons who work at this family-owned hostel—both accomplished climbers—rent equipment and offer valuable information about the mountains. Rooms s/10 per person.

La Familia Meza, Lucas 538 (tel. 726 367), between José de la Mar and Julín de Morales, one block above Luzuriaga. The staff of this very congenial hostel will treat you like family. A popular place with mountain climbers, perhaps because of the beautiful terrace that overlooks all of Huaraz. Dorms s/15 per person.

Refugio de Los Andes, Arguedas 1263 (tel. 721 694), below the Iglesia de Soledad, in an attractive house, uphill from the center of town. This *refugio* has more comforts than those found high in the mountains, including an open living room and access to kitchen facilities. Rooms s/15 per person.

Edward's Inn, Bolognesi 121 (tel. 722 692), near the stadium. Edward's Inn is an old-time favorite, which has been serving gringos in Huaraz for the last 20 years. Eduardo, the owner, offers clean, spacious rooms, a wealth of climbing information, and a parking garage. Check out the collection of signed climbing and skiing posters. Rooms US$10 per person.

FOOD

A multitude of restaurants satisfy the carbo-craving tastes of hiking enthusiasts. Look for the most diverse grub on the streets around Luzuriaga.

Siam de los Andes, Gamarrey 419 (tel. 721 294), three blocks up from Luzuriaga. The Thai chef, Naresuan, carefully prepares exquisite curry (s/16) and stir-fry (s/16-20) dishes with fresh meat and vegetables. The prices are high, but this is the best-prepared food in Huaraz. Open daily 6:30-10pm.

Fuente de Salud, José de la Mar 562, just below Luzuriaga. As the name might suggest, this is a great place to care for a sensitive stomach, altitude sickness, or whatever else might be ailing you. Common prescriptions include the *sopa de verduras* (s/7) and *arroz de jardinera* (s/6.50). Open daily 7:30am-10:30pm.

Bistro de Los Andes, Julio de Morales (tel 726 249). An eclectic mix of French and Peruvian cuisine. *Trucha a la almendra* (almond trout s/18) is the house specialty, though the menu also boasts vegetarian pastas (s/8-14). Serving excellent coffee even before the sun comes up, the Bistro is also an ideal breakfast spot for tourists who arrive in Huaraz in the wee hours on an overnight bus. Open daily 5am-1pm and 5-11pm.

Chifa Min Hua, Luzuriaga 424. This small restaurant has uninteresting decor and a blaring television. But the Chinese food is tasty, cheap, and bountiful. Try the *Tallarines en tres sabores* (noodles with three flavors s/6.50). Open daily noon-3pm and 5-11pm.

Restaurant Euskalerría (tel. 721 808), on Luzuriaga. Operated by a Basque mountain guide and his Peruvian wife, Euskalerría offers a filling *desayuno americano* (eggs, toast, *cafe con leche,* and juice s/7). They also serve a wide selection of dinner and lunch offerings. Open daily 8am-3pm and 6-10pm.

Restaurante Piccolo, Julio de Morales 632 and Luzuriaga (tel. 727 306). At this laid-back eatery you can sit a streetside table and watch Huaraz go by. The menu is fairly organic with tasty treats like yogurt with fruit and honey (s/6), a perfect way to start any day. Open daily 6am-midnight.

Crêperie Patrick, Luzuriaga 422 (tel. 723 364). Very tasty, if somewhat pricey, crepes with all sorts of fillings. Mix ingredients like chocolate, banana, and ice cream (s/2-3 per filling) to suit your own tastes. Patrick also offers more standard, non-crepe dishes such as filet mignon (s/29). Open M-Sa 8am-12:30 pm and 6-11pm.

Pizzeria Chez Pepe, Luzuriaga 570 (tel. 726 482). In case there's any confusion, the house specialty is pizza (large pies s/26-29). It's good, by Peruvian standards, but, to the discerning gourmet, that doesn't say much. Open daily 7am-midnight.

SIGHTS

EL MIRADOR DE RATEQUENUA. The *mirador* is a high mountain pass (3650m) to the southeast of town that provides spectacular views of Huaraz and the surrounding mountains. It makes for a scenic dayhike which helps many to become properly acclimatized. The round-trip takes about four hours. Some people rent mountain bikes and enjoy the speedy descent. Sadly, the pass has a dangerous reputation, and tourists are advised not to go alone or at night. *(To get there, head south on Luzuriaga from the Plaza de Armas until the intersection with Av. Villón; then take the road that starts above the cemetery, at the uphill end of Villón.)*

MONUMENTO ARQUEOLÓGICO DE WILCAHUAÍN. Discovered in 1932, this complex of Pre-Inca Huari ruins consists mainly of a temple and an army fortress dating to AD 1000. *(Colectivos marked "Wilcahuaín" (s/1) make the 7km trip, and leave from the north-bound colectivo stop across the bridge from Luzuriaga. Alternatively, it is possible to walk, either on the main road, or through the town of Huanchuc. Always open. Admission s/4, students s/2. Children will give tours in exchange for a small tip.)*

LOS BAÑOS DE MONTERREY. This complex includes two large baths and 27 smaller *pozas*, private chambers for one or two people. The water is very brown, but hordes of Peruvian and foreign tourists still flock to the baths on weekends. *(6km north of Huaraz, just off the main highway. Open daily 7am-6pm. Admission s/3.)*

LAGUNA CHURUP. A beautiful, alpine lake (altitude 4485m) at the foot of the Nevado Churup (5495m) makes for a pleasant daytrip. The lake is very popular with locals, so ask in Huaraz for more specific information. *(Camionetas to the nearby town of Llupa depart from the corner of Caraz and Lucar y Torre in Huaraz.)*

LOCAL FIESTAS. As the capital of Ancash, Huaraz hosts several regional fiestas that attract *campesinos* from the region for dancing, drinking, and singing. The most important is the **Fiesta de Mayo,** May 2-15. A whole series of events is planned, from dance festivals, to ski races, to the traditional procession of the Señor de Mayo. Another significant celebration is the **Fiesta de Las Cruces**, on September 14. Thousands of *limeños* go to Huaraz for the **Fiestas Patrias** (July 28-29), **Semana Santa** (the week preceding Easter), and the **Semana de Andinismo** (end of June). At these times, prices of transportation and lodging rise dramatically, and ordinary residents may temporarily open their homes to accommodate guests.

ENTERTAINMENT

As is the case with hostels, restaurants, and tour agencies, abundant bars and *discotecas* have sprung up in Huaraz in hopes of cashing in on the city's recent tourism boom. For those with extra energy or *soles*, these clubs are a good place to dance and drink them away.

Café Andino, Morales 753, 2 blocks up from Luzuriaga. A coffeehouse with a twist, Andino offers fresh espresso (s/5), an eclectic, multilingual library, and liquor (*cuba libre* s/9). What more could a gringo in Huaraz desire? The relaxed decor is perfect for writing letters home, playing Scrabble, or having a quiet, pre-party drink before going to El Tambo (see below). Open daily 9am-noon and 6-midnight.

El Tambo, José de la Mar 776 (tel. 723 417), 3 blocks up from Luzuriaga. It's smoky, it's crowded, and it's a really good time. Probably the only real *discoteca* in town, El Tambo is the place to go for debaucherous drinking (beer s/5, pitcher of *sangría* s/10) and dancing until dawn. No cover, unless very crowded.

Aquelarre, on Luzuriaga and Gadino Uribe. A fun bar for both tourists and Peruvians. The owner, a local artist, has decorated the place with his own interpretive paintings and sculptures—many of which have a disturbing skeleton theme. Open nightly 7pm-1am.

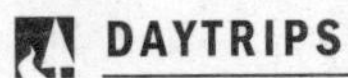

DAYTRIPS

There are numerous tourist sights which can be easily reached in daytrips from Huaraz. Predictably, there are also numerous tour operators eager to take you to see them. Packaged daytrip tours generally include round-trip transportation, a guide (who may or may not speak English), and a few hours at a particular sight. Some suggested daytrip operators are: **Pablo Tours,** Luzuriaga 501 (tel. 726 384; open daily 7am-1pm and 3:30-10pm); **Chavín Tours,** Luzuriaga 502 (tel. 721 578; open daily 7:30am-1pm and 4-9pm); and **Montrek,** Luzuriaga 646 (tel. 721 124), which also offers rafting and rock climbing. Alternatively, most of the popular destinations are also accessible by public transportation or *camioneta,* and require no special guide. Though it is rarely collected by park officials, visitors should be prepared to pay the **park admission fee** (s/5 for daytrippers).

HUARAZ CITY TOUR. This is the most generic of the tours available in Huaraz. Basically, it visits three of Huaraz's main sights: the **Museo Regional de Ancash,** the ruins of **Wilcahuaín,** and the **hot springs of Monterrey.** *(About 5hr. S/20 per person.)*

LAGUNAS LLANGANUCO. These spectacular alpine lakes lie about 60km to the north of Huaraz. Though they are more easily reached from the town of Yungay, many Huaraz tour companies offer daytrips. There are two alpine lakes, surrounded by incredible views of some of the most majestic peaks of the Cordillera Blanca, including Huascarán, towering to the southeast. The lower lake, Chinacocha, is most commonly visited by tourists. Go on a clear day, as it would be a shame to miss the incredible views because of inclement weather. *(From Huaraz, tours cost US$20-25 per person and leave frequently in the dry season. To get to the lakes independently, catch a bus to the town of Yungay. From the Plaza de Armas, round-trip camionetas to the lakes (s/20) leave frequently in the dry season.)*

PASTORURI GLACIER AND PUYA RAYMONDI. This popular excursion allows visitors to walk on a relatively flat Andean glacier. No special equipment is necessary, but it is best to be somewhat acclimatized; the altitude is 5240m. Avid skiers and snowboarders trudge their equipment up to the glacier for occasional races. Often, this trip is combined with a visit to some of the region's famous *Puya Raymondi* plants, which are found between 3600 and 4300m.

CHAVÍN DE HUÁNTAR. Finally, a popular daytrip option is to visit the famous pre-Inca ruins at Chavín (see p. 202). From Huaraz, many companies offer bus tours to the site *(s/20-30 per person, not including any individual admission fees).*

IS THAT THE WORLD'S LARGEST BROMELIAD IN YOUR POCKET OR ARE YOU JUST HAPPY TO SEE ME? Not just your average Andean shrub, the famous **Puya Raymondi** is quite a distinctive and impressive type of plant. Up to 13m tall, it consists of a low, bushy base from which a long, leafy trunk protrudes. Though its size and shape seems to fit the profile of some sort of giant, mutated cactus, the enormous plant is really a member of the **bromeliad** family, making it a distant relative of the pineapple. The Puya Raymondi, concentrated in the *Callejón de Huaylas* region of the central Andean highlands, stands in stark contrast to its surroundings and towers far above its shrubby neighbors. Recently, it has become fashionable for tour groups to visit these eccentric plants, hoping to catch one in bloom. This is harder than it sounds, as the base of each plant must mature for about 100 years before it can muster the energy to erect its central shaft. This spiky column then erupts with thousands of blooming flowers, which remain intact for several months. It's quite a magnificent reproductive ritual. Unfortunately, it's a one-time affair. The plant dies shortly after it blooms.

 MULTI-DAY EXCURSIONS

The region's spectacular multiple-day treks are what bring most visitors to the Cordillera Blanca in the first place. Fortunately, many mountain trails with breathtaking views (and elevation changes) are accessible to novice hikers without much experience or personal gear. Many of the hikes are relatively easy and there are several agencies in Huaraz that are willing to rent gear to adventurous souls. Treks may be done privately or with the aid of an **arriero,** a local mule-handler who acts as a porter and a guide. These can be commissioned at the Casa de Guías in Huaraz (see **Practical Information,** p. 204), as well as at individual trailheads. They cost about US$12 per day, plus food. Tour agencies in Huaraz and Caraz also periodically offer packaged treks along the more popular trails. In addition to the cost of equipment rental and a guide, there is a steep **park admission fee** (s/65) for multi-day excursions. The fee has not been collected very regularly, but park officials have pledged to be more vigilant in the future.

For those attempting these trips independently, there are a few essential pieces of **equipment** to bring: warm and waterproof clothing and tents, food, a camping stove and cookware, water purification tablets or a filter, and a beveled-edge compass and reliable topographic map of the region.

LLANGANUCO TO SANTA CRUZ VALLEY. Because of the incredible scenery of the route, this is the most popular trek in the Cordillera Blanca. Much of the valley is blessed with serene views of glaciated peaks, alpine lakes, and tundra-like meadows. The hike is not particularly strenuous, and there are many tempting side trails along the way. Due to the heavy traffic it receives, the main trail has recently been equipped with designated campsites and outhouses, to increase comfort and minimize the impact of human use. *(The hike generally takes 4-5 days. Both terminal nodes are accessible by camioneta from Caraz. The journey begins either at Cashapampa (2hr. from Caraz, s/15), or at Vaquería (2½hr. from Caraz, s/10).)*

FROM OLLEROS TO CHAVÍN. This is another fairly easy but much less crowded three-day trek that begins near Huaraz. The trail winds through open fields and wide valleys, providing views of the surrounding snow-capped peaks. It then pitches up to the Punta Yanashallash (a 4700m pass between two glaciers) and passes by several Quechua villages before ending up at the ruins of Chavín de Huántar (see p. 208), near the small town of the same name. *(The trailhead is in the village of Olleros, 27km south of Huaraz., s/1.50 by colectivo.)*

 MOUNTAIN CLIMBING

Huaraz is full of "cowboy" guides, who offer their services at a discount. Unfortunately, they almost never have the proper training or equipment and can be a real danger to their customers. Every year, several climbers in the Cordillera Blanca die because of human error. For serious technical climbing trips, deal with no one but **La Casa de Guías** (see **Practical Information,** p. 204). The Casa maintains a contact list of certified mountain guides, all of whom have completed a rigorous three-year course to gain their accreditation from the Peruvian Mountain Guide Association (UIAGM). The daily fee of a guide (US$40-50) is expensive by Peruvian standards, but your life is well worth it. La Casa de Guías also offers advice, a message board to seek climbing partners, and an associated hostel and restaurant list.

Huaraz is definitely the best place to find the appropriate equipment and a qualified guide with whom to attempt the many glacier climbs throughout the Cordillera Blanca. The most popular climbs are sometimes also the easiest, so climbers with little or no experience should not be discouraged. **Nevado Pisco** (5752m), **Alpamayo** (5957m), and the mammoth **Huascarán** (6768m) require little more than a sense of adventure, well-acclimatized lungs, the proper gear, and a qualified guide.

CARHUAZ

Locals like to call it *Carhuaz borrachera*, or "intoxicating Carhuaz." A visit to this small town 32km north of Huaraz proves the nickname to be no exaggeration. Though not as flashy as its big brother to the south, Carhuaz offers the same beautiful mountain scenery in addition to several quiet *casas de alojamiento*, making it is a great place to spend the night away from the comparative hustle and bustle of Huaraz. A visit during the boisterous patronal fiestas, lasting almost all of September, adds a further dimension to the town's nickname.

Carhuaz is small and easy to navigate. The **Plaza de Armas** is four blocks above the **Carretera Central,** the main road of the Callejón de Huaylas valley. Everything of importance is near the plaza. Flag down **colectivos** on the Carretera Central. They travel to: **Huaraz** (1hr., s/3); **Yungay** (30min., s/2); and **Caraz** (1hr., s/3). **Buses** also pass by occasionally. For **tourist information,** talk to Felipe Díaz, the owner of the **Café Heladería El Abuelo** (tel. 794 144), on the plaza at San Martín and La Merced. Señor Díaz designed the definitive tourist map of the region. Also, there is a three-dimensional rendering of the Cordillera to help visitors get their bearings. **Police** (tel. 794 197) are located on the Plaza de Armas. **Telephone code:** 044.

Carhuaz has several undervisited but quite handsome hostels. **Las Torrecitas,** Amazonas 412 (tel. 794 213), is four blocks uphill and two blocks to the right from the Plaza de Armas. The amicable owner offers enormous, clean rooms with parquet wooden floors, mirrors, and a black-and-white TVs. (Rooms s/15 per person.) **Las Bromelias,** Brazil 208 (tel. 794 033), is three blocks up from the Plaza de Armas. True to its name, the hostel is a comfortable and tranquil place with a beautiful flower garden. (Singles s/20; doubles s/30.) **Hostal Merced,** Ucayali 724 (tel. 794 241), is a slightly more traditional hostel option. It offers an accommodating staff, comfortable rooms, and *agua caliente*. (Rooms s/15 per person with bath).

Although it is not exactly the culinary epicenter of Perú, there are a few places to get a decent meal in Carhuaz. **Vuelva Mi Aron,** Santa Rosa 664, offers the traditional *criollo* staples in the form of trout (s/12), chicken (s/10), and *chicharrón* (s/3-7). The staff is accommodating and can prepare some simple requests that don't appear on the menu, including vegetarian dishes. (Open daily 4-11pm.) **Café Heladería El Abuelo,** San Martín and La Merced, on the Plaza de Armas, specializes in ice cream snacks (s/2-4) and tourist information, but also offers simple sandwiches and a la carte items (open daily 8am-9pm).

There is a thriving **market** every Wednesday and Sunday on the streets north and west of the plaza. Several years ago, American anthropologists found the remains of a man who lived 12,000 years ago, **"the Hombre Guitarra,"** on the other side of the valley in the hills of the Cordillera Negra. The **Chancos Hot Springs** are 4km uphill from the town of Macará, which is 7km south of Carhuaz, and 25km north of Huaraz. Take a *colectivo* and then walk or take a taxi (s/1) uphill. (Open 6am-9pm. Admission s/3.) The **Fiestas Patronales** climax on September 24 and conclude at the end of the month, but there is revelry all September long in Carhuaz.

YUNGAY

Yungay, a settlement directly under Huascarán, is best known for the massive mudslide that destroyed the town 30 years ago. Following its utter annihilation, Yungay was rebuilt about 1km north of the original site. The path that the waters took is still apparent and the buried town has become something of a tourist attraction. Besides its catastrophic past and its current status as a regional crossroads, there's not too much to distinguish the quiet Andean hamlet.

Colectivos traveling to Caraz (30min., s/2) and **Huaraz** (1½hr., s/5) leave and arrive at the **Plaza de Armas,** or three blocks downhill at the **Carretera Central.** On the Plaza de Armas, there is a **Banco de la Nación** (tel. 793 052), which will change cash and traveler's checks (open M-F 8:30am-1pm and 2:30-4pm). The **post office** is on the Plaza de Armas, next to the Municipalidad. **Telephone code:** 044.

THE WRATH OF HUASCARÁN On May 31, 1970, an enormous earthquake, measuring 7.7 on the Richter scale, caused massive chunks of rock and ice to plummet from Huascarán, the highest peak in the Cordillera Blanca. The falling debris picked up water in its descent, eventually creating a deadly *alluvia*, that smothered Yungay. More than 20,000 people, most of whom were watching the 1970 Mexico-hosted World Cup, died in the city of Yungay alone. Over 260 children, who were attending a circus, were saved when the circus tent fell, creating a protective shield. Around 90 others ran up to the cemetery to reach safety. In all, 80,000 residents of the Ancash region died in the catastrophic seismic event.

Hostal Gledel, on Arias Grazini, just two blocks down from the Plaza de Armas, offers spacious, spotless rooms with wooden floors and private hot-water baths. Traditional breakfast and dinner is served in the hostel's cafeteria. (Rooms s/20 per person.) **Hostal Yungay** (tel. 793 053), right on the Plaza de Armas, has no restaurant and offers only common baths. But, they still have hot water to chase away those misty mountain chills. (Rooms s/10 per person.)

El Alpamayo (tel. 793 214), on the carretera, three blocks below the Plaza de Armas, tends to fill up around lunchtime with tourists bound for the Llanganuco lakes. *Pachamanca* (s/10) and trout dishes (s/10) are among Alpamayo's popular specialties. (Open daily 8am-8pm.) **El Rosario** (tel. 793 154), on the Plaza de Armas, is a small restaurant frequented by locals. Pull up a seat and snack on sandwiches (s/3), *arroz chaufa* (s/15), and *bisteck* (s/8; open daily 6am-9pm.)

The **Campo Santo,** just south of the new city (a 20min. walk or s/0.50 *colectivo* ride from the Plaza de Armas) is the site of the buried town of old Yungay. There are still traces of the original settlement, like an intact cemetery, where many of Yungay's townspeople fled to escape the approaching mudslide in 1970. Now, rosebushes form a cross through the center of town and tourists wander among the ruins. (Admission s/1. Open daily 8am-6:30pm.) The access road to the **Lagunas Llanganuco** begins in Yungay. The spectacular lakes, which are nestled between the north peak of Huascarán and several other mountains, are of a dazzling blue color. Many tourists visit the lakes with a tour group from Huaraz (see p. 208), but it is probably easier to see them from Yungay, if you can find a taxi driver. Admission to the park is s/5 for the day, but the fee is rarely collected.

CARAZ

About 66km north of and almost 1000m lower than Huaraz, Caraz enjoys a lush, warm atmosphere that provides relief from the bitter cold of the high Andes. Perhaps this is why locals call it *Caraz dulzura* ("sweet Caraz"). Or maybe the sugary sobriquet comes from the super yummy *manjar blanco*, a sweet dairy concoction for which the region is famous. In any case, this tranquil terminus of the Huaylas Valley may provide the perfect remedy for exhaustion, whether it results from hectic travel, physical exertion in the nearby mountains, or the overwhelming buzz of more touristy spots to the south.

ORIENTATION AND PRACTICAL INFORMATION

The **Carretera Central** runs three blocks west of the **Plaza de Armas. Daniel Villar** and **Sucre** run perpendicular to the highway, and together help to form the plaza.

Transportation: Colectivos are the best way to travel within the region. To: **Cashapampa** (2hr., every 30min. 9am-8pm, s/6) and **Huaraz** (2hr., every 15min. until 9pm, s/6) via **Yungay** (30min., s/2) and **Carhuaz** (1hr., s/3). They leave from the market on Sucre and La Mar, 3 blocks uphill from the Plaza de Armas, and from the plaza itself. Around town, a **mototaxi** ride between 2 points should cost s/1-2.

Tourist Information: There is a municipal tourist office in Caraz, but it keeps erratic hours. **Pony's Expeditions,** Sucre 1266 (tel. 791 642; email ponyexp@pol.com.pe), on the Plaza de Armas, is a much better source of information for all types of travelers. The proprietor, Alberto Cafferata, is a great resource for information about the city of Caraz and exploring the beautiful mountains beyond. His shop rents gear, arranges transportation, and has an upstairs cafe with internet access. Open daily 8am-1pm and 7-10pm.

Banks: Banco de Crédito (tel. 791 583), just beyond the Plaza de Armas on Daniel Villar. The bank changes cash and (maybe) traveler's checks. Open M-F 9:15am-1:15pm and 4:30-6:30pm, Sa 9:30am-12:30pm.

Police: Tel. 791 335.

Hospital: (Tel. 791 031), on Leonicio Prado and Sucre.

Post Office: San Martín 909 (tel. 791 094). Mail service is quite slow from this remote location. Open M-Sa 8am-8pm, Su 9am-1pm.

Telephones: An office (tel. 791 529) is on Daniel Villar just beyond the Plaza de Armas.

TELEPHONE CODE	044

ACCOMMODATIONS

Caraz sees only a fraction of the tourists that Huaraz accommodates. This means that a comfortable hotel room is almost always available at prices that may be slightly lower. It may also mean, however, that the hostels are less tourist-friendly than the backpacker strongholds to the south.

Hostal Chavín, San Martín 1135 (tel. 791 171), on the Plaza de Armas. With its friendly staff, hot-water baths, and scrumptious breakfasts (s/5-7), Hostal Chavín is probably the best of a less-than-stellar lot. Ask the owner, Señor Sotelo, to give you his lecture about the cataclysmic 1970 earthquake, which is presented with photos, documents, and a pointer. Singles s/20; doubles s/30.

Hostal La Casona, Raimondi 319 (tel. 791 334), 2 blocks from the Plaza de Armas, is in a renovated colonial house. The pleasant, institutional-feeling hostel keeps 11 comfortable rooms with common or private hot-water bathrooms. Singles with bath s/15; doubles s/15, with bath s/20.

Alojamiento Caballero, Villar 485 (tel. 791 637). Don't be intimidated by the title, women are welcome here as well as *caballeros.* In fact, many of the homey rooms are *matrimoniales.* The common bathrooms are clean and have hot water. Ask about the delectable, down-home dining. Dorms s/10 per person; matrimonial doubles s/17.

Hotel Suiza Peruana, San Martín 1133 (tel. 791 166). There's no Swiss Miss here, though it is very popular with Peruvians. This enormous hostel has an obscene number of rooms, with or without hot-water baths. Singles s/10, with bath s/20; doubles s/15, with bath s/25.

FOOD

As is the case with hotels in Caraz, the town's restaurants are a little bit plain, producing more hearty and traditional local specialties than vegetarian-conscious innovations.

Restaurante La Punta Grande, Daniel Villar 595 (tel. 791 320), at the intersection with the Carretera Central, specializes in *comida típica* like *pachamanca* (meat, beans, and grains wrapped in leaves and baked in an earthen oven, s/12) and *cuy* (guinea pig, s/9), and offers cheap *almuerzos* (s/3.50). At lunchtime, tour groups, fresh from the Lagunas Llanganuco, fill the 40 tables. Open daily 7am-7pm.

Café de Rat, Sucre 1266 (tel. 791 642), upstairs from Pony's tours. Hopefully, the name only refers to the *cuy* on the menu. More of a full-service restaurant than a cafe, the Rat offers breakfast and serves pastas (s/8), soup (s/6), and pizza for dinner. At night, the lights dim, the music pumps, and this rodent restaurant morphs into a rodent bar. Open Su-Th 8am-1pm and 4-10pm, F-Sa until midnight.

Restaurant El Mirador, Sucre 1202, on the Plaza de Armas, specializes in serving those essential Latin American staples–chicken (s/4-24) and trout (s/9-12)–to a mostly local crowd. Open M-Sa 8am-10pm and Su 5-10pm.

Restaurante Esmeraldas, Ugarte 404, 2 blocks above the Plaza de Armas. Like a breath of fresh mountain air, Esmeraldas specializes in meat dishes. *Lomo saltado* and *bisteck* each s/10. Open daily 7am-9pm.

EXCURSIONS

LAGUNA PARÓN. The largest and deepest of the mountain lakes in the Callejón de Huaylas, Parón is located north of Caraz at an altitude of 4140m. During some parts of the year, its grandeur is somewhat diminished by a drainage scheme, which both provides hydroelectric energy and reduces the risk of water engulfing the town of Caraz—as it has its southern neighbors—in the event of a natural disaster (see **The Wrath of Huascarán,** p. 211). The lake may be visited via public transportation as a long daytrip from Caraz but is probably better enjoyed as an overnight excursion. Alternately, a *camioneta* may be commissioned in Caraz (s/100), making the trip much shorter but also much more expensive. *(Colectivos travel towards Parón from the Plaza de Armas in Caraz (1hr., M-Sa 4:50am, s/5). From the Parón sign on the road, it is another 9km and 4hr. hike up to the lake. It's possible to walk up and return to the descending colectivo (2:20pm) in 1 day, but staying overnight allows more time at the lake.)*

OTHER SIGHTS. Caraz is also a great spot from which to see the incredible **Puya Raymondi** plant, the world's largest bromeliad (see **Is That the World's Largest Bromeliad in Your Pocket or Are You Just Happy to See Me?,** p. 208), which is endemic to the region. (*Colectivos leave every day from near the market to the Paso de Winchus. From this pass, you can walk down to Pueblo Libre, where colectivos return to Caraz until 3pm.)* The **Tumshucaico Ruins,** considered to be Pre-Chavín (see p. 208) are located 1km north of Caraz, a 20-minute walk on the Carretera Central. The **Cañon del Pato,** 15km away, is a spectacular mountain highway that leads north and then to the coast. The road is flanked on each side by sheer rock faces and follows the Río Santa as it cuts between the Cordillera Blanca and the Cordillera Negra to the west. The road from Caraz to Huallaca uses 35 tunnels to travel through the canyon. *(Take a colectivo to Hualluca (2hr., s/10 round trip). A taxi should cost about s/40 round-trip.)*

ANCASH, MI AMOR The great Peruvian explorer **Antonio Raimondi** is best known as a 19th-century authority on the flora, fauna, and geography of his native country. Indeed, he relentlessly observed and catalogued the land's natural wonders, particularly in the mountainous Ancash department. Today, his name is most frequently associated with that region's gargantuan century plant, the **Puya Raymondi** (see **Is That the World's Largest Bromeliad in Your Pocket or Are You Just Happy to See Me?,** p. 208).

What most visitors, and even many natives, don't know is that Sr. Raimondi coined names for more than just burly bromeliads. Always one for melodrama, Raimondi would often personify towns that he visited by events that transpired during his stay, lending them catchy nicknames that persist to this day. During a particularly eventful 1860 visit to the *Callejón de Huaylas,* Raimondi practically renamed the region based on his personal impressions. During his stay in the town of Recuay, one of his journals was stolen, leading him to condemn the entire community as **"Thieving Recuay."** Our hero continued north to Huaraz, where he became enamored with a local lass. Unimpressed by his credentials and confident swagger, the beauty simply dismissed him. His bruised bravado and he then left **"Presumptuous Huaraz"** only to be further saddened by the intoxicated excesses on display at a fiesta in **"Drunken Carhuaz."**

Despondent and aimless, the intrepid Raimondi continued north, where his outlook finally brightened. His spirits lifted after seeing a sensational sunrise in **"Lovely Yungay."** With a new spring in his step and a rumbling in his stomach, Antonio blissfully concluded his journey in **"Sweet Caraz,"** where he nursed himself back to full health with *manjar blanco,* the caramel sandwich spread for which that town is famous.

THE AMAZON BASIN

There are no Inca ruins here. Going to the Amazon Basin means leaving behind cobblestones and grand cathedrals; the jungle's hot and humid history is not the sort that people come to see. What has been recorded concerns systematic exploitation and depletion of resources: of oil, of timber, of rubber. It was in fact the foreign rubber barons who, at the turn of the 20th century, began the modern expansion of Perú's eastern frontier: Today the pattern of exploitation continues; commercial loggers and fishermen still threaten to destroy these rainforests.

The Amazon and its promise of outdoor adventure are what lure tourists. After all, the jungle's cities—with the notable exception of Iquitos—offer little that is either culturally or aesthetically pleasing. Sadly, however, such adventure does not always agree with budget travel. Perú's rainforest hosts some 100%-guaranteed, class-act tour companies, but these cost substantial sums. Cheaper options, often in the shape of freelance guides, do exist, but it's nearly impossible to tell the gems from the con men, and thus signing up—not to mention handing over any money—can involve substantial risk. Moreover, even the "cheap" options aren't cheap—almost any jungle trip will cost upwards of US$45 a day. To top it all off, prices in the jungle tend to be slightly higher than in the rest of the country, mainly because of the difficulty of transporting goods to and from these netherlands.

Many visitors also have exotic misperceptions of what a jungle experience has to offer. The fact is you're not going to encounter some elusive animals no matter how or with whom you see the rainforest; there's simply too much vegetation for them to hide behind. Countless insects, yes. Many large mammals, no. Birds, however, do abound. At the end of the dry season, legions of brightly colored parrots flock to the macaw licks in the south to eat clay, which neutralizes the poisonous seed acids they're forced to consume when the healthy seeds run out.

The Tambopata-Candamo Reserve near Puerto Maldonado holds the world's largest macaw clay-lick (*colpa*); neighboring Manú National Park contains the area's most pristine—and most overpriced—forest. Close to Cusco, both destinations receive ample shares of visitors. Up north, lovely Iquitos fields good numbers of tourists as well but can still offer excursions more off-the-beaten-path. The areas around La Merced and Quillabamba sit ripe for exploration, well removed from the "gringo trail." *Buena suerte.* Don't forget the bug spray.

HIGHLIGHTS OF THE AMAZON BASIN

- The vast jungle around **Iquitos** (see p. 221) provides an opportunity to trek through untouched rainforest.
- Beautiful birds, monkeys, and crocodiles lurk within the **Tambopata-Candamo Reserve Zone** (see p. 226).
- Over 12,000 plants have yet to be classified in the **Manú Biosphere Reserve** (see p. 232), one of the largest and most pristine in South America.

IQUITOS

Balanced at the mouth of the Amazon, the city of Iquitos (pop. 120,000) waxes remarkably cosmopolitan for an area only accessible by boat or plane. Intricate Iberian tiles, remnants of the rubber barons' turn-of-the-century residency, decorate buildings along the avenues. Legend has it that the "Iron House" on the Plaza de Armas displays the work of Gustave Eiffel (of Tower fame). And now package

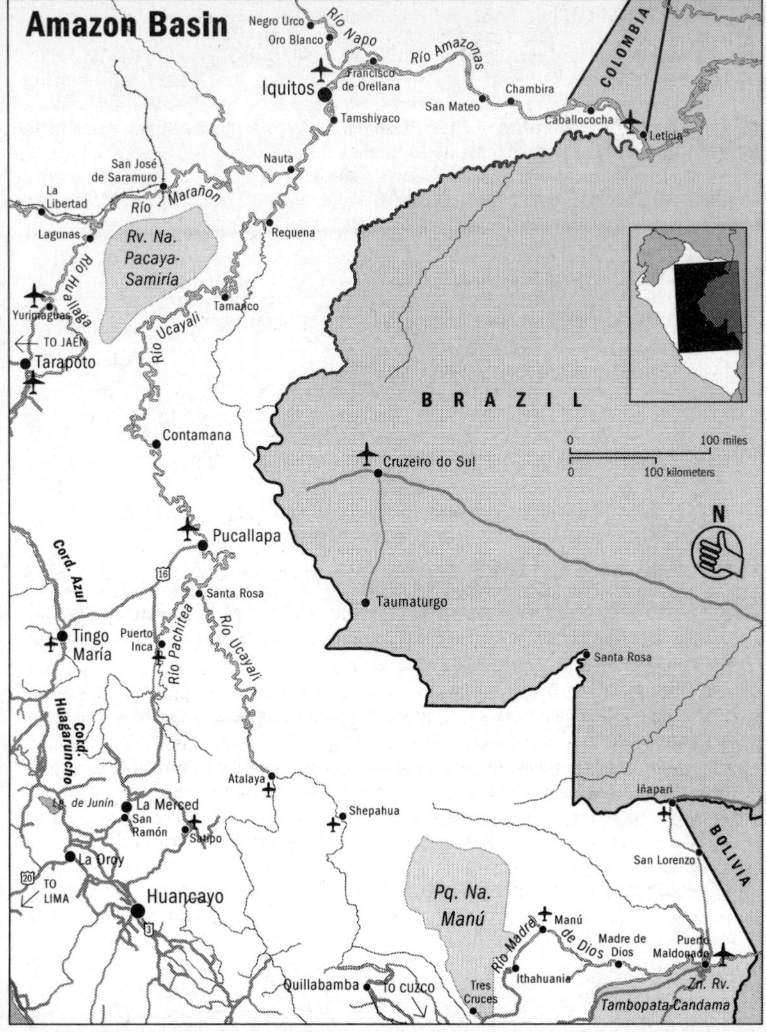

tourists from Britain and Scandinavia stroll Iquitos' streets, in transit to nearby jungle lodges—five of which are owned by Americans. The tourist bureau has grand plans to maximize this trend, estimating that Iquitos will be a "bilingual city" in several years. Inevitably, though, there are people left behind. Except for the few occasional power lines protruding from the river, the floating shanty-town of Belén, probably the city's most memorable neighborhood, could have existed several hundred years ago. As for the 61 indigenous tribes living in the surrounding forest, some of them may never have *seen* electricity at work. Ironically enough, it is the lure of viewing such ways of life—along with the accompanying flora and fauna of the "virgin jungle"—that draws ever more sophisticated (and numerous) visitors to the region. Whatever its drawbacks, however, tourism causes the rainforest less harm than alternative commerce (e.g. logging). But travelers who come so far to see the *selva* in all its glory make a mistake if they overlook the heartbeat of Loreto province: Iquitos—a diverse, charming city safe enough to be the only one in Perú where police are not required to carry guns.

ORIENTATION

Approximately 1860km northeast of Lima and technically an island, the large city of Iquitos is encompassed by rivers: **Río Mañon, Río Nanay,** and—most conspicuously—**Río Amazonas** to the east. **Malecón Tarapaca** fronts the Amazon. One block in, the main drag of **Jirón Próspero** runs from the **Plaza de Armas** eight long blocks south to the massive **Belén Market.** Many of the city's shops, services, and accommodations lie in the area between these landmarks and **Plaza 28 de Julio,** south of the Plaza de Armas, north of the market, and two blocks farther from the river. Avenues that run north-south change names as they pass the two plazas.

PRACTICAL INFORMATION

Airplanes: Aeropuerto Francisco Secada V. Iquitos (tel 260 147), 7km south of the city center, can be reached by *mototaxi* (s/6) or the frequent buses (s/0.50, children s/ 0.30) that run down Ocampo-Tacna-Grau and up Aguierre-Huallaga-Condamine. From the airport, cross the road outside the gates to catch a city-bound bus. **AeroContinente,** Próspero 232 (tel. 242 995), just south of Putumayo. Office open M-Sa 8:30am-7pm, Su 9am-noon. Offers flights to **Lima** (1½hr., 8:30am and 1:30pm, US$89). **Tans,** Próspero 215 (tel. 231 086), also just south of Putumayo, across the street from its competitor. Office open M-Sa 8:30am-7pm, Su 8:30am-1pm. To: **Lima** (1½hr.; 1:45pm, Sa-Su 8:15am also; US$59); and **Pucallpa** (1½hr.; M, W, F 1:45pm; US$59). There is an airport tax of s/12 on all domestic flights.

Boats: Boats depart from **Puerto Masusa,** off Av. La Marina north of the *centro.* Most boats that will accept passengers display signs to announce their destination and time of departure; however, few boats leave on schedule. Boats go to: **Pucallpa** (5-8 days, s/60); **Lagunas** (2-5 days, s/15); **Yurimanguas** (3-6 days, s/50); and **Leticia** and **Tabatinga** (1-3 days, s/30). Prices are negotiable.

Local Transportation: During the day and evening, buses run down Ocampo-Tacna-Grau to the airport, and then back up Aguirre-Guallaga-Condamine to Av. La Marina and the Masusa port (s/0.50, children s/0.30).

Taxis: Open-air motorcycles rickshaws known as *motocarros* or *motos,* are everywhere downtown. S/2 to anywhere in the town center, s/6 to the airport.

Motorcycle Rental: Park Motors, Tacna 621 (tel. 231 688), between R. Palma and M. Cáceres, rents motorcycles (no helmets) for s/6-10 per hr., depending on the model. Open daily 7am-11pm.

Tourist Office: Napo 226 (tel. 235 621; email turismo.mpm@tus.com.pe), on the Plaza de Armas. Offers maps, English brochures and information on jungle tours and guides. Open M-F 8am-7pm, Sa 9am-1pm.

Currency Exchange: Banco de Crédito, Próspero 22 (tel. 234 501), on the Plaza de Armas. 24hr. **ATM** accepts Visa. No commission if exchanging traveler's checks for *soles;* US$11.50 if exchanging for dollars. Open M-F 9:15am-1:15pm and 4:30-6:30pm, Sa 9:30am-12:30pm. **Banco Continental,** Sargento Lores 171 (tel. 235 421), toward the river from Próspero. 24hr. **ATM** accepts Visa. US$10 per commission on all traveler's check transactions. Open M-F 9:15am-12:45pm and 4:30-6:30pm, Sa 9:30am-12:30pm.

Market: The **Belén Market** sprawls for blocks between the river and Arica, south of G. Sanz. Open daily 3am-1am.

Laundromat: Lavandería Imperial, Putumayo 150 (tel. 231 768), between Próspero and Tarapaca, has self-service washing (s/3 per load, up to 4kg) and drying (s/3). Open M-Sa 7am-9pm. **Lavandería Express,** R. Palma 451 (tel. 234 387), between Arica and Huallaga, offers same day wash-and-dry (s/2 per kg). Open M-Sa 8am-8pm.

Emergency: Tel. 241 001.

Police: Morona 120 (tel. 231 131), near Tarapaca. Open 24hr.

Medical Services: Clínica Adventista Ana Stahl, Av. La Marina 285 (tel. 252 518), is a private facility with a **pharmacy.** Open 24hr.

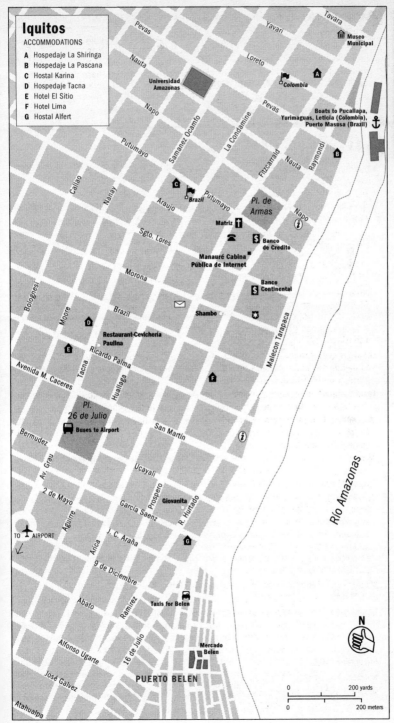

Iquitos

ACCOMMODATIONS

- **A** Hospedaje La Shiringa
- **B** Hospedaje La Pascana
- **C** Hostal Karina
- **D** Hospedaje Tacna
- **E** Hotel El Sitio
- **F** Hotel Lima
- **G** Hostal Alfert

Tavara
Yavari
Museo Municipal
Pevas
Loreto
Nauta
Universidad Amazonas
Colombia
Pevas
Boats to Pucallapa, Yurimaguas, Leticia (Colombia), Puerto Masusa (Brazil)
Napo
Samanez Ocamfo
La Condamine
Fitzcarrald
Raymondi
Putumayo
Nauta
Callao
Nanay
Brazil
Putumayo
Araujo
Pl. de Armas
Napo
Matriz
Sgto. Lores
Banco de Credito
Manauré Cabina Pública de Internet
Morona
Banco Continental
Bolognesi
Shambo
Brazil
Moore
Malecon Tarapaca
Restaurant-Cevicheria Paulina
Ricardo Palma
Avenida M. Caceres
Tacna
Huallaga
Pl. 26 de Julio
Buses to Airport
San Martín
Bermudez
Av. Grau
Ucayali
Río Amazonas
2 de Mayo
Prospero
Giovanita
García Saenz
R. Hurtado
Aguirre
TO AIRPORT
J. C. Araña
Arica
9 de Diciembre
Taxis for Belen
Abato
Ramirez
N
Alfonso Ugarte
16 de Julio
Mercado Belen
José Galvez
PUERTO BELEN
0 200 yards
0 200 meters
Atahualpa

Post Office: Serpost, Arica 402 and Morona (tel. 234091; fax 231915). Offers international fax service. Open M-F 8am-1pm and 3-7pm, Sa 7:30am-6pm, Su 9:30am-1pm.

Internet Access: Manauré Cabina Pública de Internet, Próspero 249 (tel 242 148), between Putumayo and Sargento Lores, offers access (s/4 per hr.). Open M-Sa 8:30am-midnight, Su 8:30am-2pm and 8pm-midnight.

Telephones: Central Telefónica, Sargento Lores 321 (tel. 231 047; fax 231 111), between Arica and Huallaga, also has international fax service. Open daily 7am-11pm.

TELEPHONE CODE 094

ACCOMMODATIONS

As tends to be the case with most prices in Iquitos, room rates are a bit inflated. Most of the following hostels offer such serenity, though, that the guest can almost forgive them the extra *soles*.

Hotel Lima, Próspero 549 (tel. 235 152; fax 234 111), between Brasil and R. Palma. A jaguar-print "Lima" behind the reception desk welcomes visitors while rattan-covered banisters lead them up to their rooms. Such outdoorsiness stays in the hallways, however: the small, high-ceilinged rooms are squeaky clean and all have private bath and a fan. Singles s/20; doubles/s30; triples s/40.

Hostal Alfert, G. Sanz 01 (tel. 234 105), off Ramirez Hurtado by the Amazon. The surrounding market area may not be the most savory neighborhood, but where else could private rooms, all with bath and fan, have such panoramic views over Belén? The cheerful management and effective window screens keep rooms and tiled baths very tidy. Singles s/15; doubles s/20.

Hospedaje Tacna, Tacna 516 (tel. 235 886), at Brasil. Street-side rooms can get a bit noisy, and some faulty screening calls for a double dose of insect repellent. Still, Tacna's brightly-painted floors and frescoed doors provide some colorful diversion. The rooms, all with bath and fan, vary dramatically in terms of size and light. Singles s/14; doubles; s/18; triples s/24.

Hotel El Sitio, R. Palma 545 (tel. 234 932), between Tacna and Moore. Placid, plant-lined outdoor corridors lead to impeccably kept (if un-screened and split-pea green) sleeping quarters, complete with bath and fan. El Sitio is incredibly quiet but often full. Singles s/20; doubles s/30; TVs available for s/5.

Hospedaje La Shiringa, Fitzcarrald 465 (tel. 243 293), between Yavari and Loreto. Spacious bath-and-fan rooms are relatively bare except for frilly quasi-porcelain lamps. Singles s/20, with TVs/25; doubles s/30, with TV s/35.

Hostal Karina, Putumayo 467 (tel. 235 36), between Huallaga and Tacna. Blue patterned wallpaper and navy carpets lend this ramshackle structure an air of decaying gentility. Singles s/15; doubles s/20; matrimonials s/25; triples s/35.

Hospedaje La Pascana, Pevas 133 (tel. 231 418; fax 233 466; email pascana@lima.business.com.pe), between Raymondi and the Amazon. A perennial backpacker favorite, Pascana houses 18 decent rooms, several thatched picnic tables, a book exchange, internet access (s/7 per hr.), and some English-speaking staff. Singles US$9; doubles US$12; triples US$15.

FOOD

Really, there's no need to flock to Ari's Burger on the Plaza de Armas (burger s/6-11); there are much less expensive, not to mention tastier, morsels to be had all over the city. *Chifas* line Jr. Grau on the blocks south of Plaza 28 de Julio; cheap *típicos* cluster on Jr. Huallaga north of the plaza and, farther afield, on Av. La Marina. Additionally, many stalls in the Belén market offer jungle specialties like *paiche*, a giant river fish; and *juanes* (rice, chicken, black olives and egg wrapped in a banana leaf), at their best in Iquitos. Even vegetarians suffering from the decided lack of restaurants catering to their needs can sample the hearty yellow *aguaje* fruit, sold out of buckets on street corners all over the city.

Restaurant-Cevichería Paulina, Tacna 462 (tel. 231 298), at R. Palma. The Sunday line snaking out through Paulina's tall wooden doors testifies to the popularity of her *ceviche* (s/10-18). Thankfully, the lack of weekday lines allows even the impatient to sample soups (s/7), steaks (s/16-20), and noodles (s/16-18). Open daily 7am-10pm.

Giovanita, R. Hurtado 873, between Veayali and G. Sanz. A chaotically muraled lunch spot offering tasty jungle fare. *Juanes* s/6, whole grilled fish s/6. Open daily 7am-2pm.

Don Pizza, Huallaga 204 (tel. 222 727), just south of Putumayo. The pick of Iquitos' copious pizzerias, Don's fare is served on surprisingly chewy crusts. A wooden loft escapes the dubbed American sitcoms downstairs. Vegetarian pizza s/10-30, pepperoni s/10-27, garlic bread s/3-6, jar of sangría s/18. Open daily 6pm-midnight.

Shambo (tel. 231 357), at the intersection of Próspero and Morona, also at Grau 1048 and M. Cáceres 654. A city-wide chain serving ultra-juicy popsicles made from local fruits like *uva, camu-camu, aguaje,* and *ungurahui* as well as strawberry, mango, and coconut (s/1.) Open daily 9am-midnight.

Snack Bar Antojitos, Napo 380 (tel. 234 631), near Contamine. Plain but popular, Antojitos serves salads (s/4-5), sandwiches (s/2-6), chicken dishes (s/7-15), and rich fresh juices (s/2-3) for a fraction of the prices found on the plaza. Open daily 7am-2am.

El Huaralino, Huallaga 490 (tel. 223 300), just north of Basil, is a tad pricey, but compensates with welcoming ceiling fans and an extensive *criollo* menu, which includes *picante de cuy* (s/22), *tacu tacu con pato* (s/18), and seafood dishes (s/14-20). Open daily 11am-5pm.

SIGHTS

IRON HOUSE. The rubber tycoons' century-old ambitions dominate the sightseeing in Iquitos's center. It was these grand schemes that ferried the Eiffel-designed Iron House across the Atlantic, piece by piece. The much-hyped structure looks much like a house made out of tin foil. And although the walls don't crinkle when tapped, they do emit a profoundly hollow sound, not too different from the chatter floating down from the overpriced cafe upstairs. *(At the intersection of Putumayo and Próspero, on the corner of the Plaza de Armas.)*

CATHEDRAL. The Iron House may have been designed by Monsieur Eiffel, but honestly, the pleasant cathedral's locally painted ceiling is more interesting. *(At Putumayo and Arica, on the Plaza de Armas. Hours vary. Sunday morning mass.)*

BELÉN. The impoverished floating neighborhoods of and beyond Belén hide little grandeur, faded or otherwise. The area provides a glimpse into the lives of impoverished people—many of the houses seem too small for their inhabitants, who go about their affairs on the rickety porches. Some houses float, rising and falling with the river level on rafts that must be replaced every two years; others stand on longer-lasting stilts. The squalid area closest to land, Belén proper centers around a street called **Venecia** but has little in common with its Italian namesake. Adjacent *pueblos* such as **San Francisco**—with its many lilypads—and **San Andrés** are cleaner and more tranquil. Each shelters its own church and primary school. Relatively few tourists visit this tragic yet fascinating area. "Traffic" more often consists of a *bodega flotante* than a canoe with other gringos. One can hire a canoe, but in drier times, it may be necessary to walk a fine line of boards, logs, and planks over treacherously nasty mud to reach the port. In fact, there have been times when the settlements have rested on mud alone (generally between Aug.-Nov.) making travel by canoe impossible. *(To hire a canoe (s/5 per hr.), head through Belén market along Jr. Ugarte, 2km south of the Plaza de Armas.)*

BIBLIOTECA AMAZÓNICA. This museum houses tomes on the people, animals, and plants of Loreto and a large map collection in a tiled and carved wood reading room. Tall double doors reveal the river itself, a stupendous view. The surrounding stretch of the boardwalk showcases a profusion of *azulejos*, the tiles placed on buildings during the period of prosperity that accompanied the rubber boom years. *(Malecón Tarapaca 355, 2nd. floor. Tel. 242 353. Open M-F 3:30-7:30pm, Sa 9am-12:30pm. Admission free.)*

MUSEO AMAZÓNICO DE LORETO. This relatively new museum (opened 1996) has already amassed a considerable collection of weapons, paintings, turn-of-the-century pictographs, etc. Highlights include detailed sculptures of local tribes people, made from old molds forcibly obtained from the subjects, who believed their souls would depart with the likenesses. While some exhibits could be better marked, the exquisitely restored government building is a sight itself. *(Malecón Tarapaca 386 at Morona. Open M-F 8am-1pm and 3-7pm, Sa 9am-1pm. Admission s/3.)*

MUSEO MUNICIPAL. The **tourist office** is in the process of turning the third floor of their building—which once served as city hall—into a small museum. Under imported crystal chandeliers, city scale models mingle with embalmed *paiche* (giant river fish). The curators plan much more (including an admission fee) for the future; for now, inquire at the office downstairs. *(Napo 226, across the plaza from the cathedral. Tel. 235 621. Open M-F 8am-7pm, Sa 9am-1pm. Admission free.)*

ENTERTAINMENT

A broad range of music types and dance styles—as well as much diversity in the age and class of the dancers—makes Iquitos' small club scene exciting, if not extensive. One company, **Tomis Productions** (tel. 266 638), holds moveable, weekly parties (admission s/5). They are also a good source for information about other happenings. And for those too tired to hop, the dim-lit cafes along Tarapaca (especially between Nanta and Napo) offer Pilsener, *pisco*, and breezes from the river.

Explosion, on M. Cáceres, a short cab ride (s/2) from the center of town. The current hotspot for live music and people of all ages dressed to dance rather than impress. The large, open-air pavilion can barely hold all this glee. Cover s/5. Open Sa-Su 10pm-4am.

Amanta Café-Teatro, Nauta 250 (tel. 233 109), between Raymondi and Fitzcarrald. A lavish, artsy enclave watched over by a mammoth portrait of the poet Cesar Vallejo Mendoza, this bar/theater/gallery hosts live music every night at 10pm. An enormous drink menu that includes jungle classics such as *glaro* (s/3.50) and *chuchuhuasi* (s/6) assures that any performance will be enjoyable. Open M-Sa 6pm-5am.

Noa Noa, on Pevas at Fizcarrald. Well-dressed Peruvians and gringos alike get down on Noa's many levels. From up in his glass booth, however, the DJ asks "Do you believe in life after love?" just a bit too often. Cover s/10. Open nightly from 8:30pm–collapse.

Agricobank, at the Condamine-Angel Bruzco intersection, draws a more reserved crowd, *salsa*-ing cautiously across the wide, uncrowded dance floor. Although it has lost some of its customers to Explosion, cheap beers (s/7 for 2) and lively bands sustain the energy level. Cover s/5. Open F-Su 10pm.

New Dreams, Tacna 102 (tel. 234 155), at Napo. Small and chi-chi, with dizzying lights. Particularly popular among teenagers. Cover s/15. Open Tu-Su from 10:30pm.

NEAR IQUITOS: QUISTACOCHA

Located 13km south of the city, the attractive waterside Quistacocha resort offers rest, relaxation, and a chance to see all the animals you missed on your jungle trip. In a small but well-maintained and labeled zoo, monkeys and colorful parrots frolic, a giant river otter flips for visitors, truly gargantuan *paiche* fish lurk just underwater, and beautiful pumas and jaguars yawn and pace. The complex also holds an aquarium and snake house, although both were under construction in the summer of 1999. At the pretty beach, a roped-off swimming area beckons bathers into the lake's reddish water, and trails lead off into the woods. Watch out for weekend crowds. (Open daily 8am-6pm. Beach admission s/5, children s/1.)

Transportation: A *mototaxi* to Quistacocha costs s/10, but frequent *combis* (25min., s/2) leave from the intersection of Jr. Grau and Jr. Abtao. Closer local swimming holes include Morona, Cocha, Ruococha, and Bella Vista (all about a s/5 *mototaxi* trip from the city center).

NEAR IQUITOS: SANTO TOMÁS

A few km off the route to Quistacocha, an extremely rutted dirt road leads to the village of Santo Tomás. This small pueblo is home to a coalition of 20 potters and other clay-molders, who produce magnificent *artesanía* in their home studios. The organization's current president is the knowledgeable Venacio Yuyarima Suárez, who can point visitors in the directions of various interesting crafts. To find Venacio, follow the main street several minutes to the open field; he lives and works at the house at the field's far right-hand corner. The craftspeople see few visitors, but most will gladly sell any a pot (s/10) or knick-knack (s/2).

Transportation: To reach Santo Tomás, ask a Quistacocha *combi* driver to drop you at the turn-off; it's about an hour walk or a s/2 *mototaxi* ride (s/2).

INTO THE JUNGLE FROM IQUITOS

The Iquitos tourist office delights in pointing out that the jungle province of Loreto—the capital of which is Iquitos—occupies an area roughly equivalent to the size of Germany. After all, this promise of vast virgin forest brings the city its visitors. However, the lay of the land ensures that Loreto's most pristine areas stay that way, almost entirely inaccessible. As is the case throughout Perú's *selva*, reaching anywhere even resembling untouched jungle requires lots of money and time. Your best bet lies in finding a tour that will take you at least 80km away from Iquitos and preferably—though this is harder to find—off the main riverways. Of the various protected areas near Iquitos, **Pacaya-Samiria National Reserve** and **Tamshiyacu-Tahuayo Community Reserve** provide the best look at rainforest. However, the romantic allure of "virgin jungle" should not make one forget that fascinating stuff happens all over the region. The native communities hawking goods to tourists are every bit as "real" as those who still make their clothes from tree bark. Besides, one generally doesn't encounter many animals no matter where one goes in the rainforest. Three possibilities are open to the traveler: river cruises, lodges, and trips with independent guides. No budget options exist within the first group. The second option does include some interesting options, but these are also rather expensive. Independent guides, on the other hand, keep the adventurous and budget-oriented traveler in mind.

HIRING A GUIDE

Unfortunately, of the legions of freelance guides operating in Iquitos, many have garnered **complaints:** for lack of knowledge, stealing money, sexual harassment, and, most commonly, for not completing the trip as planned. At present, visitors arriving by plane enter an airport crammed with touts, all shouting for their attention. In such confusion, it's not easy to decide whom to trust. Gerald Mayeaux, the American Rotarian who took over the tourist office last year (and has made tour reform his mission) envisions a huge billboard at the arrival gate, listing the guides with serious complaints against them. Until the inception of this billboard, it's worth taking a trip to the tourist office (see **Practical Information,** p. 216), where Mayeaux maintains a list of the deadbeats and may be able to recommend some reputable guides. Whenever deciding on a guide, try to get the trip agreement in writing, and avoid paying in full up front. Also, sign up with tours directly, instead of following the middlemen who offer to find one for you.

All caveats aside, Iquitos does harbor one guide of unblemished reputation. **Moisés Torres Viena,** the proprietor of **Expeditions and Adventure Amazon Jungle,** Brasil 217 (tel. 224 327; fax 231 111), near Próspero, has been leading tours for 45 years. An expert on anthropology and botany, Moisés also possesses a wicked sense of humor. He'll take clients trekking, fishing, and on visits to indigenous tribes for one day, six months, or anywhere in between. While Moisés only speaks Spanish, he can arrange for an English-speaking guide. (Prices average US$60 per person per day for 1-2 people, US$40 for 3 or more, but can change according to the number of days, number of people, and distance traveled. Prices include all food and lodging. Contact Moisés well in advance. Open daily 6am-10pm.)

JUNGLE LODGES

The tourist lodges offer a modicum of security not available with many of the freelance operators. Many of the affordable ones sit quite close to the city, however, and while they offer a few trails, visits to Yagua, Bora, Achuale, or Murato tribes, and sometimes even a swimming pool, any sort of jungle adventure will generally cost extra. Make sure you understand what's included (and what languages guides speak) before you sign up; food, lodging, and speedboat transport always should be included. Also, try bargaining—most people book these trips from home at set rates, but walk-in customers have far greater leverage: if the company sends a boat with spaces on it up to the lodge the next day, it's in their best interests to have more people aboard, even if they're paying half the usual rate. Since many of the less expensive companies maintain offices on Putumayo between Próspero and Tarapaca, comparison shopping requires little leg-work.

Tahuayo Lodge Expeditions, Putumayo 263 (tel. 232 738; fax 266 342; email Tahuayo@mailcity.com; www.viaexpresa.com.pe/tahuayo), on the Plaza de Armas, operates a variety of interesting programs, most of which cost the regular price. From a base lodge 120km from Iquitos, the lodge offers night hikes, "survival" trips (in which participants catch their own food and construct their own shelters), and folkloric medicine education programs, as well as the more standard tribal visits and Amazon swims. US$50 per day with 1 person, US$40 per person per day with 2, US$35 with 6 or more. Open daily 8am-8pm.

Loving Light Amazon Lodge, Putumayo 128 (tel. 243 180; email info@junglelodge.com; www.junglelodge.com), 100km from the city on the Yanayacu River. In the U.S. contact: 7016 248th Av. N.E. Redmond, WA 98053 (tel. (425) 836-9431). Loving Light can also arrange survival nights in the bush. Although partially American-run, the lodge claims a commitment to employing local guides, and a resident shaman greets arriving guests. US$70 per person per day with 2 people; group and student discounts possible. Open daily 7am-8pm.

Paseos Amazónicos, Pevas 246 (tel. 233 110), between Fitzcarrald and Raimondi. Main office in Lima: Bajada Balta 131-054 Lima 18 (tel. 241 75 76; fax 446 79 46; email postmast@p-amazon.com.pe). Maintains a variety of lodges in the area; the farthest, **Tambo Amazónico Lodge,** is 180km from Iquitos. From there, guests visit giant lilypads (Victorias Regias), make camping trips to the Pacaya-Samiria Reserve, and hope to see pink dolphins. US$100 per person per day. Open daily 7am-7pm.

Pink Amazon River Dolphin Expeditions, Pevas 116 (tel./fax 242 596; email pard-expeditions@yahoo.com), near the river. In the U.S.: 3302 North Burton Av., Rosemead, CA 91770 (tel. 572-0233; fax 572-9521; www.isptr-pard.org). This spin-off of a 17-year-old international nonprofit organization works to combat deforestation and commercial hunting and fishing as well as to provide the local native communities with means for survival, primarily through a clinic and non-disruptive co-op system. Their lodge, **Dolphin Corners,** maintains a free clinic, a 4000-acre private reserve, and an animal orphanage for wildlife that forest police have confiscated from poachers. Moreover, its location—180km from Iquitos on the Yarapa River— also helps visitors see pink dolphins Nov.-June. All guides are bilingual and the lodge features detoxifying mud baths. Week-long trips US$1400 per person for 5-10 people and US$1500 for 1-4 people, but founder Roxanne Kremer can come up with alternative transportation to help lower the price. Longer and shorter stays available. People willing to work 4-6hr. a day can pay a special rate of US$65 per day, less after a month.

Explorama, La Marina 340 (tel. 252 526; fax 252 533; www.explorama.com), the granddaddy of jungle trips in Iquitos, is extraordinarily organized, well-run, and expensive. Explorama's most unique feature is its ability to bring visitors to the ACEER canopy walkway. Open M-F 7:30am-6pm, Sa 7:30am-12:30pm.

QUILLABAMBA

A panoramic mountain view dominates the sleepy city of Quillabamba, although the humid jungle air makes a joke of the snowy hills to the south. Despite its climate, though, some travelers remark that Quillabamba doesn't feel like a jungle town; it's true that tropical vegetation in the immediate area has long since been cleared away—one has to delve deeper into the *selva* to find that. And jungle exploration is precisely the reason most visitors take the 10-hour bus trip out from Cusco. Gone are the days when the Machu Picchu train continued on to Quillabamba, however, and tourists are now few and far between. Afternoons bring children into Plaza Grau's dry fountains, shopkeepers onto its curbs, and stray dogs under the shade of the cathedral's malfunctioning clock tower. All is blissfully still, with not a camera click to be heard.

Wedged between the **Río Chuyapi** and the **Río Vilcanota** (which flows into the Urubamba), Quillabamba's small center slopes down toward the east. Two central squares orient the city: the hectic, irregularly shaped **Plaza Grau,** and the shady **Plaza de Armas,** two blocks downhill and to the north. In between the two, **Av. Bolognesi** (which borders Plaza Grau) and **Av. Espinar** (bordering the Plaza de Armas) run parallel to the hill, while **Av. Grau** (bordering Plaza Grau) and **Jirón Libertad** (bordering the Plaza de Armas) run perpendicular to the hill. The **terminal terrestre** is located on **Av. 25 de Julio,** several blocks south of Plaza Grau.

Buses run to: **Cusco** (9hr., 16 per day 8am-7:30pm, s/15) via **Ollantaytambo** (7½hr., s/12); **Abancay** (5hr., 6:30am, s/13); **Arequipa** (20hr., 6:30pm, s/35); **Juliaca** (10hr., 8am and 6pm, s/30); and **Puno** (10hr., 8am and 6pm, s/30); **Kiteni** (6-8hr., 10am and 5pm, s/10); and **Tinti** (8-12hr., 5pm, s/15). **Trucks** to **Kiteni** (8-10hr., s/7) and **Tinti** (11-15hr., s/10) also pick up passengers in the area. **Taxis** cost s/1-2 anywhere in town.

The **Banco de Crédito**, Libertad 545 (tel. 281 460), one block uphill from the Plaza de Armas, is the only place in town that will exchange traveler's checks (open M-F 9:15am-1:15pm and 4:30-6:30pm, Sa 9:30am-12:30pm). Quillabamba's primary **market** is just uphill of Plaza Grau; for food, try the market a block south of the plaza (toward the bus station), uphill from Jr. Cusco. **Emergency:** tel. 105. The **police** station, Libertad 545 (tel. 281 460), is near the Plaza de Armas (open 24hr.). The **hospital** (tel. 281 282), on General Gamarra, is at the base of Av. Grau (open 24hr., with a 24hr. **pharmacy**). **Serpost,** Libertad 115 (tel./fax 281 086), on the Plaza de Armas, downhill from the police station, has international fax as well as the usual postal services (open M-Sa 8am-8pm, Su 8am-1pm). 24-hour **internet** access is available at the pricey Hostal Don Carlos, Libertad 556 (tel. 281 150), across from the Banco de Crédito (s/10 per hr.). **Telephone code:** 084.

Quillabamba's hotels cater more to traveling businessmen than backpacking tourists, but at least they're cheap. **Hostal Cusco,** Cusco 223 (tel 281 161), half a block from Plaza Grau, features sunny and spacious—if somewhat spartan—chambers arranged around one lone palm tree in a central courtyard (singles s/15; doubles s/20; triples s/30). Quieter and less central, **Hostal Alto Urubamba,** 2 de Mayo 333 (tel. 281 131; fax 281 570), a block north (right if you're facing uphill) of the Plaza de Armas, between Espinar and Pio Concha, has a similar courtyard-centric layout and sparkling baths, both private and common. (Singles s/18, with bath s/30, and TV s/35; doubles s/25, with bath s/40, and TV s/45; triples s/35, with bath s/60, and TV s/65). Eateries line Quillabamba's streets, but many are quite dingy. **Plaza Restaurant,** Espinar 221, on the Plaza de Armas, however, has high ceilings and crisp green tablecloths. There's no set menu, but most meals cost a paltry s/3. (Open M-Sa 8am-3pm and 6-9pm, Su 8am-1pm.) A slew of juice and sandwich shops line Jr. Libertad, up from the Plaza de Armas. In the afternoons and evenings, stands selling fried chicken with french fries (s/2-3) and *chicha de mais morada* (s/0.50) fan out along the uphill edge of Plaza Grau. The main food market is a block south (left if you're facing uphill) of Plaza Grau.

The park at the base of Jr. Libertad affords a glimpse of the bubbly **Río Vilcanota;** for a closer look, try the well-kept **Sambaray complex,** 2km north of town. Although the river rushes rapidly here, some swimmers still brave the current for a dip in the

Vilcanota's shining waters. Weekends can bring crowds. (Admission s/0.50. Open daily 7am-6pm.) *Colectivos* to Sambaray leave frequently from the upper corner of Plaza Grau (15min., s/.50).

EL PONGO DE MAINIQUE

Almost 300km of rough roads and rivers farther into the jungle, El Pongo's narrow gorge and boiling whitewater rapids take a mere 15 minutes to navigate. The arduous route to Mainique along the gorgeous Urubamba passes many a burgeoning frontier settlement and then the "lawless" regions farther in. The cheapest place to find boats to El Pongo is **Ivachote,** 20km from Quillabamba and 90km from the Pongo. There are no hostels in this tiny riverside village, but as long as there are three or four of you, it should be safe to camp on the beach. (Ivachote's population is relatively transient, consisting of migrants from the mountains, and residents warn that theft could be a problem for solitary campers.) Several small shops dot the one street. Unfortunately, food tends to be expensive this far out. From Ivachote, occasional boats head to **Sepahua** (1-6 days, depending on the type of motor; 1-4 per month; s/30-100), the next large settlement beyond El Pongo. Boats back are just as infrequent, although Sepahua's small airport also offers another means of escape. In order to avoid waits longer that the duration of your visa, you can rent a *lancha* to take you through the rapids and then bring you back up (3hr. each way; the fuel for the journey costs about s/200—expect to pay more for the boatman's services). Keep in mind that the Pongo is dangerous at any time of year and that boats in Ivachote are unlikely to have helmets or life jackets for passenger use. Undeterred? Well, the gorge—30m at its widest point—is stunning indeed, with its 60m-high rock walls overhung with jungle flora.

To reach Ivachote, take a **Tinti**-bound bus (8-12hr., 5pm, s/7) or truck (11-15hr., s/10) from Jr. Palma, just off Av. Grau in Quillabamba. Alternatively, one could take one of the more frequent buses, also leaving from Jr. Palma, to **Kiteni** (6-8hr., 3 per day, s/10) and wait there (probably for a long time) for a truck to Tinti (3-5hr., s/4). Most trucks depart Kiteni between 2 and 4am when they depart at all, leaving passengers at Tinti's dock (just downhill from where the trucks stop) in time to catch a morning *lancha* (45min., s/30) to Ivachote. Most returning canoes leave Ivachote in the morning as well, and buses and trucks to Quillabamba depart from Tinti around noon. The nearest hostels lie in Kiteni. It's possible to commission boats in Kiteni for the Pongo trip, but the extra distance (and the "little Pongo" along the way) will add to the cost.

In Kiteni, the clean **Hostal Kamisea,** one of the last buildings on the road to Quillabamba, perches above an attractive river beach and features running water (although no lights: such is the case in all of Kiteni's lodgings), clean common baths, and a multitude of hanging animal skins (doubles s/12). At the other end of town, **Hostal Kiteni's** sheetless, plant-and-plastic-partitioned chambers have the advantage of a connecting restaurant with chess boards and a view of the truck and bus stop (singles s/5).

PUERTO MALDONADO

Billing itself as the "Biodiversity Capital of the World," Puerto Maldonado has built quite a name for itself in the tourism industry. The town's position as the primary jumping-off point for the vast Tambopata-Candamo Reserve Zone—which includes the Bahuaja-Sonene National Park and Las Pampas de Heath National Sanctuary—enables it to draw a larger proportion of visitors than any other corner of Perú's jungle. This heavy traffic, however, impacts the 25km of park trails far more than the town's four paved streets. So many companies whisk their clients straight from the airport to waiting boats that Puerto Maldonado's dusty languor remains largely undisturbed. Still, the boom of tourism—however transient it may be—has saved the city from the fate of other gold mining towns, like neighboring Laberinto and Boca Colorado, which fell into obscurity when the rush waned.

ORIENTATION AND PRACTICAL INFORMATION

As in most of Perú's young jungle towns, Puerto Maldonado's streets form a straightforward grid pattern, in which the major roads are paved. Busy **Av. Leon Velarde** runs from a view of the **Río Madre de Dios,** past the **Plaza de Armas** and several km farther southeast to a port on the **Río Tambopata.**

Airplanes: Aeropuerto Internacional Padre Aldamiz Puerto Maldonado (tel. 571 531), 7km outside the city. Nurses with needles eagerly wait for disembarking passengers who are not vaccinated against deadly **yellow fever. AeroContinente,** León Velarde 506 (tel. 573 702), just south of 2 de Mayo, flies to **Cusco** (30min., M-Sa 8:30am, US$59). Open M-Sa 8am-9pm, Su 9am-noon and 5-8pm. **AeroCondor,** León Velarde 545 (tel. 571 669), south of 2 de Mayo, flies small planes to **Cusco** (1hr., M-Sa 8:30am, US$39). Open M-F 7am-9pm. **Santander,** 2 de Mayo 294 (tel. 573 120), near León Velarde, also sends small craft to **Cusco** (1hr., 1 per day M-F 9:30-11:30am, US$39). Open M-Sa 8am-9pm.

Trucks: Trucks to **Cusco** (2-4 days, 4-5 per week, s/20-30) leave half a block south of the market on Ernesto Rivero.

Buses: Buses to **Caberinto** leave on Ica near Ernesto Rivero (2hr., every hr. 5:30am-6pm, s/5). From Caberinto, boats run to **Boca Colorado** (6-8hr., several per week, s/30-40) and from there to **Boca Manú** (4½hr., 1-2 per week, s/30-40).

Boats: Boats head from Puerto Maldonado's Río Madre de Dios port at the end of Jr. Arequipa to **Puerto Paldo** at the **Bolivian border** (2hr. with outboard motor, 4hr. in a peke-peke canoe; several per week; s/15-20). The **Capitania de Puerto** (tel. 571 084), at the corner of Billinghurst and Arequipa, has information about boats' destinations and departure times.

Taxis: *Mototaxis* (motorcycle taxis) cost s/3-4 from the airport, s/1-2 in town.

Moped Rental: Nearly every storefront on Prado, between Belarde and Puno, rents little blue bombers for s/3.50 per hr.

Currency Exchange: Banco de Crédito, Daniel Alcides Carrion 201 (tel. 571 001), on the Plaza de Armas, changes cash and traveler's checks. Open M-F 9:20am-1:30pm and 4:30-6:30pm, Sa 9:30am-12:30pm.

Market: Mercado Modelo, bordered by Ica, Ernesto Rivero, Fitzcarrald and Piura, bustles 8 blocks from the Río Madre de Dios and 6 from the Tambopata.

Emergency: Tel. 105.

Police: Daniel Alcides Carrion 410 (tel. 571 022), at Puno, a block inland from the Plaza de Armas. Open 24hr.

Hospital: (Tel. 571 127), on Cajamarca off Velarde (toward the Tambopata), just before the pavement cedes to dust. Open 24hr. with **pharmacy.**

Post Office: Serpost, Velarde 675 (tel./fax 571 088), at Truncoso. International **fax service** available. Open M-Sa 7:45am-8:15pm, Su 7:45am-3pm.

Telephones: Telefónica del Perú, Puno 670 (tel. 571 600), between Prado and Truncoso. Open M-F 8am-4:30pm.

TELEPHONE CODE	084

ACCOMMODATIONS

Hostal Moderno, Billinghurst 359 (tel. 571 063). At the end of Velarde, bear a half block to the left. Quiet clapboard *cabañas* near the Río Madre de Dios have no private baths, but the common ones stay clean. Singles s/10; doubles s/17; triples s/25.

Hostal Cahuata, Fitzcarrald 517 (tel. 571 526), across from the market between Rivero and Piura. Most rooms open onto airshafts that block sunshine but protect visitors from market noise. Some scuffing on the walls marks the only dirt in the place. Singles s/10, with bath and fan s/20; doubles s/20, with bath and fan s/30.

Hostal Tambo de Oro, 2 de Mayo 277 (tel. 572 057), between Velarde and Arequipa, 2 blocks inland from the Plaza de Armas. Popular despite a certain degree of deterioration—Tambo's guests socialize en route to common baths. Singles s/10; doubles s/20.

Hospedaje Español, Prado 670 (tel. 572 381), between Rivero and Piura. Lit only with the barest fluorescence, this out-of-the-way haunt distinguishes itself by having some of the cleanest common baths in the Amazon Basin. Singles s/10, with bath s/15; doubles s/20, with bath s/25.

FOOD

Über-cheap eats (*menús* s/2) hang around the market, especially around the Piura-Ica intersection. Dos de Mayo (between Velarde and Puno) plays host to numerous *braserías*. And while Maldonado might not exhibit the same wealth of jungle specialty dishes as Iquitos, the profusion of exotic fruit juices makes up for it. Keep an eye out for *cocona* (passionfruit)—it's *muy rico*.

Pizzoton, Velarde 315 (tel. 571 765), just inland from the Plaza de Armas. Basket chandeliers, some overbearing landscape paintings, and leather tablecloths somehow pull off an unusual elegance. Chase down crisp pizzas (s/11-24) and sandwiches (s/3-6) with beer (s/3-5.50) or jars of *sangría* (s/20-26). Open Tu-Su 6:30-11pm.

Marisquería Libertador, 2 de Mayo 287, off Velarde. More pleasant than most of the city's eateries, this one features an extensive traditional menu: *lomo saltado* (s/9), *picante de mariscos* (s/12), *anticucho* (s/8), *pollo con durazno* (s/9.50), and *ceviche* (s/7-10). Open daily 7am-10pm.

Wasaí (tel. 572 290), on Billinghurst near the Madre de Dios end of Velarde. The prices at this riverside restaurant reflect its affiliation with one of the swankier jungle lodges, but the thatched gazebo offers the most tranquil dining experience in the area. Chicken milanese s/16, spaghetti bolognesi s/14.50, and *pisco sour* s/6.

INTO THE JUNGLE FROM PUERTO MALDONADO

The UNESCO reserve of **Tambopata-Candamo**—its 6,000 sq. km include the Bahuaja-Sonene National Park and Las Pampas de Heath National Sanctuary—provides fields of play for the region's visitors. You probably won't see any large mammals here, but in most tours of the park you will see numerous rare beauties: the spectacular Lake Sandoval, birds such as the brilliantly colored cock-of-the-rock, macaw clay-licks, monkeys, crocodiles, and perhaps even a giant otter. If all you're looking for is a daytrip, the peke-peke canoe drivers at the Río Tambopata port can run small groups out to Lago Sandoval (s/60-100 round-trip per boat).

HIRING A GUIDE

Freelance guides can offer less crowded, more adventurous, and more flexible trips, though their services often only end up cheaper than a lodge if there's a group to split costs. As always, be very cautious about whom you pick to accompany you into the wilderness; there are lots of con men in Puerto Maldonado.

Willy Wither, Hotel Kross, Velarde 721 (email willywither@hotmail.com), is a guide with a glowing reputation. Passionate about ecology and an expert on medicinal plants and local native tribes, Willy's only weakness is in his limited English vocabulary. His 4-day trip to natural hotspots Lago Sandoval (not far into the bush) and Lago Valencia (deep within) costs US$200 for 2 people, but he's willing to go almost anywhere for any amount of time. The cost per person per day generally works out to US$25 (less with 6 or more) and includes all food, lodging, and transport but not the US$20-30 park reserve fees.

Victor Yohamona (tel. 572 613; fax at Hotel Cabaña Quinta 571 045; email yohamona@pol.com.pe) fills the well established and English-speaking niche. He leads groups on piranha-fishing expeditions, searches for medicinal plants, visits to indigenous communities, on 4-day trips to Lagos Sandoval and Valencia or the Tambopata-Candamo Reserve, 8-day trips up the Las Piedras River, and whatever else you may desire. Victor's trips for 2-3 people run US$35 per person per day to Sandoval and Valencia, US$50 to Tambopata-Candamo or the Las Piedras River (less with 4 or more people) and include food, most accommodation (though not tents for camping) and transport, but not the US$20-30 park and reserve zone fees.

Turismo De Los Angeles, Puno 657 (tel/fax 572 158), between Prado and Troncoso, helps arrange tours for a minimum of 4 people for US$40 per person per day. The English-speaking owner is very helpful. Open M-Sa 8am-1pm and 4-9pm.

JUNGLE LODGES

A slew of expensive lodges, many hosting 40-60 guests daily in July and August, dot the Río Tambopata. But there are more affordable ways to experience the area's 1,234 species of butterflies and the world's largest macaw *colpa* (clay-lick).

Bahuaja Lodge (mailing address: Tina Smith, Lista de Correos, SerPost, Puerto Maldonado). Run by British biologist Tina Smith and her Peruvian husband Hilmar Huinga, Bahuaja offers a family-run, less tour-oriented lodge option. And with its organic food, lack of electricity, and running water, and commitment to employing local guides, it operates far more responsibly than many others. Camping US$25 per person (with your own tent); beds US$35 per person per night. All meals included. Transport and expeditions to the macaw lick can be arranged at extra cost. Four-day, 3-night, all-inclusive stay US$165. Special prices may be available for Spanish-speakers willing to do manual or scientific work around the lodge for a minimum of 3 weeks.

Rainforest Expeditions, Galeón 120, in Lima, (tel. (01) 421 8347; fax 421 8183), maintains the larger and more luxurious **Posada Amazonas** lodge, in conjunction with the local Ese'eja community. While expensive, the fact that a native group both owns half of the lodge and makes up the majority of its employees sets Posada apart. Rainforest Expeditions can also arrange stays at the small **Tambopata Research Center,** 4-5hr. upstream and just 500m from the *colpa*. All-inclusive 4-day, 3-night stay at the Posada US$280; 5-day, 4-night stay (half at the Posada and half at the Research Center) US$552. Both have private baths.

Tambopata Jungle Lodge (Cusco tel. (084) 225 701; fax 238 911; www.cbc.org.pe/tambopata/tambopata.htm), is a few hr. from the *colpa* down the Tambopata River. The lodge organizes 3-5 day guided tours of the forest (US$150-230) and salt lick (US$510-630) that include transportation from Puerto Maldonado, food, lodging, and guides. Prices vary with season.

TINGO MARÍA

Where the Andes give way to the jungle rests bustling little Tingo María, best known for its thriving cocaine trade. Bulldozers roam the side streets, stirring up dust to make room for pavement. The multiple markets overflow their borders in all directions. And the suspicious BMWs sweat in the heat of this sun. Despite its reputation for ugliness and unsavory behavior, however, Tingo María does have a splendid mountain backdrop, not to mention one of the grandest caves in Perú. And give the burgeoning city a point for originality: it may well be the only one in the country without a Plaza de Armas.

ORIENTATION AND PRACTICAL INFORMATION. Cradled in a curve of the **Río Huallaga,** Tingo María's central streets (the paved ones at any rate) form a precise grid. The wide **Av. Alameda Perú** bisects both the length of the city and its primary square, the **Plaza Leonicio Prado.** Running parallel, two blocks away and next to the river, **Av. Raimondi** houses many businesses. The city's pulse, however, rests in the huge **markets,** in the southern section of town.

Tingo María's **airport** (tel. 562 003) waits on the far side of the river, 1km to the right after crossing the bridge (by *mototaxi* s/2). **TAA** (tel. 562 472), along the road to the airport, on the right, runs flights to **Lima** (1hr.; M and F 2:30pm, W 11:30am; US$75) via **Huánuco** (15min., US$26). A number of **bus** companies on Enrique Pimentel and Raimondi serve **Lima** (12hr.; 7am, 6:30, and 7pm; s/25-35) and **Pucallpa** (8-9hr., 6 per day 4-11am, s/15-18). Night buses to **Pucallpa,** however, have fallen prey to bandit attacks. **Turismo Central,** Callao 135 (tel. 562 668), runs to **Huancayo** (12hr., 5:45pm, s/25). **ETNASA,** Callao 179, goes to **Huánuco** (3hr, every hr. 8am-6pm, s/5). **Comité 5,** Raimondi 108 (tel. 563 602), sends **colectivos** to **Huánuco** (2hr., leaves when full 6am-9pm, s/10). **Transgorsa,** Raimondi 224-6 (tel. 563 186), has *colectivos* to **Pucallpa** (5hr., leaves when full 6-7am, s/30).

Banco de Crédito, Raimondi 249 (tel. 562 110), changes traveler's checks (open M-F 9:15am-1:15pm and 4:30-6:30pm, Sa 9:30am-12:30pm). For a 24-hour Visa **ATM,** try **Banco Continental,** Raimondi 543-5 (tel. 562 141). They'll also change traveler's checks. (Open M-F 9:15am-12:45pm and 4-6:30pm, Sa 9:30am-12:30pm.) **Emergency:** tel. 105. The **police,** Raimondi 413 (tel. 562 533) are open 24hr., as is the **hospital,** Ucayali 114 (tel. 563 075). The **post office,** Alameda Perú 451 (tel./fax 562 100), on the plaza, can handle international **fax** (open M-Sa 8am-8pm). **Telefónica del Perú,** Tito Jaime 405 (tel. 561 748), also works the fax circuits (open daily 7am-11pm). **Telephone code:** 064.

ACCOMMODATIONS AND FOOD. Super cheap lodgings abound in the streets around the markets—rooms for s/7 can be found there, but most are downright frightening. Far better values rest close by. **Hostal Palacio,** Raimondi 156 (tel. 562 319), near Callao, keeps its monkey and toucans caged in the garden and its ruggedly elegant interiors impeccable. Unfortunately, window frames hold no mosquito netting, and only rooms with private baths have fans. (Singles s/10, with bath s/20, with TV s/25; doubles s/20, with bath s/32, with TV s/37.) While one might not wish to spend much time in the common baths at **Hostal La Cabaña,** Raimondi 634 (tel. 565 178), between Chiclayo and Pucallpa, it's blue-and-yellow bedrooms have wooden furniture and a certain rustic charm (singles s/7; doubles s/12). The rambling **Hostal Viena,** Lamas 252 (tel. 562 194), between Benavides and Raimondi, could bed an army. Its numerous rooms feature spring or foam mattresses and open onto the courtyard or the breeze from the street. Its accommodating owner will let you keep looking until you find a room you like. (Singles s/10, with bath s/15; doubles s/15, with bath s/20; triples s/18, with bath s/25.) Finally, if you ignore the curious burnt-out structure in the courtyard, there's little to complain about at the tidy, high-ceilinged **Gran Hotel,** Raimondi 214 and Cayumba (tel. 562 217; singles s/10, with bath s/15; doubles s/20, with bath s/25; triples s/25).

The culinary front sees far less action, although run-down outdoor restaurants do pop up at most intersections with Raimondi. The market area couches several similarly decrepit *menú* places. **Comedor Vegetariano,** Alameda Perú 353, between Pratoto and Monzón, proves the one standout, with bright, fruit-bedecked tablecloths and placemats. *Almuerzos* cost s/2.50. (Open Su-F 7-10am, noon-3pm, and 7-9:30pm.)

SIGHTS. Reclining on the outskirts of the city, the **Bella Dormiente** mountain, so called because its curves resemble those of a sleeping woman, marks the location of the **Parque Nacional Tingo María.** The 18,000-hectare reserve maintains a few wooded trails, but its most popular and interesting attraction is the **Cueva de las Lechuzas.** So immense that it's rumored to be bottomless, this cave could inspire a full day of exploration, although the extreme heat, the bats, and the cockroaches crunching underfoot make most visitors turn back well before that time elapses. But even the most fearful non-spelunker can explore the cave's mouth, where wooden walkways provide security. There, magnificent rock formations hide flocks of parrots. Beyond the walkways, seemingly countless oil birds make their nests, and deeper still live the *lechuzas* (owls) for which the cave is named. Bring a flashlight and a hat to keep all their various droppings off your head. If you plan to travel beyond the walkway, wear strong shoes. The entrance to the park lies a bumpy 8km outside the city (*mototaxi* s/7 round-trip); the cave waits less than 1km from the entrance. Just before the park (on the right, coming from town) is a steamy, greenish pond that locals claim has healing abilities. (Park open daily 7am-5:30pm. Admission s/5.) Far less fascinating than the cave but worth a look if you have time to kill, the university-run **Jardín Botánico** offers shade within town limits. Though neither very large nor particularly well kept, the garden does house a few labeled trees. Its entrance is at the south end of Av. Alameda Perú; to get there, head down the boulevard with the river to your right. (Open daily 7am-4pm, though you may have to bang on the gate for someone to open it. Admission free.)

PUCALLPA

Pucallpa seems to be a city in decay, being slowly devoured by the western edge of the hungry Amazon. An abandoned amusement park languishes in a lot by the Plaza de Armas. Vultures circle silently above the river docks. Legions of smoking three-wheeled *mototaxis* queue up at traffic lights on the dusty streets (as the air above them fills with smog). Don't be misled by this rough, decrepit appearance. Pucallpa, though unsavory, is a prosperous, rapidly growing river port and an important link between the resources of the jungle and the markets of the coast and beyond. This prosperity is not betrayed by the town or its residents, for many of streets remain unpaved and the Shipibo indians who vend goods around the plaza still live in poverty.

ORIENTATION AND PRACTICAL INFORMATION

Pucallpa sits on the west bank of the **Ucayali River,** 860km northeast of Lima. Its principal avenues are **Ucayali** and neighboring **7 de Junio** (along which stretches the town's two markets). These are intersected by **Raimondi.** The **Plaza de Armas** is a block riverward from Ucayali, between Jirón Independencia and Jirón Sucre. Swampland marks the town's southern border.

Airplanes: (Tel. 572 767), 5km northeast of the *centro,* is reached by *mototaxi* (s/4). **AeroContinente,** 7 de Junio 861 (tel. 575 643), flies to **Lima** (45min., 4:30pm, US$59). **Tans,** Julio Arana 615 (tel. 575 421), flies to **Lima** (50min.; M, W, F 3:30pm; US$49) and **Iquitos** (50min; M, W, F 1pm; US$44).

Buses: Companies on Tacna, Raimondi, and 7 de Junio send buses to: **Lima** (18-22hr., 4 per day 7:30-10:30am, s/30-35) via **Tingo María** (7-8hr., s/15-20); **Huánuco** (11-12hr., s/20-25), and **La Oroya** (12-18hr., s/25-30); **Huancayo** (20hr., 6:30am, s/40) via **Tingo María** (8hr., s/15) and **Huánuco** (12hr., s/20). **Selva Express,** 7 de Junio 846 (tel. 573 219), and **Turismo Ucayali,** 7 de Junio 799 (tel. 577 158), run *colectivos* to **Tingo María** (5-6hr., leaves when full 4am-6pm, s/30).

Boats: Passenger vessels have chalkboards that announce their destination and intended date and time of departure; few leave on schedule. Boats leave almost daily for **Iquitos** (3-8 days, s/60) from the ports at La Hoyada (Dec.-Mar.), Cruze el Mangual (Apr.-July), Pucallpillo (Aug,-Nov.), depending on the height of the river. All are near each other, about 3km northwest of the *centro* (s/3 by *mototaxi*).

Taxis: *Mototaxis* should cost under s/3 to almost anywhere in town, s/4 to the airport, and s/7-8 to Lake Yarinacocha.

Moped Rental: Motos Luren, Tarapaca 228 (tel. 572 206), near Salaverry, rents bikes (M-Sa s/7 per hr., Su s/8 per hr.) Open 24hr. **Rent-A-Moto Ruiz,** at the intersection of San Martín and Tacna, does the same (s/6 per hr.). Open daily 7am-10pm.

Currency Exchange: Banco de Crédito, Raimondi 464 (tel. 571 364), at Tarapaca, has a 24hr. Visa **ATM.** No traveler's check exchange on Saturdays. Open M-F 9:15am-1:15pm and 4:30-6:30pm, Sa 9:30am-12:30pm.

Emergency: Tel. 105.

Western Union: Laser Tours, Raimondi 470 (tel. 571 120; fax 573 776). Open M-Sa 8am-1pm and 3-6pm.

Spanish Classes: The British Centre, Libertad 273-7 (tel./fax 578 682), can arrange private lessons. Open M-Sa 8am-9pm.

Markets: The larger of Pucallpa's 2 *mercados* stretches along 7 de Junio. The smaller one, bordered by Tarapaca, Portillo, 9 de Diciembre, and Huáscar, is the one that sells hammocks (s/15-30), essential for any long river journey.

Police: (Tel. 105), on San Martín between Tacna and Tarapaca. Open 24hr.

Hospital: Augustín Cauper 285 (tel. 575 209), between Diego Delunadro and Mariscal Cáceres. Open 24hr. with 24hr. **pharmacy.**

Post Office: Serpost, San Martín 418 (tel. 571 382), at Tarapaca. Open M-Sa 8am-6:45pm.

Internet Access: Instituto Superior Tecnológico Ucayali, San Martín 381 (tel. 573 896), charges s/10 per hr., s/15 for 2 people. Open M-F 9am-1pm and 4-6pm. **Vir Datacom,** Raimondi 464 (tel. 590 402), charges s/10 per hr. Open M-F 8:30am-10pm, Sa 8:30am-1pm.

Telephones: Telefónica del Perú, Tarpaca 540 (tel. 574 803; fax 590 343). Open M-F 8am-4:30pm.

TELEPHONE CODE: 064

ACCOMMODATIONS

The cheapest of the cheap cluster on Jr. 7 de Junio near the Jr. Sucre intersection. You get what you pay for... and sometimes not even that; Pucallpa's lodgings tend toward the subpar.

Hostería Del Ray, Portillo 747 (tel. 575 815), 200m off 7 de Junio away from the river, with a miniscule sign. Each high-ceilinged room has its own bath and fan, but a breezy terrace ensures that guests cross paths regardless. Singles s/15; doubles s/22; triples s/23.

Hospedaje El Triángulo, Ucayali 245 (tel. 577 211), 100m off Progreso. Would-be guests may have to ring the doorbell several times in order to gain admittance to El Triángulo's bare-bone 1-person chambers. No windows or fans, but tall ceilings make the rooms somewhat more pleasant. Rooms s/7 per person, with bath s/10.

FOOD

A **fresh fruit market** sets up shop daily along Jr. Ucayali between Independencia and Sucre. Farther along, at the intersection with San Martín, vendors sell irresistible coconut patties (s/0.50), each seemingly sweet enough to single-handedly remove the enamel from a muncher's teeth. Another block down, Jr. Raimondi (between Ucayali and Tacna) plays host to a number of burger joints.

Don José, Ucayali 661 (tel. 571 829), between San Martín and Raimondi. This 34-year-old locale isn't cheap, but its extensive menu yields large portions. Omelettes (s/1.50-10), hamburgers (s/9-12), *Tacu Tacu* (a dense dish of beans mixed with rice, onion, and other diced veggies; s/4), and fresh juices (s/1-5) are sure to please. Open M-Sa 7am-11pm, Su 7am-3pm and 6-11pm.

Icueño, Ucayali 261 (tel. 573 435), between Progreso and Libertad. The dark greenish interior harbors large crowds of patrons at all times of day; it can be hard to squeeze in at lunch. *Pollo frito* s/8, *ceviche mixto* s/13, almuerzo s/5. Open daily 6am-6pm.

NEAR PUCALLPA: LAGO YARINACOCHA

From time to time, rivers change their courses when easier routes (e.g. through topsoil weakened by floods) become available. In so doing, some leave behind reminders of their former courses: oxbow lakes, which sometimes get re-flooded in the rainy season. Such is the case with Lago Yarinacocha, a "reminder" left by the Ucayali. Located 7km northeast of Pucallpa's limits, Yarinacocha serves as a weekend retreat for the city's dusty residents. From Puerto Callao, the shore's largest settlement, one can hire boats and boatmen as guides to colorful bird haunts and various Shipibo Indian villages. The traditional crafts for sale around the lake tempt many to buy; San Francisco is one Shipibo community particularly noted for its *artesanía.* Bargain hard with the boatmen; as usual, getting a group together will lower the cost per person. There are several hostels and restaurants in Puerto Callao.

Transportation: *Colectivos* to Puerto Callao leave frequently from the Ucayali-San Martín intersection (15min., s/2).

RÍO UCAYALI

A boat ride down the Ucayali to the mouth of the Amazon near Iquitos offers as good a view of the jungle and far more—*far* more—local flavor than any tour ship. Of course, such options take time and deprive visitors of a guide's knowledgeable background chatter. The 150km boat journey from Pucallpa to Iquitos, or vice versa, can last anywhere from three to 10 days, depending on the height of the river, the speed of the current, and the strength of the vessel's engine. As most travelers have few means of gauging these variables beforehand, this trip is best not undertaken by those on a tight schedule.

FINDING A BOAT. Boats accepting passengers hang chalkboards from their bows, announcing their intended destination and departure times. However, while most reach their destinations, few depart on time. They often hang around the port for weeks, stuffing themselves with cargo; the boat that looks most ready to sink under the weight of its load will probably be the next to leave. Despite the prodigious delays, a boat sets out from both Pucallpa and Iquitos almost every day of the year, except on Sundays.

There's generally no need to arrange a "ticket" ahead of time, as these boats don't do reservations; someone will collect the standard passage fee (s/60, which includes 3 meals per day) once the boat has embarked. Special discounts, though, are far easier to negotiate beforehand with the captain, who will often agree to subtract s/10-15 for travelers who bring their own food. It's also worth going down to the port beforehand to search for a boat without your backpack; travelers who arrive at the ports with their luggage often find themselves being pulled in every direction by touts who wish to bring them to various boats. And should your chosen vessel not depart the day you board? Sling your hammock anyway and spend the night in port.

IF IT EVER LEAVES... The boats themselves usually have two decks: a lower one for cargo and an upper one for passengers. The latter features a few toilets and showers, several cramped and windowless cabins (s/10 per night; bedding is not provided), and often a canteen selling biscuits, soda, toilet paper, and the like. The kitchen can be found below, where the cook often scoops water straight from the river to prepare the rice, fish, or soup—many passengers become ill from the food, so it may be wise to bring your own. Either way, you'll need your own bowl and utensils as well as enough water to last you more days than the captain projects. Every passenger also makes use of his or her own hammock and hanging rope, which are best installed as far from the bathrooms, the entrance to the engine, and the lights, as possible. Hammocks are available in markets all over the jungle, in both string (s/15-23) and cloth (s/18-30) varieties. The cloth sort—though somewhat more expensive—provides far greater protection against intrusive elbows or feet. Other useful items include toilet paper, a chain with which to attach your bag to a pole while you sleep, a clothesline on which to hang wet towels, and a sleeping bag or blanket—the constant wind makes sleeping on deck quite chilly at night. The boat stops innumerable times en route. The three largest villages each harbor at least one basic hostel: **Contamana** lies 14 to 36 hours from Pucallpa, **Orellana** is about half-way to Iquitos, and **Requena** is located between 12 and 22 hours from Iquitos. Inconveniently located control stations in the first two towns often demand a look at foreigners' passports; your captain should be able to inform you if this is necessary and point you in the right direction.

MANÚ BIOSPHERE RESERVE

Situated by the confluence of the Manú and Alto Madre de Dios Rivers, Manú National Park has been declared both a World Biosphere Reserve (by UNESCO in 1977) and a World Heritage Site (by the International Union for Conservation of Nature in 1987) and is one of the largest reserve parks in all of South America. Its largely untouched primary and secondary forests contain 13 species of monkeys, 100 types of bats, 200 different mammals, 1,000 kinds of birds, and an astounding 3,228 named species of plants (with another nearly 12,000 species yet unlabeled). The fact that the area spans elevations from 300 to 3450m—encompassing lowland rainforest, cloudforest, and the scrubby vegetation of the high Andes—makes such a high variety of life forms possible.

No matter how one chooses to experience Manú, the following items are a must: binoculars, plastic bags to cover cameras and other electronic equipment, and, most importantly, bug repellent with DEET—the mosquitoes and sand flies are worse here than in any other part of Perú's rainforest.

HISTORY. While most people know that the Spanish never conquered Machu Picchu, far fewer realize that one of the areas of Perú not conquered by the Incas was Manú. Few ever disturbed the native Machiguenguas, Kugapakoris, Amahuacas, or Wachipaeris—all tribes who still inhabit parts of Manú—until the rubber barons arrived at the end of the 19th century. Those less-than socially conscious men decimated much of the forest and many of the communities along the riverways until the boom went bust and they left Manú to mend itself. An ambitious logging Swede built the first road into Manú almost half a century later, and the next cycle of exploitation began. The road brought not only loggers but poachers as well. Ironically, however, it was one of those poachers, a taxidermist named Celestino Kalinowski, who recognized Manú's precious biodiversity and petitioned the government to protect the area. In 1973, Perú declared Manú a national park.

WE'RE NOT IN KANSAS ANYMORE Most people's fears of the jungle focus (like Dorothy's in Oz) on lions and tigers and bears... or on jaguars and pumas at any rate. Contrary to tour company propaganda, however, one's chances of encountering a cat strolling through the rainforest past a bunch of whispering gringos are about as great as a sudden cold spell. *Friajes* blow through... but not very often. And even those few people who do spot a jaguar need not tremble, unless they're standing directly between her and her young. But don't breathe easy just yet; there are dangers in the jungle you've never even dreamed of. The skinny Fangarana tree looks innocuous enough from a distance. Get a little closer, and you may notice an eerie sort of clearing, perfectly circular, around the tree's base. Just don't get too close: a mere tap of the trunk will call out legions of **fire ants.** These tiny red critters, which pack powerful stings, make their home inside the Tangarana and work hard to protect it. They attack any parasite or animal that dares scale their tree, literally surrounding and engulfing them. In years past, the ants also served as juries: indigenous communities would strap a man accused of a crime to their tree. If he lived, he was guilty (and therefore, usually, executed). If the fire ants killed him (it's said to take 100 stings), alas! he was innocent. (For more fearful tales of bizarre jungle fauna, see **Anacondas, Bats, and Fishies, Oh My!** p. 234.)

Nowadays, three "zones" combine to form Manú: the cultural zone, the reserve zone, and what is commonly referred to as the impenetrable zone. This last area occupies the space of the original national park, and only people native to the area and scientists with special permission may access it. Aerial photographic evidence suggests that the impenetrable zone houses two tribes who have never had any (recorded) contact with Westerners. The other two zones joined Manú as buffer states at the time of UNESCO's 1977 declaration. In the inhabited cultural zone, few restrictions exist, and residents may hunt and live as they please (although the government has begun an agricultural encouragement project to lessen the depletion of the region's wildlife.) The reserve zone, though uninhabited, welcomes visitors—provided they bring with them US$65 and a licensed guide. It is this zone that offers the best chance—maybe in all of the Peruvian jungle—for spotting animals, and it is this zone that makes Manú so prohibitively expensive.

TAKING A TOUR. Independent travelers may not enter Manú's reserve zone; one must visit with a registered tour operator. While this area does rank among the most pristine forests in the world, the expense may not be worth it, especially for those seeking isolation. In parts of July and August, the reserve zone gets downright crowded. Everyone pays through the nose for a "small" group, but many companies send out multiple "small" groups at once. And since Manú's reserve zone contains only one primary waterway and a limited trail system, groups may meet frequently. Guides must rush their groups along to try to beat the others to the best campsite or to be the first boat on the river (for the best wildlife-spotting chances). And, at the busiest times, the slow groups do suffer—guides must book sessions on the Lake Salvador catamaran and the 20m Lake Otorongo observation tower when entering the reserve zone; latecomers may find themselves without a space.

Aside from the occasional rush to get there first, trips; to Manú move at a very, very slow pace. Travel time dominates the trips, many of them spend far more time in transit to the reserve than actually in it. Of course, this is guided travel time, and the hours on the river actually offer a greater chance to see animals than on a walk though the forest. In any case, trips to Manú involve a great deal of sitting still.

Finally, although Manú probably does offer the best chance to see animals in all the Peruvian jungle, chances remain slim even here. Most visitors will see tons of **birds,** with **monkeys** and **caimans** (a type of alligator that can grow to 7m) likely possibilities as well. When they're not off hunting for food, the giant **otters** in Lake Salvador often greet passersby too. But it is the bird-watcher or botanist who will most enjoy Manú, and one thing the tours' high prices do provide is very knowledgeable guides who can tell you all about the passing flora and avian life. All tour agencies operate out of Cusco (see p. 140).

GOING INDEPENDENTLY. More adventuresome travelers (with a good deal of time to spare) can explore the Manú area, even though the reserve zone remains off-limits. From **Shintuya** (the end of the road from Cusco), cargo canoes head downstream to **Boca Manú** (6-9hr., no more than s/20) about once per week from May to November. From Boca Manú, similarly frequent canoes continue down the Madre de Dios to **Boca Colorado** (6-9hr., s/20), from where it's another day's journey to **Laverinto**, right by Puerto Maldonado. One could also commission a canoe (US$400-600 for 12m) and paddles (s/25 each) in the boat-building town of Boca Manú, though this could take up to a month. None of these towns possess very desirable, if any, accommodations; it's best to have a tent and sleeping bag. Beaches far more attractive than the few available hostels speckle the river banks. **Vampire bats** do live in this region, though, so it's not so good to sleep outside.

At **Blanquillo,** a few hours downriver from Boca Manú, a series of trails winds through the jungle. Some lead to **Cocha Camungo,** on which floats a catamaran (actually more of a platform) similar to the one in the reserve zone at Cocha Salvador. As Blanquillo is unregulated, however, anyone with a few paddles can take this one out for a spin. (Do not swim: Camungo hosts both hungry piranhas and

ANACONDAS, BATS, AND FISHIES, OH MY!

Unlike in the case of the terrifying **fire ant** (see **We're Not in Kansas Anymore,** p. 232), not all of the jungle's fearsome creatures wait for you to come to them. The medium-sized **desmodus bat** may not *seem* as scary as some of its cousins whose wingspans can grow to almost a meter, provided that you're sleeping inside. This **vampire bat,** native to the Madre de Dios area, feeds on unconscious and unprotected mammals. One of the few types of bats that can walk, the *desmodus* lands near its prey and then approaches with great stealth on two legs. Its razor-like teeth cut off small layers of skin. There the bat perches, lapping up blood that pours from the wound; the anticoagulants in its saliva assure a constant flow. Their blood lust has weakened many cows and dogs; at the worst, they are rabies-carriers so slick and swift that few of their victims ever wake.

The **anaconda,** on the other hand, won't get to you without your noticing. This venomless boa constrictor, the largest snake in the world (up to 13m), kills by wrapping itself around its prey and strangling it to death. Later, he swallows it whole. People who know rainforests often warn that you watch what you touch; as snakes can resemble vines or branches—this guy looks more like a full-grown tree trunk.

But perhaps the **candirú acu,** more commonly called the **orifice fish,** holds the title of the most frightening jungle animal. This miniscule, almost invisible, river catfish has spikes on its tailfin which don't impede its swimming up into a bather's urethra but do prevent it from turning around and swimming back out. Without surgical removal, the pesky invader could cause death. Most people, however, will notice its presence before it comes to this.

territorial giant otters.) Finding the entrance to the trails can be difficult, but you may be able to find a boatman in Boca Manú who can point them out. On the downside, while independent travelers will undoubtedly spot hundreds of birds and trees, most won't understand much about them without a guide. One of Pantiacolla's most knowledgeable guides, **Tina Forster** (email tfoldspice@yahoo.com) may start running tours for independent groups through the cloudforest, Manú's cultural zone, and the Blanquillo area in 2000. Omitting the reserve zone will enable cheaper prices (7-day, 6-night tour US$320 per person with a min. of 5 people and max. of 8) and more exploratory, off-trail trekking.

ECUADOR

HISTORY SINCE INDEPENDENCE

THE EARLY REPUBLIC (1830-60)

America is ungovernable. Those who have served the revolution have plowed the sea.
—Simón Bolívar

During its early, tormented years, various rivalries plagued Ecuador, causing hostilities between politicians, ideologues, and even regions. Quito and the Sierra emerged as conservative and clerical, dominated by semi-feudal estates that still relied on indigenous labor. The cosmopolitan, commercial port of Guayaquil, ruled by a nouveau riche merchant class, had more exposure to the ideas of 19th-century liberalism. This coastal bourgeoisie favored free enterprise and anticlericalism. A common division in 19th-century Latin America, the liberal-conservative split made it impossible for Ecuadorians to agree peacefully on a national leader.

The most natural leader seemed to be **General Juan José Flores,** whom Bolívar appointed governor of Ecuador when it was part of Gran Colombia. As part of the *criollo* elite, Flores found his support among the conservative *quiteños*, while **José Vicente Rocafuerte** rose as his rival in liberal Guayaquil. For the next 15 years, the two politicians struggled for power, taking turns in the presidency. While Rocafuerte considered himself an enlightened despot, promoting civil liberties and developing the nation's public school system, Flores put more effort into commanding the military and securing his hold on power. Starting with an overthrow of Flores's regime in 1845, Ecuador experienced another 15 years of chaos. A series of coup d'états made for increasingly weak leadership and an increasingly strengthened military. One of the more powerful and influential leaders, **General José María Urbina,** ruled from 1851 to 1856. As soon as he came into office, Urbina emancipated the nation's slaves, and later played a large role in ending the indigenous population's required tribute payments. But by 1859, a year known in Ecuador as the **Terrible Year,** the country again stood in a state of near-anarchy after one local *caudillo* stirred up anger by trying to cede Ecuadorian territory to Perú.

THE CONSERVATIVE REGIMES (1860-95)

A strong leader was exactly what Ecuador needed and what it got. In 1860, **Gabriel García Moreno** came to power. He was hailed by some as the father of Ecuadorian conservatism and the country's greatest nation-builder, but by others he was condemned as its worst tyrant. During the 1840s and 50s, he watched as his country fell deeper into a pit of chaos, splitting along racial, regional, and class lines. García Moreno's diagnosis: the nation needed cohesion. At first, he tossed around the notion of incorporation into the French empire, but when France appeared more interested in Mexico, he turned to the Roman Catholic Church.

From that point on, **Catholicism** was the magic ingredient in García Moreno's social cement. After beginning his authoritarian 15-year rule in 1860, García Moreno placed state matters such as education and social welfare within the Church's domain, hoping that religious order, hierarchy, and discipline would unify the nation's population. An 1861 charter declared Catholicism the state religion, leading to a strengthening of ties to the Vatican; in 1873, the republic was officially dedicated to the **Sacred Heart of Jesus.** Ecuador deviated from the path of most other Latin American nations at the time, which had military dictatorships

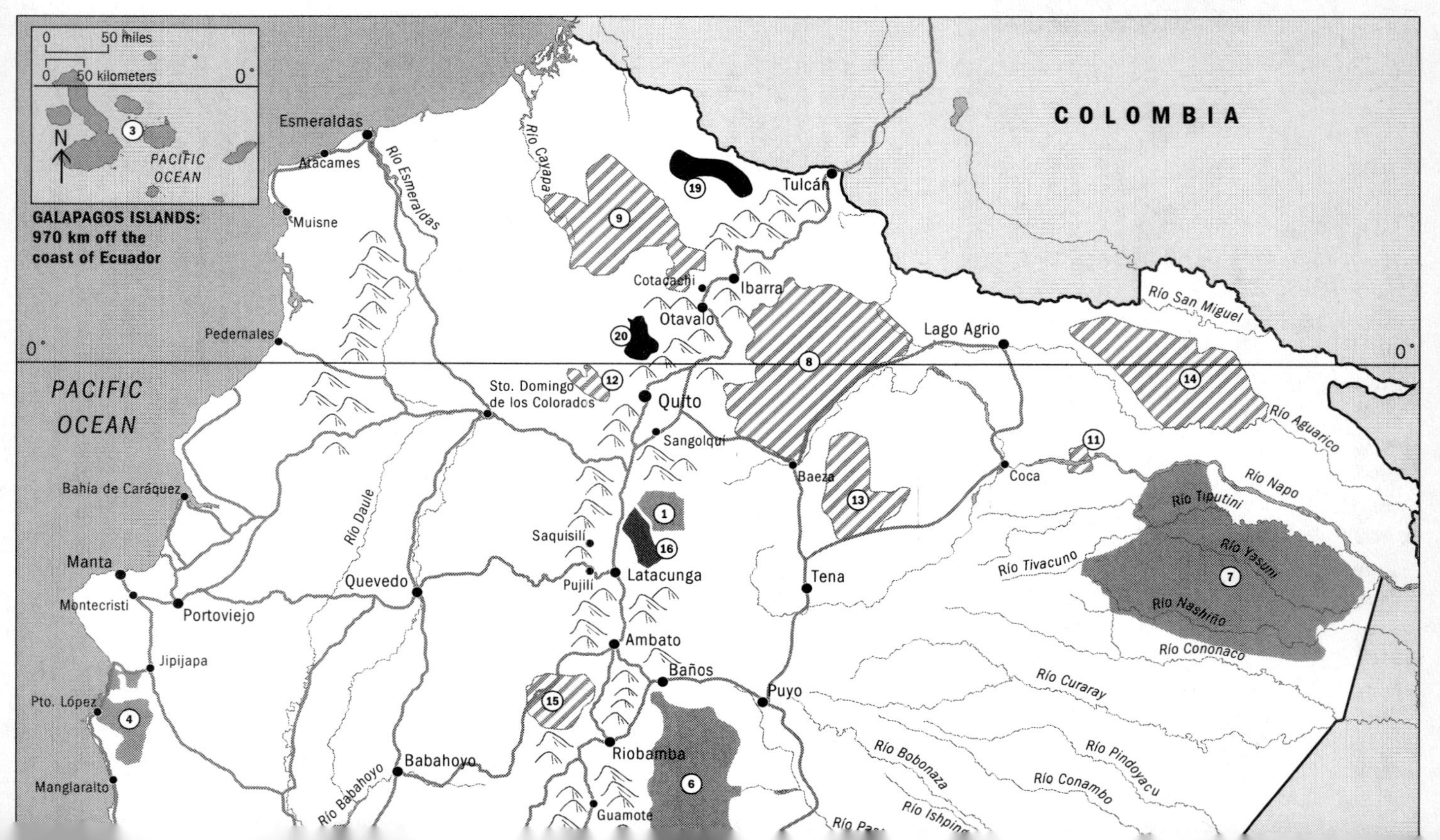
COLOMBIA
PACIFIC OCEAN
0 50 miles
0 50 kilometers
0°
N
PACIFIC OCEAN
GALAPAGOS ISLANDS: 970 km off the coast of Ecuador
Esmeraldas
Atacames
Muisne
Pedernales
Río Esmeraldas
Río Cayapa
Tulcán
Ibarra
Cotacachi
Otavalo
Lago Agrio
Río San Miguel
Río Aguarico
Sto. Domingo de los Colorados
Quito
Sangolquí
Baeza
Coca
Río Napo
Río Tiputini
Río Yasuní
Río Nashiño
Río Cononaco
Río Tivacuno
Bahía de Caráquez
Río Daule
Saquisilí
Pujilí
Latacunga
Tena
Manta
Montecristi
Portoviejo
Quevedo
Ambato
Baños
Puyo
Jipijapa
Pto. López
Manglaralto
Babahoyo
Río Babahoyo
Riobamba
Guamote
Río Curaray
Río Bobonaza
Río Pindoyacu
Río Conambo
Río Ishpingo

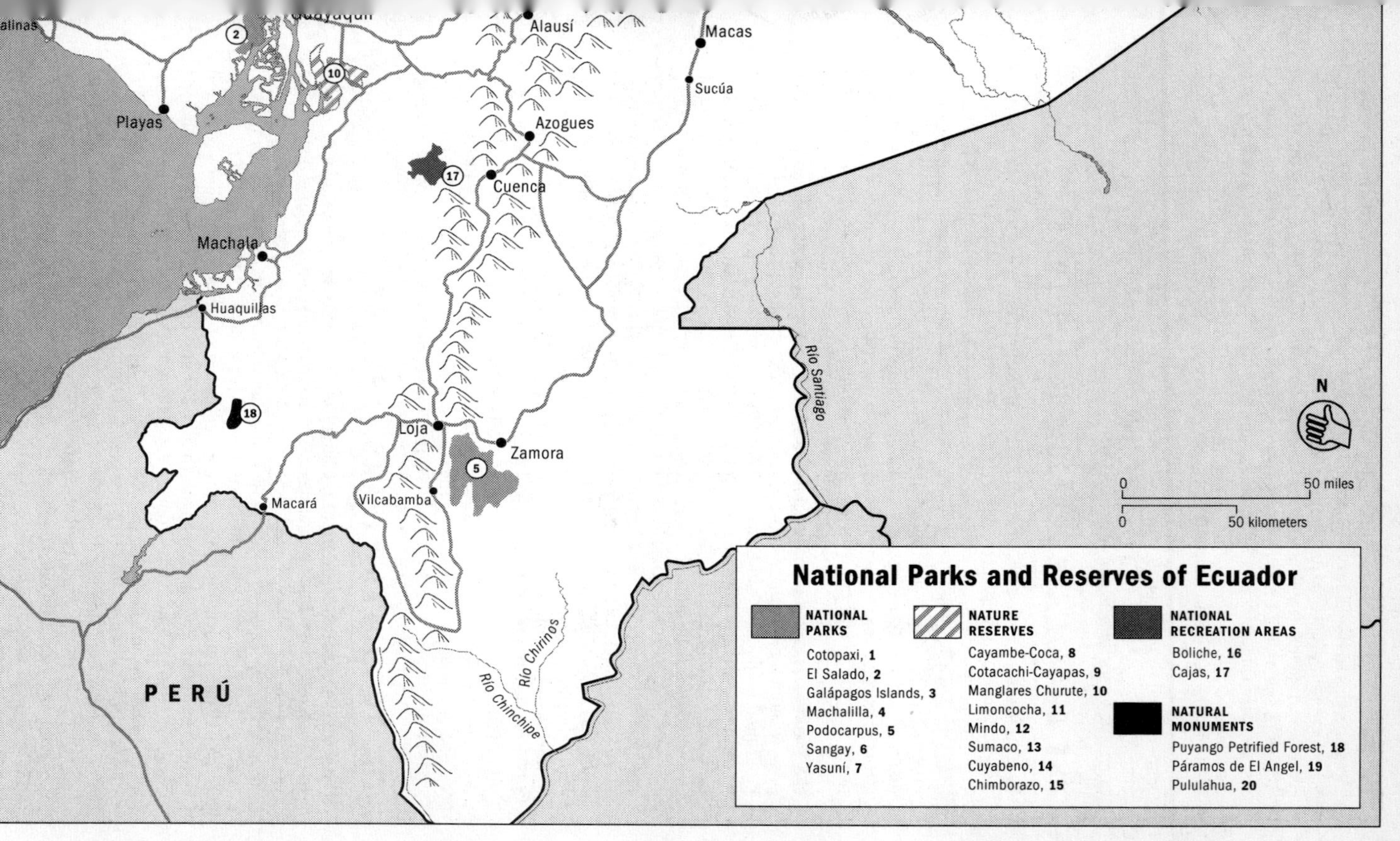
Salinas
Alausí
Macas
Sucúa
Playas
Azogues
Cuenca
Machala
Huaquillas
Río Santiago
N
Loja
Zamora
Macará
Vilcabamba
0
50 miles
0
50 kilometers
Río Chirinos
Río Chinchipe
PERÚ
2
10
17
18
5
National Parks and Reserves of Ecuador
NATIONAL PARKS
Cotopaxi, 1
El Salado, 2
Galápagos Islands, 3
Machalilla, 4
Podocarpus, 5
Sangay, 6
Yasuní, 7
NATURE RESERVES
Cayambe-Coca, 8
Cotacachi-Cayapas, 9
Manglares Churute, 10
Limoncocha, 11
Mindo, 12
Sumaco, 13
Cuyabeno, 14
Chimborazo, 15
NATIONAL RECREATION AREAS
Boliche, 16
Cajas, 17
NATURAL MONUMENTS
Puyango Petrified Forest, 18
Páramos de El Angel, 19
Pululahua, 20

that passed anticlerical measures. Yet, despite the conservative nature of García Moreno's ties to the Church, his accomplishments were often progressive: he constructed a railroad from Guayaquil to Quito, ending the isolation of the Sierra; built many new roads, schools, and hospitals; planted Australian eucalyptus trees in the highlands to combat erosion; and infused a greater sense of nationalism to the cities. Despite these accomplishments, García Moreno was **hacked to death with a machete** in 1875 by disgruntled peasants while standing on the steps of the presidential palace. García Moreno's brand of conservatism lingered for the next 20 years. By 1895, however, the progressive conservative leaders were plagued by scandal, and the liberals finally saw the chance to make their move. Led by General José Eloy Alfaro Delgado, the **Partido Liberal Radical (PLR)** stormed Quito, emerging victorious after a brief civil war.

THE ERA OF LIBERALISM (1895-1925)

For the next 30 years, **General José Eloy Alfaro Delgado** was to liberalism what García Moreno had been to conservatism. As president (1897-1901 and 1906-11), Alfaro attempted to erase anything vaguely associated with the political right. One of his first moves as president was to create a new secular constitution removing many Church privileges, exiling prominent clergy, secularizing education, and ending the nation's dedication to the Sacred Heart of Jesus. Later, Alfaro created stronger connections between Ecuador and the rest of the world by constructing ports and roads and completing the Guayaquil-Quito railroad. Because of his close ties with the United States, Alfaro was said to be "delivering the Republic to the Yankees." As it was, Alfaro's infrastructural improvements served little purpose without a profitable export to transport. The exploitation of *indígena* labor continued unchecked, and Alfaro's repression of political opponents proved just as ruthless as that of his predecessors. When he refused to step down after his second term ended in 1911, Alfaro was forced into exile in Panamá. The new president died only four months later. When Alfaro returned, a lynch mob killed him.

In the next 13 years, government changed hands four times among liberal leaders and their respective constitutions. Because executive power had been reduced after Alfaro's demise, a plutocracy of coastal agricultural and banking interests known as **La Argolla** (The Ring) called the shots from Guayaquil. During World War I and the short economic boom following, **cocoa** became Ecuador's dominant export, and the country's economy briefly thrived. Disaster struck in the early 1920s when a fungal disease ravaged Ecuador's cacao trees and the British colonies in Africa became a major cocoa-growing competitor. The resulting inflation and unemployment hit the working classes especially hard. In the **July Revolution** of 1925, a group of young military officers overthrew the government in a bloodless coup, believing they could start a new program of national regeneration and unity.

THE TURBULENT YEARS (1925-48)

Although many of the leaders of the July Revolution preached socialist ideology, they soon discovered that most army officers envisioned a new regime based more on Mussolini than Marx. The 1926-31 military dictatorship of **Isidro Ayora** seized the nation with an iron fist. Attempting economic reform, Ayora created the Central Bank of Ecuador, which took away from private banks the power to issue currency. Other reforms included the devaluation of the *sucre* to help highland exporters, labor legislation regulating hours and conditions of work, and the establishment of a pension program for state workers. Still, the living conditions of the poor did not improve. One critic said that Ayora's **public cleansing** reforms meant "prohibitions on entering markets, public buildings, schools, parks, and theaters without wearing shoes—but no reforms which gave the unshod means to buy them." With the **stock market crash** of 1929, nearly every Latin American government came crashing down, including Ayora's. Overthrown in 1931, Ayora was the first of 14 presidents to step down in the next decade. In fact, from 1931 to

1948, none of Ecuador's 21 presidents succeeded in completing a full term in office. Ecuador fared no better than the rest of the world during the **Great Depression.** The global demand for cocoa dropped drastically, the price fell by 58%, and Ecuador's exports decreased by nearly 50%. To add to the strife and instability, a four-day civil war broke out in Quito in August 1932.

The scene was perfectly set for a charismatic leader like **José María Velasco Ibarra,** who took on his first of five presidential stints from 1934 to 1935 (also 1944-47, 1952-56, 1960-61, and 1968-72). A master of 20th-century populist politics, Velasco later went on to create his own personal movement, **Velasquismo,** centered around his charisma: a carefully cultivated image of honesty and sincerity, and fiery orations. The Velasco revolution would have to wait, however, since the military overthrew him after less than a year for trying to assume dictatorial powers. The nine years before he returned were marked by fiscal crisis, political coups, and fraudulent elections. The transitory regimes represented the struggle for power between the elites, the middle class, and the military. **Carlos Alberto Arroyo del Río** claimed victory in the disputed 1940 presidential election (it was popularly believed that Velasco had actually been the victor). Arroyo del Río's government fell apart when a border dispute with Perú became a disastrous 1941 military defeat. Perú's occupation of Ecuador continued until January 1942, when both countries signed a treaty known as the **Rio Protocol,** ceding 200,000 sq. km of Ecuadorian territory in the Oriente to Perú. The Rio Protocol is still a cause of dispute between the two countries (see **Overstepping their Boundaries,** below).

Velasco returned to power in 1944 with whopping bipartisan demonstrations of support. Fine-tuning his populist rhetoric, Velasco managed to enchant the masses, transcending individual ideology. Yet instead of dealing with the country's major economic problems, Velasco obsessed over restoring Ecuador's morality and social justice. Inflation and standard of living worsened; when he was ousted in 1947, Velasco had alienated so many supporters that few rose to defend him.

THE RISE OF THE MILITARY (1960-79)

Between 1948 and 1960, Ecuador experienced something with which it had little familiarity—a period of political stability. This calm was mostly due to the onset of another atypical event—economic prosperity in the form of a **banana boom.** Ecuador became the US's main banana supplier until disease ravaged the Central American crop in the late 40s. Prosperity led the people back to Velasco, re-elected in 1952, who became so popular that he publicly referred to himself as "the National Personification." By the time Velasco began his fourth term in 1960, however, low export prices initiated a rise in unemployment and general social discontent.

The 1959 **Cuban Revolution** had profound reverberations throughout Latin America. Suddenly, the presence of communism was very real, as a threat or an attraction, and Latin American nations had to decide where their loyalties fell. Steering towards communism, Velasco began including more leftists in his government and consciously antagonizing the US. The National Congress's debate over Ecuador's ideological future became so heated that gunshots were fired in the Chamber of Deputies. In 1961, Vice President **Carlos Julio Arosemena Monroy** ousted his superior and immediately sent a goodwill mission to Washington, eager to renew favorable terms with the US. But Ecuador grew dangerously tumultuous, and with every terrorist act Arosemena was accused of weakness or communist sympathy. In July 1963, a four-man military junta seized power, vowing to implement basic reforms and to take a hard-line against communism. However, after a bloody attack on the students of Central University in Quito, the military reformers stepped down.

When in doubt, Ecuadorians could always vote for Velasco, and in 1968 this master of charisma began an unprecedented fifth term. Frustrated with the gridlock caused by an uncooperative Congress, Velasco assumed dictatorial powers with an **autogolpe** (a coup against his own government). Until his overthrow in 1972, he held onto these dictatorial powers primarily with the support of the military. The military coup in 1972 was not due to the army's lack of support for

OVERSTEPPING THEIR BOUNDARIES Wondering why this book's map of Ecuador doesn't look like the one you see in CETUR offices? That's because of a pesky little dispute over some land in the Oriente that has soured relations between Ecuador and Perú for nearly 150 years. Ecuador insists on its rightful claim to over 200,000 sq. km of Amazon basin because of its initial exploration of the great river, but most of the controversy has focused on a stretch of border in the Cordillera del Cóndor. Nobody really cared who technically owned these 78 sq. km of pure jungle until 1854, when Ecuador made an agreement with private creditors to use this stretch of the border. Sporadic mini-wars ensued for decades—and each time Perú emerged as the victor. But Ecuador refused to give in. In 1941, the issue's worldwide attention backfired for Ecuador; the **1942 Rio Protocol Treaty,** designed to end the tiff once and for all, forced the world to recognize the land as Perú's. Ever since, the border issue has aroused Ecuadorian national pride and fury, the stuff presidential campaigns are made of. Leader after patriotic leader promises to get the land back, and every January (the month the Rio Protocol was signed), the inevitable border shootings occur. On a few occasions, the catfight has erupted into full-scale war—for a few days in 1981, and for an entire month in January to February 1995. The last time, it cost Ecuador 10 lives, US$680 million, and a lot of pride—President Sixto Durán Ballén vowed "Ecuador will not withdraw," but two months later, the land was back in Perú's hands.

In October 1998, a historic peace treaty was signed by Peruvian President Fujimori and Ecuadorian President Mahuad in Brazil, delineating the border in an attempt to please both parties involved. The treaty draws the border along the heights of the Cordillera del Cóndor mountain range, giving Perú much of the disputed area, but it leaves Ecuador in control of Tiwintza, a 250-acre hill area within the Peruvian territory. This area is of great symbolic importance to Ecuadorians, since it was the site of a 1995 skirmish in which Ecuador successfully defended the land. Although many Peruvians initially responded angrily (and violently) to the treaty's provision, tensions have since calmed, and the peace process seems to be well underway.

Velasco. Rather, it was provoked by the army's fear that **Asaad Bucaram Elmhalim** might be elected after Velasco's term ran out a few months later. The leader of the populist **Concentration of Popular Forces (CFP)** and extremely popular two-time governor of Guayaquil, Bucaram was considered by both the military and business community to be dangerous, unpredictable, and unfit for the presidency. For the next seven years, Ecuador was ruled by military leaders determined to make structural changes in the country and encourage development. Yet they were not prepared for the 1970s **oil boom.** After joining the Organization of Petroleum Exporting Countries (OPEC), the minister of natural resources tried pricing Ecuadorian oil well above the world market price. Exports fell and combined with a lack of infrastructure reforms, the country's economic problems simply worsened.

The creation of a new constitution and the democratic election of a president was supposed to happen in 1976, but the process was delayed partly to ensure that Bucaram would not be elected. He was eventually barred from running, but the second-in-command of the CFP, **Jaime Roldós Aguilera,** with his reformist platform, won a run-off election in 1979 with 68.5% of the vote. **Osvaldo Hurtado Larrea,** leader of the **Christian Democratic Party (PDC),** stood as his running mate.

A RETURN TO DEMOCRACY (1979-1996)

The Roldós-Hurtado regime began under auspicious circumstances. With the country's preferential treatment as part of the **Andean Common Market,** the oil boom was finally having positive repercussions for Ecuador. Unfortunately, this new wealth only increased the domestic gap in income distribution. To make things worse, a rivalry developed between Roldós and Bucaram, and the president found himself at odds with his own party. In 1981, Roldós died in a plane crash.

Ecuador's economic luck didn't last long. Oil reserves ran dry, and massive foreign borrowing led to a debt of almost US$7 billion by 1983. The warm ocean currents from **El Niño** in 1982 and 1983 brought drastic climate changes, resulting in nearly US$1 billion in infrastructure damage. Hurtado's regime responded with austerity measures to the negative economic growth and record-high 52% inflation in 1983. Unemployment skyrocketed to 13.5%, and the **United Workers Front (FUT)** launched three riotous strikes during Hurtado's term in office.

Elected in 1984, **León Febres Cordero Ribadeneyra** supported free-market economics and a pro-US policy, trying to emulate and ingratiate his government to US President Reagan's. Understandably, Febres Cordero was not popular in Ecuador. Oil prices continued to fall, and Febres Cordero continued to face troubles with the National Congress and the military. A March 1987 earthquake left 20,000 homeless and destroyed a stretch of the country's main oil pipeline, forcing the president to suspend interest payments on Ecuador's US$8.3 billion foreign debt.

In late 1988, Ecuador's inflation grew so much and the government's austerity measures were so painful that large-scale protests ensued. The recently elected president, **Rodrigo Borja Cevallos,** made agreements with various paramilitary protest organizations, guaranteeing their civil rights in exchange for demilitarization of his government. One guerilla organization, **Montoneros Patria Libre (MPL),** refused and continued with violent action. Cevallos not only faced opposition from outside the government but from within it as well. In 1989, the vice president's plans to organize a coup were exposed. Another overthrow attempt came to public light in 1990, resulting in the impeachment of multiple members of Congress. That year also saw a rise in indigenous protests. The National Confederation of the Indigenous Population of Ecuador (CONAIE) planned a seven-province uprising, seizing oil wells and taking military hostages. Their demands included the return of various traditional community lands, recognition of Quichua as an official language, and compensation for the environmental damage caused by petroleum companies. Though the protests ended when the government agreed to consider CONAIE's demands, tensions heightened again in April 1992, when thousands of *indígenas* from the Oriente marched to Quito, demanding that their territorial rights be recognized (see **Indigenous Identity,** p. 244).

During his 1992-96 presidency, **Sixto Durán Ballén** dealt with many of these same problems on a larger scale. Austerity measures designed to cut inflation continued to cause widespread protest and general strikes, especially with a 70% price increase in fuel in 1994. CONAIE and other indigenous movements caused an even bigger stir with widespread demonstrations in June 1994, when they objected to the **Land Development Law,** which allowed commercialization of indigenous lands for farming and resource extraction. The next month, the law was modified to protect the rights of landowners. Revelations of embezzlement by top officials led to numerous impeachments and even demands for Ballén's resignation, voiced by student demonstrations throughout 1995 and early 1996.

POLITICAL UNCERTAINTY (1996-PRESENT)

BUCARAM. Abdala Bucaram (yet another Bucaram) of the **Partido Roldosista Ecuatoriano (PRE)** defeated Jaime Nebot of the Partido Social Cristiano (PSC) in the presidential election of July 7, 1996. Bucaram lost to Nebot in Ecuador's two biggest cities—Guayaquil (63% to 37%) and Quito (52% to 48%)—but overwhelmingly defeated him in the tiny towns and the Oriente. The conservative Nebot did not inspire enough confidence with his slogan, *"Primero La Gente"* (People First). On the other hand, Bucaram used the motto, *"Primero Los Pobres"* (The Poor First), and advocated mass nationalization, insisting that the country's poor would come first when rebuilding the gubernatorial structure. After Bucaram's final 54-46% victory was confirmed, revelers from poor neighborhoods caroused all night in the city streets while disgruntled members of the bourgeoisie packed their bags.

Bucaram took office on August 10, 1996, and as his first presidential measure, he devalued the *sucre* a few weeks later. From then on, his popularity entered a state of rapid decline. Hikes in gas, telephone, and electricity taxes resulted in a 300% rise in utility prices. A proposal to make the *sucre* fully convertible against the US dollar met strong resistance in Congress. Labor market reforms allowing easier dismissal of public sector employees infuriated trade unions. Surfacing reports of corruption earned the regime the nickname, "Ali Abdala and the 40 thieves." By early January 1997, public discontent began bubbling up into pockets of often violent protest, and the man of *los pobres* found himself abandoned by the very constituency that had put him into office. Tensions culminated on February 5 and 6, 1997, when the public sector unions, the left-wing political group **Movimiento Popular Democrático (MPD),** and the indigenous group CONAIE launched a united strike against the government.

Congress's response was swift and unprecedented. On February 6, 1997, the legislative branch ousted Abdala Bucaram from the presidency on grounds that he was mentally unfit. Bucaram responded by barricading himself within the presidential palace, but was forced to resign when even the military withdrew its support from the hapless leader. Bucaram, insisting that a "civilian dictatorship" had been imposed, fled the country and was granted political asylum in Panamá. He left behind charges of misappropriating or wasting US$88 million, while taking with him paintings from the presidential palace. With military assistance, Vice President **Rosalía Arteaga** immediately assumed control even though Congress voted 57-2 that congressional head **Fabián Alarcón** would serve as Bucaram's heir. Arteaga accused Congress of a "coup against the constitution" but surrendered authority to Alarcón two days later.

"¿Y ESTE HOMBRE QUIERE SER PRESIDENTE?" *"No puede ser,"* cried the television commercials of the Social Cristiano candidate Jaime Nebot before his narrow defeat at the hands of *"El Loco,"* Abdala Bucaram. With an uncanny resemblance to Adolf Hitler—mini-mustache, arm sweeps, and all—Abdala marched on the campaign path with *"una sola ideología: derrotar a la oligarquía"* (only one ideology: tear down the oligarchy). His resemblance to Hitler may not have been coincidental: Abdala (he is known by his first name) once cited *Mein Kampf* as his favorite book. However, his antics put him in his own class entirely. In his unsuccessful 1988 campaign, Abdala once emerged from a helicopter dressed in a Batman costume. Traveling with an Uruguayan rock band on the trail, Abdala would pack the working class into squares and sing *boleros* on command. But when it came to speaking, Bucaram was all business: his charismatic content matched his throaty shouts, and he somehow motivated almost all of Ecuador's poorer areas to vote for him (in the provinces of Zamora and Morona-Santiago, he won by approximately three to one). One reason may have been the female vote: Rosalía Arteaga, his running mate, was the first female vice president of Ecuador, but once elected, she seemed to have little place in the actual running of the country. Abdala's brothers also received attention: one, who was rumored to be Abdala's new Minister of Finance, had studied to be a witch doctor, and another was detained in Guayaquil the day after the election for driving a stolen vehicle. Scared members of Ecuador's upper classes fled the country the day after the results were announced (one hour late, because exit polls revealed a difference below the margin of error). Perhaps they fled for good reason. It is revealing that the man actually lost two to one in the city he was mayor of, Guayaquil. Bucaram did not last long in office and was eventually exiled (see below). In Panamá, Bucaram has been making headlines as vigorously as ever. He has cut a CD entitled, "Madman in Love," and has been seen frequenting Panamá City casinos and chatting with Ecuadorian acquaintance Lorena Bobbit, best known for slicing off her American husband's hap**piness**.

ALARCÓN. From the start, Alarcón's role was limited to the temporary. Under fire from Arteaga and others who demanded that the president be approved by popular vote, Alarcón conceded to an election scheduled for August 1998. He then focused on creating stability through his proposed plan, **El Paquetito** (The Little Shock), which would reduce the deficit, increase import tariffs and electricity rates, reinstate an 8% income tax and a 10% across-the-board budget cut, and create a task force to reduce corruption in both customs and tax collection.

Despite ambitious predictions of economic recovery, however, conditions only worsened. Growth figures for 1998 hovered around zero; inflation zoomed to 40%. Financial woes were coupled with reports of governmental abuses reminiscent of Bucaram's luckless six-month regime. Alarcón was accused of helping create 1000 phony congressional posts. His minister of the interior flew to Miami rather than face charges of misspending US$5.3 million. But in the most stinging scandal, the president was linked to an operation that diverted donated clothing away from victims of El Niño flooding and sold them off for a profit.

THE ELECTION OF 1998. In the face of such scandal Alarcón had little prospect of vindicating his rule in the election of '98. The presidential race quickly became a contest between businessman **Alvaro Noboa** and **Jamil Mahaud,** mayor of Quito. Mahaud, educated at Harvard in public administration and supported by the **Popular Democracy Party,** was favored among the educated middle class but worried some by his recent, albeit minor, stroke. Noboa, a banana mogul and member of the country's wealthiest family, belonged to Bucaram's Roldosista Party and enjoyed the backing of *El Loco* himself, cheerfully exiled in Panamá. Bucaram led an extravagant campaign, spending as much as US$100,000 per day on handouts of food and clothing and a mobile clinic to treat the sick. But many feared Noboa would pardon Bucaram, opening the path for his political resurrection, and when Ecuadorians went to the polls on July 12, they elected Mahaud by a slim margin.

THE FIRST YEAR OF THE MAHUAD ADMINISTRATION

Mahuad inherited a severely troubled economy. Inflation hovered around 40%, the government ran a budget deficit of around 6% of GDP, foreign debt was increasing rapidly, and the price of oil—Ecuador's largest export, accounting for one-third of government revenue—reached abysmal lows. Additionally, largely a result of the devastation to crops and transportation wreaked by the 1997-8 El Niño weather pattern (see p. 415), economic growth had dipped to near-zero levels.

The Mahuad administration took immediate and drastic measures. First and most easily, it eliminated subsidies for gas and electricity. More difficult was Mahuad's attempt to cut the budget deficit by instituting a 1% tax on financial transactions. To accomplish this, Mahuad, whose Popular Democracy Party had failed to achieve a majority in Congress, was forced to forge an alliance with the populist **Social Christian Party.** Finally, in an effort to revitalize lending sorely needed to pull the economy out of its economic morass, Mahaud initiated a program to overhaul the country's ailing banking system. New funds were to restore the system's liquidity and insolvent institutions were to be eliminated.

In spite of Mahuad's reforms, the economy in fact deteriorated significantly in late 1998 and the first half of 1999. Inflation sky-rocketed to over 100%, unemployment rose from below 10% to around 20%, economic growth remained close to zero, and the banking system continued to decline under the strain of the economic crisis. In early March, Mahuad declared a state of economic emergency and, still trying to reduce enormous budget deficits, raised the price of fuel over 100%. This act triggered determined resistance by the citizenry and stalwart opposition in Congress. Taxi drivers and bus companies throughout Ecuador went on strike, and, in Congress, Mahuad's erstwhile ally, the Social Christian Party, declared a "total frontal opposition" to the new policy. Mahuad's poll ratings plummeted to a miserable 16%. Not all news was bad news, however. In October 1998 Muhuad reached a settlement with Perú's **Alberto Fujimori** over a long-standing border dispute between their two countries (see p. 240).

GRASPING FOR A LIFERAFT. With the economy in ruin and ever weakening political support, the Mahaud administration is pinning all hope on the prospect of an International Monetary Fund US$400 million **rescue package.** The bailout is, however, not a sure thing. The IMF has presented Ecuador's government with a number of prerequisites that must be met before the country gets the much-needed funds: among other things, the government must slash deficit spending to below 3.5% of its GDP, liquidate numerous government-supported bankrupt financial institutions, and increase bank supervision. If Ecuador manages to meet the requirements, the IMF's US$400 million will be more than doubled by US$500 million in supplementary funds provided by the World Bank and other financial organizations. Nine hundred million US dollars could substantially ameliorate Ecuador's economic plight. So far, however, Ecuador's fulfillment of the prerequisites seems unlikely. In late April 1999, Congress passed a plan that cut deficit spending to 4.1%, short of IMF requirements. Throughout the summer the opposition party in Congress opposed bills aimed at meeting the IMF's demand for increased bank supervision.

INDIGENOUS IDENTITY

Each of Ecuador's indigenous groups has a distinct ethnic identity, and many members identify more strongly with their ethnicity than with the Ecuadorian state. This is not surprising given their status throughout Ecuadorian history: until the middle of the 20th century, the government mainly catered to the needs of the white and *mestizo* majority of its population, and hardly at all to those of *indígenas*. As in most of Latin America, this unbalanced socio-political order is the legacy of colonial times, when indigenous peoples comprised a slave labor force in *haciendas*, mines, and factories *(obrajes)* owned by the Spanish and Creole elite. This type of exploitation continued after Independence until a more liberal government in the early 1900s made a move to incorporate *indígenas* into the national community, mainly because the ruling class saw them as an obstacle to development. In the name of fighting for equality, the liberals attempted to pass legislation that would free *indígenas* from ties to the church or private landholders by dissolving their communal holdings. However, some interpreted this as an attempt by politicians to claim indigenous land and labor for themselves. Indigenous groups resisted these measures, and in 1937 two laws were enacted to reinforce indigenous rights to own land communally.

Beginning in the 1960s, various indigenous and human rights organizations began to demand changes to alleviate the subordinate status of *indígenas* in Ecuadorian society. A demonstration in Quito in 1961 by 12,000 indigenous peasants demanded social change, and in 1964 an agrarian reform bill was passed. Though the reform was more developmentalist than redistributive, it still effectively weakened the political power of the landholding elite.

Around this time, one of Ecuador's most successful and well-known indigenous groups founded the **Shuar Federation** in response to new pressures from outside forces including missionaries, colonists from the highlands, and later, oil companies. The Shuar organized into groups of about 30 families, called *centros*, which hold land communally in order to prevent the break-up and loss of indigenous property. They have also instituted a health care program and radio schooling system independent from the government. Although some criticize the Shuar adoption of cattle ranching over subsistence agriculture as dangerous to the environment and incompatible with Shuar tradition, their new practices have helped the Shuar prosper financially while maintaining their ethnic identity.

Attempts by the state to integrate local, ethnic identities into a national one have met resistance. A number of state-sponsored celebrations of popular culture, aimed at fostering national identity, have received mixed responses. Some groups recognize a government agenda behind such events and criticize them as fictionalized versions of indigenous culture. One example is Otavalo's festival of Yamor, boycotted by a group of *indígenas* in 1983 and 1984. Originally a celebration of the corn harvest, the tourism industry had begun promoting it with parades and fireworks. The offended indigenous group resented the use of the traditional ritual to satisfy outside interests.

Indígenas have developed a number of organizations to voice their desires and complaints. In 1989, these groups came together under an umbrella organization called the **Confederation of Indigenous Nationalities of Ecuador (CONAIE).** In 1990, CONAIE organized the largest indigenous uprising in Ecuador's history, paralyzing the country for a week. Their rallying cry, "500 years of resistance and survival," protested the upcoming 1992 quincentenary celebration of Columbus's landing in the Americas. Their agenda included demands to help create a satisfactory relationship between *indígenas* and the state, including more indigenous autonomy and a proposed constitutional amendment making Ecuador a multinational state. These demands ran contrary to the state's national vision, obstructing the government's plans for oil development. However, after the political debacle of February 1997 in which President Bucaram was chased from office, the interim government joined forces with CONAIE to establish **The People's Mandate.** Under this statement, a National Constituent Assembly was presented as an alternative governing body. At a first meeting in October of that same year, 400 indigenous representatives convened to discuss various indigenous issues. In January 1998, they released a suggested new constitution for Ecuador. With demands resonating with those of the original declaration in 1990, this document forged a strong foundation for the indigenous movement. Still, not all of CONAIE's suggestions were adopted in the new constitution that went into effect in August 1998, and struggles still continue between the *indígenas* and the Peruvian government. In March 1999, CONAIE led an 11-day *levantamiento* (uprising) against the Mahuad regime to protest what they saw as an abuse of power surrounding the country's economic crisis.

MODERN ART

Conveyed in a variety of styles and media, the theme that unifies the bulk of 20th-century Ecuadorian art is its indigenous subject matter, lending the movement the name **indigenismo. Oswaldo Guayasamín,** the most famous member of this school, is known for his politically charged depictions of suffering indígenas, as in his *Cabezas*, a series of portraits of anonymous heads, influenced by Picasso and the European cubist movement. Guayasamín worked with Mexican muralist José Clemente Orozco and produced some controversial murals of his own, including his 23 panels painted in the meeting hall of the Ecuadorian Congress in 1988. Next to portrayals of national historic events, Guayasamín placed a black-and-white panel of a Nazi soldier whose helmet bore the letters CIA. The US Congress responded with outrage, threatening to cut off aid, as the ambassador demanded that the letters be painted over. Diplomatic nerves eventually calmed and the mural was not touched. The best place to see Guayasamín's work today is at his museum in Quito (see **Quito Museums,** p. 263). **Eduardo Kingman,** another indigenist, is considered by some to be the trailblazer of the movement. The figures in Kingman's paintings are stylized and shadowy, depicting scenes of oppression. In *Mujeres y Santos* (1953), a downtrodden *indígena* wearing a bright blue shawl clutches an icon with Kingman's trademark gnarled, exaggerated hands. **Camilo Egas** was part of the early indigenist movement, although his style was much more varied and also influenced by French surrealist currents. In the 50s, he started painting indigenous subjects in a very different, realist style. His figures convey a feeling of strength and dignity instead of the sadness and abuse depicted by other indigenists. **Manuel Rendón,** another well-known Ecuadorian painter, was not especially indigenist, but is still considered part of the movement. He grew up in Paris, the son of the Ecuadorian Ambassador, and like Egas, was influenced by the modern art there. His works use various modernist styles, such as cubism and pointillism.

Of the more recent generation of painters, **Ramiro Jácome** is the most famous. Not a part of the indigenist movement, he instead prefers to paint abstract human figures using deep colors. Paintings by Jácome and other modern Ecuadorian artists are on display at the Casa de la Cultura in Quito.

LITERATURE

Before the advent of writing, indigenous Ecuadorians established an oral tradition of stories, songs, poetry, and theater intimately linked with religious practices. With the arrival of the Spanish and the forceful conversion of the indigenous peoples to Catholicism, much of this tradition was lost. One notable exception is the preserved story of the war between Atahuallpa and his brother Huáscar for control of the Inca Empire just before the Spanish Conquest.

The first textual works were the writings of various clergymen during the 17th century, including poetry and discourse on social and political issues in the Spanish colony. The most well-preserved authors of the following century were three Jesuit clergymen, **Gaspar de Villarroel** (1590-1665), **Antonio Bastidas** (1615-81), and **Xacinto de Evia.** In the 18th century, bourgeois professionals began to express discontent with the state of affairs that eventually led up to the independence movement. Called "the literature that did not yet have a country," these writings were the first to explicitly focus on what was to become Ecuadorian society. **Juan de Velasco** (1727-92), a historian and narrator, is considered by many to be the most talented writer of his time. A journalist, physician, and philosopher, **Eugenio Espejo** (1747-95) advocated sweeping societal reform and wrote on a vast array of topics including education, theology, politics, health, and the economy. He also started Quito's first newspaper, though it lasted only three months. **Juan Bautista Aguirre** (1725-86) is best known for his "Brief Design of the Cities of Guayaquil and Quito," which examines the still-present rivalry between the two cities.

The 19th century brought Ecuador its independence from Spain and, with that, a distinctive national literature established by the founding fathers, **Juan León Mera** (1832-94) and **Juan Montalvo** (1832-89). Though their Romantic style was influenced by Spanish literature, the content was anti-monarchical and aimed at creating Ecuadorian national identity. The most important work is León Mera's *Cumandá*, the first Ecuadorian novel. León Mera also published other short novels, poetry, and collections of Ecuadorian folklore. **Montalvo,** known as the favorite novelist of Ecuador's liberal movement, was a more political writer. His fictional *Chapters that Cervantes Forgot* narrates Don Quixote's adventures through the Americas and is dotted with criticism of intellectual and political enemies.

Since the 19th century, Ecuadorian literature has taken on a life of its own, dealing with uniquely Ecuadorian social, political, cultural, and historical topics. One of the most marked differences between the writings of the 19th and 20th centuries is the move away from a romanticization of indigenous traditions toward a more realistic portrayal of the indigenous struggle. One of the first works to mark the movement known as *Indigenismo* is the 1934 *Huasipungo* by **Jorge Incaza** (1906-78), a story of indigenous resistance to their exploitation. Another important work of the 1930s is a collection of short stories by different authors, *Los Que Se Van (Those Who Leave)*. Subtitled *Tales of Halfbreeds and Hillbillies*, the stories use crude language and themes that deviated from traditional literary norms and shocked the readers of that time. **Pablo Palacio** (1906-47) was active during the 20s and 30s, laying the foundations of a writing style that would become more widespread in the 60s and 70s. His writing is filled with irony, existentialism, psychic trauma, and a questioning of reality-subjective descriptions. Two authors of the 60s, **Miguel Donoso Pareja** and **Pedro Jorge Vera,** wrote anti-imperialist works reflecting Ecuador's frustration with its dependence on foreign powers. In 1978, the first Meeting on Ecuadorian Literature lent legitimacy to the growing literary movement, which has since continued to flourish.

QUITO

Airplanes descending towards the 2800m plateau upon which Quito rests discover a sprawling metropolis bordered on all sides by green, cloud-covered peaks. Passengers press eager faces to their window, fixing their gaze on Pichincha, a group of volcanoes to the west that conceal dangerously active lava within. From the sky above, Quito's powerful landscape steals all attention from what humans have created. But then the plane lands, and visitors, still dizzy from the altitude, look around and begin to grasp the immensity of this capital. Part thriving modern city, part decaying colonial showcase, Quito is in every way the geographical, political, and historical center of Ecuador.

With its surrounding fertile land and mild climate, Quito has long been a territory worth fighting over. Its first residents were the indigenous Quitu, Cara, Shyri, and Puruhá peoples who inhabited the area from the 6th century. The Incas conquered Quito around 1500, making it the northern capital of their empire. But things would soon change; Francisco Pizarro invaded in 1532, taking Inca emperor Atahuallpa captive. After this event, it would take the Spanish two years to successfully claim the city as their own. Legend has it that Rumiñahui, a general under Atahuallpa, set Quito aflame when he saw the conquistadors approach, preferring to reduce his native city to ash rather than see it fall into Spanish hands. Despite Quito's long legacy, the recognized date of its founding is December 6, 1534—the day Sebastián Benalcázar arrived and finally drove the Incas out. Quito was then home to 204 families; 1.35 million people live here now.

HIGHLIGHTS OF QUITO AND SURROUNDINGS

- **Plaza de la Independencia** (see p. 261) is the crowded centerpiece of the colonial city where the ornate **Palacio Presidencial** and huge **catedral** both stand.
- The nearby hill, **El Panecillo** (see p. 261), offers a stunning view of the city.
- **Museo Nacional del Banco Central** (see p. 262) holds Quito's most impressive collection of both ancient and modern artwork.
- **Fundación Guayasamín** (see p. 263) displays paintings by Guayasamín, a famed Ecuadorian artist and social activist.
- New Quito's **Nightlife** (see p. 268) defies the sierra's *tranquilo* reputation.
- **Volcán Pichincha** (see p. 269) is a popular, spectacular climb not far from Quito.
- The nearby town of **Mindo** (see p. 270) is an outdoorsman's paradise.

Quito is divided along economic and ethnic lines into two main parts: Old Town (*la parte colonial*) and New Town (*Quito moderno*). In 1978, the United Nations declared the colonial city a "World Cultural Heritage" site, prohibiting the building of skyscrapers. As a result, Old Quito's architecture has hardly changed since colonial days, although it has lost some of its polish. Streets remain narrow and cobblestoned, buildings retain their cool inner courtyards, and daily activity still revolves around the many plazas throughout. But Ecuador's worsening economy has become reflected in this section's increasingly dilapidated buildings, inhabited by a poor *mestizo* population. During the day, national and municipal business goes on in Old Town's historic buildings, while its tourist sights and plazas swell with people. But at night, politicians and tourists return to their beds in New Town, leaving the district's shady underbelly to emerge. Still, Old Quito's historic homes, churches, and Presidential Palace epitomize both the good and the bad of what Ecuador once was and what it has become.

While the colonial part is restricted by centuries-old bounds, New Quito is expanding up towards the sky and into the mountains. Its buildings clash with each other—not to mention with the surrounding landscape—but New Town is the social and commercial engine of the capital, filled with students, business people, and an increasing number of tourists. Adventuring tourists use the city as their base, returning to it after hikes through the Andes, jaunts to jungle lodges, or cruises around the Galápagos. Consequently, the streets framed by Amazonas, 6 de Diciembre, and Cordero have been converted into a *gringo* paradise where tourists sip their mango juice under thatched roofs and enjoy continental breakfasts. The usually manic speed of New Town slows down in these parts—weary backpackers settle down for weeks, planning their next South American journey.

The sun usually rises over the mountains to the east by 6:30am and sets over Pichincha by 6:30pm. The temperature in Quito usually hovers between 10°C and 25°C (50°F and 77°F) and there are hardly seasonal variations. If anything, you will experience all four seasons in a day: the morning sky, usually clear and sunny, becomes overcast by midday. Showers in the afternoon are not uncommon, and the temperature drops at night, when there is a little bite in the Andean air. If you come prepared for anything, Quito will surely not disappoint.

TRANSPORTATION

GETTING THERE AND BACK

Airport: Aeropuerto Mariscal Sucre, on Amazonas to the far north of town, near Florida. Hailing a taxi several blocks from the airport may shake hustling cabbies, but no matter what, set the fare before getting in (s/40,000) or fall victim to a taxi meter preset to go berserk. Late at night or early in the morning, taxi drivers will expect higher fares. The "Aeropuerto" bus goes to the airport from New or Old Town. Try flagging them down along 12 de Octubre or Amazonas. The trolley (*trole*) running along 10 de Agosto also goes to the airport, but you will have to transfer onto the Rumiñahui *alimentador* route from Estación Norte at the end of New Town. Upon leaving Ecuador, prepare to be slapped with an airport/departure tax of US$25.

Airlines: SAETA/SAN, Air Rep. El Salvador 880 and Suiza (tel. 254 510 or 254 511). Open M-F 8:30am-6pm. **TAME,** Amazonas 1354 and Colón (tel. 509 375). Open M-F 8am-7pm. **Ecuatoriana** (tel. 563 003), Colón y Reina Victoria, in the Torns de Almagro building, is open M-F 8am-6pm, Sa 9am-12pm. SAETA/SAN, TAME, and Ecuatoriana fly to most major cities in Ecuador.

Buses: The **terminal terrestre** lies next to a highway at the end of 24 de Mayo in Old Town. Take the *trole* to the Cumandá stop, descend the stairs on the north side of the highway, away from El Panecillo and la Virgen de Quito, and keep walking. Inside the several-story *terminal* are a police station, an ANDINATEL office, many small restaurants, an **ATM**, and myriad bus company windows. **Buses** go to: **Baños** (3½ hr., roughly every 30min. 6:55am-8:40pm); **Cuenca** (10hr., 12 per day 7:30am-10:45pm, s/90,000); **Esmeraldas** (6hr., roughly every 1½hr. 5:50am-12:30am, s/60,000) via **Santo Domingo** (3hr., s/25,000); **Guayaquil** (8hr., every hr. 5:30am-12:15am, s/75,000); **Ibarra** (3hr., every 20min. 5:40am-7:30pm, s/18,000); **Lago Agrio** (8hr., every hr. 9:30am-9:30pm, s/80,000); **Latacunga** (2hr., every 10min. 6am-7pm, s/12,000); **Loja** (15hr., every 2hr. 12:50pm-9:30pm, s/110,000); **Manta** (10hr., 16 per day 6:30am-11pm, s/56,000) via **Portoviejo** (9hr., s/56,000); **Otavalo** (2½hr., every 20min. 5am-8pm, s/15,000); **Riobamba** (3½hr., every hr. 5:30am-7pm, s/30,000); and **Salinas** (10hr., 8:50pm and 10pm, s/90,000).

Trains: A *trole* heading south goes to the station on Maldonado (tel. 656 142). Get off at the Chimbacalle stop, past Old Town. Trains are not a prominent mode of transportation in Ecuador, but the weekly departure to Riobamba offers fantastic (and frigid) mountain views at gringo prices (8hr., Sa 8am, US$15 to **Latacunga,** US$14 to **Ambato,** US$16 to **Riobamba**). For the best views, ride the roof, but beware of branches or wayward wires overhead. Tickets are sold at the station (open M-F 8am-12:30pm and 1pm-4:30pm) or at the office at Bolívar 443 and Benalcazar (tel. 582 921) in Old Town. Another route runs from Quito to **Cotopaxi** (2hr., Su 8am, US$20). A train is also supposed to go south from Riobamba to **Durán** but has only been traveling as far as **Alausí,** just before the famed "Nariz del Diablo" (4hr.; W, F, and Su 7am; US$15). Because damage sustained after El Niño in 1997-98 is slow to be repaired, call ahead to insure service to your destination. The **Ibarra-San Lorenzo** line in particular is still not running (8hr.; to San Lorenzo M, W, F, and Su 7am; returning to Ibarra T, Th, and Sa 7am; US$20).

GETTING AROUND

Local Buses: Local buses zoom every which way, all around town, and never seem to stop—because they don't. They merely slow down to 5 mph for passengers to jump on. Once the novice is both mentally and physically prepared for this task, the question is then which class to take. The cheapest are the ridiculous but ridable light-blue school-bus-style **Servicio Popular** (s/1,000); next come the crowded but more comfortable dark-blue **Servicio Ejecutivo** (s/1,400); finally the red **Selectivo,** slightly less crowded and a bit quieter, chugs along for (s/1,800). Usually, an assistant to the driver will give change for larger bills. Pay as you get off the first 2 classes, but as you get on a Selectivo. *Trole*-connecting *alimentadores* are green and white, *interparroquial* buses (to small towns just outside of Quito) are pink and white. Buses always have names of streets or landmarks on their front windows and, sometimes, numbers as well. A common route is the **Old Town-New Town pathway,** traversed by the Colón-Camal (#2) on Versalies, the San Bartolo-Miraflores (#10) on 12 de Octubre, the El Tejar-El Inca (#11) on 6 de Diciembre, and many other buses along Amazonas. From Amazonas, catch a bus to the **airport** (marked "Aeropuerto") or to the **Olympic Stadium** (marked "Estadio") on 6 Diciembre and Naciones Unidas. Keep in mind that "public transport" is comprised of private *cooperativos* competing for passengers and that each driver has a unique route, so you are better off asking if the bus goes to your destination. Getting off the bus is easier than getting on: move to the door and politely say *"gracias"* or *"parada,"* cueing the driver to stop (or at least slow down). When carrying luggage, a taxi may be a wiser choice; many public buses don't allow big backpacks or suitcases.

Trolleys: The environmentally friendly *trole* system in Quito is easy to understand, fast, efficient, sparklingly modern, and, of course, crowded. You can't miss the glass-walled, arched *trole* stops and, unlike the bus, the *trole* comes to a complete stop. The *trole* runs along **10 de Agosto** in New Town and into **Guayaquil** and then **Maldonado** in Old Town. It's hard to get lost as long as you know which direction you want to go. The C1 route runs the length of the city, from la Estación Recreó to la Estación Y. The C2 runs only the southern loop, from Recreó to Colón, while the C3 does only the northern loop, from la Y to Colón. From the final outermost destinations, green *alimentador buses* branch out into several routes. The *trole* runs M-F 5am-midnight and Sa-Su 6am-10pm; s/2,000, s/1,000 for children under 18, seniors, or the disabled.

Taxis: City-taxi (tel. 633 333), **Central de Radio Taxi** (tel. 500 600), and **Tele-taxi** (tel. 411 119) offer 24hr. service.

Car Rental: Budget Rent-a-Car, Colón 1140 and Amazonas (tel. 237 026; airport tel. 459 092). **Avis Rent-a-Car,** Aeropuerto Mariscal Sucre (tel. 440 270 or 255 890). Must be at least 25. **Team Rent-a-Car**, Amazonas 1128 and Foch (tel. 562 436), rents cars with or without drivers.

PRACTICAL INFORMATION

USEFUL ORGANIZATIONS

Tourist Office: Ministerio de Turismo, formerly CETUR, has 2 locations in Quito. The **Old Town office** (tel. 954 044), on Venezuela and Chile, accesible from the Plaza Grande *trole* stop, can provide a map of Quito and some friendly advice in Spanish, French, or English. **New Town office,** Eloy Alfaro N32-300 and Carlos Tobar (tel. 507 555), across from Parque la Carolina. Both open M-F 8:30am-5pm.

The South American Explorers Club (SAEC), Jorge Washington 311 and Leonidas Plaza (tel./fax 225 228; email explorer@saec.org.ec; www.samexplo.org). An absolutely indispensable resource for the traveler visiting any part of Ecuador. A friendly English-speaking staff can help make the most of any vacation with trip reports, listings of cultural events, volunteer opportunities, a large selection of maps, a lending library, a place to store gear, a safebox, and much, much more. Membership isn't cheap (US$40 for one, US$20 for each additional member), but is worth it if you're spending much time in the region. There are also SAEC clubhouses in Lima and Cusco, Peru. Members can check email and receive faxes and mail (mailing address: 17-21-431, Eloy Alfaro, Quito, Ecuador). Non-members are welcome to stop by once to hear about the club. Open M-F 9:30am-5pm.

British Council: Amazonas N26-146 and Niña (tel. 508 282; fax 508 283), a 5min. walk from downtown. The council offers a vegetarian restaurant and tea room (open M-Sa 8:30am-1:30pm), both an English and a Spanish language school, a photocopier (s/ 200 per copy), and email service (s/10,000 per hr.). Open M-F 7am-8pm.

Jewish Centers: The **Asociación Israelita de Quito** synagogue (tel. 502 734), 18 de Septiembre and Versalles, holds open services (F 7pm, Sa 9am, and Su 9am).

Tour Company and Tourist Information: Safari has 2 offices: one on Calamá 380 and León Mera specializing in climbing and jungle tours (tel. 223 381; email admin@safariec.ecuanex.net.ec), and the other on Roca 630 and Amazonas specializing in Galapagos trips (tel. 220 426). Reputedly the biggest climbing agency in Quito, this incredibly helpful, English-speaking company has books of hotels and tours from all over Ecuador and offers full-service itinerary planning or just some friendly advice. Tours are a bit expensive (US$180 for a 2-day guided Cotopaxi climb, US$45 for most daytrips), but less pricey adventures come up periodically, and discounts are sometimes available to SAEC members. Stopping in for ideas or brochures is welcome and costs nothing. Calamá office open daily 9am-7pm; Roca office open M-F 9am-7pm. There are a plethora of agencies in New Town offering package deals with transport, guides, and meals. While they are often rather pricey, it might be worthwhile to see what is available. Two reputable companies are **The Biking Dutchman,** Foch 714 and Juan Leon Mera (tel. 543 045; open M-F 9am-6pm and Sa 9am-1pm), and **Adventours,** Calamá 339 and Reina Victoria (tel. 820 848); open M-F 9am-1pm and 3pm-6:30pm. For peace of mind, ask guides for state certification.

Immigration Office: The **Dirección General de Extranjería** (tel. 563 327), at Paez and Carrión. The place to go for a tourism card extension. Take the *trole* to Santa Clara Stop, then walk towards Parque El Ejido and turn on Carrión towards Amazonas. Open M-F 8am-1pm.

Embassies: For the embassies of **Canada, Ireland, United Kingdom,** and **United States,** see p. 7. **Colombia,** Colón 133 and Amazonas, 7th floor (tel. 228 926 or 222 486; fax 567 766). Open M-F 9am-1pm and 2-5pm. **Holland**, 12 de Octubre 1942 and Cordero, World Trade Center, tower one, first floor (tel. 525 461 or 229 229; fax 567 917). Open M-F 9am-noon. **Israel,** Eloy Alfaro 969 and Amazonas (tel. 565 510; fax 504 635). Open M-F 8:30am-4:30pm. **Perú,** El Salvador 495 and Irlanda (tel. 468 410; fax 468 411). Open M-F 9am-1pm and 3-5pm.

FINANCIAL SERVICES

Currency Exchange: Producambios, Amazonas 370 and Robles (tel. 564 500; fax 564 753) offers the same excellent rate for both traveler's checks and cash. Open M-F 9am-6:15pm. **VAZ,** Amazonas and Roca, adjacent to Hotel Almeda Real along Amazonas, exchanges traveler's checks and cash. Open M-F 8am-6pm, Sa 9am-1pm. **Multicambio** has 4 offices: Amazonas and Santa María (tel. 561 734), Roca 720 and Amazonas (tel. 567 351), Venezuela 689 (tel. 561 734), and the airport (tel. 462 977). All open M-F 8:30am-2pm and 3-5:30pm.

Banks: Amazonas is filled to the brim with banks. Hours vary slightly, but most will only exchange cash on weekdays 9am-1:30pm. Reliable banks include: **Banco de Guayaquil** (tel. 566 800), Colón and Reina Victoria, open M-F 9am-4:30pm and Sa 9am-1pm; **Banco del Pacífico** (tel. 437 537), Amazonas and Veintimilla, open M-F 9am-5pm, Sa 9:30am-2:30pm; **Citibank** (tel. 970 100), Av. Rep. El Salvador and Naciones Unidas, open M-F 9am-4pm.

ATMs: Plentiful in New Town and virtually non-existent in Old, most will only take Visa or MC that are PIN-enabled. **ATM** cards such as Cirrus or Plus work at designated **Banco de Guayaquil, Banco del Pacífico, Banco de Prestamos,** and **Filanbanco** machines–located many places, especially on Amazonas.

Credit Card Offices: MasterCard, Naciones Unidas 825 and Av. de los Shyris (tel. 262 770). Open M-F 8am-5pm. **Visa,** Av. de los Shyris 3147 and Tomás de Berlanga at Filanbanco (tel. 459 303). Open M-F 9am-5:30pm.

American Express, Amazonas 329 and Jorge Washington (tel. 560 488; fax 501 067), sells traveler's checks and allows card- and check-holders to receive mail at the office. Open M-F 8:30am-5pm.

LOCAL SERVICES

Lost-and-Found Center: On Montúfar between Olmedo and Manabí.

English Bookstores: Confederate Books and Cafe, Calamá 410 and León Mera (tel./fax 527 890; email tommys@accessinter.net), has a great selection of used books–from a Stephen King collection to numerous old guidebooks–and serves drinks at a small outdoor cafe. Open M-Sa 10am-7pm. **SAEC** (see **Useful Organizations,** p. 249) has Quito's best selection of English guidebooks to peruse, a variety of books available for borrowing (US$30 deposit), and some used books for exchange. Some hostels also have small book exchange shelves.

Spanish Bookstores: Libri Mundi has locations at León Mera N23-83 and Jorge Washington (tel. 234 791); in Quicentro Shopping (tel. 464 473), on Naciones Unidas and Shyris; and in the Hotel Colón (tel. 550 455), Amazonas and Patria. Though not cheap, this is the place to go for fine literature (such as *Let's Go*) in Spanish, German, French, and English. Open M-Sa 8:30am-7pm; Quicentro location also open Su 10am-7pm.

Photocopies: Copies can be made at practically 2 places on every block, reflecting the curious infestation of photocopy services in all of Latin America. Among the choices are **Copifull,** 6 de Diciembre 1045 and Jorge Washington (tel. 228 473; s/300 per copy), or you might prefer to browse around bakeries, convenience stores or beauty salons, and be surprised where a copying machine might pop up.

Supermarkets: The high-quality, all-purpose **Supermaxi** chain has branches at the Multicentro on 6 de Diciembre and La Niña; the Centro Comercial America on la Gasca and Edmundo Carvajal; the airport Centro Comercial; and El Jardín shopping center. All open M-Sa 9:30am-8pm, Su 9:30am-2pm. **Bodega Mayorista** (tel. 229 156), Dávalos and Versalles, is large and well stocked. Open M-Sa 8am-8pm, Su 9am-1:30pm.

Laundry: Lavandería Lavanda Calamá, Calamá 244 and Reina Victoria (tel. 544 528) offers standard cleaning (s/4,000 per pound) and dry cleaning (s/12,000 for pants and skirts). Open M-F 8am-8pm, Sa 8am-6pm, Su 8am-noon. **One Hour Martinizing,** 12 de Octubre 1486 and Madrid (tel. 225 223), with other locations as well, does dry cleaning only (s/16,300 for pants). Open M-F 8am-8pm, Sa 8am-2pm. If you'd rather do it yourself, **Opera de Jabón,** Pinto 325 and Reina Victoria (tel. 543 995), offers self-service and will provide detergent (s/14,000 to wash or dry a load). Open M-Sa 7am-7:30pm, Su 9am-7:30pm. Many hostels also offer laundry service.

EMERGENCY

Emergency: Tel. 911. See also **Embassies,** p. 250.

Police: Tel. 101. The **Criminal Investigation Office** is in Old Town at the intersection of Cuenca and Mideros. Open 24hr.

Pharmacies: There are quite a few pharmacies peppered about town selling everything from valium to Viagra. Many pharmacists live above their stores, so you need only knock loudly in a late-night emergency. **Farmacia CYF,** Jorge Washington 416 and Reina Victoria (tel. 555 438), and **Farmacia el Sol,** 6 de Diciembre and Veintimilla (tel. 507 335), are both open 24hr.

Hospitals: Hospital Vozandes, Villalengua 267 and 10 de Agosto (tel. 263 512), on the Villaflora bus line, has English-speaking doctors and offers a **family practice center,** Americas 5650 and 10 de Agosto (tel. 439 343), staffed with some American doctors. Consultation fee s/45,000. **Hospital Metropolitano** (tel. 261 520), Mariana de Jesus and Occidental. Get there on a Quito Sur-San Gabriel bus from downtown. If you're in a hurry, a taxi should cost s/25,000. Metropolitano has English-speaking doctors.

Clinics: Private medical practitioner **Dr. John Rosenberg,** Foch 476 and Almagro (tel. 521 104; pager 227 777), speaks fluent English, German, French, and Hebrew. Also offers vaccinations for hepatitis A and B and yellow fever. Consultation fee US$20. **Dr. Wallace Swanson** (tel. 470 830) is an American doctor at the Hospital Vozandes, and though he only works a few days a week, he is very helpful and gives referrals to specialty doctors. **Clínica Pichincha,** Veintimilla 1259 and Paez (tel. 560 820; emergency tel. 529 722), is recommended for emergency care.

Dentists: The talented husband-wife dental duo, **Sixto** and **Silvia Altamirano,** Amazonas 22-227 and República (tel. 244 119), speak English and are highly competent and friendly. Open M-F 9:30am-12:30pm and 2:30-5:30pm, Sa 2:30-5:30pm.

COMMUNICATIONS

Post Office: Most hotels and hostels sell stamps and have a maildrop box, but there are also several post offices located throughout the city. **Old Town Post Office,** Espejo between Guayaquil and Venezuela, half a block towards Guayaquil from the Palacio de Gobierno. Stamps are sold inside. Mark mail *Correo Central Lista de Correos* to have it sent to this post office. Open M-F 7:30am-7pm, Sa 8am-2pm. **New Town Post Office,** Eloy Alfaro 354 and 9 de Octubre. If you want mail sent to this branch, mark it *Correo Central, Eloy Alfaro Estafeta SUC#21.* Otherwise it will be sent to the Old Town office. Stamps are sold on the 7th floor. Open M-F 8am-7:30pm, Sa 7:30am-2pm. **Packages** should be sent via **Correo Marítimo Aduana,** Ulloa 273 and Ramírez Dávalos (tel. 546 917), located next to the Santa Clara market. Open M-F 7:30am-4pm. **EMS** (tel. 569 741), Reina Victoria 1325 and Lizardo García, is faster and surer. Open M-F 8am-7pm, Sa 8am-12:30pm. **FedEx,** Amazonas 517 and Santa María (tel. 569 356), handles those truly important packages. Open M-F 8am-8pm, Sa 10am-2pm. The best place to receive mail—if you're a member—is the **SAEC** (see p. 250).

Faxes: You can send faxes from **ANDINATEL** (see below), but they charge by the page. Prices are lower on weekends and after 7pm on weekdays. It's easiest to receive faxes at the **South American Explorers Club** (tel. 225 228), Jorge Washington and Leonidas Plaza, but they can't be sent from there. You can also send faxes from some hostels but they promise to be rather expensive (s/30,000 per page). You might try sending a scanned fax from an internet cafe, but these often have poor resolution. Many copy centers offer fax services.

Internet Access: Not to be left behind in the cyber-revolution, Quito has recently spawned numerous internet cafes, which you can easily find along Calamá, Reina Victoria, and Juan Leon Mera. There is not necessarily a correlation between connection prices and speed. Expect to pay s/8,000-20,000 per hr. of internet access. One convenient place to get connected is **Planeta Net,** Calamá 414 and Amazonas (tel. 232 734). Open daily 9am-11pm. Also see **SAEC** (p. 250) and **British Council** (p. 250).

Telephones: Quito is probably the easiest place in the country from which to make international calls (which is not saying much). Nearly everything can be done from **ANDINATEL**'s 4 locations: 10 de Agosto and Colón, the airport (Mariscal Sucre), Benalcázar and Mejía, and the bus station. ANDINATEL lets you make free calling card calls from private booths, but you may have to wait in quite a line. **Payphones** can be found about town, but carry around a treasure bag of coins if you expect to carry on any sort of conversation (s/1,000 per min. for local calls). **Bellsouth** and **Porta Ale** have cellular phone booths throughout the city but require phone cards (domestic calls only s/1,450 per min.). The catch is that your card only works on phones for the appropriate company. Many stores will let you use their phones if you offer to pay (s/4,000). In general, **AT&T** (toll-free tel. 999 119) and **MCI** (toll-free tel. 999 170) calling-card calls can be made from any direct-dial phone, including those in the lobbies of most expensive hotels. Be careful the hotel you call from doesn't charge you by the minute; you should be charged a reasonable flat rate for service (s/2,000-10,000).

TELEPHONE CODE: 02

ACCOMMODATIONS

NEW TOWN

Hotels and hostels abound in New Town. Most good hostels should offer clean bedrooms and bathrooms, 24-hour hot water, and a safety box to store valuables. The main distinction between hotels and hostels is this: in hotels, single or double rooms are guaranteed, while in hostels, rooms are often shared among two to 10 people, sometimes of different genders. There is a definite correlation between price and location. Many of the hostels are gringo-run, or at least gringo-populated, and tend to congregate between Amazonas and 6 de Diciembre, bordered by Jorge Washington and Colón. Budget hotels, on the other hand, tend to lie slightly outside the main strips. Expect to pay a 10% IVA tax in addition to the cost of your room (unless otherwise stated), as well as a 10-20% service charge if you want to pay with a credit card. Also, be sure to clarify you want to stay in the *same room* for consecutive nights, so that the hotel doesn't accidentally shuffle you around.

Casa Sol, Calamá 127 and 6 de Diciembre (tel. 230 798; fax 223 383; email casasol@ecuadorexplorer.com). This bed and breakfast really shines. Centered around a sunny courtyard, rooms are brightly painted, immaculately clean, and have private baths. Though you do pay for it, the service is superior. Singles US$12, with bath US$15; doubles US$22, with bath US$26; triples US$30, with bath US$33. Discounts for long-term stays.

The Magic Bean Hostel, Foch E5-08 and León Mera (tel. 566 181; email magic@ecuadorexplorer.com). The best known of Quito's gringo hosteling hotbeds, the Magic Bean enchants with a prime location amidst New Town's activity and popular nightspots. The well-maintained, inviting, wood-paneled rooms are shared among 3 or more. The slightly expensive restaurant downstairs has a relaxed feel, with outdoor seating. Dorms US$8 per person. Private rooms with private baths also available at steeper rates: singles US$22; doubles US$26; triples US$32.

La Casona de Mario, Andalucía 213 and Galicia (tel. 544 036 or 230 129). Mario, the Argentine owner, sets guests up in his delightful house, a bit out of the way, but very social and relatively safe. Shared rooms are decked out with locally crafted weavings and cloth parrots. Patio and kitchen available for use. Rooms US$6 per person; 10% discount on stays of 15 days or longer.

El Cafecito, Luís Cordero 1124 and Reina Victoria (tel. 234 862). A paradise for any lover of the hip coffeehouse scene. Comfortable rooms with colorful wall hangings are located upstairs from a popular cafe. English is spoken better than Spanish in this Canadian-owned lodging filled with a youthful, largely European crowd. All rooms and bathrooms are shared. US$6 per person with tax.

Hostal Centro Del Mundo, Reina Victoria and García, is probably the most popular backpacker refuge in New Quito's gringo district. Guests are welcome to enjoy the cable TV with a *cuba libre,* provided they buy the booze from the hostel owners. The rooms are generally clean and comfortable, and each bed has a corresponding locking chest. Shared bathrooms have either gas or electric hot water. Dorms US$4-6; triples US$12 per person. Delicious breakfasts are served in the small cafeteria area (US$2-5).

Hostal Amazonas Inn, Joaquín Pinto E4-324 and Amazonas (tel. 225 723). This centrally located hostel offers guests comfortable rooms with private baths for very reasonable prices. Stroll out of the hostel directly into the heart of the Amazonas souvenir and handicraft strip. Some first floor rooms have balconies perfect for people-watching. Singles s/66,000; doubles s/93,500; triples s/121,000; quads s/148,500; includes tax.

Hostal Eva Luna, Roca 630 (tel. 234 799), down an alley between León Mera and Amazonas, is Quito's only women's hostel. The purplish-pink door, rickety steps, and flowers painted on the walls add to the comfortable appeal. Common room with TV/VCR and boxy cement balcony for barbecues. Rooms s/40,000 per person with tax; discounts for stays over 9 days.

Hostal Rincón de Castilla, Versalles 1127 and Carrión (tel./fax 224 312). This is the place to stay for those who came to Ecuador to explore, not lounge. Very basic rooms—with beds, table, window, and little else—are clean enough and cost next to nothing. Under 10min. from most New Town activity. Amenities include communal laundry services, living room with TV, and usable kitchen. The staff offers help in getting tickets for further travels. Rooms s/40,000 per person with tax.

Hostal Viena, Tamayó N24-77 and Foch (tel. 235 418), just a few blocks up the hill from 6 de Diciembre. An unmistakable aura of cleanliness surrounds this hostel. The white-tiled floor of the lobby and the extra-tiny, spotless private bathrooms might result in a feeling of sterility were it not for the bright bedspreads and holy shrines. Rooms s/ 55,000 per person.

Crossroads Hostel, Foch N5-23 and Juan Leon Mera (tel. 234 735; email jbrummel@vio.satnet.net). Trying to establish itself on the scene, Crossroads offers travelers a choice of either dorms or private rooms. Beds are covered with green-and-white checkered bedspreads, but rooms are basic. Staying here will get you a living room with TV, outdoor patio with fireplace, basketball court, and an opportunity to chat with the owner, Jeff, who can help you with rafting plans and other excursions. All rooms have a private bath. Dorms US$5-6 per person. Singles US$12; doubles US$20; triples US$30.

Hostelling International (HI), Pinto E6-12 and Reina Victoria (tel. 543 995). Part of the huge HI chain, this branch dutifully provides what you've come to expect: meticulous cleanliness, tiled bathrooms, and virtually identical dorm-style rooms with familiar melon-colored bedspreads and thin mattresses. Usually a safe choice, though it lacks the character of some other centrally-located New Town accommodations. Dorms US$5-12, depending on location and number of people using room; US$1 discount for HI members. Includes continental breakfast.

OLD TOWN

Hotels in Old Town tend to be lower in both price and quality than their New Town counterparts. Price is generally the biggest reason that tourists stay here, but as more budget spots open in New Town, the benefits of staying in Old Town are dwindling. Little of interest goes on in Old Town after 9pm, and safety is a concern in its budget hotel districts at night. If you choose to stay here, you'll either be confined to your room shortly after the sun sets or will face a wee-hour cab ride back to the neighborhood. (*Troles* stop at 10pm on weekends and midnight on weekdays, and buses vary in how late they run.) However, not all Old Town accommodations are as decrepit as one might imagine, and they are usually located in historic buildings. Some even prefer staying in Old Town to get a better feel for the pulse of colonial Quito.

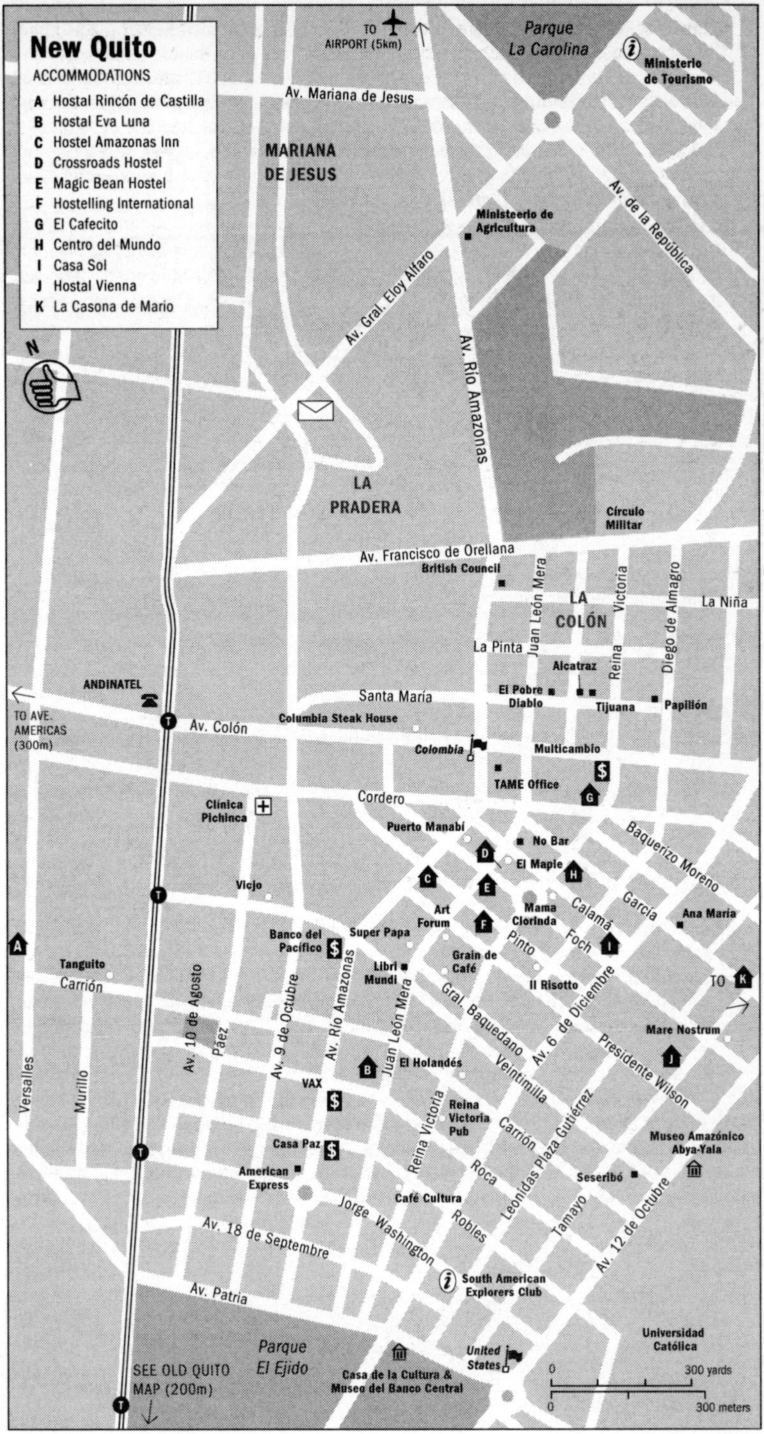

New Quito

ACCOMMODATIONS

- **A** Hostal Rincón de Castilla
- **B** Hostal Eva Luna
- **C** Hostel Amazonas Inn
- **D** Crossroads Hostel
- **E** Magic Bean Hostel
- **F** Hostelling International
- **G** El Cafecito
- **H** Centro del Mundo
- **I** Casa Sol
- **J** Hostal Vienna
- **K** La Casona de Mario

TO AIRPORT (5km)
Parque La Carolina
Ministerio de Tourismo
Av. Mariana de Jesus
MARIANA DE JESUS
Av. de la República
Ministeerio de Agricultura
Av. Gral. Eloy Alfaro
Av. Río Amazonas
LA PRADERA
Círculo Militar
Av. Francisco de Orellana
British Council
Juan León Mera
LA COLÓN
Reina Victoria
Diego de Almagro
La Niña
La Pinta
Alcatraz
El Pobre Diablo
Tijuana
Papillón
ANDINATEL
TO AVE. AMERICAS (300m)
Santa María
Av. Colón
Columbia Steak House
Colombia
Multicambio
TAME Office
Cordero
Clínica Pichinca
Puerto Manabí
No Bar
El Maple
Baquerizo Moreno
Viejo
Art Forum
Mama Clorinda
Calamá
García
Ana María
Banco del Pacífico
Super Papa
Pinto
Foch
Tanguito
Libri Mundi
Grain de Café
Il Risotto
TO
Carrión
Gral. Baquedano
Av. 6 de Diciembre
Mare Nostrum
Av. 10 de Agosto
Páez
Av. 9 de Octubre
Av. Río Amazonas
Juan León Mera
Presidente Wilson
El Holandés
Veintimilla
VAX
Versalles
Murillo
Reina Victoria
Reina Victoria Pub
Carrión
Leonidas Plaza Gutiérrez
Museo Amazónico Abya-Yala
Casa Paz
American Express
Roca
Seseribó
Café Cultura
Jorge Washington
Tamayo
Robles
Av. 12 de Octubre
Av. 18 de Septembre
South American Explorers Club
Av. Patria
Universidad Católica
Parque El Ejido
United States
SEE OLD QUITO MAP (200m)
Casa de la Cultura & Museo del Banco Central
0 300 yards
0 300 meters

Hotel San Francisco de Quito, Sucre 217 and Guayaquil (tel. 287 758; email hsfquito@impsat.net.ec). Just a block up Guayaquil from Plaza Santo Domingo, the San Francisco de Quito offers Old Town elegance at very reasonable rates. On the second floor of a recently renovated building, comfortable carpeted rooms either open onto the wrought iron balcony overlooking the charming courtyard or look out onto the streets of Old Town. Each room has a private bath (with 24hr. hot water), as well as a television, telephone, and wall speaker which plays muzak at the turn of a knob. Singles s/50,000; doubles s/80,000-90,000; includes tax.

Hotel Vega Internacional, Flores 562 and Chile (tel. 959 833; fax 954 327). With a freshly painted exterior and large courtyard, sun-filled hallways, and rooms with carpets and new TVs, this hotel offers a refreshing alternative to some of Old Town's gloomier establishments. All rooms have private bath, and the restaurant offers room service. Singles s/60,000; doubles s/85,000; triples s/110,000.

Hostel Huasi Continental, Flores 332 and Sucre (tel. 957 327 or 958 441). Usually poor lighting and an abundance of brown is a bad omen, but the spotless Huasi Continental has nothing to hide, with its immaculate, stucco-walled rooms, fairly comfortable beds, and tidy bathrooms. Ask for a back room if you want to avoid noise. Singles s/22,000, with bath s/39,000, with TV s/60,000; doubles s/40,000, with bath and TV s/66,000.

Hotel & Casino Real Audencia, Bolívar 220 and Guayaquil (tel. 952 711; fax 580 213; email realaudi@hoy.net), at the corner of Plaza Santo Domingo. Though one of the fanciest hotels in Old Town (4-star), the Real Audencia offers 5 rooms at amazing bargains. "Budget rooms" are equipped with telephones, large closets, wooden dressers, and private bath. Blow the money you save in the casino downstairs, or splurge on a gourmet meal at the scenic 3rd-floor restaurant. Rooms US$10 per night with tax.

FOOD

NEW TOWN

Predictably, New Town restaurants tend to be pricier and more upscale than their Old Town counterparts, but it's still possible to eat well on a reasonable budget here. The low value of the *sucre* means that even the ritziest joints are practically budget spots by first-world standards. Travelers can splurge and get a classy gourmet meal for the price of a snack back home. Be aware that much of the extra cost at the fanciest New Town restaurants simply covers the frills around the edges: tuxedoes on waiters, chandeliers, engraved china—the food is not necessarily better than that in the *comedor* around the corner. Don't forget that in Ecuador, meals are not rushed—there are few "fast food" joints. Just ask for the bill when you are ready to leave; it's considered rude to rush one's customers, so you may wait a while if you don't ask.

For cheap eats, hit the *almuerzo* (lunch) spots, mostly on the side streets off **Río Amazonas. Restaurant Row,** the informal name for another strip of eateries, is between León Mera and Reina Victoria, around Calamá. Pricier restaurants tend to cluster here, but there are some less expensive options as well. On Amazonas itself, **sidewalk cafes** are good for people-watching and a moderately priced drink or two, though you should be prepared to be bombarded by people begging or selling things. Be aware that restaurants charge a 10% IVA in addition to your bill and sometimes include a 10% service charge. As with accommodations, using a credit card sometimes results in an additional 10-20% service charge.

CHEAP EATS

Restaurante Tanguito, Carrión (tel. 543 565), between 10 de Agosto and Murillo. The locals know where to go, and this is where the hungry flock. Tanguito serves up an absolutely mouthwatering *almuerzo* with soup, rice, meat, and vegetables (s/8,000). The atmosphere aims to please: a congenial staff, TV, attractive green tablecloths downstairs, and mini-sofas and tables upstairs. Lively music, piles of fruit at the front counter, and even fake red flowers at each table add a special spice to this inexpensive find. Open daily 7am-8pm.

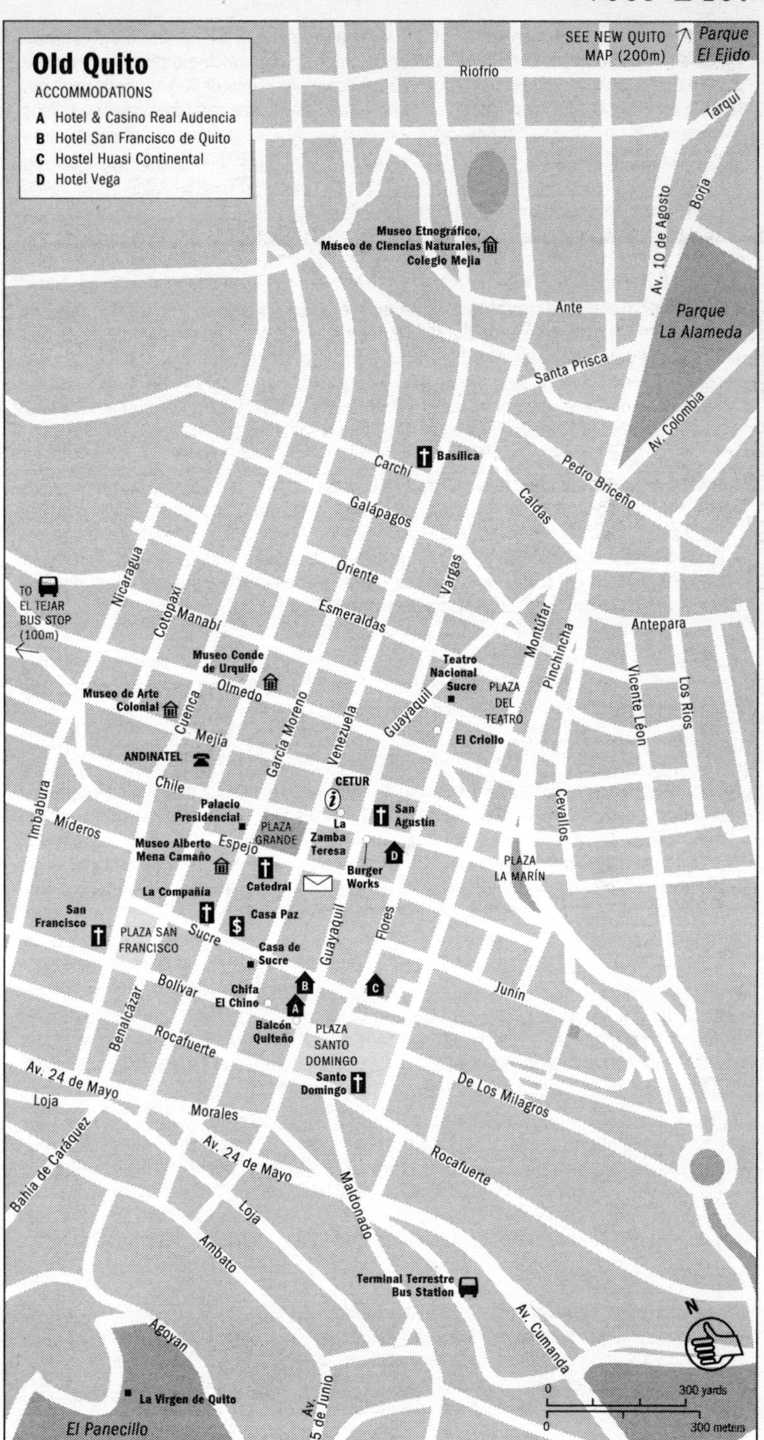
Old Quito
ACCOMMODATIONS
A Hotel & Casino Real Audencia
B Hotel San Francisco de Quito
C Hostel Huasi Continental
D Hotel Vega
SEE NEW QUITO MAP (200m)
Parque El Ejido
Riofrío
Tarqui
Borja
Av. 10 de Agosto
Museo Etnográfico, Museo de Ciencias Naturales, Colegio Mejía
Ante
Parque La Alameda
Santa Prisca
Av. Colombia
Basílica
Carchi
Pedro Briceño
Galápagos
Caldas
Oriente
Vargas
TO EL TEJAR BUS STOP (100m)
Nicaragua
Cotopaxi
Manabí
Esmeraldas
Antepara
Museo Conde de Urquilo
Teatro Nacional Sucre
PLAZA DEL TEATRO
Montúfar
Pinchincha
Vicente Léon
Los Rios
Museo de Arte Colonial
Olmedo
Cuenca
García Moreno
Venezuela
Guayaquil
El Criollo
Mejía
ANDINATEL
Chile
CETUR
Imbabura
Míderos
Palacio Presidencial
PLAZA GRANDE
La Zamba Teresa
San Agustín
Cevallos
Museo Alberto Mena Camaño
Espejo
Catedral
Burger Works
PLAZA LA MARÍN
La Compañía
Casa Paz
San Francisco
PLAZA SAN FRANCISCO
Sucre
Flores
Casa de Sucre
Guayaquil
Bolívar
Chifa El Chino
Junín
Balcón Quiteño
PLAZA SANTO DOMINGO
Benalcázar
Rocafuerte
Santo Domingo
Av. 24 de Mayo
Loja
De Los Milagros
Morales
Bahía de Caráquez
Av. 24 de Mayo
Rocafuerte
Loja
Maldonado
Ambato
Terminal Terrestre Bus Station
Av. Cumanda
N
Agoyan
0
300 yards
300 meters
La Virgen de Quito
Av. 5 de Junio
El Panecillo

Cevichería Viejo José, Ventimilla 1274 and Paez (tel. 225 187). The friendly music played at this outdoor *cevichería* encourages high spirits, which are raised even higher by meals such as *arroz marineras* (s/20,000) and delicious *la viagra criollo* (seafood soup, s/30,000). Everyone starts out with a bowl of popcorn and fried plantain chips. Open M-F 8am-9pm, Sa-Su 8am-5pm.

Puerto Manabí, Calamá 433 and León Mera (tel. 553 080). The wooden benches and fireplace give this small restaurant a homey feel. Locals and gringos alike have picked up on this cue, sometimes lounging for hours on end. House specialties are *arroz marineras* (s/15,000) and *ceviche mixto completo* (s/15,000). Open daily 8am-9pm.

RESTAURANT ROW

The Magic Bean Restaurant and Coffeehouse, Foch E5-08 and León Mera (tel. 566 181). Like the hostel upstairs, the Magic Bean eatery is a gringo stronghold. Its homey, 2-room dining area and outside seating serve an almost entirely English-speaking crowd. Coffee creations start at s/4,700. For dinner, munch on an enormous salad (s/31,000-38,500) or feast on a steak kabob (s/47,000). However, the Magic Bean is best known for its breakfast selection, featuring 8 varieties of pancakes, including pineapple (s/15,500) and granola (s/15,900). Open daily 7am-10pm.

Restaurante El Holandés, Reina Victoria 600 and Carrión (tel. 522 167). The real toucan head sticking out from a spread of its own green, red, and black feathers at first makes one question the seriousness of el Holandés's vegetarian claim, but the concern is quickly forgotten with a glance at the menu. Pineapple grilled cheese sandwiches with guacamole (s/11,000) and banana crepes (s/12,000) will please. Dutch, Indonesian, Hindu, Italian, and Greek platters start at s/21,000. Once you sample the fare, the lack of atmosphere and rushed service will seem forgivable. Open M-F noon-10pm.

Super Papa, León Mera 741 and Baquedano (tel. 239 955). Spud-lovers of all ages congregate here to celebrate the "sacred food of the Inca." Baked taters come heaped with loads of hot or cold fillings, in either *Super* or *Guagua* sizes. Avocado (s/17,500), mushrooms (s/28,000), or chicken curry (s/25,000) are just a few of the many options. Seating both inside and out. Open daily 7am-9:30pm.

Mama Clorinda, Reina Victoria 1144 and Calamá (tel. 544 362). She's the Ecuadorian *mamacita* you never had, serving traditional dishes in a room as lively and warm as mom's kitchen. A good place to try Ecuadorian specialties like cattle tongue (s/18,000) and figs with cheese (s/8,000) for dessert. Mama Clorinda also serves less adventurous meat and seafood dishes for the not-so-Ecuadorian at heart (rice with beans, lentils, and beef steak s/23,000. Open daily noon-10pm.

El Maple (tel. 231 503), Calamá and León Mera. You cannot miss the "vegetarian food" sign tempting herbivores from afar. Plenty of bamboo, plants, and bright lighting lend the restaurant's interior an atmosphere as fresh and healthy as the food it serves. Try the *Plato del Altiplano*, with rice, beets, avocado, white corn and *llapingachos* for an Ecuadorian interpretation of vegetarian food (s/22,000), or stick to more traditional plates like rice with tofu and veggies (s/17,500). All dishes are made with organically grown vegetables washed in boiled water. Open daily 11:30am-10:30pm.

Adam's Rib, Calamá 329 and Reina Victoria (tel. 563 196; fax 520 117). Given the name, the interior is not what you'd expect: blue and white tablecloths, carefully folded napkins, wicker chairs, and ivy-covered windows. The food, however, is. Selections of Texas-style barbecue include Adam's country-style ribs (s/32,300), *chili con carne* (s/20,900), and a combo rib BBQ platter (s/30,100). The BBQ sauce is so good they sell it to go. Open M-F noon-10:30pm, Su noon-9pm. Happy hour M-F 5:30-7pm.

THE BIG SPLURGE

Restaurante Mare Nostrum, Foch 172 and Tamayó (tel. 237 236). This outstanding seafood restaurant is housed in a beautifully restored 1930s mansion with stunning hardwood floors and castellar ceiling beams. Solid pewter plates, a suit of armor by the fireplace, some stained glass windows, and a small collection of canons on the wall add to the ambiance. *Paella de mariscos* (s/49,000), crab crepes (s/27,900), or a fish platter (s/37,000-s/75,000) are pricey, but order some Chilean, Spanish, or French wine and maybe the bill will seem less painful. Open daily 12:30-11pm.

La Choza, 12 de Octubre N24-551 and Cordero (tel. 507 901), diagonally across Cordero from the Swissôtel. Farm equipment scattered about, earthenware hanging from the chandeliers, and brightly painted mustard-yellow walls all contribute to the pastorally elegant dining room. Ecuadorian meat and fish entrees (s/26,000-47,000) and *caldos* (soups), with every part of the pig but the squeal, are prepared with style. Open M-F noon-3:30pm and 7-10pm, Sa-Su noon-4pm.

Il Risotto (tel. 220 400), Pinto and Diego Almagro. Put on your best (or your cleanest) and enjoy the mahogany furniture, candlelight, and fresh flowers of this elegant Italian restaurant. Tuxedo-clad waiters will treat you like royalty while you feast on home-made ravioli, gnocchi, fettuccine (6 different sauces; s/43,000), or risotto with champagne sauce (s/47,000). Open Tu-S 6-11pm.

Colombia Steak House, Colón 1262 (tel. 541 920 or 551 857), just past Amazonas. Behind a faded orange-and-brown exterior, a dark and serious meat-eating atmosphere, complete with a stuffed bull head, constitutes a steak heaven. Devour a T-bone the size of Andorra (s/28,000) and wash it down with the potent potable of your choice (s/10,000-18,000). Eleven types of enticing salads for the herbivores (s/10,000). The entryway doubles as a fast-food stop serving hamburgers and sandwiches (s/7,000-10,000). Open daily 11am-11pm.

SIDEWALK CAFES AND COFFEESHOPS

Usually small, crowded, and overflowing with trendy espresso drinks, coffeeshops can't be beat for an atmospheric meeting place. But don't come hoping for any deals—they're notoriously overpriced, and the same finger food can easily be found at any *pastelería* or *panadería*. You're paying for ambience here as well.

Grain de Café, Baquedano 332 (tel. 565 975), between Reina Victoria and León Mera, offers a huge selection of imported coffees and teas (espresso s/6,000). The bar has quite a variety as well (tequila shots s/15,000, *piña colada* s/18,500). Quiche with a salad (s/25,000), New York Cheesecake (s/12,000), and fruit with yogurt (s/15,000) round out the menu. Open M-Th noon-11pm, F-Sa noon-1am.

Café Cultura, Robles E5-62 and Reina Victoria (tel. 224 271; email info@cafecultura.com). This is the place to go for high tea complete with scones, jam, and clotted cream (s/22,000). Contemplate the vines painted with curling tendrils along the walls while sipping tea and waiting for your quiche to cool (s/29,000). Open daily 7am-7pm.

Art Forum, León Mera N23-106 and Wilson. The immaculately white building and walls lend this outdoor cafe—and the artsy, intellectual crowd that frequents it—an air of sophistication. Gather amidst canvas folding-chairs, lush plants, and umbrella-covered tables to philosophize a bit. The menus, made from popular book covers, offer a wide array of sandwiches (s/9,500-13,000), juices (s/6,000), and pastries (s/6,500). Open M-F 9am-9pm, Sa 9am-2pm.

Café Travero, Juan Mera and Joaquin Pinto (tel. 564 157). An intimate, one-room cafe whose small cluster of tables, dark wood panelling, and oversized windows invite you to sit, relax, and people-watch. Compare the antique black-and-white photos of Quito with the real thing just beyond the park. Sip from a variety of coffee drinks (s/4,000-5,500) while you nibble on a small sandwich (s/14,000-15,000). Open M-Sa 11am-9:30pm.

El Cafecito, Cordero 1124 and Reina Victoria (tel. 234 862). This coffeeshop and vegetarian cafe proves that the trendy alternative scene has hit Ecuador—the dimly candlelit room has dried flowers hanging on mustard, orange, and green walls. The menu, which is scrawled across a chalkboard, includes a soup of the day (s/10,000) and plate of the day (s/20,000). El Cafecito also offers a full bar and less-than-stellar coffee drinks. Open daily 8am-10pm, F-Sa until midnight.

OLD TOWN

Old Town's multitude of small *almuerzo* and *merienda* restaurants makes it the perfect place to look for that cheap and tasty three-course lunch. These restaurants are plentiful, similar, and change hands often. Look around for a lunch spot free of flies and filled with locals; more often than not you'll come away satisfied. Otherwise, just try one of the dependable favorites below.

Bar Restaurant Balcón Quiteño, Bolívar 220 and Guayaquil (tel. 512 711), on the top floor of the Hotel Real Audiencia on the corner of Plaza Santo Domingo. Nowhere else can you dine with such an amazing view of the colonial city. Feast your eyes on *la Virgen de Quito* as she surveys the bustle of the plaza while feasting your palate on *palta rellena* (avocado stuffed with chicken s/15,000) or *churrasco criollo* (steak, eggs, and avocado s/22,000). Open M-Sa 7:30am-2:30pm and 4-10pm, Su 7:30-9:30am.

La Zamba Teresa (tel. 583 826), Chile and Venezuela, off Plaza Grande. The bright pink walls, floral-painted booths, marble counters, and white leather chairs might make you check your map. Yes, you are in Old Quito. This is the lively little sister of the famous "La Cueva del Oso" (the fanciest restaurant in Old Town). The menu offers a nice combo of sandwiches (s/9,500-14,000), pastries (s/6,500), and traditional Ecuadorian dishes (s/22,000-30,000). Open daily 7am-7pm.

El Criollo, Flores 825 and Olmedo (tel. 219 811). A traditional Old Town restaurant with a classy touch: silverware is presented in a black basket with shiny gold rim. Gringos aplenty congregate here and, reportedly, are sometimes overcharged by the management, so be sure to check the bill before paying. *Tortillas* (omelettes s/16,500), sandwiches (s/5,000-13,000), and *almuerzos* (s/7,000) served on weekends. Open daily 8am-9:30pm.

Burger Works, Chile and Guayaquil (tel. 566 298), across the street from Iglesia San Augustín in the Centro Commercial. While the food is about as Ecuadorian as the name, the restaurant is actually in the pleasant courtyard of an historic building. The combos are a good deal and come with fries and a drink of choice (*combo works* s/15,000, *combo pollo* s/18,000, *veggieworks* s/10,000). Open daily 9:30am-7:30pm.

Chifa El Chino, Bolívar 256 (tel. 953 435), between Venezuela and Guayaquil, actually serves only a few Chinese entrees; mostly it dishes out seafood and local specialties such as beef tongue (s/13,900). Open daily 9am-10pm.

SIGHTS

With an abundance of museums and sights, there is always something to see or do in Quito. The museums are diverse—with collections ranging from ancient artifacts to local reptiles—and appeal to visitors of all ages. The city's plazas and churches, most of which are found in Old Town, display a unique mix of indigenous and Spanish baroque styles and create a striking contrast to the contemporary highrises of New Town.

LA PARTE COLONIAL (OLD TOWN)

When the United Nations declared Old Quito a "World Cultural Heritage" site in 1978, scores of 300-year-old plazas, churches, and government palaces were guaranteed both longevity and a high profile. Strict zoning and construction laws have kept much of the architecture in Old Town more or less the way it looked in the days of Spanish colonization. While exploring Quito's plazas and churches in Old Town, one must exercise caution, even by day. Pickpockets roam the streets, particularly around the market area and the *terminal terrestre.* By night the streets are even more dangerous, and tourists should retreat to New Town, as more affluent Ecuadorians do. The best way to get to the center of Old Quito is on the *trole,* which runs along Guayaquil in the colonial part.

PLAZA SANTO DOMINGO. Though there is little to do in the plaza itself, the Plaza Santo Domingo serves as a good starting place for those interested in exploring the old city. Housing an attractive gilt statue, the accompanying 16th-century **Iglesia de Santo Domingo** stands out for its elegance and simplicity *(open M-Sa 6am-noon and 4-7pm, Su 6am-1pm and 6-7pm).* Following Rocafuerte from the plaza, you'll pass by **Carmen Alto,** the home of Santa Mariana *(open M-Sa 6:30am-8pm, Su 4:30-7pm).*

PLAZA SAN FRANCISCO. The always populated Plaza San Francisco is flanked by the gorgeous and gigantic **Monasterio de San Francisco,** constructed from 1535 to 1605. (*Church open daily 7am-noon and 3-6pm. Admission free. Museum open M-Sa 9am-6pm, Su 9am-1pm. Admission s/10,000, students with ID s/5,000.)* Down Sucre a block, away from Plaza San Francisco, is the **Catedral de La Compañia.** Though the interior of the cathedral is under renovation until 2002, you can still appreciate the wonderful baroque façades, carved from volcanic rock, from behind the construction fences. *(Located at Garcia moreno and Sucre.)* Further along the right side of García Moreno sits the **Church of El Sagrario** with its large stone portico and bright, patterned interior *(open daily 8am-7pm).*

PLAZA DE LA INDEPENDENCIA. Also called the Plaza Grande, this plaza is the centerpiece of colonial Quito. The best maintained part of Old Quito, the plaza enchants with its stunning **Palacio Presidencial**—with stoic men in blue and gold holding flags—the historical **Hotel Magestic** (colonial Quito's first hotel), and the colossal **catedral**—with flashing green-and-bronze domes and a high white turret *(cathedral open daily 8-10am and 3-6:30pm).* The plaza, however, is best-loved by *quiteños* as a relaxing retreat with shady palm trees and meticulously maintained gardens. Few realize the true historical significance of this favorite rest stop. Built in 1667, the plaza's cathedral contains the grave of **Antonio José de Sucre** (see p. 47), Independence hero and namesake of the country's currency. A statue commemorating Quito's August 10th Independence Day dynamizes the plaza's center, but old men engaged in the art of people-watching make sure the plaza's energy level remains low. Weary wanderers often stay awhile to take in the air of Quito's colonial days before moving on. The **Iglesia de San Agustín** is located down the block from Plaza Grande. Containing the paintings of 17th-century artist Miguel de Santiago, it gained fame as the sight where José de Sucre declared independence. (*Corner of Chile and Guayaquil. Open daily 7:15am-noon and 3:30-6pm.)*

LA VIRGEN DE QUITO. Visible from the Plaza del Teatro, as well as most other locations on the outskirts of Old Town, the majestic statue of La Virgen de Quito surveys her domain from the summit of **El Panecillo** at the far end of Old Quito. The views to the north and south of both Quito and the surrounding mountains reveal why these hilltops have been so strategically important to the region's inhabitants for centuries. You can climb up the hill to a *mirador* just below the pedestal of the serpent-stomping virgin. The trip up El Panecillo involves a long and dangerous walk up the stairs at the end of García Moreno. Even groups get robbed frequently; a safer bet is to have a taxi take you up and wait to bring you back down. *(Round-trip, including a 20min. wait at the statue s/30,000. Open daily 9am-5pm.)*

OTHER SITES. The **Plaza del Teatro,** three blocks down Guayaquil away from San Agustín and towards New Quito, is the backdrop for the **Teatro Nacional Sucre,** constructed in 1878 and under reconstruction in 1999. *(Three blocks down Guayaquil away from San Agustín, at Flores and Manabí.)* The most awe-inspiring church is the **Basílica,** on the corner of Venezuela and Carchí. It contains a cafeteria, library, and gift shop, but the coolest thing about the basilica is the tower (115m high). Though this lookout spot offers incredible views of Quito, the long climb up a tiny spiral staircase may terrify sufferers of vertigo. *(Open Tu-Su 9am-5pm. S/15,000 to climb.)*

NOT AN ORDINARY TOURIST TRAP The notion of a women's prison in the developing world may invoke images of automatic weapons, barbed wire, and questionable human rights practices. The **Carcel de Mujeres,** las Toronjas, New Quito, is a happier, if no less shocking, vision. On visitor's day, the prison-yard becomes a circus of inmates, husbands, and children playing volleyball. One woman musically vends little bags of popcorn as two unarmed, female guards sit tranquilly knitting sweaters. Many of the women have children living in the jail with them, in blocks of rooms rather than cells. Most prisoners are poor *indígenas,* except for the handful of foreigners serving up to eight years for drug possession charges. These women—mostly from the United States—eagerly receive English-speaking visitors who often bring gifts of food, cigarettes, and books, in return for hearing some extraordinary stories. To get to the prison, take a northbound local bus on 6 de Diciembre to El Inca. Follow El Inca and take a left onto las Toronjas. Visiting hours W, Sa, and Su 10am-3pm; passport required.

MUSEUMS

Quito has so many museums that anyone who ever took the time to visit them all would end up an expert on Ecuadorian history, archaeology, culture, flora and fauna, and colonial and modern art. If you're a student, be sure to show your ID at every opportunity; you may gain entrance at a discounted rate.

NEW TOWN

MUSEO NACIONAL DEL BANCO CENTRAL. This recent consolidation of several separate Banco Central museums forms the most extensive and impressive museum in Quito. Enormous winding rooms, many dim and glass-partitioned, contain exhibits of archaeology (such as pots with faces from the Panzaleo), pre-Hispanic gold works, pre-Independence paintings, colonial religious portraits, modern art (Guayasamín, Kingman, etc.), and indigenous *artesanía. (Patria and 6 de Diciembre. Tel. 223 258. Open Tu-F 9am-5pm, Sa and Su 10am-3pm. Admission for foreigners s/10,000, with student ID s/5,000.)*

CASA DE LA CULTURA ECUATORIANA. In the same building as the Museo Nacional, this museum presents a collection of 19th- and 20th-century art, an ethnology museum, and musical instruments you can be sure you've never seen before, including the *caperazon*, made from a tortoise shell, and the *pifono*, a flute made from an armadillo tail. An Amazonian shrunken head (!) and indigenous regional garb are mixed in with the sculptures and paintings. A hangout for Quito's cultural elite, the museum also shows movies and plays from time to time. *(Patria and 6 de Diciembre. Tel. 223 392. Open Tu-F 10am-6pm, Sa 10am-2pm. Admission s/10,000, with student ID s/5,000.)* There is also a library open to the public. *(Open M-F 9am-6:30pm, Sa 9am-5pm.)* Recently, a new building opened as part of the Casa de la Cultura: the **Galería** hosts temporary exhibitions such as the Japanese flower show that takes place in late June. Call ahead to find out what the current exhibition is. *(6 de Diciembre 794. Tel. 543 748. Open M-F 10am-6pm. Admission free.)*

INSTITUTO GEOGRÁFICO MILITAR. The *Instituto* boasts the best maps for every region of Ecuador. Political, topographical, Sierra, Oriente... you name it. Many are for sale or can be copied (starting at s/2,000), but be prepared to wait around a while. There is also a **planetarium** and a **geographical museum**. Great satellite photos of Ecuador's volcanic craters are on display in the main room. Spanish is helpful for getting past the military guards at the entrance. *(On Paz y Miño, at the top of a hill. You can only reach Paz y Mino from Telm, running along the base of the hill. It is a 10min. uphill walk to the top. A taxi up costs s/5,000. Tel. 502 091. Instituto open M-F 8am-4pm. Planetarium shows M-F 9, 11am and 3pm, Sa 9 and 11am. Admission s/15,000, children s/5,000)*

FUNDACIÓN GUAYASAMÍN. The entrance to this museum opens onto a spacious garden with metal statues and several white *casas*. The collection includes an extensive exhibit of pre-Inca artifacts, all found in Ecuador, and some 18th-century colonial religious art from the *Quiteña* and *Cuzqueña* schools. The rest of the museum is dedicated to the riveting, magnificent paintings of the foundation's namesake, Oswaldo Guayasamín. A leader of the indigenist movement, his images capture the problems and pains of racism, poverty, and class stratification in South America, with plenty of references to the original Spanish conquest of indigenous peoples (see **Modern Art,** p. 245, and **Indigenous Identity,** p. 47). The 78-year-old artist was president of the Organization for Human Rights in Latin America in 1980. *(José Bosmediano 543. Take 6 de Diciembre north to Eloy Alfaro, where Bosmediano begins, and start climbing—the museum is way up the hill. Tel. 446 455. Open M-F 9am-1:30pm and 3-6:30pm. Admission s/20,000.)*

THE VIVARIUM. This is not a place for people who fear snakes and other slimy reptiles. These, as well as iguanas, a small alligator, several turtles, and some tiny poisonous frogs, are all that are on display in this reptile and amphibian zoo. Pythons, cobras, snapping turtles, and other potentially harmful animals are caged and labeled with color-coded information cards so that you can tell which are venomous, where they live, and what they eat. Ask nicely to hold the boa. *(Reina Victoria N25-68 and Santa María. Tel. 230 988. Open Tu-Sa 9:30am-1pm and 2:30-6pm, Su 11am-6pm. Admission s/20,000, children s/5,000.)*

OTHER MUSEUMS. Relatively close to each other on 12 de Octubre are two other museums, both of an ethnographic nature. The **Museo Amazónico Abya-Yala** is a large one-room exhibit on Oriente life. Exhibits about Amazonian culture, wildlife, musical instruments, and photos of oil exploitation are all on display. Downstairs in the bookstore, a huge variety of publications are available on the foundation's main interest: indigenous anthropology. *(12 de Octubre 1430 and Wilson. Tel. 562 633. Open M-F 9am-1pm and 2-6pm. Admission s/5,000.)* A few blocks north, **Museo Centro de Exposiciones y Ferias Artesanales** is Quito's only *artesanía* museum and contains a collection of handicrafts from the different provinces of Ecuador. The organization that runs the museum also sponsors several festivals throughout the year. *(12 de Octubre N24-162 and García. Tel. 503 873. Open M-F 8am-5pm. Admission free.)*

OLD TOWN

Not surprisingly, many of the museums in Old Town are of a historic nature. Colonial Quito comes alive at these exhibitions, housed at times in buildings as old as the artifacts themselves.

MUSEO DEL CONVENTO SAN DIEGO. This religious institution was established 400 years ago by Spanish colonists, and the 45min. guided tour through the complex (given in Spanish and necessary to enter the museum) reveals many intimate windows into the distant past: original murals, cooking facilities, and a chamber where bones are buried deep in the earth. The walls are decked out with religious artwork: one painting shows a rendition of the Last Supper, with the indigenous delicacy *cuy* (guinea pig) substituted for Christ's main course. *(Calicuchima 117 and Farfán. Follow Imbabura south from Old Quito until it dead-ends in the plaza in front of the convent. Tel. 952 516. Open Tu-Su 9:30am-12:30pm and 2:30-5pm. Admission s/10,000.)*

MUSEO CASA DE SUCRE. This museum celebrates Ecuador's battle for independence (The Battle of Pichincha) in the house of one of its key participants, Mariscal Antonio José de Sucre. The museum includes a free tour in Spanish of the house, giving a glimpse into Sucre's personal life—his chapel, bedroom, and even a picture of his skull after his assassination. *(Venezuela 573 and Sucre. Tel. 952 860. Open Tu-F 8am-4:30pm, Sa 9am-4pm. Admission s/6,000.)* A continuation of the Museo Casa de Sucre, the **Museo Templo de la Patria** is located up the hill of Pichincha, under the monument to the Independence fighters of Ecuador. Mariscal Sucre triumphed here and independence was won on May 24, 1822. A monument to the event, the museum contains an eternal flame. *(Tel. 952 860. Open Tu-F 8am-4pm, Sa 8am-1pm, Su 10am-3pm. Admission s/10,000.)*

MUSEO ALBERTO MENA CAMAÑO DE ARTE E HISTORIA. This museum is currently closed for renovations, but it may open by early 2000. The museum's permanent exhibit is a historical journey that descends into the maze-like basement, where wax figures lie in murdered positions, and surfaces in a courtyard near the entrance. There's also a ground-level room for temporary art exhibits. *(Espejo 1147 and García Moreno. Tel. 510 272. Open Tu-Sa 9am-4:45pm. Admission free.)*

MUSEO DE ARTE COLONIAL. The Museo de Arte Colonial contains impressive artwork from the 16th through early 19th centuries and includes a collection of miniature sculptures and carvings. Christ, monks, saints, and other religious figures abound; don't miss the 17th-century Christ figure whose heart (seen through a tear in the skin) moves when you stamp your foot. The courtyard also houses a series of plans measuring Quito's expansion from 1508 to the present. *(Cuenca 915 and Mejía. Tel. 212 297. Open Tu-F 10am-6pm, Sa 10am-2pm. Admission s/10,000.)*

MUSEO CONDE DE URQUIJO DE LA CASA DE BENALCÁZAR. Though located in the home of the founder of Quito, this museum isn't devoted to the glorification of Sebastián de Benalcázar. Instead, through the Ecuadorian Hispanic Culture Institute, the small one-room exhibit houses an extensively decorated chapel, paintings, and a collection of sculptures from the 16th to 18th centuries, donated in 1966 by the Conde de Urquijo, then the Spanish ambassador. The art is devoutly religious, and the public library devoutly intellectual. *(Olmedo 968 and Benalcázar. Tel. 288 102. Open M-F 9am-1pm and 2-6pm. Admission free.)*

COLEGIO NACIONAL MEJÍA. The Colegio Nacional Mejía houses two separate museums behind its high walls. The **Museo Etnográfico** presents a series of life-size dioramas of different indigenous Ecuadorians, as well as a taxidermy exhibit of animals that were once found throughout the country (*on Ante between Vargas and Venezuela; tel. 583 412; open M-F 8am-noon and 2-6pm; admission free; guided tours required).* The **Museo de Ciencias Naturales,** accessible via the school's main entrance, contains a thorough collection of stuffed animals, including brightly colored birds, turtles, and sharks *(same location; tel. 583 412; open M-F 7am-3pm and 5-8pm; admission free).*

NIGHTLIFE

After dark, in Quito, the wheezing of buses dies down and the deep thump of music grows louder. There are a wide range of bars and dance clubs (*discotecas*) catering to the city's flocks of young people and tourists who just wanna get jiggy with it. Stick to nightlife in New Town; not only is the scene hipper, but Old Town's streets are too dangerous for night wandering, especially if you're a bit *borracho*. However, New Town's not such a safe haven either; recent reports of robberies and assaults have put revelers of the night on guard. Follow their example, especially around Reina Victoria, and take a taxi back to your hotel.

BARS

A slew of bars around town call out to anyone interested in unwinding from a long day of sightseeing or climbing. While most bars play music, the focus is more on lounging than dancing. So, pull up a seat and name your poison.

Café Sutra, Calamá and León Mera, above Safari Tours. Follow the wooden boa winding upwards around a tree to this trendy 2nd-floor coffeehouse/bar. Soothing tunes, tapestries and Kama-Sutra-like drawings on the wall relax you before a night of deafening music in the clubs. Nightly cocktail specials (2 for s/30,000) complement healthful snacks such as hummus with pita and veggies (s/19,000). Open daily 8am-11pm.

El Pobre Diablo, Santa María 338 and León Mera (tel. 224 982). For a more relaxed evening, head to this 6-room cafe/bar. Sounds of happy chatter and a crackling fire mix with jazz, blues, and latin music make this bar both cheerful and mellow. Servers swear that the moth-like wall decorations are really human scalps... you be the judge. Good coffee (s/5,000) and Pilsener beer (s/15,000) raise spirits. Open Tu-Sa 4:30pm-2am.

Red Hot Chili Peppers, Foch 713 and Juan Leon Mera. Although this small, dimly-lit Mexican restaurant and bar is not much to look at, it does serve absolutely gorgeous mixed drinks. Share a pitcher of the best strawberry daiquiri you have ever tasted (s/15,000) or, then again, keep it all to yourself. Chips with salsa (s/8,000) or guacamole (s/20,000) complement any beverage. Bring a permanent marker and feel free to make your mark on the walls. Open daily 11am-11pm.

Reina Victoria Pub, Reina Victoria 530 and Roca (tel. 226 329). For a pint of proper ale, this is the pub you want to hit (s/20,000 for microbrew). This 3-room bar entertains patrons with a dartboard and a cozy fireplace. Serves standard pub fare like breaded fish on a roll (s/19,000) and not-so-standard banana chips (s/6,500). Try a Yellow Bird for adventure or a Beefeater Martini if you just want to get tanked (s/26,000). Open M-Sa 5pm-midnight.

Varadero (tel. 542 476), Reina Victoria and Pinto. The music at this bar is live and fun. Locals fill the scene, but anyone who appreciates rhythm and style should feel welcome. A warm glow fills the room, people dance between tables, and live Cuban music is played on weekends. Cover s/20,000 F-Sa. Open W-Su noon-4pm and 7pm-2am.

Arribar, Juan Leon Mera 1238 and Lizardo Garcia (tel. 228 545). This second-floor establishment tempts customers with a foosball table, a pool table, comfy couches, and a full bar. Cool slide projector illuminates the walls with strange shapes that come alive with cocktails (beer s/15,000, tequila shot s/12,000). Open M-Sa 5pm-2am.

DANCE CLUBS

Starting at 11pm, the dance clubs around New Town fill up with people anxious to get a groove on. Music selection is definitely mixed but usually heavily slanted towards techno and house mixes. Places playing mostly Spanish music are around, but a little harder to find. One block north of Colón, **Santa María** claims some of Quito's most jammin', traveler-friendly nightclubs, including **Tijuana, Papillón,** and **Alcatraz.** Lesbian and gay travelers have options in Quito as well, but they are often difficult to find. Ecuadorian law only recently decriminalized homosexuality (see **Bisexual, Gay, and Lesbian Travelers,** p. 35); gay hang-outs are a quiet, cautious phenomenon.

No Bar, Calamá 380 and León Mera (tel. 545 145), on Calamá's Restaurant Row. The blue-and-red sign atop the roof shouts "NO," but by all means come in to one of the trendiest nightspots in Quito. A mixed crowd of locals and travelers packs the floor. Wednesday nights are theme nights. *Cerveza* s/20,000. Happy hour M-W 6-10pm. Cover s/20,000 F and Sa nights, includes one drink. Open M-Sa 6pm-2am.

Seseribó, Veintimilla and 12 de Octubre, downstairs in the Edificio El Girón (look for the flashing pink sign). Latin music lovers will find a lot to dance to here—*salsa, merengue, rumba, or cha cha cha.* Plenty of tables and room to rest or down a *chupa* (shot) in this trendy club. Cover s/20,000. Open W-Sa 9pm-2:30am.

Ramón Antigua, Veintimilla 159 and Isabel la Católica (tel. 541 254). The excellent live music that starts at midnight is enough to convince lots of locals to pay the s/25,000 drink minimum and commit to an entire night of dancing and fun in this increasingly popular spot. As long as you have to spend the money on drinks, try something exotic like a Pink Lady with banana liquor. Open Th-Sa 8pm-2am.

Tropicana, Whymper 330 and Orellano (tel. 507 339 or 527 353). There are 2 dance floors in this multi-level club; music changes from Latin *salsa* to techno at the drop of a hat. Trendy 20-somethings (cigarette and cellphone in hand) gather and fill both floors. Cover s/20,000. Open W-Sa 8pm until the crowd goes home.

Bar-Ril, García 356 and 6 de Diciembre (tel. 226 714), past a restaurant sign that says *"Menestras."* An intimate gay bar that goes by a number of other names, this club has 2 tiny dance floors amidst cushiony benches and tables and claims a variety of dance music. Bright, red-lit, and festive. Happy hour 8-9pm. No cover. Open W-Sa 8pm-2am.

OTHER ENTERTAINMENT

SPORTS AND RECREATION

In Quito, as in all of Latin America, **fútbol** (American soccer) is sacred. Giant crowds flock to the weekend games at the enormous **Estadio Atahuallpa,** 6 de Diciembre and Naciones Varidas, near Parque La Carolina. Take a bus marked "Estadio" on 6 de Diciembre. Teams from the intra-Ecuador league compete on this field; matches between Quito and its vicious rivals from Guayaquil or Cuenca are the norm. Tickets are readily available the day of the game if you arrive a bit early (s/20,000). Ecuador isn't known for its **corridas de toros** (bullfights), but those hungry for some real bloodsport can contact **La Plaza de Toros** (tel. 246 037 or 247 850), on Amazonas and Ascaray (tickets s/20,000). If the speed demon in you gets impatient with slow buses and the *trole*, give the **Speedway** (tel. 553 105) a shot. The speedway is on Amazonas near the intersection with Eloy Alfaro, behind the Ministry of Agriculture. Work off your need for speed on this no-nonsense track populated by zooming go-carts seemingly without speed limit. (5min. s/25,000, 10min. s/45,000; discounts with ISIC. Open Tu-F 2:30-6:30pm, Sa-Su 10am-6:30pm.) If you're in the mood for some virtual racing, check out **Play Zone,** Benalcazar and Chile. Kids of all ages come here to play arcade and carnival games. (s/1,000 per game.).

Ready for an afternoon of **frisbee** and pickup *fútbol?* **Parque La Carolina,** north of the city center on Amazonas, is Quito's answer to all recreational desires. A Sunday afternoon at the park is perfect for kids, athletes, and dawdlers who can take advantage of the roller-blading park, carousels, benches, fields, courts, trees, and pond (with pedal boats). Be careful, though: in 1998, there were several armed assaults in the park, and the South American Explorers Club warned against going there in the late afternoon or night. The central **Parque El Ejido,** sandwiched between Old and New Town, has similar greenery and its own charm. **Parque Alameda** in Old Town has an observatory, some monuments to science, and a small restaurant (restaurant open daily 8:30am-5pm), but lacks the relaxed atmosphere of La Carolina. If you are hot and have some extra *sucres* to spend, go **swimming** at the **Quito Health Club** (tel. 565 946 or 520 549) on Pinzón and Colón (s/30,000).

MOVIES

The many movie theaters in Quito generally screen American movies in English with Spanish subtitles. The best movie listings are in the newspapers **El Comercio** (in the classifieds section) and **Hoy.** Some theaters have matinees, but most screen twice during the evenings. Tickets range from s/10,000 to s/30,000, with a definite correlation between price and movie quality and age. (Sometimes new releases in Ecuador came out in the U.S. six months to one year earlier.) Incredibly cheap shows are usually pornos or chintzy action flicks. Two large multiplex theaters, **Cinemark 7** (tel. 260 301), Av. Americas and República, on the Plaza de las Américas, and **Multicines,** Japan 250 (tel. 259 811 or 259 809), opened in 1998 and dominate the business. Some other high-quality theaters in

ECUADOR STRIKES GOLD July 26, 1996. It was a mild summer morning. More than 80,000 people watched with bated breath as 22-year-old Jefferson Pérez, decked out in slinky shorts and honest-to-God professional walking shoes, wobbled into the Olympic Stadium in Atlanta, Georgia, to claim the first gold medal of the 1996 Track and Field competition—**Ecuador's first Olympic medal ever.** Walking 20km in 1 hour, 20 minutes, and 7 seconds, he beat his best time by 14 seconds and the rest of the field by 25m. The closest Ecuador came to medaling before this was in 1972, when Jorge Delgado Panchama came in fourth in the 200m butterfly. In interviews, Pérez reminisced, "When I took the lead, I felt very tired, as if I was asleep. It felt like a dream. Then I thought that *this* is my dream. I have to go for it, even if I died." Back in Quito, patriots filled the streets, celebrating the momentous occasion into the wee hours of the morning. Then president-elect Abdalá Bucaram announced, "This triumph has to help the country!" and declared that a special postage stamp be issued in Pérez's honor.

New Town include **Universitario** (tel. 230 280), Américas and Vérez Guerrero at the Universidad Central; **Colón** (tel. 224 081), 10 de Agosto and Colón; **Benalcázar,** 6 de Diciembre and Portugal; and the **Casa de la Cultura,** which sometimes has film festivals (see p. 262). **Bolívar** (tel. 582486), on Espejo and Guayaquil in Old Town, is decent, though New Town films are generally of a much higher caliber.

THEATER

Although **Teatro Nacional Sucre** (see p. 261) was built to satisfy cultural Quito's dramatic desires, it has been under renovation for so long that no one can quite remember when the last real performance took place. Theatrical events have instead been relegated to a plethora of smaller theaters and *salas* around town. Check the cultural agenda in *El Comercio* for all current listings.

SHOPPING

Quito's most cosmopolitan thoroughfare, New Town's **Av. Río Amazonas,** is the most popular (but not the cheapest) place to buy souvenirs and Ecuadorian handicrafts. If you plan to buy a lot, keep in mind that markets in neighboring towns such as **Otavalo** offer both lower prices and a more cultural shopping experience. Even so, it's a good idea to visit some of the shops on Amazonas, if only to browse, check out prices, and get an idea of the *artesanía* Ecuador has to offer in a more comfortable setting than the hectic local markets. Directed at tourists, these shops aim to please, stocked with the most popular handmade Ecuadorian crafts: Panama hats, carved tagua-nuts, hand-painted pottery, and countless handwoven rugs, shawls, wall hangings, and bags. **Parque El Ejido** (p. 266) has a craft market every Sunday from 10:30am to 5pm, and here, too, is a good place to get an idea of what's out there. Unless prices are marked or explicitly stated as fixed, bargaining is expected. At the same time, squabbling over *sucres* that mean much more to the vendor can be petty. Every shopper must strike a comfortable balance. But remember: the best bargaining is done by the person who's perfectly ready to walk away if the price isn't right. For those in search of western goods, there is the new **El Jardín** mall. Across from Parque Carolina, this four-story extravaganza contains an enormous Supermaxi, as well as stores with such Ecuadorian-sounding names as ACE Hardware, Sunglasses Hut, and Harley Davidson. Still, it offers convenient and quick shopping in a street-vendor-free environment, albeit at North American prices. (Open M-Sa 10am-8:30pm, Su 10am-6:30pm.)

DECISIONS, DECISIONS... Famous for its relatively compact collection of coastal, mountainous, and jungle regions, Ecuador has long been a destination for adventurers interested in a diverse range of attractions and activities, and Quito is a convenient base for these adventures. Deciding what to do is often the most challenging part of a trip. One- or two-day trips are possible to:

Cotopaxi, p. 304, 3hr. south. Volcano climbing.
Papallacta, p. 385. 2hr. east. Thermal hot springs.
Baños, p. 311. 5hr. south. Hot springs and great nightlife.
Tena, p. 369. 10hr. southeast. Whitewater rafting.
Otavalo, p. 276. 2hr. north. Saturday market and hiking.
Atacames, p. 391. 8hr. west. Beach and bars.
Mindo, p. 270. 3hr. west. Birdwatching, biking, and more.

NEAR QUITO: BELLAVISTA CLOUDFOREST RESERVE

Though commonly known as a bird-lover's paradise, just about everyone who has visited Bellavista would probably say that it's on the stairway to heaven. Spanning 600 hectares at 1400-2600m above sea level, the lush forests are usually sunny in the morning until the clouds roll in midday, bathing the bromeliads, orchids, and moss in mist, and attracting at least 170 bird species. Come equipped with binoculars, good hiking shoes, rain gear, and snacks so that you can soak up as much as possible. An extensive network of 14 well maintained and easy-to-follow trails (one easy, 7 moderate, and 6 difficult) makes different parts of the forest accessible to visitors. Rubber boots are supplied upon request when it rains.

The **Bellavista Lodge** itself is a four-story, dome-like structure constructed with bamboo and complete with thatched roof. This is situated to offer occupants fantastic views of the surrounding cloudforest and the Tandayapa valley below. Visitors can take meals in the first floor dining area (US$8 per meal) and mimic the hummingbirds feeding just outside the windows. Some bring their own food to minimize costs and maximize time on the trails. On the second floor, rooms have balconies, private baths, and sitting areas. (Singles US$32; doubles US$27 per person; triples US$25.) Budget rooms on the third and fourth floors share baths and balconies (either floor US$14 per person). Camping costs US$5 per person. Visitors can also volunteer at the research station, which includes trailbuilding and maintaining, fence building, and light carpentry work (US$5 a day, min. 30 days). While Bellavista's remote location proves to be one of its greatest charms, it can also represent the biggest obstacle to travelers on a tight schedule or budget.

Transportation: The only way to get there with public transportation is by taking the bus to Nanegalito from the Quito *terminal terrestre*. **Cooperativo Aloag** has several buses each day (2hr., s/15,000), and any bus going to **Pacto, Puerto Quito, San Miguel de los Bancos,** or **Mindo** passes through Nanegalito. From Nanegalito, ask at **Viveres Paty** for Don Jorge Bermúdez, or just ask if anyone with a *camioneta* can take you the remaining 45 minutes up the hill to Bellavista (US$15 per truck load). Walking the 12km up to Bellavista is also an option, but it may take upwards of five hours, and it requires an early departure from Quito. Just ask the driver to drop you off at kilometer 32, just beyond **Cafe Tiepolo** but before Nanegalito. Follow the road past a couple of trout hatcheries and through the village of Tandayapa to reach the lodge. Buses returning to Quito pass through kilometer 32 until 5:30pm (2hrs., s/10,000); allow three hours for th return trip down the hill. Transportation can also be arranged through the Bellavista office in Quito but it can get pricey (US$70 roundtrip for up to 4 persons). For more information, visit the office at Jorge Washington E7-23 and Reina Victoria (tel./fax 232 313).

NEAR QUITO: VOLCÁN PICHINCHA

One of the most awe-inspiring aspects of Quito is the surrounding terrain. Perhaps the most impressive feature of this terrain is the double-cratered Volcán Pichincha. The younger, more energetic crater Gua Gua Pichincha erupted in 1660, 1881, 1931, and 1981, to name a few fiery occasions. While the volcano rumbles alarmingly close to Quito, it does not pose an enormous threat; the closer crater, Rucu Pichincha, is utterly inactive and fires off in a western direction, greatly relieving *quiteños*. As history has shown, the most severe threat to Quito itself is ash. The October 27, 1660 eruption of Gua Gua piled more than a foot of volcanic soot atop the city, causing rooftops to collapse. Despite its disastrous reputation, Pichincha's proximity to Quito makes it one of the most popular climbs in Ecuador. Less strenuous than some of Ecuador's other choice peaks, Pichincha serves as a convenient acclimatization trek before visitors venture on to higher peaks further south. Also worthwhile in it own respect, Volcán Pichincha provides fantastic views of Quito, the valley, and a slew of other mountains in the distance.

The closer crater, **Rucu,** tempts tourists to simply start scrambling straight up the hillside from the city. Theoretically this is possible but quite dangerous because of the sometimes-armed thieves from shady neighborhoods that lie at the foot of the mountain. Check with Safari or the South American Explorers Club (see **Useful Organizations,** p. 249) to hear the present state of affairs before attempting this climb. Because of the risks involved, *Let's Go* does not recommend visiting Rucu, especially with so many safer, and equally scenic, mountains nearby.

The baby **Gua Gua** outdoes the elder Rucu in altitude, scenery, and safety, though one should be wary of dogs (these are usually scared off by picking up a rock or brandishing some sort of stick). From its peak, vistas stretch to the uninhabited west and south, and when clouds don't get in the way, climbers can see down into its plummeting crater. The summit is accessed from the southern base of the volcano, through the villages of **Mena Dos** and **Lloa** (Yo-a), an hour's drive from Quito along Av. Mariscal Antonio Jose de Sucre.

LOGISTICS. In the town of Lloa, signs point the way to a road winding up to the **refuge,** which sits just shy of the crater's edge. A trip to the refuge by four-wheel-drive vehicle takes an hour-and-a-half, while walking takes five to seven hours. Inside the refuge awaits a bathroom, some rainwater barrels, and several mattresses, so those wishing to spend the night should bring a sleeping bag, candles, and plenty of food (US$3). Those planning to make it up and back in one day should start very early to beat the clouds which settle over the crater midday. From the refuge, the sometimes snow-covered summit is a one- to two-hour round-trip hike. It's cold up there—warm clothing is a must. It is prohibited, to hike down into the crater, as some climbers were asphyxiated by gaseous emissions several years ago while camping inside; a memorial has been erected at the edge of the crater. While the hike up Gua Gua is not difficult, transportation can be quite difficult to coordinate and fares may start to add up. Without a 4WD vehicle to take you to the refuge from Lloa, it will be difficult to complete the round trip in a day. It might be worth the money to hire a guide to worry about the transportation and food (see **Tour Company and Tourist Information,** p. 250).

TRANSPORTATION. To reach Lloa, take a Mena Dos bus south from the bus canopy at the intersection of Americás and Colón, adjacent to the Seminario Mayor San José, where returning southbound buses make a U-turn (45min., every 15min. 6am-7:30pm, s/20,000). Take the bus until Angamarca, the main street and bus stop in Mena Dos. From here, *camionetas* or taxis will go to Lloa for a hefty charge (s/50,000); the further up into the village of Mena Dos you walk, the less a car into the village of Mena Dos will cost. Anagmaraca leads up the hill into a street named Via Lloa, which leads to Lloa. The walk to Loja (1hr.) is not recommended because of recent muggings along the roadway. Also a possibility, at the junction of Venidores and Angamarca, *volquetas* (multicolored dump trucks) run toward Lloa (every day 5am-5pm) and drivers will often give climbers a lift for a minimal fee (s/5,000).

QUITO

NEAR QUITO: SANGOLQUÍ

While on Saturdays the town of Otavalo hosts Ecuador's most famous craft extravaganza, the prize for the best country market goes to Sangolquí's **Sunday market.** The village itself is more modern than most places of its size, mostly because it's less than 20km southeast of the capital. The outdoor market spills over several blocks into the middle of Sangolquí, starting next to the principal avenue **Enríquez,** where the buses drop their loads. The majority of shoppers are local; the market is not aimed at travelers. Vendors wait under tarps next to their goods: banana bread, rubber gloves, chicken heads, Jell-O, bras, apples, razors, and chocolate bears. The few tourists usually don't spend the night. (Sunday market 8am-8pm.)

Transportation: Buses leave Quito from the south end of **Plaza La Marín,** on the outbound side of a traffic circle along Av. Pichincha (45min., every 5min. 4am-11pm, s/2,500). The same buses return to Quito until 9pm, leaving from Enríquez.

NEAR QUITO: MINDO

The town of Mindo advertises itself with the motto "Nature and Adventure." These are big shoes to fill for a town with a population of only 1,750, but Mindo does an excellent job. Located only three hours outside of Quito, it is an easy getaway and almost another world entirely, offering visitors a taste of small town life, complemented by beautiful scenery and a variety of activities such as swimming, tubing, cliff diving, horseback riding, and, of course, hiking. Commended by Birdlife International in October 1997, Mindo has also become a favorite of avid birdwatchers. Visit and hear the many stories of those who intended to spend a day, then a week, then a month, and still haven't left.

PRACTICAL INFORMATION. Here in Mindo none of the streets have names, but no one could ever get lost. Buses enter the town on the main road, which runs the length of Mindo and dead-ends in a small plaza where the **24-hour police** station is located (open daily 9am-4pm, but may be opened in emergencies by knocking loudly). The **Centro de Salud** is on the only other road in town, which crosses the main one in front of the church and runs alongside the *fútbol* field.

ACCOMMODATIONS AND FOOD. With 17 different places to stay, visitors have plenty of options, accommodating all different budgets. An inexpensive option is **Flor del Valle,** on the small side street to the left before the church, with bare rooms, hot-water baths, and a second floor porch (s/15,000 per person). A popular option among visitors is the **Centro de Educación Ambiental,** 4km outside the town. Located on 19,000 hectares, it encompasses the **Mindo River, Nambillo River,** and **Cinto River** and contains 450 species of bird and 370 species of orchid. Excursions to Las Cascadas de Nambillo, trekking, and tubing can be arranged for guests. Prices are steeper than in the rest of the town and there is no electricity or hot water in the cabin (US$27 per person including three meals and guide, US$3 to camp). For more information on the resort, contact the **Amigos de la Naturaleza** office in Mindo, on the left hand side of the main road before the plaza, or call the office in Quito (tel. 223 242; fax 221 628). Unfortunately, dining options in Mindo are not as overwhelming. **Restaurant Francisco,** on the main road, doubles as a general store and serves large *almuerzos* (s/15,000; open daily 7am-8pm). For a satisfying meal, try **Restaurant de la Señora Niiquito,** just around the corner from the information center with buffet-style lunches (s/15,000), vegetarian food upon request, and incredible fresh-squeezed juices (open daily 7am-9pm). To learn more about Mindo prior to your visit, check out the **Centro de Información de Mindo** (tel. 458 546) in Quito, on Yumbos 133 and Cristóbal Sardoval, near the airport.

SIGHTS. The recreational options in Mindo are bountiful. Choosing between bird watching, hiking, horseback riding, tubing, swimming, cliff diving (12m), and visiting nearby waterfalls promises to be the hardest part of your visit.

Check with the center run by **Fundación Pacaso y Pacaso,** at the end of the main road just before the plaza, to gain the latest info on lodging, food, guide qualifications, and organized activities. Consider bringing good hiking boots, rubber boots, binoculars, and a bathing suit to keep your options open. Although locals swear by the power of lemons or shampoo, you will probably want to bring some insect repellent.

Hiking is a popular option, but to avoid trespassing onto private reserves and since paths are sometimes hard to find, a guide is recommended (s/40,000 for the day from info center). One popular hike is to **Las Cascadas de Nambillo,** two hours from the plaza (admission US$5, guide s/30,000). There are also several **bird-watching routes.** Choose your guide carefully, for they have varying degrees of knowledge about the local species (from s/40,000). **Tubing** in Río Mindo can also be arranged through the center (tube s/20,000, guide s/15,000). **Horse riding** is offered at the resort El Carmelo de Mindo (US$5 for 1hr). To get there, follow the road leading past the soccer field which intersects the main entry road near the blue-and-white church about halfway into town. Walking straight leads you to the Mindo River bridge where you go left and follow the signs to the resort. It takes 30 minutes to walk, but it's flat and peaceful. There is an **orchid collection** located on the road to El Carmelo (admission s/10,000). The town also boasts a **butterfly farm** with both English- and Spanish-speaking guides that take you through every stage of the butterfly's life (admission s/20,000, cost of guides varies).

TRANSPORTATION. The only bus company that goes directly to Mindo is the **Cooperativo Flor del Valle** (tel. 527 495). Buses depart from Quito at the corner of Manuel Larrea and Asunción (a few blocks west of Parque El Ejido), not from the *terminal terrestre* (2½hr.; M-Th 3:30pm, F-Su 8am and 3:30pm; s/17,000). Buses back to Quito leave from the **bus station** on the main road (M-Th 6:30am, F-Su 6:30am and 2pm). Since there are so few buses that go to and from Mindo each day, it is best to purchase a return ticket as soon as you arrive (the office is on the main road to the left as you enter the town, next to the Mindo-Nambillo office). If you don't mind the 6½km downhill hike from the main highway to the town, you can catch any bus heading toward **San Miguel de los Bancos** and ask to be dropped off at the turnoff. **Cooperativos Kennedy** at Aloag and San Pedrito runs buses every hour from the *terminal terrestre* (2hr., 8am-6pm, s/10,000). Keep in mind that if you depart from Quito after 2pm you will reach the Mindo turnoff near dark. Also, the last bus returning to Quito along the highway passes by around 4:30pm.

MITAD DEL MUNDO

Latitude 0°0'0". Yes, you're on the **equator,** the country's namesake and a popular tourist attraction. Since the equatorial monument known as Mitad del Mundo (Middle of the World) was erected 15km north of Quito in 1979, equator-mania has transformed this spot into a center for Ecuadorian culture, history, and capitalist venture. Perhaps more than any other location in the country, Mitad del Mundo has become a bona fide, First-World-style tourist attraction, visited by both foreigners and nationals alike. The overpriced tourist "village" is replete with bleach-white buildings and smooth stone pathways, a sprawling complex of museums, restaurants, and gift shops that cater to visiting equator-philes. In the center of it all, a 30m-high monument is topped by a five-ton metallic globe; this wide **obelisk** is perfectly aligned with the cardinal points of the compass. From the monument, a yellow stripe extends to denote the equator itself, and predictably, an army of tourists straddle the demarcation daily, enchanted by the notion of standing in both hemispheres at the same time.

INSIDE THE COMPLEX. As multiple inscriptions explain, the structure was built in commemoration of a multinational scientific expedition that measured the equator's location here between 1736 and 1744. The pathway through the parking lot (s/5,000 to park) on the way to the monument leads through the two rows of busts representing the 14 men (10 French, 3 Spanish, and 1 Ecuadorian) who took part in the expedition. While visiting the site itself is free, the attractions each charge for admission. Tickets to the obelisk are available from the *boletería* located directly in front of the monument's entrance on the first floor of the main info building. A ticket for the obelisk allows you to take an elevator to the top of the monument and then, on the way down, to see the **Ethnographic Museum** (tel. 394 806) surrounding the winding staircase. The museum consists of exhibitions detailing the clothing, food, dwellings, and customs of many Ecuadorian indigenous groups. The same ticket also gains you access to the **French Museum,** located southeast of the monument, which explains the history of the equator's measurement. (Free tours in Spanish and sporadically in English. Open M-Th 9am-6pm, F-Sa 9am-7pm. Admission s/10,000.)

Though these are the most high-profile, the Mitad del Mundo complex contains several more modest but interesting attractions. Back inside the complex, adjacent to the French museum, a spiffy **planetarium** (tel. 395 795) waits for at least 15 tourists to arrive before beginning its shows (38min.; open Tu-F 9:30am-5pm, Sa-Su 9am-6pm; admission s/8,000, children s/5,000). Nearby, **Fundación Quito Colonial** houses **miniature city models** of colonial Quito, downtown Guayaquil, and Cuenca. (Open daily 9:30am-5pm. Admission s/8,000, children s/5,000.) A recent addition to the complex, the monument dedicated to the **Heroes del Cenepa,** near the entrance, honors the soldiers who died in the 1995 war with Perú. A **scale** across from the post office lures weight-watching tourists to marvel at the kilos they seem to lose on the equator (usually no more than 4kg). They haven't really trimmed any inches; the equatorial bulge causes them to be farther from the center of the earth, so gravity has a weaker pull and they consequently weigh less, a bit of trivia restaurants in the area love to use to their advantage. The *plaza de toros* hosts **bullfights,** and the ever-so-popular **cockfights** take place at the *gallería* on holidays. Predictably, the major festival days in these parts are on March 21 and September 23 **(the equinoxes)** and June 22 and December 22 **(the solstices).** Come on a weekend to see live music and *baile folklórico* performed in the plaza or on a weekday for a more low-key visit.

OUTSIDE THE COMPLEX. One very impressive and entertaining site outside the Mitad del Mundo complex proper is the thatch-roofed **Museo de Sitio Inti-Ñan** ("Museum of the Path of the Sun" in Quichua; tel. 395 122), to the northeast of the obelisk. To get there follow the equatorial line through the plaza, and continue down the hill along the path just to the left of the church. After exiting the Mitad del Mundo complex, turn left and then walk up the hill again on the other side of the wall. Family owned and operated, the owners proudly guide you through exhibits on the sun's path, indigenous customs, and regional flora. There are live guinea pigs and Galápagos tortoises on site, as well as shrunken heads and bottled snakes. Also look forward to demonstrations of the Coriolis Effect (see **Straight Flush,** below) and dart-blowing. The museum also has the privilege of sitting on the current scientifically-measured latitude 0°0'0"—whereas, due to annual planetary variations, the obelisk is now at 0°0'12". So much for the straddling idea. (Open daily 9:30am-6pm. Admission s/10,000.)

TRANSPORTATION. Buses leave Quito for Mitad del Mundo from the El Tejar bus area in northern Old Town, around López and El Tejar (45min., every 5min. 5am-8pm, s/3,200). If staying in New Town, flag down the pink-and-white *interparroquial* buses along Américas—try the intersection at Colón. Returning buses leave from the traffic circle in front of Mitad del Mundo (every 5min. until 6pm).

PRACTICAL INFORMATION. Call a friend from the equator at the **ANDINATEL** office (tel. 396241) on the second floor of the main information building (open Tu-F 8am-6pm, Sa-Su 10am-5pm) or exchange money to finance souvenir shopping at the **Banco del Pacífico,** on the eastern side of the village, adjacent to the bullfighting stadium (open M-F 8:45am-5pm). Mitad del Mundo is not more than a daytrip from

travel

STRAIGHT FLUSH When 18th-century French explorers came to Ecuador in search of the "middle of the Earth," they (or rather their huffing lackeys) hauled along the finest compasses and astrolabes that the king's court could provide. Their find wasn't worth all the fuss—the Frenchmen could have done the job with a bidet. Among the odd phenomena that occur at the Earth's equator, which include feeling lighter than at any other spot on Earth and being able to balance an egg on the head of a nail, is the strange fact that toilets don't know which way to flush. A toilet in a house to the north will flush counterclockwise, while a porcelain pal to the south will flush in the opposite direction. The query: what is a poor potty to do when it's set squarely in the middle? Scientists claim that something called the **Coriolis effect** causes the swirly switcharoo, but even they can't predict which way an equatorial whirlpool will turn. Rumor has it that, in order to dispel the mystery, a group of experts has set up a laboratory of 10 toilets, one bathtub, and a lava lamp in the basement of Mitad del Mundo's equatorial monument. These gurus of bowl mechanics follow a strict daily regimen (reposition toilet, pull cord, reposition, pull cord) in search of one thing—the mythical straight flush. No one knows if they've seen it—some claim they never will—but if you want to see for yourself, head to the closest w.c. and keep on flushin'.

Quito. While there are places to stay in San Antonio de Pichincha (the town below Mitad del Mundo), tourists usually opt to return to Quito for the night. Most also choose to return to Quito to eat, but for those forced to give in to hunger pangs, there are places to find food in Mitad del Mundo—15 in fact. Cheaper restaurants can be found in the town of San Antonio, though they lack the ambience and are not as tourist-friendly as those within Mitad del Mundo.

NEAR MITAD DEL MUNDO: PULULAHUA AND RUMICUCHO

Trips to the volcanic crater Pululahua in the **Reserva Geobótanica Pululahua** (admission US$10) and Inca ruins Rumicucho can easily be combined with the obligatory Mitad del Mundo visit. Visible from the equatorial monument, the rising ridge of Pululahua offers good views of the green, checkered fields covering the depths of the crater. The crater, inactive for over 4,000 years, measures 4km across and offers two cones great for hiking: **El Chivo,** the smaller, and **Pondoña,** 2900m high.

An easy way to visit Pululahua and Rumicucho, without spending too much time at either sight, is to go through **Calima Tours** (tel. 394 796), in the main information building of Mitad del Mundo. They give visitors a ride to the sights along with all of the related details and history. Call ahead to arrange for guides in English or Spanish. (US$5 per sight, per person. Open daily 9am-noon.)

PULULAHUA. Pululahua is 5km from Mitad del Mundo. Two paths reach it and then continue as trails to the crater floor. Both are well-marked and turn off the highway between San Antonio de Pichincha and the town of Calacalí, 8km to the west. The first path begins at the Sangría Restaurant, where the buses stop for Pululahua. Follow the road up 2km bearing left at the fork (bearing right will take you to El Chivo) until you reach a *mirador* called **Ventanilla** (2900m). From this lookout point you can take a footpath that leads down into the crater. The second, less-traveled trail can be found 3km past the first among the highway to Calacalí. It is a clearly marked 15km road leading uphill through the lookout point Moraspungo (3186km) and down a very steep footpath into the crater. Make sure you bring sensible footwear; trails get muddy.

If you plan on spending the night in the crater, there is a **refuge** marked by a wooden sign to the right of the crater's main road. Ranger Jorge Guzmán speaks flawless English and makes visitors feel at home in the newly-constructed refuge (sleeps 12, s/10,000 per person). Bring food, because there are no restaurants or stores inside the crater, though the refuge does have a grill outside. Camping in the refuge is free for those who pay the admission fee to the reserve. For the most impressive views, go before noon because after that, a blanket of clouds may begin to settle over the crater. For a quick meal, head to the **Sangría Restaurant,** at the base of the road heading to the crater's entrance. By serving quick *almuerzos* (s/15,000) and selling portable refreshments, the restaurant appeals to both hungry bus drivers and weary hikers (open daily 8am-6pm). **El Crater Restaurant** (tel. 439-254), the other dining option high up on the ridge, outlooks the volcanic opening to one side and the mountains around San Antonio de Pichincha to the other. The well groomed lawns, cobblestone paths, and high stone walls provide an adequate atmosphere for high priced food (pastas s36,000-45,000, meat dishes s/45,000-68,000; open daily noon-5pm).

Transportation: There are several ways to get to the trailheads; the cheapest is the steep hike from Mitad del Mundo. As an alternative to walking, catch the **buses** that pass through Mitad del Mundo's traffic circle (15min., every 45min. 6am-7pm, s/1,400) on their way to Pululahua. Buses run back to Mitad del Mundo, often continuing to Quito, with the same frequency (5am-6:30pm). **Taxis** and **camionetas** also run tourists to the first trailhead for s/10,000-15,000 and later pick them up for the same amount.

RUMICUCHO. The other jaunt from Mitad del Mundo is to Rumicucho (meaning "stone corner" in Quichua), a set of Inca ruins atop a hill to the northeast. The roughly rectangular arrangement of rocks is barely visible from the equator lookout; locals took stones from the site to build their own homes and there are still parts remaining to be excavated, so little can be seen. The view from the ruins, which includes the **Canyon of Guayllabama,** is reason enough to take the trip from Mitad del Mundo. Free tours in Spanish are offered but are unpredictable; try after 1pm on weekdays or after 10am on weekends. If you find one, guides from the local community will walk you through the ruins, pointing out where the Incas ate, slept, and worshipped. (Open daily 7:30am-5pm. Admission s/3,000.)

Transportation: The easiest way to get there is by *camioneta* from Mitad del Mundo (s/10,000 each way), but you may be able to find a less expensive ride down the road in San Antonio de Pichincha. Walking leads through hot, dusty, and not-so-picturesque neighborhoods for over an hour. When walking from Mitad del Mundo, take Equinoccial and make a left onto 13 de Junio, the principal strip of San Antonio de Pichincha that runs north-south. Keep on the road for 30 to 45 minutes. At the Rumicucho sign, take a right; the ruins are not far.

RESERVA MAQUIPUCUNA

In the northwestern region of the Andes, just 70km from Quito, the Reserva Maquipucuna protects an ecological gem. Its borders contain 5000 hectares of land, with altitudes rising from 1200m to 2800m, 80% of which is primary cloudforest. Inaugurated in 1988 with a total of 3000 hectares, the reserve has since taken over much of the abandoned surrounding farmland. Researchers have swarmed into the reserve in its short decade of existence, and their work has produced numbers to brag about: in Maquipucuna's boundaries, next to the **Choco bioregion**—one of the world's top-ten "biodiversity hotspots"—they have found 1200 species of plants, 45 mammals, 350 birds, and 250 butterflies. The warm-blooded creatures include pumas, spectacled bears, bats, agoutis, peccaries, tapir, and deer. In addition to wildlife, Maquipucuna shelters a number of archaeological sites left by the **Yumbo,** a people who had inhabited this forest for 1,000 years before the Incas arrived.

Visitors to the reserve can look forward to hiking, birdwatching and, if weather permits, swimming in the Umachaca river (open daily 7am-6pm; admission US$5). Overnight guests stay at the **Thomas H. Davis Ecotourist Lodge,** a thatched-rooved ecotourist oasis that can accommodate 18 people and offers hot-water bathrooms and three meals per day (US$45 per person, children US$35). No camping allowed on reserve. Guides are also available through the Ecotourist center (US$10 per day). Consider bringing rubber boots, insect repellent, raingear, and binoculars along on your trip to the reserve. For more information, contact **Fundación Maqui-**

pucuna in Quito at Baquerizo E9-153 and Tamayó, P.O. Box 17-12-167 (tel. 507 200; fax 507 201; email root@maqui.ecuanex.net.ec).

Transportation: Getting to and from Maquipucuna is the hardest part. The roundabout route from Quito goes through the towns of **Calacalí, Nanegalito, Nanegal,** and **Marianitas,** 4km from the reserve's entrance. **Buses** run to Nanegal (2½hr.; M 2pm, Tu-F 1pm, Sa 9am and 1:30pm, Su 9am and 1pm; s/15,000) from the **San José de las Minas** *terminal* near Parque Alameda on José Antepara and pass through Plaza Cotocollao in north Quito 45 minutes after departure. After passing through Nangalito, get off the bus 2km short of Nanegal at the big green-and-yellow house at **La Delicia** crossing. From here, it's a 2km hike to Marianitas and another 4km to Maquipucuna (walking time 1¼hr.). From December to May, when it's excessively muddy, walking is difficult. Truck drivers can be hired in Marianitas to go the remaining 4km (s/40,000). A milk truck leaves Marianitas each morning between 7:15 and 7:45am (catch it in front of the white store) and can give you a lift to Nanegalito (45min., s/5,000). In Nanegalito, buses pass by on the way to Quito (every 30min. until 5pm, s/12,000).

NORTH OF QUITO

The further one strays from the smog-spewing buses of Quito, the more everyday life appears to slow down. Here, in the northern highlands, awaits a network of indigenous communities amidst spectacular majestic volcanoes, sparkling lakes, and thriving cloudforests. But both the people of the region and the natural landscapes find their existence endangered. In towns such as Otavalo, *indígenas* struggle to reconcile their traditional lifestyle with western values and technology. Locals speak Quichua on the street, wear the ponchos and fedoras of their forefathers, and often specialize in crafts that have been practiced here for centuries. Much of this locally-crafted *artesanía* is sold in Otavalo's famous Saturday market. Packed with tapestries, leather, wood carvings and paintings, this market draws crowds not just from Ecuador but from all over the world.

Though the man-made market goods are remarkable by almost any standard, they seem somewhat insignificant compared to the naturally-wrought cloudforests found throughout the region. These flourishing forests, including the privately-owned Intag Reserve, provide some of the last remaining havens for the most endangered flora and fauna in the northern Sierra.

HIGHLIGHTS NORTH OF QUITO

- **Otavalo's Saturday Craft Market** (see p. 280) is the most famous of its kind.
- Visit the brilliantly-sparkling **Lagunas de Mojanda** (see p. 282).
- Within the private **Intag Cloudforest** (see p. 287), visitors find live rare orchids and bromeliads, pumas and spider monkeys.
- At the southern foot of Mr. Cotacachi and resting atop a live volcanic crater, **Laguna Cuicocha** (see p. 285) offers spectacular **hiking** and wonderful views.

OTAVALO

Otavalo is one of the most prosperous and respected indigenous communities in Latin America, but its success hasn't come easily. Since the Inca invasion of 1496, the local *indígenas* have been persecuted by outsiders suffering from oppression and racism. The Spanish colonists took the brutality to grim new heights, forcing *otavaleños* to work 15-hour days under dangerous conditions in textile sweatshops called *obrajes*. Such extreme cruelty gradually became less common, and in 1964 an agrarian reform law returned much of the land to its indigenous residents. Most *mestizos*, however, still treated the *indígenas* like second-class citizens until the early 1980s, when local *indígenas* gained worldwide recognition for the beauty of their weaving and music. Now *otavaleño* products are sold internationally, and foreigners flock to Otavalo's Saturday market specifically to buy locally-crafted goods. A feast of sights, sounds, and smells, this frenzied fanfare overflows with Ecuador's largest selection of handmade handicrafts (see **Artesanía,** p. 53).

Today's Otavalo is a testament to the determination and talent of indigenous *otavaleños*. No longer solely weavers, many *indígenas* are now doctors, lawyers, and politicians. However, despite economic success, the *otavaleños* remain grounded in their traditions. Local women continue to wear traditional outfits with embroidered white blouses, blue skirts, shawls, and elegant gold necklaces; men sport calf-length white pants, dark ponchos, felt hats, and rope sandals. Though some accuse *otavaleños* of selling out to tourism, it is their adaptability that allows them to preserve their distinct identity (see **Indigenous Identity,** p. 47).

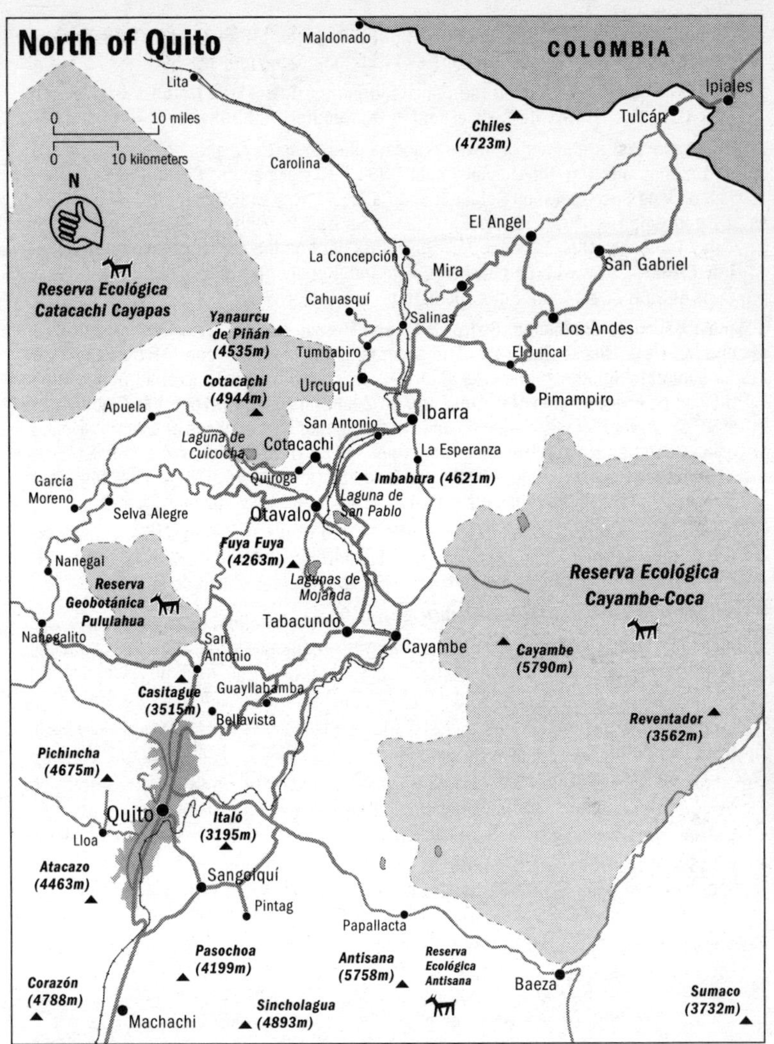

ORIENTATION

Buses usually drop visitors off in the southeast corner of town, in front of the **Plaza Copacabana,** on the corner of **Atahuallpa** and **Calderón.** Be prepared, however, to be dropped off anywhere along **Roca** (parallel to Atahualpa) or at the **terminal terrestre.** If you get a bus that only drives by the city, not through it, get off at Atahualpa and make the easy walk into town from the Panamerican Highway. **Sucre,** the major north-south avenue, runs past both **Parque Rumiñahui** and **Poncho Plaza,** the focal point of the famous Saturday market. The major east-west street is **Calderón,** which runs by Plaza Copacabana.

PRACTICAL INFORMATION

Buses: Several major bus lines are based at the *terminal terrestre* on Atahualpa and Ordoñez. Buses go to: **Quito** (2½hr., every 20min. 3:50am-7:10pm, s/15,000); **Ibarra**

(35min., every 5min. 4:50am-8pm, s/3,000); **Peguche** (30 min., every 30 min. 5am-7pm, s/1,000); and **Agato** (45 min., every 30 min. 5am-7pm, s/1,500).

Taxis: Taxis congregate around the parks and plazas. **Taxi 31 de Octubre Otavalo** (tel. 920 485). **Cooperativo de Taxis el Jordan Otavalo** (tel. 920 298).

Travel Agencies: A number of travel agencies offer tours to neighboring villages, lakes, and mountains. Day trips usually cost US$15-30 per person. Several agencies are found along Sucre between Calderón and Salinas. Check with **Diceny Viajes,** Sucre 10-14 and Colón (tel./fax 921 217). Open M-Sa 8am-6:30pm, Su 8-9am and 4-5pm. **Zulay Tours** (tel. 921 176, fax 922 969), 2nd floor on the corner of Colón and Sucre. **Inty Express,** Sucre 11-10 between Colón and Morales (tel. 921 436, fax 920 737). Open M-Sa 8:30am-7pm, Su 8:30am-1pm.

Banks: Banco del Pichincha, Bolívar 6-16 and Moreno (tel. 920 214), exchanges cash and traveler's checks. The 24hr. **ATM** accepts Cirrus and MC. Open M-F 8am-6pm, Sa-Su 8am-2pm. Another branch (tel. 921 000; fax 921 040) on Sucre and Quiroga offers the same services. Open M-F 8am-6pm, Sa 8am-2pm, Su 9am-1pm. **Vaz Cambio** (tel. 922 926; fax 923 500), Jaramillo and Pasaje Saona, also changes cash and traveler's checks and has **Western Union** service. Open M 9am-1pm, Tu-F 9am-4:30pm, Sa 8am-3pm. **Banco Previsora,** Sucre 10-07 and Calderón (tel. 921 213), doesn't change cash or traveler's checks, but does have a 24hr. **ATM** that accepts Plus and Visa cards.

Laundromat: Laundry Lavandería, Colón 5-14 and Sucre (tel. 921 267), charges s/8,000 per kg. Open M-Sa 9am-7pm. **New Laundry Lavandería,** Roca 9-42 charges s/6,000 per kg. Open M-Sa 8am-1pm and 3-6pm. Many hotels also do laundry.

Emergency: Call the **Policía Nacional** (tel. 920 101).

Police: The **Policía Municipal,** at Sucre and García Moreno, in the municipal building, serve Otavalo. Open daily 8am-12:30pm and 2-5:30pm. They have no telephone but can be seen on patrol or reached through the Comisera Municipal (tel. 920 460).

Pharmacies: Farmacia LYZ, Bolívar 1216 and Quiroga (tel. 920 344). Open M-Sa 8am-8pm. **La Dolorosa,** Calderón 3-05 and Bolívar (tel. 921 817). Open daily 8am-10pm.

Medical Services: Hospital San Luís de Otavalo (tel. 920 444; emergency 923 566), on Sucre at the northern edge of town. Open 24hr., with an ambulance service and free consultations. Emergency medical care can also be handled in the municipal building.

Post Office: (Tel./fax 923 520), Sucre and Salinas, the corner of Poncho Plaza, 2nd floor. Open M-F 8am-7pm, Sa 8am-1pm. **DHL,** Moreno 453 and Bolívar, in Intipungo Travel Office. Open M-F 9am-1:30pm and 3-5pm, Sa 9am-1pm.

Internet Access: Caffé.Net (tel. 922 969), on Sucre and Colón, offers internet access and Net2Phone, as well as scanner fax services for higher fees than you would pay in Quito (access to internet s/15,000 per 30min.). Open daily 8am-9pm. **Micro Control,** Bolívar 14-22 and Ordoñez (tel./fax 921 587) also offers access (s/1,000 per min.). Open M-F 9am-1pm and 3-7pm, Sa 9am-1:30pm. Similar service is available from **MTC Handicraft for Export,** Jaramillo 8-35 and Quiroga (tel. 922 893), right off Poncho Plaza (s/1,000 per min.). Open daily 8am-8pm.

Telephones: EMETEL, Calderón between Sucre and Jaramillo, is equipped to handle international calls, though they will charge for occupancy of the booth even on collect and calling card calls (s/350 per min.). Open daily 8am-9:45pm.

PHONE CODE	06

ACCOMMODATIONS

Most options in Otavalo are fairly congenial, inexpensive, and conveniently located in the triangle formed by **Poncho Plaza, Parque Rumiñahui,** and **Plaza Copacabana.** Unlike its neighbor Quito, most hostels include the IVR tax in their listed prices. Check with your postal to confirm this and avoid any misunderstanding.

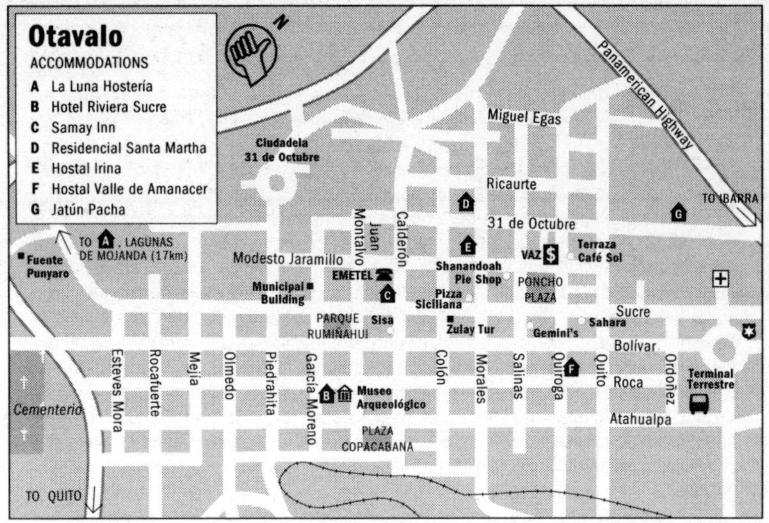

Hostal Valle del Amanecer (tel./fax 920 990), Roca and Quiroga. Constructed of avocado trees and bamboo ceilings, El Valle is a refreshing switch from the conventional plaster and cement. Quichua-named rooms are big enough to be comfortable, but still small enough to encourage mingling in the central courtyard. Great for sharing stories, a little noisy for going to sleep. The hostal also rents mountain bikes (s/35,000 a day). Rooms s/40,000, with bath s/50,000.

Jatún Pacha (HI) (tel. 922 223), 31 de Octubre and Pan-American Highway. Tucked away from the tourist center of the city, this is the most homey of Otavalo's hostels—and the most expensive. You pay more for the large rooms, polished wood floors and balconies. Other amenities include a safe, luggage storage room, and bikes for rent. Singles US$12, with HI membership US$10; doubles US$20, with membership US$16.

Hotel Riviera Sucre, García Moreno 380 and Roca (tel. 920 241). A pleasant, airy hotel with a garden/patio, ping pong room, and large guest suites. Rooms s/30,000 per person, with bath s/40,000.

Hostal Irina, Modesto Jaramillo 5-69 and Morales (tel. 920 684). Bright entry way leads you to plain but clean rooms. Telephone, laundry, shipping services, and internet access (s/1,000 per min.) are all available. Rooms s/20,000 per person.

Samay Inn, Calderón 10-05 and Sucre (tel./fax 922 871). Colorful bedspreads are the only decoration, but each room has a private bath. Rooms s/30,000 per person.

Residencial Santa Martha, Colón 7-04 and 31 de Octubre (tel. 920 147). Penny-pinchers need not look farther for the basics. Thick walls mute the outside world, and sagging mattresses make for soft slumber. Common baths only. Sleep tight and save your money for the market. Rooms s/15,000 per person.

La Luna Hostería (tel./fax 737 415), 4½km on the roadway to Laguna Mojanda. This is the place to go for a tranquil rest in the Otavalan countryside. The establishment sports a restaurant, bar, and common room with able TV. A variety of *habitaciones* accommodate different budgets. Peaceful isolation, however, will cost you in terms of transport (s/30,000 a carload to Otavalo) and meals (s/35,000 for *menú del día*). All prices per person: camping with bathroom US$1.50; dorm room with 12 beds US$3; doubles or triples with shared bath US$6; doubles with bath and fireplace US$8.

FOOD

Otavalo's restaurants offer a variety of cuisine to suit the tastes and preferences of its diverse visitors. Though you can find some spots serving traditional Ecuadorian cuisine, most places, for better or for worse, cater to a strictly gringo clientele. There are several good, moderately-priced restaurants around Ponano Plaza, but they get very busy, especially on market days.

Restaurant SISA, Calderón 409 and Sucre (tel. 920 154), 2nd floor of SISA shopping center. The immaculate entryway, wooden spiral staircase, crackling fireplace, well-stocked bar, and leather-bound menus only provide the backdrop for your fine dining experience; all-around good food provides the substance. Grilled trout (s/30,000), Brazilian chicken (s/35,000) and *lomo salsa aurora* (s/30,000) satisfy the carnivores; a salad laden with a plethora of vegetables (s/25,000) satisfies herbivores; flambeéd banana (s/10,000) and pineapple (s/12,000) for dessert satisfy everyone. Open M-F noon-4pm and 6pm-9pm, Sa-Su noon-10:30pm.

Sahara (tel. 922 212), Quiroga between Bolívar and Sucre, is all about ambiance. Most nights, the cushions and straw mats on the floor are packed with people enjoying hookah-like *pipas de agua* (water pipes) with peach, mint, apple, or strawberry tobacco. The menu is limited but certainly tasty. Falafel s/10,000. Open daily 11am-late.

Shanandoa, The PieShop/Cafeteria, Salinas 515 and Jaramillo (tel. 921 465). Really incredible pie. Enough said. Your grandma may have made great pie, but this stuff is better. Fillings include apple, strawberry, chocolate, and lemon; for a more Ecuadorian flavor, try the blackberry, pineapple, or *barbaro* (pie plain or with yogurt s/6,000, with ice cream s/12,000). Open daily 7:30am-10pm.

Gemini's Restaurant, Salinas between Sucre and Bolívar. A wall-sized painting of the sun sets the tempo for this bright, international restaurant offering various plates for different budgets and palates. Spinach crepes (s/15,000) and chicken dishes (s/30,000) fulfill the promise of "Nice Food" painted over the door. Open W-M 10am-11pm.

Pizza Siciliana, Morales 510 and Sucre (tel. 09 789 931). Offers a wide range of pies, from personals to large and vegetables to meat (s/27-80,000). The usually dim and mellow restaurant comes alive on F and Sa nights with lights and live Andean music. Open daily noon-midnight.

Mi Otavalito (tel. 917 132), Sucre and Morales, is a local favorite specializing in *criollo* delicacies, though it also serves some scrumptious international plates in its pleasant courtyard setting. The menu includes *Trucha otavalito* (s/22,000) and a modest 4-course *menú del día* (s/20,000). Open daily 8am-9pm.

Terraza Café Sol, Jaramillo and Quiroga on the 4th floor of the building adjacent to the Vaz Cambio. The terrace provides phenomenal views of Poncho Plaza and the mountains to the east of Otavalo. Watch and see how the craft vendors, fruit peddlers, and market shoppers in and around the plaza make up a lively human tapestry, mimicking the most colorful *artesanías*. Only open Sa 7am-6pm.

SIGHTS

Otavalo is best known for its brilliant and sprawling market, which is most active on Saturdays but features vendors several days during the week. Though this is the only thing that most tourists come to see, there are several other attractions to occupy the time of casual visitors on non-market days.

THE MAIN MARKET. The uncontainable fanfare of the Saturday market starts in Poncho Plaza but overflows onto the surrounding streets, stretching blocks away. **Local weavings** are concentrated in the plaza and all along Sucre, where many *indígenas* set up booths in front of their shops. **Wood carvings** and **leather goods** abound, but some of the best are sold on Sucre and in the southeastern end of the market. The fried egg, pork, and potato aroma that permeates the entire market originates on Quiroga, where streetside stands cook up **market munchies** for all. Jaramillo, the most eclectic area, sells goods such as "genuine" Air Jordans and

SUMMERTIME IN IMBABURA When summer rolls around, craftspeople and farmers alike retire from their usual routine to pay tribute to the powers that be. The well-timed visitor will marvel at extraordinary local traditions, and, as always, should show respect. Stay out of the way, and never photograph people without their permission.

The summer solstice marks the week-long purification *Fiesta de San Juan* (or **Inty Raimi**), which honors John the Baptist and the Sun God, an excellent example of the convergence of the disparate religious traditions of Christianity and local indigenous beliefs. Revelers jump into nearby waterfalls or lakes, and men parade about in all sorts of costumes (from camouflage to cowboy chaps), dance in circles, sing, and throw back *chicha,* a potent alcoholic beverage of fermented corn. Try **Peguche** or **Cotacachi** on the summer solstice (usually June 21st or 22nd) for a first-hand glimpse of this almost indescribable tradition.

Later in the season, residents of nearby San Rafael strike up the **Fiesta de San Luís Obispo** on August 19th. It's a big day for the **coraza,** the richest man in town and master of ceremonies. With hair curled, he puts on his festival mask: an elaborate warrior helmet topped by feathers and dripping with gold and jewels hanging down to cover his face. After morning mass, he mounts his horse, flanked on either side by *yumbos* (attendants) and shielded by an umbrella held over his head. Then comes the long-awaited moment of honor. Once at the plaza, the *coraza* removes his mask, and onlookers attempt to draw blood by hurling stones at his face. The good times keep rolling for the next week straight.

Levi's jeans, as well as the more traditional **jewelry** and **hand-carved pipes.** Be especially careful with valuables along Jaramillo. As the most crowded street, it attracts deviously positioned **thieves** on market day.

Most tourists begin to arrive at the market around 10am, but it is a good idea to purchase goods earlier, as bargains *(gangas)* and discounts *(descuentos)* tend to be more common before demand escalates. Another good time is just before 3pm, when most vendors eagerly try to dispose of their inventory before closing. Even more bargains are available a full day early. In most cases, the starting price offered at the **Friday market** is lower than that on Saturday, although the sheer spectacle of the Saturday affair cannot be matched. *(On market days, vendors begin selling as early as 6:30am and pack up around 3pm.)*

THE ANIMAL AUCTION. An intriguing event occurs about an hour before the main market starts. At the weekly livestock auction, pigs of all sizes, cows, sheep, goats, and who knows what else squeal and moo, waking up sleepy ears and noses. Catching the early morning auction ensures that you'll beat the crowds to the main market. *(To get to the animal auction, take Colón or a parallel street west away from town, toward the Panamerican Highway, and follow the unmistakable sounds and smells.)*

MUSEO ARQUEOLÓGICO. This one-room museum houses over 10,000 archaeological relics found in different regions of Ecuador. The pieces were collected and operated by César Váquez Fuller, the museum's curator. See material artifacts belonging to indigenous groups as far back as 15,000 B.C., including flutes made from condor leg bones, skulls shaped and manipulated at birth, models of ancient astronomical observatories, and much more. The collection and César himself are both treasure chests of knowledge about the traditions and material culture of the indigenous peoples of Ecuador *(Montalvo and Roca, on the second floor of Hostería Los Andes. Tel. 921 290. Open whenever César is there. Admission s/10,000.)*

INSTITUTO OTAVALEÑO DE ANTROPOLOGÍA. The institute has an library with anthropological information on the history and culture of Otavalo *indígenas*. *(Along Av. de las Serances on the northern outskirts of town across the Panamerican Highway. Follow Sucre north out of town until you reach the Banco International and turn left; it will be on your left. Open Tu-F 8am-noon and 2:30-6:30pm. Admission free.)*

OTHER SIGHTS. The **Parque Rumiñahui,** in front of the municipal building, at the intersection of Sucre and Montalvo, is a great place to relax under shady trees and admire the 4,609m **Volcán Imbabura** (see p. 292) towering over the town's rooftops to the east. On Saturday afternoons, the corner of 31 de Octubre and Montalvo sometimes plays host to **cockfights.** And every day except Saturday, local men come out in the afternoons to play an intense match of **handball** along Quiroga on the far end of Poncho Plaza.

ENTERTAINMENT

Though not wild and crazy by any standard, Otavalo's nightlife is most easily found in a few quality **peñas** (with live music) that can spice up any weekend night. Most tourist-friendly establishments are concentrated along Morales between Jaramillo and Sucre. **Pizza Siciliana** (see **Food,** p. 280) has live music on weekend evenings (7:30-9:30pm) to start things off, but real dance clubs don't get going until later. **Peña Amauta** (tel. 922 435), Morales and Jaramillo, wins the best atmosphere award: an underground bamboo cellar with dim lighting, massive tapestries, and a fireplace. A small dance floor and plenty of tables provide a good view of local groups. Amauta also serves the mysterious and potent brew *guayusa,* made from fermented sugarcane with a touch of lemon (s/40,000 for a pitcher; cover s/10,000; open daily 8pm-2am).

Peña La Jampa, (tel. 922 988) is at Jaramillo and Morales. Groups shake and whittle in La Jampa's outdoor courtyard, which features a lively central dance floor framed by tables for the more timid or simply tired customers. (Cover s/10,000; peña and live music Th-Sa starting around 7pm. Restaurant open daily 8am-9:30pm.) The **Peña Tuparina,** Morales and 31 de Octubre, rumbles only seasonally. Huge speakers shake the earth when local bands play, usually on Fridays and Saturdays starting around 9:30pm (cover s/10,000).

Otavalo also has some more familiar *discotecas* that pulse out techno music and spit rainbow-colored lights around the club. **Peña Tucano,** Morales 8-10 and Sucre, thumps everything from *salsa* to reggae to pop (open W-Su 10pm-2am). Right across the street, **Peña Samay** attracts those anxious to dance or thirsty for a drink (open W-Su 10pm-2am). A little out of the way, **Habana Club,** (tel. 920 493) on the corner of Quito and 31 de Octubre, boasts four levels of nocturnal diversion: dancing, drinking, billiards, and ping-pong (cover s/20,000; open F-Su 9pm-3am).

NEAR OTAVALO

The indigenous villages and Andean landscape surrounding Otavalo also offer a multitude of diversions. Peguche, Agato, Laguna Cuicocha, Cotacachi, and Lagunas de Mojanda can be visited independently, but tour agencies also lead visits to these and other destinations. Most daytrip packages include transport and guide (US$15 per person). Some agencies can also arrange guides and transportation for people interested in climbing Volcán Cotacachi (US$25 per person), though few places have the necessary equipment. Horseback riding and visits to the local pyramids in Gualimán or to Nalgumbi natural springs can also be arranged.

NEAR OTAVALO: LAGUNAS DE MOJANDA

These three peaceful lakes are tucked away between the extinct volcano **Fuya Fuya** and a range of smaller rolling mountains situated 16km south of Otavalo. On a rare clear day, the views are astounding. The **hiking** trail begins to the right of **Laguna Grande,** the only lake immediately visible from the road. The path diverges at the far end of the lake. There is an oft-used dirt trail and a less-used path through the grass; the latter is on a steep bank and leads to another dirt trail. When choosing the road more traveled, admire the spectacular scenery, but also watch the ground; many horses travel this path, and this makes all the difference. The trail that cuts to the left winds around the back of **Montaña Pequeña,** leading to an amazing view of **Laguna Negra,** named because it is tightly surrounded by cliffs that keep the waters eternally shadowed. The path to the right leads to a view of the less spectacular **Laguna Chiquita,** providing glimpses of the misty mountaintops of Fuya

Fuya and Montaña Pequeña. From there the road forks a second time. Both paths go up Montaña Pequeña to Laguna Grande, but the right-hand one, though slightly longer, is less muddy. The walk to Laguna Chiquita takes 45 minutes each way; the complete walk around the three lagoons takes four hours.

Transportation: Taxis to Mojanda charge about s/100,000 for a round-trip with up to an hour at the lakes, but this price increases rapidly the longer you make the driver wait. A cheaper option is to take a cab up to the lakes and hike back (3½hr.). One could walk the whole way, but the trip is uphill and so steep that even buses can't navigate it. **Camionetas** from Otavalo's Poncho Plaza will generally charge the same fare as taxis but will probably be more reasonable concerning the wait at the lakes. You could also visit the lake as part of a travel agency trip, but they don't spend much time at Mojanda (US$15 a day). **Hitchhiking** is possible, but *Let's Go* does not recommend it. To **walk** to Mojanda, follow Sucre west to the outskirts of the city and cross the Panamerican Highway. A cobblestone road begins at the sign for the lagoons. When the road ends, you'll be face-to-face with the immense Laguna Grande. Often, a *camioneta* or vehicle of some sort can be flagged down on the walk back, but don't spend too much time waiting—it can get very cold.

NEAR OTAVALO: PEGUCHE

Peguche is situated roughly 4km northeast of Otavalo, between the Panamerican Highway and the Community of Agato. Known for the quality of its vibrant tapestries, this indigenous community is regarded as the most prosperous of Otavalo's satellite towns. Its affluence is betrayed by the strange rumblings that emanate from the tiny homes—the sound of electric weaving machines, a luxury unheard of in poorer communities. Despite the freshly-painted houses, foreign cars, and stores with fax numbers, success has not gone to locals' heads. Peguche is still a charming Ecuadorian town, and aside from a few *borrachos* during holidays, everyone still radiates friendliness.

Peguche's quiet central plaza, **Centro Pachacutic,** is home to the **Santa Lucía Church.** Streets do not have signs. With your back to the church, the road running right to left in front of you is **Calle Cascada,** a major thoroughfare. The cross street heading directly away from you is **Calle Principal.** On the left-hand corner of Principal and Cascada, **José Cotacachi's folklore shop** sells locally-made tapestries and bags and is an unofficial one-man tourist office. José answers questions regarding the history and culture of Peguche, provided you speak decent Spanish. Ask nicely and he'll escort you to a house to observe weaving in progress.

The **bus** line **8 de Septiembre** routinely travels between Plaza Copacabana in **Otavalo** and the central plaza of Peguche (30min., every 20min., s/1,000). **Transportes Imbaburac** has buses from the *terminal terrestre* in Otavalo to Peguche (30min., every 30min., s/1,000), which usually continue on to **Agato** (s/1,5000). Peguche's **Tenencia Política,** which serves as the local authority, is found by following Principal from the plaza to the railroad tracks and heading right (open daily 8am-noon and 2-6pm). Going left along the tracks, then taking the first right, leads to the **Subcentro de Salud,** Peguche's answer to Otavalo's **hospital.** It is a white building on the left with a fence and garden in front. (Open daily 8am-4pm.)

Though Peguche lacks anything resembling a formal restaurant, the two hostels in town serve up fine meals to the hungry. **Hostal Aya Huma** (tel. 922 663; fax 922 664; email ayahuma@uio.telconet.net) is by the train tracks between Principal and Loma Pucarára; just walk down Principal from the central plaza and turn left at the tracks. Soothing sounds of a trickling stream complement friendly, English-speaking owners and bright rainbow curtains woven at the hostal. Phone/fax, email, luggage storage, laundry, a mini-library, Spanish lessons, and hiking maps are all available. (Singles US$8, with bath US$14; doubles US$12, with bath US$20; triples US$15, with bath US$27.) The restaurant serves up hearty traditional meals (US$3) and has live music on Saturday (open daily 7am-8:30pm; bar open Su-F until 10pm, Sa until 11pm). **Peguche Tío Hostería** (tel./fax 922 619; email pegtio@uio.satnet.net) is about two minutes after the train tracks on your right. Just follow Principal from the plaza until its end. The impressive multi-purpose central building serves as a reception, restaurant, and *mirador* offering stunning views of monstrous Volcán Imbatura. All 12 *cabañas* surround the garden and are equipped with fireplaces and private hot-water baths. (Rooms s/36,000 per person.) The restaurant serves traditional indigenous food (US$2; open daily 8am-8pm).

LAS CASCADA DE PEGUCHE. Peguche, a name derived from the language of the *cayapa*, roughly translates as "sweet jumping of water." This undoubtedly describes Las Cascadas de Peguche, the well-shrouded, oasis-like waterfalls near the entrance to town. Tell the bus driver to drop you off at Loma Pucará or Las Cascadas. The waterfall is straight up the hill; walk up the path/road through the corn. Once at the ruins of Bohio at the top of the hill, take a right through the archway and follow signs through the forest for the waterfalls. If coming from the central plaza in town, take the aptly-named Calle Cascada out of town and keep on it through the arch when signs for the waterfalls should appear (15min.). From the forest entrance, it's a five-minute walk until the waterfall emerges through the misty air, but there are also beautiful trails through much of the woods. **Thieves** have been known to lurk in the forest; check to see if other hikers are around in the woods before starting out alone.

NEAR OTAVALO: AGATO

At first glance, Agato seems to be a ghost town. The dusty streets of this village, 3km southeast of Peguche and 8km northeast of Otavalo, are often empty except for the usual scattering of young children, roosters, and pigs. A barrage of questions may enter your mind. Where is everybody? Whose children are these? And why is this dog sniffing my leg? The answers are simple. The parents of these children, along with the rest of the town, are either hard at work on the looms within their homes or out in the fields tending crops of wheat, barley, corn, and potatoes.

Near the center of town, the **Tahuantinsuyo weaving workshop,** Rumiñahui 9 and Atahuallpa (tel. 921 547), is run by the jovial and internationally-renowned **Miguel Andrango,** who's usually happy to demonstrate Agato's unique hand-weaving process. Locals of Agato, unlike their high-tech neighbors in Peguche, use old-fashioned sit-down and backstrap looms, or sometimes *telaros de español*, larger looms that require the use of hands and feet at once. The tapestries, blankets, and sweaters produced in Agato are more expensive but are generally considered to be more carefully crafted than those of other towns. Miguel can also be persuaded to demonstrate the process of dying wool with vegetables or chemicals. Off-white, black, or brown wool is usually natural. Miguel's goods don't make it to the market in Otavalo; his workshop in Agato is the only place to make a purchase.

Transportation: The **bus** lines **8 de Septiembre** and **Cooperativo Imbaburapaq** both go to Agato from Otavalo (45min., s/1,500), but Imbaburapaq is faster because it doesn't always stop in Peguche. The steep uphill **walk** from Peguche may be grueling, but the views are brilliant. From the central plaza in Peguche you have two options for reaching Agato on foot. One path leads out of town up the same hill leading to Las Cascadas (see Peguche, above). At the fork in the road, take the dirt path on the left up the hill. Going straight leads you through the archway on the path to the falls. When the path uphill makes a 3-way fork, keep to the far left and follow the road until you reach Rumiñahui, the main street in Agato, and turn left for the town center and weaving workshop. Alternatively, go right from Peguche's central plaza until the roadway dead ends, turn right again and follow the road up the hill until you reach Rumiñahui street and the town center. The stroll along the hill above Las Cascadas provides glimpses of glistening **Laguna San Pablo.**

NEAR OTAVALO: COTACACHI

Endowed with more leather than a sadomasochist's dream, Cotacachi is Ecuador's leather work capital. Planted 12km northwest of Otavalo under the watchful eye of **Mount Cotacachi** (4,939m), the town of the same name sells leather goods of sublime quality at relatively low prices. None of this is sold in Otavalo; the truly leather-hungry are forced to come here. The town hosts a **Sunday Market** at Parque

San Francisco which spreads out onto 10 de Agosto, but if you've just come from Otavalo, Cotacachi's version is only mildly amusing. The well-timed can visit Cotacachi during its sun festival in late June where locals, dressed in camouflage, gorilla masks, or **cardboard wizard hats,** dance for hours in the Parque de la Matriz. Use caution, though, because the dancing often erupts into fighting, and police wait ready with cans of tear gas should they become necessary.

The town's two parts, the mostly concrete **Parque San Francisco,** along **10 de Agosto** between **Tarquí** and **Rocafuerte,** and the palm tree-lined **Parque de la Matriz** along **Peñaherrera** between **Suarez** and **Bolívar,** serve as geographic points of reference for the traveler. Buses entering Cotacachi turn off the flag-lined **Camino del Sol** and enter the town along Peñaherrera passing **Parque de la Matriz** on their way to the **terminal terrestre,** just out of town at the top of 10 de Agosto.

Buses to **Otavalo** can be picked up at the corner of Sucre and 10 de Agosto, or on Peñaherrera near the park (45min., every 15min. until 6pm, s/2,000). Buses to **Cotacachi** leave from the *terminal terrestre* in Otavalo and are sent by both **Transportes Cotacachi** and **6 de Julio** (45min., every 15min. until 6pm, s/2,000). A **taxi** ride from Otavalo is faster but much more expensive (15min., s/30,000). **Banco Pichincha** (tel. 915 456; fax 915 491), Imbabura and Tarquí, just off the Parque San Francisco, exchanges cash and traveler's checks (open M-F 8am-6pm). The **Police,** Rocafuerte 10-36 and Imbabura, are just up from San Francisco (open 24hr). Up one block parallel to Rocafuerte is Av. Moncayo, which leads out toward **Hospital Asdrubal de la Toree** (tel. 915 118; fax 915 506), Moncayo and Luís Moreno, with an ambulance service and free consultations (open 24hr.). The local **post office,** Peñaherrara and Bolívar, lies to the right side of the old church in Parque de la Matriz (open M-Sa 8am-6pm). The **EMETEL** office, Sucre 1427 and Peñaherrara, is up one block from La Matriz (open M-Sa 8am-6pm).

If you decide to spend the night in town, try the centrally-located **Hostal Plaza Bolívar,** Bolívar 12-26 and 10 de Agosto (tel. 915 327). Owners Marcelo and Janet are wonderful hosts and make visitors feel at home: they even offer each of their guests a complimentary soda, coffee, or tea upon arrival. Private baths with hot water and towels, washing machines, luggage storage, and kitchen access round out the amenities. (Rooms s/25,000-35,000 per person.) If you have no other options, stay at **Hostal Bachita,** Sucre 16-82 (tel. 915 063), just past Peñaherrera. There, you'll find very modest rooms and private hot-water baths (s/30,000 per person). For a quick and affordable meal, try the **Delicia Casera,** Sucre 11-23 and 10 de Agosto (tel. 915 161). Ponder the decor, which juxtaposes a Last Supper reproduction with a poster of Pamela Anderson, while snacking on a typical *almuerzo* (s/5,000) and a mammoth soda (s/2,500). **Restaurante Inty Huasi,** Bolívar 11-08 and 10 de Agosto (tel. 915 789), serves up traditional specialties like *trucha marinera* (s/24,000) as well as more ordinary entrees (open daily 9am-10pm). **El Leñador** (tel. 915 083), Sucre and Juan Montalvo, is somewhat pricey (entrees s/17-24,000), but the good food and pleasant staff make up for it (open daily 7am-10pm).

Craft shops around town sell everything from leather jackets to purses to briefcases. Most accept credit cards, but give discounts of up to 10% to cash customers. **El Palacio del Cuero** (tel. 915 490; fax 915 286), 10 de Agosto and Bolívar, is among the largest (open daily 9am-6:30pm). If you take Moreno up from the park toward Sucre, you find Cotacachi's **Museo de las Culturas,** Moreno and Bolívar, on the left side of the road (open daily 8am-noon and 2-5pm). The museum house exhibits on the *artesanía*, traditions, customs, and myths. If you can not make it to Cotacachi to see any of the local festivals, you can content yourself here with views of mannequins frozen in contortions of ecstasy.

NEAR COTACACHI: LAGUNA DE CUICOCHA

Strange stories surround the Laguna de Cuicocha, which rests at the southern foot of Mount Cotacachi and 13km west of the town. The lake's name comes from the *cuy* (guinea pigs) that inexplicably proliferate on the two islands in the lake, even though nothing lives in the water. More mysterious, according to local lore, a monstrously large condor makes a sweeping flight to the islands between 4 and 5pm every day. Many have tried to record the creature's epic flight on film, but somehow, normally dependable cameras seem to fail when charged with this task. Perhaps part of the mystique comes from the lake's curious location inside the mouth of a live volcanic crater; locals commonly fear that the volcano will erupt and flood the surrounding area with lava and water. There's a guided boat tour of the lake that details the species of plants and animals living on the islands and gives many geological statistics (30min., s/10,000 per person, s/50,000 total for 6 people).

Transportation: The curious take a **taxi** or a *camioneta* up the hill to the lake (roundtrip s/60,000), the adventurous **walk** all the way (2½hr.), and the strong of leg (read: insane) ride **bikes** up. The least expensive option is to take the **bus** from either Otavalo (s/2,000) or Cotacachi (s/1,000) to **Quiroga,** a small town about 5km from Cotacachi, and take a taxi or *camioneta* from there (s/30,000). The **hike** around the whole lake is beautiful but can take up to six hours. Stay long enough and maybe you'll catch a glimpse of the elusive condor.

APUELA

Apuela's attractions begin with the bus ride there. As the bumpy road approaches town, the scenery becomes more and more staggering, with jaw-dropping views of western Andean cloudforests. Depending on the time of day and season, one may even peer down through the flora at the clouds below. Some locals also swear that likenesses of the Virgin Mary and Rumiñahui have been naturally sculpted by the elements on the face of the mountains. After imbibing some of the locally brewed *trago*, you might experience the miracle too—or at least gain peace of mind as the bus treads inches from precipitous mountain cliffs.

Agreeably symmetrical, Apuela is flanked by a small mountain on either side and crossed by two parallel rivers that form the town's natural boundaries. Within Apuela, two major roads run parallel to the rivers. The one entering town is officially called **Av. 20 de Julio,** although locals simply shrug and say that it's never needed a name. The dusty **central plaza** behind the bus stop has a volleyball court and a small, dilapidated **church.** Apuela's other major street, **García Moreno** (most Apuelans are confident about this name), runs parallel to 20 de Julio on the other side of the plaza. The Apuela **bus stop** is on 20 de Julio. From here, buses run to **Otavalo** (3hr., 8 per day 9am-2:30pm, s/13,500) and **García Moreno** (1hr.; 10:30am, 12:30, and 3:30pm; s/6,500) via the **Piscinas Nangulví** (s/2,000). Apuela's police station, along García Moreno, is across from the bus stop (open 24hr.). The **centro de salud** is on 20 de Julio, 30m up the road from the bus stop (open Su-F 8am-noon and 2-5pm). The **post office** is in the same building as the **police** (open M-F 8am-noon and 2-6pm). Find the only phone next door at **EMETEL** (tel. 957 657); its phone number functions as the town's **emergency line** (open daily 8am-noon and 2-6pm).

The accommodations in Apuela are so unimpressive that it's better to stay at the *cabañas* just outside of town. If matters get desperate, **Residencial Don Luís** provides a cheap night's stay and a smile. For a cold shower, go outside to the communal bathroom. (Rooms s/20,000 per person.) A 45-minute walk in the same direction as the *piscinas* (see below) will land you at the **Cabañas Río Grande** (tel. 920 442 or 920 548). Follow the main highway out of town and, after crossing the second bridge, take a left. The site is surrounded by papaya, banana, and lime trees. Spotless three-person *cabañas* have electricity and private hot-water baths. (Rooms s/25,000 per person, *cabañas* s/65,000.) There are a few places to eat in town. The **Restaurant La Estancia,** 20 de Julio across from the bus stop, is the local gathering spot. The three daily staples cost s/8,000 each and the fruit juice is fantastic. (Open daily 6am-9pm.) Just up the road, the dimly-lit **El Rincón del Buen Sabor** offers another setting for inexpensive meals.

Towering at 2000m altitude, the hills that surround Apuela are criss-crossed with paths that make for good hiking, and the rivers on either side of town are renowned for their trout fishing. One way to explore the surrounding lands is to get off the Apuela-bound bus in **Santa Rosa,** a small town at the top of a hill, and then hike down to Apuela, in the valley below.

From Apuela, a one-hour walk leads to the **Museo de Arqueología** (admission s/ 10,000) and the minor ruins of **Gualimán,** a site consisting of pre-Inca burial grounds and a small pyramid. Gualimán can be reached on foot by following the highway out of town and taking a right at the second bridge. For an easy-going day, **Piscinas Nangulví,** a set of natural hot springs, are located about 45 minutes from Apuela next to the Cabañas Río Grande. Follow the main highway out of town and, after crossing the second bridge, take a left. Locals pipe hot water from a nearby volcanic crater into three jacuzzi-like wading areas and a 15m pool. An even bigger pool is kept cold, providing a refreshing plunge for the overheated hot-tub-soaker. (Admission s/4,000.)

NEAR APUELA: INTAG CLOUDFOREST

Situated on the verdant western slopes of the Andes, this privately owned reserve protects a small portion of Ecuador's endangered cloudforests, over 90% of which have been destroyed. To combat the deforestation from agriculture and mining, proprietors Carlos and Sandy Zorilla have tried to purchase as much of the land as possible. Guests help the Zorillas' endeavor by paying rates as steep as the surrounding mountains, but the experience awaiting in the reserve is worth it.

WILDLIFE. With elevations of 1750 to 2800m and temperatures ranging from 12 to 27°C (55-80°F), Intag Cloudforest is a dynamic place. Particular combinations of clouds, fog, and constant humidity produce an incredible variety of flora and fauna. There is a plethora of **epiphytes** (plants that grow on other plants and trees), including orchids, bromeliads, and araceas. Medicinal plants such as **sangre de drago,** only recently discovered by modern medicine to cure child respiratory viruses, also grow here amongst the ferns and mosses. The mammals that live in the region—spectacled bears, pumas, spider monkeys, and mountain tapirs—tend to elude observation, as most are nocturnal and afraid of humans. Plants and animals alike are threatened by deforestation and are in danger of extinction. While mammals are a rare sight, the forest is a birdwatcher's paradise; about 180 different species of bird have been identified, including 22 species of hummingbird.

LOGISTICS. A stay on the reserve includes lodging, vegetarian meals, and a bilingual guide. Simple wood cabins have sturdy roofs and straw mats for the walls. All beds come equipped with thick blankets for those chilly mountain nights. Solar-heated water flows inside rustic outdoor showers. Carlos and Sandy only accept groups of six or more and demand a minimum stay of two nights. If lacking a group, contact them a few weeks in advance, and they can place you in one. (US$45 per person per night.) The Zorillas require reservations: write or fax them a few months in advance at Casilla 18, Otavalo, Imbabura, Ecuador (tel./fax 923 392 in Otavalo).

IBARRA

A peculiar balance between past and present exists in Ibarra. After an earthquake destroyed much of the city in 1868, the survivors were left with the monumental task of piecing the rubble back together. Whether by chance or intention, they built many of the public buildings and business centers in the southern half of the city and most of the colonial-style, white-with-red-tile homes in the northern half. This duality persists today; Ibarra's professionals and politicians race into modernity in their taxis, buses, and Mercedes Benzes, while the northern half of the city resounds with the clatter of horse-drawn buggies on cobblestone avenues. Even this provincial capital's culture has reached a balanced equilibrium. Ibarra is one of the few Ecuadorian cities where all three major ethnicities are successfully integrated: black, indigenous, and *mestizo.* Though not much of a tourist city, Ibarra does offer some peaceful parks and plazas and serves as a good stopping point on the way to or from Colombia, Quito, or Otavalo. One advantage Ibarra offers the visitor is a warmer climate than that of its Sierran neighbors, thanks to favorable meteorological patterns and a relatively "low" elevation (2225m).

ORIENTATION

Buses from Quito and Otavalo drop visitors off along **Borja** and **Vacas Galindo,** on the western outskirts of town, or along **Av. Mariano Acosta** near the market on **Av. Guerrero.** If you are not dropped off in the *centro*, walk a short distance toward Mt. Imbabura and take a left on Mariano Acosta. The immense **obelisk,** visible from a distance, serves as a good landmark. Following Mariano Acosta toward the obelisk leads you to the heart of things.

Beyond the obelisk traffic circle, the street changes names to **Av. Velasco** and intersects the parallel streets **Olmedo, Bolívar,** and **Sucre,** which host the majority of hotels and restaurants. Three blocks away from the obelisk, east-west **Flores** passes **Parque La Merced** and, two blocks to the east, **Parque Pedro Moncayo.** One block north of the obelisk, east-west **Pedro Moncayo** runs the width of the city, splitting Ibarra into two manageable halves. North of Moncayo, the city is calmer and you're more likely to find interesting architecture and historical monuments. To the south, buildings are gray and menacing, and the city is more frantic.

PRACTICAL INFORMATION

Trains: The **train station** (tel. 915 390) is the dilapidated brown building just southwest of the obelisk as you enter town (follow Espejo away from the obelisk). The train goes to **San Lorenzo** (8hr.; M, W, F, and Su 7am; US$20). It is often full, so get there early to buy a ticket; they are only sold on the day of departure, starting at 6:30am. Check after 5pm the night before to find out if the train is running. As of August 1999, damage sustained from El Niño flooding in 1997-98 combined with a lack of public funds has left the track in ill repair and the train inoperative. Check with the railroad administration in Quito to see if the line is running before trekking to Ibarra for the ride. When the train is running, the trip can take up to 12hr. depending on the number of stops, the weather, and the farm animals on the tracks. A lot of people **ride on the roof** of the train; the view is incredible, and it's especially thrilling going through tunnels and over skinny bridges. Keep your passport handy, because there may be occasional document checks along the way. As always, keep an eye on your bags.

Buses: As a provincial capital and transportation hub, Ibarra has a number of bus lines with routes serving most of the northern highlands and the Ecuadorian coast. Buses usually leave from the headquarters of their respective company—most of them lie to the west of the obelisk. Buses leave to: **Esmeraldas** (9hr., every 2hr. 6:45am-2:45pm, s/65,000); **Guayaquil** (10½hr., 8pm, s/85,000); **Otavalo** (35min., every 15min. 5am-8pm, s/4,000); **Quito** (2½hr., every hr. 1pm-10pm, s/20,000); **San Lorenzo** (6hr., 4 per day 6am-2pm, s/45,000); and **Tulcán** (2½hr., every 30min. 5:30am-7pm, s/18,000). **28 de Septiembre** runs **local buses** up and down Mariano Acosta (s/1,000).

Taxis: Can be found in parks and near bus stations. **Cooperativo Pasquel Monge** (tel. 915 415), at the train station, and **Cooperativo Los Lagos** (tel. 955 150) are 2 of the most trustworthy companies. The minimum for local rides is s/10,000.

Tourist Information: The **Ministry of Tourism** is at Olmedo 956 (tel. 958 759; fax 958 547), between Moncayo and Velasco. Open M-F 8:30am-1pm and 2-5pm.

Banks: Banco La Previsora, Sánchez y Cifuentes 10-98 and Velasco (tel. 955 900; fax 957 295), exchanges cash but doesn't accept traveler's checks. Offers a 24hr. Visa and Plus **ATM** and Visa cash advances. Open M-F 9am-4pm, Sa 9am-2pm. **Banco del Pacífico** (tel. 957 728), Olmedo and Moncayo, changes cash and traveler's check. Additionally, they have a 24hr. Cirrus and MC **ATM**. Open M-Sa 9am-3pm.

Library: Bolívar and Flores, in the municipal building. Open M-F 8am-12:30pm and 2:30-6pm.

Supermarket: Supermaxi, Mariano Acosta on the road to Otavalo. **28 de Septiembre** buses marked "San Antonio" or "Supermaxi" stop at the obelisk (s/1,000). Or take a free red shuttle marked "Supermaxi." Open M-Sa 9:30am-8pm, Su 9:30am-7pm. In the *centro*, **Comisariato del Patronato Municipal,** on the corner of Bolívar and Colón, serves your grocery needs. Open M-Sa 8am-8pm and Su 9am-1pm.

Emergency: Tel. 101.

Police: Villamar 120 and Olmedo (tel. 950 444).

Pharmacies: Can be found on almost every street in town. If you are having trouble finding a reliable one, try **Farmacia Ross,** Velasco 8110 and Narváez (tel. 952 220). Open M-Sa 7:30am-8pm, Su 7:30am-12:30pm.

Medical Services: Hospital San Vicente de Paul, Luís Vargas Torres 1-156 (**emergency** tel. 131 or 950 666; tel. 957 272). Free emergency treatment, consultations, lab work, and X-rays. Open 24hr. with ambulance service. **Clínica Mariano Acosta,** Mariano Acosta 1116 (**emergency** tel. 642 211; tel. 950 924), is a 24hr. emergency clinic.

Post Office: Salinas 664 and Oviedo (tel. 950 412; fax 958 038), has *lista de correos*. Open M-F 8am-7pm, Sa 8am-1pm. **Western Union** and **DHL:** (Tel. 957 766; fax 955 270), Rocafuerte and Flores, available in the Intipungo office. Open M-F 9am-1:30pm and 3-6pm, Sa 9am-1pm.

Internet Access: Nov@net Cybercafe, Bolívar 969 and Colón, in the lobby of Hostal Ejecutivo (tel. 956 575 or (09) 696 486), offers internet connections (s/800 per min., s/ 50,000 per hr.). Open M-Sa 9am-9pm.

Telephones: EMETEL, Sucre 4-48 and Moreno, allows international calls but charges for use of the *cabina* (s/350 per min.). Open daily 8am-10pm.

PHONE CODE	06

ACCOMMODATIONS

While there is certainly no shortage of rooms in Ibarra, high-quality rooms at moderate prices can be hard to come by. If you can rough it (i.e. cold water, cracked ceilings, and less-than-clean bathrooms), you'll be like a kid in a candy store here. Most budget accommodations congregate along Olmedo or near the train station, in prime position for you to wake up late and race to catch that morning departure. Just make sure they don't rent their rooms by the hour.

Hotel Imbabura, Oviedo 9-33 (tel. 950 155; fax 958 521), between Narváez and Cifuentes, 1½ blocks from Parque La Merced. Wood-paneled floors and simple cots decorate otherwise barren rooms. Flair can be found elsewhere: in the courtyard with an old fountain, in the lounge with an impressive mini-bottle collection, and in the invaluable information on tours and trips. Rooms s/25,000 per person.

La Casona de los Lagos (HI), Sucre 350 and Grijalva (tel. 957 844; fax 951 629), is one of the city's few remaining old hotels. Saddles line the balcony of the indoor courtyard and plants rest above the outdoor patio of this establishment. Other comforts include a tea room, pool table, and bar. Simple rooms all have private baths. Rooms s/50,000 per person, with HI cards/30,000.

Residencial San Andrecito (tel. 958 644), Cifuentes and Oviedo. Ultra-low prices, but you get what you (don't) pay for. Virtually empty rooms leave plenty of space for large backpacks. Rooms s/15,000 per person.

Hostal Madrid, Olmedo 869 and Moncayo (tel. 643 903). Unlike the Spanish capital, this Madrid is recently constructed and immaculately clean. Each room in the centrally located hostel has a private bath and cable TV. Rooms s/50,000 per person.

Residencial Magestic (tel. 950 052), Olmedo between Oviedo and Flores. Though hallways are dim and rooms slightly musty, the low price and private hot-water baths make these flaws forgiveable. Rooms s/13,500 per person, with bath s/15,000.

FOOD

Ibarra's dining options are severely limited, a sad state of affairs for a busy provincial capital. Ask Ibarrans where to find a good restaurant, and they'll be as stumped as you are. There are, however, a few options; the town is inundated with sidewalk vendors, tiny bakeries, and snack food establishments, and it's easy to find a typical *almuerzo* spot around the parks. A few exceptional eateries redeem the culinary failures of this colonial town.

Helados de Paila Rosalía Suárez, Oviedo 7-82 and Olmedo (tel. 958 772). A wooden cutout of Mickey Mouse welcomes you to this homemade ice cream shop and Ibarran tradition. Photos of Rosalía's family, the occasional supermodel pin-up, and a photograph of a former President of Ecuador (and favorite customer) co-exist on the walls. Slide down the old-fashioned fireman's pole before sitting down to a *copa* of ice cream (2 scoops s/5,000). A variety of flavors ranging from raspberry to guanabana to *leche* are all made early in the morning right in the shop. Open daily 7:30am-7:30pm.

Café Arte, Salinas 5-43 and Flores (tel. 950 806), is both a cafe and an art gallery. Little wooden menus in the shape of cupboards contain a unique combination of coffees (s/4,000-6,500), Mexican specialties (s/9-15,000), and cocktails (*Azul de Picasso* s/15,000). Cultural films and concerts on weekends. Open M-Th 4-11pm, F-Sa 4pm-whenever the crowd goes home.

El Cedrón (tel. 958 562), Olmedo and Flores. Incredibly low-priced *merienda* (s/7,000) makes this spot popular among locals. Proprietor Oscar Carvajal and family try to accommodate vegetarians by substituting an avocado—or whatever you like—for meat portions. Eat and be entertained by the latest *telenovela.* Open daily 6:30am-9:30pm.

Café Coffee Kaffee, Moreno 404 and Rocafuerte (tel. 640 438 or 951 848). This redundantly named favorite is filled with an aura of romance. The red velvet seats and slow, mellow music complement a divine cappuccino sprinkled with chocolate (s/10,000). Hamburgers (s/10,000), sandwiches (s/12,000), and other snacks also served. Open M-Th 4-10pm, F 4pm-1am, Sa 6pm-1am.

El Horno Pizzería, Rocafuerte 6-38 and Flores (tel. 959 019 or 958 508). Tasty pizzas, though lacking tomato sauce (an endless source of frustration throughout Ecuador). The "El Horno" comes with peppers, meat, onions, cheese, and tomatoes (small s/27,000, large s/42,000). Alternatively, the "Vegetarian" has cheese, carrots, cucumbers, peppers, mushrooms, and onions. Open Tu-Su 6pm-midnight.

Mr. Peter's (958 539), Oviedo and Bolívar, suits all tastes, with hamburgers (s/10-20,000), salads (s/15-20,000), and build-your-own meat or meatless soft tacos (s/18,000) as well as traditional Ecuadorian *platos fuertes* (s/20-25,000). 10% discount with ISIC card. Open daily 11am-midnight.

SIGHTS

For a city of its size, Ibarra is a bit lacking in entertainment. However, it is home to many interesting historical and architectural structures. Rising more than 30m high, the stunning white **obelisk** at Narváez and Velasco sticks out like a sore thumb in its surroundings. The landmark looks more like a monument to Cleopatra than a dedication to Miguel de Ibarra, founder of this Spanish colony (1606).

PUBLIC PARKS. Ibarra has two peaceful parks, both surrounded by outstanding architecture. **Parque La Merced,** on Flores between Cifuentes and Olmedo, exhibits a statue of Dr. Victor Manuel Peñaherrera (1865-1930), an Ecuadorian Supreme Court judge, looking quite distinguished. On the west side of the park, the **Basílica La Merced** supports a portrayal of the Virgin Mary adorned with a crown of silver. Within the *basílica* is an elaborate gold altar that reaches up to the 20m high arched ceiling. Be prepared to view it through barred windows, though; the *basílica* is only sporadically open to the public, usually early in the mornings during the week and on Sundays when mass is celebrated.

The eclectic **Parque Moncayo** is on Flores between Bolívar and Sucre. The surrounding architecture is exceptional, especially that of the **cathedral** and the municipal building. While the golden altar outshines most everything else in the cathedral, the building also houses huge portraits of all 12 apostles, painted by local artist Rafael Troya. Again, though, entrance may not be possible—be prepared to gaze upon the artistry from the outside. If you follow Moncayo to its easternmost point, you'll run right into the **Iglesia de San Francisco,** the final resting place of Ibarra's Franciscan forefathers.

ENTERTAINMENT

On weekends, the **Cine Grand Columbia,** on Moreno between Sucre and Rocafuerte, sometimes shows cultural films; stop by to check a schedule. The two-story **Baraka,** on Rocafuerte between Mospuera and Rosales, offers plenty of space for dancing as well as a pool table and full bar. Saturday nights are the wildest. (Open Th-Sa 9pm-2am) **Tequila Rock,** Oviedo 636 and Sucre, is much tighter but closer to the center of town (cover s/20,000, includes a drink.) **Café Arte** has live music on the weekends and occasional cultural movies (M and Th 8pm, Sa 4pm, Su 5pm). Both **Café Coffee Kaffee** and **El Horno Pizzería** sometimes host live singers or groups on weekends. Car-endowed Ibarrans escape to **Laguna Yahuarcocha** ("Lake of Blood") in Quichua, for some fresh air and great views of the surrounding valley. Those not too frightened by the creepy name sometimes rent canoes (s/25,000 for 30min.) or jog around the rim of the lake, only 9km north of Ibarra. The town also boasts an **autodromo** that occasionally hosts Formula 1 races.

NEAR IBARRA: SAN ANTONIO DE IBARRA

With its economy firmly rooted in exquisite **woodcarving,** San Antonio de Ibarra caters to tourists with a hankering for a carved chess sets, exquisite wooden unicorns, or religious sculptures. The town has little else to offer, but the work is of such quality that it has carved a place for itself among the South American *artesanía* elite. San Antonio's woodwork stands out because of its meticulous, stunning precision. People from across the Americas flock to San Antonio to witness the town's handiwork and buy a piece or two. Only recently has San Antonio become known for its craft worldwide, but already many shops sell pieces overseas, and the influx of foreign visitors continues to increase.

San Antonio is west of Ibarra along the Panamerican Highway. The layout is simple. **Av. 27 de Noviembre** is the main street and runs from the town center, **Parque Francisco Calderón,** to the Panamerican Highway. Most of the woodcarving galleries are either around the park or along 27 de Noviembre.

The **Hostería Nogales,** Sucre 365 (tel. 932 000), behind the dirt *fútbol* field along 27 de Noviembre on the way up the hill, is the only place to stay in San Antonio. Nogales's extremely basic rooms betray its lack of competitors. (Rooms s/15,000 per person.) The town's only dining establishment is the **Restaurante El Rancho,** on Cevallos by Parque Calderón, on the second floor. Though not much to look at, it is a great place to look from, offering a wonderful view of the park and Imbabura. It serves run-of-the-mill Ecuadorian cuisine for few *sucres* (*almuerzos* s/7-10,000; open Tu-Su 8am-4pm).

THE WOODWORKING SHOPS. The **Unión Artesanal de San Antonio de Ibarra,** at the far end of the Parque Calderón, is a set of 12 woodcarving cooperatives that sell pieces straight from the tables they're made on. This is the best place to watch the work in progress, and workshop #1 even offers occasional classes in woodworking. Many shops carry very similar carvings, but there are always a few unique pieces to be found. Though the Unión shops accept Visa and American Express, the best discounts go to cash customers. (Open daily 9am-8pm.) To the east side of the park, the **Galería de Arte Luís Potosí** (tel. 932 056) has several rooms and two floors of work a little finer and more detailed than the offerings in other shops (open daily 8am-6pm). More shops line 27 de Noviembre towards the Panamerican Highway. Some of these galleries produce larger works, some as tall as 2m, and carry a multitude of abstract, modernist carvings. The furniture shops are farther down 27 de Noviembre. (Most shops open daily 9am-7pm.)

TRANSPORTATION. Buses from Ibarra drop passengers off on the Panamerican Highway, at the edge of town (10min., every 15min., s/1,000). From here, **taxis** go directly to the heart of San Antonio (s/4,000), but the uphill walk from the Panamerican Highway to the town center only takes about 10 minutes. **Cooperativo 28 de Septiembre** and **San Miguel de Ibarra** both go up the hill to the park and can be caught on the obelisk, near the corner of Acosta and Chica Narvaz (10min., every 20min., s/1,000; sign says "San Antonio"). A taxi from Ibarra should cost s/15,000.

NEAR IBARRA: LA ESPERANZA

Life is more or less peaceful as you head out of Ibarra toward La Esperanza, 7km south. The idyllic landscape, punctuated by Volcán Imbabura and other majestic mountains, encourages clear thinking and deep breathing. This tranquility is interrupted only by the groaning of buses struggling their way uphill and the occasional truck filled with military men rumbling towards the neighboring citadel. La Esperanza really has just one road, **Galo Plaza,** which runs towards Imbabura. Nearly all attractions in the town are accessed from this cobblestone roadway.

The walk down to the Río Tahuando, which leads to Ibarra, is painless and pleasurable. Head down Galo Plaza from Casa Aida (see below), take a right at the first cross street, and continue for 30 minutes. For a more serious trek, try getting to the top of Loma Cubilche (3836m). Facing Imbabura, Cubilche is the smaller mountain to the left. To get there, head up Galo Plaza from Casa Aida, cross the dry-river bridge, and turn right immediately. Follow this road all the way to the top. (Expect a 3hr. hike up and 2hr. return.)

Die-hard climbers often use La Esperanza as a base before attempting **Volcán Imbabura** (4621m). Those who dare should leave early in the morning, as the climb takes over 10 hours. To get to Imbabura, head toward Cubilche, but turn right on the street just before the bridge. This road goes most of the way up, and various paths lead to the top. Esperanza has a few resident guides available for this hike.

A unique accommodation, **Casa Aida** (tel. 642 020) is a green and yellow building on the right, far up the hill from Ibarra. It consists of a number of traditional dormitories as well as a more exciting five-person straw hut with two beds in a loft accessible only by step ladder. Thick brick walls and blankets provide plenty of warmth on frigid nights, and the kitchen and baths are impeccably clean. Common baths have 24-hour hot water. (Rooms s/25,000 per person.) Casa Aida also has one of the only **restaurants** in La Esperanza. Outdoor dining in the vegetable garden provides a view of the grand Imbabura in its entirety, as well as of a smaller volcanic chunk that was blown off in an eruption 130 years ago. Indoor dining around the fireplace is just as pleasant, but the food is really the rage, especially the cornmeal pancakes with berry sauce (s/10,000) and Aida's veggie dishes (s/12,000).

Transportation: Buses from Ibarra to Esperanza (30min., every 20min., s/1,800) can be picked up at the Parque Grijalva on the corner of Sánchez y Cifuentes and Toro Moreno, or at the southernmost end of Ibarra, on the corner of De La Torre and Retorno. **Taxis** from anywhere in Ibarra charge about s/30,000 for the trip to Esperanza. If your boots are made for walking, the two-hour **hike** to La Esperanza is along Retorno, the main road. Exhaust fumes prove unpleasant from time to time, but the scenic walk takes you through some of Ibarra's ritzier neighborhoods, offering a glimpse of how the upperclass lives (look for the pale green replica of the Taj Mahal on the right).

TULCÁN

There are only three reasons to go to Tulcán: you are going to Colombia, you are coming from Colombia, or you know someone who lives there. Tulcán's importance lies in its crossroads status. Whether they're about to cross the border, or have just arrived, tourists here are always in transit. Colombians cross the border to take advantage of the favorable exchange rate, purchasing anything from plastic chairs to groceries to pharmaceuticals to toilet paper. For those rare few who have time to kill, there's a topiary garden within the cemetery along Cotopaxi between Venezuela and Ambato. Filled with bushes and trees pruned into arches, birds, and elephants, the garden is a magical respite from the race to the border.

ORIENTATION AND PRACTICAL INFORMATION

Most of the action can be found along parallel streets **Colón, Olmedo, Sucre, Bolívar,** and **Arellano,** which run the length of town. Right in the center of things is the **Parque Principal** (sometimes called the **Plaza Central**), between Sucre, Olmedo, Ayacucho, and 10 de Agosto. The bigger **Parque Isidro Ayora,** between Arellano and Bolívar, is two blocks southeast of the enormous **cemetery.** The **terminal terrestre** is located 1½km uphill from the *centro* on Bolívar. The **Colombian border** is northeast of town, 6km down **Av. Brazil,** which begins at the northeast end of town.

Buses: Only taxis and minivans go to the border from Tulcán (see below). All buses leave from the *terminal terrestre.* To: **Quito** (6hr., every hr. 1:30am-10:30pm, s/36,000) via **Ibarra** (3hr., s/15,000) and **Otavalo** (4hr., s/20,000).

Local Buses: Transportes Popular buses run from the *terrestre* to the **Parque Principal** (5min., s/1,000). Buses go down Sucre or Colón and return on Bolívar. **Cooperativo Carchi** vans can be picked up on the Venezuela side of Parque Ayora and go to the border as soon as they fill up (s/5,000).

Tourist Information: Ministerio de Turismo (tel. 983 892), in the CENAF building at Romicacha bridge. Open M-F 8:30am-1pm and 1:30-5pm.

Travel Agency: EcoTur (tel. 980 468; fax 980 368), Sucre at Parque Principal. National and international tours. Open M-F 8:30am-1pm and 2:30-6pm, Sa 8:30am-1pm.

Currency Exchange: Banco Pichincha (tel. 980 529), Sucre and 10 de Agosto, changes cash and traveler's checks. Open M-F 8am-2pm. A number of exchange offices and street changers congregate along Ayacucho to cater to Tulcán's shopping tourists.

Emergency: Tel. 101 or 980 101.

Police: (Tel. 981 321 or 980 345), Manabí and Guatemala, to the north. Open 24hr.

Post Office: Bolívar 53027 and Junín (tel. 980 552). Open M-F 8am-7pm, Sa 9am-noon.

TELEPHONE CODE: 06

ACCOMMODATIONS

Unless you want to spend more than s/100,000 per person, your accommodations in Tulcán will probably not be the most elegant. There are still plenty of affordable places to rest, but none glow with ambiance. Calle Sucre, just west of the Parque Principal, hops with lodgings—some ritzy, some reasonable, some dreary.

Hotel Internacional Azteca (tel. 981 447; fax 980 481), Bolívar and Atahuallpa, one block west of Parque Ayora, by a *centro comercial,* on the 2nd floor, above a *discoteca.* The cleanest rooms in town, and fluffy beds make for a deep slumber. Rooms equipped with hot-water bath, phone, and TV. Unfortunately, on weekends, a beat-pumping *discoteca* blares its tunes until 2am. Singles s/48,000; doubles s/66,000.

Hotel España (tel. 983 860), Sucre and Pichincha, has big windows (which unfortunately look out onto the unattractive Sucre), hot water in the mornings, private baths, and color TVs. Rooms s/30,000 per person.

Residencial Sucre, Junín 396 and Bolívar, near plenty of restaurants. Where there are windows at all, they face walls, making rooms pitch-black. Creaky beds and old-style fixtures furnish the rooms. Perk up in the lobby with a friendly staff, fuzzy TV, and comfy red-leather chairs. Rooms cost the same with or without bath: s/15,000 per person.

FOOD

A number of Colombian restaurants have made a place for themselves alongside the Ecuadorian establishments of Tulcán. To sample this international culinary excitement, visit eateries along Sucre and Bolívar, below 10 de Agosto.

Restaurante El Patio (tel. 984 872), Bolívar between Pichincha and 10 de Agosto. Savor monstrous plates of Colombian cuisine like the *Bandeja Paisa* (s/14,000), loaded with eggs, vegetables, rice, beans, *arepas,* avocado, and meat. A tiled indoor courtyard decorated with antiques and black-and-white photos provides a glimpse of the Tulcán of old. Open M-Sa 8am-9pm, Su 8am-5pm.

Wimpy La Verdadera Hamburguesa (tel. 983 218), Sucre and Boyacá. This streetside cheapie cures late-night munchies and afternoon hunger pangs alike. Far from wimpy, the jumbo burger comes with the works (s/10,000). Open daily 9am-11pm.

Chifa Pack-Choy (tel. 982 713), Sucre and Pichincha. Portions are large and yummy. Rice dishes s/8,500, noodle dishes s/12,000. Open daily noon-midnight.

CROSSING THE BORDER

Crossing the border *(frontera)* between Ecuador and Colombia at the Rumichaca Bridge is usually fairly straightforward. Tourists are required both to present a **passport,** to be stamped at the immigration office of each country, and to turn in and/or receive a 90-day tourist card. Very few nationalities need a visa to enter Colombia. Copies of passports, drivers licenses, birth certificates, library cards, and doctor's notes are not acceptable identification; officials are very strict about this. A **provisional passport** may be acceptable.

Occasionally, tourists (especially scruffy-looking ones) will be asked to prove that they have sufficient funds (US$20, for students US$10) for each day they plan to stay in the country. Officials may also ask to see a round-trip ticket proving that a visitor intends to leave the country within 90 days, the maximum amount of time a traveler can spend in either country in a one-year period. If you want to stay longer, you'll need to obtain a **visa** (see **Visas and Work Permits,** p. 9). Tulcán's border never closes, and the **Ecuadorian Immigration Office** (tel./fax 980 704) is open 24 hours. Ecuador charges a s/20,000 exit tax. If crossing from Colombia into Ecuador, be sure to get your passport stamped inside the Colombian immigration office. Thieves often pretend to be border officers.

THE CENTRAL CORRIDOR

The highlands of Ecuador form a valley bordered by two enormous mountain ranges running the length of the country. Almost half of the nation's population lives in this central corridor. Since pre-Hispanic times, farmers have benefited from this rich soil fed by millions of years of volcanic eruptions. Many of these fire-spewers still simmer in the northern part of the corridor, an area dubbed "avenue of the volcanoes." This still-volatile region extends from Quito down to Riobamba, flanked on the eastern side by the Parque Nacional Cotopaxi and Parque Nacional Sangay, on the western side by Volcán Chimborazo. Towns in this valley sit high among snow-capped peaks—Chimborazo's altitude exceeds 6000m.

As the road meanders farther south, very tall rocky peaks soften into very tall green hills. The towns in the southern highlands have all the charm of their northern neighbors but function at an even mellower pace. The verdant quilt of cultivated land inspires lonesome strolls through the silent, thatched-hut village of Biblián and among the church spires of Azogues. But the most spectacular scenery belongs to the routes descending from Cuenca and Alausí to the coast (El Triunfo and Guayaquil). Roads and train tracks alike dip 3000m, hugging cliffs and deep ravines as they pass through diverse vegetation zones, from mountain *páramo* to coastal jungle wetlands, dipping into layer after layer of misty cloud cover en route to their muggy destinations.

AVENUE OF THE VOLCANOES

This stretch of the Andes between Quito and Cuenca earned its fiery nickname from German explorer Alexander von Humboldt in 1802. The towering cone of Volcán Cotopaxi, the angry spew of Volcán Sangay, and other prominent fire-spitters have stunned visitors ever since. This geologically extreme section of the Ecuadorian Andes has always been characterized by cataclysmic seismic disasters. Back in Humboldt's day, the city of Riobamba had to be reconstructed stone by stone after it was demolished by an earthquake in 1797. Cotopaxi itself, the tallest active volcano in the world, has wrought havoc on Latacunga during nine separate eruptions from 1534 to 1949. But as intimidating as the volcanoes may seem, the jaw-droppingly beautiful views from misty Andean ridges somehow soften the sharp peaks. Besides, none have erupted lately. Furthermore, molten lava is not always a bad thing—the fiery interiors of Volcán Tungurahua heat the soothing mineral hot springs at Baños. If unconvinced, stick to the solemn majesty of Volcán Chimborazo—once thought to be the tallest mountain in the world and by all accounts extinct. Maybe extinct.

HIGHLIGHTS OF THE AVENUE OF THE VOLCANOES

- Along the **Latacunga Loop,** the town of **Chugchilán** (see p. 303) receives numerous visitors at the famously eco-friendly **Black Sheep Inn.**
- **Parque Nacional Cotopaxi** (see p. 304) is home to remarkable Andean beauty and the tallest active volcano in the world.
- Foreigners flock to the salubrious waters in the hot baths at **Baños** (see p. 311)
- **Volcán Chimborazo** (see p. 326) has the farthest summit from the center of earth.
- The spectacular **Devil's Nose Train** (see p. 327) chugs along down to the coast.
- Tapirs roam among the lava-spewers of **Parque Nacional Sangay** (see p. 318).

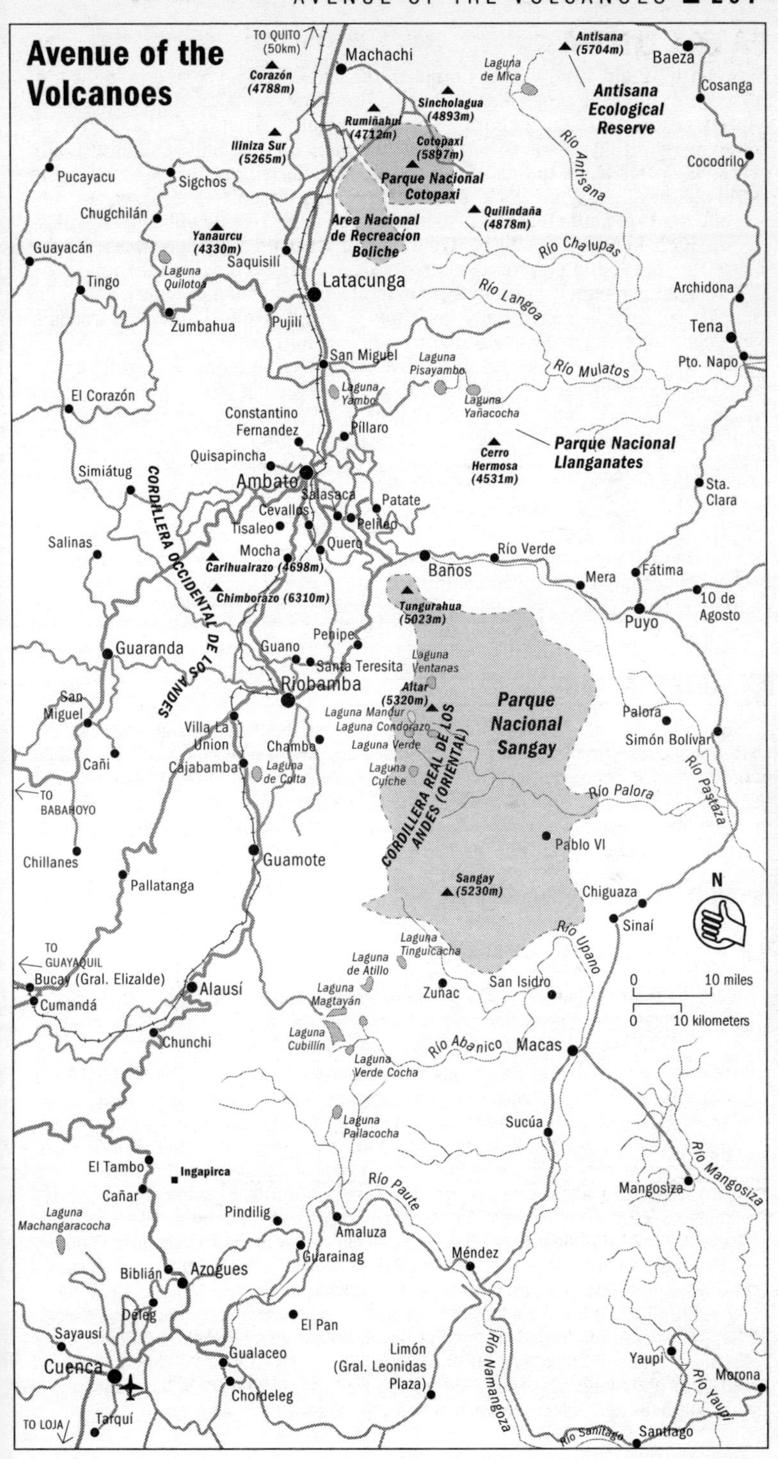
Avenue of the Volcanoes
TO QUITO (50km)
Machachi
Corazón (4788m)
Antisana (5704m)
Laguna de Mica
Baeza
Cosanga
Antisana Ecological Reserve
Sincholagua (4893m)
Rumiñahui (4712m)
Iliniza Sur (5265m)
Cotopaxi (5897m)
Parque Nacional Cotopaxi
Río Antisana
Cocodrilo
Pucayacu
Sigchos
Chugchilán
Yanaurcu (4330m)
Area Nacional de Recreacion Boliche
Quilindaña (4878m)
Río Chalupas
Guayacán
Saquisilí
Laguna Quilotoa
Tingo
Latacunga
Río Langoa
Archidona
Zumbahua
Pujilí
Tena
San Miguel
Laguna Pisayambo
Río Mulatos
Pto. Napo
Laguna Yambo
Laguna Yañacocha
El Corazón
Constantino Fernandez
Píllaro
Cerro Hermosa (4531m)
Parque Nacional Llanganates
Quisapincha
Simiátug
Ambato
Salasaca
Sta. Clara
Patate
Cevallos
Tisaleo
Pelileo
Salinas
Mocha
Quero
Río Verde
Baños
Fátima
Carihuairazo (4698m)
Mera
CORDILLERA OCCIDENTAL DE LOS ANDES
Chimborazo (6310m)
10 de Agosto
Tungurahua (5023m)
Puyo
Penipe
Guaranda
Guano
Laguna Ventanas
Santa Teresita
Riobamba
Altar (5320m)
Parque Nacional Sangay
San Miguel
Laguna Mandur
Palora
Villa La Union
Laguna Condorazo
Simón Bolívar
Chambo
Laguna Verde
Cañi
Cajabamba
Laguna de Colta
Laguna Cuiche
Río Pastaza
TO BABAHOYO
CORDILLERA REAL DE LOS ANDES (ORIENTAL)
Río Palora
Pablo VI
Chillanes
Guamote
Pallatanga
Sangay (5230m)
Chiguaza
N
Sinaí
Río Upano
Laguna Tinguicacha
TO GUAYAQUIL
Laguna de Atillo
Bucay (Gral. Elizalde)
Alausí
Zuñac
San Isidro
0 10 miles
Laguna Magtayán
0 10 kilometers
Cumandá
Laguna Cubillín
Chunchi
Río Abanico
Macas
Laguna Verde Cocha
Laguna Pailacocha
Sucúa
Río Mangosiza
El Tambo
Ingapirca
Río Paute
Cañar
Mangosiza
Laguna Machangaracocha
Pindilig
Amaluza
Guarainag
Méndez
Biblián
Azogues
Deleg
El Pan
Sayausí
Limón (Gral. Leonidas Plaza)
Río Namangoza
Yaupi
Cuenca
Gualaceo
Morona
Río Yaupi
Chordeleg
TO LOJA
Tarquí
Río Santiago
Santiago

LATACUNGA

Between 1534 and 1949, Volcán Cotopaxi, the tallest active volcano in the world, spewed its stuff nine times. Each time, the fire-spitter devastated and sometimes entirely destroyed the neighboring city of Latacunga. Each time, the citizens of Latacunga dutifully chose to return to their ruined home and rebuild virtually everything. This leads to one of the classic Ecuadorian mysteries—why in the world did they keep going back? Maybe it was the fruit, coffee, sugar, cacao, rubber, and herds of cattle that are sustained on soil made rich by millennia of volcanic ash. It could have been the gold and silver discovered and mined there. Maybe it was the incredible panorama--a crown of Andean peaks that surrounds the 2700m-high town--and the proximity to natural wonders that has made it a popular tourist base. And then again, perhaps it was Cotopaxi itself—its surreal, tranquil, white cone towering majestically on the northeast horizon.

After 50 years of geological stability, Latacunga has settled into the role of Cottopaxi province capital. As a centrally located city among more remote highland villages and the first major stop south of Quito on the Panamerican Highway, it has evolved into something of a regional transportation hub. Historically, too, Latacunga was a key center of highland commerce, first for the Puruhá and Quichua peoples and later for Spanish colonists, whose influence remains in the narrow, cobblestone streets and numerous *parques* and plazas.

Derived from the Quichua words *Llacta cunani*, the city's name roughly translates to "land of my choice"—a fitting name whether you want outdoor adventure or a relaxing sample of highland culture. While tourism has not altered the town's character, Latacunga nevertheless offers a variety of excursions to nearby villages, lakes, and, of course, to Volcán Cotopaxi.

ORIENTATION

The most heavily traveled part of Latacunga is along the **Panamerican Highway**. This strip has its selection of solid hotels and restaurants, but as the mechanic shops and Castrol Oil center suggest, its main concern is the vehicular traffic passing through. On the other side of the **Río Cutuchi** lies the main part of the city, sloping up the mountainside in a grid-like fashion. Shops line the main drag, **Av. Amazonas,** while the municipal and tourist sections are near **Parque Vicente León** on **Quito** and **Quevedo**. Buses will take you across the river into the main part of the town; if you can't find one, it's only a short walk.

PRACTICAL INFORMATION

Trains: The **train station** (tel. 800 700), M.A. Subia and J. Andrade, is on the far side of the Panamerican Highway. Trains travel only to: **Riobamba** (4hr., Sa 11am, s/80,000) and **Quito** (3½hr., Sa midnight, s/80,000). Buy tickets at departure.

Buses: The most useful bus company is **Transportes Cotopaxi** (tel. 800 752). Main offices are on the Panamerican Highway across from J. Andrade, but nearly all buses depart elsewhere, and only tickets to Quevedo need to be bought at the main office. Open M-Sa 7am-12pm, 2-6pm. Buses to **Quito** (2hr., every 10-15min. 4am-7pm, s/12,000) leave from a parking lot next to the market at Amazonas and 5 de Junio (see map). Buses to **Ambato** (1hr., every 10-15min., s/7,000) and **Baños** (2hr., every 10-15min., s/12,000) leave from the Panamerican Highway. Buses to**: Quevedo** (5hr., every hr., s/28,000) leave from 5 de Junio, 1 block west of the Panamerican Highway. Buses leave from the same location to: **Pujilí** (20min., every 5min. 6:30am-8pm, s/1,000); **Zumbahua** (2hr., every hr., s/8,000); **Pilaló** (3hr., s/18,000); and **La Maná** (4 hr., s/23,000). Buses to the loop of small *pueblos* surrounding Latacunga line up along Benavidez, next to the river, starting at Simón Bolívar go to: **Saquisilí** (20min., every 10min. 5:30am-6:30pm, s/2,000); **Sigchos** (3hr., every 30min. 9:30am-3:30pm, s/10,000); and **Chugchilán** (4hr., 10:30 and 11:30am, s/15,000). On Thursdays, buses to Chugchilán and Sigchos leave from Saquisilí instead.

Tourist Office: Latacunga doesn't really have a tourist office, but the owners of the **Hotels Cotopaxi, Estambul,** and **Tilipulo** happily provide info on the town. Susanna, at the Hotel Estambul, gladly shares her encyclopedic knowledge of local events and history.

Currency Exchange: Banco Popular (tel. 810 169), Sánchez de Orellana and Salcedo, one of 5 banks on or near the Parque León. Open M-F 9am-4pm.

Casa de Cultura: (tel. 800 983), Vela and Padre Salcedo, maintains an ethnological museum and promotes artistic activities in the community through the *Molinos de Monserrat* and an outdoor theater. Open Tu-Sa 8am-noon and 2-6pm.

Public Market: Essential to the Latacunga experience, the *mercado* lies between 5 de Junio and Clavijo. It has anything you might need to feed, clothe, or groom yourself at low, low prices. Open daily from 7am to 6pm, but Saturday is the big day. For general food supplies, try the **supermercado** next to Restaurante Rodelú.

Emergency: Tel. 101.

Police: (tel. 812 666), on General Proaño about 1km from the center of town.

Pharmacy: Farmacia La Merced (tel. 801 537), on Piño, midway between Quito and Orellana, is open 24hr.

Hospital: Hospital General (tel. 800 331 or 800 332), Hmas. Paez and Av. 2 de Mayo, has ambulance service. Open 24hr.

Post Office: Correos (tel. 811 394), Quevedo and Maldonado, a block from the Parque Vicente León and next door to the EMETEL office, has a Lista de Correos. Open M-F 8am-noon and 2-7pm, Sa 8am-noon.

Internet Access: ACCOMP (tel. 810 710; email janchat@uio.satnet.net), in the mall on Salcedo between Quito and Quevedo, offers internet access for s/1,500 per min. Open M-Sa 9am-1pm and 3-6:30pm.

Telephones: Andinatel (fax 810 410), Torres and the Panamerican Highway, near the bus stops. Open daily 8am-12:30pm, 2-6:30pm.

TELEPHONE CODE	03

ACCOMMODATIONS

While Latacunga is not tourist-swamped, it does have its fair share of hotels. Several lie conveniently along the Panamerican Highway; others are in the midst of town across the river. All are pretty cheap, though some delve into the deepest, darkest realms of the budget world in terms of quality. Be sure to make reservations or arrive early if you're coming to Latacunga on Wednesday—tourists always flock here for the Saquisilí market the next morning. Many of the hotels will arrange a day trip to Cotopaxi for US$20-25.

Hotel Cotopaxi (tel. 801 310), on Salcedo, next to Banco del Austro on the Parque León. As majestic as its namesake, comfort abounds; spacious rooms have restful beds and private hot water baths. Some rooms have excellent views of the park, and the staff is very friendly. The major drawback: the central location brings with it the continual drone of passing busses, in stereo sound. Amenities include TV upon request, luggage storage, and a safe. Singles s/40,000; doubles s/80,000.

Hotel Estambul, Quevedo 6-44 between Salcedo and Guayaquil (tel. 800 354). Situated in the "heart of the city," it offers immaculate and comfortable rooms with private bath and hot water. Self-serve manual laundry (a big tub) available. Enjoy the evening air in the courtyard, or a great view of the city from the rooftop terrace. The helpful staff provides information about local excursions. Rooms US$7 per person.

Hotel Sierra Nevada (tel. 800 407), on 5 de Junio, next to the bus stops for Ambato and Baños. Mere steps from bus transportation to the rest of Ecuador, the recessed entrance makes this hotel surprisingly quiet. Clean, well-lit rooms welcome visitors, while the private bathrooms entice them to take a hot shower. Watch some TV in the sitting room as your laundry cycles upstairs. Singles s/20,000, with bath 30,000; doubles s/40,000, with bath s/60,000.

Residencial Santiago (tel. 802 164), 2 de Mayo and Guayaquil. Large, comfortable rooms have TV, full-length mirrors, and color-coded bathrooms with hot water. There's a common reading room with vinyl easy chairs. The friendly owners live downstairs. Singles s/20,000, with bath s/30,000; doubles 40,000, with bath s/60,000.

Hotel Tilipulo (tel. 802 130), Guayaquil and Quevedo, on the corner 1 block north and 1 block west of the Parque León. A relatively new place, its wood floors and furniture still gleam proudly. Not just rooms, but actual suites–complete with bedroom, private hot-water bath, and a charming living room with TV. A small cafe downstairs serves breakfast and snacks. Singles s/45,000; doubles s/80,000.

FOOD

Latacunga's narrow streets are crammed with scores of *restaurantes típicos* that offer the standard *almuerzo* (s/12,000). Even cheaper meals can be found in the *mercado*, but hygiene is not guaranteed. There is a decent selection of fruit stalls clustered near the east end, and breads and pastries can be found at any of the dozens of *panaderías*.

Restaurant Rodelú (tel. 800 956), on Quito between Salcedo and Guayaquil, under the hotel of the same name. A departure from the ever-present *típicos* and a haven for gringos, the cozy atmosphere and fresh brick-oven pizza (s/20,000-30,000) may provide the perfect remedy for homesickness. Meat, chicken, and vegetarian pasta dishes s/19,000 and up. Open daily 7:30am-3pm and 5-9:30pm.

Restaurant Hostal Quilotoa (tel. 800 099), on the Panamerican Highway underneath the hotel of the same name. The eatery stays warm with the heat and scent of the fire, as the chickens do their slow methodical dance over red-hot coals. Filling portions of *arroz con pollo* (s/10,000) or *almuerzo* (s/8,000). Especially convenient if you're on the far side of the river. Open daily noon-11pm.

Restaurante Chifa China, 5 de Junio and Vela, just downstream from the market. The Chinese paintings of flying fish give an air of authenticity, while the food stays put on your plate. Choose from copious quantities of chow in the *mein* (chicken with vegetable s/21,000), soups (wonton s/12,000) and rice dishes (*arroz chop suey* s/18,000), all of which are available for take-out. Open daily 10am-10pm.

El Mascha, on F. Valencia away from the river, past Sanchez de Orellana. Latacungan families munch away as they watch soap operas on the big-screen TV in back. Offers chicken in every flavor, all of them tasty (s/12,000 and up). Open daily 11am-9:30pm.

SIGHTS AND ENTERTAINMENT

Admittedly, most tourists coming to Latacunga are here to see sights outside of town. However, if you're here for the night, there are a few things to keep you busy. The **Molinos de Monserrat,** next to the waterfall at Vela near Maldonado, is the center of the province's **Casa de la Cultura** organization and houses a gallery of local artwork, a museum of ethnology, a small library, and a riverside amphitheater. Built by the Jesuits in 1756 and originally used as a grain millery, this colonial building now pays homage to the culture and traditions of the area's inhabitants through paintings, artifacts displays, and colorful dioramas of local festivals. (Open Tu-Sa 8am-noon and 2-6pm, admission s/5,000).

Latacunga is home to an abundance of beautiful parks, the most prominent and centrally located is the **Parque Vicente León,** downtown at Salcedo and Quito. The park provides the perfect spot to enjoy the town's flavor or, perhaps, the flavor of an ice cream treat from nearby **Pingüino.** A block away, near Quito and Guayaquil, is the impressive **Iglesia y Convento de Santo Domingo,** whose white-washed walls are complemented by colorful garments on sale out front at the daily **artisan fair.**

The **mercado** is impossible to miss; its mammoth offerings take up several blocks from the river to Amazonas with bananas, super glue, "Calvin Klein" jeans, consumer electronics, and every piece of the cow imaginable (and unimaginable). The big day is Saturday, but the market is busy daily from about 7am-6pm.

Visitors September 23-24 can see the fiesta of **La Virgen de Las Mercedes,** in which *indígena* men dress up as black women and engage in a ceremony that involves squirting perfumed milk on bystanders. In the first few days of November, craftspeople from nearby Pujilí come to sell their pottery. Stick around for a few more days and you'll see the **Mama Negra** festival (Nov. 11), which is a repeat of the fiesta of La Virgen de Las Mercedes, except that this time white men cross-dress and paint their faces black. The Mama Negra coincides with **Latacunga's Independence Day,** which is celebrated with parades, fairs, and bullfights and commemorates the day Latacungan patriots defeated Spanish royalists in 1820.

THE LATACUNGA LOOP

The loop of less-touristed towns to the west of Latacunga is a postcard maker's fantasy come true. The small villages are hidden away among the patchwork farms and vast, jagged-rock faces of the Andean peaks. Relatively untouched by technology or tourism, life in these isolated towns has changed little over the centuries for their indigenous inhabitants. Visiting them is an excellent way to take a trip off-road and submerge yourself in a foreign world, but expect to be a pioneer of sorts in figuring your way. Bring water, sturdy but comfortable shoes, warm clothes, and a raincoat—the weather changes quickly, temperatures plummet at night, and the wind will suck you bone-dry at this altitude. Hiking will probably be required on more distant trips, as the bus service to many of these out-of-the-way places is inconvenient and inadequate. The fairly reliable bus service to Sasquisilí and Pujilí is the exception. For more information, see **Latacunga buses** (p. 298).

THE LATACUNGA LOOP: PUJILÍ

The first step in the loop, Pujilí, is effectively a suburb of Latacunga. The town's main attractions are the Sunday **market** at Rocafuerte and Pichincha and the world-famous pottery workshops at La Victoria. On the Western edge of the town, steps go up on a steep hill from which you can see Chimborazo. If the climb doesn't leave you breathless, the view will. Visitors June 3-6 witness the festival of **Corpus Christi**, which draws dance troupes from as far away as Guayaquil.

Transportation: There is frequent **bus** service to Pujilí from the corner of 5 de Junio and M.A. Subia, one block from the Panamerican Highway next to the railroad tracks in Latacunga (15min., every 5min. 6:30am-8pm, s/1,000). There is nowhere to stay in Pujilí, so make sure not to miss the last departure.

THE LATACUNGA LOOP: ZUMBAHUA

As Latacunga and Pujilí fade slowly into the distance, the scenery becomes increasingly barren and mountainous. Few communities interrupt the ride's natural splendor, until Zumbahua appears two hours later. Tourists are a rarity in Zumbahua; the only excitement the town ever sees is the **Saturday market.** During the festival of **Corpus Christi** (first week of June), alcohol flows freely, and visitors to this wind-swept town may be at risk. At other times the town is generally safe, though outsiders should always be alert. Several new hotels are trying to make Zumbahua more tourist friendly. Both the **Hostal Richard** and the **Hotel Oro Verde** are located on the market plaza and offer shared rooms with hot water baths for s/20,000. One step up, **Hostal Cóndor Matzi** (tel. 814 610), also on the market plaza, provides bright rooms with neat beds (singles s/30,000). Oro Verde and Cóndor can arrange guided tours to Quilatoa and other nearby destinations.

Transportation: catch the Quevedo-Latacunga bus on the "highway" above Zumbahua. (2 hr., every hr. until 9pm, s/8,000).

THE LATACUNGA LOOP: LAGUNA QUILOTOA

At the top of the world (elevation 3,854m), where the heavens meet the earth, lies the awe-inspiring **Laguna Quilotoa,** contained in an enormous crater which was once the colossal Volcán Quilotoa. One glance at this emerald lagoon will justify the arduous journey you endured to get here. Hikes down to the lake take 30 minutes or less, but the hike back up is quite steep and may take more than twice as long. A walk around the edge of the crater lasts about five hours—halfway around from the access road at the top of the crater, and you're already well on your way to Chugchilán. Near the access road, the town of Quilotoa is home to several family-run "hotels" which compete for the settlement's scanty overnight crowd. Because of the extremely remote location, there is no running water, and these accommodations may test even the hardiest budget traveler's standard of comfort and sanitation. The primary concern is warmth, as temperatures at this altitude plummet when the sun goes down. That said, **Cabañas Quilotoa** has common rooms with a fireplace and beds with heavy blankets (s/20,000). Not to be confused with the Cabañas, **Hostal Quilotoa** offers similar rooms, minus the fireplace (s/10,000). Both provide meals for s/15,000, and sell colorful paintings by the villagers.

Transportation: There are several ways to get to and from the neighboring towns of Chugchilán (22km) and Zumbahua (14km), none of which is especially easy or convenient. From either town, buses go to Quilotoa for s/5,000, but they leave at unholy hours of the morning. Check in town for details. Trucks from Zumbahua or Chugchilán will take tourists to Quilotoa, but rates start at s/70,000. For a little bit more, many drivers will wait an hour or two and then bring you back. Hiking all the way from Zumbahua takes about five to seven hours. The hike crosses through the **Río Toachi Canyon** and is along the road. The owners of Cabañas Quilotoa can provide maps showing a strenuous off-road hike from Quilotoa to Chugchilán

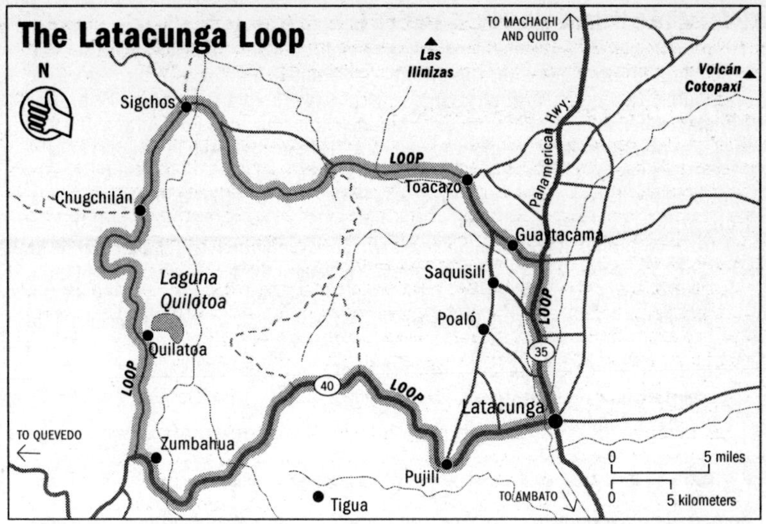

(about 5hr.; considerably longer in the other direction). Water and warm clothes are key on these walks—it gets cold at 3800m, and the weather can change quickly. For US$10 you can rent a horse to take you from Chugchilán to Quilotoa.

THE LATACUNGA LOOP: CHUGCHILÁN

An unlikely tourist destination, the *pueblo pequeño* of Chugchilán has seen more than its share of visitors in recent years. This is easily explained by a visit to the town's main tourist accommodation, the **Black Sheep Inn** (tel. (03) 814 587; email: blksheep@interactive.net.ec; www.blacksheepinn.com), located about 500m before Chugchilán on the road from Sigchos. A completely organic mountainside complex conceived and constructed by a young American couple in the early 1990s, the inn seems to be more *of* the land than *on* the land. Ducks, llamas, and even an *oveja negra* (black sheep) roam the thoughtfully planned grounds, which include an organic garden, a composting toilet, and hot-water showers with strategically-placed windows that provide soap-dropping views of the Andean countryside. The price of a room includes two home-cooked vegetarian meals, served in the comfortable dining room among other travelers. Guests can now write home about the experience via the inn's reasonably-priced internet access. (Dorm-style beds US$15; doubles US$18; triples US$17; all prices per person.) Those interested in more basic accomodations can stay at **Mama Hilda's**, right in the middle of town. Though the amenities are fewer, the view is nearly the same. She offers home-cooked meals (s/20,000) and dormitory-style rooms (s/25,000).

Because of the relative difficulty of transportation and the isolated beauty of the region, a multi-night stay in Chugchilán may be worthwhile. The owners of the Black Sheep Inn can suggest some eccentric yet excellent excursions in the vicinity. Quilotoa is not far off, and the **Río Toachi Canyon** is even closer. Following your nose in the other direction will lead to a **European cheese factory**, established decades ago by a Swiss entrepreneur and now run by local Ecuadorians. Some mysterious **Inca ruins** of the "circle in the ground" UFO variety lie three hours away by foot. For avid hikers, a one or two-day descent leads into an awe-inspiring **cloudforest** on the western slopes of the Andes. Hiking maps of the area are provided by the Black Sheep Inn and trucks and **horses** are available for hire.

Transportation: The daily bus to Latacunga leaves painfully early (4hr., M-Sa 3am, Su 6am, s/8,000). Similarly, there are occasional buses to Zumbahua via Quilotoa with a "late" departure on Wednesday morning.

THE LATACUNGA LOOP: SAQUISILÍ

One of the principle reasons for travelers to visit the Latacunga area is to shop at the acclaimed Thursday morning market of Saquisilí. Visit any other day of the week and find a quiet, ordinary village with no frills or bright hues. But come Thursday, Saquisilí explodes in living color, splashing its goods out among the various town plazas. Follow the crowds of people 1km north of the main market area to visit the livestock market, full of squealing pigs, protesting goats, and spitting llamas. Saquisilí's spanking new **San Carlos Hotel** (tel. 721 057), Bolívar and Sucre, offers princely rooms right next to the bus plaza (singles s/40,000; doubles s/ 90,000). Two blocks down Bolívar back towards Latacunga, the **Salón Pichincha** (tel. 721 247) welcomes guests like family. **La Señora Sílva** will make sure you're comfortable for an incredibly low price (US$2 per person). Hotels in Saquisilí and Latacunga tend to fill up Wednesday nights, so call ahead to make a reservation. The **police** (tel. 721 101), **hospital** (tel. 721 015), and **EMETEL** office (tel. 721 105) are one block past Pichincha heading down Bolívar away from the square.

Transportation: Frequent buses to **Latacunga** leave from Bolívar and Sucre (20min., every 10min. 5:30am-6:30pm, s/2,000).

PARQUE NACIONAL COTOPAXI

Situated about 35km to the northeast of Latacunga and 50km southeast of Quito, Cotopaxi National Park is dominated by the snow-capped monster, **Volcán Cotopaxi** (5897m), the tallest active volcano in the world. While many visitors come to scale this mammoth chunk of lava rock, the park offers more subtle pleasures as well. The flower-filled *páramo* (highland plain) surrounding the peak is home to many of Ecuador's unique species. (Park open daily 7am-6pm; admission US$10.)

WILDLIFE. The park was established in 1975 after a startling study concluded that there were fewer than 10,000 **llamas** left in Ecuador. Since that time, the park has struggled to nurture and preserve the llama population and the rest of the *páramo* residents. The park is hopping with **white-tailed deer,** who have made an impressive comeback under the watchful eyes of park management. Hot on their tails, literally, are the **Andean pumas,** whose numbers have slowly but steadily climbed since a low point in the mid-1970s. Other mammalian species, seldom seen but still alive and well in the park, are the **Andean fox,** the **Andean spectacled bear,** and the knee-high **red brocket deer.** Most visible are the herds of **wild horses** grazing on the *páramo.* Well-recognized by ornithologists the world over, the winged population of Cotopaxi fights for the attention of visitors. The park has received much attention as the last refuge of the endangered **Andean condor** (less than 100 remaining), but also nests such rarities as the **Andean hillstar,** the **Andean lapwing,** the **Andean gull,** the **great thrush,** and the tongue-twisting **carunculated caracara.** Many plants of the *páramo* have coatings of silver hairs that protect their leaves from bright daytime sunlight and help conserve heat at night. The innocent-looking **lancetilla plant** sucks water and nutrients from the roots of neighboring plants, while the **arquitecta** plant is used in traditional medicine as a diuretic.

RECREATION. Also a sanctuary for a certain two-legged mammal, Cotopaxi satisfies adventure-seekers and mountaineering enthusiasts from around the world. Without a doubt, the major adrenaline-inducing attraction of the park is the immense **Volcán Cotopaxi.** The first climbers to reach Cotopaxi's rim were the energetic German Wilhelm Reiss and Colombian Angel Escobar in 1872. Since then, thousands of world-class mountaineers and adventurers have made the icy ascent to the snow-capped summit. The climb is strenuous and requires ice-climbing gear, but it is not technically difficult. Nevertheless climbers of all abilities can benefit from a properly-qualified guide who knows the peculiarities of the ascent.

MOUNTAINEERING. Expeditions to the summit begin from the José Ribas refuge (4800m) at around midnight or 1am, to insure hard-packed snow and safer conditions. It usually takes six to seven hours to reach the top, but only about two to three hours to return to the refuge. Due to the necessity of an early start, it is imperative to stay in the refuge the night before. Though basic, the 70-person shelter has bunk beds, clean water, electricity, and a gas oven. Visitors must bring plenty of warm clothes, their own heavy sleeping bags, and nourishment. Acclimatization, another vital prerequisite, should be taken seriously (see **Environmental Hazards,** p. 19). A good acclimatization for Cotopaxi is a week in Quito, but even better is a hike around the national park or an ascent up one of the smaller peaks.

For more information on climbing Cotopaxi, check out one of the travel agencies in Quito, which are especially abundant along J. León Mera. Make sure your guide is certified by the **Ecuadorian Association of Mountain Guides (ASEGUIM),** the most respected association around. **Compañía de Guías** (tel./fax 504 773; email quismontania@accessinter.net; www.ecuaworld.com/guides), Jorge Washington 425 and 6 de Diciembre in Quito, offers a two-day summit climb (US$160 per person) complete with food, shelter, transportation, equipment, and an ASEGUIM-certified guide fluent in a number of languages (open daily 9:30am-1pm and 3-6:30pm). **Safari Tours** (tel. 552 505; fax 220 426; email admin@safariec.ecx.ec), Calama 380 and León Mera, also provides experienced, ASEGUIM-approved mountain guides fluent in a number of languages. Their two-day summit package (US$145 per person) is comparable to that of Compañía de Guías. (Open daily 9am-7pm.)

HIKING AND CAMPING. Vertigo sufferers and those sane enough not to climb a 600m ice cube can safely enjoy the park's lesser-known hiking and camping opportunities. From the plain at the base of the volcano, hikers equipped only with hiking boots, raingear, and a warm sweater can set off in almost any direction. The absence of trees and the ever-present Cotopaxi make navigation easy, while the wildlife is sure to send visitors scrambling for their cameras. A flat walk around **Lake Limpiopungo** takes about an hour and a half—slightly more adventurous hikers can extend the walk by venturing into the low hills at the base of **Volcán Rumañahui** (4712m), on the opposite side of the lake from Cotopaxi. The climb to the top of Rumañahui involves technical rock climbing. For those planning on spending the night, campgrounds within the park are about a 30-minute drive down the main road from the entrance gate. The road crosses a small river (no bridge). A sign for **campgrounds** will be on the left, and a short jaunt leads to a campsite fit for a king. Most people stay in tents, but there is a structure with four walls and a concrete floor that could, by some standards, be considered a cabin (s/2,000 per night). At least it has running water and is close to the shore of the immense Lake Limpiopungo. Up the road another 15 minutes is a second sign for **campgrounds** on the right. About as big as the other, this one provides a neck-bending view of Cotopaxi. There is a cabin here (s/2,000) but no running water.

A tiny **museum** on the path up to the campgrounds is a tribute to the National Park and is furnished with stuffed wildlife, a 3-D representation of the park, and wall-to-wall info on the history of Cotopaxi. Outside the museum, there is a helpful map of the park, which shows trails leading to the base of Rumañahui.

TRANSPORTATION. It is a good idea to have some kind of motorized transportation in the park since the main attractions are a not-particularly-scenic six-hour hike from the nearest bus stop on the Panamerican Highway (2hr. to the park entrance and 4hr. in the park). Any of the buses going between Quito and Latacunga can drop you off right at the park's southern access road or 10 minutes farther south in the town of Lasso (from Latacunga, 30min., every 10min, s/2500; from Quito, 1 1/2hr., every 10min., s/8000). Those who risk hitchhiking say that it is fairly easy to catch a ride into the park from the intersection of the entrance road and the Panamerican Highway. From Lasso, taxis and trucks take passengers into the park. If you want to go all the way to the refuge, it'll cost US$30, and you'll still need to hike about 30 minutes up from the parking lot. In Latacunga, the hotels Estambul, Cotopaxi, and Tilipulo can arrange transportation to and group tours of the park (starting at US$20 per person).

AMBATO

Nearly every Ecuadorian city claims to have miraculously survived some sort of natural catastrophe—the requisite fire, earthquake, or flame-spitting volcano. Ambato (pop. 140,000) is no exception. In 1949, a serious earthquake shook the city into a pile of rubble. Instead of simply bouncing back to its previous state, the new city far surpassed what it had been before. Many *ambateños* view the destruction of the old Ambato as the spark that fired up the spirit of its people. Half a century later, the modern mountain metropolis, resting at 2577m below the nearby peaks of Tungurahua and Chimborazo, still vibrates with this impassioned fresh start. *Ambateños* pride themselves on being productive, hard-working people who have continued the centuries-old tradition of farming the region's rich land, growing sugar cane, tobacco, coffee, fruits, and vegetables.

Ambato's cultural rebirth has been as fruitful as its economic one, particularly in the area of South American literature. Called "the city of the three Juans," Ambato has been home to novelists **Juan Montalvo, Juan Benigno Vela,** and **Juan León Mera**, as well as several other intellectual figures whose names now meet at the city's street corners and in its impressive museums. The development of tourism is evidenced by the recent proliferation of hotels, offices, apartments, and highways. Fiestas every November 12th commemorate Ambato's independence. The Festival of Fruit and Flowers, a more recently founded celebration (dating back only to 1951), occurs during the week before Carnival in February.

ORIENTATION

Ambato extends far beyond any visitor's interest or immediate comprehension. The **terminal terrestre** and **train station** are both in the northern end of the city, about 2km down **Av. 12 de Noviembre** from the *centro*, which is easily reached by taxi or bus. Turn right on the street in front of the *terminal* and walk uphill about 200m. At the first major intersection, catch the bus to the *centro* (s/1,200). A slew of budget hotels border the **Parque 12 de Noviembre.** Two other important parks are found in the downtown area: **Parque Juan Montalvo** (the center of the city's government offices and agencies) and **Parque Cevallos** (the departure spot for many local buses), bordered by a bustling commercial area. The downtown area is contained within a five-by-five block area. Many stores sell maps of the city (s/15,000).

PRACTICAL INFORMATION

Long-Distance Buses leave from the *terminal* to: **Guayaquil** (6hr., every 30min. 7am-2:30pm, s/45,000); **Quito** (2½hr., every 15min. 6am-6pm, s/19,000); **Santo Domingo** (4hr., every 1½hr. 6am-6pm, s/26,000); **Babahoyo** (5hr., every 30min. 6am-6pm, s/35,000); **Riobamba** (30min., every 45min. 5:30am-7pm, s/9,000); **Baños** (30min., every 30min. until 7pm, s/7,000); **Tena** (6hr., every hr. 6am-6pm, s/38,000); and **Puyo** (3hr., every 30min. 4am-6:30pm, s/19,000). On Sunday and Monday, when the Baños road is open to Puyo, a faster bus runs from Baños to the Oriente.

Local Buses: Buses to towns in the vicinity of Ambato depart from several places in the downtown area. From **Parque Cevallos,** buses depart to **Ficoa, Atocha, Ingahurro,** and **Pinllo** (15-30min., every 10min. 6:15am-7:30pm, s/1,000). Buses to **Picaigua** leave from Los Andes and Tomás Sevilla (10min., every 10min. 6:30am-6:30pm, s/1,000). Buses to **Pelileo** (35min., every 10min. 6:10am-6:10pm, s/3000) via **Salasaca** (25min., s/2000) depart from a "mini-*terminal*" on Carihuarazo in the suburb of Ferroviaria, up the hill from the *terminal terrestre*. Long-distance buses bound for Baños will also stop at these destinations en route.

INEFAN Office: (Tel. 848 542) Quiz Quiz Caspicara has information on the newly opened Parque Nacional Llanganates.

Taxis: Tel. 821 044, or hail one at any corner. A trip across town costs s/12,000.

Tourist Information: Ministerio de Turismo, formerly known as CETUR (tel. 821 800), Guayaquil and Rocafuerte, in front of the posh Hotel Ambato. Armed with exhaustive

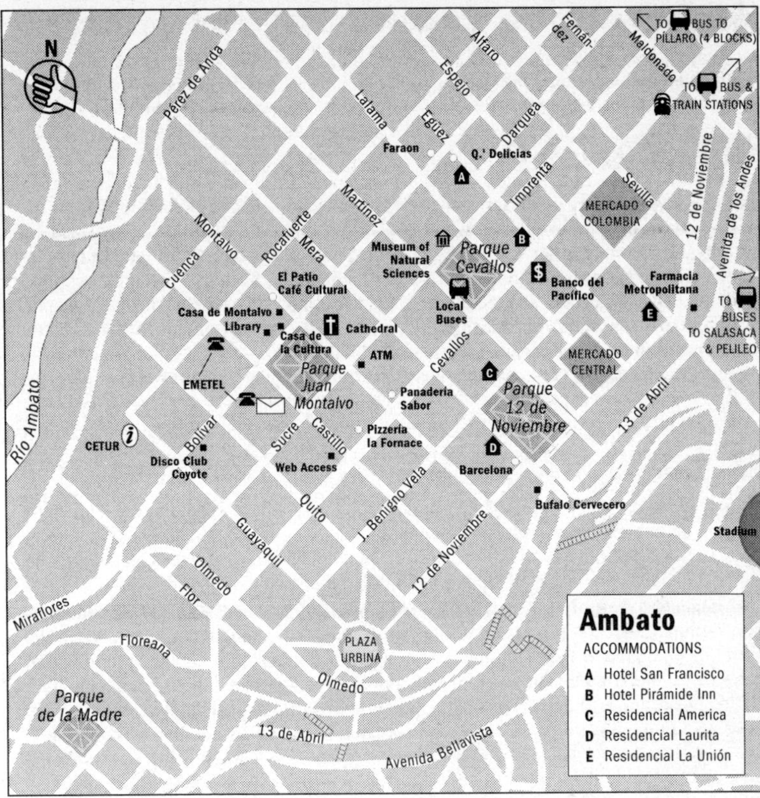

lists of local accommodations and festivals, this office provides information on Ambato in a patient, light-hearted manner—but only in Spanish. Open M-F 8:30am-5pm.

Travel Office: There is a wide choice of travel agencies, but a popular and convenient one is **Metropolitan Touring** (tel. 411 094), Rocafuerte and Montalvo, across the street from the post office. Open M-F 9am-1pm and 3-7pm.

Currency Exchange: Banco del Pacífico (tel. 844 942), Lalama and Cevallos, will exchange cash or traveler's checks until 4pm. The only Cirrus-compatible **ATM** that can reliably access foreign accounts is on Sucre and Montalvo, across from the cathedral.

Library: Biblioteca Municipal, Bolívar and Castillo, in the Municipal Building. Open M-F 9am-noon and 2:30-6pm, Sa 9am-noon.

Public Market: One of the biggest in Ecuador, sells mostly local produce and household items. Especially active on Monday. Partly indoors on 12 de Noviembre, between Martínez and Egüez, and a block up Vela in Mercado Colombia.

Laundromat: Química Automática, Vela 432 and Quito (tel. 822 888). Open M-F 8am-6:30pm, Sat 8am-noon.

Police: Atahualpa 568 (tel. 843 656 or 846 400).

Pharmacy: **Farmacia Metropolitana** (tel. 821 840), 12 de Noviembre and Espejo, open 24hr.; **Botica Bristol,** Martínez 307 and Cevallos (tel. 822 015).

Hospital: Hospital Regional Ambato (tel. 821 059; emergency tel. 822 099), Pasteur and Unidad Nacional.

Post Office: Correos Ecuador (tel. 823 332), Castillo and Bolívar. Open M-F 7:30am-7pm, Sa 8am-noon.

Internet Access: Internet Café, Castillo 5-28 and Cevallos (tel. 822 242). Offers reliable access for s/25,000 per hr. Open M-F 9am-1pm and 3pm-8pm.

Telephones: There are 2 **EMETEL** (tel. 822 122) offices: next to post office, and a block away along Castillo towards Rocafuerte. Both open daily 8am-12:30pm and 1-10pm.

TELEPHONE CODE 03

ACCOMMODATIONS

Hotel San Francisco (tel. 840 148), Egüez and Bolívar. The best suites for your sucre in town, featuring spacious rooms with private bath and TV. A few blocks from downtown, but those blocks make all the difference when it comes to noise. Call ahead to guarantee a spot, especially on Wednesday and Thursday nights—this place is no secret. Rooms s/30,000 per person, students s/25,000.

Residencial America, on Vela near Mera. Run by a friendly *ambateño* family, this place requires that its guests be of good moral standing. Passing this test entitles you to a spotless room with high, airy ceilings, hardwood floors, and large, luxurious beds. Some rooms even offer small balconies with views of the park. The shared bathrooms are clean and the agua is caliente. Rooms s/20,000 per person.

Hotel Pirámide Inn (tel. 842 092), Cevallos and Egüez, above Pollo a la Brasa. A small step up in price but a giant leap in comfort; a night at the Inn will likely cure the most severe case of budget traveler's blues. Enjoy the tidy, carpeted rooms, colorfully tiled private baths, and cable TV. Rooms s/55,000 per person.

Residencial Laurita (tel. 821 377), on Mera between Vela and 12 de Noviembre, truly screams simplicity. The graffiti on the walls provides reading material, but watch the exposed contacts when you flip on the light for a closer look. These stripped-down rooms contain walls and beds, period. The less-than-pristine shared bathrooms have hot water. The cost is bare-bones, too. Rooms s/15,000 per person.

Hostal La Unión (tel. 822 375), 12 de Noviembre and Espejo. A little bit farther from downtown and situated in the market district. Offers clean, basic rooms and hot-water common baths. There is also a sitting room with a TV. Rooms s/15,000 per person.

FOOD

El Patio Café Cultural, on Montalvo just past Bolívar, is a haven for Ambato's young intellectuals. Vegetarian salads (s/10,000) and local specialties such as *llapingachos* (s/12,000) are served amidst local artwork and *artesanía*. Poetry readings on Thursday nights if your Spanish is up for it. Live music most Fridays (s/15,000 cover); check schedule. Open daily 9am-10pm.

Panadería Sabor (tel. 825 378), on the corner of Cevallos and Montalvo. Mouth-watering pastries (s/4,500) and sugar-coated buns (s/700) will satisfy your sweet tooth. The central location makes it a convenient refueling spot. Open daily 6:30am-10pm.

Q'. Delicias, Egüez and Bolívar, next to Hotel San Francisco. *Ambateños* flock to this family-run favorite. Among other Qs, the simple menu is high on quality and quantity. *Sopa, arroz con carne* with juice s/8,000. Quick service is a given. Open M-Sa 8am-9pm.

Restaurante Faraon (tel. 821 252), on Bolívar between Egüez and Lalama. For 25 years locals have kept coming back for Faraon's excellent Ecuadorian dishes. Large mirrors on the walls let diners covertly spy on other clientele, or even check out the back of their own heads! *Desayuno* s/8,000, *almuerzo* s/19,000. Open daily 8:30am-6pm.

Pizzería La Fornace, Cevallos 17-28 and Montalvo (tel. 823 244). Don't let the classy decor scare you away—this place is Ambato's best kept budget secret. A blast of heat from the brick oven and the smell of the mini-pizzas cooked within (s/9,000-15,000) greet guests. Takeout available. Open daily noon-3pm and 4:30-11pm.

Restaurant Barcelona, Mera and 12 de Noviembre. Oddly enough Restaurant Barcelona is adorned with posters of the Eiffel Tower. The most expensive dish at this late-night diner is rice and beans (s/12,000). Open daily 3pm-4am.

THE TRASH MOUTH So you're finally starting to settle in. You've reluctantly accepted that three vehicles can fit across most any highway when necessary, and so you've relieved yourself of that vigilant, terrified gaze each time the bus driver moves to pass. But as a stranger in a strange land, the most violent culture shock probably still agonizes you: What is the *deal* with all those **clown trash cans?** In front of ice-cream shops, restaurants, and food stores, their eyes follow like a sinister painting, their gaping mouths hungry for more garbage. The original mastermind behind this ubiquitous shape lives just 7km south of Ambato in the suburb of Huachi Chico. Eighty-year-old **Victoria Pasmiño,** creator of the *basurero de payaso,* came up with the colorful trash can some 25 years ago. Though her name is far from familiar, her art is arguably the most recognized in the country. Why has she chosen garbage cans as her medium of expression? Simple: she wants to teach the children of Ecuador to put their trash where it belongs—a great idea that has yet to fully penetrate the Ecuadorian mindset 25 years later. Interested in starting a trend back home? Señora Pasmiño sells the clowns, as well as **alligator** and **Mickey Mouse** heads, for s/65,000 apiece. But make sure you're getting the real thing. By now, imitations of Pasmiño's genius are everywhere.

SIGHTS

Instituto Técnico Superior Bolívar (ITSB). The institute houses the **Museum of Natural Science**, which is by far the most arresting sight in downtown Ambato. Though the museum's admission is a bit steep, the quality of the extensive exhibits rises to the occasion. It starts slowly, with black-and-white photos of the Sierra at the beginning of the century (including a Cotopaxi eruption) and some indigenous musical instruments and clothes. The highlight of the museum, however, is its seemingly endless collection of preserved animals, including the world's largest insect species, the elephant beetle, and a regular elephant. Jaguars, birds, tarantulas, and snakes all preserve their final contorted poses, many in dioramas showing Ecuador's diverse habitats. This excellent exhibit climaxes in the back with the stuff bad dreams are made of—unfortunate **freak animals,** such as a two-headed goat and cyclops dog. (*Sucre 839, on the Parque Cevallos, between Lalama and Martínez. Tel. 824 564. Open M-F 8:30am-12:30pm and 2:30-6:30pm. Admission s/10,000.)*

MONTALVO-LAND. Ambato also provides plenty of opportunities to pay homage to its literary hero, **Juan Montalvo** (see **Literature,** p. 246). First there's the **park** that bears his name, well-groomed with bushes carved into topiary shapes. Next to the park, on the corner of Bolívar and Montalvo, is our hero's birthplace and lifelong home, the **Casa de Montalvo.** *(Open M-F 9am-noon and 2-6pm. Admission s/2,000.)* The various rooms of this open-air museum/mausoleum astound with the pure repetition of Montalvo renderings. Interwoven with these images are long articles and captions with tons of interesting information about both Ambato's and Ecuador's past. Don't worry—the Montalvo-fest isn't over yet. A couple of kilometers from the *centro*, in the suburb of **Ficoa,** lies the **Quinta de Montalvo,** Juan's country residence. *(Take the Ficoa bus, leaving from the Parque Cevallos every 15min.)*

OTHER LOCAL CELEBRITIES. Though Juan Montalvo certainly receives top billing in Ambato, several other *ambateños* may be of interest to visitors. The **Quinta de Mera** (home of **Juan León Mera**) and **Quinta de La Liria** (home of **Nicolas Martínez,** renowned mountain climber), are located near each other in the suburb of Atocha. Each house features displays chronicling the men's accomplishments over the years. *(For both, take the Atocha bus from Parque Cevallos. Both open M-F 9am-4:30pm).*

OTHER SIGHTS. Several **musical instrument shops** line the North side of Espejo, just uphill of 12 de Noviembre. Visitors can watch artisans make guitars by hand. *(guitars cost s/200,000.)* Ambato's headquarters for the arts, the **Casa de la Cultura,** is next to the *Municipio* building. The third floor houses free exhibits that change every other month. It also organizes entertaining events, such as musical concerts, which are posted in the lobby and are listed in the *Herald*, Ambato's daily Spanish-language newspaper. *(Bolívar between Montalvo and Castillo. Tel. 820 338. Open M-F 9am-1pm and 3-6pm.)* Across the way on Montalvo looms Ambato's **cathedral,** the distinguishing feature of Ambato's skyline, with its spacecraft-like spire.

ENTERTAINMENT

Business-like as always, Ambato doesn't offer much in the way of late-night revelry. Nevertheless, the weekend offers several worthwhile opportunities to join in the *fiesta* and enjoy what fun Ambato has to offer. During most nights, something is going on at **El Patio Café Cultural** (see p. 308), with poetry readings and live music promised on Thursday and Friday nights respectively. Otherwise, the **Casa de Cultura** might be sponsoring a film or a concert. One popular nightclub is the **Disco Club Coyote,** Bolívar 2057 and Guayaquil (tel. 827 886), in the city's western corner. Usually a restaurant and bar, on weekends the Coyote powers up the disco ball and blasts everything from *salsa* to rap to techno for a young, somewhat wealthy crowd. (*Cervezas* s/5,000; open F-Sa 10pm-2am.) The rest of Ambato's nightlife sits along Olmedo, just above Parque 12 de Noviembre. A popular spot is the **Bufalo Cervecero,** Olmedo 681 and Mera (tel. 841 685), which attracts a young crowd and plays all kinds of music, but leans toward techno. (Cover s/5,000. Open F-M.)

NEAR AMBATO: SALASACA AND PELILEO

The large volume of tourist traffic on the road to Baños creates great shopping opportunities along the way but provides a challenge for those who want to experience more. **Salasaca** offers a wonderful artisan fair. The Quichua who live here specialize in making woven ponchos and tapestries, with designs rich, attractive, and inexpensive enough to tempt the budget browser. The best day for the market is Sunday. (Open daily 8am-6pm.) To learn about Salasaca and the surrounding area, contact **Alonso Pilla** (tel. 09 840 125). Alonso is intent on teaching interested visitors about Salasaca, and he will gladly give tours of the surrounding countryside at rock bottom prices (s/20,000 per person for a few hours; tours in Spanish). To get to his house/workshop, follow the red signs for 600m down the highway back towards Ambato. For those looking for a party, Salasaca has its own *fiesta* in January and a well-known Corpus Cristi celebration during the first week of June.

Pelileo, a significantly larger town with a rather turbulent history, is 10 minutes east of Salasaca. Destroyed by earthquakes in 1698, 1797, 1840, 1859, and 1949, it now rests several kilometers from its original spot. After Ambato, it has the most important market in the province of Tungurahua, held every Saturday. *Chocos*, white, salted beans eaten as a snack, are a local specialty.

Transportation: Buses to Pelileo (30min., every 10min. 6:10am-6:10pm, s/3,000) via Salasaca (20min., s/2,000) leave near Av. Los Andes and Iliniza in the Ferroviaria district. Baños-bound buses, leaving Ambato's *terminal terrestre*, also stop at these towns en route.

NEAR AMBATO: PICAIGUA, PATATE, AND PÍLLARO

The smaller towns farther from Baños are less visited and more traditional. **Picaigua,** only a 15-minute bus ride southeast of Ambato, demands respect for the jackets that the locals sew and sell. The town of **Patate** lies across a stomach-churning gorge from Pelileo. This fruit-producing marvel is home to the **Complejo Turistico Valle Dorado** (tel. 870 253), featuring conference rooms, saunas, a water slide, and other diversions (admission s/15,000; open Sa-Su 9am-5pm). *Camionetas* will take explorers north to the indigenous village of **Sucre** (s/40,000). Buses to Patate leave from the market in Pelileo (25min, every 30min., s/2,500).

North of Ambato, the 2817m high **Píllaro** looks down on its neighboring metropolis without envy. This village of abundance bursts with agriculture, apples, and cattle galore. There's a big market on Sunday, but unlike other traditional villages, that's not even the most intriguing draw. Píllaro is the gateway to the brand new **Parque Nacional Llangantes,** where the emperor Atahuallpa supposedly buried his treasure. Nobody has found it—yet. To start searching, hire a *camioneta* to take you 30km north of Píllaro to **Laguna Pisayambo;** that's where the road ends. Ask at the *Municipio* in Píllaro for more information. There's only one place to stay in Píllaro: **Hostal Pillareñita** (tel. 873 220). It's the tallest building in town. (Rooms with private hot-water bath s/25,000 per person.)

BAÑOS

Long before the bus rumbles into this tiny highland town, English-language billboards appear next to the highway touting every service a tourist could want. The most popular attraction, though, needs no more advertising than the town name. The legendary **baños** consist of pools of water geothermally heated by the same fiery god that created nearby **Volcán Tungurahua.** The baths have worked wonders for the town. Many locals and tourists sport the loose and relaxed demeanor of recently emerged springs-soakers. Other aspects of the town only add to the already utopian ambience. A wall of neighboring green mountains, including Tungurahua, provides easy access to everything from pastoral strolls to vigorous hikes. The mountains loom so high and so close that, at night, the lights on top could easily be mistaken for planes flying overhead. As word has spread about Baños's stunning natural beauty, this quintessential Ecuadorian dazzler has adapted to harvest as many tourist dollars as possible. North American and European restaurants with multilingual menus are the norm. Resting in the eastern flank of the Andes, the town's popularity also comes from its status as a jumping-off point for jungle tours and exotic excursions. On every block, hotels and tour companies vie for attention, with postcard-perfect photos of past expeditions.

ORIENTATION AND PRACTICAL INFORMATION

The layout of Baños is quite simple. The main highway between Ambato and Puyo runs east-west across the northern end of town. From the **terminal terrestre** on the highway, it's about three blocks south along **Maldonado** to the **Parque Central.** The east-west street **Ambato** is the principle thoroughfare, passing the Parque Central, the municipal **market,** and the **Parque Basílica.** A lot of the town's action can be found along **Ambato** between the two parks, although plenty of stores, restaurants, and hotels can be found several blocks away as well. A huge **waterfall** on the south-east corner of town marks the location of the most popular hot springs.

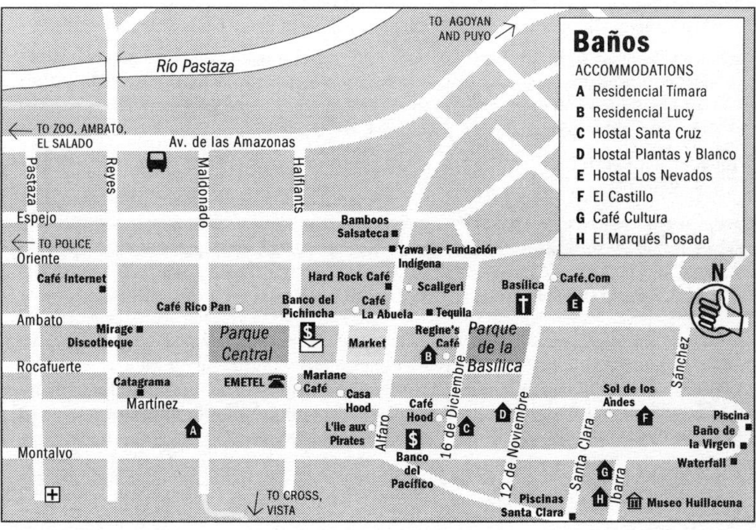

Buses: The **terminal terrestre** takes up a block between Maldonado and the main road to Ambato. Buses from the terminal area travel to: **Quito** (5hr., every 30min. 6am-7pm, s/25,000); **Ambato** (1½hr., every 10min. 4am-7pm, s/7,000); **Riobamba** (2hr., every hr. 6am-6:30pm, s/10,000); **Puyo** (2hr., every hr. 5am-7pm, s/10,000); **Tena** (6hr., s/30,000); and **Guayaquil** (11hr., 6am, s/60,000).

Taxis: 16 de Diciembre (tel. 740 416).

Rentals: Every hotel, cafe, drug store, and tour agency in Baños seems to rent some mode of transport for the tourist traffic. **Sierra Selva Adventures** (tel. 740 298), Maldonado and Oriente, charges the going rates in town (bikes s/30,000 per day; horses and guide US$15 per day). Much of what is for rent is poor quality: shop around.

Tourist Office: There is no official Ministerio de Turismo in Baños, but numerous tourist businesses (hotels, restaurants, drug stores, etc.) offer reliable information.

Currency Exchange: Banco del Pacífico (tel. 740 336), Montalvo between 16 de Diciembre and Alfaro, has a MC/Cirrus **ATM**. Open M-F 8:45am-4:30pm, Sa 9:30am-2pm. **M.M. Jaramillo Arteaga** (tel. 740 139), Ambato and Halflants. Open M-F 8:30am-5:30pm, Sa 9am-1pm. Both exchange cash and traveler's checks.

English Bookstore: Buy, rent or exchange used books in English at **Casa Hood,** Martínez, between Alfaro and Halflants. Open W-M 8am-11:30pm.

Library: Biblioteca Municipal (tel. 740 458), in the Municipio, on Rocafuerte at Halflants. Open M-F 8am-noon and 2-6pm.

Public Market: Mostly in a building boxed in by Rocafuerte, Ambato, Alfaro, and Halflants. Open daily 8am-6pm. **Sunday** is the biggest day. An open-air market specializing in produce is on Ambato and Mera, on the western edge of town. For extra-fresh organic veggies, head to the **Granja Ecológica** (see **sights,** p. 315).

Laundromat: One of the benefits of a town that caters to travelers is that laundry services are ubiquitous (wash and dry s/30,000).

Public Toilets: At the Parque Central on Halflants, across from the post office.

Police: (Tel. 740 251), on Oriente, 3½ blocks west of the Parque Central.

Pharmacy: Farmacia Baños (tel. 740 237), on Ambato between Alfaro and Halflants. Open daily 7:30am-1pm and 2-9:30pm.

Hospital: (Tel. 740 443), Pastaza and Montalvo.

Post Office: Correos Central (tel. 740 901), on Halflants between Ambato and Rocafuerte, bordering the Parque Central. Open M-F 8am-noon and 1-6pm, Sa 8am-noon.

Internet Access: Cafe Internet (tel. 740 436; email cafedos@accessinter.net), Reyes and Ambato, is the cheapest way to get on the 'net (s/1,000 per min.). Open M-Sa 9am-12:30pm, 1:30-7pm, and 8-11pm, Su 9am-2pm. **Cafe.Com** (see **Food,** p. 314) also has access, but you pay for atmosphere.

Telephones: EMETEL (tel. 740 104), Rocafuerte and Halflants, on Parque Central. Open daily 8am-10pm.

TELEPHONE CODE	03

ACCOMMODATIONS

Thanks to the high demand, Baños offers great, inexpensive lodging. The lowest-end places have comfortable beds with clean, shared baths; the tier above includes private bath as well as several other spiffy services such as complimentary breakfast. Hotels virtually pile on top of one another along Ambato, and there are also dense patches on Montalvo in the direction of the pools.

Hostal Los Nevados (tel. 740 673), right by Parque Basílica. From Ambato, take the first left past 12 de Noviembre. Los Nevados is the undisputed master of the mid-range hotel kingdom. Both the rooms and the private baths are large and spotless, with reliable, 24hr. hot water. Run by a multilingual Baños family, the friendly hostal offers complimentary continental breakfast in a rooftop cafe/bar equipped with a stereo, VCR, and TV for guest use. Los Nevados also provide a laundry service, message board, fax, in-house travel agency, and 24hr. security. The hostal fills up fast; reservations may be a good idea. Rooms s/35,000 per person.

Hostal Plantas y Blanco (tel. 740 044), Martínez and 12 de Noviembre, a block off the Parque Basílica. Besides the good location, daily cleaning, and private (though tiny) hot-water baths, there's a slew of other services: laundry, phones, fax, storage, rooftop bar/restaurant (open 7:30am-10:30pm), and most importantly, early morning "purifying" steam baths (US$3). Loads of American movies with TVs and headphones (s/ 3,000 each). Rooms US$5 per person, with bath US$6.

Residencial Tímara (tel. 740 599), Maldonado and Martínez, 2 blocks south of Parque Central along Maldonado. A reliable hotel on the budget level, Tímara includes plain rooms with psychedelic bedspreads, a clean communal bath blessed with hot water in the mornings and evenings, a sink for washing clothes, and a kitchen at your money-saving disposal. Owners are conscientious about maintaining their positive reputation among tourists. Rooms s/20,000 per person.

Santa Cruz Hotel (tel. 740 648), 16 de Diciembre and Martínez, 2 blocks south of Parque Basílica. A large central garden, open-air walkways, and big windows let in a lot of light, showing off the clean rooms. Private hot-water baths, a cafeteria, and 24hr. security round out the amenities. Rooms US$5 per person.

Residencial Lucy (tel. 740 466), Rocafuerte and 16 de Diciembre, just west of Parque Basílica. "Do you want to pet my monkey?" That's the operative question at Lucy, where, in the courtyard, Pepe *el mono* yanks his chain every which way but loose. Clean rooms come with hot water in the private bath, but only cold in the shared baths. Rooms s/15,000 per person, with bath s/20,000.

El Marqués Posada (tel. 740 053; email ivonsol@uio.satnet.net), Montalvo and Ibarra. A few blocks from the *centro* and near the mountain and waterfall of La Virgen, El Marqués offers a refuge from bustling Baños. Clean, airy rooms with private hot-water baths, a patio, and a friendly staff greet visitors. If the nearby pools aren't relaxing enough, the staff offers body massages (US$10 per hr.). Rooms s/50,000 per person.

Hostal El Castillo (tel. 740 285), Martínez and Santa Clara. Ideally located between downtown and the baths, El Castillo offers clean, simple rooms with private baths, a restaurant, and a pleasant inner courtyard. Rooms s/30,000 per person.

Café Cultura (tel. 740 083; email ivonsol@uio.satnet.net), Montalvo and Ibarra, is a good place to treat yourself to luxury lodgings. Above the Karmic and quirky Café Cultura, clean, cozy quarters contain bathtubs and fireplaces. Rooms US$7-9 per person.

FOOD

Like the hotels and just about everything else in Baños, the restaurants have been molded especially for the tourist. There are *comedores*, *chifas*, and *restaurantes típicos*, but miraculously, they're all cheap. Even better, a lot of travelers with incredible culinary skills have liked the town so much that they've stayed and set up superb international restaurants. For the socially conscious visitor, the **Quimicome** food kitchen on Martinez and Pastaza, which provides food for the less fortunate members of the community, welcomes volunteers and donations.

Ristorante Scaligeri, Alfaro near Ambato, is run by Italians—to make pasta this good, it must be. Enjoy homemade ham and mushroom fettucine just like Mama used to make (s/28,000). The *penne broccoli* (s/27,000) is also wonderful, and the list goes on. Open M-Tu and Th-F 10am-2:30pm and 5-10pm, Sa-Su 10am-10pm.

Mariane Café/Restaurant (cellular tel. (09) 837 976), Halflants and Rocafuerte. Another entry in the "authentic cuisine of the world" category. Mariane's French husband directs the production of prodigious quantities of *provençal* cuisine. Eat like a king for the price of McDonald's at home: succulent, locally-raised trout with tons of vegetables (s/26,000) and filet mignon in a peppered cream sauce with vegetables and *papas au gratin* (s/29,000) are truly incredible. A half-liter of wine (s/35,000) provides the appropriate post-meal euphoria. The food takes a while, but that's because each dish is prepared individually. Open daily 6:30-11pm.

La Abuela Café (tel. 740 635), Ambato, across from the market. This small, dark cafe is often full and for good reason. The sandwiches and pastas are delicious and affordable. Try the house specialty vegetarian lasagna (s/22,000) or the colossal *desayuno de la casa* (s/19,000). The crepes with generous ice cream and fresh fruit are a bargain (s/7,500). Open daily 7:30am-10:30pm.

Cafe.Com (tel. 740 991; email ivonsol@uio.satnet.net; www.satnet.net/cafecom), 12 de Noviembre and Oriente. This cybercafe "with a Swedish touch" specializes in a welcoming atmosphere and international cuisine. While cheaper internet access can be found elsewhere, their colossal English breakfast (s/22,000) is unique. They also serve up a tasty vegetarian quiche (s/16,000) and boast a wide selection of foreign periodicals for the international clientele. Open M-Sa 8am-10:30pm.

Sol de los Andes (tel. 740 514), Martínez and Santa Clara. Specializing in Ecuadorian food, this restaurant is anything but another *típico.* Chomp on a once-cute *cuy* (guinea pig, s/30,000; call ahead) or a slightly beefier 12-ounce steak (s/28,000). Nightly live *música folklórica* accompanies the meal. Open daily 11am-midnight.

Casa Hood, Martinez and Alfaro. The only people speaking Spanish at this popular eatery are the employees. An international selection of tourists happily consume vegetarian concoctions (mixed veggies with rice and peanut sauce s/18,000), while they watch complimentary movies or chat with the friendly American owner, Mr. Hood himself. Open Tu-Sa 8am-11:30pm.

Café Rico Pan (tel. 740 387), Ambato and Maldonado, on Parque Central. This joint's *pan* is definitely *rico.* The prosperous bakery/restaurant's selection of freshly baked breads and affordable menu items is advertised on the wall in 6 languages. Breakfast, Italian lunches (fresh pasta with mushroom sauce and juice s/15,000), and dinners available. Open M-Sa 7am-9pm, Su 7am-noon.

Regine's Café Aleman, (tel. 740 641), just moved—ask in town for directions. The friendly German owners have designed a hearty menu, full of goulash and stews, that makes their expatriate countrymen feel at home. The gypsy-spit chicken (s/25,000) is a tasty change from typically prepared poultry, and the potato pancakes (s/17,000) are a unique and wholesome way to begin any day. Open W-M 8am-3pm and 5-10pm.

Café Cultura (tel. 740 083; email ivonsol@uio.satnet.net), Montalvo and Ibarra. This cozy hostal/restaurant specializes in fireside dining with views of the waterfall. The vegetarian *llapingachos* (s/20,000) are a treat. Open daily 7:30am-9pm.

ON THE TRAIL OF DON SERGIO It seems that almost every visitor to Ecuador comes home with at least a few stories of the miracles performed by Ecuadorian auto mechanics. Following in this grand tradition of tinkerers, an old man named Don Sergio decided in the late 1970s to build his own car. Seventeen years later it was finished, and in it, a 68-year-old Don Sergio set out to travel the countryside. Constructed mostly of scrap metal and old pieces of wood, Sergio's car resembles an old corrugated shack—and with a top speed of 5km per hour, it isn't much faster. But that's OK, he's not in any hurry; he simply enjoys the freedom of traveling the road and seeing the world. When the car breaks down, as it frequently does, Don Sergio simply parks on the side of the road for however long it takes for him to fix the problem. With his toothless grin and wild, white beard, the man is as conspicuously strange as his mechanical creation, and has attracted national and even international attention. Some people consider him to be a genius; others think he's crazy.

SIGHTS

Baños is one big sight. The tourist magnets begin at the hot spring pools and radiate outwards to the volcanoes, the Oriente, and beyond. There are three hot springs in town. The locals have the right idea—they soak themselves in the salubrious springs at sunrise. Tourists who take a dip later miss the calm, clean water and the splendor of daybreak over the Andes. The pools are quietest early in the week, busiest on Fridays and Saturdays.

THE BAÑOS. The most popular spring is the **Baño de la Virgen** (tel. 740 462), at the eastern end of Montalvo. A waterfall cascades down the mountainside into this pool, but it's really the crowds and taxis that make it conspicuous. Several murky mineral-water pools, reputedly cleaned daily, are filled with the legendary hot, healing waters. *(Open daily 4:30am-5pm and 6-10pm. Daytime admission s/6,000; nighttime admission s/10,000.)* Next door, **La Piscina Las Peñas** has a slide and specializes in screaming kids and water fights. *(Open Th-Su 8am-6pm. Admission s/6,000.)* The **Piscinas Santa Clara** are at the end of the street with the same name. *(Open on weekends. Admission s/5,000.)* Two other pools, visited mostly by locals, lie outside of town. **El Salado** (tel. 740 493) is a 20-minute walk or a five-minute bus ride from the *centro*. Head west on the road to Ambato, then turn left at the sign to El Salado. Follow the road uphill until the end. Cleaned each day, the six pools include one cold, three hot, and two scalding. *(Open daily 4:30am-5pm. Admission s/6,000.)* The **Piscinas Santa Ana** lie 20 minutes by foot or five by bus on the road to Puyo. A sign points the way to the tree-enclosed pools. *(Open F-Su 8am-5pm. Admission s/6,000.)*

THE BASÍLICA. This local landmark imposes its strange, zebra-like form upon the skyline of the city. The church was built in honor of the great **Virgen de Aguas Santos,** displayed in all her lit neon glory inside the church. There are numerous stories of exactly how this plaster sculpture began working her miracles. The official version is depicted in one of the church's many murals. Apparently, during a religious procession in 1773, Volcán Tungurahua suddenly threatened to blow its top once again. The people of Baños, in a fit of religious fervor, prostrated themselves before the image of the Virgin that they had been parading around the plaza. The eruption came to a sudden halt, and the rest, as they say, is history. The murals of the church illustrate the many miracles that the Virgin has since performed to assist those that incite her name in moments of crisis. She has saved *bañeros* from every type of natural disaster; she even saved a foreign tourist whose driver plummeted off a cliff after a visit to Baños. Perhaps the words "*Sálvame Virgen de Aguas Santos!*" are worth remembering for those treacherous, cliff-side Andean bus rides. A museum in the church houses a miscellany of religious items. *(Open daily 7am-4pm. Admission s/4,000.)*

SAN MARTÍN ZOO. Along the road heading west to Ambato, the zoo detains its animal residents on the mountainside above the **Cascada Ines María.** With a professed mission to conserve, educate, and rehabilitate, the private *Ecozoológico* houses condors, jaguars, roaming tapirs, and rock-like tortoises, among other animals. Be sure not to miss the spider monkeys with their amazing tails. *(Buses leave from Alfaro at the market in Baños. Open daily 8am-6pm. Admission s/7,000, children s/5,000.)*

OTHER SIGHTS. If you've tired of its hot springs and gourmet restaurants, check out Baños's lesser-known attractions. The **Museo Huillacuna** on Ibarra, across from the Marqués Posada, houses a small collection of local artifacts. *(Open daily 9am-noon and 2-6:30pm. Admission s/5,000.)* There is more to Baños's art scene than the rows of identical *artesanía* shops lining every street. A slightly off-beat artform is practiced by several women in town: at Catagrama, on Martínez and Maldonado, amateur entomologists may browse among extensive collections of mounted insects ranging from iridescent butterflies to bird-sized elephant beetles.

ENTERTAINMENT

In spite of Baños's 2am closing law, the town has some of the wildest nightlife in Ecuador. After dinner and a movie at Casa Hood or Café Hood, tourists wander down Alfaro checking out the ample selection of bars and discos. The restaurant/bar **L'île aux Pirates** on Alfaro and Martínez encourages visitors to have a cocktail or two and then try out their French. Toward the river, **Donde Marcelo Al Paso,** on Alfaro and Ambato, blasts out the beat, while **Rodeo's** on Alfaro and Oriente switches over to live *música folklórica* for an hour at 9pm. Across the street, **Bamboos Salsateca** provides *salsa* music for dancing and a pool table for the more stationary. **Tequila,** on Ambato between 16 de Diciembre and Alfaro, also breaks out the disco ball and has a pool table.

A staple in the Baños nightlife scene, **Hard Rock Café,** on Alfaro between Ambato and Oriente, is probably awaiting a lawsuit for trademark infringement. In *peñas*, such as the one at the restaurant **El Marqués,** the authentic sounds of *música folklórica* soothe listeners. The hot bars seem to change with each new wave of tourists, so keep your ears open as you cruise the strip.

EXCURSIONS

Nestled away in the lush green foothills of the Andes and situated on the major thoroughfare between Sierra and Oriente, friendly Baños is one of the most popular and practical gateways to some of Ecuador's most amazing natural attractions. From here, you can explore nearby volcanic peaks, cloudforest, or jungle, and still be back in time for a gourmet meal and an evening soak in the hot springs.

HIKING. The steep, green hills surrounding Baños are visible from anywhere in town and beckon to hikers. To do the standard first hike, follow Maldonado toward the mountainside. Where the road ends, a path leads to the illuminated cross on top of the hill. From here, the little gringos below look like ants. The path continues beyond the cross, eventually looping back to Baños. A shorter hike to a cement virgin leaves from Mera on the west side of town and offers similar views.

To get an up-close view of some precipices, cross the main highway at the *terminal terrestre* and head toward the Río Pastaza, where the shaky San Francisco bridge crosses the churning gorge. From the other side, a path leads up the steep mountainside to the twin villages of **Illuchi Baja** and **Illuchi Alta.** For another escape from the tourist scene, take the dirt road on the right just before entering El Salado (see p. 315). Follow the path beside the river, which has views of the forest and the patchwork of farms across the valley. There is no real endpoint to the path—the hike ends at the summit of Volcán Tungurahua.

A more relaxing stroll heads to the **granja ecológica** (organic farm) of Agosto Muñoz, about 15 minutes outside of town. Just follow the road to Ouyo until the *granja*'s smiling chicken appears waving on the left. If you reach the Piscinas Santa Ana, you've gone too far. Señor Muñoz loves visitors, and he or one of his relatives will happily show you around.

BIKING. Though bicycle touring is somewhat unheard of in Ecuador, bikes can be easily and cheaply rented from many places in Baños (see **Rentals,** p. 312). A popular **bicycle** trip goes 16km down the road toward Puyo to the town of Río Verde (see p. 317). The mostly downhill ride passes over, under, and through countless waterfalls, as well as through an unlit tunnel (a flashlight might be a good idea). From Río Verde you can hop on a Baños-bound bus and put your bike on the roof (s/15,000). More ambitious cyclists can peddle back to Baños, which takes about twice as long as the trip out, or continue downhill to Puyo and catch a bus back from there. Take plenty of water, since there is none on the road, and watch out for cars going around sharp turns.

GUIDED TRIPS. Other excursions can benefit from the experience of a guide. Need transportation to a specific destination? Need a guide for a day, a week, or a month? No problem—everyone is eager and willing to take your money. Dozens of tour agencies pack the streets of Baños. Just keep in mind that relatively few of these are legitimately registered, and serious problems have been reported with a number of them. Longer, more distant excursions can be a sizeable investment, and justly so, since they may be the highlight of an Ecuadorian experience. Before spending a large sum of money, don't hesitate to ask for CETUR and INEFAN certifications from prospective guides.

One reputable agency is **Rainforest Tour** (tel./fax 740 743), right off the Parque Central on Ambato and Maldonado. General manager Santiago Herrera sets up trips to the mountains (Tungurahua, Cotopaxi, or Chimborazo), the Galápagos, and the Oriente. Jungle packages come in many shapes and sizes (US$30-40 per person per day for 3-4 days). All tours are led by guides with specific experience on that particular river or mountain. Rainforest Tour also rents bikes and horses. (Open daily 8am-8pm.) **Geotours,** on Halflants and Espejo, which is easily contacted through the Hostal Los Nevados, also offers mountain packages as well as **"jungle river rafting"** trips of up to four days.

Many **jungle tours** leave from Baños, and most are standard, *cabaña*-style excursions by jeep or motorized canoe, which may or may not include experienced guides or contact with the primary rainforest and its many inhabitants. A refreshing alternative is offered by the non-profit **Yawa Jee Fundación Indígena** (tel. 740 957; email yawajee@gye.satnet.net), at Oriente and Alfaro. The *fundación* works with several native Shuar villages in the forest south of Puyo, to promote sustainable agriculture and sanitation. They offer three- to five-day tours from Baños with an emphasis on education and cultural exchange. The residents will take you on hikes deep into primary forest, teach you about traditional plant uses, and serve you local foods. Prices are US$50 per person per day.

NEAR BAÑOS: RÍO VERDE

Midway between Baños in the highlands and Puyo in the jungle, the town of **Río Verde** seems to draw on the best of both worlds. The flash of brightly colored birds and butterflies flickering through vine- and orchid-draped trees shouts "tropics," but tilt your head back and you'll gaze upon mountain tops reaching the clouds. A convergence of tropical weather and rugged terrain have made the town and its surroundings a veritable breeding ground for waterfalls. There are over twenty *cascadas* in the area, ranging from serpentine trickles to booming cataracts. As an added perk, a number of quality cabins in the area provide bases from which to enjoy the idyllic landscape.

Transportation: Getting to Río Verde is half of the fun. The road from Baños hugs the edge of a cliff, with the Llanganates towering high above and the Río Pastaza running far below. The **Cascada Manta de Novia** and **Cascada San Jorge** provide great photo opportunities along the way. Near Río Verde, an implausible contraption, euphemistically called "the longest cable car in Ecuador," ferries fearless (foolhardy?) passengers across the abyss. Río Verde proper is nothing more than a few convenience stores along the highway; the real attractions lie outside of town. The **Río Verde** itself gushes over smooth volcanic rock at the **Cascadas San Miguel,** 250m from the highway. Surrounding the *cascadas*, **Cabañas Restaurant Indillama** (tel. (09) 785 263) provides cabins with private bath, hot water, and complimentary breakfast (US$10 per person). A **restaurant** on the premises serves *trucha frita* (s/25,000) and *espagueti vegetariano* (vegetarian spaghetti s/19,000; open daily 9am-6pm).

The ground shakes and the spray flies at the awe-inspiring **Pailón del Diablo (Devil's Cauldron),** where the Río Verde roars off a cliff to join the Río Pastaza on its path towards the Amazon. At the falls, **El Pailon Café** serves drinks and charges an admission fee (s/5,000) to help conserve the trails leading to the falls. Farther down the trail, a shaky bridge crosses the river to **El Otro Lado** (tel. (09) 820 367 or (02) 558 889; email info@ecuadortravel.com; www.ecuadortravel.com), which offers great bird-watching opportunities and deluxe cabins in the middle of 150 acres of private cloudforest (US$25-35 per person depending on group size; includes breakfast and dinner). A **restaurant** serves vegetarian, Indian, and Middle Eastern food (Hindu omelette s/15,000). To get to El Pailón and El Otro Lado, follow an easy trail for 1km from the highway to the river valley.

Transportation: To get to **Río Verde,** take one of the Baños-Puyo buses (30min., s/ 1,000). A common excursion from Baños involves renting mountain bikes (s/ 30,000 per person per day) and riding the downhill road to Río Verde. Most restaurants in Río Verde provide free bike parking. When you are ready to return, hop on a Baños-bound bus and put the bike on the roof. Following the road towards Puyo for a few more kilometers leads to the town of **Machay** and even more **waterfalls.**

PARQUE NACIONAL SANGAY

Welcome to Parque Nacional Sangay, where lava streams and tapirs run side-by-side. This unwieldy 517,000-hectare (over 5,000 sq. km) park sprawls south from Baños through five Ecuadorian provinces, falling from jagged Andean ridges in the west to the Amazon River basin in the east. The mountainous portion of the park boasts three of Ecuador's 10 highest peaks, including two active volcanoes. Excursions to Sangay's snow-capped summits and virgin forests are less commercialized than those to Chimborazo or Cotopaxi and are virtual pioneering expeditions through relatively undiscovered lands. With altitudes ranging from 5319m on the peak of Volcán Altar to 900m in the Amazon basin, much of the amazing landscape is simply impossible to traverse. This inaccessibility, combined with the park's main objective (to protect and conserve), bars visitors from reaching some of Sangay's more remote areas. First founded as a reserve in 1979, the park shelters a selection of flora and fauna almost as diverse as its geography and includes such rare and strange specimens as the endangered **Andean tapir** *(Tapirus pinchaque)*, also known as the *canta de monte.*

Though Sangay's unreachable areas may fascinate, the accessible ones are nothing to scoff at. The park is divided into two sections: the *zona alta* in the Sierra (1500-5319m), and the *zona baja* in the Oriente (900-1500m). The *zona alta* contains Sangay's main attractions; its entrance points are easily accessible from Baños or Riobamba. The *zona baja* entrance is most easily visited from Macas in the Southern Oriente. The four main attractions in Parque Sangay's *zona alta* are the relaxing **El Placer,** the towering fire-spewers **Volcán Tungurahua** (5,016m) and **Volcán Altar** (5319m), and the remote namesake, **Volcán Sangay** (5230m).

LOGISTICS. Sangay's administrative body, **INEFAN,** is a tremendous resource for those planning to explore the park. In addition to providing information, the staff offers advice for finding guides. For more info, contact them at the Riobamba office (see **Riobamba Practical Information,** p. 321). For more trip-specific information in English, consult the SAEC in Quito (see **Useful Organizations,** p. 250), which maintains members' trip reports and info on recommended guides. (Park **admission** US$10.)

EL PLACER. El Placer is a relatively low, swampy area with *aguas termales* for bathing. There is a *refugio* with amenities for overnight stays, but most make this into a long daytrip, departing for Alao at daybreak (INEFAN leaves at 4am) and returning to Riobamba at dusk. **Atillo,** a picturesque lagoon, is a two-hour drive (from INEFAN, leaves at 8am). A trail traverses the park from the Andes to the town of **Macas** in the Southern Oriente and is the best route for discovering the true diversity of the park's terrain. Some amazing species populate the park; the Andean tapir, visible from the Atillo and El Placer areas, is found nowhere else in the world. Plant and animal stalkers in the know head to **Playa de Sangay** and **El Palmar** for their observational kicks. Others take a walk on the wild side of the Oriente by heading to **Culebrillas** and the **Lagunas de Sardmayacu** *(zona baja)* in the neverending quest for still more jaguar and bear sightings. Both places are accessible from Palora and Macas (see **Tours from Macas,** p. 364).

VOLCÁN TUNGURAHUA. One of the least difficult snow climbs in Ecuador, the young Tungurahua is technically easy but physically arduous. This 10th-highest peak in Ecuador was most recently volcanically active from 1916 to 1925. The two-day excursion begins at **Pondoa** (2800m), at the base of the mountain, from where it is about a four-hour hike to the brand new, privately owned **refugio** (3800m). The shelter is equipped with a gas stove, fireplace, and mattresses, but bring your own food, toilet paper, and matches (rooms s/20-40,000 per person). Staying in the *refugio* is imperative; the four-hour ascent to Tungurahua's summit must begin at 2am, when the snow is hardest. Trails can be muddy, especially during the rainy season (June-Aug.). Crampons, ice axes, and ropes are all necessary. Non-climbers can make Tungurahua into a daytrip and simply hike to the *refugio* and back. Those planning to attempt the summit should pay the admission fee (US$10) at the control building in Pondoa.

From Baños, a *camioneta* leaves for Pondoa from in front of Residencial Party, Alfaro between Ambato and Oriente (1hr., 9am-10am, s/20,000). Alternatively, tour agencies in Baños may have extra room in their vehicles to ferry people to the park entrance. In Pondoa you can rent a horse to carry your bags to the *refugio* (s/30,000; from the *refugio*, set the animal free and it will find its way home).

EL ALTAR (LOS ALTARES). This highest mountain in the park collapsed in 1460 and is now partially covered by glaciers. Accessible from yet another park entrance at **Candelaria** (a 45min. ride from INEFAN in Riobamba), the eight-hour climb to the crater is similar to the two-day Tungurahua ascent, although there is no worthwhile daytrip to a *refugio*. Prices are similar to those of other trips, and guides are readily available in Candelaria (INEFAN officials will assist you). Again, equipment is needed for the climb to the crater. Camping is possible in a cave near the crater; you can also stay overnight at the park entrance.

VOLCÁN SANGAY. One of the most active volcanoes in the world, Sangay constantly spews ash and smoke to make sure the world doesn't forget about it. This lava-dripping monster has three deep craters at its summit. The park's mammoth namesake requires a minimum of six days to conquer it: two-and-a-half days hiking each way, and one day for the climb. Begin the hike up Sangay from the entrance at **Alao,** on the western side of the park. Hiring a guide is a must, at least for the start of the climb. In Alao, you can find a guide (s/50,000 per day) and a mule for your luggage and equipment (s/35,000 per day). You'll also need all the proper hiking and mountain-climbing equipment, plus clothing and six to eight days worth of food and water. Stock up in a Baños or Riobamba supermarket; there's not much in Alao. It is dangerous to climb all the way up to Sangay's crater; you might get in the fiery path of all that spewed ash and lava. Experience is another must, and visitors should only climb as far as guides recommend. INEFAN rides from Riobamba to Alao leave as early as 4am—call to check definite times. INEFAN officials can give advice on equipment and help you find a guide.

RIOBAMBA

Known as the "Sultan of the Andes," Riobamba (pop. 130,000) needs no elaborate show of regalia to prove that it is master of its domain. Tranquil and relatively tourist-free, this quintessential Andean city allows one to become immersed in Ecuadorian life without the fast pace and danger of a major metropolis. Cobblestone streets criss-cross plazas and parks, many with awe-inspiring views of snow-capped Volcán Chimborazo and neighboring El Altar and Tungurahua. These towering volcanoes keep watch over a city that bears the scars of its tumultuous past. After a devastating earthquake and landslide in 1797, the entire city (then the capital of Ecuador) was moved to its present site on a highland valley plain. As a result, the city's oldest architecture is neoclassical, with one notable exception: the cathedral on Veloz and 5 de Junio was transported stone-by-stone from its pre-quake location. When Quito was made the capital, many of Riobamba's wealthiest residents moved, leaving the town's grand old buildings to slowly decay.

Most visitors, however, don't come to experience the parks, plazas, and architecture. As with Latacunga to the north, Riobamba's main attractions lie outside of town. The city is known primarily as a departure point for daytrips. These include jaunts up Chimborazo, Ecuador's tallest peak, and jaw-dropping train rides to Alausí. Also common are visits to nearby indigenous villages and the Parque Nacional Sangay, home to of one of the world's most active volcanoes.

ORIENTATION

Riobamba's straightforward grid layout and clear, consistent street signs make it one of the most navigable cities in Ecuador. Activity centers around the area squared off by **Argentinos** and **Olmedo** to the east and west, and **Av. 5 de Junio** and **Angel León** to the south and north. **Primera Constituyente** and **Av. 10 de Agosto** are the city's main thoroughfares. From the **terminal terrestre,** head right (south) for 1km on **León Borja,** which turns into 10 de Agosto at **Carabobo,** or simply hop on one of the passing city buses on the **control norte** route. The **train station** is in the center of town at 10 de Agosto and Carabobo. Out of the city limits and above the clouds, Chimborazo lies to the northwest.

PRACTICAL INFORMATION

Buses: The main **terminal terrestre** is on León Borja (the western part of 10 de Agosto) and Daniela, about 1km to the northwest of the center of town. From there, buses head to: **Quito** (3½hr., every 15min. 2:15am-9pm, s/30,000); **Guayaquil** (5hr., every 30min. 2:15am-9:30pm, s/35,000); **Cuenca** (6hr., 7 per day, s/48,000); **Ambato** (1hr., every 15min. 6am-6:30pm, s/10,000); and **Alausí** (2hr., every hr. 5:00am-7:00pm, s/13,000). The **Terminal Oriental** (tel. 960 766), on Espejo and León Borja, north of town, sends buses to: **Baños** (1hr., every 20min. 6am-6pm, s/8,000); **Puyo** (3hr., 6 per day, s/20,000); and **Tena** (5hr., 3 and 6:20pm, s/40,000). The **Guano Terminal,** Rocafuerte and Nueva York (north of town), sends buses to **Guano** (25min., every 30min., s/1,900) and **Santa Teresita** (35min., every 30min., s/2,500). Buses for many nearby destinations leave 3 blocks south of the *terminal terrestre* (take the Control Sur bus from the bull-ring and get off at the 3-way intersection) and go to **Cajabamba** (20min., every 30min. 6am-7pm, s/2,500) via **Laguna de Colta** (25min., s/3,500) and **Guamote** (1hr., 6,000). Additional buses leave on Thursday for the Guamote market. Buses to **San Juan,** the closest town to Chimborazo, leave from Unidad Nacional and Prensa (45min., every 15min. 6am-6:45pm, s/3,000). Many more buses traveling the Quito-Loja route stop in Riobamba; to catch one, wait *outside* the station.

Trains: The **train station** (tel. 961 909) is at 10 de Agosto and Carabobo. Office open daily 8am-noon and 2-5pm. After a long history of track-closing repairs, the magnificent **Riobamba-Guayaquil** route was reopened in 1999, but only with limited service from Riobamba to Aluasí. Though the locomotive has now been replaced with a converted school bus, hordes of gringos still climb aboard and **ride the roof** for the best views. The "train" leaves from Riobamba 3 times per week (11hr. round-trip; W, F, Su 7am; US$15). Check the schedule, however, as it often changes. A **Riobamba-Quito** route (F 9am, s/45,000) offers fantastic volcano views from the (real) train roof. Make sure to arrive at the station by 5:30am to ensure getting a ticket. See also the **Riobamba-Alausí-Bucay-Durán Railway,** p. 327.

Local Buses: Unless you're in a big hurry, local buses are unnecessary; Riobamba is eminently walkable. There are 2 routes—Control Norte, along León Borja and 10 de Agosto, and Control Sur, running through Orozco between Carabobo and Unidad Nacional on the other end of town. Buses run 6am-8pm and cost s/1,000.

Taxis: These ubiquitous night crawlers—they're everywhere, all night long—charge a reasonable s/8,000 to go between any 2 points in the city.

Tourist Information: CETUR (tel. 941 213), 10 de Agosto and 5 de Junio, will amiably distribute city maps and brochures, as well as help any lost or querying souls. English spoken. Open M-F 8:30am-5pm.

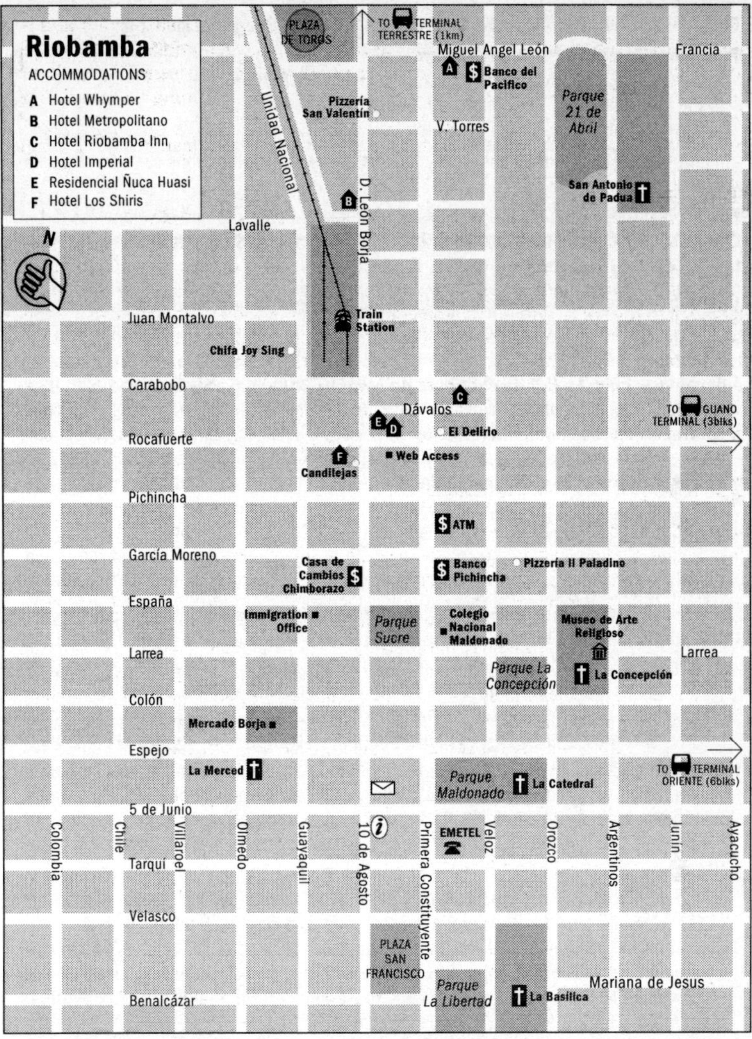

Immigration Office: España 10-50 and Guayaquil (tel. 969 844). For affairs relating to visas and tourist cards. Open M-F 8am-noon and 2-6pm.

INEFAN: (Tel. 963 779), 9 de Octubre near Duchicela, at the **Ministerio del Cultura Agrícola (MAC)** in the northwest corner of town (towards Chimborazo). Super-helpful staff can suggest numerous excursions to Chimborazo and Sangay, all using public transportation. Open M-F 8am-4:30pm.

Currency Exchange: Casa de Cambios Chimborazo (tel. 968 608), Av. 10 de Agosto between García Moreno and España, at the entrance to Hotel Monte Carlo. Exchanges dollars and traveler's checks. Open M-F 9:30am-1:30pm and 3-6pm, Sa 9:30am-1pm.

Banks: Abundant in the main section of town—look up and you'll see one. Large banks include the **Banco del Pacífico,** Veloz and Angel León, and **Banco Pichincha,** Primera Constituyente and García Moreno. Both open M-F 9am-5pm. There are 24hr. Cirrus/Plus/MC **ATMs** at Banco del Pacífico.

Emergency: Tel. 101.

Police: (Tel. 969 300), Policía and La Paz, on the Vía al Chembo. Open 24hr.

Pharmacy: Farmacia Perpetuo Socorro, León Borja 41-09 (tel. 940 808), towards the *terminal terrestre,* next to the Hotel Zeus. Open daily 8:30am-1:30pm and 3pm-10pm. In the *centro,* there's a pharmacy on almost every block.

Hospital: The **Policlínico** (tel. 965 725), Olmedo and Cuba, is the most modern and highly recommended medical facility in town. Open 24hr. Numerous private clinics are available as well.

Post Office: (tel. 966 006), 10 de Agosto and Espejo. Postcards and envelopes sold, but don't count on incoming mail. Open M-F 7:30am-7:30pm, Sa 8am-12pm.

Information: Tel. 104.

Internet Access: Café Internet, Rocafuerte 22-30 third floor (tel. 968 882; email netcafe@laserinter.net), at intersection with 10 de Agosto. Continue that online romance for s/20,000 for 30min. Open M-Sa 10am-10pm, Su 3pm-10pm

Telephones: EMETEL (tel. 969-816 or 962-001), Tarquí and Velos, offers local, long-distance, and international calling service. Allows free MCI or AT&T calling card calls. EMETEL also sends and receives **faxes** for a fee. Make calling card, make a collect call, or receive calls at local upscale hotels. Guests can receive international calls at virtually all hotels; it's usually a cheaper option than dialing home from Ecuador.

TELEPHONE CODE	03

ACCOMMODATIONS

Hotel Imperial (tel. 960 429), 10 de Agosto and Rocafuerte, right in the heart of Riobamba, is a popular backpacker refuge. Relax in spacious, airy rooms or lounge on the balcony. Large, reasonably clean beds and bathrooms that are puny but bearable. Management arranges Chimborazo excursions (US$15 per person). Some rooms have private baths and/or TVs; other's don't. The price is the same: s/25,000 per person.

Hotel Metropolitano (tel. 961 714), León Borja and Lavalle. Probably the best mid-range option near downtown, offering clean, rather small rooms with private, hot-water baths. Take advantage of the comfortable leather chairs in the spacious *sala* to watch some Ecuadorian *fútbol.* Rooms s/30,000 per person; discounts on stays of 2 nights or more.

Hotel Whymper, Angel León 23-10 and Primera Constituyente (tel. 964 575), next to Banco del Pacífico, is a bit outside the center of town. Whimper with delight at the sight of the king-sized beds. With green bedspreads and linoleum floors, it rivals Hotel Riobamba Inn for the "Best Decor from a Past Decade" award. Telephones and private bathrooms are an added bonus. The staff can arrange trips up nearby mountains, with discounts for *Let's Go* users, while the breakfast in their restaurant (s/15,000) provides fuel for the climb. Rooms s/30,000 per person.

Hotel Ñuca Huasi (tel. 966 669), 10 de Agosto between Rocafuerte and Dávalos. Around the corner from the Hotel Imperial, it offers a reasonable fall-back position–and a sexy palindromic phone number. Try to imagine this deteriorating mansion as it once was, and perhaps watching the paint peel won't seem so bad. At least the 7m ceilings mean your head is safe. Rooms s/15,000, with bath s/20,000.

Hotel Riobamba Inn, Carabobo 23-20 and Primera Constituyente (tel. 961 696), across from the Banco Central. Named with a redundant name, but boasting immense private hot-water bathrooms and spotless bedrooms. The cable TVs in each room provide something to look at other than the primary-color decor. Singles s/55,000, doubles s/100,000, triples s/135,000.

Hotel Los Shyris (tel. 960 323), Rocafuerte and 10 de Agosto, is a step above the Imperial in both cleanliness and overall room quality, but that's hard to see given the dimly-lit interior. The clean, telephone- and TV-equipped rooms (local calls s/5,000 per 3min.) seem all the larger in comparison with the tiny bathrooms. Rooms s/40,000 per person, students s/35,000.

FOOD

Riobamba, because it's the classic Ecuadorian city, has plenty of budget *almuerzo* stops with meals for s/10,000 but very little to excite the palates of travelers passing through. Most eateries serve seemingly identical meals, though their kitchens vary in cleanliness—choose carefully or you'll find yourself hopping off the Riobamba-Alansí train to "take care of business." Come dinner time, locals crowd around outdoor stands that scoop various traditional stews and meat dishes out of steaming bowls lit by little floodlights. The food can be good, but be wary—look for flies, and remember, no raw veggies. These stands cluster around Carabobo and Guayaquil, selling their goods for s/6,000. The cheapest eats, the bakeries *(panaderías)*, sell several species of bread (s/500 and up).

El Delirio (tel. 967 502), Primera Constituyente and Rocafuerte. Beautifully situated in Simón Bolívar's old house, a historical landmark, with outdoor tables in a charming patio garden under blossoming trees. If it was nice enough for the liberator of South America, it's probably nice enough for you. Entrees ranging from *cordon blue chicken* (s/20,000) to *filet mignon* (s/30,000) are a slight splurge. Ask about their daily specials. Pleasant indoor dining as well. Open Tu-Sa noon-10pm, Su noon-3pm.

Restaurant Candilejas, 10 de Agosto 27-33 (tel. 960 220), between Pichincha and Rocafuerte, is a rarity in Ecuadorian dining: it has neither background music nor a TV. Nothing distracts diners from the elegant decor and tasty food. As a concession to its foreign clientele, the menu includes Kodachrome pictures that preview your meal in living color. The owner recommends the *sopa de cebolla* (s/9,000) or *camarones al ajillo* (s/25,000). Open M-Sa 8am-8pm, Su 8am-2pm.

Pizzeria Il Paladino, Garcia Moreno 24-42 between Veloz and Orozco. César, yet another Italian-trained Ecuadorian pizza man, easily creates the best pizzas in town in his brick oven. The house specialty, pizza paladino (s/14,000), contains an entire ecosystem served from the hot oven. The salads are big and tasty (s/10,000 and up). Open M-Sa 5-10pm.

Chifa Joysing, Unidad Nacional 29-33 and Carabobo (tel. 961 285). The huge portions of savory cuisine at this typical Ecuadorian *chifa* will have you singing with joy. Creative dishes as well as old favorites. Experiment with *crema de wu chi wu* (s/8,000), or try the tasty *tallarín especial* (angel hair noodles with Chinese vegetables, chicory pork, beef, and shrimp; s/16,000). The large dining room is rather nondescript, but draws the crowds nonetheless. Open daily 10am-11pm.

Pizzería San Valentín (tel. 963 137), Borja and Torres. Though a bit pricey, this seems to be the hip hangout during the week. The young locals also enjoy the Mexican food (burritos s/20,000 and up), ice cream (s/13,000), and undoubtedly the pictures of scantily clad women decorating the bar. Open Tu-Sa 5pm-midnight.

SIGHTS

PARKS. Riobamba's scenic parks just cry out to be strolled in. One of the most compelling pleas comes from **Parque 21 de Abril,** also known as **La Loma de Quito,** perched above the rest of Riobamba. At the northern part of town, the park is boxed in by Orozco, Argentinos, León, and Lavalle. Due to its auspicious position, this park monopolizes the best panoramic views and photo opportunities in the city. Romantic and beautiful at sunset, the park also holds a church, **San Antonio de Padua,** which has stone steps leading up to its picturesque patio gardens from every direction. The **Parque Sucre,** at España and Primera Constituyente, at the center of town, graces the inland city with the next best thing to the sea—a beautiful bronze **fountain** and **statue of Neptune.** Local men gather on the palm-tree-shaded benches, socializing and people-watching. The engaging **Parque Maldonado,** Primera Constituyente and Espejo, next to the CETUR office, displays a monument to its namesake, Pedro Vicente Maldonado. This *riobambeño* historian and cartographer drew up the first political map of Ecuador. Big and bustling with weekend activity, **Parque Guayaquil,** Unidad Nacional and León Borja, provides the perfect opportunity to let your inner child roam free.

RIOBAMBANS GO NUTTY A seed the size of a chicken egg, soft and malleable when fresh, but hardened when exposed to air, the **tagua nut** has inspired a new industry in Riobamba and served as an unlikely medium of artistic expression. Local craftsmen have dubbed it *marfil vegetal* (vegetable ivory) for its pure white color and remarkably smooth texture. Before becoming an art form, however, tagua crafting mainly served necessity. Back when there was no plastic, tagua nuts were used to make teacups, buttons, and many other household items. When cheaper plastic items displaced the beloved tagua nut, the craft was nearly lost. But today, after a generation-long hiatus, a new batch of young artisans has revived the industry, creating statuettes, small animals, and even chess sets by the same techniques that their grandfathers used before them. There are at least two tagua shops in Riobamba, which has become the industry's headquarters. Both **Tagua Shop,** Borja 35-17 and Ibarra (tel. 963 694), sharing an entrance with Alta Montaña, and **Ricardo Tagua** (tel. 09 711 831), Borja at Torres, are fully functional workshops, and make up whatever they lack in creative names with the originality of the pieces they sell (s/5,000 and up). Besides, this budding industry has provided a new source of income for locals, as well as an alternative to cutting down the forest where the seeds grow. That's all wonderful, but one burning question remains: how the hell did a seed native to the coastal lowlands plant itself in the economy of the highland city of Riobamba? Even the locals can't explain that one.

CHURCHES. The city's **churches** reveal the Riobamban penchant for atypical architecture. **La Basílica,** Veloz and Benalcázar, constructed from 1883 to 1915, gained fame as the only round church in Ecuador. The main **Catedral,** Veloz and 5 de Junio by Parque Maldonado, is the oldest building in town. The sole remnant of Riobamba's pre-earthquake site, it was transported in 1797, one stone at a time. **La Concepción** (La Loma de Quito), Orozco and Larrea, and **La Merced,** Olmedo and Espejo, don't have fascinating histories, but do open for mass. *(Open M-F 6-8am and 6-8pm, Sa-Su 6am-8pm.)*

MUSEUMS. Two **museums** of note grace Riobamba. **La Concepción,** or the **Museo de Arte Religioso,** Argentinos and Larrea, has a collection of religious art and artifacts from the 17-19th centuries. *(Tel. 965 212. Open Su 9am-noon, Tu-F 9am-noon and 3-6 pm, Sa 9am-6pm. Admission s/40,000, students s/15,000.)* The **Museo del Colegio Maldonado,** also known as the Museo de Ciencias Naturales, is a tiny natural history and science exhibit inside the monumental schoolhouse at Parque Sucre. *(Open M-F 8am-1pm and 3-6pm. Admission s/3,000.)*

ENTERTAINMENT

The **Saturday market** is a *huge* affair. The entire length of every street boxed in by España, 5 de Junio, Guayaquil, and Argentinos—as well as all the space in-between—fills up with vendors, shoppers, and good old Ecuadorian energy. People from all the small surrounding villages come to join in the spectacle. Nearly *everything* imaginable is sold somewhere, from live chicks to toothbrushes, traditional Indian weaving to cow legs. More touristy items center around Parque La Concepción. On Fridays, the **vegetable market** at La Valle and Esmeraldas promises to amaze through the sheer size of mountains of plant material.

Even on the weekdays, the shopping scene stays strong. Riobamba is famous for its carved tagua nuts (see **Riobambans Go Nutty,** p. 324), which are crafted and sold at several local shops. Another well-known form of local *artesanía* is the weaving of bags called *shigras*. Market spots include Colón and Veloz, Junín and 5 de Junio, and the area around the post office at Primera Constituyente and Espejo.

Riobamba's cultural haven, **La Casa de Cultura,** Rocafuerte and 10 de Agosto, provides five floors of activities, from a museum of traditional musical instruments to Ecuador's only model-building club. Walk-ins are welcome anytime. Check the bulletin board downstairs for posted events.

Cockfights can be seen Saturdays and Sundays in a house at Almagro and Olmedo, or at the *Colizeo de Balles* at Ciudadela in the Barrio Tapi (ask at CETUR for details). Riobamba's biggest *fiesta*, **La Loma de Quito,** commemorates the city's founding. The actual holiday falls on April 21, but *riobambeños* get a headstart on the 18th and keep it up until the 22nd, a time in which fairs, bullfights, and parades swamp the streets.

Riobamba is quiet during the week, but there are several options for weekend evening entertainment. Most *discotecas* cluster around the same area—on León Borja between the *terminal terrestre* and Hotel Zeus at Duchicela—making a night of club-hopping all too easy. Some of the most dance-friendly *discotecas* are **Casablanca** and **Gens Chop** (tel. 964 325), at Borja and Duchicela. The latter has a large dance floor and UFO-style flying colored lights. Around the corner, on Duchicela, **La Che-V** (tel. 945 644) is a slightly more formal, popular local bar. At the *terminal* itself, **La Casa del Billar** entertains with pool, ping-pong, and a disco. It all gets going around 9 or 10pm and keeps on rollin' until 2 to 5am. Also popular among the younger crowd are the nearby **Vieja Guardia,** Manuel E. Flor and Zambrano, as well as **Media Luna,** Zambrano and Veloz, across from the Hotel Galpon.

The high *páramo* around Riobamba is littered with lakes, villages, and stunning vistas of the surrounding mountains. For those with well-acclimatized legs and lungs (and plenty of cash), perhaps the best way of seeing this area is from the seat of a **bicycle. Pro-Bicí,** Primera Constituyente 23-51 and Larrea (tel. 941 880 or 941 734), run by cyclist and mechanic Galo Brito, runs trips into the surrounding countryside (starting at US$25 per day.) While this does not include food or lodging, it does cover the use of a Cannondale M900 mountain bike with Deore XT components (i.e. a really good bicycle). Galo, a native Riobamban educated in the US, knows enough of the history of Chimborazo province to keep you interested for days. He and his assistant Freddy (who speaks only Spanish) keep you on quiet backroads for most of your ride.

NEAR RIOBAMBA: GUANO

Only a 20-minute bus ride from Riobamba, these tiny villages offer an intimate glimpse into a different sort of Ecuador: a rural Andean lifestyle that makes even tranquil Riobamba seem bustling. **Guano** specializes in rug-making and slow living. Numerous *artesanía* shops sell monstrous rugs, leather goods, and hemp items; many will custom-make any design that you can communicate to them with pictures or broken Spanish. The simple pleasures of all Ecuadorian towns can be found here as well—only in a smaller, quieter version. The central square houses a lovely **park** with a geometric garden, and a small **church** stands at Colón and García Moreno. It's hard to imagine an emergency happening in so placid a place, but in case of any sort of disaster, a **pharmacy** and **medical center** are at García Moreno and Ramirez.

One of the only restaurants in town, **El Oasis** dishes out chow at Hidalgo and García Moreno, near the main plaza (hours erratic). *Panaderías* and small stands throughout town offer *cholas*, buns filled with sweet stuff. If you plan to spend the night, check out the brand new **Quinta Karen Estefanía** (tel. 900 336). Slightly outside *el centro*, this resort/hotel provides the perfect place to lounge in luxury and solitude at surprisingly reasonable prices. Take advantage of the indoor swimming pool, jacuzzi, sauna, billiards room, bowling alley, and countless other diversions of the leisured class. Guests stay in suites with a bedroom, kitchen, and bathroom. Rooms s/50,000 per person, meals s/25,000, swimming pool/sauna s/20,000. Call ahead to make a reservation.

Transportation: To get here from Riobamba, catch the **bus** from Rocafuerte and Nueva York (30min., every 30min. 5am-7pm, s/1,800).

NEAR RIOBAMBA: SAN FRANCISCO DE QUITO AND GUAMOTE

San Francisco de Quito has two major sites, La Balbanera church and the Laguna de Colta. Built in 1534, **La Balbanera** was the first church in Ecuador. Plaques on the walls record the occurrence of a series of miracles related to the church in some way or another. Particularly prominent is a painting of an incident in 1959 in which the conductor of a derailed train prayed to the Divine Lady of La Balbanera—by an apparent miracle the train was saved. Beyond the church and across the road to the left sits the large **Laguna de Colta.** While the lagoon is visible from the highway, there's also a road that wanders through several beautifully framed rural villages to the back of the lake. The backwoods route reveals rural settlements with indigenous farmers working fields on the slopes of picturesque, clouded hills. Thousands of reeds growing out of the lagoon obscure much of the water from view. It's a surreal experience to watch the locals float through the reeds on their bamboo rafts. Eventually, after about a two-and-a-half hour walk around the lagoon, the road bends back around to the highway. Buses back to Riobamba or on to Guamote can be flagged down anywhere on the highway until dark.

Guamote, about a 25min. drive from San Francisco de Quito, is a very high (3056m), very pretty town, but it's probably only a worthwhile stop for the bustling and non-touristy Thursday market. The Riobamba-Alausí Railway goes right by the basic **Residencial Turismo** (s/30,000 per person) and a couple of restaurants.

Transportation: Buses bound for Cajabamba, Laguna de Colta, and Guamote leave Riobamba from the area around Unidad Nacional and Bolívar (behind the bull ring). All three locations can be reached by the Guamote bus (every 30min., s/ 2,500-6,000). More buses leave on Thursdays for Guamote's market.

NEAR RIOBAMBA: VOLCÁN CHIMBORAZO

Volcán Chimborazo (6310m) overwhelms with its sheer magnitude—leaving the climber literally teetering on the edge of the earth. Explorers once mistook Chimborazo for the highest mountain in the world, but its summit remains the farthest from the center of the earth, due to the earth's bulge at the equator. Snow-capped year-round, this dormant volcano peeks above the clouds into the silence of space. Chimborazo's second refuge (5000m) offers stunning views, and can be reached in half a day without any climbing experience, equipment, or extreme expense.

Superb scenery graces the ride up the flank of the mountain. *Comunas* and *caseríos*—tiny villages without any government administration—dot the fertile farmlands and the *cerros* (hills) in the shadow of Chimborazo. Tourists and local *indígenas* find each other equally foreign sights; schoolchildren in polychromatic shawls gape at visitors, and even the local cows stare. The rocky ascent passes through cloudforests lined with pines and tiny shrubs covering misty boulders, hills, and slopes. The cut in the mountainside created for the road shows bands of multicolored soil—each band the signature of a past eruption. Suddenly, above the treeline, the landscape takes on a lunar quality—only rocks, clouds, and snow remain. Keep your eyes peeled for *vicuñas;* about a thousand of these deerlike creatures roam the park. Look farther up than you imagine land could be, and there in the distance is the peak, which will render anyone but an Everest veteran speechless.

TRANSPORTATION. Those up for a challenging hike can ask the driver of the Riobamba-Guaranda bus if he plans to use the *Arenal* route. If so, ask to be dropped off at the turnoff to the *refugios.* From the dropoff point it's a 7km hike up a dirt road to the second *refugio.* Four-wheel drive vehicles travel this road, and some report being able to hitch-hike. Remember, hiking is much harder at this altitude. It is crucial to rest frequently and drink a lot of water. Sunglasses and sunscreen are key too, since the snow reflects sunlight. Those unaccustomed to the altitude should not hike alone. On the way back, hop on a passing bus going from Guaranda to Riobamba.

PRACTICAL INFORMATION. INEFAN recently instituted a US$10 admission fee for the park. Since there are no guardhouses along the access roads, this fee is collected irregularly. Some unscrupulous tour guides have taken advantage of the situation to collect the fee from tourists, and then pocket it. With this warning in mind, a relatively cheap way to reach the second refuge is through the **Hotel Imperial** (tel. 960 429), in Riobamba. Tell them the night before, and they'll set you up with a driver who can take you on the two-hour trip to the lower refuge (4800m). While you hike up to the second refuge, the driver will wait for a few hours, then take you back. The round-trip runs US$15 per person; trips generally leave at 7am and return between noon and 1pm. For a little more, the driver may go to the *aguas termales* north of the mountain. The drive is long, but that hardly seems to matter when you're lounging in hot water gazing past a lush pastoral countryside at Chimborazo's peak in the distance. Be careful climbing to the second refuge (5000m); though it's only an hour-long walk at most, it must be taken at a snail's pace. Frequent rest stops and water are a must, as your body will not be acclimatized to the altitude. The drive to Chimborazo can also be done by any four-wheel-drive taxi that you find in Riobamba, or by guides arranged by any of the numerous but expensive travel agencies in town.

One of Galo Brito's bicycle trips (see **Riobamba: Entertainment,** p. 324) involves driving to the first *refugio* at 4800m and then biking back to Riobamba. The roads are good enough that this isn't as crazy as it sounds, and it promises to be an unforgettable experience (trips US$45-70 depending on the number of people).

Most people stop at the second refuge, but experienced, adventurous climbers can take on the challenging ascent to Chimborazo's summit (8hr. ascent and 4hr. descent at best). Crampons, ropes, and other standard equipment are essential. Climbs leave at 1am from the second refuge; a guide is a necessity. **Alta Montaña** (tel. 963 694 or 942 215) in Riobamba can provide qualified guides. For information on guides, see **Mountaineering,** p. 305).

Both refuges on the mountain have basic food items, coffee, and tourist souvenirs. They also offer accommodations (s/60,000)—but bring your own sleeping bag, and stock up on plenty of extra water and food. If you stay overnight at a refuge, arrange for the 4WD taxi to pick you up the next day. Sleeping under a full moon high above civilization comes at a price (round-trip s/100,000). Altitude sickness can be a serious problem for those not acclimatized to heights above 3000m. For more info, see **Environmental Hazards,** p. 19. Besides its namesake, Chimborazo Park has other attractions as well. Two **Inca Ruins** and **La Chorrera Canyon** are all within hiking distance from the road, but may require some exploring. Inquire at INEFAN for details.

THE RIOBAMBA-ALAUSÍ-BUCAY-DURÁN RAILWAY

Before the El Niño storms of 1997-98, this exhilarating railway was a source of pride for Ecuadorians and a feather in the cap of railroad engineers everywhere. The line fearlessly traversed every climate zone in the land; beginning in the breathless highlands of Chimborazo province, plummeting through the páramo and cloudforest of the western Andes, and finally terminating in the steamy coastal jungle of Guayaquil. One section right after Alausí, **El Nariz del Diablo** (the Devil's Nose), was particularly inspiring. Roof-riding gringos held their breaths as the train surmounted a perpendicular cliff by means of two amazing switchbacks—quite a feat of railroad acrobatics. In under 30km, the line descended from 2347m to 1255m, with heart-stopping horseshoe twists and turns revealing magnificent views of the countryside. But, that was then...

The tracks have somewhat recovered from the decimation of El Niño and the line finally re-opened in 1999. But the journey's reincarnation is barely a hollow shadow of its former self. Sadly, the coal-burning locomotive has been usurped by its more efficient cousin, the diesel-burning converted school bus. The "train" still departs several times a week along the old tracks (see **Trains,** p. 320), which run parallel to the Panamericana until the town of Alausí. Then, it slows to a snail's pace and tenuously descends El Nariz del Diablo, the most outstanding section of the line. But this is done only to satisfy tourists, who jockey for the best views on the overcrowded roof, and the train shortly returns to the station in Alausí. Understandably, some passengers feel cheated out of the US$15 they paid for the ride.

Even without a fully functional railway, resourceful travelers can still pick the Devil's Nose. The bus to Alausí leaves at much more convenient times and offers the same views as the train. From Alausí, the splendid views of the Devil's Nose are easily within walking distance. In fact, the tracks out of town make for quite a pleasant hike, and the views may be enjoyed at your convenience. When you've seen enough, simply turn around and head back to town. You'll feel better just thinking of all the exercise you got and all of the *sucres* you saved.

ALAUSÍ

Alausí is a tranquil mountain stop in the central Sierra, where the general silence of the town's streets is disturbed only by the Sunday market and the regular chug-chugging of the train descending the "devil's nose." But with a towering, mountainside dominating everything, who has much to say anyway? At least the alpine overseer is a charismatic one, providing an amazing backdrop for Alausí's ancient buildings and sleepy streets. A beautiful setting and a slower pace of life make Alausí a worthy stop for weary travelers moving up and down the central corridor.

Plaza Bolívar and the **train station** are at the base of the *centro*, near Sucre and **Av. 5 de Junio,** the main thoroughfare in town. It takes five minutes to walk through the entire downtown area. The streets heading down the mountainside are **Sucre, Ricuarte, De Loza,** and **Av. 9 de Octubre,** though the few street signs have largely rusted into illegibility. Cross-streets are Bolívar, Villalva, García Moreno, and 5 de Junio.

Buses leave from the corner of 9 de Octubre and 5 de Julio and go to: **Riobamba** (2hr., every 30min. 4am-5pm, s/12,000); **Quito** (5½hr.; 4, 8, 10, and 11:30am; s/40,000); **Cuenca** (4½hr., 6 per day, s/20,000); **Guayaquil** (5hr., 9am, s/40,000); and **Ambato** (3hr.; 4, 8, 10, and 11:30am; s/22,000). Buses traveling the Quito-Cuenca route pass along the Panamerican Highway at all hours of the day and night. Transportation may also be arranged to **Achullapas,** from which it is a three-day hike to the ruins at Ingapirca (see p. 329). For **train** info, see **The Riobamba-Alausí-Bucay-Durán Railway,** below. The basic **Farmacia Americano** sits under the Hotel Americano. National phone calls can be made from the **EMETEL** office opposite the train station. Service is slow—it may be quicker to catch a bus to Riobamba and call from there. The **post office** is at the corner of 9 de Octubre and García Moreno. Better to hold on to those postcards for another few days—the *correo* has, let's say, a relaxed atmosphere. **Banco de Guayaquil,** 5 de Junio and Ricaurte, has good rates on dollars and traveler's checks (open M-F 9am-6pm). If you need **medical services,** you'd best return to Riobamba.

Hotel Americano, García Moreno 51 and Ricaurte (tel. 930 159), is located above the Farmacia Americano and run by the same management. In a town of unexciting hotel choices, this is probably the most appealing of the bunch. Clean, quiet, and cozy rooms have wooden floors, street views, and private baths. (Rooms s/20,000 per person.) **Hotel Panamericano** (tel. 930 156), 5 de Junio near the bus stop, may inspire a game of one-on-one basketball with its parquet floors. Just be sure not to mess up the tidy rooms and well-washed sheets when dunking. The owners can provide information about the two-day hike along the Inca trail from nearby Achupallas to Ingapirca. (Rooms s/20,000 per person, with bath s/30,000). The **Hotel Gampala** (tel. 930 138), 5 de Junio, rents similar, though somewhat run-down rooms (s/30,000 per person). All other accommodations line 5 de Junio, where the rooms have views of the mountains, but the buses below start rumbling by around 4am. The most appealing culinary choices in town are the hotel restaurants. Like the lodgings, the **Hotel Gampala Restaurant** (tel. 930 138), 5 de Junio, delivers the standard goods. (*Desayuno americano* s/12,000; *almuerzo* s/5,000. The owner claims the restaurant is open 24hr.) The **Hotel Panamericano Restaurant** has slightly cheaper *almuerzos* (s/10,000) to satisfy your appetite (open daily 7:30am-9pm).

INGAPIRCA

Ingapirca, or "Wall of the Inca," located two hours north of Cuenca just off the Panamerican Highway, is Ecuador's most notable Inca ruin site. (Ruins open daily 9am-6pm. Admission US$5, includes guided tour.) Constructed over 500 years ago, the ruins are neither as impressive nor as important as those in Perú. But, set on a highland plain in the rural hills of the south central Sierra, they still make for a worthwhile daytrip from Cuenca or the nearby town of Cañar. In the middle of June they are also the site of the world-famous Inti Raymi sun festival.

THE RUINS. The **central structure** of the ruins is called the Adoratorio, Castillo, or "Temple of the Sun." Scholars speculate that this elliptical *usnu* platform was originally used to worship the sun, but it may have had astronomical as well as religious uses. The impressively solid structure, 37.1m by 12.35m, is filled with small niches and windows. The **aposentos** (lodges) next to the Temple were most likely used in the administration of Ingapirca's religious activity. Although the trapezoidal **plaza** is eroded almost to the ground, it reveals a 20m by 10m building also believed to have been used for religious purposes. The **pilaloma** section, to the extreme south of the complex, has revealed the biggest collection of artifacts from the **Cañari** tribe, which inhabited the area before the Incas. The **intihuaico collcas** (circular receptacles for food), **ingachungana** (ceremonial spot), **bodega** (market), and many **stairways** are also worth checking out. There are free but not overly well-informed guides at the site. It may be better to hire a guide in Cuenca (see below).

Just down the road from the ruins, the small town of Ingapirca has a scanty selection of *restaurantes típicos* and *tiendas*. To avoid being at their mercy, bring enough food and water for the day. The **Hostal Inti Huasi** (tel. 290 767), which provides simple rooms with private hot-water baths and has a restaurant (singles s/30,000, doubles s/40,000, *almuerzo* s/12,000). The owners can suggest hikes in the mountains, or provide transportation to the start of the Inca trail that heads north to the village of Achupallas.

Some visitors spend the night in the nearby colonial town of Cañar, south of Tambo on the Panamerican Highway. While it may make a nice rest stop on the way to or from the ruins, it sees few tourists and only has a sparse selection of hotels. The **Hostal Ingapirca** (tel. 235 201), on Sucre just below the main square, has pictures of its namesake covering every inch of wall space (rooms s/30,000, with bath s/33,000). A number of *comedores* nearby serve standard fare, though by far the best in terms of quantity and cleanliness is **Restaurant Maderos,** on Sucre and 9 de Octubre (*almuerzo* s/10,000; open daily 8am-10pm). *Camionetas* to **Tambo** (15min., every 30min., s/2,000) leave from Av. 24 de Mayo and Sucre.

TRANSPORTATION. There are two ways to get to Ingapirca by bus. Two **direct buses** run from Cuenca's *terminal terrestre* (2hr., 9am and 1pm, s/20,000). Alternatively, Cuenca buses depart for the town of **El Tambo,** on the Panamericana between Cuenca and Riobamba (2hr., every hr. 6am-5pm, s/20,000). From there, *camionetas* and buses go to Ingapirca (30min., every 45min. 7am-5pm, s/5,000). To return, catch a direct buses from Ingapirca to Cuenca (2hr., 1 and 4pm, s/20,000) or a *camioneta* to El Tambo and catch a bus from there.

AZOGUES

Azogues (pop. 30,000), the capital of Cañar province, is set in the rolling mountains north of Cuenca. When it comes to tourist attractions, Azogues pales in comparison to its more cosmopolitan neighbor to the south, but it provides a genuine glimpse of a busy but untouristed Ecuadorian city. The capital of the Cañar province, this humbly prosperous town hosts a bustling market and is a center of Ecuador's Panama hat industry (see **Panama Hats Are Not from Panamá,** p. 406).

The **Panamerican Highway** doubles as **Av. 24 de Mayo** and forms the western boundary of town. The **terminal terrestre** is about 1km past the downtown area, just off the highway. From in front of the *terminal*, cross the highway and hop on a bus (s/1,000) to the **market,** which is one block downhill from the **main plaza** on Matovalle. Most activity centers around the plaza area at **Bolívar** and **Serrano.** Long-distance buses leave from the *terminal* and travel to: **Biblián** (15min., every 15min. during daylight, s/1,000); **Santo Domingo** (10hr., 4 per day 6:15am-7:30pm, s/90,000); **Quito** (10hr., 7 per day 7:30am-10pm, s/90,000); and **Guayaquil** (5hr., 9 per day 6am-11pm, s/50,000) via **Cuenca** (1hr., s/5,000). Super Taxis sends fancy buses to **Quito** (10hr., 2 and 10pm, s/90,000) and **Guayaquil** (5hr., 12 per day 5:30am-7pm, s/50,000) via **Cuenca** (1hr., s/5,000). Filanbanco (tel. 240 332), on Bolívar between Sucre and 3 de Noviembre, will change traveler's checks or cash, and has a 24hr. ATM (currency exchange open M-F 8:30am-3:30pm). **Emergency:** tel. 101. Other services include: the **police** (tel. 240 289), stationed at Zamuel and Sacoto, six blocks south of the *centro;* numerous pharmacies on the main plaza; the **Hospital Homero Castañero** (tel. 240 600 or 240 502), across the river; and the **post office** (tel. 240 380), on Bolívar in the main plaza, across from the church (open M-F 8am-noon and 2-6pm, Sa 8am-1pm). **Telephone code:** 07.

The **Hotel Charles International,** Serrano (tel. 241 210), between Abad and Bolívar, is perhaps the best deal in town. Slide into the slippery wood-floored rooms and shining bathrooms through an airy, plant-covered lobby. (Rooms s/40,000 per person.) The relatively new **Hostal Rivera** (tel. 248 113), on the Panamerican Highway and 3 de Noviembre, offers over-furnished rooms and perfumed bathrooms (singles s/70,000; doubles s/90,000; triples s/120,000). At the basic **Hostal Chicago** (tel. 241 040), on 3 de Noviembre and Cordero, you revert to those ubiquitous green-striped blankets and lose all extraneous furniture, but you hang on to clean sheets and a private hot-water bath (s/30,000 per person).

Restaurants in Azogues are cheap and basic. **El Padrino** (the Godfather), Bolívar 6-11 and 3 de Noviembre (tel. 241 483), suffers from the same mafia obsession as Hotel Chicago. But where's the pasta? It offers the same Ecuadorian menu you know bite by bite (*pollo* with potatoes and rice s/10,000; open M-Sa 8am-9pm, Su 8am-3pm). Dripping with ferns, **Chifa Familiar,** Rivera 6-28 and 3 de Noviembre, specializes in standard *platos* (¼ chicken s/17,000) but does offer some respite from Ecuadorian cuisine (*tallarín chop suey* s/17,000; open daily 8am-11pm).

One of the most notable churches in the region, the **Iglesia de San Francisco** sprawls out over a hill to the southeast and is visible from various places in town. Though market day is Saturday, the **main market,** 3 de Noviembre and Rivera, is active throughout the week and offers a huge selection of Panamá hats. Nearby **hat workshops** can provide a closer glimpse at the craft. To visit one, catch a bus to from the *centro* to the nearby village of Charasol and the Fundación Cañari Carlos Pérez Perasso (10min., s/1,000).

The nearby town of Biblián is the sight of the stunning and serene **Santuario de la Virgen del Rocío.** The sanctuary's white turrets evoke images of fairytale castles, and its steep hillside setting overlooking idyllic Biblián is the stuff postcards are made of. (To get to Biblián catch a bus (10-15min.) from Azogues's *terminal terrestre.* From Biblían, follow the Panamericana uphill to reach the sanctuary.)

CUENCA AND THE SOUTHERN HIGHLANDS

The southern tip of Ecuador's sierra may lack the snow-capped volcanic peaks of the central Cordillera de los Andes, but the southern highlands' natural and man-made wonders leave little to be desired. Common cloud-cover, rolling over cliff-hanging roads and the buses that bumpily traverse them, provides welcome relief from the equatorial sun. Cosmopolitan yet charmingly colonial, Cuenca is the only true city in the nation to carry out all of its real business in its historic colonial center—and this in the shadow of the most beautiful cathedral in the country.

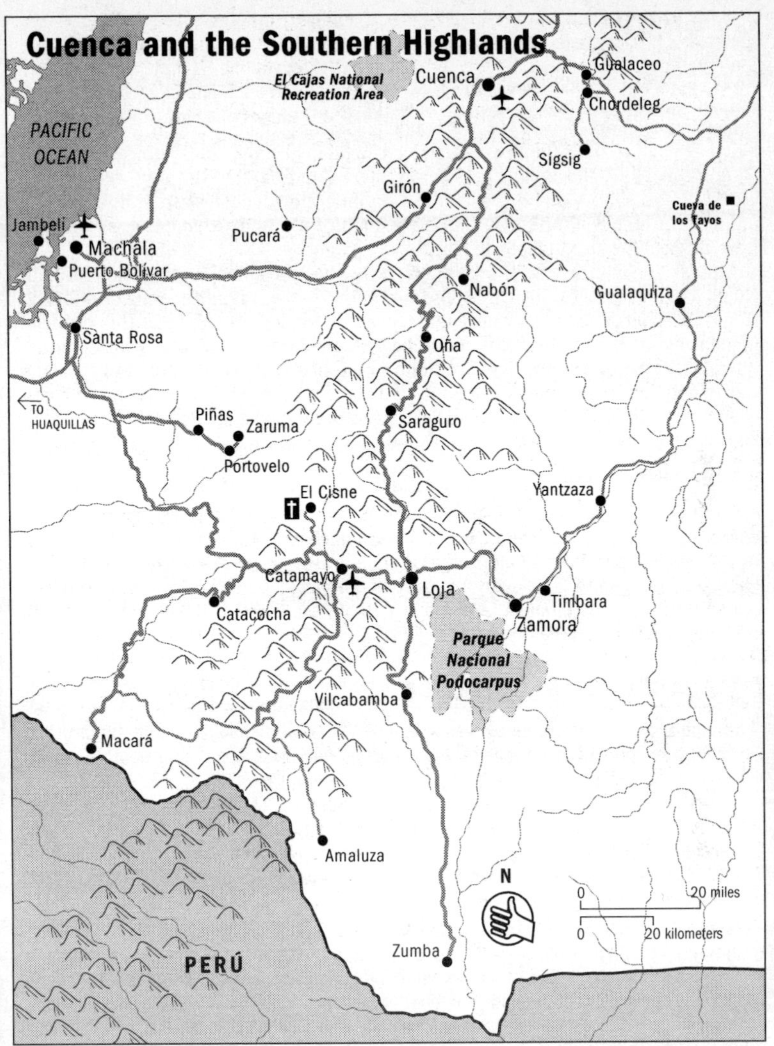

HIGHLIGHTS OF CUENCA AND THE SOUTHERN HIGHLANDS

■ Cuenca's two historic cathedrals face each other in **Parque Calderón** (see p. 337), the city's graceful and well-restored colonial center.

■ The **El Cajas National Recreation Center** (see p. 340) lures a multitude of wildlife to its highland, cloud-covered lakes.

■ The colorful **Saraguro Sunday market** (see p. 345) attracts black-robed farmers trading livestock and beautiful handicrafts.

■ Tours through **Parque Nacional Podocarpus** (see p. 349) take as long as six days to reach its remote inner regions.

■ **Vilcabamba** (see p. 351) with its horseback riding and hammock-filled lodges host crowds of foreigners looking for a place to chill.

CUENCA

As Ecuador's third-largest city, Cuenca (pop. 320,000) is seated in the Guapondélig Valley (2530m) and serves as the heart of southern highland culture and the hub of several wonderfully scenic roads. Once a prosperous indigenous city worthy of its Cañari name, *Tomebamba* (plain as big as heaven), the city was more plain than heavenly by the time the Spanish arrived. When Gil Ramirez Dávalos re-founded Cuenca in 1557, the mysteriously deserted Tomebamba already lay in ruins. Today, cobblestone streets, wrought-iron balconies, and ornate buildings ooze colonial influence. Unlike Quito, Cuenca is not a city divided between old and new; it fuses the two in historic harmony.

A lively locale bursting from the banks of the Río Tomebamba, cosmopolitan Cuenca offers tasteful brown-roofed buildings, active nightlife, and some of the finest international restaurants and museums in Ecuador. Life in this cultural mecca revolves around the old colonial center, Parque Calderón, where a blue-domed cathedral towers over tree-lined benches and communities of artisans renowned for their baskets, shawls, and Panama hats. Ever charismatic, even Cuenca's terrible traffic can't keep visitors from falling under its spell.

ORIENTATION

Most of Cuenca's activity transpires in the area framed by **Mariscal Lamar, Honorato Vásquez, Tarquí,** and **Mariano Cueva.** The **Río Tomebamba** flows through town south of the *centro*, parallel to **Calle Larga,** and its grassy banks look anything but citified. Another respite from everything urban, **Parque Calderón** lies at the heart of the colonial center. The **terminal terrestre** is a 30-minute walk, s/10,000 taxi, or s/1,500 bus ride northeast of the *centro.*

PRACTICAL INFORMATION

Airplanes: Aeropuerto Mariscal Lamar (tel. 862 203) on España, 15min. north of the city by taxi (s/15,000) or bus (s/1,500). Open daily 6am-1pm and 3-6pm. Get reservations at individual airline offices. **SAETA,** Benigno Malo 7-27 (tel. 839 090; fax 835 113), in Edificio El Galeón, next to the main cathedral. **TAME** (tel 843 222), Benigno Malo and Larga. **American Airlines,** Hermano Miguel 8-67 (tel. 831 699). **LACSA,** Sucre 7-70 and Luis Cordero (tel. 837 360). TAME flights go to **Quito** (40min.; M-F 8am and 5:30pm, Sa 8am, Su 5:30pm; s/559,000), **Guayaquil** (30min., M-Sa 6:30am, s/322,000), and smaller national destinations.

Buses: The **terminal terrestre** (tel. 842 023), on España, is northeast of the center of town. It is a bit difficult to get to and from, and a taxi (s/10,000) may be preferable to the local buses (s/1,500) that run along Sangurima and can get crowded. Many companies operate out of Cuenca, and most passengers arbitrarily gravitate towards whomever happens to be yelling out their destination. If comfort is important to you, get on one of the better buses (usually the long-distance ones), even if you're only going a short distance. Buses go to: **Riobamba** (7 hr., s/45,000); **Azogues** (1hr., s/4,500); **Quito** (10hr., every 50min. 4:15am-11pm, s/65,000); **Loja** (5hr., s/35,000); **Guayaquil** (6hr., 12 per day, s/40,000); **Cañar** (1½hr., s/8,000); **Ingapirca** (2hr., s/10,000); **Gualaceo** and (40min., every 15min. 5am-8pm, s/4,500).

Car Rental: International Rent-a-Car, España 10-50 at the airport. **Localiza Rent-a-Car,** España 14-85 (tel. 863 902). Expect to pay US$40-90 per day.

TOURIST AND FINANCIAL SERVICES

Tourist Information: CETUR, Hermano Miguel 686 and Córdova (tel. 822 058 or 839 337; email nuturaus@cue.satnet.net), offers brochures, maps of the city, a list of licensed guides, and help in English. Open M-F 8:30am-1pm and 2:30-6pm. **INEFAN,** Bolívar 5-33 and Cueva (3rd floor), is the administrative headquarters of Ecuador's 14 national nature reserves. Provides info on all of these areas and gives weak maps of El Cajas (p. 340). Open M-F 8am-12:30pm and 1:30-5pm.

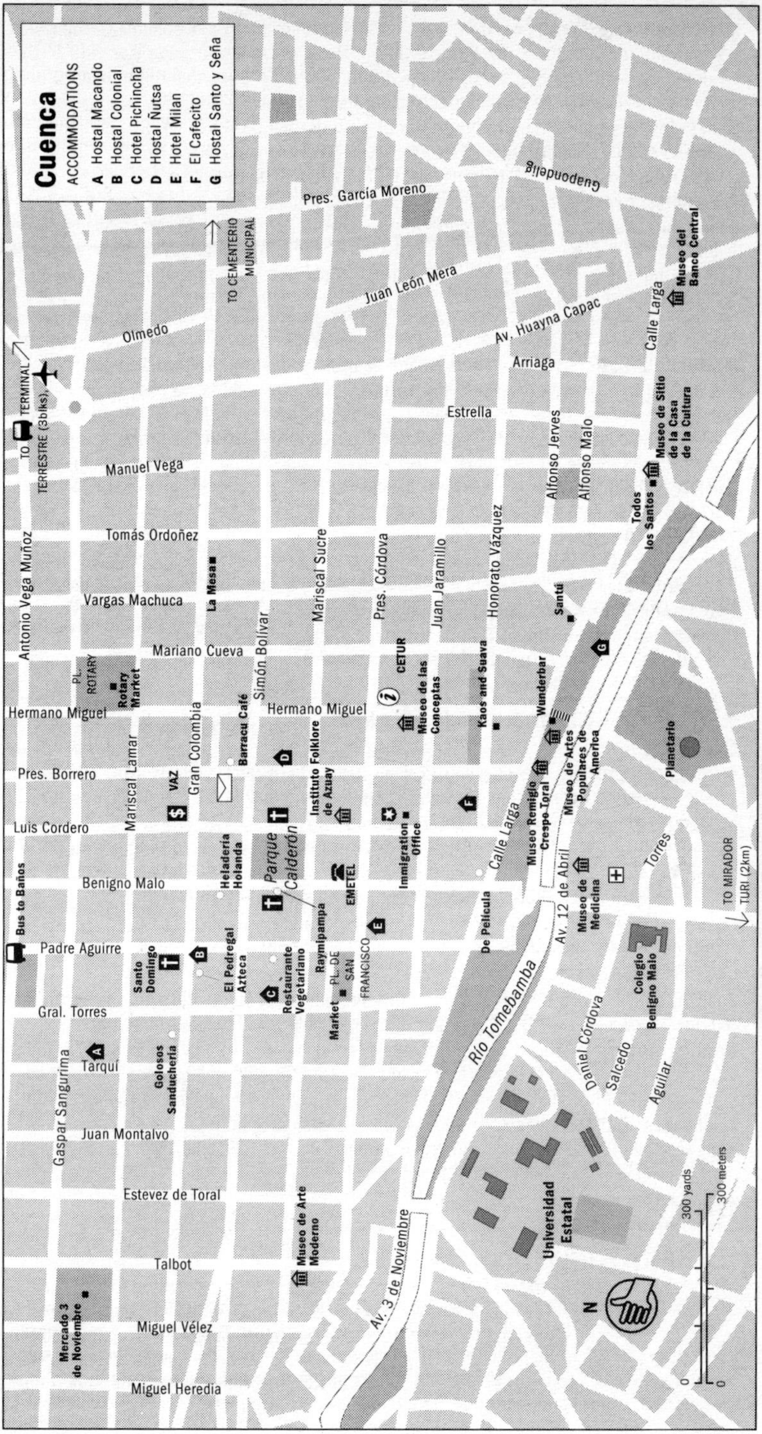

Cuenca

ACCOMMODATIONS

- **A** Hostal Macando
- **B** Hostal Colonial
- **C** Hotel Pichincha
- **D** Hostal Ñutsa
- **E** Hotel Milan
- **F** El Cafecito
- **G** Hostal Santo y Seña

Pres. García Moreno
Guapondelig
TO CEMENTERIO MUNICIPAL
Juan León Mera
Olmedo
Av. Huayna Capac
Arriaga
Calle Larga
Museo del Banco Central
TO TERMINAL TERRESTRE (3blks)
Estrella
Museo de Sitio de la Casa de la Cultura
Manuel Vega
Alfonso Jerves
Alfonso Malo
Todos los Santos
Tomás Ordoñez
Antonio Vega Muñoz
La Mesa
Mariscal Sucre
Pres. Córdova
Juan Jaramillo
Honorato Vázquez
Vargas Machuca
Simón Bolívar
Santú
Mariano Cueva
CETUR
PL. ROTARY
Rotary Market
Museo de las Conceptas
Kaos and Suava
Wunderbar
Hermano Miguel
Barracu Café
Gran Colombia
Mariscal Lamar
Instituto Folklore de Azuay
Museo de Artes Populares de America
Planetario
Pres. Borrero
VAZ
Immigration Office
Luis Cordero
Parque Calderón
Heladería Holanda
Calle Larga
Museo Remigio Crespo Toral
Torres
TO MIRADOR TURI (2km)
Benigno Malo
EMETEL
Av. 12 de Abril
Museo de Medicina
Bus to Baños
Padre Aguirre
Santo Domingo
El Pedregal Azteca
Raymipampa
PL. DE SAN FRANCISCO
De Película
Río Tomebamba
Colegio Benigno Malo
Restaurante Vegetariano
Market
Gral. Torres
Tarquí
Golosos Sanduchería
Daniel Córdova
Salcedo
Aguilar
Gaspar Sangurima
Juan Montalvo
Estevez de Toral
Universidad Estatal
Museo de Arte Moderno
Av. 3 de Noviembre
Talbot
Mercado 3 de Noviembre
Miguel Vélez
Miguel Heredia
N
0 — 300 yards
0 — 300 meters

Money Exchange: Vas Cambios (tel. 833 434), Cordero and Gran Colombia. Open M-F 9am-1pm and 3-5:30pm, Sa 9am-12:30pm. **M.M. Jaramillo Arteaga** (tel. 846 916), Hermano Miguel and Bolívar. Open M-F 8:30am-5pm, Sa 9am-noon. Both change dollars and traveler's checks and have Western Union service.

Banks: Banks are abundant in the center of town. **Banco del Pacífico,** Benigno Malo 9-75 and Gran Colombia (tel. 831 144), gives MC advances. Open M-F 9am-6pm, Sa 9am-1pm. Most banks have Cirrus/MasterCard/Visa **ATM** machines.

Consulates: Great Britain (tel. 831-996), on the Plazoletta San Alfonso, near the Plazoletta San Alfonso, in the alley connecting Presidente Borrero with Hermano Miguel. **Germany,** Huayna Capac 1-97 (tel. 835 980). Open M-F 9am-1pm and 3-7pm.

Immigration Office: (tel. 831 020), on Cordero between Córdova and Jaramillo. Open M-F 8am-noon and 2-6pm.

LOCAL SERVICES

Markets: Plaza Rotary, in the Machuca and Sangurima area northeast of the *centro*, hosts a market favored among locals, selling everything from animals to watches to clothing. A smaller, livestock-less market specializing in clothing and weaving dwells next to the Hotel Milán, at Córdova and Aguirre. Things edible can be found at **Mercado 10 de Agosto** on Torres and Larga, **Mercado 9 de Octubre** on Hermano Miguel and Lamar, and **Mercado 3 de Noviembre** on Talbot and Lamar. Thursday is the big day at these markets. The immense **El Arenal** in the Plaza las Americas, on the far west of town, is busiest on Wednesdays, and sells everything from cow arteries to *artesanía*.

Laundromat: Lavahora, Vásquez 7-27 and Cordero (next to El Cafecito) costs s/20,000 per load. Open M-Sa 9am-8pm. **Fast Klin,** Hermano Miguel 668 and Córdova costs the same. Open M-F 8:30am-6pm, Sa 8:30am-1pm.

Book Exchange: Both **WunderBar,** on the stairs to the river at Larga and Hermano Miguel, and **Centro Cultural Abraham Lincoln,** a language school at Borrero 5-18 and Vásquez, exchange English language books. Open M-F 3-6:30pm.

EMERGENCY AND COMMUNICATIONS

Emergency: Tel. 911.

Police: Central Office, Córdova and Cordero (tel. 101). Report crimes to **OID** *(Organización de Investigación del Delito),* Torres and Solano (tel. 831 041), across the river.

Pharmacy: Pharmacies work on the rotating *de turno* schedule, so one of them is always open 24hr. *El Mercurio,* the local newspaper, publishes the schedule. **Botica Internacional,** on Gran Colombia between Cordero and Borrero. Open M-F 8am-noon and 2:30-7pm, Sa 8am-noon. **Fybeca,** Huayna Capac and Jaramillo, is open 24hr.

Hospitals: Clínica Santa Ines, Córdova Toral 2-113 and Cueva (tel. 817 888), on the far side of the river, just south of 12 de Abril. **Clínica Santa Ana,** Manuel J. Calle 1-104 (tel. 814 068), southeast of the river, near 12 de Abril and Paucarbamba.

Post Office: (tel. 835 320) Borrero and Gran Colombia. **EMS** (Express Mail Service), for 3-day international mail, is next door. Both open M-F 8am-7pm, Sa 8am-2pm.

Internet Access: Several fast and cheap internet cafes are located between Parque Calderón and the river. **Cuenc@net,** Larga 6-02 and Hermano Miguel, and **Cybercom,** Presidente Córdova and Borrero, both charge s/15,000 per hour. Open daily 9am-10pm.

Telephones: EMETEL, Benigno Malo and Sucre, half a block from Parque Calderón, offers domestic (s/2,000 for 3min.) and international calls, as well as free MCI and AT&T calling-card calls. Open daily 8am-10pm.

TELEPHONE CODE	07

ACCOMMODATIONS

Hotel pricing in Cuenca is a tricky business. Though accommodations are on the expensive side—at least by Ecuadorian standards—don't just make a mad dash for the cheapest place around. For only a few more *sucres*, hotel quality shoots up drastically. Avoid ritzy hotels in town; they charge tourists twice as much as their more subtle counterparts, but are usually not worth the price.

El Cafecito (tel. 832 337; email elcafec@cue.satnet.net), Vásquez 7-36 and Borrero. An inviting sky-lit cafe by day, when the sun sets, the candles take over and the lively crowd filters in. Popular with bohemian backpackers and ultra-hip locals alike, this place has become a mecca for the young and young-at-heart. Run by a friendly, open-minded couple from Madrid, it features a full restaurant/bar, nightly happy hour (5-7pm), and occasional live music. Dorms s/30,000; singles with bath s/40,000.

Hostal Santo y Seña, 3 de Noviembre 4-71 (tel. 841 981) on Río Tomebamba. Walk down the stairs at Hermano Miguel and turn left. A new place in a beautiful riverside mansion, it features a large front-yard/garden, spacious hardwood interior, restaurant/bar, a dance floor, and live music many Thursday and Friday evenings. The owners, progressive and politically active *cuencanos*, have created a welcoming, open-minded atmosphere that is slightly more *tranquilo* than El Cafecito's and quickly becoming just as popular with young locals and travelers. Rooms are large and have private bathrooms. US$10 per person. Continental breakfast included.

Hostal Macando, Tarquí 11-64 and Lamar (tel. 840 697; macando@cedei.org.ec). Some claim this is the best hostel in Ecuador; it has all the basics—clean, comfortable rooms, friendly, knowledgeable staff, access to beautiful gardens, and the welcoming community created by American owners Steve and Maren. Kitchen facilities and capacious shared bathrooms round out the hostel's features. Singles US$8; doubles US$12. 10% tax must be paid in sucres; 10% HIYA member and ISIC discount.

Hostal Ñusta, Borrero 8-44 and Sucre (tel 830 862). A new place in an old mansion, the Ñusta is about as close to the *centro* as you can get without sleeping on a park bench. It has seven *huge* carpeted rooms for 1-6 people and amenities such as a common room with TV, a cafeteria, laundry service, and baggage storage. The open inner courtyard makes a good place for breakfast and the morning paper. US$4 per person, US$6 with bath; special group rates available.

Hotel Pichincha, Torres 8-82 and Bolívar (tel. 823 868). Dirt-cheap but dirt-free, right in the center of town. Only small sinks, mirrors, and large, clean-sheeted beds break up the whiteness of the walls. To avoid feeling as if you're living in a minimalist art exhibit, ask for a room with a window. Somewhat unappealing toilet seats make electric hot-water bathrooms less-than-inviting. Friendly common lounges on each floor have huge Trinitron TVs. Rooms s/28,000 per person.

Hostal Milan, Pres. Cordoba 9-89 and Padre Aguirre. Unpretentious, but quite comfortable. Most rooms have balconies overlooking the Plaza San Francisco. If spying on the vendors below becomes boring, there is always a color TV and a direct-dial phone in each room. The rooms with a private bathroom tend to be slightly more comfortable. The owner organizes tours of El Cajas (US$35 for one person, US$60 for two; includes US$10 entrance fee and lunch). Singles s/25,000, with bath s/40,000; doubles s/44,000, with bath s/70,000; triples with bath s/80,000.

Hostal Colonial, Gran Colombia 10-13 at Padre Aguirre (tel. 841 644; email hcolonia@cue.satnet.net). Rooms replete with refrigerator, bottled water, and fluffy wall-to-wall carpet let guests luxuriate right near the center of town. But class has a price. Singles s/70,000, two-story suite s/145,000; ISIC members get a 7% discount.

FOOD

With its attractive and diverse array of delectable diners, Cuenca is a great place to cure some hunger pangs. From the numerous *típicos* with their traditional *almuerzos* to the costly world-class cuisine at **El Jardín,** Cuenca satisfies even the most selective stomach. For picnic supplies, start out at **Supermaxi** (Cordero and Lamar). You can buy bread from a standard **panadería** on just about any block. The fruit in the markets is good, but it tastes even better when it's the filling of a crepe served at numerous restaurants.

Raymipampa Café-Restaurante, Benigno Malo 8-59 (tel. 834 159). As bouncy as its name, this lively room absolutely hops with gringos and the local elite. The view onto the Parque Calderón complements the casual, coffee-shop feel. Enjoy scrumptious dinner crepes (chicken and mushroom s/16,000, vegetarian s/12,000) and high-quality cappuccino (s/3,500), along with the requisite 3-course *almuerzo* (s/22,000). Open M-F 8:30am-11pm, Sa and Su 9:30am-11pm.

De Película, Benigno Malo 4-104 at Larga (tel. 805 049). New American/Ecuadorian fusion cuisine. Discover *el secreto de Cindy Crawford* (a cheese-and-egg sandwich, s/8,000) or try a Gandhi sandwich (strictly vegetarian, s/8,000). Live entertainment most Fridays around 10pm. Open M-Th 11am-midnight, F-Sa 11am-2am.

Bar-Restaurant Vegetariano, Padre Aguirre 8-15 and Sucre. Run by a family of local doctors, this place is clean enough for a heart transplant, much less a delectable vegetarian *almuerzo* (s/12,000). Don't be fooled by the "cheeseburger" (s/14,000) or "spaghetti with meat" (s/18,000) offered on the menu. The "meat" is made from *quinoa* grain or wheat gluten. Open M-F 9am-6:30pm, Sa 9am-2pm.

Golosos Sanducheria, Gran Colombia 11-20 and Torres (tel. 827 312), across from Hostal Chordeleg. This small lunch counter makes some of the best deli-style sandwiches in town. Hot turkey, chicken, or vegetarian subs (s/13,000) make for a nice picnic in the park. Open M-Sa 8:15am-10pm.

La Barraca, Borrero 9-68 and Gran Colombia (tel. 842 967), with a bright neon sign. Very flavorful food; the salty cream-of-vegetable soups make a good start to a plate of vegetarian spaghetti (s/22,000) or some *churrasco* (s/28,000). Barraca provides table games to while away the wait for food. Open M-Sa 11am-11pm, Su 11am-5pm.

El Pedregal Azteca, Gran Colombia 10-29 and Padre Aguirre (tel. 823 652), dishes out some of the best Mexican food in Ecuador. No bargain basement, but authentic tacos (s/22,000) and burritos (s/20,000) accompanied by ice-cold Coronas (s/12,000) are well worth the price (though portions can be small). Be prepared to dine in relative solitude–beyond the means of many locals, this dark, romantic setting can be sparsely populated. Open M 6-11pm, Tu-Sa 12:30-3pm and 6-11pm.

El Cafecito, Vásquez 7-36 and Borrero (tel. 832 337). In addition to the lively hostel and bar, they serve food all day long. The generous fruit salad, served with yogurt and granola, juice, and tea or coffee (s/11,000), is the perfect way to start the day. The lunch and dinner menu includes sandwiches, pasta, and six vegetarian options (all under s/4,000). Open daily 8am-10pm

Heladería Holanda, Benigno Malo 9-51 and Bolívar (tel. 831 449). Widely acknowledged as serving the best ice cream in town. Single cone s/3,000. The scoops get cheaper the more you have, so why hold back? Open daily 8am-7:30pm.

SIGHTS

Though the area's most compelling sights are out of town—at Turi, Ingapirca, Baños, Biblián, El Cajas, and the nearby markets—Cuenca offers more diversions than simply fine dining. With a booming *artesanía* community—concentrated on Gran Colombia between Hermano Miguel and Pres. Borrero—and almost too many museums to count on your fingers, Cuenca serves up cultural offerings as well as culinary ones. Fun-lovers also flock to Cuenca's two prominent annual festivals. During the week-long **El Septenario** (Corpus Christi) celebration beginning the second Thursday in June, the main plaza explodes with fireworks and dancing. Drinks such as the cinnamon- and *aguardiente*-filled *caneliza* help *cuencanos* let loose for unusual games of chance and wild matches of the ever-popular foosball. Cuenca stretches its Independence Day celebration into a four-day *artesanía* fair, centered around November 3. The **Pase del Niño** festival on the Saturday before Christmas features surreal parades celebrating the upcoming holiday.

MIRADOR TURI. Nobody navigates Cuenca better than the birds, and from Turi, a treacherously high lookout spot 4km south of the city center, you can experience an avian outlook as only the high-fliers normally do. A 15-minute bus ride up a steep, pothole-ridden road pays off at the top, with a breathtaking panoramic view of all of Cuenca and its surrounding mountains. A cartographic tiled painting of the city matches the view and provides a guide to the scenery. Pay-binoculars give a closer look. *(Getting up to Turi means taking either a bus, a cab, or a hike. Buses leave from 12 de Abril and Solano, south of the river (every 90min. 7:30am-4:30pm, s/1,500) and drop you off at the base of the hill upon which Mirador Turi is perched—a 30min. climb from the mirador. The Gapal bus returns from the base of the hill to Cuenca (s/1,500). A taxis cost s/25,000.)*

MUSEO DEL BANCO CENTRAL. This museum houses Cuenca's most extensive collections of art and ethnographic artifacts in a style that only Central bankers could afford. The highlights of the museum are the upstairs exhibit on indigenous cultures, featuring reconstructions of many traditional houses, and the ground floor displays of local archaeology, showing the ancient tradition of chewing coca leaves with lime. Also prominent are collections of 19th century Ecuadorian art and—reflecting the interests of the management—a history of money in Ecuador. *(Larga and Huayna Cápac, outside of the center of town at the ruins of Pumapungo. Tel. 831 255. Open M-F 9am-6pm, Sa 9am-1pm. Admission s/10,000.)*

OTHER MUSEUMS. Cuenca puts its museums where its mouth is, with enough galleries to support the city's claim to cultural significance and sophistication. Founded in 1947, **Museo Remigio Crespo Toral,** Larga and Borrero, honors the eponymous Cuencan poet with unrhymed exhibits of miscellaneous historical items *(tel. 833 208; open M-F 8am-4pm).* For the non-squeamish, there's the **History of Medicine Museum.** Equipment dating back to 1845 makes you glad you live in the age of modern medicine. *(12 de Abril 7-55, inside a courtyard next to the Military Hospital across the river. Open M-F 8:30am-noon and 2:30-5pm. Admission s/5,000.)* Just as Cuenca has more than one set of ruins, it has multiple museums to honor them. Next door to the Todos los Santos ruins, the **Museo de Sitio de la Casa de la Cultura Manuel Agustín Landivar** crams artifacts from the Cañari, Inca, and Spanish cultures into two tiny rooms *(Larga and Manuel Vega; tel. 832 639; open M-F 9am-1pm and 3-6pm; admission s/ 5,000).* Also, **Museo de las Culturas Aborígenes** sports an array of Cañari and Inca artifacts *(10 de Agosto 4-70 and Sánchez, across the river in Ciudadela Santa Anita; tel. 880 010; open M-F 8am-noon and 1:30-6pm, Sa 8am-noon; admission US$2).* Cuenca also promotes local arts and crafts through a variety of exhibition houses. The **Museo de Arte Moderno,** operating in the ancient House of Temperance, displays mainly Ecuadorian modern art and hosts a biannual international art competition *(Sucre and Talbot; tel. 831 027; open M-F 9am-1pm and 3-7pm, Sa-Su 9am-3pm; free).* **Instituto Azuayo de Folklore** exhibits a fascinating array of local and regional *artesanía (Cordero 7-22 and Córdova, third floor; tel. 830 016; open M-F 8:30am-noon and 2:30-5pm).* The **Museo de Artes Populares de America** has an equally impressive exhibit of *artesanía (Larga and Hermano Miguel; tel. 828 878; open M-F 9:30am-1pm and 2:30-6pm, Sa 10am-1pm).* An upscale *artesanía* store next door sells goods of high quality and price. For art with religious sensibilities, there's **Museo de las Conceptas,** in the 400-year-old **Monastery of the Immaculate Conception** (see **Modern Art,** p. 245). Peruse pious art and Guayasamín lithographs. *(Hermano Miguel between Córdova and Jaramillo. Tel. 830 625; Open M-F 8:30am-noon and 2:30-5pm, Sa 10am-1pm. Admission s/10,000.)*

CHURCHES. Cuenca has more churches per capita than most Ecuadorian cities, some are definitely more brilliant than others. Cuenca's two most striking churches face each other across **Parque Calderón** in the heart of town. Built in 1557 with stones from the Inca's Pumapungo Palace, the **Iglesia de Sagrario (Old Cathedral)** is currently under renovation. Across the street, the massively exquisite **Catedral de la Imaculada Concepción (New Cathedral)** towers over Parque Calderón and glows spookily by night. Designed by Obispo Miguel León Garrido but actualized by the German Juan (Johannes) Stiehle in 1885, the cathedral is one of the most recognized churches in Ecuador. Its ornate domes and brick face cover a cavernous marble interior, where brilliant rays of sunlight enter through the various windows and reflect off a four-column, gold-leaf canopy. Another church, **Todos Los Santos,** on Larga and Machuca, was the site of Cuenca's first outdoor mass. **Santo Domingo,** at Gran Colombia and Padre Aguirre, was erected in the 16th century.

ENTERTAINMENT

The large tourist contingent keeps Cuenca's bars and nightclubs open throughout the week. There's always a crowd enjoying happy hour drinks at **El Cafecito** and **Santo y Seña** (see **Accommodations,** p. 334). On the weekends, there are even more options. The hippest disco in town is **Santú,** Larga and Jerves, downstream of *el centro,* which plays techno and house (s/20,000 cover includes one drink). For lively salsa dancing, try **La Mesa,** a local favorite on Gran Colombia at Ordoñez. For the uncoordinated and lethargic, **Kaos** and **Suava,** both at Vásquez and Hermano Miguel, are a little bit more laid-back. **Kaos** has couches, a free pool table, tasty sandwiches (s/10,000), and colorful, potent, one-liter cocktails (s/30,000) to quench that deep-down body thirst. Other bars without a cover charge include **Picadilly Bar** at Córdova and Borrero, **WunderBar** on the steps at Hermano Miguel and Larga, and **Ego** on Unidad Nacional.

A haven for the performing arts, **Teatro Casa de la Cultura,** Cordero and Sucre, shows movies and houses local events such as mariachi concerts. **Cine 9 de Octubre,** Cueva and Lamar, and **Teatro Cuenca,** on Padre Aguirre between Lamar and Gran Colombia, advertise their cinematic screenings in *El Mercurio,* the local paper. All three often show quality American movies in English, but the sound is so bad that it's probably easier to read the Spanish subtitles (admission s/10,000, good for both halves of a double feature).

The area around Cuenca has long been a center of **artesanía** production for the rest of Ecuador, which makes the city itself a great place for souvenir shopping. A good starting point is the **Cooperativa Azuayana,** Malo 10-24 near Gran Colombia (don't look for a sign—they don't have one). Their small showroom is crammed with the standard *artesanía*; the real treasures are hidden next door, though, in the knitters' *bodega,* which houses one of Cuenca's best *chompa* (sweater) collections (s/60,000-s/90,000 each). You can have one custom-made if you can return in 15 days to pick it up—the design is limited only by your ability to communicate through some combination of Spanish and pictures. (Open M-F 9am-1pm and 3-7pm, Sa 9am-noon; *bodega* open only in the morning). Cuenca's artistic traditions have continued to evolve, and the city is home to numerous *talleres de arte* (art studios). Wander the streets around Jaramillo and Bordero to see what's new. Those interested in the art of hat-making can continue down Jaramillo to the workshop of **Alberto Pulla,** Tarqui 6-91 (tel. 829 399). Señor Pulla's card claims that his are the best hats in Ecuador. A bold claim, but his scrapbook full of articles about him from around the world lends him some credibility. Panama hats cost s/100,000-300,000—a lot of money, but this is "Hat as Art."

NEAR CUENCA: BAÑOS

Eight kilometers west of Cuenca, the baths of Baños are part of the **Hostería Durán** resort (tel. 892 485). The water in each of two large pools and the sauna is changed twice weekly. Bring your own towel, or you may have to buy one there. Day-trippers can enter the pools for s/25,000. Tennis, racquetball, volleyball, and a fitness center may be used for s/20,000 per hour (open daily 5am-5pm). The Hostería also offers luxury restaurants and accommodations.

Transportation: To get to the baths, take any bus for Baños passing along Muñoz (s/1,500), and get off half an hour later just before Baños's sky-blue church.

NEAR CUENCA: GUALACEO

Every Sunday, the center of activity in the Cuenca area shifts to the weekly market in this tiny village east of Cuenca, drawing bargain-hunters from neighboring mountain towns and even more rural settlements. *Indígenas* from highland farms come to town to make their living for the week. Smaller versions of the market take place every Tuesday and Friday. Despite the outsiders who frequently discover it, the market manages to maintain its local flavor.

THE MARKET. If Otavalo is the retail mall of Ecuador, **Gualaceo** is its factory outlet. In previous generations, family life in the town and surrounding area centered around the production of woolen *chompas* (sweaters), *gorras* (hats), and *tapetes* (woven carpets). In a process that has been repeated around the country, many members of the younger generation of Gualaceo have left their traditional lives for work in the city. Still, in the *barrios* in the hills around the town, old men work at their looms and women knit on their front porches. Every Sunday, production ceases and the week's output is brought into town. Heaps of handmade sweaters are sold to middlemen in the plaza by the bus station for resale in Otavalo and elsewhere. On any other day, you can visit the artisans in their homes, see the process, and buy souvenirs without any intermediary getting a cut of the price. One caveat—pressure to buy can be strong.

Only a couple of tourists can be spotted among the teeming masses of fruit- and vegetable-hawking vendors. Rows of outdoor eateries, selling every part of the pig but the squeal, make a meat-lover's paradise. Whole pigs on spits, skewered with their heads at attention and ears pricked up, get ripped apart by numerous hands as vendors drip flavorful pig fat onto delicious *llapingachos* (potato and cheese cakes, s/1,000). Look for the *Hay Rosero* ("We have *rosero*") signs in various *comedores* and ice cream stores around town. What is it? A beverage made from various fruits and fruit juices, then thickened with corn flour. The **indoor food market,** toward the bus station on Cuenca, might look cleaner. Remember not to partake of any water, ice, or raw fruits and veggies (unless peeled), as tempting as they may be. The prices don't do anything to detract from the allure. Everything is cheap; a multi-course *almuerzo* for over s/10,000 is unheard of. Non-food items lurk around the edges of the market. Practical goods from watches and toothbrushes to Panama hats abound, but don't look for baskets and shawls of the tourist variety—that's not what locals come for. *Facing uphill in the bus station, the main market lies ahead and to the right. From the bus station, head up Cordero and turn right on Cuenca, or better yet, follow the herd.*

OUTSIDE THE MARKET. If looking for a meal outside the market, there are a number of cheap restaurants near the bus terminal. Diagonally across the market, away from the bus station, lies the town plaza. Across the plaza in the same direction sits **Bar-Restaurant Don Q,** 9 de Octubre and Gran Colombia (tel. 256 578). Aiming for more ambience than other restaurants in town, it sports an indoor, skylit courtyard and hanging plants. (Entrees s/16,000-23,000; open daily 8am-7:30pm.)

For a place to stay, **Residencial Gualaceo,** Gran Colombia 3-02 (tel. 255 006), is one block from the park (away from the market). Nondescript rooms have comfortable beds and are clean enough for a night's slumber. Lounge on a communal balcony out back. (Room s/20,000 per person, with bath s/30,000 per person.) For a splurge, try the **Gualaceo Parador Turístico** (tel. 255 010) about a kilometer south of the plaza on Gran Colombia (which changes to Ave. Loja). Its white-washed, stuccoed rooms serve the few Ecuadorians who can afford its luxuries. Facilities include a pool with glorious views of the surrounding hills, sauna, outdoor athletic equipment, satellite TV, an expensive restaurant, and the ubiquitous foosball table. (Singles s/118,000; doubles s/144,000; triples s/168,000.) **Museo Artesanal de Gualaceo,** 1km south of Gualaceo off the highway toward Chordeleg, displays local artists' work (open Tu-Sa 8am-noon and 2-5pm, Su 8am-noon; free).

Transportation: Buses leave from Gualaceo's *terminal terrestre* on the main highway and travel to **Cuenca** (40min., every 15min. 5am-8pm, s/4,500), but you have to buy a ticket at the counter ahead of time. Or continue on to **Chordeldeg** (15min., every 30min. until 8pm, s/1,500) or further on to Sigsig (40min., every 30min. until 8pm, s/4,000). **Greentours** (tel. 256 603), next to the plaza at 9 de Octubre 5-00 and Dávila Chica, provides maps of Gualaceo and offers tours of the surrounding villages and countryside.

NEAR CUENCA: CHORDELEG

While Gualaceo's market specializes in the daily necessities, the market at **Chordeleg** has a lock on the luxuries. The main plaza is absolutely studded with **jewelry stores,** sparkling with good deals thanks to all the competition (be wary of some of the great deals—all that glitters is not gold or silver). Some artisan goods are also sold on the main plaza, but the best pottery shops, including the large and upscale **Centro de Artesanías** (open daily 9am-6pm), are outside the center of town, toward Gualaceo on the main road. Everything in the smaller Chordeleg is more *tranquilo* than in Gualaceo. While the plaza is generally silent, a little more activity goes on a few blocks down at the market, a small-scale version of Gualaceo's. A modern **church** is on the main plaza. To the right facing the church, three decent **comedores** of the local variety spoon out chow. The small but info-packed **Museo Comunidad** is on the plaza (open M-Sa 8am-6pm, Su 8am-4pm).

Transportation: Most **buses** heading back to **Gualaceo** or **Cuenca** leave one block uphill from the plaza (every 30min.). Buses depart for Chordeleg from Gualaceo's *terminal terrestre* as soon as they fill up (15min., every 30min., s/1,500). Buses coming from Cuenca to Gualaceo also generally continue to Chordeleg (s/6,000). The **walk** between Gualaceo and Chordeleg is a beautiful saunter past picturesque, rolling countryside and farmland. The downhill stretch from Chordeleg to Gualaceo takes about an hour; the return uphill can take one and a half hours. On blind curves, be careful of cars hugging the right side of the highway.

NEAR CUENCA: OTHER TOWNS

Other market villages in the area, including **Sigsig** and **Paute,** are accessible by one-hour bus rides from Gualaceo. Both are less touristy and more rural than either Gualaceo or Chordeleg. As with the other markets in the Cuenca area, Sunday is the best day to visit. Sigsig is also home to the paleolithic **Chobshi cave**—one of the oldest archaeological sites in Ecuador. The **tour agencies** listed under **El Cajas** (see below) offer daytrips to all of these markets (US$35-45 per person).

NEAR CUENCA: EL CAJAS NATIONAL RECREATION AREA

Water, rock, and bush are the raw materials of El Cajas National park. Their varied forms as well as the sheer magnitude of the landscape make the this 28,800 hectare park a site not to be missed. Peaks rise to a sky-scraping 4450m at their zenith, and nowhere does the altimeter dip below 3150m; sheer cliffs carved by glaciers cut through rolling highlands; and from below subterranean rivers rise near the surface and then re-submerge into fissures in the rock. Not to be outdone by the splendor of El Cajas's geological splendor, varied plants and flowers blanket the land with spring turf and splashes of color. Diminutive Quinua trees, the highest-altitude trees in the world, sprout their gnarled trunks from the *páramo* covering most of the park's area. For all it has to offer, many tourists simply pass El Cajas by since it has no single focal point. This leaves even more solitude for those who enjoy hiking, fishing, or simply relaxing in vast expanses of rugged terrain.

Virgin humid mountain forests cover the east and west ends of the area. El Cajas's unique climate makes it one of the few places where the rare *cubilán*, *chuquiragua*, and *tushig* plants flourish. Those with a little patience and luck may see some of the park's standard-issue wildlife such as deer, foxes, and rabbits, as well as the more distinctive spectacled bear, llama, puma, *huagur*, and *tigrillo* (little tiger). Bird-watchers can marvel at Andean condors, highland toucans, and hummingbirds. El Cajas wasn't always as devoid of people as it appears today. **Pre-Hispanic ruins** lie scattered throughout, and the ancient Inca Road of **Ingañan** stretches for 4km between **Luspa Cave** and **Lake Mamamag** in the center of the park. The best preserved ruins are at **Paredones,** but Lakes Luspa and Avilahuayco serve up similar slices of Inca history closer to the information center.

LOGISTICS. El Cajas's **information center,** at **Lake Toreadora** (3810m), is right next to the highway that transects the park. It offers general info and basic **shelter** with electricity but no running water. There are no beds, so bring a sleeping bag and food. (Rooms s/20,000 per person per night.) A restaurant next to the information center is open some weekends. Temperatures can drop to -5°C at night, so warm, waterproof gear is essential. Dense fog often arrives in the early afternoon, and visitors without maps, compass, and experience have been known to get lost. (Admission to park US$10, payable at the information center.)

To see the entire park really requires a guide. **Santa Ana** (tel. 832 340), Borrero and Pres. Córdoba, charges US$40 per person for private transportation and the services of an English-speaking guide (open M-F 9am-1pm and 3-7pm, Sa 11am-1pm). **Apullacta Tours,** most easily contacted through the Hostal Macondo, offers daytrips for US$35 per person, as does **Aventuras Nomadas,** Hermano Miguel 6-91 and Pres. Córdoba (tel. 820 158). Both provide English-speaking naturalist guides. Though not geared toward tourists, **INEFAN** in Cuenca (see **Practical Information,** p. 332) may be able to provide some information and maps.

TRANSPORTATION. Buses headed straight for the information center leave from San Sebastian Park at Talbot and Mariscal Sucre in Cuenca (1hr., dialy 6am, s/10,000). If traveling on a weekend, arrive well before 6am to assure a seat for the crowded ride. Those disinclined to stay up so late for the bus can catch any Guayaquil-bound bus leaving from the *terminal terrestre.* Ask to be let off at the information center. Return buses traveling the main road through the park pass by the Visitors Center throughout the day.

LOJA

Always on the move, Loja (pop. 160,000) was relocated from the Catamayo area in 1548 and was rebuilt after earthquakes twice. A gateway to the Oriente, Loja sits only a stone's throw from the most seductive and secluded spots in the southern *cordillera*—Vilcabamba, Zamora, Saraguro, and the Parque Nacional Podocarpus. Home to two universities, a law school, and a musical conservatory, this small city has developed a sense of modern culture that many other towns in the area lack, yet at the same time it manages to retain ties to its rustic origins. No buildings rise past the fourth story, and the local Saraguros, in their traditional black dress, are a strong presence throughout the city. No longer a mobile metropolis, Loja has comfortably settled into its mountain-valley home, and it offers guests a pleasant combination of relatively safe streets, traditional charm, and excellent restaurants.

ORIENTATION AND PRACTICAL INFORMATION

Loja lies along two rivers. The main one, **Río Malacatos,** runs between (and underneath) **Avenida Universitaria** and **Avenida Iberoamerica** in town. **Río Zamora** parallels **Avenida 24 de Mayo,** marking the eastern boundary of the city. The **terminal terrestre,** on Avenida Cuxibamba, is about a 15-minute walk north of the *centro* along Universitaria. Many *papelerías* sell a good city map (s/10,000).

Airport: La Tola airport, in Catamayo, is a 30-kilometer taxi ride from Loja (s/25,000). Flights depart to: **Quito** (M, W, F 7am, s/590,000) and **Guayaquil** (Tu, Th, Sa 7am; s/500,000). Loja's **TAME office** (tel. 573 030) is on the extension of 24 de Mayo and Eguiguren across the Río Zamora. Open M-F 9am-5pm.

Buses: To **Quito** (14hr., 9 per day, s/120,000); **Cuenca** (5hr., 5 per day, s/45,000) via **Saraguro** (1½hr., s/15,000); **Catamayo** (45min., every 30min. 6am-7pm, s/7,000); **El Cisne** (2hr., daily 4pm, s/13,000); **Guayaquil** (9hr., 7per day, s/70,000); and **Vilcabamba** (1½hr., 16 per day, s/6,500).

Taxis: Taxi Ruta, on Universitaria near the Gran Hotel Loja, crams 5-6 people into their cabs bound for **Vilcabamba** (50min., leaving when full, s/10,000). The ride is about twice as fast as buses to Vilcabamba and costs only a pittance more.

Tourist Information: CETUR, Valdivieso 8-22 and 10 de Agosto (tel. 572 964), provides info and maps. Open M-F 8:30am-5pm. **INEFAN** (tel. 571 534), on Sucre between Imbabura and Quito, administers **Parque Nacional Podocarpus**. Open M-F 9am-noon and 2-5pm. **Biotours,** Colón 14-96 and Sucre (tel. 578 398; email biotours@cue.satnet.net); and **Vilcatur,** Colón 14-30 (tel. 571 443; email vilcatur@loja.telconet.net), on the same block, can customize tour packages for you.

Immigration Office: (Tel. 573 600), Argentina and Bolivia, next to the police station. Open M-F 8am-noon and 2-6pm.

Peruvian Consulate: Sucre 10-56 (tel. 571 668). Open M-F 8:30am-1pm and 2-5pm.

Banks: Casa de Cambios Vigo, Sucre and Rocafuerte, changes traveler's checks. Open M-F 9am-5pm. **Filanbanco** (tel. 571 811), on Valdivieso between 10 de Agosto and Eguiguren, also changes traveler's checks and has VISA and American Express **ATMs.** Open M-F 9am-3pm. MasterCard ATMs are found at other banks around the Parque Central.

Supermarket: Tía, 10 de Agosto and Bolívar. Open daily 9am-7:30pm.

Laundromat: Maxilim (578 259), 10 de Agosto and 24 de Mayo, 3 long blocks down 10 de Agosto past Filanbanco on the Parque Central. If you're looking for a washing machine in Loja, this may be your only option (s/14,000 for a dozen items; dry cleaning prices depend on the item). Open M-F 8:30am-noon and 2:30-6:30pm, Sa 8:30am-1pm.

Emergency: Tel. 115.

Police: (Tel. 560 500), Argentina and Bolivia.

Pharmacy: There's always a pharmacy open on Bolívar. **Farmacia Loja** (tel. 570 266), on the corner of Bolívar and Rocafuerte. Open M-F 8am-10pm, Sa 8am-1pm.

Hospital: Hospital General (emergency tel. 570 540), on Isidro Ayora and Kennedy. Free 24-hour emergency treatment. **Hospital Militar de Loja,** Colón 13-28 and Bolívar (tel. 570 254). Both have ambulance services. **Clínica Especialidades Samaniego,** Imberoamerica and Eguiguren, is a private clinic with an English-speaking doctor.

Post Office: Sucre 05-85 and Colón (tel. 571 600). Open M-F 7:30am-7pm, Sa 8am-2pm. **DHL,** 14-23 Colón near Bolívar, in Metropolitan Tours. Open M-F 8am-6pm. **Federal Express,** Valdivieso 12-34 on the Parque de la Independencia, in the Centro Comercial San Sebastian. Open M-Sa 9am-noon and 2-6pm.

Internet Access: Cyber Café (tel. 573 964; email cybercafe50@hotmail.com), Bolívar and Rocafuerte, on Plaza Danto Domingo, has a moderately reliable connection (s/20,000 per hour). Open M-Sa 9am-1pm and 2-8pm. Across the plaza **Triple C,** Rocafuerte 13-41, 3rd floor, offers a more reliable connection (s/40,000 per hour). Open M-F 8:30am-1pm and 3-9pm, Sa 9am-7pm.

Telephones: EMETEL (tel. 573 050) has two branches in Loja: at Eguiguren and Valdivieso, and on Aguirre between Lourdes and Catacocha. Both allow calling card calls (s/2,000 for 3min.). Open daily 8am-12:30pm, 1-6:30pm, and 7-9:00pm.

TELEPHONE CODE	07

ACCOMMODATIONS

For a city with hardly a tourist in sight, Loja seems to have an over-abundance of hotels, most of which are clustered around 10 de Agosto and Sucre. Unless there is a local festival, most hotels have plenty of room, which can mean more flexible prices for groups or multi-night stays.

Hotel Metropolitano, 18 de Noviembre 07-51 and Colón (tel. 570 007). Single-handedly keeping local lumberjacks in business, the Metropolitano surrounds you with wood paneling: striped, zig-zagged, solid, on floors, on walls, over the ceiling. Clean, yellow-tiled, private baths have plentiful steaming water. Color TVs and quiet surroundings. Rooms s/40,000 per person.

Hostal Londres (tel. 561 936), Sucre and 10 de Agosto, next to Hotel Acapulco. Although you'll find the shower directly above the toilet in the upstairs bathrooms, the price is

hard to beat. Ask to use the larger, cleaner bathroom downstairs. Padlocked rooms have that bare, hanging-lightbulb look, but they're very clean for the money. Rooms s/15,000 per person.

Hostal Carrión, Colón 16-36 and 18 de Noviembre (tel. 561 127). Shared-bath rooms satisfy basic living needs with a bed, table, and clean sheets; significantly snazzier private-bath rooms have color TVs. Either way, Carrión will give you munchies for breakfast and useful tourism information. Singles s/20,000 per person, with bath s/35,000.

Hotel Chandelier, Imbabura 14-82 and Sucre (tel. 563 061 or 578 233). No chandeliers, but carved pillars and a tiled courtyard create the slightly-run-down-grand-old-house look. Rooms facing the street have better lighting but are noisier than interior rooms. All rooms have TVs. Rooms s/20,000 per person, with bath s/30,000.

Hotel Acapulco (tel. 570 651), on Sucre between 10 de Agosto and Eguiguren. Though not quite Mexico's Pacific coast, Hotel Acapulco does provide liveable rooms with color TV, a lacquered desk set, and floors shiny enough to use as mirrors. Many windows face the interior central hall; quieter back rooms have natural light. Rooms on the 2nd and 3rd floors escape noise from the indoor 1st-floor corridor (strangely used as a driveway/parking lot). Singles s/60,000; doubles with TV s/120,000.

FOOD

Bread seems to be unusually good in Loja, and *panaderías* diffuse warm bakery smells on every block. **Panadería La Europa,** 18 de Noviembre and Colón, sells coconut cakes (s/1,500), cheese-filled croissants (s/400), and sweet bread (s/300).

La Tullpa (tel. 570 210) 18 de Noviembre between Colón and Eguiguren. Mounted bull heads glare stonily at the indoor playground in one corner. Dishes aren't dirt-cheap, but the quantity and quality of the *criollo* cuisine justify the price. The *chuleta de chancho* (pork chop s/20,000) and *cecina* (dried meat s/25,000) are excellent. The scrumptious *almuerzo* (s/10,000) is also quite a deal. Open M-Sa 8am-10pm, Su 9am-4pm.

Cebichería Las Redes, 18 de Noviembre 10-41 and Riofrio (tel. 578 787). This net-decorated seafood joint offers more than just your average *ceviche. Ceviche de camarón* (s/21,000) is among the specialties, but the *sopa de mariscos* (seafood soup, s/14,000) is big enough for a meal and swims above the rest. Traditional Ecuadorian fare and Chinese food round out the menu. Open M-Sa 9:30am-10pm, Su 8am-3pm.

Parillada Uruguaya (tel. 570 260), on Salinas near Universitaria. Flee yon vegetarian, hasten dear carnivore. This clean, bright restaurant is a local favorite and serves some of the best grilled meat in the southern highlands. *Bife Uruguay* (thick slab of beef, s/28,000) and house specialty *lomo fino* (grilled beef s/22,000) will sate the appetite of even the hungriest meat-eater. Open M-Sa 5pm-1am, later on the weekend.

Rincón de Francia (tel. 578 686), Valdivieso and Colón. For the cheap romantic in everyone. Woo that special someone with an intimate, candle-lit dinner complemented by an outdoor courtyard, elegantly-prepared French food, and soft music. The authentic menu includes filet mignon (s/25,000), beef tongue (s/19,000), and crepes (s/10,000). Open M-Sa 9am-10pm, Su 9am-3pm.

Restaurante Vegetariano el Paraíso (tel. 576 977), Sucre and Quito, gets the prize for the simplest menu. *Desayuno, almuerzo,* and *merienda* are cheap and meat-free (s/10,000). Open daily 7am-9pm.

SIGHTS

The area surrounding Loja is so amazingly scenic that every visitor ends up outdoors, whether admiring the view from the Virgen de Loja statue or trekking in the nearby hills.

VIRGEN DE LOJA. Guarded by a terrified-looking stone lion below, the Virgin overlooks sprawling Loja from a nearby Andean hill. To visit her, head east on Rocafuerte, go uphill past the river, and follow the dirt road to the base of the statue. There is a second virgin to the west of the city, three blocks past Río Malacatos on Imbabura.

PARQUE UNIVERSITARIO LA ARGELIA. Run by the **Universidad Nacional de Loja,** the park is another outstanding outdoor experience. Full of beautifully maintained hiking trails, the park covers the hills across the Río Malacatos from the campus. Finding a good view is effortless: any way you go, you'll come to a *mirador* within 20 minutes. There is a small museum and info center at the base of the trail, and a wooden sign outside illustrates the various hikes. The warden is a helpful source of information. The trail that heads left provides a complete two-hour loop through a flowered pine forest, full of tranquil mountain streams, and (depending on the time of year) squadrons of butterflies. *(To get here take any bus headed to Vilcabamba, or take a Argelia-Capuli bus running down Iberoamerica. Argelia-Pitas buses will drop you off at the university campus. From the campus it's a 15-minute walk across the Río Malacatos and down the highway. Open daily during daylight hrs. Admission s/6,000.)*

JARDÍN BOTÁNICO. A little further down the road from the trail base, a botanical garden boasts a wonderful collection of highland and tropical plants, as well as sections devoted to medicinal plants and orchids. *(Located in Parque Universitario La Argelia. Open M-F 9am-4pm, Sa-Su 1-6pm. Admission s/6,000.)*

SIGHTS IN TOWN. A few blocks north of the *terminal terrestre*, the large **Parque de Jipiro** amuses and amazes with a zoo and a miniature reproduction of the Kremlin. *(Take a "de Valle" bus to get there.)* Loja is somewhat short on museums, but it does have the obligatory **Casa de la Cultura** and **Museo del Banco Central.** Both have free art exhibits on the ground floor, and the Banco Central has an upstairs ethnography exhibit. *(Admission to either s/3,000.)*

ENTERTAINMENT

Nighttime entertainment is a bit scarce in Loja, but the decor at the **Piano Bar Unicornio,** Bolívar 7-63 and 10 de Agosto (tel. 574 083), is amusement enough. The red velvet and zebra-striped decor are the perfect complement to the numerous exotic cocktails (s/10,000) Unicornio serves up. **Discoteque Casablanca,** on 24 de Mayo, up from the EMETEL office, offers drinks and dancing on the weekend. **Siembra,** across the river on 24 de Mayo and Segundo Cueva Celi, is a classy and romantic bar serving food and drink under a thatched roof (open Tu-Su 4pm-midnight). On the corner of a five-way intersection at 24 de Mayo and the Río Zamora, the brand new **Free Days** is cheerful and welcoming (cocktails free for women on Thursdays). Nearby, on Sani and Zamora, **D class** boasts a blacklit interior, a thumping beat, and Ecuadorian soccer matches.

NEAR LOJA: SARAGURO

A tiny stop on the Panamerican Highway between Cuenca and Loja, the town of Saraguro offers little other than typical small-town charm and untouristed solitude. Its main attraction is the *artesanía* of the indigenous Saraguros. Souvenir-hungry tourists will be able to find plenty on Sundays, when the market brings farmers into town from surrounding areas. The traditional dress you'll see at the market is unique to this region of Ecuador: men wear black capes and mid-calf black pants, while women wear black shawls with a silver pin called a *topo*. This area of the country, with its splendid scenery, clear starry nights, and unhurried lifestyle, is about as far from Guayaquil or Quito as you can get without a guide.

Everything of importance is located within two blocks of the **main plaza,** a pleasant garden with benches and trees typical of small, highland villages. For a place with such a small-town feel, Saraguro has a large number of useful services. **Farmacia La Salud** (open daily 8am-1pm and 2-10pm) and **EMETEL** (tel. 200 199; open daily 8am-9:30pm) are located along the main plaza across the street from the church. The **police** station is on 10 de Marzo on the main plaza. The **post office** is next door (open M-F 8am-noon and 2-6pm).

Transportation: Buses stop on the main plaza across from the church, heading north (toward **Cuenca**) and south (toward **Loja**) every 30 minutes or so. **Pullman Viajeros** (tel. 200 165), runs north to **Cuenca** (3½hr., 10 per day 6:30am-1am, s/30,000) and **Quito** (13hr., 3 per day 10:30am-8pm). **Transportes Sur Oriente, Transportes Union Carramanza,** and **Coop Loja** all go south to **Loja** (1½hr., s/10,000) and the **Oriente** (via **Zamora** and **Yantzaza**). Buy tickets at Pullman Viajeros before boarding the bus.

There are two hotels and a couple of eateries in Saraguro. **Residencial Saraguro** (tel. 200 286), one block from the square, is the accommodation of choice. It has comfortable beds, thick adobe walls, and a garden. A common TV and VCR provide evening entertainment. The shared bathrooms have hot water in the mornings. (Rooms s/20,000 per person.)

The **Reina del Cisne** restaurant-bar, on the main plaza on Eloro, across from the post office and police, serves some of the tastiest victuals in town. Wolf down an *almuerzo* (s/9,000) or *merienda* (s/9,000) under the Virgin Mary's watchful eye (open daily 8am-10pm). Samantha Fox's buttocks replace the Virgin at the other dining choice, **Cristal.** Despite the contrast in decor, food and prices are nearly identical. (Open daily 7am-9pm.) By night, there is little to do but relax and have a beer at one of the two bars: **Saraguro Barta-Bar** or **Picantería La Fogata.**

NEAR LOJA: CATAMAYO

Busy but uninspiring, Catamayo's main contribution to the traveler subculture is the **La Tola airport** (2.5km away), the nearest spot for flights into and out of Loja. Briefly the site of the city of Loja itself, Catamayo has been untroubled by major happenings ever since the better-known metropolis moved 30 kilometers east in 1548, two years after its founding. Though the city may be unexciting by most standards, travelers with early-morning and late-evening flights can avoid complete boredom by marvelling at the cops in straw cowboy hats striding through town or by finding shapes in the dust clouds that swirl through the surrounding roads.

Activity in Catamayo centers on the **parque principal,** between the east-west **Isidro Ayora** and **Bolívar** and the north-south **Avenida 24 de Mayo** and **Catamayo. Cooperativa Transportes,** on Catamayo near Isidro Ayora and the Parque Principal, has **buses** to **Loja** (1hr., every 30min., s/7,000). **Camionetas** to **El Cisne** leave from the corner of Ayora and 24 de Mayo (1hr., every hr., s/10,000). **Taxis** also travel to **El Cisne** from Bolívar and 24 de Mayo (s/80,000 round-trip). **Farmacia Macará** (tel. 677 149), Bolívar and 24 de Mayo, is on the *parque principal* next to the church (open M-Sa 7am-9pm, Su 7am-noon). **Police:** tel. 101. Catamayo's **hospital**, the **Centro de Salud de Catamayo** (tel. 677 146), 18 de Noviembre and Espejo, two blocks from the church offers 24-hour emergency service. **PACIFICTEL,** on Isidro Ayora, does not handle collect or calling card calls (open daily 8am-10pm). **Telephone code:** 07.

There is not much reason to spend the night in Catamayo unless you have an early-morning flight and want to sleep in a bit, rather than catching a sunrise bus from Loja. **Hotel Turis** (tel. 677 126), Ayora and 24 de Mayo, is located conveniently close to the bus stop, has private baths, and is the most affordable option around. The sunny courtyard and chirping birds in cages are compensation for the dimly lit surrounding rooms. (Rooms s/10,000 per person, s/20,000 with private bath.) Next door, at **Hotel Rossanna** (tel. 677 006), the clean, shiny linoleum-floored rooms are a pleasant surprise after the dingy cement staircase. Most of Rossanna's rooms have private baths and color TV. (Singles s/30,000; doubles s/50,000.) Restaurants in Catamayo are basic; choose a cheap *almuerzo* spot near the *parque principal* and hope it's clean. The **Bachita 2 Restaurant** (tel. 677 897), Ayora and 24 de Mayo, is both clean and bright. The menu offers *platos típicos* (*churrasco* s/16,000, *almuerzo* or *merienda* s/10,000) as well as a la carte items. (Open M-Sa 7am-10pm, Su 7am-4pm.) Centrally-located across from the park on Ayora, the **Restaurant y Cebichería La Esmeraldenita** has a lively atmosphere with loud Latin music. They serve both seafood (*ceviche* s/20,000) and traditional fare (*almuerzo* or *merienda* s/10,000; open daily 7am-11pm).

A sunny afternoon at the **Centro Recreacional Popular Eliseo Arias Carrión,** five kilometers from the *centro*, is the perfect antidote to airport claustrophobia (s/1,000 by bus from Catamayo). A popular spot for families on the weekends, the center has sports facilities, a large, inviting pool, fresh air, and appropriately enough, an airplane smack in the middle of the grounds. (Open daily 8am-5pm, pool 9am-4:30pm. Admission s/2,000, pool use s/4,000, children half-price.)

NEAR LOJA: EL CISNE

High in the hills where butterflies bounce in the breeze, snakes slither in the scorching-hot sun, and donkeys drowsily drag the day's harvest, there is a small village known as El Cisne. In this village there is an enormous cathedral with a bright, whitewashed exterior and a somewhat gothic feel. And in the cathedral there is a statue of a virgin, **La Virgen del Cisne,** looking down at worshippers from behind a plate of glass in her ornate, gold-encrusted home. Amazingly, it is this statue, not the church, town, or gorgeous mountain scenery, that draws hordes of people to El Cisne every year. For four days every summer (Aug. 17-20), following a week of *fiestas*, a river of faith led by the famous statue pours into Loja from El Cisne. The local virgin, a common postcard image, floats on the shoulders of the hearty pilgrims who clog the 80km road to Loja. Not one to settle down, the Virgin stays in Loja for only a short while; on November 1, she begins her crowd-surfing return to El Cisne. A sign of die-hard Catholicism, the Chaucer-worthy pilgrims consider the trek almost enough to merit canonization. After all, for some of them, completing the one-way trip, sometimes on their knees, amounts to a minor miracle in itself. Outside of the fascinating procession, the town's best offering is the sanctuary itself, a building gargantuan in both scale and reputation. When you're done gawking at the spectacle within, ask at the bookstore to let you into the adjoing museum. The small museum houses jewels, documents of the Virgin, and other religious paraphernelia. (Museum admission s/3,000.)

Despite regional Catholic significance, generally only the truly fascinated, the well-timed, and the imminently papal take the long daytrip between El Cisne and

Loja. Since El Cisne has no hotels, pilgrims have to proceed at least 40km back out of town to Catamayo for a bed. There is, however, no shortage of places to eat in El Cisne. Restaurants line the plaza in front of the cathedral, though options at most of them are limited to the standard *almuerzo* or *merienda* (around s/8,000).

Transportation: The easier, though less devout, route to El Cisne involves taking a three-hour bus ride from Loja's *terminal terrestre* (Catamayo Transports has one direct bus daily 4pm, F 9am, Su 7:30 and 8:30am; 1hr; s/14,000). If this schedule does not fit yours, take a bus to Catamayo to catch the erratic, unpredictable *camionetas* to El Cisne, or take the marathon trip from Loja to Catamayo to San Pedro to El Cisne, changing buses along the way. Make sure to ask about return times.

ZAMORA

Maybe Coronado was looking too far north when he searched the Wild West in vain for the mythical city of El Dorado. According to local legend, El Dorado glistened right around here in the southern Amazon Basin. Ecuador's modern city of gold, Zamora (pop. 9000), is a rustic jungle town that suddenly found itself in the center of things when gold was discovered about 20 years ago in the nearby town of Nambija. Suddenly, a mining frontier culture sprouted up alongside the Oriente vegetation and the conservationist colonies of the rainforest, and inevitable turmoil resulted. Yet Zamora has somehow adapted to these changes and come to exist between worlds: miners and conservationists, Sierra and Oriente. It has become a "gateway" city, remaining wonderfully untouristed and friendly while being home to comfortable hotels and decent restaurants, and providing easy access to the Amazon basin via the Parque Nacional Podocarpus and the Yankuam tour agency.

Some come to Zamora just for the ride. The relatively finished highway from Loja winds along cliffs and roadside waterfalls, descending from treeless *páramo* to highland cloud forests, to the leafy, palm-laden humidity of the tropical Oriente. The land is beautiful, yet encroachments are frequent and obvious; the mining equipment and tin roofs of gold-boom houses haphazardly clamber up the sides of the valley, disrupting an otherwise scenic jungle-town atmosphere.

ORIENTATION AND PRACTICAL INFORMATION. Activity in Zamora centers around the town's main park and church, Parque Pío Jaramillo, at the junction of 24 de Mayo and Diego de Vaca. The *terminal terrestre* is at the end of town, one block from Diego de Vaca.

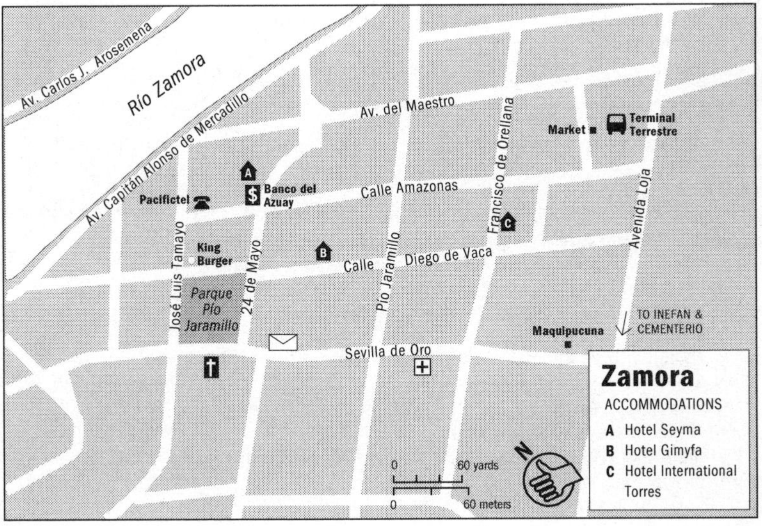

Buses leave for: **Loja** (1½hr., every 30-45min., s/15,000); **Gualaquiza** (6hr., every 3hr., s/24,000) via **Yantzaza** (2hr., every hr., s/4,000); **Machala** (10hr., 8pm, s/31,000); and many smaller towns throughout the day. For informations about Zamora try **Yankuam**, (tel. 606 147) 24 de Mayo and Diego de Vaca. They can also arrange tours to the jungle (open M-F 8am-noon and 2-6pm, Sa 8am-noon). Essential for Parque Nacional Podocarpus excursions, **INEFAN** (tel. 605 315) is on the highway before you enter town from Loja, across from the cemetery (open M-F 8:30am-12:30pm and 1-5pm). **Maquipucuna** (tel. 605 547), on Sevilla de Oro between Orellana and Loja, is a private ecological conservation foundation can which can provide information on the Parque Nacional Podocarpus. There is usually someone in the office who speaks English and can answer questions.

Banco del Azuay, 24 de Mayo and Amazonas (tel. 605 235), next to EMETEL, will change dollars but not traveler's checks (open M-F 8am-4pm, Sa 9am-1pm). **J&B Travel** (tel. 606 082), one block down Diego de Vaca from the park, exchanges dollars and also sends packages (open M-F 8am-noon and 2-6pm). **Farmacia Santa Ana,** on Amazonas toward the *terminal terrestre*, is well stocked (open daily 8am-6pm). **Hospital Julius Deepfuer** (emergency tel. 605 149), two blocks to your left when facing the church, offers 24 hour emergency service (open M-F 7:30am-4pm). **Pacifictel** (tel. 605 104), near Tamayo, one block from the main plaza away from the church, does not handle collect or calling card calls (open daily 8am-10pm). **Telephone code:** 07

ACCOMMODATIONS AND FOOD. Look for lodging and food on or around Diego de Vaca. The **Hotel Gimyfa Internacional** (tel. 605 024), Diego de Vaca and Pío Jaramillo, has an appealing, modern design. Hot water, carpeted floors, cable TV, and an underpopulated downstairs disco launch it into comparative luxury. (Singles s/60,000; doubles s/80,000.) **Hotel Internacional Torres** (tel. 605 195), on Orellana between Diego de Vaca and Amazonas, offers a unique fusion of architectural styles—modern mirrored-glass with Greek columns and a semi-classical enclosed courtyard. Hot water, cable TV, and carpeting make for an enjoyable stay. (Singles s/40,000, doubles s/60,000.) **Hotel Seyma,** 24 de Mayo and Amazonas (tel. 605 583) near the plaza, is the essence of simplicity: bare wood floors, a hanging light bulb, and shared, cold-water-only bathrooms. Many windows and a two-story courtyard lend the Seyma a traditional latin air. (Rooms s/15,000 per person.)

Restaurants and picanterías offering *almuerzos* and *meriendas* (around s/8,000) line Diego de la Vaca and Amazonas, especially near the bus terminal. **Tropy Burger,** below Hotel Gimyfa, serves burgers (s/6,000) in a simple but clean dinning room (open daily 6am-10pm). **King Burger,** across from the church on the corner of the plaza, was intended to be called Kim Burger. Señor Kim is still angry at the sign company but continues to grill beef for s/5,000. (Open daily 8am-11pm.)

NEAR ZAMORA: NAMBIJA

The gold-rush town of **Nambija,** three hours from Zamora off the road to Gualaquiza, has been a mining spot for centuries, yet was unknown outside of *indígena* communities until the 1980s. Ever since Ecuadorian miners struck upon a rich lode here, Nambija has attracted many a hopeful adventurer with pick-axe in one hand and hard-hat in the other. The traditional, isolated village was rapidly transformed into a cluster of tin-roofed shacks and clanking gold-sifting sluices perched on steep inclines and surrounded by **cloud forest.** The scruffy town is definitely daytrip material (hotels are rudimentary, and the slippery mud paths that serve as streets can be unsafe); it's a fascinating segment of rural Ecuador. Though there are several small stores and *sandwicherías* interspersed with the houses across the river, it may be safer to bring your own food. The caves and small mines in the cliffs above town are tempting, but beware of the huge pigs, dogs, and occasional armed owners guarding them.

Transportation: The bus (s/30,000) from the Namirez stop on the Zamora-Yantzaza highway winds up through waterfall-irrigated cloud forest for two hours before leaving visitors at a clearing with a ramshackle wooden building. From there, follow the muddy path along the cave-dotted cliff until the town comes into sight. When you've gawked (and been gawked at—this is not tourist country) enough, buses return to Namirez every hour until 6pm.

PARQUE NACIONAL PODOCARPUS

ZONA ALTA (CAJANUMA ENTRANCE)

Layer upon layer of rolling mist obscures the scenery in the high-altitude section of Parque Nacional Podocarpus. Miles of cliffside paths traverse this *zona alta*, a vibrant ecosystem which overcame harsh weather patterns to grow, flower, and breed at up to 3,600m above sea level. Notoriously elusive high-fliers—the toucan de altura, the quetzal, and the Andean cock-of-the-rock—hide in the fingers of fog that cloud the Podocarpan sky. Threatened Romerillo (or Podocarpus) trees dangle from the cliffs. Besides giving the park its name, they are Ecuador's only endemic conifer. It takes three or four days to reach the interior part of Podocarpus, but day-hikers need not feel deprived. Spectacled bears have been sighted near the *refugio*, and the surrounding trails have wildlife, views, and mud galore.

THE TRAILS. There are four main *senderos* (paths) through beautiful mountain terrain, all of which begin at the main *refugio* (alt. 2,750m). Mainly for children or families, **Sendero Oso de Anteojos** (Spectacled Bear Path) is a short 400-meter loop near the entrance. Although this trail gives a taste of the park's natural splendor, only the paths that go onward and upward provide climactic vistas. **Sendero Bosque Nublados** (Cloud Forest Path) climbs higher through the clouds and offers slightly larger servings of the scenic delights below. This 700-meter trail is more difficult and takes two hours to complete. **Sendero al Mirador** (Path of Views) captures the essence of Podocarpus, revealing a veritable banquet of foggy vistas along the way. The trail climbs through tangled jungle near the *refugio* and then suddenly bursts through the tree line to reveal the *mirador*. Birdwatchers can observe a feathered cabaret, and lucky hikers who smell strongly of food might glimpse a spectacled bear, mountain tapir, fox, or puma. Don't get too comfortable at the lookout; most of the hike is still to come. The trail stammers along a precarious ridge walk and then really starts to climb, reaching its apex at 3,600 meters before returning to the *refugio*. The four- to five-hour loop is muddy and misty in the summer, but clear and dry in the winter. Less ambitious hikers, whether plagued by lethargy or a stone in the shoe, can opt out of the second part of the trail and do only the one-hour hike to the *mirador* and back.

If Sendero al Mirador is a banquet, **Sendero Las Lagunas del Compadre** (Path of the Compatriot's Lakes) is an orgy worthy of the gods. The 14-kilometer trail leads to the jewel in the crown of Podocarpus—shimmering lakes buried deep in the mountain forest. The total excursion takes two or three days, and the absence of trail facilities makes proper camping equipment essential for this festival of scenery. With water everywhere, trails can be muddy during the summer and steep parts are often slippery. Huge, waterproof rubber boots are the intrepid hiker's only defense against mud-soaked footwear and pants. In January and February, grab the nearest pair of binoculars and follow the circling birds. Spectacled bears and *dantas* (tapirs) prefer to romp during November and December. At any time of year, enjoy the bamboo, orchids, and red-spiked bromeliads that line the trail.

Staying in the park for more than a few hours? Drinking a lot of water? The *refugio*, with a bathroom, several beds, and a kitchen, is the place to head. Cabins near the *refugio*, farther into the forest, are an *au natural* alternative. In either case, bring your own food and sleeping bag. A US$10 fee buys access to the entire Sierra section, including the camping cabins and resource-laden *refugio*.

TRANSPORTATION. The park entrance is at Cajanuma, a barren stretch of highway about 15 kilometers from Loja on the road to Vilcabamba. Unfortunately, buses and shared taxis heading to Vilcabamba will drop you off on the highway, leaving an 8km uphill hike to the *refugio*. On most days, a taxi from Loja will be able to reach all the way to the *refugio* (about s/150,000 round-trip).

ZONA BAJA (ZAMORA ENTRANCE)

Tropical butterflies flutter across virtually every step of the trails in Parque Nacional Podocarpus's *zona baja*, a primary tropical rainforest along the Río Bombuscara. Though some lovers of the Cajanuma forest might object, a consensus of INEFAN officials and butterfly aficionados hold that the jungle section of Podocarpus outshines its uphill counterpart. Beautifully kept trails wind past waterfalls and rainforest streams, creating an omnipresent chorus of rushing water to accompany the scenic symphonies of river views and jungle greenery. Budding botanists can explore the Universidad Nacional de Loja study area, home to a dazzling diversity of plants. Highlights include over 40 varieties of orchids and the *cascarilla* tree, the source of quinine, a key ingredient in both malaria remedies and tonic water. Colorful wildlife accompanies you on your journey through the *zona baja:* yellow butterflies fluttering with each footstep, spectacled bears rustling nearby trees (though rarely letting themselves be seen), and toucans croaking overhead. Wildlife is best in the heart of the park—farmers, miners, and other humans have shoved most creatures away from the park's edges.

THE TRAILS. Several *zona baja* trails start from the Bombuscara ranger station. A short trail from the station down a wooden staircase leads to the river itself, where you can **swim** in fresh water next to a **large waterfall.** Water clarity varies depending on recent rainfall, but take proper jungle-swimming precautions. **Los Helechos** is a trail so short that spending 30 minutes on it requires self-control. INEFAN helps the time-killing process with a brochure, available in Zamora, offering 11 points of interest along the trail. Among the labeled botanical attractions are the orchids, *guarumo*, *helechos* (huge trees), palms, and *cascarilla.* The longest path, **Sendero Higuerones,** is a two-hour round-trip trek along the Río Bombuscara. Bushwhacking, backwoods camping, and general exploring away from trails are legal, allowing the more outgoing to explore the rainforest more intimately. Bring a mosquito net if you plan to camp in the heart of the jungle. The less-intrepid can explore the *cabañas* near the station. There are also accommodations in the station itself for one or two people on research excursions. If interested, make arrangements with INEFAN in Zamora.

TRANSPORTATION. Inside the park, the station at the trail entrance is staffed 24 hours. Get a taxi from Zamora's *terminal terrestre* for about s/50,000 round-trip (arrange a pickup time with the driver in advance). Even with a car, visitors must make a 1km uphill walk to the Bombuscara ranger station. INEFAN trucks also come and go periodically, but are often full.

Another entrance to Podocarpus's *zona baja* is two hours south of Zamora at a tiny town called **Romerillos.** INEFAN officials staff a *refugio* similar to the one at Bombuscara but much smaller. **Buses** head to Romerillos from Zamora each morning (see **Zamora, Practical Information,** p. 332); ask about return times. The Romerillos entrance is not only off the tourist trail, it is also in one of the hot spots of miner-conservationist conflict.

LOGISTICS

Admission to the *zona alta* runs US$10. The *zona baja's* entrance fee reflects its good standing with the locals—twice as nice for twice the price; admission runs US$20. Buy tickets from the INEFAN office in Zamora (tel. 605 315), a 10-minute walk from town on the highway (open M-F 8am-noon and 2-5pm, see p. 348 for details). Those looking to save some sucres can buy tickets from the INEFAN office in Loja for half the price—admission tickets for either part of the park are honored at all entrances for a week after purchase date.

TOURS AND TOUR OPERATORS

All of Podocarpus is impressive, but as usual, the best parts are the hardest to reach. The easy-access fringes of the park, overrun with tourists, miners, farmers, and the occasional grazing cow, will satisfy casual plant-lovers but will disappoint hard-core botanists and animal seekers. **Tours**—to both parts of the park—are easy to find in Loja and Vilcabamba. The **Arco Iris Foundation,** Segundo Cueva Celi 03-15 (tel. 577 449; email fail@fai.org.ec), in Loja, can be reached by crossing the Río Zamora at Imbabura and heading downstream for one block on 24 de Mayo. This local non-profit conservation group provides reams of information and frequently runs jeeps to various locations in the park. If they're going your way, they're happy to take you along for a nominal fee. (Open M-F 8:30am-12:30pm and 2:30-6:30pm.) **Biotours Ecuador,** Colón 14-96 and Sucre (tel./fax 578 398; email biotours@cue.satnet.net), in Loja, has one- to six-day tours with all equipment, food, and park fees included (from US$45 per person). The company is run by multilingual conservationists who are very familiar with the park's features. Tour routes and guide style can be adjusted to suit your preferences, and the office has a huge collection of slides and info to help you choose your trip. **Vilcatur** (tel. 571 443; email vilcatur@loja.telnet.net), Colón and Bolívar, Loja, specializes in shorter, more docile tours for curious but less experienced hikers (US$20-$75 per person per day). The numerous Vilcabamba horse guides, such as Gavin's Tours (see p. 354), tend to use their favorite little-known access trails. Orlando Falco, in Vilcabamba, provides highly informative walking tours of all sections of the park (see p. 354).

VILCABAMBA

If most small towns in Ecuador are *tranquilo*, then Vilcabamba is sedated. The warm weather, beautiful scenery, and recent gringo influence have turned this sleepy town into a place like no other, where locals walk around in shorts and tank tops, every house has a hammock, and, from time to time, *fiestas* erupt in the town plaza for no reason at all. Throughout history, Vilcabamba has been seen as a mystical place, thought by the Inca, the Spanish, and, recently, travelers from around the world to possess life- and conscience-expanding properties. There are many legends about residents who lived to ridiculously old ages in the clean air, mild climate, and unpolluted surroundings of the *Valle de la Juventud Eterna* (Valley of Eternal Youth). Inca elders used to make a pilgrimage to the valley to engage in a longevity ceremony with the seeds of the local *huilco* tree. In this century, many *fiesta*-oriented foreigners have made a similar pilgrimage to sample the hallucinogenic properties of San Pedro, a psychotropic cactus endemic to the valley. But don't come to town looking to get high. Local opinion and law enforcement have recently united to decrease this drug tourism for which the town has become notorious. Because of this changing opinion, "daytrippers" may meet with a cold reception and some difficulty procuring their chemical muse. That said, Vilcabamba is still an excellent place to visit. The pleasant climate, relaxed atmosphere, and abundant attractive lodgings continue to make it one of the most popular destinations in Southern Ecuador.

ORIENTATION

Every 15 minutes or so throughout the day, buses, *colectivos*, and shared *Taxi Ruta* cars cruise in from Loja along **Avenida de la Eterna Juventud.** Activity in Vilcabamba's center crowds around a **main plaza,** overlooked by a church on one side. Standing in the plaza with your back to the church, a slew of hotels and restaurants line **Diego Vaca de la Vega** for several kilometers on the right. Most of the bars and cafes are on the lower edge of town on Diego Vaca de la Vega and **Agua de Hierro.** Street names are hard to come by—but don't worry: most of the restaurants, bars, and cafes have signs with detailed maps in the main plaza.

PRACTICAL INFORMATION

Buses: Most buses stop near the main plaza in town. All buses pass through **Loja,** but **Sur Oriente** has the most buses that go directly there (1½hr., every hr. 6am-6pm, s/6,500). From Loja, catch buses to more distant destinations.

Taxis: Taxi Ruta Avenida 24 de Mayo gets to Loja in less than an hour but crams up to 6 people in a small car (s/6,000). Taxis leave from the center of town.

Tourist Office: (Tel. 580 890), the corner of Diego Vaca de la Vega and Bolívar, on the park opposite the church. Provides helpful information in Spanish on local accommodations, tours, and restaurants. Open Sa-M and W-Th 8am-noon and 2-6pm. Diagonally across the intersection, **Aveturs,** Vega and Bolívar, is the association of the local tourism industry. Representing all the guides in town, it is a good place to book a tour and get your questions answered in English.

Bookstore: Craig's Book Exchange, a 15-minute walk up Diego Vaca de la Vega, claims to be the best book exchange in South America. It certainly has books in a variety of languages. Craig also sells cookies and handmade jewelry, and tells colorful anecdotes in English about local history.

Police: Agua de Hierro between Sucre and Bolívar. Open until 11pm.

Pharmacy: Farmacia Reina del Cisne (tel. 580 289), one block downhill from the plaza on Bolívar. Open 8am-9:30pm, 24hr. for emergencies.

Hospital: Hospital Kokichi Otani (tel. 673 128 or 673 188), three blocks away from the plaza along Eterna Juventud, offers 24hr. ambulance service. Open M-F 8am-noon and 2-6pm, 24hr. for emergencies.

Post Office: (Tel. 580 896), on Agua de Hierro, doesn't sell stamps. Open M-F 8am-noon and 2-6pm, Sa 9am-1pm. Stamps can be bought and letters mailed from the **Prima Vera** *artesanía* store on Diego Vaca de la Vega and the main plaza, or at **Las Ruinas de Quinara,** one block from the plaza, two blocks opposite the church.

Internet Access: Vilc@net (tel. 580 282; email jaramillo_angel@hotmail.com), on Diego Vaca de la Vega and Eterna Juventud. The connections are not extremely reliable, but the price is reasonable (s/20,000 per hour). Open daily 9am-9pm.

Telephones: The **EMETEL** office, next to the tourist office on Bolívar and Diego Vaca de la Vega, allows AT&T but not MCI calling card calls. Open daily 8am-12:30pm, 1-6:30pm, and 7-9:30pm.

TELEPHONE CODE	07

ACCOMMODATIONS

Due to the steady stream of tourists, Vilcabamba has a bewildering array of excellent accommodations, ranging from full-service resorts to mountain lodges. Competition is intense, and some proprietors meet each busload of tourists at the terminal. Unfortunately, not every owner provides honest information. Don't let a pushy person at the terminal sway your choice of accommodations.

Hidden Garden Pensión (tel./fax 580 281; email vilca@srv8.telconet.net), Sucre and Diego Vaca de la Vega, one block downhill from the plaza on Sucre. A well-foliated and fruit-bearing inner courtyard surrounded by a high wall explains the name. Rooms are spartan but comfortable. In the garden, there is a chilly swimming pool, a *wonderful* gas-fired shower, several hammocks and picnic tables, and, often, the friendly and talkative American owner. There is a quasi-restaurant and an honor-system guest kitchen. Singles US$6, with bath US$8; doubles US$10.50, with bath US$12.50; triples US$14.25, with bath US$16.25.

The Pole House and Ecolodge (email ofalcoecolodge@yahoo.com), near town but hidden away in the Rumi-Huilco nature reserve. Take a dirt road off of Agua de Hierro across the river, and follow the first path on the left. Check in town at the **Primavera Artesanía Shop** (on the park at Sucre and Vaca de la Vega) for directions and availability. The house is built on poles and provides a unique lodging experience for a few nights or a few months. The very friendly, bilingual Argentinian owners, Orlando and Alicia Falco, both biologists and former Galápagos guides, are experts in local flora and fauna. Home to numerous plants and trees endemic to the region, the site is of interest

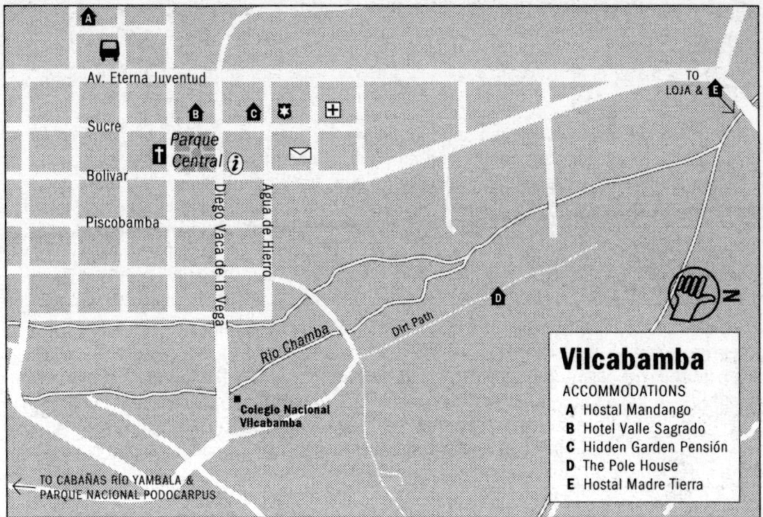

to botanists and casual observers alike. Guests are welcome to eat the fruits and vegetables grown on the property and use the well-stocked kitchen, hammocks, and fire pit by the river. Rooms US$3-7 per person, depending on number of people and length of stay; adobe cabins US$2-4 per person.

Cabañas Río Yambala, commonly known simply as "**Charlie's**." A free taxi service runs from the Vilcabamba bus station to the Cabañas. Otherwise, it's a pleasant one-hour hike down Vaca de la Vega and then along a dirt road forking to the left. The cabaña-style rooms are located in a nature preserve on the western side of Podocarpus. The amiable owners offer vegetarian meals, locally made musical instruments, and equestrian or pedestrian tours of Podocarpus. Several well–marked trails open to the public wind through the scenic grounds. Check at the tourist information center to find out about availability. Cabins s/30-50,000 per person.

La Tasca (tel. 673 186) a 20min. walk or s/10,000 taxi ride up Vaca de la Vega. Private cabins with a kitchen and a gas-heated shower provide a good lounging spot for watching brightly colored birds or gazing out across the mountains. The French-Ecuadorian owners welcome all lifestyles and run a delectable French restaurant on the premises. Rooms US$3 per person.

Hosteria Las Ruinas de Quinara (tel. 580 314; email ruinasqu@hotmail.com; www.lasruinasdequinara.com), Diego Vaca de la Vega, a 10min. walk from the park on the right. With the feel of a deluxe summer camp, Las Ruinas provides every opportunity for its guests to play and socialize. Free amenities include a pool with a slide, jacuzzi, turkish bath, direct TV and music service in every room, table tennis, a pool room, 10min. of free internet access, and complimentary water and fruit juice throughout the day. For a little bit more, get a massage, rent a bike or horse, do laundry, or place international calls. Rooms US$6 per person, with breakfast and dinner US$10.

Hostal Madre Tierra (tel. 580 269; email hmtierra@ecua.net.ec; www.ecuadorexplorer.com/madretierra), 20min. outside of town towards Loja, then 400m. up a dirt road on the left. This place is a full-service resort with more than 20 buildings across the hillside, including a restaurant and health spa—staffed by a veritable army of Vilcabambans to feed, bathe, and massage you—and plenty of *fiesta*-minded foreigners. Fee-based activities include horseback riding (s/50,000 for 4hr.); trips to Podocarpus; and a slew of health and beauty treatments such as a whirlpool bath (US$2 for 30min.), "colon therapy" (US$6 for 30min.), or the full "health and beauty package" (US$25). Breakfast is included with the price of a room. Rooms start at US$4.50 per person. Resort use US$10-17 per person. Reservations required.

Hosteria La Posada Real (tel. 580 904). On Vaca de la Vega, just before the first bridge at the edge of town. Achieving the happy medium between full-service resort and jungle lodge, this hotel provides large, comfortable rooms and private hot-water bathrooms. Set in a green field next to a river, it is *muy tranquilo,* but still only a short walk from downtown. Rooms s/40,000 per person.

Hostal Mandango, Huilcopamba and Juan Montalvo, across the street from the *terminal terrestre,* has clean, airy rooms and an inner courtyard with hammocks and chairs. Common bathrooms lack toilet seats but do have hot water. Rooms with private baths are considerably nicer. The open-air "Mirador" bar serves drinks and provides nighttime views of the city from the roof. Rooms s/15,000 per person, with bath s/30,000.

FOOD

Probably because of the recent influx of gringos, Vilcabamba offers an impressive selection of quality restaurants for such a small town. Options include tasty and affordable *típicos,* including **Restaurant Katharine** and the **Restaurant Valle Eterna Juventud**—next to each other on Sucre and Fernando de la Vega near the church—and many local hotels serve delicious, homemade meals to their guests. Several pizzerias line Vaca de la Vega as it winds out of town: **La Gioconda, Pepito's,** and **El Chozon del Abuelo** all serve tasty pies.

La Terraza (tel. 580 295), on Vaca de la Vega and Bolívar, at the corner of the plaza. The owners of Hostal Madre Tierra know how to do things with class. This new venture of theirs serves up steaming Mexican, Thai, and Italian dishes, as well as homemade brownies and apple pie. They even make their own tofu and pasta. Menu includes Thai stir-fry and chicken fajitas (s/22,000) and vegetarian lasagna (s/17,000). Open Tu-Su 2-9:30pm.

Restaurante Vegetariano, Vaca de la Vega and Valle Sagrado. This popular restaurant dishes up the cleanest, tastiest vegetarian fare in town. The breakfast crepe with banana and honey is a must (s/7,000). The three-course *almuerzo* (s/10,000) is sure to satisfy. For dinner, they offer spinach spaghetti with salad (s/18,000) and many other creative vegetarian dishes. Open daily 8:30am-8:30pm.

Restaurante Huilcopamba (tel. 580 888), Vaca de la Vega and Sucre, right on the park. Arguably the best *típico* in town, this friendly place is popular with both locals and visitors and offers outside dining right on the park. The food is oh-so-tasty and the portions giganormous. The *Cecina* (a dried-meat dish, s/14,000) is sure to satisfy even the heartiest of appetites. Open daily 7am-9pm.

SIGHTS

The countryside provides all the sights and entertainment most Vilcabamba-goers could ask for. The sunny days are easily filled with leisurely strolls, hearty hikes, and horseback rides through the land's forested terrain.

HIKES. The hike up **Mount Mandango** is a favorite. It provides several hours of strenuous exercise and Andean views. The trail starts just uphill of the bus station on Eterna Juventud and passes two crucifixes and some easily missed Inca ruins along the route. For a more forested experience, head to the opposite side of town to the **Cabañas Río Yambala** (see **Accommodations**, above). Several marked trails leave right from the *cabañas.* Following the dirt road past the *cabañas* leads into Parque Nacional Podocarpus. The tourism office, Aventurs, and Craig's Book Exchange are particularly good sources of hiking information.

HORSEBACK TRIPS. Getting a four-legged tour is as easy as falling off a horse. Most hotels can arrange tours into Podocarpus ranging from a few hours *(about US$10)* to three-day excursions *(about US$80-110 per person, depending on the season and number of people).* English-speaking guide **Gavin Moore** *(tel. 571 025)* has over 10 years of experience with "the best horses in town," and his trips include gourmet food, drinks, and two nights of lodging at his 2,500-meter-high mountain cabin in

VILCABAMBA: THE EARLY YEARS Forty years ago, Vilcabamba was much like the other villages that dot the mountainsides of southern Ecuador. Change was to come from an unlikely source: an American paraplegic hermit named **Johnny Lovewisdom**. Mr. Lovewisdom's life of isolation came to an end in the 1950s when he appeared in a *Time* magazine article and was sought out by a flock of disciples. He subsequently formed a religious sect and brought his followers down to Vilcabamba to live a spiritually pure existence—members wore only white, were sexually abstinent, and ate only fruit. Soon, however, their chaste existence was disturbed by the arrival of a new member. At first, she fit in with the sect's way of life, but before too long, she and Johnny went into "moral decline." Eventually, she fell into moral decline with just about every male member of the group. After that, things fell apart pretty quickly. Some of the original members have stuck around, though, and some say that Señor Lovewisdom himself continues to live on in the Vilcabamban countryside.

the nearby cloud forests. Cabañas Río Yambala has another set of cabins deep in the forest and offers a similar package. Horse guides advertise their trips around the central plaza and in the tourism and Aventurs offices. **Orlando Falco,** a bilingual zoologist, offers a selection of one-day cloud forest walks *(US$20 per person for groups of four or more).* He has over twenty years of guiding experience, including nine years in Vilcabamba. Tours can be arranged from the **Artesanal Primavera** shop in town on the plaza or at the Pole House.

OTHER TRIPS. If the gringos get to you, **Zumba** and **Malacatos** offer the same scenery but fewer tourists. Zumba, six hours south via a bumpy highway through the mountains, is tantalizingly close to Perú (5km), but one can't cross the guarded border here. The town caters to the military, but for heavily forested mountains, it's worth a trip. Malacatos, about 30 minutes to the north along the road to Loja, features a massive blue-domed church and the Vieja Molienda resort that seems out of place in the otherwise small town.

ENTERTAINMENT

When the sun finally sinks below the Vilcabamban hills, nocturnal life begins to stir around town. On the roof of Hostal Mandango, the **Mirador** bar lives up to its name with a thatched roof but no walls to obstruct the view (happy hour 8-9pm; cocktails s/10,000; open until 2am). The non-franchised **Hard Rock Café,** next to the bus station, offers food, drink, and coffee until the last partier leaves. **El Chozon del Abuelo,** a 15-minute walk down Vaca de la Vega, continues the thatched theme but adds multi-colored lighting and a disco ball (cerveza Nevada s/10,000).

THE ORIENTE

In the shadow of the sharply sloping eastern edge of the Andes, leafy palms hide the clusters of flat concrete buildings and tin shacks that make up the tiny, exotic villages of the Oriente. Many of these towns have only recently popped up, as Ecuador's frontier has moved eastward. Utility has governed the architecture, and one road connects all: the single treacherous Oriente "highway" traverses the land at approximately 1000m above sea level, linking sundry small jungle communities separated by stretches of untamed wilderness. These cities and hamlets dot a region blessed with lush primary tropical rainforest and the exotic wildlife that inhabits it. One traveling to the area should keep in mind that many modern luxuries (e.g. hot water, telecommunications, and electricity) may not be readily available to accommodate travelers. Nature reigns supreme in the living jungle; civilization still negotiates its lease. Beyond the small towns lining the Oriente highway lies Ecuador's last and quickly disappearing frontier. This unspoiled jungle wilderness stretches from Ecuador's easternmost urban outposts, Macas, Coca, and Lago Agrio, for more than 100km to its remote borders with Perú and Colombia. This primary-growth rainforest, which encompasses thousands of acres of nationally protected lands, is home to countless plant and insect species, as well as larger, rarer animals, including jaguars, sloths, monkeys, and crocodiles. The area is also home a number of indigenous societies; among the largest are the Huaorani, Secoya, Siona, and Shuar peoples. The jungle of the Oriente, once largely inaccessible to tourists, can now be explored with relative ease. Numerous excellent agencies base themselves in the Oriente's larger towns, offering excursions deep into the rainforest.

Tragically, over the last few decades large sections of the rainforest have been invaded and depleted by powerful corporations attracted by the discovery of valuable natural resources. In the Southern Oriente, gold deposits provide the impetus to reach deep into densely vegetated jungle. In the north it is the discovery of huge oil beds that has lured trucks and bulldozers ever eastward.

THE SOUTHERN ORIENTE

While the well-maintained, (mostly) paved **Panamerican Highway** ferries most tourists north from Loja to Cuenca and beyond, the road from Zamora through the Southern Oriente to Macas is more an of obstacle course than a highway. It's occasionally cobblestoned but usually muddy when it rains and dusty when it doesn't. If one should tire of the drive (restful as it is), there are a few uneventful but inviting small towns to stroll around in. Stopping along the way eases the trek by breaking the Southern Oriente odyssey into shorter segments.

Be aware that during the rainy season (June to August), landslides and their ilk torment the narrow, bumpy, and unpaved roads of the Southern Oriente. Don't plan too tight a schedule for yourself; buses are sometimes forced to stop and let their passengers walk a few kilometers to firmer ground. In rare cases, you may end up stranded in a town for a couple of days waiting out torrential rains..

HIGHLIGHTS OF THE SOUTHERN ORIENTE

- **Gualaquiza** (p. 357) is a tranquil jungle township.
- **Tours from Macas** (p. 364) visit the dwellings of the **Shuar** people.
- The **Southern Oriente dirt highway** (p. 356) is always an adventure.

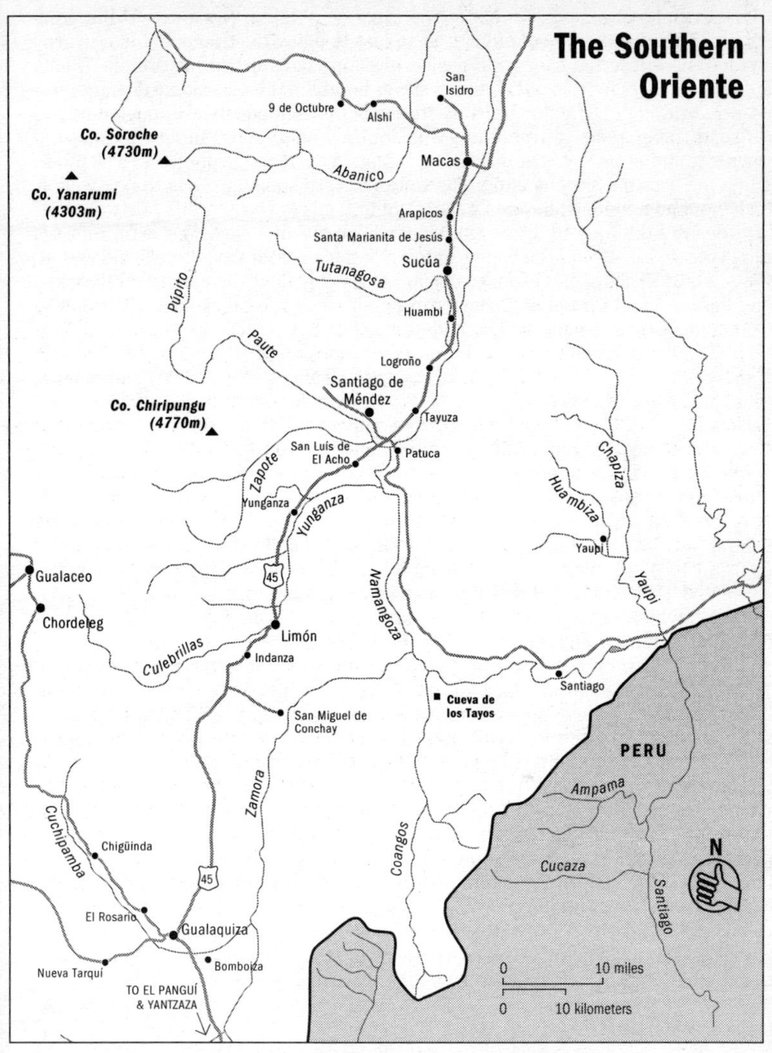

Of particular interest in the Southern Oriente are the Shuar people. Connected to the rest of civilization by little more than deep bush trails, the Shuar tribe live much as they have for centuries. Known as former headshrinkers, today they practice only a reduced version of their distinct spirituality. But the Shuar do continue to live in traditional log huts deep in the jungle and use bamboo reeds for shelter and dugout canoes for transportation. These days, lightweight aircraft carry some of the Southern Oriente's few tourists into Shuar villages from Macas and Sucúa for a look at a culture untouched by outside technology.

GUALAQUIZA

Hibernating deep in the heart of the Southern Oriente, the forgotten jungle town of Gualaquiza lies buried in a den of dramatic tropical hills. As one of the largest towns in the area, it has its share of hotels and restaurants, but as a town off the tourist track, Gualaquiza sees few foreigners walking down its cobblestone streets. The idea that people might come just to enjoy the tranquility and nearby attractions—deserted caves, a Salesian mission, undisturbed Inca ruins—elicits amused snickers from locals. Curious stares bombard the occasional deviant tourist who braves the Oriente "highway" to reach this hidden city. Although die-hard off-road travelers are attracted to Gualaquiza's remoteness in any season, the town's stunning setting is at its best from May to June and September to October, when the seasons are changing. The October-April summer tends to be swelteringly hot and humid, while June to September tends to be rainy and fairly cool.

It doesn't take long to know Gualaquiza's layout by heart. The main plaza is uncharacteristically not the center of town, but it's not far from hotels and restaurants. **Av. 24 de Mayo** and **Domingo Comín** run the length of the park on either side, and **Pesantez** and **Ciudad de Cuenca** run uphill along the other edges. Parallel to Comín are **García Moreno, Alfaro,** and **Atahuallpa. Buses** leave from the *terminal terrestre,* Pesantez and 12 de Febrero, three blocks from the plaza. They run to: **Macas** (8hr., 3 per day, s/52,000), stopping in **Limón** (4hr., s/30,000) and **Méndez** (6hr., s/35,000); **Cuenca** (8hr., 3 per day, s/50,000); **Yantzaza** (3½hr., s/16,000); and **Zamora** (5hr., s/23,000). The **16 de Agosto** company has daily trips to nearby small towns like Nueva Tarquí, Valle de Quine, and Proveduría up the river. Be forewarned that the Gualaquiza-Limón ride travels over roads that are horrible in some stretches—not for the weak-stomached. Other services include: the **police** (tel. 101), on Pesantez and 12 de Febrero, near the *terminal terrestre*; the **Farmacia Central** (tel. 780 203), on Pesantez and Alfaro (open daily 8am-10pm); the **hospital** (tel. 780 106), up toward the church and near the school (24hr. emergency service); and **EMETEL,** Ciudad de Cuenca and García Moreno, one block down from the park, which doesn't allow calling card or collect calls (open M-F 8-11am, 2-5pm, and 7-9pm, Sa 9-11am and 7-9pm). **Telephone code:** 07.

Accept it now: no hotel in Gualaquiza has hot water. **Residencial Amazonas** (tel. 780 715) has clean, airy rooms, an open courtyard, and a wonderfully aromatic bakery downstairs, but only offers communal bathrooms (s/15,000 per person, with newer mattresses s/20,000). **Hostal Guadelupe** (tel. 780 113), Pesantez and García Moreno, is better equipped, with fans, private baths, and a congenial common area offering a large color TV (s/30,000 per person). At mealtime, head to **Cabaña Los Helechos,** 12 de Febrero and Pesantez. The bamboo walls and palm-thatched roof smack of a Shuar hut, though few such abodes offer a bar with comparable selection (almuerzo or merienda s/8,000; open daily 8am-10pm). Up the hill on D. Comín, half a block from the plaza, the **Bar/Restaurant Oro Verde** (tel. 780 616) offers frog legs a la carte (s/25,000) and *almuerzos* (s/10,000) in a polished room with satellite TV (open daily 8am-10pm). **Memo's Bar/Cafetería,** on Pesantez at the plaza, is a late-night hangout where food and beer (s/10,000) glow in the aura of a huge 30-inch Sony TV, blazing nightly from 6 to 11pm.

NEAR GUALAQUIZA

Many nearby adventures await just off the beaten path. Head for the hills and explore the **deserted caves of Nueva Tarquí,** 15km west of Gualaquiza. Though some folks in Gualaquiza may know how to find them, it's easier to find knowledgeable people in Nueva Tarquí. If no one around can offer advice, just head up the hill toward the black holes. An alternative visit, the **Salesian Mission of Bomboiza,** is a bastion of New World civilization that holds its own against the jungle. This easy-to-reach daytrip destination lies just off the highway route to Zamora. Buses traveling this road can drop off passengers and often stop to pick them up. The tiny village of **Proveduría,** ideal for explorers who want to go where few have gone before (without overexerting themselves) is just up the river from Bomboiza and can be reached via bus or by foot. Play Indiana Jones for a day and make one last crusade to the relatively unexplored **Inca ruins** in the nearby town of **Aguacate.**

Transportation: These adventures start in Gualaquiza. Ask for directions at the bus station, the library (near the main plaza), or one of several pharmacies. The **16 de Agosto** bus company travels to Nueva Tarqui and Proveduría.

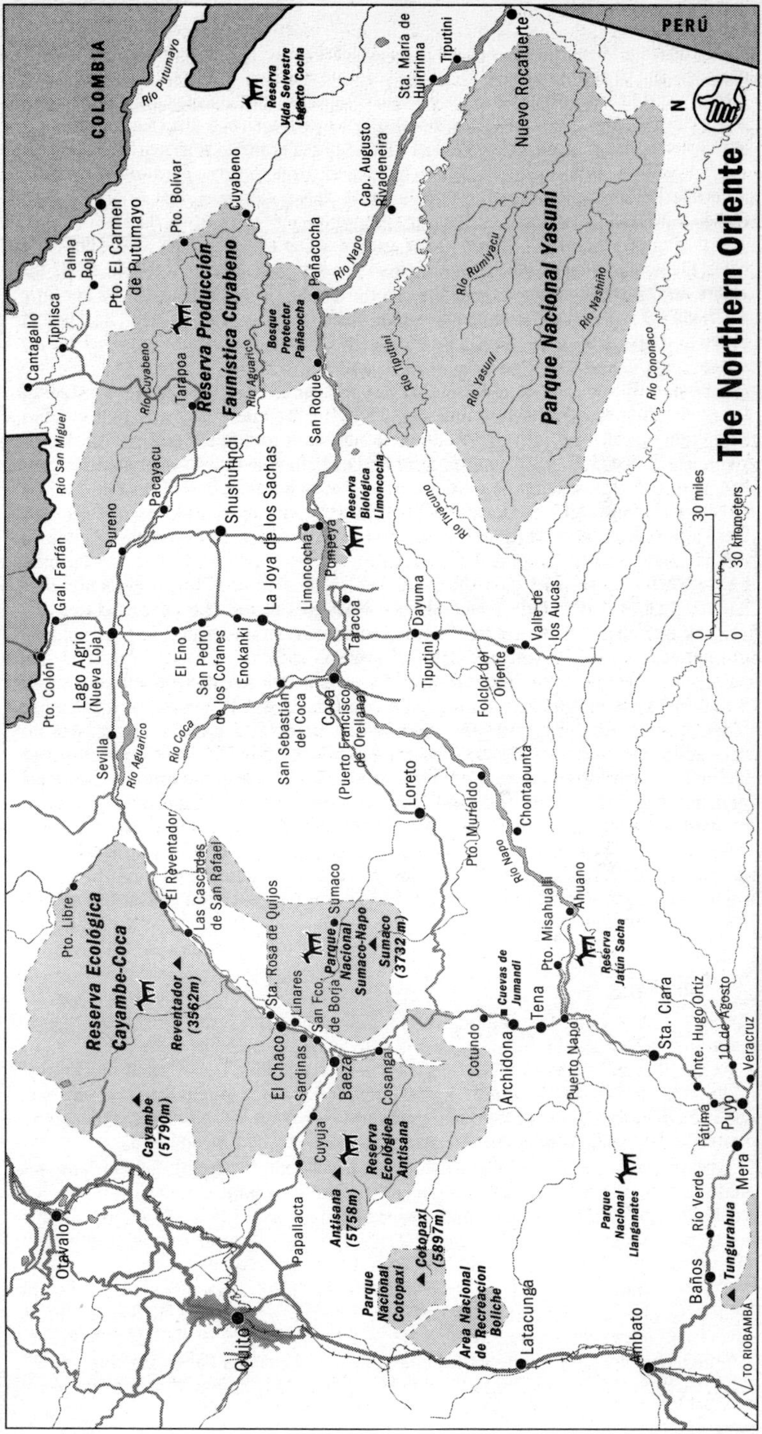

The Northern Oriente

COLOMBIA
PERÚ
N
Río Putumayo
Reserva Vida Silvestre Lagarto Cocha
Sta. María de Huiririma
Tiputini
Nuevo Rocafuerte
Cap. Augusto Rivadeneira
Cuyabeno
Pto. Bolívar
Pto. El Carmen de Putumayo
Palma Roja
Tiphisca
Cantagallo
Reserva Producción Faunística Cuyabeno
Río Cuyabeno
Río Aguarico
Tarapoa
Bosque Protector Pañacocha
Pañacocha
Río Napo
San Roque
Río Tiputini
Río Rumiyacu
Río Yasuní
Río Nashiño
Río Cononaco
Parque Nacional Yasuní
Río San Miguel
Shushufindi
Pacayacu
Dureno
Gral. Farfán
La Joya de los Sachas
Reserva Biológica Limoncocha
Limoncocha
Pompeya
Río Tivacuno
30 miles
30 kilometers
0
Pto. Colón
Lago Agrio (Nueva Loja)
El Eno
San Pedro de los Cofanes
Enokanki
Taracoa
Dayuma
Tiputini
Valle de los Aucas
Folclor del Oriente
San Sebastián del Coca
Coca (Puerto Francisco de Orellana)
Sevilla
Río Coca
Loreto
Pto. Muriáldo
Chontapunta
El Reventador
Las Cascadas de San Rafael
Sta. Rosa de Quijos
Sumaco
Parque Nacional Sumaco-Napo
Sumaco (3732 m)
Pto. Libre
Reserva Ecológica Cayambe-Coca
Reventador (3562m)
Linares
San Fco. de Borja
Cuevas de Jumandí
Río Napo
Ahuano
Reserva Jatún Sacha
Pto. Misahualli
El Chaco
Sardinas
Baeza
Cosanga
Cotundo
Archidona
Tena
Puerto Napo
Sta. Clara
Tnte. Hugo Ortíz
10 de Agosto
Veracruz
Cayambe (5790m)
Cuyuja
Reserva Ecológica Antisana
Antisana (5758m)
Papallacta
Cotopaxi (5897m)
Parque Nacional Cotopaxi
Area Nacional de Recreación Boliche
Parque Nacional Llanganates
Fátima
Puyo
Mera
Río Verde
Baños
Tungurahua
Otavalo
Quito
Latacunga
Ambato
TO RIOBAMBA

THE ORIENTE

LIMÓN

Also known as General Leonidas Plaza Gutiérrez, this tiny town has more playing children than running cars in its streets. Removed from the typical tourist track, Limón doesn't have many amenities—private baths, museums, or guided tours—but its quiet, friendly, and curious attitude toward visitors offers a window into small-town life. The area along the Río Yunganza is post-card worthy—tiny, tin-roofed houses stick up through the palms and tropical flowers, and precariously balconied houses pile over the river's bank. The residences along cobblestoned Calle Quito, the town's main street, are a creative mix of barn wood and cement.

The two major streets of Limón, **Quito and Av. 28 de Mayo,** both run parallel to the river. **El Ejército, Simón Bolívar,** and **Oriente** run perpendicular to them. **Av. 12 de Diciembre** and the **highway** are across the river. Most buses pass through the center of town via Ejército and Quito, but if you're looking for the station, head down 28 de Mayo and take a left on 5 de Junio, across the bridge; you'll find the *terminal terrestre* on your right, among *salchipapa* vendors.

Buses rumble by, heading to: **Macas** via **Méndez** and **Sucúa, Gualaquiza, Zamora, Loja,** and **Cuenca.** Most of the buses pass by in the late afternoon and evening. Shopkeepers along Quito or by the terminal can provide schedules. Across the river, the **police** (tel. 770 101) are found in a guardhouse building on 12 de Diciembre, near the highway next to the bus stop. **Botica Santana** (tel. 770 130), on Quito between Bolívar and El Ejército, will meet your pharmaceutical needs (open daily 9am-10pm). The **hospital** (tel. 770 738), to the right of the El Ejército bridge if facing the river, has 24hr. emergency treatment (emergency entrance around the back). **Pacifictel** (tel. 770 104), on Quito next to Residencial Limón, does not allow calling-card or collect calls (open M-Sa 8-11am, 2-4pm, and 7-8pm, Su 8-11am).

If taking a break from life on the road, the best rest in town takes place at **Hotel Dreamhouse** (tel. 770 166), on Quito between Bolívar and El Ejército. Clean rooms with wooden floors and new mattresses provide a comfortable setting for a night of wistful reverie. (Rooms s/20,000 per person.) Across the street from Dreamhouse, **Residencial Limón** (tel. 770 114) offers a garden courtyard surrounded by spotless rooms sporting big, soft beds. The sanitary common bathrooms, though, offer only cold water. (Rooms s/20,000 per person.) To satisfy your appetite, the **cafetería** at the Dreamhouse is probably the most attractive option. **Catilis's Restaurant,** on Quito between Orellán and Oriente, whips up speedy and cheap *almuerzos* and *meriendas* (s/10,000), as well as a la carte dishes (open daily 7:30am-9:30pm). Food stalls along Quito and 28 de Mayo or by the *terminal terrestre* may be the cheapest around, but their standards of sanitation usually aren't high.

MÉNDEZ

Another rarely visited stop along the highway and even more *tranquilo* than its southern neighbor, Limón, Méndez is worthy of a visit if you're charmed by a place that hasn't seen a tourist in months. The view from behind the bus station captures Méndez perfectly: an industrial, (sometimes) industrious village amid tropical jungle hills, drinking from the banks of the muddy Río Paute. Legend has it that a treasure of gold lies in a cave in the nearby hills, guarded by swarms of bats.

Everything of interest in this town predictably centers around the verdant **main plaza.** Adjacent to the plaza on **Cuenca,** the brilliant blue **church** is modern and strikingly angular. One major road, **Domingo Comín,** is on the left if you're standing in the park facing the church. **Guayaquil** runs parallel to Comín on the other side of the plaza, and the **Río Paute** runs parallel to Cuenca two blocks away.

The **bus station** is at the **Turismo Oriental** office (tel. 760 126), on the plaza at Quito and D. Comín. Buses head to: **Macas** (4hr., 7 per day, s/16,000) via **Sucúa** (3hr., s/10,000); **Cuenca** (7hr., 3 per day, s/45,000) via **Limón** (2hr., s/10,000). If buses aren't running, **camionetas** can make the same journeys. **Farmacia Botica Méndez** (tel. 760 149), Cuenca and Guayaquil, is on the plaza (open daily 8am-6pm and 8-10pm). All municipal offices, such as the **post office** and **library,** are on Comín at the plaza, though it may be worthwhile to take care of things in the more metropolitan towns of Limón and Macas. **IETEL,** one block up Cuenca, past Los Ceibos, allows international calls but no calling card or collect calls. (Open M-F 8-11am, 3-5pm, 7-9pm.)

If you decide to spend the night in town, **Hostal Los Ceibos** (tel. 760 133), a half-block up Cuenca from the plaza, is a first-rate choice. Chock-full of homey atmosphere, the rooms have clean sheets, ceiling fans, and TVs (with one channel) to boot. Shared, cold-water bathrooms are as spotless and painless as that deadly combination can get. (Rooms s/30,000 per person.) More primitive pensions line Cuenca, a block or so from the plaza. Eating in Méndez is easy if not savory. Try any of the small restaurants on Cuenca across from Los Ceibos, where s/15,000 will get you a complete *almuerzo* or *merienda.*

SUCÚA

The central office of the **Shuar Federation,** three blocks south of the park, is Sucúa's claim to fame. An aboriginal group of the Central and Southern Oriente, the **Shuar** lived in relative isolation until the beginning of this century. Long considered a "savage" people because of their headhunting and headshrinking religion, the Shuar of today no longer practice these legendary acts. As missionaries, colonists, and oil companies moved in, the Shuar were forced to accept modern standards of living or risk losing their land and culture all together. Unfortunately for those interested in learning about the Shuar Federation, the central office itself is more an administrative office than a cultural center. Ironically, the best place (outside of the Shuar villages) to learn about the culture is in Quito's museums. (For more information on the Shuar and their Federation, see **Indigenous Identity,** p. 244.)

Sucúa's main street is the dusty **Domingo Comín,** along which lies the small **Parque Central.** Other buildings of importance, as well as most of Sucúa's accommodations, lie along the Macas (north) end of D. Comín. Sucúa's *terminal terrestre*, a 10-minute walk down Comín (take a right at the fork), seems to get little action, since all buses go through town. **Buses** cruise up and down D. Comín, running to: **Macas** (1hr., every hr. 5:45am-6:45pm, s/6,000), and, less frequently, to more distant Oriente and sierra towns. When this close to Macas, one might as well spend the night there—but if stuck in Sucúa, the **Hotel Gyna** (tel. 740 926), D. Comín between Kiruba and Carlos Olson, offers clean rooms with private bath and hot water (s/30,000 per person, with TV s/35,000). The **Oasis Restaurant** (tel. 740 140), on D. Comín, one block north of the park, has a large selection of food (including vegetarian options) at not-so-large prices.

MACAS

In 1595 a vision of a beautiful woman known today as *la Virgen Purísima de Macas*, appeared before a family in the town that was then called *Sevilla del Oro*. If such a vision comes to you while in Macas, it's probably because you've spent too much time in one of the city's plentiful bars, or perhaps because you've been experimenting with *natem*, a hallucinogenic plant used by the Shuar in traditional ceremonies. With a population of 25,000, this capital of the Morona-Santiago province, sometimes referred to as the "oriental Emerald," is a vision of beauty even without the aid of psychotropic substances. Macas maintains the quiet friendly atmosphere of many smaller jungle towns while offering more of the amenities of a larger city, such as an airport with a paved runway or hotels with dependably hot water. For tourists, Macas serves largely as a launch pad for trips to pristine stretches of the Amazon, visits to traditional Shuar villages, and the tremendous Cueva de los Tayos. Much, however, can be learned about the surrounding area from within Macas itself. Most of the towns' inhabitants can tell fascinating tales—recounted with pride and passion—of their experiences with the jungle beyond.

ORIENTATION AND PRACTICAL INFORMATION

The **airstrip** forms the western boundary of the town. Copueno River borders on the east, behind the cathedral. **Domingo Comín**, leading up to the cathedral, is the town's busiest street, especially around the intersection with **Amazonas.** The *terminal terrestre* is on 10 de Agosto just west of Amazonas.

Airport: TAME, Amazonas and Cuenca (tel. 701 162), at the airport, has flights to **Quito** (30min.; M, W, F at noon; US$53). Open M-F 8am-4:30pm. **Austro Aero** (tel. 700 939), on Amazonas, between Tarquí and 10 de Agosto, has flights to **Cuenca** (25min., M and W noon).

Buses: **Cuenca** (10hr., 8 per day, s/60,000); **Quito** (11hr., 5 per day, s/70,000); **Morona** (10hr., 9pm, s/70,000); **Puyo** (5hr., 6 and 8pm, s/35,000); **Gualaquiza** (10hr., 12:30 and 5pm, s/50,000); **Méndez** (3hr., 10:45am and 3pm, s/17,000); and **Sucúa** (1hr., every hr. 6:45am-7:45pm, s/6,000.)

Tourist Information: Orientravel, 10 de Agosto and Soasti (tel. 700 371; fax 700 380; email orotravel@cue.satnet.net), is good for general information and also exchanges dollars and traveler's checks. Open M-F 8:30am-1pm and 2-6pm, Sa 9am-1pm. For information in English about the jungle, Sangay National Park, the Shuar, Macas, or just about anything else, see Sarah Massie at **Tsunki Tours** (see p. 365).

Currency Exchange: Banco del Austro (tel. 700 216), 24 de Mayo and 10 de Agosto. Exchanges dollars and traveler's checks. Open M-F 8am-1pm. See also **Orientravel** in **Tourist Information** above.

Laundromat: Serviclim, 24 de Mayo and Juan Salinas (tel. 701 268), several blocks past Tarquí away from the plaza, will wash and dry twelve items of clothing in 2 hr. (s/ 18,000).

Emergency: Tel. 101.

Police: There is a small police station (tel. 701 958) at the bus station.

Pharmacy: Botica Oriental, (tel. 700 388) 10 de Agosto and Soasti. Open daily 7am-10pm.

Hospital: (Emergency tel. 701 898.) There are a number of private **medical clinics** on Amazonas, near D. Comín. The **Clínica Jervés,** 10 de Agosto 7-34 (tel. 700 007), offers 24hr. emergency service.

Post Office: Correos (tel. 700 060), 9 de Octubre near D. Comín, 1 block from the central plaza. Open M-F 7:30am-6pm. **Delgado Travel** (tel. 700 595) on D. Comín between 24 de Mayo and Soasti, has a package-sending service (to U.S. only) as does **Orientravel** (see **Tourist Information,** above).

Fax Office: Above the **post office.** Open M-F 7:30am-6pm.

Telephones: Pacifictel (tel. 700 104) on Av. 24 de Mayo, between Cuenca and Sucre. International service but no collect or calling card calls. Open daily 8am-9:30pm.

PHONE CODE	07

ACCOMMODATIONS

Macas's hotels vary in price and quality. Moreover, at any hotel, the rooms of a given price may differ in quality. You might want to look at several possibilities before choosing one, especially when shopping in a lower price range.

Hotel Peñón del Oriente (tel. 700 124; fax 700 450), Amazonas and D. Comín. Somewhere between Las Vegas motel and Christian enlightenment center, Peñón del Oriente dresses its plushly carpeted rooms in red and white ruffles but tempers all this sinfulness with Bible passages plastered on the walls. After a long day of exploring Macas, the stunning views and hot showers seem god-sent, in spite of the decor. Rooms s/ 20,000 per person, with hot water s/25,000, with TV and carpet s/50,000.

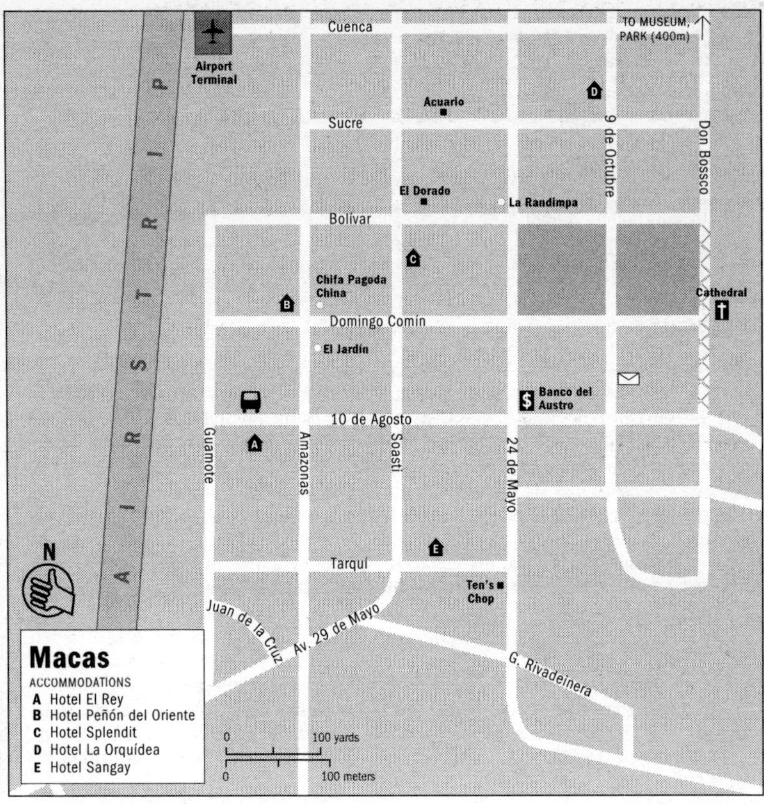

Hotel La Orquídea (tel. 700 970), Sucre and 9 de Octubre. Free of superfluous embellishment, these vibrant rooms have a simple sophistication and crisp cleanliness. Rooms s/25,000 per person, with hot water s/30,000, with TV s/35,000.

Hotel Splendit (tel. 700 120), Soasti between D. Comín and Bolívar. The new half of the hotel offers color TVs, shiny faux satin bedspreads, and reliable hot water for s/30,000 per person. The older rooms with electrically heated water, no TV, and musty smells are not quite as splendit, but are reasonably priced. Rooms s/10,000-15,000 per person.

Hotel Sangay, 6-05 Tarquí between Soasti and 24 de Mayo (tel. 700 457). With the walls painted a light, bright turquoise throughout, Sangay has a fresh, open feel. Mattresses are thin, and communal baths are not terribly clean, but the low prices and appealing atmosphere make for a great value. Rooms s/10,000 per person.

Hotel el Rey (tel. 700 529), on 10 de Agosto across from the *terminal terrestre.* Clean, spacious rooms will make you feel like a king after a long day of travel. Rooms s/24,000 per person, with bath and TV s/35,000.

FOOD

Macas's dining scene offers variety and value. In addition to the exotic jungle cuisine, a fine selection of seafood, Cuban, and typical Ecuadorian restaurants provide plenty of interesting possibilities after weeks of *almuerzos.* The best deals in town are at the simple lunch stands in and across from the market near Hotel Peñón del Oriente, where s/4,000 *almuerzos* are the norm.

Bar-Restaurant La Randimpa (tel. 700 696), Bolívar and 24 de Mayo. Cool, any way you cut it. Cuban music and food are complemented by a lively tropical ambiance. Open daily 7am-11pm.

Chifa Pagoda China (tel. 700 280), Amazonas and D. Comín. Large and clean, Pagoda China serves delicious meals to satisfy the insatiable Ecuadorian appetite for Chinese food. Try the sweet-and-sour chicken (s/26,000). Open daily 9:30am-10:30pm.

El Jardín (tel. 700 573), Amazonas and D. Comín. Provides a congenial atmosphere and a good selection of food. Prices range from s/3,000 for a cheese sandwich to s/25,000 for "fillet mignom." Open daily 7am-10pm.

Charlot (tel. 700 120), Cuenca and Soasti. Local dishes at low prices. Try the *apanado,* a sort of fried sandwich of beef, egg, and bread (s/15,000). Open daily 7am-9pm.

SIGHTS

The **cathedral** in Macas is a large, spacious modern building whose main tourist appeal is the series of twelve elaborate stained glass windows that tell the story of la Virgen Purísima de Macas, the town's patron saint. Festivals dedicated to the virgen are celebrated on August 5 and February 18. Five blocks north of the cathedral on Don Bosco, just past Riobamba, the small **Museo Arquelógico Muinicipal** contains several rooms with ceramics, tools, instruments, and other remnants of the **Upano, pre-Upano, Shuar,** and **Sangay** traditions. Behind the building is a lush, well-maintained *parque recreacional* with a view of the river below, perfect for a picnic or a leisurely stroll. Admission to the museum is free, but there are no regular hours; go in the morning when the librarian in the one-room library next door can open it for you.

ENTERTAINMENT

For those who are tired of nightlife defined by furry creatures that nocturnally prowl the wilderness, Macas rages by jungle standards. To dance the night away, try the **Discoteca Acuario**, on Sucre between 24 de Mayo an Soasti. **La Taberna El Dorado** (tel. 700 446), Bolívar and Soasti, also has a dance floor but is more popular as a bar (open M-Sa 2-5pm and 8pm-2am). **Ten's Chop** (tel. 700-280), 24 de Mayo and Tarquí, is a happening tropical bar complete with dance floor, colored lighting, a big-screen TV flickering sports and music videos, and cheap tap beer by the pitcher (s/15,000; open daily 2-6pm and 8pm-2am).

INTO THE JUNGLE FROM MACAS

Macas is the most developed and convenient town in the southern Oriente from which to begin a jungle jaunt. While the northern Oriente sees more tourists, the jungle east of Macas provides some unique opportunities. As in the north, hundreds of thousands of hectares remain undeveloped; large tracts of primary forest are still intact. Some of the more staggeringly beautiful areas remain untouched with the help of government protection, such as **Parque Nacional Sangay's** *zona baja*, the **ecological reserve** near Santa Rosa, and the caves at **Cueva de los Tayos.**

JUNGLE EXCURSIONS

This area is also home to Ecuador's second-most-populous indigenous group, the **Shuar.** While many Shuar around Macas and Sucúa have changed their traditional ways, more isolated communities in the jungle east of Macas continue to live as they have for centuries. Many of the longer (4-6 day) tours from Macas visit these communities. While the Shuar have not expressed as much distaste for this kind of tourism as have the Huaorani and other *indígenas* to the north, the visits cannot help but affect their traditional way of life. If you decide to visit one of these communities, do so with a guide who has a **contract** with the people you will be visiting and is working in coordination with a Shuar guide from that community. Only this ensures that the people there are accepting of visiting tour groups. Ask to see the contract if you are uncertain. With proper pre-arrangements made, you will find the Shuar to be friendly, welcoming hosts. Accommodations vary; some guides arrange a stay with a Shuar family, while others bring camping equipment. It will likely be possible to eat with the Shuar. If you are lucky you may even be offered **chicha de yucca,** an alcoholic drink made from the yucca plant, fermented with the saliva of an older Shuar woman.

Your hosts will have precious little experience with the amenities of modern life, something you could find refreshing or unsettling. Visitors should be sensitive to the Shuar religion and customs. Although many of the community's rites and religious festivals are closed to outsiders, some are open to observation. Among these are the ritual purifications performed in the **Cascadas Sagradas** (Sacred Waterfalls) and ceremonies that involve the ingestion of a hallucinogen the Shuar call *natem*. When visiting Shuar communities, it is polite to bring a small gift. Ask your guide for suggestions.

PARQUE NACIONAL SANGAY

For a more ecology-oriented experience, try a trip to the **zona baja** at **Parque Nacional Sangay** (Macas entrance). One of the most jungle-intensive excursions around, its trails climb hills and weave through primary tropical rainforest. At one point in the journey, cable cars cross the otherwise impassable rivers Sangay and Upano. At least one trail actually traverses the park, crossing over into the *zona alta* in the highlands near Baños and Riobamba (see **Parque Nacional Sangay,** p. 318). The trip is ideal for the jungle-obsessed: sleeping in cabins, exploration by horseback and canoe with stints of tubing and swimming—just what you came here for.

CUEVAS DE LOS TAYOS

Another commonly visited sight near Macas, the **Cuevas de los Tayos** is an enormous (85m deep), pitch-black cave that can only be explored with a guide. Its name comes from the large colonies of oilbirds (*tayos*) that reside in the cavern. These unusual birds have picked up some telltale habits from those who know caves best: the bats. Not only are the oilbirds nocturnal fruit-eaters; they also use sonar to stake out their location in the pitch-black environs. Yet another underground source of oil in the Oriente; these *tayos* used to be captured and boiled for the oil harvested from their fat-rich flesh. Many tours leaving from Macas pencil Cueva de los Tayos and other caves containing *tayos* onto their itineraries, but such caves can also be explored from **Morona,** a village on the Peruvian border with neither restaurants nor accommodations (10-11hr. from Macas).

TOUR COMPANIES

The many tour companies leading trips from Macas offer a wide variety of packages. Most guides will work with the client, and to some degree, customize the tour. Tours usually run one to eight days and can include one or more of the above attractions, some smaller attractions, as well as canoeing, hiking, horseback-riding, and fishing. The tours are usually all-inclusive (food, lodging, transport, advice, wisdom, medicinal plants, etc.), but it may be possible to hire a guide and pay for everything a la carte if you insist hard enough. Another important consideration is transportation mode. Some companies use small (and sometimes nausea-inducing) planes to conveniently and quickly transport people to remote parts of the jungle, while others rely on walking, boating, and horses.

Tour prices vary widely with group size and duration of excursion; the larger the group, the less each person pays per day (generally in the range of US$30-US$70). To arrange a tour, visit several guides to see which can best cater to your particular needs and desires. A few suggestions:

Aventuras Tsunki (tel. 700 464; email tsunki@cue.satnet.net; www.tsunki.com.ec), on D. Comín between 24 de Mayo and Soasti, builds its business on the talents of English-speaking ecologist Sarah Massie and Chilean anthropologist Daniel Castro. Congenial, knowledgeable, and dedicated to both the environment and the well-being of the Shuar communities they visit, Tsunki guides run a first-class operation. A variety of activities are offered. Prices vary with tour duration, destination, and group size (4-person, 3-day tour US$40 per person per day; 2-person, 5-day tour US$50 per person per day).

Tunkiak (tel. 700 082; fax 700 110), 10 de Agosto just west of Amazonas, in the *terminal terrestre*. Associated with Huasca Agencia de Viajes, this company is Shuar-run. Offers similar trips to Tsunki's at similar prices (see above). Also offers piranha fishing and trips to hot springs.

Ikiaam (tel. 701 690), on Amazonas next to the Hotel Peñon. Run by friendly, knowledgeable Shuar tour guides. English-speaking interpreter available. In addition to the standard offerings, guides also lead daytrips (US$35 per person).

THE NORTHERN ORIENTE

Most urbanization and colonization of the Northern Oriente has occurred, problematically at times, in the last 50 years. For centuries, even after the arrival of the Spanish, *indígenas* lived here in isolation, bothered only by occasional wandering missionaries. Only at the beginning of this century did colonists from the highlands descend upon the jungle and begin to clear plots of farmland, hunting the wildlife and intruding upon the *indígenas* who were already living there, including the Huaorani, Secoya, Siona, and Shuar peoples. The industrial growth surrounding the discovery of oil in the 1970s poses the greatest threat to these pristine natural areas and their indigenous communities. The (mostly foreign) oil companies continue to cut roads deeper into the jungle, not only destroying the forest as they go but also opening it up for colonization. Consequently, many of the jungle's original residents—wildlife and indigenous tribes—have been displaced and forced deeper into the disappearing jungle to survive.

Ironically, to facilitate the exploitation of the remote jungle, oil companies have indirectly acted to save it. The creation of an infrastructure to support employees has allowed environmentally responsible "ecotourism" to flourish from increased accessibility and inhabitability, helping in turn to preserve and promote the region's natural habitats and populations. Likewise, tourism has provided more jobs, as well as revenue that largely remains in the region rather than pouring into the pockets of multinational petroleum companies and their foreign employees. But tourism, however noble its priorities, has still had its costs. It has been particularly intrusive on the indigenous peoples, who have reportedly been exploited by some unscrupulous tour agencies. Tourists to the Oriente should consider the impact of their presence when planning a jungle excursion.

HIGHLIGHTS OF THE NORTHERN ORIENTE

- **White-water rafting in Tena** (see p. 372) is some of the best in Ecuador.
- **Jatún Sacha** (see p. 374) is one of the most impressive forest ecosystems.
- **Jungle tours from Coca** (see p. 379) visit the indigenous **Huaorani** people.
- Armadillos, river dolphins, and piranhas live in **Cuyabeno Reserve** (see p. 382).
- The hot springs uphill from **Papallacta** (see p. 385) overlook lush jungle scenery.

PUYO

At the eastern foothills of the Andes, a harrowing two-hour ride from the verdant valley of Baños, the Río Puyo passes through the town that bears its name just as it enters dense Amazonian rainforest. While wilderness has the earliest and strongest claim on Puyo, human beings go back pretty far as well. Archaeological evidence indicates that people lived in the area as long ago as 4000-3500 BC. By the time the Spanish arrived, local tribes had united into a group called the Záparos. But in the years that followed, diseases decimated the Záparos, leaving behind only 14% of their previous population.

Originally a missionary site, this present-day capital of the Pastaza province now has a population of about 20,000 people, most of whom are Quichua. Now, whether out of heartfelt pride or simply as fuel for tourism, Puyo nurtures its jungle-town image. River scenes adorn the walls of virtually every hotel and restaurant, while most tourist shops sell almost exclusively wood-carved parrots and postcards of exotic jungle fauna. Puyo itself is no more than a cluster of urban blocks that surrenders quickly to the surrounding wilderness; a very real, untamed rainforest canopy stretches east from town. Paradoxically, the jungle around Puyo is somewhat untouristed, as most travelers pass it by for more remote destinations. Thus, tourists short on time or money can see very real, very wild jungle in the surrounding areas at bargain basement prices.

ORIENTATION

The road from Baños comes in from the west to the **terminal terrestre.** From there it's a bus ride (s/1,000), taxi ride (s/8,000), or 1km walk northeast to the **main plaza.** The **centro** lies uphill from the main plaza and is defined by the east-west **Av. Ceslao Marín** and **Av. Atahualpa,** which are intersected by **Av. 9 de Octubre** and **27 de Febrero.** Most hotels, *comedores*, and various shops cluster in the area near 9 de Octubre and Atahualpa. Muddy **Río Puyo** borders the eastern edge of town. There are no street signs—give an address and you will get a blank look; name an establishment and someone can point you the way.

PRACTICAL INFORMATION

Buses: The **terminal terrestre** (tel. 885 480) is a 20min. walk or a short cab ride (s/8,000) west of the *centro.* Take 9 de Octubre downhill past the market to the traffic circle with a bronze bust, then turn right on Alberto Nambrano and follow it 1km. The *terminal* serves arrivals and departures until 6pm, after which buses drop people off downtown. Evening and night trips leave from **Transportes Touris San Francisco,** on Marín 10m west of where Atahualpa joins it. Buses go to: **Ambato** (3hr., every 30min. 4am-7pm, s/20,000) via **Baños** (2hr., s/14,000); **Quito** (5hr., 7 per day 7:30am-5:45pm, s/36,000); **Riobamba** (3hr., 8 per day 3:45am-5:15pm, s/20,000); **Macas** (5hr., 8 per day 8am-5pm, s/36,000); **Tena** (3hr., every 30min. 6am-9pm, s/20,000); **Coca** (9hr., 6:30am and 9:30pm, s/50,000); **Guayaquil** (8hr., 6:15am and 11pm, s/55,000); and **Hola Vida** (1hr., W and F-Su 5am and 12:30pm; s/6,000).

Tourist Office: CETUR (tel. 884 655), at the northwest corner of the plaza, undervisited and overstaffed, provides info on tourist facilities throughout the Oriente and a decent map of town. Open M-F 8am-noon and 2-6pm, Sa 8am-noon. The owners of **Hotel Araucano** are extremely well-informed about local excursions.

Currency Exchange: Casa de Cambios Puyo (tel. 883 219), on Atahualpa between 9 de Octubre and 10 de Agosto, changes traveler's checks and cash. Open M-Sa 8am-8pm, Su 8am-noon. **Banco del Austro** (tel. 883 924), farther down Atahualpa between 10 de Agosto and Dávila, changes traveler's checks and cash in the morning and accommodates Visa advances all day. Open M-F 8am-6pm, Su 9am-1:30pm.

Laundromat: Marthiney, 24 de Mayo and 10 de Agosto, dry cleans clothes (s/3-13,000). Open M-Sa 8am-noon and 2-7pm, Su 8am-noon. Most hotels have laundry facilities.

Police: (Tel. 883 101), 10 de Agosto, past Sucre.

Red Cross: Sucre 1540 and 10 de Agosto (tel. 885 214).

Pharmacy: Several pharmacies fill the area around the *municipio.* **Farmacia Ferr-ade** (tel. 883 892), Marín 187, just past Hostería Turingia, is open 24hr.

Hospital: Hospital de la Brigada 17 (tel. 883 131), Alfaro and Pino. In nearby Shell, **Hospital Vozandes** (tel. 795 172), Asunción, has U.S. doctors.

Post Office: Correos (tel. 885 332), 27 de Febrero and Atahualpa. Open M-F 8am-6pm, Sa 8am-3pm.

Telephones: Call home from **EMETEL** (tel. 883 104), Orellana and General Villamil, one block west of the market. Open daily 8am-10pm.

TELEPHONE CODE	03

ACCOMMODATIONS

Hotel Araucano, Marín 576 and 27 de Febrero (tel. 883 834). The management tries awfully hard for that jungle lodge atmosphere, but the buses passing outside keep reminding guests that they're in Puyo for the night. Enjoy the complimentary breakfast next to the fountain in the TV room, or do your own cooking in the well-equipped kitchen. Calling card calls are free from the lobby. Rooms are very clean and have hot-water baths. The helpful owners offer tours of their private jungle reserve (US$15 per person per day). Rooms s/25,000 per person.

Hotel Europa Internacional (tel. 885 220; fax 885 120), 9 de Octubre between Atahualpa and Orellana. This trustworthy hotel rents immense, well-furnished rooms with private hot-water baths. Ponder the seductive chainsaw and electronics advertisements that line the endless staircase and check out the jungle view from the roof. Restaurant downstairs. Rooms s/25,000 per person.

Hotel Granada (tel. 885 578), 27 de Febrero and Orellana, 2 blocks downhill from Atahualpa next to the market. A no-frills, low-cost option. Watch TV and VCR in the cozy common room. Rooms are bare but reasonably clean, with cold-water baths only. Rooms s/15,000 per person, with bath s/20,000.

FOOD

Pizzería/Restaurant Cha-Cha-Cha, Marín 249 (tel. 885 208), *(cha-cha-cha)* just past the Hotel Turingia *(cha-cha-cha)*. Say the name out loud and feel the rhythm. Enjoy pizza, vegetarian pasta, chicken, and sparkling, welcoming smiles. Tasty personal pizzas (s/30,000) and pasta with tons of veggies (s/20,000). Open daily 10am-10pm.

Mesón Europeo (tel. 883 919), on Zambrano east of the *terminal terrestre*. This open-air *hacienda* restaurant looks very fancy; cloth napkins and classy decor contrast sharply with the vacant lot next door. Bow-tied waiters complete the picture. This added luxury is complemented by reasonable prices. *Almuerzo* (s/20,000), fried chicken (s/19,000), and banana split (s/12,000). Open M-Sa noon-11pm, Su noon-4pm.

Chifa Oriental (tel. 885 467), Marín and 27 de Febrero right next to Hotel Araucano. Chomp cheap Chinese chow while ogling placemats with pictures of desserts that you won't find in Puyo. The menu is standard Chinese fare (beef and rice dishes s/13-17,000). Open Tu-Su 10am-3pm and 6pm-midnight.

Hostería Restaurant Turungia, Marín 294 (tel. 885 180), on the western edge of town. Visit the hotel's garden, pool, and pet snake before sitting down to gourmet food. Polish up your hiking boots–this is the fanciest place in town. *Almuerzos* and *meriendas* are tasty and filling (s/35,000). Open daily 7am-9pm.

SIGHTS AND ENTERTAINMENT

Though merely a pit-stop for most, Puyo does justice to its jungle surroundings. Several institutions have dedicated themselves to informing visitors about the flora, fauna, and indigenous cultures of the region.

PARQUE PEDAGÓGICO ETNO-BOTÁNICO OMAERE. This educational outdoor park speaks to the ethnobotanist in everyone, providing a wealth of information on how different indigenous groups use plants. The park itself lies on the Río Puyo, across a roped footbridge. A number of traditional *indígena* homes are scattered throughout the forest. While the park has been financed by foreigners, it serves mostly Ecuadorian schoolchildren—Spanish tours only. *(On the south end of 9 de Octubre. From the main plaza, walk 20min., or take a bus (s/1,000) headed for Obrero. Tel.*

883 001. Open Th-M 8am-5pm. Admission (s/25,000) includes a 30min. tour of the 15 hectare park given by an indigenous guide.)

HOLA VIDA. A self-service jungle experience can be found at the Hola Vida reserve. The reserve has basic cabins *(s/15,000 per person per night)* and food *(s/ 13,000 per meal)*, as well as 105 hectares of primary rain forest and a parrot who can bark like a dog. To see the area through the eyes of an experienced guide, contact Patricio Garcés, at Amazonia Touring *(tel. 883 219)*. A guide is worth the extra money. *(Located 30km south of town. Take a Tena-bound bus or a taxi (s/150,000). Admission s/10,000. Tours with Amazonia Touring US$15-20 per day.)*

ORGANIZACIÓN DE PUEBLOS INDÍGENAS DE PASTAZA (OPIP). A number of alternatives to generic guided tours exist in and around Puyo. The OPIP is an umbrella organization that can set you up directly with an indigenous guide. The advantages of contacting an indigenous guide directly are that prices tend to be lower (there is no middleman) and indigenous communities become more welcoming. Ask at CETUR or Hotel Araucano for details. *(OPIP's office on 9 de Octubre and Atahualpa. The Shuar and Huaorani tribes also have tourist offices in Puyo. Tel. 883 875.)*

OTHER SIGHTS. Continuing the botanical theme, the **Orquideario** specializes in rehabilitating exotic Amazonian plants. The owner will happily show you around, but it's a good idea to call ahead. *(Around kilometer 3 on the road to Macas, on the right in Pueblo Los Angeles. Tel. 884 854. Open daily during daylight hr.s. Admission US$5.)* After a few hundred million years of evolution, animals started to eat and reproduce amidst the plants. To see some of these newcomers, head to the **Zoocriadero.** Here semi-wild jungle creatures roam semi-free. *(Located at kilometer 15 on the road to Tena in the town of Fátima. Open daily. Admission s/25,000.)*

NIGHTLIFE. Indigenous shamans drink *ayahuasca* or *yagé* to enter a trance-like state where they see bright colors moving before their eyes. "Civilized" tourists achieve the same effect with exotic cocktails and disco lights at **New Bar** *(27 de Febrero and Atahualpa)*.

TENA

Just 197km southeast of Quito, Tena sits at the fast-flowing union of the Ríos Tena and Pano, part of the headwaters of the Amazon. East of Tena spreads the jungle, while its western panorama is dominated by the jagged silhouette of the mighty **Cordillera de los Llanganates.** Founded by the Spanish in 1560 as a daring stretch into the Oriente, this capital of Napo Province is now forging ahead with plans to become a center of Oriente ecotourism. What was once a Spanish outpost in the jungle has become a gringo one, and a budding industry of tourist possibilities meets the traveler traffic. Tena's entrepreneurs have developed a jungle playground here, with bamboo *cabañas*, spelunking, whitewater rafting, kayaking, and every other adventure a weary urbanite could hope for. The warm jungle climate and casual atmosphere also add to the city's attractiveness. But as busier destinations such as Baños attest, Tena still has a way to go in the direction of tourist services and accommodations.

ORIENTATION

On a clear day when the mountains to the west are visible, use them for navigation. Tena's most important parts are on either side of the area where Ríos Pano and Tena merge. To the west, Tena *centro* spreads as an irregular grid, from **García Moreno,** on the riverfront, to **Montalvo,** two blocks west, and from the **Main Plaza** along **Mera** to **Bolívar,** four blocks farther north. A pedestrian bridge crosses the river from Mera. East-west **Olmedo** becomes a bridge that takes a right on the opposite bank and becomes **Av. 15 de Noviembre.** The best hotels and restaurants are here, as is the **terminal terrestre,** 1km south of the bridge on 15 de Noviembre.

PRACTICAL INFORMATION

Airplanes: The **airstrip** is 3 blocks uphill from Olmedo, behind Bolívar. Flights go to **Coca** (30min., W 9am, s/600,000). While severe, it beats the bumpy, 7hr. bus ride. Flights also go to **Puyo,** but the flight schedule is less reliable.

Buses: The **terminal terrestre** is easy to miss; look closely along the west side of 15 de Noviembre, 1km from the bridges. Plenty of destinations are served, though some are affected by road closures between Puyo and Baños. To: **Sacha** (s/55,000) via **Coca** (6hr., 9 per day 9am-10pm, s/50,000); **Lago Agrio** (8hr., 6:30pm, s/60,000); **Quito** (6hr., 14 per day 9:30am-3am, s/40,000) via **Baeza** (3hr., s/20,000); **Ambato** (6hr., 9 per day 7am-9pm, s/38,000) via **Puyo** (3hr., s/20,000) and **Baños** (4-5hr., s/32,000); **Riobamba** (6hr., 2am-6pm, transfer in Puyo or Baños, s/40,000); **Misahuallí** (1hr., every 45min. 6am-7pm, s/6,000); and **Ahuano** (1½hr.; 5, 7:30am, and every hr. 9:30am-5:30pm; s/10,000).

Tourist Office: CETUR (tel. 886 536), on Bolívar near Amazonas, in the *centro,* provides helpful information on tourist activities in Napo province. A good place to check up on the record of any tour agency or report problems with one. Open M-F 8:30am-5pm. The **Consejo Provincial de Napo** (tel. 886 058), Montalvo and Olmedo, has an office devoted to divulging Napo-centric tourism information. Don't be scared off by the ominous looking building–the staff is very friendly. Open M-F 7:30am-12:30pm and 2-5pm.

Currency Exchange: Banco del Austro (tel. 886 446), 15 de Noviembre between the bridges. Exchanges cash and traveler's checks in the mornings. Also does Visa advances and has a 24hr. Visa/Plus **ATM** machine. Open M-F 8am-6pm, Sa 9am-1:30pm. **Delgado travel** (tel. 886 870), 15 de Noviembre and Tena, a block towards town from the bus station, offers the best rates but only exchanges cash. Open M-F 8:30am-5:30pm, Sa 9am-12:30pm.

Market: On Amazonas and Bolívar is the largest. Open daily 6am-5pm, busiest F and Sa.

Emergency: Tel. 101.

Police: (Tel. 886 425), on García Moreno and the Main Plaza.

Pharmacy: Farmacia Amazonas (tel. 886 495), Amazonas and Calderón, in the *centro.* Open daily 8am-10pm.

Hospital: The private **Clínica Amazonas** (tel. 886 515) is at Tena and Vasco. Walk towards the bus station on 15 de Noviembre and turn left at Banco del Pichincha. Dr. Llamuca has a solid reputation. Open 24hr.

Post Office: Correos (tel. 886 418), Olmedo and Amazonas. Open M-F 8am-6pm, Sa 8am-noon.

Telephones: EMETEL (tel. 886 105), Olmedo and Montalvo. Open daily 8am-9:45pm. Charges s/1,000 per min. to use AT&T or MCI.

TELEPHONE CODE 06

ACCOMMODATIONS

In Tena, and in most of the Oriente, your room will be musty. This is not a sign of poor upkeep—if you hung around this damp place long enough, you'd be covered in mildew, too. Otherwise, though, there's no lack of clean, comfortable, reasonably priced lodgings.

Hostal Traveler's Lodging, 15 de Noviembre 438 (tel. 886 372), next to the footbridge landing. Welcome to gringo central. Attached to a restaurant and tour agency, this reputable complex has private baths, electric hot water, hurricane-force fans, and back-friendly beds in all rooms. *El dueño,* Don Mario, and his friendly staff provide tourist info with a heavy bias towards their own **Amarongachi Tours**–a reliable company but not the only option. Rooms s/50-70,000 per person.

Hotel Amazonas (tel. 886 439), Mera and Montalvo, just off the main plaza. Clean and comfortable quarters with common cold-water crappers. Surely a safe selection when short on *sucres.* Rooms s/25,000 per person.

Hostal Indiyana (tel. 886 334), Bolívar and Amazonas, across the street from CETUR. All the comforts of Traveler's Lodging, but without the gringos and at a lower price. This brand new hostel offers private hot-water baths, cable TV, and fans in the high-ceilinged rooms. Rooms s/35,000 per person.

Hostal Turismo Amazónico (tel. 886 487), Amazonas and Calderón. Refrigerators and closets in the bedrooms, and medicine chests in the private baths make this a good choice. Tepid water only. Singles s/45,000; matrimonial s/80,000.

Residencial Alemana (tel. 886 409), Díaz de Pineda and 15 de Noviembre, next to the vehicle bridge. A sanctuary with lots of plants, Alemana is friendly. Options include hot or cold water in the private baths, and private cabins or apartment-style rooms. Rooms around s/50,000 per person, depending on room size and number of people.

FOOD

Vegetable stands and *panaderías* line 15 de Noviembre between the *terminal terrestre* and the footbridge. There are few surprises among the restaurants. Most are *típicos*, or *típicos* in disguise.

La Massilia Pizzeria, Moreno and Olmedo, next to the post office. Another *cabaña*-style joint tactfully tossing Tena's tastiest tomato-topped Italian *tortillas* (a.k.a. Sicilian-style pizzas). Whatever you choose to call them, they're scrumdidilyumptious (s/22,000 and up). If there's still room in the tummy, throw down a slice of fruity dessert pie (s/4,000). Open daily 11:30am-2pm and 4-10pm.

Kamikaze (tel. 887 616), 15 de Noviembre, just past the *terminal terrestre,* opposite the Coke distributor. Instead of suicide bombers, you'll find an open-air, *cabaña*-style eatery with funky furniture and a seafood specialty. Try the breakfast of fruit, juice, *café,* and jungle-sized pancakes (s/20,000). For lunch and dinner they offer fresh seafood (*camarones a la plancha* s/25,000). Open daily M-Sa 7am-8pm, Su 7am-2pm.

Restaurant Cositas Ricas (tel. 886 372), 15 de Noviembre, next to the footbridge. The culinary sequel to Hostal Traveler's Lodging, this open-aired hangout often crowds to capacity with tourists. Lots of American-sounding dishes (and prices) that all seem to come out a lot like *platos típicos,* but hey, it still tastes good. Veggie spaghetti (s/24,000), vegetarian *tortilla* (Spanish style omelette s/24,000). Open daily 7am-10pm.

Chuquitos (tel. 887 630), Moreno and the Parque Central, next to the police station. Enjoy hearty portions of Ecuadorian food in a tranquil setting between the Parque and the river. Don't worry; those vultures over the river aren't eyeing your *churrasco* (s/19,000). Open M-Sa 7am-9pm.

La Estancia (tel. 886 354), 15 de Noviembre, 2 blocks towards town from the *terminal.* The building is a jungle-style *cabaña,* but where's the yucca? Meat and fish dishes are a firm reminder of civilization (*lomo a la Milanesa* s/25,000, *Tilapia al jugo* s/30,000). Open daily 7am-9:30pm.

SIGHTS AND ACTIVITIES

Tena is the jungle gym of the Ecuadorian playground. Visitors swing from adventure to adventure, reveling in the rainforest. While some of Tena's attractions may exist Oriente-wide, others can be found nowhere else. Most outdoor activities require a guide of some sort, but there are hikes you can do on your own. Before setting out though, discuss the route with someone knowledgeable and leave a route plan with somebody in town. Orientation is difficult with no visual landmarks, and getting lost in the jungle can be serious business. Some report success finding a local youth near the trailhead to guide you on the trail. Agree on a price beforehand, and don't pay in full until you're safely back on the road.

PARQUE AMAZÓNICO LA ISLA. A logistical no-brainer because of its central location, this park is impressive nonetheless. An island occupying 2,200 hectares (5,440 acres) between Río Tena and Río Pano, it connects to Tena via a bamboo bridge 50m upriver from the main footbridge behind Hostal Traveler's Lodging. Monkeys and birds live freely in the park's sprawling forest, which merges with the greater jungle in the distance. Closed-in pools and cages house animals recuperating from injuries, including alligators, capybaras, tortoises, and boas. Various swimming areas dot the bordering rivers, and a lookout tower provides a panoramic of Tena. *(Open daily 9am-6pm. Admission s/13,000.)*

CUEVAS DE JUMANDI. For another challenge-free experience, visit these huge caves which lie between Archidona and Cotundo, north of Tena. The area is quite built-up (the waterslide out of the mouth of the cave is lots of fun). A resort has recently been established here and makes a convenient base for daytripping tourists who wish to explore the caves. *(Take a bus to Archidona from Amazonas and Olmedo (20min., every 15min. 6am-7pm, s/2,000) and then catch the bus from Archidona to Cotundo and ask to be let off at "las cuevas." Open daily 9am-4:30pm. Admission US$5.)*

FEATHERED SERPENT PETROGLYPH. A petroglyph of a *serpiente emplumado* is just one of dozens of rock carvings in the area northwest of Tena (CETUR has an exhaustive list). Most are on private property, and the owner will charge a nominal fee to show you around. Nobody knows much about who made these carvings or why—they're waiting for some astute visitor to unlock their secret. *(On the same road as Cuevas de Jumandi between Archidona and Cotundo. Admission s/5,000.)*

LA CASCADA DEL GRAN CANYON. Past Cotundo, a trail on the right leads up to La Cascada del Gran Canyon. This challenging three-hour hike (each way) is best done with someone who knows the trail, though the falls at the end of the trail are reported to be worth the effort. *(Buses headed north to Quito or Coca from Tena pass the trailhead: 50min., s/10,000.)*

ENTERTAINMENT

On the weekend Tena goes disco. Travelers who haven't had all their energy sucked out by the myriad jungle activities are welcome to take part. The most popular spot to boogie is **Discoteca Canambo** on Rocafuerte and the river. For other options, cruise the **Malecón Iluminado,** the area bordering both sides of the river between the two bridges, and hone in on whichever beat best suits your mood. Several dance clubs and watering holes line 15 de Noviembre towards the *terminal.* Of these, **Boli Bar,** just before the terminal, with its open-air *cabaña* feel, is most likely to bring out the jungle creature in you.

INTO THE JUNGLE FROM TENA

RAFTING. Probably the biggest adrenaline rush in Tena—and maybe all of Ecuador—comes from its killer whitewater rafting. Barely discovered by the world's whitewater enthusiasts, the river-filled region around Tena in the western Oriente is a truly amazing find. These rivers, the headwaters of the Amazon, rush through canyons, over waterfalls, and past rocky banks. While downstream, piranha-filled currents run muddy and slow, the water flows fast near Tena, fresh from the Andes' heights. Because of the unique topography and sheer volume of water, the density of whitewater rapids is higher here than almost anywhere else in the world. Even better— it's always high season; the rapids churn year-round.

Ríos Ecuador (tel. 887 438; email info@riosecuador.com) in Tena, is on Av. del Chosen, near the *terminal*, with a new office across from Cositas Ricas. The Quito office (tel./fax (02) 552 864) is at Guipuzcoa 210 and Cádiz, La Floresta. Ríos Ecuador runs trips out of Tena under the watchful eye of its owner, Gynner, a 28-year old kayaking and rafting pro with nine years of guiding experience on rivers around the world. The congenial entrepreneur is a native Ecuadorian, but he speaks better English than most Americans. Using multilingual, professional guides and modern equipment from the US, the company leads exhilarating, energetic, and safety-conscious trips for thrill seekers of all temperaments. A one-day rafting trip is US$50 per person for Class II and III rivers (novice/moderate), US$65 for Class IV and IV+ trips (advanced/expert). One-day kayaking trips are also available (US$60 per person). These prices include transportation from Tena, the guide's services, a tasty beachfront lunch, and maybe even a side trip to the enchanted **bat cave.** Ríos Ecuador also periodically offers a four-day kayaking course, including all the funky maneuvers, for US$250. Make reservations through the Quito office. Well-qualified and experienced individuals may rent their own kayaks with all the equipment and without a guide (US$30 per day).

JUNGLE LODGES. For a more tranquil wilderness experience, spend some time at one of the many *cabaña* complexes scattered along the rivers. A first-rate jungle lodge is run by the Mamallacta family through their **Fundación Izu Mangallpa Urcu** (tel. 887 487). The goals of the foundation are to preserve Quichua traditions and to protect and document the biodiversity of the area. They've also constructed a few *cabañas* to house tourists. In addition to the usual jungle walks, sons Elias and Benjamin Mamallacta lead tours through the **lava chutes** that criss-cross the family's properties. These caves, extending for many kilometers underground, contain a few fast-running underground rivers and some spectacular limestone formations. Visitors can also learn all forms of **artesanía** from the old and wise Mama Mamallacta. A vacation in paradise doesn't come cheap. Rooms run US$35 per person per day, including all tours and three glorious meals per day (made with ingredients from the family's farm). A similar experience, **Cabañas Samana Huasi** (tel. 887 424) offers excursions of three to six days to the indigenous **Pano** community, upriver from Tena on the Jatún-Yacu. The tours can be customized and include jungle hikes, traditional food, and interaction with the village. The rooms (US$40 per person per day) are a bit steep, but discounts may be available for groups of six or more. CETUR can provides a list of other tranquil cabañas hidden away along the area's waterways.

JUNGLE TOURS. There are exactly six licensed tour operators in Tena. Tours typically go by boat or car to a lodge which serves as a base for daytrips into the surrounding jungle. If yucca three meals a day doesn't appeal to you, ask to see a food list before signing up. The best known tour company, **Amarongachi Tours,** operates out of the Hostal Traveler's Lodging (see **Accommodations,** p. 370). Other reliable agencies are **Expediciones Jarrín** (tel. 887 142), though their trips all leave from Coca (see p. 376); **Limoncocha Tours** (tel. 887 583), and **Voyage Fantastic** (tel. 886 490). For information on indigenous guides, go to their headquarters at **Recancie** (tel. 887 072), 15 de Noviembre and Serafin Gutierrez, right where Av. Pano and Av. 15 de Noviembre merge. Other lesser-known tour companies are often just as knowledgeable. For more information, contact Gynner at Ríos Ecuador or ask at Safari Tours in Quito.

MISAHUALLÍ

The monkeys loitering in Misahuallí's town plaza should dispel any lingering doubts that this is *real* jungle—if the charitably-termed "road" into town hasn't done that already. A solid wall of trees lines the far bank of the muddy Río Napo, which fades into a swirling mist in the distance. Emerald parakeets and iridescent butterflies flutter among the orchids just outside of town. Except for the occasional intrusion of an outboard motor propelling camera-toting tourists to jungle lodges, the only sound to be heard in Misahuallí is the squawking of wild parrots.

No road continues downstream on the north bank of the Río Napo, and this makes Misahuallí the primary point of departure for many jungle tours. In the face of increasing tourism, the Huaorani, who used to inhabit the wilderness near town, have headed deeper into the jungle. Visitors taking excursions from Misahuallí are usually looking just to explore pristine tropical rainforest and not to encounter indigenous peoples.

The road heads into town from the west. Some hotels, restaurants, and shops congregate around the plaza. **Buses** leave the central plaza for **Tena** (1hr., every hr. 5am-6pm, s/6,000). Though Ahuano is only 15km downstream, no direct road connects Misahuallí and Ahuano. The cheapest way to **Ahuano** from Misahuallí is to cross the river in a **motorized canoe** (s/3,000), walk 30 minutes away from the river (along a dirt track) to the Tena-Ahuano road, and flag down a bus headed for **La Punta** (s/5,000). At La Punta, re-cross the river (in canoe s/2,000) and walk for 20 minutes along the road from the canoe station to Ahuano. (Who said getting places in the jungle was easy?) Alternatively, motorized canoes travel directly from Misahuallí to **Ahuano** (40min., s/350,000 split among max. 12 passengers) or **Coca** (7hr., s/2,100,000 split among max. 12 passengers). The best advice for **changing money** in Misahuallí: do it somewhere else. If in need, the Albergue Español changes cash and traveler's checks. The **maritime police** near the beach have current lists of prices. The blue-and-white Registro Curl office houses vestiges of a **police** force. Around the corner in the same building, the **Centro de Salud** functions somewhat erratically. **Doctora Mercedes Alcivar,** at the dead-end of the Tena road, has permanent hours and runs **Farmacia Misahuallí,** at the plaza (open daily 7:30am-8pm). The only phones in town are at **ANDINATEL** (tel. 584 965), by the river between Hotel Marena and the Albergue Español (open daily 8am-9:30pm).

The prices of the reasonably comfortable lodgings tend to be slightly inflated, reflecting the foreign clientele. The **Hotel Albergue Español** is on the right just before you enter town (tel. (02) 221 626). This "jungle lodge" has spacious, spotless rooms that include private bath with that elusive jungle species, *Agua caliente*. Lobby decor includes two huge, black great danes that look like Marmaduke. (Rooms US$6 per person.) The **restaurant** here specializes in high-class vegetarian dining (spanish omelette s/24,000). A sign assures that all water is boiled before use. The owners also recently acquired and renovated **Jaguar Lodge,** two hours downstream on 1,000 hectares of primary rainforest (US$30-35 per person per night). **Hotel Marena** (tel. (06) 887 584), is between the Albergue Español and the main plaza. Immaculate rooms have stained-wood furniture, hurricane-powered fans, mini-bar fridges, and kick-ass comforters. Some have hot water. (Rooms US$6 per person, students US$4.50.) Down by the plaza, **Hotel Posada** (tel. 887 444 in Tena) offers bright rooms with private hot-water baths and fans. Surprise—they also arrange jungle tours. (Rooms US$5 per person.) **Hostal Sacha** (tel. (02) 282 859), near the boat landing, has suites to suit *sucre*-savers. Shared cold-water baths are a short walk from the spare, clapboard rooms. The owner swears that it's his private swimming pool out back, though doubters might call it the Río Napo. (Rooms s/20,000 per person.) The **Posada Restaurant** downstairs, a gringo congregating spot, serves big portions of *platos típicos* (fried *tilapia* s/30,000, vegetarian plate s/30,000). The **Restaurant El Paisano,** a block down the road from the plaza to Panuno, on the left, cooks gargantuan Ecuadorian *platos* (US$3).

NEAR MISAHUALLÍ: JATÚN SACHA

Big forest. That's the Quichua meaning of the name and that's what you'll find at the Jatún Sacha Biological Station. Located 8km east of Misahuallí, right off the south bank road of the Napo River, this 2,000-hectare tropical rain forest reserve is still 80% primary growth. Refreshingly enough, Jatún Sacha is completely Ecuadorian-owned and run and was named the world's second International Children's Rainforest in 1993. It also has numerous medicinal plants, a canopy of hillside trees, plenty of reptiles, and seemingly innumerable species of insects. Founded in 1986, Jatún Sacha aims both to conserve the incredible biodiversity of the land and to provide a window into it for researchers, especially Ecuadorian ones. Thus, as **Alejandro Suárez,** the long-haired, English-speaking administrator and co-founder will readily tell you, tourists are not invited to spend the night, or even the day if they arrive in large herds. The forest is first and foremost for scientific study. Casual visitors can, however, benefit from the facilities—well-marked paths meander through the forest past an incredible variety of carefully documented flora. Maps are available from the main office, but it's a good idea to let someone there know where you plan to hike. The birds seem to love this peaceful place as well—to get a better view of Jatún Sacha's winged visitors, ask to be allowed up the station's 100-foot-high bird observation tower, or pay a visit to their canopy bridge woven (with no use of metal parts) from vines. (Admission US$6.)

LOGISTICS. The facilities can accommodate 35 visitors and 13 long-term residents at once. Bunk beds in screened **cabañas** with nearby latrines, showers, and a supply of rainwater for hand-washing make life on the reserve reasonably comfortable (rooms US$30 per person; includes admission fee and 3 meals). A new part of the complex, the **dining hall,** offers three relatively safe *and* tasty communal meals each day (s/10,000, with a vegetarian option). Those looking for an unconventional Ecuadorian experience can volunteer at the reserve for a few weeks to a few months. Volunteers work with the local Quichua community on sustainable development projects, or they help maintain the reserve, though they rarely get involved in primary scientific research unless they have a specific project in mind. (Volunteers pay US$75 per week or US$300 per month for food and lodging.) Rejected non-scientists and travelers seeking more comfortable accommodations can head to the downright luxurious **Cabañas Alinañui,** 3km down the road to the east of Jatún Sacha (follow the signs; 1hr. walk). With an office in Quito at Río Coca 1734 and Isla Fernandina (tel. 253 267; fax 253 266), the *cabañas* help fund the reserve. The eight spacious cabins, raised on stilts above a hammock-blessed patio, each have two rooms that share a hot-water bath. Conference room, bar, and library are all in the package, but the price stretches the budget boundary. (US$45 per person, plus 20% in taxes; includes 3 meals per day.) To contact the reserve, find out about the volunteer program, or make research reservations, the Quito address is: **Fundación Jatún Sacha,** Casilla 17-12-867 (tel./fax 441 592; email jatsacha@jsacha.ecuanex.net.ec; www.jatunsacha.org). The Tena address is: Casilla 15-01-218. Crafts and t-shirts sold on-site support the reserve.

TRANSPORTATION. Buses running between Tena and Ahuano can drop visitors off right in front of Jatún Sacha (1¼hr. from Tena, s/8,000).

NEAR MISAHUALLÍ: LA PUNTA AND AHUANO

With neither road access nor tourist attractions, there is actually little reason to visit Ahuano itself—it's the nearby resorts that really attract visitors. **Hotel Anaconda** and **Hotel Jaguar,** two moderate options downstream, feed on the reputations of the most exotic (but most seldom seen) animals of the Oriente. But Ahuano's most conspicuous specimen is **Hostería La Casa del Suizo.** On a bluff overlooking the Amazon rests this decadent splendor of the wealthy traveler's paradise. Use of the topaz-blue pool, polished bamboo doors, and winding wooden staircases is, as you would expect, very costly. (Over US$70 per night; includes a guided daytrip.) The well-moneyed can make reservations in Quito, at Julio Zaldumbide 375 and Toledo, P.O. Box 17-21-1608 (tel. (02) 566 090; fax (02) 236 521; email sachalod@pi.pro.ec; www.sachalodge.com). Visitors rarely stay in Ahuano, but accommodations are there for the taking. **La Posada de Mama Aida** is on the riverfront downstream of La Casa del Suizo. The namesake is an endearingly protective old woman who has four immaculate beds upstairs, above the family's *comedor*. (Rooms/ s25,000 per person.) **Hostal Samanta,** a little further downstream, is run by one of Mama Aida's nephews. It offers similar accommodations but has 12 beds. (Rooms s/30,000 per person.) The owner, Rafael García, works as a guide for La Casa del Suizo but will also take private groups into the jungle (s/350,000 per day). He can be contacted in Quito (tel. (02) 621 005).

Transportation: From the town of **La Punta,** on the southern bank of the Río Napo 10km east of Jatún Sacha, along the same dirt road, take a motorized canoe across the river (s/2,000). To avoid getting overcharged, check the price of the canoe trip with someone other than the driver. From the northern shore it's a 20-minute walk (or s/2,000 *camioneta* ride) to Ahuano.

INTO THE JUNGLE FROM MISAHUALLÍ

There's really only one reason to go to Misahuallí: the jungle tours. Trips down the river can last from a day to a fortnight and include two people or twenty. Packages are flexible, but the important part is getting a satisfactory guide. Key guide qualities include English-speaking ability, wilderness experience, familiarity with the area, and a CETUR license. Most of the guides in Misahuallí are weak on the English. Once this setback is accepted, there are a few reliable agencies to pick through. **Ecoselva,** on the plaza (with a life-size poster of a Huaorani man out front), takes the eco part of its trips seriously. Pepe Tapia González, who runs the place, speaks English. Tours visit cascades, lagoons—where you may see some alligators and piranha—and other assorted jungle stuff. In the evenings Pepe offers *charlas* (informational chats) about the local indigenous groups and jungle fauna. Itineraries can be tailored to fit a group's size and interests. Other guides, including several brothers, work for him, but if possible, try to snag the man himself. (US$20 per person per day for 1-7 days with 5-15 people.) **Clarke's Tours** (tel. (06) 887 584) out of the Marena Hotel, has 70 hectares of private rainforest downriver, including a fenced-in seven hectare **Muestrario,** where jungle animals roam in higher concentrations than they would in the wild. Some guides speak some English. Clarke's has customized three- to six-day expedition packages to their land. The trips zoom downriver in motorized canoes to thatch-roofed jungle *cabañas*. Meals are cooked using *yuca* and other native foods. Exploratory hikes pass oodles of waterfalls, squadrons of birds, and perhaps a few indigenous jungle-dwellers. Hopefully, they'll be glad to see you. (US$30-35 per day; special 4-day tour US$76.) **Fluvial River,** very visible next to the beach, is owned by Hector Fiallos. Hector has been around awhile and claims an expertise in birds. Again, try to get the man himself. (US$25-30 per person per day, for groups as small as 2.)

COCA

The easternmost urban outpost of the Orellana province, Coca (also known as Puerto Francisco de Orellana) has two histories which add up to one identity crisis. The first settlement was a tranquil jungle town seated 260m above sea level, where the Ríos Napo, Payamino, and Coca come together. This original Coca developed in the early 20th century, when its pioneer residents built a hospital, schools, and churches, and grew to a whopping population of 300. Everything changed in the pivotal year of 1969 when foreigners from the north discovered a wealth of "black gold" bubbling underground. Within a few years, Coca's population exploded and its landscape changed forever. Roads tore into the jungle and newly-erected pumps drained the land, filling the pockets of oil entrepreneurs. Whether you call them exploiters or sound economists, outsiders have transformed Coca into a gritty, dirty, riverside pit, not unlike an overgrown gas station. Recently, the unmarked streets have become muddy disasters—the soggy, sticky result of an over-ambitious water-purification project. Regardless of the city's sorry aesthetics, Coca is significant for travelers because many deep jungle tours often begin and end at this Oriente outpost.

ORIENTATION

The roughly gridded city has no street names or helpful vantage points, so orientation is a challenge. From the **terminal terrestre** in the north, **Calle Napo,** the principal mud-laden tourist drag, extends eight blocks to the **Río Napo,** the town's southern boundary. Another important north-south road is **Amazonas,** which dead-ends at the dock a block east of Napo. The parallel **Tena-Lago Agrio Road** enters the town from the north, curves around, and eventually straightens out one block east of Amazonas. It then crosses the river to the **military camp.**

PRACTICAL INFORMATION

Airplanes: The **airport** (tel. 880 046) has one runway that goes almost into downtown. To get to the terminal, follow Av. Labak for 1km as it winds out of town towards Lago Agrio. Take a taxis from the center (s/10,000), or catch the *bus urbano* which runs from downtown to the terminal (s/1,500). **Aerogal** (tel. 881 450) offers flights to **Quito** (30min.; M-W and F 10am, Th 12:45pm, Sa 11am; US$53). Tickets can be purchased at the terminal before departure. Don't be fooled by the conspicuous TAME office downtown; they don't offer flights from Coca.

Buses: The **terminal terrestre** is on Napo, 8 blocks north of the river, but night buses go to and from Napo and Bolívar, just north of the *centro*. **Trans Esmeraldas** goes to **Lago Agrio** (2hr., 8:30pm, s/20,000) and **Quito** (8:30pm, s/90,000). **Baños** goes to **Ambato** (10hr., 6:30 and 8:15pm, s/80,000) via **Baños** (8hr., s/70,000) and **Puyo** (7hr.; 12:45, 4am, 6:30pm; s/60,000).

Boats: Also known as Puerto Francisco de Orellana, the marina of Coca sees its share of boat traffic. Most tourist traffic on the river comes from organized tours, so travelers don't generally have to worry about prices or times. All boats on the river, whether coming or going, must record the names and passport numbers of all foreign passengers at the **Capitañia,** a government office right on the water at the end of Amazonas. Destinations are **Hacienda Primavera** (s/30,500); **Pompeya** and **Limoncocha** (s/43,000); **Panacocha** (s/115,000); **Tiputini** (s/156,000); and **Nueva Rocafuerte** (s/186,000). Schedules change due to variation in demand and water conditions. Hiring a boat is possible but not economical unless you're with a group.

Taxis: Some congregate outside the market 7 blocks north of the *centro* (s/10,000 for a trip in the *centro*).

Tourist Office: For the most reliable information on wilderness areas and the agencies that tour them, head to **INEFAN** (tel. 880 171), by the airfield on Amazonas and Bolívar. Open M-F 7:30am-12:30pm and 1:30-5pm. Coca's **Camara de Turismo** (tel. 880 842), Labaka and Cabrera, next to the Jefatura de Policía, is affiliated with **Expediciones Jarría** and might not be completely impartial in its information.

Currency Exchange: Hotel El Auca exchanges cash and might change traveler's checks.

Market: Fruits and veggies galore meet their fate across Napo from the *municipio,* 500m north of downtown. Open daily 6am-5pm.

Emergency: Tel. 880 101.

Police: Policía Nacional (tel. 880 525 or 880 101) is at Napo and Rocafuerte.

Pharmacies: Farmacia Oriental, on Espejo between Amazonas and Napo, is a block from the waterfront. Open daily 7am-8pm. **Farmacia Clínica Sinai** (tel. 880 362) is across the street from Hotel El Auca on Napo. Open daily 8am-10pm.

Medical Assistance: Clínica Sinai (tel. 880 362), Napo and Moreno, is costly but provides Coca's only reliable health care. 24hr. emergency care. Lab open daily 8am-5pm.

Post Office: At the southern end of 9 de Octubre, by the river, 3 blocks west of Napo. Open sporadically M-F 8am-4:30pm.

Internet Access: Available at Hotel El Auca (US$0.20 per min., 5-minute minimum).

Telephones: EMETEL (tel. 880 104), Eloy Alfaro and 16 de Diciembre, under the big tower. AT&T and MCI calls cost the same as a call to Quito (s/500 per min.). Open M-F 8am-4pm and 5-9pm, Sa-Su 8-11am and 5-8pm.

TELEPHONE CODE: 06

ACCOMMODATIONS

A few respectable hotels cluster on Napo around the Hotel El Auca. Dank, simple cheapies hover close to the waterfront. The only other frequently touristed area of the city is just down Malecón, the street that veers off to the left before the bridge, where the **Hotel Oasis** and the luxurious **Hostería La Misión** set up their quarters.

Hotel El Auca (tel. 880 127 fax 880 600), Napo and García Moreno, 6 blocks south of the *terminal terrestre.* A married couple runs this commune of red-roofed bungalows. Spider monkeys and parrots with excellent Spanish accents inhabit the garden courtyard. While it's *the* place for backpacking budget travelers to gather in the morning to form tour groups, El Auca refreshingly does not run its own tour operation. An unfortunate consequence of its mainstream status: service at the reception tends to be lackluster. *Cabañas* vary in size; all have private baths with electric hot-water showers. Rooms s/40-45,000 per person.

Hostal Oasis (tel. 880 164; fax 880 206), on Malecón on the river, 50m down the narrow left branch before the bridge. Climb up to the 2nd story of this getaway to escape the muddy quicksand of the rest of the city. Beds are fluffed, floors swept spotless, and private cold-water baths (in all rooms) well-scrubbed. Fans in all rooms. Often houses prepackaged tour groups from Quito and runs its own **Yuturi Tour** operation (See **Jungle Tours from Coca,** p. 379). Rooms are a bargain at s/25,000 per person.

FOOD

By any standard, Coca does not have a large restaurant district. Most eateries lie on **Napo** or off it on a street near the river.

Restaurant Dayuma (tel. 880 127), in Hotel El Auca, invites anyone to grab a sound portion of *comida típica.* Slightly inflated prices and quick service reflect its status as a gringo magnet. American breakfast s/11,000, *almuerzo* and *merienda* s/18,000 each. Open daily 6:30am-10pm.

Restaurant Medianoche (tel. 880 026), Napo and Rocafuerte, is open later than you would think. This immaculate and bright *comedor* is a favorite for take-out or a late-night meal. *Caldo de Gallina* s/12,000, fried chicken s/15,000. Open daily 6pm-2am.

Gran Chaparal, on Espejo, between Quito and 9 de Octubre. Full of foreigners but not tourists, this meat-and-rice joint is a favorite hang-out of imported oil workers. Large dish of meat, rice, beans, and cola only s/15,000. Open daily 3-11pm.

NEAR COCA: BOSQUE PROTECTOR PAÑACOCHA

"Cocha" is Quichua for lagoon, and *"paña"* means piranha; that should give an idea of what to expect. This sprawling 56,000-hectare swamp has enough plant and animal species to make any biologist's millennium. After motoring down the Río Napo for seven hours, visitors enter a jungle wonderland filled with giant trees and strange sounds. With a good guide, the sources of many of these sounds come into view. Commonly observed **animals** include monkeys, freshwater dolphins, crocodiles, and, with luck, a toucan or a sloth. To see the park's namesake, just toss a small piece of fish or meat into the river, and watch the water churn. Despite the abundance of piranhas, the guides swim fearlessly in the water, and often invite visitors to join them for a dip. Reportedly, the risk of getting bitten in the water is minimal, though the bacterial hazards are harder to assess. **Cabañas Pañacocha** offers housing for tours and has a high bird and wildlife observation tower. Visitors planning a tour should take into account that transportation to and from the reserve takes almost two full days. (Park admission US$20.)

NEAR COCA: PARQUE NACIONAL YASUNÍ

Coca is the push-off point to mainland Ecuador's largest national park, the 982,000-hectare Parque Nacional Yasuní. This is **Amazon Basin** country, with the Tiputini, Nashiño, Cononaco, Yasuní, and other tributaries coursing through the park's enormous expanse. Yasuní has three major habitats: dry land, sometimes-flooded land, and always-flooded land. While the rainforest is understandably wet year-round, the region's seasons still alternate between dry (Dec.-Mar.), rainy (Apr.-July), and unstable (Aug.-Nov.). Founded in 1979, Yasuní includes the greatest biodiversity in the country. The **Huaorani tribe,** first peacefully contacted in 1958, is as natural a part of the park as the wildlife. They share this land with boa constrictors, alligators, jaguars, eels, parrots, toucans, piranhas, capybaras, monkeys, sloths, and myriad other species. In spite of this precious biodiversity and the park's legally protected status, the government has chosen to ignore the recent proliferation of a newly introduced species, *Oilus maximus,* which flattens paths across pristine jungle before plunging its trunk-like mouth deep into the earth and sucking petroleum pools dry. Today, much of the park's once-pristine territory is criss-crossed by pipelines and roads for drilling. INEFAN has yet to organize a management system for the *parque;* it's simply too massive. A force of only 10 rangers controls activity within the sprawling park. To further complicate tourism, the only viable access point is at the town of **Nuevo Rocafuerte,** eight to 11 hours downriver from Coca. In order to penetrate beyond the heavily damaged northwestern section of the park, most tours last 10 days or more.

INTO THE JUNGLE FROM COCA

Coca's location, farther *al oriente* than Tena or Misahuallí, makes it an ideal base for trips to the more isolated parks, reserves, and deep-jungle communities of the indigenous **Huaorani.** The still-untamed region east of Coca is home to some of the most remote indigenous communities and densest biodiversity in the world. But as a mixed fortune, it is also home to Ecuador's most lucrative natural resource in the technological age—oil. Large petroleum companies are responsible for most of the road construction that opens the land up to further development, and, when driving through this region, the transition from jungle to iron-, rubber-, and petroleum-filled ex-jungle is painfully apparent.

Industry and nature have always been quarrelsome neighbors, and the tourist industry is no exception. Ecotourism is an important part of sustaining the jungle, as it allows the local populations to earn a living without destroying the forest. But despite universal claims of ecologically responsible tourism, the tours that stream into the jungle and down rivers and industry-made roads have negatively impacted the area (see **Ecotourism,** p. 55). On that note, if you plan to visit some of the local Huaorani villages, avoid disrupting the community by making sure your guide has received the tribe's permission to enter their land, and ask how the residents are compensated for permitting the visit.

NATURE RESERVES

In most of the reserves, unless you really know what you're doing (e.g. you're a professional ethnobotanist) INEFAN requires that you go in with a guide. A handful of villages and natural areas down the Río Napo are favorite tour destinations from Coca. A relatively short distance downstream, the **Reserva Biológica Limoncocha** and the mission towns of **Pompeya** and **Limoncocha** often make their way onto tour groups' itineraries. These days you don't even have to float to get there, courtesy of the road that the oil industry has cut past Limoncocha into "pristine oil country." *Petrolero*-inflicted damage is reported to be quite severe in this area. **Pañacocha,** another nature reserve on the Río Napo, about halfway between Coca and Nuevo Rocafuerte, is less well-known than its larger cousin to the east, **Yasuni National Park,** but has thus far avoided the heavy hand of the *petrolero.*To the west, **Parque Nacional Sumaco-Galeras** is virtually unexplored and untouched. The incongruous Volcán Sumaco soars to over 3500m in the middle of 209,000 hectares of dense vegetation and swamps where, rumor has it, man-eating anacondas lurk in the shadows. To attempt the four- to six-day summit climb, go to the village of **Huamaní** and ask for Don Chimbo. Bring enough food and gear for two guides. To the south of Coca is the village of **Tiputini,** one of the closest Huaorani communities and one of the most touristed. (Admission to protected nature reserves US$10.)

TOUR LOGISTICS

Tours offered from Coca vary greatly in price and quality. Part of the expense is the **entrance fee** (usually US$10) for each protected nature reserve on the tour. Some guides calculate their prices with this amount included, while others clearly state that it is additional. Either way, the INEFAN office in Coca (see **Practical Information,** p. 367) strongly suggests that at least one person from your group accompany the guide to INEFAN to pay the required amount. It's a jungle out there, and some guides have reportedly pocketed the park fee. Check out a number of tour companies to find one that seems reputable. Ideally, a tour should have two guides: one English-speaking naturalist and one native guide.

Several Coca-based companies offer multi-day jungle packages, most including transportation, food, lodging, jungle excursions, and maybe even piranha fishing or crocodile watching. An important factor to consider is the region. Ask to see a map, preferably one with oil pipelines, to ascertain whether you're heading to primary rainforest or oil country. The Pañacocha and Sumaco region are nearly the only virgin areas left. Most tours leave between Friday and Monday; the weekend is the best time to hook up with a group. INEFAN-recommended guides include: **Luís García,** who works out of Coca but may be contacted through **Emerald Forest Expeditions** (see below) and **Juan Medina,** who may be contacted through Baños's **Vasca Tour Travel Agency** (tel. (03) 740 147). Indigenous guide **Ernesto Juanka** and his son **Patricio** are also very good; they may be found through Hotel Auca.

Emerald Forest Expeditions (tel. 881 155; email emerald@ecuanex.net.ec; www.ecuadorexplorer.com/emerald) on Napo near the river. Most tours are organized through the Quito office, Amazonas N24-29 and Pinto (tel. (02) 541 543), but travelers may easily hop on a tour in Coca. *El jefe,* Luís García, runs all-inclusive trips to most wilderness areas, including the hard-to-reach Yasuní National Park. He speaks English well and has years of experience. The trips emphasize a responsible attitude toward the local indigenous communities and the environment. Trips run US$30-40 per person per day.

Ejarsytur (tel. 880 251), across from the Hotel Oasis, near the bridge. In Quito, at Fosch 4E 181 and Amazonas (tel. (02) 236 535). Julio Jarrín and his team of guides bring groups to his jungle lodge on the edge of Pañacocha, 7hr. downriver by motorized canoe. Great food and oodles of wildlife are a given; knowledgeable, English-speaking guides and contact with an indigenous community are not. Ask to speak with your guide before signing up. A new set of cabins on an island closer to Coca are in the works. The Pañacocha package includes boat transport, cabins, food (vegetarian options available), and hikes (US$120 per person for 4 days).

Yuturi Jungle Adventure (tel. 880 164), run out of the Hotel Oasis (see **p. 378**) but with an office in Quito, on Amazonas 13-24 and Colón (tel. (02) 504 037). Runs tours to 2 sets of *cabañas* downriver. Yarina Lodge is closer and suitable for tours of up to 3 days, while Cabañas Yuturi requires a 5-6hr. canoe ride and is best left for longer trips. Yuturi boasts a bird-watching tower, private baths, experienced guides, and good food. Five-day tours costs US$200 at Yarina lodge and US$300 at Yuturi Lodge.

Paushi Tours (tel. 880 219), best contacted through Hotel El Auca. Darwin García and his brother Edwin lead the only tours into the Sumaco region. Though the company is new, the family has been living in Sumaco forever. Spanish-only tours promise very rugged terrain, panning for gold, and stone petroglyphs, as well as standard-issue jungle wildlife. Tours for people min. are US$200 per person for 4 days, US$300 per person for 8 days.

LAGO AGRIO

A young city with a story, Lago Agrio is testament to exactly what's in a name. As late as the 1940s and 1950s this was the heartland of the Cofán, a people almost completely isolated from contact with other indigenous groups, let alone Europeans. Revered by surrounding tribes for their sophistication with medicinal and hallucinogenic plants, the Cofán spoke a language unrelated to any other. This all changed in the 1960s when Texaco hit the oil jackpot here. As bulldozers cleared the land of trees (and consequently of the Cofán), Texaco executives decided to name the new city after their first big success in Texas: Sour Lake. The Spanish equivalent, "Lago Agrio," stuck.

Though some residents lived through it, this history is almost invisible from the city today. Once numbering more than 20,000, the Cofán, their language, and their knowledge of the forest are almost gone. The few hundred remaining have moved further east, where some forest remains. Today the city consists of strips of three-story banks, hotels, restaurants, and grocery stores. Many tourists come through town on their way to the Reserva Faunistica Cuyabeno, though by far the strongest contingent of foreigners is constituted by Colombians taking advantage of the nearby border crossing to buy cheap furniture, appliances, and jaguar skins.

ORIENTATION

Lago Agrio's main road is the east-west **Av. Quito,** which runs 5km east from the **airstrip** and forks at the market, forming the northern branch of **Av. Río Amazonas.** The **market** is a triangular area formed by the fork of Quito and Amazonas, and the north-south **Av. 12 de Febrero,** one block to the west. **Francisco de Orellana** is parallel to, and one block west of, 12 de Febrero. The **terminal terrestre** is about 2km northwest of town, though many buses pick up and drop off passengers on Quito, east of the market. This is the most bustling area in town and encompasses all one needs for a (hopefully) short stay. As a border and oil town, Lago Agrio is full of young, male oil workers and displaced Colombians, which can be a dangerous combination. The downtown area is generally safe when there are people in the streets, but it's probably not wise (especially for women) to explore any secluded areas alone or at night.

PRACTICAL INFORMATION

Airplanes: The **airport** is located 5km east of the city center (s/10,000 taxi ride). **TAME** (tel. 830 113), Orellana and 9 de Octubre, has flights to **Quito** (30min., M-Sa 12:30pm, US$53). Book ahead, especially for M flights, which are often filled with package-tour groups. Open M-F 8-11am and 2:30-5pm.

Buses: The *terminal terrestre* is a short taxi ride (s/10,000) northeast of the *centro.* Daytime buses often go through downtown on their way to or from the *terminal.* Between 11pm and 6am buses only stop at their offices, all within a block of Hotel D'Mario. Buses go to: **Quito** (8hr., every hr., s/80,000) via **Baeza** (6hr., s/50,000); **Coca** (3hr., every 20min., s/20,000); and **Loja** (24hr., 1pm, s/170,000).

Taxis: Charge s/10,000 for trips within town.

Tourist Information: INEFAN (tel. 830 139), 10 de Agosto and Manabí, 6 blocks north of Quito. Open M-F 8am-noon and 1-5pm. The **Casa de Cultura** (tel. 830 264), 18 de Noviembre and Colombia, also has some tourist information and a small library. Open M-F 8am-noon and 1-5pm.

Immigration Office: Quito and Manabí, in the police station across from the market.

Colombian Consulate: Quito 441 (tel. 830 084), above Banco de Préstamos, across from Hotel D'mario. Along with the immigration office, the consulate has info concerning the dangerous Colombian border crossing 20km north of Lago Agrio at Punto Colón. Most Ecuadorians warn against crossing the border there, communicating the danger with a hand gesture across the throat.

Currency Exchange: Banco de Préstamos (tel. 830 582), Quito, 100m east of the fork, changes cash and traveler's checks. Open M-F 9:30am-3pm.

Police: (Tel. 830 101), Quito and Manabí across from the market. Considered to be more competent (read: heavily-armed) than many of their counterparts elsewhere in Ecuador because of the high, serious crime rate they are forced to deal with.

Pharmacy: Farmacia International (tel. 830 133), Quito, near 12 de Febrero, attached to Clínica Gonzáles. Open daily 8am-10:30pm.

Hospital: Hospital Lago Agrio (tel. 830 198; ambulance tel. 830 250), Quito, 500m west of the market. Local residents don't trust the local hospital; those with enough cash and concern for their own well-being should try the **Clínica Gonzáles** (tel. 830 133), Quito, near 12 de Febrero. Open 24hr.

Post Office: (Tel. 830 115), Rocafuerte, just off 12 de Febrero. Open M-F 8am-noon and 1-5pm. Some travelers have reported mail from Quito taking several weeks to arrive.

Telephones: EMETEL (tel. 830 104), Orellana and 18 de Noviembre. Calling card calls s/ 500 per min. Open M-Sa 8am-10pm, Su 8am-noon and 8-10pm.

TELEPHONE CODE: 06

ACCOMMODATIONS

Hotel D'Mario, Quito 175 (tel. 830 172; fax 830 456), 50m east of the fork. Unlike Lago Agrio itself, this hotel is clean, relatively safe, and friendly, and the street-level restaurant makes it a tourist hive. Rooms range from basic to downright luxurious, perfumed suites. Singles s/45-120,000; doubles s/60-145,000.

Hotel Secoya, Quito 222 and Amazonas (tel. 830 451), at the fork. Head up a vertiginously spiraling staircase, then re-orient yourself on the landing with patio, TV area, and rows of spacious, fan-equipped rooms. Singles s/25,000, with bath and TV s/40,000.

Hotel Guacamayo (tel. 830 601), Quito, 100m east of the fork. Guacamayo fills in the cheaper end of the spectrum, where D'Mario left off. Rooms s/15,000 per person, with bath, fan, and A/C s/40,000.

Hotel Oro Negro (tel. 830 174), Quito, across the street from D'Mario. Named for the town's crude sustenance, this hotel houses mainly tourists, not drillers. The rows of sheets drying in the cement courtyard are visible proof that the beds are clean. Fans, luggage storage, and low-ceilinged but clean communal bathrooms come at no extra charge. Rooms s/25,000 per person.

FOOD

Marisquería Delfín, Añasco and Pasaje Gonzanama, around the corner from Oro Negro. Ever-changing variety of *ceviches* and *enceballados* (s/26,000), rumored to be the best in town, are accompanied by *salsa* music. Open daily 9am-midnight.

Restaurante Los Guacamayos (tel. 830 601), on the other side of D'Mario from Hotel Los Guacamayos. Offers the same open-air sidewalk dining and menu selections as its neighbor and is quickly becoming just as popular. *Filet mignon* (s/40,000) and *churrasco* (s/25,000) for meat-loving savages. Open daily 7am-11pm.

Pizzería Restaurant D'Mario (tel. 830 172), Quito, in the hotel of the same name (see above). This sidewalk restaurant feeds most of the gringos in town. White and sanitary decor reflects the food quality. House selections include Spanish-style bass (s/ 25,000); Rice D'Mario (with chicken, shrimp, ham, and raisins s/32,000); and the usual *desayuno, almuerzo,* and *merienda* (each s/15,000). Open daily 7am-11pm.

NEAR LAGO AGRIO: RESERVA DE PRODUCCIÓN FAUNÍSTICA CUYABENO

When God created the animals of the earth, He must have stopped for a picnic in Cuyabeno. He looked at what He had made—giant armadillos, boa constrictors, electric eels, alligators, freshwater dolphins, spiders, monkeys, tapirs, land tortoises, piranhas—grabbed a beer, and said, "It's All Good." Far to the east, past the Limoncocha mission and the Pañacocha lagoon, this 603,400-hectare wildlife reserve claims a substantial chunk of the Sucumbíos province. The reserve was established in order to give Mother Nature some living space. Cuyabeno's organic orchestra perpetually plays a screeching symphony; howling monkeys and buzzing bugs replace barking dogs and roaring engines. The flora blooms and thrives as well, from joltingly colorful fruits and splashy flowers to enormous green leaves and fronds. A network of tributaries stems from **Río Aguarico** and **Río Cuyabeno,** and parades of wildlife follow the rivers as they flow into the reserve's 14 lagoons. The park also encloses the homelands of **indigenous communities,** such as the Siona, Secoya, and Shuar. The *other* human presence in the reserve has come as a consequence of the oil industry. Over the last 30 years, oil companies have been having their way with the land despite its protected status, though the damage here is reportedly less severe than in Parque Nacional Yasuní to the south. (Park admission US$20, though visitors should be certain that it is paid.)

Transportation: There are several ways to approach the park from Lago Agrio. The drive by truck or bus through Tarapoa to Puenta Cuyabeno is a rough and dusty two-and-a half hours. This method is often used to access the popular lagoons deep in the bush. Other tours launch into the Río Aguarico, then travel by water through the upper or lower regions of the reserve. If traveling by river, it's a good idea to do part of the tour by paddle canoe, since motors chopping through the rivers seem like little earthquakes to animals up ahead. For information on arranging a tour, see **Into the Jungle from Lago Agrio,** below.

INTO THE JUNGLE FROM LAGO AGRIO

For all but oil executives, Lago Agrio's charm lies not in its black, sticky oil, but in its mind-boggling natural surroundings. To the east of town, vast expanses of jungle resonate with the cries of monkeys, calls of birds, and chirps of so many insects that their diversity leaves even the most demanding bug enthusiast speechless. Rivers flow silently throughout the rainforest, swallowing the ripples left by alligators and monkey-munching anacondas. The area around Lago Agrio sees little hunting, despite the fact that several native and traditional peoples (such as the colorful Cofanes and the formerly head-shrinking Shuars) continue to make a natural living off the jungle. Some of the tours that leave from Lago Agrio visit these indigenous groups. As in other parts of the Oriente, each tourist must make the difficult decision of whether or not to take part in the interesting but unavoidably invasive practice of visiting native communities. Jungle tours often cruise the **Río Aguarico,** which runs near the city and then on to more remote areas, passing some indigenous villages along the way. The lagoons of **Lagartacocha** (Alligator Lagoon), **Limoncocha,** and **Pañacocha** satisfy visitors particularly interested in spotting wildlife; the last two are also accessible from Coca. The **Reserva de Producción Faunistica Cuyabeno,** the mother of all wildlife areas in the Ecuadorian Oriente, lies two-and-a-half hours east of Lago Agrio by truck (see p. 382).

TOUR COMPANIES. The most dependable way to plunge into the jungle east of Lago Agrio is to hire a tour guide from a reputable agency in Baños or Quito. This expensive proposition often disheartens budget travelers. A few cheaper tour operations are based in Lago Agrio; some are unlicensed or unqualified (and technically illegal). INEFAN officials have been known to check for credentials when tour groups enter nationally protected areas; unapproved tours are routinely turned away. Even if you make it into the park, a second-rate guide won't be of much use. Of the licensed companies, the current favorite in trips to Cuyabeno is **Native Life Tours,** Pinto 446 and Amazonas (tel. (02) 550 836), in Quito. Guide-owned and operated, they run five- to eight-day trips into the park. (Five-day trips US$260 per person, with a 10% discount for SAEC members.) Recent Native Life clients rave about the piranha-fishing and monkey-watching experiences but complain that the group size of 12 is a little too big for wandering in the jungle. **Kapok Expeditions,** Pinto E4-225 (tel. (02) 556 348), in Quito, is a new company that emphasizes the educational aspects of its tours (US$50 per person per day, not including the US$20 Cuyabeno admission fee). For an experience like no other, inquire at Hotel D'Mario about the **Flotel Orellana,** a floating hotel in the Aguarico reserve. For tour advice, SAEC members may consult trip reports in Quito about jungle tours in the Sucumbíos province. For the most up-to-date info and additional questions, check INEFAN offices in Lago Agrio (see **Practical Information,** p. 381), in Tarapoa en route to Cuyabeno, or at the bridge entrance to Cuyabeno.

BAEZA

Officially a part of the Oriente, Baeza puts on the convincing facade of a sierra hamlet. The quiet village sits at the junction of three roads, known as the **Y of Baeza** *("igriega de Baeza")*. One road leads northwest to Quito, one south to Tena, and the last northeast to Lago Agrio. The town itself hides along a snaking segment of the Quito-Tena road, so that travelers between the two don't even see Baeza. Not far from Quito and a pleasant pitstop on the way to or from the jungle, Baeza provides nothing to do but enjoy the coolness and scenery of the mountains. It is also a good base for those venturing to **Volcán Reventador** or the **San Rafael Falls.**

Baeza is a 40-minute walk from the Y junction, along the Quito-Tena road. First, two roads turn off to the right from the main one, leading through several old buildings to a plaza and a small church, which constitute **Baeza Vieja.** The main road twists over Río Machángara and 10 minutes later leads to **Baeza Nueva** as it becomes **Av. de Los Quijos,** which runs straight through Nueva Baeza, then turns into the Tena highway. Most people arriving in Baeza get dropped off at the Y, unless the bus is heading to Tena, in which case you should ask the driver to let you off at the Baeza Nueva bus stop. To get to Baeza from the Y, flag down one of the *camionetas* heading up the road (s/5,000). From the Y, about 35 minutes downhill from Baeza Nueva, **buses** pass by every 45 minutes heading to: **Quito** (3hr., s/20,000); **Tena** (2½hr., s/20,000); and **Lago Agrio** (6hr., s/45,000). There's no **bank** in town that can change currency. The **police** are in a white building at the Y and are supposedly always on call. The **Hospital Estatal Baeza** (tel. 320 117) is 200m downhill of Av. Quijos, near Hotel Samay. **EMETEL** (tel./fax 580 651), Quijos and 17 de Enero, past Restaurante El Viejo in Baeza Nueva, sends faxes and handles international calls (open daily 8am-1pm and 2-8pm).

Hostal San Rafael (tel. 320 114), at the bottom of new town's Quijos, on the right coming from the Y, has a clean, energetic atmosphere with tiled floors and some rarely used pool tables. All bathrooms are communal. (Rooms s/45,000 per person.) Slightly less expensive, **Hotel Samay,** on the right side of the road towards Tena, has light, wooden rooms, musty smells, and communal baths. A hot shower is available. (Rooms s/25,000 per person.) **El Restaurante Gina** (tel. 320 156), the choice dining spot in Baeza, is on the street closest to Tena in the old town. This surprisingly elegant restaurant serves up savory *desayunos*, *almuerzos*, and *meriendas* (s/10,000; open daily 7am-10pm). In the new part, **Restaurante El Viejo** (tel. 320 146), Calle Nueva Andalucía, gives special attention to travelers. Glowing wicker lamps illuminate the slightly Caribbean setting. (Meals run s/10,000.). Not far from town there are **trails** leading through the forest, past animals ranging in stature from bears to delicate butterflies. One recommended route takes off up the mountain from Baeza Vieja. Head uphill past the church to the end of town and keep going. The hike starts gradually and then heads up the mountain (4-5hr.).

NEAR BAEZA: VOLCÁN REVENTADOR

As Ecuadorian peaks go, Volcán Reventador is a baby giant. While more dormant volcanoes long ago settled into their habitat grooves, this hybrid of highland and jungle experienced some maturing eruptions in the late 1970s. The burst of magma shook the mountain so hard that it broke open, leaving slick beds of hardened lava on the floor of the wet, muddy jungle that lines its slopes. The 3562m green cone rises symmetrically between two mountain ridges, visible from Baeza, 50km to the southwest. Like its jungle companion, the isolated Volcán Sumaco, Volcán Reventador guarantees a strenuous, messy climb through thick vegetation and slippery dried lava. Just finding the trailhead is confusing. The climb begins along the Baeza-Lago Agrio road, about two hours northeast of Baeza, just beyond the **Río Reventador bridge,** or four hours west of Lago Agrio by bus. Usually hidden by clouds and nasty weather, the volcano lies to the left-hand side of the road.

THE HIKE. There are two trails that lead away from the highway. The main one begins at the sign that says "INEFAN Volcán Reventador," on the left-hand side of the road, about a 35-minute walk uphill from the Río Reventador bridge. Just behind the sign, there is a muddy path that runs parallel to a wire fence five minutes in from the trail's beginning. Shortly, a set of wooden steps leads upward for about 20 minutes until the path emerges from the woods. At the clearing, there is a pipeline with a small wooden ladder on each side to climb over it. From the pipeline, head left to the hut; then take a right turn. Continue for 10 minutes until you reach a fork in the road. Pick it up. The left-hand path goes to the **refuge** (2hr.), cutting through wet forest and mud, and is fairly obvious. The refuge is unlocked and has no satellite dish, internet hookup, or for that matter, mattresses. There is a small river nearby; the first path to the left of it leads up to the summit (4hr.). Alternatively, there is a faint trailhead about 15 minutes past the bridge, just past the yellow and black railing and marker 148 on the left. From there, follow the pipeline up to the wooden ladder; follow the previous directions from there.

The journey to the summit of Reventador is a non-technical climb that takes two to four days. Bring food and lots of water—at least four liters per person. Boots, machetes, and rain gear are key, as is a sleeping bag if you plan to spend the night near the top. Despite the hot *fumaroles*, it gets frigid up there. The South American Explorers Club can supply information from the experiences of members who have scaled the peak. The men who work at San Rafael Falls are willing to guide hikers. Those interested should find Juan or Jonidas at the hut before the falls.

NEAR BAEZA: SAN RAFAEL FALLS

Las Cascadas de San Rafael are another impressive display of natural beauty on the Baeza-Lago Agrio road. The highest falls in Ecuador dive down about 1km west of the starting point of the Río Reventador, about two hours east of Baeza or four hours west of Lago Agrio. Bus drivers generally know where to let you off if you ask for *las cascadas;* there is a sign and a little hut at the start of the road down on the right side if you are coming from Baeza. The trail descends from there, continuing past a bridge over a small waterfall and a little house marked "Guardia" where you pay an entrance fee. The attendant may not be there, but try to find him to pay—in order to further encourage wildlife conservation. The trail continues on to a group of **casitas** to rent (s/50,000 per night). Camping is also an option (s/5,000). The black arrows to the left of the *casitas* indicate where the path enters the jungle. The hike to the waterfall cuts through thick jungle, with brilliantly colored birds, armadillos, butterflies, *cabras de monte*, and other exotic species. It takes about 30 minutes to reach the top of the falls. After that, the descent through the waterfall itself is an incredible and worthwhile hike but can be difficult and slippery. (Admission s/10,000, children s/5,000; s/10,000 for a guided tour.)

PAPALLACTA

It's been exhausting and messy wherever you've been. You're dirty and drained. It's time for Papallacta. The baby-Baños of Ecuador, this steaming sanctuary hides away in a spectacular Andean valley, one hour west of Baeza and two hours east of Quito. The cloudforest greenery and blue pools of steaming hot water pretty much define Papallacta. Though the town itself may not be much to look at—worn sheet metal buildings have a tough time competing with the surrounding Andean mountains for attention—Papallactans have no trouble luring visitors from all over with their and beautiful surreal bathing facilities.

Papallacta itself is a handful of small buildings including along the main Quito-Baeza road. **Buses** to **Quito, Lago Agrio,** and **Tena** run frequently along this road and can easily be flagged down in front of the **police station**, the gray-and-blue checkpoint on the right as you walk down the hill from Hotel Quito. The **Centro de Salud,** at the bottom of town, is more concerned with vehicular traffic. If an injury or ailment is serious, you'd better head to Quito.

By far the best, and most expensive, place to stay in Papallacta is the **Hostal Posada de Montaña,** in Quito: Foch E6-12 and Reina Victoria #4A (tel. (02) 557 850; email papallc@ecnet.ec; www.papllacta.com.ec), near Las Termas. The place is beautiful, with several hot pools if guests are too lazy to walk the 45 seconds to

RIBBIT! Poster children of the fight to save the South American jungle, **Amazonian tree frogs** are doted on throughout the world for their psychedelic coloring. In the Amazon itself, animals and humans alike have learned to keep their distance from these cute little fellows—their skin contains a poisonous chemical that acts as a metabolic suppressant, slowing down the bodily functions of whatever creature has been fool enough to meddle with them. Over the years, the indigenous people of the Oriente have learned to take advantage of this powerful toxin for hunting purposes. Tranquilizer darts dipped in a concoction made with "frog skin juice" are launched through a long tubular blow gun with a carefully timed puff of air. The blowguns are about seven feet long and extremely heavy, and yet hunters often hold them up for hours, waiting for the perfect opportunity to strike. Not all of the jungle's beautiful tree *ranas* contain this potent drug, but it's best to leave them all alone, for your own safety as well as theirs.

Las Termas. A fireplace in the common room, a patio, a shared bathroom, and free passes to Las Termas are included in the deal. (Dorms US$23 per person; private rooms US$44-66 per person.) Several other, far cheaper, hotels also cluster around Las Termas and campsites are available, too (s/20,000 per night). The **Hotel Quito,** on your right as you enter Papallacta from Quito, is the best budget choice. The unexciting rooms are generally clean and safe, though the mattresses are very thin and the passing buses noisy. Hotel Quito has hot water, pumped in fresh from the hot springs, as does every building in Papallacta. (Rooms s/25,000 per person.)

For food, **La Choza de Don Wilson,** at the foot of the road to Las Termas, is the best option in town. Enjoy an *almuerzo* (s/22,000) or the local specialty—farm-fresh *trucha* (trout, s/18,000)—while sitting by the fire or watching TV in this thatched-roof, bamboo-walled restaurant. **Cafe Canela,** at Las Termas, is fancy and slightly expensive (*trucha* s/34,000), but it does have some cheaper dishes (sandwiches s/10-15,000; open daily 8am-9pm).

THE HOT SPRINGS. At the base of the town itself, piping hot **Coturpas** (blue pools) beckon through the few run-down buildings. Changing stalls, mandatory hot-water showers, and baskets for belongings are provided. (Open M-F 7am-5pm, Sa and Su 6am-6pm. Admission s/10,000, children s/5,000.) Folks might think nothing could be more perfect, unless they hiked the 2km up to **Termas de Papallacta** and **Jambiyacu,** the genuine hot springs. The road to these *piscinas* veers off the main highway to the left just before you enter the town from Quito. There is a big sign for it, but in case you somehow miss it, walk 200m up the hill from Hotel Quito and take a right up the hill at the sign and restaurants. The first half of this 1km walk is very steep, but it flattens out for the second half and is well worth it once the hot springs appear, on the far side of a Japanese-funded trout farm.

These two sets of pools have a completely different aura than the downtown Papallactan ones. Both belong to the same company and both have the same water source (38-42°C) and views. But the slate-floored Termas de Papallacta pools have a more natural, elegant feel, while the Jambiyacu ones resemble swimming pools. (Termas open daily 6am-10pm. Admission s/25,000, children s/12,000. Jambiyacu open daily 8am-4pm Admission s/11,000, children s/6,000.) The company that runs the hot springs also offers horseback riding (s/25,000 per hr.) and has several trails through the nearby mountains and cloudforest (admission s/10,000 per person; US$25 per person for a 4-6hr. guided tour).

THE PACIFIC COAST

Ecuador's diverse Pacific coast, composed of a motley combination of beaches, mangroves, estuaries, and rocky shores, stretches almost 3,000 kilometers from the town of San Lorenzo, near the Colombian border, to Huaquillas, a small town on the Peruvian border. While weather patterns are quite similar down the length of the coast (with a rainy season from December to April caused by warm water currents offshore), changes in latitude mean differences in attitude. Those looking for constant partying race to Atacames and Montañita, where nights are spent in thatched-roofed beachside bars and days are spent lying in the sun recovering. A more mellow beach experience awaits elsewhere—in Playa Escondida, Same, Canoa, Muisne, or Alandaluz—where virtually untouched beaches stretch for miles. If you can't bear to leave the city behind, head for the coastal metropolises of Bahía de Caráquez, Manta, and Salinas, where sand meets skyscrapers and the ecology sometimes finds itself sacrificed in the name of efficiency and modernization. Nature lovers can escape to the area around Puerto Lopez, a good base for the exploration of Parque Nacional Machalilla (the only coastal park reserve), which includes Isla de la Plata—a Galápagos experience without the price. A cultural awakening awaits in any of the smaller, less touristed towns, especially in the African-influenced northern coast, where the fish and shrimp are more than just food—they're a livelihood. The coast is warmer than the Sierra, so a bathing suit and sunscreen are a must. When high tides swallow up the beach or the sky clouds over for a spell, vacationers can stroll along a beachfront *malecón* (boardwalk), a lively gathering place in many coastal towns, lined with restaurants catering to those with an appetite for fresh seafood and fruit.

HIGHLIGHTS OF THE PACIFIC COAST

- **Súa** and **Same** (see p. 394) have some of the softest and least crowded beaches.
- **Atacames** (see p. 391) draws party-goers from around Ecuador and the world looking to have fun in the sun and play all night long.
- **Montecristi** (see p. 406) is the home of the famous, if misnamed, **Panama hat**.
- For all of its wildlife, **Parque Nacional Machalilla** (see p. 416) is known as the poor man's, woman's, and child's Galápagos.
- The **Alandaluz Center** (see p. 415) is a beach resort interacting with nature.
- **Montañita** (see p. 419) attracts surfers and the accompanying surf culture.
- **Salinas** (see p. 422) is the glitzy, beachside home to Ecuador's elite.

Visitors to the coast, especially the northern coast, should be ready to confront transportation problems created by El Niño and subsequent natural disasters, which have taken their toll not only on the beaches themselves but also on the roadways connecting them. Check with the Ministry of Tourism or with a travel agency to hear the latest news on coastal transportation conditions.

SAN LORENZO

Natural disasters have had an especially large impact on this northern Pacific town. Mudslides, compliments of El Niño, have paralyzed the town's primary attraction: the train ride to and from Ibarra. Without a steady and dependable flow of tourists coming to visit San Lorenzo, development of the tourism industry has screeched to a halt. Nevertheless, determined visitors armed with plenty of insect repellent and a sense of adventure can look forward to beautiful tropical forest and impressive mangroves during their stay in San Lorenzo. Many find, however, that the decrease in tourism combined with rising gasoline costs have left the price of water activities relatively high. Most people stay only one night in San Lorenzo, but there are some more rugged, little-traveled jungle areas, including several local ecological reserves, that can be explored from San Lorenzo. Inquire at SAEC or Safari in Quito, or contact Jaime Burgos (tel. 780 230 in San Lorenzo), the regional director of tourism, for more information.

Almost all services catering to tourists can be found along the town's two main streets, **10 de Agosto,** running from the park near the dock into the center of town; and **Imbabura,** stretching from the train station down towards 10 de Agosto. The restaurant **Ballet Azul,** at the intersection of Imbabura and 10 de Agosto, serves as a good point of reference for visitors. Buses go to **Ibarra** (9 per day 4am-3pm, s/40,000) from the traffic circle along Imbabura, near the train station. Buses depart for **Esmeraldas** from the dock-side park (6hr., every hr. 5am-5pm, s/48,000). **Boats** go to: **La Tola** (2hr., every hr. 5:30am-8:30pm, s/50,000); the **Colombian border** (1hr.; every day 5:30,7am, and 2pm; s/25,000); and **Playa de San Pedro** (1hr.; every day 7am, 2, and 3pm; s/20,000). Patricio can **exchange money** at the **Almacén Su Economía** (tel. 780 272), directly across the Imbabura from ANDINATEL (*almacén* open daily 7am-9pm). The **police,** by the park on 10 de Agosto, reachable by calling the bazaar down the street (tel. 780 178), have recently begun to deal with border crossings, offering immigration services such as stamping passports (open 24hr.). The **hospital** (tel. 780 188), Divina Providencia, is a short trek outside town. To get there, take a left after the train station (as you're heading into town), another left after the bridge, and then go right at the fork in the road; it will be on the left through the gates. **ANDINATEL**, on the street across the playground from Imbabura, toward the train station, allows international calls (open M-Sa 8am-10pm, Su 8am-noon and 7-10pm). To find the **post office**, walk away from the center of town, down the road past Ballet Azul, in the same direction as Imbabura. Take the second right, and it's the green building on your right. (Open M-F 8am-7pm.)

The best places to stay are located farther from the train station, so while closer hotels may pester you to stay, safety and cleanliness await farther in town. Inquire about mosquito nets. **Hotel Tolita Pampa de Oro** (tel. 780 214), Tásito Ortiz, the third left coming from the train station, is the cleanest and most modern of the options. Every room has a TV and fan, and every bed is furnished with a mosquito net. (Rooms s/35,000 per person, with bath s/40,000.) **Hotel San Carlos** (tel. 780 306), on Imbabura and José Garcés across from ANDINATEL, is another similar option (rooms s/30,000 per person, with bath s/40,000 per person). The immaculately clean **Restaurante Condorito** (tel. 780 213), Tásito Ortiz, across Imbabura from Pampa de Oro, builds customer confidence with an open kitchen visible to all patrons. Enjoy a *desayuno* (s/12,000), an *almuerzo* (s/13,000), or plates a la carte ranging from *ceviche* (s/20,000) to chicken (s/20,000; open M-Sa 7am-10pm and Su 7am-2pm). **Ballet Azul,** Imbabura and 10 de Agosto, offers seafood (*ceviches* s/22,000) and chicken dishes (s/20,000; open M-Sa 7am-10pm).

ESMERALDAS

When they first arrived on the Ecuadorian coast, the Spanish conquistadors were greeted by emerald-clad *indígenas* and concluded that the land overflowed with the rare green gem. Though they soon realized their error, the name stuck, and locals came to regard it as a compliment on the lush vegetation in the valleys and hills surrounding the city. These days, however, there is nothing gem-like about this modern city. Though an important port for the fishing, banana, and oil industries, the provincial capital has gained a reputation fouler than the smells emitted by its industrial waste. It is regarded as the most dangerous of Ecuador's major cities, and after the El Niño flooding damage of 1997-98, economic matters have worsened and tourism has practically disappeared. Still, one may end up here to catch a bus to safer and sunnier destinations. Esmeraldas is relatively safe during the day, but always exercise caution with valuables and, after dark, avoid Malecón and all streets farther downhill.

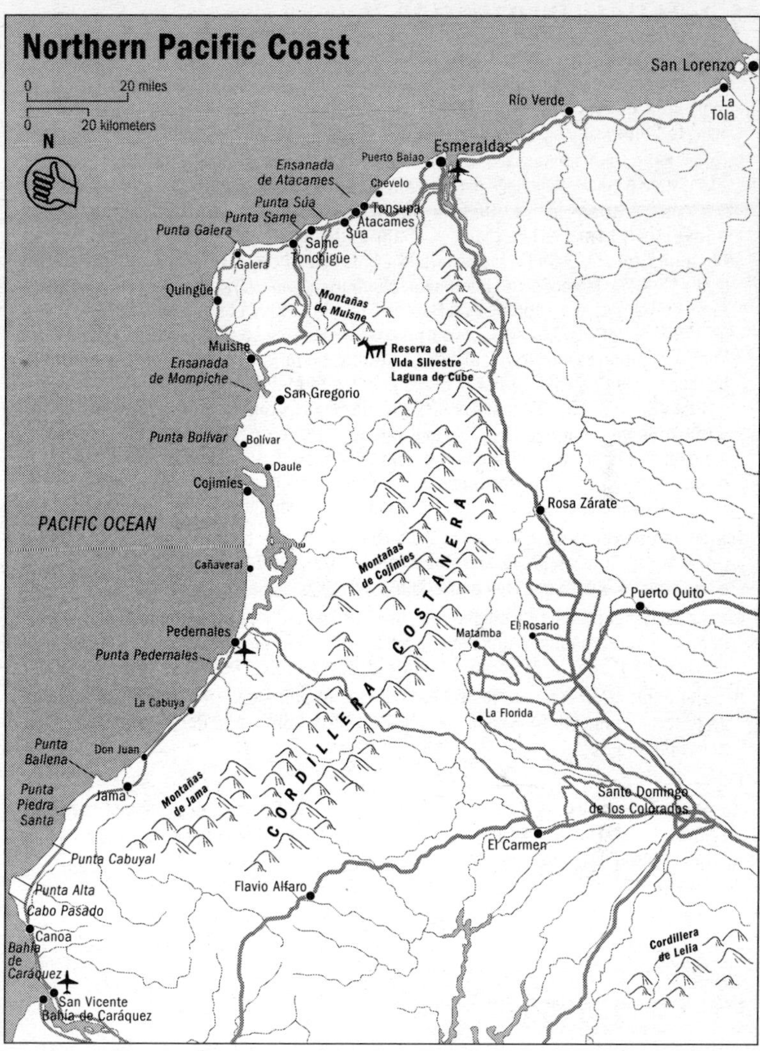

ORIENTATION

Buses coming from outside of the province usually drop passengers off at **Parque Central,** bordered by the parallel streets **Bolívar** and **Sucre, Av. 10 de Agosto,** and **Av. 9 de Octubre.** Local buses, on the other hand, tend to end up at the company bus terminals on Malecón. This is where the market is located, bordered on either side by Bolívar (slightly uphill, turning into **Libertad**) and **La Barranca** (downhill), generally considered to be Esmeraldas's **worst neighborhood.** Most of the city's attractions and services can be found along the parallel streets of Olmedo, Sucre, Bolívar, and Malecón, which intersect with the perpendicular Salinas, Mejía, Cañizares, Piedrahita, 9 de Octubre, 10 de Agosto, Rocafuerte, and Salinas. It is not recommended to stray out of this bounded area, even during the day. Ask around about safety before going out to any unfamiliar part of the city.

PRACTICAL INFORMATION

Airplanes: Aeropuerto General José Rivadeneira, 30km outside of town across the Río Esmeraldas. Taxis take advantage of the distance to charge high rates (s/50,000), so bargain or try to share a cab. **TAME** (tel. 726 863), Bolívar and 9 de Octubre, has a flight to **Quito** (30min., every day 10am, s/266,000). Open M-F 8am-1pm and 3-6pm.

Buses: There are 3 primary bus companies in town. **Transportes Esmeraldas** (tel. 721 381), on 10 de Agosto between Sucre and Bolívar, serves **Quito** (6½hr., 12 per day 6:45am-12:30am, s/55,000) via **Santo Domingo** (3hr., s/40,000), as well as **Guayaquil** (11hr., 13 per day 7:45am-12:45am, s/80,000). **Cooperativo La Costeñita** (tel. 723 041), Malecón and 10 de Agosto, and **Transportes del Pacífico** (tel. 713 227), Malecón and Piedrahita, alternate buses every hr. to **San Lorenzo** (6hr., every hr. 6am-4pm, s/48,000) via **Borbón** (4hr., s/29,000) and to **La Tola** (5hr., every hr. 5:30am-6pm, s/29,000). If you plan on making these trips, call the *cooperativo* before heading to the *terminal* to ensure that there is a vehicle. For the **southern beaches,** any Costeñita or Pacífico bus heading to **Muisne/Salto** (3hr., every 20min. 5:30am-8pm, s/15,000) passes through **Atacames** (1hr., s/6,000), **Súa** (1¼hr., s/9,000), **Same** (1¾hr., s/12,000), and **Güe** (2hr.) One popular way to bypass the city altogether is to ask the driver of a taxi from the airport or any bus approaching Esmeraldas to drop you off at the **Repsol** on the northern outskirts of town. All buses leaving the city pass by this gas station to reach the main artery running along the coast.

Tourist Information: CETUR, Bolívar 2-27 (tel. 714 528), between Salinas and Mejía. Open M-F 8:30am-5pm. **Esmeraldas Tur,** Cañizares 221 and Bolívar (tel./fax 726 875). Open M-F 8:30am-1pm and 3-7pm.

Money Exchange: Banco Pichincha (tel./fax 728 745), 9 de Octubre and Bolívar, off the Parque Central, changes traveler's checks (US$100 min.). Open M-F 8am-2pm, Sa 8:30am-2pm. 24hr. **ATM** accepts Cirrus and MC. Open M-F 9am-4pm, Sa 9am-2pm.

Supermarket: Micromercado Imperial, Bolívar 2-40 and Mejía (tel. 723 022). Open M-Sa 8:30am-1pm and 3-8:30pm. **Tía** (tel. 727 826), Bolívar and Rocafuerte. Open M-Sa 8am-8pm, Su 8am-1pm.

Police: (**Emergency** tel. 723 158 or 711 484), Bolívar and Cañizares. Open 24hr.

Hospital: (**Emergency** tel. 710 212), on the right side of Libertad as you head toward Las Palmas. Free 24hr. emergency treatment. Locals prefer **Clínica Central** (tel. 726 520), Espejo between Olmedo and Sucre. Open 24hr.

Post Office: (Tel. 726 831; fax 726 834), Montalvo and Malecón, 1st floor, in the same building as ANDINATEL. Open M-F 8am-7pm, Sa 8am-2pm.

Telephones: ANDINATEL (tel. 728 810), Montalvo and Malecón, makes international calls for a fee. Open M-Sa 8am-10pm.

TELEPHONE CODE	06

ACCOMMODATIONS

Prepare to be underwhelmed. Most hotels charge around s/30,000 for musty, cramped rooms. Hot water will be hard to come by. Few places offer mosquito nets, but many buildings have open-air vents; don't forget your insect repellent.

Hotel Costa Esmeraldas, Sucre 813 and Piedrahita (tel. 723 912 or 720 640). Large, clean rooms, private bathrooms, accommodating staff, and new color TVs make this a real find. Singles s/40,000, with A/C s/65,000; doubles with A/C s/130,000.

Residencial Sulema (tel. 712 711), Olmedo between Cañizares and Piedrahita, set back slightly from the street. One of the few budget hotels in town not downright depressing—thanks to the comical green paint job. Ceiling fans are a plus, but mattresses could be firmer and bathrooms cleaner. Rooms s/12,000 per person, with bath s/25,000.

Hostal Galeón, Piedrahita 3-30 and Olmedo (tel. 723 820; fax 723 821). Wood-paneled lobby, adorned with sea paintings and a ship's wheel, builds anticipation for ship-shape rooms, but sadly, mattresses are flimsy and showers are tiny. Friendly staff makes up for any disappointment. Private baths in all quarters. Rooms s/33,000 per person.

Hotel Sandry (tel. 726 861), Libertad (continuation of Bolívar) and Montalvo, 2nd floor. Rooms are sunny and have comfortable mattresses. TV and private *baños* for all. Unfortunately, Sandry is in an area of Esmeraldas that may be unsafe at night and noisy during the day. Rooms s/33,000 per person, with A/C s/44,000.

FOOD

A stronghold of the fishing industry, Esmeraldas naturally has great fresh seafood. There are two varieties of eateries: the sit-down type and the more informal roadside stand. Both serve the same typical regional dishes—*encocados* (seafood cooked in coconut milk), *tapaos* (meat or fish covered with plantains and wrapped in banana leaves), and, of course, *ceviche.* Olmedo has a dense concentration of eateries with inexpensive sit-down meals. For those who don't eat seafood, don't worry: chicken is everywhere.

Las Redes (tel. 723 151), on Bolívar, facing the Parque Central. Bongo drums swing from fish-net ceilings above couples sharing an intimate beachside moment and posters of the Beatles' Abbey Road. No yellow submarines here, but the seahorse garden is pretty cool. *Almuerzos* s/12,000; seafood dishes s/17,000. Open M-Sa 7:30am-6pm.

Restaurant Las Vegas (tel. 725 481), Cañizares and Bolívar, 2 blocks south of the Central Plaza. Genuinely good food served. *Salsa* music jams while ceiling fans provide a much-needed breeze. Gargantuan pasta dishes start at s/8,000, shrimp dishes s/11,000, *almuerzos* s/10,000. Open M-Sa 6am-10pm, Su 6am-4pm.

Antojo's Bar, on the corner of Olmedo and Mejía across from Parque Infantil. This open-air fruit stand/ice-cream shop attracts kids and vegetarians from afar. Fruit salad s/9,000; banana split s/15,000. Open M-Sa 8am-10pm.

Chifa Asiático, Cañizares 277 and Sucre (tel. 726 888). Slow, stoic servers roam the aisles of this institution. Large rice plates (s/13,000-18,000) and ample noodle dishes (s/16,000-18,000) help make up for the lack of personality. Open daily 11am-10pm.

ATACAMES

As the most touristically developed beach on the northern Pacific Coast, Atacames has built itself a reputation as a party destination. Some of the best maintained highways in the coastal region pump visitors into the town every weekend, filling up the town's hostels, bars, and clubs, and keeping the sarong and sunscreen vendors along Malecón very busy. By day, the crowds swim, suntan, and shop. By night, they hit the bars and clubs. At any hour, the air is filled with the beat of reggae and *salsa*, and glasses are filled with intoxicating tropical concoctions. During the week, Atacames slows down somewhat; the blenders whir at half-speed, the music dies down around 1am, and the partiers rest up for the weekend. Endless sun, swimming, volleyball, straw-roofed bars, music, and friendly (sometimes overly so) people define this party mecca. If alone, you'll make friends fast, but solitude seekers might want to plant their beach umbrellas elsewhere.

ORIENTATION

Locals refer to the road from Esmeraldas as **Principal,** or **La Carretera**. Buses drop people anywhere along this main road, but it's best to get off at the center bus stop—the one with the long white bench in front of an *helado* bar and a sign that says "*parada.*" The road splitting to the right leads to the **beach.** To reach the center of the action, walk along this road past the Nuevo Hotel and bear right at the intersection. Cross the footbridge over the **Río Atacames** and take a right. This street, which continues to the beach, is called **Calle Principal,** not to be confused with the above-mentioned "Principal." The street that runs along the beach is **Calle Malecón.** Most budget hotels, bars, and restaurants are found along this boardwalk. In town, most services are concentrated around the **plaza,** one block away from the away from the beach from the central bus stop. **La Acacia,** another important roadway, intersects La Carretera farther along Principal en route to Muisne.

PRACTICAL INFORMATION

Buses: Buses can be caught from the main stop on Principal headed toward **Muisne** (2½hr., every 30min. 5:30am-10pm, s/8,000) via **Súa** (15min., s/2,000); **Same** (30min., s/4,000); and **Tonchigüe** (1hr., s/5,000). **Transportes Occidentales** (tel. 731 276) sends buses from their office right after the footbridge when coming from the beach. They travel to: **Quito** (8hr., every day 11:45pm and midnight, s/50,000); and **Guayaquil** (8½hr., every day 11:15pm, s/60,000) via **Muisne** (2½hr., s/10,000). It is also possible to walk to **Súa** along the beach (30min.), but only at low tide.

Taxis: Standard taxis are scarce and expensive–they're all based in Esmeraldas. You can get to Esmeraldas from Atacames for s/50,000, but getting from Esmeraldas to Atacames costs around s/100,000. Self-described "ecological tours" (actually just bikes with carts) drive people all around town and the beach (s/3,000 per person and up).

Currency Exchange: Banco del Pichincha (tel. 731 029), on Principal just north of the central bus stop, away from the beach, changes cash or checks. Open M-F 8am-2pm.

Supermarket: Shops along both Principals, in town and leading toward the beach, sell everything from gallon jugs of water to sunscreen to diapers.

Laundromat: Zum Tucán (tel. 731 191), on the 2nd-to-last side street before the footbridge coming from town, washes and dries 1lb. of pound of laundry for a reasonable s/5,000. Open M-F 10am-6pm, Sa 10am-2pm.

Police: (Tel. 731 275), Acacia and Principal, in a blue and white building by the sea.

Pharmacy: Farmacia Popular, La Acacia and Malecón, on the south end of the beach. Open daily 8am-noon and 1-10pm.

Hospital: Centro Médico Quirúrgico San Andresito (cell. tel. (09) 732 494) has a number of doctors on staff as well as a **pharmacy.** Open M-Sa 24hr., Su 8am-1pm. **Doctor Vinizio Díaz** (tel./fax 731 183), 40m north of the central bus stop, also provides 24hr. emergency medical attention and laboratory/clinic services.

Post Office: Correos, off the plaza, facing the bank. Open M-F 8:30am-noon and 3-5pm.

Internet Access: Principal Librería y Papelería (tel. 731 521), off the plaza along the block between the bank and EMETEL (s/3,500 per min.). Open M-Sa 7:30am-7:30pm.

Telephones: EMETEL (tel. 731 050), 1 block beyond the bank on the plaza, 2nd floor, allows national and international collect calls for a fee. Open M-Sa 8am-10pm, Su 8am-2pm and 7-10pm.

TELEPHONE CODE 06

ACCOMMODATIONS

At first, it might seem as though Atacames has far too many accommodations. But then the weekend arrives, hotels fill with bikini-clad teenagers, and there is scarcely a room free in town. The never-ending flow of tourists could have created a breeding ground for outrageous prices, but luckily the town's quest to appeal to young people has kept them low (between s/20,000 and s/55,000 per person, usually favoring bigger groups). Midweek visitors and those who come during the low season (July-Sept.) might effectively bargain prices down and save enough for a cocktail on the beach. Despite the generally high level of comfort, the noise emitted by bars and clubs can sometimes prevent a good night's sleep.

Cabañas Los Bohios (tel./fax 731 089), at the bend in Principal, consists of several green tin-roofed bamboo cabins with TVs and clean private baths. There's also a gate and a guard to keep out late-night drunks. *Cabañas* s/45-55,000 per person.

Residencial la Casa del Manglar (tel. 731 464), on the Río Atacames, to your left after crossing the footbridge towards the beach. Only 150m from the sand, this cozy *residencial* gives you just enough distance to withdraw from Malecón's nightlife scene if you want. Relax on the terrace or in the cheery, well-decorated rooms. Rooms s/35,000 per person, with bath s/50,000.

Hotel Galería Atacames (tel. 731 149), on the beach itself, to the right after you reach Malecón. The flight of stairs past the restaurant leads to an abundance of rooms with sinking mattresses and private baths. Quads s/40,000 per person.

Hotel Tiburón (tel./fax 731 145), along Malecón just beyond Galería Atacames, sums up the Atacames experience: lots of people, noise, and fun. Simple, whitewashed rooms are situated in the back to muffle street sounds. All rooms have clean private baths. Concrete floors and high-speed ceiling fans assure a chilly night's rest. Rooms for up to 6 cost s/44,000 per person.

FOOD

While seafood dominates the menus of most restaurants, Atacames also boasts a number of places offering a diverse sampling of international cuisine. For a lighter and less expensive snack, turn to the sidewalk chefs cooking up shish kabobs and corn-on-the-cob along Malecón.

Bar Restaurant Narcisa de Jesús (tel. 731 494), on Malecón just to the right after reaching the beach from Principal. White walls highlight fluorescent poster boards that scream out the house specialties amidst snapshots of Ecuadorian landscapes and soccer teams. *Encocado de corvina* (s/22,000), *ceviches* (s/18-40,000), and lobster (s/60,000) are all very fresh. Open daily 8am-9pm.

El Mesón, to the right along Malecón just before the Hotel Galería Atacames. Step inside this white mission-style building to enjoy some delightful Spanish cuisine. Plates appeal to different sized appetites and a variety of tastes. Munch on *tapas* (s/20-25,000) or gorge yourself on a platter of *paella valenciana* (s/45,000). Open W-M 11:30am-3:30pm and 7-10pm.

No Name Pizzeria (cell. tel. (09) 821 565), 2nd floor, along Malecón just beyond Scala Club and across from Nagiba Bar. Accessible only by stepladder, this bamboo-laden balcony restaurant offers a relaxed atmosphere, great people-watching, friendly service, and good pizza. Choose from 16 toppings (large pizza s/48-75,000). Salads (s/10-16,000) and pasta dishes (s/20-29,000) are also available, plain or peppered with fruits of the sea. Open M-Sa noon-late.

Paco Foco (tel. 731 076), on Principal right before Malecón, on the left. Disinterested waiters serve mountains of coastal cuisine, such as *camarones apanados* (breaded shrimp, s/21,000) or a fruit mountain (s/10,000). Open daily 8am-10pm.

BEACHES

Though dull and gray, Atacames's beaches are unsullied, soft, and extend far enough for long walks in either direction. The ocean water is particularly warm for most of the year. First-rate views of **Punta Esmeraldas** to the north and the jagged **Isla de los Pájaros** to the south frame the enormous expanse. Though competing for the same prime beachfront space, sunbathers and *fútbol* players coexist peacefully while banana boats—for rent on the south side of the beach (s/10,000 per person)—buzz by on the blue-green water. Though the beach is generally safe in the resort area, exercise caution if exploring less-populated stretches, and avoid leaving possessions unattended. Also take care when swimming in the surf; the undertow can be quite strong. The lack of public restrooms along the beach can prove to be an obstacle, but business owners, eager to please, are usually very reasonable.

ENTERTAINMENT

Though the official drinking age in Ecuador is 18, a brief walk down Malecón on a Friday or Saturday night reveals that this law is usually not enforced. Even the youngest of travelers may feel a little over the hill as 15-year-old girls sport their favorite miniskirts and crop-tops while their male Calvin Klein-clad counterparts fail to inhale Lark Reds. Nevertheless, with 39 grass-hut bars as well as a handful of *discotecas*, there is something for everyone. Bars all offer the same laboriously prepared fruity mixed drinks, thatched roofs, music, and prices (s/10-25,000 for cocktails) and have the same hours (open daily 4pm-2am). Stroll along Malecón around during late evening and you're bound to find a happy hour somewhere. Even late into the night, Malecón is well-lit, populated, and generally safe. The beach is more dangerous; late-night walks are discouraged.

El Oasis de Nagiba Bar, just to the right of Principal along the sand, has swings hanging from the ceiling around the bar instead of bar stools. The house specialty is the *nagiba,* made from exotic Colombian fruits and rum (s/20,000). Live *marimba* Sa. Happy hour daily 8:30-9:30pm.

Scala Discoclub, just after Nagiba Bar along Malecón. Partiers of all ages cram into the beams of neon lights that illuminate walls paying tribute to Elvis, Metallica, and Claudia Schiffer. *Cerveza* s/20,000. Cover s/20,000. Open daily 8pm-2am.

El Caída del Sol, across from Scala Discoclub. Just like all the others, but for some reason more popular. Maybe it's the friendly staff or the *caída del sol* (papaya, pineapple, condensed milk, amaretto, and rum; s/25,000) they serve.

NEAR ATACAMES: TONSUPA

Más tranquilo is how locals describe this little town when comparing it to its crazy neighbor, Atacames. The beach is so quiet that even the crabs pop out of their holes and scurry across the sand. Besides a bit of beach with grass-hut bars, the couples and families that come here generally have the sand to themselves. While Tonsupa makes for a quick daytime escape from Atacames, few accommodations merit a night's stay. One commendable hotel is **Cabaña Turística Doña Emerita** (tel. 711 407), on an empty stretch of sand closer to Atacames. To reach the *cabañas*, ask to be dropped off at the *puente* of Tonsupa and take one of the bike-taxis (s/4,000) down the winding path to the shore.The *cabañas* offer spotless white-tile floors, whitewashed walls, and a solitude unmatched in the area. (Doubles s/80,000; quads s/130,000; sextuples s/180,000.) For food, head to the cheery pink-and-blue **Hotel Miramar** (tel. 731 585). In spite of its costly rooms, Miramar offers ambrosial, affordable food. Two fans struggle to cool off customers as they down lobster (s/30,000) vegetarian plates (s/15,000), available upon request. (Open daily 7:30am-9pm.) Right in the center of the beach along Malecón, the **Rincón Cloverito** serves up a great *desayuno costeño* of fish, bread, and coffee or tea (s/10,000). *Almuerzo* and *merienda* run s/12,000. (Open daily 8am-10pm.)

Transportation: To get to Tonsupa from Atacames, take the **bus** (10min., every 15 min., s/3,000) from the main bus stop, or catch a **taxi** (s/10,000). Buses coming from Esmeraldas along the highway return to Atacames. The mouth of the Río Atacames prevents a walk along the beach between the two towns.

NEAR ATACAMES: SÚA

Although not to the same extent as in Atacames, weekends still bring loads of beachgoers to Súa and banana boats still frequent the lightly littered shoreline. In addition, Súa's surrounding verdant hillsides attract hikers. There is a route that heads south of the bay along a dirt path up the side of the big green bluff. After 30 minutes of walking, a view of Atacames to the north and less-developed coastline to the south will inevitably induce a frenzied attack of photo-shooting.

Quality accommodations in Súa are relatively cheap, though prices will vary significantly on a seasonal basis. The **Hotel Chagra Ramos** (tel. 731 006 or 731 070), on the far north side of the beach, provides restful hillside villas and slightly older *cabañas*. The villas have private baths, and the screens on the windows of the basic but blemish-free rooms provide a cool, itch-free, and untroubled sleep. (Villas s/25-30,000 per person; cabins s/20-25,000 per person.) **Hotel Chagra's restaurant** serves quality seafood (s/20-35,000), salads (s/10,000), and veggie dishes (s/10,000) under the shade of droopy palm trees (open daily 7:15am-9pm).

The French-owned **Hotel Súa Café/Restaurant** (tel. 731 004) is one of the first buildings on the left coming from town. Though few seedy characters wander this hushed neighborhood, Hotel Súa takes safety seriously, with sturdy door locks and strongboxes for valuables in each room. All quarters have private bathrooms, ceiling fans, and sinking mattresses. (Rooms s/25,000 per person.) The cosmopolitan restaurant downstairs serves French (desserts s/10-14,000), Italian (spaghetti s/18,000), and local cuisine (*almuerzo* of fried fish s/15,000)—all delicious. (Open daily 7am-9:30pm.) Another reasonably priced option, the **Hotel Las Buganvillas** (tel. 731 008), farther down the beach, is a more traditional hotel, with ocean views and clean rooms that have fans and private baths (s/25-30,000 per person).

Transportation: From Atacames, take a **bus** (15min., every 15min., s/2,000), a **mototaxi** (s/15,000), or **walk** south on the beach (30min., only possible at low tide).

NEAR ATACAMES: SAME

A honeymooner's paradise, the soft shore of Same (SAH-may) waits each day to be deflowered by the first footprints to mark its untouched sands. This virtually uninhabited beach 7km southwest of Súa stretches almost 3km in length, though never more than 20m wide. Its greenish surf is said to be the best in the Atacames area and lingers at a refreshing 25°C (75°F) year-round. Graced with only a handful of low-key establishments, Same stresses quality rather than quantity, and because of the high proportion of North American and European visitors, prices are a little higher than those in the neighboring beach communities.

The **Cabañas Marinas** (cell. tel. (09) 696 713), just before the old wooden bridge to the beach, offers *cabañas* that are not as nice as the beachfront places but are more economical. Huddled together, each wooden hut has a private bath, green painted floors, and bamboo walls. (Cabañas s/50,000 per person.) The more charming seafront *cabañas* of **La Terraza Quito** (tel. 544 507) are just to your left as you reach the beach from the main road. Each comes with a private bath, a fan, and a porch with a hammock. (*Cabañas* US$5-7 per person.) In touch with its natural side, **La Terraza's restaurant** is built around a tree trunk, adorned with giant turtle shells and dug-out canoes. It's also the center of the Same social scene: an international crowd drinks *cuba libres* and exchanges stories on any given night. Try specialties such as calamari (s/38,000), pasta dishes (s/36-40,000), and *ceviche* (s/31-35,000) while sipping a cocktail. (Open daily 9am-4pm and 7-10pm.) **Restaurante Unicornio Azul,** just before Cabañas Marinas on the road to the beach, is less expensive and equally picturesque, with hand-painted menus that conceal reasonable prices (fish dishes s/20-30,000; open daily 8am-9pm). **Restaurant Sea Flower,** on the road to the beach just before La Terraza, provides a congenial ambiance to complement the elaborately prepared food. The servings and prices are similarly hefty (catch of the day platter s/45-48,000; open daily 10am-10pm).

Transportation: Same can be reached from Atacames by **bus** (25min., every 15min. 5am-10pm, s/4,000).

NEAR ATACAMES: PLAYA ESCONDIDA

Tucked away along the coast of the Esmeraldas province somewhere between Same and Muisne, Playa Escondida ("Hidden Beach") offers tranquility-seekers a unique coastal experience. Surrounded by the ocean, cliffs, and a semi-tropical forest, this is the sort of beach where you are likely to see more sand crabs than people, and where the hammocks sprinkled around the resort beckon you to just kick up your feet and relax. Situated in a little bay between two *puntas* where the Ecuadorian hills meet the Pacific Ocean, Playa Escondida is a self-described ecological refuge. Swimming in the ocean is best at high tide, but when the waters recede, visitors are treated to resort-front tidepools—home to all sorts of marine creatures—as well as stretches of firm sand and flat rocks that allow for long walks along the cliffs and coast. There is only one place to stay at Playa Escondida, and it is rustic in an endearing way. The **beach-side lodge** (cell. tel. (09) 733 368) built on a little knoll, offers visitors open-air rooms on the second floor or the larger third-story loft. Let the crash of the surf lull you to sleep as you relax on mosquito-netted beds or any of the hammocks lining the common kitchen. Camping is also possible. The common cold-water shower and outhouse, complete with compost heap, make for a rugged beach experience. (Rooms US$8-10 per person; camping US$5 per person; 10% IVA tax.) In contrast to the rooms, the **restaurant** at the lodge is anything but simple. It serves up delectable meals, but be aware: costs will quickly add up. Pancakes (s/8,000), fruit salad (s/8,000), and *batidos* (s/15,000) are sure to quench your appetite until lunch or dinner, when *platos fuertes* (s/28,000) of fish or vegetables are prepared.

Transportation: Playa Escondida is just south of the town of Tonchigüe, 12km off the main highway between Esmeraldas and Muisne, along the dirt road leading to Punta Galera. Any bus connecting Muisne and the northern beaches passes by **Puente de Tonchigüe,** where the road to Playa Escondida and Punta Galera begins, but only two buses daily can drop you off at the resort's doorstep. **Cooperativa Costeñita** sends two buses to the nearby Punta Galera from Esmeraldas (2hr., daily 12:10 and 4:10pm, s/13,000), and these buses pass through Atacames 45 minutes after leaving the terminal. In case you cannot make either of those buses, the trek from the bridge of Tonchigüe at the main highway is very straightforward but can take up to two hours. *Camionetas* occasionally offer hikers a lift for a fee (s/5-7,000). Taxis from Esmeraldas usually start at s/150,000. For more information about the resort, contact lodge owner Judith Barrett.

MUISNE

The quiet island of Muisne, 35km southwest of Atacames, remains ignorant of other beaches' tourist-driven ways. Free of cars or cares, the island can help you achieve the ultimate in relaxation. Sometimes, however, this easy-going carelessness manifests itself in poor maintenance of the town and beach. The town's bizarre weather also sets it apart from its coastal counterparts. Mornings are chilly, with a constant breeze and occasional rain; afternoons bring hot sunshine; and nights are clear with a wind so strong it howls. The lack of badgering tourist crowds allows the locals to take the time to befriend the visitors they do receive. It only takes a few days to learn the names of the beach's restaurant owners. Greet them with a cheerful *"Buenas,"* and you'll be on a first name basis in no time.

ORIENTATION AND PRACTICAL INFORMATION. Buses stop in the mainland town of **Salto,** just by the docks. **Boats** run from the docks to Muisne (3min., every 5min., s/10,000). On the docks of the island, "ecological tours" powered by boys on bicycles attached to carts, offer rides to the beach (s/3,000); otherwise, it is a muddy 15-minute walk down **Isidora Ayora,** the main street leading away from the docks. From the mainland docks, buses go to: **Esmeraldas** (3hr., every 1½hr. 5:30am-9pm, s/15,000) via **Same** (1½hr., s/6,000), **Súa** (1¼hr., s/9,000), and **Atacames** (2hr., s/12,000); **Quito** (8hr., every day 10:30 and 11:20am, s/75,000); and **Guayaquil** (10hr., every day 10pm, s/80,000). **Boats** leaving from the right of the main dock travel to **Cojimíes** (1½hr., daily 9am, s/50,000) but won't leave if there aren't enough passengers to pay for fuel; they usually hover around the harbors until they're full (often a wait of up to 2hr.). Be ready to get wet (see **Near Muisne: Cojimíes,** p. 398).

There's no official currency exchange, but Cabañas San Cristóbal (see below) will change U.S. dollars at very poor rates. The **police** are housed in a blue-and-gray building on the street parallel to the main road, just before the central park, but are most likely found roaming the streets. **Farmacia Dolorosa** is on the first major cross street after the docks, to the right of the main road. The **hospital** (tel. 480 269), on the right coming from the docks, has free 24-hour emergency care. The **post office** is on the third cross street to the left of the docks, around the corner from the municipal building (open M-F 9am-noon and 3-6pm). The **ANDINATEL** office is on the left from the docks (open daily 8am-10pm). **Telephone code:** 05.

ACCOMMODATIONS AND FOOD. While Muisne has few hotels, there's nearly always something available since so few tourists visit the island. All rooms come equipped with mosquito nets (an absolute must) and cold-water baths. The bright pink **Hotel Playa Paraíso** (tel. 480 192), to the left as you reach the beach from the main road, has English-speaking owners who treat guests like family. Rooms share well-scrubbed toilets and showers. (Rooms s/30,000 per person.) **Hotel Calade** (tel. 480 279), next door to Playa Paraíso, is the next best thing. Clean, spacious rooms are spiced up by the funky mural in the restaurant and the squawking parrot in the courtyard. The owner's son, an ecological guide, offers tours. (Rooms s/25,000 per person, with fan s/30,000, with fan and bath s/60,000.) **Cabañas San Cristóbal** (tel. 480 264), to the right of the main road along the beach, have fancy tiled rooms, but a better deal is one of the musty wooden *cabañas* that line the beach. Mosquito nets and strong locks protect guests from intruders. All rooms have private baths. (Single *cabañas* s/25,000; double *cabañas* s/40,000; rooms in hotel proper s/80,000 per person.)

Dining on this coastal isle is an exercise in patience. While seafood dishes are served at an amazingly slow pace, laid-back dining does have its advantages. Most restaurants are right on the beach, and spending up to an hour napping, reading, chatting, or sipping a beer while you wait isn't bad at all. Besides Hotel Playa Paraíso or Calade, there are several other dining options, mostly along the beach. **Las Palmeras,** two doors down from Playa Paraíso, is the local favorite. While walls are decorated with posters of royalty, the real king here is the huge *almuerzo* (s/9,000). All hail. (Open daily 7am-10pm.) On the main road just before the beach, **Restaurant Suizo-Italiano** operates out of an old building with "Pizza and Spaghetti" spray-painted on the outside. Suspicious appearances aside, the Swiss-Italian owner makes a phenomenal pizza (small s/15,000, large s/20,000; open daily noon-9pm). Though the hours and menu are slightly irregular, **Cafe Tortuga,** next door to Calade, is an option for vegetarians or those who just can't bear to eat another fishy meal. The eatery specializes in crepes (s/10-12,000) as well as a selection of teas (s/1,500-3,000) and sandwiches (s/3,500-6,000; open daily 10am-10pm).

BEACHES. Muisne's peaceful shores are endowed with heaps of soft, unspoiled sand, strong surf, and tranquility. The immense **beach** provides over an hour of walking room in either direction, and the difference between high and low tides can be as much as 70m. Though once lined with palm trees, **El Niño** did away with most of these during the winter of 1997-98. In an effort to save the beachfront establishments from further harm, the government has constructed a rather unattractive **concrete wall** along the boardwalk to keep out the menacing waves. Luckily, the wall is short enough to avoid detracting from the splendid view. The surf itself can get pretty rough, but it's the small stinging **jellyfish** that bother most people. The stings are mild and can be healed with a dab of vinegar, found at any local restaurant. Avoid the unlit areas of the beach at night; Muisne is a relatively safe town, but there has been some crime in recent years.

SIGHTS. Boating through the **mangroves** is possible and pleasurable, although there are frequent blemishes in the otherwise green landscape where *camaroneras* (shrimp farms) have sprung up. Boat rides through the mangroves either aim for a destination, such as **Isla Bonita**—with rolling green hills and rocky cliffs surrounding a sheltered beach—or they meander aimlessly around the lush vegetation. Some people camp overnight on Isla Bonita or nearby **Isla Monpiche;** others stay for a day or a few hours. If you plan to leave the sheltered area behind the island of Muisne, be prepared for rolling waves and a tottering boat. Boats with drivers can be found at the port (s/ 50,000 per hr.). Having a driver wait for hours while you hunt for seashells at Isla Bonita can add up and get expensive; arrange for a pick-up later to avoid paying for the wait.

NEAR MUISNE: COJIMÍES

Cojimíes is little more than a necessary stop during a journey along the coast. The town itself is no beach paradise due to the clutter of boats, shacks, and fishing gear covering the sand, but just south of Cojimíes a stretch of beach remains clean and beautiful, though a bit rocky in places. The only disturbance is the sound of passing *camionetas* that use the beach as a highway during low-tide.

The 24-hour **pharmacy/clinic** is just left of Principal on the second cross street. Ask for Dr. Jorge Cobos. For those who get stuck in Cojimíes, the **Residencial Manuelita,** with its cramped and dingy rooms, screenless windows, and sturdy locks, is on the left side of the main street (singles s/20,000). Dining options in Cojimíes are similarly limited, but of a much higher quality than the lodgings. There are several identical huts by the beach that serve up speedy *almuerzos* (s/12,000) and *batidos* (s/8,000) to people on the go (open daily 7am-9pm). **Flavio Alfaro,** across the road from the basketball court by the port, serves *desayuno* (s/10,000), *almuerzo* (s/12,000), and seafood dishes (fried shrimp s/14,000; open daily 7am-8pm).

Transportation: The most exciting thing about this little town is getting to it or away from it. The wet-and-wild **boat ride** between Muisne and Cojimíes (1½hr.; daily 9am from Muisne, 9 and 10:30am from Cojimíes) is in a motorized dugout climbing seven- to 10-foot swells as buckets of saltwater splash into the boat. While bags and other necessities get put away in a sealed compartment, no such protection exists for passengers—bring some kind of rain gear. Departures from Cojimíes leave from the beach in front of the plaza. If you can't find a boat to Cojimíes, take a *camioneta* from Salto to the town of **Daüle** (2hr., s/20,000), where you can catch a small motorboat to Cojimíes (15min., s/20,000). **Camionetas** to **Pedernales** (1½hr., during low tide, s/15,000) leave from the large plaza near the dock that doubles as a basketball court, or along the main street. This is another wild ride—racing along the beach in an old truck, over small rivers, around rocks, and past thick forests of palm trees—and not for anyone with a heart condition.

PEDERNALES

This bustling seaport, approximately 70km north of San Vicente and 40km south of Cojimíes, takes advantage of its position in the center of things. Pedernales hosts the largest market on the northern coast and serves as an important center for the shrimp industry. But while locals may consider Pedernales crucial, travelers searching for the perfect *playa* paradise normally look elsewhere. Coastal visitors think of the town only as a key link in the coastline's chain of transport. The famous *camionetas* to Cojimíes travel north up the coast from here, and several bus companies link Pedernales with inland and southern coastal towns.

Pedernales's **central plaza** is at the intersection of the town's two most important streets: **López Castillo,** running north-south, and **Eloy Alfaro,** running east-west. The town's lackluster **beach** is at the west end of Alfaro. Due to the fact that it also serves as a road and a dock, the sand has a grimy appearance and potent, fishy aroma. **Buses** go to: **Bahía de Caráquez** (3hr., every hr. 5:30am-11pm, s/25,000) via **San Vicente; Esmeraldas** (7hr., daily 5:20 and 8:20am, s/48,000); **Guayaquil** (9hr., daily 6am and 10pm, s/55,000); **Manta** (6hr., every hr. 4am-11pm, s/45,000) via **Portoviejo** (5hr., s/40,000); **Quito** (6hr.; daily 11am, 3, and 11pm; s/50,000); and **Santo Domingo** (3hr., every 20min. 4:30am-6:30pm, s/27,000). **Camionetas** to **Cojimíes** (1½hr., during low tide, s/15,000) leave from the north side of the plaza. There are several **banks** in town, but most don't cater to tourists. **Banco del Pacífico**, two blocks to the right and one block down from Eloy Alfaro and López Castillo (when facing the plaza with your back towards the beach), has a 24-hour MasterCard and Cirrus **ATM** (bank open M-F 9am-3pm). The **police** are located in the southeast of town, at the corner of García Moreno and Río Tachina, six blocks uphill and two blocks to the right from the plaza at Eloy Alfaro and López Castillo. The **Centro de Salud** is one block down to the right of the intersection of Eloy Alfaro and López Castillo (walking towards the beach from the plaza). **Telephone code:** 05

Given its transportation-hub status, Pedernales has few enchanting accommodations, although many are decently maintained with good security. If arriving late at night, it's probably best to find a place in town rather than stumble around in the dark down by the beach. The Hotel Pedernales, Alfaro 6-18 and Manabí (tel. 681 092), three blocks up from the plaza, offers flowery bedsheets and the occasional *"Pepe te amo"* spray-painted on the wall to brighten up the drab concrete interior. Here's to you, Pepe. (Rooms s/20,000 per person, with bath and TV s/25,000.)

Pedernales's eateries are similarly bland, both up in town and down on the beach. **El Rocío,** Alfaro 605 and Velasco Ibarra (tel. 681 337), is across from Hotel Pedernales. Wooden chairs padded with leather offer a respite from the oft-repeated white plastic chair motif. Try the *desayuno* of eggs, bread, juice, and coffee (s/10,000), or basic *almuerzos* and *meriendas* with soup, rice, entree, and juice (s/12,000; open daily 7am-9pm). **Restaurant El Pedernal** (tel. 681 248), on Eloy Alfaro, two blocks away from the beach, returns to the old reliable plastic chairs and tables and also boasts a wall-length Coca-Cola label. Fish and shrimp (s/25-40,000) are prepared every way imaginable. (Open M-Sa 8am-8pm.)

BAHÍA DE CARÁQUEZ

Bahía was the first capital of the Cara people, who conquered the area 1,100 years ago before deciding to resettle in Quito. Now, almost 700 years after the Cara made their fateful move, *quiteños* are coming back. The presidency of Sixto Durán Ballén (1992-96) inspired the government to pump a disproportionate amount of its limited funds into the leader's hometown. Several presidencies later, the town still enjoys an usually high standard of living. Glittering with clean white high-rises and tastefully arranged palm trees, the Bahía de Caráquez (pop. 20,000) attracts a good portion of Ecuador's swanky elite, many of whom have a second home by the bay. Since Bahía declared itself an "Eco-city" in February 1999, a plethora of ongoing recycling and reforestation projects have been started, demonstrating that the town is trying to be more environmentally conscious even as it develops more roadways and taller buildings. Citizens battle trash with the ubiquitous, hypnotizing town slogan, *"Bahía no tiene una copia, cuidesela"* ("There's only one Bahía, so take care of it").

ORIENTATION AND PRACTICAL INFORMATION. Boats from San Vicente drop visitors off along the docks near the intersection of **Aguilera** and **Malecón** (a.k.a. **Alberto F. Santos**), the main street in town. Most services and accommodations are found along the parallel streets of **Bolívar, Montúfar,** and **Morales,** near their intersections with **Aguilera, Ante, Ascazubi, Riofrío, Arenas,** and **Checa.**

The **Bahía Airport** (in **San Vincente**) has daily flights to **Guayaquil** (45min., 8am and 3pm, s/285,000). Visit the **AECA** office (tel. 690 377), on Aguilera and Malecón, for more precise information. **Buses** leave from the informal station along Malecón a few blocks upriver from the docks. Buses go to **Guayaquil** (7hr., every hr. 5am-7pm, s/45,000) via **Portoviejo** (2½hr., s/13,000) and **Manta** (4hr., s/18,000). **Ferries** leave from the dock on Malecón and Aguilera for **San Vicente,** where buses depart for the northern coast. **Guacamayo Baníatours** (tel. 690 597; fax 691 412), Bolívar 906 and Arenas, offers Bahía info, maps, and local tour options that are more affordable with bigger groups (open M-Sa 8am-7pm, Su 8am-2pm). Traveler's checks can only be changed at **Banco de Guayaquil** (tel. 692 205), Riofrío and Bolívar. The bank's **ATM** accepts Visa and Plus. (Open M-F 9am-4pm.) The **police** station (tel. 690 054) is at Sixto Durán Ballén and 3 de Noviembre (open 24hr.). **Farmacia San Gregorio** (tel. 690 484) is located at Ascazubi and Montúfar (open M-Sa 8:30am-1:30pm and 2:30-10pm). **Clínica Viteri** (tel. 690 429), Riofrío and Montúfar, is open 24 hours. The **post office** is at Aguilera 108 and Malecón (tel. 691 177; open M-F 8am-5pm, Sa 9am-noon). **Internet access** is available at Bahía Bed and Breakfast (s/3,000 per min.; open daily 8am-8pm). Make calls from **PACIFICTEL** (tel. 690 020), Malecón and Arenas (open daily 8am-10pm). **Telephone code:** 05.

ACCOMMODATIONS AND FOOD. Bahía wasn't built for the budget traveler. While blessed with numerous luxurious waterfront establishments, Bahía is lacking when it comes to cheaper accommodations. The very shoddiest accommodations are concentrated a couple of blocks back from the beach, on Montúfar between Ante and Riofrío. The luxury resorts begin to pop up farther north along the peninsula. Luckily, there are a few places that offer something in between these extremes. The best option is **Bahía Bed and Breakfast Inn,** Ascazubi 316 and Morales (tel. 690 146). This inviting bed and breakfast has neat, clean rooms with fans, internet access, and an affable English- and French-speaking owner. Breakfast is complimentary. (Rooms s/30,000 per person, with bath s/45,000; cable TV s/5,000 extra.) **Hostal Santiguado,** Padre Laennen 406 and Intraigo (tel. 690 597 or 691 412), 11 blocks down river from Malecón and Aguilera, offers some of the cleanest budget accommodations and bathrooms in town as well as a tasty complimentary breakfast (s/40,000 per person, with bath s/50,000). **Hotel Palma** (tel. 690 467), Bolívar and Riofrío, across the street from Banco de Guayaquil, one block up from Malecón, somehow manages to appear cheerful despite the lack of sunlight. While the "private bath" is just a corner of the room set apart by a curtain, the place is clean. (Rooms s/15,000 per person, with bath s/30,000.)

There are plenty of excellent dining opportunities in Bahía, with some economical places along the **Río Chone** by the docks. Expect the typical coastal entrees—*ceviche*, fish plates, rice and seafood dishes—along with gorgeous views of the marina and the bluffs of San Vicente. **La Terraza** (tel. 690 787), on Malecón by the docks, has a great covered terrace decorated with fake flowers and terra-cotta pots. Good seafood dishes (s/15-22,000) come with tasty salads. (Open daily 10am-11pm.) **Muelle Uno** (tel. 691 500), on Malecón along the riverfront, is across from Banco Manabí. This newly renovated spot has been taken over by Bahía bourgeoisie but still offers reasonable prices amidst shaded tables and prime water views. The menu specializes in meat dishes (s/20-40,000) and offers little for vegetarians. Cheaper, greasier food is sold at the street entrance (open daily 10am-3am).

BEACHES. The rocky shores at the western end of Malecón are a popular surfing spot. Waves break so far out that surfers are able to avoid the rocks, though sometimes they get a little too close. Though Bahía itself does not have much of a beach, there is an excellent one not too far away. The relatively long walk is only possible at low tide, but cabs in town are eager to take people there (s/20,000) and will set a time to come and pick you up.

The MCI WorldCom Card.

The easy way to call when traveling worldwide.

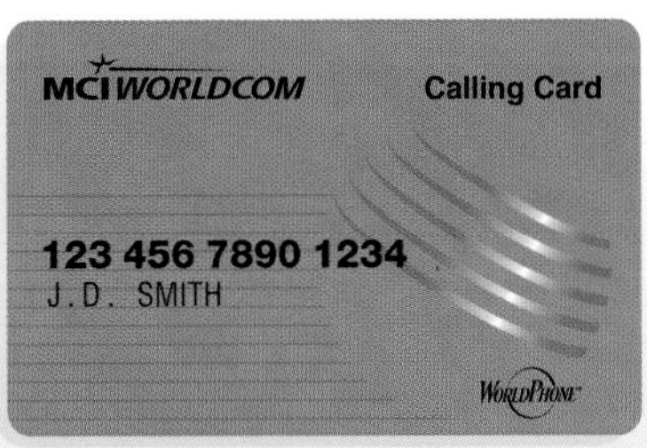

The MCI WorldCom Card gives you…

- Access to the US and other countries worldwide.
- Customer Service 24 hours a day
- Operators who speak your language
- Great MCI WorldCom rates and no sign-up fees

For more information or to apply for a Card call:
1-800-955-0925

Outside the U.S., call MCI WorldCom collect (reverse charge) at:
1-712-943-6839

COUNTRY		WORLDPHONE TOLL-FREE ACCESS #
Argentina (CC)		
	To call using Telefonica ■	0800-222-6249
	To call using Telecom ■	0800-555-1002
Australia (CC) ◆		
	To call using AAPT ■	1-800-730-014
	To call using OPTUS ■	1-800-551-111
	To call using TELSTRA ■	1-800-881-100
Austria (CC) ◆		0800-200-235
Bahamas		1-800-888-8000
Belgium (CC) ◆		0800-10012
Bermuda ✣		1-800-888-8000
Bolivia (CC) ◆		0-800-2222
Brazil (CC)		000-8012
British Virgin Islands ✣		1-800-888-8000
Canada (CC)		1-800-888-8000
Cayman Islands		1-800-888-8000
Chile (CC)		
	To call using CTC ■	800-207-300
	To call using ENTEL ■	800-360-180
China ❖		108-12
	For a Mandarin-speaking Operator	108-17
Colombia (CC) ◆		980-9-16-0001
	Collect Access in Spanish	980-9-16-1111
Costa Rica ◆		0800-012-2222
Czech Republic (CC) ◆		00-42-000112
Denmark (CC) ◆		8001-0022
Dominican Republic		
	Collect Access	1-800-888-8000
	Collect Access in Spanish	1121
Ecuador (CC) ✣		999-170
El Salvador		800-1767

FOLD

COUNTRY		WORLDPHONE TOLL-FREE ACCESS #
Finland (CC) ◆		08001-102-80
France (CC) ◆		0800-99-0019
French Guiana (CC)		0-800-99-0019
Guatemala (CC) ◆		99-99-189
Germany (CC)		0-800-888-8000
Greece (CC) ◆		00-800-1211
Guam (CC)		1-800-888-8000
Haiti ✣		193
	Collect Access in French/Creole	190
Honduras ✣		8000-122
Hong Kong (CC)		800-96-1121
Hungary (CC) ◆		00▼800-01411
India (CC) ❖		000-127
	Collect Access	000-126
Ireland (CC)		1-800-55-1001
Israel (CC)		
	BEZEQ International	1-800-940-2727
	BARAK	1-800-930-2727
Italy (CC) ◆		172-1022
Jamaica ✣	Collect Access	1-800-888-8000
	(From Special Hotels only)	873
	(From public phones)	#2
Japan (CC) ◆	To call using KDD ■	00539-121▶
	To call using IDC ■	0066-55-121
	To call using JT ■	0044-11-121
Korea (CC)	To call using KT ■	00729-14
	To call using DACOM ■	00309-12
	To call using ONSE	00369-14
	Phone Booths✣ Press red button, 03, then ∗	
	Military Bases	550-2255
Lebanon	Collect Access	600-MCI (600-624)

FOLD

COUNTRY		WORLDPHONE TOLL-FREE ACCESS #
Luxembourg (CC)		0800-0112
Malaysia (CC) ◆		1-800-80-0012
	To call using Time Telekom	1-800-18-0012
Mexico (CC)	Avantel	01-800-021-8000
	Telmex ▲	001-800-674-7000
	Collect Access in Spanish	01-800-021-1000
Monaco (CC) ◆		800-90-019
Netherlands (CC) ◆		0800-022-9122
New Zealand (CC)		000-912
Nicaragua (CC)	Collect Access in Spanish	166
	(Outside of Managua, dial 02 first)	
Norway (CC) ◆		800-19912
Panama		108
	Military Bases	2810-108
Philippines (CC) ◆	To call using PLDT ■	105-14
	To call using PHILCOM	1026-14
	To call using Bayantel	1237-14
	To call using ETPI	1066-14
Poland (CC) ✣		00-800-111-21-22
Portugal (CC) ✣		800-800-123
Puerto Rico (CC)		1-800-888-8000
Romania (CC) ✣		01-800-1800
Russia (CC) ◆ ✣		
	To call using ROSTELCOM ■	747-3322
	(For Russian speaking operator)	747-3320
	To call using SOVINTEL ■	960-2222
Saudi Arabia (CC) ✣		1-800-11
Singapore		8000-112-112
Slovak Republic		(CC) 00421-00112
South Africa (CC)		0800-99-0011
Spain (CC)		900-99-0014

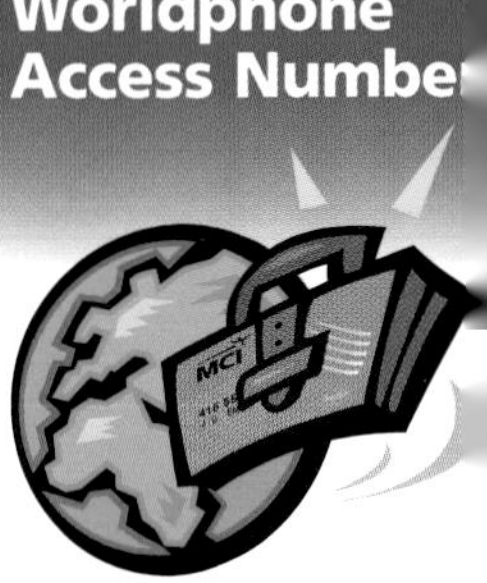

SIGHTS. The most popular excursion from Bahía is to **Islas Fragatas,** home to the largest colony of frigatebirds in Ecuador (the Galápagos excluded) as well as over 30 other species of marine bird. The best time to visit the Isla Fragatas is from August to December, the frigates' mating season. The tour usually takes three hours, and departure times vary depending on the tides. It is also possible to experience diverse coastal vegetation from Bahía. The nearby **Jororá** and **Punta Bellaca** make up all of the remaining 1% of Ecuador's tropical dry forest. From December to May, the forests are lush and green, while during the rest of the year, they become completely arid and void of vegetation, save the cactus and palo santo (its wood is burned as a bug repellent). The forests are also filled with animals and bromeliads, and are interesting to visit any time of year. A walk through the forest takes four hours. At the other end of the tropical forest are the wetlands and mangroves. These can be explored in canoes and, partly, by foot. For more information on visiting any of these sights as well as the nearby ruins of **Chirije,** visit the **Guacamayo Bahíatours** office in Bahía (tours US$12-22).

ENTERTAINMENT. Though many of Bahía's residents may be on the older side, there is plenty to do at night for the young or young-at-heart. **My House,** Teniente Rodríguez and Hurtado, a few blocks from the tip of the peninsula, is the most popular of the town's *discotecas*. Mounted bottles decorate the dull pink walls of this multi-room club. No need to worry; most of the high school aged patrons go home by midnight. (Cover s/30,000. Open Th-Sa 10pm-2am.) For a mellower night, visit the bar at the **Hostal Santiguado,** Intraigo and Padre Laennen. The music is good and the mixed drinks even better. (Open daily 7pm-2am.) For an even more low-key night, **Cínema Bahía,** Bolívar 1418 and Pinueza (tel. 690 363), shows VHS movies on a 20-inch television.

NEAR BAHÍA DE CARÁQUEZ: CANOA

While Canoa may have survived the fury of El Niño, the aftermath has left the town struggling. After the flooding of 1997-98, roads on either side of the town were left in ruin, and the already quiet tourist industry completely vanished. Regardless of weather disturbances, however, the uncrowded beaches of Canoa (17km north of San Vicente) remain beautiful and are disturbed only by a handful of shrimpers and the occasional scuttling crab. The waves draw a professional surfing competition here every February, but they usually calm enough to allow more relaxed water fun (e.g. late-night swimming with bioluminescent plankton).

There are two excellent hotels in this tiny town, one of which is **La Posada de Daniel** (tel. 691 201), along the main street in town across from the plaza where buses stop, 100m from the beach. Hillside cabins overlook the ocean in the distance, and each boasts a private bath and a balcony with a hammock. Guests can also stay in the 100-year-old main house, which offers well-kept rooms, astoundingly high ceilings, and private baths. Soft leather couches and a scattering of paperbacks, magazines, and board games make the three breezy living rooms a perfect meeting place for travelers. The amiable owner, Daniel, offers daytrips to a series of caves hidden in the cliffs of Canoa (free to Posada guests) and may even give you a lesson in surfing. (Cabins s/35,000 per person; rooms in main house s/25,000.) If you want the ultimate beachfront experience, rent a hammock from **Hotel Bambú** (tel. 753 696), at the north end of the beach (s/20,000 per person). Of course, Bambú also offers rooms with—naturally—bamboo beds. (Rooms s/40,000 per person, with bath s/60,000.) **Restaurant Tronco Bar,** 50m from the beach along the main road, offers diners a cool, laid-back environment. Dine in a hammock set on a sand floor on the ground level, or, if you prefer a chair, climb a rope-ladder to the second-floor loft. Cocktails will cost you s/10,000 and *concha* goes for s/15,000. (Open daily 9am-1am.) For a more traditional experience, **Restaurante Costa Azul,** on the main road, is 10 steps from the sand. Azul amazes with decor and ocean views, not to mention its battered fish (s/13,000; open daily 7am-8pm).

Transportation: Frequent **buses** depart for **San Vicente** (20min., every 30min., s/3,000) and **Pedernales** (2½hr., every 30min., s/20,000).

MANTA

Curiously situated on a stretch of coast running east to west and dominated by an immense harbor, Manta has long been a hub of seafaring activities. In pre-Colombian times Manta was home to an indigenous community, the Jocay, distinguished for their maritime accomplishments. Voyaging the high seas in balsawood rafts and dugouts, the Jocay made frequent excursions to Panamá and Perú; some historians assert they navigated as far north as México and south as Chile. Since the time of the Jocay, the town's location, so auspicious for sea travel and trade, has spurred speedy economic and population growth. Unfortunately, Manta's robust commerce and size (200,000 inhabitants and growing) have left its beaches dirtier than those of nearby coastal towns. Nevertheless, they do make Manta the most convenient place in the region to exchange money and stock up on supplies.

ORIENTATION

Buses enter Manta by way of **Eloy Alfaro** and present glimpses of **Tarquí,** the eastern beach, as they cross the inlet that separates it from central Manta. If you plan on staying in this part of town, you can save yourself a hike by asking to be dropped off before the **big bridge** crossing over to downtown Manta. The **terminal terrestre** is located just west of the **harbor,** not far from the bridge over the inlet. North of the bridge, Eloy Alfaro becomes **Malecón** and runs parallel to the water as it passes east of town, leading to Manta's **Murciélago** beach. In Manta's *centro*, the streets running parallel to the coast are **avenidas,** with numbers increasing the farther one gets from the water. Streets leading uphill away from the water are **calles,** numbered beginning at the Río Manta.

PRACTICAL INFORMATION

Airplanes: The **airport** is a few kilometers northeast of the *centro.* A taxi should cost s/ 20,000. **TAME,** Malecón and Calle 14, has flights to **Quito** (1hr.; M-Sa 8:10am, Su 7:10pm; s/426,000) and **Guayaquil** (25min.; M, Th, and F 11:20am; s/263,000).

Buses: The **terminal terrestre** is along 24 de Marzo just past Av. 4. A number of *cooperativos* link Manta to the rest of the coastal region as well as to the Sierra. All buses to northern destinations will pass through Portoviejo and all buses south go through Jipijapa. Buses leave from the *terminal* to: **Bahía de Caráquez** (4hr., every 30min. 5am-8pm, s/20,000); **Esmeraldas** (10hr., 5 per day 3:15am-9:15pm, s/60,000); **Guayaquil** (6hr., every 30min. 4am-7:30pm, s/34,000); **Jipijapa** (1½hr., every 20min. 5am-6pm, s/9,000); **Montecristi** (45min., every 15min. 6am-7pm, s/5,000); **Portoviejo** (1hr., every 20min. 5am-10pm, s/6,000); **Puerto López** (3hr.; every hr. 6am-noon, 3:15 and 4:15pm; s/19,000); and **Quito** (13hr., 10 per day 4am-10pm, s/ 65,000). Luxury buses go to **Quito** (10hr.; noon, 9, and 10pm; s/70-90,000).

Local Buses: The pale blue and white **colectivos** criss-cross the city (s/1,800), usually starting from the *terminal terrestre* and traveling east toward El Paseo Shopping via Tarquí or west toward the university and hospital via Malecón and the Manicentro.

Tourist Information: Ministerio de Turismo, Av. 3 1034 (Paseo José Maria Egas) and Calle 11 (tel. 622 944), provides maps of Manta. Open M-F 8:30am-5pm.

Travel Agencies: Delgado Travel (tel. 620 049), Av. 2 and Calle 13, offers car rental, an international delivery service, and currency exchange. Open M-F 8:30am-1pm and 3-6:30pm, Sa 9am-1pm. **Manatours** (tel. 621 020), Malecón and Calle 13 in Edificio Vigía. Open M-F 8am-1pm and 2-7pm. **Metropolitan Touring,** Av. 4 1239-45 and Calle 13 (tel. 623 090; fax 611 277). Open M-F 9am-1pm and 3-7pm.

Banks: Banks everywhere but most won't change foreign currencies. **Banco del Pacífico** (tel. 623 212), Av. 107 and Calle 103, Tarquí, exchanges cash and traveler's checks and has a 24hr. Cirrus/MC **ATM.** Open M-F 9:30am-2:30pm. **Filanbanco** (tel. 623 002), Av. 6 and 24 de Mayo, also offers a 24hr. Visa/Plus **ATM.** Open M-F 9am-2pm.

Laundromat: Lavamatic, Calle 11 604 and Av. 5 (tel. 610 154). Open M-Sa 9am-3pm.

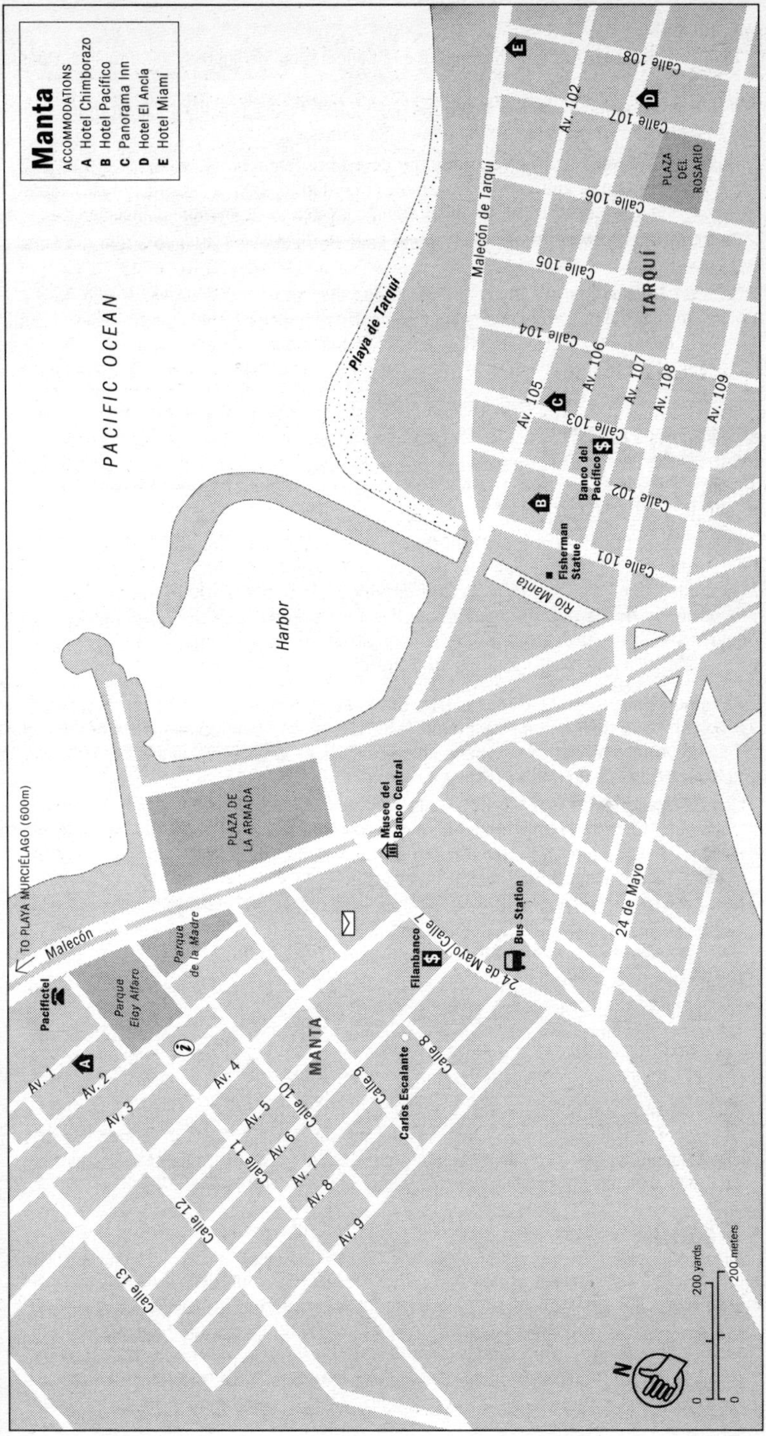

Manta

ACCOMMODATIONS

A Hotel Chimborazo
B Hotel Pacífico
C Panorama Inn
D Hotel El Ancla
E Hotel Miami

PACIFIC OCEAN
Harbor
Playa de Tarquí
Malecón de Tarquí
TARQUÍ
PLAZA DEL ROSARIO
Calle 108
Calle 107
Calle 106
Calle 105
Calle 104
Calle 103
Calle 102
Calle 101
Av. 102
Av. 105
Av. 106
Av. 107
Av. 108
Av. 109
Banco del Pacífico
Fisherman Statue
Río Manta
TO PLAYA MURCIÉLAGO (600m)
Malecón
PLAZA DE LA ARMADA
Museo del Banco Central
Parque de la Madre
Parque Eloy Alfaro
Pacifictel
Filanbanco
Bus Station
24 de Mayo/Calle 7
24 de Mayo
MANTA
Carlos Escalante
Av. 1
Av. 2
Av. 3
Av. 4
Av. 5
Av. 6
Av. 7
Av. 8
Av. 9
Calle 8
Calle 9
Calle 10
Calle 11
Calle 12
Calle 13
N
0 200 yards
0 200 meters

PACIFIC COAST

Emergency: Tel. 101.

Police: (Tel. 920 900), 4 de Noviembre and Calle 51, on the highway to Portoviejo. Open 24hr.

Pharmacies: Farmacia María Belén (tel. 620 243), Av. 3 and Calle 11, next to the Ministry of Tourism. Open M-F 8:30am-8pm, Sa 9am-3pm.

Hospital: Hospital Rodríguez Zambrano de Manta (**emergency** tel. 611 849 or 620 595), San Mateo and Calle 12, Barrio Santa Martha. Take a University bus headed along Malecón (s/1,800). Free 24hr. emergency treatment and ambulance service.

Post Office: (Tel./fax 624 402), Av. 4 and Calle 8. Open M-F 7:30am-6:30pm, Sa 8am-1pm.

Internet Access: General library of **Universidad Eloy Alfaro** along Via San Mateo. Take a bus toward the University and get out at the first entrance near the library. Access is on the 2nd floor (s/20,000 per hr.). Open M-F 9am-noon and 2-7pm.

Telephones: PACIFICTEL (tel. 622 700), Calle 11 and Malecón, charges for international calls. Open daily 8am-2:30pm and 3-10pm.

TELEPHONE CODE	05

ACCOMMODATIONS

Although most of the action is found in downtown Manta, the hotels there tend to be geared toward businessmen and wealthy Ecuadorians. Don't expect charming beachside villas; you're likely to find concrete highrises badly in need of a paint job. Malecón de Tarquí, the beachfront avenue, monopolizes the hotel market. An ocean view, no matter how polluted or obstructed, usually equals slightly higher prices; Manta's cheapest lodgings are found in the heart of Tarquí.

Panorama Inn (tel. 621 673; fax 611 552), Av. 105 and Calle 103. So maybe you wouldn't hire their interior decorator; fans, TVs, private bathrooms, and a hotel pool make up for the fact that nothing matches. Singles s/50,000; doubles s/100,000; about twice as much with A/C.

Hotel El Ancla (tel./fax 627 937), Calle 108 and Av. 105, is freshly painted with well-scrubbed rooms. Slightly pricey for singles, but doubles are a good deal. Try to avoid the windowless rooms. All rooms have private bathrooms. Singles with fan s/55,000, with TV and A/C s/90,000; doubles with fan and TV s/80,000, with A/C s/150,000.

Hotel Pacífico (tel. 622 475 or 623 584), Av. 106 and Calle 101. All rooms have turqoise and mustard walls and private bathrooms, and Pacífico offers the best price for A/C in town. Rooms s/40,000 per person, with A/C s/50,000.

Hotel Miami (tel. 611 743), Malecón and Calle 108. Welcome to Museum Miami, where living quarters are included with the price of admission. Artifacts from the indigenous cultures of Manta and the surrounding coast clutter the walls and reception area. Rooms haven't been as well preserved; showers are mildewy, lack curtains, and sometimes have drainage problems. Rooms s/20,000 per person.

Hostal Chimborazo (tel. 612 290), Av. 1 between Calles 11 and 12, is right in the center of Manta, which is fortunate since you may not want to spend time in your dark, dingy, noisy quarters. All rooms have fans and private baths. Some rooms have TVs as well, but everyone pays the same price. Singles s/30,000; doubles s/40,000.

FOOD

Most of the food in Manta once had gills. Thanks to its important seaport status, Manta has a substantial number of good eateries. Recent efforts to clean up the city's beaches have resulted in much improved beachside dining. All the restaurants clustered along Murciélago (identifiable by their matching green roofs and white walls) are referred to as Malecón Escénico. It's like a union of restaurants, all with the same menus, hours, and prices. Their counterpart along the Tarquí beach is called Parque de Mariscos. The environment here is grubbier but a little more laid-back—hammocks, plastic chairs and tables, and hundreds of Pilsener signs decorate the 19 grass huts. The claim to fame of these restaurants is that together they made the **largest ceviche in the world** in September 1997.

Beachcomber (tel. 625 463), Flavio Reyes and Calle 20, should probably be called Ranchcomber, because creatures of the sea don't appear much on the menu. The steak cut of the day (s/30,000) sends meat lovers to heaven. Small backyard patio complete with waterfall, stream, and bridge adds a romantic dimension to no-nonsense meat-eating. Open daily noon-3pm and 6pm-12:30am.

Cheers (tel. 620 779), Malecón and Calle 19, across from Murciélago. Sometimes after weeks of solo traveling, you want to go where everybody knows your name. Well, no one knows it here, but at least the food is good. Special seasonings make typical fish (s/17-24,000) and meat dishes (s/26-35,000) far less typical. Open daily noon-midnight.

Restaurante Carlos Escalante, Av. 6 and Calle 8, the small gray structure dwarfed by its neighboring buildings. Carlos never intended the place to be a restaurant; he just let some locals in for lunch one day, and suddenly his living room, which fits 6 tables at most, became one of the most popular diners in town. The *almuerzo* (s/12,000) and *ceviche* (s/12,000) merit the attention. Open M-F 9am-2pm, Sa 9am-noon.

Topi Tu Pizza (tel. 621 180), Malecón and Calle 15. Seating in the garden, on the rooftop, and along Malecón provides great views of the harbor. Pizzas are on the small side (individuals s/21-32,000). Open M-F noon-1am, Sa noon-2am, Su noon-midnight.

Picantería El Marino (tel. 610 071), Malecón de Tarquí and Calle 10, is probably the prettiest restaurant in this part of town. It also has some of the best *ceviche* (s/10-40,000) and rice dishes (s/22-28,000). Open daily 9am-5pm.

Restaurante Rey Mar (cell. tel. (09) 749 551), Malecón and Calle 16, provides some interesting Mexican reinterpretations on local foods. Everyone starts with *ceviche mexicano,* i.e. guacamole and chips, before moving on to tacos (s/12,000), burritos (s/14,000), or enchiladas (s/12,000). Open M-Sa 10am-10pm.

BEACHES

There are two stretches of beach in Manta: **Murciélago,** located in Manta just west of the *centro;* and **Tarquí,** encompassing the shores farther east. A five-minute drive or 20-minute walk west of the *centro*, Murciélago clamors with the typical assortment of *cevicherías* and sidewalk bars. The beach has a good deal of soft sand, and its proximity to the Oroverde and other luxury hotels means that it is maintained better than most public beaches. Murciélago receives the Pacific's currents directly, so there is a fair-sized surf, with up to three- or four-foot swells. Swimmers should keep in mind that the currents are quite strong. Tarquí's unpleasant, littered beach, on the other hand, could not be calmer. Placid as a lake at dawn, Tarquí's waters are a playground for **pelicans** and **frigatebirds** but offer little excitement for humans. Still, the breakneck landing tactics of the seabirds are amusing. Be sure to steer clear of the sewer outlet into the Río Manta to the north.

SIGHTS

A worthwhile walk can be taken around **Manta's harbor.** The busiest port on the central coast, Manta and its harbor teem with Old World fishing vessels and huge navy ships docked for refueling. Just over the bridge into Tarquí, across from Hotel Pacífico, is an oddly placed statue of a Manabí fisherman. It's hard to imagine how workers managed to erect the statue, since these days the stench is so strong that it's impossible to stay in the area for more than five minutes (his back is turned to the sewer outlet for a reason). The **Museo del Banco Central** (tel. 627 562), Malecón and Calle 7, in back of the Banco Central, has a small but worthwhile collection of indigenous artifacts accompanied by information on culture. The black-and-white photographs of an earlier Manta show it less populated but equally dependent on the sea. (Open M-F 9am-4pm. Admission s/10,000.)

ENTERTAINMENT

As befits an industrious city of this size, nights in Manta radiate with energy. The **Manicentro,** Flavio Reyes and Calle 24, is the focal point for a number of bars and clubs that coexist with a residential neighborhood. **K'chos,** Flavio Reyes and Calle 20, is a popular *discoteca* with two dance floors catering to very different musical tastes—*merengue* and *salsa* in the back; techno and house out front (cover s/ 30,000; open Th-Sa 8pm-5am). **Santa Fé Bar,** Calle 22 and Flavio Reyes, also heats up on the weekends. Look for fluorescent lights and a big crowd; listen for non-stop *salsa* and *merengue.* (Open Th-Sa 8pm-5am.) Another place in Manta that is always packed is **El Paseo Shopping,** on the highway to Portoviejo. A Western-style mall, El Paseo has a food court with Burger King and Kentucky Fried Chicken as well as a **Supercines 4,** which has several afternoon and evening show times (tickets M-Th s/14,000, F-Su s/28,000; stores open Su-Th 9am-8pm, F-Sa 9am-9pm).

NEAR MANTA: MONTECRISTI

Between the hurly-burly giants of Manta and Portoviejo lounges mellow Montecristi, patiently churning out its world-famous and sadly misnamed **Panama hats.** Though these high-grade hats have always been made in the countryside surrounding Montecristi, most of the ears their woven brims shelter have never heard of the place (see **Panama Hats Are Not from Panamá,** p. 406). Still, industrial anonymity has its benefits. The town's streets are tranquil and uncommercialized, with only the light traffic of grazing burros, wandering pigs, and the occasional bus.

Buses arriving in Montecristi drop passengers off along the central plaza, bordered uphill by the streets **Av. 9 de Julio** and **Av. Sucre,** and the cross-hill streets **23 de Octubre** and **San Andreas.** Buses passing by town en route to Manta or Portoviejo drop passengers off at the bottom of 9 de Julio; the plaza is a 20-minute walk from here. This tiny, shady park facing the adjacent church is home to Montecristi's practical establishments. The **police station** (tel. 606 324) is near the intersection of Sucre and 23 de Octubre (open 24hr.). The **post office** is in the same building (open M-F 8am-4pm). The **PACIFICTEL office,** on the central plaza at 9 de Julio and 23 de Octubre, has three booths for national calls (open M-Sa 8am-1pm and 2-8pm, Su 8am-noon and 2-6pm).

PANAMA HATS. Shopping in Montecristi is about as fast-paced as a ride atop one of the town's many donkeys. Montecristi's principal street, 9 de Julio, presents four or five different *sombrero* shops, all selling similar items at comparable

PANAMA HATS ARE NOT FROM PANAMÁ

Forget the name, forget your other misconceptions—Panama hats are made in Ecuador. With its origins in the ancient straw hats of the Manabí, the industry got its start in the 1830s, when the poverty-stricken inhabitants of Cuenca were forced to make hats for a living. Exports experienced a major boost after the 1855 World Expo, when King Napoleon III, and subsequently the rest of Europe, fell in love with the hat. Fifty years later, when Panama Canal workers used the hats as protection from the sun, the craze hit the States and the wrong name stuck. The industry reached its peak in 1946, when the export of 5 million hats accounted for 20% of Ecuador's earnings. Presidents and Hollywood stars alike sported the stylish *sombrero*—an integral part of 30s and 40s American fashion. Gangsters even took a liking to the hat in the 20s; to this day, a certain model is called the Capone.

Meanwhile, poor Ecuadorians worked for pennies, making hats that sold for a hefty profit in the States. The middlemen, processing factories, exporters, and retailers all took their share, leaving little for the actual artisans. These days, the hats are less popular, and imitation paper hats have taken a substantial bite out of the market. If their revenues continue to drop, the master artisans from the Montecristan countryside may have to put their straw away. So while you're in the neighborhood, help save a dying art and buy yourself an Ecuador hat.

prices. Hats start at s/20,000 for *gruesos* (made from the coarsest straw, usually taking two weeks per hat) and can get as expensive as s/400,000 for *extrafinos* (soft and delicate, taking up to three or four months to make). The best *extrafinos* can be rolled tight enough to pass through a man's ring. Prices drop steadily the more hats you promise to buy. Along with the famed Panama hats, most of these shops sell straw handbags, backpacks, and baskets.

Few hats are made in town; the *almacenes* selling goods to the public only finish the hats. To fully appreciate the labor and patience required by the time-consuming weaving process, one must head out to the surrounding countryside. If you are interested in seeing the art in process, the workshop of **José Chávez Franco** (tel. 606 343), on Rocafuerte, the street at the top of the hill running behind the church, two blocks to the right of 9 de Julio, gives demonstrations, provides a little background history, and offers some of the best prices in town.

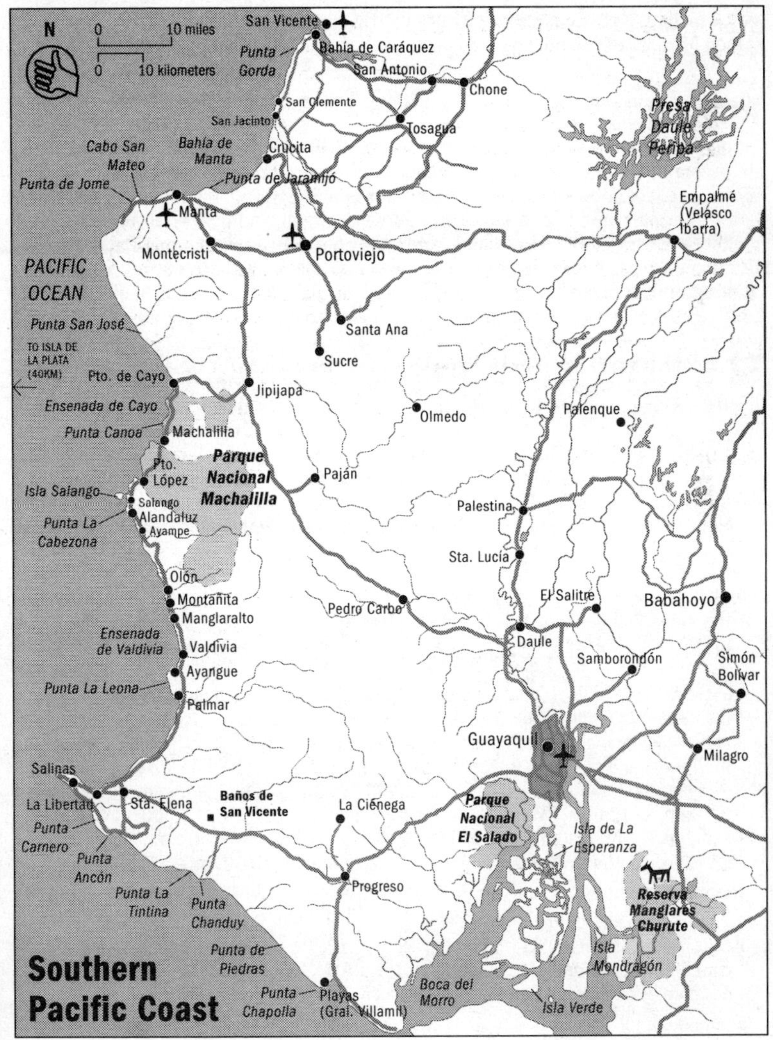

Southern Pacific Coast

SIGHTS. Aside from markets, Montecristi offers some interesting sights. The impressive church of **La Virgen de Montecristi,** on the corner of Sucre and 23 de Octubre, houses the venerated Virgin of Monserrat, said to have miraculously cured various sickly *montecristianos.* Besides being known for her medical practice, the Virgin is also known to be an avid walker, and legends describing her nighttime jaunts around Montecristi circulate through the town. There is a nice painting of the Sacred Family along the ceiling of the nave and of the Virgin above the altar. This pleasant village is home to two small museums. **Museo Arqueológico Largacha Ceballos,** 9 de Julio 436 (tel. 606 065), down the hill from the park, houses a small private collection of artifacts from the Manabí, Valdivia, and Chorrere cultures. It's a bit cluttered, but the *dueña* is happy to give detailed tours in Spanish. (Open M-F 10am-1pm and 4-6pm. Admission free.) **Casa de Eloy Alfaro,** Eloy Alfaro and 23 de Octubre, commemorates town hero and former president Eloy Alfaro with a selection of historical objects and a library. If you ask the librarians, they can give you a brief tour of the exhibit and provide you with a protracted description of Alfaro's assassination in Quito by dragging, dismemberment, and burning. (Open M-F 8am-12:30pm and 1:30-5pm, Sa 9am-4pm. Admission free.)

PORTOVIEJO

Originally situated on the coast, Portoviejo—"Old Port"—moved 40km inland to its present land-locked locale to avoid continual pirate attacks. In spite of the move, Portoviejo has retained its now-ironic name. Over the years the distance from the coast has become cultural as well as geographic. While its maritime neighbors seem more relaxed and carefree, Portoviejo's population plods along to the drone of its sober duties—commerce, industry, and education. However, although often regarded as the stiff-necked, straight-laced capital of an informal province, Portoviejo is well-respected by coastal residents.

ORIENTATION AND PRACTICAL INFORMATION

Portoviejo seems huge because the city is so spread out, but anything a tourist needs is in the *centro.* Buses entering the city usually drop visitors off along the north-south **Av. Universitaria,** at the intersection with **Ramos y Duarte,** before heading towards the **terminal terrestre** on **Av. Pedro Gual** on the western outskirts of town. From Universitaria and Ramos y Duarte, the **Parque Eloy Alfaro,** bounded by Universitaria and **Olmedo,** as well as by **Moreira** and **Alajuela,** is only two blocks away. **Sucre** and **Bolívar** bound the **Parque Central** between **Olmedo** and **Ricaurte.**

Airplanes: The **airport** is a couple of kilometers northwest of Portoviejo. **TAME** (tel. 650 000) has flights to Chile and América. **Guayaquil** (30min.; daily 8am; s/285,000, depending on the number of passengers) and **Quito** (45min.; M, W, and F 5pm; s/426,000). Open M-F 8am-12:30pm and 2:30-6:30pm.

Buses: As a major coastal transportation link, Portoviejo has a multitude of bus companies which leave from the *terminal terrestre.* To get to most places on the southern coast you'll probably have to go through Jipijapa first as a result of El Niño's damage to the roads. Buses go to: **Bahía de Caráquez** (3hr., every hr. 5am-9pm, s/13,000); **Guayaquil** (4hr., every hr. 2am-midnight, s/34,000); **Jipijapa** (3hr., every 20min. 4am-9:30pm, s/10,000); **Manta** (1hr., every 20min. 5am-10pm, s/6,000); **Pedernales** (6hr., every hr. 4am-6pm, s/40,000); **Quito** (10hr., every hr. 5am-11:30pm, s/55,000); and **Santo Domingo** (6hr., every 30min. 4:30-10:30pm, s/40,000).

Tourist Information: Ministerio de Turismo, Pedro Gual 234 and Montalvo (tel. 630 877), 3 blocks east of Morales. Open M-F 8:30am-5pm.

Banks: Filanbanco (tel. 637 550), Pacheco and Pedro Gual, exchanges both cash and traveler's checks and has a 24hr. Visa/Plus **ATM.** Open M-F 10am-2pm. **Banco del Pacífico**, 9 de Octubre and Rocafuerte, has a 24hr. MC/Cirrus **ATM.**

Emergency: Tel. 101.

Police: (Tel. 920 900), 3km outside of town along Via Crucita.

Pharmacies: Farmacia Galeno (tel. 639 748), Pedro Gual and Olmedo. Open M-Sa 8:30am-9pm, Su 9am-1pm.

Hospital: Regional Hospital de Portoviejo (**emergency** tel. 630 555 or 630 087), Rocafuerte and 12 de Marzo. Free 24hr. emergency treatment.

Post Office: Correos del Ecuador, Ricaurte 217 and Sucre (tel. 634 151). Open M-F 7:30am-7:30pm, Sa 7:30am-noon. **DHL/Western Union:** Pedro Gual 621 and Ricaurte (tel. 638 550). Open M-F 8:30am-1pm and 3-7pm.

Telephones: PACIFICTEL, 10 de Agosto and Pacheco. International calls are possible, but collect and calling card calls prohibited. Open daily 8am-9pm.

TELEPHONE CODE	05

ACCOMMODATIONS

As in many other coastal cities, visitors have to search long and hard to find a place that balances quality and economy. Most budget places are situated between the town's two parks. The more expensive places are located along Pedro Gual, especially around Chile.

Hostal Colón, Colón 212 and Olmedo (tel. 654 004), a block south of the Parque Central. The lobby looks like a beauty parlor, but pastel rooms and nice wooden furniture give off a more hotel-like feel. Don't expect to sleep late—there's an elementary school next door. Rooms with bath, TV, and fan s/40,000 per person, with A/C s/65,000.

Hotel Conquistador (tel. 651 472 or 631 678), 10 de Agosto and 18 de Octubre, 2 blocks up and 2 blocks west of Parque Central, is one of the cheaper executive haunts. Huge color TVs (with cable) take up half the room; your luggage will probably take up the other half. At least the bathrooms are scrubbed clean. Rooms with fan s/45,000 per person, with A/C s/80,000.

Hotel Pacheco (tel. 631 788) and **Hotel Victoria** (tel. 637 695), 9 de Octubre and Morales. Both share a huge maze of halls and rooms with 70 stark sleeping chambers. Super-clean rooms have super-thin mattresses. Mirrors decorate the walls; tiny skylights battle the darkness. Rooms s/10,000, with bath s/15-20,000, with TV s/25,000.

Hotel Paris (tel. 652 727), Sucre and Olmedo, right off the Parque Central. This 2nd-story hostel has collected some dust over the years, but the elegant interior design and antique finishes reveal that this establishment was once among the classiest in town. Ventilation in immense rooms is attempted with a fan and walls that sometimes don't quite reach the ceiling. All rooms have private baths. Rooms s/20,000 per person.

FOOD

The cuisine of Portoviejo is slightly different from that of its maritime neighbors. Though Portoviejo's *comedores* still offer many of the typical fish dishes, they concentrate more on beef entrees (e.g. *carne asada*) or fowl dishes (e.g. *seco de gallina*). Yogurt has become a popular snack food, and a taste for the sweet dairy treat has spawned a number of late-night, quasi-fast-food yogurt shops.

La Fruta Prohibida (tel. 637 167), Chile and 10 de Agosto, with another shop 1 block up the street, is one of the more fancy *fuentes de soda*. The fruit might be forbidden but it is fresh (fruit salads s/7-14,000). Tasty sandwiches (s/6-22,000) and shakes (s/10-12,000) keep this place full. Open daily 9:30am-11pm.

La Crema, Olmeda 204 and Sucre, right off Parque Central and under the Hotel Paris. Mirrored pillars vaguely resemble disco balls, but the financial district crowd is made up of bankers rather than clubbers. Very reasonably priced *almuerzos* and *meriendas* (each s/10,000) please everyone. Open daily 7am-8pm.

Restaurant Palatino, 10 de Agosto and Chile, 2 blocks up from Parque Central along 10 de Agosto. Palatino attempts to cater to the business community with efficient service. Fans are powerful enough to keep the tie-choked clientele from fidgeting. All plates served with a complimentary beverage. *Almuerzos* s/10,000, fish or meat dishes s/14,000. Open M-Sa 7:30am-5pm.

SIGHTS AND ENTERTAINMENT

CASA DE CULTURA. For a capital city, Portoviejo has a sad scarcity of stuff to see and do. The Casa de Cultura was flooded by a mudslide during the El Niño days. Check to see if the mud has been cleared. When functional, this center of culture hosts occasional theatrical presentations, dance performances, concerts, art expositions, and conferences. Events are held three or four times per month, with special festivities on August 9th and the week of October 9-18. *(Sucre and García Moreno, 4 blocks west of the Parque Central. Tel./fax 631 753. Open M-F 8am-noon and 3-6pm.)*

FÚTBOL. *Fútbol* fanatics might want to catch a live match while in town. The local professional team, **Liga de Portoviejo Universitaria,** is competitive within Ecuador's second-tier league and draws large, enthusiastic crowds. Games are scheduled throughout the week, so check the paper. Matches are played at the **Estadio Reales Tamarindos.** *(Stadium located on the right-hand side of Universitaria as you head north, 500m outside town. Admission s/15-20,000.)*

OTHER SITES. The town's two parks also offer visitors some diversion. The larger parque, **Eloy Alfaro,** boasts the town's largest **cathedral,** with a big earth-tone mosaic dome, beautiful inlaid stone altar and front piece, and interesting visual depictions of the Bible (like the disciple donning sunglasses in a Last Supper painting). The smaller **Parque Central** has a correspondingly smaller chapel that seems a miniaturized model of the *catedral.* By far the cleanest building in town, it presents an earth-tone mosaic dome, twin spires, marble floors, and immaculately white walls.

NIGHTLIFE. Nightlife in the city is surprisingly limited. **Barra'bas** (tel. 635 590), Pacheco and Córdoba, stands out among the few clubs, perhaps because of its bright pink paint job (open daily 7pm-2am).

NEAR PORTOVIEJO: CRUCITA

Only an hour's bus ride from Portoviejo, Crucita is the favorite beachside getaway for the capital's landlocked residents. Anyone arriving during high tide might wonder about this popularity, as there is almost no beach to be seen. But when the tide goes out, it leaves clean, firm sand bordered by relatively calm, green-blue water.

Crucita is filled with reasonably priced hotels, the best of which is the **Hostal Rey David** (tel. 676 143; fax 676 107), on the far north end of the boardwalk. The hostel is incredibly clean and nicely decorated, with new furniture, a flowery arbor, and a small pool. Unfortunately, such quality comes with a price. (Rooms s/50,000 per person.) Though some might call it tacky, **Hotel Hipocampo** (tel. 676 167), on the south end of Malecón near the road to the bus stop, has 75 rooms, all with private baths and fans, some with ocean views (s/30,000 per person). A last decent choice is **Hostería Las Cabañitas** (tel. 652 660), halfway down Malecón. Small, basic *cabañas* with dreary private baths offer little excitement, but the locally popular restaurant in front serves as a diversion. (Rooms s/25,000 per person.)

Though just about every building along Malecón sports a restaurant sign, few actually function on a regular basis. Most hostels also have a restaurants with cleanliness and quality corresponding almost perfectly to that of the accommodations. **Alas Delta #1** (tel. 676 106) or **Alas Delta #2** (tel. 676 116), both on the far south end of the boardwalk, serve very similar food at comparable prices; the only difference is the atmosphere. #1 is a sporty place decorated with hanging tennis rackets, a poster of a hang-glider in mid-flight, and plenty of flowers and palm trees. #2 is clean and serene. Christmas-colored light bulbs and a gorgeous second-floor ocean vista relax and soothe. (Both open daily 9am-9pm.)

Transportation: Transportes Crucita buses from Portoviejo (1hr., every 15min. 5:30am-7pm, s/5,700) drop visitors off at the plaza, two blocks along the dirt road from the beach.

NEAR PORTOVIEJO: BAHÍA DE MANTA

On weekends, some locals head to the tiny fishing villages situated between Portoviejo and Bahía de Caráquez, collectively known as Bahía de Manta. The two principal Bahía towns are **San Clemente** and **San Jacinto.** While they are not much as beaches, the stretches of sand extending past these towns offer plenty of solitude and an opportunity to observe a different culture.

The hotels and dining are much better in San Jacinto than in neighboring San Clemente, so come here for sustenance and rest. **Hotel San Jacinto,** along the beach on Malecón, is the most prominent building in town, and has enough space to house just about everyone who's ever visited Bahía de Manta. Cheery rooms face the ocean and cost the same as the rest. (Rooms s/35,000 per person.) **Cabañas Los Almendros,** across the street, is cheaper with plainer-than-plain rooms and baths so dark it's hard to see if they're clean (s/20,000 per person). There are a number of food stands and restaurants along Malecón. The bar-restaurant **Vanessa** is towards the middle of the beach on Malecón. The limited menu leaves the choice of seating your most difficult decision. Repose at a wood or plastic table and lounge in a hammock, beach chair, or sofa as you dine. *Desayunos* (s/8,000) and *almuerzos* (s/15,000) are cheap and filling. If you are ready for a meal immediately after an ocean frolic, head to **Restaurant Gemita,** on the highway five minutes from the beach. Scarf down enormous portions of fish, rice, beans, and thinly sliced banana chips (s/10-14,000), while keeping your eyes peeled for the bus back to Portoviejo. (Open daily 6am-7pm.)

The **San Clemente** beach has limited space, but as one walks south toward San Jacinto, the sands get much wider. Aggressive tides keep the beach smooth, damp, dark, and firm—an excellent combination for pick-up games of *fútbol* and long walks, but less than perfect for casual lounging. The beach is usually empty, and the waters are so gentle that currents will have trouble storming even the puniest of sand castles. A 15-minute walk along Malecón leads to the beach at **San Jacinto,** 3km south of San Clemente. From Portoviejo, the bus drops visitors off on the dirt road in front of the town church. Facing away from the church, head right down the dirt road, turning right at Restaurante Laurita. The beaches here offer a unique attraction: a fascinating display of tuna fishing. Seven or eight local fishermen line up a chain on the shore holding ropes and tugging with all their might at huge tuna nets. When the nets are finally dragged onshore, people descend on them, tossing the fish into the truck beds as quickly as possible while gulls and pelicans make kamikaze dives for scraps. Unfortunately, these sands sometimes become a convenient road for vehicles loaded with dead sea life.

Transportation: Buses from Portoviejo go to **San Clemente** and **San Jacinto** (2hr., every 30min. 5am-7pm, s/8,000). Any bus between Bahía de Caráquez and Portoviejo passes the turn-offs to either town; just ask the driver to stop (s/8,000 from Portoviejo, s/5,000 from Bahía de Caráquez).

JIPIJAPA

Most of the fun associated with Jipijapa ("heepy-hoppa"), 60km south of Manta, comes from its bouncy, fun-to-say name. Otherwise, this city of 60,000 only offers some of the practical facilities lacking in many coastal cities. Situated between Manta and the southern coast's primary beaches, Jipijapa chiefly serves to shuttle eager sun-seekers and anxious surfers to the sandy shores of communities such as Puerto López and Montañita. Most travelers stay only long enough to get their shoes polished in shady Parque Simón Bolívar. Stock up on sucres in Jipijapa while you can: there are very few places to change money or cash traveler's checks between here and La Libertad.

Most everything you'll need is located near the central plaza, consisting of **Parque Simón Bolívar** and a plaza overlooked by an anonymous female statue. **Sucre** on the north and **Bolívar** on the south are the east-west streets that border the plaza, while north-south **Colón** and **Av. 9 de Octubre** border it on the east and west, respectively. The **terminal terrestre** is a few kilometers west of the *centro*, near the traffic circle. **Long-distance buses** leave from the *terminal* bound for: **Guayaquil** (2½hr., every 30min. 7:30am-7:30pm, s/20,000); **Puerto López** (1¼hr., every hr. 6am-6pm, s/10,000); and **Manta** (1¼hr., every 15min. 5am-6pm, s/9,000). **Local buses** between the *terminal* and the center of town cost s/1,000; **taxis** cost s/7,000. **Filanbanco** (tel. 601 262 or 601 620; fax 600 455), Bolívar and 9 de Octubre, takes traveler's checks, exchanges cash, and has a 24-hour Visa **ATM** (open M-F 10am-1:30pm). **Banco del Pichincha** (tel. 600 472; fax 600 800), on Sucre between 9 de Octubre and Colón, changes money, but doesn't accept traveler's checks (open M-F 8am-3pm). **Emergency:** Tel. 101. The **police station** (tel. 600 444) is several blocks east of the plaza on Bolívar at Antepara. Jipijapa's streets are packed with pharmacies, including **Farmacia Manabí** (tel. 600 510), 9 de Octubre and Bolívar (open daily 8am-10pm). If you're still aching, **Hospital Cantonal Jipijapa** (tel. 600 377), Espejo and 12 de Octubre near the *terminal* in Ciudadela Paralis Igualis, has 24-hour emergency service. **EMETEL,** Bolívar and 9 de Octubre, across from Filanbanco, has no booths that make international calls (open daily 8am-10pm). **Telephone code:** 05.

Should you inexplicably find yourself staying in Jipijapa, you have a few options for accommodations and food. **Hostel Mejía**, Mejía and Colón, two blocks south of the plaza, doesn't have a telephone and is very secretive about their rooms. Don't plan on inspecting a room before paying for it. However, prices are a good deal cheaper than other options in town. (Rooms s/15,000 per person, with bath s/20,000). **Hostal Jipijapa** (tel. 601 365; fax 600 783), at Santistevan and Eloy Alfaro, provides a clean and modern experience ten minutes away from the plaza. All rooms have good fans and private bath. Also, dancers heepy-hoppa in the **disco** here on Friday and Saturday nights. (Singles s/55,000, with A/C and hot water s/88,000; doubles s/100,000, with A/C and hot water s/120,000). Not surprisingly, while unremarkable *comedores* can be found near the plaza, Jipijapa has few quality restaurants. **The Barent** (tel. 601 495), on Colón just south of the plaza, serves a la carte items (*arroz con pollo* and *churrasco* both s/15,000) as well as *desayuno* (s/10,000), *almuerzo* (s/12,000), and *merienda* (s/15,000; open daily 7am-7pm). **Rico Pollo**, on Bolívar between 9 de Octubre and Colón, is the closest you'll get to fast food in this town. Hamburgers (s/3,000) and whole-chicken-and-potato meals will feed multiple mouths (s/46,000; open 8am-11:30pm).

NEAR JIPIJAPA: PUERTO DE CAYO

Puerto de Cayo is a very sleepy beach town 28km southwest of Jipijapa. The beach is long, and the density of trash seems significantly lower than in resort towns such as Playas or Manta, but infrequent tourism has left the streets and boardwalk overgrown with weeds. It's not a particularly exciting place and it's a veritable ghost town during the *temporada baja*. As a possible base for Parque Machalilla excursions, Puerto de Cayo comes in a distant second to Puerto López. The only time of year when this sleepy town sees any action is during the December-February holiday for Ecuadorian universities. The **Hostal los Frailes** (tel. 601 365; same management as Hostal Jipijapa, above), on the Malecón, provides very clean and comfortable rooms with private bath (s/66,000 for 1 person; s/70,000 for 2 people). More expensive rooms with more amenities are also available. **Hostal Zavala's**, toward the southern end of the Malecón, has airy rooms with firm beds, private baths, and fans; some also have hot water and tantalizing ocean views (s/50,000 per person, group discounts available). Both hostels have restaurants attached, serving typical seafood dishes. Los Frailes' prices (s/24,000-50,000) are twice as much as Zavala's (s/12,000-20,000). Alternatively, in the *pueblo*, the area just north of the beach part of town accessible only by the highway, **Expedición Cayo** (Manta tel. 628 930) provides clean, spacious, oceanfront cabins with porches, hot water, and kitchens (s/50,000 per person; 10% IVA additional charge; cabins fit 2, 4, or 6). The hotel is located at the end of the main east-west street in town.

PUERTO LÓPEZ

Puerto López isn't much of a tourist-oriented town. Packs of dogs roam through its surprisingly muddy streets, and an unusual species of aquatic swine (more commonly known as the "sea pig") has been spotted along its beach. However, the brightly painted signs for travel agencies and restaurants remind visitors that this fishing town reels in tons of tourists as well, if only because of its proximity to Parque Nacional Machalilla and its famed Isla de la Plata. Although the town itself isn't much to look at, the people are friendly, the restaurants and bars are nice places to meet other travelers, and the nearby national park is worth a visit.

ORIENTATION AND PRACTICAL INFORMATION

The principal road in town, **Machalilla,** continues north to Jipijapa and south to La Libertad. Buses stop here on the corner of **Calle Córdova. Malecón,** also called **Julio Izurieta,** the street closest to the sand, runs parallel to Machalilla two or three blocks to the west. The streets parallel to Córdova, from south to north, are **Eloy Alfaro, Atahualpa, Alejo Lascano,** and **Gonzales Suárez.** The **bus stop** is located at the southern end of town, at Machalilla and Córdova.

Long-distance buses travel North to: **Manta** (3hr., every 30min. 5:30am-5pm, s/20,000) and **Jipijapa** (1¾hr., every 30min., 5am-7pm, s/11,000). South-bound buses run through town (every 30min. 5am-5:30pm) and continue to: **Salango** (15min., s/3,000); **Alandaluz** (30min., s/5,000); and **Manglaralto** (1½hr., s/15,000). The **Machalilla National Park Headquarters** (tel. 604 170), at Eloy Alfaro and Machalilla, has information and a park interpretation center (open daily 8am-noon, 2-6pm). Many tour companies in Puerto Lopez offer excursions to the park. **Exploratur** (tel. 604 123), Malecón and Córdova, has some staff with English experience (open daily 7:30am-7:30pm). Also highly recommended are **Machalilla Tour Agency,** Malecón 119 and Julio Izurieta (tel. 604 221 and 604 206; open daily); **Mantaraya** (tel. 604 233; in Quito (02) 462 871 or 447 190), on Malecón a few blocks north of Córdova (open daily 7am-8pm); and **Bosque Marino** (tel. 604 107), on Machalilla and Córdova (open daily 7am-9pm). There are no **banks** in Puerto López, so load up on *sucres* before you arrive. The **police** (tel. 604 101), are at Machalilla and Atahualpa (open 24hr.). **Farmacia Edicita** (tel. 604 122), Machalilla and Atahualpa, is across the street from the post office in the center of town (open M-Sa 7am-9pm, Su 7am-5pm). Although there is no **hospital** in town, the health center, **Centro de Salud de Puerto López,** is at the end of Machalilla, seven or eight blocks north of the *centro.* There is a sign, but it only faces north; bear right at the Tienda Rosita sign on the right side of the road. (Open M-F 9am-5pm). Around the corner from PACIFICTEL stands the **post office,** at Atahualpa and Machalilla (open M-F 8am-noon and 2pm-5:30pm). **PACIFICTEL,** Machalilla and Eloy Alfaro, only makes national calls (open M-Sa 8am-12:30pm, 2pm-5:30pm, and 7pm-9:30pm, Su 8am-12:30pm). **Telephone code:** 05.

ACCOMMODATIONS

There aren't too many places to stay in Puerto López, so it's a good idea to call ahead to reserve a spot, particularly in the busy season (June-August).

Hostal Villa Colombia (tel. 604 105 or 604 189), is on the first right off Córdova after Machalilla when heading away from the beach; the hostel is on the left. Colombia offers friendly management, hot water, inexpensive laundry service, free use of kitchen facilities, and clean, simple rooms. Dorms s/25,000 per person; singles with bath s/35,000; doubles with bath s/60,000.

Hotel Pacífico (tel. 604 147), Suárez and Malecón, is only 50m from the beach at the northern end of Malecón. The lush courtyard is laden with hammocks that swing from sun-blocking palms. Simple but clean *cabañas* with impeccable common baths are a welcome change from hostel hallways. Dorm-style *cabañas* s/40,000 per person; singles s/50,000. For an upscale splurge, fancy hotel rooms at Pacífico provide pristine tile in place of concrete and transform your communal bath into a warm private shower. Singles s/120,000; doubles s/160,000.

Hostel Tuzco (tel. 604 132), Córdova and Juan León Mera, 2½ blocks east of Machalilla. The bright color scheme and immaculate housekeeping make up for the muddy road you take to reach it. Rooms fit up to 6. Despite the hot water and a private bath, the single fan might have trouble keeping everybody cool. Dorms s/36,000 per person.

FOOD

Many of Puerto López's restaurants look (and are) surprisingly similar to one another. In addition to cheap, generic *desayunos*, *almuerzos*, and *meriendas* (s/10-20,000), a few choice restaurants serve up local delicious specialties.

Yubarta Café Bar, is at the far northern end of Malecón. Walk past Hotel Pacífico for a few blocks, cross the bamboo bridge and it's on your right. Yubarta get its natural coffee beans and cocoa from an old man who owns a small farm in the mountains around Puerto López. He grows, processes, and delivers these ingredients **by hand**. Then, Enrique and Alegría painstakingly prepare them into a pot of joe and a chocolate cake—creating one of the best desserts you'll ever eat in your life. Open daily 10:30am-until you're done eating.

Spondyllus Bar and Restaurant, Malecón and Córdova (tel./fax 604 128), serves outstanding eats in an international Latin milieu. Burlap ceiling looks like it was just shipped in from Colombia. Try the restaurant's namesake, *ceviche de spondyllus* (conch ceviche, s/25,000), or *camaron al ajillo* (shrimp in a garlic sauce, s/25,000). Hamburgers, spaghetti, and vegetarian dishes are also available. Open daily 8am-11pm, and may turn into a *discoteca* if the crowd is hoppin'.

Restaurant Carmita (tel. 604 149), Córdova and Malecón, has been around for 28 years, and the fish is as fresh as ever. Try the house specialty, *pescado al vapor,* a fabulous, non-greasy fish-and-vegetable dish (s/20,000). Carmita also offers a sizeable vegetarian menu. Open daily 7am-11pm.

SIGHTS AND ENTERTAINMENT

Puerto López is an ideal base from which to explore the marvels of **Parque Nacional Machalilla** (see p. 416). Multiple tour companies offer trips to the park and battle for tourists' bucks with bigger and better bargains (see p. 413), especially to **Isla de la Plata,** situated 40km off the coast from Puerto López. Fortunately, the prices among most of the agencies are standardized, so you don't always have to shop around to get the best deal. Exploratur and Mantaraya offer **scuba** packages as well. If you'd rather keep your feet on solid ground, Puerto López's own **beach** meets the challenge with brown, rather dirty sand. It's not the best place for sand castles, but the waters are tranquil and the pickup *fútbol* games intense.

NEAR PUERTO LÓPEZ: SALANGO

Situated 5km south of Puerto López, Salango sits patiently, like an old man with a story to tell. Salango's tale comes from beneath its sands, e home to a massive collection of **archaeological artifacts.** Dating back almost 5,000 years, six different pre-Hispanic communities thrived here, leaving behind scatterings of everyday life as well as jewelry and artwork. Many of the pieces have been excavated and now fill Salango's archaeological museum, but a large number remain trapped in the silent sand, buried beneath Salango's **fish factory.** The factory itself is the subject of another kind of story—the firing of the factory's Salangan workforce after a wage strike in 1989 and the hiring of people from neighboring towns to take their places. Salango has been hit hard by the lay-offs, and most locals have returned to unpredictable—and often unprofitable—fishing and agricultural careers.

Salango lacks accommodations, but it does support a few restaurants. A big bright sign welcomes visitors to the oft-praised **Delfín Mágico**, 200m south of the museum, which serves affordable and deliciously fresh shrimp and *ceviche* (s/22-

EL NIÑO THROWS A TANTRUM Known as the nastiest little boy to hit the Pacific, El Niño is a warm-water current that brings the rainy season to Ecuador's coastal region and the Galápagos Islands. Its deceptively diminutive name comes from its advent around Christmas, making it the second "boy child" of the season. Most years, El Niño is well-behaved, leaving on cue in late April or early May. However, in those fateful years when the child decides to act up, havoc ensues. The mention of the 1982-83 bout still brings shudders from those in the western lowlands, but the 1997-98 El Niño left a crippled and broken Ecuador in its wake, replacing its predecessor in the Ecuadorian annals of naturally-wrought suffering and destruction. The Pacific coast was devastated: rivers flooded, destroying homes and buildings, clean water became dangerously scarce, and highways and other roads collapsed. Fishing and farming were severely affected as well, damaging the livelihood and economy of the region and, in turn, the country. However, even in the first few months following the brunt of El Niño's damage, Ecuador started to rebuild with unprecedented speed. Private companies were hired to repair the coastal highway and have made remarkable progress. While buses can now pass with relative ease through the coast, and tourism continues to thrive, El Niño's wrath cannot be forgotten. Towns like Montañita are threatened by an ever-eroding shoreline. Potable water also still must be brought in by truck. One can only wait to see what Santa brings next year.

33,000). Try a fish dish in *mani* (fish in peanut sauce, s/22-33,000), a specialty of the peanut-producing Manabí province. (Open daily 8am-8pm or later.) **El Pelicano,** just down the street, is another bamboo-adorned restaurant offering a variety of local seafood and rice dishes, for similar prices (open daily 7am-10pm).

Only 15 minutes and a s/3,000 bus ride separate Salango from Puerto López. But this quick trip can take you back 5,000 years at the **Museo a los Balseros del Mar del Sur,** a well-preserved and informative collection chronicling the six cultures found at the site. The **Valdivia** culture is the oldest, subsisting from 3,000-2,000 BC, followed by the **Machalilla** (2,000-1,500 BC), **Chorrera and Engoroy** (1,500-500 BC), **Guangala/Bahían** (500 BC-AD 500), and **Manteño** (AD 500-AD 1,000). For more information, see **The Earliest Inhabitants,** p. 43. Each culture has separate glass encasements, labeled with Spanish descriptions that present various artifacts from the areas of Salango, Isla de la Plata, Puerto López, Machalilla, and Agua Blanca. The museum also has, among other things, an example of the kind of balsa raft used by some of these cultures. Reasonably-priced replicas of the artifacts and other crafts are sold in the gift shop. (Museum open W-Su 9:30am-5pm. Admission s/15,000, children s/7,000, students s/12,000.) The striking **Isla Salango** lies 2km offshore; day trippers sometimes come here from Puerto López. Although somewhat littered, Salango's sheltered cove is a very pretty spot, where fishing boats bob in the water, and green mountains loom overhead.

NEAR PUERTO LÓPEZ: PUEBLO ECOLÓGICO ALANDALUZ

Travel in Ecuador can be stressful for environmentalists: riding buses without emissions controls, using plastic bottles that will never be recycled, and spending tourist dollars that encourage unscrupulous businesses to move into fragile ecosystems. The **Pueblo Ecológico Alandaluz,** however, puts such anxieties to rest. Arranged like a garden-filled village, Alandaluz is a gorgeous beach resort just off the road between Puerto López and Montañita. It was recently rated as one of the seven best **socially responsible ecotourist projects** in the world. Constructed wholly of rapidly growing, easily replenishable materials, Alandaluz is a temple of bio-friendliness, making daily offerings to an afflicted Earth goddess. Comically, visitors can make their contribution by frequenting the bathroom, where waste is mixed with sawdust and dried leaves to speed up the decomposition process. (For more traditional flushers, there are ordinary toilets near the reception area.)

THE COMPLEX. The resort itself is set up like a tiny village. In addition to the two main buildings with regular rooms, there are several beach-front cabins, complete with bamboo patio-decks and ocean views. All of the pristine bamboo quarters are festooned with cheerful curtains and mosquito nets and are equipped with bamboo bed frames and bamboo water-bottle holders. The one exception is the **Cabaña del Arbol,** the honeymoon suite. Rather than a bamboo construction, it is built into a live tree—you can feel the structure sway as you and that special someone climb the tree-branch ladder into your lofty love nest. The center boasts plentiful amenities. Relax at a cozy bamboo **bar,** furnished with cushioned straw couches and an outdoor furnace (open daily 4pm-late). Near the bar, a first-class **restaurant** specializes in vegetable and seafood dishes. The chef uses an oven constructed of hardened fecal matter to create his pride and joy, the *viudo de pescado* (an enormous serving of baked fish served inside a bamboo cane, s/38,000), or a variety of other chicken, fish, and vegetable dishes cooked in bamboo or coconut. (*Desayuno* s/17,000, *almuerzo* and *cena* both s/30,000; restaurant open daily 8am-10am, 1pm-3pm, and 7pm-9pm). Eco-conscious extravagance has its price, though. You can either **camp** (s/20,000) or use their tent (s/25,000). For your comfort, impeccably maintained common bathrooms scattered around the grounds have both hot and cold water. From there, the prices climb. You can pay extra for private baths, ocean views, eco-toilets and/or luxury non-cabin rooms. (Singles from s/65-260,000; doubles s/95-370,000; triples s/120-450,000; quads s/135-462,000.)

Alandaluz's beach is beautiful and largely uninhabited, but the **surf** is monstrous, so a swim amounts to a salty pummeling. If you have a surfboard, and you know how to use it, however, the water is ideal. Generally slow-breaking, crumbling waves—with 5-7 ft. faces in summer and 9-10 ft. faces in winter—break in both directions. Alandaluz doesn't always have the hollow, echoing barrels of Montañita, but it also doesn't have the crowds. Alandaluz is also a convenient distance from **Parque Nacional Machalilla,** and an on-site travel agency lets visitors take advantage of its location. **Pacarina Travel** (tel. 601 203), in the main house, offers tours by land or sea into the park. Prices are comparable to those in Puerto López (US$30 per person, including lunch). Pacarina can also arrange tours to **Cantulapiedra,** Alandaluz's organic farm (1½hr., s/140,000 per person, including breakfast).

TRANSPORTATION. Alandaluz is 6km south of Salango (a 30min., s/5,000 bus ride from Puerto López). It is practically impossible to miss on the west side of the road. Even if you don't have time to spend the night, a 10-minute walk through the well-kept gardens provides an excellent feel for this unique place, and its beaches are certainly worth a visit. Reservations are recommended during the high season of July and August (tel. (09) 983 867 or Quito tel. (05) 504 084).

PARQUE NACIONAL MACHALILLA

Parque Nacional Machalilla's 55,000 hectares preserve archaeological riches, one of the most pristine cloudforests in Ecuador, and the only protected virgin dry tropical forest in South America. The arid, sometimes colorless tropical forests may not be part of the most beautiful ecosystem around, but they provide for some of the most stunning and cleanest beaches in the country. To make things even better, **Isla de la Plata** summarizes the Galápagos experience—elegant sea birds, jovial sea lions, seasickness—for only a fraction of the cost: hence the nickname "a poor person's Galápagos."

Most visits to the park take the form of daytrips that leave Puerto López early in the morning and return in the mid- or late-afternoon. From Puerto López, **buses** make the 9km trip to the Los Frailes gate (s/7,000). From there, it is a short hike to the *cabañita* and the rest of the grounds. Most sites in the park cannot be visited without a guide, but relatively inexpensive trips can be arranged through any of the tour agencies in Puerto López (see p. 413). The park admission (US$20) is good for at least a week. In general, trips are cheaper for bigger groups, so ask around at the agencies to see if a group is looking for another member. Buses leave for the park entrance from Machalilla (s/7,000) and Córdova (s/3,000). Check the schedule at the bus office in Puerto López. For more info on Parque Nacional Machalilla, visit the **headquarters** in Puerto López (see p. 413). Before embarking on a particular trip, find out what the day includes. Most land tours do not include food and bottled water—these are impossible to find inside the park. Though **camping** is allowed at San Sebastián and Agua Blanca (s/10,000), there are no facilities, so campers must provide everything themselves. Many also recommend bringing **snorkeling equipment,** as the supplies of tour agencies and boats are limited in numbers and of unpredictable quality.

PARQUE NACIONAL MACHALILLA: AGUA BLANCA

This frequently visited hamlet is called home by 43 families who still carry on many of the customs of their ancient ancestors. A short bus ride from Puerto López leads to the park entrance where a languid, dusty one-hour trail through the lowland dry forest to Agua Blanca allows for careful study of the varied flora. **Figs, laurels,** and **Kapok** trees are scattered loosely, while the lush beanstalks of the pea-like, perennially verdant **algarrobos** pierce the dry wasteland. Those dry-climate staples, **cacti,** abound in the arid terrain. The tall, spindly **prickly pear** and the **pitahaya** (which sprouts a delectable yellow fruit Feb.-Mar.) are well-represented among the spines. Agua Blanca provides an interlude to the wilderness education, with both an **archaeological museum** and the ruins of the **Manteña,** an indigenous group that resided here for the 1,000 years preceding the Spanish conquest. The museum brims with Manteña artifacts, including art, jewelry, pottery, religious pieces, and miniature replicas of their **balsa rafts.** The giant **pottery urns** on the way to the ruins were used as tombs for Manteña dead. A 30-minute walk uphill, the anticlimactic **ruins** themselves are only the basic foundations of the Manteña's homes and places of worship. Rumor has it that a dip in the **sulfur pond** on the way back to town does wonders for soreness and clogged nasal passages, but common sense maintains that these murky waters may cause skin to take on a sewage stench and emit a strange green glow. Guides are required for the trip to the ruins. (Guides US$10 per person; museum admission s/20,000, less for bigger groups).

PARQUE NACIONAL MACHALILLA: SAN SEBASTIÁN CLOUDFOREST

The trip from Agua Blanca to the cloudforests of San Sebastián almost always requires two days and is often done on horseback. The trail takes six or seven hours each way, and during the course of the hike there, the land undergoes a striking transition from dry tropical to cloudforest. San Sebastián sports many **exotic animal species,** including tarantulas, giant centipedes, scorpions, coral snakes, armadillos, howler monkeys, *guantas* (agoutis), anteaters, and numerous bird species. This tour also requires a guide, which can be arranged in a Puerto López tour agency. Less expensive guides may be available in Agua Blanca, but they might have a much more limited knowledge about the area's plants and animals and only be able to show the way. (Two-day tours cost US$40 hiking; US$50 on horseback, both per person.)

PARQUE NACIONAL MACHALILLA: LAS GOTERAS

One alternative way to explore the cloudforest without the expense and two-day time commitment is to visit the Las Goteras area (admission US$10). The entire trip takes five to six hours but is relatively difficult—the path to the cloudforest is almost all uphill, and the forest itself is a slow trek through thick and slippery mud. The walk up through dry tropical forest provides gorgeous views of the surrounding mountains and possibly, on a clear day, of the ocean far below. The vegetation gradually changes on the way up the mountain, as the trees become bigger and more lush. The cloudforest itself hosts a variety of fascinating **flora and fauna:** coffee and mango trees, bright butterflies, spiders resting on glittering webs, plentiful birds, and maybe a monkey or two. Beyond the beauty of the forest, guides can point out the varied uses of different trees and plants—everything made from brooms to roofs to jewelry—making the hike an opportunity to learn about the *indígenas* who still live in the area.

PARQUE NACIONAL MACHALILLA: LOS FRAILES

For still more environmental contrast, these secluded shores, located 2km north of the Agua Blanca gate, include **three beaches:** La Playita, La Tortuguita, and the star of the sand-show, Los Frailes. A guide is not required for the trip but is highly recommended (US$10 per person). The excursion starts at the Los Frailes gate on the road from Puerto López. About 100m past the gate, the road bends left at a *cabañita*, while a smaller dirt path leads to the right. Tickets are available for the park entrance at the *cabañita*. The two trails are the different ends of the same 3760m trail. The trail on the left leads through dry forest to Los Frailes (30min.).

Down the trail to the right, the tiny rock cove of **La Playita,** a 25-minute walk from the *cabañita*, is layered with **black sands** and lapped by calm waters perfect for waders and young children. This is also a great **snorkeling** spot, and sea turtles nest here from December to April. Walk five minutes farther and reach a cove festooned with curious rock configurations: **La Tortuguita.** Though its shallow, soft, whitish sand won't harm a soul, the two chaotic swirling swells breaking toward each other can be **dangerous.** Despite this, La Tortuguita is a popular snorkeling spot, especially just off the rocks that separate its two sand plots. However, swimming is not advised at the second beach because of the low line of rocks.

Two paths lead from here to the third beach, **Los Frailes:** the easy lower road and the overgrown high road. The high road leads to a wooden platform with a spectacular view of the beaches and ocean. The immense, almost perfectly symmetrical, rocky cove of Los Frailes waits at the end of the hike. Uninhabited except for a lining of greenery, the beach stretches in a golden arc of pure, solitary sand facing tranquil waters—perfect for sunbathing and cool dips. These beaches are also often visited by boat trips taking passengers to a variety of good snorkeling spots (min. 10 people, US$100).

PARQUE NACIONAL MACHALILLA: ISLA DE LA PLATA

The "Plata" in the name refers to the legendary lost treasure of the notorious pirate Sir Francis Drake. Supposedly, after liberating his booty from the Spanish galleons, Drake hid it somewhere on this 3,500-hectare island, which lies just 40km off the shore of Puerto López. Today, the island is more popular with tourists admiring its pristine natural environment and diverse wildlife than with scavengers looking for lost treasures.

The boat journey from Puerto López takes two solid hours, and the sea swells are often large and turbulent. Anyone even slightly susceptible to motion sickness should take the appropriate precautionary measures.

In the booby-watching Olympics, the Galápagos Islands take the gold, but Isla de la Plata is happy with the silver. The boobies in question include the outlaw **masked booby,** the nurturing **blue-footed booby,** and the small but abundant **red-footed booby.** In addition to the boobies, La Plata is home to many other species. The largest colony of **frigatebirds** in the world lives here and from April to November, the rare **waved albatrosses** wing in for fly-by-night mating season affairs. But the boobies and the other birds aren't the only wildlife to be found at this island party. A small off-shore colony of generally elusive **sea lions** is occasionally spotted sun bathing, and from July to September, the waters teem with **humpback whales.** Like the albatross, the whales prefer big love on the run, migrating here from the Antarctic to mate in the warmer waters. These amorous aquatics have complex and fascinating courting routines best seen during the rollicking boat ride from Puerto López to the island. The park office is at **Bahía Drake,** the island's only inlet and the docking point for mainland boats. From Bahía Drake, two different three-hour **trails** (each 3km) head up hills, over dales, and through nesting sites. Groups only do one of the two trails, and the decision is made in advance by the park office. One of the trails allows visitors to see albatrosses (Apr.-Dec.), blue-footed and masked boobies, sea lions, and tropical birds. The other excludes albatrosses and sea lions, but features all three booby varieties, as well as magnificent frigatebirds, pelicans, and some tropical birds. The all-day trip is a package deal, including: guide, food, and snorkeling (US$30 per person). Six-hour whale-watching tours near the island can also be arranged during mating season (US$25 per person). A slightly less expensive way to do the Isla de la Plata trip is to charter a boat yourself. This usually only requires assembling a group of eight people and arranging for food and a guide (US$15 per person).

MONTAÑITA

Situated 45 minutes south of Alandaluz and a solid 65km north of La Libertad, Montañita hops with surfers from all over Latin America and the world. During the *temporada alta* (Dec.-Apr.), the streets become a barefoot parade, flowing with long hair, bronzed, unclad torsos, and the boards that go along with them. The town calms down considerably in low season since the waves do the same, but a band of die-hard surfers resides here year-round, maintaining the mellow atmosphere that makes Montañita an excellent place to chill. Surfing life often consists of early morning (pre-breakfast) surf sessions, mid-afternoon sessions, a possible dusk session, ending just as the sun dips below the Pacific horizon, and sometimes even a nocturnal session made possible by the light of a particularly bright full moon. It's a grueling regimen, often followed by nights of beach parties, bonfires, cocktails, and general debauchery by the sea. Legends of this revelry are too intriguing to ignore and attract hundreds of non-surfers to Ecuador's all-around party town. In fact, Montañita attracts quite a bohemian crowd—nomadic artisans, left-over hippies, and trippy gringos mingle with the locals, making for an unusual demographic medley. However, tolerance is Montañita's key to prosperity. You can groove to *merengue* or Marley and will never have trouble finding other party-goers, so long as you respect a right to heterodoxy for all.

Montañita was hit relatively hard by the 1997-98 El Niño. Much of its beach eroded, and houses and hotels suffered serious damage (and in some cases, total destruction). The entire town is in imminent danger of being swallowed up by the sea. A massive fortification of the shoreline against the pounding surf can hold off the little pueblo's demise, but the *plata* for such a major project is hard to come by. Nevertheless, tourism has not suffered in the way it recently has in other coastal destinations. So long as there are still waves crashing and a patch of bonfire-worthy sand, this spunky little town has plenty to offer.

ORIENTATION AND PRACTICAL INFORMATION

Montañita is comprised of two distinct sectors separated by 1km of highway. The **pueblo** to the south houses most of the town's inhabitants, hotels and restaurants. Here, **Calle Rocafuerte** runs from the highway to the sand, while **Av. 15 de Mayo,** perpendicular to Rocafuerte, is the last street before the sand. There is a small **central plaza** on 15 de Mayo south of Rocafuerte. **Calle Chiriboga** is one street east of 15 de Mayo. **La Punta,** the other sector to the north, is named for the rocky bluffs that loom over its famous barreling break, and its one road, parallel to the beach, is filled almost exclusively with hotels and restaurants.

Montañita lacks most practical resources, such as a **hospital** or **police station,** but it is possible to make **international phone calls** at the **PACIFICTEL** on Chiriboga, near the northeastern corner of the central plaza. If you're into supporting the black market of communications, you can make **collect** or **calling card calls** (international calls s/10,000) from a private home on 15 de Mayo, four doors to the left of the plaza toward Rocafuerte (tel. 901 138; open until 10pm).

ACCOMMODATIONS

Montañita makes crashing cheaply for a week or two pretty easy. An alternative to hotels, beach houses often offer rooms for rent. Both the *pueblo* and *la punta* have a variety of great accommodation options. Many rooms are more expensive in the *temporada alta*, but almost all hotels offer discounts for longer stays. Bamboo balconies, palm-thatched roofs, hammocks, mosquito netting, clean, wood-panelled rooms, and lively, friendly surroundings are pretty much the standard.

Centro del Mundo, the towering building located on the water at the end of Rocafuerte in the *pueblo.* Like its Quito counterpart, this hostel pledges to provide the ultimate backpacker's (and here, surfer's) experience. A cozy lobby looks directly over the ocean; rooms and bathrooms are simple but immaculate. Rooms start at US$3, with private bath US$4.

Casa Blanca (email: lacasablan@hotmail.com), is, yes, that big white house on Chiriboga, 2 blocks north of Rocafuerte in the *pueblo.* The Casa features spacious, airy rooms with high ceilings, great balconies, fans and clean private bathrooms. English, Spanish, German, and French are spoken and internet access (US$5 per hr. for general public, US$2 or less for guests) and surfboard rental (US$2 per day) are available. Rooms US$5 per person, US$2 in the low season.

La Casa del Sol (tel. 901 302; email casasol@pro.ec) offers more financial, phone, internet, and other assorted services than does the town of Montañita. A bar serves up hooch every night during *temporada alta,* and you can pay for it all with dollars, *sucres,* traveler's checks, or VISA. Rooms US$6 per person, US$10 with private bath during the high season, US$3 and US$5, respectively during the low season.

FOOD

Montañita's restaurants are sure to replenish calories lost in the waves. For vegetarians, the enlightened menus are a refreshing break from *ceviche*-dodging. Better yet, these restaurants know they're cooking for many a health nut, so organic food is almost universally safe (it never hurts to ask, though). Although the hotels themselves will keep you well fed, there are many other tasty options to choose from. *Panaderías* can be found throughout the pueblo.

Rincón del Sur, on Rocafuerte near the water in the *pueblo.* Gloria serves up big, delicious crepes and *empanadas* (vegetable crepe s/10,000), as well as spaghetti and traditional dishes (around s/20,000). Open daily.

Tres Palmas (tel. 755 717), in *la punta.* This Tex-Mex restaurant is the most recommended in town. David, the owner, is from San Antonio, so he knows how an *enchilada* (s/10,000) is supposed to taste. (Veggie burrito s/20,000). Open daily.

SIGHTS AND ENTERTAINMENT

Although the chill yet wild atmosphere does its part to bring visitors to Montañita and keep them there, the **surf** is what makes Montañita what it is. The beach stretches endlessly south, but looming, jagged cliffs with peculiar rock formations contain it to the north. These cliffs bring about the consistent 3-4 ft. swells with echoing barrels that break to the right, away from the point. During the off-season, the waves struggle a bit sometimes, offering only 1-2 ft. apologies, but on good days in both seasons, waves can pitch up to over the 4.5 ft. mark. Aside from the surfing, Montañita is a well-known party spot; during the *temporada alta*, the *pueblo*'s bars are packed nightly. Ask around for the latest nightlife craze, but **La Luna Bar**, Rocafuerte next to Rincón del Sur, is a guaranteed hot spot (open year-round 7pm-whenever). Although things calm considerably in the low season, weekends often see similar levels of merriment, with music, sandy dance floors, and tropical drinks to provide strength for the next day's wild endeavors.

NEAR MONTAÑITA: MANGLARALTO

Ten minutes by bus south of Montañita and 60km north of La Libertad, an adequate surf taps the beach of Manglaralto. Though it offers a few more practical resources than the surf haven to the north, Manglaralto lacks the accommodations and drunken revelry to be found there. Quieter and gentler than Montañita, Manglaralto's streets are lined with lush, sweet-smelling trees. The beach is quiet and pretty, but has been obviously eroded by **El Niño.**

The main entrance to Manglaralto is along **El Oro,** marked by a liquor store on the south side of the street. El Oro runs east-west, and the entrance is four blocks from the **beach. Constitución** is the north-south street one block inland from the water; **Av. 24 de Mayo** is one block inland of Constitución. The town has a few **services.** The **Hospital al Manglaralto** (**emergency** tel. 901 192), 24 de Mayo and 10 de Agosto, on the left side of the street as you walk south from the center of town, provides free 24-hour treatment and has a 24-hour **pharmacy. PACIFICTEL** (tel./fax 901 100), Los Ríos and 24 de Mayo, can make international calls, but only if you pay all costs (open M-Sa 8am-7pm, Su 8am-2pm). The **telephone code** is 04.

ONE OF THOSE FEEL-GOOD PROJECTS Though tourists may run to Manglaralto from Montañita only long enough to pick up something from the pharmacy, this small town does perform a community service besides handling surfing accidents. Right next to Manglaralto's quiet beach is the headquarters of the **Pro-Pueblo Foundation,** which has worked since 1992 to buttress economic development in western Ecuador. The organization helped construct the **Museo a los Balseros del Mar del Sur in Salango** (see p. 415) and has continued to forge a connection between communities and their rich archaeological history. Additionally, Pro-Pueblo has helped bring potable water to villages and start projects of recycling and organic farming, as well as organize the sale of crafts made from recycled paper and *tagua* nuts (see p. 324). Purchase some of these crafts or find out more about Pro-Pueblo's good works at the Manglaralto office in the same building as the Las Tangas restaurant (tel. 901 208 or 901 195; email propuebl@propueblo.org.ec; open M-F 8am-12:30pm and 2:30-6pm).

Alegre Calamar, along Constitución at the northern end of town, is an acceptable hotel/restaurant, with tuna, octopi, squids, and lobsters painted on the walls. Unfortunately, the food selection is less exotic (basic fish, shrimp, and chicken dishes s/15,000). *Desayuno* is served for guests (s/10,000; open daily 7am-8pm). Basic rooms have scruffy green-marble floors but well-polished oak beds and desks. Common baths are clean enough. (Rooms s/50,000 for 1 or 2 people.)

NEAR MONTAÑITA: VALDIVIA

Just south of Montañita and Manglaralto, this pint-sized village offers little besides a bit of history and a small, quiet beach frequented mostly by fishermen. The **Valdivia people,** who lived here from 3,000-2,000 BC, were the oldest of the ancient cultures from this area. The **Museo Valdivia,** just off the main road in the center of town, displays originals and replicas of the culture's artifacts, from small figurines to funeral urns. The museum is small but attractive and well-organized. It includes stations demonstrating how replicas and crafts native to the area are created today. There is a small cafe that serves drinks, as well as a gift shop with replicas, paintings, and other crafts for sale. (Museum open daily 9am-6pm. Admission s/5,000, children s/2,000.) Also in Valdivia, on a street two blocks west of the main one, an unimpressive **Aquarium** exhibits a variety of local fish. (Open daily 9am-6pm. Admission s/5,000, children s/2,000.) A few minutes farther along the highway from the town's main entrance, the road heads straight towards a sizeable statue of an anonymous woman and child, then continues to the sand. While the calm waters make for easier swimming than at other nearby beaches, the main occupants of Valdivia's beach are **vultures** picking through the garbage.

NEAR MONTAÑITA: AYANGUE

Although Ayangue is only 5km south of Valdivia, only mountain goats ever manage the walk. With a monstrous rocky point separating the two towns, motorized vehicles provide the only reasonable inter-village transport; dropping passengers off along the highway near a few "Welcome to Ayangue" signs. The paved road heading west leads into town; it's a five-minute drive or a 30-minute walk. This road leads directly to Ayangue's **beach,** a pretty cove surrounded by high cliffs and filled with fishing boats. The currents can get strong, but when the water is calm it's a beautiful spot for a swim. During the low season, when the weather everywhere else on the coast is drearily overcast, Ayangue's cove is often magically sunny and the beach has few, if any, swimmers. There are limited food and shelter options in Ayangue. On the street parallel to the beach, **Hostal Un Millón de Amigos** (tel. 916 014) provides clean, comfortable rooms with fans and some private baths (s/ 40,000 per person). The hostal's restaurant fires its stoves up only when full pensions (3 meals and accommodations) are purchased. **Pensión 5 Hermanos** (tel. 916 029), on the main road right by the beach, has grim common bathrooms and less than impressive rooms, but does offer a breezy, open-air feel, some nice sea views, and even a resident monkey named Rocky. **Los Helechos** restaurant, down the street from Un Millón de Amigos, provides *comida típica*, with a plate of steak, potatoes, and rice for just s/15,000 (open daily 24hr).

SALINAS

In the hedonistic city of Salinas (pop. 32,000), BMWs cruise the streets, yachts rip across the harbor, and night greets the approaching dawn with the pounding sounds of the city's hopping *discotecas*. Charged with affluence, the town is packed with the luxurious vacation houses and condominiums of many of Ecuador's wealthiest residents. From December to April, Salinas is at its best: "Richie Riches" from around the continent flock to town to make the most of the seasonable weather, and, as a result, the many discos and restaurants which are closed during the low season spring to life. Though Salinas is most exciting during this high season, the city is clean, safe, and beautiful year round.

At the westernmost tip of the Santa Elena Peninsula, 150km west of Guayaquil, Salinas boasts one of the prettiest beaches around, adorned on one side by the yacht club and on the other by white high-rises lining the sky. With wealthy visitors from Chile, Colombia, Perú—and of course—Ecuador, attracted to its streets and sands, Salinas cannot help but adopt a cosmopolitan air. While the city doesn't entirely lack that typical Ecuadorian charm—chickens and dogs still roam the streets several blocks from the beach—tourists may find that it tends to lack typical Ecuadorian friendliness. Despite Salinas's high-class attitude, traditional signs of sophistication are missing. Rather than theater or ballet, Salinas presents discos and banana boats. While these may not meet everyone's criteria for high culture, they are there for the enjoyment of all the city's visitors.

ORIENTATION AND PRACTICAL INFORMATION

In case fun in the sun just isn't enough, navigating through Salinas is an action-packed adventure in itself. Seemingly caught somewhere in the middle of a reorganization of names and numbers, most of Salinas's streets have multiple names. Locals long ago gave up on figuring the mess out, so asking them won't be much help either. The **beach** cuts across the northern end of town, separated into two sections by the outcropping of land held by the **Salinas Yacht Club.** The area around the eastern beach holds most of the town's services, restaurants, and lodgings. The most straightforward street names belong to the roads running north-south, perpendicular to the water; these *calles* are **numbered** in order from lowest to highest, from west to east. The east-west streets, however, are a complete mess. The names and their numbers have been changed over the years; conflicting street

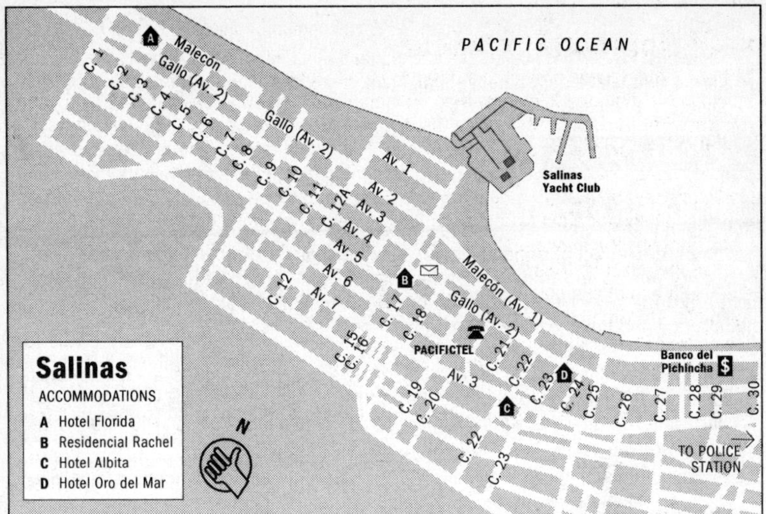

signs are everywhere. **Malecón,** the closest road parallel to the water, offers most of the dining and expensive lodgings. **General Enríquez Gallo** is parallel to Malecón and holds many of the city's important facilities. Buses from La Libertad enter Salinas along **Av. 3** *("Tercera")*, parallel to the beach, three blocks inland. From about **Calle 26** westward, Av. 3 becomes **Av. 7;** catch a bus here for La Libertad.

PRACTICAL INFORMATION

Buses: The town of **La Libertad,** a few kilometers to the east, is the peninsula's transportation hub. Buses from Salinas to La Libertad leave from Av. 3/7 every few minutes around the clock (s/1,500). Or, take a **taxi** to La Libertad, which come in 2 flavors: the blue and white-hooded kind (*taxi rutas*) jammed full with passengers (s/2,500) and the private kind which give you some breathing room but cost a whole lot more (s/15,000).

Tour Agencies: Pescatours (tel. 772 391; fax in Guayaquil 443 142), Malecón between Calle 21A and Calle 23, leads 9½hr. deep-sea fishing adventures for 1-6 people (starting at US$350). Open daily 8am-noon and 2-6pm. **Seretour** (tel. 771 065), Malecón 318 between Calles 36 and 37, leads long and expensive day tours to Isla de la Plata for whale watching during July, August, and September (4 person min. per tour, US$130 per person). Seretour also offers inexpensive land tours around the peninsula (US$12), but compared to what you could see at Isla de la Plata, these sights are mediocre at best. Open daily 9am-noon and 2:30pm-6pm.

Banks: Banco del Pacífico (tel. 774 137), Enríquez Gallo between Calles 18 and 19 changes traveler's checks and cash and has a 24hr. **ATM** that accepts MC and Cirrus. Open M-F 8:45am-5pm, Sa 9am-3pm. **Banco del Pichincha,** Malecón between Calles 28 and 30, changes cash and traveller's checks. Open M-Sa 9am-1:30pm; open later in the high season.

Police: (Tel. 778 699), Espinoza and Calle 57, on the east end of town. Follow Malecón and bear right when the road veers to the right at the Brasa Club restaurant. The police station is on the right hand side after 3 blocks.

Pharmacy: Farmacia Burbano (tel. 772 341), Malecón between Calle 25 and 27. Open daily 8am-1pm and 2-8pm. **Farmacia Sabano** (tel. 774 058), Enríquez Gallo and Calle 18. Open daily 9am-midnight, until 2am in high season.

Hospital: Dr. Jose Garces Rodriguez (tel. 776 017), in Ciudadela Frank Vargas Pazoz, in the southeast of town, has a 24hr. emergency room and ambulance service.

Post Office: Calle 17 and Av. 2A. Open M-F 8am-noon and 2pm-5pm, Sa 9am-2pm.

Telephones: PACIFICTEL, Calle 20 and Enríquez Gallo. Calling card calls possible, but not collect calls. Open daily 8am-9:45pm. Many of the ritzy hotels in town have public pay phones that accept calling cards.

PHONE CODE	04

ACCOMMODATIONS

Salinas's budget accommodations are few but not far-between. Most congregate between Calle 22 and Calle 27, on the parallel roads south of Malecón. You won't find anything lower than s/20,000 per person, but almost all rooms are well-maintained and have private bathrooms.

 **Hotel Oro del Mar** (La Libertad tel. 783 110), Enríquez Gallo and Calle 23. Large, stark rooms fill this large, stark building. Time-worn curtains redeemed by sizeable windows and partial ocean views. All rooms have private bathrooms. Rooms s/40,000 per person; 4 or more people s/35,000 per person.

Residencial Rachel (tel. 772 526 or 772 501), Calle 17 and Av. 5. A bright, plant-filled lobby and chatty parakeet greet guests upon arrival. The rooms themselves, though, are a little less tropical. Starched white sheets give them a hospital-like feel, but luckily, the hospital theme continues into the spotless, hot-water bathrooms. Rooms s/20,000 per person, with private bath and TV s/40,000 per person.

Hotel Albita (tel. 773 211, 773 042, or 773 662), Av. 7 between Calle 22 and Calle 23. Powerful fans and good window screens keep the mosquitoes at bay. Second and third floors have breezy balconies, but first-floor rooms are a tad dim. Private baths are small but generally clean. Rooms s/60,000 for 1 or 2 people; s/30,000 for each additional.

Hotel Florida (tel. 772 780), Malecón and Calle 2, offers a more tranquil experience just off the western beach. TV lounge and long hallways are comfortable and charming, and all rooms have fans and private baths. There is a restaurant downstairs (open only during the high season), which is fortunate since the hotel is 10-15min. away from the dining action of the eastern beach. Rooms s/60,000 plus tax.

FOOD

Since nothing in Salinas is particularly cheap, it follows that the food isn't a tremendous bargain, either. But if *ceviche* is your thing, you've come to the right place. Enríquez Gallo between Calles 16 and 18 is packed with *ceviche* stands, including the aptly named **Cevichelandia.** Most other food options are found along Malecón. However, like the beachfront hotels, these restaurants tend to be expen-

AND THE REST IS HISTORY Long before Salinas shone as a jewel of modernization on the Ecuadorian coast, the entire Santa Elena peninsula left its neighbors behind, hosting one of the first known civilizations in the Americas. In 1971, archaeologists discovered a site of the **Valdivia** culture who lived here from 4400 BC. Visitors can learn more about these trailblazers at the **Complejo Cultural Real Alto** (tel. 772 699 or 758 353), a museum located in the tiny fishing village of **Chanduy** (pronounced Shan-doo-ee). Forty minutes by taxi from La Libertad, the museum isn't very big (you could spend more time traveling back and forth than actually inside of it), but it's a solid introduction to area archaeology, chock full of models, artifacts found on the site, and loads of information. *(Open Tu-Su 9am-5pm. Admission s/5,000.)* Also, the village itself and the beautiful area surrounding the museum nicely complement busy Salinas and La Libertad. To get there, take a bus (1hr., s/4,500) or a taxi (s/6,000) from La Libertad.

sive. For all your carbohydrate needs (and cheap sandwiches as well), the chain *panadería* **Baguette** is located on Gallo and Calle 18.

Cevichelandia, Enríquez Gallo between Calles 16 and 17, is a *ceviche* fan's wildest fantasy come true. The Salinas version of fast food, this large plaza is filled with one *ceviche* stand after another. Although the prices and food options are similar throughout, **Don Kleber** and **Carmita** are among the most recommended. **Genesis** has a fabulous juice selection. *Ceviche* runs s/22,000; *batidos* usually s/5,000. Most stands open daily 8am-5pm, later in the high season.

Restaurante Los Helechos (tel. 773 984), Malecón and Calle 28. *Los helechos* (the ferns) hang everywhere in this simple, breezy diner, strewn with fishing nets and wood carvings. A diverse menu offers rice dishes (s/20,000), *ceviche* (s/22,000), meat and chicken (s/20-30,000), and a selection of fresh juices. Open daily 8am-midnight.

Trattoria Tony (tel. 772 609), Malecón and Calle 19. Not quite budget dining, but not a bad deal, considering its high-class crowd and prime Malecón location. The tablecloths and wooden chairs make the indoor dining a tad more charming than the plastic seating outside, but the outside diners get unhindered ocean views and breezes. The Italian menu includes pasta (s/22-36,000), individual pizzas (s/25,000 and up), and large pizzas for 3-4 people (s/45,000 and up).

Restaurante Joel, Malecón between Calles 25 and 26. The sizzling sidewalk barbecue will stop you in your tracks with the smell of its scrumptious offerings. One of the cheaper food options in Salinas, Joel still serves up tasty *chuzos* (shish kabobs, s/7,000) and rice-and-meat entrees (s/20,000). Open 4pm-late.

BEACHES

Salinas has two **beaches,** divided by a small peninsula that houses the **Salinas Yacht Club.** Salinas's main beach covers the stretch of sand to the east of the yacht club. Palm-laden and relatively unlittered, the sands are packed to capacity with sun worshippers. The water is even more congested, teeming with every kind of watercraft imaginable: expensive yachts, luxurious sailboats, time-worn fishing dugouts, banana boats, paddle boats, and jet skis, to name a few. Shallow water is safe for children and timid swimmers; the surface only stirs when a boat motors through. Join in the water diversions: a **banana boat** ride costs s/10,000. **Paddle boats** fit up to four (s/20,000 per hr.). The chronically lazy can rent junior **motorboats** to go around the harbor (s/300,000 per hr.). Requiring less exertion on your part, **tour boats** cruise the harbor as well (s/20,000 per person for 30min.). Never fear, high-speed enthusiasts, the sea's the limit on **jet skis** (s/300,000 per hr.) and **waterskis** (s/300,000 per hr.). The less busy beach on the western side of the yacht club offers few of the aforementioned diversions, but it does provide peace and quiet on its tranquil, protected shore break.

ENTERTAINMENT

When the sun goes down, Salinas's sandy carnival moves inside, infiltrating the city's bars and *discotecas.* Nightlife in Salinas means bar-hopping; just follow the teeth-rattling *discoteca* music. Frenzied dance action is restricted to the weekends during the off season, but during the *temporada alta* the city gyrates with visitors almost every night. Bars open and close frequently, especially during *temporada baja,* so ask around to find out where the party is happening.

Flintstone's Rockabar, Enríquez Gallo and Calle 25, recently renovated and better than ever. The Flintstone motif is subtle—Fred and Wilma lead the way into their respective restrooms but then leave room for a hodge-podge of other themes that somehow all fit together. Everything from American pop music to *salsa* blasts from the speakers, while

Coronas and limes (s/15,000) are consumed under the watchful eyes of movie posters and cutting-edge sports on the TVs above. The crowd is mixed; it almost looks as though the twenty-somethings could be there partying with their parents. Cover s/20,000. Open Th-Sa 9pm-at least 4am.

Pescado Mojado, on Malecón between Calles 24 and 25, is a good place to hang out and shoot some pool on any night of the week. Of course, they serve national beers (s/10,000), as well as slightly fancier Coronas (s/20,000), and some fruity cocktails. Open Su-Th noon-midnight, F-Sa until 2 am.

Choclo's Cafe and Bar, Malecón and Calle 23. The ultra-friendly owner (Choclo himself) offers a hip atmosphere, coffee drinks, and national beers (s/9,000). Open Th-Tu 6pm-midnight, F-Sa 6pm-2 am.

Entubar (tel. 773 141), Av. 2 between Calles 36 and 37. The security guard, extensive bar, and soon-to-be-completed second floor all reveal Entubar's serious commitment to partying. Jorge Israel Franco Jr., the youthful and very professional owner, brings an especially hip edge to this disco. Open Su-Th 7pm-2am, F-Sa until 4am.

El Patio, Calle 27 and Enríquez Gallo, in Hotel Salinas Costa Azul, is yet another dance bar lighting up the Salinas night (and morning). A disco ball rotates while the DJ spins *merengue, salsa,* and dance-hall hits. Cover s/20,000 includes a drink. Open F-Sa 8pm-2am or later.

Hot Beach, Enriquez Gallo and Calle 23, in the same building as Hotel Oro del Mar. This disco keeps Salinas' weekend nightlife going year-round. *Salsa, merengue,* reggae, house, and even rock and roll blast from La Playa's sound system. Open F-Sa until 2am.

LA LIBERTAD

La Libertad (pop. 50,000), glamorous Salinas's frumpy next-door neighbor, is a smaller, less modernized version of Guayaquil: it's loud, chaotic, and bustling with business and shipping. Like Guayaquil, there's no real reason for tourists to visit, but they wind up passing through to in order to depart for somewhere else.

Buses running between Guayaquil and Salinas pass through **Av. 9 de Octubre,** the main drag in town, one block inland from the waterfront. The other main street is **Calle Guayaquil,** which runs perpendicular to 9 de Octubre and houses a busy series of street-stands hawking all sorts of wares. Several bus lines are based at 9 de Octubre and Guerra Barreiro. From here, **buses** go to: **Guayaquil** (2½hr., every 15min. 3:30am-8:10pm, s/23,000) via **Progreso** (1¼hr., s/11,000); and **Quito** (10hr., 8:30, and 9:30pm, s/90,000). The **terminal terrestre** is located several blocks away from 9 de Octubre and houses the rest of the bus lines. Walk up Guayaquil and bear right at the top of the hill. When the road forks, bear slightly right again, and then turn right as soon as you can. Walk two blocks, turn left, then left again; it's on your right. From here buses go to: **Chanduy** (1hr., every 15min. 6:30am-6pm, s/7,000); **Puerto Lopez** (4hr., every 30min. 4am-4:30pm, s/27,000) via **Valdivia** (2hr., s/7,000) and **Manglaralto** (2½hr., s/11,000); **Jipijapa** (5½hr., every 30 min. 4am-4:30pm, s/38,000). Buses to **Manta** must be caught in **Jipijapa. EMETEL** and **Banco del Pacífico** are on 9 de Octubre on the east end of the center of town, near the park.

The town has few lodging options for those stuck in town. **Hotel Viña del Mar** (tel. 785 979), Guayaquil and Av. 3, offers clean rooms, sagging beds, and fans. Doubles also have balconies. (Singles s/50,000; doubles s/80,000.) A less expensive option is **Residencial Turis Palm** (tel. 785 159; fax 786 500), 9 de Octubre and Guerra Barreiro. Private bathrooms are sufficiently clean, the rooms have fans, and the hallways are breezy. (Rooms s/15,000, with bath s/30,000.) For grub, locals recommend **Savedra,** 9 de Octubre in the center of the town, a cafeteria-style restaurant serving *desayuno* (s/16,000) and a la carte items such as *arroz con pollo* (s/17,000).

NEAR LA LIBERTAD: BAÑOS DE SAN VICENTE

Situated 20km east of La Libertad, the Baños de San Vicente offer a filthy good time. Hailed as a miracle of nature, San Vicente's muddied volcanic crater is supposedly a natural panacea for such ailments as arthritis and rheumatism. Sufferers of these afflictions, as well as health-conscious pleasure-seekers, flock to San Vicente to experience this alternative physical therapy and enjoy extras including massages, steam baths, and health food. General admission to the park includes access to the **mud bath,** as well as the three indoor pools, one of which is a natural hot spring (park open daily 7am-7pm; admission s/8,000, children s/ 4,000). Park employees will tell you exactly how long one should remain in each of these areas in order to attain the maximum overall benefits. **Massages** using mud or *savila,* a natural aloe, relieve s/25,000 of tension, while **hydra-massages**—20 minutes of high-powered jacuzzi jets—soak you for s/15,000. The jets bombard bathers with surges of water that activate the surface of the skin, relaxing muscles and, it is said, improving circulation. The park also offers **internal purification,** which involves sweating away the evil build-up of everyday life in the eucalyptus and chamomile scented steam bath (s/15,000). After indulging in pleasures of the flesh, gastronomic therapy awaits at the park's **restaurant,** which has sandwiches and all-natural juices, as well as some good ol' *comida típica* such as *ceviche.* Or, if you're tired of all this health stuff, you can get something fried at a *comedor* outside of the park. Should you decide to spend the night, **Hotel Florida** (tel. 906 001), just behind the park, offers rooms with private baths and metal-frame beds (30,000 per person; 3 meals included s/120,000). The top-notch **restaurant** downstairs serves *comida típica.*

PLAYAS

As the closest beach resort to Guayaquil, Playas inevitably receives masses of *guayaquileños* during the sweltering weekends. To top it off, it's cheaper than the other major beach resort at Salinas, making Playas the sunbathing spot of choice for most of the southern Sierra. Frequent weekend invasions have left Playas somewhat in disrepair: the beach is strewn with litter, the tell-tale mark of visitors who know they will be leaving come Monday. The town itself is not terribly pleasing to the eye either. Its main streets fill with more dust than sunshine, and the view of the ocean is interrupted by bunches of *ceviche* stands. Nevertheless, for the gleeful vacationers rolling in each weekend, an affordable and almost effortless escape from the city to Playas will more than suffice.

ORIENTATION AND PRACTICAL INFORMATION

Calle Paquisha on the east and **Calle 9** on the west are the north-south streets that bound the main area of town. Most of the town's practical facilities are found along the east-west **Av. 15 de Agosto,** Playa's main street, in the area of north-south **Pedro Menéndez Gilbert,** one street east of Calle 9, and **Asiselo Garay,** one street east of Gilbert. The **central plaza** is located at 15 de Agosto and Calle 9. **Calle 9** runs south from the plaza to east-west **Calle Malecón,** Playas's shoreline drive. **Av. 2,** a.k.a. **Calle Jaime Roldós Aguilera,** runs parallel to Malecón, one street north.

Buses: Coop Transportes Villamil, Pedro Menéndez Gilbert and 15 de Agosto, goes to **Guayaquil** (2hr., every 20min. 4am-7pm, s/15,000) via **Progreso** (30min., s/5,000).

Currency Exchange: Banco de Guayaquil (tel. 760 040), 15 de Agosto and Gilbert, exchanges traveler's checks and cash. **ATM** accepts Visa and PLUS. Traveler's checks can only be exchanged on weekdays. Open M-F 8:45am-7pm, Sa 9am-6pm.

Police: Asiselo Garay and 15 de Agosto, on the right hand side of the street as you head north.

Pharmacy: Farmacia Villamil (tel. 761 607), 15 de Agosto between Gilbert and Paquisha. English and German spoken. Open daily 8am-10:30pm.

Hospital: Hospital General Villamil Playas (emergency tel. 760 328), 15 de Agosto, 1km east of town. Free 24hr. emergency treatment.

Post Office: Asiselo Garay and 15 de Agosto, next to the police station. Open M-F 9am-1pm and 3-6pm, Sa 9am-2pm.

Telephones: PACIFICTEL, (tel. 760 120), on Aguilera 800m west of town, does not allow collect or calling card calls. Open daily 8am-10pm.

TELEPHONE CODE 04

ACCOMMODATIONS

Most establishments in Playas have been around awhile and show visible signs of their age. Most budget options congregate in the western end of town, along Malecón and Aguilera, but there are a few others dispersed along 15 de Agosto. Somewhat pricier hotels are scattered along Aguilera as it runs to the east from the *centro*. Note that mosquitoes adore Playas—a fan or netting is essential.

Hotel Playas (tel. 760 121 or 760 611), Malecón and Jambelí. Its across-from-the-sand location gives this hotel an edge over its competitors. Rooms are pretty bare and poorly protected against bugs, but they do have private baths. The provided fans don't keep the mosquitoes at bay, so insect repellent might be a good idea. Rooms s/40,000 per person, plus 10% tax.

Hotel Rey David (tel. 760 024), Calle 9 and Malecón. It's not exactly fit for a king, but it's a lot nicer than many of the other hotels in the area. Clean rooms with wooden bed frames, fans, window screens, and private baths. Singles and doubles s/100,000.

Hostería el Delfín (tel. 760 125). Head east down Aguilera 1½km out of town to the sign for the hotel, then turn right. For those in the mood for a bit more luxury and a bit more exercise, Hostería el Delfín is worth the walk and the extra *sucres.* Also, its group rates are barely higher than those in town. If traveling with a group, try out one of the *cabañas*–2-room cabins fit up to 5 people and have a private bath and sizeable porch. Doubles s/100,000; *cabañas* s/250,000.

Hotel Brisas Marinas (tel. 760 324), Jaime Roldós Aguilera, several blocks west of the center of town. Like the pharmacy out front, this hotel is more functional than attractive. Rooms all have fans, private baths, and mosquito nets. Rooms s/40,000 per person.

Hotel Acapulco (tel. 760-343), Aguilera and Calle 9, offers minimalist decor. Ample quarters are barren except for the bed and solitary light fixture. Common baths are a bit rundown. Rooms s/20,000 per person, with bath s/30,000.

FOOD

Ceviche, *ceviche*, and oh-so-much more *ceviche*. Being a seaside town, Playas serves what it has. The beach is lined with nondescript seafood establishments serving standard coastal dishes (*ceviche* s/20,000). Other restaurants cluster along Malecón, Aguilera, and Paquisha near the beach. If fish just doesn't do it for you, there's a nameless establishment on Aguilera and Jambelí that serves pizza (s/12,000) and lasagna (s/40,000 for 2), among other things.

Los Ostreros, Paquisha between Malecón and Aguilera, is a strip of virtually identical *cevicherías,* complete with palm-thatched roofs and Coca-Cola billboards. A melange of fresh fruit of the sea is laid out for appraisal: conches, oysters, and clams all beg to become your *ceviche* dinner. Your standard shrimp *ceviche* usually runs s/20,000. Most open daily 7am-8pm.

La Cabaña Típica (tel. 760 464), Malecón and Jambelí on the beachfront, across from Hotel Playas. Tree-branch seats harmonize with the bamboo surroundings. Ugly, criss-crossed metal bars on the windows don't stop the cool breezes. Monstrous plate of rice, calamari, shrimp, conch, and fish s/24,000. Open M-F 8am-7pm, Sa-Su 8am-8pm.

BEACHES

Following an Ecuadorian tradition of very precise town names, this one says it all: people come for the *playas*. Most visitors spend the weekend either sweating in the sun or sprinting to the ocean in a quest for relief. Far from picturesque, the vast, treeless, litter-sprinkled sands of Playas are popular because there is room for everyone. While the beach offers no shade, many sunbathers bring immense canvases to create tents over the sand. The surf is weak and perfect for wading.

ENTERTAINMENT

Playa's nightlife is most rockin' in the *temporada*, when *discotecas* like **Mr. Frog,** on Aguilera west of the *centro*, light up the night. Choices are limited in the off-season, but try **La Cabaña Típica Discoteca,** on Aguilera, a loud club selling reasonably price *cerveza* (s/5,000; open F and Sa 9pm-2am). Across the street are **Barradisco El Madregal** and **Sonero,** two adjacent bars. Sonero plays *salsa* only while El Madregal plays a slightly more eclectic mix. (Both open F and Sa until 2am).

GUAYAQUIL AND THE LOWLANDS

The lowlands—fertile plains nestled between the Pacific coast and the western base of the Andes—have played a pivotal role in Ecuador's history. It was here that the first plantations were established during the 17th century. As agriculture grew, the endemic forests that once shaded the fertile soil here were pushed farther and farther towards the perimeter of the lowlands and, in many cases, completely out of their habitat, into extinction. Such is the price burgeoning Ecuador would pay to develop what became its most prosperous industry, bananas.

The vital importance of bananas to the region is reflected in the names of its provinces. The two major provinces of the lowlands are Los Ríos and El Oro Verde. Los Ríos, to the north, takes its name from the many rivers that spread through the region, enriching the land enough to support agriculture. "El Oro Verde" means "Green Gold"—the unripe green bananas that grow here are as precious as gold to the region's inhabitants.

HIGHLIGHTS OF GUAYAQUIL AND THE LOWLANDS

- The altar of Guayaquil's **Iglesia de San Francisco** (see p. 442) is covered with ornate gold work.
- Hopping until the late hours of the morn, Guayaquil's **Jardín de la Salsa** is the biggest and liveliest club in Ecuador (see p. 443).
- In **Machala** (see p. 446), bananas are king (and queen).
- Chill out in a hammock and savor succulent *ceviche* on the beach of **Jambelí Island** (see p. 451).
- **Macará** (see p. 457) is a charming and friendly place to cross the Peruvian border.

During the youthful era of independence, the liberal port of Guayaquil was the benefactor of newly booming agriculture. As a center of maritime traffic via the Río Guayas, the city became the economic hub of the region, the profits that poured in fueled further agricultural development. This self-perpetuating cycle of agricultural, commercial, and urban development continued well into the 20th century. The 1970s discovery of oil in the Oriente decreased the economic significance of agriculture. Today, Guayaquil and the lowlands continue to develop along same path as they have through Ecuador's history: Guayaquil acts as a commercial capital and the lowlands serve as the agricultural machine that fuels it.

GUAYAQUIL

Once an indigenous settlement, this coastal city was conquered by the Spanish in the 16th century. Legend has it that before surrendering their beloved home and, with it, their pride, the native prince and princess committed suicide. His name was Guayas, her name Quil, and from their martyrdom was born the name of the most populous city in Ecuador, now populated by over two million people.

Guayaquil, the economic capital of Ecuador, seethes with movement and energy. Though it attracts relatively few visitors from abroad, there's something very grand and exciting about a city so diverse and bustling. From the day Francisco de Orellana landed here in 1537, this port has been bombarded by commerce from the sea. Sparked by this commerce, industry exploded in the early part of this century, establishing the severe, business-oriented disposition that dominates Guayaquil's character to this day.

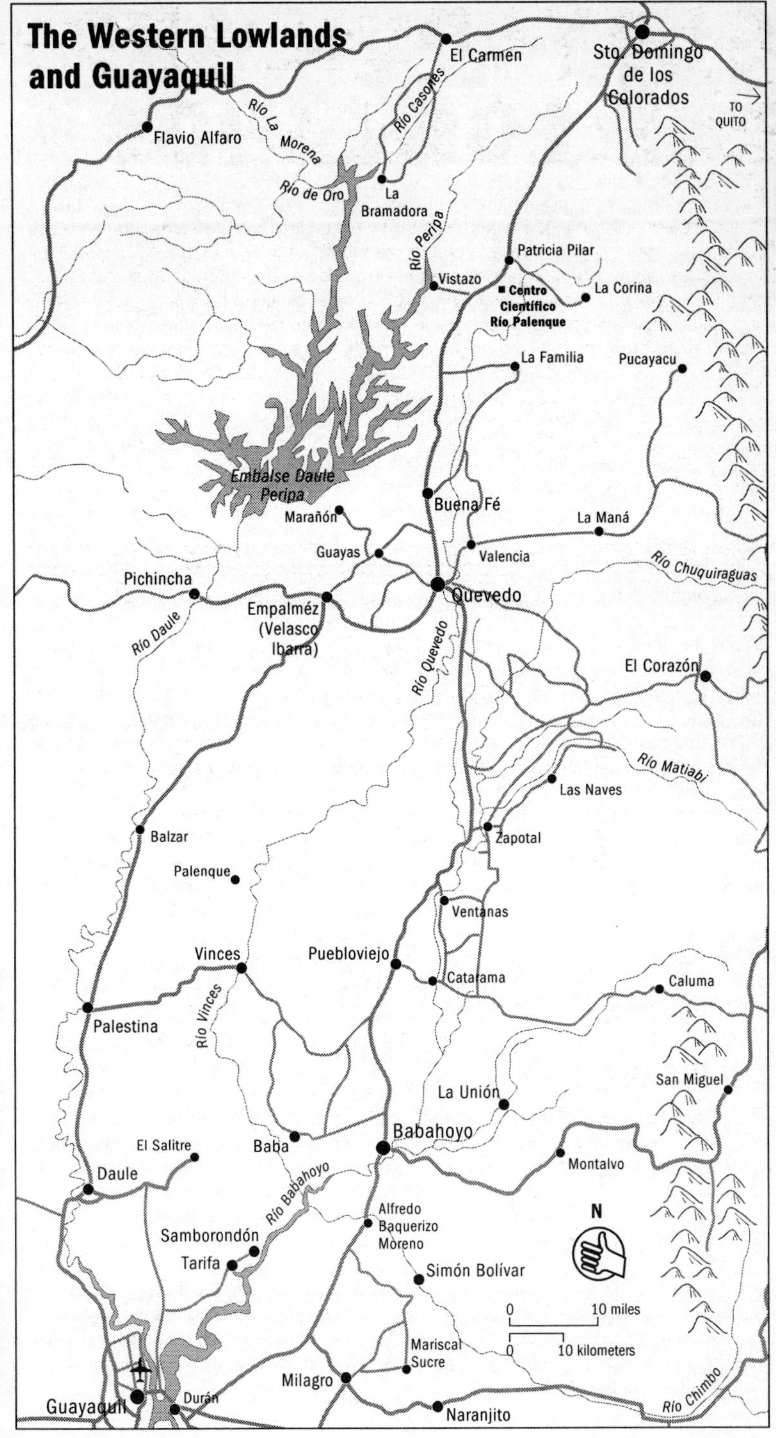
The Western Lowlands and Guayaquil
El Carmen
Sto. Domingo de los Colorados
TO QUITO
Flavio Alfaro
Río La Morena
Río Casones
Río de Oro
La Bramadora
Río Peripa
Patricia Pilar
Vistazo
■ Centro Científico Río Palenque
La Corina
La Familia
Pucayacu
Embalse Daule Peripa
Buena Fé
Marañón
La Maná
Guayas
Valencia
Río Chuquiraguas
Pichincha
Quevedo
Empalméz (Velasco Ibarra)
Río Daule
Río Quevedo
El Corazón
Río Matiabi
Las Naves
Balzar
Zapotal
Palenque
Ventanas
Vinces
Puebloviejo
Catarama
Caluma
Palestina
Río Vinces
San Miguel
La Unión
Babahoyo
El Salitre
Baba
Montalvo
Daule
Río Babahoyo
Alfredo Baquerizo Moreno
N
Samborondón
Tarifa
Simón Bolívar
0
10 miles
0
10 kilometers
Mariscal Sucre
Milagro
Guayaquil
Durán
Naranjito
Río Chimbo

PUTTING THE "QUIL" BACK INTO GUAYAQUIL Ever since the beginning of Guayaquil, the sacrifices of women have helped define the city. Three hundred years after the indigenous princess Quil immortalized her memory by killing herself for her native home (see above), another woman, **Rosa Borja de Icaza,** spent her life fighting for social justice. As one of Ecuador's first and most prominent feminists, Borja, born in 1889, began working for the poor and publishing her first poems shortly after her 1916 marriage. After spending the years from 1920 to 1923 in Germany, Borja returned to her native Guayaquil and, along with some other young and gutsy women, dedicated herself to the improvement of opportunities for her gender. In 1929, Borja supported a conference about women at a Guayaquil university, causing a ruckus among those who preferred to limit a woman's role to the home. Borja herself, in 1932, founded the **Feminine Legion of Popular Education.** In the next several years, she worked for the education and safety of women and children.

Always causing a stir, Borja continually thought up ways to change the traditional treatment of women in Ecuador while racking up important positions in the city and community to help her do even more. Late in life, she published an autobiography and other books—such as *Impresiones,* a collection of her lectures at the Feminine Culture Club of Quito. It has been said that no one else has had such an influence on the Ecuadorian social conscience.

Guayaquil's "character," however, can't truly be described as anything but a split personality; the metropolis often seems like three or four cities all rolled into one. Wealthier neighborhoods offer myriad malls, theaters, and gourmet restaurants. Near *el centro* lies the dilapidated but fascinating 400-year-old, tin-roofed Las Peñas *barrio.* In downtown are the grand government palaces on Malecón street, not to mention beautiful parks, monuments, and churches, and an assortment of interesting museums. And though *el norte*—comprised by neighborhoods north of the *centro* such as Alborada, Urdesa, and Kennedy—doesn't offer that much history or culture, it can't be ignored as part of the complicated package that is Guayaquil. The insane crowds at mega-disco El Jardín de la Salsa and the Bacchanalian revelry of the wandering *chivas* (party buses) which cruise the streets of this part of town have given Guayaquil's nightlife a reputation as the wildest, most memorable around.

Unfortunately, in addition to its reputation as *the* place to party, Guayaquil has acquired the reputation of being Ecuador's most dangerous metropolis, and this reputation is not unfounded. The busiest and thus safest parts of the *centro* are along 9 de Octubre throughout most of town and in the area bounded by **9 de Octubre, Malecón,** and **Parque Bolívar.** In general, the farther north and south you head from 9 de Octubre in the *centro,* the more dangerous the area will be. It's a good idea to stay out of places that seem somewhat isolated, to avoid walking with a lot of baggage, and to take taxis and stay in groups in the *centro* at night. In general, concentration of American fast food restaurants is a relatively good indication of area safety—albeit also of bad taste.

ORIENTATION

Guayaquil sprawls far to the north and south, but the 2 sq. km comprising the *centro* next to the river is easy enough to navigate. **El Malecón Simón Bolívar,** usually just called Malecón, is a busy thoroughfare that follows the waterfront and is lined with many hotels and offices. **Av. 9 de Octubre,** the main east-west boulevard in the city, starts at **Malecón** where **La Rotonda** stands (see **Sights,** p. 440) and passes through the central **Parque Centenario.** The T formed by 9 de Octubre and Malecón outlines the most tourist-essential parts of the *centro.*

Most places outside the *centro* are identified in terms of the neighborhood, or *ciudadela,* in which they are located. The safety of these suburbs varies a good deal. However, the upper-class neighborhoods of **Urdesa** and **Alborada** are generally safer than the downtown and can be easily reached by cab or bus.

The main strip in Urdesa, **Victor Emilio Estrada,** is packed with restaurants and shops and is Guayaquil's nightclub nexus. Alborada's main street is **Guillermo Pareja Rolando,** often called **Calle Principal.** There are fewer places of interest to tourists in Alborada than in Urdesa, but the area still has some good restaurants and bars and tends to be a pleasant place to walk around. The **Las Peñas** neighborhood is at the northeast corner of the *centro*, near the **Río Guayas**. This river, which runs east of the *centro,* is spanned by the largest bridge in the country, the **Bridge of National Unity.** On the other side of the river is the run-down suburb of **Durán,** former last-stop of the famous Devil's Nose Train and home to numerous bars and restaurants geared toward weekend daytrippers from Guayaquil.

Times are hard in all of Ecuador, and civil unrest is common. As the most populous city in the country, Guayaquil, frequently hosts **public demonstrations.** Many of these occur in the centro. Unauthorized marches are often dispersed by the police with tear gas; if you find yourself in or near a demonstration, keep this in mind when deciding whether to catch the action or head back to the hotel.

TRANSPORTATION

GETTING THERE AND BACK

Airport: **Simón Bolívar International Airport** (tel. 282 100; fax 290 018), Américas, about 5km north of the city. The airport has two terminals less than 1km apart. The larger one houses national and international flights; the smaller is the place to catch *avionetas* (smaller planes) to a national destination. **Avionetas** run to **Machala, Manta, Bahía,** and **Portoviejo.** Flights to other cities must be specifically arranged and cost considerably more. **Taxis** wait out front; from the airport to the city center, a taxi ride shouldn't cost more than s/30,000. To avoid these exorbitant prices, walk out to the highway and catch a taxi or bus there (could be dangerous at night).

Airline Offices: TAME, 9 de Octubre 424 and Ilcazacaza (tel. 310 323). Open M-F 8:30am-6pm. Flies to: **Quito** (s/570,000); **Cuenca** (s/333,000); **Loja** (M, Th, and F, s/136,000); **Machala** (M-F, s/118,000); and the **Galápagos** (every day to Baltra; round-trip Jan. 16-June 15 and Sept. 1-Nov. 30 US$290, June 16-Aug. 31 and Dec. 1-Jan. 15 US$334). Open M-F 8:30am-6:30pm. **SAN/SAETA,** 9 de Octubre 2002 and Los Ríos (tel. 296 111) flies to: **Quito** (s/570,000) and the **Galápagos** (daily to San Cristobal; round-trip Jan. 16-June 15, Sept. 1-Nov. 30 US$290, June 16-Aug. 31, Dec. 1-Jan. 15 US$334). Both fly to some international destinations as well. **Ecuatoriana,** 9 de Octubre 111 and Malecón (tel. 326 724), offers international flights. Open M-F 8:30am-6pm, Sa 9am-noon.

Trains: Due to damage from El Niño, train service out of Guayaquil is no longer available. In order to catch the Devil's Nose "express," the famous train which now operates only for adventure-seeking tourists, you will need to catch a bus at the *terminal terrestre* going to **Alausí** (4hr.). This is the closest town on the train's route to Guayaquil.

Regional Buses: Jaime Roldós Aguilera Terminal Terrestre Américas, a few km past the airport. A veritable smorgasbord of ticket counters and different *cooperativos,* the main room seems to go on forever, as do the departure times and destinations of the bus lines. Consistent prices to the same destinations spare you the task of shopping around. Buses go to: **Quito** (8hr., every hr. 10:15am-12:30am, s/75,000); **Cuenca** (6 per day 6:30am and 5pm-10:30pm, s/90,000); **Salinas** (2½hr., every 15min. 3:30am-10:30pm, s/23,000); **Playas** (2hr., every 15min. 4:30am-8:10pm, s/15,000); **Que-**

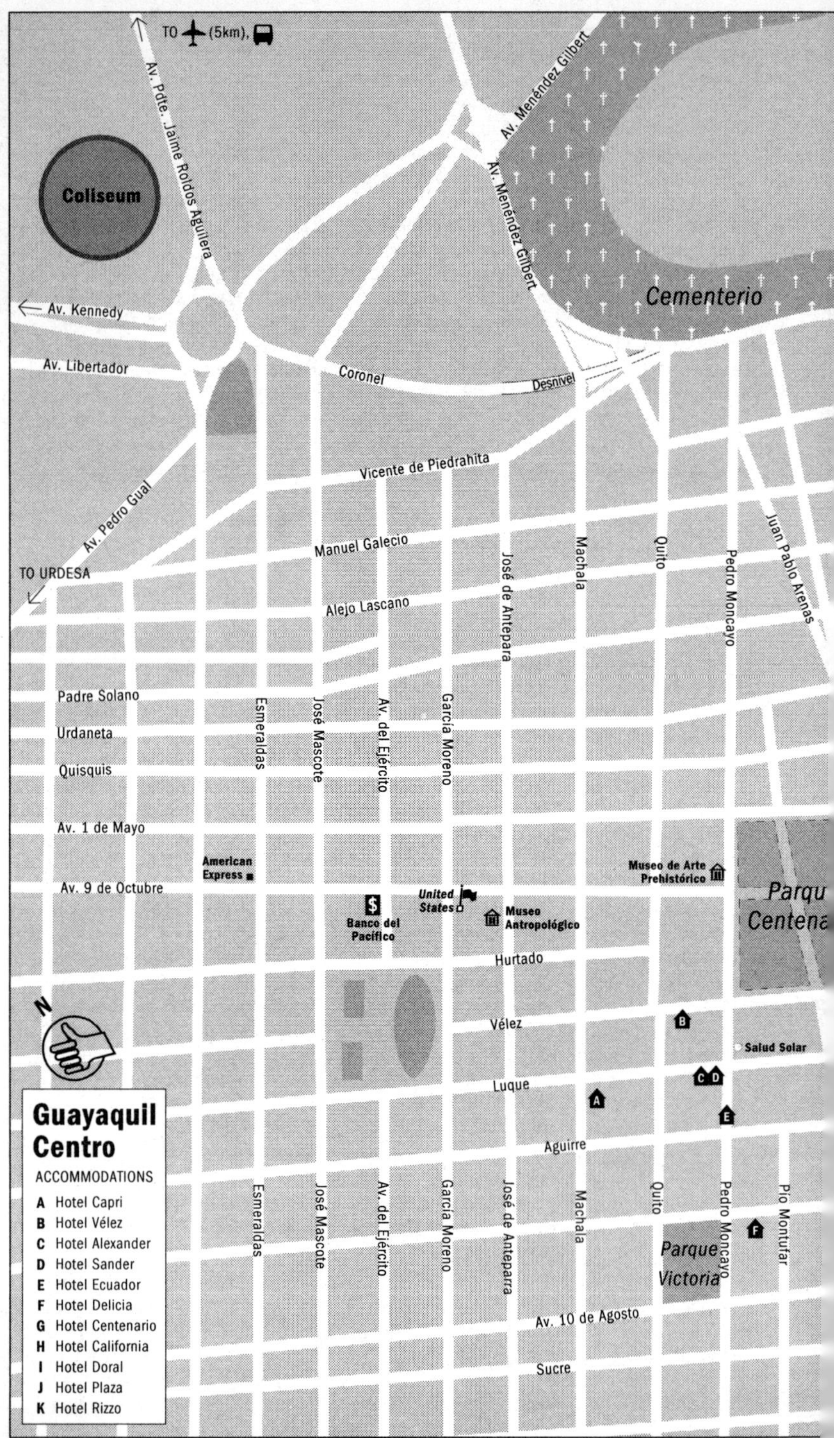

TO (5km),
Av. Pdte. Jaime Roldos Aguilera
Coliseum
Av. Menéndez Gilbert
Av. Menéndez Gilbert
Cementerio
Av. Kennedy
Av. Libertador
Coronel
Desnivel
Vicente de Piedrahita
Av. Pedro Gual
Manuel Galecio
TO URDESA
Alejo Lascano
José de Antepara
Machala
Quito
Pedro Moncayo
Juan Pablo Arenas
Padre Solano
Urdaneta
Quisquis
Esmeraldas
José Mascote
Av. del Ejército
García Moreno
Av. 1 de Mayo
American Express
Av. 9 de Octubre
Museo de Arte Prehistórico
United States
Banco del Pacífico
Museo Antropológico
Hurtado
Vélez
Salud Solar
Luque
Aguirre
Esmeraldas
José Mascote
Av. del Ejército
García Moreno
José de Anteparra
Machala
Quito
Pedro Moncayo
Pío Montufar
Parque Victoria
Av. 10 de Agosto
Sucre
N
Guayaquil Centro
ACCOMMODATIONS
A Hotel Capri
B Hotel Vélez
C Hotel Alexander
D Hotel Sander
E Hotel Ecuador
F Hotel Delicia
G Hotel Centenario
H Hotel California
I Hotel Doral
J Hotel Plaza
K Hotel Rizzo

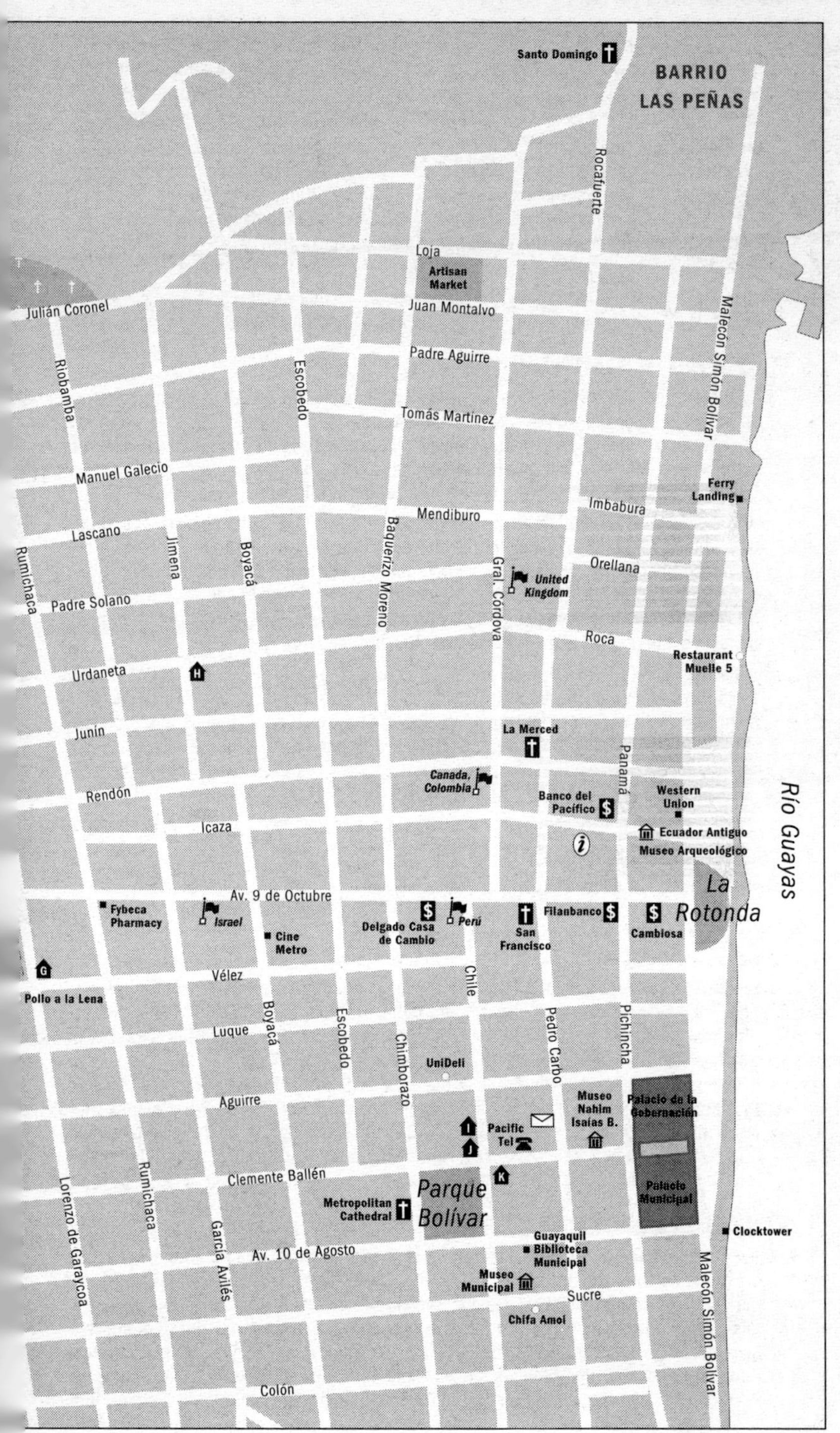
Santo Domingo
BARRIO LAS PEÑAS
Rocafuerte
Loja
Artisan Market
Julián Coronel
Juan Montalvo
Padre Aguirre
Tomás Martínez
Malecón Simón Bolívar
Riobamba
Escobedo
Manuel Galecio
Ferry Landing
Imbabura
Mendiburo
Lascano
Jimena
Boyacá
Baquerizo Moreno
Gral. Córdova
United Kingdom
Orellana
Rumichaca
Padre Solano
Roca
Restaurant Muelle 5
Urdaneta
Junín
La Merced
Panamá
Canada, Colombia
Rendón
Banco del Pacífico
Western Union
Río Guayas
Icaza
Ecuador Antiguo
Museo Arqueológico
La Rotonda
Av. 9 de Octubre
Fybeca Pharmacy
Israel
Cine Metro
Delgado Casa de Cambio
Perú
San Francisco
Filanbanco
Cambiosa
Pollo a la Lena
Vélez
Chile
Luque
Boyacá
Escobedo
Chimborazo
Pedro Carbo
Pichincha
UniDeli
Aguirre
Museo Nahim Isaías B.
Palacio de la Gobernación
Pacific Tel
Clemente Ballén
Rumichaca
Parque Bolívar
Palacio Municipal
Metropolitan Cathedral
Lorenzo de Garaycoa
García Avilés
Clocktower
Guayaquil Biblioteca Municipal
Av. 10 de Agosto
Museo Municipal
Sucre
Chifa Amoi
Malecón Simón Bolívar
Colón

vedo (4hr., every 30min., s/20,000); **Santo Domingo** (6hr., every 30min. 3am-12:15am, s/34,000); **Riobamba** (6hr., 12 per day 3am-9pm, s/40,000); **Manta** (6hr., every 30-40min., s/35,000); **Machala** (4hr., every 30min. 3am-11pm, s/30,000); **Esmeraldas** (9hr., every hr., s/70,000); **Huaquillas** (9 per day 5am-11pm, s/40,000).

Travel Agencies: Guayaquil is bloated with travel agencies. However, there are not nearly as many offering Galápagos packages as in Quito. **Galasam,** 9 de Octubre 424 (tel. 304 488), offers the most choices. Open M-F 9am-6:30pm. **Guayatur** (tel. 322 441), Aguirre between Malecón and Pichincha, might also be able to arrange relatively inexpensive tours. Open M-F 9am-6:30pm. **National Tours** (tel. 322 374), next door to Guayatar, offers tours of various classes. Open M-F 8:30am-6:30pm, Sa 9am-1pm.

Ferries: A boat leaves to **Durán** (20min.; weekday service erratic, Sa-Su every hr. 9am-6:30pm; s/2,000) from the waterfront at Malecón and Imbabura.

GETTING AROUND

City Buses: The cheapest (s/1,000-3,000) and fastest way to get around. Routes are seemingly endless in number. Many buses take 9 de Octubre or Malecón and travel throughout the *centro,* as well as to outlying *ciudadelas* such as Alborada, Urdesa, Garzota, and Sauces. Confirm that the bus stops exactly where you want to go as soon as you get on. They are usually too crowded to carry much luggage.

Taxis: Guayaquil's drivers are notorious for taking advantage of tourists, so you should decide on a fare before getting into a vehicle. Suggest a price and turn a driver away if he doesn't agree. Taxis within the *centro* should cost around s/10,000. Taxis between the *centro* and either the airport or one of the outlying *ciudadelas* should run s/20-30,000. However, as gas prices shoot up, so do taxi fares; ask locals about appropriate prices. Try the dispatch **Taxi Paraíso** (tel. 201 877 or 204 232).

Car Rental: Avis (tel. 287 906); **Budget** (tel. 288 510 or 284 559); and **Hertz** (tel. 293 011) have offices at the airport, outside the international departures entrance. Minimum age 25. A car is probably unnecessary in Guayaquil and is much more expensive than other transportation options (s/270-375,000 per day).

PRACTICAL INFORMATION

USEFUL ORGANIZATIONS

Tourist Offices: Ministry of Tourism, Pichincha and Icaza, 6th floor, across the street from Banco del Pacífico. It's good to check in here before exploring Guayaquil. The ministry offers very helpful information and advice about Guayaquil and the rest of Ecuador. Provides good maps and brochures. One employee speaks English. Open M-F 9am-6pm.

Consulates: Canada, Córdova 812 and Manuel Rendón, 4th floor, office 11 (tel. 563 580; fax 314 562). Open M-F 9am-1pm. **Colombia,** Córdova 812 and Manuel Rendón 2nd floor, office 11 (tel. 563 308; fax 568 749). Open M-F 9am-1:30pm. **Israel,** 9 de Octubre 729 and García Aviles (tel. 322 000 or 322 555). Open M-F 9am-1pm. **Perú,** 9 de Octubre 411 and Chile, 6th floor (tel. 322 738; fax 325 679). Open M-F 8:30am-4:30pm. **U.K.,** Córdova 623 and Padre Solano (tel. 560 400 or 563 850; fax 562 641; **weekend emergency** tel. (09) 723 021). Open M-F 8:30am-1pm. **United States** (tel. 323 570 or 321 152; fax 325 286; **24hr. emergency** tel. (02) 234 126), 9 de Octubre and García Moreno. Open M-F 8:30am-4:30pm.

FINANCIAL SERVICES

Currency Exchange: The first several blocks of 9 de Octubre, starting from the waterfront, are loaded with banks and *casas de cambio.* **Cambiosa** (tel. 325 199 or 517 174), on the 1st block of 9 de Octubre, has good dollar-to-*sucre* rates. Open M-F 9am-5pm. **Delgado Casa de Cambio** (tel. 510 580), 9 de Octubre between Chile and Chimborazo, also has good rates. Open M-F 8:30am-7pm, Sa 9am-5pm. There is a **Banco del Pacífico** (tel. 328 333), near Malecón at Pichincha and Icaza. There is a 2nd Banco del Pacífico (tel. 329 831), west of Parque Centenario at 9 de Octubre and Ejército. Both change traveler's checks and cash. The latter has a 24hr. Cirrus/MC **ATM.** Both offer these services M-F 8:45am-4pm. **Filanbanco** (tel. 321 780), 9 de Octubre and Pichincha, also changes traveler's checks and cash, and has 24hr. Visa/PLUS **ATM.** Open M-F 8:30am-6pm. A swarm of unofficial cash traders congregate on Pichincha near 9 de Octubre. These traders are fast but not always trustworthy.

American Express: 9 de Octubre 1900 and Esmeraldas (tel. 394 984 or 286 900), 2nd floor. Offers travel information and receives mail without charge for card- and checkholders. English is spoken. Open M-F 9am-1pm and 2-6pm. Send mail to: Ecuadorian Tours, American Express, 9 de Octubre 1900, Guayaquil, Ecuador.

Western Union: (Tel. 233 555), Malecón and Icaza. Open M-F 8am-7pm, Sa 9am-4pm.

EMERGENCY AND COMMUNICATIONS

Emergency: Tel. 199.

Police: (Tel. 101), on Américas several km from the *centro* towards the airport.

Fire: Tel. 102

Pharmacy: Pharmacies are scattered throughout the downtown area. One popular chain is **Fybeca,** with branches in the *centro* at Chimborazo and Luque (tel. 530 103; open M-Sa 8am-8pm, Su 9am-3pm); and at Rumichaca and 9 de Octubre (tel. 322 614; open 24hr.), as well as in Urdesa at Estrada 609 and Las Monjas (tel. 881 444; open 24hr.).

Medical Services: The Ministry of Tourism recommends that tourists visit **Clínica Kennedy** (tel. 289 666 ext. 470, **emergencies ext.** 100), across the street from the Policentro mall, for emergency medical attention. Another, more centrally located hospital is **Clínica Guayaquil,** Padre Aguirre 401 and Córdova (**emergency** tel. 322 308). **Red Cross** ambulance service can be called in emergencies (tel. 560 674 or 560 675).

Post Office: On the west side of Pedro Carbo between Aguirre and Ballén. Open M-F 8am-6:45pm, Sa 9am-1pm. To send packages with a bit more reliability, **EMS** (tel. 329 579) is in the same building as the post office, on the corner of Ballén and Chile. Open M-F 8am-7pm, Sa 8am-1pm. **DHL** (tel. 287 044) is on 8 Oeste near the Policentro mall. Open M-F 8am-8pm, Sa 9am-5pm.

Internet Service: Ecuanet, Córdova 1021, 6th floor of the San Francisco 300 building (tel. 562 577), near 9 de Octubre, offers full internet services (US$5 per hr.). Open M-F until 5pm. Ecuanet may be moving to a site near the Banco del Pacífico.

Telephones: PACIFICTEL, at Ballén and Pedro Carbo, in the same building as the post office. Calling cards are billed at the national rate (s/1000 per min.). International calls require a deposit (s/80-150,000). Open daily 8am-9:30pm. Pre-paid phone cards for BellSouth and Porta payphones can be purchased from stores around town.

Information: tel. 104.

Telegrams and Fax: On the 2nd floor of the building that houses PACIFICTEL is the office for telegrams (tel. 510 800) and fax (tel. 320 884) service. Allows international telegrams and faxes. Open M-F 8am-6:30pm, Sa 8am-12:30pm.

TELEPHONE CODE	04

ACCOMMODATIONS

Guayaquil has many strengths; offering budget accommodations is not one of them. There's only one true hostel in the city, and lower-end hotels aren't very cheap and don't have much character. The hotels in the busiest part of the *centro* are bursting with amenities but also are quite expensive. Many of the less expensive options cluster near the Parque Centenario, a bustling and relatively safe part of the city. As rooms get cheaper, addresses (and hotels) get shadier, so be prepared to watch your step if you really want to save on that hotel bill. Air conditioning costs extra, but in muggy Guayaquil many find that it's worth the extra *sucres*.

CHEAP SLEEPS

Hotel Centenario (tel. 513 744), Vélez and Garaycoa, on Parque Centenario. Shower-stall-type doors separate the run-down bathrooms from the coffin-sized sleeping areas. It ain't much to look at, but it's located in a better area than are most of the other hotels in its price range. Singles s/33,000; doubles with fan s/55,000, with A/C s/77,000.

Hotel Delicia, Ballén 1105 and Pedro Moncayo (tel. 324 925). Several blocks from the park, in a shadier neighborhood. The rooms hardly fit the bed, but they're clean, the staff is friendly, and the prices are right. There's a common area with TV on the first floor. Singles s/25,000; doubles s/50,000, with bath s/60,000, with A/C s/70,000.

NOT-AS-CHEAP SLEEPS

Ecuahogar (HI), Isidro Ayora (tel. 273 288 or 248 357; fax 248 341), in *ciudadela* Sauces I, 2 blocks away from the Santa Isabel supermarket, near the airport and bus terminal. Guayaquil's only true hostel, Ecuahogar has got a lot of work cut out for it, but it provides enough services to satisfy most tourists. All 4 floors of this breezy, relaxed *hacienda* are open to the not-so-fresh air; the top floor rooms open onto a terrace with a panoramic view of the city (particularly impressive at night). Amenities and services include laundry (s/20,000), international phone and fax (s/20,000-25,000), internet (US$5 per hr.), safe deposit box, attached market, and currency exchange. Light breakfast included. *Almuerzo* and *merienda* s/15,000. Rooms US$10, HI/ISIC members US$9, with bath US$12. Reservations suggested.

Hotel Sander, Luque 1101 and Pedro Moncayo (tel. 320 030 or 320 944). This place is like a tuna fish sandwich: it's plain, not too expensive, and gets the job done. The tuna is the television in every room. The bread is the plain beds and cold-water baths. Singles and doubles s/54,000; mayonnaise (A/C) s/9,000 extra. Got any chips?

Hotel Alexander, Luque 1107 and Pedro Moncayo (tel. 532 000 or 532 651; fax 328 474), between Quito and Moncayo. Almost attached to the Sander, the Alexander offers more for more. All rooms have A/C, color TV, hot-water private bathrooms, and phones. Clean, carpeted hallways and a pleasant lobby help make this hotel a soothing haven from Guayaquil's grime and bedlam. Accommodating staff stores guests' valuables in a safe in the main office. Elevators provide wheelchair access. Singles US$17; doubles US$22; luxury suite US$30; 10% service tax. Reservations suggested.

Hotel Ecuador (tel. 321 460), Moncayo between Luque and Aguirre. The name isn't very creative, and it's not a particularly exciting hotel, either, but it's less expensive than many places in the Parque Centenario area. All rooms have TV and private baths (though don't count on having a toilet seat). Attached restaurant offers inexpensive meals. Singles or doubles s/48,000, with A/C s/53,000.

Hotel Capri (tel. 517 880; or 530 093), Machala and Luque, provides plain but very comfortable rooms; marble bed frames add a bit of pizazz. The hallways and lobby are dimly-lit but pleasant and clean. All rooms have A/C, TV, and hot-water private baths. Matrimonials s/90,000; the one double s/120,000.

Hotel California (tel. 302 538; fax 562 548), Urdaneta and Jimena, is protected by an armed guard and strategically placed mirrors that let the front desk staff see visitors well before visitors can see them. It's also much more luxurious than other similarly priced hotels in town. Rooms have A/C, private bath, and cable TV. The walls are tall but have no mirrors—no pink champagne on ice, either. Cafeteria downstairs open 7am-10:30pm. Singles s/85,000, with carpeting, refrigerator, phone, and hot water 120,000; doubles s/95,000, with all the extras s/130,000.

Hotel Vélez, Vélez 1021 and Quito (tel. 530 356 or 530 311), acros from Parque Centenario. Though hot water is not available, all rooms do have telephones and TVs. Not too shabby for the price range. Singles and doubles s/57,000, with A/C s/65,000.

THE BIG SPLURGE

The most expensive hotels are in the busiest part of the *centro*. They are well air-conditioned, equipped with cable TV, offer hot water in sparkling private bathrooms, and have elevators to get you to your room. Some include breakfast. It all adds up to a great stay for way-out-of-budget-range prices (which you can pay for with any credit card, of course).

Hotel Plaza, Chile 414 and Ballén (tel. 327 140). The bright yellow-and-green exterior is much livelier than the somewhat barren hallways, but the Plaza's got all the good stuff (cable TV, A/C, hot water, telephones) for a bit less than other hotels in the area. Singles s/192,000; doubles s/225,000 including tax.

Hotel Doral, Chile 402 and Aguirre (tel. 328 490 and 324 4456; fax 327 088). Best Western-decorated lobby leads to carpeted rooms with all the amenities. Offers a tasty complimentary *desayuno*. Singles and doubles s/195,000, including tax.

Hotel Rizzo, Ballén 319 and Chile (tel 325 210). Simple rooms have linoleum floors, cable TV, and refrigerators. Singles and doubles s/192,000, including tax.

FOOD

Along the sidewalks of the *centro*, locals frequent innumerable anonymous, one-room restaurants whose few tables spill out into the streets. These *comedores*, so similar to one another that it's difficult to tell them apart, serve cheap *almuerzos* and *meriendas*. Often, though, the food quality reflects the roughly s/10-15,000 price tag attached to most meals. Many of the cheaper hotels in the Parque Centenario area offer even cheaper meals (around s/8,000). The nicer hotels usually have restaurants open for all three meals, though they won't provide the best deals in town. The fancier restaurants in the *centro* generally have a wider selection of food than the *comedores* and a lot more personality.

THE CENTRO

Restaurant Muelle 5 (tel. 561 128 or 305 753), Malecón and Roca, on the waterfront, at the site of the old Pier 5. Its wooden planks are supported by pilings on the bank of the Río Guayas. The menu includes plenty of seafood dishes (shrimp with garlic sauce s/21,000) and the usual Ecuadorian chicken and meat selections (s/20-25,000). Sip a frosty mug of *cerveza* (s/5,000) at the end of the deck while watching banana branches float toward the Gulf of Guayaquil. Open daily 10am-midnight.

Chifa Amoi (tel. 324 120), on Sucre between Chile and Pedro Carbo. This sleek *chifa* offers a variety of Chinese cuisine served by an attentive, eager staff. Fish, poultry, and beef dishes s/10-20,000. Open daily 11am-10pm.

Salud Solar, Pedro Moncayo 1015 (tel. 519 955), between Luque and Vélez, close to Parque Centenario is more commonly known as "Restaurante Vegetariano." Carrot bread (s/4,000) and a variety of fresh juices are just a few healthful treats served up between the bright yellow-and-green walls of this one-room, sidewalk restaurant. Soy substitutions make convincing replicas of traditional *almuerzos* and *meriendas* (s/12,000). Open daily 8am-10pm.

Uni Deli (tel. 327 100 ext. 1640), Aguirre between Chile and Chimborazo, a popular chain, is clean and bright, but it lacks the colorful ambiance of small, non-chain restaurants. It does, however, dish up a mouth-watering array of sweets (s/7,000) and gigantic submarine sandwiches (s/15,000). Open M-Sa 9am-8pm, Su 9am-5pm.

Pollo a la Lena (tel. 516 458), Vélez and Garaycoa, across from the Parque Centenario. The chain link fences and high ceiling are reminiscent of a giant chicken coop, but all the birds in here are rotisseried. Booming Latin tunes almost drown out the buses outside. Order at the counter for plates of lip-smacking chicken and starch (chicken, rice, potato, cheese sauce, and salad s/16,000). Open daily 10am-1am.

Sub's Miami Grill, Malecón and Orellana, attached to the Hotel Ramada. Perhaps one of the most formal delis in existence, Sub's combines larger-than-life photographs of hamburgers with smartly attired waiters to create a casually classy atmosphere. *Comida típica,* submarine and kaiser sandwiches (s/17,000-30,000), gyros, and burger combos (s/25,000) can all be found on this eclectic grill's menu. Open daily 6am-2am.

Mesón Plaza España, Baquerizo Moreno 1118 and 9 de Octubre (tel. 314 903), is a little bit of Spain tucked away behind a small arched door. Inside, Spanish music, white stucco walls, checkered tablecloths, and tuxedoed waiters make the theme a bit more obvious. Most of the food isn't particularly cheap—the house-specialty *paella valenciana* is a s/40,000 splurge—but *tortilla española* fans will enjoy this scrumptious selection for only s/15,000. Live Spanish music F nights. Don't forget to try the *sangría*. ¡*Olé*! Open M-Sa noon-whenever.

NORTH OF THE CENTRO

The eateries on the **Urdesa** strip tend to be a bit more expensive than many *centro* options, but several restaurants offer delicious food for reasonable prices. Freebies like bread before meals are almost standard, as are attentive service and attractive surroundings. **Alborada** has a high concentration of fast food joints, but a few quality restaurants can be found on Guillermo Pareja Rolando.

Lo Nuestro, Estrada 903 and Higueras (tel. 380 398 or 882 168), in Urdesa. The elegant and intimate ambiance would almost be enough to make dining here feel like a special occasion; the fabulous food just makes it better. Many seafood and meat dishes push the limit of budget dining by Ecuadorian standards (s/45,000). Open daily noon-midnight.

Bunde Abunda (tel. 640 098), Pareja Rolando near Carrión, across from Sol Banco in Alborada, proves that originality is a good thing, although the gigantic bamboo hut that encompasses this restaurant seems a tad out of place on such a commercial street. The fun just keeps coming with dishes such as chicken with pineapple and peach sauce (entrees s/20,000). Open daily 11am-midnight.

La Parrilla del Ñuto, Estrada 1219 (tel. 883 330), in Urdesa. You can't miss the gigantic sign or the smell of meat and chicken grilling on an open stove. This huge restaurant brings in scores of suburban *guayaquileños* for its grilled meat, pasta, and pizza. Servings are big; the filet mignon is a bit of a splurge (s/54,000), but the hearty portions of pizza are a bargain (s/10,000-15,000).

Hong Kong City, Estrada 1210 and Laureles (tel. 386 868 or 381 800), in Urdesa. Not unique among Guayaquil's slightly upscale *chifas* in terms of service or appearance, it is distinguished by its vegetarian selection of delicious, filling, tofu dishes (s/25,000). Also serves chicken, meat, and fish (s/20-30,000), and gigantic set meals for groups of 4, 6, or 8. Open daily noon-3pm and 7-11pm.

Bombon's Dulceria, Estrada 620A in Urdesa. A perfect after-dinner spot to indulge that sweet tooth with cake, pastries, or coffee drinks. Open daily 9am-8:30pm.

SIGHTS

Few travelers make an effort to squeeze Guayaquil into their busy itineraries, and they're not missing out on too much. Guayaquil is, however, sprinkled with parks, museums, historic buildings, and other landmarks that make for a good day or two of sightseeing.

LAS PEÑAS

The Las Peñas neighborhood, climbing the hills that begin at Malecón's northern end, contains the oldest houses in the city. The product of over 460 years of development, Las Peñas has been destroyed and rebuilt several times since the devastation of Guayaquil by fires in the 17th to 19th centuries (see above). The age of the area is exemplified by its almost complete lack of empty land or urban planning.

OF FIRES AND FORGOTTEN TIMES If it seems that an unusually high number of Guayaquil's buildings were constructed in the last 90 years or so, it's probably because only in this century has Guayaquil managed to avoid getting its behind whooped by a nasty, out-of-control fire. Although Guayaquil was struck by *incendios* in 1592, 1620, 1624, 1632, 1678, 1693... (and continued in that manner for another 200 years or so), the fire that has earned the coveted title of **Incendio Grande** swept through the city on October 5 and 6, 1896. Burning for almost 30 hours straight, it destroyed 92 blocks (a fifth of the city), including the Las Peñas neighborhood, reaching as far south as Calle Aguirre. Over half of Guayaquil's population was rendered homeless by this fire and two earlier ones which occurred in February and August of the same year. But those *guayaquileños,* being as tough and as proud as they are today, fought *incendio* with *incendio*—with a blaze of rebuilding, that is. By the end of 1896, a new Banco de Ecuador had been constructed; by 1900, the Iglesia de Santo Domingo was whole again, and a new beer factory had been built as well (first things first). By the end of 1899, the *Cuerpo de Bomberos de Guayaquil* (association of fire-fighters) had finally been established, and with the exception of two large conflagrations in 1901 and 1902, Guayaquil has been nearly fire-free ever since.

Tin-roofed homes pile onto each other, some rising majestically at the water's edge. The higher one goes, the more spectacular the views of the city and the river become. Many important Ecuadorian artists and other heroic figures were born in this neighborhood, including the composer of the Ecuadorian national anthem. A number of the houses in the neighborhood have been turned into art galleries that became important exhibition centers during city festivals. Before the road's end, a series of stairs towers up to the left. If you decide to climb them, expect an incredible view, but also get ready for lots of stares. The local Ministry of Tourism office recommends taking a guide along when exploring Las Penas, and one should never venture into this area of the city alone, since various parts of it are frequented by thieves. Contact one of the many travel agencies in town to see about a guide. Even those unwilling to attempt the climb can observe Las Peñas's distinctive architecture from most parts of the city, courtesy of the steep Santa Ana hill.

NORTH OF THE CENTRO

LA IGLESIA DE SANTO DOMINGO. There are several other notable sites in the northern part of the *centro;* visitors should remember to take caution in this area and travel in groups if possible. Near the foot of the Las Peñas neighborhood is the oldest church in Guayaquil, La Iglesia de Santo Domingo. This ornate, mauve-colored church was first built in 1548 and has been rebuilt several times since because of fires. Its most recent renovation was in 1938. *(At the end of Rocafuerte.)*

THE CEMETERY. Guayaquil's hillside cemetery, west of the Las Peñas neighborhood, faces the city from the north as well. Mausoleums and elaborate tombs crowd the slopes of this virtual city-of-the-dead like mini high-rises, and pathways wind like streets through the resting-sites. Because of its size and the preponderance of white marble, the cemetery is sometimes called **La Ciudad Blanca** (The White City). Buses from the *centro* labeled "*cementerio*" go to the cemetery, but you can also get a good look at the site from taxis or buses as they take Calle Julian Coronel in or out of the *centro.*

SIGHTS ALONG MALECÓN. Many of Guayaquil's most interesting sights can be found along Malecón. Unfortunately, a major renovation of the river parkway south from 9 de Octubre is underway, effectively eliminating up-close access to the sites along Malecón for one to three years. The sites can, however, be observed from across the street. Where Olmedo meets Malecón, a statue of **Jose Joaquín de Olmedo,** a key figure in the Guayaquil independence movement, may be found. At 10 de Agosto, a **clock tower** rises four stories above the waterfront. The Moorish-style tower traditionally called the population to prayer or to fend off attacks by scurvy pirates. A bit farther north, on the other side of the street, is the grand **Palacio Municipal,** which houses the offices of Guayaquil's mayor. A small plaza area sits between this palace and the smaller, peachier **Palacio de la Gobernación,** the headquarters of the provincial office. Much of the area right along the river is actually a small park, with grassy areas, benches, and beautiful fountains and statues. The most interesting part of the Malecón sites concludes at the august **Rotonda** at 9 de Octubre. It's hard to miss this last landmark, which commemorates Bolívar and San Martín's secret 1822 Guayaquil meeting.

CHURCHES

Some of Guayaquil's most beautiful buildings are its old Catholic churches. In addition to the Iglesia of Santo Domingo at the north end of Rocafuerte, there are some beautiful churches in the *centro* as well. The most recent version of **La Merced** was constructed in 1938, the same year as the most recent Santo Domingo renovation. *(On Rocafuerte and Rendón.)* Where Rocafuerte becomes Pedro Carbo, the *centro* opens up to a plaza dominated by the facade of the **Iglesia de San Francisco.** The altar of this impressive cathedral is covered with ornate gold work. *(Rocafuerte and 9 de Octubre.)* The **Metropolitan Cathedral** might be the most spectacular church in town, with a striking gray-and-white interior and spectacular stained glass windows. *(Chimborazo between Ballén and 10 de Agosto.)* The Metropolitan Cathedral overlooks the **Parque Bolívar,** also called the Parque Semenario. Beyond the statues, manicured lawns, sculpted shrubbery, and pleasant benches, Bolívar sports a collection of gigantic, brightly colored **iguanas** that lounge in the park.

MUSEUMS

ECUADOR ANTIGUO MUSEO ARQUEOLÓGICO. Brought to you by Banco del Pacífico, this museum has a comprehensive and comfortable archaeological collection. Detailed explanations (in English and Spanish) inform visitors about everything from the hunting and fishing techniques to the practice of keeping domestic animals in Ecuadorian cultures from 3000 BC to AD 1500. Couches and a visually pleasing exhibition hall add to the experience. One floor above the archaeological collection, the third floor is an area reserved for temporary exhibits of modern art. *(Icaza 113, between Malecón and Pichincha. Tel. 566 010 or 563 744 ext. 5390 91; fax 564 636. Open M-F 9am-6pm, Sa-Su 11am-1pm. Admission free.)*

MUSEO NAHIM ISAÍAS BARQUET. Brought to you by **Filanbanco,** this museum has two large, square-shaped halls. The first displays an interesting exhibit of regional artifacts from prehistoric Ecuadorian cultures. The other houses colonial religious painting and sculpture. Thematic music adds to the mood. English pamphlets are available, and the staff is very helpful. *(Pichincha and Ballén. Tel. 510 784 or 510 818. Open M-Sa 10am-5pm. Admission free.)*

OTHER ARCHAEOLOGICAL MUSEUMS. Across town, the **Museo de Arte Prehistórico** is perched on the western side of the sixth floor of the Parque Centenario. Unlike the other museums, this display of regional archaeological finds can only be seen at a cost. *(9 de Octubre and Pedro Moncayo. Tel. 300 500 or 300 586 ext. 102. Open Tu-F 10am-6pm, Sa 9am-3pm. Admission s/5,000.)* Larger and better displayed, however, is the **Museo Antropológico del Banco Central de Ecuador,** which contains detailed exhibits, an interactive computer display in Spanish and English, and a knowledgeable staff. *(9 de Octubre and José de Anteparra. Tel. 327 402. Open Tu-F 10am-6pm, Sa-Su 10am-2pm. Admission s/3,000.)* The **Museo Municipal** has a permanent exhibition of paintings of all of Ecuador's presidents, as well as a tiny archaeological exhibit. It also houses temporary exhibits ranging from colonial to contemporary art. *(Sucre between Chile and Pedro Carbo, attached to the library. Tel. 524 100 ext. 7401. Open Tu-Sa 9am-12:30pm and 1-5pm. Admission free.)* On a somewhat different theme, the **Armada del Ecuador Museo Naval,** traces Ecuador's naval history from colonial times until today. *(In the Palacio de la Gobernación. Open M-F 9am-4pm.)*

ENTERTAINMENT

NIGHTLIFE

As the saying goes, spend your days in Quito and your nights in Guayaquil. The city might not draw a considerable number of tourists, but it certainly lures enough locals to its wild, exciting, and ever-changing nightspots. Clubs and *discotecas* in the *centro* light the sky in shades of neon until sunrise, but the downtown area can be dangerous and considerably unpredictable. A usually safer and always thrilling option is to hit the clubs and bars out of the *centro*.

URDESA NEIGHBORHOOD

In the past, Urdesa was the place to be. The main strip, Estrada, used to be filled with scores of nightclubs. Then zoning, permit requirements, and politicians conspired to quiet the neighborhood down. Now only a few clubs remain. A few disco-bars have sprouted up in adjoining Alborada, near the plaza, but for the most part *guayaquileños* have been forced to take their nightlife elsewhere (see below). Still, there are a couple of spots in the area that you might want to hit.

Manantial, Estrada 520 and Monjosa. This lively restaurant-bar remains packed with a loud, young crown in spite of the anti-bar sentiment in the area. Pitchers of *cerveza* still cover the wooden tables and *cigarillo* smoke still fills the air. Open daily until 3am.

Chappu's Beer, on Estrada, 1 block away from Manantial, has both upstairs and downstairs patios overlooking the street. Inside, the bamboo banisters, stone walls, and a small dance floor add a touch of excitement to the relatively laid-back atmosphere. *Cervezas* s/17,000. No cover. Open M-Th 6pm-midnight, F-Sa 6pm-2am.

EL JARDÍN DE LA SALSA

Unquestionably the hottest night spot in all of Ecuador is... drum role please... **El Jardín de la Salsa,** Av. de las Americas 140 (tel. 396 083), between the airport and *terminal terrestre*. Your search for the shangri-la of *salsa* has come to an end. El Jardín, a gargantuan entertainment complex founded in October of 1998, is the place to be in Guayaquil on weekend nights. With a capacity of 6,000, this stadium-sized disco attracts young and old from Guayaquil and beyond. Sharply dressed yuppies, taxi drivers just off work, gaggles of 18-year-old girls in a rainbow of pastel tanktops, anyone and everyone with *ritmo* in their feet and *salsa* in their soul is welcome. The dance floor is practically the size of a football field (except circular) and is surrounded by multiple tiers of tables and benches where pitchers of *cerveza* can be ordered for a reasonable price (s/30,000). A well-equipped stage on the far end of the dance floor presents orchestras, singers, and dancers of both Latin and international varieties. Dancing lessons are even offered occasionally if you need some help with that fancy footwork. Live music is also frequent at El Jardín. Once you've worked up an appetite, or if you need to fuel up before busting a move, a few small kiosks serve complete meals near the entrance.

CHIVAS

Guayaquil continues its tradition of over-the-top entertainment with its *chivas*. These huge trucks carry at least 100 revelers; their bodies hang out the windows, on the hood, and off the roof where the Latin band plays. *Guayaquileños* rent these portable parties for birthdays or other occasions; although they certainly don't happen every night, travelers who happen to see them passing by can usually hop on (for a price). They can often be spotted in front of El Jardín de la Salsa. Your biggest problem might be choosing which ones to hit.

OTHER ENTERTAINMENT

Clubs are certainly the highlight, but not the entirety, of the Guayaquil entertainment experience. While Guayaquil isn't known for its artistic and cultural achievements, it does have plenty of cinemas showing slightly dated Hollywood films. Check newspapers for showtimes. The most comfortable—and expensive—of Guayaquil's theaters are **Albocines,** (tel. 244 986) at the Plaza Mayor in Alborada (tickets s/15,000); the **Maya** (tel. 386 456), Las Lomas and Dátules in Urdesa (s/15,000); **MultiCines** (tel. 831 230), in the Riocentro Shopping Plaza between the bridges to Durán (s/30,000); and **Cinemark** (tel. 692 013), in the Mall del Sol (s/20,000). Avoid taxi fees at the **Cine Metro** (tel. 322 301), downtown at Boyacá and Vélez (s/10,000). Avoid practically any fees at **Cine Foro,** 9 de Octubre and Pedro Moncayo, which shows almost-as-recent films (M, W, F 7pm; s/4,000). Aside from movie theaters, you could try to catch a **BSC** (**Barcelona Sporting Club**—Guayaquil's *fútbol* team) match while in town. Call for information (tel. 201 644 or 404 047).

FESTIVALS

Guayaquil's somewhat serious disposition is left in the dust during the yearly festivals celebrating its founding and Independence. July is an exciting month in the city, with Simón Bolívar's birthday on **July 24th** and the anniversary of the city's founding on **July 25th.** During the first week of July, public concerts and merriment anticipate the parades and celebrations later in the month. **October 9,** the anniversary of Guayaquil's Independence, is a national holiday; any *guayaquileño* will assure you that each Independence celebration is a day to be remembered.

SHOPPING

Guayaquil has all the malls and specialty stores of a big city, so if you need to buy something, it's probably here. There are plenty of stores in the area between **9 de Octubre** and **Parque Bolívar.** For a more American-style shopping experience, take a bus or cab to the new **Mall del Sol,** north of the *centro*. Practically every sign and store name is in English, and there's a food court with every kind of American fast food, an arcade, a 24-hour restaurant, and pretty much any other material thing one could wish for. The **Policentro Shopping Center** in Ciudadela Kennedy provides quite the modern shopping experience as well. An **artisan's market** provides indigenous crafts on Loja and Baquerizo Moreno near Las Peñas (open M-Sa 9:30am-6:30pm). For very cheap (often contraband) items sold in a crowded, labyrinthine street market, head to the **Bahía,** in Pedro Carbo and Villamil between Olmedo and Colón. You can get a real bargain, and exploring this endless maze can be a blast. Vendors buy counterfeit brand-name clothing tax-free in Panamá and pass the savings on to you. Both the artisan's market and the Bahía are at the outskirts of the *centro*'s tourist-safe zone, and both are crowded; don't forget to watch your back.

CENTRAL LOWLANDS

Going from Quito to Guayaquil? From the coast to the Sierra? There's a good chance you'll go through one of the towns of the central lowlands. Most travelers pass right on by; this area is frequently traveled but seldom visited. If you stop along the way, don't expect a fascinating historical journey, a mosaic of artistic possibilities, or a lively night on the town. Do expect an up-close view of typical Ecuadorian life in a small, untouristed town... and, as throughout the lowlands, expect to see lots and lots of bananas.

QUEVEDO

Quevedo's *centro,* a cluster of four-story buildings near the Río Quevedo, is pleasant, though it doesn't exactly cater to tourists. As with any non-tourist town, your uniqueness in Quevedo is a reason for caution, but its also a reason for excitement; locals will take more of an interest in you here than will be taken in more touristed areas. The five principle streets in Quevedo are: **Malecón Eloy Alfaro, Simon Bolívar, 7 de Octubre,** and **El Progreso.** The slightly run-down **Plaza de la Madre,** is between Quinta and Sexta. **Buses** in this transportation hub are generally located around **Calle Primera.** Buses go to **Guayaquil** (4 hr., every 20min. 3am-7:45pm, s/20,000) via **Babahoyo** (1 hr., s/12,000); **Quito** (4 hr., every 40min. 5:30am-5pm, s/33,000) via **Santo Domingo** (1 hr., s/14,000); **Ambato** (10 per day, 7:30am-9pm; s/24,000); and **Cuenca** (9am and 9pm, s/75,000; ticket office open M-Sa 8am-noon and 2-9:30pm). **Emergencies:** tel. 101. **Police:** (tel. 750 361) are on Novena near Progreso. Other services include: **Botica International** (tel. 750 480), 7 de Octubre and Novena (open daily 7:30am-10:30pm); **Hospital Centro de Salud de Quevedo,** Guayacanes 400 (tel. 755 031); and the **IETEL** telephone office (tel. 754 223), 7 de Octubre and Décima Tercera (open daily 8am-10pm). **Telephone code:** 05.

Hotels in Quevedo are nothing to write home about, but they tend to get the job done. **Hotel Imperial** (tel. 751 654), Malecón and Séptima, overlooks the market. Rooms provide basic private baths, sexy high-powered fans, and concave beds. All but the ones overlooking the river have both windows and a balcony. (Singles s/20,000; doubles s/40,000.) **Chifa China** (tel. 751 242), 7 de Octubre and Décima Quarta, next to IETEL at the end of the main strip, is one of the best restaurants in town and even has air conditioning (entrees s/14-25,000, a four-person, multi-course meal s/100,000; open daily 11am-11pm). **El Frutal Soda Bar** (tel. 756 332), 7 de Octubre between Décima and Décima Primera, serves incredibly cheap favorites such as hamburgers (s/5,000) and smooth yogurt and fruit blends (s/3-11,000; open daily 9:30am-11pm).

SANTO DOMINGO DE LOS COLORADOS

Before giving in to concrete urbanity, Santo Domingo belonged to the *indígenas* who gave the city the second part of its name, the **Colorados**. The scant clothing and red bowl-cuts of this tribe are commonly exploited in caricature on postcards and store signs. Although you may spot someone from an outside village still sporting the telltale coif, the city itself has little connection to its indigenous roots.

Santo Domingo's main streets are **Av. 29 de Mayo, 3 de Julio,** and **Quito.** The *centro*, bounded by **Pallatanga** on the east and **San Miguel** on the west, is the busiest section. From the eastern end of the *centro*, **Av. Tsachila** runs north, past the post office, to the **terminal terrestre** about 2km north of town. From Santo Domingo buses go to: **Quito** (3hr., every hr. 9:30am-11pm, s/23,000); **Esmeraldas** (3hr., every 1½hr. 8:30am-2pm and 5-10:45pm, s/25,000); and **Guayaquil** (5hr., every 1-3hr. 9:30am-10pm, s/35,000).

Filanbanco (tel. 758 889), Quito and Tsachila, changes dollars and traveler's checks (open M-F 9am-4pm). **Emergency:** tel. 101. The **police** (tel. 750 225) are headquartered on Tsachila, next to the traffic circle, across from the bus terminal. **Pharmacies** abound downtown. **Hospital Agosto Egas** (tel. 750 336), is off the eastern end of Quito, and can be reached by a bus along Quito marked "Chihuilpe." Make **phone calls** from the San Francisco de Asis building, 2nd floor, Quito 1200. (Open daily 8am-10pm.) **Telephone code:** 02.

ACCOMMODATIONS AND FOOD. Hotels are densely packed downtown, especially near 29 de Mayo. Most are of the you-get-what-you-pay-for variety. At the lower end of the spectrum is **Hotel Amambay** (tel. 750 696), 29 de Mayo and Ambato, with basic rooms and communal bath (rooms start at s/15,000). **Hotel Unicornio** (tel. 760 147), 29 de Mayo and Ambato, is around the corner from the movie theater (singles from s/20,000 to s/30,000 depending on your attachment to the good old *televisor)*. **Restaurante La Siesta**, Quito 606 (tel. 751 013 or 751 860), has the same aesthetic charm and foreign clientele as the attached hotel and prepares savory food for all meals (*desayuno* s/12,000; steak, chicken, and shrimp s/18-25,000 and omelettes s/8-20,000; open daily 7am-9pm). **Restaurant Elite** (tel. 763 844), Quito and Tsachila, has a cafeteria-like setting but also offers al fresco dining (chicken, fish, and meat dishes s/10-30,000; open daily 7am-10:30pm).

The nearby **Colorados** are considered the only true tourist attraction of Santo Domingo. Some live in villages not far from the outskirts of the city, along Quevedo—a kind taxi driver should take you there and back for s/20,000. Buses marked "Vía Quevedo" also travel along this route. Make sure to ask the driver if the bus goes to the "end of the line" ("a la última parada"), because certain buses on Quevedo only stay within the city limit. The **Museo Etnográfico Tsachila** (see graybox below) lies deep within one of these Colorado reserves and can be reached only by taxi or car. Expect your driver to request more for his services (s/60,000) if you make this short trip into the jungle.

NEAR SANTO DOMINGO: RÍO PALENQUE SCIENCE CENTER

The **Centro Científico Río Palenque** not only preserves dying breeds—it is one. Although it is the last tropical wet rainforest reserve in the western Ecuadorian lowlands, the Centro has been converted into a national park, leaving behind the days when it was used almost exclusively by researchers who traveled to the reserve to study what can be seen only here. Although wild animals are not frequently spotted near the Centro itself, the beautiful trails still provide ample opportunities for light hikes through the forest.

Transportation: The Centro is located halfway between Quevedo and Santo Domingo, and is an hour bus ride from each. From Santo Domingo, the entrance is 2.5km past a town called **Patricia Pílar** at the 48km mark (the 56km mark if coming from Quevedo); look for signs.

SOUTHERN LOWLANDS

On their way from Guayaquil to the Peruvian border, few foreigners pay an extended visit to this tranquil region full of coffee, pineapples, and, most importantly, bananas. But aside from the pleasures of eating entire meals consisting of *plátano* and *guineo* (a novelty that may shortly wear off), the border area offers little of purely touristic interest. Nevertheless, towns along this route allow for friendly and carefree living before the hurrying off to Peruvian points south or the more touristed areas of Ecuador to the north.

MACHALA

As the self-proclaimed "banana capital of the world," the growing town of Machala (pop. 250,000) takes its peelable yellow fruit quite seriously. The value of the banana is even listed in the daily newspapers, alongside the value of the dollar and the price of gold. Located 200km south of Guayaquil, Machala greets entering visitors with a huge statue of El Bananero, a larger-than-life banana grower carrying an eight-foot bunch. Locals extol the sacred fruit with a banana festival during the third week in September. The festivities include the selection of one lucky lady to receive the highest honor the city has to offer—the coveted title of Her Highness, the Banana Queen. Far from just tallying bananas, Machala is also capital of the El Oro province. The city celebrates its "Día de Canonización" on the 25th of June with parades, music, dancing, and drinking into the wee hours of the morning. It has no conventional tourist attractions, but its friendly, lively atmosphere and proximity to the fresh seafood and clean beaches of Puerto Bolívar and Jambelí make Machala an ideal place to stop before braving the border crossing into Perú.

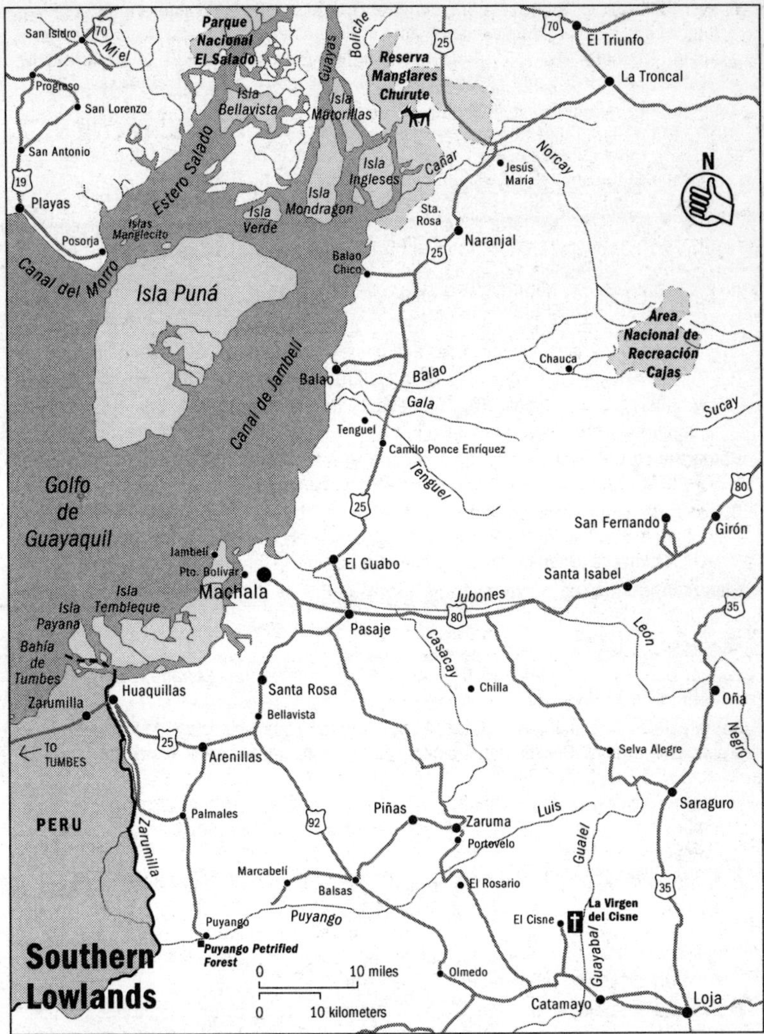

ORIENTATION

Streets in Machala use both names and numbers, but locals generally use the names. **Av. 9 de Mayo** is the main north-south strip, running past the **market** and the **main plaza,** where it intersects with the busy **Av. 9 de Octubre.** The **church** stands on the west side of the plaza; its spire can make a useful landmark. There is no *terminal terrestre;* buses arrive and leave from various places around town.

PRACTICAL INFORMATION

Airport: A few blocks west of the main plaza on Montalvo. TAME flies to **Guayaquil** (30min., M-F 8:30am and 3:30pm, s/227,000) and continues to **Quito** (1hr., s/ 568,000). The **TAME office** (tel. 930 139) is on Juan Montalvo between Bolívar and Pichincha, near the post office. Open M-F 7:30am-5pm.

Buses: CIFA (tel. 933 735), at the corner of Bolívar and Guayas, across from the Rizzo Hotel, sends buses to the Peruvian border at **Huaquillas** (1hr. direct, 2 hrs. local; every 10min. 4:20am-7:45pm; s/14,000) via **Arenillas** (25min., s/8,000) and **Santa Rosa** (40min., s/12,000) and to **Guayaquil** (4hr., every 30 min., 4:30am-7:30pm, s/30,000). **TAC,** on Colón between Rocafuerte and Bolívar, sends buses to **Zaruma** (3hr., every hr., 4am-7pm, s/20,000) via **Piñas** (2hr., s/14,000) and **Portovelo** (2½ hr., s/18,000). **Coop Pullman Azuay** (tel. 930 539), on Sucre between Junín and Tarquí, has buses constantly departing for **Cuenca** (4hr.; 1, 2:30 and 3:30am and every 20 min. 4am-10:40pm; s/35,000). **Panamericana** (tel. 931 141), on the corner of Bolívar and Colón, sends buses to **Quito** (12hr.; 7:45, 10:15am, 12:15, 3:45, 6:30, 8:30, 9:30, 10 and 10:30pm; s/85,000). **Loja Internacional** (tel. 932 030) on Tarquí between Rocafuerte and Bolívar, travels to: **Loja** (6hr., 7 per day, s/45,000); **Zamora** (9hr., 10am and 9pm, s/60,000); and **Ambato** (11hr., 10:30pm, s/60,000).

Tourist Information: CETUR (tel. 932 106), 9 de Mayo and Pichincha, 3rd fl. The Spanish-speaking staff answers questions and offers a map booklet. Open M-F 8am-5pm.

Consulate: Peruvian (tel. 930 680; fax 937 040), on Bolívar at Colón in an unmarked gray building, 2nd fl., room 102. Can supply visas, but most travelers who intend to spend less than 90 days in Perú don't need one. Open M-F 9am-noon and 3-6pm.

Bank: Banco del Pacífico (tel. 930 700), at the corner of Rocafuerte and Junín. The 24hr. **ATM** accepts Cirrus and MC. Open M-F 8:45am-4pm.

Currency Exchange: Casa de Cambio Ullauizi (tel. 931 349), Páez between 9 de Octubre and Rocafuerte; look for the man with the gun (security guard). Changes dollars but not traveler's checks. Open M-F 8am-noon and 2:30-6pm.

Supermarket: Tía, on Sucre between Guayas and 9 de mayo, is open M-Sa 8:30am-7:30pm, Su 8am-6:30pm.

Emergency: Tel. **101**.

Police: (tel. 930 449; fax 933 911) 9 de Mayo and Manual Serrano, 3 blocks past CETUR. Open 24hr.

Pharmacies: Pharmacies are almost as common as armed guards in Machala. Coincidence? Probably. Conveniently located across from the hospital, **Farmacia Imperial** (tel. 938 428) is open 24hr.

Hospital: Hospital Teofilo Davila (emergency tel. 939 099), at Buenavista and Boyaca, in front of the Parque Colón, is open 24hr. **Clínica Maridueña** (tel. 930 437), on Rocafuerte across from the park, is closer to the center of town. Open 24hr. for emergencies.

Post Office: Correos (tel. 930 675; fax 931 908), at Bolívar and Juan Montalvo, is open M-F 7:30am-7pm, Sa 8am-2pm. **DHL** (tel. 962 444), on Bolívar between Guayas and 9 de Mayo, is open M-F 8am-7pm, Sa 9am-noon. **Delgado Travel** (tel. 938 154, fax 923 334), on 9 de Mayo between Rocafuerte and Bolívar, also sends letters and packages to the US. Open M-F 8:30am-6pm, Sa 9am-1pm.

Internet: Mito-Compu (tel. 921 641) on Rocafuerte across from Banco del Pacífico, offers a slow modem connection at a steep price ($7/hr), but e-mail addicts will find this is the only place to satisfy their cravings. Open daily 9am-1:30pm and 3-7pm

Telephones: PACIFICTEL (tel. 920 050; fax 922 666), 9 de Octubre between Anda de las Palmeras and Vela, handles collect and calling card calls. Open daily 8am-10pm.

PHONE CODE	07

ACCOMMODATIONS

Because of the large number of tourists spending the night in Machala after shedding the shackles of Huaquillas, budget accommodations abound. Anyone staying overnight in Machala should check for window screens or mosquito nets, especially during the hot, wet months of January through April. Also make sure your room has a fan, or spend a few extra *sucres* and get a room with air-conditioning. Hotels closer to the center of town, while usually noisier, tend to be the safest.

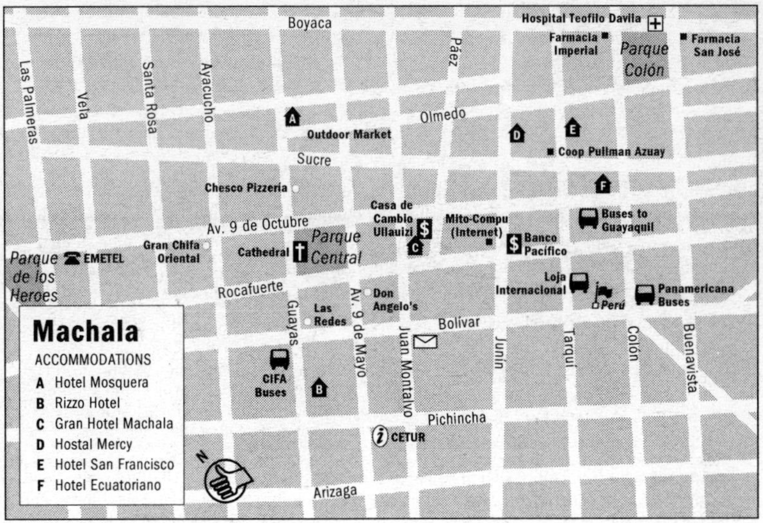

Hostal Mercy (tel. 920 116), Junín between Olmedo and Sucre, set back from the street. Tall plants thrive in the courtyard, well-maintained by the sweet, grandparent-like owners. Spotless rooms with private (cold-water) baths. Rooms with fan s/20,000 per person, with A/C s/30,000.

Hotel Mosquera (tel. 931 752; fax 930 392), Olmedo between Ayacucho and Guayas. The shining-but-basic rooms all have private (cold-water) bathrooms and TVs, which divert attention from the chartreuse-and-white walls, which give the feeling of being submerged in a bowl of split pea soup. Rooms with fan s/60,000, with A/C s/72,000.

Gran Hotel Machala (tel. 930 530), Montalvo at Rocafuerte. Bed. Chair. Fan. Nightstand. Even the name is boring. But it's centrally located and inexpensive, and an impressive iron gate puts guests at ease. Rooms s/25,000 per person, with bath (toilet. mirror. sink. water pipe/shower sticking out of wall) s/30,000.

Hotel Ecuatoriano (tel. 930 197), 9 de Octubre and Colón, above the Ecuatoriana Pullman bus station. Despite its locale, this hotel isn't any noisier than other places, unless you count the chatty receptionists. Rooms with windows to the outside are best, interior ones are a bit drearier. Rooms s/30,000 per person, with A/C and bath s/58,000.

Hotel San Francisco (tel. 922 395), Tarquí between Sucre and Olmedo. The large rose-colored San Francisco has a slick, well-furnished lobby, comfortable common area, elevator, and almost business-class rooms with phones, TVs, and private hot-water baths. Rooms with fan s/60,000, with A/C s/70,000.

Rizzo Hotel (tel. 921 511, fax 933 651), on Guayas and Bolívar, 2 blocks from the park. Treat yourself to a night of luxury in rooms with A/C, TV, and private hot-water bathrooms. Better still, Rizzo has a refreshing swimming pool and pleasant patio with reclining chairs for lounging in the sun. Other perks include 24hr. security, complimentary newspapers, and mineral water. Rooms s/150,000 per person.

FOOD

Those in search of local flavor should visit Machala's sprawling **outdoor market,** centered around Sucre between Guayas and Montalvo, where fresh fruits and meats can be found at nearly any hour. If it's seafood you're craving, join the locals at **Puerto Bolívar** (see below), only a five-minute cab ride away. In any case, bananas will likely constitute a large portion of the meal.

THE BANANA WARS Who would imagine that the innocent banana, so beloved the world over, could be the source of controversy, intrigue, and even bloodshed in Ecuador's "banana republic"? In the fertile lowlands of Southern Ecuador, the tasty yellow fruit is big business, generating more than US$600 million in annual export revenue. With all that money coming in, you'd think there would be enough to go around. But, as economists have long claimed and multinational corporations like The United Fruit Company have demonstrated, human greed knows no bounds. Therein lies the source of conflict; which has most recently taken the form of a fight between foreign fruit companies and their local suppliers over what constitutes a fair price for a box of bananas. The exporters pay growers about US$2 per box, which workers complain is unjust, since the "going price" is US$4.20. In June 1997, contractual negotiations between the two parties broke down; banana workers took to the streets, blocking highways and generally wreaking havoc. The subsequent strike was said to have cost the country US$12-16 million per week. Government mediation has temporarily restored order to this volatile region, but it is only a matter of time before the next battle in Ecuador's banana wars is ignited.

Chesco Pizzería (tel. 936 418), on Guayas between Sucre and 9 de Octubre, with a second location at Pinchincha and Ayacucho. Chesco is bright, clean, purple, white, and green. This peppy local hangout with music videos playing non-stop in the background serves the most authentic pizza in town (medium super chesco with the works s/58,000). Open M-Sa 11am-11:30pm, Su 3pm-11:30pm.

Restaurant Gran Chifa Oriental, 9 de Octubre and Ayacucho. There are *chifas* all over Machala, but this one is the biggest and the best (and probably also the most authentic). Complimenting the wide selection of rice and noodle based dishes (wonton soup s/20,000), the availability of fresh seafood from Puerto Bolívar has strongly influenced the menu (sweet-and-sour fish s/29,000).

Don Angelo's (tel. 932 784), 9 de Mayo between Bolívar and Rocafuerte. One of the most popular all-night restaurants surrounding the main plaza, Don Angelo's offers a big-screen TV and large selection of liquors to accompany your *comida típica* (s/15-25,000). Open 24hr.

Las Redes (tel. 866 199), 9 de Mayo and Bolívar, on a popular corner that also is home to the Licorería El Murciélago. Las Redes specializes in seafood (s/18,000 for a plate of *mariscos*) and also serves *almuerzos* or *meriendas*, s/9,000. Open daily 8am-9pm.

NEAR MACHALA: PUERTO BOLÍVAR

So here's land-locked Machala, absolutely bursting with bountiful bunches of bananas, but with no way to ship them out before they start rotting in the hot equatorial sun. Not to worry. Almost before the town could grasp the magnitude of its problem, the international port at Bolívar, 6km west of Machala, was born. Though originally little more than Machala's cargo zone, Puerto Bolívar's waterfront now doubles as a popular spot where savvy locals come for **scrumptious seafood** and sea-side strolls with their sweethearts.

On Friday and Saturday evenings, Puerto Bolívar comes alive with lights, music, and swarms of people. *Enamorados* (couples) stroll along the waters edge, vendors sell savory treats, and youth and adults alike circle in *salsa*-blasting autos until stopping to chat for hours while downing Pilsener after Pilsener.

Compared to the polluted harbor and inland streets, Puerto Bolívar's restaurants are refreshingly clean. Each tries to outdo its competition with a stronger superlative, but when multiple restaurants claim to make "the best *ceviche* in the world," it's hard to know where to turn. Actually, it doesn't much matter; seafood here is universally delicious, and meals everywhere usually run between s/15,000-25,000. The *ceviche de camarones* (shrimp *ceviche*) is especially popular. The **Restaurant Waikiki** (tel. 929 810), offering shade under a thatched roof, and **Pepe's** (tel. 929 505), with outdoor tables fashioned from ship steering wheels overlooking the bay, are both within sight of the dock and offer some of the best selections of seafood to be found in town, including Pepe's scandalous *Orgia de Mariscos* (seafood orgy s/30,000). To guzzle some *cervezas*, head to the popular **El Murciélago II,** near the dock (look for the Batman sign); stop inside or try the drive-thru (beer s/6,000; open Tu-Su 1pm-midnight).

Puerto Bolívar's **police** (tel. 929 684) are located on the water, at the corner of Malecón and Municipalidad, in front of the piers (open 24hr.). Puerto Bolívar is not a safe place at night. Given the dreary selection of accommodations and the town's proximity to Machala, passing a night in Puerto Bolívar should be avoided.

Transportation: To get here, hop the #1 bus from Machala's Parque Central or anywhere on 9 de Octubre, and get off when you see the large street sign for Av. Bolívar Madero Vargas (7min., s/500-1,000). Cabs cost around s/12,000.

NEAR MACHALA: JAMBELÍ

Unlike the Galápagos, the small island of Jambelí, 30 minutes by boat from Puerto Bolívar, has little in the way of exotic wildlife, unless one counts the species of Ecuadorian vacationers with a few gringos mixed in. Jambelí's palm-covered food stands and bell-ringing ice cream vendors congregate around a cement and Spanish-tiled street that runs through the center of this small beach town. While music, bamboo benches, thatched roofs, swaying palms, warm water, gentle waves, and spirited volleyball matches give Jambelí a constant summer feel, some things do change with the seasons. Hot summer months bring mosquitoes, so bring insect repellent and check hotel windows for screens. Tourists come in droves from August to October and during holidays (such as February's *carnavales*), causing prices to rise to as much as three times the normal rates.

Not all visitors are day trippers, and Jambelí has several options for those looking for a place to hang their beach hats. Despite its fun-in-the-sun atmosphere, accommodations here—while pleasant—are by no means Club Med. The largest, best-maintained rooms are at the **Cabañas del Mar** (tel. 964 113), to the right when facing the water from the main walk. The cabañas are comfortable and well-equipped—with a porch, private bath, and big windows. (Doubles s/70,000.) At the other end of the island, the popular **Las Cabañas de Pescador** (tel. in Machala, 937 710), offers doubles with shady porches (s/30,000 per person). Next door, the slightly newer **Hotel María Sol** has basic rooms with private baths (s/30,000 per person; discounts for larger groups).

Superb seafood is always the specialty of the day in Jambelí. Restaurants **El Niño Turista** and **El Pengüino** both serve fantastic, fishy, and frugal meals (s/8-15,000). After supper, grab a cool drink and watch the sunset from the hammocks or bamboo benches in front of El Pengüino.

To get to Jambelí during the week, take a **boat** from Puerto Bolívar (30min.; M-F 7:30, 9, 10am, 1, and 4pm; s/5,000). The same boats also return from Jambelí (30min.; M-F 8:15am, noon, 3, 5, and 6pm; s/5,000). On weekends, boats leave whenever they're full, though the wait usually isn't very long. Be prepared to pay the entrance fee (s/1,000) on your way into town.

NEAR MACHALA: PUYANGO PETRIFIED FOREST

The Puyango Petrified Forest, near Ecuador's border with Perú, celebrates both the living and the dead. The park's few visitors roam under the towering palms and creep through the giant ferns that grow alongside Puyango's 100-million-year-old petrified **Arcadia trees.** These stone-cold stumps have some of the largest fossilized trunks in the world; the biggest, known as "el gigante," measures 125m in length and 5m in diameter! Though they'd be hard-pressed to nest in these trees, over 130 bird species live in this small park. To fully appreciate and identify them, check out Deirdre Platt's Bird Guide (s/15,000), available in Spanish from the park administration. The trail through the towering trunks is mostly flat and well-maintained, with some tougher terrain and river crossings. Making this a daytrip is difficult, so you might want to take advantage of Puyango's simple but sufficient **accommodations** (camping US$20, s/50,000 per person for a bed in a lodge). There

HERE'S SOMETHING A'PEELING Ripe *(maduro)* or unripe *(verde)*, cooked or raw, for dinner or dessert, *el banano* (or *el guineo*) and its bigger, less-sweet cousin, *el plátano* (plaintain), have inspired countless culinary wonders in the kitchens of Machala. Here's a mere sampling of dishes prepared with these most important, abundant, and delicious of fruits:

Empanadas de verde: Empanadas with a shell of ground, green plantain.
Chirriado: Cheese, fried egg, and mashed green plantain all rolled up in a ball.
Chifles: Thin slices of unripe plantain deep-fried.
Patacones: Thick, fried slices of unripe plantain.
Maduro con queso: Grilled, ripe plantain filled with cheese.
Maduro lampiado: Slices of ripe plantain covered in egg and fried.
Colada de guineo: A juice made with ground, dry, unripe banana.
Guineo cocinado: Boiled, unripe banana, usually eaten with meat.
Torta de Guineo: Banana cake.
Choco banano: Chocolate-covered bananas.
Banano verde con Maní: Boiled, unripe banana served with *maní*, a sweet, honey-like peanut sauce.

is one basic but clean restaurant on the premises (s/10,000 for a *merienda;* park admission US$5, includes admission to small museum; park guides s/5,000).

Transportation: Puyango is worth a visit, but it is not easy to reach. From Machala, take a **CIFA bus** to Arenillas (30min., every 30min. 6:30am-6:30pm, s/ 8,000) and catch a *colectivo*, taxi or local bus from there to the park (2hr., s/ 15,000). No matter how you get to the park's entrance, you'll still have to stroll with the butterflies for 5½km from the security checkpoint to the park offices, where guides can be found, then it's another 15 minute's walk to the park entrance. Wear good walking shoes, sunscreen, and a hat, and bring plenty of water. Buses back to Machala or Loja pass by sporadically. Ask about return times when buying your morning bus ticket or you may find yourself stuck at the checkpoint drinking beer with the guards until the next vehicle passes. Finding information about the park is difficult, but the Puyango Administration Commission in Machala (tel. 930 012; fax 937 655) may be helpful.

ZARUMA

Founded in 1536, just after the arrival of the Spanish conquistadors, the mountainous, gold-mining town of Zaruma (pop. 7,000) wears its age well. Most mines were combed clean long ago, and the only sign of the international mining giants today is the surprising amount of golden hair among the local population. Nevertheless, the conspicuous number of *"Compro Oro"* ("I buy gold") signs still found around town do have a target audience: small scale miners inject cash into the local economy and, unfortunately, mercury and gold waste into the local streams. Yes, several active gold mines are located just outside of town, and with a little research and persistence, it may be possible to visit one of them. The miners love to talk (and talk, and talk) about their experiences and the fascinating but complicated politics surrounding the gold industry. Corruption, greed, and exploitation factor into the lives of people involved in this high-risk industry. But despite the gold, Zaruma is not a rich town, and its narrow streets are still lined with aging but beautiful wooden buildings from the turn of the century.

ORIENTATION AND PRACTICAL INFORMATION. Zaruma is easily accessible by bus either from Machala or Piñas. Most services cluster near the town plaza. **TAC** (tel. 972 156) and **Ciudad de Piñas** share an office on Honorado Márquez. Their buses travel to: **Quito** (12hr., 4:45 and 6:30pm, s/85,000); **Guayaquil** (6hr.; 2, 3:45, and 8:45am; s/50,000); **Cuenca** (5hr., 12:30 and 3:15am, s/50,000); **Loja** (6hr.; 4, 6, and 8am; s/34,000); and **Machala** (2hr., every hr. 3am-7pm, s/20,000) via **Portovelo** (s/3,000) and **Piñas** (s/3,000). **Coop de Azuay**, across the street, has an additional bus to **Cuenca** (5hr., 7:30am, s/50,000).

Banco de Pichincha, on Pichincha past Pacifictel, changes dollars but not traveler's checks (open M-F 8am-2pm). The **post office** is on the right when facing the church from the center of the park (open M-F 8am-4:30pm). **Pharmacies** line Bolívar just down from the church. **PACIFICTEL** (tel. 972 104), at the corner of Pichincha and Luis Crespo, past the market, doesn't do collect or calling card calls (open daily 8am-10pm). Find the **police** (tel. 972 198) on Colón. The **hospital** (tel. 972 025), on Rocafuerte, offers 24-hour emergency service. **Telephone code:** 07.

ACCOMMODATIONS AND FOOD. Both of Zaruma's hotels have sacrificed a central location for spectacular views. On the main road into town, **Hotel Roland** (tel. 972 800), is well worth the extra money and uphill hike into town. All rooms have private hot-water baths, carpeting, and TVs. Most have splendid views of the mountain valley, but latecomers might have to suffer views more reminiscent of a mineshaft. (Rooms s/70,000 per person, matrimonial doubles s/90,000). The **Hotel Municipal** (tel. 972 179), on Sesmo (just uphill from the TAC terminal) near the mountain ridge, may inspire grumbling on the hike up, but the view silences any complaints. As is the case with its classier competitor, all rooms have private hot-water baths and many have spectacular views. (Rooms s/25,000 per person.)

Zarumans eat heartily, if not always healthfully. The three-story market on 10 de Agosto is full of fruits, vegetables, meats, and noise. Small restaurants, most serving artery-clogging cheese and rice-based dishes, line Sucre and extend down along Honorado Márquez. **Mimos**, on Sucre near Bolívar, is popular among schoolchildren and adults alike (*umitas* s/2,500, *batidos* s/4,000). **Picantería 200 Millas,** on Honorado Márquez down the hill, specializes in seafood and spectacular scenery: the back porch, precariously suspended over the valley below, is worth paying for even if the food never comes (*arroz con camarones* s/15,000, *ceviche* s/15,000; open daily 7am-11pm).

SIGHTS. Grab a pick-axe and hard hat, cross your fingers, and hope to strike it rich. Just outside of town, the various active **gold mines** inspire champagne wishes and caviar dreams. Those wishing to visit or learn more about the mines should inquire at the **Asociación de Mineros Autonomos Muluncay** (tel. 972 855), just uphill from the Hotel Roland. They might also be able to hook you up with a guide to take you into one of the smaller, less productive excavations, such as the **Sesmo Mine**. **Compañía Bira** (tel. 972 227), a gold mining outpost on the road into town, is the largest mining company in the area, employing 120 miners in four shifts for maximum productivity every day of the year. The mine has been in active production since 1994, and the manager estimates that they will continue take precious ore from that location for another five years. Unfortunately, Bira is not able to take tourists into the active mine.

Those overcome with gold-plated, greedy thoughts may want to absolve themselves of their spiritual weakness with a hasty retreat to the stunning **Iglesia de Zaruma** in the center of town. Started in 1912, this intricate chapel took over 18 years to build, and the decorating still hasn't been finished. Two surprisingly life-like series of paintings have recently been added to its ceiling, depicting the creation of Adam and Eve and the life and times of Christ. Both murals end above the two-story altar that gleams with a thin, glittering layer of the very best of what Zaruma's mines have to offer. Also worth a visit are the walls of shrine-like sarcophagi at the **cemetery,** on the edge of town along Honorado Márquez. If you happen to be in town during the second week of July, enjoy the **Expo-Zaruma,** one of the town's biggest festivals.

PIÑAS

In 1825, Spanish geologist **Juan José Luis** was given a large land grant for his work in the Ecuadorian gold mines near what is now the town of Zaruma. Eager to honor his homeland, the miner called his new ranch **Piñas** after his former home in Spain's pineapple region. Eventually, his big ranch became the small town of Piñas, with a current population of about 10,000. Uninterested in pineapples, however, the people of Piñas spend their time cultivating coffee and bananas in the surrounding blue-green mountains. If you talk to anyone in Piñas about their home, the word *tranquilo* will doubtlessly come up, as it is the town's unanimously agreed-upon adjective. The laid-back Piñas of today has few ties to its historical past, with the **Virgen del Cisne** and an accompanying pantheon of saints exerting far more influence than any of Juan's kinfolk. From the cross on top of the hill to the electric candle-lit pictures of Madonna and child at roadside shrines, Piñas's piety is prominently displayed.

For a good workout and breathtaking mountain views, one need only walk the steep streets of Piñas. Many of the town's roads and walkways slope up and down as much as 45 degrees. Along these streets, the verdant, classically-designed park, vistas of the surrounding mountains, and clean, brightly colored buildings—including a simple but charming church with a tiled, oddly ventilated steeple—provide plenty to please the eye.

ORIENTATION AND PRACTICAL INFORMATION. **Loja** and **Sucre,** which merge on the Machala end of town, are the most active streets. The two **bus** companies, **Ciudad de Piñas** (tel. 976 167) and **TAC** (tel. 976 151), share an office on Sucre and Montalvo. Their buses run to: **Machala** (2hr., every hr. 4:30am-7:30pm, s/14,000); **Zaruma** (30min., every hr. 4am-7pm, s/7,000); **Loja** (5hr.; 3:30, 6 and 7:45am; s/35,000); **Cuenca** (5hr., 4:15am, s/45,000); **Quito** (11hr., 5:45 and 7:30pm, s/84,000); and **Guayaquil** (5hr.; 3, 4:45, and 9:45am; s/42,000). There is also daily **local bus** service to the **nearby villages** of Balsas, Marcabelí, Paccha, La Bocana, Moromoro, and Palosalo. The **police** (tel. 976 134 or 976 433) may be found at Carrión and 9 de Octubre, at the bottom end of town (open 24hr.). **Policlínico Reina del Cisne** (tel. 976 689), on Loja near Olmedo, is a 24-hour clinic, as is **Policlínico Los Angeles** (tel. 976 676), on 8 de Noviembre, just up the street from Residencial Dumari. There are plenty of **pharmacies** in Piñas, but if you are looking for a natural alternative, **Los Olivos** (tel. 976 292), Sucre, across from the park, has various mysterious-looking herbs in addition to standard pharmaceutical supplies (open daily 8am-6pm). **Pacifictel,** (tel. 976 105; fax 976 990), Ruminahui and Suárez, two blocks uphill from the church does not allow collect or calling card calls (open daily 8am-10pm).

ACCOMMODATIONS AND FOOD. The **Residencial Dumari** (tel. 976 118), Loja at 8 de Noviembre, on top of the hill, has the most comfortable beds and cleanest sheets in Piñas. Impeccable bathrooms, hot water, and some terrace rooms with shockingly beautiful views make the stay more enjoyable stay. (Rooms s/20,000 per person, with bath and color TV s/30,000.) **Hotel Las Orquideas** (tel. 976 355), on the corner of Calderón and Montalvo, in the lower end of town, has windows and not much else—rooms are basic, but clean and well-lit, with private baths and color TVs (s/30,000 per person, matrimonial doubles s/40,000).

It's easy to find a chicken—alive or roasted—or a plate of meat in Piñas, but other type of cuisine may be a bit harder to find. Vegetarians will want to stick to the numerous *panaderías* or visit the **market** on Loayza and Juan Leon Mera to enjoy fresh fruits and vegetables. **Punto del Sabor**, on Sucre near Montalvo, offers the standard *merienda* or *almuerzo* (s/12,000) in a cheery atmosphere with yellow curtains and baskets of fake flowers and fruit on every table. **Restaurante Las Orquideas,** next to the hotel, has sparkling glass tables, mirrors, and a very well-stocked polished-wood bar (open daily 6am-10pm). The **Soda Bar Polo Sur,** on Bolívar between García Moreno and Juan Leon Mera, has sandwiches, *umitas* (a dish of corn, cheese, and sugar s/2,000), and *batidos* (fruit milkshakes s/1,500).

SIGHTS AND ENTERTAINMENT. Even for the less devout, the **vista** at the hilltop cross is worth a visit for the spectacular view, which captures countless mountains as they fade from deep green to dark blue in the distance. Taxis in town will take you there (if you can find one); otherwise, the path is clearly visible from town. As night falls and the mist rolls in, head uphill to the **Babaros Disco/Bar/ Cervecería**, 8 de Noviembre and Kennedy, for some debauchery with Piñas youth (pitcher of beer s/25,000; open W-Sa 2pm-2am).

HUAQUILLAS

On Ecuador's border with Perú, the small town of Huaquillas enjoys a dubious fame that is strictly geographic. Unlike many of Ecuador's beautiful small towns, Huaquillas isn't a place where anyone uses up a whole roll of film, except perhaps for the obligatory "Welcome to Perú" shot. In fact, when it comes to aesthetic value, Huaquillas's dusty streets simply disappoint. Because prices in Ecuador are lower than those in Perú, the main road becomes a virtual street market, swarming with Peruvian day shoppers, money changers, and mosquitoes. In fact, the border crossing here, which can be quite hectic, has caused travelers to swap horror stories about Huaquillas. Mosquitoes certainly aren't the only thing to watch out for, as thieves lurk in the shadows and money changers are quick with their fixed calculators. The border crossing is usually a painless affair although somewhat bewildering, and most travelers opt to keep moving rather than loiter in Huaquillas.

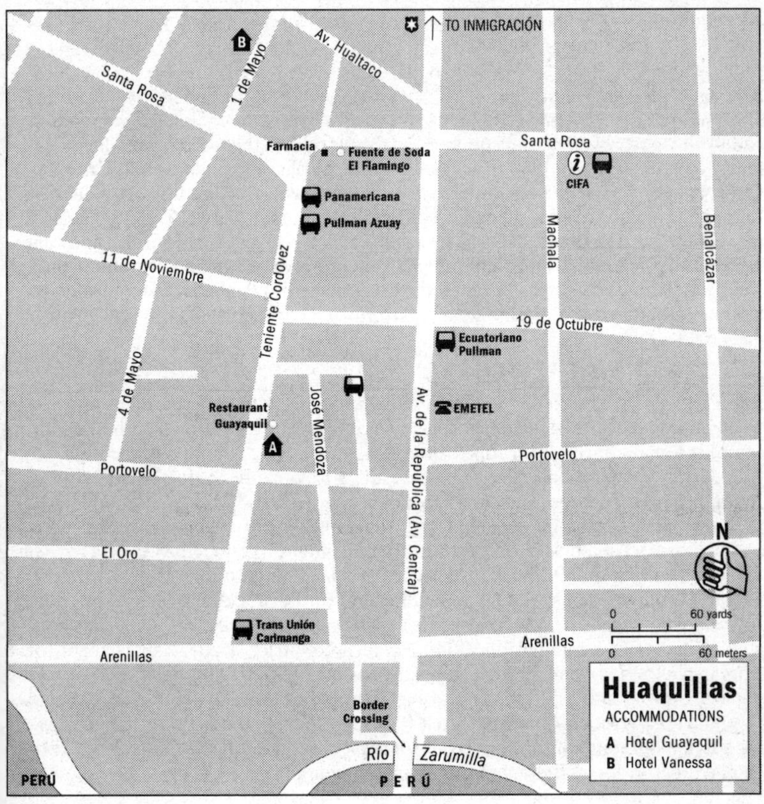

ORIENTATION AND PRACTICAL INFORMATION. Everything of any importance, including the bus terminal, border crossing, and immigration office, is along one of Huaquillas's three main dusty thoroughfares: **Av. Machala, Av. de la República** (also called **Av. Central**), and **Teniente Cordovez.**

The bus *cooperativo* **CIFA** (tel. 907 370), two blocks from the immigration office, just off República, sends buses to **Machala** (1½ hr. direct, 2hr., local; every 10min. 4:15am-8pm; s/14,000 direct, s/12,000 local) via **Santa Rosa** and **Arenillas** and to **Guayaquil** (4½ hr., 7 buses per day 3am-4:15pm, s/40,000). **Panamericana** (tel. 907 016) at the corner of Cordovez and Santa Rosa, goes to **Quito** (12hr., 6 per day 6:30am-8pm, s/95,000); **Ambato** (10hr., 8pm, s/76,000); and direct to **Tulcán** on the Colombian border (18 hr., 4:30pm, s/135,000). **Pullman Azuay**, next to Panamericana, has buses to **Cuenca** (5hr., 4 per day 6am-6:30pm, s/42,000).

For financial needs, **Banco del Pichincha** (tel. 907 015), on República, four blocks from the border, changes dollars, traveler's checks, and Peruvian *soles* (open M-F 8am-2pm). **Money changers** can also be found on the streets on either side of the border, but be especially wary of fixed calculators; carry your own calculator to double-check the arithmetic. **Police** (tel. 907 341) are ready at their station on República near the park (open 24hr.). **Telephone code:** 07.

ACCOMMODATIONS AND FOOD. Huaquillas is probably not a place where most budget travelers want to hang out. Although spending the night here is not highly recommended, and is considered dangerous by some, travelers arriving late in the evening may find it more convenient to check into one of Huaquillas's several hotels, though those near the center of town can be noisy. The main selling point of **Hotel Guayaquil** (tel. 907 303), just off República across from Pacifictel, is its proximity to the market and the border. *Habitaciones* are basic but clean. (Rooms s/15,000 per person; with private bath, fan, and mosquito netting s/25,000.) **Hotel Vanessa,** 1 de Mayo 323 and Hualtaco (tel. 907 263), is slightly off the main drag but still easily accessible. The extra *sucres* are worth it—Vanessa is one of the most reliable choices in town for safety, spotlessness, and a good night's rest. Rooms have private bath, TV, phones, A/C, and fridges. (Singles s/70,000.)

For a large, delicious platter of Chinese food, locals recommend **Chifa China Restaurante Norte,** on Teniente Cordovez near Santa Rosa. The plentiful *menú* serves up soup, chicken fried rice, and a coke (s/16,000; open daily 10am-10pm). Just around the corner, **Fuente de Soda el Flamingo** offers hamburgers (s/5,000) and fruit salads (s/7,000) in a bright rainbow-colored dining area (open daily 9am-11pm). For more traditional Ecuadorian food, you can head to **Restaurant Guayaquil,** next to Hotel Guayaquil. Enjoy simple but tasty *almuerzos* (s/10,000).

CROSSING THE BORDER

Ecuador and Perú are separated by the Río Zarumilla, which is crossed by an international bridge. In crossing the border, everyone must pass through both Ecuadorian and Peruvian immigration. Leaving Ecuador, you must pass through the **Ecuadorian Immigration Office** *(Oficina de Migraciones)*, on the left side of República, about 3km before the Peruvian border (tel. 907 755). It's a good idea to get there early, as the lines get longer throughout the day. (Open daily 8am-noon and 2-6pm.) All persons crossing the border in either direction must have a tourist **T3 card,** available at both Ecuadorian and Peruvian immigration offices, and a **valid passport.** Tourists can spend **90 days** in Ecuador or Perú within a one-year period. Anyone who wishes to stay longer must get a visa (see **Documents and Formalities,** p. 7). Citizens of a number of Middle Eastern countries, Cuba, Asia (except for Korea and Taiwan), and all African countries except South Africa may need a visa even for short stays. All visas can be obtained at the Peruvian consulate in Machala (see **Practical Information,** p. 447). Occasionally, immigration officials ask for a **return ticket** out of the country or for **proof of sufficient funds** for each day travelers expect to spend there, but this is uncommon.

MACARÁ

The border crossing at Macará may be one of Ecuador's best kept secrets. Unlike the chaotic and sometimes dangerous experience of entering or exiting Perú at Huaquillas, going through Macará is not only painless but can even be quite enjoyable. Against a gorgeous mountain background, the town's white-and-blue church sparkles in the sun, as does the water in the fountain in the central plaza. The Río Macará, forming the natural border between the two countries, is surprisingly clean; locals sometimes swim by the small "beach" on the Ecuadorian side.

The short distance between the **market** and the **central plaza** is covered by **10 de Agosto. Bolívar, Loja,** and **Veintimilla** also lead away from the plaza, crossed by **Manuel Rengel** and **Calderón. Trans Unión Carimanga** (tel. 694 047), on Loja between Rengel and 10 de Agosto, sends **buses** to **Loja** (6hr.; 12:30, 4:30, 5:30, 7:30, 11am, 1, and 3pm; s/38,000). **INEFAN** (tel. 694 280) has a small office on the corner of Loja and 10 de Agosto; they can provide information on the nearby protected forests of **Susuco** and **El Tundo (bosque húmedo)** as well as projects involving the *nogal* tree. The **Banco de Loja** in town does not change dollars or Peruvian *soles*, but the branch at the border does (open M-F 8am-1pm). Money changers can also be found in the market area in Macará. **Delgado Travel** (tel. 694 396), 10 de Agosto next to the church, also changes dollars, as well as mailing letters and packages abroad (open M-F 8:30am-6pm, Sa 8:30am-1pm). **Pharmacies** and **clinics** abound, as usual. The **Pacifictel** office (tel. 694 104), on Emiliano Correa and J. Leon Mera, does not allow collect or calling card calls (open daily 8am-10pm). **Telephone code:** 07.

The nicest lodging in Macará can be found at the **Hotel Espiga de Oro** (tel. 694 405), just off 10 de Agosto between the market and the plaza. Hanging plants and stunning views contribute to a bright and cheerful atmosphere. Fans, TVs, and private baths in every room. (Singles s/55,000, doubles s/90,000.) A ten-minute walk toward the border, the **Parador Turístico** (tel. 694 099) has a more rustic feel; simple rooms have private baths, and some have a balcony. The large hotel also includes a restaurant, bar, disco, and swimming pool. (Rooms s/42,000 per person.) For travelers on a tight budget, the **Hotel Guayaquil**, on Bolívar between Calderón and Rengel, offers bare, dorm-style rooms with common baths for (Dorms s/18,000 per person). Enjoy a plate of *camarones* (s/25,000) at the **Restaurant Colonial** (tel. 694 028) on Rengel between Loja and Bolívar (open daily 8am-9pm). Next to the hotel of the same name, **Restaurant Espiga de Oro** has a wide selection of *platos típicos* (s/20-30,000) or the standard *almuerzo* (s/15,000). The **Frigebar Central** (tel. 694 882), on the plaza across from the fountain, is indeed in a central location and is popular with the locals (hamburger "*doble grande*" s/5,000, *sandwich de pollo* s/ 5,000, open M-F 8:30am-9pm, Sa-Su 8:30am-11pm).

CROSSING THE BORDER

The bridge between Perú and Ecuador is about 3km from Macará; taxis and *colectivos* leave from the market area (ask for *la frontera*) or make the pleasant walk on foot. Although you can cross the bridge at any hour, to officially enter or exit either country you need to go to the immigration offices located on either side of the bridge for entrance and exit stamps and to surrender or receive your tourist T3 card (open daily 6am-10pm). Immigration officials are generally friendly and, sometimes, multilingual (one official on the Peruvian side speaks Spanish, English, German, and Hebrew!) From **La Tina** (the tiny settlement on the Peruvian side of the border), *colectivos* run to **Sullana** (2hr., s/8). Although there are a number of hotels and restaurants in Sullana, it is easiest to take a bus or *colectivo* from Av. Jose de Loma to the nearby, larger city of **Piura** (45 min. s/1-1.50)

THE GALÁPAGOS ISLANDS

There are few places in the world where humans are truly second-class citizens. In the Galápagos Islands, however, a national park is more than simply an isolated area within the realm of human activity; rather, 97% of the land area is protected territory, and humans can only tiptoe around this veritable miracle of nature. From the amazing amiability of the animals to the tranquil beauty of the landscape, these islands form an archipelago of fairy tale magic. On an ordinary day one might swim with sea lions or observe frigatebird courtship on sandy beaches surrounded by cliffs, volcanoes, and the shimmering expanse of the Pacific Ocean.

But just as visitors marvel at their own insignificance within the natural world, they learn all about nature's fragility. Along with discussions of unique geology and wildlife come tales of ecosystems disrupted by the carelessness of human settlers. Even after the 1959 declaration of the Galápagos National Park, whole species still remain threatened by rats that came with the earliest settlers and feral goats, which were originally brought to the islands for food.

While the interests of humans and other animals may be contradictory, the interaction between the two has been one of the Galápagos's most unique aspects. In its lava lizards and its legends, the islands seem to hold a key to the most mysterious aspects of natural history—secrets which have not gone unnoticed by its visitors. Charles Darwin made observations here that would help substantiate his then-radical evolutionary views, and 60,000 tourists now come here each year to feel a bit closer to nature. Whether it's because they've learned everything they'd ever want to about marine iguanas' mating patterns, or because they've been mesmerized by the sunset over a never-ending stretch of ocean, all who visit these enchanted islands will remember the trip for the rest of their lives.

ESSENTIALS

BUDGET GALÁPAGOS: FACT OR FICTION?

The Galápagos are not a cheap destination. Even when leaving from the relatively nearby cities of Quito or Guayaquil, it still costs US$400-$500 in airline tickets and park fees to enter the islands. Once there, tourism-inflated prices and expensive tours could easily push a two-week vacation to over US$2000. Yet the key to enjoying the Galápagos cheaply is to realize that exotic animals and landscape remain the same whether observed by the craftiest budget traveler or the guy on a US$300-a-day cruise ship. With a little savvy, negotiation, and patience, an incredible two-week adventure may materialize for around US$1000.

There are basically two ways to budget travel through the Galápagos: the inexpensive tour and independent travel. Though the independent option frees visitors from the rigidity of boat tour schedules, packaged tours usually end up a better deal in the long-run. A precious few islands are connected by public transportation and from the port towns of these islands, visitor sites are largely inaccessible. Although day trips often cost less per day than tour boats, daytrips only include lunch (while tour boats include full room and board), and daytrippers visit but one site a day (while tour boaters visit two). Although a Galápagos trip usually revolves around the sights reached primarily by boat, time spent in the towns and at attractions nearby prove an enjoyable (and inexpensive) complement to the tour boat scene. Another important key to budget travel success: the busy season is not necessarily the ideal season. Not only do airline fares increase, but the chance of finding a last-minute boat tour bargain in Puerto Ayora virtually disappears. In other words, low-season is budget season.

WHEN TO GO

The relative stability of the equatorial climate ensures a rewarding Galápagos experience year round, but there are two distinct seasons in the region. Warm ocean currents cause hot, rainy weather from January through April, the *caliente* season, while the rest of the year, during *la garúa*, the islands dry out and cool down. Neither season is completely ideal—during the rainy months, the ocean water refreshes at a comfortable 75°F (24°C), but heavy rain showers often disturb the tropical tranquility. Likewise, while rain may fall rarely during the dry months, the sky is often overcast, the water a chilly 70°F (21°C) or lower, and the waves choppy from sporadic winds. **The ideal visiting months,** climate-wise, are between seasons—March through May, when rainfall lightens, and November and December, as the climate warms up. Note also that some animals are only around at certain times, so research nesting patterns beforehand to avoid disappointment.

The Galápagos **surfing** season is between December and February. Puerto Baquerizo Moreno, on San Cristóbal, is the headquarters for the annual pilgrimage of devoted surfers during this season, and it is not uncommon for hotels to rent multi-person rooms for an affordable monthly rate.

During the busy months of July, August, and December, finding a boat becomes challenging, bargaining proves nearly impossible, and prices rise significantly—book flights well in advance. October is not a busy month, but precisely for this reason, many boat owners choose to make repairs then and put their vehicles out of commission. All things considered, the best month is May: tourism hasn't yet picked up, the climate is moderate, and the seas calm. July and August tend to be the worst times to go because tourism peaks and the seas are cold and rough—especially bad for those subject to seasickness. During the sweltering time from January to April, consider splurging on a boat with air conditioning.

The Galápagos Islands are one hour behind the Ecuadorian mainland and six hours behind Greenwich Mean Time. As on the mainland, the Galápagos do not observe Daylight Savings Time.

USEFUL ORGANIZATIONS

Charles Darwin Foundation, Inc., 100 N. Washington St., Suite 311, Falls Church, VA 22046, USA (tel. (703) 538-6833; fax (703) 538-6835; www.polaris.net/~jpinson/welcome.html). Mailing address: Casilla 17-01-3891, Quito, Ecuador. A non-profit membership organization promoting conservation, education, and scientific research in the Galápagos. Publishes a newsletter, the *Galápagos Bulletin*, 3 times a year and maintains a very informative web site.

Corporación Ecuatoriana de Turismo (CETUR), Eloy Alfaro 1214 and Carlos Tobar, Quito (tel. (02) 507 555; fax 507 564; www.cetur.org). A government-run tourist info agency with valuable facts about hotels and transportation. Provides maps and info as specific as animal mating seasons and the best sites to spot various types of wildlife. There are CETUR offices in all major cities in Ecuador, including one in Puerto Ayora (tel. 526 179) on Charles Darwin.

South American Explorers Club (SAEC), Jorge Washington 311 and Leonidas Plaza, mailing address: Apartado 17-21-431, Eloy Alfaro, Quito, Ecuador (tel./fax (02) 225 228; email explorer@saec.org.ec; www.samexplo.org). A non-profit organization with extensive info on traveling, working, volunteering, and researching in Latin America. Their "Galápagos Packet" of practical info about the islands is updated every few months. SAEC has reports on the various boats operating in the Galápagos; it's a very good idea to check them out.

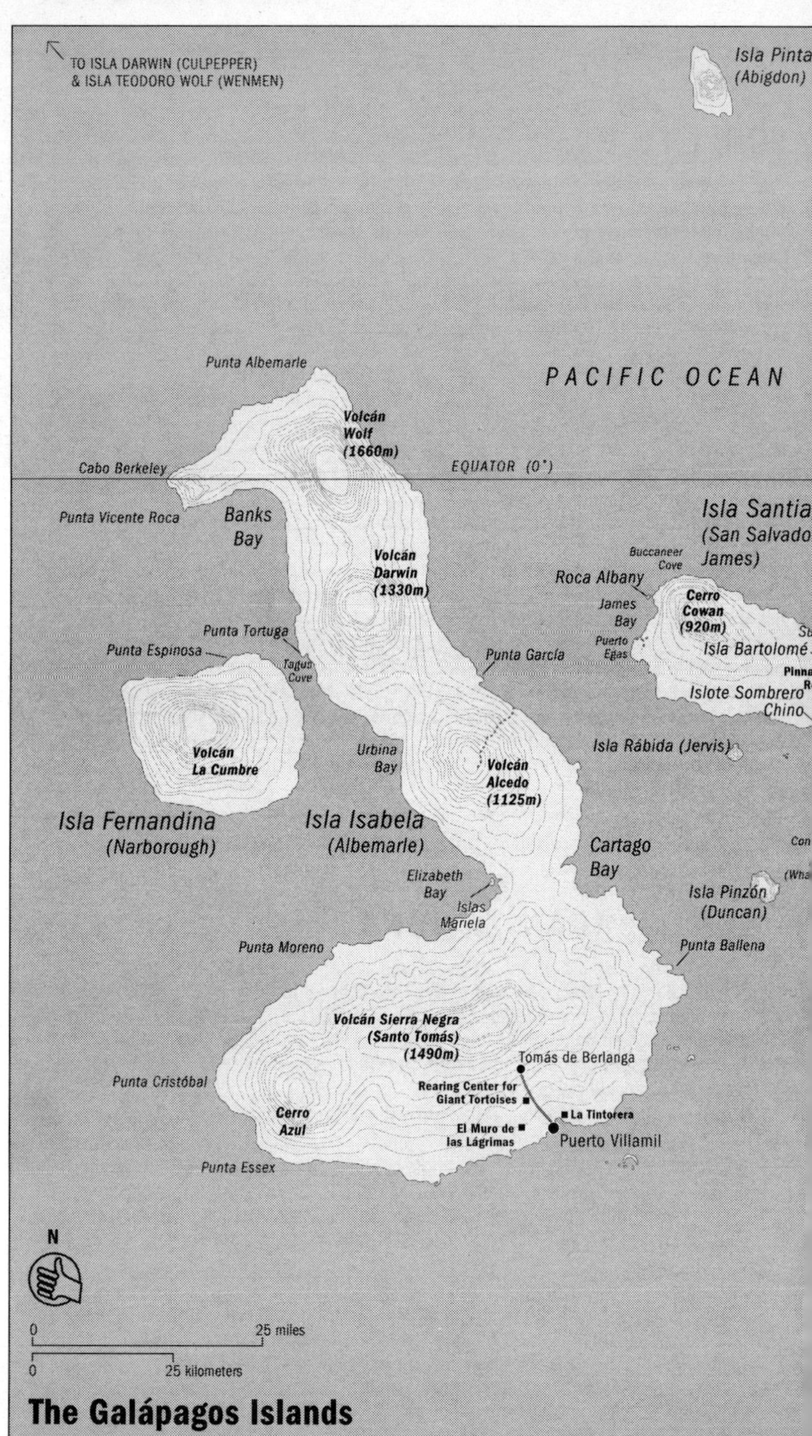

The Galápagos Islands

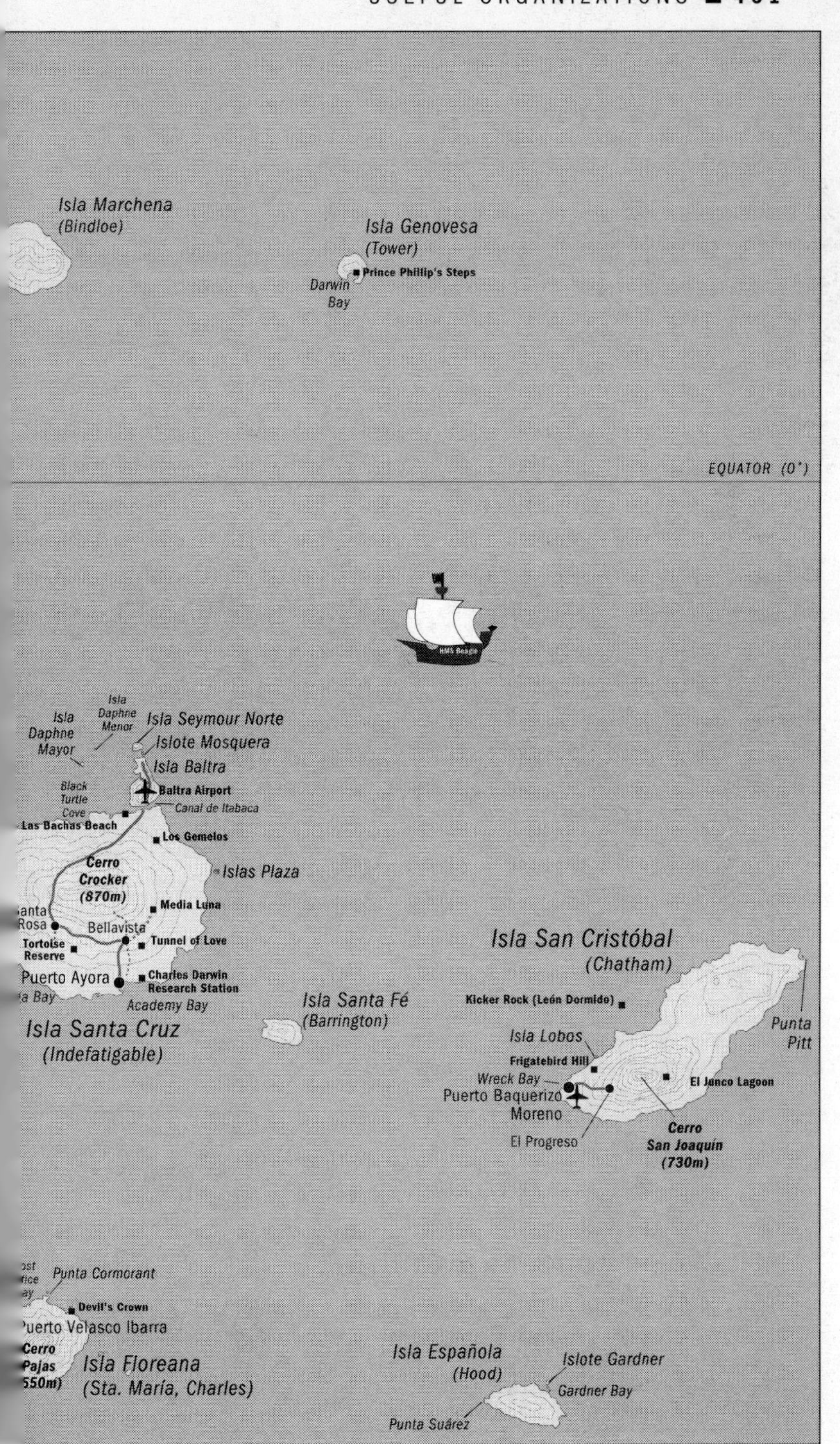

Isla Marchena
(Bindloe)
Isla Genovesa
(Tower)
Prince Phillip's Steps
Darwin Bay
EQUATOR (0°)
HMS Beagle
Isla Daphne Mayor
Isla Daphne Menor
Isla Seymour Norte
Islote Mosquera
Isla Baltra
Baltra Airport
Canal de Itabaca
Black Turtle Cove
Las Bachas Beach
Los Gemelos
Cerro Crocker (870m)
Islas Plaza
Media Luna
Bellavista
Tunnel of Love
Tortoise Reserve
Puerto Ayora
Charles Darwin Research Station
Academy Bay
Isla Santa Cruz
(Indefatigable)
Isla Santa Fé
(Barrington)
Isla San Cristóbal
(Chatham)
Kicker Rock (León Dormido)
Punta Pitt
Isla Lobos
Frigatebird Hill
Wreck Bay
El Junco Lagoon
Puerto Baquerizo Moreno
El Progreso
Cerro San Joaquín (730m)
Punta Cormorant
Devil's Crown
Isla Floreana
(Sta. María, Charles)
Isla Española
(Hood)
Islote Gardner
Gardner Bay
Punta Suárez

GETTING THERE

TRAVEL BY PLANE

Ecuador's two national airlines, **TAME** and **SAN/SAETA,** provide the only available flights to the Galápagos. All flights originate in Quito, stop in Guayaquil one hour later, then take an additional 90 minutes to reach the islands. Both airlines have similar round-trip fares, but prices fluctuate depending on the season. During the high season (June 15-Aug. 31, Dec. 1-Jan. 15), round-trip tickets cost US$378 from Quito and US$224 from Guayaquil; low-season fares dip to approximately US$324 from Quito and US$190 from Guayaquil. Passengers can pay for tickets either in dollars or *sucres;* compare the airline exchange rate and the street rate to determine the better bargain. If you don't book a boat tour in advance, getting on flights to and from Puerto Ayora can be difficult during the high season and just before and after these dates. Flights are constantly overbooked, and buying a ticket does not assure flying on a specific day. Try to get a reservation, or *cupo*, for the day you want to fly. Otherwise, you'll be placed on the waiting list, which makes getting on a flight a matter of luck (and of how early you get to the airport that morning). Always re-check flight information a few days before traveling.

TAME (tel. (02) 509 383; fax (02) 554 907), Colón and Reina Victoria in New Quito, runs the most flights to the Galápagos, departing daily from Quito at 7 and 11:30am, and from Guayaquil at 8:10am and 12:50pm. Planes land on Isla Baltra, with easy access to Isla Santa Cruz and Puerto Ayora. Returning flights leave Baltra at 9:20am and 2:20pm. TAME also offers special fares for students with valid university ID and an international student ID (tel. (02) 554 900). If you plan to arrange a tour in the Galápagos, your prospects are much better in Puerto Ayora than in Puerto Baquerizo Moreno—another good reason to choose TAME.

SAN/SAETA (tel. (02) 565 005), Colón and Amazonas, flies to San Cristóbal, not especially convenient unless your tour leaves from that island—most leave from Santa Cruz. Flights leave Guayaquil daily at 10am—SAN/SAETA does not offer service to the Galápagos from Quito.

GETTING AROUND

As may be expected, transportation around and between the islands of the Galápagos is considerably more difficult than between points on the mainland. Since most of the land is a protected national park, there are restrictions on which vehicles may travel through it. And, since there are many separate islands, trips between them must be made by boat or plane.

When arriving on Isla Baltra or Isla San Cristóbal, everyone must pay a **US$100** park admission fee in cash. Credit cards and traveler's checks are NOT accepted. There is no way around this charge, and it's a good idea to keep the receipt if traveling between islands. A passport is also required to enter the Galápagos.

PACKAGE TOURS AND CRUISES

The most practical, fun, and cheap way to get the most out of Galápagos is on a tour boat. Tours come in many lengths, from daytrips to three-week cruises. The most common are three- to eight-day trips. The SAEC recommends the following tour companies:

Angermeyers Enchanted Excursions, Foch 726 and León Mera in New Quito (tel. (02) 569 960 or 504 444; fax 569 956).

Safari Tours (tel. (02) 234 799; fax 220 426), Pasaje de Roca in New Quito, between Amazonas and León Mera.

Moonrise Travel Agency (tel. (05) 526 403 or 526 348; tel./fax 526 589), in Puerto Ayora on Darwin, facing the Banco del Pacífico.

TOUR BOATS AND GUIDES

There are three main classes of **tour boats:** economy, touristic, and first-class. Economy boats tend to be small with limited facilities, unremarkable food, and mediocre guides. Many of these boats are OK, but some are downright primitive. It's a good idea to see the boat. Ask at Puerto Ayora travel agencies if this is possible. Touristic boats tend to be a little bigger (averaging 16 passengers), with private baths, palatable food, and better guides. First-class ships are even nicer, but the comfort is reflected in their price tag. Like so many other things in life, size really does matter. Bigger boats won't rock as much in the waves, they'll have more space for privacy, and they'll handle longer voyages, which enables them to reach some of the fantastic outer islands such as Genovesa and Fernandina.

The quality of **guides** also matters; they are divided into three categories. Naturalist I is a regular guide with general knowledge of the islands' flora and fauna. Naturalist II has more in-depth knowledge and is guaranteed to speak English. Naturalist III is an bona fide biologist. A guide can make or break the experience, but a little prior study of Galápagos wildlife and history can salvage a trip ruined by a mediocre naturalist. One caveat: the best guides often work on the larger, more expensive boats—always ask what type of guide comes with a tour before signing on. Ask specific questions about the length of the trip before signing on. The first "day" of a boat tour might start after dinner and the last "day" could be a short stop at a visitor site before breakfast. It's a good idea to read up on the different islands ahead of time, in order to have a sense of which islands are more important to visit. Many of the islands have a "specialty," which may match your interests: flamingoes or red-footed boobies, mangroves or lava cacti. For example, North Seymour is excellent for frigate and blue-footed booby action, but Española, on the other side of the archipelago, is the only place to see the waved albatross. Bird fanatics might want to consider multi-day tours which hit both of these islands. For those who'd rather approach the islands in an independent manner, basing yourself in Puerto Ayora and taking **daytrips** to nearby islands is an option, although this reduces your access to more distant visitor sites.

FINDING A TOUR

When shopping for Galápagos tours, remember this principle: the closer you are to the boat when you book it and the closer the sailing date, the lower the price of the tour. Thus, someone booking a May 14 tour from the U.S. in March may pay twice as much as someone who signs up on May 13 in Puerto Ayora. The trade-off is uncertainty—those who wait run the risk of not finding a suitable boat. Yet the best deals await in Puerto Ayora, and one can usually see the boat before deciding on it. It may also be wise to compare the many agencies along Darwin and make a trip to **Moonrise Travel** before booking with one of the first places you pass. Puerto Ayora prices for economy tours run around US$80-85 per day. These prices are probably at least 50% better than what an agency would have quoted you back home. As always, these deals may be unavailable in the high season.

An alternative is to book through a travel agency in Quito or Guayaquil. These agencies can often arrange very cheap passage on boats that are set to leave in a few days but have some empty spaces. Quito is packed with travel agencies—Amazonas seems to have two or three on every block. Agencies that directly represent their own boats may be able to negotiate a lower price. Guayaquil has fewer agencies booking Galápagos tours than Quito, but with a little patience, deals may be found here as well. In busier seasons, getting an actual reservation on a TAME flight can be difficult. Boat companies usually reserve airplane seats for their passengers, yet another good reason to arrange a tour before going to the islands.

LIFE ON THE BOAT

Life on a multiple-day tour boat is very relaxed, a great time to work on your tan and pig out, but a few precautions should be taken to ensure that your trip runs smoothly. Minor theft, sadly enough, has been known to occur on some boats. Never leave valuable items within plain view in your cabin. Count your money before and after returning from island activities. Large quantities of money rarely disappear, but twenty dollars can be peeled off a large wad in a money belt, and the unsuspecting owner might never know the difference. Lock your cabin if you've been issued a key. In other words, use common sense. Again, this type of thing is very rare, and most boat tours will be fun-filled and relaxing.

Almost all tour boats (whether they have six or 100 passengers) follow a similar routine. Days start early (breakfast 7am) and generally include visits to two sites, either on the same island or on two nearby ones. Since boats cannot dock right at the shore of the islands, it's a **panga** (dinghy) ride to the shore—one quickly learns the difference between a **"wet landing"** (onto a beach—water generally about knee-deep) and a **"dry landing"** (onto a man-made or natural dock). Most days will also include an opportunity to swim or snorkel.

It is standard to tip the crew on a tour boat US$25 to US$50 per week, depending on the quality of the service. Crew members work hard and aren't paid very well (particularly on economy boats), so this is probably not the best place to economize. The guide usually gets paid about twice as much as the crew, but it is appropriate to tip the guide as well. It is best to pool together money with the other passengers and then divide it up for the crew members, but if this is awkward, give the cash to the captain to divide (and hope that it's done fairly).

INTER-ISLAND TRAVEL

BY BOAT

Instituto Nacional Galápagos (INGALA; tel. 526 199), the government-run public transportation system, offers shuttle boats between three of the archipelago's populated islands in various exciting combinations: **San Cristóbal to Santa Cruz** (Tu 8am-noon); **Santa Cruz to Floreana** (W 8am-noon); **Floreana** to **Santa Cruz** (Th 8am-noon); and **Santa Cruz to San Cristóbal** (F 8am-noon). While INGALA is the cheapest means of inter-island travel, it gives preference to residents and charges *extranjeros* (foreigners) inflated rates (s/132,000 each way). Ticket-purchasing policies differ among towns, but it is generally a good idea to buy one as early as possible. INGALA's infrequent schedule only accommodates travelers with a lot of time to spare. The **Estrella del Mar,** a municipally-owned boat based in Puerto Villamil, leaves around 7am, traveling from **Isabela to Santa Cruz** on Tuesday and returning to Isabela on Wednesday. Purchasing a ticket in Puerto Ayora is a challenge, and if you'd rather not wait at Puerto Ayora's municipal dock early Wednesday morning (we're talking 6:30am here), contact the INGALA office on Tuesday and hope they can track down the Captain, Juan Mendoza. Travel agencies in Puerto Ayora might also be able to arrange passage on the *Estrella del Mar* as well.

BY PLANE

Small planes also travel between the larger islands. **EMETEBE** (tel. 526 177 in Santa Cruz, tel. 520 036 in San Cristóbal, or tel. 529 155 in Isabela), flies between Puerto Ayora, Puerto Baquerizo Moreno, and Puerto Villamil three times per week. Although the planes are much faster than boats, one pays for the convenience (US$80 between Baltra and Puerto Baquerizo Moreno or Puerto Villamil, US$90 between Puerto Baquerizo Moreno and Puerto Villamil). Flights carry five passengers and take approximately half an hour. They are the only means of travel between Isabela and San Cristóbal.

DAYTRIP OPTIONS

Daytrips are available from Puerto Ayora to Seymour Norte, South Plaza, Bartolomé, Santa Fé, and Floreana. They cost about US$50 and include lunch and a guide (who doesn't necessarily speak English). You can book these daytrips from any travel agency in town. The Hotel Delfín also runs daytrips on its private boat, but these trips are often reserved for people staying at the hotel and are considerably more expensive (US$100). However, the boat runs some trips to nearby Rábida Island and may also visit two sights in one day, unlike the other day tours.

PRACTICAL INFORMATION

MONEY AND BARGAINING

Ecuadorian sucres are the common currency, but U.S. dollars are often accepted. Since they're aimed at rich gringos, prices in dollars are often higher than their equivalents in sucres. In fact, it is a good idea to have a large quantity of cash and traveler's checks on hand when paying for a tour after getting to the islands, since travel agents usually charge a 10-20% service charge for credit card transactions. **Credit cards** are a somewhat impractical currency on the Galápagos and very few establishments accept VISA or American Express. **MasterCard** is preferred everywhere, but still accompanied by at least a 10% service charge. Locals routinely overcharge tourists; be prepared to ask the price beforehand and **bargain,** especially in the low season. There are few places to **exchange money** and rates tend to be exploitative. It makes sense to change money ahead of time in Quito or Guayaquil; the islands tend to be relatively safe; carrying lots of cash is less of a concern than on the mainland. Currently, **Banco del Pacífico,** located in Puerto Ayora and Puerto Baquerizo Moreno, is the best place to change money. The banks' **ATMs** are convenient ways to access cash, but they do not accept VISA cards.

PACKING

Stores in the Galápagos tend to be small, expensive, and oriented towards t-shirts and souvenirs, so have everything you'll need before you get there. Carefully consider footwear since island traveling makes many demands on one's feet. For wet landings and easy hikes, a pair of sturdy **sandals** will suffice. However, **hiking boots** or sturdy shoes are a must for rockier or more difficult treks. To battle mosquitoes and their ilk, bring along some **insect repellent.** Rainy season or not, the sun's rays will likely scorch, so stock up on **sunscreen** and bring **sunglasses** and a **wide-brimmed hat.** When it cools down in the evening, a cozy **sweatshirt** and pair of **pants** will be appreciated. It's best to prepare for any kind of weather with a couple of **t-shirts,** a pair of **shorts,** and a **light raincoat.** The latter is a necessity during the rainy months (Jan.-Apr.), but may be useful anytime. Finally, for **snorkeling** or **scuba diving,** bring gear if you've got it. Most tour boats have a supply of masks on board, but there's no guaranteeing their quality (or quantity). One can also rent masks, snorkels, and flippers in Puerto Ayora. For those spending much time in the chilly water during the dry season, a **short-sleeved wet suit** may ease the plunge. Most towns in the Galápagos shut off power during the night, so bring a **flashlight**. Also, a **disposable underwater camera** may useful to capture all that close-up sea lion fun.

SCUBA DIVING AND SNORKELING

If you would find submerging yourself in fast-moving currents full of sharks, rays, and sea lions exciting, you'd probably like **scuba diving** in the Galápagos. The fish are pretty but relatively unremarkable; the reason why divers from all over the world come here is the unparalleled chance to swim with the big beasts of the sea: playful sea lions, lightning-fast schools of hammerheads, and even the elusive whale shark. Strong currents make diving here relatively difficult, and most schools will only take you out if you're experienced. No matter what you're level of experience, always evaluate the "current" situation before jumping in.

The most established diving outfit in town is **Galápagos Sub-Aqua** (tel. 526 350, in Quito tel./fax (02) 565 294 and 593-4-314-510; email sub_aqua@accessinter.net; www.galapagos_sub_aqua.com.ec), on Charles Darwin, 800m from the Darwin Center. Diveleader Fernando Zambrano is a consummate professional and friendly teacher who is licensed as a Naturalist Guide and speaks English. Sub-Aqua offers daytrips from beginner- to divemaster-level (US$75-150; including all gear, tanks for 2 dives, and a divemaster guide). "All-inclusive dive packages" include accommodations, three meals, and diving (US$70-150 per day, more if you want to dive at the remote Darwin and Wolf islands). The only diving opportunities available to non-certified divers are introductory dives at Academy Bay (US$75). Also nearby, **Galápagos Scuba Iguana** (tel./fax 526 497, in Quito (02) 253 404; email hotelgps@pa.ga.pro.ec; www.galapagos_scuba_iguana.com), is located at the Hotel Galápagos. Divemaster Mathias Espinosa, a certified divemaster/instructor and naturalist guide, speaks Spanish, English, and German. Iguana offers daytrips spanning three to seven hours (US$78-110; includes dive gear, tanks for 2 dives, a divemaster guide, and a box lunch for 7hr. trips).

Unlike scuba diving, there are no special certifications or guide companies needed for most **snorkeling** adventures. For the most part, you just need a mask, a snorkel, pair of rubber flippers, and a desire to explore the world below. Most beaches on the islands allow snorkeling, and time is usually budgeted into tour boat schedules to accommodate passengers' diving desires.

THE GALÁPAGOS: AN OVERVIEW

HISTORY

All the flora and fauna on the Galápagos mysteriously crossed nearly 1000km of ocean to reach the islands, and the first human inhabitants arrived with the help of auspicious waves as well. Pottery shards found on various islands suggest that pre-Inca *indígenas* spent time on Santa Cruz and Floreana—likely the result of their balsa rafts floating astray. But the first Galápagos tour to be recorded in history set sail around 1485, when the Inca prince **Tupac Inca Yupanqui** sent his army on an exploratory expedition. Like all Galápagos visitors, they returned loaded with souvenirs, though no tourist in Puerto Ayora picks up souvenirs like the gold treasure, bronze seat, and horse's skin and jaw that the Inca brought back.

The first Europeans on the islands were also accidental tourists. At the time, **Fray Tomás de Berlanga,** the archbishop of Panamá, and his Peruvian-bound ship didn't think it too propitious when a week-long storm and a six-day drift carried their boat so far off course. Berlanga was a bit put off by the remoteness of these arid islands, although he was struck by the tameness of the animals. This 1535 voyage is considered the official "discovery" of the Galápagos. When the islands were first included on maps 35 years later, they were given the name Galápagos (Spanish for "tortoises") after the enormous shelled specimen that Berlanga described. Numerous streets throughout the Galápagos have been named after this well-travelled *padre.* For the next few centuries, **pirates** used the islands (most notably Isla Santiago's Buccaneer Cove and James Bay) as hideaways and launching pads for surprise sea attacks. The lava tunnels that snake beneath the islands are rumored to have been preferred hiding spots for the pirates' booty—

A FISTFUL OF FINCHES

In both space and time, we seem to be brought somewhat near to that great fact—that mystery of mysteries—the first appearance of new beings on this earth.
—Charles Darwin, *The Voyage of the Beagle*

In 1831, **Charles Darwin** was a 22-year-old medical school dropout and mediocre theology student. Young Charles looked forward to a simple life as a country parson indulging in his true passion—natural history. One of Darwin's professors, **John Stevens Henslow,** recognized that the bright young man was more interested in worms than the Edict of Worms, so he hooked him up with a job as ship's naturalist on the H.M.S. Beagle and as "gentleman companion" to the captain, **Robert Fitzroy.**

The Beagle set off on a five-year, around-the-world voyage, during which Darwin's observations and collections of flora and fauna from South America, the Pacific Islands, and Australia made him something of a scientific celebrity by the time he returned to England. But young Charles had done more than observe and collect. After examining multiple, disparate ecosystems, Darwin began to see a certain set of patterns. An eager reader of **Charles Lyell's** *Principles of Geology,* Darwin was willing to see the natural world as a product of constant change. Evolution was not a new idea—geologists had developed the fossil record sufficiently by the 18th century to see convincing evidence for change. What Darwin provided was a mechanism. His idea that the brutal competition to survive and reproduce writes its story in the offspring of the victor—the survival of the fittest—was as insidiously persuasive as it was an anathema to conventional views on natural history and man's place in the universe. Upon the 1859 publication of *The Origin of Species,* a scientific and social firestorm broke out across the literate world, altering biology and philosophy forever. His notebooks later revealed these cryptic words: "In July opened first book on 'transmutation of species'—Had been greatly struck from about one month of previous March—On character of South American fossils—and species on Galápagos Archipelago—These facts (especially latter) origin of all my views."

keep an eye out for buried treasure while spelunking. Raiding and pillaging can be hard work, and when hungry pirates discovered that the Galápagos tortoises could survive for months with little food or water, they began storing them in their ships to use as a fresh meat source on voyages. When this trend caught on, the tortoise population began to dwindle at an astonishing rate; at the time of **Charles Darwin's** 1855 visit, he reported that pirate ships would take as many as 700 tortoises with them at a time. In subsequent years, hunters continued to harvest the animals for their meat and the oil prepared from their fat for use in Guayaquil's new street lamps.

Darwin only stayed in the Galápagos for five weeks, but his visit would ultimately determine the historical path of the archipelago and its precariously endangered namesakes. Darwin's writings about the islands and their purported impact on his theory of evolution eventually gave the archipelago a high profile worldwide. Ecuador had claimed the islands only a few years before Darwin arrived and used them as a penal colony at first. But due to the Galápagos's fame and importance in the scientific and ecological world, a few areas were declared wildlife reserves in 1934, and in 1959 all non-colonized areas officially became the **Parque Nacional Galápagos.** In the following decades, tourism steadily increased. In the 1990s, the islands have hosted 60,000 visitors each year, at least 75% of them foreigners. It appears that many of the tortoise populations will continue to survive, despite their difficulties, because of a selective advantage that Darwin could never have foreseen: people, their one-time enemy, now respect and protect them.

GEOLOGY

BACKGROUND

The first Galápagos island was formed over 4 million years ago, and new islands have been forming ever since. The islands were never part of the mainland, but instead were formed by underwater volcanoes that expelled lava onto the ocean floor, building themselves higher and higher until they finally broke the water's surface. Volcanically active islands such as Fernandina have continued to add new territory even within the last decade. The volcanoes of the Galápagos were formed by basaltic lava, which has a relatively fluid consistency. For this reason, the Galápagos volcanoes are more inclined to vent their fury in the form of lava flows than enormous explosions, which is why they tend to look more like domes than the perfectly shaped, conical volcanoes most people imagine.

Tectonic theory proposes that the surface of the earth is made up of a number of **tectonic plates** that are suspended on the **magma** (molten rock) that lies below them. These tectonic plates are constantly moving, each one being pushed and pulled by the plates around it. The Galápagos are located on the **Nazca plate,** which is being pushed towards the southeast by plates to the north and west of it. The "hot spot," a stationary area beneath the Galápagos, melts the Nazca plate into magma that bubbles onto the surface of the earth, usually through a volcano. These volcanoes formed and continue to form the islands. Other famous hot spots are responsible for the Hawaiian Islands and the geothermal activity of Yellowstone National Park in the United States. While the Galápagos hot spot remains stationary, the Nazca plate is moving to the southeast, taking the older islands with it and leaving the hot spot to form new islands to the northwest. As a result, Isla Española in the southeast is the oldest island in the archipelago, while Fernandina and Isabela to the northwest are the youngest and most volcanically active.

ATTRACTIONS

While most people come to the Galápagos to see the unique wildlife, the geology is some of the most interesting in the world. Newly-created land formations abound, since the islands themselves are so young (4 million years is a blink of an eye, geologically speaking). On the island of Santa Cruz, you can lose yourself in the **lava tunnels** of love (see p. 482). These were formed by lava flows that hardened on the outside but remained liquid and continued to flow on the inside, eventually forming a rocky hollow tube. On Isabela, visit one of the largest **calderas** (collapsed volcanic crater) in the world (10km in diameter) on the summit of Volcán Sierra Negra (see p. 494). Also on Isabela, witness the steamy, vaporous emissions of the **fumaroles** (steam vents) of Volcán Alcedo (see p. 496). The 6.5km-wide and 900m-deep *caldera* of Volcán La Cumbre is the fiery heart and soul of Isla Fernandina (see p. 497). The island grows larger and larger with every eruption; a 1975 eruption caused the uplift that formed Punta Espinosa to the northeast, and an eruption in February 1995 caused a lava flow that created a new cape on the island's southwest end. While this recent flow is not yet open to visitors, many slightly older lava flows are, including the beautiful *pahoehoe* flows at **Sullivan Bay** on Isla Santiago (see p. 498). Isla Bartolomé's sweeping, crater-filled lunar landscape (see p. 499) is another spectacular by-product of the Galápagos' fiery disposition.

FLORA AND FAUNA

BACKGROUND

One fine day around 4.5 million years ago, some bacteria carried by wind and water happened upon a steaming clump of volcanic rock, newly emerged from the sea. These microorganisms, simple but resourceful, settled on that rock to do what bacteria do: process minerals and sunlight into energy, creating more bacteria to do the same. Thus, the first life-forms on the primordial Galápagos were hardly elegant—prokaryotes rarely are—but they were essential to all life on the archipelago. These bacteria did two important things: they broke down the hard volcanic rock and left the remains of their bodies (minerals and organic compounds). The result was an accumulation of a substance resembling soil.

Indeed, seeds, brought from great distances by the wind, the currents of the sea, or even a passing seabird, found their way to little crevices in the rocks where they could sprout. These plants, capable of living with little water or nutrients, further broke up the rock and added to the organic mass of the islands, allowing larger plants to survive. Pioneering plants like these still may be found on the islands' many lava fields. Birds and insects, blown to the islands by strong winds, found that the larger plants could provide food and shelter. Animals arrived by flying, swimming, or rafting, and either found a way to live on the barren islands or died: an extreme instance of survival of the fittest. It is probable that for every creature that made it on the islands, hundreds or thousands died a hot and salty death.

The animals that prospered found a large area with lots of land and fish and little competition. Isolated from the mainland by about 1000km and each other by up to 200km, the islands of the archipelago provided the perfect environment for rapid species expansion. Darwin could not have found a better laboratory to demonstrate the geographical distinction of species that results from varying selective pressures. The time scale was such that the changes from the mainland ancestors were obvious, yet was not so great that the connections were undetectable.

The life forms that arrived had a few traits in common. They had to be able to make the voyage in the first place; therefore, the sea lion had a chance while the llama did not. Once on the island, they had to be able to survive the vigors of the sea and extreme deprivation of fresh water; water-efficient reptiles thrived while wasteful mammals hardly stood a chance. With the advent of boats, however, mammals have been popping up with greater frequency, inflicting massive, rapid change on the islands' ecosystems. Humans and our retinue of goats, horses, cats, dogs, and rats have upset the ecological balance considerably, both by consuming the food of the aboriginal animals and the animals themselves. Humans have done their share, too, feeding on the helpless tortoises that inhabit many of the islands.

Ecological awareness and a very active park service, however, have largely stopped the contamination of the ecosystems (although humans continue to arrive). The purity that remains is unique and extraordinary. The biological distinction between life forms on the islands is apparent upon first observation, and continued examinations reveal complex interconnections, remarkable adaptations, and fascinating communal behaviors. Perhaps more pleasing to the visitor is the unbelievable amiability of the animals. They are sometimes described as tame, but this is inaccurate: they are wild animals entirely unafraid of humans, a phenomenon which provides some of the most exhilarating natural observations on earth. Preserving this purity is the responsibility of all who visit the Galápagos.

RESPONSIBLE ECOTOURISM

The islands' ecosystems are fragile. The regulations of the National Park Service are designed to protect those areas for future generations and should be followed: stay on the trails, don't molest the wildlife, don't take or leave anything, and if your guide tells you not to do something, don't do it. The importance of following these rules can never be over-emphasized. The perfect photograph is not worth the insidious damage which clumsy feet and harassment will have on the animals.

Remember the stories about the time traveler who wandered from the path for only an instant and changed the course of history? That could be you. This admonition extends to your purchases: don't buy souvenirs made of animal parts (particularly black coral) and, when you sit down for dinner, think twice about ordering lobster, which has recently been overharvested. At the most basic level, the mere presence of tourists on the islands contributes to their contamination; recognize that these islands are a unique natural treasure as well as an opportunity for the adventure of a lifetime (for more info, see **Ecotourism,** p. 55).

BIRDS

The Galápagos are well-known for their birds, the most prominent and diverse type of animal on the islands. In fact, many of the feathered residents found here, having evolved into their own unique species, are endemic to the islands and can't be found anywhere else in the world. The different species of birds found in the Galápagos are presented here grouped by habitat.

BIRDS OF THE SEA

Undeniably a seabird, the endemic **Galápagos penguin** is an aberrant member of its cold-water family. These shy birds (long-lost relatives of the penguins of southern Chile and Antarctica) live mainly around the Bolívar Channel between the western coast of Isabela and Fernandina. They are also found in various places near the Isla de Santiago. Some of the most well-known birds in the Galápagos are the **boobies,** of which there are three types: the **blue-footed, red-footed,** and **masked.** The boobies, like the frigatebird and cormorant, are related to the pelican, members of the order *Pelicaniformes*. They use their large and sometimes colorful feet to incubate their eggs and to swim through the water after a dive-bombing fishing foray. The highest concentration of red-footed boobies is on Genovesa. They are the only boobies that nest in trees or bushes. Blue-footed and masked boobies nest on the ground, surrounding their territory with a circle of *ejecta* (bodily waste). The identity of masked boobies is given away by the black mask that contrasts with their otherwise white bodies.

Another famous endemic seabird, the **flightless cormorant** is found only on the westernmost islands of Fernandina and Isabela. These cormorants were originally a flying species, but lack of predators or food on land meant that big wings were a waste of energy; selective pressures favored the strongest divers. Those with webbed feet, powerful legs, and small wings survived, and the species conformed through the millennia. Today, the birds rely mostly on their powerful legs for swimming. Flightless cormorants have also developed a rather strange habit to assist them in their fish-finding efforts. Cormorants have light bones—appropriate for flying but not for diving deep down into the water. Therefore, in order to weigh themselves down sufficiently to reach deep, fish-filled waters, flightless cormorants swallow small stones which give their light bodies the extra ballast needed to get down deep. Cormorants nest in small colonies on sheltered shorelines, and they have some rather odd domestic habits, too: every time a bird returns to the nest, it brings some new sort of decoration. By the time the chicks are grown, the nests are eclectic masses of seaweed, stones, and shells.

Some of the largest and most notable birds on the islands are the black **frigatebirds.** Both humble species (the **great** and the **magnificent**) are **cleptoparasites,** which means that they make a living by stealing the food of other birds, usually by harassing them in midair and forcing them to give up their catch. Since they spend so much time in the air, their wingspans have grown up to 2.3m—they have the highest wingspan-to-weight ratio of any bird. Also, their cleptoparasitic ways have preempted the need to get their feathers wet, and they have consequently lost the ability to produce the oily secretions that protect the feathers of other seafaring birds. This adaptation has reinforced their need to steal fish instead of fishing for their own. One of the most outstanding features of the frigates is the enormous red pouch beneath their beaks, which males inflate when courting the ladies. To witness this sensual display, visit the colonies on San Cristóbal and Genovesa during the mating season (March and April) or on North Seymour Island anytime. Perhaps the rarest bird in the Galápagos, the **waved albatross** is endemic only to Isla Española. The largest birds in the archipelago—weighing over 4 kilograms with a wingspan of 2.5m—they only stay on the island from April to December; they spend the rest of the year in various places around the South Pacific. Other seabirds include the ever-present **brown pelican,** the **swallowtail gull,** the **lava gull,** and five kinds of **petrels.**

BIRDS OF THE SHORE

Of the shorebirds, the **flamingoes** are by far the most famous. These guys are fairly rare, with an estimated 700 specimens currently inhabiting only a few lagoons around the islands. They feed on small, bright pink shrimp larvae and pink marine insects that live in the silt and shallow water of the lagoons. This unusual diet gives the birds their colorful appearance. The flamingoes are true shorebirds, building nests of mud right near the water. They can be seen on Isla Rábida, in lagoons near Puerto Villamil on Isabela, at Punta Cormorant on Floreana, and at Espumilla beach on Santiago. Although an up-close flamingo sighting will always excite camera-happy tourists, be careful not to get too close—these less-than-people-friendly birds are easily frightened.

A much more common shorebird is the **heron,** of which there are several types in the Galápagos: the **great blue, lava,** and **night herons,** to name a few. These long-legged waders feed on all kinds of small animals, from beach creatures to lagoon-dwellers. A more specialized shorebird is the **oyster catcher.** The size of your average heron, this bird is not as common due to its particular habits. It is mostly brown with a black head and red eye ring, and it feeds primarily on shellfish such as abalone and sea urchins. Other shorebirds include **egrets, gallinules, turnstones, stilts,** and **whimbrels.**

BIRDS OF THE LAND

Because of their isolation from other landbird populations, the residents of the Galápagos compose the greatest percentage of endemic species (76%). Most famous are **Darwin's finches,** of which there are 13 types. Tiny sparrow-sized birds, they all look extremely similar and can only be differentiated by beak morphology and feeding habits; Darwin himself didn't recognize them as distinct species until after he'd left the archipelago. While some live simply on seeds or fruits, the **carpenter finch** uses a stick to dig insects out of trees, and the **"blood-sucking" finch** of Wolf Island actually uses its sharp beak to suck the blood of red-footed and masked boobies. Other notable endemic landbirds include several sociable mockingbird species, the **Galápagos hawk** (the largest land predator on the islands), the **Galápagos dove,** the **Galápagos martin,** and the **Galápagos rail.** Some of the more striking land birds are non-endemic. The **vermillion flycatcher,** a red-and-black bird found in the humid highland forests of the central islands, is a favorite, as is the nearly universal **yellow warbler.** Lastly, as surprising as it may be, some pioneering, adventurous owls must have made the trip from the mainland long ago; the islands are now populated by two subspecies of **barn owl** and **short-eared owl.**

REPTILES

TORTOISES AND TURTLES

The namesake of the islands and the undisputed king of the Galápagos reptiles is the **giant tortoise.** These are the animals that really set the islands apart from other parts of the globe (only one other island in the world has a tortoise population). How the tortoises first came to inhabit the islands is a mystery to this day. Their closest relative is a species of tortoise native to Argentina; it is possible that the big guys (up to 250kg) got stuck on some floating vegetation that carried them out to sea and eventually to the Galápagos. Whatever their origin, the anomalous giants have been appreciated (and exploited) for centuries by pirates, whalers, and now, tourists from around the world.

As a result of human interference, the tortoises aren't as plentiful as they once were. Three of the original 14 sub-species are now extinct, and introduced animals such as rats and dogs continue to threaten the remaining populations. While each animal can live to be over 150-years-old, they do not reproduce often, and when they do, it is not guaranteed that the vulnerable hatchlings will ever reach maturity. The **Galápagos National Park** and the **Charles Darwin Research Center** (see p. 479) are doing what they can to prevent predation. The organizations are also trying to boost the head count by harvesting eggs, raising the hatchlings to four years of age, and then releasing them back into their natural habitat. The **largest tortoise population** is found on Isabela, concentrated around the crater of Volcán Alcedo. Elsewhere in the islands, wild tortoises can be observed at the **tortoise reserves** on Santa Cruz (see p. 482) and Española (see p. 503). Captive tortoises can be viewed at the Darwin Research Center on Santa Cruz (see p. 479) and the **Breeding Center for Giant Tortoises** on Isabela (see p. 494).

Back in the sea and on the beaches, **marine turtles** are also common. These animals float easily on the water's surface and can therefore travel great distances across the seas with great ease. Four of the eight species of marine turtle have been seen on the Galápagos, but none are endemic (given their great mobility). The **black turtle,** a sub-species of the Pacific green turtle, is the most common. They lay their eggs in nests on the beach, burying them to incubate in the hot sun. While they can lay their eggs year-round, it is most common from January to June. For a day or two after the eggs are laid, visitors may observe tracks leading from the sea to the nest and back again. Night visitors may even catch a turtle in the process of laying eggs. In these cases, it is fine to watch quietly, but do not disturb the animals, especially not with the beam of a flashlight.

IGUANAS

One of the most bizarre and unique reptiles of the Galápagos is the **marine iguana,** the only aquatic iguana in the world. Related to the land iguanas of the American mainland, marine iguanas have evolved to eat green algae that grows underwater. They are capable of doing this because of a few strategic biological adaptations, including the ability to swim to a depth of 20m and to stay under water for up to one hour at a time. They are also able to rapidly discharge excess absorbed salt out of their unusually square noses, and they have a tail tailored for efficient swimming. The largest marine iguanas (on Isabela) can grow to be a meter long. Like other reptiles, these strange creatures are **ectothermic,** meaning that their body temperature is determined by the temperature of their surroundings. Consequently, they are often seen piled on top of each other in big groups, sunning their big, black, spiny bodies on rocks. Darwin called the marine iguana "a hideous-looking creature, of a dirty black color, stupid and sluggish in its movements," but many people think they're cute, or at least fascinating to look at.

Two species of **land iguanas** also inhabit the islands; while their genus is endemic to the Galápagos, the land-loving lizards seems less exotic than their water-borne counterparts. They can also grow to 1m in length, but their noses are more characteristically pointed. Their diet varies depending on their particular habitat. They eat insects and scavenge for other meaty meals, but they also love to eat grasses, cacti, fruits, and flowers, particularly the big yellow blossoms of the **opuntia** cactus.

OTHER REPTILES

Long ago, through some heroic feat of seamanship, **snakes** also reached the islands. On land, the non-poisonous Galápagos **land snake** slithers hither and yonder in search of small prey that it can crush with its constrictive power. Found on all but the northernmost islands, these brown or gray snakes have yellow stripes or spots and may grow to 1m in length. On a smaller scale, seven species of **lava lizard** are also endemic to the islands. Reaching up to 25cm, they feed primarily on plants, with an occasional insect thrown in for variety. They are gray, and females typically have eye-catching red-orange throats. While they are very territorial, most confrontation takes the form of bouncing up and down on the forelegs; fights between lizards are seldom serious.

MAMMALS

The most prominent and strangest mammals of the Galápagos inhabit the islands of Santa Cruz, San Cristóbal, Isabela, and Floreana, though some may be found on other islands from time to time. Social animals, they live in big groups, primarily by the ocean, but also in more fertile and moist regions of the islands. Their bodies are quite strange in form and vary greatly in size. At night they usually gather around unknown sources of strange rhythmic sound and consume various quantities of liquid that alters their behavior dramatically, causing some of them to make more noise and others to regurgitate and eventually lie still, presumably in a state of dormancy. While these **Homo sapiens** have arrived only recently on the islands, they have had a great impact on the ecology. The number of individuals in the population fluctuates regularly but continues to rise steadily. It is unclear whether the population can continue to grow at this rate without damaging the islands beyond repair. Humans have also increased the mammal contingent of the islands by introducing varieties of dog, cat, goat, and rat, which have multiplied faster than their primate counterparts.

A less disturbing large mammal found in astonishing abundance in the Galápagos is the endemic **Galápagos sea lion.** Relatives of the sea lions of California and Perú, they live in colonies on the beaches of most of the islands. Males are much larger than females and can reach up to 250 kilograms. They are highly territorial, holding their turf and the females that come with it for a month at a time and aggressively defending them from any kind of intruder (usually other males). Mating occurs in the ocean, but females give birth on land, and the pups are suckled for up to three years before being weaned. The animals are playful and are commonly seen surfing or showing off for tourists.

Another related but quite distinct species found here is the **Galápagos fur seal (or fur sea lion).** Technically, fur seals are not seals at all but rather a species of smaller sea lion with pointed ears and an extra layer of fur. In fact, their appearance makes it clear why they are sometimes called Galápagos sea bears; their short snouts and thick necks actually make their faces resemble a bear's. These features result from these sea lions' ancestors having come from the south of South America, where their small surface-area-to-size ratio and extra layer of insulating fur kept them warm in the chilly waters. The rich pelt of these animals was once very much desired and caused them to be hunted nearly to extinction by European fur traders; one boat in the Galápagos killed 50,000 in a period of three months. The little "bears" are much more shy than their personable sea lion cousins, most likely because of their unpleasant history with humans. These timid creatures are also prey for sharks; when the moon is full and visibility high, you'll find them seeking refuge on dry land.

The only other mammals on the islands that were not introduced by man are **bats** and **rats.** Two species of bat comb the islands of Santa Cruz Floreana, Isabela, and San Cristóbal for insects, while the brown rice rat scurries across the islands in search of vegetation. Lately, the rice rat population has been decreasing due to the introduction of the black rat, which competes with the rice rat for food. Before the black rat's arrival on the island, there were seven species of endemic rice rat; today, there are two.

MARINE LIFE

The waters of the Galápagos are truly tropical, teeming with just about every form of marine life. The islands are fed by three nutritious **currents:** the Humboldt, the Cromwell, and El Niño, which bring a bounteous supply of species and nutrients from all over the Pacific. Sixteen species of **whale** and seven species of **dolphin** have been sighted around the Galápagos, with a particularly high concentration off the west coast of Isabela where the Cromwell current brings plankton and other delectable organisms to the surface. Whale species include sperm, humpback, blue, and killer whales. The most prevalent species of dolphins are the common and bottle-nosed dolphins.

Twelve species of **shark** also inhabit these waters. By far the most common is the white-tipped reef shark, but black-tipped reef sharks, hammerheads, Galápagos sharks, and tiger sharks are common as well. Also sharing these waters are five species of **ray,** including stingrays, eagle rays, and manta rays. Before the most recent visit of El Niño, **coral reefs** used to surround many of the islands. But the inhospitable temperature extremes caused by this pesky weather phenomenon resulted in the destruction of most formations. Galápagos marine life is resilient, however, and numerous species such as lobster, crab, squid, octopus, starfish, and shellfish of all kinds abound. The sea cucumber, a sluggish echinoderm, continues to struggle against its status as a delicacy in Japan.

Because of this great diversity, the waters in and around the Galápagos, an area of 70,000 sq. km, form part of a marine reserve established in 1986. While the area is protected and fishing is often frowned upon, regulated commercial fishing of certain species is still permitted: before snagging a saltwater snack for yourself, consult the locals or your trusty tour guide.

PLANT LIFE

The Galápagos support **seven vegetation zones** that are home to over 600 species of plant, approximately 170 of which are endemic. The zones range from dry and low to high and moist. The area right on the coast—the **littoral zone**—is dominated by plants that have adapted to the presence of salt, such as **mangroves.** The **arid zone** is the driest region and comes just above the littoral in altitude. Generally on the side of the island opposite the prevailing winds, this region is dominated by cacti and other dry-weather plants. The **opuntia cactus,** with bright yellow flowers, is the only endemic species of cactus and also happens to be the most common. It often grows like a shrub, except on islands where it is threatened by herbivorous animals; there, these cacti can grow trunks up to 5m tall. The **Palo Santo** tree is also native to this zone. Producing only small leaves during the wet season, the branches of these stark gray trees are often burned for their incense-like odor. The tree (its name means "Holy Stick") is so named because its small white blossoms that appear around Christmas time.

The next highest zone, which is also more humid, is the **transition zone.** The most common inhabitants are the Palo Santos, again, and the **pega pega** (which translates literally as "it sticks, it sticks"), which has spread-out branches and a short trunk. When those damn leaves stick to your clothes, you'll understand the name. The next zone is very humid and has been called the **scalesia zone** for the endemic scalesia trees that are so common here. In addition to scalesia trees, which can grow up to 10m tall, many mosses, ferns, and grasses thrive here. The scalesia forest of the Santa Cruz highlands is the best place to see such vegetation. The three remaining zones are the **brown, miconia,** and **pampa zones.** The brown is named for the prominent **brown liverwort mosses** found here. The miconia zone gets its name from the endemic and shrubby **miconia plants,** which look somewhat like flowering cacao plants. The highest and wettest vegetation zone is the **pampa,** dominated by mosses, ferns and grasses; few trees or shrubs grow in this hyper-humid region.

ISLA SANTA CRUZ

Known also by its English name of Indefatigable, Isla Santa Cruz's never-ending diversity—its myriad wildlife, radically varied geology, and scores of international visitors—is indeed tireless. Tourism in the Galápagos revolves around this hub close to the geographical center of the archipelago. Nearly every visitor stops here, whether to schmooze with the tortoises or just to stock up on supplies. After all, Puerto Ayora is the largest and most developed town on the islands, and Santa Cruz is a conveniently close first stop if you arrive at the Baltra Airport.

The trip from the airport to Puerto Ayora serves as the perfect introduction to the islands. Baltra looms barren and powerful, and the entire landscape is covered with lava rock, cacti, and wind-blown trees. After a boat ride across shimmering, turquoise waters, visitors enter the central highlands of Santa Cruz, where the bus jostles its way through vegetation that seems all the greener in comparison to the desertscape before it. From there the bus descends to the relaxed port town.

Good news for land lovers—Santa Cruz is one of the few islands in the Galápagos where many sites can be reached without a boat. In addition to offering the Charles Darwin Research Station and the beautiful beaches near Puerto Ayora, the lush scalesia forests of Santa Cruz's highland region provide ample opportunities for horseback-riding, hiking, and exploring Santa Cruz's geology and wildlife.

HIGHLIGHTS OF ISLA SANTA CRUZ

■ The **Charles Darwin Research Station** (see p. 479) is the first authority on everything in the Galápagos archipelago.

■ At the **Tortoise Reserve** (see p. 482), humans can mingle with *tortugas* in the wild.

■ The romantic caverns in the **Tunnel of Endless Love** (see p. 482) resulted from ancient lava flows on Santa Cruz.

ISLA SANTA CRUZ: PUERTO AYORA

The constant influx of tortoise-happy tourists has given the port town of Puerto Ayora a vaguely cosmopolitan air, a high standard of living, and a happy-go-lucky attitude. However, it has also made Puerto Ayora more expensive than mainland Ecuador and converted part of it into a string of souvenir shops and bars. Despite the number of Galápagos t-shirts and sea lion figurines for sale along Darwin, however, the town maintains a very genuine feel. The fresh-off-the-bus tourists, hopping between tourist agencies with their backpacks and bags, blend well with the locals, who gather each afternoon for volleyball games in the park on the waterfront. Puerto Ayora also seems to enjoy a good parade. They are fairly common, and if one happens to march by, take time to observe the local color. Dancing sea horses are a common sight in these processions. Puerto Ayora exudes a feeling of subdued contentment—the streets bustle, but only with people strolling casually. In the bars at night and in the streets and restaurants during the day, locals and tourists mix and mingle, and everyone seems to appreciate the friendliness of the people and the beauty of the surroundings. The first town in the Galápagos to have 24-hour electricity, Puerto Ayora has not given up its simpler charms—where else can you stare through a bank window at pelicans relaxing in a turquoise bay?

ORIENTATION AND PRACTICAL INFORMATION

While street signs are located on the corners of Puerto Ayora's buildings, few locals will recognize the names. Get a free map at the Ministry of Tourism if you need directions. However, virtually everything of importance is located on **Av. Charles Darwin** (where else?). The other busy street is **Av. Padre Julio Herrera**.

Airport: To get to Puerto Ayora from the **Isla Baltra airport,** take the free shuttle bus to the boat that goes to Santa Cruz (10min., s/4,000). A bus takes passengers across Santa Cruz to Puerto Ayora (50min., s/20,000). Buy bus tickets at the airport. The bus back to the airport leaves from the center of town in front of the CITTEG sign (6:45, 7:15, and 11:30am). Get there early (as if it's not early already).

Airlines: TAME (tel. 526 165), Darwin and 12 de Febrero. Tickets and flight reservations can be arranged here. It's a good idea to try to reserve return flights as soon as possible, especially in the high season. Open M-F 7am-noon and 1-4pm.

Inter-Island Boat Travel: Find the **INGALA** office (tel. 526 177), 15min. up Herrera, in the same building as the post office. Boats go to Floreana (4hrs., W 8am) and San Cristóbal (4hrs., F 8am), though the schedules are subject to change. Be there by 7:30am, buy tickets 1-4pm the day before (s/132,000 adults, s/66,000 children).

Inter-Island Plane Travel: EMETEBE (tel. 526 177), in the same building as INGALA, flies to **San Cristóbal** and **Isabela** (30min., US$80-$90 one way). Schedule varies.

Tourist Information: For all those pesky Puerto Ayora-related questions, visit the **Ministerio de Turismo** (tel. 526 174), on Darwin between Berlanga and Binford. Answers are always up-to-date and usually in Spanish. Provides informative (though somewhat blurry) maps of Puerto Ayora and general literature about all of the islands. Open M-F 8am-12:30pm and 2-5pm. Next door to the Ministerio, **CAPTURGAL** (tel./fax 526 206; email cptg@pa.ga.pro.ec) gives info about boat companies and tours but has some general Puerto Ayora information as well. Open M-F 8am-noon and 2-5:30pm, Sa 9am-noon. A unique tourist resource, the **Charles Darwin Research Station** (tel. 526 189; fax 526 190; email png@ga.pro.ec) is less than 20min. from town on an easy trail, just past Hotel Galápagos. The station is a worthwhile stop and can answer nearly any question about the national park. Open daily 7am-noon and 1-4pm.

Travel Agencies: Several travel agencies in town arrange boat tours, daytrips, and inland excursions. **Moonrise Agencia de Viajes** (tel. 526 348; fax 526 403; email sdivine@pa.ga.pro.ec), on Darwin across the street from Banco del Pacífico, is a very helpful English-speaking agency recommended by the SAEC. Open M-Sa 8am-6pm. **Galapagos Discovery** (tel./fax 526 245), is on Herrera in front of the hospital and **Galapatour** (tel. 526 581), on Darwin across the street from the park both have English-speaking staffs as well.

Bank: Banco del Pacífico (tel. 526 282; fax 526 364), on Darwin just beside Hotel Sol y Mar, changes traveler's checks and dollars at the best rates in town. The **ATM** accepts Cirrus and MC. MC cash advances can be arranged as well. Open M-F 8am-3:30pm, some services Sa 9:30am-12noon.

Market: Proinsular (tel. 526 120), on Darwin, across from the dock, is the closest thing Puerto Ayora has to a real supermarket. Open M-Sa 8am-8pm, Su 8am-2pm.

Restrooms: Public restrooms are located on Darwin near the park.

Laundromat: The **Peregrina B&B,** on Darwin, runs a *lavandería* (s/10,000 per kg, including dryer service). Open M-Sa 8:30am-6pm.

Police: (Tel. 526 101), by the water off 12 de Febrero, beside the Lobo del Mar. 24hr.

Pharmacies: Farmacia Edith (tel. 526 487) is open daily 7am-11pm. **Farmacia Vanessa** (tel. 526 392) is open daily 7:30am-1pm and 2-10:30pm.

Hospital: Puerto Ayora Hospital (24hr. **emergency** tel. 526 103), on Padre Julio Herrera, less than a block from the center of town.

Post Office: The **Correo Central** (tel. 526 575), in the Proinsular shopping center on Darwin, near the dock. Postcards and stamps available. Mail to the US should arrive in 3 weeks. Open M-F 8am-1pm and 2pm-6pm, Sa 9am-noon.

Telephones: PACIFICTEL (tel. 526 104 or 526 105), on Herrera, handles international phone calls, faxes, and telegrams. Few lines are available to call outside of the islands, so be prepared to wait. Since all calls out of the islands go through the mainland, there is an additional charge per min. for collect and calling-card calls. Open daily 7am-11pm. You can also make international collect or calling card calls from **Moonrise Travel** (see **Travel Agencies,** above) but also must pay an additional charge per min.

Internet Access: The **Banco del Pacífico** (see **Bank,** above) offers access for US$0.25 per min. **Moonrise Travel** (see **Travel Agencies,** above) also has a connection.

PHONE CODE	05

ACCOMMODATIONS

The selective forces of the fertile coastal environment have led to the development of several hotels, although given the large price discrepancies, one wonders if they really could have evolved from a common ancestor. Always ask to see a room before sleeping in it; besides doing a quick cleanliness check, look for netting or window screens to keep out mosquitoes—while not usually a problem, they can be murder during the wet season. Know ahead of time that the prices for *extranjeros* can be twice as much as those for Ecuadorians. In general, more money means more luxury, leaving thrifty travelers listening to the sounds of the local disco rather than waves gently lapping outside their door. Yet, as can only happen in the Galápagos, the rare "hybrid" hotel does exist, combining luxurious ocean views with affordable prices.

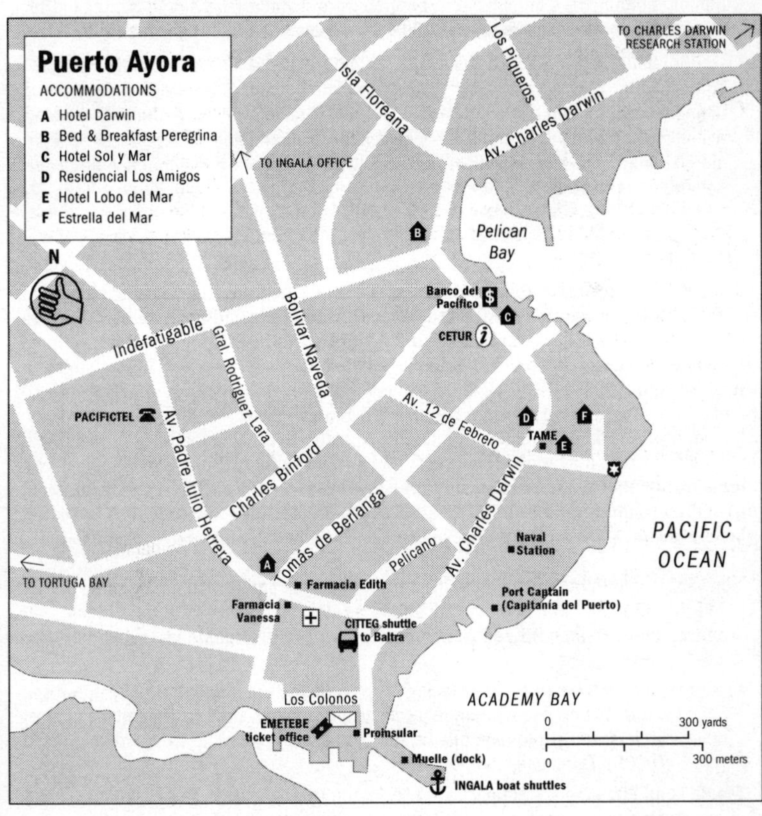

Hotel Lobo del Mar (tel. 526 188; fax 526 569), 12 de Febrero, just off Darwin, next to the police station. The Sea Wolf provides a TV lounge for your enjoyment and gorgeous views from second and third floor rooms. It's the best deal in town, hands down. Singles and doubles s/50,000; triples s/75,000.

Estrella del Mar (tel. 526 427), right next to the ocean. Make a left at the end of 12 de Febrero and follow the flower-trimmed path. One of the prettiest hotels in town, this *estrella* twinkles with airy rooms, extra clean baths, a lounge with TV, and fantastic ocean views from the balconies. Hot water in cold weather. Rooms without ocean view US$7 per person, with ocean view US$10 per person. Group discounts available.

Bed and Breakfast Peregrina (tel. 526 323), off Darwin, past the bank. Homey atmosphere and continental breakfast make up for the BYOT (towels and toilet paper) policy, but the management will provide towels if you happen to forget yours. Shared rooms have minor partitions and private baths. There is also a laundry service (s/10,000 per kg). Rooms s/45,000 per person, with A/C s/55,000 per person.

Residencial Los Amigos (tel. 526 265), Darwin and 12 de Febrero, is the island's answer to the youth hostel, with communal bathrooms, rustic bedrooms and some of the most affordable prices in town. The social atmosphere and a roof-top deck are added perks. Singles s/30,000; doubles s/40,000; triples s/60,000.

Hotel Darwin (tel. 526 193), Herrera, past the hospital, 1 block from the ocean. With the cheapest rates in town, the hotel has a weathered, palm frond-covered patio separating guests from Av. Herrera's traffic and commerce. Darwin has survived the natural selection of Puerto Ayora's hotels, but its bathrooms and thin mattresses betray their years, despite their cleanliness. Singles s/20,000; doubles s/40,000; triples s/45,000.

Hotel Sol y Mar (tel. 526 281; fax 4 471 701), on Darwin, across the street from CAPTURGAL. A lot pricier, but you get what you pay for: clean, elegant ocean-view rooms, dining with sun-soaked iguanas on the oceanfront patio, and private hot-water baths. According to Jimmy Perez, the friendly owner, more affordable rooms with less spectacular views are under construction. US$25-$45 for 2 people, US$5 for each additional person. Group discounts available.

FOOD

Not just diving pelicans abound on Darwin—so do restaurants. Those on the first few blocks are moderately priced; most restaurants around here and on Herrera are open most of the day and serve a set *desayuno*, *almuerzo*, and sometimes *merienda* (usually s/15,000). Perhaps because these places tend to attract the timid tourists fresh off the boat, the patio furniture has become a great spot to meet other visitors and arrange boat tours. Farther down towards the Research Station, more expensive restaurants cater to tourists ready to splurge. For typical fare, check out Charles Binford, just off Herrera, where locals get cheap, fresh meals from small wooden kiosks. Of these, **William's** comes highly recommended. For a cheap, yummy dessert, try a soft-serve ice cream cone (s/4,000) at (of all places) the **hat store** on Darwin between Bolivar Naveda and 12 de Febrero.

Servi-Sabrosán, Herrera, right in the center of town. This eatery offers a big-screen TV for your favorite Latin American variety shows and a bamboo-covered patio. Serves set *almuerzo* and hearty, affordable *meriendas* (s/20,000). Open daily 11am-4pm and 6pm-9:30pm.

El Rincón del Alma (tel. 526 196), facing the park on the waterfront, has both indoor and patio seating. The exposed bar reveals eclectic decorations and is a great place to meet other travelers. *Desayunos* and *almuerzos* are served and there is a full dinner menu (s/15-40,000). Open daily 8am-9pm.

Media Luna Pizza, on Darwin past the turn for the Darwin station. This half-moon serves up delicious pizza (small s/24-38,000) and sandwiches (s/18-25,000), including the stellar avocado sub. Locals, tourists, and families alike appreciate the homey feel and incredibly friendly staff. Open W-M noon-10pm.

La Garrapata, Darwin, adjacent to La Panga *discoteca*. Although a bit on the expensive side by Puerto Ayora standards, Garrapata's romantic and relaxing ambiance are worth the price. An eager-to-please staff and high-quality food combine to make it the best deal among Puerto Ayora's pasta-and-meat dinner establishments. The pasta with mushrooms (s/40,000) and gigantic T-bone steak (s/45,000) are both out-of-this-world. A well-stocked bar, which attracts a noticeably sophisticated crowd, stays open well after dinner service ends. Open M-Su 7-10:30pm.

Capricho, on Darwin past the turn for (and on the way to) the Research Station. Capricho unabashedly caters directly to tourists, but its numerous vegetarian dishes, cappuccino, and English, German, and French book exchange are welcomed by travelers who've long gone without such luxuries. Pasta (s/35-40,000), very good omelettes (s/19-30,000), a variety of drinks, and box lunches "for take away" (s/45,000) round out the menu. Open F-W 7am-10:30pm, Th 7am-7pm.

Panadería La Selecta, Herrera across the street from PACIFICTEL. Before getting on a boat, grab a bite to eat here, where bread starts rising with the sun. Though the selection is limited, these sweet treats are the cheapest meal you'll find in all of Puerto Ayora. Open daily 6am-11pm.

Cuatro Linternas, on Darwin after the turn towards the Research Station. The place to take that cute iguana in your life. Lanterns throw soft lighting on Italian cuisine, but the atmosphere doesn't quite obscure the hefty price tag for pizza (s/50,000) and pasta (s/44-52,000). Open M-Sa 6:30-10pm.

SIGHTS

Though rather small city, Puerto Ayora is the center of much Galápagos-related activity. Therefore, it has a fair amount of sights to offer the interested tourist.

THE CHARLES DARWIN RESEARCH STATION. Less than 20 minutes from town on an easy trail, just past Hotel Galápagos, the Research Station is a veritable complex of Galápagos and conservation-related information, as well as the headquarters of the **Galápagos National Park.** The trail leads first to a national park information booth and the park's administrative headquarters. The helpful **Office of Tourism** as well as the office of the conservation program are here. This is also the place to pay the US$100 National Park fee for those who arrived on boats and didn't pay at the airport *(Tel. 526 189 or 526 511; fax 526 190; email png@ga.pro.ec. Information booth open daily 7am-noon and 1-4pm. Office of tourism open M-F 7am-4pm.)*

Further along the main road and up a short path is the **Van Straelen Exhibit Hall,** which contains information on the islands' natural history and focuses particularly on threats to the ecology of the islands and current efforts to counteract them. This is a great place to beef up on facts and figures which, while interesting in themselves, will make the next stop on your tour of the station far more rewarding. A six-minute video about conservation programs is available and shown to anyone interested. The center is run by a small but enthusiastic staff who can usually be found in the Hall's adjacent office. *(Open M-F 7am-12noon and 2pm-5pm.)*

Just beyond Van Straelen is the station's **tortoise rearing center.** A shady path leads past pens containing baby giant tortoises, from newborns to kids just a couple of years old. To get a good look at the cute little *galapaguitos*, visit between 7am and 4pm on a weekday, when the covers of their pens will be open. The big boys are just around the corner and their corral is open to the public. All of the tortoises in the pens are bachelors, so don't expect to find scenes of blissfully domestic *tortuga* life as you wander among them. For many, this is the only chance to see a Galápagos tortoise. The animals in this area were originally kept by islanders as pets, so they really do like people and very rarely retreat into their shells like the wild ones do. Even though it's alright

THE GALÁPAGOS

to get close enough to the tortoises to pose with them for those priceless pictures, touching them is a big no-no. Also, be careful not to walk across or stand on the tortoise feeding platform (a large cement slab covered with partially chewed vegetation), as this may contaminate their food with harmful organisms. There are many informative signs throughout the area to enhance your tortoise-viewing experience.

For more info about the Galápagos, the Research Station, and its projects, visit the station's **library.** Although its resources are used by students and researchers much more than by tourists, the library is open to tourists interested in learning about Darwin, Galápagos history, and more. If you have a specific interest or question, this is a good place to find Gail Davis, the station's extremely helpful librarian who came to the islands years ago on a research project and never left. This area also has a tiny but beautiful **beach,** where sunbathers lounge and others simply gaze across the turquoise waters of the harbor. While swimming doesn't appear too inviting on this pebbly cove, a wealth of coral and seashells have washed up on the shore, making a dry beach excursion rewarding. *(To get there, walk down the main road past the turn-off for the Exhibit Hall until you reach the hub of the Research Station. Make a right when you see an administration building which has a prominent "Charles Darwin Research Station" sign in front. Library open M-F 7:30am-4pm. Beach open daily 7am-6pm.)*

TORTUGA BAY. Pristine white sand, a scenic, rocky background, and a foreground filled with giant cacti and yellow finches all combine to make this perhaps the most beautiful beach in the Galápagos. This seaside eden gets its name from the large number of sea turtles that come here to lay their eggs. Sharks and marine iguanas also call Tortuga Bay home. When swimming, be careful of the unusually strong currents, and make sure you swim only in the designated swimming area—Baywatch doesn't patrol these waters. Also watch for iguanas lounging on the sand and crabs darting out of their perfect little holes. *(Getting to the beach takes about 45min. Walk past the hospital on Herrera to Binford, turn left, and follow the dirt road out of town for 200m to a Galápagos National Park sign and an observation tower standing high on a sheer rock cliff. Before starting the pleasant 2½km hike to the beach, check in with the guard—the passport numbers and names of all visitors must be recorded. The beach is open until 6pm.)*

LONESOME GEORGE George is an 88kg tortoise who lives at the Charles Darwin Research Center... but George isn't like all the other tortoises. He isn't like any other tortoise anywhere—sadly, George is the last of a dying race.

Found in 1971, George was the first **Pinta tortoise** *(Geochelone elephantopus abingdoni)* to be seen in 65 years. Tragically, the story of George's race is all too reminiscent of tales of endangered species the world over; exploited by man until they were nearly extinct, the tortoises were left with an uphill battle for survival. The dwindling Pinta tortoise population suffered another blow when introduced goats drastically affected the island's habitat, further contributing to the demise of George's tragedy-stricken race.

Some think that George, who is probably 60 or 70 years old (halfway through his expected life span), should live out the remainder of his days on his home island of Pinta, now goat-free. Currently, George remains at the research center, comfortably housed with two lovely lady tortoises from Isabela, genetically his closest relatives. But sadly, George is apparently far too depressed to think about sex; the females just don't arouse his interest. Researchers are offering a US$10,000 reward to anyone who can supply a female Pinta tortoise, so keep an eye out. Unfortunately, the Pinta is not the only tortoise species in danger. Of the 14 species that originally inhabited the Galápagos Archipelago, five others are in danger and may soon join the three extinct species.

To catch a glimpse of Lonesome George, it is best to come early in the morning, for as the day becomes hotter, he tends to retreat under the trees and out of visitors' sight.

OTHER SIGHTS. If you're not the snorkeling or scuba diving type but want a taste of what underwater Galápagos has to offer, the **Bote con Fondo de Vidrio** (glass-bottomed-boat) gives views straight down into Academy Bay and surrounding waters. *(Three-hour tours leave from the Municipal dock twice daily at 8:30am and 2:30pm. Contact Academy Bay Tours (tel. 526 234) for more information. The trip costs US$25.)*

ENTERTAINMENT

Oodles of happy-go-lucky tourists and the high standard of living in Puerto Ayora have combined to make this port town an exciting place once the sun goes down. On almost any night of the week, visitors and locals are ready to get down. **Galapasón,** just off Darwin at the turn to the Darwin Station, is *the* place to be in Puerto Ayora. Inside, you'll find a pool table, slide, foosball table, tropical decor, and freely flowing specialty drinks. (Open M-Sa 6pm-midnight.) Closer to the center of town is **La Panga,** a *discoteca* at Darwin and Tomás de Berlanga, which attracts both endemic and migratory Galápagos residents; it's the standard late-night dance spot (open M-Th 8:30pm-2am, F-Sa 8:30pm-3am). **Barba Negra** (soon to be renamed **Chique Macho**) is a promising *discoteca* smack-dab in the middle of town. Its expansive dance floor (reached by the obligatory smoke-filled, winding stairs of any self-respecting club) and bassed-out sound system hearken back to the thumpin' atmospheres of mainland nightlife. Getting the big crowds to do justice to such a set-up seems to be this disco's only problem—but if your party's big enough, maybe you can get your very own, private rave going. The other half of Puerto Ayora's nightlife consists of slightly mellower bars scattered up and down Darwin. These relaxing environments pass on the latest D.J. remixes, opting for more mature, time-honored classics like Eric Clapton, U2, and everyone's island hero, Bob Marley. **Tambulero's Pub,** near the Darwin Station, across the street from Galapasón, is a small roof-top bar with breezy, pleasant outdoor seating (open M-Sa 8pm-1am). **Cafe Limón,** on Darwin and 12 de Febrero, always has a large crowd sipping Pilseners beneath its thatched roof and grooving to the endless classic rock on the sound system (open daily 6pm-midnight).

SANTA CRUZ: THE HIGHLANDS

For those who haven't quite gotten their sea legs yet, never fear—the verdant interior of Santa Cruz offers a multitude of land-based outings. Many of these places can be visited independently of tour groups or guides, though arranging trips through tour companies is, predictably, more convenient and more expensive. The small towns of **Bellavista** (6km north of Puerto Ayora) and **Santa Rosa** (8km northwest of Bellavista), though lacking hotels and most anything else, are ideal departure spots for nearby hikes. Two popular hiking peaks are **Media Luna,** a crescent-shaped volcanic cinder cone 5km from Bellavista, and **Cerro Crocker,** 3km beyond Media Luna. There is a hill near Santa Rosa **(el Mirador)** that offers an impressive view of the southern coastal area, although one side is blighted by a nearby mine.

Guided tours of the highlands can cost US$20 per person—more if the guide speaks English. Some charge a flat rate for the car and guide, so if you put together a group and haggle, it may be quite cheap. Compare the deals between different agencies. **Camionetas** (pickup trucks) are an alternative mode of transportation to various sites in the highlands and can be found almost anywhere in town, especially near the park and the CITTEG office. They are expensive but charge a flat rate for the truck—bigger groups might end up getting a fairly good deal.

The most stylish way to see the highlands is atop your very own **horse. Amalca Horse Trekking** offers several horse trips: through a **finca** (highland farm), up Cerro Crocker, and to Garrapatero when trail conditions are good. Contact the Moonrise Travel Agency (see **Travel Agencies,** p. 476) in Puerto Ayora to arrange a trip. (Trips US$15-25, plus an s/80,000 *camioneta* ride to get to their ranch.)

While there are no hotels or hostels in the highlands, **camping** is available at the **Butterfly Ranch** (admission US$3) near Santa Rosa. As an added bonus, Galápagos tortoises are frequently sighted in this area. To arrange camping anywhere within the park grounds, contact the National Park Office (tel. 526 189 or 526 511).

To reach the highlands via bus, you'll need to purchase a ticket to the Baltra airport ferry from the CITTEG office in the center of town on Darwin. Passengers may get off the bus at any point on the route, so just let the driver know where you'd like to be let off. Unfortunately, lower fares to Bellavista and Santa Rosa do not exist, so if your group is large enough, finding a *camioneta* might be cheaper. (Buses depart at 6:45, 7:15, and 11:30am; s/20,000.) One shouldn't depend on taking this shuttle back to town, as it is often full with new arrivals and might not stop. Though Let's Go does not recommend hitchhiking, it's not unusual for trucks to stop and pick up passengers for a fee (approx. s/60,000). It is a good idea to head out early in order to catch a ride back into town before dark.

SANTA CRUZ: OTHER SIGHTS

THE TORTOISE RESERVE

Chilling with the *tortugas* at the Darwin Station is fun, but it can't match the visceral satisfaction of meeting these guys on their own turf. Here, the reptiles are as wild as 250kg tortoises can get, which is evidenced by their trails—although slow, these reptiles are powerful green bulldozers, leaving behind flattened vegetation and collapsed fences in their path. A guide is now required to visit the reserve, and shelling out the extra sucres for a knowledgeable one is highly recommended. These beasts are incredibly elusive and tortoise sightings cannot be guaranteed, but a good guide will know where to look. The tortoises tend to move around according to weather conditions, and at the wrong time and place, one could spend all day without seeing any. The trails also can be confusing and many lone tourists have lost their way, which is another reason why guides are required.

Hiking through all the dense, low-growing vegetation of the reserve can be a challenge. Highland tortoises have gradually developed large, dome-shaped shells that enable them to burrow through Santa Rosa's plant growth; for those without such natural advantages, wearing sturdy shoes/boots and long pants helps tremendously. Tortoises are often seen in two areas of the reserve: **La Caseta** and **El Chato.**

LOS GEMELOS

These "twins," on either side of the road to Baltra, just outside of Santa Rosa, are a pair of crater-shaped magma chambers, each approximately 30m deep. They are filled with lush vegetation, most of which is endemic scalesia forest, and are truly monstrous. The vicinity around Los Gemelos is home to Darwin's finches, the striking vermillion flycatcher, and the occasional short-eared owl. The National Park Administration has recently declared Los Gemelos a site that can be seen only with a guide. Inquire at the National Park Office (see p. 479) or at one of the travel agencies in town to arrange a tour.

THE LAVA TUNNELS

The island of Santa Cruz is riddled with **lava tubes** *(los túneles)*, the remains of ancient magma flows that helped to form the Galápagos. The outer crust of these molten streams hardened as they cooled, but the liquid magma within continued flowing. When the flow ceased, these enormous, hollow tubes were left behind.

There are several tunnels around the island, but the most frequently visited is Bellavista's **Tunnel of Endless Love,** named not for what could potentially go on in its dark chambers, but for the heart-shaped hole in the tunnel's roof. Though the tunnel is only 800m long, it begins to seem endless the further you explore. The entrance is draped with romantic, leaf-covered vines that filter the sun's rays and soften the idyllic singing of the birds outside. A rickety banister provides support, but visitors must tread carefully over the loose rocks on the descent. The pathway inside is littered with large but easily navigable piles of rubble. The sheer enormity of this tunnel in addition to the strange, magma-carved designs on its inner surface serve as reminders of Mama Nature's creativity. The number of tubes and caves open to the public varies. The Bellavista tunnels are 7km outside of Puerto Ayora—take the Baltra shuttle to Bellavista and ask for directions, or take a *camioneta* (s/20,000) which will get you directly there. (Admission to the tunnels costs s/25,000; rent flashlights for s/5,000.) Another set of lava pathways are **Furio's Tunnels,** off the road to Baltra in between Bellavista and Santa Rosa. The tunnels are lit, but a flashlight may be useful anyway. The tunnels are divided into different levels, connected by slime-coated ladders. Wear sturdy shoes and prepare to get dirty. (Admission US$4. The tunnels may be reached by the Baltra shuttle.)

The pretty but expensive **Restaurante de Furio** lies at the mouth of the tunnels and prefers that you contact them a day in advance if you plan on eating there (lunch US$14-18). They don't have a phone, but hotels and travel agencies in Puerto Ayora will be able to radio them.

NORTHWESTERN SANTA CRUZ

The far northwest side of Santa Cruz boasts beautiful bays and beaches that can be reached by boat. Some daytrips to these areas leave from Puerto Ayora, but they are more often visited as part of larger, multi-day boat tours.

Las Bachas Beach, near the Baltra Airport, makes for a refreshing swim. Bring bug repellent, though, to ward off stinging flies. Many visitors are happy simply lounging in the sand amidst the small outcroppings of lava rock that jut into the ocean. However, those who just can't get enough of Galápagos fauna can try to catch a glimpse of a flamingo or two in the nearby saltwater lagoon. A variety of other wading birds, such as black-necked stilts, can also be seen here. Marine iguanas and sally lightfoot crabs scamper along the beaches as well. On the way to the lagoon, visitors can see the remains of two barges, which were beached and abandoned by a sore United States military when its attempt to occupy Baltra was cut short by Ecuador's president back in the 1940s.

Conway Bay and **Ballena Bay** (Whale Bay) lie on Santa Cruz's west coast, though there are not many animals to be seen there, so neither is often visited. **Cerro Dragón,** on the northwest coast between Las Bachas and Conway Bay, is a recently-opened visitor attraction that gets its name from the imposing hill that resembles a bumpy green dragon. Tour boats too large to visit tiny islands such as South Plaza often stop here. Its summit is a 2km hike up, and the more commonly used trail winds through scrubby vegetation and reveals dragons of another sort—monstrous, cactus-eating land iguanas. Visits to Cerro Dragón are often made as part of trips to Isla Rábida, an island to the northwest of Santa Cruz.

THE CENTRAL ISLANDS

HIGHLIGHTS OF THE CENTRAL ISLANDS

■ Female **sea lions** greet visitors to **South Plaza Island** (see p. 483).

■ **Isla Santa Fé** (see p. 485) is the home of those teasing **land** and **prickly pear iguanas** and offers fantastic snorkeling in it's beautiful **cove.**

■ **Isla Seymour Norte** (see p. 485) hosts the largest colony of **magnificent frigatebirds** and up-close glimpses of **blue-footed boobies.**

THE CENTRAL ISLANDS: ISLAS PLAZAS

Of the tiny twin islands off the eastern coast of Santa Cruz, only **South Plaza** (a mere 1.3 sq. km) is open to visitors. **North Plaza** remains off limits due to mysterious scientific research (and the high rocky cliffs surrounding the island). While one can only guess what is transpiring on the north island, the desert-like interior of South Plaza can be viewed from the rocky trail that winds its way up and around the sloping island. Reddish, low-lying shrubs dot the landscape, but **prickly pear cacti** dominate the vegetation on this arid rock, assuming the role reserved for water-guzzling hardwoods in most ecosystems. The cacti are reputed to have grown over 8m tall—much larger than those found elsewhere in the world. But for some reason, South Plaza's succulents are now nowhere near this tall, perhaps as a result of El Niño's tumultuous treatment of the Galápagos.

Gargantuan **land iguanas** often lurk beneath these cacti. The male iguanas and cactus fruit bear the same bright yellow hue, and the two share a scintillating tale of evolutionary intrigue. Centuries ago, these reptilian culprits voraciously devoured low-growing flowers. The only cacti able to reproduce were the taller, tree-like plants with large trunks that the chubby iguanas weren't able to climb. Today, the sky-scraping prickly pears prevail, and the diminutive dragons must wait for their succulent treats to fall to the ground. If you're lucky, you might see the iguana population during lunch time, a truly amusing spectacle.

THE SEA LION COLONY

After a dry landing, travelers to South Plaza are greeted by barking female **sea lions** and their pups, basking in the sun and frolicking in the surf. The sea lion population on South Plaza, as on most beaches, is very territorial. During the **mating season,** which begins in May, the bulls join the females on the northern shore, each controlling a harem of females, fighting with other males over their territory, and constantly patrolling his turf. The Spanish term for sea-lion bulls is, fittingly, *los machos*. As a rule, visitors should stay far away from bulls (and should not approach sea lions in general). In fact, sea lions bite several tourists each year, making them statistically more dangerous than sharks. After the tiring mating season, during which the bulls often do not even take sufficient time to nourish themselves, they retreat to the **bachelor colony** on the southwestern side of the island, where cliffs tower over the ocean waves. Although all of this is common behavior, the bachelor colony on South Plaza is particularly well-established, mainly because it is one of the largest in the Galápagos. Though visitors should be careful not to get too close to the gigantic and often violent bulls, the bachelor colony is a fascinating part of the island. The bulls bask in the sun and climb up high, rocky cliffs, a feat which seems to defy the physical capacity of their clumsy bodies. They also engage in full-fledged shouting matches; evidence of their physical confrontations is seen in the gashes from each other's fangs.

OTHER ANIMALS

South Plaza is also replete with its fair share of **birdlife.** Blue-footed and masked boobies may be seen perched on the cliffs of the sea lion bachelor colony, a spot which provides the perfect opportunity to snap a photo of everyone's favorite winged species. These cliffs are also a perfect place to watch red-billed tropical birds swooping through the air. Frigatebirds and lava gulls reside here as well. Keep a lookout for the swallowtail gull, with its striking white-and-gray body and large orange eyes. Glance over the cliff to see how easy it is for diving birds to spot schools of fish in the water, but don't get too close to the edge—even the best boots don't grab limestone the way boobie feet do!

Besides the land iguanas which frequent its rocky interior, South Plaza's physical layout makes it the best place in the Galápagos to see **hybrid iguanas**—the result of male marine iguanas (which are smaller with black skin) and female land iguanas overcoming their habitat differences and getting down and dirty. The geography of South Plaza leads specifically to this phenomenon. The gradual, rocky coastline, with cacti very close to the shore, brings land iguanas near the water. When marine males decide to come onto shore, they use their comparatively large and strong tails to stand their own against land iguanas defending territory. Hybrid iguanas are difficult to find; keep an eye out, and maybe you'll get lucky.

THE CENTRAL ISLANDS: ISLA SANTA FÉ

Isla Santa Fé keeps its treasures well-hidden. Unlike on many of the other islands, a simple walk along the beach here hardly assures sighting much, if any, animal life. Though sea lions and pelicans are hardly discreet as they glide through the water and air surrounding this small island, the elusive Galápagos hawks and snakes, as well as the endemic land iguanas and rice rats, don't often advertise their presence.

One of the best-concealed island creatures, the crested *Conolophus pallidus* species of **land iguana,** is found nowhere else in the world. Hide-and-seek champions with a little patience and time to spare stand the best chance of spotting one of these devious creatures. It's important to walk quietly along the island's trails, since the loud stomps of human feet can easily scare away the iguanas. Your guide may toss a tempting piece of prickly pear cactus to a nearby iguana, enticing it to leave a cozy resting spot and expose itself to camera-happy tourists. Charles Darwin himself had a similar method of seizing the attention of these creatures: "I several times threw a piece [of cactus] to two or three of them when together; and it was amusing enough to see them trying to seize it and carry it away in their mouths, like so many hungry dogs with a bone." The **prickly pear iguanas** found on South Plaza also call Santa Fé home, but here they are a richer golden color than those on other islands. These gargantuan reptiles commonly measure 1m long, with some giants growing much larger.

To experience Santa Fé to its fullest, take one of the two easy hiking trails. There is a short 300m path and a longer 1½km trail that extends into the highland region. Both are somewhat rocky but accessible to most visitors. The longer trail has a relatively steep uphill part that might be difficult for inexperienced hikers; however, this trail offers a better chance of spotting the iguanas, as well as a breathtaking view of the rest of the island and the shimmering ocean below. The trail is also an excellent place to birdwatch and to look for the **Galápagos snake** and **rice rat.** Large **Galápagos hawks** frequent the area, as well as a variety of finch species and curious **Galápagos mockingbirds** who have been known to land on startled visitors' hats. Santa Fé features a beautiful, sheltered **cove** in its northeast bay. Snorkeling here is no more difficult than hiking, though for safety, you should bring a friend for both. Sea lions often join snorkelers' fun or swim up close to anchored boats. Even if you don't get to snorkel with these friendly creatures, the flashy, fluorescent fish that make this cove an exciting place all by themselves.

THE CENTRAL ISLANDS: ISLA SEYMOUR NORTE

North Seymour Island, just north of Baltra, is a common tour boat stop that features not-so-common wildlife. This island is a must-see for any devoted ornithologist, professional or amateur. The largest colony of **magnificent frigatebirds** in the Galápagos nests here, and Seymour is also one of the spots where both fabulous subspecies (the magnificent and the smaller **great frigatebird**) nest side-by-side. At first glance it's hard to tell these two birds apart, but there are a few simple distinctions. Magnificent female frigates have blue rings around their eyes, while great female frigates red ones. For the males, magnificent frigates have a purplish sheen in the feathers on their back, while great frigates have a greenish gloss. Also, magnificent frigates make only clicking, rattling, and grunting sounds, while great frigates' calls are more high-pitched. Like many magnificent or great humans in history, the tyrannical frigates prove that they can bully the smaller and weaker. Because their feathers aren't waterproof, frigates don't dive into the sea to collect fish. Instead, they harass smaller diving birds who are returning from the sea; when a startled booby or gull drops its fish, the speedy frigates zoom down and scoop it up. Nesting mothers are also favorite targets; a frigate will wait until the bird is feeding her wide-mouthed babies, then swoop down and stick its large beak right into the booby's mouth to snatch a regurgitated fish. North Seymour also boasts a variety of wildlife common to the central islands. As visitors make their (dry) landing on the shore of the island, they can hear the barking of **sea lions** announcing their presence. Visiting Isla Seymour Norte is one of the best opportunities to get up close and personal with **blue-footed boobies.** These charming creatures are usually found here during the dry season, when there is less vegetation and more ground space for them to nest. **Snorkeling** near Seymour Island is always a treat, with plentiful schools of brightly colored fish, the occasional stingray, and, of course, those somersaulting, freewheelin', wild and crazy sea lions.

THE CENTRAL ISLANDS: ISLOTE MOSQUERA

So small that it is often referred to by the diminutive "islet," Mosquera hides quietly between Isla Baltra and Seymour Norte. Its proximity to Baltra Airport, however, makes it a convenient first or last stop for tour boats. Reached via a wet landing, the island lacks hiking, swimming, or snorkeling options, but it does provide ample opportunities to get up close and personal with its large sea lion colony. Keep an eye out for the dominant bull, known as the "beach-master," as he swims up and down the shore barking loudly in defense of his territory.

ISLA SAN CRISTÓBAL

Isla San Cristóbal, despite its airport and status as closest location to the mainland and the administrative capital of the islands, is perpetually a distant second to Santa Cruz as headquarters for Galápagos tourism. Although many of its attractions are mediocre by Galápagos standards, it's one of the islands you can adequately explore without being on a tour boat. Possibly the oldest of the islands, San Cristóbal was formed by the towering volcano Cerro San Joaquín (730m high) and low-lying lava flows that fill out the southern regions of the island. The northern part of the island is dry and rather barren, but the lowlands are kept moist by humid winds from the south. The island's first settlers founded the towns of Puerto Baquerizo Moreno and El Progreso in this area to take advantage of the fertile soil and favorable climate. Today the island boasts a naval base and the Galápagos' first radio station. Puerto Baquerizo Moreno has plenty of comfortable places to stay, though nothing particularly luxurious. Interesting daytrips can be made by boat to Isla Lobos, León Dormido, Punta Pitt (the easternmost point in the Galápagos), and several other sites on the island as well.

HOMEMAKING HUBBIES In addition to their unusual methods of acquiring food, **frigatebirds** have adopted some pretty unorthodox practices when it comes to home life. The male of the species is entirely responsible for the assembly and maintenance of the nest as well as for the attraction of a female. Once a satisfactory home has been built on top of a sturdy tree or bush, the male focuses his attention on attracting a suitable mate with whom he may share his new home. This is done through an extensive display of his masculine, seductive attributes—his crimson pouch inflates to full capacity, and he proudly flaunts his enormous wing span. This behavior will hopefully attract a female to his liking, since the choice of a mate is entirely his. If only human males were so progressive...

However, after one year of home and hearth, the male leaves the nest to begin a new life with a new mate. However baffling it may be, this behavior sadly seems a good deal more familiar to our species.

ISLA SAN CRISTÓBAL: PUERTO BAQUERIZO MORENO

Far fewer tourists stay in Puerto Baquerizo Moreno than in Puerto Ayora. But then, San Cristóbal has always had to work just a little bit harder to attract people—its first residents were convicts who revolted and killed their overseer, and it's always hard to correct a bad first impression. The island is more peaceful today; indeed, this ancestral violence seems completely beyond the capacity of Puerto Baquerizo Moreno's 3,000 laid back residents. Some of them even refer to rival Puerto Ayora as the Guayaquil of the Galápagos—a mainland town known for its crime—in contrast to Baquerizo Moreno's small size and peaceful disposition.

Though Puerto Baquerizo Moreno is the political capital of the Galápagos, it hardly feels like a bustling political center. Instead, visitors are struck by the courtesy and relaxed nature of the town; though offices may say they are open throughout the day, don't try to buy an airline ticket during the afternoon *siesta*, and don't forget to say a *buenos días* and *bien provecho* to everyone you meet. The small but lively town overlooks Wreck Bay, a smooth harbor with a rough name. Note that the power goes off at midnight, so have your flashlight ready.

PRACTICAL INFORMATION

Airplanes: SAN/SAETA office (tel. 520 156), at the airport at the end of Alsacio Northia, offers daily flights to Quito via Guayaquil. Non-discount TAME tickets are interchangeable with SAN tickets. Office open M-Su 8am-4pm.

Taxis: Cooperativa de Transporte y Turismo "Lobería" (tel. 520 243), next to the ocean across the street from the police station, runs *camionetas* to: **the airport** (s/9,000); **El Progreso** (15min., s/18,000); and **La Lobería** (15min., s/25,000).

Inter-Island Transportation: INGALA, on the road to El Progreso (taxi s/9,000 to get there), sends boats to **Puerto Ayora** (4hr., Tues. 8am). Buy tickets on Monday afternoon before 3pm at the INGALA office and arrive at the tourist *muelle* at least 30min. early. Open M-F 7:30am-12:30pm and 1:30-4:30pm. **EMETEBE** (tel./fax 520 036), at the airport at the end of Alsacio Northia past the radio station, flies to: **Puerto Villamil** (35min., US$90) and **Baltra** (20min., US$80). Schedules change frequently. Open M-Sa 8am-1:30pm and 3-5:30pm.

Tourist Information: CETUR, on Charles Darwin at the center of town; look for the unmistakable pink and blue box topped by a life-sized, smiling gray whale. Like the whale, this office is more cute than useful. Hours and days of operation are irregular.

Bank: Banco del Pacífico (tel. 520 365; fax 520 368), on Charles Darwin near Jose de Villamil, next to the ocean. Changes dollars and traveler's checks at worse rates than on the mainland and has Master Card cash advances. The **ATM** does not accept VISA. Open M-F 8am-3:30pm, Sa 9am-12:30pm.

Laundry: There is an expensive *lavandería* (tel. 520 333) on Alsacio Northia near the cathedral. US$6 per basket for wash and dry. Open daily 9am-9pm.

Police: Policía Nacional (24hr. emergency tel. 520 101 or 520 129), Darwin and Española. In a blue and gray building. Open 24hr.

Pharmacies: Farmacia Jane (tel. 520 242), on Darwin between Teodoro Wolf and Española. Open M-Sa 8am-noon and 12:30pm-9:30pm, Su 9am-1pm. **Farmacia San Cristóbal,** Jose de Villamil, 1½ blocks from Banco del Pacífico. Open M-F 7:15am-1pm and 3-10pm, irregular weekend hours.

Hospital: Hospital Oskar Jandl (24hr. emergency tel. 520 118), Quito and Alsacio Northia, near the Cathedral and museum, offers 24hr. emergency care and ambulance service. It is usually quite busy, so be prepared to wait for a while. Open daily 7:30am-noon and 1:30-5pm.

Post Office: (Tel./fax 520 373), at the end of Darwin just past the municipal building, provides fax service. Open M-F 7:30am-noon and 2pm-5:30pm, Sa 8am-2pm.

Telephone: Central Telefónica San Cristóbal (PACIFICTEL; tel./fax 520 104), Quito, 4 blocks past Darwin. Look for the mural of blue-footed boobies and a bikini-clad girl holding a cellular phone. All calls go through the mainland; even collect and credit-card calls have an extra per-min. charge. Provides fax service. Open daily 8am-10pm.

PHONE CODE	05

ACCOMMODATIONS

Although foreign tourists rarely take advantage of them, Puerto Baquerizo's hotels offer a decent alternative to cramped ship's quarters. Camping is permitted, but only at the beaches at the Galapaguera. Check with the **National Park Information Site,** just out of town on Alsacio Northia towards the Cabañas de Don Jorge, for specific camping information.

Hotel Mar Azul (tel. 520 139 or 520 107), head away from the waterfront and turn right on Alsacio Northia (in the direction of the airport); it's the white and blue one-story building on the right. While the hot water bathrooms aren't as sparkling as they could be, the price is right for these otherwise tidy rooms with ceiling fans. Two courtyards provide shade under their large, leafy trees. Rooms s/35,000 per person.

Cabañas de Don Jorge (tel./fax 520 208; email cterena@ga.pro.ec), on Alsacio Northia on the east side of town; follow Alsacio Northia as it veers to the left out of town. These ecologically-inspired cabins are popular with Isabela's Dec.-Feb. surfing pilgrims, but they also provide excellent accommodations for families or those interested in extended visits year-round. Each cabin is unique and surrounded by palms, cacti, and hibiscus-draped seating areas. Private bathrooms have hot water. Singles US$10; roughly US$7 for each additional person. US$150/month for longer stays. Breakfast US$2. Call or email for reservations.

Hotel San Francisco (tel. 520 304), on Darwin just across from Banco del Pacífico. One of the best values in town, Hotel San Francisco has a cluttered indoor courtyard filled with murals, plants, and winding staircases reminiscent of an M.C. Escher drawing. Rooms have private baths, fans, and black-and-white TVs. Just s/25,000 per person.

Hostal Northia (tel./fax 520 041; email hnorthia@telconet.net), Alsacio Northia and 12 de Febrero, offers clean rooms as plain as the building's gray exterior. All rooms have fans, hot water, balconies, and firm mattresses. Some also have TVs. The ground floor houses a restaurant and TV lounge. Singles US$20; doubles US$25; triples US$30.

FOOD

Puerto Baquerizo Moreno may suffer from a lack of many things, but its streets are lined with restaurants. Cheap *almuerzos* are available on almost every block, juicy morsels abound in the many fresh fruit stands scattered across town, and bread-lovers can start their day with cheap, delicious goodies from a *panadería*.

Restaurant/Pizzeria Bambú, Villamil and Ignacio de Hernández. Whether or not you're in the mood for *comida típica,* head on down to Bambú for the best of both worlds. This friendly, comfortable restaurant features a traditional *almuerzo* (s/15,000), as well as tasty, vegetarian-friendly pizzas (s/25-28,000) and pasta (s/25-30,000). Bambú also serves homemade ice cream (s/10,000). Open daily for most of the day.

Genoa, on Darwin next to the *municipio* building, set back from the street. This tin-roofed restaurant serves a la carte *comida típica* in hearty portions (s/35-50,000). Open daily 9am-noon and 6pm-midnight.

Restaurante Rosita (tel. 520 106), Villamil and Ignacio de Hernandez. Approaching near-cult status in town, Rosita has been a part of Puerto Baquerizo Moreno's restaurant scene for over 50 years. Unfortunately, it has recently jumped on the tourism bandwagon with higher menu prices than elsewhere in town (*almuerzo* US$3). Although it's not on the menu, *arroz con vegetales* (rice and vegetables, US$3) may be cooked to order as a vegetarian option. Dine indoors, or outside under the palm-frond awning. Open daily 7am-10:30pm.

Miconia, on del Armada next to the naval base. One of the fancier establishments in town, this airy eatery offers savory appetizers (garlic bread s/8,000), numerous seafood/pasta dishes (s/30-50,000), and a subdued ambiance perfect for those Galápagos twilight hours.

Soda Bar Nathaly (tel. 520 018), 2 blocks up Jose Vallejo, off Alsacio Northia. A bit out of the way, but charming with its tree-trunk tables and hanging plants. The hamburgers (s/8,000) and weekend barbecue are the biggest attractions (barbecue chicken dishes s/18,000). Wash it all down with a frothy *batido* (s/7,000). Open daily 8am-11pm.

SIGHTS AND ENTERTAINMENT

A cold drink under a palm tree is all the entertainment most tourists experience in this small town. However, slightly more ambitious tourists can be rewarded with several enlightening and intoxicating experiences.

INTERPRETATION CENTER. This impressive, relatively new complex is one of San Cristóbal's biggest attractions, by far surpassing the educational offerings in Puerto Ayora. The architecture and environment of the center are treats in themselves: wooden walkways wind through beautiful, modern buildings and amidst lush plant life and ocean views. The center's informative exhibits trace the geological and human history of the islands and effectively combine an appreciation for human life in the archipelago with a concern for the islands' conservation. The stories of human history are fascinating, and the information about wildlife and weather will keep nature lovers happy as well. *(Down Alsacio Northia past the Cabañas de Don Jorge. Tel. 520 358. Open daily 7am-6pm.)*

MUSEUM OF NATURAL HISTORY. The museum provides a somewhat, er, different Galápagos experience. Compared with the live goods outside, the poorly preserved Galápagos wildlife that constitutes the museum's main exhibit is just depressing. Fortunately, the admission price also lets you chill with the tour mascot, Pepe the Tortoise. *(On Alsacio Northia next to the cathedral. Open M-F 8:30-11:30am and 3:30-5:30pm, Sa 8:30am-noon. Admission US$1)*

NIGHTLIFE. For those seeking overpriced beer and a slamming beat, Puerto Baquerizo Moreno's *discotecas* are sure to please. **Blue Bay**, across the street from CETUR near the tourist dock, is the most happenin' disco in town. *Salsa*, techno, and reggae attract multitudes of locals to this chromed and upholstered dancing mecca. The nearby **Neptunus,** above the **Casablanca Restaurant and Bar** (a good pre-club drinking establishment itself), provides a very similar scene, but doesn't attract Blue Bay's large crowds. While these discos are open sporadically during the week, Friday and Saturday nights are by far the best nights to get down. In fact, clubbing on any other night is almost a waste of time.

NEAR PUERTO BAQUERIZO MORENO: FRIGATEBIRD HILL

This site, which used to involve a challenging two-hour hike, was recently equipped with several sets of wooden steps that make the climb much more leisurely. The view from the top is breathtaking (literally and figuratively)—the red roofs of Puerto Baquerizo Moreno stretch out to one side, with views of bright white sand and lava rock beaches on the other. Both the magnificent and great **frigatebird** nest here. With wingspans of about 2.3m and bright red, inflatable pouches, they actually do live up to their names. Since these birds only frequent the hill at certain times of year and certain hours of the day, there's no guarantee you'll spot one; in the end, it all depends on luck.

Transportation: To get to Frigatebird Hill, start at the Cabañas de Don Jorge and continue along the same dirt road for five to seven minutes. Two trails lead off from an opening in a stone wall on the right-hand side at the end of the road, both of which eventually lead to the summit. The first one wanders through the woods before reaching the foot of the hill, while the second heads briefly through woods and then along a beach. Several trails snake around the area, but it's not difficult to stay oriented—just check if you're walking in the direction of the hill or away from it. Parts of the path are rocky, so hiking boots are a good idea. The stairway leads to various platforms, each boasting stunning views of the town and the bays and cliffs below. The hike to the top should take 20 to 40 minutes.

NEAR PUERTO BAQUERIZO MORENO: LA LOBERÍA

Located just outside of Puerto Baquerizo Moreno, this rocky beach abounds with the sounds of oodles of sea lions. Swimming is not permitted, and all trash and foodstuffs from picnics must be packed out. Those who choose to linger until sunset can watch the water darken from crystal clear to bright blue to deep purple. To get here, follow directions to Hotel Mar Azul, and then take the road out of town towards the airport. Turn left at the airport and then stay to the right at any forks in the road. It's about a 30-minute walk altogether. Taxis from town (s/25,000) are available if you'd rather not walk.

NEAR PUERTO BAQUERIZO MORENO: EL JUNCO LAGOON

Earth, wind, fire, and water came together to form the elemental extravaganza that is known as Junco Lagoon. A road winds up the verdant sides of an extinct volcano, until, at the summit, it reaches a beautiful mist-enshrouded lagoon formed by hundreds of years of rain water collecting in the *caldera*. If at first the fog is too heavy, never fear—one of the wispy zephyrs which sweep across this mountain top will soon come along, lifting the haze and revealing the erstwhile hidden lagoon. Frigatebirds use the lake as a bathtub, gliding through the mist and cleaning themselves in the fresh water. A narrow trail winds its way around the rim, past numerous land and sea birds, and overlooks nearly all of San Cristóbal, including León Dormido to the north and Punta Pitt to the northeast. A small portion of the coastline is obstructed, however, by the looming **Cerro San Joaquín** (at over 700m, the highest mountain on San Cristóbal). Despite rumors to the contrary, visitors do *not* need to be part of a tour group to visit the highlands, though tours can be arranged in town (ask at Restaurant Rosita).

Transportation: The highlands can be reached by foot or by hiring a truck in town (it shouldn't cost more than s/150,000 round trip). To reach the lagoon by foot, head out of town on Quito or 12 de Febrero and follow signs to the town of **El Pro-**

EL PROGRESO'S PROGRESS In the 1880s, El Progreso was founded by **Manuel J. Cobos** as the first settlement on Isla San Cristóbal. Cobos imported a group of convicts to serve as laborers on his sugar plantation, halfway between the highlands and the current capital of Puerto Baquerizo Moreno. His ruthless supervision and slave-labor policies quickly incited an infamous mass-mutiny in which rebellious workers took his life. These days the memory of Cobos lives on, immortalized by the street signs scattered around the island which bear his name. The small agricultural town he founded also survives, easily accessible by hike or taxi from Puerto Baquerizo Moreno. Though it's small, El Progreso boasts one of the only restaurants around. There's never a dull moment at **Quita d'Cristhi.** The rambling grounds of this eating/entertainment establishment are popular with locals, but tourists are a rare sight. Quita d'Cristhi usually has *fútbol* games, arm-wrestling matches, and particularly heated card games. (Open weekends.) El Progreso also offers a great deal of outdoorsy stuff to do, and you can bring the kids for a romp on the playground. For a Tarzan-esque sleeping experience, try **La Casa del Ceibo** (tel. 520 248), a large bamboo cabin built 12m off the ground in a gigantic 200 year-old *ceibo* tree. Visitors enter via a rickety suspension bridge made of vine-covered bamboo. The two-story house is completely furnished with two bed mats, a hot-water bathroom, a refrigerator, and a soda-and-beer bar. (Rooms s/25,000 per person per night; tours US$1.)

greso. From here, it is 10km farther to El Junco. Follow the highway until you can make a right onto an uphill dirt road (which is really just two tire tracks). The hike up the hill is very steep, but it's short and the view at the top makes it all worthwhile. Another impressive view of the highlands may be seen from the **Mirador de la Soledad**. Reaching this point is quite easy; since it lies right at the side of a road just outside of El Progreso.

ISLA SAN CRISTÓBAL: OTHER SIGHTS

The most popular excursions are to the islands of **Isla Lobos** and **León Dormido** (also called **Kicker Rock**) and to **Cerro Brujo** beach, off San Cristóbal's western shore. These nearby sites are accessible by boat, either as daytrips from Puerto Baquerizo Moreno or as longer tours from other islands. **Isla Lobos,** the first of the two islands, is about one hour northeast of Puerto Baquerizo Moreno. Separated from San Cristóbal's shore by a small channel, the tiny, rocky island has a white sand beach where blue-footed boobies nest and sea lions sunbathe. Humans, however, only observe the habitat from the 850m trail that cuts across it from east to west. Snorkeling around the island lets you watch the underwater antics of the carefree sea lions. Just stay away from the big males—they're not interested in fun and games. **León Dormido,** another hour northeast of Lobos, gets its name from its resemblance to a sleeping lion. Whoever named it must have had one mighty imagination; it looks more like a monstrous rock sticking straight up out of the ocean, with a gigantic splinter to one side. Scuba diving and snorkeling here are prime and Galápagos sharks are often seen. Still, watch out for dangerous currents. To the north, Cerro Brujo is a beautiful beach made from finely ground white coral. It also has an eroded tuff cone where boobies, pelicans, and gulls hang out.

The easternmost point in the archipelago, **Punta Pitt,** is another of San Cristóbal's notable sights. Located on the far northeast corner of the island, it takes quite a while to reach from Puerto Baquerizo Moreno. But booby fanatics won't think twice about making the trip; red-footed, blue-footed, and masked boobies all call Punta Pitt home. Compared to spots on other islands, though, Punta Pitt offers few chances to get close to the birds, so bring binoculars if you want a good view. Beyond the landing at a sandy cove, a trail leads up the mountain, weaving through booby territory and providing lofty views of the rocky shore below. The trail takes only about 20 minutes to hike each way, and the views are amazing.

One final attraction in the mountains of San Cristóbal, **La Galapaguera,** is just down the shore from Punta Pitt. Here, giant land tortoises roam free, making it very similar to the Tortoise Reserve on Isla Santa Cruz. The hike takes two hours each way, which shouldn't be a problem for hard-core *tortuga* fans.

Since all these spots can only be visited with a guide, you need to arrange daytrips with organizations in Puerto Baquerizo Moreno. The travel agencies affiliated with and located above Rosita's Restaurant both provide day tours to these locations, as well as to nearby **Isla Española.** The trips generally cost US$70-80 (larger groups of 8 people or more are preferred.) Trips to the nearby attractions generally hit more than one of these sites in a day. Visiting them on multiple-day tours may be more economical if you have the time and funds for an extended boat trip.

THE WESTERN ISLANDS

When the *Beagle*, carrying Charles Darwin on his fateful journey, crossed the Bolívar Channel between Isla Isabela and Isla Fernandina, Darwin marveled at what he called the "immense deluges of black, naked lava, which have flowed either over the rims of the great caldrons, like pitch over the rim of a pot in which it has been boiled, or have burst forth from smaller orifices on the flanks." This channel remains an exciting place for boats to pass through as they visit the still volcanically active Western Islands; steaming volcanic *fumaroles* sometimes flare up, and groups often see dolphins and whales surface from this region's deep waters.

The Western Islands of Isabela and Fernandina are usually only visited by large or fast boats, or those on extended (10+ days) tours, as the visitor sites are far away from each other and from the rest of the archipelago. However, like many of the harder-to-reach islands, the Western Islands are rich with unique geological and living wonders which will amaze visitors as much as they did Darwin.

HIGHLIGHTS OF THE WESTERN ISLANDS

- The **volcanoes** of **Isla Isabela** (see p. 492) have been active as recently as 1991.
- *Tortugas* grow up at Isabela's **Breeding Center for Giant Tortoises** (see p. 290).
- **Isla Fernandina** (see p. 497) is a good place to observe the **flightless cormorant.**
- **Isla Bartolomé** (see p. 499) has some of the Galápagos' most stunning rock formations and spectacular vistas.

THE WESTERN ISLANDS: ISLA ISABELA (ALBEMARLE)

Although Isabela is strikingly big and beautiful and one of the few islands inhabited by humans, it still doesn't get much attention. Its lack of a true airport or developed town makes it an unlikely base for tour boats, and usually only big and fast boats are able to access its widely dispersed visitor sites.

Much of Isabela's attraction derives from its powerful geology. The island, comprising over 58% of the archipelago's land mass, resulted from the fusion of six volcanoes by lava flows. Few of these volcanoes have lost their steam; eruptions have occurred on **Volcán Wolf, Sierra Negra, and Volcán Alcedo** in recent decades, and in September of 1998, **Cerro Azul** erupted with a blaze of red-orange magma and fire. From various sites on the island, and from as far away as Santiago and Rábida islands, the series of giant volcanoes looms grandly between the ocean and sky. Besides the western-coast visitor sites on Isabela, there are several exciting places to see, all accessible from the southern town of **Puerto Villamil.**

PUERTO VILLAMIL

In Puerto Villamil (pop. 1,500), which is relatively free of commercialization, there is no Ministry of Tourism, there is no supermarket, and, in lieu of a newspaper, people make announcements from a loudspeaker in the center of town. Prickly pears substitute for fence posts, and only the moon and stars light up the town once midnight rolls around. Like many small towns, Villamil gossips and gawks. Outsiders are an uncommon sight in this distant town, so be prepared to receive many a curious look as you stroll along the sandy avenues. The people are quite friendly, though. Don't be surprised if an islander invites you in for a bit of conversation; everyone here has a story to tell. Life in Puerto Villamil is not complicated; four walls, a roof, and a spot on a fishing boat more than suffices. A stroll at sunset along Puerto Villamil's coconut-lined beaches makes the exploitative t-shirt shop scene of Puerto Ayora seem a world away.

PRACTICAL INFORMATION. There is no tourist office, but hotel proprietors can generally help with any question. Town information and maps are available at the Hotel Ballena Azul and at various shops in Puerto Ayora (s/10,000). Sometimes, free town maps are available at the CETUR office in Puerto Ayora. The **airport/landing strip** is 3km outside of town, and while hitchhiking is not recommended by Let's Go, some travelers take trucks into town (s/15,000). Finding a willing truck is not guaranteed, so be prepared to hoof it. Captain Juan Mendoza takes passengers by his **boat,** the *Estrella Del Mar*, to Puerto Ayora (Tu morning, s/184,000). Purchase tickets in the municipal offices on Mondays. The **Capitania** (tel. 529 113), in the center of town across from El Municipio, knows when boats are leaving (supposedly open 24hr.). If you have to get back quickly or don't like boats, the **EMETEBE** office (tel. 529 155), located on the corner of Las Frigatas and Conocarpu, across the street from the Capitanía, arranges flights to: **Baltra** (20min., Tu, Th, and Sa, US$80) and **Puerto Baquerizo Moreno** (35min., M, W, F, US$80), but schedules are subject to change. If the phones aren't working, the office can contact TAME or SAN via radio. (Open M-F 7am-noon and 2-6pm, Sa 7am-3pm.)

In an **emergency,** call 529 101. The **police** are across the street and are theoretically on call 24 hours but don't appear to be particularly busy. There is no hospital on Isabela, but Puerto Villamil does boast a **health center** (emergency tel. 529 181) on 16 de Marzo and Antonio Gil, a block away from the police station (open M-F 8am-noon and 2-6pm). Make calls from the **PACIFICTEL** office, on Las Escalecias, three blocks away from the beach.

ACCOMMODATIONS. Lodging in Puerto Villamil is good, verging on excellent. **Hotel Ballena Azul** and the adjacent **Cabañas Isabela del Mar** (tel./fax 529 125 for both; email isabela@ga.pro.ec; www.pub.ecua.net.ec/isabela), on Conocarpus at the edge of town, are easily two of the best places to stay in the Galápagos. The large, rustic rooms at Hotel Ballena Azul, complete with hot water, wooden walls, mosquito netting, and ocean views, would have made Hemingway's "Old Man" content to simply *look* at the sea. Dora, the Swiss mistress of the house, loves to sit down and chat (in English, Spanish, French, or German). The hotel also has an inexpensive laundry service. (Rooms s/40,000, US$7 with bath.) **The Cabañas Isabela del Mar** are spacious and spotless. Each private cabin, equipped with a private hot water bath and a ceiling fan to ward off mosquitoes, fits two or three people. (US$8 for one person; US$7 each for 2 or 3 people). The nearby **Hotel Tero Real** (tel. 529 106) is conveniently located on Tero Real; look for the red roofs. The two-story bungalows with refrigerators and private baths house four to five people each. (Bungalows s/30,000 per person.) **Hotel San Vicente,** (tel. 529 140 or 529 180), Cormorantes and Pinzón Artesano, offers basic, clean rooms with private baths. They also allow free **camping.** (Singles s/30,000; doubles s/25,000.)

FOOD. The restaurant at the **Hotel Ballena Azul** definitely serves up the highest quality food in town. Join Antonio and Dora for great local and international food that borders on gourmet. The menu includes a breakfast of fresh fruit, bread, homemade jam, and coffee (s/10,000, with eggs s/15,000); lunch and dinner offerings include rice, meat, salad, and vegetables (s/15,000, s/20,000 with soup). For smoother sailing, give advance warning if you plan to have lunch or dinner. Your only other option is to eat in one of the restaurants near the Municipio. **Ruta, Costa Azul,** and **Rosita** are the most highly recommended; all serve *desayuno*, *almuerzo*, and *merienda* (s/12-15,000 each). Costa Azul also has a la carte items (*pollo* dishes s/35,000, *ceviche de langosta* s/40,000).

IT'S NOT THE NBA, BUT... In a town that lacks a real supermarket or post office, visitors to Puerto Villamil might initially be startled to see a disproportionate number of basketball courts along the quiet dirt roads. In Ecuador, *fútbol* reigns supreme, but basketball has become quite the Isabelan craze. Every summer, Puerto Villamil hosts a month of basketball "play-offs" for local teams. On the newly painted court at the local *escuela,* eight teams (five men's, three women's) from the community at large alternate playing against each other, with about two games going on under the lights every Saturday night. The crowd is loud, the energy high, and the players manage to ignore the number of dogs chasing the action on the court. For additional local flavor, before the games, each team marches out with its *madrina* ("godmother"), a woman or young girl sporting a silky beauty-pageant-esque sash, who presents her team to the cheering crowd. No one knows how long this tradition will last, but in the meantime, it's making for some lively Saturday nights in little Villamil.

ENTERTAINMENT. Nightlife in Puerto Villamil is unpredictable, but depending on the night of the week, there just might be some serious *salsa* going down. **La Barca Discoteca,** on Conocarpas between Escalecias and Opuntia, is recommended by the locals. However, Puerto Villamil nightspots tend to go in and out of fashion rather often, so ask around to find out what's going on.

NEAR PUERTO VILLAMIL

Though not much is going on in the sleepy town of Puerto Villamil, there is plenty of excitement awaiting the curious visitor. This is the Galápagos at their most feral, and the real attractions must be visited in their natural habitats.

VOLCÁN SIERRA NEGRA (SANTO TOMÁS). After two hours of bruising your fanny on the back of a horse, the mist parts, your jaw drops, and you tell your bum that it was worth it. The dark, ominous **caldera** extends in all directions, refusing to be framed by even the widest angle lens. Volcán Sierra Negra is the oldest and largest of Isabela's six volcanoes; with a diameter of 10km, it is the second-largest volcanic crater in the world.

Adventurous travelers may follow a trail westward along the crater rim to the **sulphur mines.** Just inside the crater, three levels of sulphur formations bubble and steam. The trip to the sulfur mines is longer and more difficult than the daytrip to Sierra Negra alone, and those who are planning on doing both might consider **camping** at the crater rim, which will allow ample time to see everything. Before camping, it's a good idea to talk to the park officials in Puerto Villamil (tel. 529 178), on Antonio Gil. Remember, fires are not permitted and trash must be carried out. Tents can be rented from Hotel Ballena Azul, though other items (including rain gear) should be brought along. It's really not a safe idea to visit the volcano without a guide; the area is very easy to get lost in, especially due to the often-heavy mist. However, the people who rent the horses to visitors will send someone who knows where he's going along with the group. Bringing long pants, long sleeves, and a rain coat is advised.

Transportation: Day trips to see this monstrosity can be arranged through Hotel Ballena Azul and also can include a visit to neighboring Volcán Chico (*camionetas* s/230,000, horses s/20,000, guides s/60,000). This trip is much more affordable in large groups.

LA GRIETA DE LOS TIBURONES. This marine attraction is a 10-minute *panga* ride from Puerto Villamil. After a short walk, the rocky black lava trail approaches a large channel beside a lagoon. Small fish swim around the narrow channel entrance, but farther up lurks a bigger catch—**white-tipped reef sharks.** Far from aggressive, these docile creatures glide in and out of the channel in groups. Only 2 ft. from the trail, cliques of 30 or more bask in the shallows. Some daredevils jump in with the sharks; while this may not be dangerous for the humans, it is for the sharks. They scare easily, at times cutting themselves on the sharp lava rocks in their attempt to avoid running into clumsy tourists. It's better for the sharks when people swim in the adjacent lagoon, where sharks swim among smoother rocks. If lucky, you could also see a **sea turtle** or **spotted eagle ray.** The trail continues to a small beach area where **sea lions** often rest in the shade of the mangroves just up from the water. **Penguins** also reside in this area.

Transportation: You might be able to find a *panga* willing to take you, but chances are it will be difficult, so it's better to arrange it through Hotel Ballena Azul. A group should cost approximately s/180,000-200,000. This includes a two-hour stay and a boat ride back to town.

THE BREEDING CENTER FOR GIANT TORTOISES. For more crazy tortoise action, check out this breeding center. Run in conjunction with the National Park Service, the center provides up-close looks at Galápagos tortoises in every size from small to extra-extra-large. The center focuses on the rearing of two breeds of Isabelan tortoise. *(Follow Antonio Gil past the health center to the edge of town, where a sign points to the station, 1km away. National Park Office tel. 529 178. Open daily 7am-6pm.)*

EL MURO DE LAS LÁGRIMAS (THE WALL OF TEARS). This wall, in accordance with its name, commemorates Isabela's past as a penal colony. In June 1946, then-President José María Velasco Ibarra decided to move 300 prisoners and 30 guards from Guayaquil to the base of a hill called La Orchilla, 5km outside of Puerto Villamil. With no other means of employing the prisoners, the penal colony's chief decided to construct a jail with the only substance available—lava rocks, piled on top of each other without cement. The extreme variety in the shapes of the rocks prevented efficient stacking, so the result was a tall pile 9m high with sloping sides. The grueling hours in the sun and back-breaking labor broke many men's spirits, stealing away their wills to live. Over time, it came to be known as the place "where the cowards died and the brave wept." Construction of this "wall of tears" ceased when the sadistic chief was transferred and the colony moved to the highland agricultural area. The colony was abolished in 1959 after a major rebellion in which prisoners seized the camps and fled to the continent in a stolen yacht. *(To get to the Wall of Tears, follow Antonio Gil past the health center to the outskirts of town. From there, signs guide the way. The walk takes 2hr.)*

OTHER SIGHTS. There are various other spots for snorkeling and swimming near La Grieta—ask at the Hotel Ballena Azul for details. On the other side of town from La Tintorera are several lagoons filled with flamingoes, ducks, and other birds. One is right in town on Flamencos (of course). A road goes all the way around this lagoon, so the wildlife can be seen from all angles. Another generally well-stocked lagoon is on the left side of the road that leads to the Tortoise Breeding Center. There are several nice lagoons and beaches on the way to El Muro de Las Lágrimas, including the particularly secluded and aptly named **Playa de Amor**.

TAGUS COVE AND PUNTA TORTUGA

Tagus Cove is the most frequently visited attraction on Isabela, and, conveniently, it gives a taste of much of what Isabela has to offer. It is reached by a beautiful *panga* ride along Isabela's cliffs past cormorants, penguins, iguanas, and pelicans. The graffiti near the landing site indicates just how popular the spot has become since the turn of the century, when sailors scratched their ships' names on the cave walls—today, travelers are encouraged *not* to add their own marks. Up a series of wooden steps begins the upward path that eventually overlooks **Darwin Lake,** a body of water with a higher salt content and water level than the sea. The view just keeps getting better and better as the trail continues. At the trail's summit, if visibility is good, one can see Volcán Darwin and Volcán Wolf–which lies on the equator–to the north and Sierra Negra to the south. Isla Fernandina also looms in the distance. Near Tagus Cove, the rarely visited **Punta Tortuga** boasts the only habitat in the world that supports the **tool-using mangrove finch.** Endemic to Isabela and Fernandina, these talented birds explore tree bark using sticks or cactus spines held in their beaks. When they find a particularly good tool, they stash it away for later use. Although a trek through the mangrove swamp does not assure a rare bird sighting, the challenging terrain provides other exciting bird-watching opportunities and some good exercise to boot.

URBINA BAY

Urbina Bay's attractions are big and tough. First, there's some gigantic wildlife—monstrous land iguanas frequent this area, as do those slow-but-steady *tortugas*. The tortoises come down from nearby **Volcán Alcedo** in the rainy season to lay their eggs, so they normally can't be seen here once the dry season hits. Enormous herds of feral goats roam the area, and their pounding hooves have transformed large patches of shore into dusty wastelands—an example of how damaging introduced animals can be. Urbina Bay also has some big coral formations that arose from the sea when it was uplifted by tectonic shifting in 1954. In fact, this entire area was underwater until that year. The trail, which begins with a wet landing on a black beach, is easily navigated during the dry season, but visitors may need to wade through water during the rainy months. Eventually, visitors reach a second beach which, before the uplift, was the shore of the island. Though no one was present at the time of the uplift, **skeletons** of marine turtles, sharks, and even entire schools of fish were found here when a crew of Disney filmmakers arrived on the scene a few days later. The fast-moving animals didn't even have time to escape, testimony to how quickly the event occurred. From this point, groups may either return to the landing site via the same trail or continue on a longer path past the coral heads and along a stretch of the (new) beach.

ELIZABETH BAY

On the western side of Isabela is Elizabeth Bay, a marine neighborhood rife with aquatic and land-based activity. There are no landing sites, so get out those binoculars and hope for a clear day. To the north of the bay lie the **Mariela Rocks**—a landscape of rugged cliffs and gnarled Palo Santo trees frequented by penguins and *pangas* alike. Some tours offer snorkeling around these rocky isles, and oversized star fish and fishing *pinguinos* are the reward for plunging into the freezing water. The average temperature of the ocean in this part of the archipelago is a few degrees lower than elsewhere–a result of the cooler Cromwell current coming in from the open sea. While "a few degrees" doesn't sound like much of a difference, you will definitely feel it. Boats continue past the Marielas into an aquatic **mangrove forest,** which creates a labyrinth of watery channels that wander lazily among the lush green leaves and red roots of the mangroves. The beauty and serenity of the environment can only be described as something out of a sappy romantic movie. The dense mangroves serve as breeding grounds for several types of fish and green sea turtles, and rays and white-tip reef sharks often make rounds in search of a quick meal. The bay is a favorite spot for other seafaring wildlife as well; sea lions and some sea birds, like the **Flightless Cormorant,** sunbathe and dine among the partially submerged rocks which dot the bay's shallow, sandy bottom.

PUNTA MORENO

Punta Moreno can be one of the most memorable stops on an entire tour. The juxtaposed craggy lava rocks and small, idyllic lagoons scattered across the landscape are home to a variety of birds—including blue herons and flamingoes—that flock to these watering holes. If you visit around mating season, the flamingoes' coloration is particularly vivid, with some birds sporting uncharacteristically dark red feathers. The colors that greet visitors' eyes are practically unreal—the black lava field is dotted with holes of blue water, each surrounded by a ring of green vegetation and speckled with pink flamingoes. The journey to the watering holes from the landing site traverses fields of jagged lava rocks, and their reflection of heat often leaves the air very dry. Bring plenty of water and sturdy hiking shoes; sandals definitely won't do for this one. Near Punta Moreno some groups might visit a series of coastal pools, one of which is known as **Derek's Cove.** While it is illegal to go ashore, these pools are an excellent place to observe sea lions and a large number of sea turtles from a boat.

VOLCÁN ALCEDO

For many years, Volcán Alcedo was the height of Galápagos adventure for mountain-climbing visitors. The 10km climb led to fantastic views and a 7km *caldera* housing the largest population of tortoises on the islands (five species, 4,000 individuals). Recently, that strength was tested by an invasion of voracious goats, driven onto the volcano by Isabela's packs of savage dogs. The dogs have been eliminated, but the goats, at home on the scrubby, mountainous terrain, continue to breed. Their exploding population has taken a toll on Volcán Alcedo's vegetation, depriving the tortoises of food and shelter from the sun. The national park has closed the site while its team of expert goat assassins brings the shaggy horde down to size. With limited funds and inhospitable terrain, the eradication program may take years. The volcano cannot be re-opened to visitors until the ecosystem is stabilized—so unless you're a biologist with an uncanny knack for shooting goats, Alcedo will have to wait until your next trip.

THE WESTERN ISLANDS: ISLA FERNANDINA

An island of superlatives, Fernandina is the newest island in the archipelago, the westernmost link in the Galápagos chain, and the most volcanically active. The last eruption, in January 1995, was of a smaller volcano on the island's southwest corner, **Volcán La Cumbre.** One of the parasitic cones—the smaller volcanoes which sprout from the sides of larger volcanoes—could erupt again anytime. Perhaps most notable is Fernandina's lack of introduced plants and animals, a distinction that prompts many to award it the most impressive superlative of all: "the most pristine island in the world." In light of other islands' colonization by goats, rats, and dogs, Fernandina's purity is surprising. The fact that fishermen have been illegally using Fernandina as a campsite has biologists biting their rat-fearing nails.

PUNTA ESPINOSA

Fernandina has only one visitor sight, **Punta Espinosa.** A geological baby formed by tectonic uplift in 1975, it is reached by a wet or dry landing, depending on the tide level. Be careful—the algae covering many of the island's rocks makes them extremely slippery. Penguins, flightless cormorants, herons, and other friendly wildlife are often spotted sunning themselves near the landing spot. The area also boasts the largest colony of lava cacti in the Galápagos.

Several different visitor paths jut out from the national park monument near the landing, none of which are particularly long. To the left, a path winds its way over and near dry fields of *pahoehoe* and *aa* lava, which take their names from similar flows in the Hawaiian islands. The *pahoehoe* is also called "ropey" lava, since it dries in a ripply formation resembling cords of thick rope. The *aa*, or rugged lava, cools down much faster than the *pahoehoe*, breaking in pieces and resulting in very sharp formations. The *aa* fields are consequently not explored during land tours but are easily seen from adjacent *pahoehoe* fields. The lava fields are also very hot during the day, so don't forget to hydrate yourself adequately before venturing out on this sea of undulating black rock. A huge, rusty engine from an old boat also appears mysteriously down this path, proving that even this remote island has not remained untouched by humans.

On the path to the right of the monument, hoards of abnormally large **marine iguanas** are often seen basking in the sun. These anomalous reptiles are much larger than their brethren on other islands. Marine iguanas are voracious eaters—after gorging themselves on a meal of algae, these social animals stretch out next to (and on top of) their neighbors to dry out, warm up, and digest their food. They are excellent swimmers; if forced, they can stay underwater for over an hour. Darwin's "Imps of Darkness" have one more trick up their scaly sleeves. They have evolved a unique way to excrete the salt they unavoidably consume from their algae main courses—they blow it out of their noses in a sneezing action. Years ago, pirates thought this "poisonous spit" was an acid. Even though it's only salt water, it can pack quite a punch—the excreted salt often shoots 3 or 4 ft. Watch out; iguanas may also do this when pesky humans come too close.

The iguana nests lie on either side of a very narrow sandy path, where blue herons, Galápagos hawks, and other predatory birds look to make a quick meal of their hatchlings. Be careful where you step; any visitor that strays from this path can kill the iguanas before the birds even get a chance. Nesting sites are well concealed and quite fragile; the weight of a human being could easily crush an entire nest. Not too many visitors seem to have strayed from the straight and narrow, though; just beyond this trail hundreds of iguanas often doze in the sun. This prodigious outpouring of animals results not only from reptilian hormones, but also from Fernandina's lack of introduced predators. This is what all the islands must have been like years ago. This path also leads to the best place on the island for viewing the rare **flightless cormorant.** The cold Cromwell current that brings nutrient-filled waters into this part of the archipelago makes the ocean here particularly rich with fish. Snorkeling around Fernandina is superb. Numerous **sea turtles** gracefully glide about the underwater volcanic rock formations. The small **horn**

shark can also be seen here. When observing these timid creatures, don't swim frantically in pursuit: this will only spook them. Rather, try to imitate their fluid motions, use your plastic flippers as they use their exquisitely evolved appendages, and you too will attain the zen serenity of Galápagos marine life. Fernandina's breathtaking landscape truly makes it seem more pristine than many of the islands. The turquoise of the water is slightly brighter here, the white sand seems to shine even more than usual, and the waves crashing against the shore compete with Volcán La Cumbre in the distance for the attention of all visitors to the area.

THE WESTERN ISLANDS: ISLA SANTIAGO (JAMES OR SAN SALVADOR)

Santiago's history has been less than serene. Human commercialism and a great deal of volcanic action have disrupted the island time and again, making it one of the most interesting, and thus frequently visited, in the Galápagos. Santiago's volcanic cones, beachfront lava spires, gentle *pahoehoe* lava flows, and black sand beaches are reminders of the island's explosive past. The first humans to inhabit the island were 16th-century pirates hiding out in the sheltered coves. It wasn't until the 1880s, when four rather amorous goats were abandoned on the island, that irreparable damage was done. Their population ballooned to over 100,000, and the gluttons ate everything in sight. Since then, environmentalists with voracious appetites for conservation (and goat stew) have managed to keep the population in check. Many a tour boat is rumored to still serve Chivo de Santiago (Santiago Goat). The island was further sullied in the 1920s and 1960s by two commercial salt mines that unsuccessfully attempted to profit from the island's salt-lined crater. Despite its turbulent past, there is much to see and do on Santiago. Its central location makes it easily accessible, so most Galápagos boat-trippers will get a taste of all that Santiago has to offer (whether or not they try that goat stew).

PUERTO EGAS

Puerto Egas, located on Santiago's western shore, packs it all into one fun-filled visitor site. A black beach, the remnants of the area's human history, amazing geology, and unique wildlife all cluster in Santiago's **James Bay.** The brown, layered tuff stone and black basalt volcanic rock that make up most of the landscape form a masterpiece of apertures, crevices, and natural bridges. The resulting alcoves are perfect siesta spots for sea lions seeking refuge from the glaring equatorial sun.

The visitor's trail first leads along the coastline to one of the best tide pool areas in the Galápagos. The black lava towers, basins, and craters are filled with crystal-clear sea water. As with all tide pools, the marine treasures of Puerto Egas' are only visible when the tide is out. Sea birds, such as great blue herons, lava herons, ruddy turnstones, oyster catchers, and terns, often gorge enthusiastically on the tasty shellfish, crustaceans, and small fish which reside in these easy-access tide pools. The lava rock along the tidal area is very slippery: be careful when walking.

Past the tide pools visitors come to what, for many, is the highlight of a trip to Isla Santiago: the **grottoes.** These deep pools, which all belong to a connected system of collapsed lava tubes, are constantly filled and refilled by the open sea. One pool, appropriately dubbed **Darwin's Toilet,** fills with a particularly noisy flushing force. The grottoes are an especially good spot to find the elusive **Galápagos fur seals.** Once hunted to the brink of extinction for their thick, insulating fur, these diminutive sea lions have made an impressive comeback. They reside in large numbers but are much more timid than their sea lion cousins, probably because of their traumatic history of human contact. They are also excellent climbers, and use the shady ledges of the grottoes to keep the sun off their extra-thick fur and would-be harassers at a distance. The impact of human activity on Santiago is quite apparent in both the historical and current uses of Puerto Egas. The remains of buildings and equipment from the salt mine companies stand among the lava rock and vegetation along the shore.

PLAYA ESPUMILLA

Espumilla Beach, reached via a wet landing at the north end of James Bay, was a good spot to see flamingoes until the 1982-83 El Niño. Since that time, flamingoes can no longer be found in the saltwater lagoon behind the beach, but the 2km inland trail is still a good place to observe other bird species; look out for **Darwin finches, Galápagos Hawks,** and **flycatchers.** The long, sandy beach is also a great swimming spot, but be careful where you step; sea turtles often lay their eggs here.

SULLIVAN BAY

The beach of **Sullivan Bay** is quite unlike the sandy areas lining many Galápagos shores. Instead, the shore of eastern Santiago is made up of a fresh (100-year-old) *pahoehoe* lava flow, producing solid black fields of rock. Pockets of gases trapped beneath the surface of the lava, known as *hornitos* (little ovens) have erupted as "mini volcanoes," producing the wrinkles breaking up the smooth, black span. Also notice the *kipukas*, tuff cones that were once their own autonomous rocky isles before the sudden attack from all sides by Santiago's quick-flowing lava. A trail loops around the bay and takes about one-and-a-half hours to hike.

BUCCANEER COVE

An impressive reminder of the renegade pirates that used to dwell here, Buccaneer Cove is located at the northwest end of Isla Santiago. Pirates frequented this cove in the 1600s and early 1700s, later followed by visiting whalers. Fresh water was often available in depressions in the lava rock, and the cove was also a convenient place to maintain boats. Although today tour boats don't land in the cove, many take the time to pass by slowly, letting passengers enjoy the area's towering cliff walls and impressive rock formations. The shoreline is now populated by feral goats that do as much damage to the landscape as the pirates did on the high seas. Its rock formations are remarkable—sailors watched the passing pinnacles and outcroppings with the same imagination people use when looking at clouds. Keep an eye out for "The Monk" and "Elephant Rock."

THE WESTERN ISLANDS: ISLA BARTOLOMÉ

You know that picture of the Galápagos in which a wind-sculpted spear of rock juts defiantly over a blue sea with a white-crescent beach underneath? That's Bartolomé. Although only 1.2 sq. km in size, the island's striking geology makes it one of the most visually stunning to visit—deep reds, blues, and shimmering blacks mingle and shift, creating a kaleidoscopic landscape. Dominated by an ancient volcano of stark and imposing beauty, this barren island consists of ash and porous lava rock on which colonizing plants are just beginning to grow. The *isla* boasts two visitor sites: the **summit** of the volcanic cone and the **twin crescent beaches,** home to the only colony of Galápagos penguins this side of Isabela.

THE SUMMIT

The trail to Bartolomé's summit begins as a dry landing at a set of stairs that sea lions often claim for their own. Farther along the trail, lava lizards dart back and forth, rarely stopping long enough to allow spectators to get a good look. The main part of the trail is a wooden staircase (over 370 stairs) built by the national park in order to limit the island's erosion. Although the climb can be somewhat tiring, the view from the top on a clear day enables climbers to grasp the immensity and uniqueness of the archipelago. North Seymour, Daphne Major and Minor, Santa Cruz, Sombrero Chino, Bainbridge Rocks, Baltra, Rábida, and Santiago can all be seen. A 180-degree turn while standing on this same peak will reveal why Bartolomé itself is often compared to the surface of the moon—unearthly craters coated with black ash surround the volcano. Nearby, the various colors of the **lava cactus's** banana-shaped stalks show the relative ages of the different parts of the plant—the oldest are gray, the younger green, and the youngest bright yellow. **Tiquilia** is another plant that has adapted to Bartolomé's severely arid climate. The green plant appears white because of the small hairs on the surface of the leaves which provide shade and hold water droplets for the leaves.

THE TWIN BEACHES

Double your pleasure with Bartolomé's twins, which lie on either side of the island. Many groups visit only the North Beach, where **swimming** is permitted. Powerful tides and currents, wandering sharks, and stingrays make the South Beach daunting for swimming but top-notch for nature-watching. Look for nesting sea turtles from late December to early March and great blue herons year-round.On the North Beach, the massive **Pinnacle Rock** (the one most often photographed) points majestically to the sky. This "rock" is made up of tightly packed sand shaped by the wind and sea. As with everything in the Galápagos, Pinnacle Rock is still changing; the Swiss-cheese holes caused by the wear-and-tear of the elements will eventually send the rock crumbling into the sea. Before this happens, take a moment while swimming to stop beneath the rock and stare at its immensity from below. Snorkeling is gorgeous at Bartolomé; brightly-colored tropical fish and the occasional white-tipped shark can be seen wandering among the submerged rock formations here. The oceanside base is also a popular place to try to spot the **Galápagos penguin,** an endemic bird markedly smaller than its Antarctic cousin. Though shy when it comes to nesting, the birds let people get close in water; snorkelers in the bay get quite a sight of these slippery sun worshipers swimming by.

THE WESTERN ISLANDS: ISLA RÁBIDA (JERVIS)

Though Isla Rábida, just south of Santiago, is certainly not conspicuous in size, its striking color, central location, and variety of wildlife keep it from being easily forgotten. After a wet landing, the northern beach glows a deep maroon color, and visitors usually encounter sea lions and marine iguanas resting on or close to shore. The salt bush area behind the beach is a nesting site for the brown pelican, one of the largest birds in the Galápagos. Behind this vegetation lies a small lagoon occasionally inhabited by **Galápagos flamingoes.** However, their population on the Galápagos is very small (approx. 700 birds total), so spotting these dainty creatures is a bit of a challenge. Rabida's lagoon, however, allows visitors to get closer to flamingoes than at those on many other islands; take the opportunity to watch the motor-like motion of the flamingoes' filtering action as they separate their bright pink yummies from sediment and water. While captive flamingoes are fed a mixture of shrimp and red dye to achieve their characteristic color, Galápagos flamingoes' tint is naturally maintained by their diet of bright pink shrimp larvae and pink marine insects. A visit to Rábida is not complete without a chance to check out the unique landscape from above. A short trail from the beach leads to a viewpoint overlooking the ocean, lagoon, and striking scarlet cliffs. This portion of the island is a great place to watch **blue-footed boobies**. Snorkeling off of Rábida's beach is also enjoyable: the water is clear, the fish are exceptional, and elusive sharks and manta rays are occasionally seen.

THE WESTERN ISLANDS: ISLA SOMBRERO CHINO

Isla Sombrero Chino, a tiny island off the southeastern coast of Santiago, is so named because of its uncanny resemblance to a Chinese hat. Though it is not visited as frequently as many of the other central islands and is not a daytrip destination, Sombrero Chino's proximity to various islands makes it possible for even those visitors who do not stop there to appreciate its unique landscape from a distance. Sombrero Chino's wet landing site is a beautiful, white beach where sea lions once again form the greeting party. Because of the fragility of the lava rock making up most of the island, the visitor's trail does not go to the summit of the volcanic core. The trail is thus short but heads up to a point where visitors can "ooh" and "aah" at the waves. Keep your eyes peeled for penguins here, especially while enjoying the snorkeling in the area between Sombrero Chino and Santiago. White-tipped reef sharks also frequent this area.

THE SOUTHERN ISLANDS

Española and Floreana, the southernmost islands in the archipelago, each have several visitor sites, providing full days of boat-tripping fun. Española is conveniently accessible by a daytrip from San Cristóbal, but Floreana usually appears on multiple-day tour boat itineraries. The Hotel Delfín in Puerto Ayora does have Saturday day trips to Floreana for US$100 (twice the cost of daytrips to other islands), but space on their ship is often limited to hotel guests. It's usually not difficult to find a tour that does both islands, and visitors tend to appreciate going down south for a couple of days.

HIGHLIGHTS OF THE SOUTHERN ISLANDS

■ **Isla Floreana** (see p. 501) wins first place for having the wackiest human history in the archipelago.
■ If the mainland's postal system looked bad, see how long it takes to send a letter home from **Post Office Bay** (see p. 502).
■ **Isla Española** sports one of few nesting sites for **waved albatrosses** (see p. 503).

THE SOUTHERN ISLANDS: ISLA FLOREANA (CHARLES)

Although Galápagos visitors today may distinguish the islands from one another mainly by their animals and landscapes, the various legends that have arisen since the discovery of the archipelago give many of them a unique personality beyond the number of boobie species nesting there. Floreana, the first inhabited island, does not allow its history to be easily forgotten. The remains of a Norwegian fish cannery at Post Office Bay and the well-known and sordid saga of the island's German colonists (see **Sex, Lies, and Dentures,** p. 502) loom over Floreana to this day.

PUERTO VELASCO IBARRA

The town of Puerto Velasco Ibarra (pop. 70) is sometimes visited by tourist ships, but if you want to spend the night (or eight nights) here, you'll have to take the INGALA-operated boat from Puerto Ayora which leaves port on Wednesdays at 7:30am sharp and returns to Puerto Ayora on Thursdays at 7am. Latecomers have to wait until the following week for the next boat. The small **Pensión Wittmer** (tel. 520 150, in Guayaquil (04) 294 506) is the only place to stay on Floreana. Rooms with private baths, hot water, and an ocean view are priced far below their more popular competitors on other islands. Breakfast (s/15,000), lunch, and dinner (s/20,000) are also served. Four Wittmer generations, one of the original German families to inhabit Floreana, may be found under this friendly hotel's roof. Pensión Wittmer also sells autographed copies of original inhabitant Margret's book, *Floreana*, and stamps letters for the post office barrel. (Rooms s/40,000.)

Just outside of Puerto Velasco Ibarra is the **Asilo de Paz,** the site of the island's original settlement town. A number of mysterious, hand-carved "caves" were hewn out of this mountainside by the German settlers when they arrived, but exactly what they intended them for is uncertain. Perhaps they were primitive dwellings meant to heighten the idealistic colonists' communion with Nature. Or, perhaps they might just be the product of the settlers having too much time and a whole lot of mountain on their hands.

POST OFFICE BAY

In 1793, a British whaling captain erected a post office barrel on the quiet bay of an uninhabited island. The island was later named Floreana; for a long time its barrel was the only postal facility for hundreds of miles. Whaling ships from around the world left their letters in the barrel and picked up those that they could deliver in their travels. Although the first post-barrel is now long gone, the tradition is kept up by the island's many visitors each year. Visitors get to the bay via a wet landing at a brown beach on Floreana's northern shore. Today's barrel is quite different from the original one: no longer content to leave letters, numerous visitors have added signs, pictures, and other wooden messages to this growing piece of public art. Drop off a postcard, letter or hastily written note and see if any are addressed to an area near you. When you get home, deliver them personally if you can.

PUNTA CORMORANT

Though Floreana's history is somewhat notorious, Punta Cormorant takes on more conventional hues: glistening green stones, red mangroves, gray hillsides, pink flamingoes, white sand, and blue water. Visitors arrive here via a wet landing at the northern end of the island, on a beach littered with thousands of small, green beads. This unique crystal, known as olivine, was formed centuries ago as a volcanic by-product.The olivine gives the sand a greenish tinge; scoop up a handful and you'll easily see the smooth, green crystals. Because of its volcanic origin, the beach is classified as inorganic. A short walk inland leads to one of the largest **flamingo** lagoons in the Galápagos. Because of the minimal flamingo population in the Galápagos overall, large flocks cannot be seen here, but the shrimp larvae that are the primary attraction for the few birds present tint the muddy lagoon with their pinkish color. The rare *Leococarpus Pimatificles*, or **Cutleaf Daisy,** can be seen here as well. This unusual flower grows nowhere else in the world, so take a moment to appreciate this unassuming wonder.

Another site at Punta Cormorant, **Flour Beach** gets its name from its strikingly soft white sand, which is made of ground-up coral, making this an organic beach. Shadowy gray **ghost crabs,** bright red **sally lightfoot crabs,** and green **sea turtles** fre-

SEX, LIES, AND DENTURES On September 19, 1929, a ship arrived on Isla Floreana with two people and a whole lot of boxes: the island hasn't been the same since. **Friedrich Ritter,** a German doctor and devoted follower of Nietzsche, retreated from society with **Dora Strauch,** his patient and lover. Their goal? To create an untainted community of two, dedicated to the healing powers of the mind. Before coming to the island, Ritter insisted that both he and Dora have all their teeth removed and **stainless steel dentures** made; one pair was soon lost, so the couple had to share. Over the next five years, more and more Germans moved to the isolated isle. The temperamental **Baroness von Wagner de Bosquet** blew into Floreana like a hurricane, dressed in riding pants and tall leather boots, with a revolver in one hand and a **whip** in the other (presumably to keep her lovers in line). Of course, she could have used it to crack the tension in the air when she proclaimed herself **"Empress of Floreana,"** a declaration that enraged Ritter and his dreams of intellectual isolation. But in 1934, the Baroness suddenly disappeared with one of her lovers, and the body of another was found on the beach of Isla Marchena, mummified by the sun. Soon after, Dr. Ritter, a vegetarian, mysteriously died from poisoned chicken. Onlookers say he cursed Dora with his dying breath; she moved back to Germany and lived only long enough to write the book *Satan Came to Eden* before falling victim to that curse. Today, one of the less eccentric of Floreana's original residents, **Margret Wittmer,** still lives on the island. Nobody ever proved any foul play, but ask Margret if she ever picked up on any fishy smells during the whole sordid mess.

quent this beach. The latter come at night to lay eggs, but only one out of 100 newborns survives, as frigatebirds and other predators anxiously await the turtles' birth. Finally, keep an eye on the shallow waters of Flour Beach's quiet cove; large numbers of stingrays come here to feed. Because of the sometimes-dangerous rays, Flour Beach is not a swimming or snorkeling spot, but Floreana's Devil's Crown fulfills these needs and more.

DEVIL'S CROWN

At one time, this underwater formation, just off the coast of Punta Cormorant, was a submerged volcano. Subsequent eruptions and the powerful ocean have eroded the cone into a jagged ring of black lava spires rising from the sea floor. Yield to the temptations to descend into this dark world of devilishly good underwater delights. Thanks to currents that bring in tons of fish, Devil's Crown offers some of the best snorkeling in the islands. But these same currents can be dangerous; snorkelers should be cautious. **Sharks** are perhaps the biggest attraction of the Corona del Diablo. The probability of seeing the elegant creatures is relatively high—both white-tipped reef sharks and hammerheads frequent the area. While hammerheads have been known to attack humans elsewhere in the world, the abundance of food in the Galápagos makes the sharks in these parts uninterested in, and even wary of, curious snorkelers. For the best odds of seeing a shark, remain calm, quiet, and close to your guide, keeping an eye on deeper waters where groups of sharks sometimes cruise past. While the chance of seeing something big gets the adrenaline flowing, visitors realize that the often-ignored world of the small is equally amazing as soon as they see schools of beautiful fish rushing past.

THE SOUTHERN ISLANDS: ISLA ESPAÑOLA (HOOD)

The southernmost island in the archipelago, Española's distance from the rest of the chain may well be its greatest asset. Its remote location has largely prevented genetic flow between Española and other islands. Thus, many of its animals are found nowhere else in the archipelago (or the world). Española's most unique fauna are its birds; the waved albatross itself makes many tourists glad to have made the trip. Don't let Española's distance deter you; a visit to this remote island is the highlight of many an island tour.

PUNTA SUÁREZ

Boats reach Española via a dry landing on Punta Suárez, an area covering the island's western tip. A large colony of **sea lions** loll about on the sandy beaches here, sometimes playfully posing for pictures, sometimes barking at pesky humans who disturb their peace and quiet. **Marine iguanas** are often found warming themselves on the black rocks that separate the sections of beach. Those endemic to Española are the only species that change color during breeding season. Though young iguanas are all black, adults have a reddish tinge and take on an additional greenish hue during the breeding season.

The endemic **española** or **hood mockingbird** boldly greets Española's visitors in a display of inter-species camaraderie and friendship, or so it seems. This welcome wagon is actually more interested in those crystal-clear, gleaming bottles of universal solvent attached to your knapsack. Española has no natural source of drinkable water, so the mockingbirds do everything they can to quench their thirst, including trying to steal a sip from the human camels that visit their territory. Slightly larger than its relatives on other islands, the Española subspecies also has a longer, curved beak and is the only carnivorous mockingbird species; they feed on sea lion placentas, sea turtle hatchlings, and insects. They've even been known to peck at and drink the water-rich blood of baby boobies.

A TIDIER TORTUGA TALE The giant tortoises of Isla Española came dangerously close to the same sad end as Pinta's Lonesome George (see p. 480). However, some luck and raging tortoise hormones have brought about a much happier ending to this story than to that of George and his poor Pinta pals. Feral goats had been doing their usual damage to the tortoise population on Española. Over two decades ago, only two male and twelve female tortoises were found on Española, and these were taken to the Darwin Station in Puerto Ayora. None of the tortoises, however, were reproducing. Just when scientists were beginning to fear extinction, an Española male was miraculously identified in the San Diego Zoo. This Californian had a mysterious—and fortunate—effect on the rest of the pack, since shortly after his arrival many of the tortoises began to reproduce. Now that the Española goats have been eradicated, some of the tortoises have been returned to their island, leading to more happy news: Española has become the first island on which repatriated tortoises have begun to reproduce in the wild, perhaps boding well for future programs to reverse the damaging effects of introduced animals.

Continuing along the recently-renovated pathway, visitors can see more of the unique bird species which distinguish Española. **Blue-footed boobies** (grayish, duck-shaped birds) caress the rocks with their sensuous blue feet, honking and whistling. These birds nest on the ground and normally raise two eggs annually, for which the male and female share the incubation responsibilities. Males and females look quite similar but are still distinguishable. Female boobies have larger eyes and voice their opinions by honking, while beady-eyed males answer with an unmistakable whistle. Sex distinction becomes crucially important when watching the boobies' mating dance, which not surprisingly focuses on those unforgettably sexy feet. The **swallow-tailed gull** also can be seen along this path; the charcoal-and-crimson beauty is one of five seabirds species endemic only to the Galápagos.

The most famous wildlife spot on the island, however, is the nesting area of the **waved albatross,** another endemic seabird whose habitat can be found nowhere else in the world. Albatrosses breed here between mid-April and mid-December. This striking bird combines elements of grace and ungainliness in a way only the albatross can. The topography of Isla Española contributes directly to the fact that the birds nest here. Española's steep cliffs serve as convenient runways for albatrosses to start their legs moving, pick up speed, spread out their wingspan (up to 2.5m), and finally glide gracefully through the air. Accustomed to life in the air and at sea, the albatross lands a less elegantly and more comically. Watch them glide to the cliff's edge, put their feet down, and stumble to a halt. Albatrosses mate for life but only spend time with their mate during the breeding season. Thus, in order to identify their mates each April, albatrosses re-perform their specific **mating dance,** a spectacle which can last five days and involves strutting, stumbling, honking, and a good deal of beak-fencing. They say it's better than dating.

One of the trails from Punta Suárez provides a prime view of the island's famous **blowhole.** A seaside cliff on the south end of the trail provides the perfect vantage point to watch wave-powered spray soar over 25m into the air, as incoming waves are forced out of a narrow volcanic fissure in the rock. The rainbow-colored mist produced by this spectacular geyser sends tourists' cameras crazily clicking.

GARDNER BAY

While Punta Suárez's animal attractions are Española's biggest draw for tourists, tour boats often visit Gardner Bay, located on the northwestern side of the island. Although white sand, white sand, and more white sand is the majority of what you'll find here, the beach is far from humdrum. Waves crash and sea lions dance themselves into a frenzy in desperate competition for an audience. Divided into two sections by an outcropping of lava rock, the long, open shoreline is one of the few places in the Galápagos that is completely safe to explore without a guide. Visitors planning to walk the entire length of the beach should bring sturdy shoes. Snorkeling is possible in Gardner Bay but is usually more rewarding nearby at the aptly named **Tortuga Islet,** which gets its name from being shaped a lot like everyone's favorite Galápagos creature. Look for sea turtles, stingrays, and colorful parrotfish while you're under water.

THE NORTHERN ISLANDS

The distant northern islands are rarely visited by one-week touring boats, because the sail here from the central islands takes at least six hours and the seas are usually rough. **Isla Genovesa** (often known as **Tower Island**) is the only one of these islands visitors can set foot on; **Pinta** and **Marchena,** as well as **Darwin** and **Wolf** to the far northwest, are visited only by diving tours. However, a visit to Isla Genovesa is definitely worth the trip.

THE NORTHERN ISLANDS: ISLA GENOVESA

Genovesa has two major tourist sights, both accessible via **Darwin Bay** on the east end of the island. This gigantic bay, which often gives visitors the impression that they are completely surrounded by land, is a partially submerged **caldera,** or collapsed volcanic crater. Most boats choose to enter and leave the bay in daylight, as only a small segment of the opening is deep enough to allow boats to pass. In order to assist boats in this complicated maneuver, two solar panels and lights have been installed across the bay from the opening. Boats can only enter the bay at an angle that makes these two panels line up perfectly.

DARWIN BEACH

Most of Darwin Bay is lined with 20- to 30m-high cliffs, making the small, white-coral-covered **Darwin Beach** stand out prominently near the middle of the bay. After a wet landing here, many visitors are amazed by the sheer number of birds that glide over the shore and rest on the rocks and vegetation on the beach. Although the birds on Genovesa are rarely frightened by people, it is still important to remain at least 2km away from them, so as not to interfere with them or their nests. Isla Genovesa's remote location has prevented it from being a home to land iguanas, lizards, or snakes, transforming it into a bird-lover's paradise. **Masked boobies** whistle, and **great frigatebirds** display their gigantic red pouches near the landing site, while **mockingbirds** dart along the sand. Boobies and frigates here have a less-than-peaceful relationship. Since they compete for nesting space, boobies destroy frigates' nests, while frigates steal boobies' eggs. After leaving the landing site and passing a tidal pool, the trail enters a wooded area of salt-bushes and mangroves, which is home to a **red-footed booby** colony. Bird-watching fun just goes on and on; Darwin Beach is the place to see **sharp-beaked finches, large ground finches,** and **large cactus finches,** as well as **Galápagos doves** and **swallow-tailed gulls.**

PRINCE PHILLIP'S STEPS

Genovesa's other visitor site, **Prince Phillip's Steps,** is also an excellent bird watching area. This dry landing leads to a steep set of natural stairs which are the only access (besides winging it) to the high cliffs that surround Darwin Bay. The rocky trail winds its way through several colonies of nesting sea birds to a wooded area of lush green **lava morning glories,** stark **palo santo** trees, and the occasional green and yellow **lava cactus.** Among the vegetation on the interior of the island, red-footed boobies, nests, and some species of **Darwin finches** can be seen as well. Eventually, the trail leads to a flat, rocky area formed by lava flows. Here, the air is filled with small black-and-white **storm petrels,** which nest in cracks in the hardened lava. Look for the elusive **short-eared owl,** which, in the absence of hawks, feeds diurnally. These birds, however, are well-camouflaged and difficult to find.

Genovesa is also a popular destination for **scuba** divers. As is the case in much of the Galápagos, the current here is quite strong; only highly experienced divers should explore the depths. A memorial to two missing divers who never surfaced from a dive off Genovesa reminds visitors to the island of the humbling power of Nature and the respect which explorers must always take care to accord her.

APPENDIX

HOLIDAYS AND FESTIVALS

Consult the **South American Explorers Club** (p. 18) or the tourist offices in each city for the dates of art exhibitions, theater and music festivals, and sporting events. Throughout Ecuador, CETUR can provide specific information. Where possible, *Let's Go* lists specific 2000 dates in individual cities. Be aware of them, as hotels fill up quickly and banks, restaurants, stores, and museums may all close, potentially leaving you homeless, broke, and hungry. Regional holidays listed below are only a small sample of the many fiestas that take place in different parts of Perú and Ecuador almost every week.

NATIONAL HOLIDAYS

DATE	FESTIVAL	ENGLISH
January 1-6	El Año Nuevo	New Year's Day, with festivals throughout the week
January 6	Festividades de los Reyes Magos	Festival of the Three Kings (Epiphany)
February 12	Aniversario del Descubrimiento de los Ríos Amazonas	Discovery of the Amazon River
February 27	Recordación de la Batalla de Tarqui, Día del Civismo y la Unidad Nacional	Commemoration of the Battle of Tarqui, National Unity Day (Ecuador)
March 6-7	Carnaval	Carnival
April 17-23	Semana Santa	Holy Week
April 20	Jueves Santo	Holy Thursday
April 21	Viernes Santo	Good Friday
April 23	El Día de Pasqua	Easter
May 1	Día de Trabajador	Labor Day
May 24	Fiesta Cívica Nacional	Battle of Pichincha (Independence Day, Ecuador)
June 11-13	Corpus Christi	Corpus Christi
July 24	Nacimiento de Simón Bolívar	Birth of Simón Bolívar
July 28-29	Fiestas Patrias	National Holidays (Independence Day, Perú)
August 10	Aniversario de la Independencia de Quito	Independence of Quito (Ecuador)
August 30	Fiesta de Santa Rosa de Lima	Celebration of Santa Rosa, patron saint of Lima (Perú)
October 8	Fiesta de Angamos	Battle of Angamos (Perú)
October 9	Aniversario de la Independencia de Guayaquil	Independence of Guayaquil (Ecuador)
October 12	Aniversario del Descubrimiento de las Americas	Discovery of America
November 1	Día de los Santos	All Saints Day
November 2	Día de los Difuntos	All Soul's Day
November 3	Aniversario de la Independencia de Cuenca	Independence of Cuenca (Ecuador)
December 6	Aniversario de la Fundación Española San Francisco de Quito	Foundation of San Francisco de Quito (Ecuador)
December 8	Concepción Inmaculada	Immaculate Conception (Perú)
December 25	La Navidad	Christmas Day
December 28	Los Santos Inocentes	All Fool's Day
December 31	Incineración del Año Viejo	New Year's Eve

REGIONAL HOLIDAYS

DATE	FESTIVAL	ENGLISH
January 18	Aniversario de la Fundación de Lima	Anniversary of the Foundation of Lima
February 2	Fiesta de la Virgen de la Candelaria	Festival of the Virgin of the Candelaria (Puno)
last week in Feb.	Verano Negro	Black Summer (Chincha)
May 4-10	Fiesta del Durazno	Peach Festival (Gualaceo)
April 19-21	Feria Agrícola, Ganadera, Artesanal, e Industrial.	Farming, Cattle, Handicraft, and Industrial Fair (Riobamba)
May 2-3	Fiesta de la Cruz	Festival of the Cross
May 11-14	Feria Agrícola e Industrial de la Amazonía	Agricultural and Industrial Festival of the Amazon
June 24	Fiesta de San Juan/Inti Raymi Fiesta del Maiz y del Turismo Gallo Compadre, Vacas Loca, Castillo, y Chamiza	Saint John the Baptist's Day/Festival of the Sun (Cuzco) Corn and Tourism Festivals (Sangoloqui) Rodeo Day (Calpi)
June 29	Festividad de San Pedro y San Pablo	Saint Peter's and Saint Paul's Day
July 16	Celebración de la Virgen del Carmen	Celebration of the Virgin of Carmen
July 24	Fiesta del Chagra	Festival of the Chagra (Machachi)
July 23-25	Aniversario de Fundación de la Cuidad de Guayaquil	Anniversary of the Foundation of Guayaquil
August 3-5	Independencia de la Cuidad de Esmeraldas	Esmeraldas's Independence Day
August 5-7	Fiesta de la Virgen de las Nieves	Festival of the Virgin of the Snow (Sicalpa)
August 10	Festividades de San Lorenzo Fiesta de San Jacinto	San Lorenzo Festivities (Pillaro) San Jacinto Festivities (Yaguachi)
August 12-20	Aniversario de la Fundación de Arequipa	Anniversay of the Foundation of Arequipa
August 19-25	Fiesta de San Luís Obispo	Festival of San Luís Obispo
September 2-15	Fiesta de Yamor Festividades de la Virgen del Cisne	Festival of Yamor (Otavalo) Festivities for the Virgin of El Cisne (Loja)
September 20-26	Feria Mundial del Banano Festividades de la Virgen de las Mercedes	Banana's World Fair (Machala) Festivities of the Virgen of Mercy (Latacunga)

TELEPHONE CODES

To call Ecuador or Perú from abroad, dial your country's international code, the country code, the regional code, and the telephone number. Drop the zero from the regional code when calling from abroad.

TELEPHONE CODES	
Ambato	03
Arequipa	054
Cajamarca	044
Cuzco	084
Esmeraldas	06
Galápagos	05
Guayaquil	04
Ibarra	06
Latacunga	03
Lima	01
Loja	07
Macas	07

TELEPHONE CODES	
Machala	07
Manta	05
Otavalo	06
Piura	074
Portoviejo	05
Puyo	03
Quito	02
Riobamba	03
Tena	06
Trujillo	044
Tulcán	06
Tumbes	074

COUNTRY CODES	
Ecuador	593
Perú	51

LANGUAGE

Even if you speak no Spanish, a few basics will help you along. Any attempts at Spanish are appreciated and encouraged, and you'll find that many people in the tourism industry and in larger cities understand some English. Learn the vocabulary of courtesy as well; you'll be treated more kindly if you are polite to those around you (see **Customs and Manners**, p. 49). Those who know Castillian Spanish will notice some idiomatic differences in Ecuadorian and Peruvian Spanish. You are likely to hear *indígena* languages such as Quechua and Aymara as well.

Pronunciation is very regular. Vowels are always pronounced the same way: *a* ("ah" in father); *e* ("eh" in escapade); *i* ("ee" in eat); *o* ("oh" in oat); *u* ("oo" in boot); *y*, by itself, is pronounced like i. Most consonants are the same as English. Important exceptions are: *j* ("h" in "hello"); *ll* ("y" in "yes"); *ñ* ("gn" in "cognac"); *rr* (trilled "r"); *h* is always silent; *x* has a bewildering variety of pronunciations.

Let's Go provides phonetic approximations for particularly tough town names. Stress in Spanish words falls on the second to last syllable, except for words ending in "r," "l," and "z," in which it falls on the last syllable. All exceptions to these rules require a written accent on the stressed syllable.

SPANISH GLOSSARY

aduana: customs
agencia de viaje: travel agency
aguardiente: strong liquor
aguas termales: hot springs
ahora: now
aire acondicionado: air-conditioned (A/C)
ají: red Peruvian chili used in criollo cooking
ajo: garlic
a la plancha: grilled
albergue (juvenil): (youth) hostel
al gusto: as you wish
almacen: (grocery) store
almuerzo: lunch, midday meal
alpaca: a shaggy-haired, long-necked animal in the cameloid family
amigo/a: friend
arroz: rice
arroz chaufa: Chinese-style fried rice
artesanía: arts and crafts
avenida: avenue
ayllu: a kinship-based Inca clan
bahía: bay
baño: bathroom or natural spa
barato/a: cheap
barro: mud
barrio: neighborhood
batido: n: a shake (fruit and milk); adj.: whipped or beaten
biblioteca: library
bistec/bistek: beefsteak
bocaditos: appetizers, at a bar
bodega: convenience store or winery
boletería: ticket counter
bonito/a: pretty/beautiful
borracho/a: drunk
botica: drugstore
bueno/a: good
caballero: gentleman
caballo: horse
cabañas: cabins
cabildos abiertos: colonial era town councils
cajeros: cashiers
caldera: coffee or tea pot
caldo: soup, broth, or stew
caldo de balgre: catfish soup
caldo de pata: hoof soup
calle: street
cama: bed
camarones: shrimp
cambio: change
camino: path or track
camioneta: small, pickup-sized truck
campamento: campground
campesino/a: person from a rural area, peasant
campo: countryside
caneliza: a drink made from boiling water, aguardiente, cinnamon and lemon juice
canta de monte: Andean tapir
cantina: drinking establishment, usually male dominated
carne asada: roast meat
caro/a: expensive
carretera: highway

carro: car, or sometimes a train car
casa: house
casa de cambio: currency exchange establishment
casado/a: married
cascadas: waterfalls
caseríos: hamlet/small village, often unregulated by govt.
casona: mansion
cena: dinner, a light meal usually served after 8pm.
centro: city center
cerca: near/nearby
cerro: hill
cerveza: beer
ceviche/cebiche: raw fish marinated in lemon juice, herbs, veggies
chica/o: girl/boy
chicha: a liquor from the Oriente made from fermented yucca or maize plant and human saliva
chicharrón: bite-sized pieces of fried meat, usually pork
chifa: Chinese restaurant
chuleta de chancho: pork chop
chompa: sweater
churrasco: steak
churriguerresco: rococo (in the style of the 18th century Spanish architect Churriguerra)
ciudad: city
ciudadela: neighborhood in a large city
coche: car
colectivo: small municipal transit bus or shared taxi
coliseo: coliseum/stadium
colonia: neighborhood in a large city
colpa: macaw lick
combi: small bus
comedor: small restaurant (Ecu.); dining room (Perú)
comida criolla: regional, Spanish-influenced dishes
comida típica: typical/traditional dishes
con: with
consulado: consulate
correo: post office
cordillera: mountain range
corvina: sea bass
criollos: people of European descent born in the New World
cruz roja: Red Cross
cuadra: street block
cuarto: a room
cuenta: bill/check
cuento: story/account
curandero: healer
cuy: guinea pig
desayuno: breakfast
descompuesto: broken, out of order; or spoiled/rotten food
despacio: slow
de turno: a 24hr. rotating schedule for pharmacies
discoteca: dance club
embajada: embassy
emergencia: emergency
encebollado: stew flavored with onions
encocados: seafood cooked in coconut milk
encomiendas: estates granted to Spanish settlers in Latin America
estrella: star
extranjero: foreign/foreigner
farmacia: pharmacy
ferrocarril: railroad
fiesta: party, holiday
finca: a plantation-like agricultural enterprise or a ranch
frontera: border
fumar: to smoke
fumaroles: hole in a volcanic region which emits hot vapors
fútbol: soccer
ganga: bargain
gordo/a: fat
gorra: cap
guatita: grilled stomach
guineo: banana
habitación: a room
hacienda: ranch
hervido/a: boiled
iglesia: church
impuestos: taxes
indígena: indigenous, refers to the native population
jirón: street
jugo: juice
kilo: kilogram
kuraka: the chieftan of an Inca clan (see p. 37)
ladrón: thief
lago/ laguna: lake

lancha: launch, small boat
langostino: jumbo shrimp
larga distancia: long distance
lavandería: laundromat
lejos: far
lente(mente): slow(ly)
lista de correos: the general delivery system in most of Ecuador and Perú
llapingachos: potato and cheese pancakes
loma: hill
lomo: sirloin steak
mal: bad
malecón: pier or seaside thoroughfare
máneje despacio: drive slowly
mar: sea
mariscos: seafood
menestras: lentils/beans
menú del día: fixed daily meal often offered for a bargain price
mercado: market
merienda: late afternoon snack/early dinner
mestizo/a: a person of mixed European and indigenous descent
mirador: an observatory or look-out point
mita: a system of forced labor imposed upon indigenous communities by the colonial Spaniards
mordida: literally "little bite," bribe
moto/mototaxi: small, 3 wheeled taxis adapted from motorcycles
muelle: wharf
muerte: death
museo: museum
nada: nothing
obra: work of art/play
obraje: primitive textile workshops
oficina de turismo: office of tourism
paiche: jungle fish
palta: avocado (Perú)
pan: bread
panadería: bakery
panga: motorboat
parada: a stop (on a bus or train)
parilla: various cuts of meat, grilled
paro: strike
parque: park
parroquia: parish
paseo turístico: tour covering a series of sites
payaso: clown
peligroso/a: dangerous
peninsulares: Spanish-born colonists
peña: folkloric music club
pescado: fish (prepared)
picante: spicy
pisco: a traditional Peruvian liquor made from grapes
pisco sour: a drink made from pisco, lemon juice, sugarcane syrup, and egg white
plátano: plantain
playa: beach
policía: police
pollo a la brasa: roasted chicken
pueblito: small town
puerta: door
puerto: port
rana: frog
reloj: watch, clock
ropa: clothes
sala: living room
salchipapa: french fries with fried pieces of sausage
salida: exit
salsa: sauce (can be of many varieties)
salsa/merengue: Latin dances
seco de cordero: pieces of lamb in a flavorful sauce
seco de gallina: pieces of chicken in a flavorful sauce
seguro/a: n.: lock, insurance; adj.: safe
selva: jungle
semana: week
Semana Santa: Holy Week
shaman/chaman: spiritual healer
SIDA: the Spanish acronym for AIDS
sillar: white, volcanic rock used in construction
sol: sun/Peruvian currency
solo carril: one-lane road or bridge
soltero/a: single (unmarried)
sucre: Ecuadorian currency
supermercado: supermarket
tarifa: fee
terminal terrestre: bus station
tienda: store
tipo de cambio: exchange rate
trole: trolley (Quito)
trucha: trout
vicuña: a usually-wild animal in the cameloid family

SPANISH PHRASEBOOK

BASICS

ENGLISH	SPANISH	ENGLISH	SPANISH
Hello	Hola	**Goodbye**	Adiós/Hasta luego/ Chao
Good Morning/Afternoon	Buenos días/Buenas tardes	**Good Evening/Night**	Buenas noches
Yes/No	Sí/No	**How are you?** (formal)	¿Cómo está Usted?
I don't know	No sé	**How are you?** (informal)	¿Qué tal?
Sorry/Forgive me	Lo siento	**Cool!/Awesome!**	¡Chévere!
Please	Por favor	**Thank you**	Gracias
Excuse me	Con permiso/discúlpeme	**You're welcome**	De nada, a la orden
Who?	¿Quién?	**What?**	¿Qué?
When?	¿Cuándo?	**Where?**	¿Dónde?
Why?	¿Por qué?	**Because**	Porque

PHRASES

ENGLISH	SPANISH	ENGLISH	SPANISH
My name is...	Yo me llamo....	**I am from...**	Soy de....
What is your name?	¿Cómo se llama?	**It's a pleasure to meet you**	Mucho gusto concocerle
What's up?	¿Qué pasa?/¿Como está la vaina?	**Pardon/me**	Perdón/perdóneme
How much does this cost?	¿Cuánto cuesta?	**Let's Go**	¡Vámonos!
Go away/Leave me alone	¡Déjame en paz!	**Stop/enough**	Basta
Could you tell me?	¿Podría decirme?	**Is (Lara) available?**	¿Está (Lara)?
I don't understand	No entiendo	**Could you please repeat that?**	Otra vez, por favor/ ¿Podría repetirlo?
Please speak slowly	¿Podría hablar más despacio, por favor?	**How do you say...?**	¿Cómo se dice...?
Could you help me?	¿Podría ayudarme?	**Help!/Help me!**	¡Socorro!/¡Ayúdame!
I am hot/cold	Tengo calor/frío	**It's hot/cold out**	Hace calor/frío
How old are you?	¿Cuántos años tienes?	**Where do you live?**	¿Dónde vives?
Are there rooms?	¿Hay habitaciones?	**Are there student discounts?**	¿Hay descuentos para estudiantes?
I love you	Te amo/Te quiero	**No poking**	No empujar
I want/would like...	Quisiera/Me gustaría...	**I like chocolate**	Me gusta chocolate
I have...	Tengo...	**I'm looking for...**	Busco...

DIRECTIONS

ENGLISH	SPANISH	ENGLISH	SPANISH
(to the) right	a la derecha	**(to the) left**	a la izquierda
next to	al lado de	**across from**	en frente de
straight ahead	todo derecho	**to turn**	doblar

ENGLISH	SPANISH	ENGLISH	SPANISH
near	cerca	**far**	lejos
above	arriba	**below**	abajo
traffic light	semáforo	**corner**	esquina
street	calle/avenida/jirón	**block**	cuadra
How do I get to...?	¿Cómo voy a...?	**How far is...?**	¿Qué tan lejos está?
Where is...street?	¿Dónde está la calle...?	**What bus line goes to...?**	¿Qué línea de buses tiene servicio a...?
When does the bus leave?	¿Cuándo sale el autobús?	**Where does the bus leave from?**	¿De dónde sale el autobús?
I'm getting off at...	Bajo en...	**I have to go now**	Tengo que ir ahora
Where is the bathroom?	¿Dónde está el baño?	**I'm lost**	Estoy perdido(a)

NUMBERS

ENGLISH	SPANISH	ENGLISH	SPANISH
one	uno	**twelve**	doce
two	dos	**fifteen**	quince
three	tres	**twenty**	veinte
four	cuatro	**twenty-five**	veinticinco
five	cinco	**thirty**	treinta
six	seis	**forty**	cuarenta
seven	siete	**fifty**	cincuenta
eight	ocho	**one hundred**	cien/ciento
nine	nueve	**five hundred**	quinientos
ten	diez	**one thousand**	un mil
eleven	once	**one million**	un millón

FOOD

ENGLISH	SPANISH	ENGLISH	SPANISH
breakfast	desayuno	**lunch**	almuerzo
dinner	cena/merienda	**dessert**	postre
drink	bebida	**water (purified)**	agua (purificada)
bread	pan	**rice**	arroz
vegetables	legumbres/vegetales	**chicken**	pollo
meat	carne	**milk**	leche
eggs	huevos	**coffee**	café
juice	jugo	**tea**	té
wine	vino	**beer**	cerveza
ice cream	helado	**fruit**	fruta
cheese	queso	**vegetarian**	vegetariano(a)
soup	sopa/caldo	**cup**	una copa/taza
fork	tenedor	**knife**	cuchillo
spoon	cuchara	**Bon Apetit**	Buen provecho
napkin	servilleta	**the check, please**	la cuenta, por favor

TIMES AND HOURS

ENGLISH	SPANISH	ENGLISH	SPANISH
morning	la mañana	**afternoon**	tarde
evening	tarde, noche	**night**	noche
today	hoy	**yesterday**	ayer
tomorrow	mañana	**week**	semana
month	mes	**year**	año
midday	mediodía	**midnight**	medianoche
early	temprano(a)	**late**	tarde
open	abierto(a)	**closed**	cerrado(a)
What time is it?	¿Qué hora es?	**When is it open?**	¿Cuando está abierto?

OTHER HELPFUL WORDS

ENGLISH	SPANISH	ENGLISH	SPANISH
embassy	embajada	**consulate**	consulado
post office	correo	**hospital**	el hospital
alone	solo(a)	**friend**	amigo(a)
good	bueno(a)	**bad**	malo(a)
happy	feliz, contento(a)	**sad**	triste
hot	caliente	**cold**	frío

INDEX

A

B

C

INDEX

D

E

N

O

P

Q

R

S

T

U

V

W

Y

Z

INDEX

ABOUT LET'S GO

FORTY YEARS OF WISDOM

As a new millennium arrives, *Let's Go: Europe*, now in its 40th edition and translated into seven languages, reigns as the world's bestselling international travel guide. For four decades, travelers criss-crossing the Continent have relied on *Let's Go* for inside information on the hippest backstreet cafes, the most pristine secluded beaches, and the best routes from border to border. In the last 20 years, our rugged researchers have stretched the frontiers of backpacking and expanded our coverage into Asia, Africa, Australia, and the Americas. We're celebrating our 40th birthday with the release of *Let's Go: China*, blazing the traveler's trail from the Forbidden City to the Tibetan frontier; *Let's Go: Perú & Ecuador*, spanning the lands of the ancient Inca Empire; *Let's Go: Middle East*, with coverage from Istanbul to the Persian Gulf; and the maiden edition of *Let's Go: Israel*.

It all started in 1960 when a handful of well-traveled students at Harvard University handed out a 20-page mimeographed pamphlet offering a collection of their tips on budget travel to passengers on student charter flights to Europe. The following year, in response to the instant popularity of the first volume, students traveling to Europe researched the first full-fledged edition of *Let's Go: Europe*, a pocket-sized book featuring honest, practical advice, witty writing, and a decidedly youthful slant on the world. Throughout the 60s and 70s, our guides reflected the times. In 1969 we taught travelers how to get from Paris to Prague on "no dollars a day" by singing in the street. In the 80s and 90s, we looked beyond Europe and North America and set off to all corners of the earth. Meanwhile, we focused in on the world's most exciting urban areas to produce in-depth, fold-out map guides. Our new guides bring the total number of titles to 48, each infused with the spirit of adventure and voice of opinion that travelers around the world have come to count on. But some things never change: our guides are still researched, written, and produced entirely by students who know first-hand how to see the world on the cheap.

HOW WE DO IT

Each guide is completely revised and thoroughly updated every year by a well-traveled set of over 250 students. Every spring, we recruit over 180 researchers and 70 editors to overhaul every book. After several months of training, researcher-writers hit the road for seven weeks of exploration, from Anchorage to Adelaide, Estonia to El Salvador, Iceland to Indonesia. Hired for their rare combination of budget travel sense, writing ability, stamina, and courage, these adventurous travelers know that train strikes, stolen luggage, food poisoning, and marriage proposals are all part of a day's work. Back at our offices, editors work from spring to fall, massaging copy written on Himalayan bus rides into witty, informative prose. A student staff of typesetters, cartographers, publicists, and managers keeps our lively team together. In September, the collected efforts of the summer are delivered to our printer, which turns them into books in record time, so that you have the most up-to-date information available for your vacation. Even as you read this, work on next year's editions is well underway.

WHY WE DO IT

We don't think of budget travel as the last recourse of the destitute; we believe that it's the only way to travel. Living cheaply and simply brings you closer to the people and places you've been saving up to visit. Our books will ease your anxieties and answer your questions about the basics—so you can get off the beaten track and explore. Once you learn the ropes, we encourage you to put *Let's Go* down now and then to strike out on your own. You know as well as we that the best discoveries are often those you make yourself. When you find something worth sharing, please drop us a line. We're Let's Go Publications, 67 Mount Auburn St., Cambridge, MA 02138, USA (email: feedback@letsgo.com). For more info, visit our website, http://www.letsgo.com.

READER QUESTIONNAIRE

Name: ____________________
Address: ____________________
City: ____________ **State:** _____ **Country:** ____________
ZIP/Postal Code:__________ **E-mail:** ______________ **How old are you?**____
And you're...? in high school in college in graduate school
employed retired between jobs
Which book(s) have you used? ____________________
Where have you gone with Let's Go? ____________________
Have you traveled extensively before? yes no
Had you used Let's Go before? yes no **Would you use it again?** yes no
How did you hear about Let's Go? friend store clerk television
review bookstore display
ad/promotion internet other: __________
Why did you choose Let's Go? reputation budget focus annual updating
wit & incision price other: __________
Which guides have you used? Fodor's Footprint Handbooks Frommer's $-a-day
Lonely Planet Moon Guides Rick Steve's
Rough Guides UpClose other: __________
Which guide do you prefer? Why? ____________________
Please rank the following in your Let's Go guide: (1=needs improvement, 5=perfect)

packaging/cover	1 2 3 4 5	food	1 2 3 4 5	maps	1 2 3 4 5
cultural introduction	1 2 3 4 5	sights	1 2 3 4 5	directions	1 2 3 4 5
"Essentials"	1 2 3 4 5	entertainment	1 2 3 4 5	writing style	1 2 3 4 5
practical info	1 2 3 4 5	gay/lesbian info	1 2 3 4 5	budget resources	1 2 3 4 5
accommodations	1 2 3 4 5	up-to-date info	1 2 3 4 5	other: ________	1 2 3 4 5

How long was your trip? one week two wks. three wks. a month 2+ months
Why did you go? sightseeing adventure travel study abroad other: __________
What was your average daily budget, not including flights? ______________
Do you buy a separate map when you visit a foreign city? yes no
Have you used a Let's Go Map Guide? yes no **If you have, which one?** ________
Would you recommend them to others? yes no
Have you visited Let's Go's website? yes no
What would you like to see included on Let's Go's website? ______________
What percentage of your trip planning did you do on the web? ______________
What kind of Let's Go guide would you like to see? recreation (e.g., skiing) phrasebook
spring break adventure/trekking first-time travel info Europe altas
Which of the following destinations would you like to see Let's Go cover?
Argentina Brazil Canada Caribbean Chile Costa Rica Cuba
Morocco Nepal Russia Scandinavia Southwest USA other: ________
Where did you buy your guidebook? independent bookstore college bookstore
travel store Internet chain bookstore gift other: ________

Please fill this out and return it to **Let's Go, St. Martin's Press,** 175 Fifth Ave., New York, NY 10010-7848. All respondents will receive a free subscription to ***The Yellow-jacket***, the Let's Go Newsletter. You can find a more extensive version of this survey on the web at http://www.letsgo.com.